A HISTORY OF THE JEWISH WAR

A conflict that erupted between Roman legions and some Judaeans in late A.D. 66 had an incalculable impact on Rome's physical appearance and imperial governance; on ancient Jews bereft of their mother-city and temple; and on early Christian fortunes. Historical scholarship and cinema alike tend to see the conflict as the culmination of long Jewish resistance to Roman oppression. In this volume, Steve Mason re-examines the war in all relevant contexts (e.g., the Parthian dimension, Judaea's place in Roman Syria) and phases, from the Hasmoneans to the fall of Masada. Mason approaches each topic as a historical investigation, clarifying problems that need to be solved, understanding the available evidence, and considering scenarios that might explain the evidence. The simplest reconstructions make the conflict more humanly intelligible while casting doubt on received knowledge.

Steve Mason is Distinguished Professor of Ancient Mediterranean Religions and Cultures in the Faculty of Theology and Religious Studies at the University of Groningen. A former Canada Research Chair (in Greco-Roman Cultural Interaction) at Toronto's York University and Visiting Fellow in Oxford and Berlin, he has published several monographs and scores of essays on Roman Judaea, Josephus, Flavian Rome, Christian origins, and historical method. He edits the multivolume international project *Flavius Josephus: Translation and Commentary*.

A HISTORY OF THE JEWISH WAR

A.D. 66–74

STEVE MASON

University of Groningen

CAMBRIDGE
UNIVERSITY PRESS

32 Avenue of the Americas, New York, NY 10013-2473, USA

Cambridge University Press is part of the University of Cambridge.

It furthers the University's mission by disseminating knowledge in the pursuit of education, learning, and research at the highest international levels of excellence.

www.cambridge.org
Information on this title: www.cambridge.org/9780521853293

First published 2016

Printed in the United States of America

A catalog record for this publication is available from the British Library.

Library of Congress Cataloging in Publication Data
Mason, Steve, 1957- author.
A history of the Jewish War, AD 66-74 / Steve Mason, University of Groningen.
     pages   cm
Includes bibliographical references and index.
ISBN 978-0-521-85329-3 (Hardback)
1. Josephus, Flavius–Criticism and interpretation.   2. Jews–History–Rebellion, 66-73.
3. Josephus, Flavius. De bello Judaico.   I. Title.
DS115.9.J6M377 2015
933'.05–dc23   2015016873

ISBN 978-0-521-85329-3 Hardback

CONTENTS

ILLUSTRATIONS

TABLES

ACKNOWLEDGEMENTS

A decade of wandering while preparing this book has left me with debts to various universities, agencies, groups, and individuals.

My former employers, York University and the University of Aberdeen, allowed me to be away for periods of research, while the University of Oxford and Wolfson College, the Humboldt University of Berlin, and the University of Groningen made their excellent research facilities available to a nomad. Canada's indispensable Social Sciences and Humanities Research Council provided both research funds and support of my Canada Research Chair until 2011. The Kirby Laing Foundation then funded my Aberdeen Chair from 2011 to 2015. A *Forschungspreis* from the Alexander von Humboldt-Stiftung made possible a valuable year in Berlin (2013), and Groningen's new Dirk Smilde Fellowship gave me the first half of 2014 there—now *here*.

A number of academic groups gave me a patient hearing and what seemed friendly critique: the Collaborative Program in Ancient History (Toronto and York: ColPAH), York's Graduate Programme in History, the SBL Josephus Group/Seminar, Aberdeen's New Testament seminar, Edinburgh's Christian Origins workshop (which heard much of the book *in nuce*), the ancient history/classics seminars of Newcastle and St. Andrews, King's College London's postgraduate workshop in early Christianity and ancient Judaism, Trinity College Dublin's Jerusalem conference (2013), The Parkes Centre at the University of Southampton, University of Leiden (ancient history/classics), the student archaeologists and colleagues of Ben-Gurion University of the Negev, and the sponsors of a 2011 conference on Jewish historiography in Brussels. In all cases the feedback was useful, at least in challenging me to be clearer.

Many colleagues and friends in these places and elsewhere have generously shared their wisdom, encouragement, and/or challenges. I offer my sincere gratitude to Jonathan Edmondson, Ben Kelly, Andreas Bendlin, Martin Goodman, Erich Gruen, Danny Schwartz, Zuleika Rodgers, Nora Chapman, Hindy Najman, Joan Taylor, Helen Bond, Sarah Pearce, Haim Goldfus, Motti Aviam, Peter Fabian, Dudi Mevorach, Tommaso Leoni, William den Hollander, Reuben Lee, Stephen Ford, John Lowery, Marijn Vandenberghe (who also prepared the indices), Jamie McLaren, Jens Schröter, Cilliers Breytenbach,

Bernie Hodkin, Myles Schoonover, Onno van Nijf, Erin Wilson, Wout van Bekkum, and Mladen Popović.

It remains to thank the staff of Cambridge University Press in New York. Although they commisioned a compact book for a series and received a huge manuscript, they adjusted nimbly, waiting as I cut four chapters and trimmed the rest. Thanks to Beatrice Rehl for her patience and prudence, to the Press's anonymous referees for an academic counterpart to tough love, and to Ezhilmaran Sugumaran's expert production team.

My father, siblings, and grown children (Cara and Ian) are my harbour. My mother Grace, whose love made everything possible, left us when this book was in production. I dedicate it to her memory.

PART ONE

Contexts

CHAPTER ONE

A FAMOUS AND UNKNOWN WAR

> Ambition sighed: she found it vain to trust
> The faithless column and the crumbling bust, . . .
> Convinced, she now contracts her vast design,
> And all her triumphs shrink into a Coin.
> A narrow orb each crowded conquest keeps,
> Beneath her palm here sad Judaea weeps.
>> Alexander Pope, *To Mr. Addison,*
>> *Occasioned by his Dialogues on Medals* ll.19–26

Of all the scents, the balsam is the best. The only land to which it has been given is Judaea, where formerly it grew in two gardens. . . . This tree was displayed to the city [of Rome] by the *imperators* Vespasian and Titus. . . . This tree is now enslaved, and pays tribute along with the nation to which it belongs. . . . The Judaeans used to vent their fury on this tree, just as on their own lives. The Romans defended it against them, and battles were fought on behalf of a tree!
> Pliny the Elder, *Natural History* 12.111–13

A provincial revolt in Roman Judaea and the campaign that suppressed it in A.D. 67–70[1] received unprecedented publicity. The modest achievements of Vespasian and Titus in Judaea came at an unusually dangerous period for the capital. In the domestic turbulence that followed Nero's suicide (June 68), their claim to have conquered a foreign enemy gave them unique *bona fides* as men capable of uniting Rome in peace. Their supporters promoted this

---

[1] Although we usually date the revolt from 66 to 73 or 74 (the fall of Masada), for Flavian Rome the war began with the Flavians' arrival (spring 67) and ended with Jerusalem's fall in September 70.

narrative with tireless energy. In the eighteenth century still, Alexander Pope could assume his readers' familiarity with the coins issued to celebrate Jerusalem's defeat: *Iudaea Capta!*

The Flavians and their backers left no stone unused in publicity. But was any of this meant to help people understand what had happened over there? Soon after he arrived in Rome, Pliny's younger contemporary Flavius Josephus began complaining about an inverted fame-to-ignorance ratio: so much fuss, so little truth (*War* 1.1–8). The remaining chapters of this book will explore what lay beneath the fuss: what really happened in the war. In this first chapter we need to understand the fuss itself. It began in Josephus' day and has continued well into modern times.

The outcome of the Judaean-Roman war affected the course of Western history in three quite different ways. Jewish responses were the most complex, because the loss of mother-city and temple required the reshaping of Judaean culture with a vitality that would enable its survival, eventually as *Juda-ism*, through the centuries ahead.[2] In Rome, the Flavians' exploitation of success in Judaea was critical to the establishment of their regime, which laid the foundation for a peaceful succession through the second century. Most consequentially, early Christian groups quickly assimilated Jerusalem's fall into their self-understanding and self-representation. Of these three directions of impact, Jerusalem's destruction was of course felt most keenly by Jews, but they did not celebrate and propagate it. We shall focus here on the two groups that did.

1. FLAVIANS DEFEAT THE EASTERN MENACE! FAME ESTABLISHED

There used to be a monumental arch in Rome's greatest entertainment facility, the Circus Maximus, southwest of the Palatine Hill and Forum. If a ninth-century visitor copied it accurately, it honoured the emperor Titus (ruled A.D. 79–81) in the following terms:

> The Roman Senate and People:
> for the *Imperator* Titus Caesar Vespasian Augustus, son of the Deified Vespasian,
> *Pontifex Maximus*, with *tribunicia potestas* for the tenth time, *imperator* for the seventeenth,Consul for the eighth, *pater patriae*, their *princeps*,
> Because on the advice and counsel of his father, and under his auspices, he subdued the nation of the Judaeans (*gentem Iudaeorum domuit*). The city of Jerusalem, either attacked in futility or left entirely untried by all the leaders, kings, or nations before him, *he* destroyed (*urbem Hierusolymam . . . delevit*).[3]

---

[2] On the rabbis and the temple, see Cohn 2012. On Titus, see e.g. *b. Gitt.* 56b.

[3] *CIL* 6.944. As I write, Tommaso Leoni (York University Toronto) is completing a PhD dissertation on this arch. In the meantime see Ciancio Rossetto 2000: 1.108–9.

Every informed person knew that the last lines were nonsense. To speak only of Roman conquerors: Pompey the Great besieged and occupied Jerusalem in 63 B.C. A generation later (37 B.C.) Gaius Sosius, Syria's governor under Marc Antony, repeated the exercise to remove Jerusalem from the Parthian sphere and install King Herod. Both generals received triumphal processions, memorialized on a marble record in the Roman Forum, fragments of which survive.[4] Pompey's abundant coins featured Judaea's submission alongside that of other nations in Syria, and Antony's coins proudly co-opted Sosius' victory.[5] Those were only the *Roman* conquerors. Half a millennium earlier, the neo-Babylonian Nebuchadnezzar had destroyed Jerusalem, and between 586 and 63 B.C. Jerusalem had passed to Persian, Ptolemaic, and Seleucid imperial powers before Rome's. Titus was very far, then, from being Jerusalem's first conqueror. Yet he was still being feted as such in the 90s: "By war he destroyed the fierce tribes of Palestine!" (Silius Italicus 605–606).

Overdone rhetoric was hardly rare when it came to emperors' achievements. A lost arch created for Claudius boasted of his British campaign (A.D. 43): "[H]e first brought the barbarian peoples across the Ocean under the authority [or sway, *indicio*] of the Roman people."[6] Writing just before that triumph, Pomponius Mela professed joy at *finally* being able to describe Britain accurately: "Look: the greatest of emperors is opening up what for so long lay closed, the conqueror of nations that were previously not only ungovernable but indeed *were unknown!*"[7] But Britain's tribes had been clients of Rome for decades before Claudius,[8] and Pomponius' accuracy was not noticeably improved by Claudius' invasion. Then again, Silius Italicus flatters Vespasian as the first to open up "unknown" areas of Britain (597–98), while Tacitus claims that his father-in-law was the first to subdue Britain properly (*Agr.* 10). The model emperor Augustus had set the pace for such exaggerated claims to primacy: "The Pannonian peoples, whom before I was first citizen the army of the Roman had people never approached, were conquered . . ." (*RG* 30).[9]

---

[4] In the *fasti triumphales*. See Degrassi 1954: 108 for Pompey's triumph (61 B.C.), 110 for Sosius' (34 B.C.). In Pompey's case time has effaced the wording, but the context makes his record clear. For cautions in using the *fasti* generally, see Beard 2007: 61–80.

[5] See Hendin 2010: 404–5.   [6] Barrett 1991: 12.

[7] 3.49: *quippe tamdiu clausam aperit ecce principum maximus, nec indo-mitarum modo ante se verum ignotarum quoque gentium victor.* Romer (1998: 2–3) proposes a pun on Claudius' name in the participle of *claudo* (*clausam*): "closed."

[8] See Strabo 4.5.3; several decades earlier, recounting relations with Rome after Julius Caesar's British small conquests (55 B.C.), celebrating the wealth that has flowed in trade duties from what is "virtually Roman property."

[9] The Pannonians were an Illyrian (Balkan) tribe, and Illyria had been among Rome's first concerns in its eastward expansion. Although the Pannonii were somewhat inland, south of the Danube in the Sava and Drava river valleys (toward Budapest), the Romans had engaged them militarily from the late second century B.C., and the governor of Macedonia may have encountered them when he fought in the region between 75 and 73 B.C. (see *OCD*[3] "Pannonia").

People cannot remember everything, and Rome's residents were accustomed to giving rhetoric a wide berth. It is not shocking that the Senate of the 70s would invite the populace to imagine Titus' Jerusalem victory as unprecedented. It only hurt if one thought about it.

In the absence of modern-style media, Rome's leaders had three principal means for advertising their achievements:[10] a magnificent procession for the home constituency (senators and people); the construction of public monuments, arches, statues, temples, and public facilities, ostensibly funded from the new wealth generated by the foreign conquest; and an empire-wide distribution of coins. Literary propaganda was also possible, but lengthy historical narratives were not well suited to that task, being open to varied and uncontrollable interpretations and risking mischief on the part of clever authors or audiences.[11] For the simple points that needed making, spectacles of overwhelming impact, along with images and brief statements on stone and coin-metal, were most reliable.[12]

Even before Jerusalem's fall, the Flavians and their supporters began exploiting all three media. Monuments and celebratory coinage they took to with an energy matching that of predecessors who had actually conquered large new territories. Building and minting coins required no evidence from the conquered territory. These were zones of free creativity; the Flavians could craft any imagery that suited them. Only the triumph, in principle, required material from the conquered territory. In the second century B.C. Polybius, a long-time Greek resident of Rome, explained triumphs as occasions on which "the vivid representation of the deeds of the generals, accomplished by their hard labours, is brought to the citizens by way of this spectacle" (Polybius 6.15.8). Consuls who had made conquests in far-off lands demonstrated their achievements by placing before Rome's populace the captured royals, soldiers, weapons, and piles of wealth that were now at their fellow-citizens' disposal. In theory, success justified such display. Mary Beard wryly comments, however: "The triumph was about display and success – the success of display no less than the display of success."[13]

Triumphs in context: foreign conquest versus civil war

In the passage just cited, Polybius was explaining the Republican Senate's power to award triumphs. By the time of this ninth emperor, however,

---

[10] See Hart 1952; Hölscher 2006; Vasta 2007.
[11] Stover 2012 interprets Valerius Flaccus' *Argonautica* as a reconfiguration of familiar myth in the service of the new regime. Convincing though the study is, it illustrates the complexity of interpreting literary texts: Stover must argue even for a Vespasianic date. On the perils of interpreting texts under autocracies, see Rudich 1993, 1997.
[12] E.g., Favro 1996, 2005; Galinsky 1996; Wallace-Hadrill 2005: 78–81; Beacham 2005.
[13] Beard 2007: 31.

experience had taught senators that it was in their interest to enable each new autocrat. The formal role senators retained in awarding triumphs took the edge off the perception of autocracy, leaving the senators crumbs of status in a mutually beneficial back-scratch. The august chamber still had to vote the honours, and a curmudgeon or two could get away with grumbling about it *in camera*, as long as the monarch's requirements were met.

As soon as it was clear that Vespasian's forces had defeated those of Vitellius (December 69), and months before the commander would arrive personally in Rome, a Senate wearied by years of civil turmoil eagerly recognized his supremacy by issuing a *Law concerning the Imperium of Vespasian* (*lex de imperio Vespasiani*).[14] This was a series of ostensible "permissions," which amount to *carte blanche*: Whatever the dear leader does, says, thinks, orders, or has done is valid and excellent. One of the few specific privileges granted Vespasian in this document was the right "to extend and move forward the boundaries of the *pomerium*" whenever he should see fit.[15] The *pomerium* was Rome's sacred boundary, the delimited zone creating a *templum* in which auspices – reading omens from the flight of birds – could legitimately be taken.[16] It was marked by small inscribed stones, or *cippi*. Altering it did not affect the city's walls, but given the importance of augury (taking auspices) to Rome's public life, being one of the few men ever permitted to extend the sacred boundary was a huge honour for Vespasian. This right was extended to a conqueror as a local miniature representation of his expansion of Rome's power (*imperium*) abroad through the capture of foreign territory.[17] Triumph and extension of the *pomerium* were thus a natural pair. They had most recently been granted to Claudius for Britain, and the grant to Vespasian cites Claudius as most relevant precedent. That is particularly fitting also because Vespasian had played a pivotal role as legionary commander in Claudius' invasion. Now the protégé was receiving the honour for provincial Judaea's (still-imminent) "conquest."[18]

---

[14] *CIL* 6.930. For the date see Hellems 1902: 2; Levick 1999: 85–86.

[15] This bronze-tablet inscription, which is missing text at the beginning and may be the second of two parts, was discovered in fourteenth-century Rome. It is published as *CIL* 6.930 (among other places); English translations are in Hellems 1902: 3–6; Sherk 1988 no. 82.

[16] Aulus Gellius 13.14; Platner and Ashby 1929: *s.v.* "Pomerium."

[17] Tacitus is speaking of Claudius when he says that, by ancient custom (though one hardly used before), "to those who expand the *imperium* it is given to extend the limits of the city" (*Ann.* 12.23). Cf. Aulus Gellius in 13.14.3: "[T]hey had the right to enlarge the *pomerium* who had increased the [space of] the Roman people *with land taken from enemies*."

[18] Some scholars have linked the *pomerium* grant to another achievement, apparently because a connection with (already provincial) Judaea would stretch credulity. Levick (1999) is hesitant even to connect *the triumph* with Judaea for that reason ("*Probably* the suppression of the Jewish revolt was the main theme," p. 71, emphasis mine). As justification for the *pomerium* grant, she proposes "Q. Petillius Cerialis' campaigns in Britain" (p. 71) and "[s]uccesses, probably those that continued Claudius' work in Britain" (p. 130). Because Levick agrees with the standard dating of the *lex* to early 70 (pp. 85–86), before those successes, she seems to

Several discovered *cippi* show that Vespasian exercised this privilege in A.D. 75, the same year in which he dedicated the Temple of Peace, also largely in celebration of Judaea (below).[19]

On hearing of Jerusalem's eventual fall to Titus (September A.D. 70), the Senate went farther and authorized commemorative arches in anticipation of the two men's arrivals and the extravaganzas to follow.[20] These arches have disappeared with time, although a decorated arch depicted inside the southern relief panel of the standing Arch of Titus, built a decade later (Fig. 1), may be one of them.[21]

The arches, triumph, and *pomerium* grant show the Senate's collusion in the pretence that suppression of a provincial disturbance could be reckoned a new foreign conquest.[22] Roman tradition was clear about what constituted a proper war (*bellum iustum*). A special college of priests, the *fetiales*, had the principal task of making treaties and declarations of war, both of which were possible only with foreign peoples not already part of Rome's empire.[23] In spite of Josephus' incidental remark that Vespasian landed in Syria when "war had been declared" (*War* 7.46), it seems impossible to imagine this fetial process having been conducted in the case of Judaea, which had been part of Roman Syria since Pompey's famed conquests.[24]

Scholars' efforts to find a loophole for the Flavians by suggesting that Judaea had become effectively independent, and the Flavians "had reconquered a small rebellious province,"[25] founder on the definition of *Judaea*. If there had been a province of Judaea before the Flavians, its capital would have been

---

mean that the Senate made the grant as a wild card, interpreting the word "as/when he saw fit" (*censebit*) to include both justification and timing. But the right seems to assume a one-time extension (Why would the Senate say: for any pretext you like, but *once only*?), and Vespasian's grant is compared with Claudius', which was based on alleged conquest. Irrational though it may be, the centrality of the Judaean victory for the Flavians is overwhelmingly attested. Cf. Newton 1902: 5.

[19] See Newton 1902: 4–5.   [20] Dio 65/66.7.2 (Epitome).

[21] So Kleiner 1990: 130. Its upper decoration, with two triumphal chariots and a figure on horseback, matches Josephus' description of the later joint triumph, with young Domitian alongside (*War* 7.152). Or perhaps it was the standing Triumphal Gate. See the discussion in Davies 2004: 184–85 n. 30. See Pfanner 1983: plates 54–56 for gate detail. An engraving by P. S. Bartoli showing the detail still visible ca. 1685 is at http://bellori.sns.it/bellori//TOC_1.html (= Bartoli and Bellori 1685: *Arco di Tito, Pompa Trionfale* plate 5).

[22] Mommsen 1894: 5.538–39 ("such an inevitable victory over a tiny, long-subjected people," my translation); Mattern 1999: 191–94; Millar 2005: 102; Goodman 2007: 438–44.

[23] Wiedemann 1986 assesses the college's functions to the late Republic. See Augustus *RG* 7.3 for his membership, and Dio 50.4.4–5 with Suetonius, *Aug.* 31, as context for his revival of many old rituals and priesthoods.

[24] Josephus' language perhaps reflects the fact that the Flavians had declared this a *war* when they became involved. The unsystematic nature of such language is clear from *War* 2.284, which dates *the beginning of the war* to Artemisius/Iyyar in the spring of 66, two months before even Cestius' tribune visited and reported on the city's peaceful disposition (Chapter 5).

[25] Levick 1999: 71; cf. 2: "Judaea was still in revolt."

FIGURE I. Spoils relief in the south panel as it looks today. Courtesy of the Arch of Titus Digital Restoration Project, Director Professor Steven Fine. Note the arch being entered to the right.

coastal Caesarea, and it would have included Samaria, western Galilee, and some of the coastal plain. During the Flavian conflict, however, those regions remained steadfastly loyal. The Judaea in question, evidently, was the ethnic hinterland of Jerusalem and not a formal province (Chapter 4). On any account the Flavians were engaged in political malarkey. But malarkey was the order of the day in political life. How much has changed in that respect, readers may decide.

Many questions about Roman triumphs remain uncertain, and no ancient guide survives. The processions we hear about are described in vague and contradictory ways, usually by writers remote from the events.[26] If we assumed a coherent system, we might well ask: What did someone *do* to earn a triumph? But evidence from the Republic shows that senators debated the merits of each case, sometimes denying a triumph even to a great conqueror because of political conditions, or changing their minds, or forcing the man to choose between a triumph and a consulship, or offering a compromise that fell short of a full triumph.[27] The criteria that some scholars have proposed are

[26] Beard 2007 (e.g., 57–58, 72–106) gleefully dismantles common perceptions. On the remoteness of our accounts see Itgenshorst 2005: 13–41.

[27] Pelikan Pittenger 2008. Livy 22.21 describes the denial of a triumph to M. Claudius Marcellus, a great hero who had triumphed twice, personally killed an enemy chief, and (211 B.C.) taken much of Sicily from Carthaginian sympathizers (cf. Plutarch, *Marc.* 21–22). Livy 28.9 describes a compromise: A joint triumph was awarded to deserving generals, but only

merely cobbled together from those debates over particular cases, but already in the Republic it is easy to find exceptions to any imagined rules.[28] Even the eminent Cicero could not contrive a triumph for himself.[29] Under the Empire, autocratic rulers basically did as they pleased, although to be sure they must have weighed considerations of prestige, seemliness, and political need – or what they could get away with – in consultation with advisors.

The Imperial triumph seems to have retained faint overtones of a boundary-crossing purification ritual. In Republican times the event had supposedly welcomed back citizens-in-arms from wild territory abroad to the world of order inside Rome's sacred boundary.[30] Purification may sound primitive, but a modern military analyst laments the absence of such rituals today. It is important, he maintains, "to purify the warriors or soldiers so as to help their transition back from a situation in which almost anything was permitted to one in which a great many things are not."[31] If the purificatory idea still applied to the armies of the early Empire, however, it could have done so only abstractly. The legions that had fought in Judaea, for instance, did not "return" to Rome, but were ordered back to their bases on the empire's northern and eastern frontiers.[32] Overtones of purification may have retained important symbolic meaning for the commanders themselves and a token parade force, signifying that the bloodshed was over.

The components of the triumph most famous from historical dramas (red-painted faces, a slave reminding the general to remember his humanity) are among the elements most open to doubt. We can say, at least, that it was

one was permitted to ride in the chariot. Even Pompey was turned down at first by the Dictator Sulla, who later yielded to the young man's intimidation (Plutarch, *Pomp.* 14).

[28] For a neat list see Zaho 2004: 14 ("specific qualifications had been laid down: a just war ... originally sanctioned and declared as a war ... must have killed at least five thousand ... must return with prisoners and trophies ... war must have been brought to a complete end"). For demolition see Beard 2007: 200–14.

[29] Cicero, *Ad Fam.* 15.1–6 describes the rhetorical dance between a proud man obliquely requesting a triumph and the upright Cato the Younger obliquely denying it.

[30] So the second-century Festus, *Lexicon* (epit. Paulus), "Laureati" (p. 104 L) with Laqueur 1909; Ehlers 1939: 495–96. A Republican rule required that returning generals not cross the *pomerium* until they had gone through the ritual (Plutarch, *Pomp.* 44.1). Pliny reports (disagreeing) the notion that the triumph's laurel wreaths were chosen "for fumigation and purification after the slaughter of the enemy" (*Nat.* 15.135); cf. Laqueur 1909: 226–36; Warde Fowler 1913: 49–51; Zaho 2004: 13–14. Bonfante Warren (1970: 49) thinks the triumph developed from a purification ritual to a "purely honorific ceremony" focused on the *auctoritas* of the victor. Versnel (1970: 152–63) rejects the purification model, asking why only those victorious in war would have needed purifying. He sees the triumph as an entry-rite evolved from Greek ceremonies for welcoming home victorious athletes; cf. Künzl 1988: 42–44. Beard (2007: 246–47, 332–33), without discounting purificatory overtones, proposes that the ritual had come to mean many things at once. Esler (1995: 239–58) emphasizes the honour–shame dialectic that played out in a triumph, with useful observations on the Flavian event.

[31] van Creveld 2008: 161.   [32] Josephus, *War* 7.5, 18–19, 117.

normal for the procession to form up in the military zone northwest of the city called the Field of Mars (Campus Martius). After prayers and sacrifices, the parade passed through a ceremonial gate and wound its way through Rome's public spaces. The procession displayed foreign rulers and generals, enemy soldiers, Roman dignitaries, artistic representations of the foreign countryside and battle scenes, and representative legionary units. The day-long event might culminate with the execution of an enemy general. It concluded with a solemn sacrifice outside the temple of Jupiter Optimus Maximus on the Capitoline hill, overlooking the Forum. Joyous feasting for the populace, with a rare meal of excellent roasted meat, concluded the festivities.

In planning their big event Vespasian and Titus had glorious precedents to live up to. Leaving aside the luminaries of the distant past, there was the unavoidable shadow of Pompey the Great, the man who really had brought Judaea under Rome's *imperium*. Pompey celebrated a triumph for each continent (i.e., Africa/Numidia, Europe/Spain, Asia/Syria) – a veritable world conqueror and arguably Rome's greatest general.[33] His last triumph, held over the two days that included his birthday in 61 B.C.,[34] celebrated his eastern victories: defeat of Mithridates VI of Pontus and the conquest of some fourteen nations in Syria, including the Judaeans.

Plutarch relates of Pompey's triumph that, "even though it was divided into two days, the time was still insufficient and most of what had been prepared had to be excluded from the spectacle" (*Pomp.* 45). Although he had enough plunder for several days, Pompey held back for decency's sake. Large inscriptions nevertheless listed the newly subject territories: "Syria, Cilicia, Mesopotomia, the area around Phoenicia and Palestine, Judaea, and Arabia, as well as the whole pirate operation he had dismantled by war." Pompey claimed to have seized more than a thousand fortresses and nearly 900 cities. Income from the provinces had previously amounted to 50 million drachmas, but inscriptions explained that "just from what he had acquired for the city, they would now receive 85 million drachmas, *and* he was bringing into the public treasury 20,000 talents [524,000 kg, 1.155 million lbs] in silver and gold coin and vessels." Appian writes in a glowing tone: Pompey's last triumph saw 700 enemy ships brought to Rome's harbour and more than 75 million drachmas of silver coin, along with assorted enemy kings including the Judaean Aristobulus (*Mithr.* 116–17).

Pompey halted his conquests at Egypt's frontier. This left the completion of the Mediterranean circle to Augustus as a function of his war with Cleopatra and Antony. His triumph was another precedent that the Flavians could hardly ignore. From August 13 to 15, 29 B.C., two years before he accepted the title

---

[33] Deutsch 1924.   [34] On this paradigmatic and much-discussed event see Beard 2007:7–41.

Augustus, Octavian held a three-day triumph for, respectively, Dalmatia/Ill-yricum (35–33 B.C.), the defeat of Cleopatra at Actium (31 B.C.), and the annexation of Egypt (30 B.C.).[35] Dio writes (51.21.7): "Also the other [two days'] processions were resplendent *because of the spoils from there [Egypt]*: they were so plentiful as they were accumulated that they were enough for all the [three] processions, but the day for Egypt itself was by far the greatest in the display of wealth and magnificence." The dearth of plunder from Actium's naval battle and the rough tribal areas of Illyricum was masked by the eye-watering wealth of Egypt.

From Augustus' time onward, triumphal spectacle was too potent to be permitted a general other than emperor or his approved family members. A man capable of flooding Rome with new wealth from foreign conquest would certainly become the city's darling, building new temples, monuments, and public structures with the proceeds. Whereas the Republican system had enabled Rome's leading men to compete for such glory, under the monarchy such rivalry would put the top man's pre-eminence at risk and so could not be tolerated.

Even in the Republic there had been no simple correlation, we have seen, between battlefield success and triumphal honours. Imperial rule severed even a notional link.[36] Some impressive successes, such as that of Corbulo over the Parthians in A.D. 63, went without a triumph (Chapter 5). A successful general might be given the "ornaments" of triumph or a low-key *ovatio* in quiet gratitude for his deeds, but the spotlight had to remain on the emperor. The *ovatio* was a triumph-lite, lacking the crucial display of domination that under-pinned the grander event.[37] Claudius' commander in the British campaign, Aulus Plautius, deserved a triumph if anyone did. He had conquered foreign nations and created a province in the feared island "across the Ocean." But the emperor, with no skin in the game, stole a march and triumphed before Plautius returned to Rome, leaving the general the consolation of an *ovatio*.[38] At least he had the grace to walk beside Plautius in that ceremony.

---

[35] Gurval 1995: 25–31.   [36] Hölscher 2006 has many astute observations.

[37] Plutarch (*Marc.* 22) traces the *ovatio* to Latin *ova* (sheep), arguing that the sacrificial animal – over against the ox in a triumph – determined the name. He also proposes that the *ovatio* signifies a conflict won by strategy and persuasion, rather than by direct force and bloodshed as in the triumph. Four times the *fasti* mention a triumph "on Mt. Alban," an even lower-key, quasi-private ceremony conducted outside Rome.

[38] Suetonius, *Claud.* 24 and Dio 60/61.30.2. According to both Tacitus (*Ann.* 11.20) and Suetonius (*Claud.* 24.3), Claudius was over-generous with triumphal *honours*, handing them out to a future son-in-law while still a lad and to commanders who had undertaken engineering works (including Corbulo, later denied a triumph by Nero for serious military success). The future emperor Galba received triumphal honours from Claudius for two years of dogged effort in repelling attacks from across provincial Africa's frontier (Suetonius, *Galb.* 7–8.1), Pomponius Secundus for opposing foreign invaders (the Chatti) from across the Rhine (Tacitus, *Ann.* 12.27–28).

What had the Flavians actually achieved for Rome? Their enablers declared the Judaeans a foreign enemy, whose mother-city had finally been conquered. In reality, Judaea had for more than 130 years belonged to Roman Syria. Nero sent Vespasian to Syria only because his legate there, Cestius Gallus, had lost the emperor's confidence (*War* 3.1–5; see Chapter 5). Had Cestius been successful, in either the brief expedition he undertook or a planned follow-up, *he* could not have triumphed. Nor do we have reason to suppose that Nero, who did not triumph even for Corbulo's settlement of Armenia, would have done so for Judaea. One of Nero's successors in 68–69, Galba, Otho, or Vitellius, might have held a triumph, in a desperate effort to shore up their teetering regimes – if Vespasian had been willing to serve them and completed the Judaean campaign before they died. But if they had done so, it would have been an obviously desperate move, given that there was no foreign people, army, or king to be conquered in Judaea, certainly no new wealth to be brought home.

Why, then, all the fuss? The simple if shocking answer is that Vespasian needed this. He had achieved a much more important military victory for Rome, but it was one that dared not speak its name: in the *civil war* following Nero's death. That was of far greater concern to Romans than anything happening in Judaea, 2,500 km (1,500 mi) away, on soil that few Romans would ever see or care about.

We call A.D. 69 "the year of the four emperors," but just as impressively it was the year of at least fifteen consuls. Consuls held the highest magistracy in Rome, and their office was vital to the city's functioning. In the Republic the consulship was an annual elected magistracy of great prestige, and the two consuls were memorialized by giving their names to the year. The early Empire began to see truncated terms, with replacements ("suffects") installed part-way through to expand the sphere of imperial patronage. But a year with fifteen or more consuls revealed deep divisions, as each new supremo installed himself alongside a friend, and each Senator tried to align himself with changing realities.[39] Rome was in chaos. That civil war witnessed the mutilation and beheading of 70-year-old Galba in Rome's Forum, of his 30-year-old successor Piso at the entrance to the temple of Vesta, and of Vespasian's older brother Sabinus in front of Vitellius' palace. Vespasian's immediate predecessor Aulus Vitellius was killed on the very Capitol steps, from where his killers dragged his remains by hook to the Tiber River for disposal.[40] Warring Romans also burned down the city's most revered temple, for Jupiter Best and Greatest.[41]

---

[39] Townend 1962.
[40] Suetonius, *Galb.* 19–20; *Otho* 9–11; *Vit.* 16–18; Tacitus, *Hist.* 1.18–44; 2.56, 60; 3.21–22, 27, 32–34, 55, 83–86. For detailed analysis, see Wellesley 2000; Morgan 2006.
[41] Tacitus, *Hist.* 3.71–73.

Open warfare inside Rome's sacred boundary was rare, the presence of armed units inside the *pomerium* being forbidden. Tacitus' account of this period reflects his distaste for the mob, so disgustingly fascinated with the bloodshed around them as though it were entertainment. They gawked at the violence while scoffing down meals and enjoying the baths undeterred (*Hist.* 3.83). Josephus claims that Vitellius "made all of Rome into a military camp and filled every house with armed soldiers" – in improvised billets. Having never seen the delights of such a city, his German soldiers allegedly went wild with violence and rapine (*War* 4.586–87). As well as terrorizing the city of Rome, the civil war had brought legions into direct conflict on Italy's battlefields, costing tens of thousands of citizen lives. Dio's figure of 80,000 casualties in just the first Battle of Cremona must be a considerable exaggeration (*Epit. Dio* 63/64.10.3), but losses from the repeated clash of these professional armies surely exceeded by far those in Judaea, where Flavian legions faced minimal resistance and the conflict amounted to a series of sieges (Chapter 3). Anyway, hardly any of the Judaean dead were Roman citizens.

Vespasian's decisive victory in the civil war was therefore what really mattered in Rome. The problem was that removing Vitellius and his Roman army furnished no glorious basis for a claim to power. In Graeco-Roman thinking, civil strife was the most detestable political disease.[42] As Vespasian's immediate predecessors had shown, victors over fellow senators were unavoidably covered in the mire. Further challenge and conspiracy from rivals and aggrieved supporters of their victims were unavoidable. A strong man might suppress this for a while, as L. Cornelius Sulla and Octavian (Augustus) had in the previous century, but the lingering bitterness of senatorial rivalry and divided armies would likely result in further bloodshed. Public celebration for a victory in a civil war would have been unseemly, a triumph out of the question.[43]

The only safe way to disperse the adrenaline and war-weariness, to unite the Roman community after years of deep partisan hatred and fear, was to funnel that destructive energy onto a foreign scapegoat. (The tactic has not lost its appeal.) The legions existed to secure Rome's *imperium* and conquer foreign enemies, under commanders who should be duly rewarded for their perils, not

---

[42] Dionysius of Halicarnassus (*Pomp.* 3) attacks the much-admired Thucydides for his choice of subject, a shameful war among Greek *poleis* (a war that should never have happened and a shameful story best left untold) in contrast to the morally uplifting story of Herodotus, concerning Greeks against barbarians. On *stasis* in general as the worst political disease, see Thucydides 3.82–4 (at Corcyra); Herodotus 1.59.3, 60.2, 150.1; 3.82.3; 5.28.1; 6.109.5; Isocrates, *Paneg.* 4.79, 114, 174; Plato, *Leg.* 1.628c, 629c-d; Aristotle, *Ath. Pol.* 5.2–3; 13.1; *Pol.* 1265b; Diodorus 9.11.1; 11.72.2, 76.6, 86.3, 87.5; Plutarch, *Mor.* 16.813a, 32.823f-825b; Dio Chrysostom, *1 Regn.* 1.82; Pausanias 3.2.7; 4.18.3; Lintott 1982; Gehrke 1985; Molyneux 1993; Henderson 1998.

[43] Cf. Beard (2007: 123): "a triumph in civil war ... was a contradiction in terms."

to fight each other. A real triumph, for a foreign victory, could put a line under civil conflict and thus put the exhausted city on a path toward reconciliation. It was all the better if the conqueror had not personally been present in Italy during the bloodbaths, but away fighting the foreigners. These political imperatives in Rome from December 69 were not shaped by anything happening on the ground in Judaea. No one cared what had caused the upheavals *there*. Politicians are not historians.

As with most aspects of Roman politics, Augustus had shown the way. Everyone knew that his rise to power brought an end to devastating civil wars: between Julius Caesar and his rivals, between Caesar's assassins and his friends, and between two leaders of that circle friends, Octavian and Antony.[44] Yet in the celebrations that inaugurated Octavian's bright new day, those internal-Roman hostilities went carefully unmentioned.[45] Dio comments that he flooded Rome with so much money and promise of well-being that "the Romans forgot all the disagreeable events and looked on his victory with pleasure, as if those who had been defeated had all been foreigners" (51.21.4). His triumph had to focus on foreign conquests, especially on Egypt's Cleopatra, *sans* Antony, and the resulting acquisition of Egypt's wealth. Cleopatra foresaw the humiliation in store for her and killed herself to evade it, but Octavian needed her too badly to accept that. He had her children brought to Rome along with her own royal couch, which could carry a mannequin of the deceased queen in his triumphal procession (Dio 51.21.8). The foreign enemy was indispensable as a conduit for popular hatred.

Only near the end of his long rule would Augustus acknowledge that his accession had ended *both* external and civil war, although still without naming Antony (*RG* 1–4).[46] Decades later Seneca could write for his young ward Nero about Augustus' clemency – *after* he had filled Actium's waters with citizen blood and exhausted himself in murdering Romans. Nero should pass over that bloody phase and move straight to the clemency.[47]

So compelling was the scapegoat tactic that during the civil strife of 69 Vitellius tried to co-opt Vespasian's Judaean campaign as *his* foreign war.[48] Vitellius' coins intersperse messages of peace, concord, and the "agreement of the armies" with images of Victory fastening her shield to the palm

---

[44] The classic study is Syme 1939; Eck 2003: 16–23, 34–45 is a readable overview, and Levick 2010 is particularly sharp on the image/reality distinction.

[45] See Gurval 1995: 25, 28.

[46] Cf. Velleius Paterculus (writing under Tiberius) 2.89.3–4 on Augustus' ending of civil strife, and Lucan's *Bellum Civile*.

[47] Seneca, *Clem* 1.11.2–3 with Braund 2009: 61–63.

[48] According to Tacitus (*Hist.* 2.4), by the spring of 69 the war was essentially over, delayed only by Jerusalem's topographical situation and the population's irrational persistence. The survival of more than one issue of Vitellius' "Judaean" coins suggests that some appeared after July 1 and Vespasian's acclamation by eastern legions.

tree that symbolized Judaea.[49] This was chutzpah, but born of political necessity. Vitellius had also needed a distraction from Roman bloodshed, and the dispatch of a multi-legion Roman force to deal with a conflict on the eastern periphery offered as good a prospect as any.

Vespasian, having been entrusted with the campaign by Nero, was happy to continue under his first successor, the aged blueblood (and anti-Nero) Galba, whom he knew from Claudius' court (Chapter 5).[50] But when Galba was murdered after just a few months, Vespasian was not at all ready to yield the precious commodity of this rare military campaign to young Otho, Nero's former friend and cuckold; much less to Vitellius, recent commander of legions in Germany, also his junior and widely seen as a repugnant fellow riding a distinguished father's coat-tails.

When Vespasian's partisans had finally done away with Vitellius (December 69), he reused Vitellius' coin types, declaring to the capital that the genuine article – the real commander whose glory Vitellius had tried to steal – was about to arrive in person.[51] While Otho and Vitellius were busy killing other Romans, Vespasian had been risking his life against real, foreign enemies. (It was inopportune to bring up the devastation wrought by his armies against Vitellius' legions on Italian soil.) His was the kind of old-fashioned virtue that Rome needed. He was not going to let this message be lost.

By a happy coincidence, the Flavian celebration in the summer of 71 fell in the hundredth year after Augustus' triumph in 29 B.C.[52] Centenaries were and remain heavy with potential meaning.[53] Septimius Severus would delay his triumph for Parthia by a couple of months (to 28 January, A.D. 198) so as to have his son Caracalla acclaimed co-emperor on the centenary of Trajan's accession.[54] The century from Augustus to Vespasian, although we hear nothing of it in ancient sources, must have attracted notice. Counted exclusively, a century from Augustus would have fallen in 72, but that would have been too late for the urgently needed triumph for Judaea. Vespasian reached Rome only in October A.D. 70, although the Senate had confirmed his

---

[49] E.g., the coins ref. 1920,0325.7, 1933,0711.1, and R.10275 in the British Museum (www.britishmuseum.org).

[50] Josephus, *War* 4.498–99, and Tacitus, *Hist.* 1.10; 2.1–4.

[51] See Hart 1952: 191–92 and coin ref. 1872,0709.482 in the British Museum.

[52] On Augustus' exploitation of victory see (from an ocean of studies) Sutherland 1951: 14–26; Kellum 1982; Zanker 1988; Gurval 1995; Castriota 1995; Galinsky 1996; Eck 2003: 46–54; Rich 2009; Hölscher 2009. On the Flavians and Augustan resonances see Boyle & Dominik 2003: 1–68 et passim; Panzram 2002: 170–71 (who, unusually, notes the century); Millar 2005.

[53] E.g., Feeney 2007: 145: "the century of one hundred years was a crucial link in the chains of significance that were forged between past and present." The interval from −29 to +71 is not a full 100-year span because there is no "Year 0" in the alignment of the Roman-Julian calendar with our Gregorian.

[54] Lusnia 2006: 294.

supreme power in December 69. And he antedated his reign to July 1, 69, retrospectively erasing most of Vitellius' term (from 16 April). The inclusive century from Augustus' triumph would therefore have to do. It was close enough for providential reverberations.

Imperial triumphs: performance anxiety and sham

To understand the Flavian triumph itself, we need to bear in mind the great models, especially the two mentioned above, which must have been in the minds of Flavian planners and informed Romans alike. Our reports of the Republican events should not, of course, be mistaken for factual reporting. They likely include false memories of "the good old days" and various kinds of literary embellishment long after the fact. But they are still valuable for giving a sense of what a proper Roman triumph was imagined to be.

Describing Aemilius Paullus' big event after defeating Perseus of Macedonia in 167, Plutarch has him begin in grand style, sailing to Rome in Perseus' magnificent galley with sixteen banks of oars (*Aem.* 32.4–34.1). Then:

> The procession being allotted three days, the first hardly sufficed for the captured statues, paintings, and colossal figures, brought along on 250 chariots, which made quite a show. On the next day the finest and costliest of the Macedonian weapons were presented in many wagons [carefully arranged to look terrifying]. ...After the weapon wagons walked 3,000 men carrying coined silver in 750 three-talent [80-kg, 276-lb] containers, each carried by four men; others had silver wine-bowls, drinking horns, bowls, and cups. ... On the third day ... came those bringing the gold coin, distributed in three-talent containers like the silver, though the number of these containers was only 77. ... Following all these were the chariot and the weapons of Perseus, and his diadem sitting on top of his weapons. ... Behind the children and their attendants walked Perseus himself. ...

After the bar had been raised even higher by the monumental triumphs of Pompey and Augustus, first-century emperors understandably felt perform-ance anxiety. Their withdrawal of triumphs from field commanders who might become rivals, politically necessary though this was, placed enormous pressure on themselves. Each man had to appear supremely deserving of all the honour he was hoarding. But what could a serving emperor triumph *for*? Going to war could get him killed. Second-century emperors would decide they had no choice but to become a "fellow-soldier" if they hoped to keep the army's loyalty and pre-empt challenge from popular commanders,[55] but the Julio-Claudians had not yet embraced this reality. Tiberius had commanded

---

[55] Campbell 1984: 49–55, 65–69.

armies before coming to power (A.D. 14) and triumphed as Augustus' heir,[56] but not as emperor. In A.D. 17 he (via the Senate) awarded his nephew Germanicus a triumph, merely for crossing the Rhine and recovering a legionary standard from the Germans. Germanicus had to withdraw without securing any new territory.[57] Tacitus' account of the "triumph" is sardonic:[58] a few prisoners and some spoils, yes, but mostly arts and crafts (*simulacra*) made in Rome. Creative artists were summoned to portray Germany's mountains and rivers and the battles over there to impress the home audience. Although Germanicus had not won an actual war, the triumph said otherwise and that was all anyone needed to know (*Ann.* 2.42). Concerning Claudius and Britain, similarly, Suetonius remarks that although the emperor's personal involvement was negligible (*modicam*), he triumphed with all possible dazzle (*maximo apparatu, Claud.* 17.1–2).

Mary Beard has shown both how problematic the triumphal ritual is for us, because we know so little, and how ironic the ordeal could be for Roman observers, who knew too much. She describes widespread murmuring about these great parades, fuelled in part by the shenanigans alleged of certain emperors:

> According to Suetonius, to celebrate his triumph over the Germans, Caligula planned to dress up some Gauls to impersonate *bona fide* German prisoners. . . . [H]e was going to get them to dye their hair red, learn the German language, and adopt German names. . . . Much the same story is told of the triumphs of Domitian, but he is credited also with a bright idea for the fake spoils: according to Dio, he raided the palace furniture store.[59]

Beard's book is a tonic against the "glory that was Rome" tradition. I demur on two points, which are small in the context of her comprehensive study but important for us. First, she associates triumphal fakery with such "transgressive" emperors as Gaius and Domitian, whereas I shall argue that the triumph of the highly respected Vespasian and Titus was basically an exercise in deception and misdirection. Second, she takes Josephus to be a well-fed Flavian apparatchik, shilling for the regime on their big day, whereas I shall argue that Josephus was fully alert to Flavian sham. When Domitian paid for his make-believe triumph in the early 80s (Dio 67.7.4), in other words, he was taking a page from the

---

[56] Suetonius, *Tib.* 20–21.

[57] Tacitus, *Ann.* 1. 1.55 (the award of a triumph came early, before Germanicus had launched a second campaign and recovered another standard); 2.26, 41; Suetonius, *Cal.* 1.1; Velleius Paterculus 2.129.2.

[58] See also Beard 2007: 109–10.

[59] Beard 2007: 185–86. The Caligula story is in Suetonius, *Gaius* 45–49. He did not fight, except in mock combat with his own soldiers; he allegedly had them collect sea-shells for his triumphant return. Cf. Dio 67.6–9 on Domitian.

family playbook.[60] The same people who produced *Flavian Triumph I: Judaea* were on hand for *Flavian Triumph II: Germany*, and sequels are rarely as good as the originals.

Josephus' triumph account

The only surviving description of the Flavian triumph resides in the last book of Josephus' *War* (7.121–57). Nearly every historian who has written about that event has inferred from circumstantial evidence – after all, Josephus was preserved and housed by the Flavians – that his account delivers the regime perspective.[61] Some doubt that he was even present for the parade itself, suggesting that he dutifully copied an official source.[62] This is not the place to retry Josephus on the old Flavian-lackey charge.[63] Even Martin Goodman, though he shares the general view today that the *War* hardly answers to the needs of imperial propaganda, finds the triumph narrative disconcertingly Roman – out of step with the rest of the work.[64] By contrast, I shall anticipate Chapter 2 and argue that the triumph episode bears the stamp of Josephus' perspective on Rome throughout the *War*, which may be roughly character-ized as resigned skepticism and gentle irony. We could only view Josephus' account of the triumph as a Flavian statement if we detached it from the body that gives it its life and meaning. He did not expect his audience to begin reading or listening in the last book.

Read as part of the work, the passage suggests a certain bemusement. A sense of awe too, no doubt. This *was* a once-in-a-generation spectacle, and everybody loves a parade. But foreign visitors could gush over the 2008 Beijing Olympics, not to mention their 1936 precursor in Nazi Berlin,

---

[60] See Jones 1992: 50–71, qualifying an older view (based in Dio 67.2.1–3) that Domitian repudiated his brothers' and fathers' friends. Jones shows that virtually all the senators and equestrians known to have been close to Vespasian and Titus remained in place, although Domitian installed his own domestic staff of powerful freedmen.

[61] Weber 1921: 282–83; Künzl 1988: 9–29 (9: Josephus stood "already on the side of the Romans and no longer on that of his people"); Itgenshorst 2005: 28–29; Beard 2003: 543, 556 ("we are probably getting as close as we ever can to the 'official version'"), 558 (Josephus was "besotted with the Flavians").

[62] Weber 1921: 282–83; Michel-Bauernfeind 1969: 2.2: 242; Künzl 1988: 14–15; Itgenshorst 2005: 26–27.

[63] The old view was mostly a creation of the early twentieth century. Telling blows were landed by Lindner 1972, and the *coup de grace* came (in principle) with Rajak 1983 and Bilde 1988. See also Mason 1991: 55–75; 2003a, 2003b; Barclay 2006; den Hollander 2014: esp. 68–138. The tendency of Josephus scholarship in the past two or three decades has been to emphasize the differences between his outlook and that of the regime, but the only study of the triumph I know from this general perspective is Eberhardt 2005.

[64] Goodman 2007: 445 ("the description of the ceremony is remarkable for its consistently Roman viewpoint") and 452.

without admiring the sponsors.[65] As a statesman and practised dissembler himself, Josephus must have recognized the need of the Flavians and a pliant Senate to manipulate the masses. He and his peers had done much the same in Judaea and Galilee, routinely giving the people what they wanted in practised forms of deception. What else was one to do with an untutored and impulsive mob: reason with them? Teach them truths they could not handle? The notion that political leaders *ought* to tell the truth to the masses was far from the ancient horizon. Josephus' self-assigned literary task in Rome, as a Judaean nobleman and historian, was to tell the moral truth about what had really happened over there, for audiences experienced in such political complexities. His avowedly Judaean account is unavoidably at cross purposes with the agendas of Vespasian and Titus at certain points (see Chapter 2). There is no reason to suppose that Vespasian and Titus would have minded, however, unless they believed their own propaganda. He was only disclosing what every informed person knew.

Nearly half of his *War* by weight (Books 1–2) is a detailed account of Judaean-Roman relations from their origins, beginning with the alliances initiated by the brave Hasmoneans in the glory days of the Roman Republic (1.38, 48). Josephus dwells there on the conquests of Jerusalem by Pompey (1.127–58) and Sosius, the latter forming the central event of Book 1 (1.327–57). He details the close friendship between King Herod (37–4 B.C.) and Augustus and the continuing friendships between Herod's descendants and subsequent emperors, the current examples being Agrippa II and Berenice with Claudius and Vespasian/Titus.[66] The Judaean pair were well known in Josephus' Rome: Agrippa II received the ornaments of a praetor, and Berenice was Titus' lover around the time Josephus was writing.[67] Not only did the Flavians not *conquer* Judaea, his narrative makes clear, but the nation has never been opposed to Rome. The origin of the recent conflict is a complicated story, which takes him seven volumes to explain.

In his account of the triumphal spectacle in his final volume, Josephus' bemusement is detectable in various barbs, but especially in the pervasive

[65] E.g., the *Western Morning News* of Devon, UK (Sat. 1 Aug. 1936, p. 9): "Berlin's Olympic Games Fervour, Herr Hitler to Perform Opening Ceremony, Great Spectacle." Cf. the *Aberdeen Journal* (3 August 1936, p. 6): "Signor Mussolini has endeavoured to give architectural expression to the spirit of Fascist Italy in the magnificent new public buildings that have been erected in Rome. . . . Herr Hitler's counterpart is the wonderful arena in the no less wonderful Olympic Village near Berlin. . . . The pomp of ceremonial and the perfection of the arrangements are the new Germany's gestures *to a watching and watchful world*. . . . Jews will be received without question or distinction on account of their race" (emphasis added). The moral reflections that follow do not detract from the clear sense of awe.
[66] *War* 2.178–87, 204–20, 223, 245, 252, 335–37, 406, 420–21, 500–502; 3.29, 443, etc.
[67] Suetonius, *Tit.* 7.1–2; Dio 65/66.15.3–5.

language of "manufacture, creation, production, fashioning, adornment, [*Roman*] expense, and cover." Rather than displaying captured kings, armies, and treasures as the triumph expects, this procession screams out "Made in Rome." Impressive though it is in an age of no triumphs, this is not the old Republican sort of triumph but one of the new Potemkin type. It is a political necessity, though, for establishing the new dynasty. Let us walk through Josephus' account, taking special note of the details he brings forward.

1. It is part of *War*'s detached style that Josephus reserves his character's appearances for star turns. He bursts on the scene as a fully formed "general," with no past but entrusted with the command of Galilee (2.562–84), and he remains in focus only as long as he is a brilliant commander and then a gifted seer with occult powers. He all but disappears after his capture, except to deliver a couple of brilliant speeches. His autobiography mentions, however, the honour he enjoyed as Titus' chosen companion on the crossing from Alexandria to Rome (*Life* 422–23). That would explain his claim in *War* about the pleasant voyage and Titus' warm reception in Rome, which he mentions omnisciently (7.119–20). He was evidently on hand, and he may have been consulted for Judaean realia as the parade was being staged. Where he sat during the procession itself is an intriguing question.[68] A reserved seat in the bleachers of the Circus Maximus seems more likely than either walking with the humiliated captives or accompanying the Roman conquerors and dignitaries. But we have no idea.

2. Surely he did not need to fight for a spot with the unwashed. He relates (7.122):

> When the day for the procession that would follow on their victories was announced beforehand, none of the countless rabble in the city was left at home. They all went out ahead of time, determined to find places to stand. These they secured, leaving only the narrowest possible thoroughfare for what they were about to watch.

Matching Plutarch's comment that security guards had to keep a space clear for Aemilius' parade (*Aem.* 32.3), this also conveys Josephus' typical disdain for the crowd. It is not a hostile view exactly, but more pitying: The common people are *so* predictable, lacking dignity and driven by impulsive response-mechanisms. One scholar has estimated that 300,000 to 400,000 might have turned out for the Flavian parade.[69] That could be. Anyone aged 30 or younger in the summer of A.D. 71 could have had no memory of this

---

[68] Scholars of the triumph who have taken Josephus' silence about vantage-point as evidence of absence from the triumph (e.g., Weber 1921: 246, 283; Michel-Bauernfeind 1969: 2.2: 242; Künzl 1988: 14–15; Itgenshorst 2005: 26–27) do not reckon with the same phenomenon throughout *War*.

[69] Künzl 1988: 72.

quintessentially Roman ritual. It *was* an extraordinary event. Josephus' observation also drives home that the biddable populace was the main audience for an event calculated to bond the people, army, and Senate with the new rulers.

3. His potentially sharpest barb comes just before this line, where he remarks that the Senate offered separate triumphs to father and son, but they opted for a joint affair (7.121). This sounds just like humility. But a moment's thought leads one to ask: How would a separate triumph for Vespasian have looked? Most everything mentioned in their shared triumph came from Titus' achievement after Vespasian had left the region: the temple furnishings, prisoners from Jerusalem, and even the chief culprits Simon and John. According to Josephus, Vespasian faced only one significant adversary in Galilee: himself. Otherwise, the old soldier dealt with some unpleasantness in eastern Galilee and the Golan on behalf of Agrippa II (Chapter 6) and burned a number of villages as he tightened the cordon around Jerusalem in the south. If Vespasian had triumphed alone, would he have exhibited wagonloads of Dead Sea bitumen? Pliny made much of the balsam trees (see chapter head), but greatly valued though it was, balsam was not quite up to the standard of great triumphs. Did he uproot some date palms for the trip to Rome? Bitumen, dates, and balsam were the region's famous products (Tacitus, *Hist.* 5.6), but these had long been available to Rome from subject Judaea and Idumaea.[70] Josephus even remarks that Vespasian *prided himself above all* on the temple spoils, which he would later put on permanent display in his Forum of Pax, after taking some home (*War* 7.161). But that was all Titus' work.

The joint triumph seems not to have been so much a generously shared event, therefore, as it was the father's co-opting of the son's accomplishments. Vespasian as regime founder needed the good stuff, and so he must have been relieved to be able to parade with Titus. Still it was all they could do *together* to fill a single day with their haul, in contrast to Aemilius, Pompey, or Augustus.

4. Describing the forming up of the army before the parade, Josephus writes (7.123):

> While it was still night, the entire soldiery had proceeded out in their companies and ranks and under their commanders, around the gates – not those of the palaces above but rather [the gates] near the Temple of Isis, because that is where the imperators were staying during that night.

This incidental reference to the Temple of Isis, part of a compound in the Field of Mars that included a matching Temple of Serapis, has seemed implausible to many historians because of its non-Roman air. Some have proposed that the soldiers assembled near the Temple of Isis because the

---

[70] Cf. Virgil, *Georg.* 3.12 (with M. Servius Honoratus, *In Virg. Georg.* 3.12.1, 4); Martial, *Ep.* 10.50.1; Silius Italicus 3.600; 7.456.

Flavians were also staying *near there*.[71] That would be a strangely elliptical way to write. The natural reading, identifying the Egyptian sanctuary as their overnight accommodation, makes better sense. Scholars who have accepted that much have usually traced the curious choice to Vespasian's gratitude for Domitian's escape from Vitellius' forces by dressing as a priest of Isis.[72] That may be right, although it is difficult to see how an observer of the event would have caught such a specific allusion from the many possibilities.

The Isis cult was enormously popular at the time, as temples in Rome and well-preserved specimens in Pompeii, Libyan Sabratha, and elsewhere show. More generally, such evocations of Egypt as pyramids and obelisks appeared throughout the city from the time of Augustus. The cult of Isis had its ups and downs – enthusiastic patronage by Gaius Caligula not helping. The short-lived emperor Otho was rumoured to be a devotee.[73] But Vespasian and Titus had strong and specific connections with Egypt and its cults.[74] The legions of that province had acclaimed Vespasian emperor long before the Roman civil war was settled (*War* 4.617), and Egypt's prefect, Tiberius Julius Alexander, would serve as Titus' executive officer, with a force that also included thousands of legionaries based in Egypt (5.46).[75] The most important omens of imperial honour had occurred in Egyptian temple settings, and Vespasian may have been personally initiated in the Egyptian cult of Serapis.[76] Egypt was a critical source of grain and other goods for Rome, and Vespasian resided there for about a year after he left Judaea, precisely to secure it as a base of power. Titus also lingered there, for a shorter time, pausing to offer a traditional Egyptian sacrifice in Memphis before returning home.[77] When we recall that Vespasian would produce coins featuring this Temple of Isis, in a coin programme that was overwhelmingly triumphal,[78] we can hardly avoid connecting the coins and the overnight stay with larger Egyptian themes and overtones in the triumph.

In short, Judaea was being presented to Romans as the anchor of a much larger, albeit rather vague, *eastern* settlement.[79] Romans tended to imagine a close ethnic relationship between Judaeans and Egyptians anyway.[80] In putting

---

[71] E.g., Zaho 2004: 16. See Beard 2007: 95–96, discussing the hypothesis that they actually stayed in the unnamed *villa publica* complex, a more spacious area where foreign visitors were sometimes housed.

[72] The story is told by Suetonius, *Dom.* 1.2; cf. Tacitus, *Hist.* 3.73. This is Beard's preferred explanation (2007: 95).

[73] See Köberlein 1962 (on Gaius, generally thought to have built the Isaeum on the Campus Martius, though Barrett 1989: 219–22); Roullet 1972: 37–52; Bricault and Leclant 2001; Bricault, Versluys, and Meyboom 2007; Bricault 2013.

[74] Levick 1999: 69, 228 n. 14.   [75] Turner 1954: 62–64.   [76] See Curran 2007: 86–88.

[77] See Suetonius, *Vesp.* 7; *Tit.* 5.   [78] E.g., the coin ref. 1852,0609.1 in the British Museum.

[79] Agreeing with Curran 2007: 85–91, by a very different route.

[80] E.g., Diodorus 1.28.2–3, 55.5; Tacitus, *Hist.* 5.2–3 (trans. Clifford H. Moore): "Some hold that in the reign of Isis the superfluous population of Egypt, under the leadership of Hierosolymus and Iuda, discharged itself on the neighbouring lands; many others think that

it about that they had sewn up the Egyptian half of the empire, enjoying the favour of Egypt's deities in the process, the Flavians were insinuating themselves further into the company of Augustus (with Egypt) and Pompey (with Syria) as the men who had handled the eastern menace.

5. If their choice of accommodation was a calculated innovation, Josephus presents the rest of the morning's preliminaries as reassuringly Roman (7.124–31). Whatever Vespasian and Titus were doing overnight in the Isis compound, they emerge early in the morning dressed in the traditional purple robes with gold-leaf laurel crowns, and this is how they receive the appropriate greetings from the city's senators and equestrians. Sitting on the traditional ivory chairs of senior magistrates (the *sella curulis*), they accept the time-honoured acclamation as conquering generals (*imperatores*) from the soldiers present. They offer customary prayers in the standard posture, toga drawn up over the head. Vespasian gives a "brief talk" – as a true Roman and man of few words, not like that Greekling Nero – before giving the soldiers breakfast while he and Titus continue with customary sacrifices by the renowned Triumphal Gate. From there the procession will cross the sacred threshold and move through the city's public heart via unidentified theatres (7.131). The Circus Maximus could seat about a fifth of the population, and Josephus' Roman audiences would have assumed that it was a prime viewing spot.[81]

A modern reader of Josephus' entire *War* must be struck by the rupture between this very conservative performance on the part of Vespasian and Titus, so redolent of great past triumphs, and the story that the Judaean author has been telling. The commanders now thank every God *except* the one who, they know according to Josephus, gave them their victory. Josephus makes it a theme that the Judaean God used the Romans to purge his temple, a feat they could not have accomplished otherwise.[82] Just a few paragraphs before this account, Titus himself, after getting a close look at Jerusalem's mammoth walls and towers, confesses: "God was the one who brought the Judaeans down from such defences, for what could human hands or machines have achieved against these towers?" (*War* 6.411). Yet here he is in Rome, conveniently forgetting all that for the sake of the necessary show. Having told his own truth at length, Josephus does not need to stop at each point to say "Now of course *that's* not right." His writings give every indication that he understands political

they [Judaeans] were an Egyptian stock, which in the reign of Cepheus was forced to migrate by fear and hatred." On Tiberius' expulsion of "the Egyptian and Judaean worship," see Tacitus, *Ann.* 2.85; Suetonius, *Tib.* 36; with Seneca, *Ep.* 108.

[81] See Millar 2005: 103–7. For the Circus Maximus, Dodge 1999: 237. She estimates that with Trajan's later renovations the Circus could seat 350,000 (a third of the estimated population), in the Flavian period perhaps half that number.

[82] E.g., *War* 2.390; 3.293, 351; 4.366, 370; 5.19, 39, 278, 343, 368, 378, 396–98; 6.38, 101, 110, 371, 399; 7.319, 323, 333.

necessity. This is what the Flavians had to do. But their show has little connection with what (they know) really happened.

6. Given *War*'s detailed history of Judaea as a long-held Roman territory in Books 1 and 2, the next part of the triumph is particularly interesting. What will Vespasian and Titus do for the mounds of foreign plunder that are supposed to front the procession? Josephus is duly impressed by the display produced, but this is not because he recognizes it from Judaea. He cannot say: "Oh look: the silver plate from the high priest's residence," or "See the gold from Sepphoris and jewels from Tiberias!" Instead he turns vague and repetitive, declaring how "amazing and expensive" and "rare" the exhibited stuff is (7.133–37, 140). But what *is* it?

His covering statement is that the Flavians put on display "the vastness of the Roman *imperium*" (7.133). Heading the parade were "silver, gold, and elephant [i.e., ivory], *fashioned* in every kind of way" (7.135), "woven carpets in the rarest purple ... and vividly accurate representations, embroidered in the Babylonian technique" (7.134). Then came precious translucent stones, some set in gold crowns (7.135). This language suggests broadly eastern themes. "Accurate representation" of either human or animal life was certainly not a Judaean trait, because it was taken to violate one of their most distinctive laws – a point he has made repeatedly.[83] Are these *Judaean* spoils at all, then? There is no good reason to think so. He has mentioned *one* Babylonian-style curtain in Jerusalem, hanging before the temple sanctuary (5.212–14), as a one-off wonder, but *many* such curtains are on display here. The diaphanous stones are particularly intriguing (7.135). Ancient authors use that expression (λίθοι διαφανεῖς) for pearls or topaz, which they associate not with landlocked Judaea but with the Red Sea and points east.[84]

The gold crowns evoke the luxury of eastern potentates, or perhaps Roman largesse, not the scenes of Flavian prowess in rural Galilee or Peraea or the capital Jerusalem. Josephus has mentioned gold crowns five times, but mostly when describing gifts of Roman provenance.[85] The only Judaeans who might own such crowns, the Herodian royals, were already close friends of the Flavians and allies in the war.[86] If their jewels were on display, it would have been a friendly loan for the occasion. Josephus does not even suggest that the

---

[83] *War* 1.649–59; 2.5–13, 170–71, 185–95.

[84] Theophrastus, *Lap.* 36; Agatharchides, *Mari eryth.* 96; Strabo, *Geog.* 16.4.6; Athenaeus, *Deipn.* 3.45 [Kaibel].

[85] Sosius dedicates one to the temple (*War* 1.357). The deceased King Herod is laid out with crown, diadem, and sceptre (1.671). Josephus notes that the headgear of the high priest included a sort of gold crown (5.235). The Parthian king Vologaeses presents Titus with a gold crown (7.105). Multiple gold crowns appear only when Titus distributes them to his soldiers – along with spears, standards, and other Roman ornaments of victory (7.14).

[86] *War* 2.181–82, 206–15; 3.29, 443–45; 4.498–500; cf. Dio 65/66.15.

jewel-encrusted specimens come from Jerusalem. Anyway, it seems that no monarchs were harmed in their appropriation.

Also catching is his repeated reference to "elephant" (ἐλέφας 7.136, 141, 151), not the derivative for "ivory," which he uses for the ivory chairs (above) but the whole beast for the part. This again suggests general eastern-exotic realms rather than elephant-free Judaea. He encourages the surmise that the parade organizers scavenged whatever they could to dazzle Rome's populace, who were neither art critics nor historians.

7. Next come "statues of their Gods, amazing in size and *of formidable craft*, not one of them lacking *an expensive covering* of some kind" (7.136), accompanied by "animals of many kinds," lavishly decked out and accompanied by attendants in *rich costume*. "Their Gods" invites a satirical reflection. The supposedly divine beings are carefully fashioned and richly accessorized (οὐ παρέργως πεποιημένα . . . ἧς ὕλης τῆς πολυτελοῦς). The honour bestowed on these pint-size productions contradicts everything that *War*'s reader knows about what really happened at the Judaean God's omnipotent orchestration.

The animals are a puzzle. Josephus does not explain whether they are supposed to represent rare and exciting wildlife from Judaea or locally recruited victims of the usual kind for the coming sacrifices (7.155). "Many kinds" might suggest the former, but Judaea lacked exotic beasts to compete with those that Romans could see in frequent entertainments: elephants, giraffes, hippos, bears, crocodiles, and so on.[87] On the restored Arch of Titus, high up beneath the architrave that has largely survived on the east face, is a small frieze depicting this part of the procession. It includes many animals, although not many *kinds,* not even the traditional Roman trio of boar, ram, and bull. They all seem to be bulls or oxen headed for sacrifice, with decorative banners draped over them. Their attendants are half-naked and wield axes. Every part of this looks to be from Rome.[88] Josephus' emphasis is on the dress-up (κοσμέω) involved, especially that of the attendants in their expensive purple laced with gold – a Roman contrivance for the occasion and not from Judaea.

In the same vignette comes the mass of Judaean prisoners, also "fully decorated" (οὐδὲ . . . ἀκόσμητον). Josephus reflects that their attractive clothing together with their personal beauty "concealed from sight the ugliness of the injuries on their bodies" (7.138). We should not miss the pathos here, for the preceding story explains just who these prisoners were. After Jerusalem's

---

[87] Livy 39.22; 44.18; Pliny, *Nat.* 8.96.

[88] See Pfanner 1983: plates 79–87 (*kleiner Fries*). Detail of this small frieze below the architrave is clearer in S. P. Bartoli's seventeenth-century engraving (Bartoli and Bellori 1685: *Arco di Tito, Pompa Trionfale* plates 1–4, http://bellori.sns.it/bellori//TOC_1.html). Note the river-god carried on a *ferculum* and sacrificial bulls with attendants.

fall, Titus allowed his soldiers to kill and plunder for several days. Only when they were "tired of slaughtering" did he order thousands of enemy survivors to be corralled in the temple's Court of Women. The soldiers were now instructed to kill only those who resisted, while carefully preserving the youngest and fittest for Roman use (6.414–15). Titus entrusted the portfolio to his friend Fronto, who found grim ways to quietly lighten his burden, while dutifully saving "the tallest and most attractive for the triumph" (6.417). From this group Titus made a final selection of 700 for the voyage to Rome (7.118; cf. 36). We may be confident, from antecedent probability and Josephus' notices alike, that these men were maltreated at every point, apart from wounds they may have sustained in combat. Josephus emphasizes again that the triumph was an exercise in image-making and the concealment of simpler truth.

8. But the most spectacular cover-up comes next (7.139–47):

> What produced the greatest amazement was *the construction* that held up the scaffolds, for on account of their size there was alarm over the unconvincing stability of the foundation. Many of them *had been built* to three or even four storeys in height, and the *luxuriousness of the construction* was *intended to generate pleasure* – albeit mixed *with terror*. On many of them were *woven carpets* laced with gold, and all *were framed in carefully wrought* gold and elephant [ivory].
>
> Through several *representations* [possibly counterfeits: διὰ πολλῶν δὲ μιμημάτων; cf. Latin *simulacra*], the war, now all divided up into segments, *produced a vivid spectacle of itself*, running from one scene to the next. *On display* were: a prosperous countryside being ravaged; entire phalanxes of the enemy being killed, some running away and some being taken captive; walls of great height and thickness being wrecked by machines; the strongest of fortresses being stormed; the most populous city compounds on the tops of hills being seized; an army pouring inside walls; every place filled with slaughter; the hands of the impotent raised in supplication; fire engulfing temples; the destruction of houses on top of their owners; and after much wasteland and gloom, rivers flowing – not over cultivated land, or as drink for man or beast [i.e., they had been in the past], but through a land aflame on every side.

Josephus makes clear the scale of contrivance and production. The regime's people have created a show for the masses, with gigantic picture-books. Their clear message dovetails with the inscription on the Circus arch mentioned above: Titus and his armies did what no one else had, dominating this alien enemy. The whole picture contradicts Josephus' narrative at every point (Chapter 2).

Josephus' literary audience, who are men of affairs and cognoscenti, must know or strongly suspect this. From his descriptions in *War* 2–6, if nowhere else, they should understand that the rivers criss-crossing the Judaean countryside, populous hilltop cities, varied fortresses (the desert fortresses had not yet been part of the fighting; Chapter 9), and varied sacred sites are imaginary. In Josephus' main geographical excursus (3.35–58), the only river is the Jordan, which marks Judaea's eastern edge and plays no role in the war (3.51). The Flavians made a great deal of rivers, however, as we shall see. In Josephus' account, the closest parallel to an army's "pouring over the walls" of a hilltop city comes in the siege of Gamala (*War* 4.19–38). But there, when legionaries indeed pour over the walls, at the *misguided* direction of Vespasian, they face catastrophe before Titus arrives to rescue them (4.70–71). It is they, not Judaeans, who find themselves caught on collapsing rooftops and die in the rubble. And the notion that Roman machines could have wrecked Jerusalem's wall has just been dismissed by Titus himself (6.411).

If the triumphal portrait does not mirror the real conflict in Judaea, it does fit neatly with the recommended way of portraying a captured city in art. According to Quintilian, Vespasian's favoured teacher of rhetoric, one is entitled to take liberties in elaborating the kinds of things that *always* happen when cities are taken, in order to move an audience: "flames will appear spreading over houses and temples, and the crash of falling roofs . . . there will be wailing of women and children . . . the pillaging of sacred and profane treasures, the hurrying of the plunderers back and forth."[89] Perhaps Quintilian advised on the triumph.

Pure inventions too are "entire phalanxes of the enemy." In Josephus' *War*, as in any conceivable reality, the Judaeans are prudent enough not to face legionary columns in battlefield array. Not being a foreign power with an army, they have no Macedonian phalanxes or Parthian cavalry. It is true that Josephus, aggrandizing his role as Galilean general, claims to have recruited a force of 100,000 (2.576–84). But the claim is absurd, and even he seems quickly to forget about it. This crack force vanishes even before the Flavians' arrival (Chapter 6). Otherwise, the very few Judaean rebels who fight do so guerrilla-style, raiding and ambushing and mainly retreating to inaccessible caves or walled towns or fortresses. The Flavians' production team have dreamed up the wrong war. But facts are not their concern, and those who know the facts (including Josephus) understand the programme.

Another curiosity is Josephus' remark that on top of each scaffold, perhaps 9–12 m (30–40 ft) high on unstable structures, "was stationed the general of the captured city – in the manner in which he was taken" (7.147). Who *are* these men? No cities with generals come up in Josephus' account of the Flavian campaign. Their toughest site before the siege of Jerusalem, aside from his own redoubt in Galilee's Iotapata, is Gamala in the territory of Agrippa II

[89] Quintilian, *Inst.* 8.3.67–70. Cf. Chapter 7 for Josephus' own parallels with Quintilian's prescriptions.

(Chapter 6). But Josephus insists that Gamala's rebel leaders died there with nearly the whole population (4.65–69, 81–83). Galilee as a whole falls rapidly and without notable fighting, aside from Iotapata, and those unlucky enough to be caught in postures of resistance died. Josephus himself survived only through a unique string of lucky circumstances (Chapter 2). In Judaea proper, by his account, the Flavian army rampaged more or less at will, finding most towns empty except for those unable to flee – women, children, and aged men, whom the Romans killed or enslaved.[90] That leaves only Jerusalem. But Simon and John, the two leaders caught in the besieged capital and held chiefly responsible, do not seem to have been set atop the floats (cf. 7.154). The only other *generals* in the story – King Agrippa, regional kings, Tiberius Alexander, and legionary commanders – worked with Vespasian and Titus.

Josephus' language suggests that these generals up on the scaffolds were live human beings, in stress positions that do not bear thinking about. Perhaps they were prisoners forced to play enemy general for a day. But other triumphs depicted generals artistically, in capture-poses,[91] and Josephus' words could conceivably mean that each float was topped by the *image* of a supposed general. The whole production would then be a sort of cartoon, without the complications of living actors.[92]

The most flagrant mismatch between Josephus' triumphal representation and his account comes in the Flavians' portrait of total legionary domination, with Judaeans running in fear or begging for mercy. Because that is the image we also see on the coins (below), we have good reason to believe that it was a theme of the triumph. But again it contradicts one of Josephus' root themes: the Judaeans' innate courage, resourcefulness, and contempt for death, by means of which they regularly upset the legions (Chapter 2).

If doubt remains about the fabricated nature of the triumph as Josephus presents it, the "large number of ships" should settle the matter (7.147). Pompey and Augustus had won great naval battles, but landlocked Judaea was not suited for that kind of thing. Vespasian would nevertheless produce coins featuring Victory on the prow of a ship, with the legend *Victoria Navalis*. Assuming that the triumph's producers had some sense of reality, scholars have imagined that these coin motifs must allude to Vespasian's control of the sea

---

[90] *War* 4.440–50, 486–90, 550–55 with Chapter 7.

[91] Appian, *Mithr.* 117, on Pompey's depiction of his deceased enemies in fighting pose, as beaten, and then as running away.

[92] The Greek reads (7.147): τέτακτο δ᾽ ἐφ᾽ ἑκάστῳ τῶν πηγμάτων ὁ τῆς ἁλισκομένηςπόλεως στρατηγὸς ὃν τρόπον ἐλήφθη. The first verb (τάσσω) is naturally taken to mean that an actual "general" was stationed or assigned there. But it can mean, in artistic and literary contexts, to position the elements of a composition (2.130; *Ant.* 1.30; 4.197; *Apion* 2.148). Given the fabricated scenes on the floats otherwise (7.139–46), the truncated final phrase ("what manner he was taken"), and the other issues mentioned, we must wonder whether the generals are also artistic creations.

lanes from Alexandria, which cut off Vitellius' supplies.[93] But that would not easily explain ships in the triumph against the foreign enemy in Judaea, and we should prefer to explain similar evidence in the same way if we can.[94] The small frieze on the arch beneath the architrave depicts a river-god image, seeming to confirm that the Flavians made an issue of naval victory in the Judaean War itself.[95]

Josephus mentions only one waterborne conflict, on the Sea of Galilee (Kinneret). Rebels against King Agrippa II had fled from Taricheae in boats. Vespasian ordered his men to build rafts and pursue them. The day ended in a slaughter of the fugitives (3.497–31). Explaining S. P. Bartoli's engraving of the river-god tableau, the seventeenth-century antiquarian G. P. Bellori assumed that it represented this battle (or slaughter) on the Kinneret, through which the Jordan River flowed, given the ships in the triumph and the later coins. It is hard to disagree with his thinking.[96] To look more Pompeian-Augustan, it seems, the Flavians either greatly magnified the lopsided lake skirmish or simply fabricated a real naval victory.[97] Either way, it is hard to imagine where the ships – prows? – on display in Rome came from. Local manufacture or expropriation is infinitely more likely than the salvage and transport of Galilean fishing boats.

9. The only components of the parade that Josephus unambiguously connects with Judaea, aside from designer prisoners and got-up generals, are "those that had been abandoned in Jerusalem's temple" (7.148–52), namely: the golden table and lampstand from the inner sanctuary as well as "the Law of the Judaeans." The last may have been donated by Josephus himself.[98] In contrast to his vagueness about other matters, he provides a detailed description of the menorah on display here, its design being so different from lamps in common use. Finally, he reaches items that he well recognizes, to which he feels a close attachment. Whatever preconceptions we may have of our priestly reporter, we must imagine that he felt moved to see these hallowed objects from the temple, the centre of his life and identity, paraded in Rome under such circumstances.

---

[93] Such coins are British Museum specimens, ref. 1913,0614.105, 1929,0716.5, 1929,0716.8, 1930,0407.8, 1931,1006.10, R.10549, R.10550, R.10559, R.10560, R.10668, R.10709. For the proposed explanation see Mattingly and Sydenham 1966: 7.

[94] See Kokkinos 2010: 9–11.   [95] Knight 1896: 73–77.

[96] Bartoli and Bellori: 6 (commentary to Arch of Titus pl. 4): *Tariclaeis ad lacum Genesar navali proelio devictis, simulacrum lacus ipsius in triumpho ducitur. . . . at Iosephus navium rostra tantum in haec pompa exhibita memorat. Extat nummus Titi cum inscriptione VICTORIA NAVALIS.*

[97] Smallwood (1981: 309 n. 65) thinks the naval coinage too abundant to be traceable to "the minor Roman naval action on the Sea of Galilee." This is entirely sensible, but it assumes *their* concern for proportionality and historical truth.

[98] In *Life* 418 Josephus claims that he, when permitted by Titus to seize what he wished from the ruined temple, rescued "sacred volumes."

In this case we have the rare luxury of corroborating an event mentioned by Josephus with material remains, for the Arch of Titus also takes the temple spoils to be the heart of the procession (Fig. 1).[99] Ancient monuments were usually painted in vivid colours, which have since faded to leave the false impression of a stone-coloured world. The Arch of Titus was originally colourful, with the reliefs of the golden furniture painted in a suitably eye-catching hue.[100] When we put together this panel with Josephus' emphasis on the temple furniture and Vespasian's pride in it (7.160–61), as well as the absence of anything Judaean in the small upper frieze, we have reason to suppose that the temple spoils were objectively the highlight of the day. But then, the Flavians' resort to the temple spoils as their main plunder seems pathetic, whether we think in terms of the idea of the triumph or in relation to the practice of other conquerors.

In *War's* ring-compositional structure, many elements in Book 1 find a reprise in Book 7 (cf. Chapter 2). That structure underscores the contrast between Pompey's conquest in Book 1 and the Flavian celebration in Book 7. Pompey reportedly strode into the temple sanctum and saw the gold structures, as well as a very tempting 2,000 talents [52,400 kg, 115,000 lbs] of gold. But Josephus makes clear that *Pompey did not touch these holy items*. On the contrary, he virtuously directed the priests to purify the temple and resume their customary sacrifices (1.152–53). The great general did not need temple furnishings for his triumph, which is not described by Josephus but was famous in Rome, given the embarrassment of riches he took while conquering the whole foreign territory for Rome. Josephus' *War* ascribes Pompey's caution to political wisdom; *Antiquities* explicitly commends his piety (14.72). The later work furnishes a contrast to Pompey in the despicable King Antiochus IV: "he had seen much gold in the temple . . . so he stripped the temple bare and carried off the very vessels of God: the golden lampstand, the golden altar, the table, . . . and did not hold back even from the curtains, which were made of fine linen and scarlet" (*Ant.* 12.149–50). Now, which sort of conqueror do the Flavians resemble?

As soon as he has finished describing the temple furnishings, which are indubitably from Judaea, Josephus quickly reverts to the language of manufacture: "Many people were carrying statues of Victory; everything was *constructed* of elephant [ivory] and of gold." The Roman statues of Victory so prolific in this triumph are endemic also on Flavian coinage (see "coins" below). Last of all come the conquering father and son in their triumphal chariots. Young Domitian "rode alongside, himself magnificently decorated" (7.151–52).

---

[99] For a minute analysis of the spoils depicted, in connection with other evidence also, see Yarden 1991.

[100] A Yeshiva University team led by Steven Fine is using recent technology to recover the colours without further damaging the monument. See Povoledo 2012.

It was a day of unstinting expense and decoration, then, a remarkable show put on by Senate and palace, for which all the available chariots, purple, and gold in Rome were pulled out of the storerooms. The city's artisans must have worked furiously. With the notable exception of the temple spoils, however, the production had little to do with Judaea, and nothing to do with the addition of new territory.

10. "Now the end [or goal] of the procession," Josephus writes (7.153–54):

> was at the shrine of Capitoline Jupiter. Having reached that point they stopped, for it was an ancient tradition to remain there until someone announced the death of the enemy general. This was Simon son of Giora. Having been in the procession among the captives, at that point – after being covered with a harness and being tortured by those who were leading him – he was dragged to the spot in the Forum: it is a law with the Romans that this is where they kill those condemned to death for criminality. When it was announced that he had met his end, everyone shouted for joy and the sacrifices began.

The other 700 Judaean prisoners, including John of Gischala, will not be killed today. Simon's ritual death is the cue for jubilant banqueting, inaugurating the new Flavian era of peace (7.153–57).

Read as part of Josephus' story, the Flavians' choice of Simon as enemy general is a shrewd one. In the narrative he is anything but a representative Judaean: a nogoodnik of the first water, hated by everyone, and not even from Jerusalem. A callous troublemaker by nature, he brutally handles everyone he meets: distinguished Judaeans, innocent villagers of Idumaea and Samaria, Cestius Gallus' legion, or Zealots in Jerusalem. The *sicarii* of Masada keep him at arm's length.[101] The only reason Simon is able to enter Jerusalem is that desperate Jerusalemites, suffering horribly under another interloper from outside, consider him the only poison strong enough to neutralize John from Galilee. To their horror, however, they end up with two tyrants (Chapter 7). One would surmise from Josephus that he and most other surviving Judaeans – including the other rebels – would have danced at Simon's demise. For all we know, Josephus might have advised Vespasian on this choice.

The selection of Simon as scapegoat underscores the make-believe nature of a triumph supposed to be for the conquest of a foreign people. None of the Judaean elite, from Agrippa II and Berenice to Josephus or the surviving members of the priestly aristocracy, is punished. Simon's death satisfies Roman popular blood-lust and removes a man who would be inconvenient for Judaeans of all types if he remained alive.

---

[101] E.g., *War* 2.521, 652–64; 4.503–44; 5.11, 21, 105, 248–55; 6.114; cf. 7.263–66.

By diverting the residual anxiety from Rome's crippling civil war to an alleged foreign threat, the regime could hope to consolidate loyalties orphaned by the civil war. The Judaean conflict was not ideal for this purpose, but since it was the foreign-ish conflict they had on hand, they pressed it into service. It was left to the outsider Josephus to observe that the triumph actually celebrated both a victory abroad *and* the end to internal evils (*War* 7.157) – which he also recounted at some length (4.491–663). We cannot say that the Flavians' machinations were politically misguided, for they laid the foundation for more than a century of peaceful transition in Roman governance. By any measure, however, their triumph was a *tour de force*.

Monuments

Having met the challenges of the triumph, which required material evidence from abroad, the Flavians and their backers entered a zone of imaginative freedom in crafting more permanent reminders of their achievement. With the buildings and coins they could tell whatever story they pleased. Grand public facilities, monuments, and statues are usually well received, no matter what nonsense motivates them. Coins are needed anyway, and something has to be on them. The new regime had a blank slate for imperial imagination.

Of the monumental buildings issuing from the triumph, the most famous is the 50,000+-seat Flavian Amphitheatre, known since the eighth century as the Colosseum.[102] It was begun by Vespasian, opened by Titus with lavish celebrations in A.D. 80, and completed by Domitian. The famous remains we know today are the result of major restorative work in the early nineteenth century, because the structure had become a teetering danger after centuries of neglect and earthquakes.[103] The silhouette of the restored ruin continues to embody Rome's tourist appeal.

Conservative in its own ways, Rome did not yet have a permanent amphitheatre in 71. According to Suetonius (*Vesp.* 9.1), Vespasian knew that Augustus had hoped to build one and so he realized his predecessor's dream – although Vespasian may have put the dream in Augustus' head posthumously.[104] In any case, this was Rome's first, and an architectural and technical marvel it was. Building began soon after the triumph.[105] The Haterii tomb relief (Fig. 2) and Titus' coins show that the main entrance was surmounted by a triumphal chariot, connecting the building with the dominant theme of victory in Judaea.

---

[102] For a compact introduction to the amphitheatre as a signature Flavian creation, see Sear 1982: 134–45; Panzram 2002: 171–73. Fuller studies include Coarelli and Gabucci 2001; Hopkins and Beard 2005; Welch 2007.
[103] Jokilehto 1999: 77–87.   [104] See Coleman 2002: 69–70.
[105] So the common view. Sear (1982: 134, 139) maintains that it could not have begun until 75.

FIGURE 2. The Haterii tomb relief, showing five Flavian monuments couched in triumphal themes.
Courtesy of Scala/Art Resource, New York (ART145852).

Virtuoso sleuthing by Geza Alföldy in 1994 revealed, to the satisfaction of many scholars, that this Flavian facility originally boasted signs to the effect that it was "[built] from the spoils of war."[106] Alföldy determined this after examining letter-holes beneath a fifth-century inscription. He argued that the original letters were 20 cm (8 in) high and executed in gold-plated bronze, to be unmissable. Although he discovered only one example, which he took to be from the lintel that had stood over the main southern exit, he argued that comparable signs must have surmounted all four main exits. Moreover, because the recovered inscription is terse, abbreviated to fit those small stones, a much larger version must have graced the ampitheatre's central podium.[107] That inscription would have spelled out Titus' honorific titles and gratitude to his father, possibly making fuller mention of the conquest (in Judaea) that had made this construction possible.[108]

Given the boldness of the Flavians' claim, Alföldy concluded straightforwardly that the facility *was* built from the spoils of war, and this has been the general assumption of scholars who agree with his reconstruction.[109] I would urge caution.[110] Political leaders do not always tell the truth. Given that the triumph was fraudulent in fundamental ways, and that a central pillar was the illusion of a wealth-generating foreign conquest, why should we not suspect that any such claims about the great amphiteatre were part of the charade? It is difficult or impossible to imagine that the Flavians funded that magnificent structure with new Judaean spoils – from a remote region of an existing province comprising mainly desert and villages.[111] Perhaps "wealth from Jerusalem" paid for a dressing room or inscription in the facility, and they extrapolated.

[106] See Alföldy 1995: 195–226. Feldman (2001: 20–31, 60) is a glossy and highly readable account. For contextual interpretation, see Millar 2005: 117–19. Hopkins and Beard 2005: 32–34 are among those skeptical of this reading.

[107] Alföldy 1995: 223–26.

[108] The name was reduced to almost coin-like brevity: "Imp. Caes. Vespasianus Aug." Because father and son shared the name Titus Flavius Vespasianus, and the inscription used only *Vespasianus*, Titus' people needed only to cram in a T to update the benefactor (Alföldy 1995: 208–13).

[109] Alföldy (1995: 226): It can "also be understood as a monument to the victims whose tragedy was the cost of this grandeur"; cf. Feldman 2001 (already the title). Cf. Panzram 2002: 171–73. Coleman (2002: 69–70) wonders whether "Jewish prisoners-of-war had provided the staple work-force in the construction of the amphitheatre that was funded by the plunder from their own nation." Josephus' narrative, however, which accounts for the captives in ostensible detail, gives no hint of involvement, although the possibility cannot be excluded. The suggestion may originate, however, with an eighteenth-century visitor who imagined 12,000 Jewish workers (representative of the twelve tribes?) enabling Titus to build the structure in a year; see Linder 2009: 372–73.

[110] Cf. Hopkins and Beard: "*Some* of it [the funding to build], *almost certainly*, [came] from the mass of precious spoils that flowed into Rome ..." (2005: 32, my emphasis), although one must still wonder about the source of this mass.

[111] Hoping to show how Jerusalem's wealth *could have* funded the Colosseum, Coleman (2002: 69–70) cites Josephus' *War* 6.387–91 (a priest and temple treasurer smuggle temple stores for Titus in exchange for their lives: gold, spices, curtains), *War* 5.550 and 6.317 (*soldiers* kill and

We do not know where the Flavians found the resources to rebuild Rome with a verve not seen since Augustus, but the perception of an infusion of Judaean wealth counted more than any reality. Rebuilding the city was partly a practical necessity after the devastation caused by the fire of 64 and especially the civil war. In part it was a political necessity to erase the memory of Nero's tyranny and create the feeling of a secure new dawn. The bare decade of Vespasian's and Titus' reigns (71–81) would not suffice for all the needed construction. Domitian, longest-ruling Flavian (81–96), completed family projects and initiated many of his own. He had to deal with another fire during Titus' reign (80), which destroyed some of the new structures. He showed his devotion to the family business by converting their old residence into a temple-cum-mausoleum of their Flavian *gens*, a grand marble and gold affair dominating the aristocratic neighbourhood near the temple to Quirinus (Romulus).[112]

Domitian completed not only the amphitheatre but also the surviving Arch of Titus, executed in flawless white marble imported from Mt. Pentelikos and Paros in Greece. The structure commemorated his brother's posthumous ascension among the Gods.[113] It was probably topped by a statue assembly in bronze, with Titus driving a triumphal chariot (*quadriga*), perhaps with elephants rather than horses pulling the chariot.[114] The great beasts would have contributed to the general eastern-Egyptian atmosphere.[115] The remarkable thing for us is that, after a decade of Flavian rule and the deaths of the first two

rob refugees before the city's fall and later plunder with abandon), and Qumran's *Copper Scroll* (69: "A mere fraction of the wealth invested in the Temple can be estimated from the stash of Essene treasure"). There are many problems here. No one knows, for example, what the *Copper Scroll* means (Wolters 1990; Brooke and Davies 2002). It purports to be a list of treasures hidden at 64 (or 61) sites, but its date and provenance are unclear (post-70, or utter fantasy, or describing the *first* temple's treasure?), and no one has been able to find the treasure sites—not for lack of trying. Soldiers' plundering should *subtract* from any imperial haul available from Jerusalem. And Coleman's evidence at best reflects the peak potential of the temple treasury, not the situation in late 70 after: the depredations of Nero's procurators, which sparked the revolt; Jerusalem's four-year isolation from its neighbours, brutal civil war, and the legions' encirclement from 68, which all saw the flight of private capital and exhaustion of resources for survival (cf. Chapter 8 on coinage during the revolt); the six-month siege and famine of 70; the likelihood that much of what remained went to bribery or securing food; the burning of the temple, which consumed metal and stone; and the soldiers' plundering of hidden private wealth for some time after the city's fall.

[112] Davies 2004: 24–27 summarizes the evidence for this lost temple.   [113] Davies 2004: 23.

[114] Davies 2004: 22 makes the suggestion in view of a remark by the sixth-century Cassiodorus (*Var.* 10.30.1) that the Ostrogoth king ruling Rome in the 530s ordered the restoration of bronze elephants that were about to fall onto the Sacra Via. Where else would bronze elephants be found in a lofty place along that route?

[115] To be sure, elephants had a wider use in memorial imagery. Titus honoured his deified father on coins showing Vespasian's chariot drawn by elephants with riders (e.g., British Museum coin ref. BNK,R.144 of A.D. 80–81).

Flavians, this arch shows that Judaea remained the family's great achievement and signal testament to Titus' character.

In Republican tradition, the most important monuments to issue from a triumph were temples, vowed by the Roman commander on campaign.[116] Pompey transformed this tradition (55 B.C.) when he erected a huge temple to Venus Victrix (Conqueror) in the Campus Martius. His architects cleverly blended it with Rome's first stone theatre, the seats of which doubled as temple steps. Adjacent was a colonnaded park for viewing the statues and symbols of the nations Pompey had conquered – including Judaea.[117] There is a further Judaean connection in that Pompey's theatre was reportedly built in his name by his rich freedman Demetrius, who came from Gadara (Umm Qais) east of Judaea (Dio 39.38.6). Pompey had restored Gadara after its devastation by Judaea's Hasmoneans (Josephus, *War* 1.155; Chapter 4). That theatre was therefore already a kind of triumphal monument to conquest of Judaea.

In 46 B.C. Julius Caesar started another trend by dedicating a smaller forum with a temple on more expensive land near the central Forum Romanum. Slightly longer than a football field, his Forum Iulium was anchored by a temple to Venus Genetrix, mother of Rome and of his *gens* (Iulian family). Four decades later, Augustus began his reign by ostentatiously restoring eighty-two temples (*RG* 20.4). He complemented Caesar's forum with the nearly adjacent Forum Augustum. Abutting Caesar's on the northeast, Augustus' forum hosted a temple to Mars, God of masculine virtue (*virtus*) and war, here in his aspect as the Avenger (Ultor). Augustus also built a Portico of the Nations, which identified with statues and inscriptions the many nations he now ruled.[118]

Vespasian was not going to fall short on the temple front and undertook at least three projects. First, the duty of rebuilding the Capitoline Temple fell to him. This ancient centre of Roman life and politics had burned in 83 B.C. and was rededicated in 69 B.C.[119] Like Jerusalem's temple, however, it lay in ruins now, reportedly because of accidental fire late in the civil war.[120] Vespasian arranged for its reconstruction while he was still in Egypt. Tacitus describes the elaborate rituals by which the site was purified and consecrated on June 21, A.D. 70 (*Hist.* 4.53). Vestal Virgins and other auspicious groups attended. Sacrifices were performed and gold and silver nuggets were sprinkled into the foundations. When Vespasian returned in the autumn of 70, he personally helped to clear debris and initiated a search for copies of the temple's precious diplomatic records (Suetonius, *Vesp.* 8.5).[121]

---

[116] For example, Camillus after taking Etruscan Veii in 396 B.C., following a ten-year siege (Livy 5.23). For vowed temples in the Republic, see Orlin 2002: 11–75.

[117] Beard 2007: 18–31.   [118] Pliny, *Nat.* 36.39.   [119] See Flower 2008: 74–92.

[120] For the Temple of Jupiter see Tacitus, *Hist.* 3.71–72; Josephus, *War* 4.646–49.

[121] Cf. Josephus, *War* 1.200; 2.216; *Ant.* 12.416; 14.36, 144; 16.48.

Flavian coins proudly picture this rebuilt shrine, with its distinctive six-column front and statues of the divine triad.[122] We do not know when it was finished, perhaps in 75 along with the Temple of Peace.[123] The ill-fated structure burned down again under Titus (A.D. 80), which may have seemed to some Jews divine vengeance, though Domitian's replacement would last nearly four centuries.[124]

Vespasian's second project was the temple for the deified emperor Claudius on the Caelian hill, which had been initiated by Claudius' widow and Nero's mother Agrippina (Suetonius, *Vesp.* 9.1). Vespasian had reasons to honour Claudius. They had shared the consulship of A.D. 51[125] and Vespasian enjoyed a life-long love affair with Caenis, a freedwoman of Claudius' mother Antonia. Titus was raised in Claudius' court with the emperor's son Britannicus and did not forget his friend's untimely death (A.D. 55) – at the hands, it was widely believed, of Nero.[126] Titus' first wife was the daughter of the Praetorian Prefect who had proclaimed Claudius emperor, and Vespasian appointed the same man's son as his Praetorian Prefect.[127] Domitian married the daughter of Corbulo, another Claudian stalwart and victim of Nero.[128] In many ways, then, the consciously old-fashioned reigns of Claudius and Vespasian formed bookends around the fiasco (as they saw it) of Nero,[129] a consideration that might help us think about other personal connections relevant to the Judaean War (Chapter 5). Vespasian's rebuilding of Claudius' temple was a rebuke to Nero's neglect or abuse (Suetonius, *Vesp.* 9.1).

Finally, Vespasian made his own impressive addition to the imperial forums with the Peace Compound (*Forum Pacis*), which he sited as near to Augustus' forum as then seemed practicable. He used the site of Rome's central market-place (*macellum*), which had burned in the great fire (64), creating a new public space in contrast to Nero's hubristic Golden House. Nearly square, about 1.5

[122] E.g., ref. 1872,0709.480 and 1872,0709.480 in the British Museum.

[123] The coins continue through Titus' reign: see Mattingly and Sydenham 1966: 74 no. 496 and 82 no. 577, plate 2 nos. 34 and 37.

[124] Stamper 2005: 151–56.   [125] Gallivan 1978: 409, 414.

[126] Suetonius, *Tit.* 2, confirmed by coins of Titus honouring Britannicus 25 years after his death at 13 (e.g., British Museum coin ref. 1872,0709.447).

[127] Tacitus, *Hist.* 3.66; Suetonius, *Vesp.* 3; *Tit.* 2, 4, 6; cf. Jones 1992: 4–14; Levick 1999: 14–22. The Praetorian Prefects connected with Claudius and Vespasian were both named M. Arrecinus Clemens, and Titus' first wife was Arrecina Tertulla. Although the office of Praetorian Prefect was understood to be for equestrians, Claudius innovated in requesting a Senate seat for another of his, Rufrius Pollio (Dio 60.23.2–3; Talbert 1984: 160). Titus would go much further, as both senator and heir to the throne, in assuming that post through much of the 70s.

[128] Syme 1970b: 38–39. Corbulo had been governor of Lower Germany and proconsul of Asia under Claudius.

[129] E.g., Claudius had revived the old office of Censor in 47/48, and in that capacity had adlected a few men to the Senate. The next adlections come from Vespasian and Titus, who again assume the office of Censor in 73–74 (Talbert 1984: 15).

football fields in length and width, this walled garden was surrounded by colonnades. The temple to Pax was embedded in the outer colonnade, rather than in the centre, which meant that visitors could enjoy unobstructed walks. In this public museum Vespasian displayed works of Greek art from Nero's private collection alongside spoils from Jerusalem, the latter being the ostensible reason for the site.[130]

Augustus had long before made *pax* his governing theme, as his massive Altar of Peace (*Ara Pacis*) reminds us.[131] Vespasian picked up this theme with energy, issuing beautiful *pax* coins in gold and silver, often with the Augustan slogan "[throughout] the circle of the world (*orbis terrarum*)."[132] Peace is accompanied, however, by the Goddesses Victoria and Nemesis, the latter signifying remorseless retribution.[133] There may be a subtle reference here to the civil war, for the cult of Nemesis had been established in Alexandria by Julius Caesar after his defeat of Pompey.[134] At any rate Vespasian's temple to Pax was the *yin* to Mars Ultor's *yang* in the Augustan forum nearby.[135] As Honora Chapman has proposed, the Flavian site might well have acquired a certain sanctity among Jews, even attracting Judaean pilgrims, because of the temple furnishings there.[136]

The restored Arch of Titus in the Forum provides an anchor for our survey of Flavian triumphal construction. John Stamper has pointed out that the bay of this arch was a virtual lens through which the main Flavian projects could be seen in a unifying vision: amphitheatre to the east, Capitol to the west.[137] This unity, grounded in the destruction of Jerusalem, seems to be confirmed by the Haterii tomb relief. In 1848, a richly decorated tomb belonging to a wealthy freedman named Haterius was discovered in Rome. The tomb honoured his departed wife Hateria. A dedicatory inscription names members of the Q. *Haterius* family. Among its various decorative elements, the object of our interest is a panel nearly 1.6 m long (5 ft 2 in) and 42 cm (16.5 in) high, which depicts five monumental structures.[138] This relief dates from the end of Domitian's reign (ca. 90–96), and all five monuments may be Flavian

---

[130] Platner 1929: 220–227, 386–88; Panzram 2002: 173–78; Stamper 2005.

[131] Favro 1996: 129–30, 262–68; Castriota 1995; Rossini 2006.

[132] See the coins ref. 1864,1128.39 andR.10329 in the British Museum (www.britishmuseum .org).

[133] See e.g. the following coins in the British Museum online catalogue (www.britishmuseum .org): R.1874,0715.16, R.10350, R.10487, R.10484, 1926,1205.1, 1912,0710.19, R.10485, R.10491.

[134] Hornum 1993: 13–16.

[135] John Stamper has argued that Vespasian's signature temples were mirrors of each other, the one for Jupiter and the one for Pax being about the same width and sharing design motifs. He contends (2005: 19–32) that the temple of Jupiter was about 50 percent smaller than usually thought (132, 157–58).

[136] Chapman 2009: 107–30.   [137] Stamper 2005: 168.   [138] See Jensen 1978: 347 n. 189.

creations or restorations.[139] From left to right they are: an unknown arch with three bays labeled the *Arcus ad Isis* ("Arch at [the something of] Isis"); the Flavian Amphitheatre; another arch, either four-way (*quadrifons/tetrapylon*) or standard and viewed side-on;[140] the Arch of Titus (called "the arch on the summit of the Sacra Via"); and a temple to Jupiter.[141]

Unsurprisingly, historians have differed over the identity of the Haterius family, the identification of these monuments, and their interpretation in this funerary context.[142] The well-attested *nomen* Haterius illustrates the problem.[143] At least three freedmen of the late first century had this name. The two best candidates are Q. Haterius Tychicus, known from a statue-base of Hercules as a public-works contractor (*redemptor*), and the Haterius Fronto who participated in Titus' council concerning the Jerusalem temple's fate (Chapter 8) and was perhaps the man (above) placed in charge of Judaean prisoners.[144] The most durable hypothesis holds that the monuments are landmarks on the route of Hateria's funeral procession, although that requires reading them from right to left.[145] That reading would not easily explain the prominent depictions of Flavian triumphal imagery, which seems too real-world to represent the victory of the deceased over death.[146]

[139] Discovered south of the Via Casilina in the Centocelle area, the tomb is now housed in the Vatican's Museo Gregoriano Profano. For detailed analysis, see Jensen 1978: e.g., 150–51, 225–43 on the date, 269–304 on the status of the Haterii.

[140] For the standard *quadrifrons* interpretation, see Jensen 1978: 97–99. Frothingham (1912: 37–80) proposed that this is a profile view of the triple-bay structure that would become the Arch of Constantine (fourth century), reading the final clause of the inscription as "an arch famous for its *triumphs*" (*arcum triumphis insignem,* 374–75), which suggests frequent reuse. After Domitian's *damnatio* and the removal of his distinguishing marks, he argued, the Senate was left with this Flavian arch as a blank "bulletin board" as advertising space for later emperors (370). Alice Walton (1924: 169–80) argued rather that it is a standard single-bay arch viewed in profile (171). If it is Flavian, another candidate would be the lost Arch of Titus in the Circus Maximus.

[141] In private communication, Prof. Eleanor Leach (University of Indiana Bloomington) has suggested that this might be the temple of deified Vespasian.

[142] For a summary of interpretations to his time, see Jensen 1978: 103–5.

[143] Ten cases appear in *PIR²* among senators and upper freedmen. Haterianus and Aterianus are derived *cognomina*: Kajanto 1982 (1965): 148. In the late first century we tend to think of former slaves of the very well-connected Q. Haterius Antoninus, consul of 53, who would have taken their patron's first two names on becoming freed. For summary discussion of the name see Coarelli 1984: 175–76.

[144] For these two candidates see respectively *CIL* 6.107 and *War* 6.238, 242.

[145] Jensen 1978: 133–51, reviving one of the earliest hypotheses. See now Leach 2006: 1–17. The Temple of Jupiter would be that of Jupiter Stator near the Arch of Titus, which burned in 64 (Jensen 1978: 150; Tacitus, *Ann.* 15.41). The Isis-related arch would be near a Temple of Isis on the city's east side and near the tomb. For debate about the location of this arch, see Coarelli 1993: 1.97; also 386 fig. 52.

[146] See Jensen 1978: 142–48 on triumph over death. But Leach 2006:11, acknowledging "something vaguely triumphal in the reading from left to right. . . . But what have these civic monuments to do with a burial of a Roman freedwoman?"

An alternative hypothesis takes the monuments to be major Flavian constructions, with their triumphal motifs, in which the tomb's owner had a
stake of prestige, whether as a participant in the war or as a building
contractor in Rome.[147] The left-hand arch would then be near the famous
Temple of Isis in the Campus Martius, which the Flavians honoured so
conspicuously, and the right-side temple to Jupiter would be the one rebuilt
by Vespasian on the Capitol.

   We need not solve all these problems to observe the striking fact that the
Flavian theme of conquest – of Judaea – also pervades this panel. The
triumphal chariot (*quadriga*) is conspicuous over the entrance to the Colosseum, which has been shrunk to accommodate it. The presence of such a
structure is confirmed by Titus' coins.[148] Occupying the Arch of Titus,
moreover, is the Goddess Virtus (Masculinity) in her characteristic pose, with
one foot raised on the prostrate enemy, accompanied by Mars and Victory in
the side panels. The tenants of the three bays in the first arch ("near [the
temple of] Isis") are led by Minerva with helmet, shield, and spear. Domitian
was a devotee of Minerva, who also leads Titus' *quadriga* in the north panel of
the Arch of Titus.[149] In the side bays here are Isis herself, holding the telltale
sistrum (rattle), and her dog-headed companion Anubis, apparently, on the
left.[150] Above the left-hand figure is the basket (*cista*) usedin various
mystery cults.

   Sealing the connection between all this triumphal imagery and
Judaea is the series of triumphal symbols along the top of the left-hand
arch.[151] Looking toward the *quadriga* are kneeling, bound prisoners
surrounded by palm trees and trophies. These motifs match those on both
the Flavian coinage and the Sabratha cuirass (below), and unmistakably
indicate Judaea. Why did the artist trouble to include such a small – about
5 cm (2 in) high – frieze here? Its position at the starting point of the
sequence (top left) indicates that this victory is the basis for the triumphal
imagery that follows. Victory in Judaea undergirded the Flavian building
programme.[152]

---

[147] E.g., Spano 1906; Castagnoli 1941: 59–69; Coarelli 1984: 176–79. Cf. Condor 2010.
[148] Cf. the coin ref. 1844,0425.712 in the British Museum.
[149] Suetonius, *Dom.* 13.2; cf. 5–6. Domitian was said to be embarrassingly fond of arches and
     monuments, inspiring a punning graffiti-artist to write: *arkei* – meaning "it's enough!" in
     Greek, but sounding like "arches" (*arci*) in Latin.
[150] Jensen 1978: 89–92.   [151] Hart 1952: 180–81.
[152] A recent study acknowledges "something vaguely triumphal in the reading from left to
     right" but fairly asks, "But what have these civic monuments to do with a burial of a Roman
     freedwoman?" (Leach 2006:11). Because the artist chose real structures rather than mythical
     scenes, it is not too much to suggest that he selected monuments that the woman's family
     had built or otherwise had some stake in.

Coins

Monuments could be found throughout the provinces, but their dispersal precluded the strong contextual thematizing that was possible in Rome. In the provinces, coins offered the most comprehensive medium for imperial propaganda. Across the empire from Spain to Syria, accordingly, the Flavians minted celebratory issues in all denominations and in gold, silver, and bronze: "For Captured [or Defeated] Judaea!" That they could not wait to exploit their victory is shown by a gold *aureus* apparently produced in the western empire (Tarraco) in A.D. 70 – during or immediately after the siege of Jerusalem. *Judaea* sits helpless before a trophy of Roman armour.[153]

Production of Judaea-related coins commenced on a scale unparalleled after actual conquests of new territory, and it continued through the reigns of Vespasian and Titus, if not longer.[154] Alongside the famous *Iudaea Capta* coins, others developed triumphal themes without spelling out the cause: a Flavian driving a *quadriga*, the triumphal procession (see also Chapter 7), military trophies above the fallen enemy, Victory and Peace, even the alleged naval victory mentioned above. Particularly graphic is a bronze from the early 70s depicting Titus on horseback, spearing a fallen eastern-style enemy.[155] When Titus succeeded his father in 79, he honoured Vespasian for their shared victory while also asserting his distinctive role.[156]

Judaea was, for the Flavians, the gift that kept on giving. Every emperor had been itching to claim a foreign military victory, but only Vespasian and Titus had done it – at least plausibly enough. As real men who had risked life and limb for Rome, they formed an exclusive club of two. The glory that radiated from them obliterated the puny claims of recent pretenders or any rivals then on the horizon.

Even Roman Africa was touched by their glory. Due south of Sicily, in the coastal city of Sabratha (near Tripoli, Libya), excavation of the forum turned up a headless marble statue.[157] Because it was found next to an identified statue of Titus, and in view of its imagery, it seems to represent Vespasian. Statues with cuirasses bearing symbolic decorations were common, and several hundred are known.[158] On this one the vivid images resemble those on Flavian coins and the Haterii relief. Winged Victory prepares to write on a shield

---

[153] Coin ref. 1864,1128.38 in the British Museum (www.britishmuseum.org).

[154] For the *Judaea Capta* coins and the question of Domitian's continuation of them (with a negative answer) see Meshorer 2001: 185–93.

[155] Coins ref. R1874,0715.15 and R1852,0607.1 in the British Museum (www.britishmuseum.org).

[156] E.g., a gold *aureus* with the head of deified Vespasian but, on the reverse, a riot of Titus' triumphal imagery (British Museum refs. 1864,1128.254) and gold and silver coins of Titus' first year with the full array of titles usually reserved for inscriptions, still based in his Judaean victory (ref. R.10948, R.10744).

[157] Vespasian had a presumably forgettable connection with Sabratha: His first wife had reportedly been the lover of an equestrian who lived there (Suetonius, *Vesp.* 3.1).

[158] Gergel 1988: 5.

fastened to palm tree (Fig. 3). Nearby are prisoners in simple garb, one standing with hands cuffed behind him.[159] The other sits on a pile of discarded shields, in the trousers (*bracae*) associated with easterners, begging for the mercy that is apparently being granted.[160]

In Rome of the 70s and 80s, then, Judaea was forced to play a mute role in the drama of Flavian power. Domitian, although too young to have participated, continued to celebrate the family victories by completing the triumphal monuments, in the verse that he enjoyed composing and in melding his purported achievements with theirs.[161] He may even have continued to issue Judaea-related coins.[162]

The Flavians would perhaps not have been pleased that the modern surveys *Warfare in the Classical World* and *The Great Battles of Antiquity* do not include Judaea. The former gives it four sentences under "armed insurrections,"[163] while the latter does not mention it at all.[164] These modern historians are right, however. Notwithstanding the tens of thousands of soldiers involved, and the historic destruction of a great city, this was not a real war but a revolt within a well-established province that was, unsurprisingly, suppressed. Josephus had his own literary reasons for describing the conflict as "the greatest war ever joined, not only of those in our times, but almost the greatest even of those about which we have received report" (*War* 1.1). Incompetent writers in Rome who had taken triumphal propaganda too seriously and lacked the political nous of the leaders were propagating nonsense in shoddily obsequious accounts (1.1–8). Josephus, who wrote to put them right, could have had no idea that his effort would turn out to be the decisive link between that temporary Flavian exuberance and a much more enduring Christian exploitation of Jerusalem's fall.

II. FAME ASSURED: CHRISTIANITY, SUPERSESSION, AND THE ABUSIVE RELATIONSHIP

The Arch of Titus provides a surprisingly stable reference-point for the transition to Christian promotion of Jerusalem's fall. Those vivid reliefs in the

---

[159] See Hart 1952: 172–73.

[160] Gergel (2001: 197–98) argues for a male with barbarian leggings. Hart (1952: 172–73 n. 6) cited correspondence from J. M. C. Toynbee in support of his view that the figure is female, albeit in male dress.

[161] So C. Valerius Flaccus, *Argonautica* 1.12–14: "Your offspring unfolds a verse on Idumaea— for he is well capable—with his brother blackened by the ashes of Solyma, scattering firebrands as he rages in every tower." This is addressed to Vespasian; the ash-blackened brother is Titus; Domitian is the wordsmith (cf. Suetonius, *Dom.* 2.2). For his role in the triumph compare Suetonius, *Dom.* 2.1 with Josephus, *War* 7.152. For the family shrine see Suetonius, *Dom.* 1.1.

[162] Hendin (2010: 403–59) argues that numismatic celebration for Judaea may have continued to Nerva's time.

[163] Warry 1998: 259.   [164] Gabriel and Boose 1994.

FIGURE 3. Decorated cuirass from presumed statue of Vespasian in the forum of Sabratha (mod. Libya). Copyright Brian J. McMorrow.

protected area inside its bay would become a literal touchstone in Christian interactions with Jews. New Testament scholar B. F. Westcott, who was Lord Bishop of Durham in 1896, wrote in his introduction to a book on the Arch of Titus: "It is no exaggeration to say that the Fall of Jerusalem is the most significant national event in the history of the world."[165] The criteria of significance invoked by both author and Bishop, however, were not those of the Flavians, Josephus, or recent military historians. This book was a reissue (from 1867) by the Religious Tract Society of a careful study of the Arch, which was already framed as proof of Jesus' predictions.[166] Writing at the height of the British Empire's (Christian) confidence, Westcott was affirming the age-old view that Titus' destruction of Jerusalem was punishment for the Jews' rejection of Jesus. It was the necessary basis for the growth of Christianity and the transfer of the biblical heritage to gentiles, who became one with the few Jews who accepted Christ:

> That which had been in the past the shrine of the Presence of God among His people [the temple] was necessarily doomed to final desolation when "the more perfect Tabernacle" had been faithlessly and fatally violated [in Jesus' crucifixion]. . . . [T]he destruction of the Temple was the condition of the establishment of the Catholic Church. As long as the Temple remained, a Catholic Church was impossible.[167]

Westcott goes on to speak of the way that God "fulfilled His will through Roman armies," and describes the Arch of Titus as portraying "the last scenes of Jewish national life," even declaring that "[t]he prophecies of the Lord and the narrative of Josephus combine to form one picture."[168] Westcott was a Protestant, but his perspective has roots in ancient and mediaeval Christianity. After the Reformation, this outlook was the shared property of Catholics and Protestants.

You know you are a supersessionist if: Christians and the fall of Jerusalem

The notion that Christian faith superseded Jewish law and life is suggested already in Paul's first known letter (40s A.D.), which is the first known Christian writing:

> They [the Jews] killed the Lord Jesus and the prophets, and they persecuted us, and they are not pleasing to God, and they stand against all of humanity, hindering us from speaking to the nations [or gentiles] so that

---

[165] In Knight 1896: 9. Holders of the Durham bishopric traditionally style themselves with the Latin *Dunelmensis* in place of their family name. Westcott signs the Introduction "B. F. Dunelm."

[166] Knight 1896: 13–17, 121–26.   [167] Knight 1896: 9–10.   [168] In Knight 1896: 10, 12.

they might be saved – in all of this relentlessly filling up the measure of their sins. Well, finally the [divine] *wrath has overtaken and fallen on them*! (1 Thess 2:15–16)

This claim fits the events of A.D. 70 so well that some scholars have considered it a post-70 interpolation.[169] Whether it was, or whether Paul referred to some event in the 40s – Agrippa I's premature death in A.D. 44 or a famine – as condign punishment, the logic had been set in motion. Paul's later letters (Gal 3–6, Rom 9–11) elaborated the other side of the equation, that God had "grafted" Christian believers into the ancient biblical heritage lost by (unbelieving) Jews. Dying some years before Jerusalem's destruction, Paul did not require that event as support for his claims. He maintained that Moses' covenant, a temporary project from the start, had ended with Christ's arrival.[170] The authors of Hebrews, the gospels, and the *Epistle of Barnabas*, along with Ignatius of Antioch among many others, held similar views.[171]

For Christians of this mindset, A.D. 70 came as a godsend. The *Epistle of Barnabas* can thus declare that the destroyed sanctuary in Jerusalem has been replaced by the community of Christian believers (16:1–10). Similar views are already found in Matthew and Luke, which scholars usually date to A.D. 80 or later.[172] Jesus attributes the temple's destruction to the city's rejection of himself: "Jerusalem, Jerusalem – the one killing the prophets and stoning those who have been sent to her. . . . Look: your desolate house is abandoned to you!" (Matt 23:37–38 = Luke 13:34). Luke 19:42–44 has him predict: "[Y]our enemies will infest you with fenced camps and encircle you and control access to you from every side . . . and will not leave one stone on another inside you, *because* you did not recognize the time of your inspection." As recently as 1955 these laments prompted the building of the *Dominus Flevit* church on the Mount of Olives, from which Christians could look down on forsaken Jerusalem.[173]

Jesus (d. ca. 30) may have spoken critically of the temple or its administration, but some sayings in the gospels reflect post-70 knowledge. The clearest

[169] E.g., Pearson 1971; Boers 1975–76; see the survey and rejection in Collins 1984: 97–124.
[170] Phil 3:3–11; 2 Cor 3; Gal 3:15–4:7. The stronger current in New Testament scholarship today locates Paul within a "Judaism" broadly defined. The question has something to do with the contexts and categories one finds available in the ancient world (e.g., ethnicity, religion, Judaism; cf. Mason 2007) and something to do with the evidence, especially one's understanding of Romans (cf. Mason 2009a: 283–328).
[171] Heb 1:1–5; 3:1–6; 4:14–5:14; 7:11–10:25; Ignatius, *Magn.* 10; *Phil.* 6; *Barn.* 2.5–6; chaps. 6–15. On Abraham's 318 soldiers (9.7–8; cf. Gen 14:14), the number being TIH in Greek, the author of *Barnabas* says: the I and H, with values of 10 and 8, obviously represent the first two letters of "Jesus" (ΙΗΣΟΥΣ), and the T for 300 is self-evidently a cross.
[172] The passage is commonly assigned to the lost sayings source Q, normally dated no later than the 60s, although the clear reference to the temple's current state of destruction suggests a post-70 date.
[173] See Roth 1973: 11–13.

example is Matthew's reworking of a simple parable. The simple form, found in Luke and the *Coptic Gospel of Thomas*, tells of a wealthy man who threw a banquet and, when it was ready, sent a slave to alert his well-to-do friends. They, citing busy lives and commitments, excused themselves one by one. The indignant host ordered his slave to rush out and bring in the poor, crippled, blind, and whomever else he met. *They* would be grateful. The point of the story does not seem extremely obscure. Luke has the host conclude openly that "none of those men who were invited will get to taste the meal," while *Thomas* sharpens the class emphasis: "buyers and merchants do not enter the places of my Father."[174]

In Matthew, however, this potentially timeless parable becomes a specific, pointed, frightening allegory. The host is now a *king* who throws a *wedding* banquet for *his son* – ominous changes all. The guests are not content to excuse themselves, but actually *beat and kill* the host's messengers (plural). If that seems excessive, the response is shocking: "[T]he king became enraged. He sent *his armed forces*, destroyed those murderers, and *burned down their city*" (Matt 22:2–8). What city did the king's guests occupy? Evidently Matthew's Jesus is speaking allegorically about Christ, Jerusalem, and divine retribution. This fits with that author's supersessionist refrain that the Reign of Heaven has been taken away from its natural heirs and offered to gentiles.[175]

Whereas modern scholars conclude that the gospel writers reformulated Jesus' sayings with Jerusalem's fall in the past, early Christians assumed that Jesus had predicted the event in such terms,[176] sealing the nexus between Jerusalem's destruction and Christian inheritance. When the emperor Julian (A.D. 361–363) undertook to rebuild the temple, partly in order to undermine such Christian claims, but died prematurely, Christians interpreted his death as a divine verdict on such attempts to tamper with salvation history.[177]

Supersessionist Christianity was, it should be said, not the only kind. An exasperated John Chrysostom wrote, in fourth-century Antioch: "I realize that many (Christian) people revere Judaeans and regard the present-day society/constitution of those people to be worthy of awe (1.3.1)." Chrysostom

[174] The simpler version is in Luke 14:16–24 and Coptic *Gospel of Thomas* 64.
[175] Matt 8:11–12; 21:33–41; 22:12–13.
[176] There is a parallel here with biblical Daniel. The work purports to be from Babylonian/Persian period, and so ancient Jews (as Josephus, *Ant.* 10.269–281) and Christians were genuinely amazed at the accuracy of its predictions. But the third-century philosopher Porphyry (cited by Jerome, *Comm. Dan.* praef.) anticipated modern scholars in concluding from Daniel 11 that the work was completed around 165 B.C.: everything described until the detailed career of Antiochus IV is accurate and therefore past; the mistaken description of that king's imminent death is genuine prediction.
[177] Julian, *Ep.* 51 (298a) and the fragment 295c. For the context of this initiative in Julian's life, see Theodoret, *Ecclesiastical History* 3.2–4, 15–22, and for analysis, Bowersock 1978: 88–90, 120–22.

thought that "if the ways of the Judaeans are great and worthy of reverence, ours are false. But if our ways are true ... theirs are full of deception" (1.6.5). The Christians he censures obviously viewed things differently. Treasuring Judaean law and custom, as they understood Jesus to have done, they had no investment in the temple's destruction.[178] On the opposite pole, some Christians understood their faith as utterly unrelated to Judaean law and culture, a tendency detectable in earlier texts but powerfully articulated by Marcion of Sinope in the second century[179] – and notoriously revived by the "German Christians" of the interwar and Nazi periods.[180] Unlike the Nazis, Marcion was happy for Jerusalem and its temple to continue, but felt that they had nothing to do with Christian faith.

The supersessionist outlook prevailed in Christian circles, perhaps understandably because of the need for a respectable heritage, and the vulnerability of these new associations without one.[181] Some Christians lumped Roman authorities and Judaeans together as the cause of their difficulties.[182] Tertullian wrote in early third-century Carthage:

> In the past the Judaeans were in favour with God, and notable for the justice and loyalty of their ancient founders. ... But how badly they failed ... their final predicament [exitus] nowadays would prove, even though they would not own up to it themselves. Scattered, wanderers, exiles from their own sun and sky, they roam the earth without a king either human or divine. ... While holy voices were threatening them

[178] For Judaizing Christianity, see, e.g., Paul in Gal 1:6–24; 3:1–5; 4:10, 21; 5:2–6; 6:12–16; Ignatius, *Magn.* 10; *Phil.* 6; Hippolytus, *Ref. haer.* 9.9 [one Elchasai insists on circumcision and Torah observance, also that Christ was born in the normal way]; Eusebius, *Hist. eccl.* 3.27; 6.17; John Chrysostom, *Adv. Iud.* 1.1.5 ("Some [of us] are going to watch the festivals, and others will join [the Judaeans] in keeping their feasts and observing their fasts"); 1.3.1–5; 2.1.1–6; 3.1.1; 5.1.3–7. From a vast literature I particularly recommend Wilson 1995: 143–68; Paget 2010: 1–76, 149–84, 289–382.

[179] Wilson 1995: 207–20; Moll 2010.

[180] Preludes came with Chamberlain (1910: 1.187–250), who insisted that Christ was not a racial Jew but represented the "negation" of Jewish religion (221) and with neo-Marcionite Assyriologist Friedrich Delitzsch, who was indignant that his call for separation was taken for anti-Semitism (1921: 2.3–4 and n.★). In his view, Yahweh was the exclusive national God of Israel, comparable to the deities of other Near-Eastern peoples (13). He wished "to see off the 'Old Testament' from school and church, and to give back to Christianity the figure and teaching of Jesus, pure and unadulterated" (4).

[181] E.g., Justin Martyr, *Dial.* 40, 46.1; Minucius Felix, *Oct.* 10, 33; Melito, *Pasch.* 94–99; cf. Wilson 1995: 241–56; Broadhurst 2005.

[182] Hippolytus, *Comm. Dan.* 1.15–29; 4.50.3. Hippolytus allegorizes the story of Susanna and the Jewish elders (in Dan 13, absent from Jewish and Protestant Bibles). Susanna, who would become a saint in some Christian traditions, is harassed by two lecherous and scheming elders, who receive their just deserts thanks to Daniel's intervention. One elder represents the Jews, says Hippolytus, the other the gentile authorities. The story was widely represented in early modern art, for reasons having nothing to do with Jews and Christians, but in the twentieth century it became a vehicle for racial stereotyping: Günther 1930b: 246–47 with photograph.

severely with this, all were constantly declaring that in the final courses of time God would choose for himself much more faithful worshippers, from every race, people, and place [i.e., Christians], to whom he would transfer his favour.[183]

Hippolytus, a dissident Bishop of Rome (d. 235), and Origen of Alexandria (d. 254) held similar views.[184]

Within a century of Tertullian, Hippolytus, and Origen things would dramatically change. The leaders of the empire had in the meantime become Christian or Christian-curious, and official anti-Christian measures had ceased from about A.D. 311. Far from bringing an end to supersessionist claims, however, the spokesmen of established Christianity tended to propound them with increased stridency. Such a man was Eusebius, Bishop of Caesarea, biographer and theological advisor of the emperor Constantine. Eusebius' ten-volume *Church History* would be a fundamental authority for more than a millennium.

Its preface announces as a central theme "the things that immediately overtook the whole *ethnos* of the Judaeans because of their plot against our saviour" (*Hist. eccl.* 1.1). Eusebius returns to the point often, for example in claiming that Jerusalem's Christians were directed by an oracle to flee the doomed city, leaving only unbelieving Jews to be punished (3.5.3).[185] For the gory details of the siege, he refers readers to Josephus' *War*, quoting generously from its graphic depictions of famine, starvation, death, and cannibalism (3.5.4–6.28). Eusebius' take-away could never have been imagined by Josephus, however: "This was the payback for the Judaeans' crime against the Christ of God and their impiety" (3.7.1). This is how Josephus' works came to be preserved by the Christian West. Josephus had established himself among Graeco-Roman authors as the source *par excellence* for matters Judaean,[186] and

---

[183] *Apol.* 21; cf. *Marc.* 3.23. For Tertullian, see Barnes 1971, best read alongside the sometimes caustic reviews by Frend 1974: 72–76, Momigliano 1976: 273–76, and Wright 2000.

[184] Hippolytus, *Adv. Iud.* 1 ("Well then, Jew, bend your ear to me. . . . You have often boasted about having sentenced Jesus of Nazareth to death. . ."); 6 ("you poured out his blood in indignation. . . . 'Let their habitation be desolate' – that is, their famous temple"); 7 ("Why. . . was the temple made desolate? . . . it was because they killed the son of their Benefactor.). Although authorship of this tract is not certain, its sentiments accord with Hippolytus' views elsewhere, e.g.: *C. Haer. Noeti* 18.3 (God nailed to a cross by the Jews); *Ref. haer.* 9.25, although to be sure these were not unique views. Hippolytus thought that restoration of the temple would be the work of a Jewish Antichrist: *Antichr.* 6, 25, 30, 49 with *Ref. haer.* 9.25; *Comm. Dan.* 4.49. On this theme in the Middle Ages; cf. Burr 2004. Cf. Origen, *C. Cels.* 4.22.

[185] On the alleged flight of the Christians from Jerusalem to Pella, see Lüdemann 1980; Koester 1989.

[186] Josephus was known to Suetonius (*Vesp.* 5.6) and probably Tacitus (given *Hist.* 2.101 and the close similarities of 5.1–2, 10–13); Dio (65/66.1.4); and Porphyry (*Abst.* 4.11–14). Even the Epitome of the second-century Aelius Herodian cites Josephus about thirty times for place

Christians were hesitant at first to make much use of his Judaean interpretation of the war, which tended to undermine their claims.[187] But in the new conditions of the fourth century, Eusebius felt confident enough to co-opt Josephus while ignoring his own themes and structures. For him, Josephus furnished decisive independent proof of the Christian narrative about Jerusalem's suffering, and for this purpose it was important that Josephus was not a Christian (*Hist. eccl.* 3.5.4, 9.2). His account of Jerusalem's fall and eventually his detailed accounts of Judaean and Galilean life would remain precious to Christians. The late nineteenth century still saw many Christian babies baptized with the name Josephus.[188]

In A.D. 401 Sulpicius Severus produced his *Chronicle* of world history, which draws heavily from the Bible, Josephus, Tacitus, and other authorities (Chapter 8). His conclusion about the destruction of the temple combines the elements we have seen (*Chron.* 2.30):

> [T]he temple was demolished three hundred and thirty-one years ago. This latest overthrow of the temple and harshest captivity of the Jews, which sees them refugees from their ancestral land and scattered across the earth, are a daily proof to the world of their having been punished for nothing other than the impious hands they laid on Christ.

This emphasis on Judaean homelessness as perpetual witness to Christian truth would have dire enough consequences through the later Middle Ages and early modern periods. But with the rise of a new nationalism coupled with "racial science" at the end of the nineteenth century, it took on a particularly sinister hue. Because every nation and race was expected to have its own place, as in ancient ethnographic models but with markedly stronger ties to blood and soil, writers became preoccupied with "the Jewish problem."[189] It is more

---

names in Syria: text in Lentz 1867. E.g., Part 3 vol. 1 (*Herodiani technici reliquiae*), pp. 76, 87, 91, 93, 192, 207, 243, 252–53, 390, searchable via www.tlg.uci.edu.

[187] Fundamental studies are Schreckenberg 1972; 1977; Deutsch 1986; Feldman and Hata 1987; 1989; Hardwick 1989; Schreckenberg and Schubert 1992; Liebl 1997; Whealey 2003; Yeager 2004: 70–102; Kletter 2005; Inowlocki 2006. An Oxford-based research project now focuses on Josephus' reception-history (www.orinst.ox.ac.uk/research/josephus/home, accessed 25 May 2013).

[188] E.g., Woodrow Wilson's Secretary of the Navy was Josephus Daniels, as his father had been (1862–1948). Christian-devotional author Grace Livingston Hill (1865–1947) married *Flavius Josephus* Lutz. Newspaper archives of the nineteenth and early twentieth centuries turn up thousands of hits for "Josephus" (www.britishnewspaperarchive.co.uk: 10,000+; www.fold3.com: 3,428), mainly in reference to contemporaries rather than the ancient writer.

[189] Herzl 1896 (subtitle: "attempt at a modern solution to the Jewish question"). Herzl stresses that Jews have done everything possible to be committed citizens of their European homelands, seeking only to preserve their ancestral *faith*; the states in which they live will not allow them because they see Jews as an alien *Volk*. The solution of a Jewish state follows logically. Cf. Günther 1930b: 292–95 ("Die Judenfrage," advocating Zionism from the other side).

than paradoxical that Christians, whose ancestors had been vulnerable in Graeco-Roman society because they were *not* a nation (*ethnos*) with a city (*polis*), had become so deeply nationalized in late nineteenth-century Europe that they could embrace concepts of race-based nationhood, which transformed traditional Christian images of Jewish wandering into a problem calling for state-level remedies.

Arch enemies: the sequel

I mentioned earlier that the Colosseum survived because of major restorative efforts in the early nineteenth century. Likewise the Arch of Titus would not be available to us today if Pope Pius VII had not sponsored its restoration in 1818–1823. What was his interest in doing so?

The Jewish experience under Christian rule is familiar in its main lines, though no less disturbing for that: restrictions on land and slave ownership, public offices, professions, housing districts, and interactions with Christians.[190] Beneath such official positions, to be sure, Jews often found ways to live alongside real-life Christian neighbours, and the Renaissance (thirteenth to sixteenth centuries) brought tentative green shoots even in official practice. But Martin Luther's decisive turn against the Jews[191] and the Counter-Reformation had further dreadful consequences.[192] In his brief term of office (1555–1559) Pope Paul IV felt the need to demand stringent adherence to the official position, lamenting the laxity of his predecessors in allowing Jews to mingle with Christians. His papal bull *Cum nimis absurdum* begins with such legal-sounding *whereases* as these . . .

> Since it is absurd and improper that Jews – whose own guilt has consigned them to perpetual servitude – under the pretext that Christian piety receives them and tolerates their presence should be ingrates to Christians . . . considering that the Roman Church tolerates the Jews in

---

[190] Classic studies include Graetz 1949 [German 1862] vols. 3–5; Marcus 1999 [1938]; Roth 1946; Milano 1963. Important recent work, from a profusion, includes Stow 1977, 1992, 1995–1997, 2006, 2007; Glick 1999; Segre 2001; McMichael and Myers 2004; Chazan 2006; Elukin 2007.

[191] The early Luther wrote *That Jesus Christ was Born a Jew* (1523) in the hope of making Christianity more attractive to Jews ("If I had been a Jew and had seen such dolts and blockheads govern and teach the Christian faith, I would sooner have become a hog than a Christian"). Twenty years later, the lack of Jewish response even to his brand of Christianity led him to write *The Jews and Their Lies*. This tract proposed measures (Part XI) in Germany that were more draconian than those of the Popes: forced labour; burning of homes, schools, and synagogues; and execution of rabbis who persisted on preaching.

[192] These are crude categories, but even Hudon 1996, while stressing that point in his review of scholarship, accepts that Paul IV broke with centuries of increasing tolerance (1996: 794 n. 26). Cf. Vivanti 1995: 323–24.

testimony of the true Christian faith ... [and] as long as they persist in their errors, they should recognize through experience that they have been made slaves while Christians have been made free through Jesus Christ ...[193]

It goes downhill from there. The fifteen measures that follow include nullifying previous concessions, even by Popes, reinstatement of distinctive Jewish clothing for ease of identification, a blanket prohibition on fraternization with Christians, forced sale of Jewish real estate to Christians, and the creation of a walled-off district to house Rome's Jews. This Ghetto, coincidentally built in the ancient Campus Martius where the Flavian triumph had begun, would last more than 300 years.

From the twelfth to the nineteenth centuries, Popes took advantage of the nearby Arch of Titus to remind Rome's Jews of their merely tolerated status. They instituted a bizarre sort of game: the "encounter" ceremony. On special occasions such as Easter or a Papal coronation, representatives of the Jewish community would be summoned to greet the Pope, presenting a copy of the Torah for his approval while hyperbolically expressing loyalty. The Pope would approve of the Torah itself while castigating the Jews for failing to recognize that the Messiah had come. From at least the sixteenth century, such ceremonies often assumed a more aggressive tone. Jews would stand before the Arch of Titus holding placards in Latin and Hebrew verse, exuberantly contrasting the Pope's virtues with those of Titus, himself a supposed model of clemency.[194] This was a situation ripe for irony, and we would like to know how Jewish leaders managed it.

In the early 1700s, Adriaan Reelant marveled that Providence had preserved the arch's interior scenes until his time, whereas most Roman monuments had long gone.[195] By 1800, however, these ancient friezes were near the point of collapse. Only the central bay and eastern face of the architrave (with the Senate's inscription for Titus) remained from Domitian's memorial to his brother, and they had suffered from centuries of rebuilding around them, large cracks now marring the old stones (Fig. 4).

This was the context in which Pope Pius VII (Pope 1800–1823) undertook to shore up the arch, along with the imperilled Colosseum. It was at first a modest effort to prevent collapse. The decisive impetus for renovation came from his nemesis Napoleon, who had a more secular love of the eternal city and its emblems of empire. In the brief period during which Napoleon controlled Rome (1808–1814) he initiated ambitious plans to restore the entire

---

[193] Trans. Stow 1977: 294–98. Cf. Roth 1946: 294–302 and Segre 2001: 41–74. For cautions about assuming direct practical effects from such harsh rhetoric, see Ravid 2012.
[194] Lerner 2002: 14; Linder 2009: 334, 340–48, esp. 366–72.   [195] Reelant 1716: 1, 3.

FIGURE 4. Engraving of the Arch of Titus (*Veduta dell'Arco di Tito*) by Giovanni Battista Piranesi, ca. 1760. The ancient elements were then embedded in brick structures north and south. This side of the freestanding Flavian structure has all but disappeared, although the spoils relief is intact and visible. Metropolitan Museum of Art, New York (OpenAccess Scholarly Content provision): www.metmuseum.org/collection/the-collection-online/search?ft=64.521.4.

Forum, along with these structures,[196] having bundled Pius VII off to a roving French imprisonment.[197] The similarities between the Arch of Titus and Napoleon's Arc de Triomphe in Paris, three times the size, are not

[196] Jokilehto 1999: 83–85.
[197] Cf. his encyclical *Il trionfo* ("The Triumph") of 4 May 1814 (www.papalencyclicals.net, accessed 15 May 2013).

accidental.[198] Napoleon himself was soon gone, however, and the restored
Pius VII resumed work on the Arch. Taking a sharply conservative turn after
Napoleon's abolition of church claims and institutions, he reinstated the Index
of Prohibited Books, the Roman and Spanish Inquisitions, the Jewish Ghetto,
and compulsory sermons aimed at converting the Jews.[199] His restoration of
the Arch of Titus, hardly the fruit of a simple love of antiquity, was part and
parcel of this religious programme.

On its upper west side, opposite the Senate's dedication to Titus on the east
face, Pius honoured himself with a revealing inscription. His text imitates the
ancient lettering and number style of that for Titus (Fig. 5). In subtle language
it declares that the current *Pontifex Maximus* – a title the Pope shared with
Titus – ordered this decaying monument, "impressive for religion and art
alike," to be "secured and saved (*fulciriservarique*) by means of new works
imitating the ancient model." The Pope could not have been expressing a
fondness for Titus' religion. He can only have meant that the structure was
important for *true* religion: Christianity. Pius' engraver dates this inscription to
the twenty-fourth (and final) year of his *sacred principate*, rather than the
expected *pontificate*,[200] evoking his status as *princeps*, another ancient epithet
for emperors. The Pope was positioning himself as Titus' latter-day Christian
successor, building (Christianity) on what his ancient forebear had torn down
(Jerusalem and Judaism).[201]

Pius' architects reconstructed the arch so expertly that today we easily forget
how thorough their restoration was. Controversially at the time, they had to
dismantle the ancient elements, further damaging some in the process, in order
to free them from the adjoining material and rebuild the detached structure in
a conjectured frame including much modern stonework.[202]

---

[198] Note especially the coffered arch ceilings, internal side reliefs, spandrels, and triumphal-
processionfrieze beneath the architrave, in Napoleon's case for success in Egypt. The most
recent heir of the Flavian arch is apparently Atlanta's Millennium Gate: Jonsson 2008.

[199] Pius VII must have known the fifteenth-century *Book of the Popes* (*Liber Pontificalis*), which
gives as the only ruling of the first Pope Pius (A.D. 140–155) that Jewish converts should be
welcomed and baptized (Loomis 1916: 14–15).

[200] E.g., in the two encyclicals at www.papalencyclicals.net, Pius VII gives the years *del nostro
pontificato*.

[201] Although he is not responsible for this paragraph, I am indebted to Bill Thayer, the most
generous *diakonos* of Classics on the web, for his reflections at http://penelope.uchicago
.edu/Thayer/E/Gazetteer/Places/Europe/Italy/Lazio/Roma/Rome/Arch_of_Titus/
inscriptions.html (accessed 28 May 2013).

[202] Mariana Starke reported immediately after the reconstruction (1828: 140): "This Edifice was
nearly destroyed [in the Middle Ages], that its ornaments might be placed elsewhere: but
enough remains to prove that that it was the most beautiful building of its kind ever erected
at Rome. . . . [I]t has been recently and judiciously repaired; for the modern work is of such
a description that it cannot be confounded with the ancient." Cf. Octavian Blewitt in 1837
(1850: 349): "In the time of Pius VII, the building was greatly ruined, and would have

FIGURE 5. Arch of Titus in mid-twentieth century, looking east to the Colosseum. This west-face inscription (1823) identifies Pius VII as the saviour of Titus' monument and continuator of his work. Courtesy of the Deutsches Archäologisches Institut (D-DAI-ROM-36–507: H. Behrens).

After its restoration by Pius, the Arch for Titus became a potent symbol again. Not long after Westcott laid out his perspective, another paragon of the British elite, Lord Redesdale,[203] wrote a fulsome introduction for H. S. Chamberlain's notorious *Foundations of the Nineteenth Century* (1910). After ten massively popular German editions, this would become a Third Reich staple. Contextualizing Chamberlain's treatment of the Jews, from which he partly demurred, Redesdale wrote in the spirit of civic Christianity at the time. His point was not markedly different from the Bishop's, however, and he cited the New Testament in support:

> In the destruction of Jerusalem by the Romans one sees the hand of Providence. . . . [The Jew] was a continual thorn in the side of his chosen rulers, and his final subjugation and dispersal became a necessity. Had the

perished but for the judicious restorations then made. It is easy to distinguish these modern additions. . . ."

[203] Redesdale's title, like Westcott's, obscured his identity. He was Algernon Bertram [Freeman-] Mitford, graduate of Eton and Oxford and adventurer. He served the Foreign Office in Russia, China, and Japan before entering the civil service and later serving as MP for Stratford-on-Avon. Made Baron Redesdale in 1902, he wrote several popular books, especially *Tales of Old Japan*. His fascist-friendly son, the second Baron Redesdale, bought a gold mine in (coincidentally) Swastika, Ontario, Canada, and one of the son's daughters (Unity) became an acolyte of Nazi leaders. Another (Diana) married British fascist Sir Oswald Mosley, in the home of J. Goebbels. Another (Jessica), however, was a communist who became a renowned American writer.

Jew remained in Jerusalem, Christianity would have become a mere sect of the Jews. . . . In destroying the stronghold of Judaism the Romans, though here again they knew it not, were working for the triumph of Christianity.[204]

Supersession and its implications have loomed large in the history of Jewish-Christian relations. There were always undercurrents of protest, from those few Christians who saw the Jewish people as kindred heirs of biblical tradition. Just a year before her death in 1846, the vehement Protestant Charlotte Elizabeth (Tonna) excoriated "our Christian historians" for holding "that Jerusalem had been visited with final destruction, her wrecks being left merely as monuments of divine vengeance," and "that the Jews, as a nation, are cast off, at least so far as to render any future restoration contingent on their embracing the faith of the gospel."[205] As in many aspects of her life, Elizabeth was swimming against the tide.

Supersessionist assumptions are well captured in a large canvas painting from 1846, on the brink of the nation-state explosion. In *Titus' Destruction of Jerusalem*, by Wilhelm von Kaulbach, court artist of the Bavarian King Ludwig I, the prophets Isaiah, Jeremiah, Ezekiel, and Daniel stand above, authorizing what is happening below as they themselves fade away.[206] To the upper left is the burning temple, with Simon bar Giora and John of Gischala in front. To the right are angels with flaming swords who oversee the Roman conquest. Upper right is Titus, calmly executing his task and surrounded by emblems of Roman authority. Although the Romans think they are in control, they are players in a divine tableau: In the lower centre, Jews are being killed or taking their own lives, their gold coins spilling out according to stereotype. Some cower while the figure of "the eternal Jew" flees the Furies pursuing him. To the right Mary and Joseph with the infants Jesus and John the Baptist emerge bathed in light, as an angelic escort holds high the sacred chalice. The scene blends in motifs from Jesus' triumphal entry (palm fronds, donkeys). The faithful group exits right, searching Jewish scripture for their foundation.

Given the importance of Titus' Jerusalem campaign for nascent Christianity and later Western history, it is not surprising that the old Flavian boast featured again, now reversed, in the symbolism of modern Israel. *The Hope (Ha-Tikvah)*, its lyrics revised for service as Israel's national anthem, declares: "The hope of *two thousand years* never faded: to be a free people in our land." In the state's

---

[204] In Chamberlain 1910: xxiii.   [205] Elizabeth 1845: 15.
[206] Wilhelm von Kaulbach, *Die Zerstörung Jerusalems durch Titus*, 1846: large canvas (5.85 x 7.05 m [19 x 23 ft]) now in the Neue Pinakothek, Munich. For interpretation see the Munich art historian Albert Ottenbacher (www.albert-ottenbacher.de/kaulbach/).

FIGURE 6. Postcard from Trani Displaced Persons Camp, September 1949. The main Hebrew banner reads, "May you be inscribed for a good year!" (year 5710). The smaller caption below: "Long live our homeland Israel!" Courtesy of the United States Holocaust Memorial Museum (#24609).

self-representation, the triumphal imagery of the Arch of Titus and Flavian coinage for *Iudaea capta* has finally been undone by *Israel liberata*.[207] A striking example comes in a postcard for Rosh Hashanah 5710 (Jewish New Year, September 1949), created with meagre tools in a Displaced Persons camp in Bari, Italy.[208] Between Moses on the left and a map of the new state of Israel on the right is a toppled Arch of Titus with its potent spoils relief. Two millennia of Judaean displacement are finally set right, the symbols cry (Fig. 6).

CONCLUSIONS

My aim in this chapter has been to explore the fuss that has been made for nearly two millennia about the first Judaean-Roman War. Given the massive size of the canvas, I have only been able to rip it open at a few revealing spots – the Flavian triumph, some Christian interpretations, the Arch of Titus as touchstone – to expose the frame beneath.

[207] E.g., from the Israel Mint: www.israelmint.com/?
section=518&product=2768&lineItem=748.For the Arch of Titus see the 1965 gold medals at www.mcsearch.info/search.html?search=similar%3A402233#0
[208] I thank Dr. Zuleika Rodgers for alerting me to this postcard.

Two main conclusions emerge. First, the fall of Jerusalem was important to many people other than the Jews, who lost their mother-city, and it was the others who had reasons to advertise it. The Flavian regime and later Christians each had powerful, although entirely different, motives for propagating Jerusalem's fall. Second, however, all the fuss they created leaves us none the wiser about the actual nature of the war, its causes, and its course. It was not their aim to invite historical curiosity; indeed, they packaged the war in ways that stifled inquiry. Flavian propagandists conjured up Jews as a foreign enemy with a great army, or as a nation in revolt. Christians portrayed them as the people that had crucified God and so faced eternal punishment. That was all anyone needed to know. Even Josephus' account of the war does not invite further inquiry, for different reasons. In the spirit of most ancient historiography, it provides a wealth of material, for which we must be grateful, in an elegant synthesis that reveals as little as possible of the elements that went into its construction (Chapter 2).

The result is that we have no one *to rely on* for this war. This is no bad thing for historians. It throws us back on a basic question, which we may take as the central problem for our inquiry: What happened in this war? More basically: How can we go about finding out what happened? Before we proceed to Chapter 2, which frames and then begins our inquiry, I would like to savour a methodological point that has now become clear.

We have seen that events do not declare their own meanings. The fall of Jerusalem to Titus' legions did not come with a self-extracting explanation. *We* construct the meanings of events, by bringing our experience and insight to bear on the surviving evidence. In recognizing this much we already begin to unpack three related contrasts, or polarities, which will remain with us throughout the following study. First is the contrast between an event and its exploitation. Billions of things happen every day.[209] Who decides which are important, how to contextualize the important ones, or what story to tell from them? In the second century B.C. Polybius observed: "*The Senate* has the power to make a big production of the general's successes and inflate them or, again, to fade and shrink them" (6.15.7). It is a more general and abiding truth that *someone* has to explain events; they cannot do it themselves.

Second and related is the polarity between *force* and *power*. We have suspected already in this chapter that Rome's application of physically coercive force against enemies, at the hands of the legions, was both expensive and risky. It could not be repeated constantly. Like other rulers, the Flavians had to leverage the little they had actually accomplished by physical force in southern Syria to generate the vast political power they needed in Rome.

---

[209]   Hölscher 2006 is full of relevant insights.

The third polarity underlies these two. It affects each of us every day, even as we watch the evening news. It is the contrast between the chaos of what is really going on in the world and any attempt to represent that reality in a meaningful way: reality over against representation. These polarities drive us on to Chapter 2. What, then, is history?

CHAPTER TWO

UNDERSTANDING HISTORICAL EVIDENCE
Josephus' Judean War *in context*

And yet it should be obvious that, for the very historical purposes for which the book is now chiefly studied, it is misleading and dangerous to use what is plainly one of the most sophisticated products of ancient historiography without constant regard to the plans and purposes of its author.[1]

D. A. Russell wrote this in 1966 concerning Plutarch's *Lives*. Others have issued similar warnings about trying to extract raw facts from texts while ignoring their nature, structures, and themes.[2] In principle all survivals from the past, material or literary, need first to be understood for what they are if we are to use them to answer other questions. Recognition of this in the case of Josephus' *War* and *Antiquities–Life* has been recent and partial.[3] This chapter is

---

[1] Russell 1966: 139.

[2] E.g., Luce 1977 for Livy; Sacks 1990 for Diodorus; Habicht 1998 [1985] and Alcock, Cherry, and Elsner 2001 for Pausanias.

[3] An early effort to study Josephus' language was Brüne 1913; Moehring 1957 (and later) called attention to Josephus' narrative art. Still, these studies made no effort to interpret each work as a composition. Nor did the various explorations of Josephus' theology or religion or worldview (Schlatter 1910, 1932; Montgomery 1920–21; Foakes Jackson 1930; Lindner 1972; Rajak 1983). The biblical paraphrase (*Ant.* 1–11) was the first section of the corpus to attract sustained literary analysis, although the focus remained on those volumes only (Attridge 1976; Sterling 1992; Begg 1993; Spilsbury 1998; Feldman 1998b) or even on micro-traits within them (Franxman 1979; essays in Feldman 1998a). In a thorough 1988 survey, Bilde could find little if any research on the structures, audiences, and themes of Josephus' works (1988: 71, 92, 118). In the last quarter-century, although the study of Josephus has blossomed, little attention

mainly an effort to understand Josephus' *War*, because it is the most important literary source for the following chapters. We need to begin, however, by clarifying where the interpretation of evidence fits in the larger project of historical investigation. And this requires us to think about the surprisingly difficult question: What is history?

History and interpretation

Historians are often impatient with theory.[4] We feel that we know what we are doing, and abstract philosophizing can get in the way. We should just get on with the hard work. Going theory-less, however, can create miscommunication. In the final months of preparing this book I have heard professional historians express such views as these: History is the past or an authoritative account of it; historians must *follow the evidence* and avoid speculation; history concerns itself with elite literary texts and neither material evidence or the life of ordinary folk, which are the province of archaeologists; historians are either maximalists or minimalists, realists or postmodernists, left-wingers or conservatives, or they fall in some other two-kinds-of-people scheme. A problem relevant to this chapter is the notion that those who care about the meaning of texts must be literary types unconcerned with the actual past.[5] And these positions are held by historians. If we include more popular ideas about history, including those espoused by political leaders and school boards, the picture becomes bewildering.

This is not the place, my publisher insists, for a head-on discussion of the nature of history. Dedicated discussions of the problem are easy to find, even if I cannot recommend one that perfectly matches my outlook. Here I can only hope to clarify the most basic principles underlying this inquiry into the Jewish War.

1. Outside the academy, history seems most often to be equated with the past itself or with supposedly authoritative records.[6] We all say of obsolete conditions or relationships "That's ancient history." The poor soul who cannot recall what she learned about 1066, we say, "does not know her history." History, in this sense, is first of all a set of discoverable and learnable facts, which are found in "the history books." And those books, wherever they are,

---

has gone to overall interpretation. Grünenfelder 2003 is an exception for *War*; Semenchenko 2002 for *Antiquities*; cf. Mason 2003: 55–146 is an attempt at addressing the corpus.

[4] See Jenkins 1995: 64–66 (on G. R. Elton): Clark 2004: 9–28.

[5] E.g. Freyne 2009: "Yet not everyone, I suspect, will be prepared to accept Mason's artful and literary Josephus to the exclusion of any interest, however partisan, in the historical events that his texts evoke and reflect." Cf. Bernett 2007: 20–21.

[6] This usage has sometimes been abetted by academic handbooks (e.g., Garraghan and Delanglez 1946) that defer to authorities for confident knowledge of the past.

are not mere records. According to politicians, at least, they are bursting to teach us – if only we would heed what they call the "lessons of history." The same mentality leads politicians to warn us about "how history will judge" some action or other, as though history were an intelligence outside of ourselves.

But if we ask in simple faith where history's facts, opinions, and lessons are filed, we quickly discover a problem. Namely, they do not exist. If history means the past, then it cannot exist now by definition – the past being the past. As for the lessons of the past, if we actually open some historical studies, we find patently competing, schematic, hypothetical reconstructions that frequently disagree with each other. Take, for example, one of the most basic "facts" one could learn about the Jewish War: the years in which the conflict began and ended. Recent years have seen both dates vigorously debated.[7] Histories of the far better documented twentieth-century wars fare no better in this respect. Although the advertising for each new book might hail it as the definitive one, my drooping bookshelves tell a different story. Each historian uncovers a new angle and offers it as a better key to understanding, but this very activity of constant reimagining means that we are not in a position simply to *learn* the facts and lessons of history. We are required instead to *think, explore*, and *judge*: not to hear what the past is itching to *tell us* but to investigate for ourselves.

History, then, is the *process* of methodical inquiry into the human past. Inquiry is of course the root meaning of Greek *historia*, the word that became English "history." Herodotus was known in antiquity as history's father,[8] although no one imagined that he fathered the past. But Herodotus realized that if he wanted to *know* what had actually transpired in the recent Persian-Greek wars, he could not rely on such stories, which in his region tended toward Greek triumphalism and ignorance of the other side. He would need to travel, explore, and investigate all sides for himself.[9] This is what made him the father of history: his applying the prestigious language of research (*historia*), which was being used for establishing reliable knowledge in other fields, to the human past. He was soon heavily criticized, as pioneers usually are, for not fulfilling this ambition very admirably. His successor Thucydides, who would become the gold standard for historians, even avoided the word *historia* for his work, presumably because he thought it tainted by Herodotus' indulgence and lack of critical acumen. He preferred simply to stress his own rigour, veracity,

---

[7] The war is usually dated A.D. 66 to 73. But Kokkinos (1998: 386–95) argues for 65 as the first year, and Masada may have fallen in the spring of 74 (see Chapter 9).

[8] Cicero (*Leg.* 1.1.5), citing a commonplace, although Cicero (also *à la mode*) thinks Herodotus full of fabulous tales.

[9] E.g., Herodotus 1.24.7, 31.1; 2.19. 3, 22–23, 19.1–2, 34.1, 44.1–5, 54.1, 113.1.

precision, skepticism, methodical doubt, testing, and proof.[10] Between the two of them, at any rate, they entrenched the idea that anyone who wanted to know the past in any meaningful sense could not simply learn it. He had to work very hard indeed to figure it out by comparing and explaining evidence.

Most historians today would agree that history is the methodical investigation of human activity in the past, but the many possible paths from that starting point defy simple summarization. One consequence of our agreed starting point is that the historian's default stance in relation to any given question about the past – in advance of a successful investigation into it – must be one of ignorance.[11] As historians, that is, we cannot claim to know what happened unless we can show colleagues how we acquired this knowledge, and we can only do that after a systematic investigation. This point is often neglected. Historians either feel compelled to believe something ("Until someone can show otherwise, I am happy believing X. . . .") or the public expects us to believe things, as though not knowing what happened were a moral failure. But belief is the province of religion, not history. Ancient historians must make their peace with uncertainty because that is where the nature of surviving evidence requires us to live much of the time. Our job description is to investigate responsibly, not to know what happened.

Another consequence of understanding history as methodical inquiry is that we must receive all *claims* about the past, whether ancient or modern, with skepticism and methodical doubt, kicking their tires and looking for their limitations in relation to the questions we are pursuing. They will have limitations, and so there is never a prospect of declaring any ancient source adequate or "reliable" for our inquiry. This lesson was hard to learn when the great Thucydides and Livy were knocked off their pedestals as "authoritative" accounts. It remains a problem in areas of ancient history with religious connections (#3 below). But history, as one application of critical thinking, must rest on ceaseless probing, questioning, and therefore doubt about what has been given.

When a historical argument survives scrutiny and is thought to explain a range of overlapping, independent evidence better than other hypotheses, our acceptance is only ever provisional. We then look for ways to connect it with other provisional scenarios, constantly comparing and revising our views of whole and part to see what needs refinement or complete rethinking. The human past itself cannot change, of course. It is truly finished. But history

---

[10] E.g., μαρτύριον (evidence) in Thucydides 1.8.1, 33.1, 73.3; 3.11.4, 53.4; 6.82.2; τεκμήριον (convincing proof) in 1.1.3, 20.1, 21.1, 34.3, 73.5, 132.5; 2.15.4, 39.2, 50.2; 3.66.1; 6.28.2; ἔλεγχος (testing, testable evidence) and cognate verb in 1.132.1, 135.2; 3.38.4, 53.3, 61.1, 86.1. For analysis, see Hornblower 1987:100–107.

[11] Note the catchy subtitle of J. Neusner's *Rabbinic Literature and the New Testament* (1993): "What we cannot show, we do not know."

understood as the *critical investigation* of that past changes without rest. Popular and schoolbook images of history as something fixed, standing outside us and seeking to instruct us, do not reflect the real world.

2. Although many historians would agree on this much, principled disagreements among them create other fissures. Some of this has to do with changing trends, some with personal taste, background, and influences, and some with one's areas of research. The kinds of history one can attempt for ancient Parthia or Galilean village life in the first century B.C., for example, will be different from research into World War II or British trade unions in the 1980s, for which we have abundant written, material, and probably audiovisual evidence. But enduring differences of historical philosophy are also a factor.

As soon as we give it serious thought, history presents real conceptual challenges. (a) Because the past itself does not exist, what can we study? (b) What is the relationship between surviving evidence and the real past as it was once lived? (c) What is the intellectual justification for studying the past, especially the remote past? (d) How sure can we be of our results – and does this matter? (e) Are some ways of studying the past more legitimate than others? (f) Is *knowledge* of the past possible, and if so in what sense?

One gateway to such problems is the famous book entitled *What Is History?* by E. H. Carr, a historian of Soviet Russia, comprising his 1961 G. M. Trevelyan lectures at Cambridge University. Because of its lively style, compact size, and appealing title, this paperback remains a favourite among history students. But if undergraduates imagine that it lays out generally accepted foundations, Carr is quick to disabuse them. He begins by showing how contested the principles of historical research were even in 1961. He defends his positions ably, but in the process shows that they are far from being universally held.[12]

Although he is deservedly respected, Carr makes two propositions that, if we were to accept them, would preclude much of what follows in this book. First, he considers *social forces* alone to be history's proper object, rejecting any concern with individuals as such:[13] "The facts of history are . . . facts about *the relations of individuals to one another in society*. . . ."[14] The convention Carr has in view is an inheritance from the mid-nineteenth century: a quasi-scientific perspective on the past, which we might call positivist (see next paragraph).[15] A history restricted to social forces would place out of bounds the unique

---

[12] Carr 2001 [1961]: 3–4. For an overview of the work's impact, see R. Evans in pp. ix–xlvi of this Jubilee edition.

[13] Carr 2001: 25–49.   [14] Carr 2001: 42, 46, 49, emphasis mine.

[15] Carr mentions positivists only to distance himself, because they take all "facts" to be of equal value, whereas he selects only those that are "on the side of history" (Carr 2001: 2–4). But his preoccupation with social forces, predictive laws from the past, and humanity in the aggregate puts him at least in the larger positivist family. Cf. I. Berlin (2002: 20): "Carr is . . .

situations and decisions of Gessius Florus, Cestius Gallus, John of Gischala, Josephus, or Simon bar Giora, who will all be important individual actors in our investigation (Chapters 5–9). Equally difficult is Carr's view that only what endures *in retrospect* from a given period is worthy of historical investigation. He dispenses with mere *chance events*, considering only those that subsequently prove to be revealing of social forces worthy of the historian's time.

> Just as from the infinite ocean of facts the historian selects those which are significant for his purpose, so from the multiplicity of sequences of cause and effect he extracts those, and only those, which are *historically signifi-cant*; and the standard of historical significance is his ability to fit them into *his pattern of rational explanation and interpretation*.[16]

Although Carr has a way of sounding reasonable, this is a remarkable position, first in its assumption that the historian gazes on an ocean of usable *facts*, which require only selection and rearrangement. But what makes them facts? Second, only those facts that yield or express general laws, such as "Wars begin for reasons X, Y, and Z," deserve the historian's time.

Both Carr's belief in the existence of ready-to-use facts and his preoccupation with laws that arise from these facts and aid prediction justify including him with the tradition I have labelled *positivist*. Since the early nineteenth century, partly because of our insecurity about the status of history in the university, there has been a powerful tendency to refashion history to make it look more like the prestigious natural sciences. Only if we abandoned the intuitive, often rhetorical and moralizing narratives long associated with history, trading them for a cold hard look at the human species in the aggregate and in ways that invite statistical analysis could we hope to pass muster as a worthy discipline. Alas, when the dawn of the twentieth century saw natural scientists begin to seize history-writing from seemingly soft-headed humanists, they produced cold hard studies indeed, purporting to show the racial basis of human progress, a framework deeply ingrained since the rise of positivism but made ever more respectable with the apparent aid of biology.[17] That sanguine kind of law-generating history, merging with the prevailing science, at least supported various expressions of national competition and attempted racial

essentially a late positivist, in the tradition of Auguste Comte, Herbert Spencer and H. G. Wells."

[16] Carr 2001: 99–100, emphasis mine.

[17] For stronger scientific claims for history see Comte 1896 [1830–1842]: 1.2; 2.299–333; 3.1–5 (already with racial overtones); Buckle 1903 [1857]: 1.2–7; Spencer 1896 [1872]: v, 31; Marx 1904 [1859]: 11–12; Hempel 1942. For the growing racial-biological enthusiasm (and criticism of soft humanists), Chamberlain 1910: xcvii, 2.200–211; Grant (Chairman, New York Zoological Society; trustee of the Natural History Museum) 1916: 7–14, 59, 79, 100 (cf. the introduction by a Professor of Zoology at Columbia, vii–ix); Gobineau 1915 [1853]: xv, lxvi; Dalberg-Acton 1907: 240–41.

purification. It has all but disappeared since the 1940s and humanists, who had never left the room, were able to reassert their right to history. But deep insecurities remain and may be growing again in a world dominated by technocrats, about the purposes, methods, and value of historical research.

More enduring and wholesome quasi-scientific directions emerged from Karl Marx's interpretation of societies at different stages of economic evolution. From about the 1920s, although the inclination is older, historians have found ever new ways of exploring the past "from the bottom up." Reacting equally against conservative histories of "great men" and their political institutions and a dehumanizing concern with vast schemes of racial-national progress, they have been interested in the real-life social and economic conditions of the majority of people: the voiceless poor, slaves, common soldiers, artisans, labourers, women, and children. Lacking evidence for specific individuals outside elite circles, social historians investigate such questions as family structures, infant mortality, water and food supply, farm labour, the internal workings of the ancient or mediaeval city, incidence of disease, women's occupations, slave tasks, or life in a military camp. For the study of such ongoing social conditions, which do not change abruptly, it does not matter if the evidence comes from different places over a span of decades.[18]

Alongside the social-scientific, collective approaches to the past, some kinds of investigation still require that we attend to individuals, not because they are the "great men" who have shaped world history but simply because individual choices and actions are important for the events. This is the case with our inquiry into a single war led by unique protagonists in a particular place within just a few years. Each chapter includes consideration of long-span conditions and Chapter 3 is devoted to them, but certain figures also demand attention. Just as in Rome Cicero and Catalina, Caesar and Pompey, or Octavian and Marc Antony had much in common as to class and status, yet must be studied as individuals, so also in the Judean War a great deal turned on the particular contexts and actions of men of the same general type and class, who were however not interchangeable: on one side Cestius Gallus, Vespasian, and Titus; on the other side Josephus, John of Gischala, and Eleazar ben Hanania (Ananias).

In other words, the following inquiry in the humanistic tradition. Even as social-scientific history increasingly drew our attention to groups, types, models, and patterns of behaviour, historians from Thomas Carlyle and J. G. Droysen to R. G. Collingwood and Isaiah Berlin remained resolutely

---

[18] Highly productive and enduring examples of ancient social history include Braudel 1958: 725–53 and e.g., Saller 1982, 1994; Hopkins 1983; Edmondson 1987; Harris 1989; Parkin 1992; Cribiore 2001; Harlow and Laurence 2002; Harland 2003; Scheidel 2004; Scheidel and Friesen 2009.

interested in individuals and their particular situations.[19] If we want a label for this approach, to weigh against positivist history on the aggregate side, we might call it *historicist* (from German *Historismus*), although both terms are used with disconcerting variety.

In spite of the ongoing debates among historians about the nature of our craft, we may press forward with wise words from Marc Bloch, the co-founder of the social-historical *Annaliste* school who would fall victim to the Gestapo in 1944:

> The word [history] places no *a priori* prohibitions in the path of inquiry, which may turn at will toward either the individual or the social, toward momentary convulsions or the most lasting developments. It comprises in itself no credo; it commits us, according to its original meaning, to nothing more than "inquiry."[20]

3. Finally, all historical research is shaped by modern contexts,[21] and the study of Roman Judaea is no exception. Contemporary political, social, and religious concerns can shape discussions in ways both obvious and subtle. For one thing, scholars who specialize in this field do not uniformly work in departments of history or classics, as historians of other parts of the Roman empire usually do. Their departmental homes are just as likely to be in religious studies, Jewish studies, archaeology, biblical studies, or theology. If even those who understand themselves to be historians and nothing else differ significantly in method, the potential for disagreement over aims and methods is likely to be all the greater in this field. On top of that lie all the potential stakes in this period held by Jews and Christians of various kinds, religious and non- and anti-religious scholars, Zionists, post-Zionists, and anti-Zionists.

Consider two examples of what might seem innocuous debates about semantics, which can both create misunderstandings of a kind not found in the study of Roman Egypt or Britain. First is the spillover of concerns about the Bible and its authority. Only in this area do we encounter debates over what are styled *maximalist* and *minimalist* approaches to ancient history. These categories extend disagreements about the usefulness of biblical accounts for Israelite history to involve the post-biblical and "New Testament" or even later periods.[22] Minimalists are said to nurture what their opponents consider

---

[19] E.g., Isaiah Berlin (2002: 18–30; cf. 94–165), here p. 26: "[A]nyone concerned with human beings is committed to consideration of motives, purposes, choices, the specifically human experience that belongs to human beings uniquely. . . ."

[20] Bloch 1992 [1941]: 17.

[21] This is true even of the history established in the University of Berlin (in a Prussia dominated by Napoleon) as rigorously free and scientific, soon to become the Western model. Cf. Iggers et al. 2008: 71–76.

[22] E.g., Sandgren (2010: 3–4), introducing a survey from the sixth century B.C. to the seventh century A.D.: "There are two contemporary and competing approaches to historical

an unhealthy "hermeneutic(s) of suspicion," a failure to trust sources that have done them no harm and do not merit suspicion.

These debates cause confusion to no purpose. If history means disciplined inquiry into the human past (above), then we investigate problems by interpreting and explaining whatever evidence is available, all of it but no more than that. Methodical doubt of all claims, our own as well as others', is the animating principle of critical inquiry. R. G. Collingwood (1926) rightly called it "a working hypothesis without which no historian can move a single step."[23] From this perspective, maximalism and minimalism have no useful meaning. As for the "hermeneutics of suspicion," which is a term of opprobrium in these discussions, Paul Ricoeur most famously used it to express his view of language, as both concealing and revealing.[24] Language is our medium of thought and communication, but we should never imagine it to be simply revelatory. We should be duly suspicious. Ricoeur's "masters of suspicion," a term of respect, were Nietzsche, Marx, and Freud – *not* people who doubted the accuracy of ancient texts, but great thinkers alert to what language could and could not say.[25]

A second special impediment in our area of history is a kind of dependence on the tag-team of archaeology and Josephus' works. It is often assumed that if Josephus tells a story and we can "check" it with archaeology, or conversely if an archaeological find can be "confirmed" by Josephus, then little remains to be done.[26] Josephus' master narrative should be doubted when it concerns himself or the Flavians, the thinking goes. But when archaeology supports his factual accuracy, this formidable pair pushes history out of the ring, making it superfluous.

When history is thought to have a function, its remit may be oddly reduced to the study of *elite literary accounts* – effectively the works of Josephus for most of this period. Whereas historians like the smell of old books, archaeologists are out in the fresh air before the crack of dawn to study *real life*.[27] In popular perception and to an extent in academic work, the sunkissed science has the

---

investigation. . . . One is called minimalism, the other maximalism. . . . The minimalist applies the so-called hermeneutic of suspicion to our sources. Every witness has an ulterior motive, or may be outright lying, unless it can be proven otherwise. . . . The maximalist leans in the other direction. . . . Some call this approach a hermeneutic of trust." Cf. Garfinkel 2011.

[23] Collingwood 1994 [1946 with earlier material]: 378.   [24] E.g., Rorty 1989.

[25] Ricoeur 1970: 32. Cf. Stewart 1989: 296–307; Leiter 2004: 74–105.

[26] E.g., the chapter "Archaeology and Josephus" in Meyers 1999: 109–22. This dialectic is standard: throughout Yadin 1966; Broshi 1982: 379–84; with Cohen 1982: 385–405; Avigad 1983; Ben Zeev 1993: 215–34; Rappaport 1994: 279–89. Occasional criticism (Moehring 1984; McLaren 1998: 178–218, 226–36; Mason 2009a: 103–37) may gradually be having a small impact.

[27] E.g., Leon 1960 and Kadman 1960 devote chapters to "the historical record/background," by which they mean the literary accounts, before turning to material evidence.

decisive edge in this relationship,[28] its political uses providing an even glossier sheen of prestige.[29] Although most questions that people ask about the ancient past are by definition historical, history often seems to be a guest in the house of the more vigorous archaeology.[30] This is understandable in popular culture, given the spectacular achievements of archaeology over the last half century in Israel and Palestine. On a dig one can certainly get the exhilarating feeling that excavation brings the past immediately to life. It is as though Lazaruses were popping out of their tombs everywhere, hungry for dinner and ready to tell their stories.

That impression is a mirage, however. Finds in the ground, like literary texts, have no voice to declare their meaning and significance. All survivals require interpretation: What *are* they and what might they mean for various kinds of investigation? That is why debates persist about the interpretation of even the famous remains at Qumran or various inscriptions, coin symbols and legends, and even tableware. These finds do not come with manuals explaining their meaning. Much less do they solve *our* investigative problems for us.[31] Just as philology interprets textual survivals, so archaeology interprets material remains. Papyrology, epigraphy, ceramic studies, numismatics, art, and architecture are among the subspecialties that study classes of archaeological finds together in catalogues of coins, inscriptions, or monuments from certain regions and periods.

So I shall use *history* to mean simply the investigation of the human past. This includes both the interpretation of surviving evidence and the imaginative reconstruction of scenarios that might have created this evidence. Investigation

---

[28] Cf. Magness (2002: 4–5): "although both archaeologists and historians study the past. ... Archaeologists learn about the past through the study of the material remains left by humans, whereas historians study written records (texts)." But cf. Wilamowitz-Moellendorff, who concluded a 1921 survey of the discipline of ancient history (*Philologie*): "research of this kind entails a descent to the masses from the rarefied atmosphere of polite society in an effort to understand unliterary, irrational, unsophisticated humanity" (1982: 177). Zunz 1985: 3–10 likewise describes the most common kinds of *history* today – social history – as something much like Magness's archaeology.

[29] Cf. Hallote and Joffe 2002; Rabinovich 2011, citing then-president of the Israel Exploration Society Y. Aviram (e.g.: "archaeology was a major instrument of nation-building" before 1948).

[30] The deservedly popular *Biblical Archaeology Review* hosts many historical investigations, as does *The Naked Archaeologist* television series: http://en.wikipedia.org/wiki/The_Naked_Archaeologist#Season_1_.282005.29 (accessed 15 June 2013).

[31] Woolf (2006: 93): "Modern historians who specialize in the Roman provinces have a bad habit of treating ancient authors as if they are research assistants. ... [O]ur 'witnesses' are not colleagues, their texts are not responses to our research questions, and at least some apparent resemblances between their texts and the products of modern scientific research are profoundly misleading." Cf. Syme 1970b; Walbank 1972; Luce 1977; Woodman 1988; Plass 1988; Eckstein 1995; Feldherr 1998; Mellor 1993, 1999; Kraus and Woodman 1997; Champion 2004; Pitcher 2009.

begins with the formulation of a problem.,[32] Much like a detective, the historian is an investigator who imagines and test possibilities against the evidence.[33]

In case this all sounds too insubstantial, I would stress two points. First, our constant reimagining of what we cannot see, which is the basis of progress in science, does not mean that all scenarios are equally plausible. We imagine so that we do not overlook what might actually have happened to create our evidence, and our scenarios remain answerable to the evidence. Second, we will prefer a scenario that explains the most with the smallest investment of assumption and supposition. This preference for economy is also basic to scientific thinking. Although it is *possible* that a person with a headache has a brain tumour, physicians cannot send everyone with a headache for expensive scans, because tumours are rare in comparison with other causes of headache. Only when they have ruled out common causes can doctors justify tests for what is rare. In somewhat the same way, although it is possible that all Judaea was charged with messianic fervour through several generations, that Romans harboured a unique and irrational hatred of the Jews over the same period, or that Simon bar Giora was possessed of a frenzied messianic consciousness, we should turn to such possibilities only if there is evidence that does not yield to explanations from more common human experiences.

As we close this overview of historical foundations for our inquiry, I am aware of having condensed much and omitted more. In distinguishing the interpretation of evidence from the imagining of what produced it, for example, I would not want to be misunderstood as having installed a turnstile between them, as though one could only move to imagining real life when one had finished completely with interpretation. Interpretation does have a certain *logical* priority over reconstructing the lost past, because we would waste a lot of speculating if we did not have a clear idea of the evidence, but this does not translate to a rigid chronological priority. The act of formulating a problem about the real past requires that we have already thought about some possibilities, and most historians probably begin with hunches. But if we are to avoid becoming like the southern sheriffs of film and song, who know what happened without needing to investigate, we must recognize the interpretation and explanation of evidence as a separate exercise from our free imagining. This is something that Lord Acton (1862) got right: "The absence of a definite didactic purpose is the only security for the good faith of a historian."[34] We must accept that the evidence may not be amenable to our hunches and be willing to adjust course throughout our investigation.

---

[32] Collingwood 1994 [1946, here 1926]: 269; Momigliano 1977: 368–69; Ginzburg 1991.
[33] Collingwood 1994: 266–82.   [34] Dalberg-Acton 1922 [1907]: 236.

The remaining chapters will offer many examples of the principles I have tried to sketch here. Before we proceed with the interpretation of Josephus' *War*, which is a large part of the evidence that will need explaining, let us recapitulate.

1. History means above all the methodical investigation of the human past. Without investigation we cannot know the past, in a historical sense.

2. Because history is a method, the chief requirement of a historical inquiry is that it be transparent and in principle repeatable by others.

3. Whether enough evidence has survived to support confident results is not our responsibility. That depends on *force majeure* and the accidents of transmission and discovery. Our task is to investigate our problems responsibly. In our control are the formulation of those problems, the construction of the inquiry, the interpretation of evidence, and our willingness to imagine and test explanations.

4. Historical investigation requires two distinct modes of thinking: interpreting remains from the past that interest us and imagining scenarios that would explain this evidence as it bears on our investigation.

Interpreting Josephus' War

Josephus' earliest and most famous work is not the only survival relevant to our inquiries, but it is the single most important one and so we need to have an idea of what is actually in it. We need to do this in particular because false impressions abound. To begin with the obvious, the *Jewish War* by Josephus is a vestige from an long-gone and alien world, whose elite members communicated in a particular kind of Greek discourse that is far removed from our sensibilities. When Josephus speaks of the *polis* and challenges faced by *polis* leaders, or the sacred precinct (*to hieron*) within the *polis* and its dangerous pollution (*miasma*), we cannot immediately relate to these categories. To understand his work we must step outside the comfort of our language, values, and social-political assumptions to think in terms of the Greek discourse that he shared with his audiences.

Let us begin by scouting some of the core values imparted by rhetorical culture in the first century, which shaped the writing of history and all other literature, the ways in which books typically came into being, and the categories assumed in ancient discussions of society, politics, and piety.

I. CONTEXTS: HISTORY-WRITING, CHARACTER, AND RHETORIC

In the early third century the senator Cassius Dio had the courage to stare historical uncertainty in the face, and the honesty to spell out the difference between real events and literary representations (53.19.4–6):

Much that does not actually happen gets endlessly repeated, while much that really does happen remains unknown, and in more or less every case there is a difference between what happens and what gets reported. Certainly, too, the size of the empire and the number of things going on make accuracy in these respects a very slippery prospect. In Rome a great deal is happening, and much in the subject territory [provinces] too, and with the enemy it is always something or other – every single day, you might say. When it comes to these things, no one beyond the circle of those immediately involved can easily get a clear picture, while most people do not even hear the first thing of what happened.

With this in mind, I shall explain everything in sequence, as much as needs to be said at any rate, *as it has been made public here and there, whether it really happened like that or in some other way.* Something of my own perspective will certainly be added to the mix, to the extent that is acceptable, in those cases where, instead of what gets endlessly repeated, I have been able to confirm a different account from the many things I have read, heard, or seen.

Such a rare disclosure from one of our "authorities" deserves pondering. Dio concedes that much of the time he does not know what happened – and nor does anyone else. For the sake of a compelling narrative, however, he will unabashedly retell stories about which he is uncertain.

We might well ask: "Why write at all if you are so uncertain?" Dio obviates this question by highlighting his personal authority, in the process exposing central values of his time. History has lessons for men who think about political affairs as he does, and these moral lessons are more important than knowing exactly who did what to whom, when, and why.

A century and a half before Dio, Josephus enrolled himself in the list of statesmen and military commanders writing history in retirement. Such men rarely put the matter as clearly as Dio, but they often signalled how difficult it was to know things. Decades before Josephus, Strabo had tried to immunize his lost *History* and surviving *Geography* against picayune criticism on that score by directing attention to the moral-political weight of his work (*Geog.* 1.1.23, emphasis added):

So, after we had made our *Historical Outlines* – beneficial, we reckon, *for moral and political philosophy* – we resolved to supplement them with the present composition [the *Geography*]. It has the same form and is *for the same men,* particularly those *in high positions.* Still another similarity is that, just as that other work [the *History*] brings to memory the lives of illustrious men and *leaves aside what is small and inestimable,* so also here we must disregard what is trivial and inconspicuous, and concern ourselves with *what is distinguished and grand,* wherever we find that which is practically useful, conducive to memory, and pleasurable. Just as with colossal structures *we do not examine each little bit meticulously,* but take in the parts as a whole and [ask] whether *the whole* works well, this is also how one should reach a judgement about these present volumes. For this [*Geography*] is a sort of colossus in the making, *explaining large matters and wholes*, except where some small item is able to stimulate the lover of learning and *the practical leader*. These remarks were made in order to say that the work at hand is serious, and *suitable for a philosopher*.

A reader impertinent enough to ask, "Are you sure that *x* occurred precisely then and there?" would have been met with a roll of the eyes. There are truths more important than mere facts.

History was another vehicle through which elite men asserted their moral authority. They were not expected to make original discoveries about what happened on a given day and show how they knew this to be so; they did not expect scrutiny on that mundane level. After Herodotus, they rarely paused to explain even roughly how they knew things – beyond making general claims about their hard work in research or, if possible, eyewitness status. If they named sources at all it tended to be in support of an overall evaluation of the source's character: completely reliable, as Josephus with Judaea's holy books, completely unreliable because of some unacceptable bias, or only polemically usable.[35] Authors postured as men of trustworthy character exercising their uniquely keen moral judgment in weighing up the evidence. There was no point in laying out that evidence for scrutiny by others who lacked their insight. They expected to be judged by the prevailing cultural values. These were instilled by years of training in rhetoric, which was about more than mere words.

Rhetoric

Rhetoric – the ability to persuade others in the courtroom, in speeches deliberating political or military policy, in varied social contexts, and in writing across genres – was the umbrella subject of the ancient curriculum. Philosophy was a theoretical competitor, but by the first century it had been largely assimilated to the rhetorical programme. Society's leaders had to seem familiar with the teachings of the main philosophical schools (Platonists, Stoics, Epicureans) about life, death, and moral action, and such virtues as simplicity, self-control, contempt for luxury, and death. But real devotion to a philosophical school fit awkwardly with the practical, compromising ethos of public life.[36] Leading men might be called upon to serve as defence advocates and prosecutors, judges, military commanders, councilmen, senators, priests, landowners, and writers on every subject of public utility. Intensive training and

---

[35] For one early episode, Polybius prefers Aratus over Phylarchus – whose account is simply *false* because of the author's political allegiances (2.56–63).

[36] See Marrou 1956; MacMullen 1966.

practice in rhetoric was the best formation for these tasks, and the goal to which lower levels of grammatical and literary study led.[37] Odd though it may seem now, the assumption that the most important subject for a society's leaders was the accumulated wisdom of its classical texts endured well into the modern period (see Chapter 3 for military applications).

Ancient students not only committed great texts to *memory*, which was the most fundamental skill. They learned to take famous episodes from the Greek or Roman past, rewrite them in various ways, reargue military and political decisions made centuries earlier, and extract an endless variety of moral lessons. To develop mental agility they practised arguing both sides of a criminal case, adducing opposite moral conclusions from the same evidence, so that once they were active in public life they would be capable of making whatever case the occasion required.[38] They would need such dexterity to lead the mass of common people. Versatility was the name of the game.[39] In the rhetoric-teacher Antiphon's *Tetralogies* a character complains about the difficulties facing the man who would stand up for simple truth in the face of potent speakers who are able to twist matters however they wish (*Tetr.* 2.2.2). But of course, a claim to care only about the truth – "Unaccustomed as I am to fancy talk, I want to say this from the heart..." – was rhetoric's trump card.[40]

Cicero embodied this rhetorical spirit when he boasted that he was able to "inspire in the judge a feeling of angry indignation or move him to tears, or indeed sway his feelings *in whatever direction the situation* demanded" (*Brut.* 93.322). Not everyone was enamoured of such rhetorical craft, however, and this is important for understanding Josephus. The reputation of the old Greek sophists for being able to make bad arguments appear good ones made some people uneasy.[41] A surviving critique of Cicero accused him of lacking moral principles: "Whom do you hold as a friend, or as an enemy?. . . . Your thinking about the Republic changes as you stand or sit."[42] If rhetoric could make people believe anything, was it not dangerous?

---

[37] Cribiore 2001 provides vivid evidence from Egyptian papyri of school exercises, if mainly in a period somewhat later than ours.

[38] Cf. the *progymnasmata* (Theon, *Prog.* 62–64, 107–10; Quintilian, *Inst.* 1.9.2; 10.5.4–11) and other manuals: Marrou 1956: 194–205, 284–91; Hock and O'Neil 1987: 35–37; Cribiore 2001: 56–57; Kennedy 2003.

[39] Sprague 1968, 1972; Ballif and Moran 2005: 146–57.

[40] Cf. Paul in 1 Corinthians 1:18–2:13; 2 Corinthians 10.

[41] E.g., Plato, *Gorg.* 449a–461e on the lack of connection between rhetoric and virtue (455a, 458a: rhetoric persuades on the level of belief/opinion only; it does not educate one in the truth); Quintilian, *Inst.* 2.16.3–4.

[42] *Inv. Cic.* 4. The essay was transmitted with Sallust's writings, although scholars have guessed that it was by M. Porcius Latro. It may itself be (as perhaps Ps-Plutarch on Herodotus) a rhetorical exercise: If one were to attack the great Cicero, how would one do it?

Teachers of rhetoric had a ready answer: "Rhetoric doesn't hurt people; people hurt people. The best remedy for a bad man using rhetoric is a good man using rhetoric."[43] Plato in the *Gorgias*, Aristotle, and Josephus' contemporary Quintilian agreed that rhetoric was a potentially dangerous tool, but they held that it should (or could) be used only by *good* men. Good and bad men were in their view clearly recognizable characters.[44] This view also seems to underlie Josephus' autobiography. He presents pre-war Galilee as a scene of perpetual dissembling by rival leaders, both good and bad. His opponents are congenital liars, but he also constantly dissembles to the common people.[45] What distinguishes him from his adversaries is not skill in deceptive rhetoric, which they share, but *the character* and motives of the one deceiving.[46] Good leaders do it only for the public welfare, whereas demagogues conscript an unwary public for their self-serving schemes.

Rhetoric had many principled detractors, including philosophers, Spartans, and Romans of the old school. Philosophers advised people to speak little and modestly and to focus on moral action.[47] Even the Athenians reportedly banned sophists from their courtrooms for a time in the fourth century B.C., because people spoke so compellingly on all sides of an issue that audiences despaired of figuring out the truth.[48] In classical Sparta, contempt for Athenian-style rhetoric meant that citizens-in-training learned to speak in pithy aphorisms, which we still call *laconic* after Sparta's territory Laconia.[49] Many philosophers in turn admired Sparta as a nearly ideal society; some even wore the rough Spartan cloak.[50] Elite Roman culture included a Spartan strain, and Polybius pointed out parallels between Roman and Spartan

---

[43] Aristotle, *Rhet.* 1355b: "If [it be objected that] one who uses such power with words unjustly may cause enormous injury, well, this is a common trait of all good things, except virtue [good by definition]. . . . Whoever uses these justly has the potential to do the greatest good; but unjustly, to do harm."

[44] Plato, *Gorg.* 460a–e; Quintilian, *Inst.* 2.16.11: rhetoric means speaking well (*bene*), which only a good man (*vir bonus*) can do.

[45] His enemies: *Life* 37–40, 217–22, 236, 280–89; Josephus: 126–44, 148, 163, 169, 223–25, 265, 379.

[46] E.g., *Life* 36: Justus of Tiberias was "longing for revolutionary activities, intending to manufacture power for himself." 134: Jesus of Tiberias was "a wretched person whose nature was to disrupt important affairs, a sedition-fomenter and revolutionary like no other."

[47] E.g., Aesop, *Fab.* 22.1–3; Thucydides 1.39.2, 69.5, 128.3, 144.2; 2.65.9; 4.67.1, 70.2, 87.1; 7.48.3; 8.46.3; Seneca, *Ep.* 20.2; Dio, *Or.* 68, 70.3; Epictetus in Arrian, *Diatr.* 3.26.8–23; Lucian, *Herm.* 9–19; Josephus, *War* 1.288; 5.361, 457; 6.200; *Ant.* 2.253, 272; 3.306; etc.; *Apion* 2.12, 169–72, 182, 241. Wardy 2009 gives a nuanced account of the relationship between philosophy and rhetoric.

[48] Philostratus, *VS* 483; cf. Quintilian, *Inst.* 2.16.4.

[49] Plutarch, *Lyc.* 19–20. An admirer, Plutarch writes not only the biographer of the Spartan lawgiver but separate treatises on their institutions and on the pithy sayings of their men and women.

[50] Demosthenes, *Con.* 34; Plato, *Symp.* 219b; *Prot.* 335d; Arrian, *Diatr.* 3.1.34; Diogenes Laertius 6.13; cf. Tertullian, *On the Pallium.*

values.[51] Cato the Elder remarked that "Among the Greeks, words issue from the lips; among the Romans, from their hearts." Dionysius tells the story of a consul on a diplomatic visit to a Greek-Italian city who, on being ridiculed for his imperfect Greek diction, promised to return not with words, so beloved of Greeks, but with blood.[52] Training in oratory taught the projection of a strong masculine voice, gait, gestures,[53] but this did not prevent Spartan, Roman, and philosophical detractors from disparaging it as an effeminate Greek pursuit unworthy of dignified men.[54]

Josephus aligns his Judean people with the more masculine, action-not-words value system. He opens *War* with a stinging attack on others who are writing about the Judean conflict in a "sophistic" way – all style and no hard substance (1.2–6). His own work has been criticized, he says, by certain "Greek wordy-men" in Rome, who are pleased with themselves as they brilliantly retail useless tales of old Greece in fine style, while they ignore more important recent events (1.13). They may have superior *speech-craft*, he concedes, but they care nothing for *truth* (1.16). *Antiquities* takes a number of swipes at Greek word culture, and Josephus' last known work, the *Apion*, ramps up the anti-rhetorical rhetoric.[55] Josephus remarks that, although he himself has worked hard at learning Greek literature, his people "do not look favourably on those who have mastered the languages of many nations, and deck out their speech with elegance of styles, because they consider such a pursuit to be perfectly common" (20.264). Even slaves can do that sort of thing. His literary nemesis Justus of Tiberias, he says derisively, is a man with "the Greek sort of education" who can overcome better arguments with "a kind of guile through words" (*Life* 40).

Josephus assumes that fancy talk is the refuge of rascals. Virtuous men must possess oratorical skill, alas, because the masses may need a barnstorming speech to move them, and Josephus' *War* includes perhaps ten substantial orations.[56] Chapter 9 will examine one (or two?) of the most famous, by Eleazar at Masada. Here I can offer only summary remarks on *War*'s speeches as a class.[57]

---

[51] Polybius 6.10–11, 50–51; Wardman 1976: 90–93; Kennell 1995: 80–82.

[52] Plutarch, *Cat. Mai.* 12.5; Dionysius, *Ant. rom.* 9.5.1.

[53] Gleason 1995; Corbeill 2004: 122, 134; cf. Richlin 1992a, 1992b; Williams 1999; Ferris 2000: 1–62; Deacy and Pierce 2002.

[54] E.g., Cicero, *Mur.* 29; Valerius Maximus 3.2.22; 4.7.4; 9.1.5; Pliny, *Nat.* pr. 24–28; 24.4; 29.14; Tacitus, *Dial.* 15; *Ann.* 14.20; Juvenal 3.60; 6.185–99. For contexts, Syme 1970b: 504–19; Wardman 1976: 110–34; Balsdon 1979: 30–38.

[55] *Ant.* 1.15, 121, 123–24, 129, 168; 2.3; *Apion* 1.4–7, 12–15, 20–21, 28. Cf. *Ant.* 19.209: the hated emperor Gaius abandoned concern for justice and good government, being obsessed with rhetorical practice and "how to appear instantly more persuasive than anyone else."

[56] Agrippa II against war (2.346–404), Josephus against suicide (3.361–91), Ananus II against Zealots (4.163–92), Jesus against Idumaeans (4.238–69), Simon the Idumaean (4.271–283), Josephus outside Jerusalem (5.361–419), Titus to faltering troops (6.33–53), Josephus' final appeal (6.97–112), Titus' final speech (6.327–53), Eleazar at Masada (7.341–88).

[57] See Lindner 1972: 21–39; Runnalls 1997; Price 2008; Mason 2008: 265–68; 2011; 2012a.

(1) Of the three recognized functions of oratory – forensic/judicial (debating guilt for past actions), deliberative (pondering future action), and epideictic (display) – all are deliberative. They are given in moments of crisis and urgently advocate courses of action. Genuine deliberative speeches were rare in the early empire, because cities under Roman rule had little freedom to make important decisions. It seems that *War*'s powerful speeches, with life and death hanging in the balance, would have engrossed and moved a willing audience.

(2) The speakers are not before a council that welcomes different opinions.[58] Addressing a resistant or even hostile segment of the public, they have the difficult and dangerous task of dissuading them from their course and persuading them of the speaker's alternative.

(3) Each speech is a *tour de force*, in which the speaker simplifies and somewhat distorts realities known to Josephus' literary audience: as with Agrippa's claims about the acquiescence of Rome's provinces or the character Josephus' proposition that Judeans had never succeeded in armed conflict.[59]

(4) In spite of their contextual urgency, most of the speeches include strangely abstract, debating-school elements that pursue oddly remote philosophical, historical, or exegetical questions: Agrippa surveying the Empire's legionary dispositions, Josephus sermonizing on biblical stories, and Eleazar exploring nuances of Indian philosophy as the gates of his hilltop redoubt burn.

(5) Josephus can highlight the manipulative nature of the speech. He sometimes has the speaker first attempt a brief rational argument, which fails, and only then realize that he must resort to high-flown oratory. The effectiveness of grand speeches with commoners appears as an unfortunate fact of life.

(6) Although rhetoric can momentarily stir the needed impulses, it cannot change political-military realities.[60]

(7) When scholars read Josephus' work mainly as a compilation of sources, some looked to the speeches as the parts most likely to reveal his worldview or theology, because few doubted that he had composed these parts.[61] The considerations above cast doubt on this logic. Although the speeches are his and do include recurring themes, he configures each one for its occasion and speaker, who must often bend reality for his purpose. The speeches are not

---

[58] An exception is *War* 2.25–36, a pair of speeches before Augustus' *consilium* on Herod's succession, which I do not include above because of their relative brevity and remote location. In 4.238–83 we have dueling speeches concerning the Idumaeans, but these are in the form of mutual abuse rather than pleading before an audience.

[59] Mason 2008: 265–68 and commentary following.

[60] Successes: 2.404; 3.387–91; 4.193–95; 5.420–22; 6.54–59. I differ from Price (2008), who proposes that the decisive framework is Thucydidean contrast between the failure of rational speech and the success of irrational. NB: Eleazar's speech succeeds explicitly as the triumph of *reason over emotion*, although this is ironic.

[61] Lindner 1972: 1–39.

stable repositories of Josephus' personal ideology, but we shall also see that
there is no reason to regard the rest of his work as borrowed.

The ancients recognized that writing history was not the same as composing
speeches for the public square or drama, which freely indulged emotion.
Unlike orators or playwrights, historians were constrained by *the truth*. But
the truth in question turns out to have had more to do with moral tone and
gravitas than proofs concerning events and facts. The idea was: "We can tell
that this historian is speaking the truth because of his sober masculine tone, free
of feminine emotion or embellishment."[62] Strikingly, however, the most vocal
advocates of a supposed "law of history" that would exclude emotional or
tragic display were among its most blatant transgressors. They mentioned such
a law only to explain why they felt compelled to violate it at some crucial
moment: "What I'm about to say is *so* compelling that I must suspend the laws
of history, which of course I otherwise follow."[63] The audience should think:
How bold, how courageous, how *truthful*!

As Strabo suggests above, the same elite men were usually writing for the
same audiences, in any genre they chose. Aside from the division between
poetry and tragedy on one side and history and philosophy on the other,
genres were not clearly defined. Writers incorporated generous amounts of
history in geography, ethnography in history, and botanical or philosophical or
dramatic or violent colour wherever they liked.[64] Cicero's Atticus demands
that history show a sobriety different from rhetoric's playfulness (*Brut.*
85.292–93), but still requires that it be written by orators – for only they know
how to exploit moral *exempla*, which history furnishes (*De orat.* 2.35–36).[65]
Even the sober Polybius, after denouncing rhetorical and tragic intrusions into
others' history, stresses the importance of varying scene and tone – in keeping
with rhetoric's mandates (38.5–6). Dionysius uses rhetorical criteria generously
himself and also prescribes: "[I]t is necessary to relieve monotony by introducing appropriate changes, for change [ἡ μεταβολή] is the stuff of pleasure *in
every endeavour*" (*Comp. verb.* 12, my emphasis). His criticism of Thucydides
derives equally from stylistic preferences (*On Thucydides*) and from a moral

---

[62] See Polybius 2.56.8 on "the sordid [or low-born] and feminine project" of Phylarchus, and
Lucian, *Hist. conscr.* 8–10, ridiculing the prevailing drama-queen style as unmasculine (hence
untrustworthy and wrong).

[63] Josephus, *War* 1.11; 5.20; Cicero, *Leg.* 1.5; *De or.* 2.62; *Fam.* 5.12; Dionysius, *Thuc.* 8; cf. the
rhetorician Lucian, *Hist. conscr.* 7–9, 39–51 (42, on Thucydides' law of truth).

[64] Clarke 1999. Cf. Pliny, *Ep.* 7.17.3; Tacitus, *Dial.* 3; Aelius Theon (*Prog.* 70; cf. 60): "training
in exercises is absolutely useful not only for those who are going to practice rhetoric but also
if one wishes to undertake the function of poets or historians or any other writers." Examples
of such multigenre writers are Julius Caesar, Dionysius, Strabo, Pliny Elder and Younger,
Plutarch, and Tacitus. See Marincola 1997: 19–33.

[65] For discussion of the passage, see Cape 1997; on rhetorical values and historiography
generally Woodman 1988, Marincola 1997.

objection to Thucydides' theme: the disgrace of civil war (*Pomp.* 3). Evidence and facts do not appear.

Rhetoric's mandate meant that historians who needed to retell the same events did not simply repeat verbatim. That would have been boring. Gwyn Morgan shows how Tacitus, Plutarch, and Suetonius all borrowed sayings from a source for the year 69, but freely assigned them to different situations and even speakers, a phenomenon paralleled somewhat in the gospels.[66] Josephus retold stories more than any surviving ancient historian, his *Antiquities* 13–20 with appended *Life* rehashing much of *War* 1–2, and he had no problem making drastic changes the second time around (see Chapter 6). Whereas we view consistency as an index of truth, because of our preoccupation with what actually happened, Josephus was innocent of such prejudice.[67] He and his contemporaries were entirely capable of noting inconsistencies in others' work, but this usually had to do with moral-aesthetic concerns, as in his tirade against Justus of Tiberias (*Life* 335–67). An error with a date or location mattered if it could serve to expose larger moral failings, but not in and of itself.[68] Polybius, likewise, sounds as though he is concerned with facts when he rejects Phylarchus as a source, until we see that his real gripe is the historian's failure to properly credit Polybius' home city (2.56–63).

Ultimately rhetoric was about assessments of character. School exercises taught practitioners to identify types of people and situations.[69] These commonplaces – *topoi* in Greek, *loci* in Latin – could be tapped to bring an instant sigh of audience recognition: "Ah yes, we know that type!" Tyrants are savage, masses fickle, old men cautious, young men hot-headed, women emotional, and so on. Common situations included everything from hunger during sieges to a general's quick-witted stratagems.

A modern editor of Dio's *History of Rome* complains that the historian substitutes the unique details of battle scenes, which we would love to know, with mere commonplaces. He is preoccupied with the *effects of his narrative*, showing little or no concern for what actually happened.[70] The editor is right, although it seems unfair to blame ancient authors for following the norms of their time. Readers of Josephus' *War* find *topoi* and stereotypical groups everywhere. He singles out only a few actors for more rounded treatment (e.g., Herod, himself, Ananus, Titus), and also in their cases his descriptions are shaped by rhetorical convention. If we cannot recover the real human beings even with such prominent figures, what are we to make of his reckless youths,

---

[66] Morgan 2006: 287–89. In gospel research, the "sayings source" Q is hypothesized mainly because the sayings of Jesus found in Matthew and Luke are very similar internally, but placed in very different life-contexts (e.g., the lament over Jerusalem in Chapter 1).
[67] Pelling 2000: 44–60.   [68] Marincola 1997: 12–13.   [69] Cf. Marincola 1997: 128–74.
[70] Cary 1914–1927: I.xv–xvii.

wailing women, tyrants, and bandits? The answer is that if *we* are nosy enough as to insist on knowing what happened 2,000 years ago, a concern that has not afflicted most civilizations and Josephus could not have anticipated, we have brought the problem on ourselves.

To understand Josephus' *War*, in sum, we must reckon first with the rhetorical framework of ancient history-writing. Although we instinctively want to separate what is historical-factual from the "merely rhetorical," that is impossible. Like his contemporaries, Josephus wrote every word and phrase (as long as he was on the ball) according to the prescriptions of rhetoric. Figuring out the consequences of this value-system for understanding his text, let alone for investigating the events beneath it, is no simple matter.

Producing history in Rome: the author's public

One important function of rhetorical culture in Rome was the production of a book such as Josephus' *War*. How did books make their appearance? Much useful research has explored these processes in depth.[71] I shall pull together the points that seem most relevant for understanding Josephus. To begin with, we must abandon modern notions of *publication*.

When I finish writing this book, I shall send it from my study, which has shifted from Toronto to Aberdeen, Berlin, Groningen, Jerusalem, Oxford, and Exeter, to the publisher's office in New York. Then various editors, designers, and printers in different countries will work for months to create the bound volume or digital text you are reading. When the book is deemed ready to meet its public (i.e., you), it is the publisher's responsibility – beyond my reach and not my concern – to find this public among the world's billions of inhabitants. As I was researching and writing the book in various locales, moreover, no one around me had any notion of I was doing. The work was not *for them*. My location and my envisaged audience had no connection.

None of these conditions were possible for ancient writers. The public envisaged by the ancient historian, the only people whose knowledge-base and tastes he could reliably anticipate, were those living around him. He knew many of them well, and others were acquaintances of friends.[72] Authors often read aloud sections of their work in social gatherings and gave friends partial drafts to read or to have read aloud by a slave (Pliny, *Ep.* 7.17). The only way to retain control over the content of one's work was to confine its

---

[71] E.g., after Birt 1882: van Groningen 1963; White 1975, 1978; Ogilvie 1980: 12–14; Saller 1983; Starr 1987; Harris 1989: 222–29; Salles 1992; Fantham 1996; Marincola 1997: 19–33; Wiseman 1998; Potter 1999: 23–44; Pelling 2000: 1–17; Nauta 2002: 328–35; 2004: 87–119; Johnson and Parker 2009; Johnson 2010.

[72] Johnson 2010: 3–73.

dissemination to these immediate social circles, and that is as far as many books went. Only the very wealthy could hope for *both* wider distribution *and* content control.[73] Peter Wiseman argues that the stupendously rich Julius Caesar, when he wanted his *Gallic War* to be widely known, had to replicate the local-social model in several cities. Since he could be in one place only, he looked for surrogates with fine voices, nominated by city councils, to read out authorized copies to large audiences.[74] Most writers, lacking Caesar's resources, expected only the public where they resided. Those were the people they wrote for. For authors living in Rome, like Josephus, this was no great limitation. They had access to culturally diverse and multilingual literary circles in the capital.[75] They had no publisher, however, to whom they could hand their finished manuscript in the expectation that the marketing department would locate the book's worldwide audience and ensure that copies were available internationally.

Writing was usually a social exercise in the local community. The poet Virgil directed that, on his death, his works be consigned to the flames to prevent their distribution without his control. He had already reached the public he cared about. Happily for us, Augustus countermanded his wishes.[76] In Josephus' Rome, Quintilian, after teaching rhetoric for more than twenty years, discovered that student-made copies of his lesson notes were circulating against his wishes (*Inst.* pr. 7). When he was preparing a summary manual of his teaching as a gift for a friend's son, someone else begged him to allow this to be copied by some booksellers, so that unknown others could learn from him (*Inst.* pr. 1, 6). Quintilian agreed very reluctantly, because he worried about the changes the work might suffer "in the hands of people generally."[77] Imagining it as a little ship headed for dangerous waters, he figuratively raised the sail and prayed that it would fare well (*Inst.* pr. 3). It was a similar story with the physician Galen, who was unsettled to find his lectures being distributed.[78] The issue was not loss of income to the author. Distribution beyond one's own social circle broke the usual bond between the author and his work – an expression of his authority (*auctoritas*). The text by itself was a lifeless thing, no longer part of a direct communicative process but subject to constant misunderstanding and misuse.[79]

---

[73] Cf. Birt 1882: 352–54 on Varro and Cicero.

[74] Wiseman 1998: 5–7. Wiseman remarks: "Publication was the public performance; the written text was for 'consultation by the educated.'" (p. 5, quoting Lucian, *Apol.* 3). By publication he means literally the making-public of a work.

[75] See Noy 2000 for social diversity, Salles 1992 for the reading cultures.

[76] Birt 1882: 347; Pliny, *Nat.* 7.114.

[77] Quintilian, *Inst.* letter 3: *in manus hominum*; cf. Cicero, *De orat.* 1.94; Pliny, *Ep.* 7.17.15 for similar language, concerning a book that slips out of the author's grasp into a wider public.

[78] Galen, *Ord. libr.* 19.49–50 [Kühn]; with van Groningen 1963: 1–3.

[79] Johnson 2010: 75–91; cf. Martial 7.72.12–16; Saller 1983: 247.

History was subject to the same conditions as other literature. The younger Pliny's letters are a trove of insight into elite Roman society a couple of decades after Josephus was writing his *War*. He responds good-naturedly to a friend's criticism that he has used their literary meetings (attended by Tacitus) to recite *speeches* he had already given. Pliny responds: If *history*, tragedy, and lyric poetry can be recited, why not speeches?[80] Irrespective of the genre involved, he wants criticism from friends in order to build his confidence as he publicizes the speeches to larger audiences (17.7–8). He describes the feeling of terror when he appears before an audience unsure about his material. That fear of live embarrassment, he says, is the best stimulus to good writing in advance (17.8–13). (University lecturers understand this.) In addition, he wants to be sure that whatever he leaves behind him for posterity will be a worthy legacy (17.15). When he complains of the poor behaviour of others at long recitals – people entering only near the end of a book or leaving early – he has histories partly in view, for he mentions as an example of better times the recitation of the historian M. Servilius Nonianus, whose reading drew in the emperor Claudius (*Ep.* 13.1–5).

In Lucian, two generations after Pliny, we meet a harsh critic of the histories he has heard recited. Lucian mentions a number of occasions on which, while travelling through Greek cities, he would enter a hall to hear someone's history and stomp out in a marked manner because of its incompetence.[81] History was part of the common literary culture of local, social book production.

When an author had shared his work with his chosen public, he could either leave it there, as many did, or give up control of it and offer a copy to a bookseller. If he chose the latter course, as we have seen, his motive was not likely to have been financial considerations, which play a role in modern publishing.[82] More likely, he wanted to be sure that work circulating under his name represented his own authorized version – rather than early drafts, copies made by others, or outright frauds. Such a book trade as there was is mainly attested within Rome. It was thus an extension of the local-social model. The seller had somehow come into possession of a variety of rolls, which could be made available for copying at a price – for him, not the author. As far as we know, there was no organized provincial distribution system.[83]

---

[80] Pliny, *Ep.* 17.3–4.   [81] Lucian, *Hist. conscr.* 5–6, 14–15, 19, 23, 24, 29

[82] Birt (1882: 353–55), observing that booksellers usually retained profits from their sales, proposed that Cicero's interest in the wide dissemination of his books indicates a financial interest. That is not clear, however. Most academics would like their work widely known, irrespective of compensation. Martial, a constant supplier of guilty-pleasure epigrams (1.1; 6.60; 11.16), apparently received ad hoc honoraria from those who disseminated his works *in Rome*, which he deemed insufficient (10.74.7), but this may have been an arrangement uniquely suited to the genre and the man. Birt reasonably suggests that if money changed hands in the case of a book, it would have been a virtuous bookseller's purchase of an authorized copy, not some kind of royalty.

[83] Starr 1987: 221.

These circumstances help to explain the ancient tendency to understand historical truth as mainly *impartiality*.[84] Because history involved the characterization of individuals, the risk of offending important people in one's environment, especially in Rome where the most important people gathered, was palpable. Pliny relates that a historian friend had to cancel his scheduled recitations because something he had said in his first outing offended the friends of "a certain person" (*Ep.* 9.27). Tacitus opens both his histories by reassuring audiences that he is able treat his characters "without hostility or partiality" – because they are dead: "Those who make a claim to incorruptible truthfulness must speak *without favour or hatred*."[85] This implies that he could not have spoken freely, and it explains why he did not write, while Domitian lived. The inevitability that writers would conciliate the powerful gives a sharp edge to the Thucydidean principle (Thucydides 1.22.4) captured in Lucian's advice for historians: "Keep your gaze not on those *who are hearing you now*, but on those who will encounter your work in later times" (*Hist. conscr.* 40). Writing with an eye on posterity did not mean that authors wrote into a void, with no audience or communicative purposes in mind. It meant that in writing for such audiences, which was a given of ancient book production, they had to look beyond these local and passing relationships. The test of impartiality (or truth) was that, notionally, someone of a later generation could profit from the work, not dismissing it as merely a composition for the pleasure of some no-longer existing group. But of course it was impossible to apply such a litmus test. It was the ideal that mattered for historians, of not writing for momentary needs alone.

Scholarship has tended to ignore the real-life conditions of ancient book production and to read Josephus' *War* in a modern bookish way, as a timeless collection of data for a vaguely conceived readership all over the empire.[86] Once we ask the question of Josephus' manner of writing *War*, however, we can find plenty of evidence that he produced it in the normal way: in the first instance for local audiences in Flavian Rome, but aspiring to enduring grandeur. Once we know what to look for, his preface already reveals a lively literary culture in reborn Rome that required sharp elbows and thick skin.

Josephus claims to have heard other writers on this war, whom he dismisses as ignorant flatterers of the Flavian regime (1.2). His own claim to truth rests on absolute impartiality and a courageous refusal to pander even to the imperial family. He writes for the world and posterity, not merely for the local situation (1.7–9). That lofty goal does not spirit him away from social realities, evidently. He indicates that he has taken criticism from certain Greek pedants in Rome.

---

[84] Woodman 1988: 70–116; Marincola 1997: 158–74.   [85] Tacitus, *Hist.* 1.1; *Ann.* 1.1.
[86] E.g., Laqueur 1920: 126–27; 255–56; Thackeray 1929: 27–28; Rajak 2005; Huitink and van Henten 2009.

Because they know each other's work in preparation, he can give back as good as he gets in criticism of their efforts (1.13–16). We get a vivid glimpse of his social context in this remark: "I shall not conceal any of my personal calamities, since *I am about to speak to those who know* [them/me]" (μέλλων γε πρὸς εἰδότας ἐρεῖν; 1.22). This confirms the audience's personal knowledge of Josephus and, it seems, his oral recitation of at least part of the *War*.

In later works Josephus elaborates, if not as fully as we would prefer, on the social context for *War*'s production. He mentions certain collaborators on the work (*Apion* 1.50), for example, and refers to drafts of individual volumes that he shared with King Agrippa II as well as their exchange of information in personal meetings (*Life* 362–67). After presenting his work to local audiences, he concluded that period of controlled dissemination by arranging for copies of his "authorized version" for Vespasian, Titus, members of the Herodian family, other cultured Judeans, and Roman commanders involved in the conflict – all or most of them apparently part of the local Roman scene.[87] Josephus gives no indication that he gave copies to booksellers, although curiously he may have sold a few copies himself.[88] He claims that Titus ordered the work to be made publicly available, apparently by expert copying and deposit in imperial libraries (Eusebius, *Hist. eccl.* 3.9): Titus allegedly did for him what Augustus had done for Virgil (*Life* 363). The book's further dissemination was in any case beyond Josephus' control. Any interested party could now secure a copy without his knowledge.

Recognizing Josephus' local public in Rome helps us to think about interpretative possibilities we might have overlooked if we imagined the *War* as a mere factbook brought by the stork without human gestation. The Roman context, for example, suggests criteria for what Josephus omits, includes, or emphasizes, such as his programmatic link between Roman and Judean civil war (1.4). *War*'s preface also includes a detailed prospectus

---

[87] *Life* 361–63; *Apion* 1.50–51.

[88] In *Life* 362 Josephus claims to have *given* a copy to Agrippa II, whereas *Apion* 1.51 includes the king among the Judeans of Greek learning to whom he *sold* (ἐπίπρασκον) copies. Scholars have highlighted the contradiction, Laqueur (1970 [1920]: 21–23) suggesting that writing was Josephus' business, later jeopardized by Justus. But it is hard to imagine that Josephus sold *War* to the king. Even if we assume a correct manuscript reading, the sentence is complicated. After citing Vespasian and Titus as witnesses to his accuracy (1.50), he relates that he had given copies to them first, then to unnamed Romans who had fought in Judaea, and then he had sold copies to "many" compatriots of sufficient Greek education. Then comes the small relative pronoun "among whom" (ὧν . . .) and the names of three distinguished (as he stresses) Herodian princes. Although the grammar puts these three in the sales category, we all know that it is easy to make grammatical mistakes. Perhaps he meant to say that these three were *among the notable recipients*, the main point of what precedes, and not in the third category. Given the terrible state of the *Apion* manuscripts (Leoni 2009: 170–75), we cannot even be certain that Josephus himself wrote "sold." NB: Birt's main examples of authors selling their wares come from the Christian period, and even then the circumstances were unusual (1882: 109–11).

(1.19–30) that seems tailored for a Roman audience (Table 1): It glides over large and important stretches of the narrative concerning Judean life and culture. It ignores the Hasmoneans, the arch-tyrants of the war (Simon, Eleazar, and John), and their high-priestly opponents (Ananus and Jesus), and even Josephus' generalship. Instead it shines the spotlight on Vespasian and Titus, Nero, Cestius Gallus, Varus, Sossius, Pompey the Great, and Roman affairs generally, although these are incidental to the Judean story. Particularly striking is the prospectus for Book 4 (*War* 1.22–23), which flags only the few paragraphs near the end concerning *Rome's* civil war.

Josephus appears to be signalling Roman audiences that he will be their sensitive and accessible guide. He will delay his introduction of Judaica until he has warmed them up, as it were, foregrounding the Hasmoneans' Roman alliances and featuring compelling stories of Herod the Great – famously close friend of Marc Antony (and near victim of hated Cleopatra), Augustus, and Marcus Agrippa. At a trivial level, he sometimes employs Latin forms (*Magnus, Augustus*) rather than the Greek equivalents we would expect.[89] One might even ask whether there is something Roman about his approach to history. Although it is not possible to draw clear lines between Greek/Hellenistic and Roman historiography, the focus of Roman historiography on exemplary personal character, assessed by ancestral tradition (*mos maiorum*), has clear parallels in Josephus and may dovetail with his Roman-Spartan posture toward Greek rhetoric.[90]

Although his *War* is unmistakably Judean and redolent of Greek culture, Roman corpora offer suggestive parallels. Caesar's *Gallic War* (50s B.C.), initially written in seven volumes like this war monograph, similarly combines ethnography, autobiography, reference to the author in the third person, and an exotic setting on the fringes of the empire. Both authors emphasize their resourcefulness and their battle scenes and speeches are often similar.[91]

Another example is the work of Sallust (86–ca. 35 B.C.), Roman senator and historian in retirement. In Josephus' time, he was hailed as a model historian who had written in a masculine style.[92] Surviving fragments of Sallust's *History of Rome* focus on individual characters and their failings,[93] and his speeches are largely about the character of others: "the lowest of all criminals" (*Hist.* 1.67.3), "a bandit with a few goons and cut-throats/assassins (*sicarii*)" (1.67.7), "fond of sedition" and "a lover of war" (1.48.16), a "contemptible female slave, the corruption of all honours" (1.48.7–25 [21]). In Sallust as in Cicero, *latro* (bandit) and *sicarius* (knife-assassin) are terms of

---

[89] *Magnus* at 1.127; 5.409; *Augustus* at 1.20; 2.168, 215, in spite of Greek *Sebastos* at 2.167; 5.562 and throughout *Antiquities*.

[90] Hölkeskamp 1996; Comber 1997; Kraus and Woodman 1999: 1–9; Mellor 1999: 10–11; Yardley and Heckel 2001: 6–12; Timpe 2011; cf. Sallust, *Cat.* 5.9–13.5; Livy 1. praef. 6–9.

[91] Cf. *War* 2.635–36 with *Bell. gall.* 7.45.

[92] Seneca, *Contr.* 9.1.13; Quintilian, *Inst.* 2.5.19; 4.2.45.

[93] Sallust, *Hist.* 1.8. See McGushin 1992, 1994.

TABLE I. *Comparative table: Josephus' prospectus of* War*'s contents (1.19–30) for Roman audiences* versus *the actual narrative contents.*

Prologue Reference	Narrative Correspondence (or Not)
1.19 MATCHES	1.31–40 (**Hasmonean** revolt), 117–58 (factions and **Pompey**), 269–357 (**Herod** and **Sossius**)
BUT IGNORES	Hasmonean dynasty, Herod's early years in Galilee, his political skill and military campaigns, his domestic troubles
1.20 MATCHES	1.647–73 (illness and death of **Herod**), 2.39–75 (revolt under **Q. Varus**), **Nero's** principate and beginning of war (2.284–332), defeat of **Cestius Gallus** (2.499–555), first assaults of trained Judean army (2.562–84; 3.9–28, 61-3, possibly 3.141–288).
BUT IGNORES	Herod's sons and governors of Judaea, three Judean schools (featuring Essenes), Agrippa's speech, internal Judean problems, temple closed to foreigners, local causes of violence, reprisals and massacres.
1.21 MATCHES	2.572–76, 648 (fortifications), 3.1–8 (**Vespasian** appointed by **Nero**), 3.29–34, 64–9, 115–542; 4.84-120 (Galilean campaign of **Vespasian** and **Titus**)
BUT IGNORES	Josephus' defence of Galilee, brilliance as general, his fateful surrender at Iotapata: the main content and focus of Book 3
1.22 MATCHES	3.70–109 (training of **Roman** army), 3.35–44 (two **Galilees**), 3.48–56 (Judea), 3.294–306, 329–39 (suffering of **Galileans**)
BUT IGNORES	Most of Book 4: Gamala, Tabor, Gischala, factional strife in Jerusalem, Idumaeans, murder of Ananus and Jesus, rebel crimes against sanctuary—though all crucial.
1.23 MATCHES	4.491–93 (**Nero's** death), 4.486–91, 588 (**Vespasian** near Jerusalem), 4.491–502 (**his** call to empire), 4.491–96 (**Roman** civil war)
BUT IGNORES	Socuses on Roman affairs in few paragraphs of Book 4, passes over John of Gischala, Simon bar Giora, Disciples, Idumaeans, and Jerusalem leaders.
1.24 MATCHES	4.592–604, 616-20 (acclamation of **Vespasian**), 4.656-58 (**his** withdrawal to **Alexandria**), 5.1–38 (the [unnamed] Judean tyrants and their differences).
BUT IGNORES	Everything but activities of Vespasian and Titus at end of book 4 and beginning of Book 5: detail about Jerusalem's internal *stasis*.
1.25 MATCHES	4.658–63 (**Titus** marches from Alexandria), 5.39–70 (**Titus'** forces), 5.98-105, 248–57 (Judean factionalism in general—leaders unnamed), 5.136–55 (topography of **Jerusalem**), 5.156–206, 238–47 (defences of the city).
BUT IGNORES	Examples of Judean courage, unity, and partial success (5.71–97, 109–35).
1.26 MATCHES	5.184–226 (temple and altar measurements), festival customs (seven purities and priestly services anticipated but *not* in later narrative), 5.228–37 (clothes of high priest), 5.207-19 (nature of Holy Place).
BUT IGNORES	Thematic examples of Judean unity, courage, and success—and of legions' disarray (5.258–330).
1.27 MATCHES	5.248–57 (unnamed) tyrants' brutality; cf. 5.423–45, 527-33. 562–72; 6.193–213), 5.318-30 (Roman desire to spare Judeans and temple; cf. 5.348–55, 359–61, 456, 519; 6.124–31, 214-16), distinction between consequences of famine (5.511-15) and of bandits (5.115–18; also 5.342–48, 379–74, 418, 424-38, 454).
BUT IGNORES	It is unclear which parts of the narrative are in view: many passages correspond, though the closest matches break sequence. OMITS Josephus' own major speech (5.362–419).
1.28 MATCHES	5.29–30, 421-24 (misfortunes of deserters; also 447–48, 452–53, 548–61; cf. 4.377–80, 410, 490; 6.366–67), 5.446–51, 45 (prisoners of war), 6.228, 236–66 (sanctuary fired against **Caesar's** will), 6.387–91 cf. 7.148–52 (temple treasures),

TABLE I. (*cont.*)

Prologue Reference	Narrative Correspondence (or Not)
	6.392–413 (final capture of the city), 6.288–315 (bad omens), 6.432-34 cf. 7.26–36 (fate of tyrants), 6.414-34 cf. 6.383–86 (numbers of dead, imprisoned, enslaved).
BUT IGNORES	Romans' long hard struggle to take Jerusalem, delayed by Judean courage (6.12–92, 129–92), Josephus' final speech (6.99–110) and transmission of Titus' speech (6.124–128), and Maria's cannibalism (6.193–219).
1.29 MATCHES	7.163–215, 252–58, 275–406 (capture of last outposts), 7.19–62, 96–115 (**Titus'** travels in region), 7.116–62 (**Titus in Rome** and triumph).
BUT IGNORES	Vespasian's arrival in Rome and revolt of Germans/Gauls (7.63–95), hardships of Judeans, Commagene and Parthia (7.216–51), problems in Egypt and Cyrene, destruction of temple at Leontopolis, accusations against Josephus (7.407–53).

political invective.[94] This is all familiar from Josephus, whose taste for the Latin term *sicarii* in a Greek composition is intriguing (Chapter 4).[95] Sallust's surviving works amount to history as biography. His portrait of the conspiratorial senator L. Sergius Catilina (*Cat.* 4.5), which was recycled by Livy in describing Hannibal (21.4.5–9) and by Tacitus for Sejanus (*Ann.* 4.1.3),[96] seems to underlie Josephus' description of John of Gischala (*War* 2.585–90).[97]

Although it is mainly about Judean affairs, *War* assumes no Judean knowledge on the part of the audience. Josephus must explain even basic customs and laws concerning sabbath, Passover, and the prohibition of images, for example, as well as the geography of Judaea, Jerusalem and its temple, and Galilee.[98] Such famous personalities as the Hasmoneans and King Herod are carefully introduced.[99] In striking contrast, he assumes the audience's knowledge of Roman and Italian geography, personalities, customs, and events.[100] Thus he can describe the freedman-governor Felix as "the brother of Pallas," which only works if the audience knows of Claudius' notorious freedman Pallas. Similarly, he gives a compressed list of key figures in Claudius' reign, relying on audience knowledge, and avoids elaborating on Nero's

---

[94] See van Hooff 1988: 111–15; Habinek 1998: 69–87; Grünewald 2004: 73–76. Galen would call some of his Roman medical colleagues "bandits" (Eichholz 1951: 64).

[95] Men behaving as women: *War* 4.561–62; 5.565. On Josephus' *sicarii* see Chapter 5.

[96] Ramsey 1984: 69.   [97] Thackeray 1929: 119–20; cf. Villalba i Varneda 1986: 70–71.

[98] *War* 1.146 (sabbath), 270 (high priest must be free of defects), 650 [again 2.170] (law forbids images of living creatures); 2.10–11, 42 (feasts of Passover, Shavuot), 213 (nazirite vow explained); 4.317 (law requires immediate burial of corpses).

[99] *War* 1.36–37, 181, 203–204.

[100] E.g., 1.183: "Now after Pompey fled with the Senate across the Ionian Sea, Caesar. . .." Cf. the figures of Messalla (Corvinus, the renowned orator, mentioned in rhetorical context), Varus, Marcus Agrippa, Augustus' daughter Julia, and her son Gaius: *War* 1.243, 284; 2.25.

recent reign because it is well known to his audience and has received detailed coverage by both Greek and Latin authors.[101]

In arguing that Josephus wrote first for his local Roman audience, I must stress that I am not talking about ethnicity or even citizenship. It is not that Judeans or Egyptians were barred from his recitations. I mean simply that he seems to have brought out his book in the normal way, for Greek-speaking groups with sufficient leisure and learning around him in Flavian Rome.

Josephus and his audiences had high expectations of each other. As part of a broad cultural revival in his time, cultured Greeks were trying to bring back the canonical Attic dialect from fifth-century B.C. Athens, which had long since given way to a simplified *koinē*.[102] There was no simple set of criteria for the revived Attic, although critics were ready to pounce on perceived defects. When we see Josephus making gestures toward Attic purity, however, we must conclude that he thought his audience would value such eforts. His opening sentence is a convoluted Greek period of some 264 words, which features atticizing elements more densely than the remainder of the work.[103] Recall his assumption that only those with Greek learning among his own people would appreciate such a work (*Apion* 1.51). We do not know exactly who constituted Josephus' public in Rome, it is true, and his literary circle left no trace outside of his works. That is not terribly surprising, however. We have no other direct information about Rome's literary circles in the 70s, where such traces might have turned up.

First-century categories: ethnos *and* polis, *Jews and Judeans*

Early drafts of this book included a chapter exploring the categories that elite Mediterranean writers assumed and shared to communicate with each other. Space limitations required the excision of that chapter. I must nevertheless note the most important points for understanding Josephus' assumed categories.

The classical paradigm was rooted in three terms that appear every few pages in most Greek-language authors, including Josephus: *ethnos*, *polis*, and words connected with piety and sacrificial cult. *Ethnos* (plural *ethnē*): The ancients viewed the world not in terms of countries with borders, but of populations with distinctive physical traits, laws (often from a famed lawgiver), customs, diets, dress, Gods, and holidays. Each people's distinctive laws and customs tended to be connected with its unique environment. In the simplest model,

---

[101] *War* 2.247, 249, 250–51; 4.496; cf. *Ant.* 20.154.
[102] See Swain 1996: 17–64. Disappearing Attic features included dual forms, optative mood, participles and adjectives definite articles as noun equivalents, spelling conventions (e.g., double τ replaced by double σ), avoidance of *hiatus* (vowels ending and beginning words), and complex sentence structures (periods).
[103] Following the standard Niese punctuation. Some editors end the sentence at 1.3, which would still give it 113 words.

everyone belonged to an *ethnos* and this was their primary group allegiance. The picture was complicated by an awareness that new *ethnē* could derive from older ones and that individuals or populations could create new ethnic identities or affiliate with other peoples, although this last might be seriously frowned upon.[104] *Polis* (plural *poleis*): The small citizen-state was the quintessential concentration of an *ethnos*, the home of its central institutions, and the primary source of identity for most people. Usually no bigger than 3 km^2 and walled, a *polis* typically housed the population's council building, courthouse, civic temples, gymnasium, market, shops, baths, theatre, public spaces, while a much larger territory (*chōra*) provided land for farming, grazing, and living. The reality was again more complicated than the simple picture of one *polis* for one nation would suggest, because larger *poleis* of the first century had mixed populations, sometimes with a majority of noncitizens (foreigners, women, slaves), and they might experience internal unrest because of the resulting tensions.[105] *Cult*: Represented by a range of related terms, the provision for temples, altars, and bloody animal sacrifice (also offerings of wine, grain, and incense) was central to ancient life – politics, family, festivals/holidays, military campaigning, business, education, athletics, and entertainment.[106]

This classical paradigm would gradually dissolve in the fourth and fifth centuries, as Christianity's triumphant leaders closed altars and temples while sidelining *ethnos* and *polis* as crucial fonts of social identity. These they replaced with systems of *faith/belief and practice*, or –isms, translocal and interethnic *religious* communities under the authority of bishops. The Emperor Julian (A.D. 361–363) made a rearguard attempt to re-establish the classical model, but died before he could reverse the trend, which resumed with a vengeance. After much evolution through the Middle Ages, when the Enlightenment had rejected claims to revealed truth in favour of a universal reason, the Christian paradigm would itself gradually be displaced by modern identity-discourses deriving from nation-states, a biological conception of race, religion (something separable from other political and social life), and even radical

[104] E.g., Herodotus 2.2–182; 4.59–82; 7.85; Thucydides 6.1–6 on the *ethnē* connected with Sicily and Syracuse; Ps-Hippocrates, *Airs, Waters, Places*; Aeschines, *Fals. leg.* 116; Ps-Scylax, *Voyage*; Polybius 2.49.6; Diodorus 11.6.3; 15.26; Strabo, *Geography*; Pliny, *Natural History*; Plutarch, *Mor.* 761d; Barth 1969: 9–37; Hartog 1988: 34–60; Bar-Kochva 1992: 10–13, 192–219; S. Jones 1997: 56–83; Hall 1997: 1–33; 2002: 9–29; Thomas 2000: 75–134; Bloch 2002; Cartledge 2002a: 133–66; Funke and Luraghi 2009 (especially Morgan 2009b: 148–82); Ulf 2009.

[105] E.g., Jones 1940, 1971; Bowie 1970: 3–41; Delia 1991 (Alexandria); Millar 1993: 236–56; Hansen 1993a and b; Swain 1996: 65–100; Habicht 1998: 19–20, 23; Cartledge 2002b; Hansen and Nielsen 2004; Scheidel 2004; Hansen 2006; Krause and Witschel 2006; Harland 2006; Vlassopoulos 2007: 56–60; Revell 2009; Morgan 2009a and b; Carlsson 2010; McEvedy 2011.

[106] E.g., Burkert 1985; Bremmer 1994; Turcan 1996, Baumgarten 2002, Larson 2007, Dignas and Trampedach 2008; Knust and Varhelyi 2011; Faraone and Naiden 2012; Naiden 2013.

individualism.[107] With this crude sketch I intend nothing more serious than to highlight the remoteness of the ancient *ethnos-polis-cult* paradigm assumed by Josephus from our modern categories.

One point emerging from the ancient paradigm merits comment because of its potential to generate needless controversy. From this chapter onward I shall translate Greek *Ioudaioi* as *Judeans* rather than *Jews*. This is not because I have any quarrel with the use of *Jews*. That is the familiar translation, and I have used it until now. But our aim is to understand ancient ways of thinking, and in my view *Judeans* better represents what ancients heard in the *ethnos-polis-cult* paradigm. That is, just as Egypt (Greek *Aegyptos*) was understood to be the home of Egyptians (*Aegyptioi*), Syria of Syrians, and Idumaea of Idumaeans, so also Judaea (*Ioudaia*) was the home of Judeans (*Ioudaioi*) – the only place where their laws and customs were followed. Jerusalem was world-famous as the mother-*polis* of the Judeans, and Judaea was Jerusalem's territory. That is why Judeans (like other immigrants) did not enjoy full citizen rights in Alexandria, Antioch, or Ephesus and could face curtailments of privileges or even expulsion. With other non-natives, and like foreigners in Jerusalem, they lived outside the homeland on sufferance.[108] This was also the case in Caesarea, Gaza, Ascalon, Dora, Ptolemais, Scythopolis, and other *poleis* (plural) surrounding Judaea. We need to take on board *ethnos-polis* language not only for the sake of interpreting Josephus, but also to help us re-imagine daily realities in the region and the origins of this war (Chapter 4).

Some scholars accept part of this, but argue that unique conditions in the Judeans' case – long residence away from Judaea or adoption of Judean law by others – rupture the ethnographic paradigm and recommend that we speak of *Judaism* as a "religion" and *Jews* as its adherents.[109]

I disagree. First, Juda-*ism* was not an available category, and we do not find it in pre-Christian authors with a couple of exceptions. The closest Greek word (*Ioudaismos*) only became popular as a Christian term indicating the reduction of Judean culture to a mere –*ism* or belief system in the Christian mould.[110] Second, the classical model accommodated the complexities just

---

[107] Thomas Paine's *Age of Reason* (1793) is a powerful statement by a key figure. For implications in the study of religions see, e.g., Fung 1948: 1–6; Smith 1963: 61–64; Masuzawa 2005; Cavanaugh 2009; Josephson 2012; Nongbri 2013.

[108] Rome granted subject *poleis* different degrees of autonomy (Richardson 1976: 49–52), but the principle held that each *ethnos* belonged somewhere and not elsewhere, although they might reside abroad for generations (Rüpke 2007: 18; Revell 2009: 53). For Alexandria, see Delia 1991; Capponi 2005: 5–64; Harker 2008 with Claudius' letter of A.D. 41 (P. Lond. 1912 = *CPJ* 2.36–60 [no. 153]). For Antioch, see Josephus, *War* 7.103–10. On the decrees enacted to protect Judeans abroad from vulnerability to local law and custom, see Pucci ben Zeev 1998.

[109] E.g., Cohen 1999: 78–81, 92–137; Dunn 2003: 263; Schwartz 2007; 2008: 360–61.

[110] See Mason 2007.

mentioned: derivations, reaffiliation with another *ethnos* (usually considered reprehensible, however), and multiple identities. Ancient writers never changed their language to speak of "religious conversion" or the like.[111] Living abroad for generations was also common enough not to shatter the paradigm. If Egyptians and Syrians remained such after generations in Rome or Alexandria, why should we need a new word for *Judeans* outside their homeland?

In sum, it is not wrong to speak of ancient Jews and Judaism from our perspective. If our goal is to understand *ancient discourse*, however, I think we lose too much if we assimilate their usage to familiar, Christian-influenced categories. My aim is to try to enter their world, not to domesticate them in ours.[112]

Date of the Judean War

In discussing Josephus' writing environment earlier in this chapter we have already gone some way toward establishing *War*'s date of composition early in the Flavian period. The clearest indicators are statements in his later works about his correspondence with Agrippa II, apparently not long before the king's arrival in Rome in 75, and his presentation of copies to Vespasian and Titus "when the deeds were barely out of view."[113] His rhetorical strategy in *War*'s preface turns on the honour of both Flavian rulers, which seems to assume that both are alive. He charges that his dimwitted rivals unwittingly deprive the Flavian rulers of honour (present tense: αὐτοῖς ἀδοξοῦσιν, 1.8) by belittling their Judean enemy.[114] Given that Vespasian died on June 23, A.D. 79, and the last datable event in *War* is the dedication of his Temple of Pax in the summer of 75,[115] the most explicit evidence favours a completion date between the summers of 75 and 79.

That is the simple case, but scholars have complicated matters. First, in his opening sentence, portraying himself as the exotic eastern nobleman, Josephus twice mentions his own earlier writing(s) on war "in the native/ancestral

---

[111] Herodotus 4.76–80; Thucydides 1.132.1–2; Diodorus 1.95.4–5; Tacitus, *Hist.* 5.5; Lucian, *Scyth.* 8; Philo, *Mos.* 1.34; *Virt.* 102–103; Josephus, *Ant.* 20.17–96.

[112] "Emperor" is an example. Although fine for general use, it would be badly misleading if we understood it to suggest an inheritable office marked by a coronation date, rather than the assembly of roles and prerogatives first assembled by Augustus. I encourage students to use the ancient terms such as *princeps*, *imperator*, and *Caesar* for precision. For the sake of this book, where the mechanics of Roman rule are not our focus (although I had begun with *princeps*), *emperor* will do but Judean(s) yields a better sense of *Ioudaios*.

[113] *Life* 361, 366 (with Dio 65/66.15.3–5); *Apion* 1.50–51.

[114] Barnes (2005: 139) mistakenly says that the preface "names only Titus, not Vespasian," for the father is treated fully and flatteringly in 1.21–24. Titus is named alone in the earlier section (1.10), certainly, because there Josephus is talking about Jerusalem's fall, at which only Flavius Jr. was present.

[115] *War* 7.158–62 with Pliny, *Nat.* 36.102; Suetonius, *Vesp.* 24; Dio 65/66.15.1.

language," which he now claims to be "bringing over" or "recasting" in Greek for the Graeco-Roman world (1.3, 6).[116] Scholars of earlier generations, assuming that our Greek text more or less translates this "lost Aramaic," speculated that the Semitic-language original held the key to Josephus' aims in writing. Since they could only imagine a Semitic-language version sent to the Parthian world as propaganda from the Flavian court to discourage the Parthians from conflict with Rome, that must be the explanation of our Greek *War*.[117] Josephus was writing Roman propaganda.

The problem is that our *War* is thoroughly Greek in language (it is not translation-Greek), historiography, rhetorical assumptions, speeches and digressions, crafted diction (including word-play), sentence construction, and literary models, with apparent Latin influences too. It looks like an original composition. A comprehensive Aramaic source text would also be hard to square with Josephus' later reflections on his writing process, his reception in Rome, and the drafts shared with Agrippa.[118] Even *War*'s preface is quite vague about this Aramaic precursor. Josephus uses it as a rhetorical springboard to highlight his exotic connections but then seems to forget about it. Assuming that he really had some kind of Aramaic precursor in mind, it *might* then have been no more than a few notes or letters drafted while he was still in the East – having nothing to do with the Flavians. Whatever it was, it cannot explain our present Greek work. Given the preoccupation of earlier scholars with the Aramaic text, it is remarkable how completely recent scholarship ignores it as largely irrelevant for understanding the Greek text we have.[119] There is no need to push *War*'s date later to accommodate an Aramaic project that took precedence for Josephus.

A more current complication concerns Book 7. Scholars have given reasons for detaching this volume, or much of it, from the trunk of *War* and dating it later. Some would push even Books 1 to 6 to Titus' reign (A.D. 79–81), because of their perceived favour of that ruler, and postpone most of Book 7 to Domitian's time (A.D. 81–96) or later. Reasons for the latter move include: a sense that Josephus' history of the war was formally complete with Jerusalem's fall in Book 6; perceived changes of tone and interest in Book 7, which are taken to match those of the later *Antiquities*; seeming flattery of Domitian in

---

[116] *War* 1.3: "having recast what I had formerly recounted in the ancestral [language]." 1.6: "the Parthians and Babylonians, the most remote of the Arabs, our own compatriot bloc over the Euphrates, and Adiabenians ... know precisely, through my diligence, why the war began, through what mutations it passed, and the way in which it came to an end."

[117] Laqueur 1920: 125–28; Thackeray 1929: 127–29.

[118] *Life* 360–65; *Apion* 1.50–51. For criticism of scholars' use of the Aramaic as key to understanding *War*, see Hata 1975; Rajak 1983: 174–84, 233–36.

[119] Brighton 2009 does not mention it; Mader (2000: 153 n. 6) and Landau (2006: 211 n. 24) relegate it to footnotes.

War 7.85–88; and Josephus' reference to the death of Catullus, governor of Cyrene, in the same volume (7.451). We lack the space even to lay out all the issues here.

Several recent studies that offer an analysis of *War*'s date agree that Josephus' apparent placement in the latter half of Vespasian's rule remains most satisfactory.[120] To the issues they discuss I would add that singling out Titus for praise was quite possible even while his father lived,[121] that structural symmetry and anticipations of Book 7 earlier in the work suggest at least an original *plan* of seven volumes, that rhetorical prescriptions recommended the inclusion of both antecedents (= Book 1) and aftermath (= Book 7) in accounts of wars,[122] and that a severely truncated original Book 7 would be hard to imagine.[123] Some of these points will become clearer as we consider *War*'s structure.

II. AIMS AND STRUCTURES OF *THE JUDEAN WAR*

In Chapter 1 we explored the post-war context in which Josephus was writing. We observed the nonsense being proclaimed by the regime's enablers – that this was a war against a foreign nation, which Titus was the first to conquer, and that the Flavian amphitheatre was built from foreign spoils. Josephus must have understood the Flavians' political needs; anyway, there was nothing he could do about that. It was a different matter, however, when his peers in Rome, to whom he considered himself far superior, began transforming the regime's myth-making into pretended histories. It appears that they were

---

[120] For Thackeray (1929: 35), the fall of Jerusalem was the "natural stopping point" and the style and diction of Book 7 better suited *Antiquities*. Cohen agreed (1979: 87–89), adding that Josephus' charge against John of Gischala in 7.264, focused on halakhic purity, was written (like *Antiquities*) with an eye on the rabbis of Yavneh, and that the flattery of Domitian in 7.85–88 suggests that he was then in power. S. Schwartz raised the stakes with his contention that Catullus, "governor of the Libyan Pentapolis" (7.439), who paid for his crimes with a tormented death "not long afterward" (7.451–53), was L. Valerius Catullus Messalinus (*cos. ord.* 73), who died after 93 (1986: 375–77; Tacitus, *Agr.* 45.1). That identification has been overturned, however, and most recent studies find little reason to doubt the work's unity or earlier date: Rajak 1983: 195; Paul 1993; Jones 2002; Cotton and Eck 2005; especially Brighton 2009: 33–41 and Siggelkow-Berner 2011: 25–33. Barnes 2005: 136–39 is an exception, supporting a date spread under Titus and Domitian.

[121] Paul 1993 elucidates Josephus' techniques for enhancing Titus's figure while assuming a Vespasianic date (56). After all, nothing that Josephus says of Titus exceeds the praise lavished on him by Pliny (*Nat.*, praef.: *iucundissime imperator*) in 77.

[122] Theon, *Progymn.* 119 (Spengel).

[123] *Ant.* 20 is uncommonly short at just 9,367 words, but even that is 30 percent *fuller* than a truncated Book 7 would have been. The brief *Apion* volumes, at 11,742 and conjectured 11,265 (8,765 Greek + 2,500 behind Latin) words, would have been nearly twice the length of the hypothesized stump of Book 7. The shorter such a hypothetical volume becomes, the harder it is to understand why Josephus would not have included it in Book 6.

historicizing the triumphal motifs (1.1–3). Perhaps they saw an opportunity to bond with the new regime and create life-chances for themselves:

> Those who did not happen to be at the events, but are collecting random and incoherent tales through hearsay, are writing them up sophist-like, while others who were there are misrepresenting the events, *either through flattery toward the Romans or through hatred toward the Judeans*. Their compositions comprise denunciation [of Judeans] in some cases, encomium [of Romans] in others, but nowhere *the accuracy of history*. So I, Josephus son of Matthias, a priest from Jerusalem, who myself fought against the Romans at first and eventually happened to be among them by necessity, have set myself the task of providing a narrative in the Greek language for those under the Roman *imperium*. . . .

We do not know how accurate this characterization of his environment is, of course, but Tacitus also mentions hack Flavian historians who curried favour (*Hist.* 2.101). Decades later, shortly after a Roman campaign in Parthia, Lucian would similarly complain about the flurry of histories at that time: "[M]ost of them neglect to investigate what actually happened, but elevate their own leaders and generals to the sky while tearing down those of the enemy beyond all proportion" (*Hist. conscr.* 7). It is a predictable tendency, and Josephus' complaint is plausible enough.

He further accuses these other writers: "They dare to entitle those books 'histories,' in which there is nothing sound, so that they seem to me at least to miss their target. For although they want to portray the Romans as great, they always vilify and belittle the Judean side" (1.7). He does not challenge the regime's claims in the political arena, but rather these scribblers whose eye is on their main chance. Against *them* Josephus has every advantage, and he is going to drive it home. He can easily demolish their vapid accounts with his authoritative knowledge. Who could challenge an actual Judean commander, preserved by the ruling family, who has intimate knowledge of the war theatre?

Scholars have proposed two main explanations of the *War*. The stronger stream since the nineteenth century, which occasionally still trickles past the dams that should have stopped it, takes the work to be commissioned propaganda. This view rests equally on suppositions about the lost Aramaic and a perceived flattery of the Flavians in our Greek text (below in this chapter).[124] The more common view today holds that Josephus was trying to absolve his nation, above all the priestly class and particularly his good self, from war guilt by deflecting blame onto a small band of rebels, tyrants, and malcontents.[125]

---

[124] Laqueur 1920; Weber 1921; Thackeray 1929 with dozens of stops until Beard 2003, 2007 and Curran 2007. The main dam was built by Rajak 1983. See Chapter 1.

[125] E.g., Luther 1910: 15; Rhoads 1976: 12, 56; Rajak 1983: 78–83; Goodman 1987: 20–21, 166–68; Bilde 1988: 77–78; S. Schwartz 1990: 15; an early Mason 1991: 64–67; Price 1992: 32–33, 187; McLaren 1998: 55–56; Mader 2000: 10–17.

These proposals will come up again in relation to specific passages, but already here in our overview we have reason for initial doubt.

First, multivolume works of history do not make good propaganda. They are not like inscriptions or even argumentative essays. Covering many locations, events, persons, and groups, with periodic digressions, histories are too diffuse to be efficient as propaganda.[126] Robert Connor writes of Thucydides' *Peloponnesian War*, one of Josephus' inspirations:

> The work cannot be summed up as advocacy of Periclean rationalism, the law of the stronger, a tragic pessimism, or any of the other formulations so popular in Thucydidean scholarship. It defies reduction and resists simplification ...[127]

The same is true of Josephus' *Judean War*.

Second, as I have stressed above, our interpretation of the *War* will affect the way we use it. If we assumed that Josephus tried to impose a single thesis on recalcitrant material, for example, we might consider whatever seemed at odds with such an intention particularly valuable for history: If it violates his own programme, he could not have invented it.[128] We see this problem when scholars attribute to Josephus a simple agenda and then complain about his sloppiness in realizing it ("a second-rate propagandist").[129] After berating him, however, they often declare his alleged incompetence a blessing: His biases are *so* clumsily executed that he leaves plenty of low-hanging fruit uncontaminated by their pestilence, for the historian's picking.[130] Before unleashing our mechanical harvesters on Josephus' orchards, however, we might ask ourselves why there is so much that does not fit his alleged biases or purposes. Perhaps it is we who have misapprehended them.

No one doubts that historians had motives and purposes. But given that they chose a genre spectacularly ill-suited to establishing simple propositions, it seems pointless to isolate a few statements from thousands and identify everything that does not conform to these as unassimilated. The ancient historian's most important *message* was more likely to have been the implicit one that he, the creator of such a literary monument, was a man to be reckoned with, a paragon of moral insight and authority.[131]

By declaring his credentials in lofty dismissal of competitors (1.1–3), Josephus quickly establishes a tone of moral seriousness. Against the rampant cheap

---

[126] Cf. Yavetz 1975: 431–32.   [127] Connor 1984: 249.   [128] See Mason 2009a: 103–37.
[129] Curran 2007: 77.
[130] Curran (2007: 90): "The historian ... is still, I think, entitled to some confidence in Josephus. ... It is the very weakness of Josephus as an artist that provides this confidence." Cf. Goodman 1987: 20–21 (many passages "contradict the main thrust of his apologetic"); Price 1992: 33, 186 (many "uncooperative details").
[131] See Marincola 1997: 128–74.

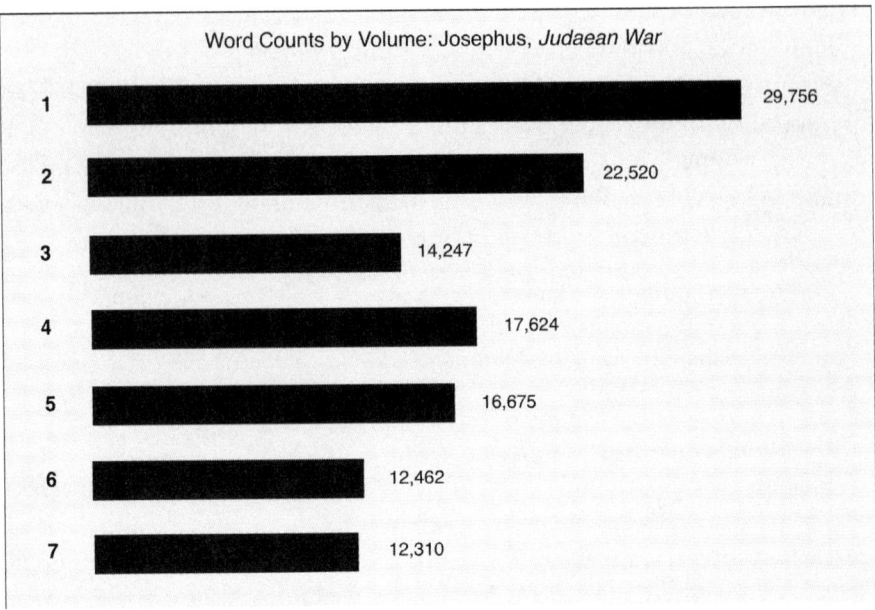

FIGURE 7. Word counts for each volume of the *Judean War*.

partisanship, he stresses the need for moderation and *balance*: "I certainly have no intention of contending with those who heap praise on the Romans' deeds by exalting those of my own compatriots. No, I go through the actions of both sides with precision" (1.9). His handling of the political chestnuts of freedom, piety, tyranny, civil strife, and monarchical succession should reveal a man of political experience and wisdom. He postures as a keen observer of human foible and self-delusion, able to digress with equal confidence on moral-philosophical questions, sacred spaces and purity, flora and fauna, military manoeuvres, or the motives and fears of those facing battle and siege. If the *War* has a single overriding *message*, it lies beneath the surface: "I am a Judean priest-nobleman. In spite of the lies being spread about us, I am a better man, political analyst, and historian than any writer on this war."

A glance at the size and disposition of *War*'s seven volumes also makes it difficult to support the standard interpretations (Fig. 7). In a work of about 125,600 words (Niese text), distribution in volumes is conspicuously uneven. Josephus' book-rolls across the corpus average 15,000+ words – *Antiquities*' twenty volumes remaining remarkably close to this average.[132] But in *War* only the middle volumes approach it. Book 1 is double strength and Book 2 has a 50 percent bonus, whereas Books 6 and 7 fall well below the standard.

---

[132] In *Antiquities* (ca. 306,488 words) each volume is close to the mean of 15,324 words, the appended *Life* having 15,835 words. Cf. *Apion* 1.320 on the need to finish one roll and begin the next.

Given that Josephus created his own book divisions,[133] we infer that he wanted seven volumes, no matter how disparate their size, each containing whatever he considered necessary. *Chronological* proportion could not have been among his criteria, for Book 1 covers 167 years, whereas most later volumes describe a few months only. Moreover, given that he could easily have included Books 6 and 7 in a single roll that would still have been only 80 percent of Book 1's length, he must truly have wanted seven volumes.

One neglected point emerges clearly from this outline: Books 1 and 2, accounting for 42 percent of *War*'s content, must be important. Many of Josephus' hearers/readers would presumably not have not lasted beyond the first volume. There must be enough in it already to establish his main purposes – long before the war or the appearance of the Flavians. Most of the other Roman-period histories have reached us in fragmentary form (Polybius, Livy, Dionysius, Diodorus, Tacitus' *Histories* and *Annals*), and in those cases the first volumes are the ones most likely to be intact, which may suggest that they were read most often. Martial jokes that only writers of epigrams, like him, might include are read all the way through (1. praef.). Ancient and medieval teachers focused their exercises on the opening volumes of canonical works, perhaps assuming that a work's opening material was most important.[134] Historians today would happily trade surviving early material in Polybius, Livy, or Tacitus for what is lost from later volumes. But beginning volumes were clearly important for establishing a work's themes and perspectives. Any interpretation of Josephus' *War* that requires us to begin reading in Book 3 or 4, halfway through, will be implausible.

To help us get a sense of *War*'s overall shape, let us survey its entire contents.

1. = ca. 170–4 B.C. From the conflict that created Onias' temple in Egypt and the Hasmonean Revolt to the funeral of Herod the Great, with a preview of the succession problem. A compact Hasmonean history (1.31–122) foregrounds that family's friendship with Rome, rapid acquisition of territory, and political agility. These themes continue with Herod, a force of nature and loyal friend of successive Roman great men. It is a tragic story, however: Herod's brilliant success is undone by his inability to escape passions and domestic intrigue.

2. = 4 B.C.–A.D. 66/67. From the Herodian succession struggle to Josephus' command of the northern defences in expectation of Roman retaliation for the assault on Cestius Gallus, with a preview of later Jerusalem. Succession hearings in Rome, punctuated by disturbances in Judaea (4 B.C.), dominate Archelaus' story. Josephus interweaves regional politics and conflicts with Roman experiments in governing Judaea from Jerusalem or Caesarea. Outrages committed by Samarians, auxiliaries, and Nero's later governors and the

---

[133] Cf. *Ant.* 13.298; Eusebius, *Hist. eccl.* 2.21.3; 3.6.1, 20; 9.3.   [134] Cribiore 2001: 194–209.

failed effort to remake Caesarea as Judean generate violence: massacres of Jerusalem's auxiliary cohort and of Caesarea's Judeans. The legate Cestius intervenes from Antioch and loses a legion, forcing the Judeans to prepare for retaliation. Josephus is dispatched to prepare Galilee.

3.   = spring to autumn, A.D. 67. From Nero's appointment of Vespasian to the fall of Galilee, including suppression of Agrippa II's restive *poleis*. Gamala, Tabor, and Gischala remain untaken. After a survey of Rome's allegedly invincible and terrifying military, the narrative savours the few weeks of Josephus' brilliant defences before his divine revelation, surrender, and prediction.

4.   = late 67—December 69. From the remnants of Galilee and Golan to the Flavian domination of Judaea, featuring civil strife there and simultaneously in Rome. Vespasian and Titus subdue Gamala for Agrippa, Tabor and Gischala as remnants of their campaign. John uses a feint to flee Galilee for Jerusalem, soon becoming a tyrant there. He arranges for Idumaean fighters to enter the city and kill the native nobles; this episode forms the centre of both this volume and *War*. Simon bar Giora's entry in the latter half generates unstoppable civil strife and tyrant-rivalry. Rome's bloody civil war following Nero's suicide (June, A.D. 68) is interwoven. Despicable Vitellius begins ruling there as Simon enters Jerusalem (= April 69). Vespasian leaves Judaea to assume imperial power.

5.   = ca. December 69–June 70. From newly intense factionalism in Jerusalem to the horrors of murder and famine after Titus renews the siege, punctuated by a digression on Jerusalem's topography and a speech by Josephus. The narrator moves back and forth between Judean and Roman sides. Titus gradually hardens, his persistent alternation of carrots and sticks bringing little success.

6.   = ca. late June–early September 70. From Titus' redoubled siege effort to Jerusalem's fall. The work's climax brings many threads together. Temporarily dispirited Romans recover energy and discipline against the ever-resourceful Judean foe. Besieged Jerusalem's miseries reach their nadir in crushing famine, violence, and the refugee noblewoman Maria's resort to cannibalism. Hearing of this Titus determines to bury the city, though he is trapped in a divinely orchestrated story. He later resolves to spare the temple but it burns in spite of him.

7.   = September 70–ca. July 75. From the days following Jerusalem's fall to the closure of Onias' temple in Egypt, with a glance at Josephus' post-war life. Book 7 contrasts the dire aftermath for the Judeans of Syria and Egypt and the Roman triumph, on the one hand, with compelling stories of Judean resourcefulness (Machaerus) and disaster (Masada). These remaining desert fortresses are captured by Roman governors with a legion at their disposal. The closing of Onias' dissident temple and a reminder of Josephus' towering virtue close the work's narrative arc.

If we consider this content in the context surveyed in Chapter 1, one point jumps out forcefully. Josephus' narrative thoroughly dismantles the edifice constructed for the Flavian triumph, now being cast as history by regime flacks. By beginning his story with the establishment of Judean-Roman relations in the mid-second century B.C. (1.38), two centuries before the Flavians' campaign, by describing in detail the conquests of Pompey and Antony's general C. Sosius, and by exploring Herod's intimate friendships with the great Augustus and Marcus Agrippa, Josephus renders absurd any notion that the Flavians conquered a foreign enemy. Because Judaea has been paying taxes from of old, and its elite have always enjoyed such close connections with Roman officials, there is no prospect of spoils from "conquered Judaea" flooding Rome's coffers. Moreover, by focusing on Roman *civil war* and Vespasian's very personal conflict with Vitellius, which the Flavians were not keen to discuss, Josephus exposes the real meaning of their victory – over *Roman* rivals. Judaea, the story explains in various ways, is misunderstood and misused by regime historians.

This overview also suggests some basic structural devices. In most volumes, Josephus frames the central subject matter inside opening and closing panels on different subjects. The pattern appears at least in Book 2 (opening in Rome and closing in Josephus' Galilee with a central narrative of equestrian government and regional strife in Judaea), Book 3 (opening with the Roman army and closing with Agrippa's cities, the central narrative on Josephus at Iotapata), and Book 4 (opening in Galilee and closing in Rome with a central section on John, the Idumaeans, and the coup in Jerusalem).

Another device is Josephus' frequent use of narrative anticipation. Book 1 opens with Onias' temple in Egypt and a promise to explain more, which he fulfills only at the end of Book 7. He sprinkles Book 2 with anticipatory notes about Eleazar son of Yair, "who would later exercise tyranny at Masada" (2.447; cf. 7.253–401), and Simon bar Giora (2.652–54). Although they are marginal to this volume, Josephus' literary audience would know of their later importance (6.434; 7.36, 154). John of Gischala receives a full preview in Galilee (2.584–87), aside from his crucial role in Jerusalem. More subtly, the story of Simon of Scythopolis anticipates Masada, when he runs through his parents, wife, and children before making a recognition speech and killing himself (2.469–76; 7.332–36). In Book 5 Josephus refers to the reversal of fortune that King Antiochus of Commagene, then at the peak of success, will suffer (5.461); Josephus lets that other shoe drop only in 7.232–43. These notices heighten suspense and raise expectations, even if everyone knows basically how the story ends.

In several volumes Josephus almost seems to spool or coil the narrative around a central spindle and then, on reaching a pivotal moment, lets it begin to unravel. In Book 1 the central episode is Herod's capture of Jerusalem (1.340–57), from which apex the story will soon fall away to end in the king's distress and death. In Book 2 the end of the fateful Caesarea conflict (2.292) falls around the halfway point (at 10,269 of 22,520 words). And the nearly precise halfway point of Book 6 (12,462 words) is Titus' declared intention to bury the city after Maria's cannibalism (2.219 at 6,202 words). Given Josephus' general fondness for A–B–A concentric patterns, this kind of structuring seems unlikely to be mere coincidence.[135]

Indeed, it seems that the entire work exhibits a large-scale ring structure. In the 17,624 words of *War*'s middle volume (4), the precise halfway point (in the standard text) comes at 8,812 words. Just one sentence before that is the whole work's turning point: the narrator's eulogy on the murdered chief priests of Jerusalem: Ananus and Jesus (4.325). Josephus' encomium – "the capture of the city began with the death of Ananus, and from that very day came the overthrow of the walls and the ruin of the Judean commonwealth, on which they saw the leader of their own rescue slaughtered in the middle of the *polis*" (4.318) – makes this pivotal role clear. A retrospective passage in *War* 7 confirms it (7.267). Book 4 itself furnishes this episode with a grand frame. John and the Zealots invite Idumaeans into Jerusalem to assist with this horrible deed (4.224–313), but after accomplishing it, the Idumaeans realize that they have been misled and storm out of Jerusalem in disgust (4.345–65). Except that they do not. Their quietly continuing presence shows that the entry-murder-departure sequence is an artificial literary frame highlighting the central deed.[136]

All of this alerts us to watch for other signposts of symmetry along the way, and there turn out to be many.[137] Such patterning is not a matter of mathematical precision, much less of any mysterious codes. Placing near the beginning episodes that would be reprised toward the end was a common artistic

---

[135] Cf. the passage on the "three schools" at 2.119–66. The twelve initiates' oaths occupy the centre (2.139–142), while the rare mirrored verbs "reckon in" and "reckon out" stand guard on either side (2.138, 143). Moving outward are reverence for the sun-deity (2.128, 148), the rare phrase "make it a point of honour" (2.123, 146), and the rare *nomen agentis* "despiser" – of wealth or the terrors of death (2.122, 151) – until we reach the outer ring, with corresponding references at beginning and end to women, children, sex (2.119–121, 160–61), and then Pharisees and Sadducees (2.119, 162–66).

[136] *War* 4.566; 5.248–50; 6.381.

[137] E.g., an Antiochus Epiphanes (at 1.31–40; 7.219–44; cf. 5.460); anachronistic Medes (1.50, 62; 7.244–46); Masada (1.175–82; 7.252–406, 455); *Pascha* with its "many sacrifices" (only 2.10; 6.423); heaping of corpses worse than foreign war (2.30; 6.259, 421); souls of the good enter "most refined ether" (2.152; 6.47); "pseudoprophet" misleads the people costing many lives (2.261; 6.285); burning of temple porticoes, with Judeans or Romans above dying five ways (2.229–30, 405; 6.233); Agrippa's and Titus' speeches ("Don't foolishly rely on…"; 2.362; 6.328–32); Josephus imprisoned, predicts Vespasian's rise; prediction fulfilled his release (3.387–408; 4.622–44).

device.[138] Concentric structures assisted comprehension and memory while reinforcing the narrative shape and sense of compositional balance. Josephus plainly says at the beginning of the *Antiquities* that he omitted Judaea's ancient past from *War*'s beginning because it would have led to imbalance. "I separated that work by itself and *measured off a balanced composition*, with the beginnings and the ending proper to it" (1.6–7). His use of the verb συμμετρέω suggests the coordination of architectural elements.[139] He gave *War*'s seven volumes a consciously proportionate structure.

III. THEMATIC CLUSTERS

Given that Josephus' *War* is not reducible to a thesis, the best way to come to terms with the work in an overview may be to sample its thematic repertoire and narrative colour. What is the difference between a theme and a thesis? By *theme* I mean words, phrases, and situations that reoccur in many places and lend coherence to the story, without representing a simple idea, proposition, or claim. They sustain an atmosphere, as in a novel or a film, but can be turned and twisted in complex and unexpected ways to create tension and texture. In *War* these themes are drawn from the shared *langue* of Josephus' time. If we insist on asking, "But what is he *trying to say*? How would we state it in a Twitter post?" we shall go away frustrated.

Different readers would characterize *War*'s themes differently. I suggest four large thematic clusters, which are present from beginning to end and thus reveal the work's most durable fibres. These have to do with (1) the character of the Judean *ethnos*; (2) familiar problems of managing a *polis* in distress; (3) tragic situations in human and inter-*polis* relations; and (4) the Jerusalem temple cult, its pollution, and purification. By no means a central theme, but requiring attention because it has so often been declared the key to understanding *War*, is Josephus' treatment of Vespasian and Titus.

The character of the Judean ethnos (and of Josephus)

War's opening sentences complain that contemporary writers are "always pushing down [denigrating, vilifying] and diminishing [reducing, humiliating]" the Judean side (1.7: καταβάλλουσιν δὲ ἀεὶ τὰ Ἰουδαίων καὶ ταπεινοῦσιν). It seems likely that those lost historians began with accounts of the origins, geography, and national character of the Judeans. Rhetoric assumed that a person's or nation's origins revealed their character, and Tacitus began his account of Jerusalem's fall by declaring that one should begin with the city's

---

[138] See Myres 1953: 89–117; Duckworth 1962; Whitman 1965 (Homer); Beck 1971 (Herodotus); Wood 1972; Welch 1981; Conte 1994: 266.

[139] E.g., *War* 1.411; 5.192; *Ant.* 8.74.

origin (*Hist.* 5.2–13). In that section he acknowledges the hardihood of Judaea's people and the excellence of their palms and balsam trees, but stresses the deadness of their national body of water and the surrounding land. He speaks of the Judeans' "perverse and foul customs, which get their strength from their grotesque nature," although senatorial prejudice permits him a degree of sympathy for their burdens under Roman equestrians and freedmen.[140]

If the sober Tacitus could write of Judaea thus, we can only imagine what nonsense the Flavian hacks (whom he criticizes) were propagating. Their ill-informed and likely mischievous portraits of Judaea's origins would explain why Josephus planned to include these subjects (*War* 1.17), before shunting them to *Antiquities* (*Ant.* 1.6–7).

Analogies may also help us to imagine the lost Flavian accounts. Karen Welch describes the general imperial mentality when portraying conquered foes:

> Under the Empire, scenes of battle in Roman art became more ideologically charged than ever before. . . . Enemies were no longer Greeks but uncultivated or "effeminate" barbarians. . . . Romans are always shown with impassive faces, while their weaker enemies are shown with un-Classical physiognomies, often contorted and terrified in appearance. Romans are always shown winning; foes are always shown losing, begging for mercy, being subjugated, appealing, being killed. . . . Enemies of Rome are never shown as worthy opponents.[141]

This sounds just like the presentation of Judeans in the triumph (Chapter 1) and like the Flavian histories that Josephus writes to correct.

Indeed, Romans often portrayed their serious eastern enemy, the Parthians, as feminized. Parthians appeared on carved table-legs in upper-class Roman households as Ganymede or Peter Pan types.[142] In military contexts it was (and is) common to taunt one's enemies as effeminate, flattering the victors' masculine dominance. A famous Athenian wine pitcher from the 460s B.C. portrays a naked Athenian about to penetrate a defeated Persian, bent over in front of him.[143] Plutarch's account of Crassus' defeat with seven legions at Carrhae (53 B.C.) illustrates the theme. The victor Surena chose a captive who resembled the dead general, dressed him in royal woman's purple, and with savage sarcasm assigned him Roman-style lictors. From the rods carried by the lictor – in Rome a symbol of über-masculine *imperium* – he suspended women's purses. And behind this conscripted actor came a procession of musicians "who sang many scurrilous and ridiculous songs about the effeminacy and cowardice of Crassus" (*Crass.* 32).

---

[140] Tacitus, *Hist.* 5.1–13, quotations and references in order: 5.6–7, 8 (*superstitionem . . . taeterrimam gentem*), 5 (*instituta, sinistra foeda, pravitate valuere*), 9–10.

[141] Welch 2006: 11–12.   [142] Schneider 1998: 106–10.

[143] Summary discussion in Ferris 2000: 7.

A temple from Nero's reign in Aphrodisias (modern Turkey) sported a football-field-sized promenade along which imperial victories over the world's *ethnē* were portrayed. On the northern façade were statues of some fifty nations; by chance the inscription for the *"ethnos* of the Judeans" is one of the few to have survived. The southern façade hosted mythical scenes portraying the emperors.[144] In one, a heroically naked Tiberius escorts a bound prisoner half his size. In another Claudius, naked as a God, looms over a supine and helpless Britannia, grabbing her long hair as she struggles beneath him, one of her breasts exposed. Another scene features Nero towering over naked and distraught Armenia.[145] These are potent images,[146] but such representation reached a new level with the column of Marcus Aurelius, built by Commodus *in memoriam* (ca. A.D. 192). Under the philosopher-emperor's gaze enemy soldiers lie dead, dying, and headless. Women, disheveled after implied rape, desperately try to protect their children.[147]

The small surfaces of coins required cruder insinuations of these themes. We have examples from Augustus' reign of reused Republican images: a Roman soldier dragging Sicily, portrayed as a naked and helpless woman (cf. Chapter 2).[148] The *Iudaea Capta* coins are not as graphic as that, but many represent *Judaea* as a confused woman or puny male, helpless and in sharp contrast with the towering, confident Roman, whose left foot rests on an enemy helmet (Fig. 8). Domitian and Trajan would use similar techniques.[149] Size discrepancies became extreme in statues of Hadrian, who was given gigantic proportions as he stepped on the backs of tiny foreigners.[150]

We do not know exactly how the Flavian historians were "belittling and degrading" the Judeans, but the general tone seems clear from Josephus' response. He stresses his nation's virtue (*aretē, virtus*): a concept grounded in masculine prowess.[151] After introducing the theme in his opening sentence (1.1–8) he develops it immediately with the courage of the Hasmoneans and King Herod (Book 1), tracks it through virtuous Essenes, various political leaders, and his own character (Books 2 and 3), and traces it even in some of his political enemies to certain *sicarii* in Egypt (end of Book 7). Against the characterizations prevailing in Rome, he would prove Judeans to be innately tough and virtuous.

---

[144] Smith 1988: 51.   [145] Erim 1982: 277–81.   [146] See Ferris 2000: 56–59 and plate 12.

[147] The slaughter is portrayed vividly, the rape suggested by the women's reactions, postures, and dress. See Ferris 2009: 97–150; on still later monuments, Lusnia 2006: 272–99.

[148] On the British Museum coin ref. 1850,0330.13 the Augustan moneyer L. Aquillius Florus recalls ancestral exploits in suppressing the slave revolt of Sicily (101 B.C.), and a coin image re-used for the Spartacus revolt of 70 B.C. The imagery of provincial domination is our concern.

[149] E.g., coins R.11365 and R.7740 in the British Museum.

[150] See Opper 2008: 66 fig. 49; cf. Ferris 2000: 85–86 and plate 19; coins ref. 1860,0330.13 and 1983,0723.1 in the British Museum.

[151] Kennell 1995; McDonnell 2006.

FIGURE 8. Example of *Iudaea Capta* bronze *sestertius* from Vespasian's A.D. 71, severely miniaturizing conquered Judaea.© Trustees of the British Museum (ref. 1872,0709.473). See also coins 1952,0105.4, R.10570.

In support of this theme Josephus often employs the Spartan language of training, discipline, order, courage, endurance, manly prowess, and contempt for death – this last turning up more often in *War* than in any other known ancient text.[152] Josephus' much-discussed passage on the Essene "legion" (*tagma*; 2.119–61) has the highest concentration of Spartan language in his corpus. Its longest (and least-discussed) section concerns this order's contempt for death: "Smiling in their agonies and making fun of those who were inflicting the tortures, they used to cheerfully dismiss their souls" (2.151–58). The theme continues in *War* as we watch common people baring their necks to the sword rather than violating ancestral law (2.174, 196). Vespasian is amazed by the courage of a captured Judean who, holding out under every kind of torture, finally "met death with a smile" on a cross (3.320–21).

Although he can observe the bravery of individual Romans,[153] scrupulously honouring his promise of balance, Josephus' programmatic emphasis on Judean valour often comes at a cost to Roman self-regard. He typically portrays the storied legionaries as fearful, confused, impulsive, undisciplined, and overmatched in the face of a Judean enemy.[154] A few examples give the flavour. When Vespasian rests his soldiers in coastal Caesarea (4.89–90), Josephus reads his thoughts:

[152] *War* 2.60, 151, 377; 3.356, 475; 5.458; 6.33, 42; 7.406; *Ant.* 6.343; 11.130; *Apion* 2.294 (θανάτου καταφρόνησις).

[153] E.g., *War* 6.55, 81, 148, 161–63, 187.

[154] E.g., *War* 3.471; 5.55–58, 76–79, 86–87, 109–27, 285–88, 291–95, 322–30, 336–41, 466–72, 480–85, 490, 548–61; 6.9–14, 31–38, 88–89, 169–71, 179, 190, 252, 257, 260.

> For he saw that a good deal of work remained in the vicinity of
> Jerusalem. ... Both its natural strength and built walls presented a
> challenge of no small proportion. And he reckoned that even without
> walls, *the determination of the [Judean] men and their daring actions would be
> difficult to cope with*. So he trained his soldiers just like athletes for contests.

At 5.315–16:

> The *Judeans, for their part, careless of their sufferings,* were intent solely on
> the damage they could inflict, and *death itself seemed to them trivial* if it
> meant attacking and killing just one of the enemy. Titus, by contrast,
> took as much care for the security of his soldiers as for their success.
> Saying that the reckless charge was foolish, and that it was only valour if
> accompanied by forethought and avoiding the risk of casualty, he
> directed his side *to show their masculinity in ways that did not involve risk to
> themselves.*

During the siege of Jerusalem (6.11–14) Josephus expresses compassion for the
exhausted legionaries, while highlighting the Judean valour that is causing
them such grief:

> Their [legions'] bodies were by now falling under their labours, their
> souls in the face of repeated reverses. ... But the biggest [concern] was
> finding out that *the Judeans had a fortitude of spirit* that rose above not only
> civil strife but also famine, war, and so many disasters. They began to
> reckon that *the charges of these men were unstoppable,* that their joy even in
> distress was *unconquerable.*

He comments on an engagement in which both Roman and Judean forces
behaved out of character (6.17–18):

> With the Judeans, the characteristics of the *ethnos* were all lacking: daring,
> spirit, the simultaneous charge, and never retreating even when faltering.
> And the Romans were *unusually well coordinated,* drawn up in a tougher
> formation than normal.

Even as the Roman force nears victory, Titus must address his dispirited
soldiers, nearly undone by Judean determination (6.42–44; cf. 6.33):

> How shameful if the Judeans, for whom defeat carries no real shame since
> they have learned to be slaves, should ... *hold death in contempt* and
> repeatedly strike at our middles – not in the hope of victory, but *for the
> raw demonstration of masculine courage* – whereas you, who control more or
> less all the earth and sea, for whom not to be victorious is a disgrace,
> should *not even once venture into the enemy's ranks.* ...

Although Josephus usually allows even those he accuses of political folly to
share the Judean character, he makes an exception for John of Gischala. John
practised the atrocities typical of tyrants: murdering, stealing, and figuratively

drinking the people's blood.[155] And deep down, John and his gang were not real men at all (4.561–62):

> Without shame and insolently they began behaving effeminately – styling their hair, dressing in women's clothes, dousing themselves with perfume, and applying eyeliner to improve their beauty! It wasn't only women's fashion they imitated, but also their passions. In an extreme of wantonness they thought up new illicit pleasures. They wallowed around the city, as if in a brothel, and polluted the whole place with their unclean activities.

With this exception, however, Josephus can recognize valour even in Simon bar Giora (4.503) or the fighters loyal to Simon and John (6.81–90). Likewise, the first character he credits with contempt for death in *War* is the wretched shepherd Athrongeus, who led a revolt after Herod's death: "Strength of body and *a soul that held death in contempt* commended this hope to him" (2.60).

Failure to follow Josephus' distinction between admiration of the innate Judean character and disparagement of those who make foolish political choices has, I suspect, produced some futile debates, especially about whether Masada's inhabitants or the "fourth philosophers" were *really* heroes or villains for Josephus (see Chapter 9).

Polis affairs in dangerous times

Citizens of modern Western countries have an ideal that political leaders should reach office on the strength of their ideas and policies. They should govern fairly and transparently, state their principles forthrightly, and follow through with appropriate actions. This kind of thinking, which presumes a literate populace and democratic structures, could not exist in first-century *polis* leadership. The prevailing political ethos, even in formal democracies of various kinds, was aristocratic.

Consider Plutarch's *Precepts of Statecraft*. Writing for a young friend entering *polis* leadership, Plutarch emphasizes the need for constant duplicity because the impetuous and querulous rabble are unable to bear frustration of their hopes. The wise leader's task is to listen and learn the people's character so that he can then win their trust by saying what they want to hear, as he subtly steers them in his direction (*Mor.* 3.799b–800a). He must possess oratorical skill to "soften by persuasion and overcome by charms the fierce and violent spirit of the people" (801e). Given the inevitability that the masses will dislike their leaders at times, the *polis* leader must sometimes resort to cunningly manipulative schemes. For example, he might arrange for colleagues to pretend to speak in the assembly against a measure they actually favour, so that the pretend

---

[155] *War* 5.439–45: arch-tyrants John and Simon act in much the same way.

dissenters can appear to be won over by better argument and bring the people with them (813a–c, 818e–819b). Modern politicians might feel much the same way, but few would dare to spell it out thus.[156]

Plutarch, in explaining strategies of manipulation, does not seem to hold the common folk in contempt. He speaks more from pity and concern for their welfare, given their lack of understanding. It is the simple reality that they need the cultivated leadership of his class. That is why he insists that, should the *polis* find itself in crisis, the statesman must never abandon the ship of state. He remains responsible for the people's welfare "even though he had no share in the wrongdoing of the masses, taking the dangers upon himself for their sake" (*Mor.* 815d). Plutarch sees the life of the political leader in the noble terms of self-sacrifice: going on embassies and hazarding sea travel, although it is the last thing he wants, and generally risking his life for the safety of the *polis*.

Under Roman rule, the statesman's most important task is at all costs to avoid internal conflict (*stasis*), to keep Roman forces from becoming involved (814f–816a): "The most excellent thing is to make provision so that they never fall into civil strife, and to regard this as the greatest and noblest function of the statesman's art, if you will" (824c). In Josephus' account it is precisely what he describes as a major *stasis*, which virtuous leaders fail to head off at the cost of their lives, that brings Roman arms to Jerusalem.

The charter text of political values for men of Josephus' type, and one of his inspirations, was Polybius' "pragmatic history," apparently the first written by a Greek statesman under Roman rule.[157] When Rome advanced into the Greek mainland and defeated Perseus of Macedon (168 B.C.), Polybius held a senior position in the Achaean League. The Romans were not pleased by the League's actions and took a thousand members of their elite to Rome, including Polybius. He moved to Rome at about the same age as Josephus (his mid-thirties) and likewise spent much of his adult life there. Polybius became a mentor to the young Scipio Aemilianus, who later presided over the destruction of Carthage with Polybius at his side (146 B.C.)– much as Josephus accompanied Titus outside Jerusalem.

Two points about Polybius' work are particularly relevant for understanding Josephus. First, he does not offer a simple view of Rome, as merely good or bad. Rome's growing power is the result *both* of fortune or chance (*tychē*) and of Rome's perseverance *in spite of fortune*, by virtue of her excellent

---

[156] Cf. Mearsheimer 2011. His theme is interstate lying, which he argues does not happen often, but (e.g., 6–10, 45–62): "Leaders . . . lie to their own people, and they do so because they believe it is in the best interest of their country. And sometimes they are right."

[157] For analysis relevant to our questions, see especially Eckstein 1995. Complementary, although more theoretical, is Champion 2004. A highly readable general introduction is McGing 2010, alongside the classic studies of Walbank 1972, 2002. For Josephus' debts to Polybius, see Eckstein 1990.

constitution, national character, and army (1.1–4; 3.2–4). Scholars have long debated Polybius' ideas about Rome and fortune, but his narrative resists reduction.[158] Fortune, he says, "always makes new things" and "aggressively interposes herself" in human affairs (1.4.5). In the opening paragraphs, a Roman general brings Carthage to the point of submission (255 B.C.), only to face abrupt reversal of fortune and defeat (1.35.2). Polybius acknowledges "how apt fortune is to envy men, and how she especially puts forth her power in cases where we think that our life has been most blessed and most successful" (39.8.2 [40.12.19]). Such comments suggest that Rome's unprecedented fortune might be her undoing.[159] As the narrative progresses, indeed, we meet strong hints of Rome's decline. Near the end, Polybius describes Scipio's dread at the destruction of Carthage (38.20.1–10) on the ground that Rome's doom would follow one day. Polybius endorses that observation, noting the extreme "slipperiness" of fortune (38.21.1).

An essay on *The Fortune of the Romans* by Plutarch emphasizes that Rome has indeed been favoured by fortune – *but* that the wheel of fortune continues to turn.[160]

Second, Polybius' many-sided treatment of Rome's power shapes the political aims of the history he writes for statesmen such as himself (1.2.8). The statesman's art was necessary because there was rarely one obvious course to take in response to foreign power. *Poleis* leaders always faced conflicting priorities and competing demands. They had to steer a safe course among various dangerous shoals, and this required putting aside rigid ideology, narrow nationalist sentiment, or reflexive emotion in response to slights. The fundamental and abiding tension was between the need to preserve the dignity and traditions of the *polis* and the requirement to survive under the greater power – a tension that recalls Thucydides' polarization of *justice* and the pragmatically *advantageous course*.[161] Polybius could respect any statesman who sought to preserve as much independence as possible, as long as he acted in a prudent manner.[162] Unacceptable positions were extreme ones: craven abandonment of *polis* interests (24.8–10) or pointlessly rigid opposition to Rome, which could only lead to a disaster such as Corinth's destruction in 146 B.C.[163]

---

[158] E.g., Fowler 1903; Shorey 1921; von Fritz 1954; Walbank 1972: 60–65; Eckstein 1995: 254–71.

[159] Cf. Eckstein 1995: 257–58; Champion 2004: e.g., 100–169.

[160] Cf. Plutarch, *Phil.* 17.2 (on the Romans of Polybius' day): "[T]heir strength in all areas advanced mightily, with the aid of the divine spirit, and that end was near, which it was necessary for *the rotational movement of fortune* to reach."

[161] Thucydides 1.42.1–2, 76.2–3; 3.44.2–4; 3.56.3, 6; 5.89–113 (Melian dialogue); 6.87.2–4. Cf. among many studies Zagorin 2005: 100–107.

[162] Eckstein 1995: 206. Cf. Polybius 24.10.4, 11.12; 27.15.10.

[163] Most instructive is the debate in the Achaean Council (24.11–13) between Aristaenus, who advised submission *for the benefit of the Greeks*, and Philopoemen, who thought that leaders

When we read Josephus, I suggest, we should likewise be impressed by the degree to which Judean leaders' motives (as his own) lack reference to pro- or anti-Roman ideology, although this is what scholars often look for. Front and centre are rather the Polybian notions of honour, safety, wisdom, and the attitudes of statesmen toward their *polis*. Josephus' assumptions draw from this common fund of elite conceptions.[164] But whereas his contemporaries Plutarch and Dio worked to *prevent poleis* from falling into civil strife and trouble with Rome, Josephus' *polis* had undeniably plunged over that cliff. His narrative shows, however, that Jerusalem was not uniquely tumultuous, not more than Alexandria for example. It faced the same pressures as any other *polis*. But in Jerusalem's case the provocations of equestrian governors, simmering tensions with neighbouring cities, the readiness of hot-tempered youth to aggravate matters, the appearance of self-seeking demagogues, and the violent removal of Jerusalem's own virtuous leaders resulted in a loss of control, which sent the glorious ancient *polis* tumbling toward catastrophe.

It was not for lack of effort. *War*'s Judean leaders understand the grievances and the passions of their people. Seeking remedies, they send letters and embassies, give brilliant speeches, issue forceful cautions about unintended consequences, and when things become desperate use the small military force at their disposal (King Agrippa's cavalry), before Roman officials finally find it necessary to intervene. Even when the revolt gathers unstoppable steam, the best of them do not abandon ship, seeking their own preservation, but try to harness and steer the people to a safe harbour. Alas, their efforts are overwhelmed by popular sentiment, whipped to a lather by charismatics and militants who enter Jerusalem from elsewhere seeking short-term personal glory. By the time the populace understands the futility of the course they have taken and the real motives of the demagogues, it is too late.

Josephus portrays leading aristocrats, not least himself, as concerned chiefly with honour and the people's well-being. Of his own character in Galilee he writes in the third person (3.136–40):

> He could see to what a fall Judean affairs were headed, and he knew that they had but *one route to safety*: if they could reverse course. Even though he himself could expect pardon from the Romans, he would rather have died many times over than betray his homeland. . . . . Therefore, he decided to write to those in charge in Jerusalem, describing the situation with precision. . . . *If they were opting for treaty terms*, they should write back to this effect immediately, whereas *if they had*

---

had to resist where Greek traditions or dignity were at stake. Polybius respects both (Eckstein 1995: 202–3). Plutarch wrote a glowing biography of Philopoemen, whom he understood via Plato's figure of the statesman as pilot of the ship of state (*Phil.* 17.3–4).

[164] Compare Eckstein's portrait of Polybius' worldview of (1995: 28–236).

decided to continue fighting they should send him a force that was equal
to combat against the Romans.

In this presentation, we notice, either fighting on (with adequate troops) or
immediate surrender would be an equally acceptable moral choice. Irrational
and immoral behaviour would be to sustain the conflict without a viable force
and watch the nation destroyed for no purpose.

The high priest Ananus II likewise, in Josephus' portrait, represents elite values
rather than some pro- or anti-Roman ideology. While preparing for war of
necessity (given popular sentiment and the recent ambush of Roman forces),
Ananus' hope is to steer the populace toward a safe path (*War* 2.648–51):

> In Jerusalem, Ananus the chief priest and those of the powerful men who
> were not minded toward the Romans were preparing the walls and many
> war machines. Throughout the whole city, projectiles and body armour
> were being forged... *Ananus, nonetheless, harboured the intention of bending
> the insurgents and the recklessness of the so-called Zealots to the more
> beneficial course*, as *he gradually sidelined the preparations for war.* But he
> succumbed to the violence. ...

Compare Plutarch's "nudging them gently towards the better course and
handling them with mildness" (*Mor.* 800a–b).

The same values-based alternatives appear in the speech of the chief priest
Jesus as he addresses the Idumaeans who have arrived outside Jerusalem's walls
(4.248–50):

> It was possible for us either not to revolt at the outset or, having revolted,
> quickly to fall in line while the surrounding territory was still unravaged;
> whereas now, *even for those wanting a cessation of hostilities it is no easy matter*,
> when a submissive Galilee has made them [the Romans] contemptuous
> of us, and trying to solicit their favour now when they are so close would
> bring *a disgrace* worse than death. As for me, *although I would certainly value
> peace above death*, now that I am at war and have joined the fight, I'd
> prefer *noble death to shameful living.*

Jesus is not concerned about whether one *should* oppose Rome or cooperate,
as an abstract principle, but about political wisdom and honour given the
present circumstances. We could and probably should have surrendered honourably at some earlier point, he says, but we cannot do so here and now – not
with honour anyway.

In Josephus' obituary on Ananus II, most clearly, character and political
wisdom rather than ideology take centre stage (4.319–21):

> For he was indeed *a man of dignity and unsurpassed justice* in every area: along
> with the *gravity resulting from his noble birth, status, and the honour he had
> achieved*, he eagerly accorded equal *honour* to the humblest folk; unique in

his *love of freedom, and a partisan of democracy*, he invariably *placed the public advantage* —and in every case *making peace – above his private rewards.*

For he knew that what the Romans had was irresistible. But still he made careful preparations even for war, of necessity: so that *if the Judeans should not be able to resolve the matter, they should distinguish themselves with skill.* To say it briefly: with Ananus alive, they would certainly have resolved matters, for he was *forceful in speaking* and also in persuading the populace; he was already taking in hand those who were obstructing him. *Or, in the case that war continued, they would have confronted the Romans with a long-protracted attrition* under such a general!

In Josephus' narrative, Judean leaders operate from a commitment to the *polis*-leadership values scouted by Polybius, identifying themselves wholly with the people's welfare. Eschewing ideology and emotion, they recalibrate their responses as circumstances change, finally throwing themselves into the defence of the people when under attack while always hoping to salvage as much as possible.

In other words, they think strategically. The essence of strategy is the pursuit of a goal, not from ideology, emotion, or reflex, but by the rational means most likely to secure it. The great strategist Sir Basil H. Liddell Hart wrote of politics:

History bears witness to the vital part that the "prophets" have played in human progress, which is evidence of the ultimate practical value of *expressing unreservedly the truth as one sees it.* Yet it also becomes clear that the acceptance and spreading of their vision depended on another class of men – "leaders" – who had to be philosophical strategists, *striking a compromise between truth and men's receptivity to it.* . . . The prophets must be stoned; that is their lot, and the test of their self-fulfillment. But a leader who is stoned may merely prove that he has failed in his function through a deficiency of wisdom, or through confusing his function with that of a prophet.[165]

Scholars often seem to have the idea that Jerusalem's leaders, including Josephus, should have behaved like prophets. If they were for or against the revolt, they should have declared themselves and acted accordingly. In this way of thinking, the fact that Josephus prepared Galilee's defences and Ananus prepared Jerusalem's already shows these men to have been committed rebels and anti-Romans. Josephus' later claims that they did not want war must therefore be his empty whitewashing after the fact: Their actions tell the true story. But we have seen that ancient political writers viewed things differently from academics in modern democracies. And here is the methodological problem. Josephus' account of his and his peers' behaviour – regardless of whether it

---

[165] Liddell Hart 1941: x–xi.

reflects reality, which we cannot know – is not implausible on its face. It fits the strategic mindset we find everywhere in his time. He tells a coherent story and mentions these leaders' actions in that context. Extracting the presumed actions alone, while ignoring much of what he says even about them, and holding some core of them to the prophetic standard, will not plausibly recover what happened in this war.

Central to the idea of the *polis* were notions of freedom (*eleutheria*), self-sufficiency (*autarkeia*), and self-regulation (*autonomia*). In classical Greece, *poleis* made and broke alliances in pursuit of optimal freedom. Under the empires of Alexander and his successors, kings motivated subject *poleis* by conferring the honorary status of *free*, or *holy and inviolable*.[166] Freedom was a highly charged but highly malleable slogan for conquerors – or "liberators."[167] In the Roman period, a special "free" status held by a *polis* under the Hellenistic kings was usually honoured, although the Romans applied their own grid of ordinary (fully taxable), free (with higher autonomy and perhaps the right to mint coins), and allied (ostensibly independent) *poleis*.[168] Rome's small-footprint style of provincial administration relied on *poleis* and their established leaders. Rome's governors depended on local elites for the empire's drudge-work.

Rome thus founded many new *poleis* and also transformed towns into privileged autonomous colonies for Roman military veterans.[169] In southern Syria, *poleis* such as Tyre, Ascalon, and those of the Decapolis had high levels of freedom in principle, although it varied with circumstances. The status of Jerusalem fluctuated dramatically, from that of a uniquely privileged ally and regional hegemon to that of an ordinary and vulnerable *polis*. This fluctuation was, I shall suggest, a significant factor in the regional hostilities that generated the war (see Chapter 4).

Josephus' *War* may be read as a kind of meditation on the meaning of political freedom – and slavery. In Book 1, the Hasmoneans, and Herod after them, gain spectacular heights through nimble alliance-making, carving out a sphere of independence and regional dominance for Jerusalem.[170] When Herod dies, various notions of freedom are propounded. His sons, contending before Augustus over the succession, are ironized by absurd tyrant-figures contending for power in Judaea. A delegation of elders from Jerusalem pleads

---

[166] Rigsby 1996.

[167] Green 1990: 414–15; Walbank 1992: 39, 43, 53, 93–94; Green 2007: xvii–xviii,33–34.

[168] Richardson 1976: 49–52.

[169] Stevenson 1949; Boatwright 2000: 8–15; Meyer-Zwiffelhoffer 2002 (224–25 on taxes, with Millar 1967: 81–103); Revell 2009: 40–79; Rogan 2011. On *polis* rivalry for status, see Dio Chrysostom's speeches, e.g., *Or.* 38.3–7; 48.7; 39.4.

[170] *War* 1.38, 48, 50. Herod and his father make agreements with Pompey (1.127–31), Crassus (1.179), Pompey's enemy Caesar (1.183), his assassin Cassius (1.218–20), Caesar's avenger Marc Antony (1.242), and Antony's enemy Octavian, Herod's *closest* friend of all (1.386, 400).

that Jerusalem will realize its optimal freedom as part of Roman Syria, liberated from native (Herodian) tyrants.[171] Throughout the narrative Josephus returns to the paradoxes of extravagant freedom promises:[172]

> For the enchanters and bandits came together and kept inciting many to defection [from Rome], cajoling them toward "freedom," *threatening death* to those who submitted to the Roman *imperium* and saying that *they would forcibly eliminate those who willingly chose slavery*.

Josephus accepts that Jerusalem's external condition, like that of all *poleis* under Rome's *imperium*, amounts to *slavery*.[173] But from a Polybian, Stoic-like perspective he explores how a *polis* can best create a zone of virtue and freedom *within* this reality. The utopian sort of freedom train that promises radical independence has a certain destination. Its terminal station is announced by Eleazar, tyrant of Masada, as he cajoles his reluctant comrades to the final "free" act of killing their families and themselves (cf. Chapter 9). For Eleazar, this is preferable to a life of "slavery" (7.385–86). For Josephus, it is a *reductio ad absurdum*.

He gives full play, finally, to fortune's blessings and dangers. Along with Rome's constant upheavals (*War* 1.5, 23) he brings forward the reversals suffered by Jerusalem (1.11), by various Macedonian, Seleucid, Hasmonean, Herodian, and Roman rulers,[174] and by his own character (3.394–96). Describing this last, he says that Titus was moved: "Recalling the former combatant, and seeing him now in the hands of his enemies, he turned to reflect: how powerful was fortune, how abrupt was collapse in battle; human affairs were simply not stable" (3.396).[175] Like Polybius, Josephus connects Rome's current power with fortune even as he highlights fortune's instability.[176] Fortune can also support the Judean fighters, although only for brief moments.[177] Herod cautions his soldiers, "For among humankind neither misfortune nor its opposite is stable, but one can see fortune exchanging one side for the other" (1.374). Vespasian also knows that fortune "stands along one side and then the other" (4.40–42). With Polybius and Plutarch, Josephus strikes an intriguing note of provisionality when speaking of Rome: "For fortune had passed over to them from everywhere else, and God, who was taking the rule around, nation to nation, was *now* over Italy" (5.367).[178]

[171] *War* 2.1–111, esp. 2.22, 80, 90–91; cf. 1.169–70.
[172] *War* 2.264; cf. 4.159, 175–78, 185, 258, 347, 389, 510; 5.28; 7.255.
[173] *War* 2.349, 355–58, 361, 364–65, 368, 373–79.
[174] E.g., *War* 1.95, 270, 282, 353; 2.113, 360.
[175] Cf. 2.184, 250, where the bad emperors Gaius and Nero who abuse or outrage fortune, neglecting their Polybius.
[176] *War* 2.373, 387, 494; 3.71, 100, 106 [the last three a rhetorical exception], 354, 359; 4.622; 5.88; 6.57, 413; 7.203.
[177] *War* 3.9; 4.238, 243; 5.78, 120–22; 7.7.   [178] Cf. Lindner 1972: 89–94.

Tragic themes

Reversals of fortune straddle the spheres of politics and tragedy. *War*'s preface introduces powerful notes of pity,[179] compassion, and lament over the fate of his beloved *polis* (1.9–12). These word groups persist throughout the work:

> [O]n top of the events I do overlay language related to my personal disposition, and I have *permitted my own feelings to mourn over the calamities* of my native place. ... Now, in case anyone might recklessly impugn what we say accusingly against the tyrants and their bandit bloc *or our groaning over the misfortunes of our native place*, let him grant indulgence *for this feeling*, which goes beyond the "law of history." For indeed it happened that *our polis, of all those under the Romans, reached the most complete happiness, then in turn fell in the worst of calamities*. At any rate, *the unfortunate things* that have happened to all [nations] since time immemorial in my opinion pale in comparison with what has happened to the Judeans. And since no foreigner was the cause of these things, it was *not possible to keep control over one's lamentations*. If, however, anyone should be too rigid a judge for *compassion*, let him assign the events to the historical work, the *expressions of mourning* to the writer.

Josephus may beg to be excused, but these emotions lend poignancy to his account and draw the reader in.[180]

Polybius had attacked his predecessor Phylarchus for confusing history with tragedy (2.56.6–9, my emphasis):[181]

> Being keen to elicit *pity* in his readers and generate *sympathy* by his words, he weaves tapestries of women and disheveled hair and the slipping out of breasts. To these he adds *the tears and lamentations* of both men and women being led off [to slavery] – all together with children and aged parents. He does this throughout his whole history, always trying *to place the horrors in each situation before our eyes*. Forget about the fact that his chosen procedure is *unworthy and womanly*; let us consider how far it is *proper or useful for history*. It is certainly not the business of a writer to use history to thrill his readers with such wondrous tales; nor should he *like the tragic playwrights* pursue words assumed to have been spoken or work out all the implications of incidental matters. ...

---

[179] Aristotle famously made pity and fear the hallmarks of tragedy (*Poet.* 1449b, 1452b, 1453a–b, 1456b).

[180] On the place of emotions in history, see MacMullen 2003; Marincola 2003.

[181] But ancient writers hardly observed rigid generic boundaries. See Clarke 1999 and Shahar 2004 on history and geography. Aelius Theon (*Progymn.* 103–4 [Patillon, from the Armenian] in Kennedy 2003: 68) distinguishes six kinds *of history*, but his categories appear to be ad hoc and unsupported by any known practice. For ubiquitous tragic influences in historiography, see McDonald 1975: 4; Marincola 2003.

In this respect Josephus parts company with Polybius, for his *War* is pervasively and unabashedly tragic.[182] He may allow his audience to see only men's bared chests (*War* 2.322), but the work includes the other features that Polybius abominated. Weeping women and children abound.[183] King Herod, dominating the first book, is a proud protagonist undone by fortune's reversals.[184] Josephus signals his literary stagecraft by using the word *drama* ("stage action") and its compounds (1.471, 530, 543). *War* is a story of the *misfortunes* of the Judeans (1.11–12), and Josephus has constant recourse to the tragic lexicon of calamity, pity and fear, dirge, lament, mourning, and cries of despair.

Given the Flavian triumph and its boundless afterglow, Josephus' Roman audience knows how the story ends – just like viewers of tragic plays. That knowledge imbues *War* with dramatic irony. Every Judean character who celebrates a victory or sheds the blood of fellow citizens, as the supposed price of "freedom," becomes a pathetic figure fuelling the train to disaster.

Even incidental-seeming words may evoke tragedy. The noun *to ptōma* was mainly used in the sense of "downfall, collapse, or catastrophe." The secondary and specific meaning of a fallen *person*, hence a *corpse*, is far less common and associated with tragic plays, especially those of Euripides.[185] Josephus uses this word fourteen times, thirteen in *War* and eleven of these in his descriptions of the dire civil conflict of *War* 5 and 6. In all but two cases (1.594; 6.30) he gives the word its tragic Euripidean meaning of a corpse, although he can artfully play with both senses (below). Similarly, the verb *mudaō*, suggesting the moistening caused by eyelids or gums or rainstorms, does not find much use before Josephus,[186] but the tragedian Sophocles had used it for the "oozing" of Polyneices' corpse.[187] All three occurrences in Josephus, in *War*'s middle section, have to do with oozing corpses.[188] For a literate audience these tragic resonances would have been clear.

Recent research has exposed Josephus' use of visualization language to create a virtual spectacle before his audience's eyes.[189] This vivid representation (*enargeia*) was a cardinal virtue of historical writing, under the influence of rhetoric.[190]

---

[182] Cf. Landau 2006: 10–12, 59–60 *et passim*.

[183] Cf. *War* 1.97; 2.192, 198, 307, 395, 400, 475; 3.113, 261; 4.71, 79; 6.351, 384; 7.228, 321, 362, 380, 382, 385, 386, 391, 393, with Chapman 1998; Ullman and Price 2002; Landau 2006: 76–78, 107–8, 194–98 (note her qualifications: 80–81).

[184] *War* 1.204, 354–56, 386–93, esp. 429–32, 556.

[185] Aeschylus, *Suppl.* 662, 797; *Prom. vinc.* 919; Euripides, *Or.* 1197 [var.]; *Heracl.* 77; *Herc.* 1228; *El.* 575, 686; *Phoen.* 1482, 1697; *Troi.* 467; Sophocles, *Ant.* 1046.

[186] Theophrastus, *Phys.* 12; Polybius 6.25.7; Dioscorides Pedanius, *Mat. med.* 1.7.4, 24.1.

[187] Sophocles, *Ant.* 410; also in a variant reading at 1278.   [188] *War* 3.530; 4.383; 5.519.

[189] Chapman 1998.   [190] See D'Huys 1987; McDonald 1975: 4.

Although Greek literature is *War*'s most obvious background, his education was fundamentally Judean[191] and his tragic language happens to mesh also with the lamentation tradition associated with biblical Jeremiah.[192] Anyone familiar with the Bible could not miss such connections in Josephus, even if he had not explicitly compared himself with Jeremiah (5.391–92). His Greek-speaking audience in Rome would not have required such a background, however, to recognize the pervasive tragic atmosphere.

Temple, pollution, purification

Classical tragedy sometimes invokes a case of pollution and the need for its removal.[193] In Sophocles' *Oedipus the King*, most famously, Creon reports from Pythian Apollo that a pollution (*miasma*) is parasitic on the land and must be expurgated (97–99). He specifies banishment or "the atonement of murder for murder, since it is blood [guilt] that holds the *polis* in a storm" (100–103). Pollution and purification provide a bridge from tragedy to our final thematic group. In Josephus' *War*, pollution and purity arise mainly in connection with the unique sanctity of Jerusalem's temple priesthood and sacrificial system. The God who watches over the sacred place will use Romans to purge it from the blight of compatriot bloodshed.

Temple and pollution are signalled as programmatic themes in the preface (1.10):

> That domestic factional strife brought it [Jerusalem] down, and that the Judean tyrants drew both the Romans' unwilling hands and the fire upon the shrine, Titus Caesar – the very one who destroyed it – is witness.

Early in Book 2, pilgrimage festivals become the *loci* of violence. Those who have come from afar and undergone ritual purification in order to make animal sacrifice become themselves victims of slaughter.[194] Passover is particularly charged in this regard. Because *Pesach* is the ultimate celebration of national *liberation*, as Josephus plaintively reflects, it provides an evocative backdrop for raising issues of freedom and slavery (*War* 4.402; 6.428). On the pretext of promised freedom, rebel leaders turn their fellow citizens into Passover

---

[191] *Ant.* 20.264–65; *Life* 1–6.   [192] Cf. Lindner 1972: 32–33, 136–40.

[193] E.g., in Aeschylus, *Prom. vinc.* 868; *Eum.* 169, 177, 195, 281, 378; *Choe.* 650, 859, 944, 967; Euripides, *Cycl.* 373, 677; *Alc.* 22; *Med.* 266, 1149, 1183; *Heracl.* 71, 264, 558; *Hippol.* 25, 35, 317, 946, 1379; *Andr.* 335, 615; *Hec.* 24, 1173; *El.* 87, 322; *Herc.* 1155, 1219, 1232–33; *Troi.* 282, 881; *Iph. taur.* 383, 946, 1047, 1168; *Ion* 1118; *Hel.* 1000; *Phoen.* 816, 1050, 1052; *Or.* 517, 524, 1563; *Bac.* 1384; *Iph. aul.* 1364, 1595; Sophocles, *El.* 275, 492, 603; *Oed. tyr.* 97, 138, 241, 313; *Ant.* 172, 421, 746; *Trach.* 987, 1009; *Oed. col.* 1374.

[194] *War* 2.10–13 with 30, 197, 402. A rough parallel in Dio (78.23.2) confirms the universal force of the human/animal victim trope.

victims.[195] As Thucydides observes of a *polis* torn by discord, words take on opposite meanings (3.82.3–6).

Cultic purity has deep roots in the Bible. Along with the Torah's detailed prescriptions, Jeremiah, Lamentations, and Daniel are rich in images of temple pollution and divine purging through foreign hands.[196] The language of "bandits" or "robbers" polluting the temple, which is common in *War*, has a striking precedent in Jeremiah 7:11: "Has this house, which is called by my name, become a den of robbers in your eyes?" But again Josephus' configuration of these themes would have made sense to a literate audience in Rome that knew nothing of the Bible. Rome's most important sanctuary had also recently burned in civil conflict (Chapter 1), and Tacitus' reflection recalls Josephus (*Hist.* 3.71–72):

> Since the city's foundation, this was the most deplorable and disgraceful event. . . . *Facing no foreign enemy*, and with the Gods propitious if only our behaviour permitted, the seat of Iuppiter Optimus Maximus, founded by our ancestors with auspices as pledge of *imperium* . . . was destroyed by the madness of our own *principes* [those contending for rule].

I noted that Josephus brings Roman and Judean civil strife into conversation. In telling the story of Claudius' accession (A.D. 41), for example, which brought conflict between the Praetorian Guard and the Senate, he has Claudius remark: "It was necessary that an area for the fight be pre-approved outside the city, for it would not be holy for the sanctuaries of their native land *to be polluted by internecine slaughter* on account of their [the Senate's] bad counsel" (2.210).

Josephus' orchestration of civil strife, bloodshed, pollution, false freedom, and atoning purification become intense in *War* 4 and 5 (Chapters 7–8). He describes the murder of eminent priests thus (4.150): "Having glutted themselves with their injustices toward men, they transferred their insolence to the Deity and with polluted feet entered the sanctuary." Members of the Zealot faction desecrate the sacred pavement while chief priests complain that scum from outside have arrived – "bandits polluting even that inviolable pavement in their excess of impiety."[197] Two comments by Josephus express the flavour of the narrative:

> For their most eminent men . . . kept prodding them . . . to punish immediately the destroyers of liberty and to purge the sanctuary of the murder-polluted men. . . . He [Ananus the high priest] said, "It would have been better indeed for me to have died before watching the house of God being filled with such gross abominations, and these inviolable and hallowed spaces being crowded by the feet of murder-polluted men." (4.159, 163)

---

[195] *War* 2.209, 264, 443; 4.177–78, 394 with Colautti 2002.
[196] Cf. Lindner 1972; Mason 1994; Spilsbury 2003.   [197] *War* 4.201, 215, 242, 323; 5.10.

And:

> Those who had hurried from the ends of the earth to this renowned sacred
> site fell before their sacrifices themselves, and honoured an altar universally
> revered by Greeks and barbarians with a libation *from their own slaughter*.
> Foreign bodies kneaded themselves together with the local dead, com-
> moners with priests, and the blood from corpses of all provenance flowed
> into pools in the divine precincts. Most miserable city, what have you
> suffered comparable to this from the Romans, who came in purging with
> fire your own internal defilements? For neither were you still God's place,
> nor could you even endure after becoming a grave for indigenous bodies
> and making the shrine a cemetery of civil war. (5.17–19)

Even Titus enjoins John of Gischala "no longer to pollute the sanctuary and
offend against the God" (6.95; cf. 127). Josephus, mocking the rebel claim to
have God as ally (6.99), adds: "God himself, with the Romans, is effecting a
purging of it with fire, and is wiping out the city that is filled with such great
pollutions" (6.110).

A special case of pollution would later become *War*'s most famous episode,
when Christians began using Josephus to prove that God had punished the
Jews (Chapter 1).[198] In *War* 6.193–200 Josephus describes the hunger in
besieged Jerusalem and the atrocities committed by armed men as a result.
He highlights the case of Maria, a wealthy refugee to the capital (6.202–205):

> Whereas the tyrants had ransacked the rest of her possessions, which she
> had packed up and brought with her from Peraea, the armed thugs
> would grab whatever was left of her valuables and any food she had
> thoughtfully preserved, when they burst in on a daily basis. So a fearsome
> indignation possessed the little woman, and by constantly abusing and
> cursing the plunderers, she kept trying to provoke their anger against her.
> Yet since no one would . . . actually do away with her, and she grew tired
> of finding bread for other people, . . . and the famine worked its way
> through her inner organs and bone marrow, . . . she took the combined
> counsel of rage and necessity and proceeded [to an act] contrary to
> nature.

Although he is about to describe a horrid atrocity, Josephus does not pour
abuse on this woman, as Christian authors would in the retelling. Rather, her
tragic plight elicits a measure of sympathy (6.205–208):

> Now, she had an infant who was breast-feeding. She took him and said,
> "Miserable baby, given this *war* and *famine* and *civil strife*, what should
> I preserve you for? [Life] among the Romans would mean *slavery*, should
> we survive until they come, but *famine* is precluding even slavery, and *the*

---

[198] Schreckenberg 1972: 186–203.

insurgents are harsher than both. So come: be food to me, to the insurgents an avenging fury (ἐρινὺς), and to the living a story (μῦθος) – the only thing missing from the calamities of the Judeans." After saying this, she kills her son. Thereupon she roasts him and devours one half. The rest she concealed and guarded.

Maria speaks in matching triads, evoking the three ills anticipated in *War's* preface (1.27) and adding a compact exegesis.

The dead child becomes immediately effective in his role as avenging fury (2.209–12):

> Presently the insurgents appeared and, when they caught the smell of the illicit sacrifice, threatened that if she did not *show* them what she had prepared, they would cut her throat on the spot. But she had kept a fine cut for them, she said – and disclosed the remainder of the child. Horror and stupefaction seized them immediately, and they froze at the sight. But she said, 'This is my own natural child, my own issue. Eat, for I have feasted! Don't be softer than a woman . . . ! But if you are all pious and repulsed by my sacrifice, . . . well leave the rest for me too!" At this they went out, trembling – cowards in this one instance only, though indeed scarcely conceding even this food to the mother.

Here we see tragic irony and a reversal of immense power. The bandits *know* that the woman has been cooking and arrogantly demand a share. But in an instant of recognition these hard men flee, broken and trembling. The emaciated woman, until now their frail and helpless victim, rises to supreme confidence. Josephus remarks (6.212): "Immediately the entire *polis* resounded with the abomination, and each person, placing before his eyes this case of suffering as if it had been dared by himself, shuddered."[199]

Josephus then fuses his tragic and political themes (2.214–16):

> This instance of suffering (*pathos*) was quickly reported to the Romans. (a) Some of them did not believe it, while (b) others were moved to *pity*, but (c) for most it had the effect of increasing their *hatred* of the nation. Caesar [Titus] absolved himself also of this before God, declaring that he had offered the Judeans peace and self-government, as well as amnesty for everything they had committed: "whereas they (i) are choosing *civil strife* in place of concord, (ii) *war* in place of peace, and (iii) *famine* instead of plenty and prosperity. And with their own hands they set fire to the sacred precinct that was being carefully preserved by us. They deserve such food!"

---

[199] Josephus' designation of Maria's action as *mysos* (abomination), which Titus reprises (6.217), intensifies the tragic tone. There may be a word-play with *mythos* (6.207), and a play with the *misos* that soon follows (6.214) seems clear (Chapman 1998: 96–97): the heinous act of pollution (*mysos*) calls forth hatred (*misos*).

Titus thus reinforces Maria's triad, from the preface. But whereas she saw no escape from the dismal trinity, Titus charges that the Judeans have *chosen* these ills rather than the benefits he has offered. Josephus concludes Titus' view (6.217):

> Certainly it fell to him to bury this abomination of child-eating with the collapse (or *corpse*? *to ptōma*) of their homeland itself. A *polis* must not be allowed to remain in the civilized world, for the Sun to look upon, in which mothers are nourished this way.

Verbal plays invite all kinds of associations, by suggestion rather than argument. Josephus' noun for child-eating (τεκνοφαγία) is highly resonant. Although the word is first attested here, it appears routinely from the second century onward and so is not likely his coinage. Elsewhere it usually evokes the original child-eater of Greek myth, the Titan Kronos, who swallowed his own children to thwart a prophecy that one of them would overthrow him (Hesiod, *Theog.* 452–62).[200] Lucian, the next known author to use τεκνοφαγία, criticizes a dim-witted pantomime dancer for confusing that story with the different one of Thyestes' eating his children *unawares* (*Salt.* 80).[201] These well-known myths would have come to mind with any dramatic story of eating one's children.[202]

Again, however, Josephus' biblical heritage dovetailed neatly with Greek culture. Deuteronomy specifies as a penalty for failing to observe the commandments (Deut 28:15, 49–53) that "... the Lord will bring against you a far-off nation. .... They will besiege you within your gates ... and you will eat the fruit of your own body, the flesh of your sons and daughters." The curse is realized in the Babylonian conquest with the first temple's destruction (586 B.C.): "I shall make them eat the flesh of their own sons and daughters" (Jer 19:9); "The hands of compassionate women have boiled their own children, who became their food in the destruction of the daughter of my people" (Lam. 4:10; cf. 2:20); and "Therefore fathers will eat their children in your midst, and children will eat their fathers" (Ezek 5:9–10). The Bible also includes a story of siege-related cannibalism (2 Kgs 6:26–31). Honora Chapman has pointed out that Philo fuses the biblical and Greek traditions when he says of Deuteronomy's curses: "[T]he Thyestian business is child's play when compared to those extremes of calamity, which the times will

---

[200] Lucian, *Salt.* 80; Theophilus, *Autol.* 1.9; 3.3; Ps-Justin, *Or. gent.* 38c [Morel]; Gregory of Nyssa, *Virg.* 3.10; Ps-Nonnus, *Schol. myth.* 4.89. Cf. Gantz 1993: 41.

[201] Atreus and Thyestes are cursed and exiled for conspiring to murder their step-brother Chrysippus. When Thyestes seduces his brother's wife, Atreus takes revenge by inviting Thyestes to a sacrificial banquet – of his sons – and Thyestes curses Atreus' descendants in response. See Aeschylus, *Ag.* 1191–93, 1219–22, 1583–1611; Gantz 1993: 546–47.

[202] See Erasmo (2004: 39, 50–51) on the prominence of Greek tragedy in Rome.

produce in abundance" (*Praem.* 134).[203] Surely Josephus would have made the same connection.

Turning from myth to lived reality, cannibalism under siege was a familiar if ghastly prospect. The first-century satirist Petronius has the *nouveau riche* Eumolpus promise his greedy hangers-on that he will leave them millions – *if* they promise to eat his corpse. When they recoil, he ridicules their squeamishness and cites well-known examples of cannibalism during siege or famine (*Sat.* 141.17): "And when Numantia was taken by Scipio, mothers were found who were clutching the half-eaten bodies of their own children to their chests." The sources of the episodes he mentions are lost,[204] but cannibalism under siege was not unheard of. After all, starving the enemy into desperation was a primary aim of siege warfare (Chapter 3). During the 900-day German siege of Leningrad (1941–1944), as in Josephus' description of Jerusalem, people were reduced to eating peat shavings, sawdust, shoe leather, bark, insects, wallpaper paste, and household pets.[205] Some 226 were later charged with cannibalism, and it seems likely that many more consumed human meat without asking questions. Whatever the real basis of the Maria story may have been, it is entirely plausible that the long Roman siege of Jerusalem brought acts of cannibalism.

The Flavians

Scholars of earlier generations were largely convinced that Josephus wrote his *War* to advance Flavian interests, and still today it is easy to find the view that "[h]is depiction of Vespasian is adulatory and that of Titus little short of sycophantic."[206] Our survey of *War*'s more enduring themes has, I hope, incidentally raised questions about such an interpretation of the whole work. We might ask, however, what the Flavians saw in it and why Titus authorized its dissemination (*Life* 363). One might doubt that he did so, but it would have been a bold claim for Josephus to invent in Flavian Rome, and *War*'s reception suggests that the work was well known.[207] Let us take up that question of Titus' interest after reviewing Josephus' actual presentation(s) of the Flavians.

---

[203] Chapman 1998: 72.   [204] See Chapman 1998: 94 and notes.

[205] Roberts 2009: 172. In the final days of Ottoman rule in Jerusalem (1917), when supplies from the east had stopped and the British had not yet established their supply lines from Egypt, starvation exacerbated by typhus and cholera killed tens of thousands: "Izzat Darwazza ... wrote that that there were women who ate the flesh of their babies" (Segev 2000: 22).

[206] Curran 2007: 77. Cf. Künzl 1988: 9–29; Beard 2003: 543, 556, 558 ("besotted with the Flavians").

[207] Eusebius (*Hist. eccl.* 3.9.2), who quotes extensively from *War*, claims that Josephus' works were deemed worthy of deposit in an imperial library and that a statue of him was erected in the city.

Not only do they enter the story late, close to the halfway point, but Josephus presents the two leaders as markedly different in character, not as "The Flavians, Inc." He gives the two men very different profiles and suggests the shortcomings to which each character tends, once again quietly distancing his outlook from that of the shared Flavian triumph.[208]

Context can help us establish suitable criteria for assessing attitudes toward the Flavians at the time. Pliny the Elder (d. 79), a level-headed military man and polymath, was writing in Rome at precisely the same time as Josephus. While Vespasian was in power, Pliny composed a study of all three Flavians, but he declined to make public it from fear of being considered ambitious, which is to say sycophantic toward the powerful. Although he did not make that work public, he let Titus know about it in the glowing dedication of his *Natural History* to the younger ruler. He calls Titus "Most pleasant/agreeable *imperator* – an address that truly represents *you*, while for your ageing father it should be *greatest*." And later, "[I shall] let everyone know the modesty with which you exercise the *imperium*. Sharing a triumph, a censorship, the consulship six times, and tribunician power . . ., all this you do for the republic" (*Nat.* praef.). Let us be clear from the start that Josephus has nothing like this, and it is difficult to imagine him writing a fawning biography of the Flavians.

Or consider Tacitus, who is generally seen as jaded toward the principate and who insists that he has nothing to gain or fear from deceased Flavians (above). Still, for him "Vespasian was a keen soldier who would march at the front, select the camp site, and whether it was night or day throw his skill against the enemy or indeed, if the situation called for it, his own arm" (*Hist.* 2.5). Again, "Vespasian personally went the rounds, exhorting, praising those who did well and stimulating the indolent by example rather than by force" (2.82).[209] Tacitus has no problem speaking either about "the character of Titus himself being fully equal to his abundant fortune, the beauty and also majesty of his countenance" (*Hist.* 2.1). Most famously, gossipy Suetonius opens his biography of the younger man thus: "Titus . . . was the love and darling of the human race; such was his capacity for winning the favour of all" (*Tit.* 1). It is from these writers too, and not from Josephus (aside from his prediction, below), that we hear about the "omens of empire" preceding Vespasian's rise.[210] Yet he is the one who attracted the charge of sycophancy. Strange.

Josephus is also far from the gushing Flavian poets, although some of their oilier lines may be examples of persiflage.[211] In any case, Josephus never wrote

---

[208] The same point underlies den Hollander 2014.   [209] Also Tacitus, *Hist.* 2.80; 4.3.

[210] Tacitus, *Hist.* 2.78; Suetonius, *Vesp.* 5.

[211] Cf. Statius, *Silvae* Bk. 4 (over the top for Domitian); Silius Italicus 3.597–629 (on all three: "a heavenly virtue will soar to the stars").

as effusively about the Flavians as any of them, although he is the one who became thought of as a shameless regime lackey.

I mentioned Tacitus' reference to fawning historians of the Flavian period. In their eagerness to praise Vespasian, he complains, they attributed his bid for power to "concern for peace and love of the republic," whereas his real motives were personal (*Hist.* 2.101). Was Josephus among the writers Tacitus disparages? Let us see. What does he say about the Flavians, especially about Vespasian's rise?

Vespasian's active role in *War* is restricted to Books 3 and 4, and much of what he says is at least potentially critical.[212] The scholar quoted above for Josephus' "adulatory" treatment of Vespasian cites only one scene in support: Vespasian's grant of freedom to Josephus (4.622–29). But that episode praises *Josephus*, not Vespasian. Only after the army has acclaimed Vespasian emperor, a full year after he has thrown Josephus in chains and grudgingly spared his life, does the commander *finally* give credence to Josephus' foresight, accept that he is "a minister of the voice of God" (4.626), recall the Judean's brilliant generalship at Iotapata, and hear Titus' plea that Josephus be released in a meaningful ceremony. The conclusion makes the point: "And so *Josephus received this recognition of his predictions* as a reward for now, and *was considered trustworthy* [from then on] concerning what would happen in the future" (4.629).[213] The story is about Josephus. Vespasian merely provides a famous back for Josephus to stand on while preening. *Even* that famously tough soldier was forced to acknowledge the Judean's gifts.

That happens to be *War*'s final mention of Vespasian as field commander. To understand it, we need to recall how things came to this pass. In Book 3 Vespasian figures prominently after Nero gives him the forces to invade Galilee (3.1–5). This makes him Josephus' enemy and a worthy foil for our author's exploits.[214] A minor injury to Vespasian, gleefully inflicted by Josephus' fighters, throws the legions into disarray before Vespasian calms them (3.236–39).

In Josephus' extended account of his surrender, which sets up the release episode just described, Vespasian appears as an inveterate liar, or at best a savvy trickster. He sends two tribunes to pledge safety "and persuade him [Josephus] to come up" from his cave (3.344). Josephus is too shrewd for such an obvious ploy. Sure that he will in fact be tortured or killed, he refuses (3.345). The frustrated Vespasian sends the tribune Nicanor, whom our author somehow

---

[212] Vespasian is mentioned by name 116 times in *War*: twice in the preface (1.21, 23), twelve times as contender in the civil war or recalled as general (from 4.630), and nearly a dozen times as reigning emperor (from 6.269), leaving ninety-one references to him as field commander in Judaea from 3.4 to 4.629.

[213] So also Rajak 1983: 188 ("such enthusiasm as there is centres on his own brilliance").

[214] E.g., 3.176, 207, 213: see chapter 6.

knows. Nicanor dilates extravagantly on the Romans' kindness, insisting that Vespasian is a huge admirer and solicitous of Josephus' well-being – chocolate cake with cherries and cream await! Even as he lies as ordered, the tribune can barely restrain his soldiers from burning Josephus' cave with him in it (3.346–51). Also with Nicanor, Josephus cannot believe a promise of safety under such circumstances and will not come out (3.350). When he finally surrenders, it is *only* because – in the story – he feels assured of a divine mission and heavenly protection from Vespasian. So he entrusts his fate to God, *not* to Vespasian, who he is sure wants to kill him (3.351–54).

After extricating himself from his own soldiers at Iotapata and going with Nicanor into the Roman camp, Josephus finds that Vespasian's promises are just as empty as he had assumed. The commander shows not the slightest interest in him, now that he is in chains. Enraged legionaries try to lynch the Judean immediately, and Vespasian is not about to stop them. Other commanders, however, are impressed by the man's youth and vulnerability. Providentially for Josephus, Titus is one of those who has a sudden *change of heart* (i.e., he too had not thought of sparing) and manages:

> *to bring over* most of them to his view, to have pity for Josephus. Indeed, he [Titus] became the greatest factor in *influencing his father to save his life*. All the same, Vespasian ordered that Josephus be guarded with the tightest security, as he was going to send him shortly to Nero.   (3.397–98)

This is how Josephus came to be in chains, to be released a year later, again with Titus' intervention. So much for Vespasian's admiration and lying promises.

Having consented to spare Josephus for the moment, Vespasian's first thought is to dispatch him to Nero. This is the context of Josephus' prediction and the message from God, which would become such damning evidence of betrayal for later readers.[215] Josephus has no reason to mention it here, for his audiences know his life story (1.22), but he had already travelled to see Nero once, a trip from which he may have returned just a year or two ago. He had every reason to want to avoid going back to Nero. On the first trip, he nearly drowned in a shipwreck. His mission to free Judean aristocrats detained by Nero was successful only through astonishing luck: the intercession of Poppaea, whom Nero has in the meantime murdered (*Life* 13–16). Recently, Nero has been summoning even senior governors to Greece, where they have a habit of dying (Chapter 5). So it is hardly surprising that Josephus balked at the prospect of going to Nero now, as a chained enemy

---

[215] Laqueur 1920: 253 (Josephus betrayed the movement he had led); Thackeray 1929: 14–15 (more sympathetically); see Rajak 1983: 185–90 for a survey of problems and possibilities.

fighter, and that he would try everything possible to divert Vespasian from this course.

Cassius Dio delights in recalling – or scripting – foreigners' appraisals of Nero as a soft woman-man and their amazement that self-respecting Romans were tolerating him as ruler. Having come to power as a lad through his mother's manoeuvres, and now on a concert and athletic tour of Greece, the 28-year-old was an absurd product of hereditary monarchy. His lyre-playing, singing, and obsession with personal appearance offended elite male standards, leading Dio's Boudica to claim that British women had more testosterone than he, "a man in name, a woman in behaviour."[216] The Parthian-Armenian king Tiridates, after meeting the emperor and grovelling as diplomacy required, was reportedly disgusted by his get-up and wondered how a general like Corbulo could be the slave of such a person (Dio 63/64.6.4).

Against this background, it was an obvious strategy for Josephus to say to the grizzled Vespasian: "*You're* going to send me *to Nero*? Why would you do that? . . . *You* are a real Caesar, Vespasian, you and this son of yours! By all means tie me up more securely if you like, but keep me here for yourself" (3.401–402).

In Josephus' account Vespasian assumes that this is merely a lifesaving tactic. They understand each other. This is the reason for Josephus' year-long shackling and eventual release, after Vespasian is acclaimed emperor and a prediction by an exotic eastern priest can have propaganda value (3.403). Nothing suggests that Josephus was scandalized by Vespasian's dissembling – deceit being normal in war and politics[217] – but the extended surrender episode in the narrative hardly amounts to flattery of Vespasian.

Indeed, Josephus' consistent image of Vespasian is of a tough poker-player of a general, who deceives people congenitally. At the end of Book 3, after capturing anti-Agrippa rebels at Taricheae, Vespasian promises them their lives if they leave town unarmed. A cordon of soldiers conveys them southward to the stadium of Tiberias an hour away – where Vespasian proceeds to cut them down in violation of his pledge (3.532–42). Josephus adds the mitigating note that he yielded to his friends' Thucydidean advice to choose the advantageous course over the merely proper (3.536). But he was responsible and this is not adulation. In Chapter 1 I proposed that the same readiness to deceive underlay Vespasian's approach to the Roman triumph, in which he not only fabricated a conquest of Judaea but appropriated Titus' modest achievement in the bargain.

---

[216] Dio 62/63.6.2–5: "May this She-Nero/Domitia no longer reign over me or you [British] men. Let her sing and be a master to the Romans – they are worthy to be slaves to such a woman. . . ."

[217] For Josephus' own dissembling in crisis, see 3.193–206; *Life* 21–22, 126–28, 141–44, 226.

Scenes in which Vespasian is prominent in Book 4 tend to expose the darker, ignoble hues in his character. First, he leads his soldiers to "unprecedented disaster" by a rash assault on Gamala, which Titus must salvage (4.20–53, 39, 70). Later, on a trip to witness the famed buoyancy of the Dead Sea, he orders that certain men *who cannot swim* be thrown into its deepest part, with hands cuffed behind them (4.476–77). They float and survive, although one has the feeling that Vespasian would have been happy either way. There *may* be a certain diplomacy in Josephus' toning down of indications in other writers (Tacitus, *Hist.* 2.74; cf. 1.46, 50) that Vespasian began calculating his imperial chances quite early, from the time of Vitellius' accession. According to Josephus, Vespasian had to be drafted, but not in the flattering tones of a Cincinnatus reluctantly called to duty.

Vespasian actually seems rather passive-aggressive, to use a modern concept: convinced of his superiority to Vitellius and incandescent with rage at this man's rise to power, yet also paralyzed by his fears – of winter travel over long distances, of the risks of a military confrontation, and even of the dangers of public life should he succeed. These fears his officers force him at sword-point to overcome (*War* 4.591, 602–604). How flattering is that?

Josephus also blatantly contradicts the official chronology, which gave the day of Vespasian's acclamation by Alexandria's legions (July 1, 69) as the date of Vespasian's rise. Josephus ruins the scheme by having him acclaimed first in Caesarea and strategically contriving support in Alexandria (*War* 4.616–21).[218]

No one should doubt that Josephus presents the current emperor as a tough, disciplined, and capable general. His questionable behaviour passes without overt criticism, any potential for censure left entirely between the lines. It is nevertheless difficult to find anything approaching adulation in these passages. Josephus expresses even his gratitude to Vespasian for dealing with his would-be accusers in Rome with a surprising matter-of-factness – and again a nod to Titus' influence.[219] The Vespasian that emerges seems realistically human, internally coherent and matching other writers' portraits, inspiring of respect and sometimes fear, but not an object of panegyric.

Josephus' prediction before Vespasian has been the single biggest blot on his own character, although he may be a victim of his extraordinary posthumous

[218] For the official date see Suetonius, *Vesp.* 6.3; Tacitus, *Hist.* 2.79. Nicols (1978: 72–73), like most who considered Josephus a Flavian mouthpiece, did not explain the mismatch. Weber (1921: 168–69 n. 1) consigned it to a footnote focused on the underlying events rather than the text's meaning and suggesting that the complexity of events in both Caesarea and Alexandria meant that they would have overlapped, although he conceded Josephus' version suited his perspective. Lindner most clearly recognized Josephus' independence of outlook (1972: 65), the Judean linking Vespasian's rise with scripture (*War* 6.313–15 with 3.352–53).

[219] *War* 7.450; *Life* 423–28.

fame. With the enormous popularity of his work through two millennia, this episode was flash-frozen for posterity to scrutinize and, especially in modern times, to contrast with the purest ideals of ethical action. In real life, however, commanders of invading armies have always received exuberant affirmation from fast-thinking natives, their welcome often being full of providential overtones. "It's not just our city council that considers you marvellous, Your Excellency; you are *the One* for whom our people have been waiting!" Local elites who make such claims are expressing overt loyalty, but more importantly they are asking that their community be spared and protected by the conqueror. In Chapter 6 we shall see a diverse range of *poleis* rushing to welcome Vespasian and his army before he reaches Galilee, for just such reasons.

Rajak cites the example of Ibn-Khaldun and the Mongolian Tamerlaine,[220] and we may add others. Napoleon was regarded by Europe's long-suffering Jews as a Davidic-Messianic liberator (*Cheleq Tov*), who made real again the biblical Song of the Sea (Exod. 15:1–15).[221] He encouraged this. A century later (October 29, 1898), Kaiser Wilhelm II was exuberantly welcomed in Ottoman Jerusalem, by its Jewish community among others. The first of three arches along his "triumphal procession" was the Jewish one, decked out in silk and carpets with gold letters, even though he came as a self-conscious Crusader who was claiming the city for Christian Germany. An enormous eagle mounted over the Jaffa Gate greeted him as he entered to plant churches and other signs of German culture. Still the legend on the Jewish arch declared in Hebrew and German, "Blessed is he who comes in the name of the Lord! We welcome you from the house of the Lord" – the line from Psalm 118 cited in Jesus' triumphal entry[222] – as Jewish school-children sang these words (Fig. 9). The Kaiser also received a parchment scroll inside a Torah case that read in part: "Be sure, O Kaiser, radiant with Heaven's noble consecration, that the sons of Judaea also approach you rendering homage, greeting you reverently from their innermost bosom." An accompanying prayer affirmed God's choice of the Hohenzollerns to rule in righteousness.[223]

Not even two decades later (December 11, 1917), however, the British General Edmund Allenby would be similarly welcomed at Jaffa Gate by Jews, Muslims, and Christians – as the city's redeemer from Ottoman-German rule. His surname invited the transliteration *Allah an-nabi* (prophet of God) among the Arab population, which British propaganda delighted in exploiting.[224] There was supposedly an old Arab prophecy, recalling the one that Josephus

---

[220] Rajak 1983: 187–88.   [221] Schechter 2003: 194–234.

[222] Ps 118:26; Mark 11:9; Matt 21:9; Luke 19:38; John 12:3.

[223] Roth 1973: 13–15 with Mountford 1898 and *HaMigdal* (The Tower of David Museum of Jerusalem, special edition). Oct. 2012.

[224] Halsey 1920: 10.91 (with some confusion about the Arabic); Segev 2000: 55; Bar-Yosef 2001: 98–99.

FIGURE 9. The triumphal arch built by Jerusalem's Jewish community for Kaiser Wilhelm II and Kaiserin Augusta Victoria, October 1898, complementing municipal and Muslim arches. Detail from photograph in the American Colony Archive digitized by the Library of Congress (www.loc.gov/pictures/item/mpc2004007274/PP/), declared public domain.

made famous, that a prophet from the West would enter Jerusalem's Golden Gate when Nile water reached Palestine (cf. Allenby's pipeline from Egypt). The British government toyed with having Allenby enter via the long-sealed Golden Gate, but drew back from practical complications and the wish to avoid *kaiserlich* pomp.[225]

No one alleges craven betrayal in such events. The Kaiser's *Eingriff* in Jerusalem was the subject of a 2012 display in Israel's Tower of David Museum at the Jaffa Gate. That Josephus' comparable sophistry lives on to convict him seems not quite fair. Whatever we may speculate about his character, he was one of the very few who faced Roman legions in combat, putting himself in harm's way (Chapter 6). The prediction episode he retails is in any case not *Flavian*. It crowns his self-portrait as a resourceful commander, seer, and all-round extraordinary fellow, who gave the Romans their toughest time in the north.

[225] Bar-Yosef 2001: 98. Ottoman officials had filled in Jerusalem's moat, changing the city's topography forever so as to create an entry road for the imperial party, but these radical optics were not to be repeated.

Josephus' Titus is a different creature from his father. Josephus portrays him warmly, it is true, often sounding like Polybius describing Scipio. Still there is restraint and nuance. Josephus' richest statement comes in a speech of his to the rebels, where he asserts that a spring in Jerusalem had increased its yield with Titus' arrival (5.409). But that speech is riddled with rhetorical mischief.

There may have been genuine affection between the two men. Titus did preserve Josephus' life after all, and Josephus allegedly returned the favour during Jerusalem's siege. He portrays Titus as a fine if rather sensitive young man, personally courageous and everyone's would-be saviour. Titus' valour usually comes to the fore when he is forced to rescue his own undisciplined, frightened, and/or outmanoeuvred legionaries, which at least makes the story impossible to read as *Roman* propaganda. Josephus' Titus is also usually clement toward prisoners and tries to save Jerusalem from its own tyrants. But this remarkable mildness creates its own kinds of mismatch with the picture of the all-conquering hero in the triumph.

Young Titus is said, for example, to have been hoodwinked by a "clever trick" of the sinister John, who evades his grasp at Gischala in a blindingly obvious ruse, to cause him enormous grief later in Jerusalem (4.103, 116). Titus is nearly tricked again by a common Judean fighter who fakes a surrender to trap the gullible Romans (5.317–30). "Titus, in his simplicity, believed him" (5.319) – unlike shrewd Josephus, who sees through the con and has to protect the Roman. When Arab soldiers take to cutting open Judean deserters to find secreted gold pieces and some legionaries join in, Titus is appalled – but characteristically helpless (5.548–61). At the story's dramatic climax, in spite of Titus' firm resolve to spare the temple, it goes up in flames, because his soldiers ignore his orders. He is reduced to waving his arms and screaming impotently (6.233–66). A very nice man, then, but hardly the Dominator portrayed on thousands of victory coins.

Josephus' Titus does not use carrots only. Even he can lose patience and become violent. When his exasperation reaches its peak, he orders the crucifixion of first one prisoner and later hundreds, although only those who have fought against him (5.289, 446–51). Even this uncharacteristic harshness backfires on him, however (Chapter 7).

This brief survey should suffice to cleanse our palates from the old cheese of imputed Flavian propaganda, so that we can taste the story's real flavours again. It is an account by a proud and cultured nobleman of Jerusalem. Although it certainly shows respect for both Flavians (there was no option), they serve his narrative aims. Why, then, might Titus have promoted Josephus' work?

Titus was reportedly a man of the arts and letters (Suetonius, *Tit.* 3.2). Pliny's dedication of his *Natural History* declares Titus an excellent judge of literature, with unmatched ability in oratory, letters, and poetic composition.[226] Granted Pliny's hyperbole, such interests might suffice to explain some level of support for his protégé turned author Josephus. Titus recognized quality when he saw it, and might have preferred Josephus' obviously knowledgeable account to the thin agitprop of the Flavianist hacks.[227] Second, the obvious independence of Josephus' *War* could have been useful. After all, Christians would exploit Josephus' work precisely *because* it was so clearly Judean that it could not be suspected of bias toward them (Chapter 1). Third, after the war it was in the rulers' interest to rehabilitate Judeans, the dominant and traditionally stabilizing *ethnos* of southern Syria (Chapter 4). Would not such a mature political analysis by one of the region's prominent aristocrats, written from realist premises, help everyone to settle down? Titus' endorsement and broader dissemination of Josephus' *War* could help to tamp down lingering hostilities and unproductive reprisals as in Alexandria and Antioch (cf. *Ant.* 12.122–24).

IV. SOURCES AND HISTORICAL USE OF *THE JUDEAN WAR*

We cannot close our effort to understand Josephus' *War* without asking about its sources, which have played such a central role in research. When critical research on Josephus gathered steam in the mid-nineteenth century, it had become axiomatic for many scholars that to understand almost anything meant first to know its origins and antecedents. With texts this meant excavating their sources. Scholars were bullish about the possibility of doing this with Josephus and with many classical and biblical works. Whatever dressing he had added to his sources was hardly worthy of study. The following notions were expressed or assumed in various permutations.

1. As "prophet of the new Caesar," W. Weber confidently explained, Josephus copied the spine of *War* (Books 3–7) from a Flavian court history.[228]

2. Josephus, like the stereotypical news anchor, was at best a lovable dope who never let a thought about the world pass between his ears. He could not speak without someone else's script in front of him.[229]

3. Josephus' work contains three kinds of material, and these are still more or less visible to the trained eye: Most was directly copied from literary sources of a much higher calibre than he could have written; some material originated in

---

[226] See Pliny, *Nat.* praef. 5–11.

[227] The usual assumption is that if Titus authorized the work, he must have been in power (A.D. 79–81) when the final version appeared.

[228] Weber 1921.

[229] Cf. R. Laqueur's complaint (1920: viii) about "source criticism, which until now has made Josephus into a stupid copyist [*zu einem stumpfen Abschreiber*] of the sources lying directly before him" (cf. 132 on the prevailing source-stratification method).

"oral traditions," conceived as discrete parcels transmitted by others; and some final touches, added by the incompetent editor Josephus, promoted (in *War*) the interests of the Flavian regime.[230]

4. The principle "earlier sources are more truthful/reliable" was complicated by the recognition that "earlier sources can corrupt." Josephus' sources often obscured what he could have known more accurately, as a Jerusalemite, if he had bothered. His use of a court history for a war that he largely witnessed (so Weber), or of Alexandrian sources for Judaea's "philosophical schools," although their members lived around the corner from him, or of partisan sources on the Herodian royals, pushed aside whatever personal perspectives he might have had.[231]

5. This tension was complicated further by the scholarly tendency at the time to read real human motives and emotions out of literary portrayals.[232] Hence the search – not entirely abandoned today — for a "reliable source" that would allow us to lay down the critic's burden of defensiveness and suspicion, to simply trust and follow.

I hope that the effort to interpret Josephus' *War* in this chapter will have shown why these older assumptions do not withstand scrutiny. We have found instead a thoughtfully structured and thematically coherent text with features that could not be explained by an assemblage of sources, much less as the reproduction of a regime history.

Nevertheless, one must still ask about the basis of Josephus' knowledge. Given the length of this chapter already, I offer four summary observations.

1. Although *War* says nothing about source material, and Josephus makes his unique personal knowledge the basis of his authority (1.3), most of the content cannot have come from his direct observation. Everything that occurred before he was fifteen or so (A.D. 52: *War* 1.31–2.244), or about a third of the work, he could not have meaningfully observed. Nor could he have witnessed the civil strife inside besieged Jerusalem (Books 5–6), the struggles in Rome after Nero's death (end of Book 4), or the reduction of the desert fortresses and Oniad temple in Egypt, while he was in Rome (Book 7). He might have been present for the subduing of Agrippa's cities and Gamala, but if so he did not see what was transpiring inside them, which he nevertheless describes.

---

[230] Hölscher 1916 is the classic statement. It remained a key reference throughout much of the twentieth century. Cf. D. R. Schwartz 1990: 2–3, defending much of this approach against newer whole-composition approaches.

[231] Bergmeier 1993 is the most detailed disambiguation of Josephus' alleged sources for Essenes, although the notion that he used sources (perhaps for all three schools) is pervasive; cf. Collins 2009.

[232] E.g., Schürer-Vermes 1.324 (Antipater "wanted total power and could hardly wait for his father to die"), 332 ("Sabinus, whose conscience was uneasy..."); Williamson 1964: 145 (Gessius Florus was "heartless, dishonest, disgusting"); Rogers 1992: 18–20.

For the earliest part of *War*, Nicolaus of Damascus' massive *oeuvre* was one major source. That is clear from the likelihood that he would have turned to Herod's aide and biographer for this period, from the prominence of Nicolaus as a character at the transition from Book 1 to Book 2, from *Antiquities'* later naming of Nicolaus as a main source for Herod, and from correspondences with excerpts of Nicolaus that survived by other means.[233] For the later material, the *Apion* offers clues. After being freed from his bonds in Beirut, Josephus went with Titus to the siege of Jerusalem (*Apion* 1.48), where not a single thing reportedly escaped his knowledge (1.49, 55). In the Roman camp, he saw and recorded everything, and he was the only one who could understand Judean deserters (1.49). This is obviously generous exaggeration. Josephus' direct knowledge of goings-on in the camp must have been severely limited to the space around his physical presence. And as soon as there were other Judean deserters, they could have interpreted for the Flavians, as could King Agrippa and his staff. I have mentioned his allegedly full correspondence with Agrippa. He also plausibly claims also to have consulted the field notes (*commentarii*) of the commanders, especially those of Vespasian and Titus, presumably in Rome.[234] Whatever he gathered from these official sources must have been supplemented by rumour and hearsay, of the kind that brought him the Maria story (above).

Removing the material Josephus *could not* have witnessed leaves a surprisingly small core of what he *could possibly* have experienced in the best case: the latter two-thirds of Book 2 and about 80 percent of Book 3, with occasional episodes from Book 4 onward. We still do not know that he *did* see most of this. His location during the upheavals under Florus or Cestius' expedition, for example, is unclear.

Where did the material that he did not witness originate? Some of it came ultimately from written and oral sources, of unknown kind in unknown ways. *War's* set-piece speeches and shorter dialogues, moralizing and philosophical asides, and geographical excursuses likely come from Josephus' general knowledge, experience of the region, sense of the plausible, and literary imagination. All of it comes from Josephus in the sense that he chose what to include and how to structure and compose it.

2. Knowing that Josephus did not directly observe much of the content behind *War* does not get us far in recovering sources because the resulting narrative is such a coherent fusion. The notion that we could ascribe one sentence to him and the next to a source dissolves under study of the work's language and themes. How much then should we trace *ultimately* to Josephus'

---

[233] So *Ant.* 94, 159; 7.101; 12.126; 13.250, 347; 14.9, 68, 104; 16.183, 289. For other sources on Herod see *Ant.* 15.174.

[234] *Life* 342, 358, 366; *Apion* 1.56.

general knowledge of his homeland and culture, to specific and immediate oral reports (e.g., from Agrippa), to "traditions" (or gossip) partly remembered, or to written sources – sitting before him in full as he wrote, or formerly read and hazily remembered, or mediated by a précis, notes, or excerpts?

Older scholarship simplified the problem by imagining, in a bookish way, only full written sources laid out before an author and certain remarkably robust and self-contained oral traditions. But once we think in realistic human terms about the ways in which both written texts and oral reports might become part of our own thinking, and about the considerable overlap between these two in the first century, the prospects of recovering intact sources become very dim. Josephus' general knowledge has been a neglected factor in these discussions. Most American adults can probably list the presidents since World War II, or even World War I, perhaps with party affiliation and wife's name in some cases. Even if we disregard Josephus' academic boasts (*Ant.* 20.263; *Life* 7–12), it seems likely that such a member of the Jerusalem elite would have "known" a good deal, in the way that we think we know general cultural phenomena.

Indeed, authors tend write about subjects in which they are broadly know-ledgeable – and then undertake extensive research to supplement, refine, and correct what they know. Pliny claims to have researched 2,000 volumes by 100 authors, but still his encyclopaedia is "slanted where possible towards his own experience," his style and choices being "highly individual."[235] Josephus knew his subject far more intimately than Pliny knew his. There is no reason to doubt that he felt in control of the narrative, even though he relied on countless reminders and oral or written sources.

This fusion of observed events with things heard and read is not a matter of speculation. In *Antiquities* 1–13, where we basically know his biblical and post-biblical sources, we can still watch him energetically and thoughtfully reworking this material to make it his own.[236] Another test case involves the excerpts from Nicolaus of Damascus in the tenth-century collection *On Virtues and Vices* made for the Byzantine Emperor Constantine VII. When we exam-ine those that overlap with Josephus' *War*, for example on the Herodian succession hearings,[237] we can immediately see the differences. Nicolaus wrote with a focus on his own brilliance in overcoming insurmountable hostility toward his man, in the process winning personal commendation from Augustus.[238] When Josephus uses Nicolaus, understandably, he reshapes the

---

[235] Purcell 1996: 1197. For Pliny's outlook and integration of sources, see Beagon 1992; Murphy 2004.

[236] Begg 1993; Feldman 1998a and 1998b.

[237] See Dindorf 1870: 143–44 (=Müller 1841–1870: vol. 3, p. 354, frag. 5 lines 70–102).

[238] Müller lines 87–95; Dindorf 143, lines 18–32.

material for its new home in *his* work, rinsing out Nicolaus' egocentrism. It would not be possible to reconstitute Nicolaus, or any other such source, from Josephus' account.

3. In keeping with the old models, scholars have tended to assume that sources determined the proportions of Josephus' work. Thus *War* 1 is full *because* he had plentiful material there, while the period from A.D. 6 to 66 in Book 2 is skimpy *because* of a dearth of material.[239] This assumption, with its consequence that Josephus did not know much apart from specific source material, seems disprovable.

Comparison of *War* 1 with the corresponding material in *Antiquities* 14–17 suggests that Josephus knew much of the later material while composing *War* but chose not to include it.[240] Both of his Herod accounts are indebted to Nicolaus, yet they differ greatly in structure, perspective, and often content. The *Antiquities* version is usually considered closer to the source, because it lacks the obvious compacting and structuring devices of *War* 1. But we have not always pondered the implication of this, that *War* 1 is therefore a taut précis.[241] This would meant that the proportions of *War* were not dictated by available material. Consider also the rapid-fire summary of Herodians and Roman governors in *War* 2.218–22:

> [Agrippa] began to surround Hierosolyma with a wall. . . . *But he fore-stalled the work before it reached its height, having expired in Caesarea.* . . . Claudius again *made the kingdoms a province and sent Cuspius Fadus, thereafter Tiberius Alexander, who [both] preserved the nation in peace by disturbing nothing of the local customs.* After these events the *Herod ruling Chalcis as king also expired*, having left behind *two children* from his niece Berenice – *Bernicianus as well as Hyrcanus* – and from his *previous [wife]*, *Mariamme, Aristobulus.* A *different brother of his [Agrippa's] also died, a private citizen [named] Aristobulus*, having left behind a *daughter, Iotape.* . . . The *family line of Alexander reigned as kings of Greater Armenia.*

Josephus knew much more about each of these statements. *War* 5.147–55 elaborates on Agrippa's wall, and *Antiquities* develops all of them.[242] Available material did not, therefore, determine the content or structure of *War*. He selected and shaped his material to suit his purposes.

4. Finally, with respect to events that Josephus may have personally witnessed, we need to avoid the "I know because I was there" fallacy, which

---

[239] E.g., Grabbe: "*Josephus's knowledge* of the period between Herod's death and the 30s was extremely skimpy," and the new material in *Antiquities* represents "welcome additional information" (1992: 370–71, emphasis mine).

[240] Cf. Cohen 1979: 24–66.   [241] *War* 1.400–431 well illustrates such compression.

[242] *Ant.* 19.326–52; 20.1–16, 97–104; 18.130–42. Other examples include *War* 2.245, noting Agrippa's presence in Rome (cf. *Ant.* 20.135), and 2.248–51, a rapid overview of Roman affairs showing that he *must* have known much more than he wrote.

Josephus himself commits (1.1–8). In real life, none of us understands much about what is going on around us. In moments of political crisis or especially the heat of battle, this general ignorance becomes more pervasive.

Captain Cavalié Mercer commanded a British horse-artillery troop in the Battle of Waterloo (1815). He diligently kept a diary, the notes of which he expanded fifteen years later. He did not intend this for publication, but it surfaced two years after his death. Such an account seems like it should be an outstanding source, intended to deceive no one. For that reason it illustrates the problems of historical reporting, in two ways.

First, we have Mercer's own wise observations. Even in writing for his own amusement he carefully restricted his claims to knowledge:

> A scientific relation of this great struggle [with Napoleon] . . . I pretend not to write . . . – just what happened to me and mine, and what I *did* see happen to others about me. Depend on it, he who pretends to give a general account of a great battle from his own observation deceives you – believe him not. He can see no farther (that is, if he be personally engaged in it) than the length of his own nose; and how is he to tell what is passing two or three miles off, with hills and trees and buildings intervening . . .?[243]

His candour encourages us to treat what he *does* relate as reliable, because we imagine him to have been so restrained. But now the second problem arises. A modern postscript shows that even what Mercer thought he saw was often illusory. He laments the loss of 140 horses, whereas only sixty-nine died. He describes men falling dead around him at an alarming rate, but the battle killed only three.[244] Since we have no reason to accuse Mercer of mendacity, his case provides a valuable caution about all eyewitness claims. The biggest problem of all is the understanding of high-level motives, strategies, and ambitions, which Mercer realizes he knew nothing about. Neither did Josephus know about the many groups and individuals whose inner thoughts he nonetheless describes.

Josephus *was* undoubtedly a significant eyewitness-participant in the Judean War and uniquely well informed, as he claims. Precisely because he was involved, however, he could see little and he understood less – at the time it was happening. His sophisticated synthesis a few years later required considerable research and reflection, along with innumerable decisions about selection, structure, narrative register, voice, literary register, and characterization, resulting in endless choices about diction and sentence structure. Books do not write themselves.

---

[243] Mercer 1999 [1870]: 162.
[244] So Philip Haythornthwaite's afterword in Mercer 1999 [1870]: 395. Mercer also claims that his troop expended 700 rounds *per gun*, whereas a post-battle inventory gave that figure for all six guns.

CONCLUSION: WHY JOSEPHUS' *WAR* IS NOT RELIABLE

The most important point of this chapter is the distinction between real life, in our case the boundless complexity of lives interacting in the 60s and 70s of the first century in southern Syria, and the meagreness of any survivals from that period. This distinction holds even for the best possible case: a seemingly detailed and full ancient monograph written at the time by an intelligent eyewitness to all sides. That happy situation, for which we can only be grateful, does not change the reality that a narrative is an entirely different thing from real events.

Josephus' *War* was not immaculately conceived. It was incubated in the quotidian reality of Flavian Rome. There, in a lively but unforgiving literary culture, Josephus wrote as the spokesman of the defeated nation. Judeans had been humiliated in the Flavian triumph and local scribblers were now converting the themes of Flavian propaganda into historical prose. Josephus, a prominent aristocrat from Jerusalem with unique knowledge of the subject, wrote to stake his claim. Dismissing the others as cheap polemicists, he could reasonably posture as a statesman of uncommon *gravitas* and moral-political insight. Authoritatively tracing Roman-Judean relations from their origins until the recent conflict, he sought to elevate the character of his nation and such leaders as himself in Roman esteem. Rather than advancing a thesis, he worked to create an atmosphere of understanding among like-minded elites concerned with *polis* affairs. His literary character together with his flesh-and-blood presence in Rome provided the medium and chief moral *exemplum*.

It should now be clear why this literary effort could never be *reliable* for us. We might as well ask whether a song or a mountain is reliable. When scholars declare Josephus unreliable, they usually do so to complain about him. They mean that his *War* is *biased* or *tendentious*, *sloppy* and *careless*, filled with *gaps*.[245] The criticism assumes that he should have written with either no biases or better ones. I hope to have shown that such a longing for safe, unskewed *data* is not only a mirage but a recipe for misery. A realistic approach to Josephus' work is far more interesting.

Josephus, like Tacitus or Dio, did not write for us. We could not share *his* values and interests even if we wanted to. We cannot meaningfully speak of curses incurred by polluters of Jerusalem's sanctuary, about the moral quality of various *ethnē*, or about his degree of insight into *polis* leadership. We can only

---

[245] E.g. Cohen 1979: 20–21, 51, 77, 111, 132–33, 143, 181 ("That Josephus provides enough data to refute his own account is a sign of sloppiness and incompetence"), 233, 240 ("Those sections of the Josephan narrative . . . may, of course, be true and may derive from unbiased sources"), 270; S. Schwartz 1990: 8, 15, 121, 132, 140 n. 100; Price 1992: 19 ("we must simply admit ignorance due to gaps in the evidence"), 72, 186, 188, 291; Berlin and Overman 2002: 1 ("an invaluable though, as has often been noted, tendentious historical source").

try to understand his work as a product of its time. Our task is different: to formulate and investigate our problems, such as: Who was Cestius Gallus and what did his expedition intend? Or, what were the Flavians' aims in Galilee? No ancient historian formulated these problems as such; much less did they methodically investigate them. We must conduct our inquiries and let Josephus rest in peace. Although we should be pleased that he wrote as much as he did, so well and so durably, our *historia* is our responsibility.

CHAPTER THREE

PARTHIAN SAVIOURS, SIEGES, AND MORALE
ancient warfare in human perspective

Most of us, happily, do not need to think about surviving combat. Because the remaining chapters of this book explore episodes of lethal confrontation, therefore, we should pause to condition our thinking. We do not yet know which Judaeans fought Roman soldiers or why. Whatever we decide about that, some Judaeans plainly did fight Rome, and legions were unleashed against them. Our research questions will be sharper, and our imagining of scenarios more plausible, if we take time to think about the nature of this kind of warfare in the Roman period.

Rome's legions have acquired the mystique of an unstoppable machine driven by a cool, purely military discipline, whereas Jewish-Judaean rebels appear in film (*Ben-Hur, Life of Brian*) as motivated by wide-eyed religious-nationalist fervour. On both sides, we easily forget the human conditions that affected both and their largely shared values. Obviously, they were in very different situations, one side boasting a well-armed professional force of empire and the other lacking even a standing army. But the alternation of guerrilla and siege warfare created by this situation brought challenges for both. Even if Rome's ultimate victory was not in serious doubt, we can only hope to grasp the hard choices their commanders faced if we lay aside "the glory that was Rome" and think more realistically. Helmet shapes, armour, and ammunition are certainly part of the story, but they need not detain us here. Countless academic and popular books as well as websites and even re-enactment clubs devoted to the Roman army are readily accessible.[1] Nor should we assume that strategy and tactics, the hobby of our pipe-smoking forebears in their drawing rooms, are the most important considerations for understanding this war.[2] Because the Judaeans lacked a trained army, our conflict does not compare with the great battles of the Roman Republic at Cannae, Cynoscephalae, or Carrhae. In those cases military historians can diagram opposed columns, using symbols and colours to mark unit types and arrows to trace their movements. That is all exciting from the distance of two millennia. A conflict such as ours, which saw no such set-piece confrontations, invites different questions.

After a preliminary sketch of the Roman army, highlighting some relatively neglected aspects, this chapter asks about the extent to which Judaeans could have looked to the Parthian empire as a guarantor or balance against Rome. Promised aid from that quarter would have been the greatest possible well of morale. We proceed then to consider other factors that might have boosted or sapped morale on both sides, from city walls to disease and desertion, bearing in mind always the radically asymmetrical nature of the conflict.

1. ROME'S ARMY: THE SHARP END OF PIETY

Because of the vast expanse of the empire, we have much more evidence for Roman than for Judaean fighters. This includes the remains of legionary forts, camps, and battle sites throughout Europe, North Africa, and the Near East; portraits and reliefs of soldiers and enemies in typical (if idealized) situations and dress, such as those on Trajan's column; funerary and other honorary inscriptions; documents, including diplomas issued to auxiliary troops upon discharge; papyrus letters from Egypt or Masada; literary accounts by Julius Caesar, Plutarch, Josephus, Arrian, Appian, and others; manuals of generalship from the first to the fourth centuries; and the partial remains of weapons and armour at numerous sites. I am making final revisions of this book in Exeter, where quite by accident I am sitting above the long-buried camp of Vespasian's *Legio II Augusta*, from a decade before his dispatch to Judaea. Although this abundant evidence might seem to have settled most questions, new studies of the Roman army continue to appear at a prodigious rate. Many

---

[1] See the *Journal of Roman Military Equipment Studies*. The basics and much more are covered by Ritterling 1925; Parker 1928; Watson 1969; Webster 1985; Le Bohec 1994; Goldsworthy 1996; Keppie 1998; Gilliver 1999; Erdkamp 2007: 181–476; Roth 1999, 2009. Important complementary studies from various angles include Cheesman 1914; Mann and Roxan 1983; Campbell 1984; Roth 1999; Dąbrowa 1993; Alston 1995; Kennedy 1996; Pollard 2000; Le Bohec and Wolff 2000; Phang 2001.

[2] The Judaean War has not benefitted from much large-scale military analysis, other than Bloom 2010. When scholars have analyzed episodes from military perspectives (e.g., Bar-Kochva 1976; Gichon 1981, 2000), their emphasis has been on terrain and tactics rather than on questions pursued here.

studies and certainly re-enactment exercises omit such weird or illegal practices as animal sacrifice, however, an omission that exposes crucial differences between the Romans' world and ours.

Let us begin with a basic conception of Rome's legions, the heart of its armed forces. Latin *legio* means selection or levy. The term goes back to a time in which male citizens meeting a property requirement were conscripted for a summer's campaign led by one of Rome's two consuls, after which they would return home to life in the city (Polybius 6.19). They were truly Rome's citizens in arms. The legion's two key officer ranks, tribune (*tribunus*: "tribal chief") and centurion (*centurio*: "division man"), are vestiges of the Republic's 35 *tribes* and 350+ *centuries* – two kinds of voting assemblies. By the second century B.C., Rome's growing foreign entanglements were placing unbearable military burdens on the citizenry, who might need to be on campaign for unsustainably long periods. In 107 B.C., seeking an effective way to deal with various military challenges, the consul Gaius Marius invited Rome's poorest citizens to enlist voluntarily. His guess that they would have a stronger motivation to sign up for multi-year enlistments proved correct, and legionary ranks swelled with volunteers from Rome's lower economic strata.

Consuls in the middle Republic enrolled up to four legions in a season to deal with foreign threats, but this number grew exponentially during the civil wars of the first century B.C. Needing legions that would be loyal to them personally, powerful senators looked to Italian and even provincial manpower, facilitating immediate citizenship when necessary. By the time Octavian (soon to be Augustus) faced Marc Antony at Actium in 31 B.C., sixty or more legions may have been enrolled.[3] As sole victor of that conflict, Augustus quickly pared the number to about twenty-eight,[4] three of which would be lost to an ambush in Germany near the end of his life (A.D. 9). Successive emperors occasionally added new legions, so that when Vespasian and Titus entered Judaea there were around twenty-eight again. Vespasian's three and Titus' four legions in the Judaean campaign, with detachments of others, thus represented a sizable portion of empire's entire legionary capability.[5]

With no more than 150,000 men all told, that citizen (legionary) army had to protect an empire stretching from Spain and Britain to Syria and from the Rhine-Danube to North Africa. To put these numbers in perspective, consider that the tiny state of modern Israel, defending a small territory that had *no*

---

[3] See Appian, *Bell. civ.* 5.53: Octavian had 40.

[4] Although not given clearly in ancient texts, this is the generally accepted number for explaining diverse material and literary evidence. Tacitus gives twenty-five legions under Tiberius (*Ann.* 4.5). See Ritterling 1925: 1215–18, challenging Mommsen's proposals (of eighteen and later twenty-six). Keppie (1998: 134–36, 142–43) lists the proposed twenty-eight with creation dates; Roth (2009: 146) unusually posits thirty-one.

[5] Ritterling 1925: 1363–64.

legions before A.D. 67, has a larger active-duty force (176,500) than the entire legionary army – not to mention a reserve nearly three times that size and advanced weaponry.[6]

Plainly insufficient for preclusive *defence* of the empire or "border patrol," Rome's legions were concentrated in a few places: More than half were based in Britain, Germany west of the Rhine, and northern Syria. This means that most provincial subjects never saw legions, which was probably just as well. They were a deterrent force, meant to pacify by intimidation, although they were available when needed for overwhelming retaliation against selected targets.[7] Given the usual conditions of peace, many legionaries before the late 60s apparently served their twenty years of active duty without seeing serious combat.[8]

The first-century province of Syria, of which Judaea was a part (Chapter 4), hosted a standing garrison of four legions, totalling about 20,000 men at paper strength. Based far in the north, more than two weeks' forced march from Judaea, they were complemented by perhaps thirty-two auxiliary cohorts of about 500 each (16,000+ total). These cohorts were distributed throughout the province, including Palestine-Judaea.[9] I shall propose in Chapter 4 that our war began chiefly from conflicts between Judaeans and these local antagonists, who enjoyed official backing whatever their shortcomings.

Until a decade before the Judaean War, the legions in Syria were *III Gallica*, *VI Ferrata*, *X Fretensis*, and *XII Fulminata*.[10] The first three were positioned near the middle-Euphrates frontier with Parthia, whereas the Twelfth was farther south at Raphaneae. The last site is hard to find now because there is no modern town there, but it is roughly at the western point of a triangle joining modern Syria's Hama (Epiphaneia) and Homs (Emesa), on a latitude halfway between them. The Twelfth may have been placed so far south in part to monitor the bandit haven of Ituraea (modern Lebanon).[11] Nero's efforts to

---

[6] So Israel's Institute for National Security Studies 2012: http://inss.web2.moonsite.co.il/uploadimages/SystemFiles/israel-2012.pdf

[7] Luttwak 1976: 7–50. The number and positioning of the legions would evolve much in the second through fifth centuries.

[8] Roth 2009: 172.

[9] Auxiliary service-completion diplomas from A.D. 88 indicate at least nineteen infantry and eight cavalry cohorts in Syria (Butcher 2003: 412), by then a separate province from Judaea. That may be an increase from the pre-70 period, if it includes recently absorbed allied forces (e.g., from Commagene). If not, we might add the 3,000–3,500 auxiliaries based in Caesarea, Sebaste, and Jerusalem for a pre-70 estimate of 17,000 auxiliary soldiers in Syria.

[10] Tacitus (*Ann.* 4.5) places those four legions in Syria under Tiberius (A.D. 14–37).

[11] Josephus (*War* 5.44) and Philo (*Leg.* 207, 259) portray Syria's legions as "guards" of the Euphrates frontier; cf. Wheeler 2007: 242; Edwell 2008: 7–20. Slight literary and epigraphical evidence might suggest that only one (*III Gallica*) was based right on the river in the mid-first century, perhaps at Zeugma (in modern Turkey), the others inland at Cyrrhus (*X*, Tacitus, *Ann.* 2.57) and Apamea (Afamia) on the Orontes, or even at coastal Laodicea (Ritterling

deal with Armenia in the late 50s and 60s required adjustments to the Syrian garrison. These efforts were entrusted to his special representative Cn. Domitius Corbulo as legate of Cappadocia and Syria.[12] Although Josephus nowhere mentions Corbulo, that commander's presence must be a factor in any historical reconstruction of Cestius Gallus' career, and we shall need to ask about him (Chapter 5).

In spite of their reputation as killing machines, we should not think of the legions as more robotic or homogenized than any other army. Two of those based in Syria, *X Fretensis* and *XII Fulminata*, differed greatly in unit history and ethos, and that difference may help to explain their different roles in the Judaean War (below here and Chapter 5).

Alongside legions and auxiliary forces were the armies of allied kings. Men such as King Herod, his sons and grandsons, and the kings of Chalcis, Emesa, and Commagene farther north in Syria maintained independent forces of 5,000 to 20,000 soldiers. When their kingdoms fell under the Syrian legate's direct administration, a reversible arrangement in principle, selected cohorts from their armies continued as auxiliary units in the same part of the province.[13] Because the allied forces had already modelled themselves on Rome's legions and often seconded experienced legionaries as commanders, it is not clear how dramatic the change from allied to auxiliary unit would have been in practical terms for most of them, although units lost the prestige that had attached to a notionally independent royal army. In Judaea the change was major because it came with a shift in command centre from Judaean Jerusalem to Roman Caesarea (Chapter 4).

In this period, allied/auxiliary soldiers usually remained near their homes, although they could be sent abroad if they had special skills needed elsewhere. Eastern units typically excelled in cavalry and archery. The mountain tribesmen of the eastern Balkans – the Thracians of Spartacus fame – were famous for exceptional skill in archery. While still serving in an allied kingdom in A.D. 26, they were ordered abroad in the service of Rome and violently resisted (Tacitus, *Ann.* 4.46–51). Within a few decades, however, we find Thracian cohorts among Syria's auxiliary.[14] Specialists from Ituraea (Lebanon) and Emesa (Homs) were used in much the same way.[15] In southern Syria around Judaea, auxiliary cohorts were recruited mainly from Samaria/Sebaste and Caesarea. They remained in place throughout our period, with dangerous consequences.

1925: 1525, 1589), as well as Raphaneae. After the war, the Twelfth would be moved to the eastern front (Melitene) as punishment for ineptitude (*War* 7.18).

[12] Ritterling 1925: 1257–59, 1521–22; Dąbrowa 1996; Vervaet 2003: 441–42.

[13] Cheesman 1914: 15–19, 57–65; Kraeling 1942: 265–74; Schürer-Vermes 1.364–66; Webster 1985: 141–56; Keppie 1998: 156.

[14] Cheesman 1914: 19, 60; Pollard 2000: 120–24.   [15] Cheesman 1914: 67–85.

Legions and auxiliaries were never hermetically sealed from each other, and by the late second century they would become barely distinguishable.[16] In the East, Greek seems to have been the everyday language for both, Latin being restricted to command-level communication and certain traditional rituals.[17] Citizenship grants to auxiliary veterans and their children gradually blurred the citizen/non-citizen divide, as did legionaries' informal relationships with local women. Career progression also knitted the two forces together. An experienced legionary soldier might accept promotion to a centurial auxiliary post, while a legionary centurion might be offered an auxiliary prefectship – commanding 500 instead of 80 – before returning to the legion as a tribune, a post he might leave again to command an auxiliary cavalry troop.[18] This movement back and forth helps to explain why we find Latin-named tribunes, prefects, and centurions among the auxiliary cohorts in Caesarea and Jerusalem.[19]

In pre-70 Syria, nevertheless, legions, auxiliary cohorts, and allied royal forces were still fundamentally separate, with different roles. As the primary vehicle for Rome's projection of power, legions apparently remained together as wholes in this period, so as to be rapidly movable when needed. Corbulo and Vespasian could take whole legions from the Danube provinces for their eastern conflicts. The half-legions used by Cestius and Titus were apparently ad hoc divisions created by military need rather than a collection of already dispersed cohorts.[20]

Auxiliaries had supporting roles in Rome's projection of power, to be sure, but a different ethos. They had lower entry standards, were paid less

---

[16] On the many factors in this gradual interweaving see Parker 1928: 171–72; Keppie 1998: 181–85; Pollard 2000: 152–59; Phang 2001: 296–392. Phang doubts that legionaries' children by local women were retroactively legitimized, whereas Pollard (2000: 152–53) applies the auxiliary grant of citizenship (at retirement) for children and wives also to legionaries *a fortiori*.

[17] Pollard 2000: 134–38, although leaning on auxiliary evidence (from Dura) for both legions and auxiliaries.

[18] See Watson 1969: 24–25; Webster 1985: 112–13, 145–50; Le Bohec 1994: 26, 46; Parker 1928: 188–90, 204 for evidence that auxiliary cavalry commands could be ranked more highly than the legionary tribuneship.

[19] E.g., *War* 2.52, 291, 298, 450. See also Acts 22:27–28, where the auxiliary *tribune* Claudius Lysias (23:26) is a Greek-speaking provincial who has acquired Roman citizenship in his course of promotion. Acts assumes that the commander of Jerusalem's garrison was a *tribune* (21:31–37; 22:24–29; cf. John 18:12). Josephus uses that title for Cumanus' (Roman-named) tribune Celer: *War* 2.244; *Ant.* 20.132, 136.

[20] The late first and second centuries would see legions broken up for broader coverage within a province, I take the evidence for the East to support Luttwak (1976: 40–50) and Wheeler (2007: 241) in seeing a tendency until the 60s to keep legions whole and concentrated. Goldsworthy (1996: 39–75) argues for a much more tactically diverse norm, and Butcher (2003: 411) proposes the compromise of (Syrian) fragmentation in *peacetime*, the legionary bases mentioned in sources being little more than administrative headquarters as detachments roamed the large province on specific tasks. If Syria includes Judaea, this picture would face the objection that we do not see legions there (Chapter 4), and Cestius' moves appear to suggest intact legions ready for movement (Chapter 5).

(apparently five-sixths),[21] were less well trained, had fewer privileges in service and on discharge, and were commanded by equestrians rather than senators. Their local identities and lighter equipment did not generate the same awe, and their 500-strong cohorts could never match the spectacle of 5,000 legionaries formed up (Vegetius, *Epit.* 2.2). Auxiliary duties involved much more in the way of local policing and population control, although in certain settings legionaries might do similar things. The legionaries also provided a check and balance against auxiliary forces, whose local allegiances might lead to grievance and rebellion.[22] For Tacitus and Josephus, at any rate, the legions were Rome's *real army*. Both authors were well aware of auxiliary forces, but a province without legions was "without an army" (*inermus*).[23]

Rome's use of the legions to project power brings us to the distinction between force (*vis*, δύναμις) and power (*imperium*, ἡγεμονία), which seems already to have been articulated in antiquity.[24] In modern usage (influenced by physics), force is energy applied whereas power is latent and potential. Thus Rome used force when its armies defeated or coerced others into submission at a particular time and place. Power was the timeless *capacity* that accrued to Rome from such applications of force. Using force always risks diminution, with the loss of men and materiel, and the risk can only be accepted when it is low and/or replenishment is possible. Roman planners well understood that military adventures risked catastrophic loss, no matter how confident their leaders might be, through reversals of fortune such as those suffered against Carthaginians, Parthians, and Germans. Given the vast size of Rome's empire and the meagre resources capable of applying force, the human resources of the legions therefore needed careful husbanding. Using them in open-ended conflicts or reflexive expressions of anger would have been foolish.

Power, in direct contrast to force, can grow without limit. Every successful experiment with any combination of force and psychological coercion grows the pie. Fortunately for Rome, situations that called for displays of force were few. A single, short sharp application could generate massive amounts of power. Modern terrorists know this also and try to leverage a single beheading into worldwide fear. For Rome, the application of force was not constantly required, because power – the appearance of *being able* to apply effective force – could be expanded just as effectively by diplomatic means.

That is because force does not automatically generate power. A clear military thrashing could undermine a state's power, for example, if it served to exacerbate grievances and steel the resolve of the defeated for another round, perhaps with the help of more potent allies or by means of an interminable,

---

[21] Phang 2001: 181–87. Earlier estimates had been only one-third.   [22] Luttwak 1976: 42.

[23] Tacitus, *Ann.* 4.5; *Hist.* 2.81; Josephus, *War* 2.362–87, esp. 366; 3.70–109.

[24] Cf. Luttwak 1976: 33, 195–200; Mann 1979; Eckstein 2006: 244–316.

morale-sapping guerrilla conflict. Force is reliably converted into power only where it is accompanied by the skillful cultivation of the affected parties. The victor must convincingly construct the meaning of the event for outside observers, engage in active diplomacy and restoration of the defeated as far as possible, integrate the defeated leaders into a programme of hope, and exploit all nonmilitary inducements to elicit respect and willingness to cooperate.

No one has ever doubted that Rome was adept in applying force, but the Hellenistic kingdoms and Parthia were no different in that respect. What distinguished the Romans, as Arthur Eckstein has elaborately argued, was their unique talent in the *political exploitation* of force with an arsenal of psychological and diplomatic techniques, including the innovative extension of their citizenship to selected foreigners.[25] As we have seen, on the more basic level of impression management the Flavian triumph and programmes of building and coinage (Chapter 1) were a clinic in the conversion of minimal, locally applied force into empire-wide power.[26]

Although they did not formulate the distinction in just this way, Roman-era writers used language in strikingly similar ways. Josephus uses the phrase "Roman force" (Ῥωμαίων δύναμις), for example, mainly to indicate actual Roman military units and their physical capabilities.[27] Characters in his narrative then describe this deployed force for those who have not seen it, in the expectation that merely hearing about it – without the need for a visitation – will encourage submission. That is *power*. Dio and Plutarch likewise tried to persuade their audiences to behave peacefully on the strength of Rome's *reputation* for force.[28] In Josephus, the legate Petronius describes Roman force (τήν τε Ῥωμαίων διεξῄει δύναμιν) and also the threat by the emperor Gaius to bring it into Judaea (*War* 2.193). Judah Maccabee seeks a treaty with Rome because he has *heard* of their force (ἀκούσας περὶ τῆς Ῥωμαίων δυνάμεως) – meaning their many conquests from Carthage to Asia Minor (*Ant.* 12.414). The Adiabenian Izates, having heard about Rome's force and good fortune, uses that reputation to dissuade the Parthian king Vardanes from challenging them (20.69–71).[29] King Agrippa's great speech puts the matter most vividly. Because of what they have achieved by *force*, he says, the Romans can keep proud nations in check with tiny garrisons or even none at all (2.384–87):

> And why is it necessary to give examples of the Romans' force [τὴν Ῥωμαίων ὑποδεικνύναι δύναμις] from remote places, when it is so easy

---

[25] Eckstein 2006: 244–316.   [26] See Hölscher 2006: 27–48.

[27] E.g., *War* 2.519, 550; 3.8; 4.417, 549; 5.50; 6.149; 7.275; *Life* 285–287, 378, 407.

[28] E.g., Plutarch, *Mor.* 815b; Dio, *Or.* 31.125; 79.7–10.

[29] Cf. *Life* 60, where Philip ben Iacimus persuades Gamala to remain peaceful by relating how great the Roman force is, and 175, where Josephus confides to his opponents that he understands the force of the Romans as well as they do.

with neighbouring Egypt? Although extending all the way to Ethiopia and Arabia Felix ... and having 7,500,000 people ..., it does not scorn the Roman *imperium* [ἡγεμονία]. ... Two legions stationed by the *polis* effectively bridle both deeper Egypt and the nobility of the Macedonians [i.e., Alexandria].

Rome sustains its *imperium* with an extreme economy of force because of the fear arising from demonstrated violence: "You will find no place of refuge, if you survive, with everyone else having – or afraid to have – Romans as masters" (2.397). Those who are afraid to have Rome as masters are formally outside the empire: the Parthians. But even they send their sons to grow up in Rome, showing that they are just as much under Rome's power (*imperium*) as the direct subjects of empire.

Let us return to the constitution of a legion. The smallest unit was the eight-man squad (*contubernium*), whose members lived in the same tent or room, cooked meals together, and shared a pack animal. Material remains of forts and camps from Scotland, Wales, Holland, Germany, and Masada preserve the structures of barracks with such small rooms.[30] These must have been cramped, even if the legions were chronically undermanned and if they used a hot-bed system for sentry and other night duties.[31] Ten *contubernia* made up the eighty-man *century*, six centuries the *cohort* of about 500 (480 plus officers and specialists), and sixty centuries (= ten cohorts) the legion. The forts and camps often have ten squad-rooms in a row, with a larger apartment at the end for the centurion. The six centuries of a cohort likewise remained together.

First-century legions reportedly kept a cavalry escort of 120 (*War* 3.120). This was mainly for scouting and messenger duties, however: chasing down refugees from the battlefield and perimeter checks during sieges.[32] The Romans had given up on developing a tactical cavalry of their own.[33] In a time when horses were unshod and riders lacked stirrups or modern-style saddles, the advantages of a cavalryman's height and speed in battle could be neutralized by his vulnerability if he lacked expertise.[34] In many situations that legions were likely to encounter, such as counter-guerrilla operations in hills and caves, or siege warfare outside city walls, horse units had little tactical use anyway. In steep and cramped ascents or descents they could be a dangerous hindrance (Chapter 5). But Rome had acquired plenty of eastern and western allies, whose men had grown up on horseback. So there was little point in training legionaries to master such skills. Putting up a sub-par Roman cavalry

---

[30] Nash-Williams 1940; Richmond 1962; Boon and Williams 1967; Webster 1985: 167–230.
[31] Roth (2009: 174) notes that sentry duty would have kept two men outside at all times. Still, I share the privately communicated view of Dr. Haim Goldfus, excavator of the camps at Masada, expressing doubts as we looked at the site that even six men could fit in each room.
[32] Dixon and Southern 1992: 20–30.   [33] Cheesman 1914: 9–10.
[34] Gagniart 2007: 87–88.

against Parthian riders would only play into their hands. It made much better sense to look to auxiliary or allied units for these skills.

The Judaean War provides examples of Rome's variable force configurations, combining legionary, auxiliary, and allied components (Chapter 5). If we are seeking a realistic picture of warfare, we should not neglect the perennial problem of inter-unit rivalry that such combinations must have created. Tensions are inevitable in all such alliances, especially where unit loyalties are particularly strong and in situations of high danger, where one's life depends on trusting colleagues.[35] Tacitus tells a story that finds echoes in every age. Among Vitellius' coalition force in 69, a legionary and a Gallic auxiliary soldier challenged each other to a fight. When the auxiliaryman got the better of the legionary, soldiers on each side leapt into a ferocious brawl. It was quelled, temporarily, when the legionaries annihilated two cohorts (*Hist.* 2.68, 88). Vegetius refers to the natural hostility between infantrymen and cavalrymen, a problem the Romans addressed by housing cavalrymen in infantry squads, rather than as a unit. They also rotated soldiers and centurions from one cohort to another to avoid the hardening of loyalties (*Epit.* 2.21).

It is not part of Josephus' interest to explore such differences, but he tells a story about "the Arab rabble and the Syrians," fighting on the Roman side. They took to cutting open Jerusalem's refugees in search of the gold pieces these desperate people were rumoured to have swallowed. Josephus claims, not quite convincingly, that the barbarians led the Romans astray (*War* 5.551) and that Titus had to reprimand legionary commanders because "some of his own soldiers were also implicated" (5.554). Josephus relates the episode for other reasons – to illustrate old Judaean-Arab hatred, the growing horrors of a siege, and Titus' ineffectual decency, as well as to arouse fear and pity in the audience. But we need to consider such basic and well-attested issues as inter-unit conflict when we attempt textured reconstructions of events, even if we have no clear evidence in this case.

Josephus expands on the violent conflicts among Judaean groups. Although much of their early disagreement has to do with diverse reactions to the same provocations, he attributes the gradual hardening of positions to individual "tyrants" who put themselves above the collective interest in their pursuit of power. Josephus' Vespasian, a keen observer of such inevitable strife, exploits it fully. In *War* 4.366–77 his senior officers propose striking while the Zealot faction is killing its rivals and the city is in turmoil. Vespasian replies that there

---

[35] For major fissures among the Nazis, who used to be considered ruthlessly efficient and homogeneous, see Mazower 2008 and Evans 2005: 42–55; for differences on the German side at Cassino, von Senger und Etterlin 183: 327–39. For American-British tensions at the level of units and men, exacerbated by differences in rations, weapons, tactics, and unit cultures, see L. Clark 2006: 237–38. For the view from command level, M. Clark (2007 [1950]: 182–83, 212–13, 243), and for larger suspicions and tensions among the Allies, Burleigh 2010: 334–59.

is no need to attack while such bloodshed is underway, and appeals to the economy of risk (4.370): "For God is certainly better at general's work than he [Vespasian], as he delivers the Judaeans to the Romans without requiring any effort, and without risk to the Roman army."

The notional infantry strength of a legion, at 60 centuries of eighty men, was 4,800. We have evidence in the material remains of legionary camps from the 80s onward that the first cohort was larger: only five centuries, but each of double strength (160 each), for a total of 800 rather than 480.[36] If the first cohorts were enlarged already before A.D. 70, that would add 320 soldiers to the 4,800. If we should add the officers (at least sixty-six), the 120 cavalrymen, and assorted central administrators and specialists, we come close to a theoretical total of about 5,400 per legion. But in peacetime it is likely that most functioned somewhat below full strength.[37]

The legionary cohort seems to have had no special commander. Perhaps the highest-ranking centurion within each cohort doubled as *de facto* commander. The most visible legionary officers were those sixty centurions, who wore distinctive uniforms and with crested helmets stood high above common soldiers. The next ranks were well below them: each century's *optio* (adjutant/enforcer) and *signifer* (standard-bearer). Most centurions had come up through hard service in the ranks, although they could be directly appointed to this rank with no experience (below).[38]

Among the centurions there was a clear hierarchy. Cohorts and centuries were both numbered in order of precedence, and the centurion of the first century in the first cohort, called the *primus pilus* ("first file"), enjoyed immense honour. His fellow-centurions of the first cohort shared next-highest status as *primi ordines* ("first ranks").[39] This hierarchy had material consequences: The *primus pilus* earned perhaps four times as much as other centurions and more than sixty times as much as a private soldier.[40]

The legion's commanding officer, who may or may not have had much military experience, carried mainly political weight. Selected by the emperor as his personal representative (*legatus*), he was entrusted with keeping this precious force loyal and ready for action. In consultation with his tribunes and camp-prefect the legate planned overall operations and training, maintained

---

[36] Keppie 1998: 174–76; Gilliver 1999: 18–22. Vegetius (*Epit.* 2.6) would later describe the first cohort as larger still.

[37] Cf. Roth 2009: 135. In *War* 3.65–69 Josephus implies a complement of 6,000, but he also seems to assume cohorts of 600 and perhaps centuries of 100.

[38] Parker 1928: 199–201, 277–84.

[39] On centurions' promotion lines see Parker 1928: 277–86.

[40] See Parker 1928: 214–24. The chart on the last page shows the *primus pilus* receiving 15,000 *denarii* p.a. against a legionary's 225 *denarii*. If a modern private were paid $20,000 annually, the same ratio would give a centurion $1.34 million. Cf. Phang 2001: 181–87.

discipline, fitness, and morale, oversaw sacrifices and the taking of omens (with specialists assisting), gave appropriate speeches, dispensed rewards, and executed punishments. Except in Egypt, from which senators were barred and legions were commanded by equestrian prefects,[41] the legion's commander had normally served in Rome as *praetor*, an important senatorial magistracy. Augustus had lowered the qualifying age for the fourteen to eighteen annual openings in this post from 40 to 30 (effectively 29).[42] So a legionary legate was likely to be in his 30s, *en route* to a stellar career if he did not blunder too badly. Even if he did blunder, like Caesennius Paetus (below), his career might be salvaged by auspicious family relationships and/or imperial favour.

Provinces usually hosted either two or four legions,[43] in which case their legates reported to the ex-consul, higher up the senatorial ladder, who governed the province as the emperor's *legatus*. As both supreme military commander and governor, he wore a uniform and sword.[44] This again shows how different the Roman army was from modern counterparts. Rank was a social-political-military fusion, reflecting one's status in Roman society, not a mark of professional military achievement.

The legionary legate was assisted by the six *tribunes* mentioned above. Of these the highest-ranked would be a young nobleman of about 20. Called the *laticlavius* ("of the broad stripe"), he was *en route* to a senatorial career. His year-long stint or so was likely to be free of undue strain, but was an essential rung on the political ladder.[45] Tacitus reflects common views of these young tribunes when he claims that his late father-in-law, when he was a *laticlavius*, had used neither his status nor his youth as an excuse to shirk labour – unlike many others in that position (*Agr.* 5).

The other five tribunes, "of the narrow stripe" (*angusticlavii*), were older men with more military experience but lower, equestrian status. Some may have begun their service on a fast track, entering as centurions (below). Applying simple arithmetic, we might be tempted to divide the legion's sixty centuries by the six tribunes and conclude that tribunes were something like colonels, each responsible for ten centuries (ca. 800 men). Greek authors rendered Latin *tribunus* as "commander of a thousand" (*chiliarchos*), an older

---

[41] Parker 1928: 193–96.   [42] Talbert 1984: 16–21; Harlow and Laurence 2002: 114.

[43] Tacitus, *Ann.* 4.25 (only Spain had three). The exception in mid-first century was the Province of Africa. It was the only public-senatorial province to host a legion, and it had only one: initially under the ex-consular governor, but from Gaius' time onward stationed outside the capital and commanded by an ex-praetor who reported to the consular governor. Judaea after 70 seems to have been innovation: a single-legion imperial province in which the same ex-praetor was legionary and provincial legate (Franke 1996: 236).

[44] Dio 53.13.6.

[45] Scions of the few noble families called *patrician* could, however, bypass *laticlavius* assignment (Talbert 1984: 14).

title from Greek armies.[46] But the well-attested division into ten 500-man cohorts rather than 800-strong regiments frustrates any such inference. And the tribunes appear in our sources working mainly as a senior council, together supporting and advising the legate.[47] Josephus calls Cestius Gallus' tribunes his companions (*hetairoi*), of whom he selects one for a sensitive diplomatic mission (*War* 2.334–41; Chapter 5). It seems that tribunes did whatever the legate asked, which could include commanding a cohort or some number of legions for special tasks, but that they did not hold regular positions as in a modern chain of command.

The other crucial figure at the top of a legion was the Prefect of the Camp (*praefectus castrorum*). As the man likely to exercise command in the legate's absence, he was effectively second in stature, although his equestrian status was below that of the young *laticlavius* tribune. He was the legion's quartermaster, with responsibility for all logistics including food, material supplies, and siege preparations. This officer was also a likely candidate to spy for an emperor who trusted his equestrians more than the senatorial legate.[48] Two camp prefects play important roles in Josephus' *War*, commanding large secondments ("vexillations") from legions that did not participate as wholes. It is a camp prefect who fatefully persuades Cestius Gallus to leave Jerusalem in the autumn of 66, precipitating the war (*War* 2.531; 6.238; Chapter 5).

A major difference between Roman legions and modern armies is the proportion of the force dedicated to support, logistics, and services. In the Pacific theatre of World War II, U.S. forces had about eighteen support personnel for every combat soldier. Other western armies averaged 8:1, although the notoriously Spartan Japanese boasted a 1:1 ratio.[49] In Vietnam the service-and-support proportion of the U.S. military reached about 86 percent.[50] Supplies and logistics were no less important to the legions,[51] but they required far less technical maintenance.

The legions prided themselves on being self-contained and self-sustaining. All soldiers were taught to gather and transport supplies and live off the land, and all learned basic engineering tasks for building roads, ramps, and camps. This common on-the-job training meant that they could take care of themselves with extreme efficiency.[52] They certainly had no qualms about conscripting menial labour from a local population, but legionaries handled mission-critical tasks such as building siege walls and ramps.

---

[46] For many such problems, see Mason 1970: 157–58.
[47] Cf. Tacitus, *Ann.* 1.37, 44, with Parker 1928: 188–90; Webster 1985: 112–13; Le Bohec 1994: 39.
[48] Parker 1928: 192–96; Le Bohec 1994: 39.   [49] Burleigh 2010: 360.   [50] Geier 1999.
[51] Vegetius, *Epit.* 3.2–3; cf. Roth 1999.
[52] See Vegetius, *Epitome* Book 1, for a vivid and perhaps *roughly* representative picture, written three centuries later than our period but based on a study of much older information.

Of course there was more to a soldier's life and morale than military tasks. On the march, when circumstances permitted, they were trailed by many hundreds of followers in civilian camps (*canabae*), who provided an array of goods and services, including prostitution. Officers of equestrian rank and above could marry and live with their families, in their winter quarters at least. Financially comfortable centurions were attended by slaves and valets to help with their burdens.[53]

In the Julio-Claudian period it seems that legions were typically on manoeuvres from spring to early autumn. During these months they lived in temporary camps, which they built and dismantled regularly as a perpetual training in mobile self-sufficiency.[54] As winter approached, nature drove them back to their settled quarters, whether as billets in cities or in purpose-built fortified camps. Ancient writers mention these winter quarters (*hiberna*) as the legions' fixed bases.[55]

Length of legionary service ranged from sixteen years' active duty followed by four in the ready reserves, under Augustus, to twenty plus five in our period. Typical enlistment age seems to have ranged from 17 to 23. On retirement legionaries were given the stupendous lump sum of fourteen years' pay, accompanied by tax exemptions, housing, and sometimes land in colonies purpose-built for veterans, where they could enjoy their golden years with comrades.[56] These colonies must have been an intimidating presence, if also an economic boon, for nearby populations.

In A.D. 45 the emperor Claudius established a colony for veterans of Syria's four legions at Ptolemais (modern Akko, Israel), just west of Lower Galilee. This was far south of those legions' customary zones of operation, and even of the older colony in Beirut (established 15 B.C.).[57] A coin from Nero's time depicts the foundation scene: a toga-clad priest ceremonially marking out with oxen the sacred boundary (*pomerium*), inside which auspices could be taken.[58] Syria's legions are indicated by standards bearing their numbers: *III, VI, X, XII* (as earlier mentioned).[59] A decade later Nero ordered a 400 km (250 mi) road built to connect the new colony of Ptolemais with Syria's capital Antioch.[60]

---

[53] Phang 2001: 115–33.

[54] Pollard 2000: 22–23. Cf. *War* 3.72–93, although it is unclear whether the camp construction and demolition (with burning) described there was the norm in peacetime. Evidence for permanent legionary forts is Flavian and later.

[55] Caesar, *Bell. gal.* 1.54.2; 2.35.4; 4.38.4; [Hirtius] 8.4.1, 46.3; Sallust, *Bell. iug.* 97.3; 103.1; Livy 9.28.2; 21.5.5, 15.6; 22.32.1 (and often); Velleius 2.107; Pliny, *Nat.* 10.16; Suetonius, *Gaius* 8.1; Tacitus, *Ann.* 2.57; esp. Suetonius, *Vesp.* 6.4; cf. Josephus, *War* 1.297, 302; 3.412; 4.442.

[56] See Parker 1928: 212–14; for the payout, Keppie 1998: 148.

[57] Pliny, *Nat.* 5.75. Cf. Ritterling 1925: 1519–20; Millar 1990, 1993: 65; Isaac 1998: 92; Hall 2004: 44–49.

[58] On the *pomerium* of a Roman city see Chapter 1.   [59] *RPC* 4749.   [60] Goodchild 1949.

Given that Claudius created this southernmost colony in the year following Agrippa I's death (A.D. 44), he may have been responding to the explosive regional tensions unleashed by that king's passing, which reportedly disturbed the emperor greatly (Chapter 4). In any case, Ptolemais would become the common staging area for expeditions into Judaea. Unlike coastal Caesarea, the seat of Roman administration in the south, which would receive the status of colony immediately after the war, Ptolemais was thoroughly Roman in character. We have no evidence of Judaean, Samarian, or Idumaean minorities there.

Roman military life, from daily camp routines to special preparations for a campaign or demobilization ceremonies, was shot through with cultic rituals of divination and worshipful sacrifice.[61] In this the legions resembled all ancient armies. The Spartans, memorialized for their martial devotion and skill alone, were known in antiquity for their utterly scrupulous observance of divine rites. On campaign they would sacrifice a goat before battle.[62] Rome was no different in this respect. The fine friezes on the memorial columns and arches of Titus, Trajan, and Marcus Aurelius highlight sacrificial rituals.[63] In his function as highest priest, the emperor on campaign oversees the traditional sacrifice of a pig (*sus*), sheep (*ovis*), and bull (*taurus*) – the *suovetaurilia* – to purify the army before the killing begins.[64]

In his work *On Agriculture* (*Agr.* 142), Cato the Elder had prescribed the ritual of the *suovetaurilia* in the nonmilitary context of purifying land, although even then it included prayers to war-God Mars. Like the taking of auspices by an augur and the reading of animal entrails by ritual specialists, this quintessentially Roman ritual accompanied the citizen army everywhere it went.[65] Judaeans would likewise have offered sacrifice at the temple in Jerusalem, in hope and thanks for military victories.

Pompey the Great, arguably Rome's greatest general, illustrates the fusion of military life and piety. Before his great campaigns he would offer a massive public sacrifice (Plutarch, *Pomp.* 26.1). Most revealing are the coins he issued in Rome after his three triumphs. Around his portrait are key symbols of his *priestly office* as augur – the libation jug and staff with coiled end, the latter preserved by Christian bishops.[66] Imagining a Napoleon, Rommel,

---

[61] See Webster 1985: 275–81; Bohec 1994: 236–54; Herz 2002: 81–100 (with a valuable effort to recover concrete procedures); Stoll 2007: 451–76.

[62] E.g., Burkert 1985: 59–60.

[63] On the Beneventum arch see Beard 2007: 126–28; for Titus' arch see Chapter 1.

[64] Cf. the sketch of a lost Roman relief by an mid-sixteenth century Italian artist in the British Museum (ref. 1947,0319.26.154), which resembles scene 53 on Trajan's Column, spiral/panel 8b on drum 6–7, in the *McMaster Trajan Project* (http://cheiron.mcmaster.ca/~trajan).

[65] See Ferris 2009: 67–69.

[66] See the coins ref. 1867,0101.584, 1860,0328.155, and 1862,0415.8 in the British Museum.

Montgomery, Patton, Westmoreland, Schwarzkopf, or Petraeus begging to be photographed in clerical garb, or framing his battlefield maneouvres in elaborate rituals and vowing to build a monumental church, exposes basic differences between the role of "religion" in modern society and the roles of cult, priesthood, and sacrifice in theirs.

Modes of combat available to the legion were many. By the first century Rome's leaders had decided that their strength lay in the uniformly trained and equipped core of heavy infantry. Their preferred style was "shock and awe." Each legion carried on campaign about sixty-five precision, torsion-driven machines, refined from Hellenistic inventions, for firing large arrow-bolts from *catapultae* and grapefruit-size balls of stone from *ballistae* (*War* 3.166; Vegetius, *Epit.* 2.25). These projectiles could fly over four football-fields' distance. An enemy planning a frontal assault should have been thoroughly unnerved, if not physically devastated, before even making eye contact. In the Judaean conflict, with no field army to face them, the legions used these machines to escalate the terror level of enemies trapped in walled towns and fortresses.[67] To carry such machines, along with replacement parts, ammunition, and other supplies, each legion kept a baggage train of hundreds of mules.

Each legionary soldier was kitted out with two javelins (*pila*) of nearly 2 m (± 6 ft) length. These were designed for the lethal penetration of wooden shields and any flesh they caught. In facing an opposing field army, as their ranks came within about 25 m (80 ft) of the enemy, they would hurl these javelins in volleys. Once disencumbered of them, they would rush forward with their 75-cm (30-in) swords drawn for hand-to-hand combat. The swords were designed for deadly thrusting, rather than a less efficient hacking and slashing. For protection, legionaries carried a large curved oblong shield (*scutum*), which could be joined with others to create a hard shell around the unit (*testudo*), supplementing their personal helmets and body armour.[68]

Everywhere we look in surviving evidence, we see Romans trying to minimize the risk to legionary bodies while maximizing the likelihood of enemy collapse. In the case of Judaea, Roman commanders had to think of the best ways to overcome this poorly equipped enemy without facing them in open confrontation on the field.

As provincial subjects, the Judaeans had no army. Their territory, comprising mainly difficult inland terrain, frequently changed in size during the century before A.D. 70 (Chapter 4). Judaeans had served as mercenaries in Egypt of old and with Hellenistic armies,[69] and their Hasmonean forebears had

---

[67] Marsden 1969: 174–98; Bishop and Coulston 2006: 88–90.
[68] See Goldsworthy 1996: 191–247.
[69] Cf. the fifth-century B.C. Judaean military colony at Elephantine; 2 Macc 8:20; and *Apion* 1.192; 2.35–36, 44 with Barclay 2006.

been renowned for martial ability. Herod's army, commanded from Jerusalem, seems to have had a preponderance of Judaean units (*War* 2.52). He stationed expert mounted archers, Judaeans brought from Babylonia, in Batanaea and Trachonitis to the northeast, where those units would later pass to his son Philip and eventually to his great-grandson King Agrippa II (*Ant.* 17.23–31). Herod's Judaean and Idumaean units largely defected, however, in the turmoil following his death, and we do not know what became of them or their familial traditions of military service (Chapter 4).

The Idumaeans are a particular puzzle. In Josephus' narrative they suddenly appear outside Jerusalem's walls in A.D. 68, as a tough and well-equipped army of 20,000, in units commanded by "generals" (*War* 4.224–32; Chapter 7). Although they preserve old martial traditions (2.55) and play a decisive role in Jerusalem during the siege, they do not appear to have a stake in the larger Judaean struggle.[70] At least they do not show up in the story before this point. If that narrative absence reflects real events, it may have had something to do with the inter-ethnic nature of the conflict between Judaea and its neighbours (Chapter 4), which was not the Idumaeans' fight as a partly distinct *ethnos* having its own issues with Judaea. Their own territory had been repeatedly ravaged by Judaeans, some of whom seem to have regarded them much as Samarians (*War* 4.511–35). It is intriguing to ponder the issues that might underlie the Idumaeans' reported commitment to Jerusalem's temple, although we may not get beyond speculation.

The results of archaeological excavation in the few small sites of Judaean-Roman conflict have been impressive. Jerusalem, Masada, Gamala, and Iotapata (Yodefat) preserve the clear scars of this war, as we shall see in due course. Still we lack much evidence for the size, organization, strategy, tactics, and morale of Judaean forces. Our only significant source is Josephus, who touches on these matters in the pursuit of his literary purposes. When *War* 2 describes his creation of a regular army of 100,000, for example, his presentation is so bizarre and disharmonious with his accounts elsewhere that we can do little with it (Chapter 6).

Otherwise, he gives the odd flash of detail, for example, when mentioning preparations for war in Jerusalem: "Throughout the entire city, while arrows and full kits of armour were being forged, the mass of the youth were in occasional exercises, and everything was full of clamour" (*War* 2.649). Judaeans must have taken some such measures as soon as Roman revenge for the ambush of Cestius was inevitable (Chapter 5).

We would like to know much more about the Judaeans' training, organization, command structure, and equipment. We do have slight evidence confirming the assumption that their military leaders rode horses and that their fighters often wore

---

[70] For a sensible, if unavoidably speculative, effort to join the dots of Idumaean martial history, see Appelbaum 2009: 11–19.

armour and carried swords.[71] And Josephus assumes a distinction, which rings true because it is familiar from other conflicts, between Judaeans who knew one end of a weapon from the other and ordinary folk who felt terrorized by the presence of fighters.[72] Did the fighters have concealed training camps where they learned hand-to-hand combat, practised bow shooting, and mastered obstacle courses? It seems plausible but we do not know.

Rome's enjoyment of overwhelming military superiority in dealing with a provincial revolt is no less important for being blindingly obvious. Since ancient times it has nevertheless been clear that ethnic-national or political-religious groups with a strong will to fight need relatively few resources. They can be endlessly inventive in conjuring up ways to damage the enemy. As the Romans understood and as Josephus' narratives assume, capacity for armed conflict ultimately comes down to will and morale, not mere numbers. Polybius, as he enthused about Rome's legions, was critical of mercenary armies precisely because of their doubtful morale and reliability in a crisis, in spite of the inflated force they created (1.70.3–7; 11.13.1–7; 34.14.4).

Two centuries later, the legions themselves had become a quasi-mercenary army. Their oath was to the emperor rather than the state, and he personally paid them.[73] This shift was intended to ensure stability, by cutting senatorial legates out of the picture to prevent their amassing of loyalty and personal power. But the paradoxical consequence was that soldiers became all the more susceptible to the appeals of a contender who could command their respect and/or offer a better financial deal – a Galba, Otho, Vitellius, or Vespasian.[74] We might well ask how morale in the legions, motivated by material reward and devotion to the remote patron in Rome, stacked up against that of Judaean irregulars fighting for survival, family, and homeland.

II. MORALE I: OUTSIDE HELP? PARTHIA, ROME, AND JUDAEA

Within its empire Rome held an emphatic monopoly on armed force. Subject nations contemplating revolt, especially if they lacked trained auxiliary forces, looked for outside help. It is no coincidence that revolts in the early empire occurred along the frontiers, where non-Romanized tribes across the frontier could assist: in Illyria, Germany, Africa, Batavia, and Britain.[75]

---

[71] E.g., *War* 3.434; *Life* 293, 303. Cf. the finds of armour at Masada (Chapter 9).

[72] *War* 4.19–97, 233–35, 293, 306–307.   [73] Campbell 1984: 34, 152, 190.

[74] Augustus, *RG* 3.3; Epictetus in Arrian, *Diatr.* 114. Campbell 1984 charts the emperor's evolving relationship with the army. Galba was respected personally and because his agents offered bonuses. When as emperor he righteously declined to buy his army, the writing was on the wall.

[75] For the revolts in question see Dyson 1971; Pekáry 1987, although their focus is not on outside help.

Did Judaean rebels expect or receive such outside help? The large kingdom of Nabataea to the south and east was a possible ally theoretically, but that kingdom's relations with Judaea had been abysmal since the time of Herod (they had killed his father), and Nabataea's kings proved reliable allies of Rome.[76] The only great power that could plausibly assist Judaea in a conflict with Rome was Parthia.

There is fleeting evidence in Josephus that some rebels pursued Parthian assistance and that Rome was concerned about this.[77] It was a long shot, in the first place because the *Judaea* that revolted – Jerusalem's hinterland – was ringed by cities, nations, and tribes loyal to Rome: Nabataea east and south, the Decapolis cities north and northeast, the ancient *poleis* all along the Mediterranean coast, Samaria directly north, the remaining allied kingdoms, and Tyre. Even had it wished to do so, Parthia could not simply pluck Judaea out of its geographical context. To bring Jerusalem into its own sphere it would have had to occupy Arabia and at least southern Syria, perhaps the entire Levant. In Chapter 7 we shall discuss the involvement of individual Adiabenians from the Parthian world in the Judaean conflict. Here our concern is with the larger prospect of a central Parthian intervention.

The Roman empire was a hollow ring around the Mediterranean (*mare internum* or *nostrum*), bisected by the Italian peninsula. This geography provided the capital with extraordinary natural defences: the sea on three sides and the Alps guarding the north. At the same time, the sea provided efficient transportation for grain and spices, which could be carried in wide-hulled merchant ships from Egypt and North Africa. This geography also brought disadvantages, however. The hazards that made the sea a difficult prospect for attackers also rendered the transportation of food and goods perilous at times. Ship traffic hugged the coastlines to mitigate these dangers. Those who had to take land routes for long distances, for example in winter, faced often circuitous and mountainous journeys. Moreover, administering provinces on the three continents of Europe, Africa, and Asia, with their profound cultural differences, presented many challenges of governance.

Rather than an internal sea, the Parthian empire was built around large deserts. Parthian Arsacid conquerors had moved from their northern home in Parthava to drive out the withering Seleucid empire. By the first century B.C. they had a capital at Ctesiphon on the Tigris, about 35 km (21 mi) south of modern Baghdad and across the river from the Greek centre of Seleucia, which they preferred to monitor closely rather than coerce into subjection. Their

---

[76] See Bowersock 1971; 1983: 28–75 for Roman Arabia as a trustworthy ally of Rome (and province from A.D. 106); on Arabian-Judaean relations, *War* 1.277–78, 371–88, 574–77; 2.68–70, 76, 362 [Arabians assumed as local enemy]; 3.68, 262; 5.551, 556.

[77] E.g., *War* 1.4–5; 6.343 and Chapter 7 on Adiabenians.

empire comprised three huge zones, corresponding roughly to modern Iraq, Iran, and Afghanistan. By the first century the Iraqi zone in the west had become their base, thanks to the rich alluvial plain between the Tigris and Euphrates. To the east, on the north side of the Persian Gulf, two large mountain ranges provided a left-hand frame for the rest of the empire: the Zagros range running southeast and Elburz running east. The right-hand frame was provided by mountain ranges in Afghanistan. These ringed the vast eastern deserts, far from the Parthians' Hellenized centre of power and wealth in the west.

Roman fascination with Parthia is clear not only from their literature but also from artistic representation in monuments, coins, reliefs, table legs, and sculpture. No other people had such a ubiquitous presence in Roman art, or such a variety of representation.[78] R. M. Schneider discusses the prominence of Parthians in the "Grand Cameo of France," a triplet of scenes finely cut in sardonyx, declaring the majesty of the Julio-Claudians.[79] Each of its three panels highlights Roman glory by contrasting submissive Parthians. Schneider sees Parthia as an alternative universe (*alius orbis*) for the Romans, imagined as the home of decadent luxury and gruesome savagery along with other alien values. Because the Romans knew little about real Parthian culture, they leaned on old Greek stereotypes of the Persians.

Today, literary survivals from Parthia are virtually nonexistent, although we have inscriptions, coins, and other archaeological finds. The coins are often difficult to sequence because of dynastic rivalries as well as the stereotyped portraits of rulers – all bearing the dynastic name of Arsaces (*Arashk*). It is striking that rulers used Greek on their coins and that some even called themselves "lover of Greek."[80] We have no clear picture, however, of the distribution of Greek, Parthian-Pahlavi, Aramaic, and local dialects in the eastern empire.[81]

To judge from independent and overlapping descriptions by outside observers, the Parthian empire was a quasi-feudal conglomeration of regional dynasties and aristocracies, each more powerful than any western counterparts in relation to Rome.[82] In addition to the seventy-two administrative districts indicated for the Seleucid period (Appian, *Syr.* 62), most of which continued as Arsacid satrapies, there were at least eighteen quasi-independent client

---

[78] Schneider 1998.   [79] Schneider 1998: 116–17.
[80] Debevoise 1938: xlii, 270–71; Gregoratti 2012: 129.
[81] For different perspectives see Beyer 1986 and Schmitt 1998.
[82] For the main outlines of Parthian history, we depend mainly on western writers: Plutarch, Appian, Cassius Dio, and Josephus. Scholarly syntheses, taking into account coinage and other slender material remains, include Debevoise 1938; Frye 1962, 1967; Colledge 1967; Colpe 1974; Schippmann 1980; Yarshater 1983; Wolski 1993; Campbell 1993; Kennedy 1996; Rajak 1998; Lerner 1999; Schuol 2000; Curtis and Stewart 2007; Grajetzki 2011.

kingdoms clustered in the west (Pliny, *Nat.* 6.112–14). Adiabene was one of these, in the area that had been home to the Assyrian empire (modern Iraqi Kurdistan in Irbil/Arbel). Others included Greater Media, Media Atropatene, Hyrcania, and Armenia – this last the main bone of contention with Rome (below). Relationships between each substate's monarch and the central Parthian King of Kings (*shah-an-shah*) seem to have been in constant flux.[83]

Dynastic rivalry in the central Parthian court combined with the substantial autonomy of the client kingdoms to create a decentralization unknown in the Roman world. The Roman Crassus was defeated by *the Parthians*, we say correctly. But the commander who achieved this, Surena, was actually a vassal king from Parthia's Sacastan/Sistan region far in the east. A year after his memorable achievement, Surena was rewarded with execution by the perpetually insecure "King of Kings" Orodes, who was himself soon to die by the hand of his rival son (Plutarch, *Crass.* 33.5). A century later, King of Kings Artabanus III was forced to take refuge from usurpers in his court with his ostensible client, Izates of Adiabene.[84] And when the Adiabenian king needed to protect his son from local dangers, instead of sending him to the imperial capital as Rome's allied kings would have done, he entrusted him to another petty king like himself who was farther from the danger (Josephus, *Ant.* 20.22).

Josephus reflects this perpetual turmoil in the East. He has Artabanus III remark (30s A.D.) that some of his satrapies are in open rebellion while the others are contemplating it (*Ant.* 18.330). The Judaean brothers Anilaeus and Asinaeus reportedly carved out an independent fiefdom in southern Babylonia through much of that king's reign (*Ant.* 18.310–79). Greek Seleucia, visible across the Tigris from the Parthian capital, managed to maintain its effective independence until Artabanus tried cautiously to assert his influence.[85] When Artabanus died in A.D. 40, his empire seems to have dissolved into civil war and dynastic murder (Tacitus, *Ann.* 11.8), the succession remaining unsettled for more than a decade. After this chaos Vologaeses (*Valakhsh*) I took the throne. Because his relatively stable reign (A.D. 51–77) spanned the Judaean War and the rise of Vespasian, who also brought order from chaos, he is the king who interests us most.

Given these internal dynamics, it would seem that Parthia's top men were too beleaguered to have had any ambition, much less the capacity to challenge Rome, even to meddle seriously in Judaea in the mid-first century.[86] Dio observes, moreover, although in a later time, that Parthian armies were suited

---

[83] Colledge 1967: 57–76.

[84] So Josephus, *Ant.* 20.45–6. Although he may here have inflated Izates' prestige and generosity, he mentions a similar incident incidentally elsewhere (*Ant.* 18.100).

[85] Gregoratti 2012.

[86] Cf. Debevoise 1938: xlii–xliii; Frye 1962: 187–97; 1967; Colledge 1967: 57–76; Schippmann 1980; Wolski 1993; Lerner 1999; Schuol 2000 – on Characene.

only to defence. Their strength lay in their expert mounted archers, who could operate to devastating effect in Parthia's plains and hot dry climate, where their bows worked optimally. But Parthia had no real capacity in infantry, logistics, or engineering, areas in which Rome excelled and which would be needed for campaigns far from home (Dio 40.15).

Indeed, the main conflict between Parthia and Rome arose not because of Parthian aggression but from the misadventures of Roman senators pursuing glory over there: Lucullus (69 B.C.), who aborted his attempt; Licinius Crassus (55–53 B.C.), who lost his life with that of his son and half his 40,000 legionaries – another 10,000 being taken prisoner along with their standards; Julius Caesar (45 B.C.), who was planning a campaign of revenge when he was murdered in Rome; and Marc Antony, whose generals followed through on Caesar's plan (36 B.C.) and lost nearly half of their 100,000 soldiers. Augustus ended this adventurism for more than a century, although in the early second century Trajan would again find the temptations irresistible.

Augustus put Roman–Parthian relations on a stable footing by characteristically finding a way to claim great military victory and enhance Roman power in relation to Parthia without the actual hazards of warfare. By the late first century B.C., Rome had become implicated in Parthian affairs in various ways. Rivals for the Parthian throne would appeal to Rome for recognition to enhance their credibility. In a particularly bold gambit, one unsuccessful claimant, Tiridates, kidnapped the son of his rival (Phraates IV) and sent him to Augustus. The unimpressed emperor restored the lad to his father.

This was the context when, in 20 B.C., Augustus visited Rome's easternmost province with the future emperor Tiberius.[87] The people of Armenia – a Parthian client kingdom north of Syria and east of Roman Cappadocia – appealed to the Roman emperor to support a king other than the man the Parthian king Phraates had designated. Augustus, apparently feeling that Armenia's proximity to his empire gave him a stake, sent Tiberius with a force to install his choice, a brother of Phraates' appointee. By the time the replacement arrived, the Armenians had already done away with Parthia's man. At this delicate moment, the Parthian king Phraates wisely chose diplomacy. With such powerful Roman forces nearby and having no choice but to yield on Armenia, he initiated a lasting peace with Rome. As a sign of goodwill, he handed back to Tiberius the military standards lost by Crassus and Antony along with all the surviving Roman soldiers in captivity.[88]

Although the initiative seems to have come from Phraates, Augustus used the recovered standards and men to prove his humiliation of the mighty Parthians and the restoration of Roman honour. He declined a triumph for

---

[87] See Campbell 1993.   [88] Suetonius, *Aug.* 21; Dio 54.8.

this, but still celebrated with monuments, games, and a triumphal arch, issuing an array of coins "For captured Armenia!" This series became a precedent for Vespasian's equally dodgy *Iudaea Capta* coins. Augustus' memoirs gave the decisive spin (*RG* 29): "The Parthians *I forced* to give me back the spoils . . . and to request the friendship of the Roman people *as suppliants*." The recovered standards were showcased in Augustus' temple of Mars Ultor, God of war-vengeance (cf. Ovid, *Fasti* 5.579–96). A famous statue of Augustus, from Prima Porta, features a kneeling Phraates giving up the standards.

This was of course for the home audience. Dealing with the Parthians themselves, Augustus made clear his lack of military ambition. When his man in Armenia, Tigranes, died in 7 B.C., the Parthian ruler thought he might reassert his control, and considerable unrest in Armenia followed. Augustus finally sent his 21-year-old grandson and prospective heir, Gaius, to sort things out (A.D. 1–2). With his advisors, young Gaius negotiated a diplomatic solution that recognized the legitimate interests of both sides. Armenia would remain part of Parthia's empire and Rome would not try to control it, *but* the Parthians would accept Rome's nominee as king. An elaborate ceremony on the Euphrates River symbolized this historic agreement (Velleius II.101).

The balance of interests and recognition of the power differential underlying this agreement would more or less endure through the Judaean War. In the intervening decades Parthian rulers would send their young sons to grow up in Rome and ask the Senate to recognize their central monarchs.[89] Some might well have coveted Syria, considering themselves the natural rulers of Oriental populations up to the Mediterranean littoral in keeping with the model of older eastern empires. But the fragmented condition of their empire and Rome's legionary deterrent in Syria made any such dreams, if they existed, impracticable.[90] On the Roman side, too, the Julio-Claudian emperors showed no interest in invading Parthia.[91]

Armenia remained a special case, bordering Roman Cappadocia and Syria, and a potential flashpoint.[92] In the mid-30s A.D., when a Rome-endorsed king died, Artabanus III again chanced his arm by giving the kingdom to his son. This provoked a sharp Roman response. Tiberius enlisted the king of Iberia (modern southeast Georgia), who had his son seize Armenia's throne on behalf of Rome (Dio 58.26.1–4). The indignant Artabanus reportedly planned to attack Roman forces in Syria, under L. Vitellius, boasting absurdly that he

---

[89] Tacitus, *Ann.* 2.1–4, 56, 58, 68; 6.31–7; 11.8; 12.10–14.   [90] See Kennedy 1996: 73–74.

[91] For example, in A.D. 49 Claudius dispatched, at the request of a Parthian delegation, a member of their royal family who had grown up in Rome, Meherdates, and the Roman governor Cassius escorted him to the Euphrates. Once in Parthia, however, he was confronted by the other king's forces, and his ears were lopped off (Tacitus, *Ann.* 12.12–14). Tacitus notes (12.14.3) that this was "a disgrace for us."

[92] Cf. Günther 1922; Ziegler 1964; Colledge 1967: 36–56; Sonnabend 1986.

would recover the old Persian empire. Vitellius quickly outmanoeuvred him, and it came to nothing. Vitellius drove the point home by forcing Artabanus to sacrifice to the deified Augustus and to the current emperor Gaius (A.D. 40)[93] – another exercise in the conversion of negligible physical coercion into enormous political power.

Roman rulers remained alert to the prospect that their Semitic subjects and allies near the eastern frontier might drift into unwholesome collusion with Parthia. When Herod's son Antipas made a bid for kingship after long decades as tetrarch of Galilee, his nephew Agrippa (I) accused him of conspiring with Artabanus and storing equipment for 70,000 soldiers. Antipas allegedly confessed, remarkably enough, and Gaius exiled him (*Ant.* 18.250–52). Not long afterward Agrippa himself, after his friend Claudius had made him king in Jerusalem, faced perpetual suspicion of conspiracy from the watchful legate in Syria, Cn. Vibius Marsus (*Ant.* 19.326–27, 338–42). On the Parthian side, however, Artabanus' disposition and rhetoric seem to have been more in the way of pique than a live threat. When new Armenian problems erupted early in Nero's reign (54), they landed in the lap of the Parthian king (Vologaeses) as a result of strictly regional politics.

The story goes that in the year of Vologaeses' accession (A.D. 51), the king of Iberia to the north had a problem with his son Radamistus. The popular young man wanted to rule. This was inconvenient for the father, who turned the lad's gaze to Armenia, where his brother and Radamistus' uncle (also father-in-law) Mithridates was in power – as Rome's appointee, supported by Roman garrisons. The father plotted that Radamistus should ingratiate himself into his uncle's court, gradually foment conspiracy, and finally oust the older man. Something went wrong, however, and Radamistus quickly found himself facing Roman garrisons, which he managed to expel as he seized power. The shrewd legate in Syria, Ummidius Quadratus, was not greatly troubled by these events. He assured Claudius that he was defending Rome's interests in the region, writing a display letter demanding that Radamistus yield. But in fact he turned a blind eye – on the sound principle, says Tacitus, that such conflict among foreigners was a gift for Rome (*Ann.* 12.44–49; cf. Chapter 4).

Now things became interesting, however, because Vologaeses did not enjoy (or perhaps understand) this game. He had been obliged to accept Rome's man Mithridates as part of the longstanding arrangement, but he was not going to tolerate little Iberia's usurpation. If the Romans did not care about who was in power, Vologaeses' dignity required him to assert Parthia's claim and install his own brother Tiridates (*Ann.* 12.50). So he did, marching with him into Armenia and seeing off young Radamistus.

---

[93] Tacitus, *Ann.* 6.32, 36–7; Dio 59.27.3–4.

This was roughly the situation when Nero came to power in 54: a pro-Roman neighbour taking advantage in Armenia without Rome's consent, Rome's own king ousted, and Parthians flexing their muscles. Syria's legate Quadratus might be content with a quiet game, but Parthia's intervention challenged the balance of power. Advisors to the 16-year-old Nero insisted that the situation required a firm response. It was a test of the young emperor's mettle.

Nero dispatched the respected ex-consul Corbulo to Cappadocia in A.D. 55 with special authority to secure Rome's interests in Armenia. Corbulo took a good couple of years to prepare his army for such potentially serious warfare across the frontier. In 58 he marched into Armenia, and before long he was accepting the surrender of the kingdom's two main cities. In Dio's words (62.20.1), Corbulo "imposed on Vologaeses, though he was a formidable presence, agreements that befitted the dignity of the Romans." Nero also sent a new king for Armenia (A.D. 60), to displace Vologaeses' brother. The new Tigranes happened to be the 40-year-old great-grandson of King Herod, and he had lived mainly in Rome.[94] Although he was given a sizable Roman security detail, however, Tigranes quickly ran into serious trouble. For some reason he was not content with occupying his throne but was soon attacking other Parthian possessions, including Adiabene – now ruled by Monobazus II, whose family had adopted Judaean law since the 30s (*Ant.* 20.17–96). A furious Monobazus complained to Vologaeses, and the pair of them tried to eject this new Roman-Herodian choice for Armenia.

Corbulo, after ensuring Tigranes' installation, had withdrawn across the Euphrates, where he soon became Syria's provincial legate (A.D. 60). With the new problems brewing and Corbulo now occupied with Syria, Nero sent L. Caesennius Paetus to assume Corbulo's old position – Cappadocia's governorship with special powers for Armenia. Caesennius arrived in 62. Vologaeses was prodded to action by Monobazus and Tiridates, the ousted brother who was furious at being removed from Armenia. Vologaeses sent emissaries to Nero to try to resolve the issue diplomatically, but the men were rebuffed. So he decided to attack the Roman who had imposed Tigranes on Armenia: Corbulo, now in Syria. It is unlikely in the extreme that he hoped to take the huge province of Syria for Parthia. More likely he wanted to make a point with a show of force, to create a stronger hand in negotiations over Armenia.

Meanwhile, Caesennius had arrived in Cappadocia and – in stark contrast to Corbulo's careful preparations – almost immediately crossed into Armenia. Later reports portray him as arrogant and boastful. We have no idea of his personality. But once on the Parthian side he was quickly disoriented, perhaps

---

[94] *Ann.* 14.26. On Tigranes see Kokkinos 1998: 248–50.

by severe weather. Having failed to make proper logistical provisions, he had to beat a retreat to the north side of the Arsanias River in Armenia to minimize his vulnerabilities. There he allegedly confirmed his reputation for laxness and incompetence by dismissing thousands of soldiers to leave and failing to fortify his position.

Vologaeses had set out with the large army that would be needed to teach Corbulo a lesson. But when he noticed such a lightweight newcomer in such a vulnerable position, he seized the opportunity for a low-risk, high-reward victory and swung his cavalry north toward Caesennius. Caesennius, caught completely off guard, made the further mistake of dispersing the forces he still had, from the Fourth and Twelfth legions – inviting their encirclement on the enemy side of the river at Rhandeia. Seeing his likely doom, he sent a courier to Corbulo in Syria requesting emergency help. Corbulo assembled a force but could not reach Rhandeia in time. He was still three days away when the panicked Caesennius capitulated to Vologaeses. The forward elements of his Fourth and Twelfth legions had been destroyed, the survivors fleeing to Syria.

In a bid to spare the remaining Romans' lives with his own, Paetus gave away the store. He promised Vologaeses that Rome would evacuate all its garrisons from Armenia, renounce all interests there, and allow Vologaeses' brother Tiridates to rule undisturbed. To rub the Romans' faces in this unexpected victory, Vologaeses ordered them to build a bridge for him and then ostentatiously declined to use it (Dio 62.21.4). As soon as he was able, Caesennius reportedly fled speedily (Tacitus, *Ann.* 15.1–17). Suetonius mentions this "disgrace in the Orient," where legions were made to pass under a symbolic yoke of slavery and the province of "Syria was retained on its deathbed" (*Ner.* 39.1).

I have surveyed these events of the early 60s because they provide important context for the Judaean revolt, even though Josephus does not mention them. Concerning Parthia's possible involvement in Judaea, or Judaean aspirations in that direction, three points deserve mention. First, a central figure in these events was the Adiabenian king Monobazus II (above). Members of his family had long been living in Jerusalem, and some of them would take a prominent role in anti-Roman activities (*War* 2.520). Second, the humiliation and depletion of the *Legio XII Fulminata* under Caesennius may be significant for understanding that legion's role in the coming events in Judaea (Chapter 5). Third, in the accounts we possess, neither the Parthian Vologaeses nor his senior allies such as Monobazus appear in the least bit servile toward Rome. On the contrary, they come across as strong and rather disdainful, obliged by common sense and statecraft to accept peace with Rome but eager to assert their pride and power at every opportunity.

These attitudes seem to be reflected in the final settlement of the crisis that soon followed. In 63, Nero removed Corbulo from the legateship of Syria, replacing him with Cestius Gallus, who would play a key role in the Judaean revolt (Chapter 5). Corbulo was ordered to salvage the situation created by Caesennius' bumbling. Leaving the disgraced Fourth and Twelfth in Syria, he had four other legions at his disposal, as well as detachments from other provinces and allied and auxiliary units. Vologaeses prepared for war and Corbulo's forces caused some mayhem east of the Euphrates, but once again diplomacy prevailed. The matter apparently came to a quick and bloodless end when Vologaeses and Tiridates sued for peace, a sign of their respect for Corbulo. He, understanding that Vologaeses was no real threat to Rome, dictated generous terms. Vologaeses' brother Tiridates would be an acceptable king to Rome *if* he could be visibly presented as Rome's man. To achieve this, he should ceremonially remove his diadem before an effigy of Nero there in the East and to take it up again as Nero's gift – prostrate before the emperor in Rome. Tiridates agreed, grumbling that he had not actually been defeated (Tacitus, *Ann.* 15.25.4–30.2).

Tiridates and Vologaeses chose the setting for this meeting with Corbulo –at Rhandeia, the scene of Caesennius' recent debacle. They also proposed the terms for Tiridates' long journey to Rome. He would not leave for a couple of years, dispelling any appearance that he was rushing to obey a Roman summons. When he finally did go, Tiridates would take his sweet time – nine months – and travel by land, possibly for religious reasons but also to enjoy the hospitality of many dignitaries en route. He expected to be feted in a style befitting his eminence, to meet all the provincial governors and never be kept waiting, and to wear his royal scimitar. Once in Rome, he had to be accorded the same honour as a Roman consul (*Ann.* 15.31). Vologaeses himself refused to make the trip, angering Nero with his insistence that the Roman ruler was welcome to visit him any time he wished (Dio 63.7.2).[95]

Our Roman accounts are no doubt jaundiced, but the basic terms and itinerary of the settlement are not in doubt. Nero was using Tiridates for his political purposes, to display his grandeur and supposed conquest, but the Parthians may have had the best of it. For the Roman celebrations in the spring of 66 we have only Suetonius (*Ner.* 13) and the epitome of Dio (63.1–7). The latter grumbles that the festivities cost Rome hundreds of millions. The *defeated* ruler even finagled to take Roman tradesmen back with him to help him rebuild his capital Artaxata (cleverly styled "Neroneia"). It was a fair question who had won this conflict.

Fragmentary though our picture of Roman-Parthian relations is, it is enough to make us wary of any sentence beginning "The Parthians wanted to …" In particular we should guard against the assumption that the

---

[95] Wheeler (2007: 242–43) sees Nero's triumph as dressing up a diplomatic failure: the *de facto* loss of Armenia.

rapprochement of 63–66 meant the end of Parthian grievances. That is usually not the case with high-level treaties between age-old rivals. Vologaeses and Tiridates had spared their people a pointless bloody war. But they achieved most of their aims, and possibly more, through skillful diplomacy: Tiridates' little kingship was immeasurably enhanced by the grand tour in lavish style funded by Rome.

Opportunistic and spiteful actions against Roman interests remained a possibility: for Vologaeses, his successor, and the disgruntled Adiabenian-Judaean Monobazus II (A.D. 79–81). And Rome remained wary of this potential, in spite of the grand settlement. Just three years after the big event, as Vespasian was planning his bid for empire in 69, he felt the need to send emissaries to Vologaeses and Tiridates to satisfy himself that they would not take advantage of his absence (Tacitus, *Hist.* 2.82). As Gwyn Morgan puts it, "there was no telling whether the king had learnt his lesson or was thirsting for revenge."[96] Within two years of Vespasian's accession, Caesennius had failed upwards to become the new emperor's legate in Syria (72–73). Once there, he was able to persuade Vespasian that King Antiochus of Commagene, an ally of previously unimpeachable loyalty, was plotting with Parthia. Vespasian took the report seriously enough that he removed Antiochus and annexed Commagene to the Province of Syria. The king's outraged sons mounted a brief resistance before fleeing to Vologaeses, who received them with open arms, again giving substance to Roman suspicions (*War* 7.219–43). Note incidentally that Josephus' insistence on Antiochus' innocence is another point of divergence from the Flavian version (Chapter 2).

In the early 70s the Parthians reportedly faced an invasion from their north, linking up with internal secessionists. It was a dangerous moment, and Vologaeses pleaded with Vespasian for help. But the Roman coldly refused, perhaps following L. Vitellius' principle of encouraging tensions among potential enemies (*War* 7.244–51). It is conceivable that Vespasian had arranged the invasion, taking a leaf from Tiberius (*Ant.* 18.96–97). According to Suetonius (*Dom* 2.2), Vologaeses flatteringly suggested that one of Vespasian's sons might lead a Roman force, and Domitian was eager, but still Vespasian quashed the idea.

That rebuff may have provoked a brief conflict. We hear nothing clear about this, but in Pliny's adoring speech for Trajan in 100 he observes (*Paneg.* 14.1; my emphasis), "You were hardly more than a boy when your success in Parthia enhanced your father's glory ... when you checked *the savagery and pride of the Parthians* by the mere sound of your approach." When was this? Trajan, born in A.D. 53 to a father who had served as Vespasian's legionary

---

[96] Morgan 2006: 186.

legate, would have been the age of a *laticlavius* tribune (above) in 73/74, around the time of the tensions we have been discussing. A minor confrontation with Parthia might have been enough for Pliny's flattery.

Finally, the Epitome of Dio claims that Vologaeses' successor Artabanus IV, whose brief rule overlapped with that of Titus (79–81), was at odds with the young destroyer of Jerusalem. He not only gave shelter to a "false Nero" of that period, Terentius Maximus, upsetting the populace of Flavian Rome, but supposedly tried to get the man a hearing in Rome (Dio 66.19.3). This story and a similar one told by Suetonius (*Ner.* 57.3), whatever their historical merits, assume lingering animosity and suspicion.

If we pull all such clues together, the complex Parthian-Roman-Judaean relationship in the 60s seems to have been along these lines. On the one hand, for desperate Judaeans seeking help with their plight, which we have yet to explore, the great empire of Parthia was the most plausible ally, whether the hope was for a radical reconfiguration of the eastern Mediterranean, merely for military-logistical support and "advisors," or for diplomatic cover of some kind. The well-established Judaean population in the Parthian world and the influential Adiabenian family, who had both close ties with Jerusalem and issues with Rome, made Parthia a particularly attractive source of aid. In Chapter 7 we shall review the scattered indications of actual appeals to Parthia in the context of Adiabenian involvement.

On the other hand, a Parthian assault on Rome was out of the question, and the possibility that Parthians might have mounted a serious effort to take Syria from Rome could not even be called a long shot. They were in no position to intervene on that scale. Such efforts would have destroyed the hard-won settlement over Armenia. The Parthians could never have held Syria even if they had managed to seize it in a rapid and lucky campaign. The Judaeans would have had to settle, at most, for quiet moral support and energetic assistance from Adiabene's royal family. Some likely *hoped* for more. It would not be the first time or the last that a vulnerable population was fatally disappointed while hoping for aid from a great power.

III. LEADERSHIP AND THE ETHOS OF COMMAND

In our times we have finally come to believe, at least officially, that competence and merit are the only rational criteria for advancement in work and society. Our umbrage when this does not happen reveals our assumption that it *should*: It is only fair. We ridicule old boys' clubs, "who-you-know" scenarios, privilege based on ancestry, influence peddling, and patronage. Equality of opportunity and before the law are axioms for us.

The ancient world knew nothing of this. Roman society had developed from the monarchy and Republic, the latter led by wealthy land- and slave-holders.

The few men at the top had the attributes necessary, they were sure, to manage the state's affairs. In the absence of government-run systems, schools, universities, policy centres, welfare, or disinterested enforcement of "human rights," the animating force of social cohesion and safety alike was the patronage of the elite classes.[97] In the period we know as the Empire (from 31/30 B.C.), the decisive change was the incarnation of the top-most source of privilege in one man: the *princeps* or emperor. Prominent senators such as Pliny the Younger continued to be powerful benefactors for lower-level friends, but even the more significant benefits Pliny wished to dispense as a function of his high status could be granted only by the master of the world.

Nowhere was imperial patronage clearer than in the army. We expect that an emperor would appoint the commanders of his twenty-eight legions, but his personal involvement with lower ranks is surprising. Trajan intervened even in the case of an auxiliary soldier.[98]

It has been estimated that of the ninety openings for centurions that occurred in an average year, about 10 percent were filled by men with no military background but of social standing, whom the emperor directly appointed by his grace and favour.[99] Pliny mentions a letter that he wrote to Trajan hoping to secure a high-status centurionate for a man from his town (*Ep.* 6.25). Cassius Dio portrays Maecenas advising Augustus that men of equestrian rank should be able to aspire to membership of the Senate, but of course only those who "began their service with the rank of centurion," who were thus unsullied by private soldiering (52.25.6–7). We have epigraphic evidence of 18- and 19-year-olds being appointed centurions, posts for which others would sweat for long years.[100] Juvenal satirized this kind of direct appointment – as a way for fathers to find honourable work for troublesome sons (*Sat.* 14.193–99). We might compare the well-regarded solicitor in eighteenth-century London who secured a commission in the British East India Company as a remedy for his dissolute, embezzling son, William Hickey. Not knowing even the regiment in which he would be made an instant officer, young William had half a dozen uniforms made.[101]

---

[97] Classic studies are Saller 1982 and Millar 1977.   [98] Campbell 1984.

[99] Campbell 1984: 101–109, esp. 102; Birley 1989; Goldsworthy 1996: 31–32; Gilliver 2007:190–92.

[100] An inscription records that Sex. Pilonius Modestus died aged 37 – after 19 years *in the centurionate* (from age 18) – and one Ti. Claudius Fatalis died at 42 after 23 years as centurion (from age 19). His inscription was found in Aelia Capitolina (formerly Jerusalem); his final posts had been with *XII Fulminata* and *X Fretensis*, both earlier involved in the Judaean War. See Birley 1989: 115 (*ILS* 2654 = *CIL* 3.1480; *AE* 1939, 157). Frontinus may have had such a person in mind when he related that Vespasian, on hearing of a young (*adulescens*) officer completely unsuited to military life, cashiered him with a bonus (*Strat.* 6.6.4).

[101] The son's memoirs became a literary classic – Hickey 1995 [1810]: 68–71.

Most legionary legates, aristocratic tribunes, and directly appointed centurions were probably competent,[102] for the life training of a young aristocrat put a premium on basic horsemanship and physical fitness as well as the study of great battles and military writers. Some legates, such as Vespasian or Corbulo, had gained combat experience in a series of commands. But even they were not like modern generals, and most legates lacked anything approaching their military experience. The basis for selection was first of all moral, and tied up with status and character. Was the candidate a "good man" – of the leading classes, with the appropriate ancestry, culture, and general education? Such a man, the assumption was, would learn whatever he needed for any leadership position, military or political.

If the idea of instant commissions sounds bizarre, we should recall that an aristocratic officer corps remained standard in much of Europe through the seventeenth and nineteenth centuries. In the British army, the majority of commissions were purchased.[103] A man of great means could enter service near the top, through the proprietor-colonel system "in which some notable – a man of standing in the county, but not necessarily with military experience – would be contracted to field a regiment of specified strength. ... They were ... clothed, fed, and paid by the colonel."[104] The rank of general was beyond purchase, because the monarch needed "men of proven worth" who could actually provide experienced counsel.[105] But ranks as high as colonel could be bought as late as 1871.[106] Long after the formal abolition of the purchase system, gentleman status remained an expectation of the officer class. As in Roman times, the assumption continued to be that officers required *character* traits, which could not be learned without a certain bloodline and cultivation. Such men were expected to identify themselves with the state (*polis, ethnos*) in ways that lower classes could never do. Their independent means should also put them beyond suspicion of grubby personal gain.[107] This is also why the core of aristocratic education into modern times continued to be the Greek and Roman classics.

What kind of officers did such omni-competent gentlemen prove to be? Results were mixed. The Charge of the Light Brigade (1854) is perhaps the most famous disaster.[108] Lords Raglan, Lucan, and Cardigan lacked field experience when they faced the Russian army in the 1850s, and more than a third of their force became instant casualties. A *New York Times* editor expressed bafflement at the consequences for officer competence and soldiers'

---

[102] See Eck 2001. Eck attempts to qualify the influential study by Brunt 1975, among others, that showed that *specialized* knowledge was not a criterion for appointment in Egypt.

[103] Holmes 2011: 126–55.   [104] Mallinson 2010: 52.   [105] Mallinson 2010: 54.

[106] In the *Army Regulation Bill* (Holmes 2011: 155). Artillery and engineering officers, because of the technical knowledge required, had always required special training.

[107] Holmes 2011: 137–38.   [108] Mallinson 2010: 204–209.

morale of aristocratic command.[109] Yet the same system produced prodigies. Arthur Wellesley, reluctant Irishman and Professor of Music, took advantage of free commissions and the willingness of friends to pay his way. By the time of his first command in India (1798), it seems that he was a colonel without having served in a regiment. This future Duke of Wellington would fight some sixty battles, however, capping an illustrious career by defeating Napoleon at Waterloo (1815)[110] – before serving as Prime Minister twice and in the House of Lords. The Duke of York, who "had ten thousand men" and introduced important military reforms during the 1790s, was Commander-in-Chief at just 32 by virtue of being King George III's son.[111] We might compare him to 30-year-old Titus, who had legionary experience but nothing like modern officer or general-staff training, when his father gave him the siege of Jerusalem.

In ancient Rome as in Britain, concern with character and bloodline could go to absurd lengths. Britain allowed a 1-year-old ensign, a captain by age 6, and a 13-year-old ensign who made lieutenant-colonel by 20. These extremes are unattested in Rome, but neither system prevented eminent men from holding commands well into their golden years.[112] Corbulo, Cestius Gallus, and Sulpicius Galba were all active – donning armour and riding on horseback for long days – into their late 60s or 70s, and in the service of a teenaged emperor.

Just as the Roman commanders were senators, equestrians, and men of royal/elite lineage (Agrippa II and Tiberius Julius Alexander), the first Judaean commanders were chief priests and wealthy laymen, esteemed above all for their general abilities to lead the temple cult, the holy city's affairs, and teach the divine laws. On both Roman and Judaean sides, the war's leaders were members of the political echelon that led society in peacetime, except that the Herodian royals had little choice but to assist Roman forces (*War* 2.562–68).

In later chapters we shall get to know a few commanders. Here a quick summary will make the necessary points about their political-social positions, absence of professional training, and kinds of forces led.

The crucial decision to sever Jerusalem's ties with foreigners was taken by the temple commandant Eleazar, an aristocratic younger priest and son of the high priest Ananias (2.409–18). All the factions of those willing to fight someone seem to have been led at first by men of social status. Eleazar's high-priest father was killed by a rival faction led by Menachem (reportedly

---

[109] Anonymous, "Money vs. Merit" (1855): "The British Army . . . closes, for the most part, that competition by talent and merit, which has been found so greatly to elevate the *morale* of the military service, out of England." A strident English critique is in Maude 1907: 158–59.

[110] Holmes 2011: 146–47.   [111] See Mallinson 2010: 135–38.   [112] Holmes 2011: 138–39.

the son of the prominent Judas in A.D. 6), and Eleazar took revenge by killing Menachem (2.443–49). This chief priest also directed the slaughter of Jerusalem's auxiliary garrison (2.450–56). He disappears from Josephus' narrative thereafter, although his associates Ananias Sadouki and Judas the son of Jonathan, cultivated men and possibly priests, remain in the coalition government (2.628).

The next armed leaders named are those who lead the daring raids on Cestius Gallus' force (late 66). Most prominent here are the young relatives of Monobazus the Adiabenian king (2.520; cf. *Ant.* 20.71), along with Niger the Peraean and Silas the Babylonian. Niger may have been a Roman citizen, given his Latin name ("black [beard?]"). He became part of Jerusalem's wartime administration at the same time as Josephus (2.566), but later met his death for being insufficiently radical (4.359–64). Silas' name might also be Latin (*Silva*, *Silvanus*) or Aramaic. He seems to have been prominent in the Babylonian-Judaean military community settled by King Herod east of Galilee (*Ant.* 17.23–31). Eleazar son of Simon, denied a leadership position at first (*War* 2.564), emerges as a factional leader of the most famous, priest-based *Zealot* faction (4.225; 5.5–7, 250–51; Chapter 7).

These were evidently men of social-political standing, as were those whom Josephus names as leaders of Jerusalem's earliest coalition government: Joseph son of Gorion, a prominent Pharisee, and Ananus son of Ananus, former high priest (2.563). The former fades from the story as Ananus becomes paired with a fellow chief priest, Jesus son of Gamalas (4.238). These two are killed in a single operation by a Zealot-Idumaean alliance in *War*'s pivotal episode (4.233–56; cf. Chapter 2). Another Gorion, perhaps Joseph's father or son, or Joseph himself if the story has become garbled, is killed when the Zealots move against the "reasonable/moderate ones" (4.358).[113] The high-priest/Pharisee coalition then appoints "generals" for Judaea, Idumaea, Peraea, and Galilee. This is the context in which our 30-year-old priest and aristocrat Josephus, with diplomatic but not military experience under his belt, is given a quasi-military command in the north (2.566–68). Like the Romans, Judaeans assumed that "men of quality" were society's natural leaders, whether in law, administration, sacrifice to the Gods, or war.

With these basic conditions of ancient warfare in view, we return to consider factors aside from Parthia's participation that might have affected morale on both sides.

---

[113] A further curiosity is Gorion son of Nicomedes at 2.451, who anticipates the Nakdimon son of Gorion of rabbinic literature, a wealthy figure from this period (*b. Ketub.* 65a–b, 66b, 67a; *Git.* 56a; *Avod. Zar.* 25a). At 4.358 a distinguished leader named Gorion falls to the Zealots – the same man as Joseph or one of the family. See Ilan and Price 1993–1994: 200–203 for discussion. It seems most likely that the Gorion family, like the Gamaliels, were Pharisees.

IV. MORALE II: STRATEGY AND TACTICS IN ASYMMETRICAL WARFARE

Given the lack of statistics concerning morale among the legions, Adrian Goldsworthy invites us to ponder S. L. A. Marshall's famed studies of infantry combat in World War II. Marshall startled the U.S. military establishment by claiming that in an average company only about 15 percent "would take any part with the weapons" – *any* part.[114] In elite companies the number barely reached 25 percent. Although things might have been different in times when hand-to-hand fighting was required, Marshall allowed, in terms of reluctance to fight and kill he considered his statistics a fact of "human nature."[115]

Goldsworthy cites anecdotes from Roman sources to suggest that the ancient situation was little different,[116] bringing healthy skepticism to the common picture of the legions as machine-like killers. I would add that the civil servant who wrote a manual of military principles in the late fourth century, P. Flavius Vegetius Renatus,[117] frequently notes differences in levels of courage and readiness: "[V]ictory is usually attributable to a small number of men," and that is why only "picked men" should be placed in critical positions (*Epit.* 3.20). Again, "Nature produces few brave men; good training and hard work yield many [NB: not *all*]" (3.26). The assumption that only "picked men" are suitable for critical operations[118] supports the picture of great variety even in combat units of similar experience.

Marshall's sobering analyses were debated, but the U.S. military took no chances. They introduced more aggressive training methods, which raised the level of reflexive weapon use to 55 percent in Korea and a staggering 95 percent in Vietnam[119] – the last paradoxically in a cause with far less popular support. We might suspect that Marshall's statistics would not hold for such guerrilla fighters as the ancient Judaean rebels. Of modern warriors he observed that "The really active firers were usually in small groups working together,"[120] and small-group operations characterize guerrilla fighting. A different approach to risk-taking would be expected, given that the professional soldier's incentives such as pay and promotion do not apply. This obvious difference might help to explain Josephus' thematic contrast between the death-defying Judeans and risk-averse legionaries (Chapter 2).

Thinking about morale leads to questions of strategy, the ultimate aim of which is to increase morale on the home side and destroy that of the enemy.

---

[114] Marshall 1947: 54–57.   [115] Marshall 1947: 60.   [116] Goldsworthy 1996: 219–22.
[117] Milner 1996: xiii–xli; Allmand 2011: 1–4.
[118] E.g., Josephus, *War* 1.162, 351; 2.535, 588; 3.95, 120, 331, 470; 5.47–48, 52, 82, 258, and *passim*.
[119] Jordan 2002; Spiller 1988; Smoler 1989. I am indebted to Rickard (2003: 37) for these references and a summary.
[120] Marshall 1947: 56.

Strategic reflections can bring a dose of realism to our analysis, if we avoid entanglement in the artificial terminology of grand strategy, strategy, and tactics.[121] Although these words have Greek roots, modern uses of them were unknown to the ancients.[122] *Stratēgia* meant for them simply "being a general" and everything that went with it: generalship.[123] The adjective *taktikos* (something "arranged, drawn up") referred most often to troop and column formations, not what we call tactics.[124] It was a general's responsibility to come up with ruses, deceptions, or "general's manoeuvres" (στρατηγήματα): undermining walls when besieging, building extra walls from within a siege, launching surprise sorties, misleading the enemy about the state of one's food and water supplies, making siege ramps slippery.[125] These tricks approach our category of tactics.

Several writers, including Josephus' contemporary Frontinus, produced manuals of "general's devices" (*Stratagems*), illustrating with examples from the past. Certainly Josephus delights in recalling, or inventing, his own stratagems.[126] Because deception was central to ancient notions of what generals do, secrecy was paramount. Luring traitors was therefore a primary concern, and scenes of both secret instruction and betrayal of cities appear frequently in ancient narratives.

When we imagine Roman legions fighting mere irregulars, we easily forget two points. First, even commanders of massive armies such as Rome's needed to plan operations and logistical support carefully in order to play to their strengths and avoid conditions chosen by the enemy. The need for a general to control the terms of combat is a central theme in Vegetius' manual (*Epit.* 3.9–13). Basil H. Liddell Hart suffered injury in World War I and watched lines of British soldiers marching into enemy fire because of the generals' commitment to a dogma about the need to attack an enemy's "decisive point." Studying examples from Greece and Rome through Hitler's early successes, he wrote in 1941 that the whole concept of strategy required intelligent

---

[121] Liddell Hart 1941: 184–88. 189–90.

[122] Liddell Hart 1941: 194–96; Luttwak 2001: 267–70. The latter jettisons standard terminology, proposing instead five mutually interacting levels of strategic thinking (87–205): *technical* (weapons, armour, transportation); *tactical* (battlefield manoeuvres); *operational* (coordination of battle zones); *theatre-level* (e.g., the Pacific or European theatres of World War II); and *grand strategy* (overall war policy and planning).

[123] E.g., *War* 2.568, 627; 3.137; 4.617; cf. Thucydides 5.26.5; Plutarch, *Per.* 16.3.

[124] Xenophon, *Cyr.* 8.5.15; so Anaeas' *Tactics* [fourth century B.C.]; Ascleopiodotus' *Tactics* (on the Macedonian phalanx, first century B.C.); Aelian's *Tactical Arrays of the Greeks* [second century A.D.]; Arrian's *Art of Military Formations [Tactica]* and *Array Against the Alans* [second century A.D.].

[125] Such tactics, which appear in concentrated form in Herod's siege of Jerusalem (37 B.C.; *Ant.* 14.470–75) are elaborated in Josephus' defence of Galilee (*Life* 64–412; *War* 3) and the siege of Jerusalem (*War* 5–6).

[126] *War* 2.604, 630; 3.176, 190; *Life* 148, 163, 169, 265, 379.

thought, on the assumption that unexpected and indirect approaches must be preferable to open frontal assault. The commander must use every means to keep the enemy off balance and dislocated, doing what is least expected in the hope of meeting the least effective resistance.[127] This was the kind of thinking that produced Churchill's insistence on attacking Germany via North Africa and Italy, not to mention the Allies' extravagant feints and decoys before the D-Day Channel crossing in June 1944.

Second, and the other side of the same coin: Strategy is by nature risk-averse. Liddell Hart wrote: "Strategy ... has for its purpose the reduction of fighting to the slenderest possible proportions," and "[t]he perfection of strategy would, therefore, be to produce a decision without any serious fighting."[128] This is in part a practical matter of maximizing limited resources, but even more important is morale. If the enemy are dislocated and psychologically overwhelmed, they will be in no position to fight *irrespective* of the resources potentially available. On one's own side, success allows soldiers to feel that the inevitable casualties are not for nothing (Vegetius, *Epit.* 3.9).

High casualty rates cause despair not only among the soldiers in the field, who may quickly lose faith in a strategy deemed too costly or ineffective,[129] but also among government leaders and the home citizens. After Claudius' invasion of southeastern Britain in A.D. 43, his triumphal arch boasted that eleven kings had submitted to him with little bloodshed (Chapter 1).[130] *That* was the mark of great generalship and indeed of Roman power: The mere sound of the legions' name produced submission, without the risk of fighting. Rome celebrated violent conquest, to be sure, but most of her provincial territory, including Syria with Judaea (*War* 1.141–54), had been taken by intimidation and manoeuvre with very little bloodshed.

There have been modern exceptions to the economy-of-force principle, especially in the period from the Napoleonic wars to World War I when conscription and mechanization gave planners "a blank cheque on the bank of man-power."[131] States with massive human resources, a political doctrine favouring the collective, or an ideology that warfare purifies the citizenry, could sacrifice millions.[132] But the Romans lacked any such

---

[127] E.g., Liddell Hart 1941: 190–99.   [128] Liddell Hart 1941: 190.

[129] This was the problem in the Cassino campaign of World War II. After the 36th Division took 2,000 casualties, their survivors persuaded Congress to open hearings on the leadership of Gen. Mark Clark. From his point of view, the problem lay with subordinates who lacked the *will to fight* (Clark 2007 [1950]: 182–87, 220).

[130] *CIL* 6.920; for discussion see Webster 1978: 55–57.   [131] Liddell Hart 1941: 140.

[132] Before World War II Stalin had executed more than 22,000 officers in a purge (Burleigh 2010: 345). Both Mussolini and Hitler believed that ongoing warfare was necessary for the purification of the citizenry.

ideology,[133] and mass conscription and mobilization were not on their horizon. They had little choice but to maximize the capacity of their precious legions and secure their objectives as far as possible by the exploitation of power rather than through force.

Liddell Hart observed many paradoxes in strategic planning. For example, the aim of planning for war is to *reduce fighting*, and one can often achieve the most effective concentration by dispersal.[134] Edward Luttwak goes farther, arguing that strategic thinking is paradoxical *in every possible way*. Winning is losing – in a sense. An army that penetrates deep into enemy territory (winning) is unavoidably becoming more vulnerable (losing), if there are no powerful compensating factors. The army's very success requires it to extend supply lines far into hostile terrain, while the "losing" enemy enjoys the advantages of concentration, decreasing supply lines, increasing support on home soil, and a resolve stiffened by the need to defend home and family.[135]

These paradoxes are germane for us. Cestius Gallus (Chapter 5) and the Flavians (Chapters 7–8) planned their expeditions in consultation with Agrippa II and other local allies. They must have had some kind of aims and perhaps post-conflict scenarios and configured their forces to achieve these aims. Leading an army of tens of thousands into the Judaean hills, once the region had become obviously hostile, was not something to be undertaken lightly. The larger the force, the more difficult it would be to maintain and feed. No one doubted that a 5,000-strong legion would intimidate its enemies when formed up on a field facing them. But it could only be in a position to do that if the terrain permitted, if careful attention had been given to logistical support, and if the enemy obliged.[136]

The larger the force marched into the Judaean hills, again, the greater the risk of natural disaster – from disease epidemic, weather or terrain-based catastrophe, loss of commanders to accident or illness, or lucky ambush. Any such embarrassments would greatly encourage the enemy without actual combat.[137] Strategic thinking is always relational, therefore. It must be able to evolve quickly in view of the other side's aims, resources, and movements. It requires constant attention and the readiness to exploit weaknesses that appear momentarily – as when Cestius' huge force had to move quickly through the Beit-Horon bottleneck and Judaeans pounced (Chapter 5).

The ultimate purpose of strategy is of course to break the enemy's will to fight. Liddell Hart is quotable again:

---

[133] Some writers did lament (esp. Sallust, *Bell. jug.* 41; *Bell. cat.* 10) that the loss of enemies had weakened Roman virtue (cf. Dawson 1996: 159–66) but this is a common reflection ("We don't have the virtues we had when we were at war") and not a call to perpetual warfare.
[134] Liddell Hart 1941: 197.   [135] Luttwak 2001: 1–86.   [136] Roth 1991.
[137] Liddell Hart 1941: 193.

It is thus more potent, as well as more economical, to disarm the enemy than to attempt his destruction by hard fighting. For the "mauling" method entails not only a dangerous cost in exhaustion but the risk that chance may determine the issue. A strategist should think in terms of paralysing, not of killing. Even on the lower plane of warfare, a man killed is merely one man less, whereas a man unnerved is a highly infectious carrier of fear, capable of spreading an epidemic of panic. On a higher plane of warfare, the impression made on the mind of the opposing commander can nullify the whole fighting power that his troops possess.[138]

According to ancient handbooks, similarly, the commander's goal was to disorient and demoralize. Especially in siege warfare, to which Frontinus devoted the last of his initial three books, the contest for morale was zero-sum: One side gained it inevitably at the other's expense. Whether it had to do with preserving or stealing secret plans, dispelling fears generated by bad omens, sowing panic among the enemy, or deceiving them about the strength of one's forces, the fighters' mental and emotional dispositions were decisive.[139] These considerations figure prominently in Josephus' *Judean War*.

V. ASYMMETRICAL WARFARE: WHOSE ADVANTAGE?

Guerrilla tactics are an effort to answer the question: *How can the weak make war against the strong? . . .* As Mao wrote, "The strategy of guerrilla war is to pit one man against ten, but the tactic is to pit ten men against one."[140]

Overwhelming force cannot by itself win wars. One analysis of asymmetrical warfare shows that between 1800 and 1998, in cases where there was a greater than 5:1 difference in paper strength the *weaker side* won nearly 30 percent of the time. And their odds have been improving. In the most recent half-century (i.e., post–World War II), those who should have realized that they were overwhelmed, in theory, have prevailed more often than they have lost.[141] How can this be?

In the magnificent speech that Josephus crafts for Agrippa II, with Thucydidean logic the king argues that a nation may have every just cause for war, but if it is *unable* to mount a credible fight, it must submit to a stronger force (*War* 2.350–57). That sounds prudent, but powerfully disaffected groups often persevere in spite of negligible resources. As Mearsheimer vividly puts it, "for every neck, there are two hands to choke it."[142]

---

[138] Liddell Hart 1941: 298; cf. 202.

[139] Onasander, *Strat.* 13.1–3; 14.3; 28; 42; Frontinus, *Strat.* 1.7, 12; 2.4, 6–8, 11; 3.3, 5, 8; Vegetius, *Epit.* 3.4, 10–11, 25–26.

[140] Joes 1996: 4.   [141] Arreguin-Toft 2001: 96–98.   [142] Mearsheimer 2001: 31.

At the very time that Polybius was extolling the manoeuvrable legion's advantages over the inflexible Macedonian phalanx, a Celtiberian named Viriathus was waging a successful, eight-year guerrilla campaign against Rome's *relatively inflexible* legions in Lusitania (147–140 B.C.). Although vastly outnumbered, his nimble fighters killed reported thousands in well-planned ambushes. Holding the Romans in contempt, he played havoc with them, demoralizing those he did not kill. With such determination he was able to conclude "a very hard war for the Romans" in his favour, reaching an agreement that secured his people's land. Having earned their respect, he even became the Romans' friend for a time – until another commander, who felt that this arrangement was unworthy of Roman dignity, renewed the fight (Appian, *Hist. rom.* 6.69–70). Noteworthy in Appian's account are his comments on differences of character among Roman commanders: The timid Quintius hides in the camp, whereas bold Aemilianus forces Viriathus to respect Romans (6.66).

In spite of Josephus' perhaps mischievous claim that legions had never been bested by human or natural foe (*War* 3.105–107), everyone knew of their terrible defeats. Shortly before this laudatory passage, Josephus himself has described their loss of a legion (2.499–555). This suggests that he deliberately hyperbolizes the legions' invulnerability in order to exalt Judaean fighters for being able to inflict so much pain on them (Chapter 6).

In his *Grand Strategy of the Roman Empire*, Edward Luttwak argued that the composition, equipment, training, and ethos of early imperial legions made them lethal in "high-intensity warfare," such as pitched battles or when seizing heavily defended strongholds. Their engineering skills were particularly impressive. "By the same token," he went on, "the relatively slow-moving legionary infantry was unsuited for guerrilla (or counter-guerrilla) warfare, and indeed for all mobile warfare against elusive enemies."[143] Adrian Goldsworthy takes a nearly opposite view, arguing for the imperial legions' increased flexibility. This arose, he argues, from their new focus on the cohort as an independent tactical force and from the use of specialist allied and auxiliary units, configurable to the needs of each campaign. He contends that the Romans were more adaptable than their enemies, many of whom (notably the Germans and Gauls) could not sustain low-intensity conflicts as the Romans could with their superior logistics. Their need for quick victories forced the Celts into open battle and defeat.

These proposals highlight different aspects of the same reality. Goldsworthy is right that Roman commanders could configure their forces to suit requirements (Vegetius, *Epit.* 3.9) and display a nearly inexhaustible versatility of manoeuvre. But Luttwak is onto something when he observes that the training and equipping of legions continued to assume pitched battles or sieges. The

---

[143] Luttwak 1976: 40–41.

African campaigns confirm this, for Tacitus emphasizes the inability of Roman forces to deal with Tacfarinas' ambushes and the latter's avoidance of the open confrontation the Romans desired (*Ann.* 3.20.1). They must learn guerrilla warfare (*Ann.* 2.52.1–5): "As long as that remained the barbarian's method, he mocked with impunity the thwarted and exhausted Roman" (*Ann.* 3.2.4–5, trans. A. J. Woodman). The Roman proconsul Q. Junius Blaesus gradually learned to adapt, but there were no staff colleges in which he could teach what he had learned and it is far from clear that his experience brought changes to legionary training. In Josephus' narratives, as we have begun to see, Roman soldiers appear lost and vulnerable when they cannot rely on practised column-based manoeuvres.

Vegetius' insistence that an army should fight only where it controls the terrain is illustrated by other first-century conflicts. In Tacitus' description of the Batavian Revolt (A.D. 70), the rebel Civilis faces tens of thousands of Roman legionaries across the marshy plain that he has formed by damming the Rhine. This creates a highly advantageous situation for his men, who are lightly armed, good swimmers, and taller than Romans. When the bravest legionaries charge ahead toward his force, panic ensues as those behind watch their heavily armed comrades disappearing into the water. The advantage cannot be sustained, however. When the legionaries extricate themselves, the Germans must retreat. Tacitus observes that both commanders emerge determined to renew the fight: Civilis to exploit soaring morale and the Roman Cerialis to erase the humiliation (*Hist.* 5.14–15). Boudica's Iceni likewise enjoyed stunning early victories (A.D. 60), but only as long as they fought on their terms. One fateful afternoon she saw her army cut to pieces by a disciplined Roman infantry finally able to fight on its terrain.

In the same way, although the Judaeans' opportunistic ambush of Cestius' expedition supercharged their morale, it meant little for the contest ahead, in which the Romans controlled virtually all of the fighting. The campaign led by Vespasian and Titus from early 67 amounted to a succession of sieges, with brief follow-up operations to chase down those who retained even a possible will to fight – for any reason. The few who had such a will may have seen their best hopes in opportunistic guerrilla strikes against small units, the flank or rear of a column, a baggage train, or a depot, but we have little evidence of this activity against the Flavian forces. Those Judaeans who did not capitulate seem mostly to have retreated to fortified cities, desert strongholds, or caves. What were their prospects in these fortified sites?

VI. SIEGE WARFARE: WHOSE ADVANTAGE?

When the U.S. general (later president) Andrew Jackson took Florida's Pensacola from the Spanish in 1814, he declared that if *he* had been defending it, with the same 300 men who surrendered to him, he could have defied a siege by all the European powers combined.[144] Beyond the bravado, his boast reflects a truth easily forgotten, that the outcome of sieges is rarely a foregone conclusion. Romans and Judaeans alike realized that Rome's campaign in Galilee and Judaea would boil down to a string of sieges. That is why Josephus describes his first activity in the north as fortifying Galilee's towns (*War* 2.573). In the flat, open, and fertile landscape of Lower Galilee, which lacked real fortresses, the arrival of Vespasian and Titus with a 60,000-strong force may have created a foregone conclusion (see Chapter 6). But once the conflict moved to Judaea's hills, conditions became much more daunting for the attackers.

In explaining why Scipio Africanus was not quick to besiege Carthage when he arrived in Africa in 204 B.C., Liddell Hart comments on the rarity of favourable conditions for sieges:

> Unless there is opportunity and favourable prospect for a quick surprise assault, a siege is *the most uneconomic* of all operations of war. When the enemy has still a field army capable of intervening, a siege is also the most dangerous – for until it is crowned by success the assailant *is progressively weakening himself out of proportion to his enemy*.[145]

The last point is important. Many sieges have ended in humiliating departure for the besiegers or a victory scratched out after many failures. A classic case concerns Napoleon's *Grande Armée*, trying to take the port city of Acre (Akko/Ptolemais) in 1799 from the Ottomans, then supported by the British. Bonaparte expected to seize this "heap of stones" quickly, but two months and 5,000 casualties later he beat a reluctant retreat. He was undone by many factors: his army's reputed brutality at their previous stop (Jaffa), rumours of which stiffened the resolve of Acre's defenders; a plague that ravaged the besiegers; access of the besieged to provisions from the sea; and their unexpectedly effective tactics – accurate sniping, surprisingly bold sorties outside the walls, and the construction of an internal wall, which deflated the French attackers after they had penetrated the main wall.[146] Jerusalem's ancient defenders anticipated the same moves, and the Romans must have known going in that a siege of that great city such as Jerusalem in Jerusalem's hills would be far from easy.

Consider ancient examples. In 414 B.C., the Athenian army began a siege of Syracuse in Sicily. Although they were well-equipped and confident, they could not prevent the arrival of the enemy's allies, who thwarted their effort to complete a containment wall. Thucydides remarks of the Athenians: "[T]hey were beaten at all points and altogether" (7.87.6). This victory gave Syracuse

---

[144] Remini 2001: 161.   [145] Liddell Hart 1941: 38 (my emphasis).
[146] Lanfrey 1886: 1.292–300; Fournier 1903: 141–51.

the reputation of being unconquerable until the Romans took it in a later century, after many setbacks caused by Archimedes' anti-siege devices. Even they finally succeeded only with the help of a traitor from inside – a common figure in successful sieges.[147]

The island-city of Tyre and coastal Gaza both refused to submit to Alexander the Great. In the end he took both and exacted brutal vengeance, but it cost him seven months for Tyre and two for Gaza. Another commander might have weighed the costs differently. In 305 B.C. Antigonus the One-Eyed, one of Alexander's successors, sent his son Demetrius to besiege the island *polis* of Rhodes. Nicknamed "the Besieger" for his prowess, Demetrius brought 200 warships, 120 supply ships, another thousand privately owned ships, 40,000 infantry plus cavalry, and abundant supplies. But the morale of the island's residents was high, and they took measures to increase it: appealing to Antigonus' rivals for help, manufacturing their own weapons and armour, and expelling all but their most able fighters to reduce food consumption and risk of betrayal. After a year of energetic effort, and in spite of his patented "city-taker" (*helepolis*) engine, Demetrius had to withdraw (Diodorus 20.81–88, 91–100). Rhodes even managed to exact favourable terms: They would remain autonomous and free to use their revenues rather than paying him tribute (Diodorus 20.99).

Did those who promoted Jerusalem's resistance hope for some such accommodation? This is hard to imagine, but easier than believing that they expected to achieve radical independence from Rome, landlocked and surrounded as they were.

The well-fortified city of Saguntum in northeastern Spain is another suggestive case. Besieged by 28-year-old Hannibal at the beginning of his career (219 B.C.), this city under Rome's protection had no intention of yielding and appealed to Rome for aid. Not yet knowing Hannibal, the Senate dithered for months with fact-finding embassies, while Hannibal squeezed the city. Still the Saguntines' resolve held out. Hannibal was motivated not only by Saguntum's strategic value but also by rumours of its immense wealth. To neutralize this incentive, the besieged citizens gathered up their gold and silver and melted it together with base metals to convince their foe that it would be unusable. But Hannibal did not relent. The besieged undertook brave defensive and offensive activities, even incapacitating Hannibal for a while with a leg wound. Still he did not leave. When starvation finally threatened them after eight long months, they felt they had nothing left to lose. Their men charged out at night and killed many Carthaginian soldiers in their sleep. When they were finally overwhelmed, they tried to destroy their property before taking their own lives – rather than face capture with its likely horrors.[148]

---

[147] See Plutarch, *Marcellus* 13–19.   [148] Livy 21.5–15; Appian, *Hist. rom.* 6.7–12.

Although the details of what happened at Saguntum vary in our accounts, that siege offers many parallels worth pondering for Jerusalem, Machaerus, and Masada (Chapters 7–9).

Carthage is famous for having been comprehensively destroyed by Scipio Aemilianus in 146 B.C. But that destruction came only after the city had defied earlier Roman sieges over three years. According to Appian, things began to go well for the Romans only when Scipio brought a new approach (8.97–108). Goldsworthy observes: "The siege illustrated once again the extreme difficulty of capturing a large and well fortified city. ... The final collapse in the defenders [sic] morale came very suddenly."[149]

Frontinus, who had gained military-political experience in Britain under the Flavians, gives eleven tactical suggestions for besiegers along with seven for the besieged, citing famous examples of success *from both sides* (*Stratagems*, Bk. 3). Again we see the position of besiegers as inherently vulnerable. They would normally undertake a siege only if they felt able to end it quickly. In the best case, thousands of troops massed outside would provoke a rapid surrender. After all, they needed only a few of those inside to open a gate. It was in the besiegers' interest to conclude the matter quickly and avoid risking depletion of manpower, disease, changes of weather, loss of food or water, or other setbacks that fortune might dish out. Until the moment of surrender, the besiegers were anxious and ramped up the pressure in every way possible: ostentatiously securing their supply lines, beginning assault ramps and possibly containment walls, using artillery and archers to keep defenders from the ramparts, and randomly bombarding those inside with stones, bolts, and arrows. They might try to undermine the walls (removing crucial support stones), to batter the wall with rams at weak points, or even to scale less-well defended areas (escalade).

They had to work quickly because nature made their position risky. In the Mediterranean summer, aggressors camped outside the city faced relentless heat and sun exposure. They lacked the stone-cooled shade and buildings enjoyed by those inside. Whereas walled cities were normally well supplied with food and water in their stone-cut cisterns, springs, and warehouses, the besiegers often had serious worries about water and other basic necessities. An army of 50,000 – smaller than that reportedly assembled by Vespasian or Titus – required *each and every day* some 50 tonnes (55 U.S. tons) of grain, 12,500 litres (3,300 gal.) of wine, and possibly 50,000 litres (13,200 gal.) of water, along with piles of meat, butter, salt, and lentils. That was for the soldiers alone. Horses and pack animals required possibly 20 litres (5.3 gal.) of water *each per day*, along with massive amounts of grain.[150] Getting all this to a siege site in rugged hill country was no small feat. It required a secure

---

[149] Goldsworthy 2000: 355.   [150] See Roth 1999: 165–213.

supply chain in perpetual motion, supplemented by local requisition and foraging where possible.

Contaminated food and/or water would spread illness quickly. Even if it happened by accident, tainted food and water was a highly effective demoralizer. Dysentery worried all besiegers. If they had to remain stationary for long periods, the soldiers' waste, sewage, and drainage problems rapidly increased. The hills around Jerusalem offered few options for shifting camp locations. Although a modern understanding of hygiene was far from the horizon, hygiene was no less of a problem. People knew to stay away from human waste, rotting things, and foul air, but these could be hard to escape where tens of thousands of men camped. Drinking water was a problem especially in regions such as North Africa and, according to the Epitome of Dio, outside Jerusalem. This author plausibly claims that besieged Judaeans made tireless efforts to spoil the Romans' precious water supply (Dio 65/66.4.5).

The perils of contagious disease for the besieging (Roman) army are not elaborated by Josephus, but the silence of ancient historians about such matters may be due to the ubiquity of disease in life generally and to a lack of analytical tools or language for these problems. They often mention a general *plague*, such as Josephus describes in Jerusalem (*War* 6.421). What does plague mean? Cassius Dio criticizes Marc Antony's choice of a camp location at Actium on a low-lying broad plain near the coast (50.12.8). The site was better for fighting than for camping, he observes, because it bred disease (νόσος), especially in summer. Antony's eagerness to give battle was frustrated for months because, although his army was larger, he kept losing men to disease – and desertion prompted by disease, in part – before any fighting had occurred (50.11.2). Dio also recounts an ill-fated expedition into Arabia in which the legions won all their battles but had to abandon the field because disease ravaged their force (53.29.3–8).

Such stories do not tell us what was happening in medical terms, and the study of ancient epidemiology is an enormous challenge because of the lack of evidence. It requires a knowledge of both medicine and the ancient texts, languages, and history. The present writer lacks any medical competence, but high-quality research along these lines is beginning to appear.[151]

Southern Syria shared the environmental challenges of the Levant, some of which have endured to modern times. For example, the levels of infant mortality we hypothesize for antiquity were still found among poor populations in the early twentieth century – more than 20 percent in the first year of life.[152] When Western travellers began visiting the Holy Land in significant

---

[151] E.g., Scheidel 2001; Sallares 2002, the latter on malaria in ancient .Italy.

[152] Sufian 2007: 8–9 with n. 14. Aside from contagious disease, leprosy has been common in the land since biblical times, although the Bible includes other diseases under the same name. Cf. Martineau 1848: 500.

numbers in the nineteenth century, they found it heaving with typhus, typhoid, cholera, dysentery, and malaria. Beset by fleas and mosquitoes wherever they lodged, explorers were more likely to die of mysterious fevers than from the perils for which they had prepared: lack of food or water or armed attack.[153] Malaria, whose intermittent fevers were not traced to the parasite-hosting anopheles mosquito until the late 1800s, generated staggering rates of infection before British-Mandate and Zionist health authorities drained the swamps that hosted the mosquito, began widespread medical examination and distribution of quinine, and eventually sprayed DDT.[154]

Although we cannot be sure what conditions were like in the first century, the environment that made malaria endemic – Palestine's topography, climate, rainfall, and natural drainage lines (which could also be blocked by nature, creating lagoons and swamps)[155] – was presumably there. It is possible that canals, built in the Roman period for other reasons, incidentally mitigated the problem of swamp-based malaria.[156] But Crusader accounts of malaria (thought to issue from exposure to "bad air"), which General Allenby read in preparation for the British campaign to dislodge the Ottomans in 1917, show that the problem was severe a millennium ago. So there is no reason to doubt its presence in Roman times.[157] Josephus also mentions potentially lethal cases of fever, some recurring in three- or four-day cycles and suggesting malaria, such as the disease that felled Alexander Jannaeus while he conducted a siege east of the Jordan.[158]

When Allenby's force entered the region in 1917, they enjoyed logistical support that would have made the Romans envious. The British general devoted major and targeted resources to preventing malaria. He placed an antimalarial squad in each unit. Even still, the proportion of his soldiers that fell ill from malaria, diarrhea, dysentery, and venereal disease was an astonishing

---

[153] E.g., Napoleon's army outside Acre ("the plague, which we had brought from Jaffa, was raging in the camp"; Lanfrey 1886: 1.296); the fever that gripped members of the U.S. Naval expedition to the Dead Sea led by Lt. William Lynch in 1948, which claimed Lt. John Dale (Jampoler 2005: 234–45); or the mysterious fever that struck Ernest Renan and his sister Henriette in Beirut, which he alone survived (Renan 1898: ix–x). In general, see Martineau 1848: 472–74.

[154] Sufian 2007: 63–98.   [155] Sufian 2007: 70–79.

[156] Conder and Kitchener 1881–1884: 3.183 [this item dated 1874]: "'The climate of Jericho would seemingly have changed since the days of Josephus, or more probably the surplus irrigation was not then, as now, suffered [i.e., allowed] to become stagnant pools, causing malaria and fever."

[157] Sufian 2007: 84.

[158] Josephus, *War* 1.106 (= *Ant.* 13.398) on Jannaeus' fatal quartan fever (tertian by inclusive counting); *Life* 48 on Philip son of Iacimus' incapacitating sudden fever. Cf. Plato, *Tim.* 86a on recurring fevers; Hippocrates, *Prog.* 20 and *Morb. pop.* [*Epid.*] 3.3.12 on "the many and varied" recurring fevers, typically in (inclusive) four-day cycles; also Galen *On the Different Fevers*.

75 percent per year. Non-battle casualties were ten times as frequent as those from fighting.[159] In the period from October to December 1918 alone, Allenby's army recorded 20,000 cases of malaria, and prisoners of war had an infection rate of 60 percent.[160]

Exacerbating the effects of disease was the simple discomfort of any military action in harsh environments. A relatively well-provisioned British officer of 1917 complained in a letter home: "Am writing in a beastly tent the temperature being 106 in the shade. . . . Before sitting down to write I had to chase a small snake out of the tent. . . . I'm one mass of bites and blisters already."[161] We can only imagine how the tens of thousands of legionaries under Titus fared, camped for months in close quarters outside Jerusalem, without customary baths and enduring hard physical work under an uncaring sun.

Although a siege by tens of thousands of heavily armed soldiers was undoubtedly terrifying for those inside the city, then, they enjoyed advantages in the short term and had some reason for hope, if they could keep their heads. Their city was sited in the first place for its defensive qualities. In southern Syria, fortified towns and cities typically had steep precipices on three sides (cf. Iotapata, Gamala, Jerusalem, Machaerus, Masada), leaving only one line of access as the focus of defensive efforts. For this reason Jerusalem was nearly always attacked from the north.[162] In his truncated description of Jerusalem's siege, Tacitus dilates on the fortress-like character of the city, ringed with multiple thick walls and its temple creating an internal fortress (*Hist.* 5.8, 11–12). Jerusalem's founders anticipated wars, he offers, and "had built at every point as if they expected a long siege" (*Hist.* 5.12). The residents had storage facilities for large amounts of food and water as well as a prolific spring. This was the Roman view, which Tacitus found in his sources. Although their forces could overlook Jerusalem from Mount Scopus and the Mount of Olives, Roman artillery could not cover anything like the intervening distances, and there was no chance of crossing the valleys to assault Jerusalem's towering walls from below.

The prospect of digging beneath a besieged city's walls, whether to get out or to gain access, appears to have been something of a draw for besiegers and besieged. The multi-tonne ashlars laid on bedrock for Herod's temple enclosure doubled as the city wall on the east side. They also provided a formidable obstacle on the north, where they were buttressed by the thick

---

[159] Mitchell 1931: 208–17; cf. Falls 1928–1930: 3(= 2.2).596–99. [160] Sufian 2007: 85.

[161] Letter from Capt. William Hine to Hilda Gosling (Sept. 5, 1917), cited by Segev 2000: 24.

[162] David's capture of the city from the Jebusites came from the south, through infiltration of a water tunnel (2 Sam 5:6–10), but the Jebusite city was located on the southeast hill. The Assyrians, Babylonians, and Romans (63 B.C., 37 B.C.) have attacked mainly from the north. Modern mechanization and weapon systems, of course, make such considerations mostly irrelevant.

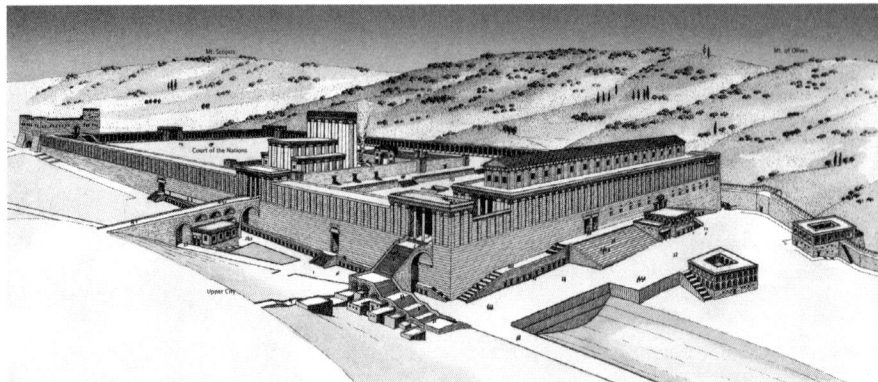

FIGURE 10. A classic reconstruction of Jerusalem's Temple Mount.© and rights reserved by L. Ritmeyer, used with permission.

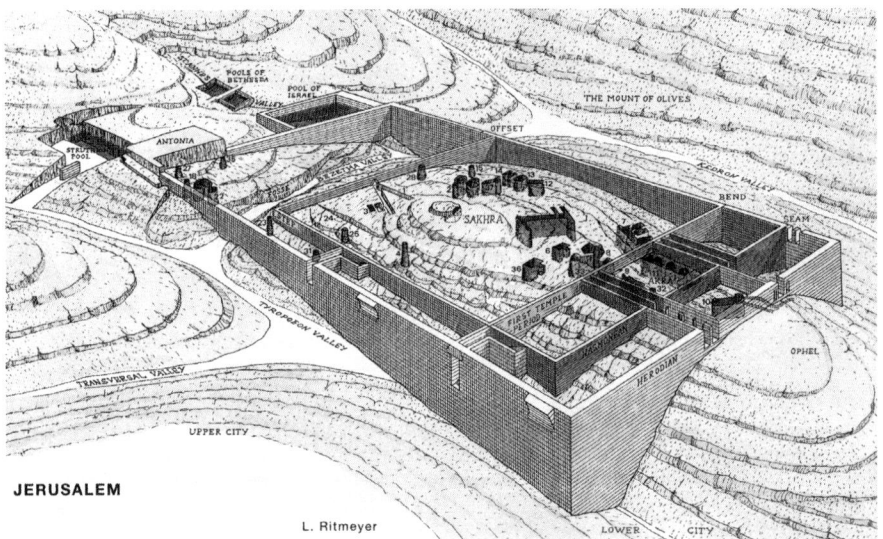

FIGURE 11. Cutaway view of the building stages of the Temple Mount, the largest area being Herod's retaining wall, and showing the bedrock.© and rights reserved by L. Ritmeyer, used with permission.

walls of the Antonia fortress and the Pool of Israel. Because they sat on bedrock, those temple-platform walls could hardly be undermined (Figs. 10–11).

The Epitome of Dio relates that the Judaeans had many tunnels, dug through the soil under parts of the (western) city wall, which did not sit on bedrock, and opening a considerable distance off in the countryside (65/ 66.4.5). These were the routes they used to contaminate the Romans' water supply. When Titus found the tunnels, he closed them. Underground caverns and tunnels figure in Josephus' *War* from the siege of 37 B.C., where legions assisted Herod (1.348–50; 2.428). The missionary-architect Conrad Schick, enjoying unique access beneath the ancient temple mount (*haram as-sharif*) in the 1870s, identified some forty-five cisterns along with other chambers and cavities,[163] created by the Herodian vaults that supported the temple platform. In the siege of 70, both the cisterns below the temple compound and the caverns and tunnels below the Upper City were heavily exploited as hiding places.[164]

Tunnels also provided a means of permanent escape. In 2007 a long drainage tunnel, 3 m (10 ft) high in places, was discovered beneath the main north-south street of pre-70 Jerusalem, running from the west side of the temple mount southward to the Pool of Siloam (Fig. 12). The road above was found broken through in places, matching Josephus' description: "[T]he Romans searched for those in the underground spaces and, tearing up the ground, killed all those they found" (6.429).[165] Ancient accounts of other sieges describe besiegers digging tunnels under the walls *to get in*, only to be met by counter-measures. In a famous case, bears, other large animals, and bees were sent to greet the enemy sappers.[166]

In the early days of a siege, as long as food and water stores remained plentiful and disease contained, the greatest problem inside the walls was likely to have been morale, given the thousands of hostile soldiers tens of metres away. Movement inside would have been restricted, especially if the population had swelled with refugees, as was normal when nearby villages were evacuated. Unaccustomed proximity to crowds under highly stressful conditions can be explosive, and constant fear of projectiles landing randomly – even if these were nonexplosive *ballista* stones and bolts – must have heightened tensions immeasurably. Stress would have been compounded by urgent dis-agreement about the best course of action. The longer the siege lasted, as food supplies diminished, water evaporated, sickness and death became more wide-spread, and external aid was clearly not forthcoming, spirits would naturally have plummeted. Fear and hatred might even produce such irrational actions as the spiteful burning of stores (*War* 5.24–26).

All such problems within obviously served the besiegers outside. Where possible, they would exacerbate internal strife by means of propaganda, per-haps offering privileged terms to one group or trying to remind them of their mutual distrust. As life inside became increasingly untenable, chances increased

[163] See Gibson and Jacobson 1994: 150.
[164] Cisterns: *War* 5.102–104; Caverns and tunnels: 6.370, 392, 402, 433; 7.26, 35, 215.
[165] The find under the southern part of the road was announced on August 9, 2007, after discovery by R. Reich and E. Shukron. See Reich and Shukron 2011 with Steinberg 2008: 20; Anonymous 2010.
[166] Campbell 2005: 18, discussing the defence of Mithridatic forces against Lucullus at Themyscira; cf. Campbell 2006: 139.

FIGURE 12. The drainage tunnel excavated by R. Reich and E. Shukron, extending from the southwestern edge of the Temple Mount to the Pool of Siloam. This photo shows the steepness of the descent in places. Author 2013.

that some influential figure(s) would find a way to bolt, further diminishing morale, or contrive to let the besiegers in, "betraying" the city. This was all predictable and common.

Just as the besiegers could not usually afford to remain idle outside, it was psychologically impossible for those inside merely to sit and wait for the enemy's moves. Constant initiative and at least the appearance of small victories were necessary to keep hope alive as weeks turned into months. That psychological necessity helps to explain Josephus' and Dio's references to death-defying sorties outside Iotapata's, Machaerus', and Jerusalem's walls. Such references are conspicuously absent, however, in the case of Masada (Chapter 9).

In sum, the arrival of Roman forces, as terrifying as it must have been for those inside walled Jerusalem, was by no means yet a *fait accompli*. That some Roman soldiers reportedly fled to join the besieged Judaeans (below) confirms that the situation was not entirely one-sided. For those inside, defiance remained an enormous gamble. But so was attempted flight or surrender. How long would it last? Would it end like Tyre against Alexander, in the besieger's ferocious vengeance, or like Rhodes with Demetrius? Given Josephus' repeated reference to the confidence placed in Jerusalem's walls,[167] it may be that some residents felt fairly confident at first. Perhaps they imagined that they could negotiate terms, given formerly strong relations with Roman officials.[168] What such terms could have entailed is far from clear. It seems most likely that key leaders persisted because they felt they had passed a point of no return, after which the expected horrors of capture or surrender mandated a fight to the end.

VII. MORALE III: INTIMIDATION AND DESERTION

Having surveyed factors that might have affected morale for both Judaeans and Romans, we may finally address the central question of morale in this conflict. Compare the following three texts: a Roman military manual of the fourth century, American psychological-operations warfare doctrine from 1994, and a Canadian military perspective. From the ancient manual:[169]

> No one challenges, no one dares to strike at someone he knows will best him if he fights. . . .

---

[167] *War* 2.378; 5.136, 153, 247, 374.
[168] Cf. Goodman 2007: 424–25 (they may have sought autonomy under a native king, as under Agrippa I).
[169] Vegetius, *Epit.* 3.praef., 10, 26.

It is a wise commander who *sows the seeds of discord among his enemies.* For no nation, no matter how small, can be entirely destroyed by its enemies *unless it devours itself in feuds.* . . .

In all combat the principle of the campaign is this: *what benefits you harms the enemy, and what helps him always hinders you.* Therefore we ought never to effect or to neglect anything *at his determination,* but should *do only what we judge useful to ourselves.* . . .

It is *better to subdue an enemy by famine, raids, and terror than in combat,* where fortune tends to have more of an effect than bravery. . . .

In soliciting and receiving enemy soldiers, if they come over in good faith, enormous confidence arises [on our side], because *deserters shatter the enemy much more than casualties.*

Some U.S. Air Force psychological-operations principles from 1994:[170]

- Persuade enemy and neutral nations that the strength and determination of the United States and its allies will ultimately defeat the enemy.
- Weaken and demoralize the enemy population and key influential groups so they lose the will to continue hostilities.
- Divide enemy alliances.
- Deter enemy operations in designated areas and discourage the enemy from escalating the conflict or weaponry.
- Isolate the enemy from sources of foreign support.
- Weaken the enemy's ability to generate, field, and support armed forces by subverting the loyalties of enemy citizens, promoting sabotage, and lowering morale in the enemy country.

And a Canadian military analyst in 2003:[171]

Army doctrine has evolved past its Cold-War fixation on fighting the close battle in Europe to the point where we envision winning battles by attacking the enemy's moral cohesion and will to resist through manoeuvre warfare.

As we have seen, psychological manipulation was built into every aspect of Rome's outlook. To observe an endless legionary column on the march, three to six armed men across with resplendent horsemen riding the flanks, was to be impressed for good or ill. Like all pre-modern military uniforms, that of the legionary proclaimed domination: His height increased several inches by a shining helmet, sometimes topped by a crest, his width enhanced by armour, senior officers wearing a cuirass formed as defined musculature. The helmet provided nearly complete protection for his head, neck, and face. His

---

[170] USAF PSYOP Doctrine (1994) 4.2. Online at www.fas.org/irp/doddir/usaf/10–702.htm (accessed October 10, 2008).

[171] Rickard 2003: 33.

blood-red tunic and polished spear-tip, sword, and dagger inspired fear without needing to be drawn. Even his hob-nailed boots – thick sandals with cleats in the soles – created alarm by their clack on hard ground and provided traction on earth. (They could become a problem on wet or polished cobblestones: *War* 6.85–88.)

Estimates of the average height of adult males in the Roman period, based on skeletal remains, range from 166 to 170 cm (5 ft 5/7 in); of women, about 148 cm (4 ft 8 in). Judaeans fell in the same general range. Elite military units in Rome required above-average height, and nations such as the Germans had a reputation for unusual size.[172] Josephus appears to say that the Judaeans of Caesarea were bigger and stronger than their Syrian-Greek neighbours, which is possible (*War* 2.268). Vegetius remarks (*Epit.* 1.5), however, that in his day (ca. A.D. 400) it was impossible to meet the earlier imperial legionary recruitment standard of 5 ft 7.5 in (172 cm, Roman 5 ft 10 in), and especially the preferred 5 ft 10 in (6 Roman feet). Because environment and nutrition play a role in one's size along with genes, the perception that those raised in physically challenging environments were bigger than the city-bred might reflect reality.

The heights mentioned appear to have remained averages into the twentieth century. By then, the advantage of height for military needs was becoming less relevant. A British manual from 1912 observes that:

> Tall men had, in the days of close formations, a distinct moral [i.e., morale-related] value when it was a question of close quarters and shock tactics. The comparatively small man, on the other hand, is quicker, as a rule more active, gets more value out of his ration, and does not knock himself about to the same extent as the bigger men on rough ground.[173]

Physicians of this time felt that taller men were "ordinarily the first to fail" in combat and "commonly suffer from diseases in greater proportion to the others."[174] The British army therefore imposed height *limits* in some units.[175]

---

[172] Detailed discussion is in Roth (1999: 146–57), who favours the higher number. Palaeopathologist J. Zias in private correspondence (Sept. 6, 2008) says that average heights in antiquity generally were 5 ft 5 in (166 cm) for males and 4 ft 8 in (148 cm) for females. For the perception that the *Germani* were bigger than most, see *War* 2.376; 6.331; Tacitus, *Germ.* 4, 20. Rives (1999: 129) cites measurements of ancient German skeletons at an average 5 ft 6 in (167.5 cm) for males and 5 ft 2 in (157 cm) for females – males thus at the upper end of average, females significantly larger.

[173] Melville 1912: 24.   [174] Myerly 1996: 16.

[175] Melville (1912: 24) reports that the minimum standard for infantry was 5 ft 4 in. (as against only 5 ft 1 in. for continental armies), lower for "departmental [non-combatant] corps," whereas field and garrison artillery required 5 ft 7 and 8 in, respectively. The elite Grenadier, Coldstream, and Scots Guards demanded 5 ft 9 in, and the Household Cavalry (the sovereign's personal bodyguard, used also for parade duties) 5 ft 11 in. Mounted units had upper height limits: a maximum of 6 ft 1 in the tallest of them. (Later paratroopers faced

Only parade and bodyguard units continued to need the intimidating effect of unusual height.[176]

The modern shift helps us to imagine the ways in which Romans used every opportunity to exploit the appearance of their superbly equipped army, massed in rank and file. Opportunities were few during a siege, but Josephus describes Titus using such a tactic just after taking Jerusalem's second wall. Instead of continuing the assault immediately against the city's innermost, oldest, and strongest wall, he staged an elaborate payday parade over four days. Legionaries were paid three times per year, and this may simply have been the scheduled time, but Josephus portrays it as a tactic to intimidate. The legions parade in full uniform, their polished swords drawn. Even the horses are decked out in armour and shiny decorations, the bright sun giving the whole scene an otherworldly radiance. "The broad area in front of the city gleamed with gold and silver, and nothing was more exhilarating than this spectacle to themselves, or more terrifying to the [Judaean] enemy" (*War* 5.348–55). The city's north wall is crowded with spectators craning their necks, and Josephus characteristically reads their minds: "dire consternation overtook even the most daring, as they observed this force all massed together and the fineness of the weapons and the good order of the men." He has the Jerusalemites admit that they would have surrendered right then and there, *had they not gone too far* to expect clemency.[177] The last remark is important, and we shall return to it in coming chapters.

While the Romans relied on such overt displays in combination with periodic assaults, the Judaeans' only hope for instilling terror required stealth and *invisible* actions. Before the sieges these involved ambush, sabotage, and lightning forays against flanks, rearguards, and baggage trains. As we have seen, their fighters must have worn armour and used swords, spears, arrows, and slings.[178] No doubt they collected the gear of fallen Romans when possible (*War* 2.553–54). Their inability to use captured artillery without the help of Roman deserters, however – reportedly tried only in the final siege[179] – highlights the difference. *They* had to be quick and as light as possible. They wanted Roman soldiers to worry about a ghost-like menace appearing from

---

similar limits for practical reasons.) The average height of British recruits in 1909 was 5 ft 6.5 in, says Melville, and that was a half-inch taller than in the previous decade.

[176] Cf. Mountford 1898: Kaiser Wilhelm II entering Jerusalem had "a body of picked German hussars in high, shining helmets that made them look still taller and bigger than they are, although it is said that every one of them is seven feet tall."

[177] Note the same rationale at Masada, Chapter 9.

[178] *War* 2.56, 434, 649; *Life* 22, 29, 293, 303.

[179] At *War* 5.267 Simon bar Giora tries to use the artillery that his group had taken from Cestius (cf. 2.521) and from the auxiliary garrison of the fortress Antonia. At 5.359 he mentions an astonishing 300 bolt-throwers and 40 stone-throwers. See Campbell 1986: 122–25. Given Josephus' general exaggeration of figures, it is easy to imagine that he inflated these numbers to give the defenders a more credible chance.

nowhere. Even during the siege of Jerusalem, they had to unnerve the enemy through rapid, unexpected strikes, then disappear (Chapter 7).

The single most effective tool for unnerving an enemy is the enticement of deserters, whether they come to your side or simply flee. Desertion pays double dividends, at once leeching the morale of the donor side and immeasurably strengthening that of the beneficiary. Success in enticing desertion depends, however, on fighters' weighing of their current trauma against the chances of surviving flight and their likely reception by the other side if they either cross over or are caught.

Niall Ferguson argues that "Surrender was the key to the outcome of the First World War."[180] In its final three months, the Germans inflicted much higher casualty numbers on the British than the reverse (ca. 65,000 to just 28,500). Yet the British took more than 157,000 prisoners, many more than the Germans and nearly as many as in the previous four years combined. Ferguson concludes: "Once the Germans lost their fear of surrendering to the Allied armies, the war was over" – because Allied soldiers did not lose *their* fear of surrendering.[181] Ferguson argues that something changed in 1918 to radically mitigate German soldiers' fear of surrender.[182] Both sides had a well-earned reputation for executing enemy soldiers, and both applied lethal discipline to their own "cowards" caught attempting to flee. But both sides had photographers ready to publicize their humane treatment of enemy prisoners for display. Officers on the ground were not always so alert to the needs of impression management. Many preferred to unburden themselves of hated enemies who would require food and medical attention. Anyway, bad experiences might recommend not taking the risk of receiving a bogus surrender, which could be a deadly trap (cf. Dio below).

Plutarch relates that the Roman consul Marcellus, en route to Syracuse in Sicily, first took the city of Leontini. There he treated the residents with scrupulous care, with an eye on his image as he moved toward the capital where he hoped to encourage rapid capitulation. His Carthaginian adversary Hippocrates recognized the strategy, however, and pre-empted it by sending urgent word to Syracuse of alleged atrocities committed by Marcellus' army in Leontini. The deception was effective in persuading the Syracusans to resist Marcellus with everything they had – and to welcome Hippocrates (Plutarch, *Marc.* 14). We have noted Napoleon's problems taking Acre, in part because his army's behaviour in previous towns had removed surrender from the options of the besieged. It has been argued that Germans' cruelty toward the 3.6 million Russian prisoners they captured in the first months of World War

---

[180] Ferguson 1998: 367.   [181] Ferguson 1998: 371.
[182] The U.S. entry into the war is an obvious reason, although Ferguson offers grounds for doubting that they treated prisoners any better on the whole (1998: 387).

II's Operation Barbarossa similarly removed any incentive for surrender among Russians and thereby undermined Germany's effort.[183] The Soviets, for their part, devoted about 400,000 soldiers to loss prevention, and the victims of these blocking units, who simply machine-gunned deserters, numbered an estimated 200,000.[184] At Stalingrad alone, the defending general had 13,500 wavering men shot – "to stiffen morale."[185]

Desertion and surrender are basic concerns in all military conflicts. Some soldiers (and many civilians) who find themselves in constant peril will flee when they can, irrespective of the noble ideals claimed by their side. We tend to forget that even in World War II, the most righteous of all wars from the Allied side, British forces lost some 100,000 soldiers and the Americans about 50,000 to desertion.[186]

Josephus portrays Jerusalem in A.D. 68–70 as a scene in which the besieged population were unwilling hostages to their militant leaders. Although they lacked machine guns, these "tyrants" would unhesitatingly cut down would-be deserters (Chapter 7). This was to be expected – to stiffen morale indeed.

According to the Epitome of Dio, when Titus first arrived outside Jerusalem, he offered respectful terms if the Judaeans would give up the city. Only when they refused did he proceed with the siege (65/66.4.1). Later, when he saw how costly it was going to be to take Jerusalem's second wall, he offered immunity to all those who would surrender even then (65/66.5.3). Similarly, Josephus has Titus approach Jerusalem pre-emptively in the hope of a quick surrender. He presents this bid as the fruit of intelligence reports reaching the young commander – perhaps from Josephus – that most of the population, feeling tyrannized, would happily to flee to safety. With Titus' massive force nearby, they would surely take courage and let him deal with their native tyrants (War 5.52–53). Josephus presents these offers as expressions of Titus' magnanimous character,[187] whereas Dio assumes that it was merely sensible strategy to terminate the conflict quickly.

There is no reason to doubt that Titus made such offers. Titus presumably did hope for a quick submission, as Vespasian had two years earlier (Chapter 7). In modern warfare, no one considers offers of safe passage mere sentimentality. In World War II both Allied and Axis forces relentlessly targeted the morale of enemy soldiers with radio broadcasts and "bombs" that dropped flyers in the enemy soldiers' native languages. Those dispatched by the Germans reminded British soldiers of their wives and girlfriends at home, where large numbers of U.S. soldiers lingered with time and money on their hands – exploiting a very real tension. At Monte Cassino, the defending Germans offered Polish troops

---

[183] Roberts 2009: 164.   [184] Roberts 2009: 183; Burleigh 2010: 360.
[185] Burleigh 2010: 348–49, the quoted words from the latter page.   [186] See Glass 2014.
[187] E.g., War 1.10; 6.345–346.

passage through their lines to assist their families at home, now suffering under harsh Soviet rule.[188] Titus' appeals to the Judaeans, we may imagine, struck similar notes – whatever had a chance of working – just as Vespasian had tried to winkle Josephus out of his cave with empty reassurance (Chapter 2).

In the face of such appeals, how to deal with loss prevention? The first-century philosopher Onasander observed: "There is no army from which slaves and free men alike do not desert to the other side, on the many occasions [or pretexts] that war furnishes" (*Strat.* 10.24). He counseled commanders to keep their plans concealed from the lower ranks, because "worthless scoundrels desert at just such crucial times, when they reckon they will receive honour and reward from the enemy by divulging and disclosing things." On the other hand, a commander must treat the enemy's traitors conspicuously well and fulfill promises of reward made when the surrender was invited. The purpose is not to reward the moral failure that surrendering soldiers represent, of course, but to encourage others to do the same: "for *he* is not the avenging judge of the wronged city, but the general of his own homeland" (*Strat.* 38.7–8). Frontinus also devotes an important section of his manual to the solicitation and exploitation of traitors (*Strat.* 3.3).

In spite of the severe punishment that Roman *transfugae* (deserters) faced if caught – execution preceded by horrendous torture – desertion was a well-known problem.[189] Military law made even a soldier who fell asleep on watch or lost a weapon on the battlefield guilty of capital desertion (Polybius 6.37.10–13). Josephus relates that a cavalryman who lost his horse to the Judaeans was executed at Titus' order (*War* 6.155). In another case, Judaean fighters captured both an infantryman and a cavalryman. The former they dispatched immediately, and they were about to kill the trooper when he made a daring escape, although blindfolded and cuffed. Josephus makes it a sign of Titus' extraordinary clemency that he did not execute this man simply for having been captured. Titus merely dismissed him from the legion on the spot, although this was a disgrace worse than death (6.358–62; cf. Polybius 6.37.4).

Nevertheless, desertions occurred. In the final struggle for Carthage in 146 B.C., which the Romans famously won, some 900 legionaries reportedly took refuge in Carthage's temple of Asclepius.[190] When the end came, they preferred to die in the flames than to face their comrades. The Numidians Jugurtha and Tacfarinas, as well as the Dacian king Decebalus, supposedly recruited their best soldiers from Roman fugitives,[191] and such renegades figure prominently in Appian's *Roman History*.[192]

---

[188] Bytwerk 2005 gives examples from a single day at the end of the Cassino conflict.
[189] Campbell 1984: 303–4.   [190] (Appian, *Hist. rom.* 8.130–31; cf. Polybius 38.20.4.
[191] Cf. Goldsworthy 1996: 113.
[192] Appian, *Hist. rom.* 5.2.2 [2.4]; 6.73 [308]; 7.43 [186], 51 [218]. Cf. Polybius 21.30.3.

We do not have much evidence of *Roman* desertion during the Judaean War, but we have enough to confirm that it happened. The Epitome of Dio gives comparable space to desertion on both sides. Some Roman soldiers, it says, becoming dispirited at the long siege and suspecting that Jerusalem might turn out to be impregnable after all, absconded. Those who did so were conspicuously well treated by the Judaeans, "as a demonstration that they [the Judaeans] too were receiving deserters" (65.5.4). It could be that Dio or his epitomizer had little knowledge and imagined mutual desertions for the sake of rhetorical balance. But the scenario is not implausible.

Josephus gives no explicit attention to Roman desertion, perhaps because it was a relatively marginal phenomenon, although he obliquely confirms that it happened when he notes that Simon bar Giora's faction, trying to use captured Roman artillery in besieged Jerusalem, needed to be trained by "the deserters" (*War* 5.268). These might have come from any element of the Roman side: Agrippa's allies, auxiliaries, and/or legionaries. But in view of Dio's remarks and typical siege situations, it may be that dispirited legionaries discovered a fascination with Hebrew. For this to have worked, the Judaeans must have found a way to overcome enemy fears after the earlier massacre of the auxiliary garrison and the ambush of Cestius' legion (*War* 2.449–55, 540–55). Given the circumstances of Metilius' preservation in the former episode, perhaps Roman defectors were spontaneously offering to undergo circumcision as proof of sincerity.[193] But now we are freely speculating.

Whereas we catch only glimpses of Roman desertion, Josephus thematizes defection from inside Jerusalem.[194] We noted his later claim (*Apion* 1.49) to have relied on information gleaned from deserters when later composing *War*. He also thematizes Roman clemency toward refugees, except in moments near the end when Titus becomes occasionally exasperated.[195] Many of the Roman commander's actions are said to have "encouraged still more to

---

[193] *Ant.* 13.257, 318; 20.38–48, 139, 145; cf. *Life* 112–13.

[194] E.g., *War* 4.377–80, 410–11, 490; 5.420–23; 6.115–16, 229–31, 282–84, 345, 366–67, 380–86. See Price 1992: 95–101, 135–42, 255–63, 292–97. Price argues that the desertion theme serves Josephus' putative interest *in distancing himself from the war*. I would suggest that Josephus makes no such effort – indeed his authority chiefly depends on his role in the war (1.1–8) – but repudiates the dishonourable leaders of the tyrant-led *stasis* in Jerusalem that, in his view, caused the city's destruction by their stubbornness. Price perceptively argues (a) that, although Josephus gives various reasons for the waves of defection (e.g., a powerful speech), they are more convincingly connected with steady Roman success, and (b) that Titus treated deserters according to their circumstances of their departure and social rank, thus acting from practical considerations and not from a feeling of clemency.

[195] This decision results from the rebel leaders' alleged request to be allowed to leave the city and head for the desert (6.351–54). Titus immediately relents in the case of Adiabenian royalty (6.356) and soon gives a general amnesty to tens of thousands, confusingly described: Women and children were sold into slavery, whereas more than 40,000 "citizens" deemed not culpable were free to go wherever they wished (6.382–86).

desertion" (5.422). The contrast with the rebel leaders' vigilance in preventing or killing deserters, except when individual guards succumb to bribery, serves his minor theme of native-tyrant barbarity. But as we have seen, the prevention of desertion is every bit as predictable in real life as the encouragement of it by the enemy.

Josephus explores the semiotics of desertion when he describes a tactic used by Titus that backfired. Titus was caught in the standard bind of being unable either to maintain or to free the hundreds of captives taken each day, the standard excuse for killing prisoners.[196] The Roman commander had ordered his men to arrest any Jerusalemites found gathering food outside the walls. Josephus claims that such people would happily have fled entirely, but for the punishment that would fall on their families inside the city from the tyrants. He explains, with who knows what levels of irony, that the captives' "resisting out of necessity" prompted Titus to crucify them – or gave him a needed pretext (*War* 5.449). Titus' message to those watching from the walls was altogether too complicated: They should surrender because *if he were forced to take them prisoner*, this is what would befall them too. The more obvious lesson was of course that Rome was killing Judaeans. Exploiting that, the rebel leaders in the city were able to remove desertion from the horizon of hope, because the besieged felt they had no alternative but to fight to the death (*War* 5.449–55). Similarly Titus' later generous decision to transfer elite deserters to the countryside invited the surmise that he had callously done away with them (6.116).

In balancing the flow of deserters from both sides, Dio's epitomator gives different motives to each side. The bold Judaeans, he says, had no intention of actually surrendering. They pretended to do so only to get close to the enemy, so as to destroy their supplies, pollute their water, and/or kill them. Titus therefore stopped accepting deserters, according to this author (65.5.1–3). Such a picture might have supported Josephus' theme of Judaean resourcefulness, evoking Hannibal's fake deserters at Cannae (Appian, *Hist. rom.* 7.22–23), but he has nothing like it. The visceral outrage that bogus desertion inspires and the dire consequences for sincere deserters are well known from all periods of warfare.[197] Perhaps Josephus considered it morally counterproductive to write that Judaean men would fake surrender – in light of the suspicion of treachery that he says clung to him personally in the Roman camp (*Life* 416).

He does portray some surrender-related ruses, but these are in the vein of possibly admirable, possibly humorous clever tricks. Some besieged rebels

---

[196] Napoleon reportedly shot and bayoneted 2,000 or more Turkish soldiers captured at Jaffa (1799): "To dismiss them was to furnish the enemy with certain recruits; and to detain them was to keep useless mouths" (Lanfrey 1886: 1.289–90).

[197] E.g., Burleigh 2010: 380–81.

release through one of Jerusalem's gates a group pretending that they were the only committed fighters remaining and so have been expelled from a city now eager to surrender. Judaeans on the ramparts play Oscar-winning supporting roles, hurling rocks and abuse at these men while pleading with the Romans to enter quickly. Titus, rightly suspicious, orders his men to stand fast. Some officers, however, characteristically disobey him and surge forward, straight into an ambush. Titus is furious while the Judaeans are jubilant at their easy manipulation of naïve Romans (5.109–29). But Titus can also be fooled (cf. Chapter 2). When his troops approach the wall with a battering ram, some Judaeans who have positioned themselves nearby jump out with arms out-stretched, begging for clemency. Josephus remarks that poor simple Titus trusted them (5.319). But when an earlier Judaean deserter steps forward to welcome his brothers, these actors hurl a boulder at him (*War* 5.317–30). Titus can only respond with one of his pointless "Why, I oughtta . . .! No more Mr. Nice Guy!" declarations.

CONCLUSIONS

We have not yet begun our specific inquiries into the Judaean War, which begin in the next chapter. My aim in these three chapters has been to offer frameworks that will help to refine the problems underlying the following investigations, to understand the relevant evidence, and to imagine the scenarios that might have produced the survivals. This contextualization has involved becoming acquainted with our main narrative source in its historical situation and, in this chapter, thinking about the nature of warfare in first-century Judaea.

We have assumed only what is undeniable: that some Judaeans fought Roman legions to the death. Many refused to leave Jerusalem and some aggressively defended it when it was besieged by Titus' army. We have probed various considerations that might have come into play and affected morale on both sides: the distant prospect of major external assistance, hunger and disease, internal conflict, inducements to surrender, and the prevention of desertion.

We have yet to consider how it was that so many Judaeans found themselves committed to defying Rome's armies in the final siege of Jerusalem, or how legions came to be in conflict with Judaea in the first place. To these questions we now turn, beginning with the causes of the conflict and the surprising evolution of a Roman-Judaean antagonism.

PART TWO

Investigations

CHAPTER FOUR

WHY DID THEY DO IT?
Antecedents, circumstances, and "causes" of the revolt

States should not start wars that they are certain to lose, of course, but it is hard to predict with a high degree of certainty how wars will turn out.

John J. Mearsheimer[1]

When ancient Jewish and Christian writers discussed the Judaean War in retrospect, their interests tended to be theological: "*Why did God allow* (or cause) his house to be destroyed? What help does biblical tradition offer in understanding the catastrophe?"[2] Josephus shared those concerns, but fortunately for us, he historicized the problem by marrying cosmic drama with concrete personalities, incidents, and situations (Chapter 2). His account leaves countless loose ends, to be sure, and inexhaustible food for thought. One simple question that he does not pose in a systematic way, although he narrates much relevant material, is: Why and how did this war begin?

In this chapter we re-examine the war's beginnings, as a foundation for the rest of our inquiry. We should not assume that early grievances remained the same throughout, but having an idea about how Judaeans came into lethal conflict with Rome's legions will help us to understand later developments.

In exploring the war's causes, we need to avoid seductively simplistic paths. Because Rome and Judaea ended up at war, it has usually seemed obvious that

---

[1] Mearsheimer 2001: 211.
[2] So *4 Ezra* and *2 Baruch* at the end of the first century, and the later rabbinic reflections in *b. Shabb.* 119b; *Yom.* 9b.

the Judaeans must have had serious grounds for complaint. For such a humble David to have taken on such a Goliath, these grievances must have become intolerable and finally popped the cork of rational restraint. In 1893 the eminent Heinrich Graetz put it thus:

> In their native land, and especially in Jerusalem, the yoke of the Romans weighed heavily on the Judaeans, and became daily more oppressive. . . . The last decades exhibit the nation as a captive who, continually tormented and goaded on by his jailer, tugs at his fetters, with the strength of despair, until he wrenches them asunder.[3]

Although scholars have refined their explanations in countless ways, this picture has remained more or less intact. Leading military historians take it for granted that: "Judaea caused incessant trouble to the Romans. . . . The people defended their religious identity and culture from the efforts of provincial authorities to impose Greek and Roman culture. . . ."[4] The image of a Judaea seething with anti-Roman fervour has filtered out from scholarship into the best-researched novels and films, from Lew Wallace's *Ben-Hur: A Tale of the Christ* (1880) to Monty Python's *Life of Brian* (1979), Boris Sagal's *Masada* (1981), Mel Gibson's *The Passion of the Christ* (2004), and the television series *Rome* (2005). Who does not *know* that Judaeans, devoted to worshiping their God and following his Law in their land, could not abide Roman rule?

Although Roman legions undeniably came into lethal contact with Judaeans, deducing origins from outcomes is a well-known historian's fallacy.[5] I shall propose rather that the beginnings of this war had little to do with long-term antagonism. The great power favoured Jerusalem as regional broker of its *imperium*, and Judaean leaders turned habitually to Rome for support, nearly always with success.[6] Judaea's real, and finally existential threats, were local. When Rome proved an unreliable protector of its interests, late in Nero's reign, Judaeans predictably resorted to armed self-help – against the neighbours. Because Rome demanded a monopoly on armed force, and Judaea's most virulent enemies were protected as auxiliary forces of the empire, when the Roman legate in Syria finally intervened, he had no choice but to act against those Judaeans who had taken up arms. Even still, his pacification measures were narrowly limited. But it is not possible to control the outcome of armed interventions, and one thing led to another.

As always, my purpose is not to advocate a single, exclusive truth about the war's causes, but to invite the reader to think with me about the evidence and its plausible explanations. The inquiry is the thing (Chapter 2). Any

---

[3] Graetz 1949 [1893]: 2.233.
[4] Dąbrowa 1993: 9. Cf. Isaac 1992: 55: "[I]t is usually agreed, Rome encountered an unparalleled scale of continuous opposition."
[5] See Fischer 1970; Taylor 1979.   [6] For examples, see McKechnie 2005.

reconstruction will have little traction without context: In scholars' explanations of the war, a review of the second volume of Josephus' *War* and its *Antiquities* parallels, analogies from other times and places, Rome's tendencies and preferences, and the identity of the *Judaea* that revolted. In the available space we can only sprint through these fields as we collect perspectives for an adequate picture of the war's origins.

I. SCHOLARS' EXPLANATIONS

With Graetz, older scholarship assumed that there must have been an innate national-religious conflict between Judaea and Rome, spearheaded by a "zealot" movement in Jerusalem, which perhaps wished to keep the Holy Land free of foreign idolaters and polluters.[7] Emil Schürer entrenched this view in his influential and oft-revised *Textbook (Lehrbuch) of New Testament Background History* (1874). Unlike King Herod and his sons, he proposed, the Romans lacked understanding of Jewish sensibilities. That is why the transition to direct Roman administration in A.D. 6 created tensions that would prove unbearable: "[I]t was almost only a question of time as to when this inner contradiction would ignite."[8]

A noteworthy exception to this trend was the Victorian writer, Protestant-Orange crusader, and proto-feminist Charlotte Elizabeth. Simply from reading Josephus, she concluded that Nero sent the Flavians into Judaea because of a specific crime: the massacre of the auxiliary garrison in Jerusalem. But even that was "an act into which the Jews were goaded by the really unprovoked wrongs and cruelties inflicted on them by the savage Roman procurator, Gessius Florus." Florus "pursued an undeviating course of treachery, cruelty, and murder against the people committed to his charge." They, after making every effort to conciliate him and crying out for Roman protection, finally agreed with the priest Eleazar's decision to declare war on Rome by halting the daily sacrifice for the emperor.[9] It is remarkable that Elizabeth considered this Josephus' account, for recent scholars have made similar claims about *the historical reality* while suggesting that they are liberating us from Josephus' very different account. These disparate perceptions reinforce the need to think carefully about what he actually says (Chapter 2 and later). Elizabeth blotted her copy by going on to explain Florus' misdeeds as the work of Satan. But she was onto something, and her insights have been largely neglected.

---

[7] E.g., Graetz 1949: 234 ("not merely for liberty . . . but had likewise a religious character"); Bentwich 1914: 11–36 ("a struggle for national liberty . . . an episode in the more vital conflict between Hebraism and paganism"); Laqueur 1920: 251 ("brewing persistently, and the battles between Jews and Romans did not cease"). Smith 1971 is a learned and entertaining review of key scholars.

[8] Schürer 1874: 249.   [9] Elizabeth 1845: 18–22.

The post–World War II generation of scholars, while generally assuming the old picture of growing conflict, brought considerable refinement to their analyses. A 1949 Cambridge seminar inspired W. R. Farmer to inspect parallels between Hasmonean and Roman-period zealotry, a connection that had only been cursorily noted.[10] His resulting 1956 monograph strengthened the picture of deep Judaean-Roman opposition by rooting it in the self-understanding of the Hasmoneans two centuries earlier, who had thrown off the menace of Seleucid rule (167–164 B.C.).[11] First-century Judaeans, Farmer argued, looked to these forebears for inspiration. Although the revolt of 66 proved unsuccessful, it was the expression of an "age-old Jewish nationalism, . . . which in the Maccabean period reached heights never attained before or since."[12]

Soon after Farmer's monograph came M. Hengel's *Die Zeloten* (1961), which deepened and broadened the same path.[13] Adding teutonic tonnage in documentation with many small insights, Hengel charted the pulse of a "Jewish freedom movement," which appeared variously as the Fourth Philosophy, the Zealot movement, and the *sicarii*. These were all heirs of the Bible's call for *zeal for the Torah* and the exclusive lordship of God, paradigmatically realized in the biblical character Phineas and later embodied by the Hasmoneans. This ongoing resistance movement of the Hellenistic-Roman period finally launched a holy war in 66.

Having recovered what they considered the truth about Jewish motives in the war, Farmer and Hengel characterized Josephus as a serial obfuscator. Although he must have known the truth, they said, he took every opportunity to deny the rebels of 66 a noble heritage, ascribing their motives only to the basest criminality if not madness.[14]

The combined impact of Farmer and Hengel on scholarship was considerable, especially after the latter's translation into English (1989).[15] In 1970 S. G. F. Brandon considered it accepted wisdom that:[16]

> From the first imposition of Roman rule in A.D. 6, Jewish reaction had been adverse. . . . For subjection to Rome affronted the most cherished belief of their religion: that they were the Chosen People of their god Yahweh, who had given to them their Holy Land as their unique heritage. The only polity that could be consistent with this faith was a theocracy, in which Israel would be ruled for Yahweh by a godly high priest. . . . This ideal had been proclaimed in A.D. 6 by Judas of Galilee, the founder of Zealotism.

For these authors and many others, therefore, the revolt began *in principle* in A.D. 6. All that really changed in 66 was that the Zealot impulse found an

---

[10] See Smith 1971: 1–5 for an expert survey of earlier work.   [11] Farmer 1956: 8.
[12] Farmer 1956: 12.   [13] Cf. Goodman 1987: 11–16, 76–108.   [14] Farmer 1956: 11–23.
[15] See R. Deines' review of Hengel's impact in Hengel 2011: 403–48.   [16] Brandon 1970: 38.

effective champion in Eleazar, a priest finally willing to declare war on Rome.[17]

We lack the space to review the many international contributions from this viewpoint.[18] Two German studies go farthest. E. Baltrusch's monograph on the "conflict-filled history" of Roman-Judaean relations argues that the whole Judaean worldview, forged in the return from Exile, required that religious and political autonomy go hand in hand. This could have no conclusion other than war with a power such as Rome.[19] M. Bernett extends Baltrusch's approach into the imperial period by arguing that Judaea's rejection of the putative demands of imperial cult, a problem delayed but not solved by Herod's finessing, could only have led to war.[20]

The systemic character of these approaches is clear in their treatment of Judas of Galilee, famous for leading an abortive revolt in A.D. 6. For most scholars who share this perspective, the slogan that Josephus attributes to Judas – "No ruler but God!" – truly captures the core issue: Judaism could not tolerate submission to foreign (or any human?) rule.[21] In a Hegelian sense, Judas embodied the spirit (*Geist*) of his time and *Volk*. Whereas Josephus' *War* includes only three or four sentence fragments about Judas, and *Antiquities* a few more, Hengel wrote a chapter of fifty-five pages about the man, building the character from the *Geist*.[22]

This ideologically grounded thesis of holy zeal found its antithesis in studies that highlighted instead material, socioeconomic conditions as the war's chief causes. A comprehensive answer to the West German idealist Hengel came from the East German H. Kreissig. His book, *The Social Relations of the Judaean War: Classes and Class Struggle* (1970), found its data chiefly in the Talmud, secondarily in Josephus and other post-biblical literature. Kreissig used these on a *longue-durée* basis to identify Lenin's economic classes and class struggle in Roman Judaea.[23] Although such an explicitly Marxist construction (and in German) found little uptake, economic and sociological explanations of the war would proliferate from that period.[24] In recent decades, purely theological

---

[17] Brandon 1970: 38–39.

[18] E.g., Bohrmann 1989: 280 ("antagonism between ideologies," "clash of their two cultures"); Hadas-Lebel 2006: 21.

[19] Baltrusch 2002. That his analysis more or less ends in 55 B.C. (125–47) shows the degree to which he considers long-term structural conditions, and no single events or personalities, the cause of the eventual war (149–57).

[20] Bernett 2007: 310–51.   [21] *War* 2.118, 433; 7.323, 410 (cf. 7.418–19); *Ant.* 18.4–10.

[22] Hengel 2011: 93–149; cf. Farmer 1956: 24–40, 67–69.

[23] Kreissig 1970: 17–87; esp. 54–55, 73, 80–82 (classes defined in relation to the means of production).

[24] Notably Brunt 1977 (an inventory of socioeconomic indicators in Josephus, which was a new perspective in English-language scholarship); Faulkner 2004 (a rarely comprehensive study of the war on quasi-Marxist premises).

constructions have mostly faded or fused with social issues in a new synthesis, which tends to be driven by the social-economic engine.

The most influential work in this vein is in a series of studies by the New Testament scholar R. A. Horsley. He has applied E. Hobsbawm's research on social banditry to ancient Judaea and Galilee, translating what Josephus excoriated as out-and-out "banditry" into a common sociological response to imperial imposition. For Horsley, "the Jewish revolt against Roman domination may be the most vivid and best attested example from Antiquity of a major peasant revolt preceded and partly led by brigands."[25] More generally:

> The lifetime of Jesus and his followers was framed historically by widespread popular revolts against both the Romans and their client rulers. . . . Again thirty-some years after Jesus' mission, after multiple provocations by insensitive or arrogant Roman governors and predatory practices of the high-priestly families, widespread revolt erupted.[26]

Notice Horsley's alignment of Romans, client rulers, and priestly aristocrats over against the common people and Jesus, a widely accepted association that is open to doubt (below).[27]

Although Horsley's conception of a Robin-Hood sort of banditry in Galilee and Judaea has not fared well among historians, because of doubts about its plausibility in ancient agrarian conditions,[28] his emphasis on social realia over against purely theological-exegetical motives has become indispensable to the field. The point is accepted even by the editor of Hengel's posthumously revised work.[29]

A landmark study by D. M. Rhoads in 1976 fused the ideological and material issues. Rhoads argued that in the ancient world "religious" issues were inextricable from political, social, and economic conditions. He insisted that it was this amalgam of oppression, for which Judaeans held Rome responsible through their own elite class, that caused the war. Rhoads also complicated the standard picture of steadily building tensions. Because the central issues were not purely ideological, they could be managed pragmatically and often were. Under Pilate in the 20s, Judaean resistance was peaceful and issued in successful diplomacy. After King Agrippa's death in 44, however, violent Judaean reactions to the incompetence or venality of Roman officials raised the stakes to deadly levels. Rhoads thus rejected monochromatic explanations

---

[25] Horsley 1979a: 61. Cf. Hobsbawm 1972.

[26] Horsley 2008: 81; cf. Horsley 1979b, 2003; with Horsley and Hanson 1988.

[27] So already Graetz 1949 [1893]: 2.234–36 (Herodians as the worst examples of the pro-Roman immorality affecting "aristocratic families" and eschewed by "the wise and vigilant among the nation").

[28] Contextualization and exigent critique are in Blumell 2008, which in part applies the seminal study by Shaw 1984. Horsley is an ongoing negative foil for Grünewald 2004: 11–13, 92–106.

[29] Deines in Hengel 2011: 446.

and introduced much welcome nuance. But he still assumed that the irritants – however one should label them precisely – were bilateral between Judaea and Rome.[30]

Two distinguished studies of the 1980s pursued Roman-Judaean relations in still newer ways. T. Rajak devoted a chapter of her 1983 classic on Josephus to his "Account of the Breakdown of Consensus."[31] The consensus in question was between the Jerusalem elite and Roman officials, which in her view depended on the Judaean leaders' ability to control their people. Understanding the breakdown of this consensus to be a theme in Josephus, Rajak tracked his account in *War* – while quietly smuggling in important material from *Antiquities*. She pronounced his account of the breakdown basically valid, with corrections needed mainly for his failure to register the failings of his own elite class.[32] She found him to be blaming the war on a combination of bad Roman officials and the Jews who responded unwisely to their provocations.

Rajak is surely correct that communication between Jerusalem's elite and Rome broke down. Her proposal that Josephus thematizes this breakdown in *War* presents difficulties, however. Does her inclusion of so much material from *Antiquities* not put this in question?

In his first important monograph of two on our subject (1987), Martin Goodman largely agreed with Rajak about Josephus' portrait of growing bilateral tensions, but he considered that account *unreliable* because of its lack of attention to the ruling class, a point Rajak had noted but Goodman took to be crucial. After reviewing seven causes for the war offered by historians – governors' incompetence, oppressive Roman rule (in taxation especially), Jewish religious sensitivity, a freedom movement with messianic expectations, culture-conflict with Hellenism, class tension, or trouble with the neighbouring populations – he found them all wanting.[33] In part this was because such explanations assumed a unified Jewish outlook, whereas the *varieties* of Judaism (s) had come to the fore in scholarship of the 1980s. More importantly, Goodman argued that such longstanding irritants could not explain the outbreak of revolt *in 66* or the absence of revolt in other provinces facing similar indignities. Why Judaea, and why 66?

Looking for specific triggers, Goodman turned to what he saw as a uniquely artificial and incompetent ruling class in Judaea, which lacked the established position of its counterparts in other provinces because Herod had destroyed the ancient aristocracy. This newer, half-baked elite would struggle and finally bring the house down under the particular stresses in the 60s. Deprived of popular support because of their fealty to Rome, and of Roman support because of their inability to control the populace, in desperation they threw

---

[30] Rhoads 1976: 1.   [31] Rajak 1983: 65–77.
[32] Rajak 1983: 65 ("this very theme"), 75–77.   [33] Goodman 1987: 5–25.

in their lot with popular sentiment and led the revolt as a last-ditch effort to recover legitimacy. In a sense their revolt ended up being comparable to those in other provinces, which tended to be led by aristocracies or parts thereof.[34] Josephus is guilty of obscuring the war's real causes. In blaming a few nasty types, he misleadingly exonerates his class and himself.

In contrast to the general tendency of scholarship to seek systemic explanations, whether ideological or material, Goodman shows a historicist's interest in particular. For him it is pointless to speak of *the high priests* or *the aristocracy* without specifying which families, at which times, and in what situations. His handling of Judas of Galilee in A.D. 6 is revealing. Against the tendency to see Judas to be the embodiment of the zealot spirit, Goodman asks for evidence of this particular man's influence. Finding none, but still accepting Josephus' description of the "No ruler but God!" motto, he concludes that Judas must have been a mere curiosity in his time, and not the founder of a potent school. He taught an impractical anarchy, which had no impact.[35] We shall return to Judas.

An important contribution in a similar vein was James McLaren's *Turbulent Times?* (1998). He was concerned to free scholars from the iron grip of what he took to be Josephus' portrait of a gathering storm that led to war. In sharp contrast to Charlotte Elizabeth's reading, he thought that scholars had been seduced by Josephus in this regard, with the result that:

> Judaea is almost exclusively portrayed as being a place of intensifying turmoil throughout the first century CE. Conflict between Jews and Romans, among Jews and between Jews and Syrian-Greeks continued to escalate until the inevitable explosion came in 66 CE with the Jewish revolt.[36]

Josephus could only have come up with such a (putative) view in hindsight, McLaren argues. In real time, the events he mentions on the road to war each had its own context and potential. They were not yet part of a causal narrative, and no one could have seen what was coming. As a "trailer" to this argument, McLaren selects three episodes as case studies. He wants to exploit their potential when read by their internal logic, freed of Josephus' colouring.[37] At the same time he hopes to show that Josephus' (putative) interpretation is implausible.[38]

---

[34] Goodman 1987: 165–68, 231–51. Compare Goodman's own summary in Berlin and Overman 2002: 17.

[35] Goodman 1987: 93–96.   [36] McLaren 1998: 128.   [37] McLaren 1998: 68–126.

[38] McLaren 1998: 264–88 (288: "[T]he actual situation in the three incidents examined differs quite substantially from how Josephus has directed his readers to understand what is happening").

McLaren makes a valuable contribution by highlighting, for our field, what D. H. Fischer has in general labelled *the* historian's fallacy: freighting events with meanings that are only possible in hindsight.[39] His constructive proposals are harder to follow, however, because the case studies are still excerpts from Josephus' narrative, not freestanding or neutral reports. When we try to make sense of them "on their own," it is like trying to make independent sense of clips from a film such as Ridley Scott's *Gladiator*.[40]

The last study I shall mention in this survey is Goodman's magisterial *Rome and Jerusalem* (2007), which goes even farther in the historicist direction. In spite of the subtitle ("the clash of ancient civilizations"), Goodman emphasizes that systemic cultural or religious differences between Rome and Jerusalem *could not* have generated war. Rather, "a series of incidents, none particularly serious in itself," led to a rupture of trust between the Judaean elite and the Roman governor, Gessius Florus. When the crisis came, Jerusalem's leadership broke into two camps: one abandoning the city to its fate, the other, including an initially defiant Josephus and the chief priest Eleazar, choosing war. Until Cestius' intervention in late 66, Rome's responses were in the nature of police actions. But once Cestius had lost legionaries to a Judaean ambush, both sides knew that war was on. From that point until Jerusalem's fall in 70, Goodman proposes, Judaea was an independent rebel state.[41] Finally, the political needs of Vespasian and Titus, who took control of the conflict after Cestius and quashed the revolt, elevated the conflict to the status of a monumental war.

As will be clear from Chapter 1, I agree independently with much of Goodman's refreshing approach. He and McLaren are surely right to ask that we understand events as they looked when they were happening. A basic question that remains open, however, is: Where did the energy that propelled such bold Judaean actions, eventually attracting harsh Roman reprisals, *come from*? Florus' behaviour by itself does not provide a satisfactory answer, unless Elizabeth were correct that he was possessed by Satan. As Agrippa's speech points out, the procurator would soon be replaced. Why not wait him out, as the Judaeans had tolerated Ventidius Cumanus?

For significant numbers of Judaeans to expel their king and massacre both an auxiliary garrison and much of a legion, they must have considered their situation extreme in some ways. If armed self-help seemed the only possible

---

[39] Fischer 1970: 209–12; cf. 177–78 (the identity fallacy).

[40] McLaren gives the impression that these are freestanding events available to the historian by (a) intermingling passages from *War* and *Antiquities-Life* and (b) linking them with the *year 66* rather than with a narrative (1998: 21–22, 261, 264–68, 286). He never clearly addresses the problem that they are in fact parts of Josephus' narrative, included and structured and composed to serve their narratives, as scenes in a film.

[41] Goodman 2007: 422–45. On the notion of an independent state see also Goodblatt 2006: 121–39.

recourse to many, in spite of its manifest dangers, the situation must have been dire. The best explanation of these choices, I shall argue, lies in the combination of deep regional resentments, the new failure of Roman officials to protect Judaeans, and the underlying assumption of what we now call "realist" assumptions about the interactions of nations.

In the proposals canvassed earlier, two assumptions have remained almost completely stable. The first is that the war's principal cause was a failure of bilateral Judaean-Roman relations – even with Goodman and McLaren, the final breakdown is between these two sides. The second assumption is that, however the truth about the war's origins should be described precisely, Josephus obscured it while seeking to exculpate himself, his class, and the Judaean populace. In Chapter 2 I offered initial reasons to doubt this understanding of Josephus' *War*. Here I shall focus on Books 1 and 2 in an effort to clarify what Josephus does and does not say about the origins of the conflict before returning to the historical question: How did Judaeans end up at war with Rome?

II. JOSEPHUS' *WAR* 1–2: A CLOSER LOOK

A younger version of me supported the consensus view that Josephus furnished *War* with what amounts to a thesis statement on the conflict's origins (1.10–12):[42]

> That *domestic civil strife* (στάσις οἰκεία) brought it down, and that *the Judaean tyrants* drew both the Romans' unwilling hands and the fire upon the shrine, Titus Caesar – the very one who destroyed it – is witness. Toward the populace, kept under guard by the insurgents, he showed pity throughout the entire war; and often … gave opportunity even during the siege for a change of mind *on the part of those responsible*. Now in case anyone should haul us up for what we say, *accusing the tyrants and their bandit bloc*, or for our groaning over the misfortunes of our native place, let him grant indulgence … *Since no foreigner* was the cause of these things, it was not possible to keep control over one's lamentations.

This has seemed to many readers a covering statement for the whole work. Thus Farmer: "But whatever the Romans did to help bring on the war, Josephus is careful to make clear that the responsibility rests ultimately upon the shoulders of *the seditious elements among the Jews*."[43] And Rhoads: "Josephus defended Judaism in *The Jewish War* by placing the blame for the war *not on the whole nation but on those misguided revolutionaries* among the Jews who had

---

[42] Mason 1991: 64–65 ("Thus the paragraph §§ 9–12 constitutes something like a 'thesis statement' for *War*"); cf. 67.

[43] Farmer 1956: 14, my emphasis.

instigated the war. . . ."[44] Also Rajak: "His interpretation of the war, as far as he has one, is that a rift between Jews and Romans had been opened by *bad governors and was widened by various criminal or reckless types* among the Jews themselves. . . ."[45] McLaren similarly takes this passage to explain "why the war took place," and grounds his understanding of Josephus' view here: "What happened in 70 CE was inevitable. The events narrated are explained as part of the process which culminated with *God punishing the 'godless' generation*."[46] Goodman places particular weight on Josephus' putative thesis and uses it as a criterion to push against:

> Josephus' declared intention was to explain the outbreak and course of the war from 66 to 70. . . . Far from omitting causes of conflict, he might be expected to make as much as he could of all the cases he could conceivably cite. . . . [T]he reason he could not describe any more blatantly revolutionary behaviour *to support his picture of a decline into war* was that no such revolutionary behaviour occurred. In fact, once *Josephus' historiographical purpose* is recognized, what is striking is how little specific evidence he could cite of Jewish hostility to Rome before 66.[47]

But what if we are labouring under a misapprehension, and the reason *we* discover a series of disconnected events rather than a linear descent into war in Josephus, is that this is what Josephus intended to say?

Subsequent research has persuaded me that complex histories do not have essay-like theses (Chapter 2). In this passage, the "it" that was brought down by the tyrants is clearly *Jerusalem* with its temple, and the "tyrants" in question are those responsible for that catastrophe, namely Eleazar, John, and Simon. But these men become prominent only from Book 4. The preface is here anticipating *War*'s climactic volumes, concerning the *stasis* and the siege, which are indeed full of the terror and violence it mentions. Books 1 and 2, by contrast, where Josephus explores the war's deep background, are a tyrant-free zone.[48] They have a different feel from the unrelenting misery of the later volumes, which emerges after the narrative fulcrum in the middle of Book 4.

---

[44] Rhoads 1976: 12, 56, 175, my emphasis.

[45] Rajak 1983: 78, my emphasis. Cf. 107: the "dynamic element" in *War* "is the civil conflict between zealots (in the broad sense) and the rest of the population"; 79–82 (on the importance of the preface as interpretative key); 83 ("three main points": Rebels are cruel, sinful, and divisive, the last being "the most crucial to the argument of the *Jewish War* as a whole"). Elsewhere, however, Rajak hints at the unconnected and episodic nature of the narrative: 116 ("as though by chance").

[46] McLaren 1998: 80, 88, my emphasis.

[47] Goodman 1987: 412–13 (emphasis mine); cf. 413: "Josephus' description, in the second book of his *Jewish War*, of a society heading inexorably to its doom."

[48] "Tyrant" (τύραννος) and cognates appear seventy-two times in *War*: five in the preface, looking ahead to the latter half; eight in the lengthy Book 1, although not speaking of Judaeans (except abstractly in 1.202); fourteen in Book 2; zero in Book 3. The vast majority

It is worth reminding ourselves of what is in these important opening volumes. The story begins with Judaea in crisis. Ptolemies and Seleucids are contending for the part of Syria that includes Judaea. The Judaean nobility must choose sides, creating an immediate instance of programmatic civil discord (στάσις, 1.31–33). The Sixth Syrian War (169–168 B.C.) must be in view, because Josephus names Antiochus IV and Ptolemy VI as antagonists, although if so he is mistaken about the events.[49] Jerusalem had been under Seleucid control since about 200, whereas he implies that a siege to capture the city generated Antiochus' wrath when he finally took possession. That is why he threatened the *ethnos*' existence, forcing Judaeans to abandon their ancestral customs and assimilate to the Hellenistic culture (1.34). In *War*, this is the supposed crisis in which the Hasmonean family arises, fighting with brilliant success for national survival (1.36–37).

Josephus does not offer overt political analysis in Book 1, which includes many thematically relevant diversions but no arguments. Two broad movements deserve interest, however, by way of contextualizing the later war: (a) the steady expansion of Judaean territory under the Hasmoneans and Herod and (b) the political savvy shown by both.

(a) Because Josephus moves so rapidly through the Hasmonean succession, what he chooses to foreground and emphasize should attract our notice. Simon's reign he deems excellent (1.50) *because* of the many places he conquered. John Hyrcanus' enviable success (1.67) is again praised in terms of the *poleis* of Syria that he captured. Josephus gives particular attention to Samaria, pausing to comment on *Argarizein* (Mt. Gerizim), its temple, and the siege and destruction of the Samarian capital (1.64–65), along with the annexation of Idumaea in the south (1.62–64). In both content and tone this account highlights the vitality of the Hasmoneans and their rapid domination of the region, although in reality this was a decades-long process.[50] Even for Aristobulus' year-long tenure we

(45) fall in Books 4 to 7, all but three times indicating Judaeans and usually Simon and John – simply "*the* tyrants." Of the fourteen in Book 2, the first three are accusations against Herod (retrospectively) and Archelaus (84, 88), one a demurral by emperor Claudius (208), one an accusation against Florus (276) and one against Josephus (262); three are brief anticipations of the *later* tyranny of Eleazar of Masada (447), Eleazar ben Simon (564), and Simon bar Giora (652). That leaves five references to Judaean tyrants in Book 2. But two of these refer to the vanishing figures of Menachem (2.442, 448) and the Egyptian (262). The other two describe the situation under Albinus, where Josephus uses a tyrant simile for anonymous figures (2.275–76). *War* 1–3 thus has no significant or programmatic tyrants of the kind anticipated in the preface, who do weigh heavily on the latter half of the story.

[49] In the Sixth Syrian War Antiochus IV stopped Ptolemy's forces at the Egyptian-Palestinian frontier, whereas Josephus gives the impression that Jerusalem was in Ptolemaic hands until Antiochus IV took it by siege.

[50] Roman alliances: 1.38, 48. Achievement and success language (κατόρθωμα, εὐπραγία): 1.36–37, 39, 44, 50, 55, 66–67, 89. Failing Seleucids: 1.46–47, 65 *et passim*.

read incidentally of a military campaign in Galilee (1.76). Josephus' compact account of Alexander Jannaeus' reign is mainly devoted to his regional conquests (1.86–89, 103–105). Most Hasmonean acquisitions are removed by Pompey and Gabinius (1.155–57, 165–70), although Rome gradually returns them to Jerusalem's control under Antipater/Hyrcanus II and his son Herod (1.396–400).

(b) As for political agility, *War* I offers a dizzying ride. Like all good statesmen, these Judaean leaders are both quick to adapt and cool in handling surprises that come their way. The Hasmoneans Judas and Jonathan make it a priority to become treaty friends of Rome (1.38, 48),[51] while Jonathan does not scruple to take even the son of Antiochus IV as his ally (1.48). The Hasmoneans align with one Seleucid rival after another to improve their position, while carefully nurturing the prestigious (if practically useless) relationship with faraway Rome. None of this involves *ideological or programmatic affinity*, we see clearly. The sole criterion is the welfare of the nation.

Herod and his father show the same dexterity in spades. Against the background of Rome's bloody civil wars of the 40s and 30s B.C., they nimbly latch onto one Roman strong man after another, all the while steadily enlarging their power and Jerusalem's *chōra*.[52] Josephus dwells on the poignant scene in which Herod, recently the devoted ally of Marc Antony, effects a perilous transition to friendship with Antony's mortal enemy Octavian/Augustus (1.386–95). Josephus has a sophisticated take, in other words, on Judaea's greatest generation. Proudly tracing his own ancestry to the Hasmoneans (*Life* 1–6), and treasuring their conquest of neighbouring territory as proof of vigour and virtue, he stresses their political nous in achieving what is practical and dealing with any power that will enhance the nation's condition.

If we ask why Josephus should begin *War* with the long and complex Book 1, one reason must be that it lays out the contours of the regional situation behind the later war, beginning from the earliest contacts between Rome and Judaea. In this account the Judaeans quickly transform the region from one of mortal danger for themselves under Antiochus' rule from Antioch to one of Jerusalem's political dominance. Their brief humiliation after Pompey's arrival is fully redressed by the Judaean King Herod's unchallenged primacy. This gives substance to Josephus' observation in the preface (1.11) that Jerusalem had reached *the pinnacle of success* before its recent destruction. After the Hasmonean

---

[51] *War* 1.38, 48; contrast 1 Macc. 8.1–29; 14.24, 40.

[52] Herod and his father make agreements in turn with Pompey (*War* 1.127–31), Crassus (1.179), Pompey's enemy Julius Caesar (1.183), Caesar's assassin Cassius (1.218–220), Caesar's avenger Marc Antony, who arranged Herod's kingship (1.242), and finally Antony's mortal enemy Octavian, who would allegedly become Herod's closest friend in spite of the connection with Antony (1.386, 400) – to the benefit of Judaeans everywhere.

conquests and Herod's reign, Judaeans were by far the most populous and prestigious *ethnos* in southern Syria.

This pre-history carries its own implicit critique of the recent rebels. They tout Hasmonean precedents in their dreams of "freedom" but do the opposite of their great pragmatic forebears by turning inward and cutting Jerusalem off. Acting from irrational emotion and lacking either the smarts or the courage of their ancestors, they box themselves into besieged Jerusalem and drive their incomparably great *polis* into the ground.

The first sixth of Book 2 (1–116) takes up the succession hearings in Rome after Herod's death (4 B.C.). Obvious questions emerging here have to do with the Hasmonean-Herodian legacy. Having lost the towering figure of King Herod, what is next for Jerusalem? Josephus provides no answer but visits many related issues while observing the constantly changing modes of governance in the area. Augustus awards Archelaus a probationary ethnarchy in the Judaean heartland. Although this includes only the inland strip of Idumaea, Judaea, and Samaria plus coastal Joppa and Caesarea, the very young son of Herod makes a hash even of this. He manages to offend both his main constituents, Samarians and Judaeans, whose double-barreled appeal to Augustus persuades him to exile the young royal in A.D. 6 (*War* 2.111). What next?

Following is an overview of Josephus' narrative, representing the period from A.D. 6 to 66. I emphasize with italicized bold script those episodes that occupy ten or more Niese sections as a rough indicator of emphasis. There are large digressions on Judaea's philosophical schools (2.119–66) and the speech of Agrippa (2.345–406). They are entertaining and thematically relevant, the Essene "legion" providing a stunning example of Judaean masculine virtue and the speech displaying the statesman-author's command of political affairs. But they are digressions all the same, which require space by their nature, and not points of *narrative* emphasis.

117 Judaea becomes a Roman province. Brief mention of a disturbance led by the sophist Judas. [Digression on the schools, especially Essenes.]

167 Governments of Philip and Antipas; territories of Livia; accession of Tiberius.

169 Pilate, a procurator sent by Pilate: standards and aqueduct episodes with ensuing disturbances.

178 Agrippa and Antipas accuse each other before Tiberius and Gaius. Antipas exiled.

184 Mad Gaius' effort with the statues, thwarted by God and the legate Petronius.

204 Accession of Claudius through the skillful assistance of Judaean Agrippa I.

214 Agrippa I, allied monarch ruling grandfather Herod's territory, dies quickly.

220 Judaea a province again, enlarged though fragmented post-Agrippa. Its two first governors.

223 *Procurator Cumanus and the threats facing Judaeans.* Several incidents of Samarian aggression, as auxiliary soldiers and procurator align against Judaeans. Judaean vigilantes (under Eleazar b. Deinaeus) respond. Legate Quadratus intervenes. Claudius hears the case in Rome, young Agrippa II advising. Severely punishes Samarians, procurator, and auxiliary tribune.

247 Claudius puts Felix over Judaea, Samaria, Galilee, Peraea; enlarges Agrippa II's territory in the northeast; Claudius dies.

250 Insane Nero. In early years adjusts Herodian territories, giving Agrippa II significantly more (continuing Claudius' direction).

253 *Procurator Felix deals effectively with problems:* long-time bandits ravaging the countryside, urban knife-assassins, apocalyptic visionaries, Egyptian pseudoprophet who plans to become Jerusalem's tyrant, and a radical freedom group that kills and plunders Judaeans.

266 *Caesarea: civil strife* caused by *an effort* to make the *polis* Judaean.

271 In contrast to briefly mentioned Festus of admirable energy, procurator Albinus takes bribes while promoting banditry and local strongmen.

277 *Procurator Gessius Florus* in the vein of Albinus but much worse.

280 Legate Cestius Gallus from Antioch visits Jerusalem, hears complaints about Florus, and promises help.

284 *Caesarea II:* Nero's affirmation of its Greek character aggravates Judaeans and emboldens non-Judaeans. Ferocious fighting ensues. Florus takes payment from Judaeans in exchange for help but exacerbates problem.

293 *Gessius Florus II: outrages in Jerusalem.* Takes huge sums from the temple, violently suppresses protestors, sets up tribunal in the city; auxiliary soldiers exceed orders with violence and plunder, commit atrocities; Queen Berenice's life imperiled, her appeals disregarded. Florus tries to take still more from temple treasury but is thwarted by protesters and broken colonnades. As he withdraws, the populace demands and receives a change of garrison.

333 *All parties write to Cestius in Antioch, who sends a tribune with Agrippa II on a fact-finding visit.* The pair confirm Jerusalem's peaceful disposition *toward Rome* but hatred of Florus.

342 *The people demand an embassy to Nero to assure him of their fidelity* and to accuse Florus. Agrippa II cannot oblige them; instead gives brilliantly irrelevant speech *against war with Rome*. [Speech of King Agrippa II.] The king is driven from the city for his uselessness.

408 *Armed factions begin to form – to defend against auxiliary and Samarians – and some priests close the temple to foreign gifts and sacrifices.* This move denounced by elder priests and Pharisees, for the antisocial image of Judaea and because it is a dangerous insult to the emperor, the daily sacrifice for him being included in the boycott.

418 Jerusalem leaders appeal to Florus and Agrippa for immediate help against armed factions. Agrippa sends a cavalry troop, which briefly restores leaders' control. Leaders and cavalry are soon overwhelmed, however: hide in tunnels, Herodian palace, and Antonia.

430 Militants attack Antonia, kill auxiliaries, besiege palace. Terrified populace of Jerusalem *does not want soldiers massacred*; factionalism among militants, arms gathered from Herodian stores at Masada. Menachem's group kills Eleazar's father; Eleazar's group kills Menachem. Agrippa's (Judaean) troops released. Auxiliary garrison, pledged safety, is massacred on appearance – except its Roman prefect, who promises to Judaize.

457 Simultaneous massacre of Judaean minority in Caesarea. Widespread vigilante retaliations by Judaeans follow in "the Syrians' villages and adjacent *poleis*": Decapolis and coastal cities as far as Kedesa in Upper Galilee. Syrian *poleis* retaliate against Judaean minorities. Turmoil grips *all Syria*. Tragedy in Scythopolis. A few *poleis* do not harm their Judaean minorities.

481 Plot against Judaeans in Agrippa's kingdom while king is absent, by viceroy Noarus. Agrippa discovers it and removes the man.

484 Judaean militants seize Herodian desert fortresses from auxiliary (?) garrisons.

487 Long-time ethnic strife in Alexandria is ignited by Judaeans' intrusion in city's planning for embassy to Nero. Alexandrians kill three Judaean intruders. Judaeans gather fuel for a massive retaliation. (Judaean) governor Tiberius Alexander urges them to desist. They refuse and slander him; he unleashes two legions. Cestius Gallus decides to move into Judaea (see Chapter 5).

This overview prompts a few observations. First, Josephus' most consistent interest is political: Who was governing what and when? As a Polybian-style statesman-historian he describes the shifting political arrangements as fortune also makes her unpredictable moves. He illustrates each kind of governance with exemplary incidents.

Second, in southern Syria his interest is all but exclusively in Jerusalem's relationship with Caesarea and neighbouring cities. Although Galilee, Peraea, and Idumaea are largely Judaean in piety and demography, *they play no role* in these rising tensions.

Third, both scene (Judaea, Rome, Alexandria) and level of "zoom" constantly change. The prospect of a governing *thesis* is rendered all the more implausible by these constant shifts in angle and perspective.

Nevertheless, fourth, recurring thematic complexes have to do with (a) close ongoing cooperation between high Roman officials and Jerusalem's elite and (b) troubled relations between Judaeans and their neighbours.

Fifth, the legates based in Antioch are, to a man and to the end (including Cestius), concerned with maintaining good relations with Jerusalem and ensuring that the equestrian procurator does the same. This pattern briefly falters only under Quadratus with procurator Cumanus, whom Claudius punishes severely, before Nero's abominable agents Albinus and Florus.

Sixth, the most consistent aggravating factor in Jerusalem's environment is the Caesarea–auxiliary axis.

Undetectable in *War* 2, as far as I can see, is any hint of blameworthy rebel-tyrants among Judaeans or any significant anti-Roman feeling. Rather than assigning blame in such simple ways, the narrative seems designed to make the audience feel the dilemmas and paradoxes faced by Judaeans and their leaders. They are provoked (and who would not be?) when the auxiliaries tasked with law and order them rudely expose themselves with nasty insults above the crowd, in the courtyard of their sanctuary on the holiest festival days. Again, what would we expect to happen when Samarians murder Judaean pilgrims *en route* from Galilee, and the procurator not only fails to punish them but aggressively pursues Judaeans who retaliate? And why is Nero's man Florus allowed to behave with such gross disrespect even to Judaean royalty, while using his willing auxiliary as muscle to raid the temple? What is the legate Cestius' problem? He plainly cares about good relations with Jerusalem and has legions at his command, so why will he not intervene as his predecessors had done? Why is Nero so cold toward Jerusalem?

The story of Books 1 and 2 together is about a region always in potential crisis, because of inter-ethnic relations, and the struggles of *polis* leaders to keep control through quick thinking, letters, embassies, crowd-calming speeches, days of mourning, or ostentatious tokens of submission. *War* 2 shows people trying to go about their business while also acting out typical roles: Young men rush impulsively to action when humiliated, some dying in the process; elders urge restraint and attempt conciliation in spite of their humiliation and profound sorrow; women wail and mourn their losses while cradling orphaned children. The audience should feel the fear and pity and be distraught.

In contrast to what comes later, however, we are struck by the nearly complete absence of overt moralizing from our narrator. Josephus' detached-observer tone is evident right from the succession hearings (2.1–111). Judaean elders voice damning criticisms of Herod's violence (2.84–87). But should we believe them, because they are credible aristocrats, or not – because Josephus has narrated nothing like what they are claiming? He describes Archelaus as extremely careful to avoid wearing the diadem or making any royal-like decisions before Augustus has approved his kingship (2.2–13). Yet the prince's accusers tell Augustus that arrogant Archelaus has done precisely these things (2.26–32, 89–90). Who is right? We do not know and can only experience the tension.

The significance of the two matching Pilate episodes (2.169–77) has been much debated. But this, I suggest, is largely because Josephus refrains from moralizing. Pilate introduces standards at night and under special covers. Does he intend to aggravate the populace or the opposite? They respond with outrage, but is this justified by the act? He then builds an aqueduct for Jerusalem. Surely that is a good thing? For some reason not explained, the project exhausts the treasury. How did that come about, and was it his fault? Many Judaeans die protesting, but mainly from trampling each other. Both incidents occasion "great disturbances" in Josephus' dramatic world, but who was responsible? *We* want to know whether Pilate was a good or bad man, but our narrator is a worldly observer. His story is often all the more powerful because of his restraint. He repeatedly observes cases of missed communication with tragic consequences, but without knitting together any neat picture of moral blame and causation.[53]

Even while inviting his audience to feel the Judaeans' plight, Josephus does not present either his people as mere victims or the *poleis* around them as purely evil. Judaeans boldly try to alter the established Graeco-Roman identity (cf. 1.407–14) of Caesarea, igniting a predictably violent reaction. Josephus never explains their motives, but emphasizes that elders *on both sides* tried to restrain their youth (2.267). Who was in *the right*? He does not say. Violent Judaean raids against nearby Samarian villages that had no part in the murder of Judaeans, or against *poleis* that had no role in the Caesarean massacre similarly sit there without moral interpretation. Josephus does not criticize the Judaeans – one can understand their rage – nor does he justify their actions. His narrative suggests only that this is how people behave when they are outraged and threatened. Again, when the Judaeans of Alexandria attempt to incinerate everyone in the stadium after three of theirs are murdered, are they *right*? They react as people do, with neither praise or blame from Josephus. The closest Josephus comes to moralizing, perhaps, is with Simon of Scythopolis, who must pay an awful penalty for compatriot bloodshed (see Chapter 2). But even there the "curse" that Simon supposedly incurs is a tragic one, for the reader understands that he had little choice but to join other Scythopolitans in defending their *polis* from outside Judaean assaults.

My understanding of *War* 1–2, then, is along these lines. In trying to provide a responsible account of the recent war, against the claims of simple-minded Flavianist hacks (Chapter 2), Josephus traces Judaean-Roman relations to their origins. He describes with pride and detail the great national success and continuing prosperity Judaea has enjoyed as Rome's friend and ally, under leaders of great political skill. Book 2 shows that this bond has never

---

[53] Significant studies of Pilate include Kraeling 1942; Winter 1961: 41–51; Lémonon 1981; Krieger 1995, 1998; Bond 1998; Scheidgen 2002; Jaroés 2002; Taylor 2006, with Frova 1961; Schwartz 1992: 182–217; Alföldy 1999; Lönnqvist 2000 for dates and material evidence. Also relevant is the trunk full of studies of Jesus' trial, which usually give Pilate considerable attention.

disappeared; there is no steady "breakdown of consensus." Yet Rome's experiments in governance after Herod created a hazardous landscape for Jerusalem. Bad things happened in the city's relations with its neighbours. For the most part, wise legates in Syria with the aid of Judaean royals and an emperor such as Claudius kept things in check. Only during Nero's final years did things fall apart. This is something that an audience in Flavian Rome, where Nero's memory was hated, might understand.

Again, this summary does not reflect a *thesis* or a set of propositions on Josephus' part. I am trying to pull together some highlights and inclinations of a story that is chiefly designed to convey atmospheric richness through its recurring themes (Chapter 2).

Because I am about to make a historical case for the regional origins of the conflict, I must now stress the differences between that case and Josephus' narrative. I am not deducing this argument from his narrative. Nor do I suppose that if we could cross-examine Josephus, he would recognize much of what I am arguing. His interests and emphases – in tragic and fortune-related themes – were different. If he had wished to make the case that I shall offer, he could have explained much more clearly: the background to the Judaean initiative in Caesarea, which he declares important but does not explain (2.284); the nature of the auxiliary army; and the relationship between Judaea's local enemies and the auxiliary. *War* usually calls the auxiliary soldiers *Roman*.[54] That is not wrong, for they were part of the Roman system (Chapter 3), and actions against them were challenges to Rome's *ordo* and *imperium*. For his retrospective purposes it makes sense to highlight that side of the coin. But if *we* want to understand the thoughts and motives of Judaeans *at the time*, who acted against the auxiliary and went so far as to kill its Jerusalem cohort, we might pay attention to quite incidental remarks in *War* such as this: "the bulk of the Roman [= auxiliary] force there were recruited from Syria and so, just as one would expect of relatives, were eager to lend assistance [to local adversaries]" (2.268) – and also look for information and analogies elsewhere.

III. "IF I AM NOT FOR MYSELF...": ANCIENT REALISM AND REGIONALISM

To help us gain purchase on our historical questions, I propose that we review common ancient assumptions about inter-*ethnos/polis* relations. These anticipate a modern approach to international relations that today we would call *realist*. For us, however, realism is one stream of political thought, contrastable

---

[54] *War* 2.224, 262–63, 268, 296, 320, 326, 329, 408, 438, 450.

with alternatives we call liberal, internationalist, and idealist, as well as purely isolationist. Modern political realism includes a heavy theoretical component as it seeks to provide a basis for the foreign policy. I intend none of this by invoking the term. The ancients knew no alternative to what seemed the inexorable, grim, and tragic, laws of nature concerning the way peoples interacted. These ancient views remained the only ones available until institutions grounded in notions of international law were advanced as a consequence of World War I.

Presentations of similar material to academic audiences have made me cautious. I realize that I risk diversion into pointless discussions of the nature of realism today and *its* applicability to ancient conditions. But I would stubbornly suggest that attention to the *ancient* assumptions I am calling realist help us in at least three ways. First, even the oldest of us living in the West today has grown up with the language and values of universal/international human rights, justice, and law all around us. Our socialization in these modern values can obscure our reading of ancient evidence, which knew nothing of them. Second, laying aside modern scruples can help us to understand Judaean behaviour from the Hasmonean expansion to the revolt against Rome in a coherent way, without the need for exceptionalist ideological or economic superstructures proposed by some of the research reviewed earlier. Third, realism redirects our attention from ideas and ideals, about national Chosenness or an evil foreign empire, to the immediate threats on Judaea's doorstep, which are amply evidenced if we think to ask this question.

What gives (political) realism[55] its name is the core observation that certain *realities* are simply there, no matter what we prefer to think or hope. The harshest of these realities is that the nation (*ethnos*, *polis*, or *basileia*) provides the highest meaningful possibility of government (ἀρχή), law, and justice. Beyond that threshold can lie only *anarchy*, the absence of any meaningful government. No matter what values we may cherish in our internal legal and judicial systems, be they monarchic, aristocratic, democratic, we all face the same reality in dealing with other nations. No one can control those realities through laws or constitutions. Namely, each nation must attend to its own survival and well-being, because no one else will. Fear is the common and perpetual motivator, even for the strongest.[56] Security is best assured through the expansion of a nation's territory, wealth, military capability, and influence.

---

[55] Classic American realist studies are Niebuhr 1932, Morgenthau 1954, and Waltz 1979. Noteworthy recent contributions on the broader subject (among many) include Griffiths 1992, Beer 1996 (3–6 for a summary of principles), Donnelly 2000 (6–9: summarizing principles gleaned from many studies), Crawford 2000, Mearsheimer 2001, and Craig 2003.

[56] Mearsheimer comments on the conflict between Russia and the Ukraine (2014, my emphasis): "*Because there is no world government* to protect states from one another, major powers are acutely sensitive to threats – especially near their borders – and they sometimes act

Most of the time that will not be possible, and in such cases the nation's leaders must seize upon beneficial alliances. These are not ideological but based on advantage under current conditions and are therefore always changeable. Indeed, settling into a status quo is never a safe option. Each nation's leaders must constantly decide when to seek new friends and leave old ones (whose interests will have changed direction), embark on diplomatic initiatives, or take advantage of new chinks in a rival's armour. In the last resort, every nation that is unwilling to perish must be willing to resort to violent self-help or the credible threat of it.

The underlying logic begins from a perceived law of nature. Each individual has an imperative to survive and so will if necessary repel physical attackers with lethal force. Everyone has always recognized the right of self-defence. But humans are social creatures, the ancients accepted, who find the optimal conditions of a happy life in society. Society extends the principle of self-protection through the family and clan to the voluntary social unit of the *polis* and its dependent zones, or the *ethnos*.[57] In exchange for the huge communal benefits of a *polis*, members entrust much of their protection and well-being to shared laws, courts, and enforcement mechanisms. One need not live each day in mortal fear about food and protection, as an individual would in the wild, because the consent for interdependence and effective mechanisms of redress take away most of that daily concern. Even still, in exceptional situations of imminent threat, one is justified in resorting even to lethal self-help. All of that is clear up to the level of the *polis* or the notionally kinship-bound society.

Beyond the political community, however, there was in ancient perspective no realistic basis for meaningful government. Philosophers might have worked out that all human beings were divine sparks in material form or that there were such things as a true, natural, and universal justice realizable in individual characters and *polis* constitutions, but these ideas were best realized in the best kind of *polis* and could have little traction in the relations among *poleis*. Who could enforce justice between *poleis*? Everyone belonged to a family, *ethnos*, and *polis*, and these affiliations defined their identities. So there was no prospect of a judge on earth who would care equally for all. International government was an oxymoron. Given very different national characters and constitutions, moreover, which fascinated the ancients, the notion of a single *politeia* (citizenship and constitution) for all would have been absurd. Every nation had to face the reality that survival lay in its own hands.

---

ruthlessly to address potential dangers. *International law and human rights concerns take a back seat when vital security issues are at stake.*"

[57] See the first two books of *Republic* (*Politeia*)—NB: 1.339a (refuting Thrasymachus' idea that justice is indistinguishable from the *polis* government's advantage) and *Laws*; Books 1 and 3 of Aristotle's *Politics*.

What about empires? By Josephus' time everyone in civilization lived under one empire or another. How states dealt with Rome's growing empire is the theme of Polybius' great history (Chapter 2). He provides no simple answer, other than the imperative to deal with it. In realist terms, empire meant the great success of one *polis* (Rome) in dominating others with resulting strength and prosperity, hence the failure of the others to protect themselves. But prudent imperialists, realizing that mere domination created instability, gave selected elites among the subjects a stake in their project and couched their dominance in the language of *alliance* and *friendship*. Although the form of international law imposed by empires did not escape realist principles (it was not truly international; one nation called the shots), an empire such as Rome's nourished itself on the paradox that it could indeed provide a level of peace and security – albeit predicated on its own interests in stable revenue and the monopoly of force – they could never have achieved by trying to secure their own interests. There could be freedom, perhaps maximal freedom, in slavery. The subject peoples needed only to reconcile the situation with their own dignity, and Rome suggested that their leaders view themselves as Rome's *friends*, if it would make them feel better. In truth, it was not always a one-way street. If we think of Agrippa I's role in Claudius' accession (A.D. 41) or Agrippa II's assistance to Cestius and the Flavians, or his sister Berenice's love affair with Titus, it is clear that the prospect of actual friendship was possible, at least for a nation's highest elite.

So empire, although itself an expression of realist assumptions, also offered a kind of remedy for the plight that realism predicted. It is also an extreme illustration of the fact that realist assumptions about perpetual rivalry and suspicion did not mean that nations were in open conflict or actually fighting. Far from it. Everyone feared the destructive potential of war and political leaders worked assiduously to avoid it through nimble diplomacy. Where there was no empire, they talked constantly, seeking nonaggression pacts and alliances of mutual benefit. The Greek *poleis* had long before established traditions of hospitality toward visitors, truces for central games, resorting to third-party mediation, and ever-changing alliances as mechanisms for ameliorating the fearful conditions of unavoidable rivalry.[58] These mechanisms did not come close to modern institutions of international law and justice. Stronger powers exploited their ability to *compel* advantageous alliances, preferably without bloodshed, and the Romans innovated by extending their citizenship.[59] Realism does not mean fighting, then. It means, simply, that each nation must take care of its interests because no one else will and that this self-help will take whatever form is possible or necessary in the circumstances.

---

[58] See Bederman 2001 for elaboration of the measures, Eckstein 2006: 37–78 for qualifications.
[59] Eckstein 2006: 244–316.

Although there is reason to think that Thucydides lamented realism's grim logic, his *Peloponnesian War* continues to serve as the realist's Bible. It lucidly articulates realist positions, even if the author's purpose was to expose their perils and criticize Athens' realist behaviour.[60] At the heart of the war, he explains, was Sparta's *fear* of Athens' growing power (1.23.6). He has Corinthians chide Spartans for failing to respond energetically to regional changes (1.69–71), on the ground that any self-respecting *polis* must do this if it is to secure its own position. He portrays Athenians dismissing complaints about their power from the weak: Justice, schmustice, they say. No one ever cried "Justice!" who was able to impose his will (1.76; 5.89).[61] Justice becomes relevant only among powers of comparable strength, because one cannot control the other. In the famous dialogue between Athenians and Melians (5.86–11), Athens insists that Melos immediately submit to its domination, not least because of Athens' own *fear* of what will happen if other *poleis* think they can brush them off with impunity (5.91). Athens' emissaries reflect (5.105):

> Concerning the divine we accept the common opinion, but concerning humanity we know for a fact that it *is a necessity of nature* that, wherever they *can* dominate, they rule. We did not make this law .... Having found it already there, and expecting to leave it intact forever after us, we are merely using it now, knowing that you and others would do exactly the same thing – if you had the force that we have.

Polybius' later *Histories* are a manual of realism for Rome's empire, showing how Rome's *archē* grew to dominate the Mediterranean and how other *poleis* made their peace (or failed to do so) with this reality (1.1–4; 3.1–4).

Josephus and his audiences knew their Thucydides and Polybius. Josephus' cheery descriptions of Judaean-Hasmonean conquest and of Rome's arrival in the region with Pompey rest on the same assumptions. Judaea had its day in the sun, not very long ago, and will do so again. The speeches he writes for Agrippa and his own character do not sugar-coat Judaea's present "slavery" under Rome. On the contrary, they recognize "a firmly established law, as potent among animals as it is among humans: to give way to those who are stronger, and that domination belongs to those who are at their peak in arms."[62]

That these ideas were in the air is confirmed by a speech that Cassius Dio writes for Julius Caesar. When his officers are unable to summon the

---

[60] The key texts are collected in Brown, Nardin, and Rengger 2002: 34–60. Cf. Forde 1995; Crane 1998; Donnelly 2000: 6–42 (esp. 12); Boucher 1998; Freyberg-Inan 2004: 19–36. Thucydides' canonical role has been qualified or doubted (e.g., he does not present Athens as a model of political intelligence): cf. Ahrensdorf 1997; Lebow 2003: 65–178; Monten 2006. For our purpose, it is enough that he articulates realist ideas, to which there were no real alternatives before modern times.

[61] Thucydides 1.23.6, 69–71 (peace comes only through willingness to use power), 76 (cf. 5.89).

[62] *War* 2.355–57, 385; 5.364–67.

motivation to fight the Gaul Ariovistus, Caesar enjoins them not to think of
foreign relations as though they were private affairs in the *polis*, in which the
safest course would be to mind one's own business and defer to common
justice. It is completely different with external relations:

> A *polis*, at all events *one with ruling power*, would rapidly be undone by
> such a course. *These are laws established by nature herself*, not by human
> beings. They have always existed, they exist now, and they will exist as
> long as the race of mortals remains viable. With these things in mind,
> none of you should at this moment be thinking about what is personally
> agreeable and safe, but rather about *what is fitting and advantageous for all the
> Romans* (38.36.1–3).

It is easy to forget how recently, fitfully, and partially the West has embraced a
liberal discourse based on notions of international law and justice for the
weak.[63] Before World War I we find mostly enthusiastic articulations of realist
principles.[64] Although one might imagine that Christian thinkers would have
favoured universalist principles in view of its non-nationalist and cheek-
turning origins, and Anabaptists through Leo Tolstoy and beyond have taken
such positions, more often Christianity has accommodated itself to the realist
predicament of nation-states, perhaps most clearly in the "Christian realism" of
Reinhold Niebuhr. Francis Wayland (1796–1865), philosopher, pastor, and
president of Brown University argued that nations, like individuals, should
suffer wrong rather than fight, for "There is not a nation in Europe that could
be led on to war against a harmless, just, forgiving, and defenceless people."
Major-General Wager Halleck had no trouble dismantling Wayland's case
with an array of Christian, biblical, and natural-law arguments. Ultimately
he fell back on realist foundations: "But nations do not resort to tribunals, like
individuals, to settle their differences" – any such tribunals being mere vehicles
of powerful sponsors and affording no disinterested justice. Compare Lord
Acton's remark in a 1891 preface to Machiavelli's realist classic, *The Prince*
(1532): "Most successful public men ... approve Lord Grey's language to
Princess Lieven: 'I am a great lover of morality, public and private; but the
intercourse of nations cannot be strictly regulated by that rule.'"[65]

On the eve of World War I, British, French, German, and American writers
sounded remarkably similar in marrying realist principle with the new

---

[63] For an entertaining history of British realism see Meyer 2009.

[64] Halleck 1846: 1–83 (69–70). Halleck's critique may have had an effect, for Wayland came to
accept limited just war (cf. Murray 1891: 204 n. 1).

[65] Acton 1907: 219. Lord Charles Grey (Second Earl Grey, of tea fame) was Prime Minister
from 1830–1834. Dorothea Lieven, wife of the Russian ambassador in London (1812–1834),
was a notoriously influential princess, socialite, and unofficial diplomat. Acton's quotation
slyly alludes to her intimacy with Grey and others.

evolutionary science to conclude that healthy nations must look constantly for ways to expand, unavoidably at the expense of the less worthy. We like to blame the Germans for such views, and General Friedrich von Bernhardi provides fuel with his insistence that war was a "biological necessity" and part of the divine order.[66] But British Colonel F. N. Maude wrote in very similar tones: "Unless, as I believe, war is the divinely appointed means by which the environment may be readjusted until the ethically 'fittest' and 'best' become synonymous, the outlook for the human race is too pitiable for words."[67] Maude valued Christianity for inculcating the virtue of self-sacrifice for the community, even as he deplored mass education for encouraging young men to question this. In 1915 (before the United States entered the war) the U.S. Navy League's official publication expressed barely distinguishable views:

> There should be no doubt that even with all possible moral refinement it is the absolute right of a nation to live to its full intensity, to expand, to found colonies, to get richer and richer by any proper means such as armed conquest, commerce, diplomacy. Such expansion as an aim is an inalienable right and in the case of the United States it is a particular duty, because we are idealists . . .[68]

Only when the cost of pursuing naked national interests with horrifying means of mass killing became vivid on the battlefields of Belgium and France (ca. 1915–1917) did urgent pleas emerge to rethink the whole basis of international relations. While Stanford professor Edward Krehbiel published a hasty point-form conspectus of the horrors that realist thinking was producing in Europe, the Dutch jurist Daniel Josephus Jitta wrote a detailed case for an entirely new basis of international law, in which he gave legal grounds for viewing *humanity* as a single juridical constituency.[69] The institutions that eventually grew out of this kind of thinking, only after the further horrors of World War II,[70] reflected new ways of thinking hard won. Now many hoped for a truly international law passed by the world's constituencies, meaningful concepts of universal human rights, and enforceable global justice.

Even after the World Wars there was great skepticism of such transnational efforts because of the utter novelty of the concept, also because of fear that the

---

[66] Bernhardi wrote several popular works in 1911–1914 (1914a–c) to prepare Germans for coming conflicts. See 1914: 18–32 and 99: "We need not concern ourselves with any pacific protestations of English politicians, publicists, and Utopians, which, prompted by the exigencies of the moment, cannot alter *the real basis of affairs*"; also 103: "Since the struggle is, as appears on a thorough investigation of the international question, *necessary and inevitable*, we must fight it out, cost what it may."

[67] Maude 1907: 18. cf. vii, xiv, 20, 37, 105, 155, 168, 243–47.

[68] Navy League of the United States, *Seven Seas* 1915: 27–28.

[69] Krehbiel 1916: 227–55 (before America's entry into the war); Jitta 1919.

[70] van Creveld (2008: 158–59) sees 1948 as decisive, when the new UN finally outlawed the use of war to acquire territory, the norm since antiquity.

new Bolshevism sought to dissolve cherished national identities in global *class* conflict. The successful arguments of U.S. Senator Henry Cabot Lodge for keeping the United States out of President Wilson's League of Nations rested on realist principle. Only the United States could determine American interests, with which no foreigner could be entrusted.[71]

My point in recalling all this is that many of our ingrained sensibilities and categories such as international law and human rights are very recent innovations, which had no possibility of emerging in the ancient world.

The ancient assumptions that I am calling realist also direct our attention to the local scene, which is where a nation's survival and well-being were truly in the balance. Rome's destruction of Corinth in 146 B.C. and war with the Numidian Jugurtha, for example, both grew from longstanding *local* conflicts into which Rome was drawn, and not from Corinthian or Numidian hatred of Rome.[72] I am proposing a similar kind of explanation of the Judaean War's origins.

With few exceptions, research has neglected these local factors. In his earlier monograph, we have seen, Goodman considered regional antagonisms as conceivable factors, but his dismissal was complete:[73] They were merely local squabbles and such bickering "could have continued indefinitely without necessarily ending in revolt *against the suzerain power*."[74] In a rarely noticed 1981 essay, however, Uriel Rappaport portrayed the Hasmonean expansion as the root cause of the region's unrest, which left "bloody accounts to settle between Jews and their neighbors."[75] Roman administrators understood the problem, Rappaport suggested, and tried to mollify one side or the other – mostly the other – but "the most insoluble problem was the pagan-Jewish conflict in Palestine." It was a time-bomb that would explode on the Romans in the revolt.[76]

In 1988 and 1990 came A. Kasher's *Jews, Idumaeans, and Ancient Arabs*, and *Jews and Hellenistic Cities in Eretz-Israel*, which gave full weight to regional conflicts, but from a singular perspective that I do not consider so helpful.[77]

---

[71] Henry Cabot Lodge, "Speech Against the League of Nations," 1.1172: "But it is well to remember that we are dealing with nations every one of which has a direct *individual interest* to serve, and *there is grave danger in an unshared idealism*. . . . Internationalism, illustrated by the Bolshevik and by the men to whom all countries are alike provided they can make money out of them, is to me repulsive. National I must remain. . . ."

[72] On Numidia see Sallust *Jug.* 5–15; Plutarch, *Mar.* 12; on Corinth see Gruen 1976; Green 1990: 447–52 with Pausanias 7.7–16 (from Polybius' lost Book 37).

[73] Goodman (1987: 13 n. 23) cites a Hebrew article concerning regional strife in connection with Gaius' statue and then Schürer-Vermes' survey (2.85–183) of the Greek cities around Judaea, although that survey, focused on each site's history and government, is in no way an argument for regional conflict as the cause of the war.

[74] Goodman 1987: 18, my emphasis.   [75] Rappaport 1981: 85.   [76] Rappaport 1981: 95.

[77] Kasher 1990: 225–312 for the period from A.D. 6.

Kasher minimized the possible role of Hasmonean expansion as a *grievance* because he traced the root hostilities back to Israelite times, when the invading Israelites were commanded to drive out Canaanite/Philistine idolatry and immorality – a noble aim, in his presentation, that Hellenistic and Roman authors perversely failed to appreciate.[78] Their accounts, for example, in complaining about the Hasmoneans, contain little more than libel and calumny. Even Josephus "is absolutely pro-Roman."[79] In Kasher's dualistic scheme, Hellenistic and Roman authority was all but uniformly ranged with the pagan *poleis* against the righteous Judaeans-Jews.[80]

Of these studies it seems to me that Rappaport's is closest to the mark in explaining the evidence. His account was extremely brief and suggestive. But let us now try to draw together the evidence from this perspective, bearing in mind the ancient assumptions about national self-reliance we have considered .

IV. TOUGH NEIGHBOURHOOD: JUDAEA IN SOUTHERN SYRIA

From vulnerability to primacy

For Josephus and his contemporaries, *Syria* meant the eastern littoral from Anatolia/Turkey to Egypt. The region took its name from the Phoenician trading capital of Tsur or Tyre on the Lebanese coast. Tyre's massive hinterland was thus *Tsuraya*, which came into Greek and Latin as Syria.[81] Tyre had been prominent on the biblical authors' radar. They regarded it as a major alien presence, whether as a wealthy foreign power friendly to Kings David and Solomon or as an object of divine wrath.[82] Throughout the Persian and Hellenistic periods, Tyre and its old rival Sidon maintained colonies throughout Syria, down the coastal plain to the Egyptian frontier and across Upper Galilee to Mt. Hermon.[83] Although Tyre's wealth, power, and *chōra* were much reduced in Roman times, it was still considered an ancient, "free" and "inviolable" city of considerable prestige. When its interests aligned with those of the inland Greek *poleis*, it could still be a thorn in the Judaeans' side.[84]

---

[78] Kasher 1990: 1–13 ("Guidelines for the Evaluation of Historical Sources and Their Tendentiousness") and 313–17.

[79] Kasher 1990: 8–9.

[80] Kasher 1990: 313–14: "The basic identity of interest between the cities and the authorities . . . (i.e., the governors appointed by the Hellenistic kingdoms, and later the Roman procurators) inevitably resulted in a rift between the local Jewish population and the authorities."

[81] Wright 1985: 1.5; Rawlinson 1889: 45. Tsur ("rock") gave its name to the city. Greek lacks the Semitic *ts* letter: It used Tyros for the city and Syria for the region.

[82] Josh 19:24–29. Good times, thanks to wealthy King Hiram: 2 Sam 5:11; 2 Kgs 5:15; 7:1. Bad times: Isa 23:1–17; Ezek 26:2–15.

[83] Berlin 1997a and b.   [84] See *Life* 44 with *War* 2.459; 4.105; *Apion* 1.70.

Alexander's successors (from 323 B.C.) well illustrated realist assumptions. As they seized all the territory they could, the frontiers of their kingdoms were repeatedly challenged. The Battle of Ipsus in 301 brought a provisional settlement. Seleucus I, based in Antioch, would hold the vast territory from Pakistan through most of Turkey, while Ptolemy I in Alexandria would control the smaller but rich and unified territory of Egypt. Ptolemy was quick to spot an opportunity, however, and annexed Syria as far as Lebanon before anyone had time to object.

The term Coele (*koileh*: "hollow")-Syria referred narrowly to Lebanon's Bekaa Valley,[85] but in common use it came to include the whole of southern Syria, including Palestine, Idumaea, and Judaea (Strabo 16.2.21), which had no other collective name. Polybius often mentions Coele-Syria with this meaning as the bone of contention between Ptolemies and Seleucids.[86] In an inscription from the second century A.D., residents of Scythopolis near Galilee still see themselves as "one of the Hellenic *poleis* of Coele-Syria."[87] The Ptolemies retained Coele-Syria until 200 B.C., although only by repeatedly fending off the Seleucids. Finally, the Seleucids defeated them convincingly enough at the Battle of Panias (200 B.C.), to annex the coastal plain from Sidon down to Gaza, with its many Greek *poleis* and inland territories including Samaria and Judaea.

Both Ptolemies and Seleucids liked to convert ancient Aramaic-speaking settlements into substantial, walled, *poleis* in which the trappings of Greek culture fused with the older cultures. A famous example is the town called *House of Shan* (Beit-Shean) south of Galilee, a wonderfully situated settlement since about 4000 B.C. Under the Ptolemies it was called the *Polis of Scythians* or Scythopolis, honouring the God Dionysus – Nysa-Scythopolis – and was decked out with temples, baths, and public squares. Similar things happened in Gaza, Ascalon, Dor, and Ptolemais on the coast, and inland with Philoteria, Hippos, Pella, Gadara, Gerasa, and Philadelphia (previously Amman-Rabbah, modern Amman).[88]

Maps of *ancient Judaea* or *Palestine in New Testament Times* sometimes confuse the issues we are investigating. They typically show the whole region south of Lebanon as a kind of natural whole, even if divided up among Herod's sons.[89]

---

[85] It has been suggested, however, that the term originated from misunderstanding Aramaic *kol* (all), from the Persian term for the large administrative district "across the river": Cohen 2006: 38.

[86] E.g., Polybius 1.3.1; 3.1.1, 2.8; 4.2.11, 37.5; 5.1.5, 9.7, 31.1, 34.6; 16.39 [Batanaea, Samaria, Abila, Gadara, and Jerusalem are part of it]; 28.1.2 ["the *poleis* of Coele-Syria"]. "The war for Coele-Syria" (from the Fourth Syrian War) provides one of his fixed starting points. Cf. Josephus, *Apion* 1.1225, 179 (Judaeans are from Coele-Syria, a subset of Syria).

[87] *SEG* 37:1531 with Foerster and Tsafrir 2002: 75. Cf. for Philadelphia as part of Coele-Syria *IGLSyr* 21.2.23 (late second century) and 21.2.24.

[88] See Hoffmann and Kerner 2002.

[89] Recently Lykke 2012. Notwithstanding her refreshingly integrated approach and recognition of the complexity of the region, she defines the region as *Palaistinē*, "at least to be equated

The map for "pre-70 Judaea" in the venerable *Cambridge Ancient History* illustrates this (Fig. 13). Those who lived in the region understood *Judaea* to be the central part of the internal highland, between Idumaea to the south and Samaria to the north (Fig. 14), which is to say Jerusalem's hinterland (*chōra*). The rapid expansion and contraction of the territory dominated by Jerusalem created grievances.

Although Polybius often uses Coele-Syria to mean southern Syria in the early second century B.C., he rarely names any constituent parts. He observes that Raphia (modern Rafah) south of Gaza is "the first city of Coele-Syria next to Egypt" (5.80.3), and he seems to assume that Samaria was the most prominent centre. For when Antiochus III pushed southward from Antioch in the Fifth Syrian War, in which he finally seized Coele-Syria from the Ptolemies, he reportedly took Gadara east of the Jordan, which Polybius calls the strongest *polis* of that region, along with Abila, Philoteria, and Samaria to the west, installing a 5,000-strong garrison in Samaria to guard the south (5.70–71). Polybius' extant text mentions Judaea just once (16.39), and that is in a passage preserved only by Josephus, quoting Polybius. Shortly after Antiochus III's major conquests, it reads, "those Judaeans who reside around *the temple [τὸ ἱερόν] called Jerusalem* surrendered to him." In calling Jerusalem a temple, Polybius apparently thought of the site, toward the mid-100s B.C., as a very small town mainly devoted to maintaining the national shrine.[90] Samaria was the military-administrative centre of Coele-Syria.

Samaria was a natural site for such a garrison. Perched on the western edge of the central highlands, at 450 m (1454 ft) above sea level, it commanded the coastal plain to the west with a gradual, open ascent and large summit. Contrast the ascents to Jerusalem farther south, especially via Beit-Horon, which were steeper and more hazardous (Chapter 5). In the Persian period Samaria had also been the primary city, with a governor (Sanballat) and army that tried to hamper Jerusalem's restoration.[91] It is unclear what became of Samaria under the Ptolemies, but under Antiochus III and IV it was likewise a

---

with the nucleus of the ancient *Land of Israel*, the Hebrew *Eretz Israel* used in the Hebrew biblical scriptures for the area compassing the native Jewish land" (p. 10), which has "natural borders" at the Mediterranean, the Jordan, Mt. Hermon, and the Negev (p. 11); hence the map of this *Palestine* on p. 19.

[90] Josephus, *Ant.* 12.135–37. Josephus attributes to Polybius the intention to say more "about the manifestation/presence that had come into being around the temple" (περὶ τῆς γενομένης περὶ τὸ ἱερὸν ἐπιφανείας). Although editors ascribe this to Polybius, it is suspect because: (a) *Antiquities* thematizes the divine presence with similar language (esp. 8.119; cf. 2.339; 3.310; 9.60); (b) we might have expected Josephus to have credited such language to Polybius if he had seen it there; and (c) he himself frequently postpones subjects, sometimes without ever returning to them (e.g., 4.198). For the population of Persian and early Hellenistic Jerusalem, see Finkelstein 2008 (he proposes only about 100 adult males).

[91] Neh 2:10, 19; 3:33 [4:1]; 4:1 [4:7]; 6:1–5, 12–14.

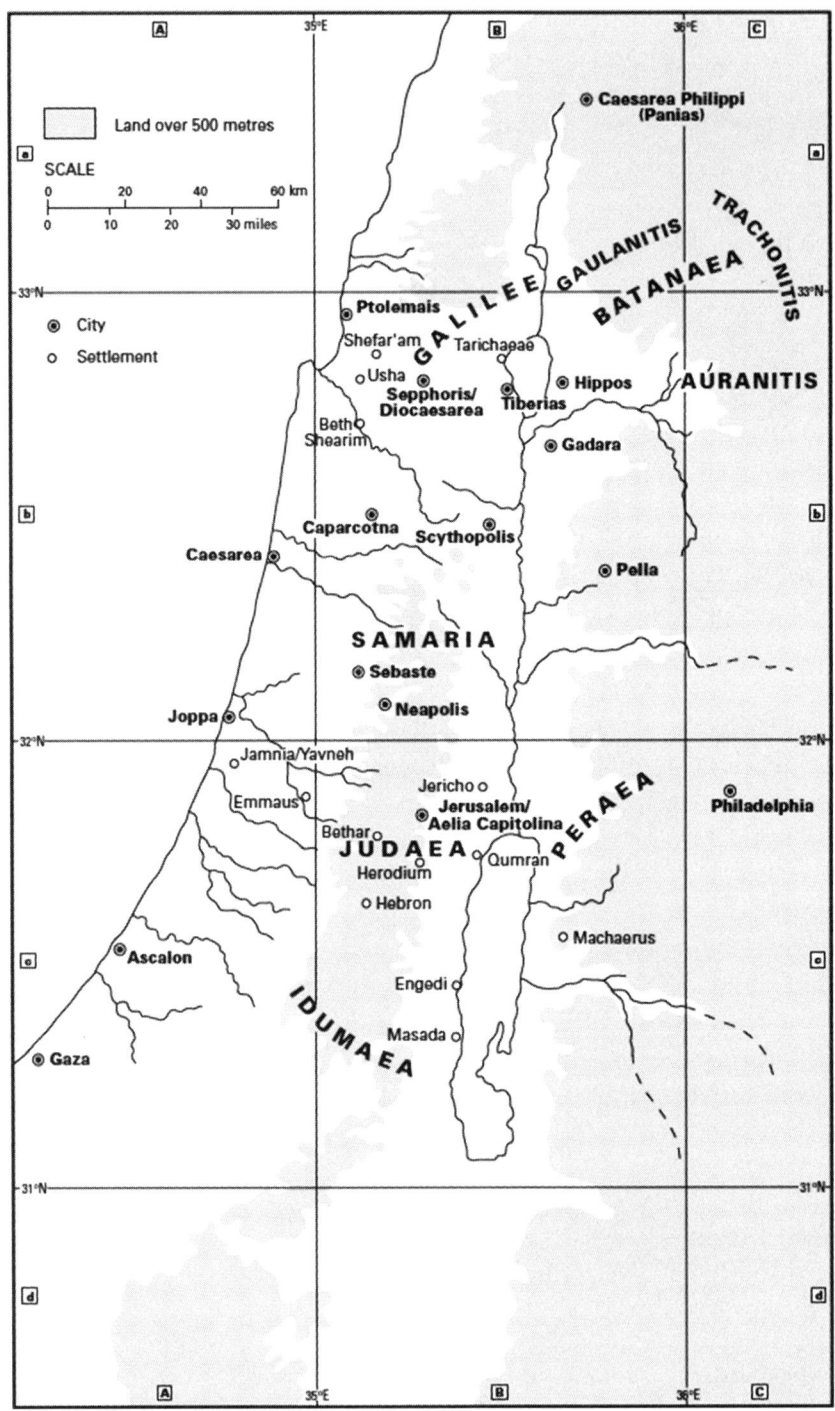

FIGURE 13. Map of pre-70 "Judaea" in *Cambridge Ancient History* 10, p. 738

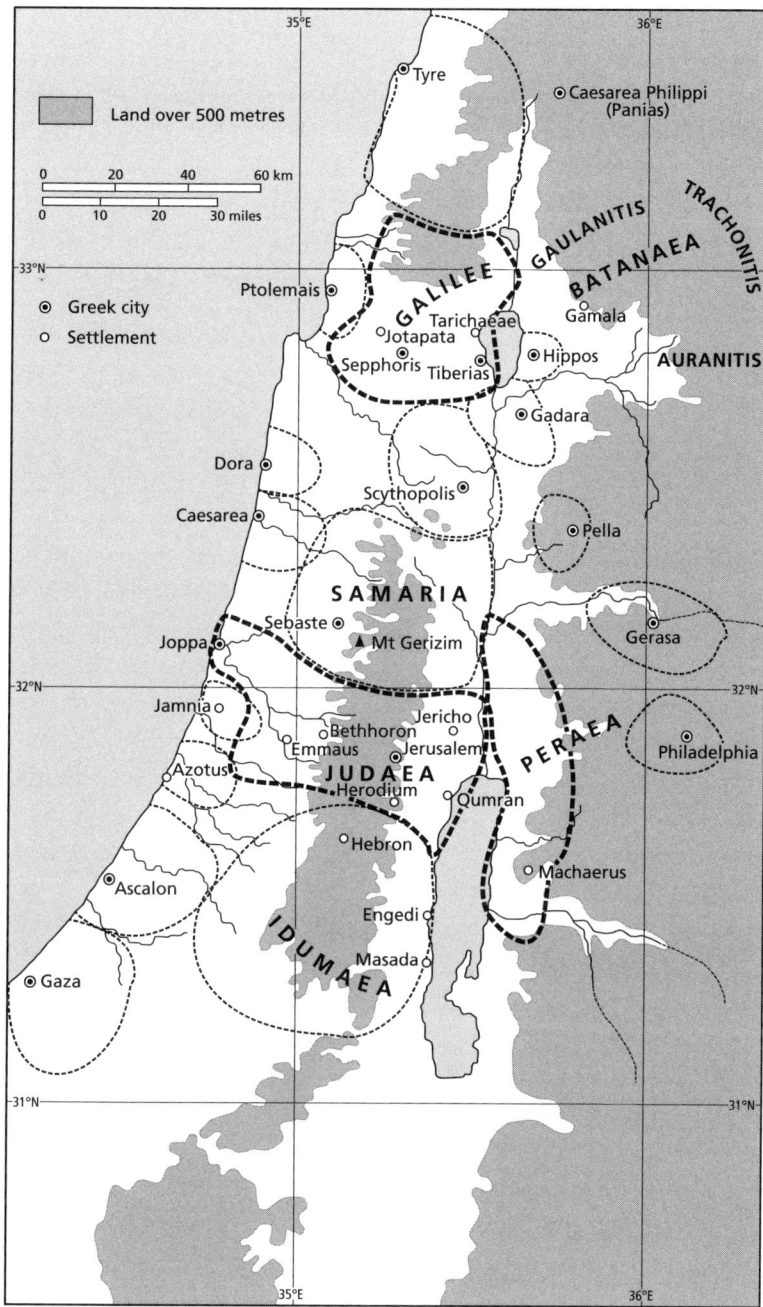

FIGURE 14. Map of pre-70 Judaea in regional context, indicating the main ethnic zones, *poleis*, and their territories. Judea proper and areas of predominantly Judaean habitation, recognized by Rome soon after Pompey's conquest, are indicated by a thick line.

prominent centre. After Antiochus III took Coele-Syria (200–198 B.C.), Samaria was the capital of an expanded *chōra* – Greater Samaria or Samaritis – which may have included smaller Jerusalem and possibly Galilee.[92] And when Antiochus IV moved to suppress the Hasmonean revolt, he had his general bring in "a large force from Samaria" (1 Macc 3.10).

In keeping with standard local-elite behaviour toward a new conqueror, Samarian and Judaean leaders were eager to cooperate with Antiochus III, who rewarded them accordingly. Says Josephus (*Ant.* 12.133):

> Once Antiochus had subjugated those *poleis* in Coele-Syria that [Ptolemy's defeated general] Scopas had taken, hence Samaria, the Judaeans voluntarily put themselves at his disposal. They welcomed him into their *polis* and furnished his army and his elephants unstintingly. They also joined enthusiastically in the fighting when he besieged the garrison that Scopas had left behind in their citadel.

This appears to suggest that once Greater Samaria was in Antiochus' hands, its constituent elites, including those of Jerusalem, appealed to their new king. In gratitude Antiochus helped Judaea, like the others, recover from the ravages of the preceding wars. His benefactions there targeted the priests, whom he exempted from taxes. The temple itself he funded lavishly for repairs as well as sacrifices (12.134–46). His benefactions for Samaria were on a larger scale.

Archaeological work on the soaring Mt. Gerizim (950 m, 3,100 ft above sea level) suggests that this period was the city's apogee. Samarian origins are murky and much debated,[93] but we need not figure them out. It now seems that Samarians had built a temple to YHWH on Gerizim by the fifth century B.C. – nearly as old as the Judaeans' postexilic temple – and that the early Seleucid period saw a major expansion of their temple precinct and community. At perhaps 10,000 strong, the hilltop settlement itself would have been larger than Jerusalem, and it was supplemented by Shechem down the hill. Half a million animal bones found on Gerizim, coupled with the absence of images or other "pagan" objects, suggest a thriving temple-based community scrupulously observing biblical prescriptions. Hundreds of donor inscriptions from the Seleucid period attest the temple's wealth and prestige at this time.[94] Finally, two marble inscriptions from the Greek island of Delos document Samarian colonies abroad. We read of people calling themselves "Israelites on Delos who pay dues to [or support sacrifices of] the holy sanctuary Argerizein [Mt. Gerizim]," who honour certain foreign benefactors on the island for

---

[92] Dušek 2012: 69–70, synthesizing several scholars' analyses.
[93] Pummer 1987, 2010; Crown and Pummer 2005; Kartveit 2009; Dušek 2012: 74–81.
[94] See Berlin 1997a: 15; Hjelm 2004; Magen, Misgav, and Tsefania 2004; Magen 2008; helpful summaries in Magen undated and Hjelm 2010.

helping to fund Samarian community facilities.[95] Similar foreign benefaction toward Judaean communities abroad is well known.[96]

Relations between Seleucid rulers and local elites in Coele-Syria remained close. When Antiochus IV took power in 175 B.C. the local elites appear to have understood that he would welcome new initiatives expressing their loyalty and solidarity. Informed people knew that the Seleucid empire was falling apart, with the Parthians eating away swaths in the east and the Romans encroaching from the west. One scholar has proposed that Antiochus IV, having reached maturity as a political hostage in Rome, tried to consolidate the remains of his empire by imitating Roman diplomacy and extending the citizenship of his "Antiochene republic" to other *polis* elites.[97] It could be.

Whatever happened exactly, both Samarian and Judaean elites were quick to express their support and the other *poleis* of the region were just as keen.[98] In Jerusalem priests asked the king's permission to introduce Greek customs into Jerusalem in order to make their *polis* more like the regional norm.[99] The Samarian elite likewise asked for permission to follow Greek ways, even renaming their Gerizim sanctuary, which had borne no divine title, in honour of "Greek Zeus."[100] Evidence comes from Josephus in one of his anti-Samarian passages, admittedly, and its authenticity has been doubted because the letter-writers call themselves "Sidonians in Shechem."[101] But there were Sidonian colonies throughout the area, also at Jamnia-on-the-sea and Marisa (Maresha) in Idumaea, so this is perhaps not a strong objection.[102] If it represents an authentic core, the letter would suggest that Sidonian colonists in Shechem, proud of both their ethnicity and their adopted home, had come to identify with Samaria's traditional cult and felt confident to speak for it.

That would not be as strange as it might seem, given the general confusion of ethnic-cultic allegiances and possibility of multiple loyalties, which we find also among Idumaeans and Judaeans. A few decades later, the large colony of Sidonians in Idumaean Maresha/Marisa, if they remained in place during Hyrcanus' invasion, presumably adopted Judaean law, giving them a triple

---

[95] Kartveit 2009: 216–24; Dušek 2012: 75–81.   [96] Brief summary in Mason 2007: 478–79.

[97] Goldstein 1984: 84–123, 227, 359–64 etc.

[98] Hoffmann (2002: 109–10) dates Gadara's Zeus temple to the time of Antiochus III–IV, noting that Zeus was the state deity of the Seleucids.

[99] 1 Macc 1.11–15; 2 Macc 4:7–50.

[100] Zeus Hellenios: Josephus, *Ant.* 12.257–63 with Dušek 2012: 101–107. 2 Macc 6.2, by contrast, claims that Antiochus *punished* Jerusalem and Gerizim by imposing the names of Zeus Olympios and Zeus Xenios (Friend of Strangers) on them. It is easier to understand both as names requested by the "foreignizing" elites, for sanctuaries of the nameless and ineffable God, than as Antiochus' impositions (Kartveit 2009: 99).

[101] See Kartveit 2009: 96–100, 137–38 (against Bickerman's and Goldstein's support for authenticity).

[102] Berlin 1997a: 15; Dušek 2012: 101–104.

identity. We have noted foreign benefactors of Samarian communities on Delos and benefactors of Judaean and Idumaean communities abroad. A later inscription from Delos shows "Praulos the Samarian" making a dedication to a temple of Serapis.[103] Flexibility in benefaction and devotion is certainly known among early Judaean communities in Egypt.[104] And just 10 km (6 mi) northwest of Mt. Gerizim, the *polis* of Samaria – Coele-Syria's administrative centre and military headquarters[105] – hosted temples to Serapis and Isis while under Egyptian rule, then to Korē under the Seleucids.[106] Cultic flexibility and adaptation were common. This point is important when we think about who the first-century "Samarians" or Sebastenes were who bore such a durable grudge against the Judaeans.

What happened next I may summarize quickly because it is more familiar. Whereas the Samarians' initiative toward Antiochus IV paid off in protection for their renamed cult on Mt. Gerizim, unique aggravations in Jerusalem (e.g., 2 Macc 5.11) elicited the king's wrath, for reasons we can no longer recover with clarity. His anger brought a series of harshly punitive measures (169–167 B.C.). These included prohibition of Torah observance and the violent implementation of this decree.[107] These measures sparked the Hasmonean Revolt (167–164 B.C.), the purification of the temple, and the reinstitution of Judaean ancestral law. These were quickly followed by the steady expansion and growing autonomy of Jerusalem's *chōra* under a series of priestly strongmen based there, the Hasmoneans (or Maccabees).[108]

The Hasmonean expansion makes perfect sense on realist assumptions. Having found itself extremely vulnerable, tiny Jerusalem now took every opportunity to expand its territory and wealth, so as to prevent a recurrence. According to *1 Maccabees*, the Hasmoneans took their first three sites (Ephraim, Lod, and Ramataim) *from Samaria*,[109] confirming the latter's regional primacy.

Although excellent news for Judaeans, this reversal of fortune and gradual expansion soon became terrible news for the neighbours, and particularly for Samaria. To be sure, the expansion was more gradual than it seems in long

---

[103] Kartveit 2009: 220.

[104] See Bickerman 1988: 237–45 on the fifth-century Jews of Elephantine with their own temple to YHWH, which, however, acknowledged other Gods. Centuries later the deeply observant Judaean Philo, although often ridiculing the games and spectacles of Alexandria's theatre, makes it clear that he has often been there (*Ebr.* 177), which might seem to have required compromises with the Gods that other Judaeans would have abhorred. Josephus feels comfortable saying in *Antiquities* (20.100) that Philo's nephew Tiberius Alexander "did not remain with the ancestral customs," as his prominent father had, but we have no clear idea what this means or how Alexander himself saw the issue.

[105] Cf. 1 Macc 3.10; 2 Macc 15.1 with *Ant.* 12.261–62: Apollonius is the governor of Coele-Syria, apparently based in Samaria with an army, and Nicanor was a royal official.

[106] Magness 2001.   [107] Goldstein 1984: 89.   [108] Schwartz 1993.

[109] 1 Macc 10.30, 38; 11.28, 34; cf. Dušek 2012: 71.

retrospect, with bursts of intense activity over three generations. But the momentum was all in the direction of steady growth. Simon (143–134), John Hyrcanus (134–104), Aristobulus (104–103), and Alexander Jannaeus (103–76 B.C.) eventually brought nearly all of Coele-Syria under Jerusalem's rule.[110]

What did this look like in practice? Making it a priority to secure a port for Judaea's landlocked *chōra*, Simon reportedly expelled the populations of Jamnia, Gazara, and Joppa in a 20-km (12.5-mi) arc by the sea, and colonized those towns.[111] Hyrcanus captured cities east of the Jordan River. Most fatefully he destroyed both the Samarian temple on Gerizim (112/111 B.C.) and the Samarian capital, letting his two sons lead that operation: "After conquering the city, they utterly destroyed it and reduced its inhabitants to slavery" (*War* 1.65). Hyrcanus also required the Idumaeans to accept Judaean law, which entailed circumcision for adult males, or to flee for their lives.[112] A number seem to have fled, for a substantial Idumaean community appears in Egypt around that time: an inscription from 112 B.C. honours an Egyptian official for building a temple to the Idumaean God, Qos-Apollo.[113] Aristobulus I then ranged 200 km (125 mi) north to the Bekaa Valley, where he forced the Ituraeans to accept Judaean law or flee, joining their land also to Jerusalem's *chōra*.[114] Scholars have usually surmised that this was the time when Galilee became Judaized.[115]

---

[110] For the revolt and early events we depend mainly on 2 Maccabees, the abridgement of five-volume work by Jason of Cyrene, and 1 Maccabees, a court history written soon after Hyrcanus I's death. For the later dynasty we depend on Josephus, *War* 1.31–127; *Ant.* 12.234–13.432 by way of literary accounts. Hasmonean coins provide valuable evidence, along with occasional archaeological traces.

[111] Cf. Semple (1931: 12): "Every city state, every dwarf principality, every far-flung colony, every pirate league faced seaward towards the Mediterranean. Inland countries were left out in the cold, condemned to poverty and provincialism. Highland Judea tried again and again to secure a foothold upon its shore." Jonathan had already taken Joppa and installed a garrison there (1 Macc. 10.75–76; 12.33–34; *Ant.* 13.180). But the description of Simon's campaign, led by Jonathan son of Absalom, has him driving out the inhabitants (1 Macc. 13.11, 43–48; Josephus, *War* 1.50; *Ant.* 13.215).

[112] Josephus, *Ant.* 13.254–58.

[113] *OGIS* 737. The inscription joins other documentary indicators of Idumaean communities in Egypt. They were apparently organized, like other ethnic communities (including some Judaeans), as military colonies, which gradually incorporated others as they also lost their military functions, especially under Rome. Cf. Rappaport 1969; Fraser 1972: 1. 280–81; Thompson Crawford 1984; Thompson 1988: 99–105; Honigman 2003.

[114] Josephus, *Ant.* 13.318–19, quoting Strabo quoting Timagenes.

[115] Schürer-Vermes 2.3–8; Smallwood 1981: 14. According to 1 Macc. 5.14–23, Judaeans living in Galilee at the time of the Hasmonean Revolt were a small minority vulnerable to attack from Ptolemais, Tyre, and Sidon. Simon took 3,000 soldiers to evacuate them back to Judaea. *War* 1.76 remarks that Aristobulus' brother Antigonus had recently acquired impressive armour and military decorations *from Galilee*, which scholars have taken to suggest that he fought (although they are not named) alongside Aristobulus. For skepticism, see Kasher 1988: 79–84, and for the problems of reconciling literary indications with archaeological evidence, see Chancey 2002: 37–47; Myers 2010: 24–30.

Aristobulus' long-ruling son Alexander Jannaeus (103–76 B.C.) marked the zenith of Hasmonean hegemony. He besieged and stormed the remaining coastal cities except Ascalon: Raphia, Gaza, Anthedon, Strato's Tower (later Caesarea), Dor, and Ptolemais.[116] He crossed the Jordan River and captured prosperous Gadara, Gerasa, Pella, Gaulanē, Seleucia, Gamala, Dium, and Esebonitis, as well as Scythopolis west of the river.[117] Josephus claims that Pella was destroyed because its residents "refused to embrace the ancestral customs of the Judaeans" (*Ant.* 13.396) and that Gadara was likewise demolished (*Ant.* 14.75). Archaeology seems to attest the destruction of Gadara's wall in about this period.[118]

Paradoxically, the vigorously Judaizing Alexander achieved these victories with the aid of mercenaries from Asia Minor. They were needed because he faced implacable opposition from Judaeans in his capital Jerusalem. Some had become horrified that such a violent commander was clinging to the high priesthood, an office requiring constant purity (Num 19:13). Josephus alleges that Alexander killed some 57,000 Judaean opponents.[119] Although that number must be hugely exaggerated, there was evidently a civil war of some scope at this time.[120]

If Hasmonean expansion came at the direct expense of Samaria and the Greek *poleis*, another casualty was Seleucid authority. Some Seleucid kings were willing to yield land parcels in exchange for Judaean military support in their dynastic struggles. They gave territory and tokens of independence while making a show of maintaining overall control, and they could become outraged if Hasmonean leaders appeared to defy them.[121] So Hasmonean and Seleucid fortunes remained intertwined for decades. As late as about 90 B.C., disaffected Judaeans hoped that a Seleucid would remove their king Alexander

---

[116] It is possible that Alexander threatened Ascalon but was repulsed with the aid of Ptolemy IX Lathyrus from Egypt, for the Ascalonites celebrated their freedom and autonomy from what happened to be Alexander's first year. Rigsby 1996: 519–21.

[117] See Josephus, *Ant.* 13.324–37, 356–64, 395–96.   [118] Hoffmann 2002: 104–105.

[119] *War* 1.89, 91, 97; *Ant.* 13.373–76.

[120] Opposition to the Hasmonean priesthood is evident in rabbinic literature (*b. Ber.* 48a; *Kidd.* 66a), where Yannai (= Jannaeus) is often used as a generic name for these rulers (cf. *b. Ber.* 29a). This agrees with Josephus' claims about opposition already to John Hyrcanus, whom he nevertheless admires (*War* 1.67; *Ant.* 13.288–298). Cf. the *Habakkuk Commentary* among the Qumran Scrolls, which identifies the "wicked man" of Hab 1:4 as a certain "wicked priest" who held power in Jerusalem and drove out the "Righteous Teacher" and his group (*1QpHab* 8.8; 9.9; 11.4; 12.2, 8).

[121] 1 Macc 13.36–14.5 takes the Demetrius II's grant of freedom from tribute (142 B.C.) as the beginning of independence, but in 139 B.C. Antiochus VII is still speaking as though he holds the cards: "I permit you to fashion your own currency..." (1 Macc. 15.5–9), and the king soon rescinded his grants in anger because of Hasmonean interference in "my kingdom" (15.27–29), whereas Simon claims to be taking only what belonged to his forefathers (15.33). It is only the death of Antiochus in 129 that gives Hyrcanus leisure to act with impunity (*Ant.* 13.274).

Jannaeus.[122] The rule of Alexander's widow Alexandra Salome (76–67) seems to have been the final period of relative stability, alhough her death created a standoff between her two sons, and this had regional complications.

Pompey's arrival in 64–63 B.C. made Judaea's inclusion under Rome's *imperium* all but certain. His conquest of southern Syria was made infinitely easier, however, by Hasmonean dominance of that entire zone. Jerusalem was the only address he needed and the lynchpin for the rest. Urged on by friends and advisers connected with *poleis* that had fallen to Jerusalem, Pompey quickly removed Aristobulus II, the younger son of Alexander and Alexandra, installed the grateful older brother Hyrcanus II, and promptly stripped away Jerusalem's vastly expanded *chōra*. Josephus writes:[123]

> After depriving the [Judaean] *ethnos* of the cities in Coele-Syria that it had conquered, he assigned these under a Roman commander appointed for that purpose [i.e., M. Aemilius Scaurus], and confined it [the *ethnos*] *entirely within its proper borders*. He also rebuilds Gadara, which had been destroyed by the Judaeans, as a favour to one of his own freedmen, Demetrius.[124] So he liberated from them the cities in the interior, at least those they had not already razed to the ground: Hippos, Scythopolis, Pella, Samaria, Jamnia, Marisa, Azotus, and Arethusa, likewise also the coastal cities of Gaza, Joppa, Dora, and Strato's Tower. ... All these *he gave back to their legitimate [*or native, proper*] citizens* and designated them *for the Syrian province.*

Josephus can wax nostalgic about Judaea's dramatic losses: "For we tossed away our freedom and fell under subjection to Rome, and the territory (*chōra*) *we had acquired by force of arms, removing it from the Syrians, we were forced to give back to the Syrians....*"[125]

Pompey and his successors did not entirely return the area to the pre-Hasmonean *status quo*, however. An early proconsul of the new province of Syria, Aulus Gabinius (57–55 B.C.), could see that there were now Judaean majorities outside Jerusalem's old *chōra*. Along with three administrative centres in older Judaea, therefore, he named Sepphoris, leading *polis* of Galilee, and Amathus across the Jordan River in Peraea (i.e., "Over [the River]") as Judaean centres also. Not long afterward, Joppa was returned to Judaean control as their only outlet to the sea.[126] Both Hasmonean colonization and later migrations in the Herodian period help to explain why, upon the outbreak of war in A.D. 66, Judaean minorities would be found in many *poleis* of Syria.

---

[122] Demetrius III Eucaerus: *War* 1.89–97; *Ant.* 13.372, 376, 380.

[123] *War* 1.155–57; cf. *Ant.* 14.74–76.

[124] See Chapter 1 on this man's role in honouring Pompey in Rome.

[125] *Ant.* 14.77; cf. *Life* 1–6 on Josephus' Hasmonean ancestry.

[126] This is affirmed in an edict attributed to Julius Caesar (Josephus, *Ant.* 14.205), presumably in the early 40s, although we do not know the background.

The Hasmonean Judaization of Coele-Syria created antagonisms that would remain potent until the time of our war. Several *poleis* celebrated their liberation from Jerusalem by making dating their civic "Year 1" to Pompey's arrival – a rebirth.[127] Gadarenes would proudly style themselves "Pompeian"[128] for centuries to come. One impression of perceived Hasmonean belligerence comes from the Augustan-era writer Pompeius Trogus:[129]

> He [Antiochus VII Sidetes, 138–129 B.C.] also reduced the Judaeans, who during the Macedonian rule under his father Demetrius [I Soter] *had recovered their freedom by force of arms*. Their strength was such that after him they would submit to no Macedonian king. Rather, electing rulers from their own people, *they harassed Syria with fierce wars*.

Trogus complained that, after securing their own liberation from foreign oppressors, the Judaeans became oppressors to their neighbours (Justin, *Epit.* 36.3.8). The surviving prologues to his lost volumes confirm that he said much on the subject that has not survived. The prologue to Book 39 promises a description of how Arabs and Judaeans "molested Syria with banditry on its lands" (*Syriam ... terrestribus latrociniis infestarint*).

In a similar way, the geographer Strabo (early first century A.D.) mused that the Judaeans' admirable beginning, with Moses' good laws, turned rancid when they became belligerent (*Geog.* 16.2.37): "For some broke away and ruined the territory (*chōra*), both [theirs] itself and that of their neighbours; others ... seized what belonged to others and subdued much of Syria and Phoenicia." Strabo makes clear which Judaeans he has in view (16.2.40):

> With Judaea under tyrannical rule, Alexander [Jannaeus] was the first to put himself forward as a king instead of a priest. Hyrcanus along with Aristobulus were this fellow's sons. While they were having a dispute over the rule, Pompey went over and dismantled their [regime]. ...

Strabo's sympathies are clear when he describes Joppa, an ancient Greek *polis* famous from the myth of Andromeda and Perseus. He observes that its elevation is high enough that "Jerusalem, the mother-city of the Judaeans, is visible from it." Then some acid: "To be sure the Judaeans have made use of this port ... but it is clear that the ports of the bandits are bandit-nests" (16.2.28). He has a similarly dyspeptic remark about Gadaris, home of many

---

[127] Meimaris 1992: 74–135. The evidence is collected and analyzed in Schürer-Vermes 2.97–183; the Decapolis cities, 125–60.
[128] For the later Gadarene coins, see Schürer-Vermes 2.134.
[129] My emphasis. Trogus' work is lost, but it is preserved in a selective synopsis by the early third-century A.D. writer Justin. This passage is from Justin, *Epit.* 36.1.9. On Trogus and the relationship between his work and Justin's, see Yardley and Heckel 1997: 1–19.

world-famous men,[130] "which the Judaeans also appropriated for themselves" (16.2.29).

If such impressions lingered for so long in these writers, we must imagine that Judaea's actual neighbours bore their grievances more bitterly. Poseidonius of Apamaea (in Syria), a contemporary of the later Hasmoneans, commended Antiochus IV's attempt to eradicate what he saw as Judaean superstition.[131] Tacitus agreed. Although writing in the second century A.D., he could still speak of the Hasmoneans (*Hist.* 5.8),

> who, driven out by the fickleness of the rabble, their despotism regained by force of arms, having ventured on the flight of citizens, the overthrow of cities, the murder of brothers, wives, and parents, and the other usual deeds of tyrants, fostered their superstition by appropriating the dignity of the priesthood in support of their power.[132]

The Idumaeans' forced adoption of Judaean law particularly intrigued writers because of the resulting ethnic hybrid. Strabo says that Idumaeans (a) are considered one of four distinct *ethnē* in southern Syria, alongside Judaeans, Gazans, and Azotians (16.2.2), but (b) are actually Nabataean Arabs who, (c) after being expelled because of civil strife, "went over to the Judaeans and began to share in their laws/customs" (16.2.34). Two centuries later, a grammarian named Ammonius wrote a work *On the Similarities and Differences of Words*, in which he discussed hundreds of pairs of similar words.[133] He has an entry on *Ioudaios* and *Idoumaios*, in which he quotes a certain Ptolemy.[134] Ammonius tries to explain:

> Judaeans and Idumaeans differ, as Ptolemy affirms in the first [book] of *On Herod the King*, for whereas *Judaeans* are such by origin and naturally,

---

[130] Strabo seems to be confusing biblical Gezer/Gazara, 6.5 km (4 miles) NW of Ammaus/Nicopolis in the coastal plain, with Gadara of the Decapolis, although both were taken by the Hasmoneans.

[131] Assuming that Diodorus (34/35.1.1–4) is here elaborating material from Poseidonius (ca. 135–51 B.C.), whose writings did not survive as such, but who was a principal and oft-named source of Diodorus.

[132] There is a striking parallel in Pompeius Trogus (in Justin, *Epit.* 2.4), who marvels (with less vitriol) at the Judaeans' fusion of priestly and political roles, to which he attributes their unbelievable power.

[133] E.g., Athens differs from Attica in that the former indicates the *polis*, the latter both *polis* and *chōra* (*Adfin. voc.* 15).

[134] Ptolemy of Damascus (Nicolaus' brother, *War* 2.20–21) or of Ascalon? A critical edition of Ptolemy's work on the same theme as Ammonius' was published by Heylbut (1887: 388–410). Some scholars argue that this is not Ptolemy's work but a crib of Ammonius (see the dense discussion in Schürer-Vermes 1.27–28) – although the two works had different structures and contents. Cf. Kokkinos 1998: 90–92. Ptolemy of Ascalon's authorship of a Herodian biography is important to Kokkinos' argument concerning Herod's Ascalonite origins (1998: 103, 105, 123, 343–48).

Idoumaioi are not such [or not *Ioudaioi?*] by origin, but rather Phoenicians and Syrians.

But having been overpowered by them [Judaeans], and having been forced to undergo circumcision and to pay taxes into the *ethnos*, and to follow the same laws/customs, they were called Judaeans [or Idumaeans].[135]

Josephus' own description of Idumaean Judaization is remarkably matter-of-fact and realist (*Ant.* 13.257–58):

Hyrcanus also captures the [Idumaean] *poleis* of Adora and Marisa, and when he had taken all the Idumaeans in hand, he let them stay in the *chōra* if they circumcised their genitals and if they were willing to live by the Judaeans' laws (τοῖς Ἰουδαίων νόμοις χρήσασθαι θέλοιεν). In their yearning for their ancestral land they patiently submitted to circumcision and to practising the very same regimen of life in other respects as the Judaeans. Given what happened to them at that time, from then onward *they were Judaeans* (ὥστε εἶναι τὸ λοιπὸν Ἰουδαίους).

Dio may have had Idumaeans in mind when, describing Pompey's entry into *Palaestina* and observing that the region also had the name *Judaea*, he continues (37.17.1): "Just when this [Judaea] designation came into use I do not know, but it holds also for other persons, all those who emulate (*zēloō*) their legal precepts, *though being of different ethnicity* (ἀλλοεθνεῖς ὄντες)."

Although the ancient writers broadly agree that the Hasmoneans conquered Idumaea in the ways reported, scholars have shown much more reticence about what they usually call a *forced conversion*, which would be so repugnant to later Judaism. Some have argued that Idumaea must already have been so Judaized, given its proximity to Judaea, that any force involved has been greatly exaggerated.[136] There is little doubt that Idumaeans would have cultivated ties with Judaea (and earlier Yahud) over centuries, and some may have already adopted the Judaean cult.[137] But it also seems clear that Idumaeans generally had preserved a distinctive culture and cult. The independent and long-lingering perceptions of Hasmonean compulsion, in authors of entirely different outlook and date (using different source material), would be difficult to explain if no such thing happened.

Perhaps part of the problem is our anachronistic category of *religious conversion*. In ancient realist terms the conquest of the neighbouring territory is not

---

[135]   The Teubner edition reads *Idumaeans* at the end: Idumaeans did not begin as such, unlike the Judaeans (Nickau 1966). But given that Judaeans were widely believed to have originated from Egyptians, and that the other circumstances described fit the Hasmonean conquest of Idumaea, most scholars prefer the variant *Judaeans*.

[136]   A thorough analysis and survey of scholarship to that point, arguing against forced "conversion," is Kasher 1988: 46–77. For a synopsis see Chapman 2006: 137–43.

[137]   For the Persian period see Edelman 2005: 243–76.

surprising, unpleasant though it must have been for the conquered. Other nations' conquests and resulting domination were no picnic either. Because religion was not an isolable category, however, there was nothing especially *religious* about these moves (see Chapter 2). They were ethno-political. A modern parallel might be the Treaty of Frankfurt in 1871, which required residents of nearly 1,700 communities in Alsace-Lorraine to embrace a new German identity and citizenship or leave. Whichever path they chose, their loyalties would remain doubtful – the clearest example being the relocation of the Dreyfus family to Paris at this time, setting the stage for the notorious prosecution of Albert Dreyfus in the next generation.[138]

When did Judaea separate from Syria?

Pompey's conquests brought Judaea into Rome's new province of Syria. When, then, did Judaea become a province? This question is basic for understanding relations among the region's inhabitants and between Jerusalem and the legate in Syria. Did the coastal cities, Caesarea, Samarians, and the inland *poleis* see themselves as part of *Judaea*? In 66, was Judaea a province in revolt? We have a secure terminus, for no one doubts that Judaea was a province, under an imperial legate of ex-praetor rank who commanded its resident legion (*X Fretensis*), after the Flavian war. And from about A.D. 117, Judaea's legate was an ex-consul with two legions (also *VI Ferrata*).[139] But what was Judaea's status in the period of our interest, between A.D. 6 and Vespasian's arrival in 67?

The standard view is that Judaea was a distinct province; scholars have even suggested that this province of Judaea revolted in 66.[140] The importance of the question demands a closer look. I have mentioned Schürer's 1874 *Textbook*, an extraordinary reference work that went through several German and English editions, eventually enjoying a major centennial refit by an Oxford-based team in the 1970s as *The History of the Jewish People in the Age of Jesus Christ*. It is a tribute to Schürer's research and writing that the revisers could still often follow his wording in the main text, while greatly expanding the notes. Judaea's political status is one of the issues, however, that has morphed noticeably through successive editions.

In the first outing Schürer offered a tidy view. Until Vespasian's arrival in 67 Judaea was part of Syria. That is why Schürer included a survey of *Syria's*

---

[138] McGillicuddy 2011: 15–62; on the Dreyfuses, Read 2012: 16–25.
[139] *War* 7.5, 17, 163 with *Life* 420; Eck 1970: 5; Smallwood 1981: 331–34; Capponi 2010: 499.
[140] E.g., Mommsen 1887: 2.200–203; Stevenson 1949: 46; Schürer-Vermes 1.357–98; Smallwood 1981: 144–80; Levick 1999: 71 ("the Flavians had reconquered a small rebellious province"); Sicker 2001: 115–20; Schäfer 2003: 105–109.

governors from Pompey to Vespasian: because Palestine obviously "shared the fortunes" of the province to which it belonged.[141] When Schürer described the equestrian procurators in Caesarea, he reiterated that Archelaus' former territory was incorporated *into Syria* and so became the legate's responsibility. The equestrian in the south had strictly limited tasks, when the legate was not available.[142]

This is no longer the textbook position, however, and Schürer's changing view was instrumental in changing other minds, given his great influence. Through evolving editions, puzzlingly, Schürer intensified his conclusion to the list of Syrian governors – saying that it was *only* with Vespasian's arrival that Palestine became separate (*abgetrennt*)[143] – while also giving the southern equestrian a much larger role, amounting to virtual independence of action. The holders of the post in Caesarea, we now read, enjoyed the same freedom as other provincial governors, with the sole qualification that the northern legate would interfere *if* he saw problems.[144] The growing tension between Schürer's conflicting claims was definitively resolved by the Oxford revisers in the direction of Judaea's independence. Josephus' remarks about incorporation into Syria, they say, "must be taken with a grain of salt. Judaea remained until A.D. 70 an administrative unit with its own provincial government." It is part of the revised work's British charm that it retains the list of Syrian governors *with Schürer's rationale*: The legate in Syria was responsible for Judaea.[145]

These various formulations are possible because the evidence does not clearly point in one direction. Important recent studies are returning toward Schürer's original formulation,[146] however, and I have come to agree that pre-70 Judaea is best understood as an ethnic zone of Syria, anchored in Jerusalem, not as a Roman province with Caesarea as capital. Let me indicate as briefly as possible the points that seem to me most telling.

---

[141] Schürer 1874: 144 = 1890: I.242. He was agreeing with A. W. Zumpt (1859: 105), who in a chapter on Roman Gaul had offered Judaea as the best documented case of the principle (as in Raetia, Noricum, and Thracia), as he thought, that procuratorial governors were subordinate to nearby imperial legates. Mattingly (1910: 143–45) disagreed that this was a principle, but saw Judaea-Syria as an exception: The equestrian *was* practically dependent although theoretically independent.

[142] Schürer 1874: 249–50.   [143] Schürer 1890: I.272–73.   [144] Schürer 1890: I.379–81.

[145] Schürer-Vermes I.360 (the equestrians "seem to have been subordinate to the legates . . . only to the extent that. . ."); cf. I.243, 266. The Oxford revisers, while otherwise translating Schürer precisely (1874: 144), made a subtle adjustment (I.243). He had stressed that Palestine *was* under Syria's oversight, *wenn es auch nicht unmittelbar der Provinz Syrien einverleibt war* ("even if [i.e., at the times when] it was not directly incorporated into the Province of Syria"), which became: "Palestine, *although not directly annexed* to the province of Syria, was nevertheless subject to . . . the Roman governor of Syria").

[146] Brunt 1983: 55–56; Ghiretti 1985; Franke 1996: 236–37; Cotton 1999; Eck 2003: 98; 2007: 1–54; Sartre 2005: 103–4, 127; 2008: 635–39; Bernett 2007: 188–89; Labbé 2012 (entire monograph). Eck 2007: 38 (my translation): "The *praefectus Iudaeae* was responsible only for the region Judaea within this great province [Syria]."

1. Ancient writers unanimously understand Judaea as Jerusalem's, not Caesarea's, territory.[147] It is an ethnic region, not a province.

2. Sometimes a "province" is not a Roman province. Just as Latin *imperium* does not mean territory first of all, but controlling power, and βασιλεία suggests rule or kingship before territory, so *provincia* has first to do with the person wielding authority.[148] Josephus can speak of allied kings' "provinces" (ἐπαρχίαι)[149] and call Upper Galilee the "province" of John of Gischala (*Life* 73). It would be easy to understand the equestrian in Syria being said to have a special portfolio or responsibility within the province of Syria. The appointment of a prefect to handle a particular tribe, city, or region within a province was not strange.[150] As to the language itself, Josephus mentions a "procurator of Judaea" – the same word as that for Pilate and others [151] – reporting to Titus, the imperial legate of the time. A "procurator of Judaea" could work alongside a legate.

3. An inscription fragment discovered in Caesarea in 1960 identifies Pilate as "prefect *of Judaea*," who dedicated a *Tiberieum* there: *[Pon]tius Pilatus/[Praef]ectus Iuda[ea]e.*[152] The fourth line (after "of Judaea") is almost entirely gone, removing possibly valuable context.[153] Although the inscription confirms Pilate's role as prefect of Judaea, it does not say that he governed a province called Judaea. His task could be understood simply as the "Judaean portfolio," given Jerusalem's unique importance and long primacy in the region. It might even be that the equestrian in Caesarea was understood to be minding the area when there was no Herodian king on Jerusalem's throne.

4. The main apparent conflict in the evidence is between Josephus' *War*, which says that Archelaus' territory *became a province* in A.D. 6,[154] and his *Antiquities*,

---

[147] Especially Josephus, *War* 3.51–54; *Apion* 1.60; Tacitus, *Hist.* 5.1–13. Josephus' 274 references to Judaea are not perfectly consistent, especially if measured against a rigorous logic (e.g., if a "procurator of Judaea" based in Caesarea must imply that Caesarea is the capital of Judaea). Some problems have to do with momentary rhetoric, just as when he wishes to claim Ptolemais for Judaean Galilee (*War* 2.187–91), although he knows that it was outside (*War* 3.29/38; *Life* 105, 118, 213–15, 342). *War* 3.53 (Judaea is not bereft of the sea's delights, for it "reaches out" to Ptolemais) can be reconciled with *Apion* 1.60 (not a maritime country, built far from the sea), for example, if we take the former to mean that Judaeans enjoy the delights of the sea *because it is visible from their land*, as Strabo suggests.

[148] On the Latin terms see Sherwin-White 1963: 11–12; Shatzman 1999:53; Richardson 2008 with the corrective review by Shatzman 2010.

[149] *War* 2.247; *Ant.* 15.349, 352; 19.343 and next note.

[150] Mattingly 1910: 134, 144; Brunt 1983: 155.

[151] *War* 2.169; *Ant.* 15.406; 18.29, 35, 55, 89; 19.366; 20.2. 5, 97, 101, 102, 105, 107, 137, 142, 160, 162, 185, 197; cf. Philo, *Legat.* 299–305 on Pilate. Suetonius (*Claud.* 28) has Felix in charge of "the cohorts, cavalry wings, and province of Judaea."

[152] Cf. Frova 1961; Schürer-Vermes: 1.358 n. 22; Boffo 1994: 217–233 (no. 25).

[153] Recent speculation about the nature of the Tiberieum include Alföldy 1999 (a rebuilt lighthouse-tower on the east side of the harbour entrance) and Bernett 2007: 205–14 (a sacred site for the cult of Tiberius).

[154] *War* 2.117; 2.220.

which says clearly and repeatedly that it was joined to Syria.[155] The logic of *Ant.* 17.355–18.2 requires that the legate Quirinius included Judaea in his property registration of A.D. 6 *because* it was now part of Syria, his province. Importantly, *Ant.* 18.2 and 29 also mention Coponius, whom *War* 2.117 presents as Judaea's first governor, as an equestrian *sent with Quirinius* "to govern the Judaeans with all authority" – while explaining that Judaea "was made an appendage of Syria." *War*'s information about Coponius can thus be understood in light of *Antiquities*' bigger picture, but the bigger picture cannot be squeezed into *War* 2.117. *War* also mentions Quirinius' census, incidentally in retrospect (2.433; 7.253), says of Raphia (Rafah) that for travellers from Egypt "this *polis* is the beginning of Syria" (4.662), and assumes throughout the responsibility of Syria's legates for Judaea. So we must conclude that Josephus knew Judaea to be part of Syria, and that perhaps his tight focus on Judaean affairs in *War* produced misleading language there.

5. Strabo (17.3.25) and Cassius Dio (53.12–15) both offer explanations of Augustus' provincial system, which would endure throughout the first century. In Dio, provincial governors are either ex-praetors or ex-consuls and either imperial legates or public-senatorial proconsuls, Egypt's Prefect being the sole equestrian exception, for reasons peculiar to that province (53.13.2, 14.1). Strabo omits the possibility of an equestrian governor. Imagining an equestrian governor of Judaea would require us to see him as somehow comparable to Egypt's prefect, a comparison that would not explain Dio or Strabo. When Strabo describes southern Syria, moreover, he treats Judaea merely as one of the region's ethnic zones: Judaeans are comparable to Idumaeans, Gazans, and Azotians (16.2.1–2, 21–27).

6. Pliny the Elder has a similar perspective, independently. The opening index for his encyclopaedia promises to describe, after Egypt, "Idumaea, Syria, Palaestina, Samaria, Judaea, Phoenicia, Syria-Coele, Antiochene Syria, and the Euphrates area" (1.5a). When he reaches that section of the work, he says that Syria adjoins Egypt (*Nat.* 5.66–90), and that Syria *used to* include (before the Flavians?) "Palaestina, which is what the part touching on Arabia was called, *and Judaea, and Coele, then Phoenicia* and moving inland, the territory of Damascus" (5.66). Then again, "those who make finer divisions have Phoenicia surrounded by Syria. And so it goes: maritime coast of Syria [next to Egypt], of which *Idumaea and Judaea are a part*, then Phoenicia, then Syria" (5.67). Pliny mentions the coastal cities and concludes: "This is the frontier of Palaestina," after which come Phoenicia up the coast and Samaria inland (5.69). His final passage (5.70–73) portrays a Judaea "above Idumaea and Samaria" – apparently referring to elevation. Judaea is clearly not a province

---

155 *Ant.* 17.355; 18.1–2.

in this description of pre-Flavian conditions, but an ethno-geographical region like the others he mentions *in Syria*.

7. Pomponius Mela, writing in the 40s, who was one of Pliny's sources, paints a similar picture. He mentions a bewildering array of names he has heard for internal parts of Syria: "for it is called Coele, Mesopotamia, the Damascus region, Adiabene, Babylonia, Judaea, Commagene, and Sophene" (1.62).[156] Within Palaestina he knows three historic cities: Gaza, Ascalon, and Joppa (1.64), again precluding a province of Judaea. Likewise Lucan, the poet of Roman civil war, includes Damascus, Gaza, and Idumaea with Tyre and Sidon as *Syrian* population centres.[157]

8. King Agrippa II's great speech (*War* 2.344–404) includes a tour of the provinces, their resources, and legionary garrisons (2.364–87).[158] The king stresses that *right next door* a wealthy and proud nation submits to Rome: Egypt "your neighbour" (2.384). The striking omission is the great province of Syria, which would have been an obvious neighbour to mention if Judaea were separate from it. The simplest explanation of the omission is that speaker and audience assumed they were *in* Syria.

9. Philo (d. ca. 50) was well informed about Judaea and had visited Jerusalem at least once.[159] His large corpus mentions Judaea just ten times, however. Fully eight of these references fall in a single passage, concerning Caligula's statue (*Leg.* 199–299), where the point is that Jerusalem's *chōra* (Judaea) is world famous for banning human statues or images. Philo is not speaking of a province, certainly not one headquartered in Caesarea, but of the ethnic zone based in Jerusalem. When Philo speaks of the larger area he uses terms going back to Herodotus: Palaestina-Syria, Syria-Palaestina, or simply Palaestina. Along with Phoenicia and Coele-Syria, he says, those are the *current* Greek designations for the ancient land of the Canaanites.[160] Philo even locates the Essenes in *Palaestina–Syria* (*Prob.* 76).

In a particularly revealing passage Philo describes Judaean leaders (in Sidon) negotiating with Petronius, legate of Syria, about Gaius' plan to place his statue in Jerusalem's temple (*Legat.* 230–31):

> Petronius, we are peaceful both by nature and by choice. ... When Gaius received the imperial power, *in all of Syria we were the first to join the celebration*. Vitellius, whom you succeeded as

---

[156] I translate the Latin of Ranstrand 1971. The translation by Romer 1998 (p. 52) lacks the third to fifth names. For our purposes it does not matter.

[157] Lucan, *Bell. civ.* 3.214–17.   [158] See Mason 2008 *ad loc.*

[159] Cf. Eusebius, *Praep. ev.* 8.14.

[160] Philo, *Abr.* 133; *Mos.* 1.163; *Virt.* 221. Josephus speaks of the land from Gaza to Egypt as "what the Greeks call Palaestina" (*Ant.* 1.136), roughly equating current Judaea with ancient Canaan (1.134, 160).

governor, was in our *polis* at the time, and letters were brought to him about this. So the news was happily proclaimed from our *polis*. . . .

This passage says a great deal. The Judaean elite understand their *polis* to be part of Syria and therefore take their concerns to the Syrian legate. They cite as proof of their loyalty the visit of the legate's predecessor to Jerusalem, when they led *all of Syria* in celebrating Gaius' succession.

10. Both of Josephus' histories portray the governors of Syria working hard to maintain ties with Jerusalem as one of the major *poleis* in their purview. This does not change from the Republican proconsuls Gabinius and Sosius to the imperial legates. These senators in Antioch come and go as they wish, making a special effort to be in Jerusalem for Passover and giving no hint they are entering another province.[161] On the road to doubt about Judaea's integration in Syria, Schürer 2.0 proposed that Vitellius and Quadratus had unusual authority and that is why they freely entered Jerusalem,[162] but the Tacitean texts he cited do not suggest this.[163]

11. Several fourth-century historians had the impression from their sources that the province of Judaea was a Flavian creation.[164] Eutropius says: "Under this man [Vespasian] Judaea and Jerusalem, which was the most distinguished city in Palaestina, were added to the Roman empire" (*Brev.* 7.19). Aurelius Victor has the new province formed from "[that part of] Syria whose name is Palaestina and [from] the Judaeans" (*Caes.* 9.10).[165] This would explain Pliny's remark in the mid-70s that Syria *used to* include the south. Although Victor makes a number of errors, for this period they are not many and he even corrects Suetonius.[166] He considers the formation of provinces revealing of a ruler's character, and finds Tiberius and Gaius deficient on this point (*De Caes.* 2.3; 3.11). Presumably he would have credited Augustus or Claudius with a *provincia Iudaeae* if he had known of such a thing.

---

[161] *War* 2.243, 280; *Ant.* 15.405; 18.90; 19.340, and the Philo passage mentioned earlier. On Cassius Longinus (legate 44/45–50), Josephus has him come to Jerusalem with a military force in support of the procurator Fadus' implementation of Claudius' decision to undo the grant of custody over the high priest's garments (*Ant.* 15.405–406; 20.6–7). Sulla's *Lex Cornelia de maiestate* (81–80 B.C.), apparently confirmed by the *Lex Iulia de repetundis* (59 B.C.) of Caesar's consulship, viewed a governor's departure from his own province as *prima facie* treason (Cicero, *Pis.* 50).

[162] Schürer 1890: 1.380–81 – citing for Vitellius, who removed Pilate, Tacitus, *Ann.* 6.32; for Quadratus, who removed Cumanus, *Ann.* 12.54.

[163] In *Ann.* 6.32 Tacitus is talking about Parthian affairs and Tiberius' measures to control them, including the delegation of authority for the East to the then-virtuous legate of Syria, L. Vitellius. *Ann.* 12.54 merely describes Quadratus' intervention in an alleged (but evidently garbled) squabble between Felix as Samarian champion and Cumanus.

[164] See Bird 1994: xii–xxii.   [165] Cf. the anonymous *Epitome of the Caesars* 9.12–13.

[166] Suetonius (*Tit.* 11) gives Titus' age at death as 41; Victor correctly has 39 (*De Caes.* 10.5).

12. The strongest evidence in my view is the Flavian celebration of Judaea's conquest (Chapter 1). The Judaea they were so proud to have added cannot have been known as an existing province. In the words of one Flavian poet, Titus "destroyed by war the fierce tribes of Palestine!"[167] Making a province of a reduced territory was normal, and it made sense for the Flavians to create the province and install a legate and legion after their claims of conquest. It is hard to imagine how this could have made sense to anyone if Judaea had long been known as a province. When Hadrian suppressed the Bar-Kochba Revolt (A.D. 135), in what was then clearly a consular two-legion province of Judaea, even though the fighting was much more sustained and intense than in the Flavian first revolt,[168] a triumph was out of the question for him. The Flavians had made so much fuss about adding Judaea that a similar claim from him would have been ridiculous. No longer indebted to the Flavians, Hadrian went his own way by building Aelia Capitolina over Jerusalem's ruins, at once erasing his predecessors' memory and exalting his family. After the war he renamed the Flavian province, which could no longer be meaningfully named for *Jerusalem's* hinterland of Judaea, the old Herodotean Syria-Palaestina.[169]

A.D. 6: *The census, Judas the Galilean/Gaulanite, and the sicarii*

We have seen that scholars usually treat A.D. 6 and Judas the Galilean's protests as the beginning of Judaea's freedom movement and the progression toward war. Solomon Zeitlin put the standard view succinctly: "The Sicarii were the followers of the Fourth Philosophy which was founded by Judas of Galilee in the year 6 CE."[170] To untangle the knot of assumptions behind this, we must reconsider the evidence. Fortunately, there is little.

---

[167] Silius Italicus 605–606.   [168] Eck 1999b; Capponi 2010.

[169] Cf. Burrell 1993. This change has been explained by Hadrian's alleged hatred of Jews, "the aim being to obliterate the Jewish character of the Holy Land, and the implication being that the province was not really the land of the Jews but was basically Syrian and Hellenistic" (Feldman 1990: 15). But Hadrian was an enthusiastic city-builder who established "pagan" temples in Judaean Tiberias and Sepphoris, as on Mt. Gerizim (Smallwood 1981: 462). Only this case apparently ignited a revolt (Dio 69.12.1; Schäfer 2003: 45–47). Although any phase in the project – temple (perhaps originally for Jews in 117; cf. Capponi 2010), city beginning in 117, renamed province from 135 – might have had anti-Judean motives, that seems an unnecessary hypothesis. In choosing the provincial name, Hadrian followed the convention that whereas *poleis* were personal (Aelia, Julias, Caesarea, Sebaste, Iotapata, Tiberias), provinces indicated ethnic constituencies. Because Judaea was the famous *chōra* of *Jerusalem*, but Jerusalem was gone, and anyway Judaea was the Flavian's display province, that would have been a very odd choice. *Syria–Palaestina* was logical as the other old, informal ethnic name.

[170] Zeitlin 1965: 316.

War 2.118 notes very briefly that when Archelaus was deposed and the equestrian governor arrived, "a certain Galilean fellow by the name of Judas" tried to incite rebellion. In Josephus' disparaging portrait, this "eccentric sophist" was "censuring the local people, that they would put up with paying tax to the Romans, thus tolerating mortal masters besides God." In a forced segue, Josephus insists that these fringe elements had nothing to do with Judaea's three philosophical schools, especially the amazing Essenes, which he raptly describes at length – without further reference to A.D. 6 (2.119–66).

Josephus knows more about Judas but does not see fit to mention it here. Later will he note incidentally that two factional leaders at the time of the war were a son and a descendant of *that Judas who had called for rebellion at the time of the census* (2.433; 7.253). Even the census had not appeared in his brief reference to Judas and A.D. 6.

Antiquities elaborates considerably. There the legate Quirinius conducts a property census when Judaea is annexed to Syria (17.354; 18.2). The people of Jerusalem spontaneously balk at this demand and protest. The high priest Joazar mollifies them long enough to conduct the census (18.3), but then Judas – now called a Gaulanite and teamed with the Pharisee named Saddok – denounces the registration as tantamount to slavery.[171] "The people heard what they said with pleasure," Josephus remarks (18.6), and the two men thus inaugurated a "fourth philosophy." This philosophy, which Josephus did not mention in *War*, here provides a literary frame (18.9, 23) for the three respectable philosophies (18.11–22). It is obviously a literary creation for this

---

[171] Many scholars have assumed from the coincidence of name and mention of Galilee – with the authority of Schürer-Vermes (1.381; already Schürer 1874: 251 [*sicherlich identisch*]) and Hengel (2011: 329–32; bibliography n. 101) – that this Judas is the same one who agitated in Sepphoris in 4 B.C. (*War* 2.56), son of a Hezekiah killed by Herod before the latter was king (1.204). Cohen (1979: 111) is so sure that he charges Josephus with sloppiness for introducing the *same man* twice. For Price (1992: 20–21, bibliography in n. 69), the only reason *not* to identify the men is Josephus' failure to do so; "his calculated silence" serves the literary purpose of fragmenting the rebel tradition, which conceals the truth. Historical method is unclear in such cases. (a) Josephus' portrait of Hezekiah as a "bandit-chief" who had been raiding Syrian property around Galilee suggests a problem with neighbours rather than Rome (*War* 1.204; 2.56; *Ant.* 14.159–60). And his son Judas was reportedly occupied with rivals for power *in Sepphoris* (*War* 2.56; *Ant.* 17.271–72). Of course he *might* be the same fellow as Judas of 6 in Jerusalem, but why should we think so? (b) Because Judas is among the most commonly attested names of the time, there is no reason to identify any two Judases just because they have a link of some kind with Galilee – or the Golan. (c) Josephus does not try to *obscure* dynastic-rebel links. *War* pointedly connects Menachem and Eleazar ben Yair with Judas of 6, while *Antiquities* adds sons executed by Tiberius Alexander (*War* 2.433, 447; *Ant.* 20.102). Josephus' mention of these chronologically problematic links suggests a half-hearted effort *to affiliate* them. (d) Scholars who doubt the identification bear no burden of proof but nevertheless have offered cogent reasons, especially in relation to chronology: the patriarch Hezekiah (d. 47 B.C.) having a son vigorously leading a revolt 53 years after his death, and his son doing the same 60 years thereafter (Kreissig 1970: 114–16; Smallwood 1981: 153 n. 40).

context. It could not have worked in the structure of *War* 2, where the events of A.D. 6 are quickly left behind. Judas and Saddok's rejection of not only *foreign* domination but any rule other than divine seems directed against those Judaeans who would cooperate with the annexation and census, not against the Romans (18.4–10, 23–25).[172]

Focusing on *Antiquities*' literary construction, scholars have imagined the historical Judas as the crystallization of virulent anti-Roman ideology:

> The hardening of Jewish nationalist feeling into a militant resistance movement at the very start of the period of Roman rule [in A.D. 6 with Judas] was the fundamental cause of the recurrent disturbances of the next sixty years and of the revolt which was their climax.[173]

But the eminent scholar quoted here knows that Roman rule had been in place for seventy years (Chapter 1). What was new in A.D. 6 that caused such problems?

Let us sharpen this question with another. Would the Judaeans of Jerusalem have had cause to protest, before Judas and Saddok intervened, if Archelaus had not been removed? What if he had continued in office for decades as his brothers Philip and Antipas did in the north? The large Judaean populations in their tetrarchies were not subject to annexation and had no mentioned role in these protests of A.D. 6.[174] This suggests that there was no Judaean-Roman problem, but that only the changes facing Jerusalem in A.D. 6 drew a storm of protest there. Some scholars have suggested that this was just the final explosion of a hatred *against Rome* that was for some reason free to express itself with Archelaus' removal.[175] But that would not explain the description in *Antiquities* 18.

If we read Josephus' account contextually, we find Jerusalem's unhappy populace, who are only later urged on by Judas and Saddok, rejecting the longstanding effort of the city's elders to free Jerusalem *from a Herodian monarch*

---

[172] That Luke-Acts also features the legate Quirinius' census, rebellion, and Judas the Galilean (Luke 2:1–2; Acts 5:37) suggests literary influence from Josephus.

[173] cf. Applebaum 1971: 158–60, 166; Smallwood 1981: 153–55 (here 155); Vermes 1981: 40–42 ("The struggle against the Empire"); Schürer-Vermes 1.381–82; Goodman 1987: 93–96 (accepting Judas' militant anti-Romanism, *but* seeing it as marginal among the war's causes); most elaborately the third chapter of Hengel 1989 [1961], as still 2011 (with Deines' concluding essay, 403–39); Schwier 1989: 137, 150–51, 259 (with cautions); Price 1992: 15, 20–27; Horsley 1993: 80–89 (emphasizing the social and community-organizing expressions of the ideology); Jossa 2001: 63–67; Labbé 2012: 238 n. 1.

[174] Schürer-Vermes 1.405.

[175] So Applebaum 1971: 158 (the revolt both anti-Roman and anti-Herodian); Horsley 1993: ("The harshness of Herodian client kingship, continued by Archelaus, may well have been a factor, provoking as it did a high level of critical resentment against the Roman imperial situation generally"). Horsley sees direct taxation as the main concern. Goodman (1987: 93) rightly observes that Judas' ideological slogan (rejection of *all* mortal rulers) should *logically* have applied equally to Herodians and others. That is surely a clue to its artificial nature as a product of Josephus' rhetoric.

and see it *annexed to Syria* (*Ant.* 17.300–314). They did not get their wish in 4 B.C., but it has finally been granted with the removal of Archelaus in A.D. 6. The popular protest only now, upon that annexation to Syria, suggests that the people had been relatively content with Archelaus, much as their compatriots in the north were content under Philip and Antipas. The change they were protesting was *the removal* of a ruler from Jerusalem and the annexation to Syria.

Although the implementation of the census may have been unpleasant and intrusive,[176] it is unlikely that the main cause of such vehement protest was either a percentage of tax increase or an ideological aversion to census-taking, much less a belief that Judaea could tolerate no earthly ruler. No one has ever wished to pay taxes, but it is doubtful that these were going to increase greatly in A.D. 6, or be higher than other provincial levels, and the issue does not arise in Josephus.[177] As for the prospect of a census, the biblical book of Numbers opens with one, and Judaeans must have submitted to many such registrations during long centuries of foreign rule.[178] The possibility that Judas and Saddok

---

[176] We cannot be sure of the mechanics. Josephus indicates that the legate entered Judaea as part of his province. The high priest Joazar's role suggests broad local-elite cooperation. Quirinius may have ordered legionary tribunes, the prefect in Caesarea, and auxiliary officers to assist. A copied Latin inscription honouring Q. Aemilius Secundus, prefect of an auxiliary cohort in northern Syria, mentions that he was entrusted by Quirinius with the census of Syrian Apamaea in A.D. 6 and recalls the number of persons registered (*CIL* 3.6687; *ILS* 2683; discussion in Kennedy 2006). The Babatha Archive offers a possible parallel, recording her property declaration before an equestrian military officer after moving from Arabia (*P. Yadin* 16). The census of A.D. 127 in Arabia is evidenced by fragments of property declarations among the documents of other Judaeans fleeing Arabia at the time of the Bar Kochba Revolt (Cotton 1991).

[177] Whether Herod or Archelaus paid tribute to Rome is uncertain. In principle all subject territory was liable to tribute or indemnity, but Rome dealt with client kings flexibly (Braund 1984: 63–66; Lintott 1993: 70–96). As one who enjoyed a possibly unique relationship with Augustus, Herod supplied assistance when needed (Richardson 1996: 229–34; Shatzman 1999: 81–82). Did this exempt him from tribute? Pompey had placed Judaea under tribute along with the rest of Syria (*War* 1.154), and Julius Caesar required it from Hyrcanus II (*Ant.* 14.200–10 with Smallwood 1981: 33–40; Pucci ben Zeev 1998: 33–40). Taxes were apparently lightened by Caesar in the mid-40s B.C., but still reportedly amounted to 25 percent of produce – not counting the tithe to native rulers (*Ant.* 14.200–206; cf. Pucci ben Zeev 1998: 85–88). Appian (*Bell. civ.* 5.75.318–19) seems to have Herod assessed some kind of tribute, at least by Marc Antony (or one time only?) for Idumaea and Samaria (Pastor 1997: 109–10). *Ant.* 17.308, although in a highly rhetorical speech accusing Herod, claims that the king made heavy annual exactions from his subjects and expected extravagant gifts from the elite. For the tax burden under Herod and Archelaus see *War* 2.4, 84–86 and Herod's gestures toward tax relief (*Ant.* 15.365; 16.64; 17.25), with Schalit 1969: 262–98; Braund 1984: 63–66; Lintott 1993: 70–96. Tacitus mentions an appeal to Tiberius from Syria and Judaea for tax relief in A.D. 17 (*Ann.* 2.42), whereas Josephus has Agrippa II emphasize Judaea's relatively light burden in relation to other provinces (*War* 2.382–86).

[178] Num 1:2; 4:2, 22; 14:29; cf. Exod 30:12; 38:26. The Ptolemies, who ruled the area from about 300 to 200 B.C., kept records down to the village level. The story of David's census, which for some reason becomes a sin, is odd, as the Chronicler recognized in changing the

would recognize no mortal ruler is a problem first because the popular unrest preceded their involvement. Second, such a platform would explain neither the previous five centuries nor the timing here.

It seems rather that the popular protests, which the charismatic pair reignited, were reactions to the changes that came in A.D. 6 with Archelaus' removal, involving annexation to Syria and property registration. What these represented most obviously, in realist terms, was Jerusalem's dramatic loss of status. The *polis* that had controlled much of Coele-Syria, even in the rump version of Archelaus' rule, was about to become just another *polis* under Roman officials: the legate in Antioch (Antiochus IV's capital of old), an equestrian official in Caesarea, and an auxiliary army under the latter's command, recruited from Jerusalem's enemies. The Hasmonean and Herodian achievements that had given Jerusalem unmatched prestige in the region, though circumscribed under Archelaus, were now to be completely extirpated. Jerusalem was returning to a state of pre-Hasmonean vulnerability. Annexation would mean the loss of the right to administer its own finances and take revenue from the region, and perhaps most importantly the loss of the regional military garrison, which along with the rest of the administrative apparatus was catching the last train for the coast.

These losses furnished compelling reasons for the population of Jerusalem to worry, as events would soon show.

A central but neglected figure in these developments was the high priest Joazar, son of Boethus. He was the one, according to Josephus, who managed to quell spontaneous popular agitation. What was his angle? Joazar and his peers had apparently lobbied long and hard for this change. If so, they would have been delighted that it had come to pass. I mentioned the delegation of Judaean elders that travelled to Rome in 4 B.C., begging Augustus to free them from native monarchy.[179] This desire is not surprising, given the contempt with which Herod had treated the priestly elite.[180] Why would they want another round under Herod's twenty-something son, who might be in place for another thirty or fifty years? They were desperately hoping to have their status restored under the high priest Joazar, Herod's final appointee. But Augustus' decision to install Archelaus put their hope on ice for a decade.

Commagene in northern Syria provides an illuminating parallel. When its king Antiochus III died A.D. 17, there was a split reaction and two delegations went to the emperor Tiberius. The nobles pleaded to be incorporated into

---

instigator from God (2 Sam 24:1) to Satan (1 Chron 21:1). It provides no obvious basis for imagining a national antipathy to census.

[179] *War* 2.80–91 (esp. 90–91); cf. *Ant.* 17.300, 304–14.

[180] See Goodman 1987: 29–48, 109–33 for Herod's evisceration and re-creation of the ruling class.

Syria without a king, while the common people begged for a new king – as befitted their proud ancestral customs and status. In that case Tiberius accommodated the elite perspective and incorporated Commagene into Syria. Gaius Caligula restored native rule under Antiochus IV in 38, however, before it was lost again in 72.[181] What happened in Judaea after Herod's death looks very similar. The difference is that Augustus went the other way and appointed Archelaus as a provisional monarch, perhaps partly in deference to Herod's will and partly because Herodian control of Coele-Syria had been so productive for Rome. After a decade of Archelaus, however, he had seen enough. Now accommodating the aristocrats' wishes, he banished Archelaus and annexed Judaea to Syria. It was the people's turn to complain.

Joazar was a brother or a son of the long-serving high priest Simon, son of Boethus (served 23–6/5 B.C.),[182] whom Herod had brought from Alexandria to Jerusalem. Herod had fallen for Simon's daughter, Mariamme II, and appointed her father high priest to ennoble her pedigree. When he divorced Mariamme II near the end of his life, suspecting her of intrigue, he ousted the father too and appointed Matthias, who was married to Simon's sister or a different daughter (6/5–4 B.C.; *Ant.* 17.78). Matthias was also gone soon, for seeming to sympathize with the teachers whose students pulled down Herod's eagle (*Ant.* 17.164–65). Herod's final shot at the high priesthood was Joazar. The king died shortly after appointing him.

Joazar seems to have had two terms as high priest, if Josephus' account is not badly confused. He was a new high priest when Archelaus as king-designate supposedly began a listening tour, inviting his father's subjects to state their grievances and desires in an effort to keep them calm before his confirmation hearings. The people took up this invitation to candour and called for the punishment of those Herod had honoured, including his last high priestly appointment Joazar. In the story, this demand does not seem connected with anything that Joazar had done. They simply demanded a new high priest untainted by Herod, who would be chosen for his commitment to the laws and not as a political move. Archelaus promised support for their demands but declined to act before his confirmation, avoiding executive decisions that might seem presumptuous. Once confirmed as ethnarch by Augustus,

---

[181] Tacitus, Ann. 2.52 (end) with Josephus, *Ant.* 18.53.

[182] Smallwood (1962: 15) thinks it more likely that Joazar was a brother to Simon and uncle to Mariamme II. That would make the best sense of 17.164, according to which Joazar (a son of Boethus like Simon) was brother to Matthias's wife – an unnamed daughter of Boethus on this reading. If Simon (presumably 40 or older, for his daughter to marry Herod), a sister, and brother Joazar all came from Alexandria in about 23 B.C., Joazar might have been rather old by A.D. 6, nearly thirty years later. If he was a son of Simon and brother to both Mariamme II and the sister married by Matthias, the chronology (including opportunities for Matthias to marry a young sister) becomes easier to imagine.

however, he indeed removed Joazar. Josephus curiously comments that the pretext was alliance with "the seditious."[183] How does this connect with the people's demand for his removal as Herod's appointee?

Josephus' language is vague (he did not expect our scrutiny), and Archelaus had at least two groups of opponents that might qualify as seditious: the energetic members of the elite who had pleaded with Augustus not to appoint him and the popular leaders who were demanding a pious high priest. There may have been occasional opportunistic collaborations between the groups. Joazar's predecessor Matthias was reportedly removed on suspicion of supporting popular pietists, although it seems implausible that he, a member of the super-elite, shared principles with those pietists. Perhaps Joazar had made tactical moves in finding common interests with such charismatic leaders. Or perhaps Josephus' "sedition" is a contentless, generic reason for a monarch to dismiss a high official, to cover the monarch's mere capitulation to popular demand. Or perhaps Archelaus dismissed Joazar in 4 B.C. for associating with the *anti-monarchical* elite – those who had appealed to Augustus against him and therefore posed an ongoing threat.

However Joazar's first removal played out, Archelaus appears to have reinstated him at some point, for he is high priest again when the ethnarch is removed in A.D. 6. Joazar now manages the whole transition away from monarchy, persuading the people to accept annexation and census. How did he come to be so involved?

Circumstantial evidence suggests a simple answer: Joazar had led the movement to oust Archelaus and so this was the fulfillment of his fondest wishes. His high standing certainly placed him among "the principal men" of the Judaeans – and Samarians – who had lobbied Augustus for Archelaus' removal in A.D. 6; he may well have been their conductor.[184] Augustus' decision to support the aristocrats now makes good sense, given that their cooperation was important to the province's administration, that the appeal was inter-ethnic, and that he had disappointed Jerusalem's elite for a decade.

Josephus claims that Joazar briefly won the people over, long enough to effect the transition and census. That success did not protect him, however, when popular disquiet was stoked by Judas and Saddok. The ordinary folk did not share the interests of Joazar and his elite friends. They had walked taller for decades because of Jerusalem's lofty position as Rome's leading ally and regional broker, the military and financial centre of southern Syria. Those had been salad days for Judaean culture in the region. Now Joazar and the aristocrats were eager to trade all this away for their own aggrandizement.

---

[183] *War* 2.7–8 // *Ant.* 17.207–209 (209: Archelaus' refusal to implement the demands), 339 ("removed Joazar son of Boethus . . . accusing him of banding together with the seditious").

[184] *Ant.* 17.342; cf. *War* 2.111.

Popular contempt for Joazar became so strong under Judas and Saddok that Quirinius had little choice but to depose him – "the common lot (ἡ πληθύς) having rebelled against him" (*Ant.* 18.26).

I am not suggesting that this reconstruction is obvious, much less inferable from Josephus. His notices, which were clear enough for his purposes, leave large gaps covered by vague language for us who want to know exactly what happened. I am proposing a hypothesis that would explain his various indications, contextually and by analogy, as we try to figure out what was at stake in A.D. 6.

Scholarship has tended, we have seen, to assume a split between ordinary folk and the elite. But in Commagene things were more complicated: The elite was divided as nobles wished to be free of monarchs. Josephus' account seems best explained by similar conditions in Judaea. Some priestly aristocrats, perhaps mainly Sadducean (*Ant.* 13.297–98; 18.15), considered themselves to be Jerusalem's proper leaders, and so they lobbied Augustus to end monarchical rule.[185] Against them were the royal family, court hangers-on, the masses, and popular charismatic leaders such as Judas or the Pharisee Saddok. Close bonds between monarchs and masses were common in antiquity. Autocrats typically curried popular favour as a bulwark against the nobility, who were usually the main threat to monarchy.[186] Agrippa I and II, having learnt lessons from their forebears, seem to have worked particularly hard to strengthen ties with both the people and the chief-priestly elite, although the tensions appear even in those cases.[187]

If we put the pieces together along these lines, then the issue for Judas, Saddok, and company concerned not *Roman rule* but rather Jerusalem's position in southern Syria.[188] Since Hasmonean times Jerusalem had been

---

[185] For the base of Sadducees in wealthy priestly circles, contrasted with popular support for the Pharisees, see *Ant.* 13.297–98; 18.15, 17.

[186] In Rome, the emperors Gaius (Suetonius, *Gaius* 15–21; Josephus, *Ant.* 19.115: "honoured and loved by the folly of the populace") and Nero (Suetonius, *Nero* 53, 57; Tacitus, *Ann.* 1.4; 2.8; Josephus, *Ant.* 20.154), although hated by the elite and hence in western tradition, were reportedly very popular with the masses even as they acted brutally toward members of the Senate. A classic case is Domitian. See Suetonius, *Dom.* 4 (extravagant benefactions to the populace), 10, 13 (measures against the aristocracy), 23 (senators' rapture at his demise).

[187] Agrippa I reinstated the high-priestly house of Boethus, appointing two high priests from this family, which was last seen with Joazar (*Ant.* 19.297, 342); cf. Goodman (1987: 43–44) and Agrippa II's close relations with Jerusalem's leaders in this chapter and the next.
A notable case of tension was priestly indignation at Agrippa II's construction of a porch from which he could watch the priestly service in the temple.

[188] Pondering what the rebels of 66 could reasonably have hoped for, Goodman (2007: 424–25) proposes that experience of autonomy under Agrippa I several decades earlier might have inspired them to seek that status again. Open resistance toward Rome would not seem the safest way to win such an imperial concession, and Goodman's insight might better suit A.D. 6 and 44, moments when the loss of that status was imminent.

pre-eminent.[189] The people were unhappy and fearful about relinquishing that, especially in view of the grievances that neighbouring populations had stored up under Jerusalem's dominance. The dangers of this change were palpable, but neither ideological nor anti-Roman. The greatest practical risk was that the foreign remainder of Herod's army, which had been commanded by Archelaus in Jerusalem, would now be moved to its ethnic recruiting grounds and under the command of those whose behaviour was unpredictable. This was uncharted territory.

The aristocrat Josephus, unsympathetic to monarchy at the best of times,[190] had no great interest in fairly explaining Judas' or the people's pro-Archelaus views. He was content to ridicule Judas, saddling him with the absurd platform of tolerating no earthly ruler and making him sound like a petulant teenager. If divine sovereignty or theocracy *had* been their goal, Judas and Saddok should have been delighted with the monarch's removal and the arrival of priestly-collegial governance.[191] Judas' real concern and that of the people he inspired was, we have reason to think, more serious and more practical than Josephus suggests.

The execution of Judas' sons by Tiberius Alexander might be illuminated by this reconstruction. Claudius' installation of Agrippa I (A.D. 41) must have seemed a godsend to those who lost in A.D. 6 and longed for the restoration of Jerusalem's status – those who shared the worldview of Judas and Saddok. Conversely, the king's early death in 44 sparked unseemly celebrations among the other side, the relieved Samarians and Caesareans. *Antiquities* mentions that Ti. Julius Alexander crucified two of Judas' sons in A.D. 46–48, on charges unspecified (20.102). The date raises the possibility that they were involved in the turmoil following Agrippa's death and the renewed shift of power from Jerusalem to Caesarea. Perhaps the swagger of the auxiliary and their Samarian relatives, which portended new dangers for Judaeans, became too much to bear. Judas' sons might have had concerns like those of their father about the perils of Jerusalem's loss of status. If they became involved in confrontations with Samarian auxiliary soldiers, Tiberius Alexander would have had little choice but to punish them. This is highly speculative, of course; I am trying to show what the hypothesis advanced here might explain.

On such a reconstruction, the prevailing view of Judas as a voice of popular discontent would be correct, with the major qualification that Roman rule was not the concern. Goodman would be also correct (against the general view) about Judas' lack of impact in the years following A.D. 6, but this would not be because Judas was an irrelevant eccentric. Rather, Judas faded from view after A.D. 6 because his moment had passed. Once Jerusalem had fully rejoined

---

[189] Pliny, *Nat.* 5.70 ("the most illustrious/glorious city of the east"); Tacitus, *Hist.* 5.2.
[190] Mason 2009b, 2012b.   [191] *Apion* 2.164–65, 184–87.

Syria and the auxiliary army had been established in Caesarea, there was no yield in continuing to protest a *fait accompli*. Protests would be renewed, however, perhaps by Judas' sons and others, when Agrippa's death brought a repeated and more alarming shift of power to Caesarea.

This is the best place in our investigation to tackle the related problem of the *sicarii*. As we have seen, scholars who trace an anti-Roman freedom movement to Judas also consider him the original *sicarius* if not also a "Zealot."[192] Some of the doubtful assumptions behind this view have been challenged by others,[193] so I shall focus on the issues as I see them in the context we are developing. The crux is a thorny passage near the end of *War*, which some have read as enrolling Judas among the *sicarii*.[194]

This passage comes when Josephus is introducing the siege of Masada (A.D. 73/74) and he remarks that the site was occupied by *sicarii* led by Eleazar (from A.D. 66), "a descendant of the Judas who persuaded many Judaeans not to involve themselves with the property registrations when Quirinius was sent into Judaea as assessor, as we formerly explained." He continues (7.254–55):

> For at that time (τότε γὰρ) the *sicarii* joined together against those who were willing to submit to the Romans and handled them in every way like enemies: seizing their possessions, rustling their cattle, and setting fire to their homes. For they declared them no different from foreigners, who ignobly gave up the liberty so hard-won [or prized] by Judaeans, having capitulated and chosen slavery to the Romans.

The lofty claims of the *sicarii* were only a pretext, Josephus charges, for their savagery. When others were persuaded by them "and participated in the revolt and joined the war with Rome," these followers suffered terribly at their hands. "Indeed, that period (ὁ χρόνος ἐκεῖνος) had somehow become productive of every kind of baseness among the Judaeans" (7.259). Josephus concludes by describing the *sicarii* as the first to turn on other Judaeans with violence, before proceeding to excoriate John, Simon, the Idumaeans, and the Zealots, who surpassed the *sicarii* in their evils.

---

[192] Hengel 2011: 16, esp. 51, also 82, 85, 88–89, 381–89. Cf. Zeitlin 1965: 302 ("The Sicarii were members of the Fourth Philosophy who had been organized by Judas…"), 316; 1967: 259; Smith 1971: 18 ("Judas' sect survived, continued its opposition to the Romans, was led by his descendants, and in the mid-fifties, … made itself notorious by a series of murders. … These won this party the name of 'the Sicarii'"); Schürer-Vermes 2.602 ("the Sicarii were organized by Judas at the census, and … they remained loyal to his descendants").

[193] See especially Brighton 2009, for *War*.

[194] On disambiguating *sicarii* and Zealots see already Lake 1917: 57–62, who also kept the *sicarii* distinct from Judas and A.D. 6; cf. Zeitlin 1965, 1967; Smith 1971; Black 1974. Hengel (1989: 380–404) knew the criticisms yet still imagined a unified freedom movement that could be conveniently labelled Zealot.

To what period does the first "at that time," in the block quotation, refer? Hengel saw no ambiguity, taking it as self-evident that Josephus dates the *sicarii* to *Judas'* time of A.D. 6. But we have reason for doubt. Is Josephus elaborating *on the time of Judas* just mentioned or, having intended only briefly to mention Eleazar's ancestry from Judas, has he quickly returned to his main subject: the rogues' gallery of John, Simon, Zealots — *at the time leading up to the recent war?*

Although the phrase is admittedly ambiguous on its own, and Hengel's reading would be plausible if we focused on what immediately precedes it, the larger context favours the latter reading.[195] *War* first introduced *sicarii* — under Felix's governorship in the mid-50s — as then a new and "different species of bandit," as people who killed their Judaean neighbours with concealed weapons (2.254–55). In that same context Josephus makes much of a *new claim* then being aired, that submission to Rome's *imperium* amounted to voluntary slavery.[196] That is also the context in which the burning and plundering of fellow Judaeans' homes first occurs in his narrative (2.265), which he describes as a characteristic activity of *sicarii* (4.400–403). These points are all brought together in the *War* 7 passage. In 7.257–58, Josephus' references to the people who were persuaded by the *sicarii* and *joined the revolt against Rome*, moreover, and again to "that period" as the time of John, Simon, and the Zealots, show that he is speaking of the 50s and 60s and not A.D. 6. Although his first dating phrase could have been clearer (Who will cast the first stone?), he seems to be identifying Eleazar of Masada in two ways: (a) as a descendant of the Judas who was active in A.D. 6 and (b) as a *sicarius* of the type that arose under Felix. There is no reason here to see Judas as a *sicarius*.

Contrary to widespread impressions, it should also be stressed, Josephus gives the *sicarii* no role in the war against Rome. *War* mentions the group fifteen times, *Antiquities* four times, and both narratives date the appearance of this phenomenon to the 50s.[197] But *sicarii* do not appear in *War* 3 to 6, from the arrival of the Flavians to Jerusalem's fall, except for incidental references to their activities *against fellow Judaeans* around Masada, away from the conflict with Rome (4.400, 516). Their activities at Masada and in Egypt and Cyrene we may postpone to Chapter 9. Here I offer two concluding observations on *sicarii*.

First, although some of Josephus' phrasing suggests that they constituted a distinct group or faction,[198] and so this is the general scholarly assumption,[199] in most cases he seems to be using a name that signifies a *mode* of killing – like

---

[195] So too Brighton 2009: 100.
[196] *War* 2.264; cf. 4.159, 175–78, 185, 258, 347, 389, 510; 5.28.
[197] *War* 2.264; *Ant.* 20.186 (τότε μάλιστα ἐπλήθυον).
[198] *War* 2.425; 4.400, 516; 7.410: e.g., "they were called *sicarii*."
[199] Brighton (2009: 1–22) surveys the scholarship.

shooter, hitman, or assassin – rather than a group or faction with card-carrying members. Most impressive in this regard is *War*'s first description of *sicarii*. These *kinds of bandit*, it says, would murder people in the city, day or night and especially at festivals, by concealing daggers under their clothes. The murder of the high priest Jonathan by this means began an epidemic, with the result that Jerusalemites would not only keep their enemies at a safe distance but became suspicious even *of friends* who might be carrying (*War* 2.254–57). Fear was pervasive. If so many people could be *sicarii*, however, we are not looking at a political group, or a group at all – any more than the larger category "bandits" defined a political faction.

The *Antiquities* parallel portrays Jonathan's murder as a special contract killing arranged by the procurator Felix, who paid one of Jonathan's friends for the deed, and he in turn hired bandits who used concealed daggers. Because these criminals got away with their bold technique, they returned to the city often to do away with other enemies of theirs or to kill for other people under paid contract (*Ant.* 20.162–65). *Antiquities* does not yet call these men *sicarii*, postponing the use of that label for a recurrence of the same type of crime (20.185). But none of these passages suggests an anti-Roman rebel faction called *sicarii*.

If that is so, we do not need to find heroic ways of linking the *sicarii* of Alexandria and Cyrene with those of Masada.[200] There need be no organizational connection, only Josephus' choice of language. But why would he use this Latin term so often, while writing in Greek? *Sicarius* does not appear in any surviving Greek text before Josephus and the New Testament. Byzantine lexicographers who mention the term – perhaps because of Josephus and Acts – emphasize that it was a *Roman* expression for assassins who used concealed curved daggers[201] – not for a political faction. The Latin word was indeed well known in Rome because of a law passed under Cornelius Sulla (81 B.C.) against *sicarii* and poisoners, and the courts established to try cases under that law (*inter sicarios*).[202] Twenty-seven-year-old Cicero made his reputation defending an accused *sicarius* – actually a wealthy target of Sulla – in the first known trial (*Pro Sex. Roscio Amerino*). Cicero uses the term *sicarius*, which he glosses as "a brazen man often involved in murder" (*Pro Rosc.* 39), dozens of times, sometimes to characterize his elite adversaries (*Verr.* 2.1.9). In the third century, however, the Christian Origen [*C. Cels.* 2.13] was still using the term for a specific crime in Roman law.

How are we to account for Josephus' heavy use of *sicarii*? The common explanation is that it was a name given by "the Roman authorities" to a

---

[200] See *War* 7.410–15, 437, 444 with Brighton 2009.
[201] John of Lydia, *Mag.* p. 98; Photius, *Bib.* Σικάριοι ("a class of bandits. The Romans call curved swords/daggers *sicae*, thus those using them were called *sicarii*").
[202] Justinian, *Inst.* 4.18.5; cf. *Dig.* 1.2.2.32; 4.8.32.6; 29.5.3.13.1, 25.1; 47.9.3.8; esp. 48.8.

Judaean rebel group, which then took it as a badge of honour (cf. Protestant or Huguenot).[203] But if Roman law used the term for a mode of killing, why would Roman officials think to fasten it on a political faction in Judaea? And which officials would they be? Those who came east spoke Greek in their dealings with locals and with auxiliary soldiers. Finally, if there was a group that officials for some reason called *sicarii*, what did the group members call themselves and why does *their* name appear nowhere, even in sarcasm (cf. Zealots in Chapter 7)? However we answer such questions, the biggest problem is that Josephus obviously does not reserve the tag for a particular group. He uses it in the usual Latin/Roman way, to indicate a style of insidious murder and people unafraid to threaten such violence.

The simplest explanation of his usage is that Josephus employed a familiar scare-word *in Rome* to make the violence in Judaea vivid for his local audience. On the meter of fear, the threat of sudden knife-blade attack was akin to that of poisoning, both being achieved by stealth. Only Latin possessed the *mot juste* for this kind of thing, and *sicarii* would evoke the desired response even for Greek speakers in the capital.[204] After finding the term useful for the rash of stealthy knife crime that allegedly broke out in the 50s, Josephus occasionally returned to it. Perhaps he chose it for the troublemakers in Egypt and Cyrene in *War* 7 because it was still in his mind from Masada.[205] At any rate, there seems no reason to think that first-century Judaeans would have answered a call for *sicarii*.

It would be a problem for this explanation if other texts from the period independently attested Judaean *sicarii*. Among remotely contemporary texts, however, only Acts 21:38 uses the term. A tribune asks Paul whether he is not "the Egyptian who was agitating some time ago, and led the 4,000 men of the *sicarii* into the desert." But this passage brims with problems, has nothing to do with anti-Roman behaviour, and seems best explained as a mangled recollection of Josephus.[206] Rabbinic literature, from centuries after the war, has scattered references to *siqra* and *siqarin*, sometimes with doubtful manuscript support, but these terms may be explained without reference to *sicarii*.[207]

---

[203] Hengel 2011: 395 with support cited.

[204] Ancient Greek had no particular word for assassins or cut-throats.

[205] This analysis intersects with Brighton 2009: e.g., 141–44, although he connects *sicarii* more programmatically with literary themes in *War*.

[206] For "the Egyptian [X]" (NB: The lack of a proper name seems more likely one author's literary choice than two independent characterizations) near *sicarii*, see *War* 2.254–61; *Ant.* 20.169–72, 186, with Mason 2003: 277–81. Such confusion would match Luke's famous use of the census under Augustus and Quirinius (featured only in *Antiquities*) to date Jesus' birth (Luke 2:1–2), impossibly, as well as his apparent reversal of the chronology for Judas and Theudas (a rare Greek contracted name, Acts 5:36–37).

[207] *M. Maksh.* 1.6 has Jerusalemites hiding fig cakes (presumably in the siege-induced famine) because of *sikarin*. *B. Git.* 56a mentions Abba Siqra (אסקר), nephew of Yohanan b. Zakkai,

Who were the Sebastene–Caesarean auxiliary?

I have proposed that regional tensions in southern Syria underlay the conflict that eventually brought legions in arms to Jerusalem and that these conflicts featured the auxiliary cohorts. Now we must try to clarify who these soldiers were.[208] In Chapter 3 we saw that auxiliary cohorts were typically the successors of allied armies when the territory fell under direct Roman rule. Subject populations remained subject to conscription whenever the Romans considered it necessary.[209] What about southern Syria?

King Herod (37–4 B.C.) had gradually built an army that fluctuated between perhaps 18,000 and 25,000 men. Although it had a Judaean majority, it included elements from around his kingdom – Greeks, Galileans, Ituraeans, Idumaeans, and especially Samarians, the other main ethnic constituency with Judaeans.[210] When Herod died, the intervention of the Syrian financial procurator Sabinus in his financial affairs, with a legion supporting the man's investigations, precipitated a crisis. Herod's army, torn between their loyalty to the deceased king and a new direct obedience to such Roman masters, reportedly broke up. Judaean units joined their compatriots in resisting the procurator's virtual invasion.

Some 2,000 Idumaean veterans reportedly defected, went home, and sought independence – whether for Idumaea or Judaea–Idumaea is not clear (*War* 2.55). After Herod's cousin Achiav persuaded them to give up their protests, some of their commanders were executed by Augustus in Rome (2.76–78).

A core of 3,000 Samarian–Sebastene soldiers, however, at least partly under Roman officers, remained in service, happily supporting the Syrian procurator's humiliation of Jerusalem (*War* 2.39–52). Apparently, these units became the heart of Archelaus' army. Judaean units may have remained through this period, given the army's reportedly eager support for the ethnarch and the continuity of some commanders from Herod's time (*War* 1.652; 2.3, 9). If they did remain that long, they seem to have disbanded in A.D. 6 with the transfer of this force to Caesarea. At this point the five or six remaining infantry cohorts and a cavalry wing[211] apparently became Rome's auxiliary army. It would function as a regional police force under the equestrian prefect.[212]

---

who ran a group of *biryoni* (thugs, bandits) at the time of the war. These passages would not match Josephus' account, however, because his *sicarii* had left Jerusalem by then. The rabbis used many Greek and Latin loanwords and might independently have borrowed an apt Latin term for murderers (again, no specific faction is suggested). As for the latter passage, *siqra* (with or without ') appears a number of times in rabbinic literature meaning scarlet or vermilion (*b. Zeb.* 53a; *Bech.* 17b; *Shabb.* 104b; *Meg.* 18b; *Men.* 97b).

[208] The main evidence is laid out in Schürer-Vermes 1.361–67.   [209] See Chapter 3.

[210] *War* 1.290–94. Rocca 2009: 10–22 gives a fresh survey of the evidence and crisp analysis in dialogue with the major study by Shatzman 1991.

[211] See *War* 3.66 (five cohorts from Caesarea and one cavalry wing supported Vespasian) and *Ant.* 19.364: five infantry cohorts from Sebaste and Caesarea (2,500 soldiers).

[212] *War* 2.39–52, 55, 77–78.

From the beginning of his reign, Herod had built up Samaria as a counter-weight to sometimes hostile Jerusalem: This was the key component of his regional "balancing programme."[213] He would resort to Samaria whenever Judaean antipathy became dangerous.[214] It was there that he married Mariamme I, and Malthace, the mother of Archelaus and Antipas, was herself Samarian. In 27 B.C. Herod grandly restored the Samarian capital, which had been destroyed by Hyrcanus and partially repopulated under Gabinius (*War* 1.166), renaming it Sebaste in honour of Augustus. Continuing this military city's tradition of cultic adaptability, he built there the first known temple to the cult of Augustus and Rome, a magnificent structure. He populated the *polis* with both local Samarians and a reported 6,000 of his veteran soldiers.[215] Together with opulent Caesarea on the coast, which became effectively Samaria's port, Sebaste was the proud home and recruiting base of the post-Archelaus auxiliary.

Among the cohorts and cavalry wings attested in literary and material evidence, which include Ituraean, Sebastene, and Caesarean cohorts in a slightly later period, we find no Judaean units.[216] This might be an accident of the evidence, but we have no indication anywhere that Judaean units made the transition to auxiliary service, and strong hints that they did not. We might wonder why.

To begin with, a blanket exemption from conscription had been granted to Judaeans by Julius Caesar, which seems to have been honoured thereafter.[217] It solved a real problem. Conditions for Judaeans who would serve alongside age-old enemies, near the others' home towns and away from Jerusalem, would have been unappealing in itself, aside from the challenges of observing Judaean law in relation to sabbath, festivals, and diet on foreign territory. The situation under Herod and even Archelaus would have been ideal for Judaean soldiers, by contrast, with their monarch commanding forces from Jerusalem and their position prestigious as members of the dominant group. Perhaps those Judaeans who wanted to remain in military service in A.D. 6 moved to the tetrarchies of Philip or Antipas.

This background explains why Josephus assumes (but does not explain) the close relationship between Judaea's regional enemies, especially Samarians, and the auxiliary. Josephus can call this force both Roman and Sebastene, but Sebaste *was* ancient Samaria. As we shall now see, this ethnic bond appears clearly in his account of events after Agrippa I's death, then a few years later under Cumanus, and again in Caesarea just before the war. The aristocrats who favoured annexation to Syria in A.D. 6 perhaps did not foresee such dangers. Perhaps they were so confident in the accustomed good will of emperors,

---

[213] For the phrase and much useful discussion see Bernett 2007: 66–98.
[214] *War* 1.303, 314, 344, 551; *Ant.* 15.292–96.   [215] *War* 1.403–404; *Ant.* 15.292, 296.
[216] Cf. Cheesman 1914: 57–101.   [217] *Ant.* 14.204; Schürer-Vermes 1.362–63.

Syrian legates, and equestrian governors, which they expected to cultivate, that they assumed this would mitigate any hazards. Most often it did.

V. DEADLY CONFLICT IN SOUTHERN SYRIA

The general scene

After Pompey brought Syria under Rome's *imperium*, he and his successors faced the problem of how best to govern this enormous area with its diverse cultures and traditions. The southern two-thirds of Syria were protectively ensconced by the newly allied Nabataean kingdom, with the forbidding Arabian desert beyond. The north of the province (modern Lebanon and western Syria) was the obvious place to focus Rome's military strength. One-seventh of the empire's legionary capability would go there, in garrisons radiating out from the capital Antioch to the Euphrates frontier with Parthia.

For internal governance the Romans had many options, which they seem to have selected according to certain governing instincts or values rather than a calculated grand strategy.[218] These principles included (a) economy of Roman investment and risk, exploiting provincial resources as fully as possible; (b) cultivating existing local elites in a province's *poleis*; (c) rewarding their friends and displaying trust, albeit with healthy suspicion; and (d) keeping each *polis* and ally separately dependent on Rome, to preclude any pooling of grievances or resources. We have discussed (a). Principles (b) and (c) were exemplified by Rome's innovation in offering its citizenship, sometimes even equestrian or senatorial status, to important friends.[219] In a model widely imitated since, local elites would do the heavy lifting of empire (tax collection and maintenance of local order). The governor supported their efforts as he toured his *poleis* and kept lines of communication open.[220] Juvenal's advice to young Ponticus about treating provincials well (*Sat.* 8) reflected the enlightened self-interest of the empire.

---

[218] Luttwak 1976 animated the debate with its effort to define Rome's evolving strategy over the centuries, although Millar 1977 has had a greater impact with its model of an early empire in crisis-response mode and no strategy. Luttwak was challenged especially for his analysis pertaining to the second century and later (e.g., Gruen 1978; Mann 1979; Isaac 1992 and Whittaker 1994). For the period of our interest, Luttwak makes valuable proposals about the logic behind the distribution and functions of the legions – as rapid responders, punishers, and image-enhancers. For the values in question, see Lendon 1997; Mattern 1999; Barton 2001; Meyer-Zwiffelhoffer 2002.

[219] See Dionysius, *Ant. rom.* 2.16–17; Aristides, *To Rome* 59–63; Lendon 1997; Ando 2000; Eckstein 2006: 312–13.

[220] Stevenson 1949; Lintott 1993; Swain 1996: 227–29 on assize centres; concise overview in Burton 2002: 423–39; full elaboration in Meyer-Zwiffelhoffer 2002.

Principles (b) and (c) produced the allied monarchies in Asia Minor, Syria, Nabataea, and North Africa.[221] These could be an ideal arrangement under the right conditions. In that case, Rome needed only one regional address for a large, alien, and inhospitable territory. Even better, the local potentate could be relied upon to pursue his own ambitions, and in the best case Rome could marry these with theirs, riding his ambition to enhance their assets. So it was with Herod, the Nabataeans, and the Commagenians.

The problem with a system based on friendships, of course, is the inevitability of death and succession. Emperors tried to keep the party going by having the spawn of their allied monarchs grow up in Rome, to forge strong social bonds, absorb Roman values, and prove their character.[222] But the kings first appointed, such as Herod, had earned their *gravitas* and political skill from hard work. Their children, growing up *as royals*, had no chance to develop such governing intelligence. By the end of the first century A.D., therefore, Rome had taken most allied kingdoms under their direct administration. Still, the principle of rewarding favourites remained a part of provincial governance.

The yin to this yang was (d), the principle of fragmentation. Local elites should be cultivated as spokes of a wheel, each dependent on the centre (cf. Machiavelli, *Prince* chap. 3). Subject peoples must not be tempted toward other unions or loyalties, especially those of shared misery. Tacitus expressed the idea when describing German tribes in violent conflict with each other: "May it always continue and remain with these nations, I pray: if not love for us, at least hatred of each other" (*Germ.* 33). Again, speaking of the nations in Britain (*Agr.* 12): "Our greatest advantage in coping with tribes so powerful is that they *do not act in concert*. It is rare that two or three cities join together to repel a common threat. So as long as they fight individually, they are beaten as one."[223] The same principle held for allied kings. When a Syrian legate was tempted to intervene in a local dispute, his advisors counselled non-interference on the ground that "every foreign crime should be regarded as welcome; in fact, the seeds of hatred should actually be sown" (*Ann.* 12.48.2). We have seen Josephus' claim that Tiberius arranged for Parthia to be attacked by neighbours to encourage its bond with Rome.[224] Sowing discord among enemies has remained a lynchpin of psychological warfare ever since (Chapter 3), and is embodied in the retroactive Latin slogan *divide et impera*![225]

---

[221] Braund 1984.

[222] Braund 1984: 9–21; cf. Roller 2003: 59–90 on the illustrative experience of King Juba II of Mauretania.

[223] For discussion see Stevenson 1949: 34–35, 39, 102–103.

[224] Josephus, *Ant.* 18.96–98; 19.338–42.

[225] The Governor of Bombay after the great mutiny of 1857: "*Divide et impera* was the old Roman motto, and it should be ours." Cited in Stewart 1951: 54; cf. Sutherland 1932:

When we consider Rome's government of southern Syria in these terms we reach surprising conclusions, against the tendency of research to see Judaeans as Rome's unique victims. In view of the background we have been developing, we may now survey the evidence crisply under two heads: first, the *uniquely close* Roman-Judaean bond and increasing hostility to Judaea from its neighbours; second, the sudden collapse of this protective balance, which led many Judaeans to choose armed self-help – in keeping with realist assumptions.

Roman favour – and local hostility – toward Jerusalem

Throughout the 130 years between Pompey and the war, Rome conspicuously favoured Jerusalem. Herod ruled Coele-Syria from Jerusalem for a quarter of that period. His sons, grandsons, and relatives then ruled significant sections of it: Archelaus, Antipas, Philip, Agrippa I, Herod of Chalcis, Tigranes, and Agrippa II. These men were by far the most prestigious allied-royal family in the region. Long after Herod's death, Agrippa I and II remained personal friends of Gaius and Claudius, whereas Agrippa II would be greatly honoured by the Flavians. No Ascalonite, Gadarene, or Samarian enjoyed anything close to this level of influence and practical impact.

It is not surprising that Jerusalem's renewed domination of southern Syria under Herod would irritate the neighbours. Although Josephus does not advertise these grievances, memories of disaffection survive. When Augustus' lieutenant Marcus Agrippa visited Asia Minor in 22 B.C., the renowned *polis* of Gadara, which Augustus had "given" to Herod a few years earlier, sent an embassy to accuse the king, along with grumpy delegates from other Decapolis cities, Samaria, and Gaza.[226] Refusing to hear complaints against his friend, however, Agrippa shackled the emissaries and sent them to the king, who magnanimously released them (*Ant.* 15.351). This did nothing to appease them. When Agrippa visited Syria two years later, "most" Gadarenes reportedly rushed to complain that Herod "was being too harsh in his orders, and tyrannical" (15.354). This time they were supported by Nabataeans and one Zenodorus, who had lost his territory north of Galilee to Herod. Again Marcus

---

231–32. Similarly Carnaticus, "General View of our Indian Army," *The Asiatic Journal and Monthly Register for British India and its Dependencies* 11 (1821): 429–39 (437), "*Divide et impera* should be the motto for our Indian administration, whether political, civil, or military." A search of British newspapers from 1600 to 1950 (including those of colonial America) turns up 366 instances of the phrase, a political maxim. For British imitation of Greece and especially Rome, see the editorial "Our Colonial Policy" in *The Colonial and Asiatic Review* 1 (1852): 1–10 (esp. 1–2). For doubts about the aptness of the model, see Brunt 1965. For applications elsewhere, Antonius 1938: 54, 69, 371–72; Basu 1927: 74–79; in British Palestine Rashidi 2006: 30–64.

[226] *War* 1.396; *Ant.* 15.217.

Agrippa ignored them. He soon visited Judaea and made his sympathies clear by funding a hecatomb (technically 100-animal) sacrifice, providing a lavish feast for Jerusalem's populace (*Ant.* 16.14).

I mentioned earlier the flight of Idumaeans who could not accept Hasmonean domination. But those who remained were not for that reason free of all hostility. King Herod, an Idumaean on his father's side, tried to integrate Idumaeans in his rule from Jerusalem. He made use of Idumaean troops where special toughness was needed, posting 3,000 to deal with banditry in Trachonitis (*Ant.* 16.285). Early on he made his brother-in-law Costobar governor of Idumaea and Gaza. Costobar's ancestors had been priests of Cos/Qos (*Ant.* 15.253), his own name preserving the honour of that deity.[227] According to Josephus, Costobar exploited his position to attempt secession from Jerusalem, outraged that a man of his noble ancestry should be taking direction from the commoner Herod. When Herod's sister learned of her husband's disloyalty, she both divorced and reported him (*Ant.* 15.253–66). It has been speculated that Costobar hoped to create a Hasmonean-Idumaean alliance against Herod linked with Cleopatra's Egypt.[228] However that may be, the story confirms ethnic unrest under Herod's rule from Jerusalem. Other opponents found mileage in calling Herod only a Half-Judaean (*Ant.* 14.403). We should assume that the few incidents we happen to hear about were the tip of a lost iceberg.

When Herod died, according to a fragment from Nicolaus, the Judaean *ethnos* rose up against the neighbouring Greek *poleis*.[229] We do not know the precise causes, but it is clear that old hostilities had not gone away. In Rome, according to Nicolaus, Greek leaders begged Augustus to free them from Jerusalem's domination.[230] It may be that the appeal of Joazar and the priestly elite to be free of monarchical rule was motivated in part by concerns about this hostility with the neighbours.[231]

No antagonism is better attested than that between Judaeans and Samarians. This is largely because of the gospels, especially the Parable of the Good Samaritan (Luke 10:29–37), which assumes that it was considered shocking for a Samarian to help a needy Judaean. The story of Jesus and the Samarian woman in John 4 makes the same assumption. She is shocked that "You, a Judaean, are asking for a drink

---

[227] It has been suggested that his name was actually *Cos-gever* ("Cos's man"), on the analogy of *Cos-melekh* (Cos's king) attested in an inscription: see Ronen 1988: 214–215.

[228] See Ronen 1988.

[229] The fragment of Nicolaus' autobiography is preserved in a tenth-century collection *On Virtues and Vices* put together by the scholar-emperor Constantine VII. We are concerned with the passage in Dindorf 1870: 143–44 (= latter half of frag. 5, lines 70–102 in Müller 1841–1870: vol. 3, p. 354).

[230] Dindorf 1870: 143 lines 13–18: αἱ ὑφ' Ἡρώδῃ Ἑλληνίδες πόλεις αἰτούμεναι τὴν ἐλευθερίαν παρὰ Καίσαρος.

[231] *Ant.* 17.342.

from me, a woman of Samaria?" (4:9). She offers Jesus a history lesson: "Our ancestors once worshipped on this mountain [Gerizim], and yet you say that one must worship in Jerusalem!" (4:20). Tacitus has garbled information, but he also knows of violent strife between Judaeans and Samarians, "who had longstanding hostilities, and now [in the 50s] curbed their hatreds even less" (*Ann.* 12.54).

Josephus everywhere assumes lethal hostility between the groups. Pilgrims travelling from Galilee to Jerusalem would typically avoid the much quicker route through Samaria for this reason (*Life* 269). When Josephus himself had to send a delegation from Galilee to Jerusalem, although 500 soldiers would accompany them, he still needed ask "friends in Samaria" for help with security (*Life* 268). Similarly, Jesus is said to have sent scouts into Samaria to secure his passage. When his party was rebuffed *because he was heading to Jerusalem*, he took the long way via the Jordan valley (Luke 9:51–56). The Judaeans' destruction of the great Samarian temple had occurred more than a century earlier, but such events are not easily forgotten, and Samarians had remained subject to Jerusalem in the meantime.

Let us now survey known expressions of this conflict between A.D. 6 and 66, to see how it could have generated direct conflict with Rome.

1. Bones in the temple. With Archelaus' removal and Jerusalem's loss of status, Samarians wasted no time in testing the new situation. At Passover in the spring of A.D. 7 or 8, while Coponius was settling into Caesarea and an auxiliary cohort was supposedly watching Jerusalem, Samarians entered the temple precinct at night and scattered human bones in the colonnades and Court of Nations. Because this defilement rendered the sacred precinct unusable, the priests had to evacuate everyone, purify the site (perhaps losing the major festival that year), and institute better security measures. This may be the origin of the office of temple commandant/general (στρατηγός) and guards who reported to him on temple-mount activities.[232] A later holder of that position of commandant, one of the chief priests, will cut the temple off from foreign connections and move Jerusalem decisively toward war. In this case the auxiliary garrison at the very least turned a blind eye, if they did not facilitate the Samarian raid (*Ant.* 18.29–30). The first prefect in Caesarea, Coponius, was recalled to Rome "shortly after" (18.31).[233]

This episode contains the main ingredients of the next six decades of conflict: simmering Samarian-Judaean antagonism, (arguably) a pro-Samarian auxiliary, and the risk that an equestrian governor would either go native with

---

[232] For the guards see *War* 6.294: οἱ τοῦ ἱεροῦ φύλακες; cf. John 18:3 (Judas came for the arrest of Jesus with "a cohort and officers from the chief priests and the Pharisees . . . with weapons").

[233] The text has at least one lacuna. The best discussion, also of some proposed implications of this episode, is in Pummer 2009: 222–25.

his troops or be insufficiently sensitive to Judaean interests. But in this case, higher Roman authorities intervened and the incident blew over.

2. Pontius Pilate's focus on Jerusalem. The most famous equestrian prefect in Caesarea, Pontius Pilate, dominated the first half of the period we are reviewing. Appointed by Tiberius in either 18/19 or 26, he served under three, four, or five Syrian legates. And when he finally left his post, it was not on a normal rotation, but because the legate L. Vitellius ordered him back to Rome in 37.[234] Vitellius was moved by a complaint from *Samaria's* council that Pilate had been showing repeated brutality toward Samarians. The last straw came when a Samarian leader organized a pilgrimage up (temple-less) Mt. Gerizim. His flock was armed because, he claimed, Pilate's cohorts had a history of harassing them (*Ant.* 18.85–89). This episode shows that the Samarian auxiliary could be turned against Samarian pietists, perhaps in the way that modern states turn their forces against internal extremists.[235] But what does the incident say about Pilate's general orientation?

Pilate's long tenure, long whether it lasted a decade or eighteen years, appears to suggest that most of the time he successfully avoided seriously antagonizing his main constituents. The incidents we happen to hear about show a consistent attitude of care toward Jerusalem. The gospel accounts famously minimize his involvement in Jesus of Nazareth's death for theological reasons,[236] to the point that he passively does the bidding of the city council. But in general Pilate must have worked closely with the priestly elite, as Rome's governors were expected to do.[237]

When Pilate's effort to bring a cohort with their military standards into Jerusalem – in the dark of night and covered up – sparked a protest, he yielded and removed the standards.[238] In an apparently different episode, he allowed a cohort to install *imageless* votive shields in the Herodian palace, where they could offend no one. Although perplexed that even these proved offensive, and he may have been reluctant to move them from concern for the soldier's feelings, a harsh directive from the emperor Tiberius brought his rapid compliance there too.[239] Both the concealment of images in the one case and the

---

[234] On Pilate's dates see Schwartz 1992: 182–217 and Mason 2008: 139 n. 1054.

[235] Cf. U.S. authorities and the Branch Davidians at Waco (1993), Egypt and the Muslim Brotherhood, and Israel in relation to some settler groups (e.g., in the evacuation of Gaza, 2005).

[236] The trend is clear already in 1 Thess 2:14–16; Acts 2:23; 3:13–15; 4:10, which (in spite of 4:27) minimize Pilate's role and blame Judaeans. On Jesus' trial itself: Mark 15:1–44; Matt 27:2–65; Luke 23:1–52; Josephus, *Ant.* 18.63–64 (although it includes Christian traits). See Winter 1961 for a forceful presentation.

[237] On Paul's trial: Acts 21–26.

[238] *War* 2.169–74; *Ant.* 18.55–59. The *Antiquities* version unambiguously accuses Pilate of intending provocation, but this not at all clear in *War*'s version or in the reported action.

[239] Philo, *Legat.* 299–306.

use of blank standards in the other suggest Pilate's concern not to offend. Finally, he initiated an aqueduct project for Jerusalem. This was a mark of enormous prestige – analogous to building a first-class communications tower today – in addition to its obvious practical benefits.[240]

Each of these episodes has been scrutinized from many angles, and our dramatic literary accounts conceal more than they explain.[241] But these few reported incidents from a long tenure, taken with Pilate's eventual removal when he crossed the line in harassing Samarians, suggest a determination to conciliate Jerusalem's leadership. Philo uses harsh language about Pilate, but Philo is using him as a negative foil for Tiberius' unstinting beneficence toward Judaea (*Legat.* 302). The only action Philo can mention in support of his denunciation is Pilate's aborted dedication of blank shields. Even if the equestrian did occasionally side with his soldiers against Judaean cultural norms, a requirement to support to protect Jerusalem seems clear.

The coins issued by Pilate and others in his post appear to confirm this. Y. Meshorer included these in his catalogues of *Jewish coins* on the ground that, unlike usual provincial coins portraying the emperor's image, these "appear to be Jewish coins bearing Jewish symbols."[242] The minor symbols of Roman cult that complement ears of barley and wreaths on Pilate's later coins have been read as intentionally offensive or worse: as part of a programme to impose imperial cult on Judaeans.[243] That very strong interpretation of such bland symbols is implausible. When we consider that he and the auxiliary were based in a thoroughly non-Judaean *polis*, the regional home of imperial cult, also that the coins circulated in Sebaste and elsewhere, these rather anodyne symbols at most hint at a modicum of civic pride outside Jerusalem – while they remain conspicuously attentive to the Judaean abhorrence of animate images.[244]

3. Syria's legates and Jerusalem. Whatever Pilate may have felt about Jerusalem, Philo and Josephus agree that the legates based in Antioch worked

---

[240] *War* 2.175–77; *Ant.* 18.60–62.   [241] See the studies listed at the first mention of Pilate.

[242] Meshorer 2001: 167–76, plates 73–76. Coins were only produced as needed: in the early years of the Prefectural arrangement (6–12) and on Augustus' death/Tiberius' accession in A.D. 14 (Kokkinos 2012: 93). Importantly, Kokkinos 2012 establishes that those produced under Augustus use an era from 27 B.C. rather than the Actian era (from 31 B.C.) that is widely assumed, also by Meshorer.

[243] Bernett (2007: 199–204) sees in Pilate's coins an attempt to impose imperial cult. Cf. Kokkinos (2012: 101), for whom the symbols were "strikingly foreign to Jewish culture and must have left a bad taste, if not directly offended by promoting the imperial religion of Rome in a religiously exclusive Judaea." I do not understand where this religious exclusivity is supposed to have existed under the prefect's purview. Bond (next note) points out the rather stronger "pagan" symbols even on Hasmonean and certainly on Herodian coinage; cf. Lykke 2012: 121–57.

[244] Bond (1998: 19–23) reviews the debates and makes a compelling case; so also Meshorer 2001: 171–72; Goodman 2007: 417.

assiduously to cultivate Jerusalem's leaders. In a passage already mentioned (*Legat.* 231), Philo puts L. Vitellius there when the news of Gaius Caligula's accession arrived. The 24-year-old Gaius came to power effectively on March 16, 37, on Tiberius' death, although his accession may not have been ratified until April 21.[245] Josephus locates Vitellius in Jerusalem for Passover, which in 37 seems to have begun in mid-April,[246] and makes this visit a watershed event for the city. This happens also to have been the year of Josephus' birth. Perhaps he grew up hearing about these momentous events.

Josephus describes Vitellius' memorable visit in three different passages. Each adds important information, and together they confirm the legate's concern to keep strong ties with Jerusalem. The first passage claims that Vitellius, being "magnificently received by the masses" in Jerusalem, offered them a favour in gratitude. They requested that the high priest's robes be returned to their priestly control (*Ant.* 15.403–405). Since Hasmonean days the high priest's ceremonial clothing, worn during the three great festivals and Yom Kippur, had been kept in the fortress next to the temple. Under Herod that custom continued, the fortress now being his rebuilt Antonia, and the same custom continued under Roman administration. *Ant.* 18.90–94 explains that the commander of the auxiliary cohort on duty and Jerusalem's leaders would make a ceremony of the transfer, using matching seals to ritualize each act of storage and removal.

The tradition had apparently become irksome in recent years, however. With no Judaean monarch in Jerusalem, it was a different and humiliating business to ask foreigners to store and retrieve these core symbols of *polis* identity. So Vitellius wrote to the emperor. Receiving a green light from Tiberius, he jubilantly reported the news in Jerusalem – at a subsequent Passover in Jerusalem.

After removing Pilate, according to the second passage, Vitellius appointed a friend named Marcellus to Caesarea, as he himself headed back to Jerusalem for Passover, where again he was "received in majestic fashion" (*Ant.* 18.90). It was on this visit that he not only brought news of Tiberius' decision about the robes but also freed the people from certain taxes and installed a new high priest at their request. Vitellius must therefore have made *two* successive and warmly welcomed Passover visits: one in 36, his very first opportunity after arriving as legate (summer A.D. 35),[247] and again for the next Passover in 37.

---

[245] See Barrett 1989: 71–72.

[246] There was a new moon on April 4 of 37 (http://eclipse.gsfc.nasa.gov/phase/phases0001.html, accessed 30 Sept. 2013), which would be Nisan 1 that year, making the day of Passover preparation (counting from the 5th to allow for moon sighting) around April 18.

[247] See Schürer-Vermes 1.262–63: Vitellius had been consul in 34.

The third passage concerns the visit of 37 and is even more interesting. Josephus backtracks to tell of a quarrel between Herod Antipas in Galilee and King Aretas (IV) of Nabataea. The dispute arose when Antipas cheated on his wife, who happened to be King Aretas' daughter, during a trip to Rome. Hearing that he planned to marry that other woman (his own sister-in-law), the wife fled to her father. Aretas' fury led to a battle, fought by the two rulers' generals, which Antipas lost badly (*Ant.* 18.109–15). The Judaean people considered this fitting retribution for such disgraceful behaviour, but Antipas boldly complained to Tiberius about being attacked by a Roman ally. Tiberius took the Judaean ruler's side, and with a vengeance. He ordered his legate Vitellius to march with legions to Petra and send him either Aretas or the king's severed head (18.115).

Rushing to obey an imperial order, Vitellius reached Ptolemais with his army, but he was intercepted by Judaean leaders requesting that he not pass through their land with his army's image-bearing standards. Vitellius readily obliged. He ordered the army directly eastward, through the Jezreel to the Jordan Valley so as to skirt Judaea. He personally headed to Jerusalem, with Antipas at his side, to join in the Passover sacrifices. That, we now learn, was the setting for the happy visit of 37, during which he also heard of Tiberius' death and Gaius' accession. That news required him to call off his revenge expedition (he may have been hugely relieved) ordered by Tiberius, which no longer had imperial authorization. So he opted to linger in Jerusalem and lead the populace in celebrating Gaius' accession and also taking an oath of loyalty to the new emperor.

These three partial accounts, which do not serve any connected story or purpose on Josephus' part, seem to require the following historical background. Vitellius paid an inaugural Passover visit to Jerusalem at his earliest opportunity, while Pilate was prefect, because it was a crucially important *polis* in his province. After a warm reception, he worked on the robes issue with Tiberius and planned to return with good news at the next Passover. During the intervening year (36–37), however, Antipas and Aretas came to blows, and he also felt compelled to dismiss Pilate after the Samarian complaints. Tiberius ordered Vitellius to punish Aretas, which would entail another spring visit to Jerusalem en route to Petra. Even when he rerouted his army to oblige the Judaean request, he was determined to visit Jerusalem personally, with a small entourage that included Antipas. He happened to heard of Gaius' accession while there, and so stayed on for convivial celebration. Evidently, this important legate viewed Jerusalem as a key *polis* in his province and went out of his way to develop good relations with its priestly leaders and people.

With a legate of this kind, the move by Joazar and his colleagues to bring Jerusalem under the Syrian governor's direct responsibility must have looked wise to many Judaeans. Vitellius' successor (A.D. 39), Publius Petronius, was little different. Philo and Josephus write independently glowing accounts, portraying this legate in almost heroic terms as he courageously prevaricates in spite of Gaius' order to install imperial statues in Jerusalem's temple.[248] Both authors portray Petronius engaging in protracted and highly respectful discussions with Jerusalem's leaders. Philo claims even that Petronius was personally fascinated by Judaean law. More pragmatically, the legate understood the uniquely large distribution of the Judaean *ethnos* in Syria, Asia, and farther abroad, which made provocation by the emperor seem foolhardy.[249]

4. Judaean royals and emperors. With Herod's descendants Agrippa I, Berenice, and Agrippa II, we see the clearest evidence of Rome's preference for rule from Jerusalem. If emperors generally valued the relationships they had forged with Herodians of Judaea, Agrippa I was a spectacular case. When he was only 5 or so, his widowed mother Berenice took him and his siblings to Rome (ca. 5 B.C.), where they were welcomed into the powerful court circle of Antonia Minor: daughter of Marc Antony, later Tiberius' widowed sister-in-law, emperor Gaius' grandmother, and Claudius' mother. Antonia's circle included leading Alexandrian-Judaeans and also such future Roman stars as Vespasian (see Chapter 5).[250] Young Agrippa remained in Rome for more than thirty years and was supremely well connected there.

From a young emperor Gaius Agrippa first received a starter kingdom in the north/northeast. But he remained in Rome during much of that reign, where his astonishing role in the accession of Claudius after Gaius' murder yielded a much larger and more prestigious kingdom, from imperial gratitude. Based in Jerusalem, this enormous territory matched that of his grandfather Herod. It also abutted the smaller kingdom of his older brother Herod in central Lebanon (*War* 2.217–18). Aged only about 50, Agrippa might have been expected to rule for one or two decades, after which his then-teenage son would succeed him. For Judaeans praying for a renewal of Jerusalem's regional ascendancy, things must have looked rosy.

The sudden death of Agrippa I created a situation related by Josephus, mentioned earlier, that is among the most revealing for our inquiry (*Ant.* 19.356–58):

> But when it became known that Agrippa had departed this life, the Caesareans and Sebastenes, forgetting his kindnesses, took a position of extreme hostility. They hurled slanders at the deceased that would be unseemly to relate. *Those of them who were serving in the military* at that time, and *there were many*, went off to his house and seized the statues of the king's [three] daughters. These they brought en masse into the brothels, and set them up on the roofs, and proceeded to indulge their

---

[248] Philo, *Legat.* 207–60, 333; Josephus, *War* 2.185–203; *Ant.* 18.261–309.
[249] Philo, *Legat.* 213–17, 245.   [250] D. R. Schwartz 1990: 39–45 and Chapter 5.

desires in every possible manner, doing things too shameful for narration. They turned public places into feasting halls and held banquets for everyone: putting crowns on their heads, dousing themselves with perfume, pouring libations to Charon [mythical ferrymaster of the dead], and drinking toasts to one another over the king's last breath.

We must allow for much embellishment in this retelling, but an explosion of joy at Agrippa's unexpected death matches what we would expect in this situation. For a generation since Archelaus' removal, Samarians had enjoyed an improved position out from under Jerusalem. Agrippa's monarchy brought them back to Jerusalem as an allied force under his command. This must have chafed. When Agrippa died so quickly, leaving a 16-year-old son who could not yet succeed him, it would have been surprising if the auxiliary and the inhabitants of Samaria and Caesara generally had not erupted in celebration.

So indignant was Claudius when he heard the news, reportedly, that he was on the verge of sending young Agrippa II in spite of his youth. Talked down from that hazardous course, he sent a trusted equestrian (Cuspius Fadus) to Caesarea with responsibility for an enlarged area that now included the tetrarchies of Herod's other sons. Josephus claims that Claudius did this in part to keep the legate Vibius Marsus, who had been Agrippa's bête noir, out of his late friend's business. He also recalled Marsus and instructed Fadus to read the riot act to the exuberant Caesareans and Samarians. Claudius allegedly told him to arrange the transfer of their auxiliary cohorts to the Black Sea, to be replaced by legionaries from northern Syria (*Ant.* 19.361–66).

We may doubt that Claudius really had such a plan.[251] In any case it failed to materialize, reportedly because the Samarians (via embassies) promised to be on their best behaviour. *Antiquities* remarks tellingly – the episode is not in *War* – that these cohorts "became the foundation of great calamities for the Judaeans, and sowed the seeds of the war after the war in the time of Florus" (19.366). This work also notes that Vespasian would finally realize Claudius' abortive plan, when he moved the auxiliary to other provinces and installed Syria's most trustworthy legion, the Tenth, in Judaea (*Ant.* 19.366). I suggested in Chapter 3 that Claudius' creation of a military colony at Ptolemais in A.D. 45 (Pliny, *Nat.* 5.75) might have been Claudius' reaction to the turmoil following Agrippa's death, so that legionary veterans could keep a closer watch on the auxiliary.

---

[251] *Could* the better part of a legion be withdrawn from the Euphrates frontier? Could it be placed under an equestrian procurator, with legionary cohorts rotating in and out of Jerusalem? And how did Josephus know what Claudius had planned or said to his advisors? Although we cannot know the truth, Josephus had motives to exaggerate Claudius' outrage and to invent or inflate such plans.

For some reason Claudius now decided to undo Tiberius' decision about the high priest's robes. A new legate, Cassius Longinus, characteristically understood the gravity of this decision and allowed a four-man Judaean embassy to seek redress from the emperor. They were leaning against an open door, it turned out, because Claudius was being advised by the late Agrippa's brother Herod and son Agrippa II. He not only relented quickly on the robes (*Ant.* 20.6–14) but granted the deceased king's brother Herod authority over all temple activities and the appointment of high priests (20.15–16), a right that would devolve to Agrippa II when his uncle died.

Claudius' next choice as prefect was a member of Alexandria's most distinguished Judaean family, Tiberius Julius Alexander.[252] Josephus has no complaints about either Fadus or Alexander, who both punished Judaean vigilantes. The motives of those vigilantes were apparently regional conflicts and not anti-Roman sentiment. For example, a border dispute flared up between the *chōra* of Philadelphia (Amman) and Judaean villages in Peraea. Josephus claims that Judaeans armed themselves and killed some Philadelphians. Fadus was angry that they had turned to self-help rather than coming to him. He executed one and banished two. Another Judaean was harassing Idumaea and frontier areas with Nabataea, and thus was executed as a bandit (*Ant.* 20.2–5). Tiberius Alexander, we saw earlier, also executed two sons of Judas (20.100–102) – perhaps for vigilante activity in the ethnic strife following Agrippa's death.

5. Cumanus and Quadratus: the revolt in a nutshell. After that period of relative calm in the late 40s, both Josephus and Tacitus portray the governorship of Cumanus (A.D. 48–52) as a time of turmoil *because* Samarian-Judaean tensions reached new heights.[253] This was the Judaeans' nightmare scenario: a prefect in Caesarea corrupted by his auxiliary army and either looking the other way or actively encouraging them against Judaea. The survey of *War* 2 includes the incidents. An auxiliary soldier's provocative insults to Passover pilgrims in the temple court incites Judaean youths to rock-throwing, which gives the soldiers a pretext to react with force. In a search for Judaean bandits in the Judaean countryside after a Judaean robbery, an auxiliary soldier finds a copy of the Torah and burns it. One or more Galileans travelling to Jerusalem is/are killed in Samaria near modern Jenin (Ginae).

The last of these incidents produces a microcosm of the war fifteen years later. Outraged Judaean leaders plead with Cumanus to punish the Samarian murderers. Recall Fadus' insistence that Judaeans bring grievances to him. So they do. For whatever reason, however, Cumanus is perceived as doing

[252] See Turner 1954.
[253] Josephus, *War* 2.223–46; *Ant.* 20.103–36; Tacitus, *Ann.* 12.54. Curiously, Tacitus has Cumanus take the side of Galileans against Felix (not yet present in Josephus' account) and the Samarians.

nothing (*War* 2.233). When Rome's protection fails, the Judaeans turn to self-help, for they cannot allow Samarians to attack them with impunity. They are not about to travel deep into Samaria looking for the particular culprits, however, so they burn the Samarian villages nearest to Judaea instead (*War* 2.234–35). Only when he notices this escalation does Cumanus finally intervene (20.122): "[H]e took the cavalry wing of Sebastenes and four infantry cohorts [i.e., most of his auxiliary army] and, *after arming the Samarians*, went out *after the Judaeans*." This language might seem to suggest that Cumanus armed Samarian civilians. More likely Josephus is speaking of the army and calling *it* Samarian. Arming an army sounds redundant, but at 20.177 he will speak in similar language of arming the auxiliary before an operation. Either way, the close connection between the auxiliary and Samarians remains clear.

Further prefiguring the later war, Jerusalem's elders plead with their compatriots to stop attacking Samarian possessions, from fear of *Roman* retaliation. Samarian and Judaean elders then both appeal to the legate Quadratus. His initial intervention suggests that he assumes the Judaeans to be responsible, because he executes ringleaders of the raids. But he soon dispatches representatives from both parties to Claudius, along with Cumanus and the auxiliary tribune most closely involved (*War* 2.243–44). Agrippa II's presence at Claudius' side is credited by Josephus with another favourable verdict for the Judaeans. Cumanus goes into exile while the tribune is sent back to Judaea, reportedly to be tortured and lynched by the Judaeans (*War* 2.245–46). Claudius also executes three of the Samarian delegation (*Ant.* 20.136), as he had executed Alexandrian emissaries who accused Alexandrian Judaeans.[254] Judaean elites could usually rely on the highest level of Roman support.

It seems that "the Jewish revolt against Rome" could have begun there and then in the early 50s, if Judaean vigilantism against Samarians had escalated as it would a decade later. Quadratus might then have needed to intervene with a legion, and he might have been ambushed at Beit-Horon. In that case it would have been clear that the war arose from regional aggravations. It is difficult to see much difference between the conditions of the early 50s and those obtaining when the war actually broke out in 66. The decisive change was in the different response from a very different emperor, Nero, and from his officials on site.

6. Happy family: Felix, Drusilla, and Agrippa II. Following the debacle of Cumanus, Claudius sent another trusted representative as prefect. Felix (52–58/ 60) was the brother of Claudius' close advisor Pallas, whom he had inherited from his mother Antonia, as part of that eastern circle that included prominent Judaeans.[255] Josephus came to maturity in Jerusalem while Felix was prefect. He

---

[254]   Harker 2008: 39–45 (on the *Acts of the Alexandrians*) with *CPJ* 2.66–81 (no. 156a–d).
[255]   For his dates, see Schürer-Vermes 1.460 and Kokkinos 1998: 385. For his support, see Barrett 1996: 126–27.

claims that the high priest Jonathan had lobbied Claudius for Felix's appointment (*Ant.* 20.162), another sign of Judaean-elite influence with legate and emperor.

The single most important point about Felix's term in Judaea may be that he soon married Drusilla, daughter of Agrippa I and sister of Agrippa II. In considering the political import of this union, we should not be distracted by Josephus' moral criticisms of it (*Ant.* 20.141–44). A Roman official's marriage to a Judaean princess must have sent a message to the region, especially to Samarians and auxiliary forces: Felix would *not* be another Cumanus. He would return to the main tradition of Pilate, Fadus, and Tiberius Alexander.

It may be that Claudius had been grooming Agrippa II to take his father's place. Josephus plausibly claims that the lad was not old enough for rule at his father's death (*War* 2.220; *Ant.* 19.362). But he was still only 20 when his uncle died and Claudius gave him the small kingdom of Chalcis in Lebanon (*War* 2.223), along with the rights to manage the temple and appoint high priests (*Ant.* 20.103, 179). At 24 he received an enhanced version of his father's first kingdom (*War* 2.247). It may be that in sending Felix – now Agrippa's brother-in-law – Claudius was using him as a capable caretaker until the young Herodian was ready for the monarchy to Jerusalem. If that had been Claudius' plan, it died with him. The 16-year-old Nero followed Claudius' lead at first, further expanding Agrippa's kingdom with lucrative cities in Galilee and Peraea (*War* 2.252). But Nero would soon go in a different direction, and Agrippa advanced no farther before the Flavians took power.

In Josephus' accounts of Felix's term, the longest since Pilate's, he mentions no instances of Samarian or auxiliary overreach. This governor acts with energy and success against "bandits." Throughout his term there are signs of a groundswell of popular Judaean agitation against the neighbours, quite possibly because of the ugly turn under Cumanus and before that, the fallout from Agrippa's death. An Egyptian-Judaean prophet promised to oust the hated auxiliary garrison, for example, but Felix cut down his followers (*War* 2.263). Josephus does not blame Felix for failing to suppress all such disquiet; he comments approvingly on his efforts to do so (*Ant.* 20.168, 177).[256] The unrest appears still to be inter-ethnic in nature.

7. A Judaean bid for Caesarea. Caesarea, although home of the auxiliary forces, imperial cult, and equestrian governor, hosted a sizable Judaean minority. It had been a cauldron of inter-ethnic violence for some time, although this was kept in check by the military presence. Under Herod, Archelaus, and Agrippa I, Judaeans there and elsewhere had been members of the region's ruling *ethnos*. When Caesarea became the seat of administration, in 6 and 44, Judaeans

---

[256] *War* 2.252–70; *Ant.* 20.160–78.

resident in Caesarea must have felt vulnerable, especially during the raucous festivities held there after the death of Agrippa I.

The Judaean minority's attempted remedy, beginning from the late 50s, was bold, creative, and implausible. First by internal mechanisms and then by a direct appeal to Nero, they apparently tried somehow to have Caesarea redesignated or rechartered a Judaean *polis*, which would follow Judaean laws and customs. At least that is the clear import of both Josephus' narratives, which otherwise differ considerably.[257] Both state clearly that Herod founded Caesarea as a *non-Judaean* harbour city, open to the world and marked by colossal statues, temples, theatres, and quinquennial games (*War* 1.408–15), and dedicated to the Province of Syria, sailors on the Mediterranean, and Augustus (1.414).[258] In light of the serious tensions of the 40s and 50s, it seems, the Judaean minority made a bid to change this. Josephus' accounts agree that their initiative sparked predictable violence:

> The Judaeans of the *polis*, emboldened by their wealth and for this reason looking down on the Syrians, hurled insults at them in the hope of provoking them. Though indeed inferior in resources, the others prided themselves on the fact that *most of those drafted by the Romans for military service there were Caesareans and Sebastenes*, and so for a time they likewise abused the Judaeans with words. After that, they took to throwing stones at each other, until many were wounded and some fell dead on both sides – although usually the Judaeans would win.[259]

In *War*, Caesarea's Judaeans try to buy up land at many times its market value. The others refuse to sell, however, in one case driving their point home by building out to the edges of their property, crowding the Judaeans because they had built to the edge of *their* property in the expectation of purchasing the adjacent land. There the local youth could provoke the Judaeans, who had to walk close by them to enter their synagogue, with displays of bird sacrifice (*War* 2.285–89). The auxiliary commanders, Josephus remarks, arrested ringleaders on both sides. Felix intervened only when he observed that the Judaeans were winning most of these brawls and would not desist as he had ordered. Finally, he sent in auxiliary troops, who killed a few but arrested many. Felix gave the auxiliary soldiers leave to plunder the Judaeans' homes.[260] In *Antiquities*, all this leads to an apology from the Judaean leaders and a promise of peace in the

---

[257] Acutely Levine (1974: 387): "Thus we find a Jewish community daring to seek control of a Greco-Roman city, an attempt without parallel in antiquity." Unparalleled perhaps in the sense that an internal minority led the move, although many cities changed their legal-political identities for various reasons, undergoing refoundation by kings or rechartering as military colonies, for example.

[258] Cf. Beebe 1983.   [259] *Ant.* 20.175–76; cf. *War* 2.267–68 (my emphasis).

[260] *War* 2.270; *Ant.* 20.178.

future, which settles the issue for a while (20.178). In *War* Felix dispatches delegates from each side to make their cases before Nero (2.270).

These peculiar-sounding stories might make sense on realist assumptions. Many *poleis* of the region had changed legal and political identity over the previous two centuries. The Judaeans of Caesarea felt secure enough in this vitally important city to ask for its rebirth under their laws. Perhaps they realized, after Cumanus, that they could not count on the resident prefect's goodwill and energy. If Jerusalem was not going to be the seat of regional government, they would try to engineer more favourable facts on the ground. Caesarea was a ticking bomb, a nursery of hostility populated by their armed and officially backed enemies. Prosperous Judaeans there saw the need to rebalance these political dynamics by diplomacy.[261] Thinking of the issue this way, we can understand why Nero's eventual rejection of their appeal, which may have prompted him also to cancel the Judaeans' existing exemptions and rights in this non-Judaean *polis*, was in Josephus' view a foundation of the coming war.[262] Caesarea encapsulated the Judaean predicament after Jerusalem's loss of status. Had they secured Nero's permission to Judaize the *polis*, whatever that would have meant concretely, the auxiliary army and prefect would have been constantly aware of Judaea's regional primacy, even without a monarch in Jerusalem. Nero's support would have sent a strong message in continuity with the Judaeans' historic position. His emphatic refusal dramatically increased the Judaeans' peril and energized their enemies.

8. A perfect storm under Nero. When Nero dispatched Gessius Florus to Caesarea in 64, the elements of a perfect storm were gathering. Florus' mandate for ruthless revenue collection from Jerusalem's temple with its world-famous wealth (Chapter 5) made the nightmare scenario a reality. Judaeans now faced an auxiliary army itching to have free rein against them, with little constraint from the equestrian prefect if they resisted his efforts to seize temple funds, which they would inevitably do (*War* 2.277–344). Florus appears to have fully exploited the existing hatreds to intimidate and silence Judaeans or worse.[263]

The auxiliary's aggravating role under Florus percolates throughout Josephus' narratives, although he does not thematize the inter-ethnic dimension that I am offering as substructure. After a series of deadly confrontations,

---

[261] Quadratus has remained governor all this time. Either he was also involved in approving the delegations and Josephus does not mention it or a new dynamic after Nero's first years in power (next chapter) encouraged him to let the freedman Felix deal with it.

[262] *War* 2.284: Nero refuses to make the change, after the delegates have been in Rome for years. *Ant.* 20.182–84: The issue is provisionally settled by Felix, but Judaeans from Caesarea then bring charges against him in Rome (unspecified: perhaps because of the auxiliary). Then Greek-Syrian notables from Caesarea bribe a trusted secretary of Nero's to annul even such equality (*isopoliteia*) as they already enjoyed.

[263] *War* 2.305, 332.

Jerusalem's leaders persuade Florus to exchange the cohort in Jerusalem, because it has blood on its hands (*War* 2.332). Florus' compliance might suggest that he understands their grievance at some level. The Jerusalem garrison's violent behaviour explains why Judaeans eventually massacre them in the summer of 66, bringing Roman retaliation and war.

Shortly before that massacre comes an episode often viewed as an effective Judaean declaration of war against Rome. Priests led by the temple commandant (security chief) Eleazar son of Ananias resolve "to accept no gift or sacrifice from any outsider" (2.409). Other members of the elite plead with them not to do this, insisting that the temple has always accepted gifts, sacrifices, and votive offerings from other nations (2.412–13). There is no reason to imagine that this measure was directed against Rome, much less that it was a declaration of war *with Rome*. Josephus as narrator draws out implications for relations with Rome in retrospect, as a logical corollary: If you cut off ties with *foreigners*, that will include ending the sacrifice for the emperors (2.402–403, 410). Snubbing Rome itself cannot have been the priests' intention, but they are so incensed about the lack of effective Roman assistance (from the legate or Nero) for their conflict with Samarians and auxiliary that they are willing to risk offending Rome. Perhaps they are convinced that senior Romans no longer care, and so they must take care of matters.

The bi-play between Jerusalem and Caesarea comes to a violent conclusion, according to Josephus, in both cities at once. On the very same day that Jerusalemites massacre their auxiliary garrison, the Caesarean majority massacre much of their Judaean minority and drive out the rest (*War* 2.452–57). Naturally we prefer to imagine that one atrocity prompted the other, but we have no way of knowing.

Both, at any rate, attracted harsh reprisals. The massacre of Jerusalem's garrison could not go unpunished by the Syrian legate, because whatever the regional aggravations may have been, the auxiliary was part of Rome's army. Before the other shoe could drop in that regard, however (Chapter 5), Judaean vigilantes responded to the Caesarean violence with furious attacks throughout southern Syria: against possessions of the Decapolis, Golan, northern Galilee, and such coastal *poleis* as Caesarea and Sebaste (2.458–60). Outraged in their turn at these unprovoked attacks, those cities turned against their Judaean minorities, enlarging the death toll and bringing regional unrest to a boil. Did armed Judaean mobs really hit such strong and distant *poleis* as Gerasa and Gadara? Archaeology suggests that around this time their city walls were breached and their temples to Zeus badly damaged.[264] It seems that even now, well into the year 66, the drivers of intense conflict were the old regional antagonisms.

---

[264] Seigne 2002: 13–14, 22; Hoffmann 2002: 109–12.

Similar things now happened farther afield. Judaeans in Tiberias attacked Gadara, Hippos, and Scythopolis. John of Gischala was radicalized in northern Galilee by attacks from Tyrians, Gadarenes, and Soganians. These attacks, not rebellion against *Rome*, caused him to fortify Gischala (*Life* 42–45). Eleazar ben Deinaeus and Simon bar Giora began their militant activities with border skirmishes against Samaria, Simon following an earlier Tolmai in also overrunning Idumaea and parts of Arabia (*War* 2.652; 4.503–37).

Then there is the remarkable story of Noarus. The details are reported differently in *War* and *Life*, but the main outline seems recoverable.[265] Noarus belonged to Ituraean royalty, his father having ruled a petty kingdom in Lebanon to which he was presumptive heir. When the father died in 49, the kingdom went back to the Province of Syria. Claudius allowed Noarus a provisional rule (as tetrarch) therefore, before deciding to gift this territory instead to his rising star, the Judaean Agrippa II (ca. 53). Agrippa graciously or self-protectively took Noarus on as a senior advisor. But while he was away from his kingdom in the summer of 66, having entrusted affairs to Noarus, the latter moved swiftly against prominent Judaeans in the territory. Agrippa removed him when he heard, but Noarus' attempted purge had lingering effects, above all in Judaean mistrust of the king and the flight of many to Gamala (Chapter 6). This fascinating story illustrates both the widespread inter-ethnic hostility and the resentment of Judaeans because of their ascendant position and Rome's favour.

In *War*'s final speech, Eleazar ben Yair signals the complexity of Jerusalem's regional conflicts, even with Judaeans elsewhere: "You well know that there is not a *polis* in Syria that has not killed its Judaean residents, who were much more hostile to us than to the Romans" (7.367).[266] But these conflicts were local. Even after their opportunistic ambush of Cestius' invading force (next chapter), their first priority was a fierce assault on Ascalon, "an ancient *polis* . . . that had always been hostile to the Judaeans" (*War* 3.9–10). Philo confirms: "There is among the Ascalonites, who are neighbours, an inveterate and irreconcilable hostility toward the Judaeans residing in the holy *chōra*" (*Legat.* 205).[267]

---

[265] See Tacitus *Ann.* 12.23 and Dio 59.12.2 on Noarus' father Sohaemus; *War* 2.247 on Agrippa's receipt of Noarus' (Varus') territory; and *War* 2.481–44 with *Life* 52–61 (with incompatible details) on the plot.

[266] Following the available manuscripts (ἡμῖν πλέον ἢ Ῥωμαίοις ὄντας πολεμίους). A widely accepted emendation drops the final ς from "Romans" to make it nominative ("more hostile to us than the Romans are"), but the emendation seems to be based on assumptions about Judaean-Roman hostilities.

[267] This hostility endured for centuries. Cf. *Lamentations (Eicha) Rabba* 1.39: Two Ascalonite prostitutes fall out. One tells the other she looks like a Judaean, so cannot hope for business. Cf. *Song of Songs Rabba* 7.3.

CONCLUSIONS

Our driving question in this chapter is about the source of the energy for lethal conflict between Judaea and Rome. What could that source have been? Against the nearly universal assumption of either innate hostility or unbearably mounting grievances between Judaeans and Rome, I have argued that the Rome-Judaea bond was closer than any other we know about. This emerged not from philo-Judaean sentiment but from a combination of political pragmatism and carefully nurtured personal relationships: Monarchy in Jerusalem seemed an efficient tool of empire. When a monarch in Jerusalem was not available, emperors, imperial legates, and prefects worked to maintain harmonious relations with the Judaean capital while supporting Herodian princelings in other parts of Syria.

Jerusalem's renewed expansion and dominance after Pompey's brief removal of Hasmonean gains provoked residents of the old and proud coastal cities, Samaria, and the Decapolis. Their antagonism, however, was usually manageable. The greater danger lay with the Samaria-based auxiliary army after A.D. 6, which would seek opportunities to flex its muscles against the Judaean capital. When power shifted from Jerusalem to Caesarea, those opportunities expanded. Everything would depend on the character of the equestrian prefect, the energy of the legate in Antioch, the vigilance of the Herodian royals, and ultimately the emperor's level of concern.

Most of the time these checks and balances worked for Judaeans. At moments when they found themselves alone and vulnerable, however, they were quick to arm themselves for self-help. Margins of survival were thin. They could not allow the pent-up hatreds of surrounding populations to congeal and explode if the prefect and legate did not intervene quickly. Events under Cumanus in the early 50s were a foretaste of what *could* happen if the prefect were to go native and the legate, Judaean royals, and the emperor were either slow or distracted. As we shall see in the next chapter, this was the perfect storm that occurred in Nero's final years.

The Judaean War was not the revolt of a "province of Judaea" *against Roman rule*. Judaea was not a province but the ethnic zone around world-famous Jerusalem. Its people and elite found themselves in the autumn of 66 awaiting Roman retribution because they had recently acted against the local apparatus of administration – Caesarea, its resident prefect, and the auxiliary force. The regional tinderbox had been set alight when Nero both sent his equestrian procurator Florus with the single-minded purpose of extracting revenue from Jerusalem, with the auxiliary's help, and paralyzed the legate and Judaean royals.

In this reconstruction I am not ignoring occasional literary expressions of anti-Roman sentiment, nor ruling out the possibility of long-running social, economic, or religious grievance, which some Judaeans (with some Samarians or Gadarans) might have blamed ultimately on Rome. All of that seems likely in some measure. Even modern Western democracies generate dissent and grievance, occasionally apocalyptic and potentially militant. Much of the world's population today blames its woes on American or former British or French hegemony. But evidence of sustained or militant anti-Romanism of a kind that could generate the Judaean War is exceedingly hard to find, whereas evidence abounds for singular Judaean success under Rome's tutelage. Of course this was success for the elite first of all, but presumably also for traders, craftsmen, and producers.

The Qumran Scrolls, although sharply dualistic, are by and large quietist and in that sense Danielic, concerned above all with the purity of the community over against the rest of Israel (*1QS, CD*). Partial exceptions are the *War Scroll* and oblique references to Romans as *Kittim* (a category not created for Rome), but nowhere do we find an anti-Roman manifesto.[268] Of the so-called pseudepigrapha, some chapters in the *Psalms of Solomon* express anti-Roman sentiments, but these come from the years immediately following Pompey's conquest. In that context, in Judaea's first moments of subjection after decades of Hasmonean independence, they are not surprising.[269] Notwithstanding a powerful current in New Testament scholarship, which seems to find "anti-imperialist" rhetoric under every olive tree,[270] early Christian texts portray Rome's representatives and institutions very favourably on the whole, or as mere scenery. Certainly they assume harmonious relations between Roman officials and Jerusalem.[271] The clearest hostilities that appear in Christian texts are again those between Judaea and its neighbours, especially the Samarians.[272] Missing is any sharp *anti-Roman animus*.

Finally, one might ask whether the Flavian settlement after Jerusalem's fall suggests anything about their understanding of the revolt's origins. Vespasian was well positioned to understand the causes of the conflict, in spite of his triumphal charade about conquering barbarians. He had knowledgeable and trusted sources in Tiberius Alexander, King Agrippa II, and Berenice, not to mention Josephus. His postwar settlement in Judaea seems telling in two respects. First, he conspicuously punished only those who had persisted in defying Titus during the siege of Jerusalem: Simon and John. He seems to have distinguished between the origins of the conflict, which he might have been

---

[268] Collins 1997: 91–109.   [269] Atkinson 2004.
[270] Diehl 2011 and 2012 survey the main contributions.
[271] E.g., Rom 13:1–7; Matt 22:17–21; 27:18–19, 23–24; Luke 23:4, 14, 20; Acts 10:1–48; 13:7–12; 18:7, 12–17; 21:31–22:30; 23:16–35; 24:27; 25:24–27.
[272] E.g., Mark 7.24–28; Matt 10:5–6; Luke 9:51–56; 10:13–14, 29–37; John 4:4–26; Acts 12:20. When Jesus declares that it will be more tolerable for Tyre and Sidon on the day of judgment than for Bethsaida and Chorazin (Matt 11:21–22; Luke 10:13–14), evidently Judaeans in Galilee assume that Tyre and Sidon will burn.

happy to attribute to Nero's indifference and maladministration, and the unaccountably stubborn defiance that Titus faced (*War* 6.415–20). Josephus remarks in a neglected passage that Vespasian and Titus were angry with those "who did not hand over their weapons, but continued making war *until the very end*" (*Ant.* 12.122–24).

Second, I have proposed that Vespasian created the province of Judaea, with a legion and imperial legate, as a kind of trophy – to seal the message of his triumph by this "addition" to the empire. But he may have had a practical motive for installing the Tenth Legion. I mentioned Josephus' notice in *Ant.* 19.366 that Vespasian did in 70 what his mentor Claudius had threatened to do in A.D. 44. Namely, Vespasian decoupled Rome's military prestige from the toxic ethnic entanglements, installing a legion as the principal military force and shifting the existing auxiliary cohorts elsewhere, while bringing in new cohorts to supplement the legion. From the Flavian period, Ascalonite and Sebastene cohorts and a Sebastene cavalry wing are attested in other provinces.[273] Even if some remained in the south for a time, they were displaced by the legion. In spite of their reputations, Vespasian and Titus may have been concerned to ensure that a local auxiliary embedded in ethnic conflict never again create such problems for Roman rule in Judaea.

---

[273] Schürer–Vermes 1.364 n. 52; Pollard 2000: 120–34 with *CIL* 03.02916; 16.00106; *AE* 2005.1730.

CHAPTER FIVE

NERO'S WAR I: THE BLUNDER OF CESTIUS GALLUS?

He who has been beaten in an engagement with a standard battle array – although even there, design is of great advantage – can nonetheless in his defence accuse fortune. But he who has suffered a sudden attack, ambushes, or traps cannot deflect his own blame, because he could have avoided these things or, by means of competent scouts, discovered them in advance.

Vegetius, *Epitome* 3.22

One of the great puzzles of the Judaean War is the event that set it in motion: the expedition to Jerusalem by the legate C. Cestius Gallus, in September–October of A.D. 66. Until that time, as we have just seen, Judaeans had been in conflict only with the largely Samarian auxiliary (Chapter 4). Now Cestius marched south with a reported force of 30,000, anchored in the Twelfth Legion, with auxiliaries and regional allies from the north plus ad hoc recruits (*War* 2.499–502). Within two months, most of that being travel time, he was back in Antioch, disgraced and disconsolate after losing an alleged 5,300 men. Even if the real number were much smaller, he suffered a serious humiliation. No one could doubt that this would swiftly be avenged. Judaeans began preparing for that retaliation (*War* 2.562–79). But how did Cestius come to such grief? What was he intending, and was he so utterly incompetent to see it through?

Assuming that Judaea was already in open revolt against Rome and that Cestius' objective was to crush Jerusalem, analysts have found his behaviour baffling. His apparent dithering *en route* and abrupt departure from Jerusalem, capped by the catastrophic ambush in the Beit-Horon pass, have seemed evidence of staggering ineptitude. The successful ambush gave an incalculable boost to Judaean morale (*War* 3.9). And because it clearly demanded revenge, more than any other single event it created the Judaean-Roman War. Josephus' formulaic repetition of "the blunder(s) of Cestius" brings this episode into the orbit of "the Varian disaster" (*clades Variana*) of A.D. 9, in which an emeritus legate of Syria lost three legions and his own life in Germany.[1]

Cestius lived long enough to suffer the ignominy, but not long enough to redeem his reputation. A generation later Tacitus reflects that "he suffered varied fortunes and met defeat more often than he gained victory" (*Hist.* 5.10). Suetonius mistakenly heard that Judaeans killed their prefect (*praepositus*), apparently meaning Florus,[2] and that when the consular (Cestius) arrived, they defeated him and stole his legionary eagle (*Vesp.* 4.5) – an enormous disgrace not mentioned by Josephus. Suetonius may have been wrong about the eagle,[3] but it confirms Cestius' reputation in Rome as a loser. And Josephus portrays Nero, as he sends Vespasian to Syria, grumbling about Cestius' poor generalship (*War* 3.1–2). The Cestius affair joined the Varian disaster and the Parthian defeat of Crassus in 53 B.C. on Rome's roll of shame.

The legate's ancient infamy lingers in modern scholarship. A standard text on Roman Judaea expresses amazement at his failure: "Such an army should have been more than adequate to subjugate the small and unorganized Jewish levies."[4] According to the authoritative *Cambridge Ancient History*:

> An attempt by Cestius Gallus, the governor of Syria, to suppress the rebellion with military might in November 66 failed (the reasons for his withdrawal were inexplicable to contemporaries as they are to us), and Nero had to embark on a regular war to restore Roman control over Judaea.[5]

---

[1] The *Clades Variana* was proverbial: Seneca, *Ep.* 47.10; Suetonius, *Aug.* 49.1; *Tib.* 17.2; *Cal.* 3.2; 31.1; Frontinus, *Strat.* 3.15; 4.78; Tacitus, *Ann.* 1.10, 57; 12.27. Greek πταῖσμα, a near synonym, turns up in various forms in Josephus: *War* 1.21 (τοῖς Κεστίου πταίσμασι); 3.1 (τὰ κατὰ τὴν Ἰουδαίαν πταίσματα); 5.41 (τὸ πάλαι σὺν Κεστίῳ πταῖσαν δωδέκατον [τάγμα]); *Life* 24 (τὸ Κεστίου πταῖσμα). *Clades* is "a shattering" and in warfare a decisive defeat/destruction, overthrow, or massacre; πταῖσμα is more of a slip or mis-step as in wrestling; in military contexts, though, it is often a blunder that leads to catastrophic defeat.

[2] Cohen (1979: 251) suggests the auxiliary prefect Metilius as a better candidate for the prefect whose death prompted Cestius' intervention. The logic works better, except that Josephus makes much of Metilius' lone *survival*.

[3] Suetonius was apparently wrong about Florus' (perhaps auxiliary prefect Metilius') death and about the cause of Cestius' intervention (see *War* 2.531, 558). His claim that Judaeans rebelled against Rome *because* an old prophecy had said that men from Judaea would come to supreme power (cf. *War* 6.312–15) seems only to reflect Flavian propaganda, not independent knowledge.

[4] Smallwood 1981: 296 ("Gallus marched on Jerusalem"), 297 ("disunity inside Jerusalem encouraged Gallus to believe that he could take the city").

[5] Wiedemann 1996a: 251.

A historian of the post-Neronian civil war writes:

> the governor of Syria, Gaius Cestius Gallus, had bungled his attempt to nip the movement in the bud. . . . [Nero] had to find a governor for Syria too, as a result of Cestius Gallus' incompetence.[6]

Goodman speaks of the legate's "apparently incompetent generalship,"[7] while a reference work on the legates of Syria, after glowing summaries of Cestius' predecessors, belabours him mercilessly: "Failures began to multiply" as he neared Jerusalem, but "worse still" was his bizarre retreat: "The final balance of the campaign was disastrous."[8]

Scholars who have studied Cestius' Judaean expedition from a military perspective have echoed these judgements. Imagining that Judaeans were in "full-scale revolt," Brandon is perplexed that Cestius delayed for precious months, when "swift punitive action by the Syrian legate might have been effective."[9] But "[t]he crux of the problem lies in the legate's decision to withdraw from the siege of Jerusalem."[10] Bar-Kochva also assumes that Cestius' aim was "to try and subdue the Jews," which makes it incomprehensible that he "lifted the siege when only six days had elapsed."[11] Goldsworthy assumes that Cestius intended to march "straight to the head of the rebellion and country," but unaccountably failed to follow through.[12] Gichon concurs: "From the moment Cestius decided to intervene, *his aim obviously was to make a quick and direct move on Jerusalem*, since his first concern must have been to quench the uprising in its bud there, before it could spread."[13] And yet, "[i]nstead of the swift move on Jerusalem demanded by the circumstances, Cestius interrupted his progress four times," because "caution got the better of him."[14] Thus, "All his actions, beginning with the first confrontation with the Jews, are marked by initial hesitation and inability to make up his mind quickly." Gichon's damning verdict is that the legate took up this "first high command without sufficient training" and was "not naturally gifted for high command."[15]

This is scholarship's unanimous judgment. "The blunders of Cestius," we still sigh.

It may be that Cestius Gallus was singularly witless, but we should hesitate to draw that conclusion about such a little-known and yet eminent figure. It would help if we had a clearer idea of what he thought he was up to. Josephus' *War* is no diary or even documentary. He includes only a few items that are

---

[6] Morgan 2006: 174.

[7] Goodman 2007: 16. Also 580: "his incompetent withdrawal after he had almost captured the city."

[8] Dąbrowa 1998: 57. [9] Brandon 1970: 39–40. [10] Brandon 1970: 44.

[11] Bar-Kochva 1976: 18. [12] Goldsworthy 1996: 88.

[13] Gichon 1981: 42 (emphasis added); cf. 40–41. [14] Gichon 1981: 46.

[15] Gichon 1981: 60.

useful for his narrative. He says not a word about Cestius' political context or his strategy. He expresses the regret of hindsight, in *War*'s customarily tragic vein: "*If only* Cestius had persevered and found a way to enter Jerusalem and remove the rebels, the city would have been spared its later destruction" (paraphrasing *War* 2.531, 539). That is no doubt true. Writing retrospectively, Josephus was alert to all the moments at which the later catastrophe *might have been* averted, except that it was not.

We all think in similar ways after traumas: "If only I had not turned at that intersection." "If only I had kept my mouth shut." But *at the time* of course we acted as we did with no inkling of the consequences. Whatever Cestius was, he was not a prophet, and we have no real basis for accusing him of incompetence merely because of what followed. Much less can we distill his aims from Josephus' mournful retrospective. The questions we would need to answer to make a responsible assessment of Cestius' expedition are not explored by Josephus.

On the Roman side these include the following. Who was Cestius Gallus? What was the nature of his commission (*mandatum*) from Nero? Did he have clear instructions concerning Jerusalem? Once he was in post, how were his relations with Nero and with senatorial peers, especially with Corbulo in neighbouring Cappadocia? What were his aims and constraints in responding to the growing turmoil in the south? How were relations with Nero's equestrians in Caesarea: Lucceius Albinus (60–63/64) and Gessius Florus (63/4–67)?[16] What roles did Agrippa II, Berenice, other royals, and Jerusalem's elite play in shaping his understanding? What motivated his timing, choice of route, and force configuration? Did he achieve *any* of his aims?

On the Judaean side: How did those who were willing to fight the Samarian auxiliary feel about conflict with legions? How many groups were there and how unified or diverse were they? Why did they attack Cestius' legionaries? Had his army done anything to deserve this? How much was reflexive, impulsive, or opportunistic, and how much part of a larger plan? What was the role of outsiders, whether Judaeans from abroad or non-Judaeans? What was the state of Judaean morale before and during Cestius' campaign? How far in advance did they know of the expedition's approach to Jerusalem? If the rebels had a strategy, how successful were they in realizing it?

Although Josephus probably *knew* something about some of these issues, he found no reason to write about them. Any relevant observations he makes are woven into the fabric of the story he crafts for his own reasons. As always, the shortfall between our questions and his narrative is not his fault. We are the ones with the problem. No matter how ingeniously we analyze his narrative,

---

[16] The dates are usually given as 62–64/5 and 64/5–67 (Schürer-Vermes 1.465–66 n. 42), but Kokkinos (1998: 385) offers reasons for earlier dates.

we cannot transform it into an all-sufficient source of data. We can only pursue our questions by all possible means and make some tentative proposals.

Let us begin with a preliminary analysis of the episode as Josephus presents it, so that we have a clearer picture of what needs explaining. What might have happened, that allowed him to configure the episode as he does? Then we shall return to our questions.

I. JOSEPHUS' ACCOUNT

To understand the story in Josephus we need to have its context in view. Our way of thinking makes us want to start with maps and a clear timeline. Although neither was not available to Josephus' audiences, I shall cheat and alert the reader here that Figure 17, in this chapter, offers a chronological reconstruction. But first I give the gist of Josephus' account. I use the present tense to emphasize that I am summarizing the existing narrative, not the actual past.

When Gessius Florus arrives as procurator in Caesarea, he is even more offensive than his predecessor Lucceius Albinus. Josephus' boilerplate accusations of "plunder and torture" (*War* 2.277) begin to unfold in disturbing detail. Florus takes large sums of money from wealthy Judaeans and from the temple, citing the emperor Nero's needs as justification (2.293–94). He brooks no opposition and badly mistreats any who challenge him.

The legate Cestius comes to Jerusalem, as legates are wont to do, for Passover in the spring of 66. Although this is otherwise a pleasant encounter, he gets an earful about the hated Florus. He promises to rein in his procurator, who himself dismisses the charges and accuses the Judaeans of rebellion against Roman authority (2.280–83). As soon as Cestius leaves, Florus escalates his assaults, targeting the temple's resources with redoubled energy and defrauding Caesarea's Judaeans of a huge sum (2.284–93). In silencing the inevitable protests, with the over-eager Samarian-auxiliary cohorts at his disposal, he goes as far as crucifying members of Jerusalem's elite, some of whom are Roman citizens or even equestrians, an unprecedented enormity (2.301–32).

In this explosion of violence, Florus and Jerusalem's elite both write urgently to the legate Cestius. Florus alleges rebellion against Rome, a charge he hopes will provoke legionary suppression, while Queen Berenice and Jerusalem's leaders plead for his immediate removal. Weighing both appeals, Cestius rejects the advice of his commanders, who instinctively support Florus, and resolves to find out more for himself. Perhaps, in the story, this caution is influenced by his recent pleasant visit. So he sends a trusted tribune to visit Jerusalem and furnish a report (2.333–41). This man, Neapolitanus, meets up with King Agrippa II for a fact-finding tour, and soon returns to Antioch with another favourable assessment. The Jerusalemites cannot tolerate Florus' violence and sacrilege, but they have no problem with Rome or the legate.

When Neapolitanus leaves Jerusalem, Agrippa stays on. This is the occasion for his great speech (Chapter 4), which deflects the people's demand *for* an embassy to Nero – *to insist on their peaceable intentions* and accuse Florus. The king's inability to help with the Florus problem leads Jerusalem's exasperated citizens to expel him from the city, although he and his sister Berenice have until now been their trusted advocates (2.342, 407).

As we saw in Chapter 4, various groups in Jerusalem begin to arm themselves at this point, because they despair of Roman or royal help against Florus and cannot simply be slaughtered. This is the context in which young priests led by the commandant Eleazar close the temple to interactions with non-Judaeans. Jerusalem's terrified elite appeal to both Florus and Agrippa. Only the king responds, dispatching a cavalry force to Jerusalem. Arriving quickly, it momentarily secures the Upper City for the elite council, but the leaders soon find their position untenable. The newly armed factions besiege the auxiliary garrison, which they had already overwhelmed and chased into the Herodian palace, *and* Agrippa's troopers in the same place, along with key city leaders.

Although Agrippa's cavalry and the auxiliary are both elements of Rome's military, the insurgents draw a clear distinction. They allow the royal (Judaean) troop to leave whereas, after giving a pledge of safety, they massacre the auxiliaries (2.454–56). At the same time the Judaean community in Caesarea is slaughtered, which sparks the Judaean reprisals and counter-reprisals (Chapter 4; 2.457–98).

This is when Cestius intervenes. But why and to what end?

Josephus' account of the expedition (*War* 2.499–555) is too long to quote, but we need a fairly full summary. The Beit-Horon pass, a narrative gateway to and from Jerusalem, frames the central story. A characteristic ring composition also highlights the role of Gabaon (Giv'on, el-Jib) as the Romans' camp and Mt. Scopus as forward base. So the story falls naturally in three parts: from Antioch to Gabaon via Beit-Horon; from Gabaon to Jerusalem and back; and from Gabaon back to Antioch via Beit-Horon.

1. From Antioch to Gabaon via the Coast and Beit-Horon (2.499–516)

Leaving Antioch (499–502). Cestius proceeds from his capital with the Twelfth Legion "plus 2,000 select soldiers from each of the others," six auxiliary infantry cohorts, four cavalry wings, 5,000 allied archers (2,000 mounted and 3,000 infantry) from Antiochus of Commagene, nearly the same number (with fewer cavalry) from Agrippa II, and 4,000 from Sohaemus of Emesa (modern Homs). Then (with my emphasis):

> Large numbers of auxiliaries were also recruited from the cities, inferior to the soldiers in expertise, of course, but compensating for their lack of skill with *feelings of eagerness and hatred against the Judaeans*. [King] Agrippa himself was present with Cestius, in charge of the route as well as general support.

Notice the strong current of inter-ethnic hatred.

From the rendezvous at Ptolemais (503–506). Cestius attacks "a stalwart city of Galilee, Chabulon, which is called '[the City] of Men,'" a beautiful and prosperous town on Galilee's western edge. Finding it deserted, he burns it and allows his men plunder, as with the surrounding villages. The local people remain hidden as long as Cestius is present. When he departs with his legionaries, however, leaving those angry new recruits to plunder Judaeans, the latter attack them and kill 2,000.

Caesarea and Joppa (507–509). Cestius moves rapidly down the coast to Caesarea and sends forces ahead to Joppa, by sea and by land. In Joppa, "They ... did away with them all, including their families, and after they had plundered the city they set it on fire. The number of those slaughtered was 8,400." The cavalry he allows to charge around the countryside of Narbata, burning and pillaging Judaean assets.

Brief Galilean operation (510–13). Cestius sends the legate of the Twelfth Legion with a select force back north to Galilee, where "the most stalwart *polis*" of Sepphoris eagerly welcomes him, inspiring Galilee's other towns to do the same. This isolates "the factious and bandit-like element" in Galilee, which takes urgent refuge in the highest nearby mountain, Asamon, just across the valley from Sepphoris (Chapter 6). These rebels hold the Romans off briefly, but the latter attack them from above, with the cavalry ready to chase those who escape on the plain. Having killed 2,000 rebels, the legionary commander Caesennius Gallus declares Galilee peaceful. He rejoins Cestius Gallus in Caesarea.

Antipatris to Gabaon (514–16). The autumnal feast of *Sukkot* (Tabernacles, from 15 Tishri) is now beginning, so many Judaeans are heading to Jerusalem. As Cestius advances, he burns their largely empty villages, especially Aphek Turris and Lydda (Lod). He brings his force up the steep pass of Beit-Horon and establishes camp at Gabaon, 50 *stadia* (10 km, 6 mi) north/northwest of Jerusalem.

2. Gabaon to Gabaon, via Jerusalem (2.517–44)

First Roman-Judaean contact: head-on (517–20). Realizing that a Roman attack is imminent, many Judaeans "quit the festival and went to their weapons," in spite of the sabbath rest. Straining for the fight:

> [T]hey attacked the Romans with such fury that they tore through their ranks and advanced through their middle, devastating them. Had the cavalry not supported the slackening infantry column by coming out and around, along with that part of the infantry that was not becoming desperately weary, Cestius with his entire force would have been imperiled.

The Romans lose 400 infantry and 115 cavalry, the Judaeans only 22. Most effective among the Judaean fighters are "the relatives of Monobazus, the king of Adiabene, named Monobazus and Cenedaeus," Niger the Peraean, and Silas the Babylonian, the last a defector from Agrippa's cavalry.

A Judaean attack from the rear (521–22). Whereas the head-on attackers are driven back to Jerusalem by Cestius' massive force, "Simon son of Gioras attacked the Romans from behind as they were ascending at Beit-Horon and mauled much of their rearguard." He is able to seize "large quantities of the baggage train." Cestius consolidates his camp at Gabaon for three days.

Agrippa's attempt at parley (523–26). Cestius' local expert King Agrippa II, seeing the emerging peril, sends two of his closest companions ahead as negotiators: Borcius and Phoebus. (Presumably his recent expulsion from the city makes it pointless for him to go personally.) These emissaries are authorized to announce an absolute pardon for all militants who desist. But Jerusalem's insurgent element, realizing that these envoys will persuade the people if they are permitted to enter, charge out on horseback (apparently) to intercept them. Phoebus they kill before he can say a word, whereas Borcius escapes back to Gabaon severely wounded. Much of the populace has accompanied the militants, outraged at their behaviour toward these heralds, who should be sacrosanct, and trying themselves to make contact with their king, but the militants herd them back into the city.

From Scopus to Jerusalem's walls (527–32). Having confirmed his initial assumption that most of Jerusalem welcomes him, but understanding that the people are harassed by a small number of militants, Cestius brings his force up on Mt. Scopus – just 1.4 km (0.87 mi) northeast of the city, Josephus notes. There he waits for three full days before leading the army down into Jerusalem's northern suburb (New City). Terrified at the advancing army, the people in that suburb retreat to the strong walls of the temple and main city. Cestius burns the New City, then camps north of the Upper City – the wealthy quarter that shares Jerusalem's western hill with the Herodian palace. Josephus reflects, "If only he had been willing at that very hour to get inside the walls by force, he would instantly have had the city." Josephus alleges that the camp-prefect Tyrannius Priscus, chief advisor on logistics (Chapter 3), along with most cavalry commanders, had been bribed *by Florus* – who has otherwise disappeared from the story – not to pursue the assault and end the conflict.

Efforts on both sides to link up (533–39). Trying to arrange an agreed moment to open the gates, a few members of ruling class call out to Cestius from the walls. But he, steaming with anger at his treatment thus far and disinclined to trust them, misses this fleeting opportunity. The militants notice the plot, pull these men down from the ramparts, and install guards to prevent it from happening again. Cestius devotes another week or so to a few test assaults: five days against the old wall of the Upper City, and a brief effort with hand-picked men against the temple compound's northern wall. Under constant fire from protected colonnades above, these men resort to the famed tortoise (*testudo*) manoeuvre, but they have no chance of access through that wall.

The Judaean militants, not realizing that Cestius' massive force is in despair, assume that their end is near. Some of them flee the city through hidden passages. The peaceful populace, greatly encouraged by this, expect Cestius to make a decisive push. Dramatic tension reaches a peak because, tragically, Cestius has no idea that many militants have fled in fear. Again Josephus laments, "If he had just persevered a short while with the siege, he would indeed have quickly taken the city."

From Scopus back to Gabaon (540–44). Angry and frustrated, Cestius returns his troops to Scopus. Their departure the next day fully restores the militants' flagging morale. They feel bold enough to pursue the legionary column and make sporadic attacks on its rear. According to Josephus, the legionaries

> did not have the courage to turn themselves toward the men who were wounding them from behind, supposing that some countless horde was chasing them. . . . Whereas they were heavily armed [i.e., encumbered] and anxious about breaking ranks, they had seen that the Judaeans were lightly armed and capable of sudden raids.

So the Roman force incurs losses again, including the commander of the Sixth Legion's cohorts, who might be the same man as Cestius' camp-prefect. Badly shaken, the army "barely made it to their former camp at Gabaon, *after abandoning the bulk of their equipment.*"

3. Gabaon back to Antioch via Beit-Horon – and Disaster (2.545–55)

Plans for a tactical retreat (545–46). Flummoxed by these developments, Cestius keeps his force at Gabaon for two days while pondering his options. In this newly hostile environment, each day becomes more perilous. Because his priority is to save his soldiers, he orders them to destroy "whatever was dragging the army down," including mules, donkeys, and pack animals along with their loads. They will keep only the animals carrying their precision-made artillery pieces, which must not fall into enemy hands. Much lightened, they head rapidly for the coastal plain the way they came, via the Beit-Horon pass.

The ambush (547–50). Judaean militants, realizing that this is the only plausible escape route, trap Cestius' force. They cannot achieve much in the open spaces, but as the column bunches up to descend the pass it becomes vulnerable. Some Judaeans advance to block the exit, while others keep pressure on the column's rear and still others take a position above a section of the road from which they can lob projectiles down. The Roman cavalry is unable either to descend the narrow pass, with the infantry below them, or to turn around and ride back through the infantry behind. Leaving the narrow road on either side would mean death. The Judaeans are able to kill thousands. Indeed they could have "taken" (ἀναρπάζω) the entire force, including Cestius, had it not turned dark. The surviving Romans find an overnight reprieve in Beit-Horon (upper or lower?) while Judaeans watch them closely.

Final trick and partial escape (551–55). Knowing that his exit route to the plain will become deadly after daybreak, Cestius exploits the only kind of surprise left to him: timing. He chooses 400 brave soldiers and has them call out the watchwords all night long, to convince the Judaeans that everyone is tucked in bed – while he leads his main force away in quiet darkness. Now they must abandon even their precious artillery pieces. By daybreak they have gained a 6-km (3.75-mi) head start, which puts them safe in the open plain. The Judaeans give chase but soon realize there is no point. So they go back and rob the corpses, collect the abandoned haul of artillery, and return to Jerusalem in triumph. Suffering negligible losses, they have killed a legion's worth of infantrymen plus 480 horsemen. "This was all accomplished, then, on the eighth of the month Dius [= Cheshvan], in the twelfth year of Nero's *imperium.*"[17]

II. PRELIMINARY ANALYSIS: SCENES AND SUSPICIONS

Before we can use Josephus' account we need to see what it is made of.

Getting there

Roman commanders had several possible routes for the march to Jerusalem from Caesarea. If they needed surprise or felt endangered, they might go out of their way via Samaria or Gophna to the north, or even via the Jordan Valley to approach from the east. Titus would later use those routes, given that resistance was by then expected and in view of Cestius' experience (*War* 5.39–43). For routine travel with no anticipated problems, however, it was much more efficient to follow the coastal road south and then turn east. One could go all the way to Joppa before making a right-angle turn left, but the quicker route veered eastward from Caesarea, skirting the plain on a hypotenuse to Antipatris (Aphek) or Lydda (Lod), and ascending there. This is the route Cestius chose.

---

[17] Nero's twelfth year ended on October 12 A.D. 66. Dius/Cheshvan straddles October–November, moving progressively earlier against the solar year until a second month of Adar is pushes it back. In 66 it appears from NASA's moon-phase tables (http://eclipse.gsfc.nasa.gov/phase/phases0001.html) that 1 Cheshvan was at its earliest point (Oct. 7) before the new moon would have fallen in September (in 67), necessitating the insertion of Adar II the next year. In 66, therefore, 8 Cheshvan would have fallen on October 15. A modern perpetual Jewish calendar (www.hebcal.com) puts it on October 13. Either way, Josephus' mistake is assigning this to Nero's twelfth year. Most scholars align 8 Dius with a much later Gregorian date (see table in Levick 1999: 40), hence well into Nero's thirteenth year (cf. *War* 2.284). Whereas most nevertheless take the Cestius passage to be in error, Kokkinos (1998: 368–95) argues that this notice is correct, and on that basis redates the beginning of the revolt to Nero's *eleventh* year (= spring of 65).

From Lydda two routes were still available: one southerly through Ammaus, Ayalon, and Kiryat Yearim – roughly the modern Tel Aviv-Jerusalem Highway 1 – and the other via Modein, Lower and Upper Beit-Horon, and Gabaon (Gibeon) – roughly today's Route 443.[18] With Agrippa advising him (2.502), Cestius chose the latter. This clearly suggests that they were expecting no serious trouble in the Judaean hills.

No matter which route Cestius took, it was no trivial task to move tens of thousands of soldiers and a massive baggage train of pack animals from the coast to the Judaean plateau. The ascent had to be made somewhere, and even without enemies the direct passes into Judaea were potentially dangerous. Among the difficult options the Modein/Beit-Horon route offered several advantages. Between Lower Beit-Horon (modern Beit-Ur al-Tachta), emerging from the plain to the west, and the upper town 3.3 km (2 miles) to the east (Beit-Ur al-Fawqa), the road ascended some 230 m (755 ft). The rise was steep and narrow only in its final short segment, however.[19] In addition to being the shortest overall route, it limited the vulnerable part of the journey to that brief climb, after which the column would be home free on the plateau (ca. 660 m above sea level). Moreover, a force that held Upper Beit-Horon could see out to the Mediterranean in a wide arc taking in the coastal plain north and south (Fig. 15).[20]

Although the modern road has mostly concealed ancient Roman engineering, nineteenth-century explorers could find segments of the Roman ascent.[21] These confirm that the steepest part comprised steps cut from the bedrock, about 3 m (10 ft) wide, for more secure footing. Rabbinic lore would recall that it was not safe for two camels to walk side by side in this pass (b. Sanh. 32b).[22]

The legions were used to adapting their marching formation to the terrain and security environment. Josephus claims that they normally marched six across, although he gives evidence of three-file formations. In the second century, Arrian describes his army marching in four files, which could rapidly thicken to eight against a cavalry charge.[23] Ancient texts give no fixed amount of space from man to man, but a column of 30,000, marching six across and with 1 metre from one man's back to the next, would occupy 5 km (3 mi) of road. Marching four abreast they would take up 7.5 km (nearly 5 mi), in three

---

[18] Har-El 1981: 14–17.   [19] See Har-El 1981: 15–16.
[20] The crusaders built a manor house, which may have functioned as an observation post, in the upper town. We have no remaining evidence of Roman structures.
[21] See maps and discussions in Bar-Kochva 1976: 14; Fischer, Isaac, and Roll 1996: 73–79, 135–39.
[22] See the nineteenth-century engraving in Wilson 1881: 1.191, which shows the steepest part of the pass (looking inland) and the narrow, perhaps rock-cut road.
[23] Josephus, War 3.124; cf. 2.173; 5.131; Arrian, Ectasis 4–5, 15–17. For analysis, Goldsworthy 1996: 180–83; Gilliver 1999: 46–48.

FIGURE 15. Commanding view westward to Mediterranean from Upper Beit-Horon (author 2009).

files 10 km (6 mi).[24] Allowing for a large number of mules and cavalry horses and for breaks between units, the length of a column of 30,000 might reach 14 or 15 km (8.7–9.3 mi) in three files. That is a quarter of the entire distance between Jerusalem and the Mediterranean coast: an imposing sight but also a temptation to flank attack in constricted spaces, especially in the rear.

While in the coastal plain, that is for most of the expedition, Cestius' force may have marched six across, with horse patrols on the flanks (cf. *War* 3.124) to keep the column compact. This was not possible in the pass, however. They might just have been able to maintain three infantry files, but the rock-cut steps would have made it difficult to protect the pack animals and their attendants. Normal practice was to keep the baggage integrated in the column, with a rearguard of mercenaries, armed infantry, and cavalry to chase off any challengers (*War* 3.125–26).[25] But leading pack mules up a long series of steps with hundreds or thousands of soldiers behind them was an invitation to

[24] Assuming a 0.75 m space (pace) for each soldier, Gichon (1986: 303–308) proposes that the army later commanded by Vespasian, roughly twice the size of Cestius', reached 28–30 km (17.4 to 18.6 miles) on the march. Noting the practical difficulties this would pose, Gilliver (1999: 47) suggests that in suitable terrain the column might have marched in parallel or even triple lines – one on the road itself and one on each side – also to facilitate rapid communications along the line. Even if Cestius did some such thing in the plains, however, this option was unavailable to him in the ascent through the Judaean hills.

[25] See also Vegetius, *Epit.* 3.6; Gilliver 1999: 38–46.

mishap. That may be why, as Josephus implies, Cestius placed his baggage train in the rear with little protection (*War* 2.521), which would again suggest a high level of comfort and confidence.

Roman tacticians were well aware of hazardous topography and they had standard procedures for managing it. Scouts went ahead to ensure that a route was passable. They were followed by lightly armed, rapid-response units to preclude or confront ambushes, then by engineers for clearing and straightening roads as needed (cf. *War* 3.116–19). Then came the advance force to occupy the heights preclusively (Vegetius, *Epit.* 3.6). Military discipline prescribed such precautions *always*. Given that Cestius' main column reportedly reached Gabaon without incident (*War* 2.516), we might guess that he took these routine precautions.

Nor was Gabaon randomly chosen as a camp site. It is a hill nearly 800 m (2,600 ft) above sea level, with a commanding view of the surrounding countryside. Just 2 km (1.25 mi) farther south is the very highest point in the region (1,000 ft [300 m] above sea level), known today as Nebi-Samwil ("Prophet Samuel"). A large Roman base on Gabaon presumably had sentries if not units camped on the higher hill.

Josephus' account of the first skirmishes (2.517–22) presents many difficulties. Passing uneventfully through Beit-Horon, Cestius reaches Gabaon about 9 km (5.6 miles) beyond. That concludes a hard day's march (about 32 km, 20 mi) from Lydda. Camping at such a high place, now only half a day's march from Jerusalem, would have made sense. In the story, however, it is only now that those in Jerusalem *hear* of the expedition and charge out to confront it. Their furious attack somehow breaks Roman infantry ranks (2.517–19). But where and how could this happen?

The story reads suspiciously like a set-piece engagement: "[T]hey [the Judaeans] tore through their ranks and advanced through their middle" (*War* 2.518). Cavalry wheeling around and infantry supporting a collapsing centre were classic field manoeuvres.[26] But how could they apply where there was no battle between massed forces? Because Cestius' army had made camp at Gabaon (*War* 2.516), we might assume that this encounter occurred the next day. But was it a pitched battle or a series of Judaean attacks on the front and rear of a *marching column* (2.521)?[27] Judaean guerrilleros normally refrain, sensibly, from confronting legions in pitched battle (cf. *War* 2.547). We must suspect that Josephus has conventionally dramatized whatever actually

---

[26] Cf. Webster 1985: 145–47; Goldsworthy 1996: 228–44; Warry 1998: 246; Gilliver 1999: 110–12. Josephus improbably claims that he drilled his Galilean recruits in these column manoeuvres (*War* 2.579; Chapter 6).

[27] Everyone knew that armies were most vulnerable when on the march (e.g., Vegetius, *Epit.* 3.6.1).

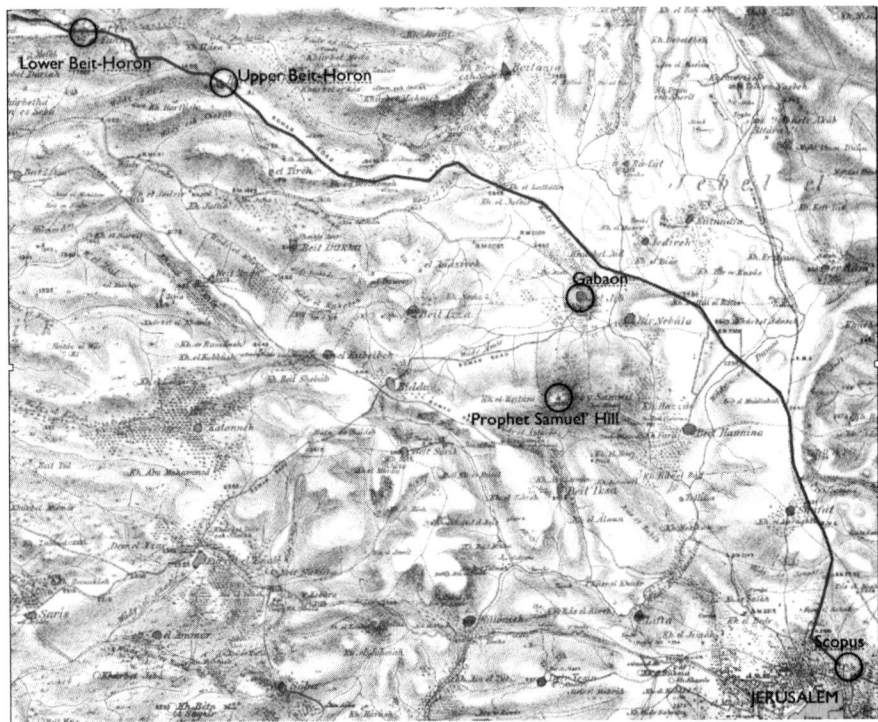

FIGURE 16. Map from Conder, Kitchener, and Warren 1881–1884, Sheet 17: the Roman Road from Jerusalem to the Beit-Horon Pass via Gabaon (el-Jib).

happened with little concern to explain to his audiences in Rome the real timing and topography – if he knew them.

Difficulties increase as the story progresses (*War* 2.521). Whereas the Judaeans are repulsed *at the front*, Simon bar Giora leads a successful attack on the rear and baggage train "as they were going up at (*possibly* upon or back to) Beit-Horon," carrying off vast quantities of plunder. Yet Cestius holds his position for three days at Gabaon as Judaeans occupy the hills between him and Jerusalem (2.522). How is it possible that the column's rearguard and baggage train are attacked while ascending Beit-Horon, if the army has already established camp 9 km (5.6 miles) ahead? If the column occupied 14 or 15 km (8.7–9.3 miles), even at a speed of 5 km (3 mi) per hour[28] the rear would have arrived about three hours after the van. Even crawling on hands and knees they should have cleared Beit-Horon by the time *camp had been set up* on Gabaon. Finally, if the men in Jerusalem hear about the Romans' arrival only when the front reaches Gabaon (*War* 2.517), how are they able both to confront those soldiers (where?) *and* reach the rearguard ascending Beit-Horon?[29]

[28] Gichon 1981: 42 n. 16.

Imagining realistic scenarios requires us to ignore or fiddle with at least some of Josephus' language. This is not very disturbing in view of ancient historiographical values (Chapter 2), but it highlights the problem with trying to milk a literary source for data. Bar-Kochva's picture of a simultaneous attack on the head and tail of a very long column still on the march would explain some things, but must neglect Josephus' plain statement that camp had been established.[30] Assuming Josephus to be "reasonably accurate and trustworthy," Gichon thinks that Cestius must have separated his baggage train from the column, to arrive "many hours after the main body."[31] Another possibility is that Simon's attack on the rear is an undeclared flashback, having occurred before camp was established at Gabaon, although he thinks to mention it only later. Further, the Jerusalemites must have known about Cestius' expedition days if not weeks before Gabaon. The legate's arrival in Galilee or at least in the Caesarea region, and at the very least his destruction of Joppa, must have prompted messages to Jerusalem. If that happened, perhaps a guerrilla group had *prepositioned* itself near Beit-Horon awaiting the column? Because Josephus explains little of the context, almost anything is imaginable.

Underlying standard analyses is an assumption of Josephus' geographical accuracy. Bar-Kochva avers that "Josephus, however, inaccurate [sic] and tendentious as a historian, is highly reliable in his topographical excursuses."[32] In my view, however, it is hard to imagine Josephus consciously separating the tasks of geography and history (Chapter 2). Think of his dramatically exaggerated claims about being unable to see the valley floor from the heights of Iotapata (*War* 3.158), or from Jerusalem's walls (*Ant.* 8.97; 5.412), or his schematic and misleading description of Masada's topography (Chapter 9). The problems with Beit-Horon are of a similar kind. His audiences did not have maps in their laps and his priority was to tell them a compelling story – even a true one but not overly concerned with facts (Chapter 2).

Cestius' baggage train is another example. Like Mary Poppins' bag, it is continually emptied and yet remains full. Josephus claims that Simon's men carried off "large numbers" of pack animals (συχνὰ τῶν σκευοφόρων; 2.521) in the first assault. Then, with Cestius' withdrawal from Scopus, attacks *on the rear* cost the Romans "*the bulk* of their baggage" (τὰ πολλὰ . . . τῶν σκευῶν; 2.544). They must have precious little left, we think. But a few sentences later Cestius decides to jettison *the baggage*, ordering all the "mules, donkeys, and

---

[29] An alternative route is conceivable. A Hellenistic/Hasmonean road from Lydda to Gabaon was identified in the 1980s, from Lower Beit-Horon via Khirbet Jifna (not the more famous Jifna [Gophna] north of Ramallah), Beit Duqu, and Adasa. See Fischer, Isaac, and Roll 1996: 108–10, 331, 334. Conceivably, Simon's group used some such path. But still the rear of the column should have cleared the pass well before news could reach Jerusalem of the camp at Gabaon.

[30] Bar-Kochva 1976: 18.　　[31] Gichon 1981: 39, 53.　　[32] Bar-Kochva 1976: 18–19.

pack animals" destroyed, *except* those carrying artillery (2.546). He really must have *nothing* left but artillery, then. Yet after the final flight the Judaeans collect a harvest of discarded spoils (τήν τε ἀπολειφθεῖσαν λείαν, 2.554).

Josephus' indication that Cestius and Agrippa registered the dangers of their situation only once they had reached Gabaon (2.522–53) may be important, however, and it agrees with other indications. Before the confrontations at Beit-Horon, they had seemingly anticipated an easy passage to Judaea and entry into Jerusalem. The newly changed circumstances make Agrippa realize that he had better prepare for their arrival at Jerusalem, and that is why he decides to send envoys.

Violent treatment of heralds was a serious breach of etiquette. Spartans and Athenians knew that they had incurred a blood-debt – paid in the carnage of Thermopylae – when they killed Persia's emissaries (492 B.C.).[33] Arthur Eckstein shows why envoy immunity was important as one of the few checks on constant warfare, but also why such men might be killed. If they were seen not as good-faith ambassadors – the moral basis of their immunity – but simply as instruments of "compellence diplomacy," they represented an insult and deserved treatment as such.[34] Josephus' claim that the rebels cut down Agrippa's heralds because they would have appealed to the people seems plausible in the situation.[35] That was after all why Agrippa sent them, still confident in his close friendships with city leaders and his personal understanding of the conditions.

Cestius in Jerusalem

Did Cestius *besiege* Jerusalem? Josephus' language is admittedly loose. He uses the word "siege" (2.539: "if he had persevered with *the siege*" [εἰ ... τῇ πολιορκίᾳ προσελιπάρησεν]) and refers to those in the city as "besieged." If Cestius did initiate a real siege, his abrupt departure would be "strange behaviour."[36] Brandon assumes that Cestius burned the northern suburb "to clear the area for his siege operations."[37] Gichon imagines that he began a siege but suddenly remembered that he lacked the hardware because of the raids on his baggage and so had to abort.[38] An embarrassing senior moment if ever there was one.

---

[33] See Cartledge 2002b: 102, 104.   [34] See Eckstein 2006: 37–78, esp. 58–64.

[35] Journalists, writers, and other opinion shapers are always vulnerable in politically unstable situations.

[36] Quotation from Gichon 1981: 56 (cf. 54–55). Cf. Bar-Kochva 1976: 18 ("started a siege on the Upper Town and Temple . . . lifted the siege when only six days had elapsed").

[37] Brandon 1970: 41.

[38] Gichon (1981: 56): "Since our narrative does not mention heavy siege artillery, . . . it is clear that Cestius lacked the necessary siege train to sustain his assault. At least part of his siege

But we should be wary of taking a fundamentalist approach to Josephus' language. One could use siege language in loose, figurative, or even psychological applications in antiquity, just as we use English equivalents.[39] As soon as an army appears outside a walled city, there is a "siege" if those inside feel unable to leave (cf. 2.529). Josephus does not indicate that Cestius initiated an actual siege, however, and the story as a whole suggests that he never imagined the need for such a thing.

Josephus knew sieges. He described them in detail at Iotapata, Gamala, Jerusalem, Machaerus, and Masada. The familiar elements are all missing here. Contrast Iotapata (*War* 3.161–70): Vespasian's generals first decide on a siege in council, then have their men gather wood and stone from all around, build screens to protect their siege works, excavate earth, build ramps, and commence artillery and archery covering fire to keep the besieged off the walls. In the spring of A.D. 70, Titus only gradually comes to see the need for a siege of Jerusalem after his efforts to secure capitulation fail (Chapter 7). In Cestius' case there is no hint of any such decision or preparations. We do not even hear about his siege engines until they are captured, in their crates, after the ambush (2.553). Evidently a siege was never in the cards.

The notion that Cestius planned a siege runs against the drift of Josephus' account. He is in ongoing consultation with Agrippa II and Jerusalem's elite. Their assumption that they will be admitted to the city explains their surprise at the attacks, Agrippa's dispatch of emissaries, Cestius' long waits at Gabaon and on Scopus, and his rage *at not being admitted* (2.528–34). There is no room here for a planned siege. The fires that Cestius sets in the northern suburbs are not (in Josephus' story) to clear ground *for siege ramps*. Like the other fires he sets (2.504–5, 508–9, 516), their purpose is to terrorize and intimidate. Watching from the north wall as thousands of heavily armed soldiers set the northern suburb's wood-emporium ablaze, choking on the smoke as ash clouds fill the sky, Jerusalem's militants *should have* been scared into submission. It was shock and awe.

Finally, Cestius could not have been intending to begin a siege of Jerusalem, a city whose walls and climate he and Agrippa knew well, in October. When cold, rain, and even snow threatened, it was time for winter quarters and not sieges outside such remote places without full logistical preparation.

The only military manoeuvre that Josephus describes furthers our suspicions about his use of clichés. This is the *testudo*: the shell that a legionary unit created by interlocking shields. Cestius' picked soldiers, banging away at the north wall, have no hope. The hail of arrows from the colonnade drives them back until they think, "Wait a minute, we are legionaries. *Testudo!*" This brilliant tactic enables them to

---

equipment had been lost to Bar Gioras, and moreover, he did not give himself the time to procure the materials needed for constructing heavy machinery. . . ."

[39] E.g., Plato, *Alc.* 2.142 and LSJ *s.v.* πολιορκέω.

remain close to the wall for a few hours, but to what end? They would have prevailed, Josephus alleges, if Cestius had not withdrawn them. But this sounds just like malarkey, driven by Josephus' sorrow rather than the reality of the circumstances. Our narrator implies that the *testudo* should have been Cestius' key into the city, but this ignores his own theme elsewhere of Jerusalem's impregnability.

The north wall of the temple platform was about three football fields in length, one-third of that occupied by the Antonia fortress with its imposing glacis (*War* 2.430). It towered above the legionaries to their right. The eastern third was taken by the Pool of Israel, which likewise projected far northwards with a strong wall. Cestius' men were thus in a tactically impossible situation, pressing ahead into the U-shaped middle, where the wall could not be undermined because it sat in bedrock. Only divine intervention, Josephus will later claim, would enable even *Titus* to overcome such defences, after a carefully planned and prolonged siege.[40] It was not going to happen for Cestius, tortoise or no tortoise, on that October afternoon.

Josephus mentions the *testudo* again in an equally doubtful passage, illustrating his own anti-siege measures at Iotapata (3.270–75). This was a celebrated technique of the legions, perfecting a Hellenistic tactic.[41] In Josephus' battle of wits with Vespasian, he relates, the *testudo* enables the Romans to charge against his excellent walls. But their clever manoeuvre pushes Josephus to even greater resourcefulness. His men conveniently have cauldrons of boiling oil on hand. He orders these to be poured down on the tortoise, then delights to describe the effects of his chemical-weapon attack: the burning oil flowing unstoppably under the legionaries' armour, which they could not release, and devouring their skin. If anything like this happened, we can understand why Vespasian was eager to get Josephus in his hands and why his soldiers were ready to lynch the prisoner (Chapter 2: *War* 3.392–97).

At the Upper City's wall to the west, where Cestius and his troops spent the bulk of their time, prospects were no better. Josephus elsewhere describes this wall as "very hard to capture" (5.142). It was anchored on the west by Herod's Hippicus tower, 40 m (130 ft) high with a solid 12 m (40 ft) square stone base (5.163–65). The wall was interrupted by Jerusalem's "second wall," which somewhere projected north and then east to join the Antonia. This left little space for Cestius' great army to manoeuvre against the Upper City's wall, and some of that space was occupied by a large pool. When Josephus later describes the months-long efforts of Titus' legions to build siege ramps here, he

---

[40] *War* 1.4–12 with 4.127; 5.136–89; 6.9–13, 330–31, 409–13. Cf. Tacitus, *Hist.* 5.11–12.

[41] Polybius 9.41.1; 10.31.8 (Macedonian military uses); Aeneas Tacticus 32.11; Onasander, *Strat.* 20; Livy 44.8; Cassius Dio 49.30–31 (Roman adaptations); cf. Parker 1928: 256; Gilliver 1999: 134–36. The formation is pictured on both Trajan's and Marcus Aurelius' columns (plates in Gilliver 1999: 136; Goldsworthy 2003: 194.

mentions this *Amygdalon* or Towers Pool, which *X Fretensis* also had to contend with (5.468). The size of a shortened football field (73 m [240 ft] by 43 m [140 ft]), it is now dry and enclosed by buildings in the Old City.

In short, there was no chance of a successful siege and no reason to suppose that Cestius imagined such a thing. He expected to be admitted in the usual way, with the city leaders pouring out to greet him – on Scopus if not earlier. When that did not happen, he waited and incrementally raised the level of intimidation until his glittering army was just metres away from the population, great fires blazing behind them. His aggressive posture could not be sustained, however. The militants, even if relatively few (we have no idea of proportions), needed only to control the few gates to hold out until Cestius found his position untenable. Because he had not prepared for a siege, that would not be long. When he was not admitted after a week, the sensible option was to leave and plan a very different kind of operation for the spring.

Josephus claims that Cestius' decision to leave Jerusalem was influenced by the camp-prefect Priscus (2.531). Accusations of bribery are convenient because unprovable.[42] Such an effort by Florus is unnecessary and sounds doubtful. The Camp Prefect was responsible for siege preparations, and we can imagine that his unbribed expert opinion was that beginning a siege now would be unwise. Josephus' need to have Priscus bribed may be revealing in other ways, though. It tends to confirm that Cestius had not planned an assault on Jerusalem. Discussion of a siege would only have come up with the surprise of Jerusalem's closure. If this Priscus was the one killed in the withdrawal, he was in no position to defend himself against Josephus' accusation (*War* 2.544).

Ambush at Beit-Horon

Rebuffed outside Jerusalem, Cestius had to move. To remain much longer, for a siege or otherwise, he would have had to establish high-volume supply chains and build secure shelter. The foraging his army had done during their week of waiting was only a temporary solution to their exclusion from the city. If they could not get in, they had to leave.

Reprieve behind Gabaon's walls and ditches was also temporary because Cestius was now vulnerable, in a remote highland environment turned hostile (*War* 2.545). He sensibly lightened his burden for a dash to the coast. In desperation, it seems that he had no time to secure the heights of Upper Beit-Horon, as we imagine him to have done on the ascent.

---

[42] Note examples from Josephus' own career: *Life* 195–96; cf. 73, 80. He accuses the Jerusalem leadership of having been bought by John and alleges that his priestly colleagues in Galilee were in John's pocket, while he himself was incorruptible.

However we look at it, this part of the story presents yet more problems. The first concerns the length of the column. Even if it was only 10 km (6 mi), it would have occupied the entire road from Scopus to Gabaon, or Gabaon to Upper Beit-Horon. Bar-Kochva suggests that the Judaeans allowed the front sections to pass unmolested to create a false sense of security before launching attacks on the rear.[43] That may be, although Josephus' description assumes a more compact column. We should also reckon with the possibility that Cestius brought a much smaller force than his original 30,000 (if *that* number is not greatly inflated) into the hills, perhaps only the legionaries with a cavalry escort. He had left a garrison at Sepphoris and presumably others at Joppa, Lydda, and other places he had taken along the way. The marching line might have stretched only 3 or 4 km (9,000–12,000 men in three files) or even rather less, which could make the scene easier to imagine.

The climactic ambush scene (2.547–49) is also difficult to match with the topography. Gichon wryly remarks: "If we do take his description at face value, we have the picture of a true alpine landscape."[44] The site has no yawning chasms, hills towering over roads, or deadly steep ravines off the side as Josephus implies. The steep part of the ascent was dangerous, not because of cliffs but because of the narrow steps, outside of which was steep and sloping ground. Scholars recognize the mismatch but still insist on Josephus' accuracy. For Bar-Kochva, "we must assume that it [Josephus' language] accords with the topography of the Ascent."[45] Why must we? Bar-Kochva notes that the modern road has altered the ancient landscape, the terracing of hills mitigating the ancient declivities. Still, he and Gichon prefer to locate some of the action east of Upper Beit-Horon, where parts of the terrain offer better prospects.[46]

The fame of the pass between Upper and Lower Beit-Horon has led most scholars to assume that it was the lower town that Cestius reached when darkness fell, but Gichon rightly observes that Josephus does not distinguish Upper from Lower Beit-Horon. So he proposes that Upper Beit-Horon is a better candidate for the site reached by nightfall, which would mean that the overnight was down the pass and possible because it was hidden from view.[47] These are interesting suggestions, although problems would still remain in matching story with land.

I cannot see the reason for assuming Josephus' geographical accuracy in the first place. It seems more likely that he dramatized this landscape as he does the rest of his narrative. Spectacular scenery was more important to this pivotal episode than fidelity to a nature unknown to his audiences. This is a good place to remember how much Josephus omits, which is almost everything, and why it is futile to suppose that we can recover the past from him. For example, King

---

[43] Bar-Kochva 1976: 20.   [44] Gichon 1981: 58.   [45] Bar-Kochva 1976: 18.
[46] Bar-Kochva 1976: 19; Gichon 1981: 57–59.   [47] Gichon 1981: 58–59.

Agrippa II is a central figure in the early phases of this account, then he vanishes without a trace, to reappear telekinetically in his territories (2.595, 632–33). We would like to know what became of him and King Sohaemus of Emesa with his army (*War* 2.501). Were they also caught in the ambush? Or did they return northward by a different route? Or did the militants give Agrippa special consideration? We want to know, but Josephus does not say. He can include only slivers and glints from the complexity of real life in his narratives.

III. CHRONOLOGY

Chronological considerations (cf. Fig. 17) suggest that Cestius' campaign was hurriedly planned, reluctant, and meant to be quick, also that its aims did not include a siege of Jerusalem.

Problems with reconciling ancient and modern calendars are well known.[48] Happily we may speed past most of them. Josephus uses Macedonian month names throughout *War*. Macedonian months had originally been lunar (*moonths*), derived from the Babylonian calendar and beginning with the sighting of a new moon. By the late first century B.C., some eastern cities had aligned their Macedonian months with those of Rome's solar calendar, as reformed by Julius Caesar. Judaeans, however, continued to reckon by the Hebrew-named lunar months that remain in use today. When Josephus uses Macedonian months, it is not immediately clear which alignment is assumed: Has he accommodated his months to the Roman solar calendar or do they represent Hebrew/Babylonian lunar months? The answer to that question can alter significantly the plotting of his dates on our solar calendar.

Fortunately, Josephus provides enough evidence to indicate that he normally identifies Greek months with Hebrew-lunar equivalents.[49] His reference to "the new moon of Panemus" shows that a lunar month is in view, for example, just as his dating of Passover to 14 Xanthicus shows that Xanthicus is equivalent to Hebrew Nisan. Knowing that he normally uses these equivalents is valuable because we can rediscover the moon's phases in antiquity by astronomical calculation, and therefore can trace the *theoretical* lunar months of each year.[50] There are wrinkles, to be sure. Lunar calendars that need to remain coordinated with the seasons, such as the biblical-Judaean (Passover must be in spring, Booths/Sukkot in autumn), insert a double month every

---

[48] See Samuel 1972; Bickerman 1980: 9–91; Stern 2001; Hannah 2005; Feeney 2007.

[49] E.g., *Ant.* 1.81; 2.311; 3.201, 248; 8.61, 100; 11.109; 12.248, 319; Schürer-Vermes 1.587–99; J. Price 1992: 210–30; S. Stern 2001: 34–38; Hannah 2005: 71–97, 135–88.

[50] See http://eclipse.gsfc.nasa.gov/phase/phases0001.html. (accessed August 1, 2012). In the Judaean calendar the intercalated month fell seven times in each nineteen-year cycle. As it happens, NASA's table corresponds within several days to Jewish perpetual-calendar models (e.g., www.hebcal.com).

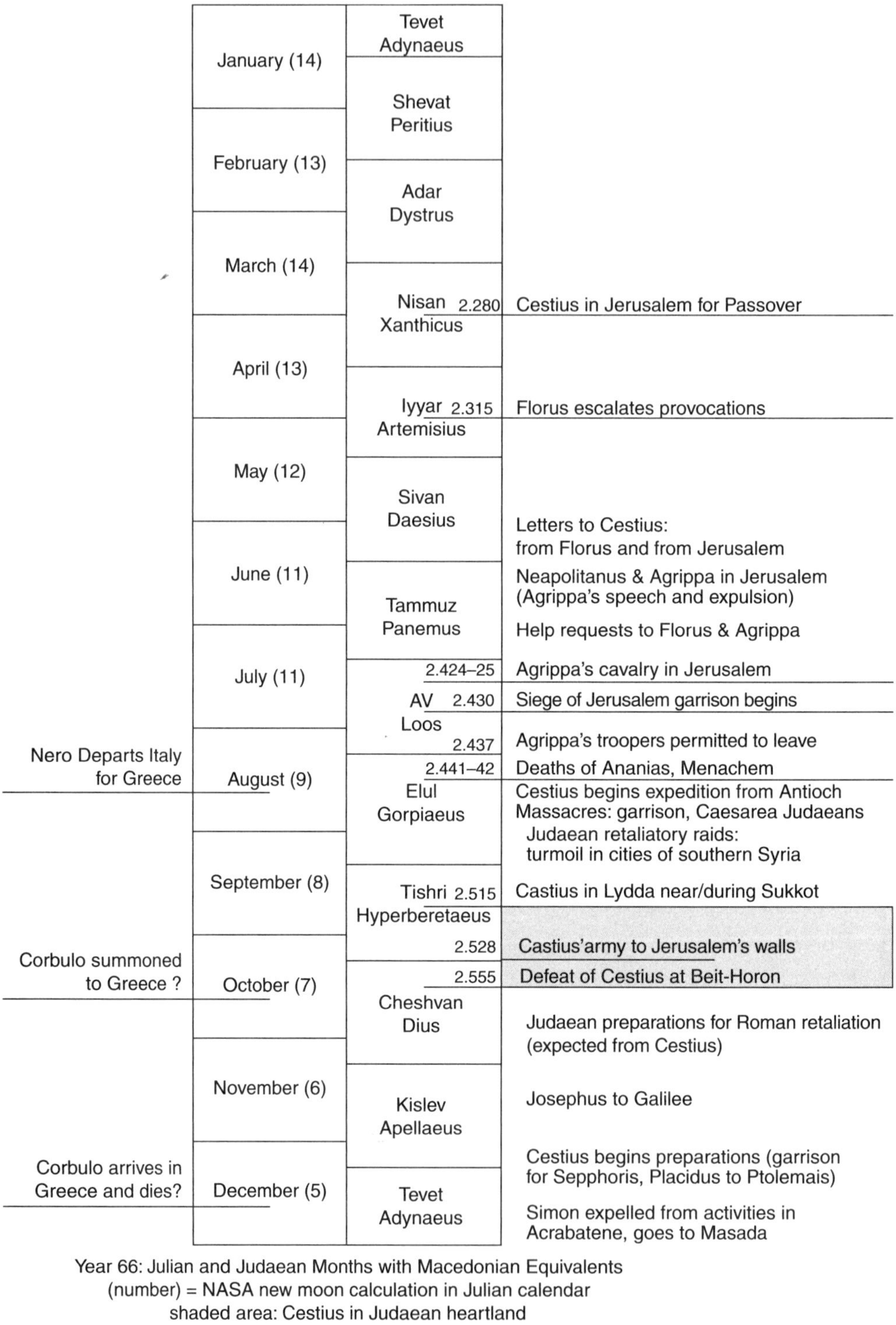

January (14)	Tevet Adynaeus	
	Shevat Peritius	
February (13)		
	Adar Dystrus	
March (14)		
	Nisan 2.280 Xanthicus	Cestius in Jerusalem for Passover
April (13)		
	Iyyar 2.315 Artemisius	Florus escalates provocations
May (12)		
	Sivan Daesius	Letters to Cestius: from Florus and from Jerusalem
June (11)		Neapolitanus & Agrippa in Jerusalem (Agrippa's speech and expulsion)
	Tammuz Panemus	Help requests to Florus & Agrippa
July (11)	2.424–25	Agrippa's cavalry in Jerusalem
	AV 2.430 Loos	Siege of Jerusalem garrison begins
	2.437	Agrippa's troopers permitted to leave
Nero Departs Italy for Greece	2.441–42	Deaths of Ananias, Menachem

August (9)	Elul
	Gorpiaeus
		Cestius begins expedition from Antioch
		Massacres: garrison, Caesarea Judaeans
		    Judaean retaliatory raids:
		        turmoil in cities of southern Syria

September (8)	Tishri 2.515 Hyperberetaeus	Cestius in Lydda near/during Sukkot
	2.528	Castius' army to Jerusalem's walls
Corbulo summoned to Greece ?	2.555	Defeat of Cestius at Beit-Horon
October (7)	Cheshvan Dius	Judaean preparations for Roman retaliation (expected from Cestius)
November (6)	Kislev Apellaeus	Josephus to Galilee
Corbulo arrives in Greece and dies?		Cestius begins preparations (garrison for Sepphoris, Placidus to Ptolemais)
December (5)	Tevet Adynaeus	Simon expelled from activities in Acrabatene, goes to Masada

Year 66: Julian and Judaean Months with Macedonian Equivalents
(number) = NASA new moon calculation in Julian calendar
shaded area: Cestius in Judaean heartland

FIGURE 17. The year 66: Julian solar months (left) aligned with Hebrew and Macedonian months. (Numbers) in the left column indicate the day of the solar month on which the new moon fell according to NASA calculations. On the right is a timeline for Cestius' involvement in Judaea, the shaded area representing his actual presence in Judaea.

few years to check the forward momentum against the solar seasons of a purely lunar (e.g., Muslim) calendar. These intercalary months can usually be calculated, however, because we know that the second month of Adar (= Dystrus) is added in years when the lunar months would otherwise leave their seasons.

This does not yet mean that we can be precise in making Julian-calendar dates from Josephus' notices.[51] He might have had mistaken information, or been inconsistent in aligning Macedonian months, or followed a source that used a different scheme, or redated an event for his dramatic reasons.[52] Moreover, the beginning of the month was defined not by the new moon's physical occurrence, in a theoretical way, but by *observation* and reporting, which could mean a lag of days. With all of those qualifications, we have a reasonable basis for plotting Josephus' dates, broadly speaking, against the Roman solar calendar (Fig. 17). This is enough to make his dates look familiar to us, without adding the complication of our own Gregorian calendar. In any case, it is customary when speaking of first-century dates to plot them on the Julian calendar.

Most other published research in our area dates the events in 66 later than I shall propose.[53] This disparity illustrates the uncertainties of ancient history. I may be wrong. Were those later dates correct, however, they would make it *even less likely* that Cestius envisaged a military assault on Jerusalem, and they would thereby strengthen my case. My real concern is not with absolute dates, which I offer for reference, but with the sequence of events *within* each lunar month, irrespective of where these fell in the Roman year 819 A.U.C. (= A.D. 66). It is the compression of these lunar dates that exposes the problems in Josephus' account of cause and effect and so requires us to rethink Cestius' aims.

Cestius passed the spring/summer/early autumn campaigning season of 66 monitoring the problems in the south, but seeing no reason to intervene with a force. It was a long trip to Judaea and his Passover visit in April, supplemented by Neapolitanus' report of late June, showed that Jerusalem was not *in revolt*. Only toward the end of campaigning season did Cestius feel

---

[51] It is customary to use the Julian calendar for ancient dates, because there is little point adjusting those dates to our Gregorian calendar.

[52] In *War* 4.654 Josephus dates Vitellius' murder to 3 Apellaeus (Kislev). This month falls in the November/December range. In the five years I have charted for the following chapters (66–70), Kislev *ends* no later than Dec. 24. In 69 it seems to have been near its earliest position, putting 3 Kislev around November 5. Yet even from Josephus (4.499, 548, 652) it seems that that Vitellius died on 20/21 December 69 (cf. the meetings of the Senate on Jan. 1: Tacitus, *Hist.* 4.39–40). For other mistakes about Vitellius' time in power see Epit. Dio 64/65.22.

[53] Levick 1999: 40 provides a table with three options for each of Josephus' dates, all weeks later than those I give in Fig. 18. Goodman, however (2007: 4–5, placing Cestius' defeat in October), seems to agree with the alignment proposed here.

that he had to march southward, although Jerusalem would soon be turning cold and wet. Why?

Whatever he intended, the expedition was brief. When he reached Lydda, the population had gone to Jerusalem for Sukkot, which begins on 15 Tishri (*War* 2.515).[54] They might have left days before his arrival, but Josephus mentions that Sukkot was underway when the Romans made camp at Gabaon the next evening (2.517). After stops of three or four days each, there and on Scopus, Cestius is inside the New City for 30 Tishri (*War* 2.522, 528). He spends about six days around Jerusalem (2.535, 541) and several more at Gabaon again before fleeing. Josephus dates the ambush to 8 Cheshvan – Dius (Oct. 15; 2.555) – a mere eight days after Cestius was outside Jerusalem.

Josephus may have massaged his dates to make festival or sabbath connections, or he may have bad information. But his dates are incidental, not foregrounded, and coherent with each other. So we have reason to suppose that the entire operation, from ascent into Judaea's hills to descent, lasted no more than three weeks. Given that this included unexpected delays, Cestius might have *planned* a stay of ten or fewer days in the Judaean hills. In light of the tradition of Passover visits by legates, including his own earlier that year, we might imagine that he hoped to arrive for the major autumnal festival of Sukkot. He would confirm Agrippa II's authority with the king alongside, strengthen his bond with the city's leaders, punish the troublemakers identified to him by the leaders, especially those who had killed auxiliary soldiers, and make a grand speech drawing a line under the unpleasantness. His army's presence (even if only 2,000–3,000 strong) would drive home that armed self-help was neither necessary nor permissible. He might even have attempted a public display of rebuke for Florus and the auxiliary.

However that may be, the expedition must have been hurriedly planned. Cestius would first have had to prepare for at least a month, a preparation period not included by Josephus. Second, even with that extra month, his large expedition would have been hastily assembled. Third, Cestius used every option other than legionary intervention in Judaea, acting decisively once those options were exhausted.

1. Cestius must have begun planning earlier than Josephus implies because, if we burrow forward from events before the expedition and backwards from the expedition, each tunnel requires too much time for us to join them up. With the aid of Figure 17, let us first look ahead from the summer. Agrippa's cavalry are in Jerusalem no later than 7 Av, because they control the Upper City for a

---

[54] The physical new moon was on September 8. Rather than counting that as 1 Tishri, for argument's sake I am allowing an intervening night for it to be seen and reported, making 1 Tishri September 9. The precise beginning of the month makes no difference, however, to the relative chronology.

week before losing it to militants on the Feast of Wood-carrying (14/15 Av).[55] The siege of the auxiliary garrison lasts at least three weeks, during which Agrippa's troop is released as the rebel factions fight each other and rearm (2.437). That violence claims Ananias on 7 Elul (Aug. 16) and Menachem a few days later (2.440–46). The massacre of the auxiliary follows on a sabbath (2.456), on or near 13/14 Elul (August 23 was apparently a Saturday). In Josephus' account, however, the events that stirred Cestius to action are still some way off.

War 2.457–99 then describes Judaean reprisal attacks on faraway *poleis* (2.458–60) and their responses (2.461–98). All this would seem to require a good four weeks, given the distances involved and movements of people and news, actions and reactions. Even a minimum of three weeks would push us a week into Tishri (= late September). But if Cestius decided to intervene only after hearing about *these* events, he could not have reached Lydda from Antioch by 15 Tishri. A great deal had to happen in the meantime: the news reaching Cestius, his planning and assembling of a force, the march southward with various detours, and the move up into hill country.

It is about 400 km (250 mi) from Antioch to Ptolemais, or fifteen days' marching at a fast pace (27 km = 17 mi per day). Then it is two days to Caesarea (52 km [32 mi] from Ptolemais) and and another two to Lydda (55 km [33 mi]). That makes at least nineteen days of *steady marching* from Antioch to Lydda, with no time for recuperation or adjustment.[56] The delays and special operations (northern recruitment, Galilee visited twice, Joppa, Aphek Turris) presumably needed another ten days. This would require at least twenty-nine days counting backward from Lydda, making 10 Elul (Aug. 19) Cestius' *latest possible* departure date from Antioch and suggesting an earlier date. But even 10 Elul was before the massacres in Jerusalem and Caesarea (ca. 13 Elul) and well before the reprisals and resulting turmoil. Cestius could not have been responding to those events.

Before Cestius could depart from Antioch in early Elul, he needed time to organize. Allowing three weeks for that would make *early Av* the latest date for his decision to travel south. Syria's legions were deployed not in Antioch itself but hundreds of kilometres away: perhaps near Zeugma on the middle-Euphrates, Cyrrhus on the Afrin River, and Apamaea southwest on the

---

[55] 2.430 puts the feast of wood-carrying, when Agrippa's troops lost their Upper City stronghold to rebels, the day before 15 Av. *M. Taan.* 4.5 gives nine dates for wood-carrying, of which five fall in Av, and 15 Av is the major one; *Meg. Taan.* 5 (Av) mentions only 15 Av (though possibly in light of this incident). It is curious only that Josephus, perhaps clumsily, dates it to 14 Av.

[56] Similarly Gichon (1981: 42): fifteen days from Antioch to Ptolemais. See his n. 16 for various kinds of comparative data.

Orontes or Laodicea on the coast.[57] The Twelfth, we have seen, was far south at Raphaneae. Cyrrhus, Zeugma, and Commagene's capital Samosata are about 100, 200, and 300 km (60, 120, 180 mi), respectively, northeast of Antioch, meaning three, six, or nine days of marching. There must have been at least one round of communication to prepare their movements. Allowing a minimum of time for strategizing with his commanders, then, the first week of Av seems the latest time that Cestius could have made his decision and begun rapid planning – if he reached Lydda by 15 Tishri.

Thus, Josephus' claim that Cestius intervened because of the reprisals and counterreprisals after the massacres makes for compelling drama, but does not work chronologically. The same kind of mistake is common in our world, however. We often assume that a U.S. president's trip to some foreign capital is a response to a crisis, but the White House points out that it was planned long before.

What did stir Cestius to action, if it was not the turmoil following the massacres? Among the events mentioned by Josephus, one stands out as a likely stimulus. The beginning of Av was when Agrippa dispatched his cavalry in response to the Jerusalem envoys' pleas. The events that generated this appeal and Agrippa's response provide a plausible trigger for Cestius' expedition, with which Agrippa's had to be coordinated. Let us take a closer look.

With armed factions rapidly forming (2.408) and the temple commandant isolating the sanctuary (2.409–17), the city's leaders send messengers to Agrippa and to Florus (2.418–21):

> Once they comprehended that they themselves could not contain the civil strife and that the danger from the Romans would reach them first [i.e., they would be held accountable], the elite tried to offload the responsibility and therefore sent envoys: some to Florus, ... others ... to Agrippa. They pleaded with both to come up into the city with a force and amputate the civil strife before it became uncontainable. To Florus, such awful news was a welcome report, and since he had resolved to kindle the war he gave no answer to the emissaries. Agrippa, on the other hand, ... sent 2,000 cavalry. ...

If Agrippa's troop reached Jerusalem by about 7 Av (2.424–25), the envoys could have left Jerusalem no later than the end of Tammuz (July 10/11).[58] But they could not have left much earlier, given Neapolitanus' happy departure from the city to Cestius around mid-Tammuz.

---

[57] Some hints about the legions' locations are in Tacitus, *Ann.* 2.57.2, 79.2; Josephus, *War* 7.17–18. Cf. Parker 1928: 128. See also Chapter 3. At *Ann.* 15.3.2, Tacitus describes Corbulo moving the remaining Syrian legions up to the Euphrates as an emergency measure in A.D. 62.

[58] This part of my chronology agrees with that of Gichon 1981: 61, although we work from different assumptions in many respects (e.g., the next note).

Josephus puts the worst interpretation on Florus' response (2.420), but we may imagine less nefarious motives. The procurator must have realized by now that he and his Samarian-Caesarean auxiliary were an object of hatred (Chapter 4). For him to impose the same auxiliary force on the populace now could only have *escalated* the violence. It is understandable that he declined. Extracting revenue with violence at Nero's direction was one thing; visibly exacerbating the conflict risked his own position. He may have referred the emissaries who visited him to Cestius.

Agrippa's dispatch of cavalry around 1 Av must have had Cestius' agreement at least, if it was not the legate's own initiative. Agrippa was not king *of Jerusalem*, and anyway he was not at liberty to intervene militarily in a *polis* under the legate's authority. Josephus remarks in another context that Agrippa was consulting with Cestius in Antioch before this expedition (*War* 2.481), in continuation of their usual close collaboration (2.335). This note seems important for understanding Cestius' aims and Agrippa's action.[59] Our need to backdate the expedition planning to early Av for chronological reasons meshes with Agrippa's dispatch of cavalry in consultation with Cestius.[60]

Agrippa's absence from his kingdom around this time was what allowed his lieutenant Noarus to act against the Judaeans (Chapter 4). When was Agrippa away? The possibilities are constrained by his visit to Jerusalem with Neapolitanus and expulsion just after the middle of Tammuz, on one side, and on the other by his dispatch of cavalry around 1 Av. Josephus remarks that, when Agrippa was driven out of Jerusalem, he "withdrew into the kingdom" (2.406–407). Even if he had wished to sulk, the king would have needed to confer with Cestius about such an ominous development post-haste. After Neapolitanus' comforting report, Agrippa could not have kept quiet about the new dangers he had just experienced in Jerusalem.

Whether we reckon forward from Neapolitanus and Agrippa's visit or backward from the expedition, then, we end up in much the same place. Cestius and Agrippa began planning their expedition around the end of Tammuz / 1 Av. After his banishment from Jerusalem (mid-Tammuz), Agrippa headed to Caesarea Philippi or another part of his kingdom long enough to deputize Noarus, then went immediately to see Cestius. At some point in all of this he sent four cavalry squadrons to meet the Jerusalem leaders' urgent request.

---

[59] Emphatically Gichon (1981: 41): "[N]either G. Florus nor Agrippa II felt at ease about . . . notifying C. Gallus. . . . Agrippa feared that serious disturbances would delay his becoming king over all Judaea. . . . Therefore, his aim was to try and stem the revolt with his own forces and without having resort to the *Legatus Syriae*." Gichon also seems to overlook Cestius' dispatch of his tribune on the fact-finding trip with Agrippa.

[60] Josephus was presumably not free to play around much with Agrippa's activities, given the king's membership in his publishing circle and favour in Flavian Rome (*Life* 361–67).

Where did Agrippa meet Cestius? Antioch is where Josephus locates their consultation (2.481), and the expedition leaves from there (2.500). *Life* 49, however, mentions that Agrippa and Berenice went to see Cestius in Berytus (Beirut). This would help to explain the chronology. This ancient Phoenician city was now a veterans' colony for Syria's legions, founded by Marcus Agrippa in 15 B.C.[61] Cestius might have been making his usual rounds, but Berytus was a particularly convenient site from which to monitor Judaean affairs, far south of Antioch. It had been a site of Herodian benefaction, most spectacularly with Agrippa II. He seems to have made Berytus a kind of home, after his capital and Jerusalem. He built a theatre, sponsored shows and fine statues, and subsidized the city's grain and oil (*Ant.* 20.211–12). If Cestius happened to be there while on his circuit, that would have been a godsend for Agrippa, who needed to confer with him urgently. Berytus was just two or three days' travel from his territory, sparing him the extra trek of 330 km (205 mi) to Antioch.

The simplest hypothesis, then, is that Agrippa and Berenice met Cestius in Berytus. After reviewing the situation and Jerusalem's appeal for help, around 1 Av Agrippa dispatched a cavalry force from there as an immediate response. Planning a larger intervention, however, they hurried to Antioch. They might well have assumed that 2,000 cavalry would suffice for the immediate crisis, confident that they would have no difficulty entering Jerusalem. So far they were correct. Josephus claims that the troopers were indeed welcomed by the leaders and initially succeeded in pacifying the city (2.422–26). The militant factions were few and small enough to be handled by such a professional force. Soon, however, the militants were able to outmanoeuvre the newcomers, knowing the cramped urban space with its internal walls, and confine them to one area.

If Cestius and Agrippa could send a force of 2,000 soldiers and expect it to enter the city without difficulty, they must have assumed that with thousands of legionaries behind them they would have no difficulty when they arrived. Therefore, only a short sharp visit to Jerusalem would be necessary. Cestius at would depart before the weather turned inhospitable, perhaps leaving a legionary detachment. Agrippa might stay and consolidate his relationships with the leaders after the removal of factional troublemakers. This is speculation, but the logical consequence of our reconstructed chronology.

2. Such rapid planning at the end of Tammuz and beginning of Av also confirms that Cestius had not seen the need for military intervention before Agrippa's expulsion. All his experience that year had confirmed the city's typical friendship and loyalty, now disturbed only (if seriously) by the serious aggravation of Florus and his auxiliary.

---

[61] Hall 2004: 45–58; Millar 2006b [1990].

Cestius had no thought of attacking Jerusalem, then, because he thought he understood the situation well. He assumed that he could visit the city to resolve recent problems. He knew that Judaean vigilantes had been reacting against Nero's callous revenue collection. This Judaean violence was unacceptable no matter what, and it had to be stopped. Those who killed auxiliary soldiers had to be executed. But none of this made Jerusalem or its leaders enemies of Cestius or Rome. Just as his general Caesennius Gallus would be welcomed in Galilee's major *polis* of Sepphoris, in spite of militants there who had to be punished, so Cestius and Agrippa expected to be welcomed in the mother-city, even as they dealt with identified militants there.

IV. THE SHAPE OF CESTIUS' ARMY — AND CORBULO

Three aspects of the force that Cestius assembled might throw light on his aims: its overall structure, the choice of *Legio XII Fulminata*, and the supporting units.

On the first question, compare Cestius' force with that of the Flavians a few months later (Chapter 7). Although there are points of difference, partly because the Flavians had learned from Cestius, their expeditions have much more in common than their different results would suggest. Table 2 compares Josephus' descriptions of their force structures.

If these numbers are anywhere near accurate, or at least proportionate, Cestius' army was about half the size of Vespasian's. The added size is explained by Vespasian's need to ensure that he would not suffer Cestius' fate and by his realization that he might face hard Judaean resistance. Nevertheless, the structures are roughly the same: a legionary core (*possibly* equal in size) supplemented by auxiliaries and allied specialists in horse and archery.

The differences are worth noticing. First, Cestius used only 5,000 of perhaps 21,000 Syrian auxiliaries at his disposal, whereas the Flavians would use most of them. Cestius apparently wanted to leave most of the Syrian army in place. Second, he seems not to have used auxiliaries from the south, as Vespasian would (3.66). Because these soldiers would have had the best knowledge of the terrain, this suggests that Cestius left them out because he knew that they had created the present troubles. At the same time, third, he inflated his force with a "very large number" of — at least 2,000 — angry fighters with no training. Fourth, Cestius used nearly the same number of allied specialists (13,700 against 15,000) as the Flavians, meaning that cavalry and archery were relatively prominent in his expedition. Fifth, Cestius took allied support only from the northern kings (Antiochus of Commagene, Sohaemus of Emesa, and Agrippa II), not from the Nabataean Arabs as the Flavians would (3.68). Three considerations might explain that. (a) He was in too much of a hurry to coordinate with distant kings. (b) He did not see this as a *war* requiring all hands. (c) The

TABLE 2. *Comparison of Cestius' and Vespasian's forces.*

Cestius Gallus (*War* 2.500–502)		Vespasian and Titus (*War* 3.65–69)	
LEGIONS (heavy infantry)		LEGIONS (heavy infantry)	
XII Fulminata	5,400 [6,000]	*V Macedonica*	5,400 [6,000]
3 × 2,000 others	6,000	*X Fretensis*	5,400 [6,000]
	11,400 [12,000]	*XV Apollinaris*	5,400 [6,000]
			16,200 [18,000]
AUXILIARIES		AUXILIARIES	
6 × 500 [1,000] infantry	3,000 [6,000]	10 × 1,000 infantry	10,000
4 × 500 [1,000] cavalry	2,000 [4,000]	13 × 600 infantry	7,800
	5,000 [10,000]	13 × 120 coh. cavalry	1,560
		6 × 500 [1,000] cavalry	3,000 [6,000]
			22,360 [25,360]
ALLIES		ALLIES	
ca. 5,000 cavalry	5,000	3 × 2,000 archers	6,000
ca. 8,700 infantry	8,700	3 × 1,000 cavalry	3,000
	ca. 13,700	1 × 1,000 cavalry	1,000
... of whom at least 9,000 archers		1 × 5,000 inf. archers	5,000
			15,000
OTHER FIGHTERS		OTHER FIGHTERS	
2,000? ad hoc recruits	2,000		
TOTALS		TOTALS	
Cestius' Entire Force	**32,100 [37,700]**	**Entire Flavian Force**	**53,560 [58, 360]**
Minus irregulars	30,100 [35,700]	(Josephus: 60,000)	

Nabataeans were fierce enemies of the Judaeans and this hatred could be destabilizing – as it would be for the Flavians.[62]

We might ask why Cestius chose *XII Fulminata* as legionary core. As we saw in Chapter 3, the later practice of breaking up legions for peacetime duties appears not yet to have been established. Corbulo reportedly considered the legions' fragmentation in Syria a sign of lassitude, which he remedied (Dio 62.19.1). Why then did Cestius not summon a second legion alongside the Twelfth, rather than 2,000-strong contributions from the others?

Cestius lacked the special *imperium* of Corbulo and Vespasian to bring in legions from outside Syria (cf. *War* 7.117). He had to work with units already in the province. Perhaps he worried about a problem that had arisen in the Pannonian Revolt (A.D. 6–9): "[W]hen legions were withdrawn from one sector to meet a threat on another . . . enemies beyond the border were liable to take the opportunity to rebel against Roman rule or to raid imperial territory."[63] Instead of removing a whole legion from the frontier, taking

---

[62] For the situation under Herod, leading Varus to remove the Arab contingent of his army, see *War* 2.68–69, 76. For their atrocities under Titus' command, 5.551, 556.

[63] Luttwak 1976: 48.

cohorts from several would leave Syria's deterrent intact and visible, with most of the auxiliary also still in the north.

Why the Twelfth? Based in Raphaneae (*War* 7.18), it was by far the closest to Judaea and farthest from the Parthian frontier. It was also not far – a long day's march (36 km, 22.4 mi) – from Sohaemus' kingdom of Emesa (Homs), which contributed 4,000 troops.[64] Accompanied by 4,000 from the north-eastern legions and the 5,000 from Commagene, Cestius could hope to leave Antioch with relative speed (cf. 2.481). Perhaps he ordered the Twelfth, along with the detachment from Apamaea and Sohaemus' 4,000, to meet him in Tripoli. From there the column could gather up the volunteers from the coastal cities before the whole force mustered in Ptolemais (2.500). Then they could begin joint exercises in confidence-building and muscle-flexing on Galilee's fringe.

But Cestius might also have been thinking about the Twelfth's combat readiness. Corbulo had used the inexperienced *XII Fulminata* and *IV Scythica* to strengthen them, leaving his more seasoned legions (*III, VI, X*) in place on Syria's frontier. He wanted to harden *XII* and *IV* with a moderate intensity of combat experience.[65] Under the leadership of Caesennius Paetus in 62, however, both legions performed abysmally and were largely destroyed (Chapter 3). Corbulo sent the Twelfth's dispirited remnant far from the front. So Cestius' choice of the same disgraced Twelfth now, four years later and with many new soldiers, might reflect a principle spelled out by Vegetius: Weakened and humiliated units need opportunities to rebuild confidence in combat, but of a relatively safe and manageable kind (*Epit.* 3.25; cf. 10–12).[66] The same principle has been followed until modern times.[67] If this were part of Cestius' calculus, it would further confirm that he saw his expedition as a police action – not as a war or as an assault on rebellious Jerusalem.

---

[64] The unmarked ancient site lies between the modern villages of Baarin and Nisaf. The Deutsches Archäologisches Institut (DAI) has been surveying there since 2005: see Gschwind 2006–2011, especially 2008 and 2011. Ground Penetrating Radar has exposed the lines of the legionary camp beneath the ground, as well as a sanctuary, tombs, a quarry, and the route of the road to Tripoli: see www.dainst.org/en/project/raphaneae?ft=10.

[65] Tacitus, *Ann.* 15.3, without naming the legions in question, but see Ritterling 1925: 1256.

[66] Cf. Plutarch, *Marc.* 13, on Claudius Marcellus' efforts to restore those who had fled Hannibal's forces at Cannae and been dismissed by the Senate to Sicily. They pleaded for the chance to re-establish their honour as soldiers, a request he understood and supported.

[67] Cf. Roberts (2008: 287): "[T]his was one of the reasons that the invasion of France was postponed to 1944, until victories had been won over the Wehrmacht in the lesser theatres of North Africa, Sicily and Italy" – although Italy proved anything but a confidence-builder. Until 1942, British forces faced a series of humiliating defeats at the hands of Germany, which Churchill and his generals attributed to inferior fitness levels, training, and morale (Roberts 2008: 124–25).

Of the many other questions we might ask about Cestius' force, two require attention. First, why include such a large allied-specialist (cavalry/archery) component? Second, what was Cestius' relationship with the great Corbulo?

Josephus knew the distinctive roles of cavalry and infantry, which he mentions often. In this campaign he highlights the ways in which Cestius used the cavalry for rapid movement across open plains. Outside Jerusalem's walls, however, or on the narrow cobbled streets inside, mounted fighters were of little added value.[68] Ascending and descending the Beit-Horon pass they could be a liability. (Agrippa had sent cavalry because that was his force specialty, and they could arrive quickly.) We may hypothesize from Cestius' inclusion of an alleged 7,000 horsemen that operations along the coastal plain were an important component of his plan, which were therefore not a careless diversion as scholars have surmised.

The question of Cestius' military relationship with Corbulo is tied up with Josephus' remark that Cestius brought 2,000 soldiers from each of "the other" legions. Scholars have proposed that the donor legions were as few as two or as many as six.[69] Josephus names only *VI Ferrata* – because its commander Priscus was killed (2.544; cf. 531). The underlying issue is Corbulo's activity at this time and how many of Syria's legions he controlled. As we saw in Chapter 3, Corbulo returned to Cappadocia-Galatia when Cestius was commissioned as legate of Syria in 63, with a special remit for Armenia.[70] Tacitus remarks that Cestius "was given administrative authority in Syria, Corbulo the military forces" (*Ann.* 15.25: *Syriaeque executio Cestio, copiae militares Corbuloni permissae*).

The issues are too complicated for us to disentangle fully, but we cannot understand Cestius' mission historically without some consideration of Corbulo. Understanding Tacitus to mean that Cestius had no military authority while Corbulo was present, Emil Ritterling reasoned that Corbulo must have been out of the picture by the time of Cestius' expedition in 66.[71] But he dated Corbulo's recall by Nero to August/September of 66, and "the beginning of Cestius' expedition" to October/November. We have seen, however, that Cestius must have begun planning by early Av (mid-July) in 66, while most scholars agree that Corbulo was not summoned until the end of that year.[72]

---

[68] Agrippa sent mounted troops presumably because they were an elite force that could reach Jerusalem quickly. Once inside Jerusalem, their horsemanship was of little value.

[69] Parker (1928: 138) has only *IV Scythica* and *VI Ferrata*, apparently on the assumption that *X Fretensis* and others were assigned to Corbulo. Ritterling (1925: 1257) and Campbell (1986: 124) assume that, with Corbulo gone, Cestius controlled as many as seven legions.

[70] Vervaet 1999, 2000.   [71] Ritterling 1925: 1257.

[72] Xiphilinus' Epit. Dio 62/63.17 provides the main account. It gives no date but suggests that Nero has been involved in his Greek projects for some time when he summons his legates to their deaths. Dio locates the event at Corinth's port of Cenchreae, and Bradley (1978: 72) has him in Corinth only from about October (if at all), after participating in games elsewhere. Hence the common views: Syme 1970a: 27 ("In the winter of 66/7 Nero summoned

Cestius therefore acted with military freedom in Syria while Corbulo was still present in Cappadocia. M. Gichon and F. Vervaet solve the problem by arguing that Corbulo's special *imperium* lapsed once the Armenian problem was solved, when Tiridates left for Rome in the autumn of 65 (Vervaet) or when Nero received him in spring 66 (Gichon).[73]

Those are plausible suggestions, but Tacitus' remark need not mean that Cestius had *exclusively* civic responsibilities. That would seem peculiar for a sword-bearing *legatus pro praetore* in a prestigious frontier province.[74] Tacitus goes on to say that "the tetrarchs, kings, prefects, procurators, and praetors" were also directed to submit to Corbulo, but this does not mean that *they* lost day-to-day control of their forces. The idea may simply be that all regional forces were at Corbulo's disposal for Armenia from 63. Josephus makes a similar statement about Vespasian in 67: Nero "sends this man to assume command of the armies in Syria" (*War* 3.7), although in fact Vespasian took only the Tenth and auxiliary cohorts from Syria. The new legate Mucianus retained control of Syria's legions, even if he used them mainly to support Vespasian's imperial bid (Tacitus, *Hist.* 2.83). It is simplest to suppose that Corbulo's authority over all regional forces for the sake of Armenia did not prevent governors and kings from using their armies in normal ways when he did not need them, and indeed that once Armenia had been resolved, that higher requirement became practically irrelevant.

Figure 18 summarizes what seems to have been the military relationship between the legate of Syria and the legate in Cappadocia with special command for Armenia.[75]

On "the other" legions contributing 2,000 each to Cestius' force, then: In the absence of contrary indications, we would assume that Josephus was referring to Syria's ordinary garrison of four legions. Although we cannot be certain which were present in late summer 66, the best candidates are *IV Scythica*, *VI Ferrata*, and *X Fretensis*.[76] Cestius took the Twelfth as a whole plus the equivalent of a second legion from the other three.

Corbulo"); Griffin 1984: 178 ("winter of 66/67"); Alston 1998: 100 ("late 66 or early 67"); Levick 1999: 25 (summoned October 66); Vervaet 2002: 158 (left in province until "end of 66"), 170 ("arrived [in Greece] early in 67"); likewise 2003: 437.

[73] Gichon 1981: 44, 62; Vervaet 1999, 2000.

[74] *Annals* 15.25.3 could be understood as a correction of the situation during Corbulo's first tenure in Cappadocia. That earlier arrangement, a division of Syria's legions between Corbulo and Quadratus, had led to their bickering and even confrontation (*Ann.* 13.8–9). To preclude such problems, it made sense for the emperor to declare which man had the higher rank for military affairs: Corbulo. In 62 Corbulo dismissed *IV Scythica* and *XII Fulminata* to Syria (*in Syriam translatis*; *Ann.* 15.26). Surely, then, they at least would have fallen under the Syrian legate's command, unless Corbulo needed them again.

[75] Fundamental work has been done by Ritterling 1925: 1255–59; Franke 1991; the various authors in Le Bohec and Wolff 2000. I draw here from Vervaet 2003: 437–42, who bases himself mainly on Franke, as a recent overview of our particular issue.

[76] Vervaet 2002: 169 n. 148.

Imperial Legate in Syria (Antioch)	Legate in Cappadocia (for Armenia)
1. A.D. 54/55 – 60 Ummius Quadratus *X Fretensis, XII Fulminata* (*Ann.* 13.40)	Cn. Domitius Corbulo *III Gallica, VI Ferrata* A.D. 56: *IV Scythica* > Moesia (*Ann.* 13.5.2) A.D. 58: vexillation > *X Fretensis* (13.40)
2. A.D. 60: initial success in Armenia, Nero's man Tigranes appointed king. Corbulo to Syria as legate. *III, IV,* and *VI* rejoin *X* and *XII* (1,000 legionaries remain in Armenia).	No legate with Armenian portfolio No legions in Armenia except vexillations, with 3 infantry cohorts and 2 cavalry wings to protect Tigranes
3. A.D. 61: new troubles in Armenia. Corbulo as legate of Syria sends *IV* and *XII*, untested but under trusted commanders. *III, VI,* and *X* remain with Corbulo in Syria.	*IV* and *XII* under commanders Verulanus Severus and Vettius Bolanus (*Ann.* 15.3). Parthian Vologaeses cooperative. Legions to Cappadocia for winter (*Ann.* 15.6).
4. Late 61: Nero sends Caesennius Paetus. Corbulo, still legate of Syria, has legions *III, VI,* and *X* (*Ann.* 15.3).	L. Iunius Caesennius Paetus commands Armenian campaign. Has *IV* and *XII* from Cappadocia plus *V* *Macedonica* from Moesia.
5. A.D. 62: disastrous rout of Caesennius; Corbulo vainly tries to remedy, bringing *III* and *VI* to aid (*Ann.* 15.12.3).	Caesennius Paetus: Leaves *V* in Cappadocia. Leads *IV* and *XII* to disaster in Armenia.
6. A.D. 63: C. Cestius Gallus legate of Syria. Disgraced *IV* and XII plus reliable *X* remain in Syria.	Corbulo given renewed command over eastern armies. Corbulo leads *III* and *VI*, with *V* and now *XV* *Apollinaris* from Pannonia. Quickly reaches compromise with Vologaeses over Armenia.
7. A.D. 64–66: post-settlement. Cestius Gallus has *IV, X, XII* with *VI* (sent back from Corbulo) in Syria.	Corbulo retains *III, V,* and *XV* until his recall in ca. October of 66. At that point, *XV* is dismissed to Alexandria.

FIGURE 18. Comparison: legates of Syria and Cappadocia (for Armenia) with their forces.

More important for our investigation is the question why, if Corbulo was available nearby, Nero did not send *him* into Judaea. The legions drafted for Corbulo's use in Armenia from the Danube (*V Macedonica* and *XV Apollinaris*) remained on deployment; Vespasian would take them over. Corbulo could have brought them into Judaea without disturbing the Syrian deterrent at all, and then Nero might never have needed to involve Vespasian.

The simplest answer seems to be that Judaea was part of Syria and therefore Cestius' responsibility. No one viewed this as *a war* of the sort with Armenia that would necessitate Corbulo's high-powered intervention. By the time that Cestius failed, further, Nero likely thought that Corbulo had quite enough glory, and Corbulo himself will have seen the wisdom of inaction. This brings up our final set of contextual considerations, which have to do with Cestius' political context, before we draw these threads together in a reconstruction.

V. CESTIUS THE POLITICIAN

The political and social realities of Cestius Gallus' life are opaque, but we are not without suggestive contextual clues. Nero's final years were marked by financial emergency, deep conflict with the senatorial elite, and conspiracies against the emperor. Pondering Cestius' place in all of this may add colour to Josephus' portrait, given that his Roman audiences would have known some of this, and refine our thinking about the real-life Cestius' intentions in relation to Judaea.[77]

Finances and fears

In the early 60s Nero's financial crisis was becoming severe, and his taxation regime in the provinces ever harsher.[78] His need for funds had something to do with the costs of the Armenian–Parthian campaign and something to do with personal largesse, including the sponsorship of lavish Greek-style entertainments. When the tight-fisted Galba succeeded Nero, he would deploy fifty procurators to recover the 2.2 billion sesterces that his predecessor had squandered.[79] Already in 59/60 we find Nero's procurator in Britain calling in supposed *loans* made by Claudius, although the Britons, taking them to be gifts, had spent them. At the same time Seneca was recalling his loans to British leaders to the tune of 40 million sesterces (Dio 62.2). It seems that Seneca was hoping to retire from public life and to use the cash to obviate any suspicion of disloyalty. Nero preferred to see the glass of loyalty as half empty. A retired Seneca would attract too much sympathy and so the emperor rejected his resignation (*Ann.* 14.53–56). This was the context in which Nero had sent Albinus to Caesarea.

The financial crisis was real enough. In 62 Nero appointed a panel of three ex-consuls to review expenditures, while criticizing his predecessors – as one does – for *their* recklessness (Tacitus, *Ann.* 15.18.1–3). In 62 or 64 came Nero's

---

[77] See Campbell 1984, in several relevant sections.   [78] See Wiedemann 1996b: 248–49.
[79] Suetonius, *Galb.* 15; Plutarch, *Galb.* 16. This is more than half a billion *denarii* – a single *denarius* being a decent day's wage for a manual worker. For discussion see Morgan 2006: 47–48.

reform of gold *aureus* and silver *denarius* coins, which reduced the weight of the latter by about 7%. Although his motives are debated, he was saving these metals.[80]

Two events in the following years had serious economic ramifications. First was the settlement with Parthia with its expensive consequences. The nine-month procession of Tiridates with his retinue, costing the imperial treasury 220 million sesterces, looked to critics like a foreign triumph over Rome.[81] The other comet that struck the treasury was the great fire of A.D. 64. Spreading rapidly from the Circus Maximus over the Palatine hill, the blaze left just four of the city's fourteen districts untouched. Nero was away and reportedly rushed back to assist the populace, but suspicion still attached to him because of the alacrity with which he made lemonade from these lemons. He planned a complex of parks and massive buildings from the Palatine to the Esquiline hills, covering prime real estate east of the Forum, including the space where the Colosseum now stands. Anchoring all this would be his vast Golden House. Rumour had it that he planned to rename Rome "City of Nero."[82]

Tacitus describes the consequences of Nero's financial crisis in terms that seem relevant for Judaea (*Ann.* 15.45.1–2):

> Meanwhile, for the sake of financial contributions Italy was being laid waste and the provinces ransacked, even allied peoples and those cities that are called "free." The Gods, too, were implicated in that plunder, as the ravaged temples in the City [Rome] were emptied of gold.

Tacitus gives examples from Asia and Greece, where Nero sent his freedmen to collect revenue aggressively. He mentions the plundering of temples and the seizure of costly divine images. The Epitome of Dio says that no one could count the number of offerings Nero stole from temples in Rome, while in Greece he did away with prominent men in order to seize their wealth – and their freedmen, wives, and children to preclude any rival claims to the property (62/63.11).

Some of this may be exaggeration. But when we consider that Nero dispatched Florus to Caesarea at the height of the crisis and while he was beginning to rebuild Rome (A.D. 64), we can see why this procurator would have felt confident in showing unprecedented aggression in collecting taxes.[83]

The context explains not only Florus' behaviour but also his untouchable status. In contrast to the legate Cestius Gallus' political world, in which good

---

[80] Sutherland 1984: 3–5, 133–48. Cf. Pliny, *Nat.* 33.47 (Nero set a standard of 45 *aurei* to the Roman pound, changing the early Augustan standard of 40, although the decline had been gradual before his time). On Nero and silver see Comparette 1914.

[81] Dio 63.1.2 gives the figure of 800,000 sesterces per day for nine months.

[82] Tacitus, *Ann.* 15.38–44 in general, 15.39 with Suetonius, *Ner.* 55 on the name.

[83] See Eck 2011: 61–65 for a sensible contextual treatment.

relations with subject *poleis* were crucial for success,[84] the equestrian's career horizon was determined entirely by his success in executing Nero's orders. Lacking Cestius' connections, status, or legions, Florus was also well placed to inform against the senator and be believed. If Florus did his job satisfactorily, he could look forward to the sort of benefits enjoyed by his predecessor, Lucceius Albinus. After Judaea (62–64) Albinus received the pleasant province of Mauretania Caesariensis (northern Algeria and part of Morocco), where he commanded twenty-four auxiliary units. He would die backing the wrong man in the coming civil war (Tacitus, *Hist.* 4.58–59).

Florus' untouchable status has another twist. According to a note in *Antiquities* (20.252), he was a Greek from Clazomenae (near modern Izmir, Turkey). Whereas Felix had been requested by the Judaean high priest (Chapter 4), Florus won his post thanks to his wife Cleopatra's friendship with Poppaea Sabina, Nero's wife from A.D. 62. Nero is alleged to have killed her in a moment of rage, along with the baby she was carrying, but also to have mourned her inconsolably for the rest of his life.[85] Persuading Nero to remove Florus and his wife in the year following Poppaea's death might have been too delicate a proposition for Cestius.

Tacitus considered it one of the "mysteries of *imperium*" – that is, a reality not openly discussed – that imperial freedmen and equestrians had become more important than senators to the running of the empire under emperors such as Nero.[86] Even under Claudius, when the people of Bithynia-Pontus accused their procurator and senatorial legate alike of extortion, the emperor's freedmen-advisors secured the condemnation of the senator alone. The procurator's term was extended. On the advice of Claudius' freedman Narcissus, he even managed to win the insignia of a consul.[87] It was perhaps an inevitable function of Rome's ever more explicit monarchy that emperors would increasingly bypass senators, who were likely to resent the monarch and might have the means to foment dissent, and lean ever more heavily on freedmen and equestrians.

Nero's revenue drive, at any rate, fell mainly to such men. The case of Hispania Tarraconensis, where the old ex-consul S. Sulpicius Galba was legate,

---

[84] Compare the relative independence of action shown by Cestius' predecessors Quintilius Varus, L. Vitellius (with respect to Antipas and the Parthians), P. Petronius (undermining Caligula to maintain local relations), C. Cassius Longinus, Ummidius Quadratus, and even Cestius himself in deciding how to proceed with the southern affairs.

[85] See Tacitus, *Ann.* 16.6; Suetonius, *Nero* 35.3; Cassius Dio 62.27.4. For a compelling assessment of Nero's responses to her death, see Champlin 2003: 104–107.

[86] At *Hist.* 1.4 Tacitus uses the phrase in the singular: One secret of *imperium* was that an emperor could be created outside Rome by military power. The much-cited plural (*arcana imperii*) comes from *Ann.* 2.36. For interpretation see Syme, e.g., 1995: 303.

[87] The fates of these provincial officials, noted by Syme 1995, are described in Dio 60.33.6 (procurator) and Tacitus, *Ann.* 12.21–22 (procurator and proconsul).

provides a suggestive parallel to Syria.[88] Plutarch writes that "when that man's [Nero's] abominable procurators were savagely and cruelly harrying the provinces," Galba "had no way to help them, but he made it clear that he felt their pain and shared in their distress and grievance at wrongdoing" (*Galb.* 4.1). This was reportedly of some comfort to the provincials, "who were being condemned and sold into slavery." Even if not from simple compassion, Galba might have felt affronted that a man of negligible social rank was interfering in his province. Suetonius claims that the distinguished senator nevertheless adopted a safe posture of "sloth and sluggishness" (*Galb.* 9). He did not want to seem vigorous and effective – and attract Nero's attention.[89]

Likewise in Syria, although the procurator sent to Judaea was not merely a revenue agent but had governing (praesidial) duties, Cestius could not remove Nero's freedman in spite of the man's low rank – even though the legate's predecessors had sent such men packing. Like Galba, Cestius preferred not to challenge the emperor's man. He no doubt hoped to maintain quiet in his province with as little display as possible.

Conspiracies

In tandem with the economic crisis, political life was entering a dangerous new phase. When his colleague Burrus died in A.D. 62, Seneca – feeling vulnerable to accusations from Nero's younger friends – decided it was time to fade from public life. When Nero refused his resignation, he began to feign illness as a tactic for staying out of sight (*Ann.* 14.56.3). Burrus, who had been sole Praetorian Prefect, was replaced by a more traditional pair, Faenius Rufus and Ofonius Tigellinus. Ancient writers portray Tigellinus as Nero's diabolical counselor and make his appointment the beginning of rapid decline. Under his influence Nero began hearing accusations from informers (*delatores*) concerning treasonous talk, a precedent from earlier emperors that he had avoided at first. Convicted senators were expelled or executed. A convicted man's estates fell to the imperial fund, and an attractive reward accompanied successful prosecutions. An informer could make a killing, literally, from just one success. Two men received 5 million

---

[88] Coincidentally, when Josephus describes Cestius reluctantly turning to action (Κεστίῳ δὲ οὐκέτι ἠρεμεῖν ἐδόκει, *War* 2.499), his language parallels Suetonius' description of Galba (*in desidiam segnitiamque conversus est*; *Galb.* 9.1).

[89] Passivity may have been a deliberate strategy to avoid danger, after Galba had confided his support to the local leaders (much as Agrippa seems to have made it clear that he felt for his people's humiliation, even while trying to calm the waters and dissuade them from angry response). But passivity too might be interpreted by Nero's agents as opposition. I am indebted here to Vervaet (2002: 173–74), who credits private correspondence with A. Giovannini, for drawing attention to Galba's situation. Neither deals with Cestius or Judaea under Florus.

sesterces each when they prosecuted the free-thinking and philosophical Thrasea Paetus in the spring of 66 (Tacitus, *Ann.* 16.33.2).

It was not so much Nero against *the Senate*, then, as it was Nero against senators who could be successfully accused by their colleagues.[90] In slight defence of the *delatores* (informers), not being an informer brought the constant worry of showing up on someone else's target list. Many senators found it prudent to "do unto others" pre-emptively. In any case, Tigellinus' appointment plainly began a series of high-profile executions and assassinations, including those of bluebloods in exile.[91] Formerly trusted freedmen were also executed. In 62 Nero did away with his long-suffering bride Octavia, after exiling her twice. This freed him to marry Poppaea, who was widely suspected of being behind Octavia's end (*Ann.* 14.60–66).

The time of Cestius' and Florus' appointments (A.D. 63/64), then, was one of great fear and uncertainty in elite Rome. Tacitus claims that Nero's actions instilled fear in the upper classes and that they in turn supported intrigues against the emperor, who was still only 25 after nine years in power (*Ann.* 14.65). In 65 the senator C. Calpurnius Piso – wealthy, handsome, a powerful orator of distinguished ancestry – attracted a constituency of disaffected senators, equestrians, legionary tribunes, and centurions (*Ann.* 14.65). They plotted a coup, but Nero's discovery of it brought their deaths and many others, including those of the poet Lucan and his uncle Seneca. The city was filled with funerals (*Ann.* 15.71).[92] Then Nero killed his pregnant wife Poppaea.

Tacitus continues the list of victims through early 66 (*Ann.* 16.18), until Nero tried "to extirpate virtue itself" by bringing trumped-up charges against the senators Thrasea Paetus and Barea Soranus. Nero tried to bury their executions in the hoopla surrounding Tiridates' visit that spring (*Ann.* 16.23.2). Then in August 66 another conspiracy failed. This was apparently led by Corbulo's son-in-law, Annius Vinicianus, who had accompanied Tiridates to Italy. An effort to ambush Nero at Beneventum faltered, and Annius and his group met their doom. The attempt occurred as Nero was leaving Italy for his tour of Greece from August 66 to December 67.[93] Vespasian was among Nero's companions on the tour, and it was from Corinth that he was dispatched in early 67 to Judaea (Chapter 6). The Greek

---

[90] Tacitus (*Hist.* 4.40–44) portrays a kind of truth-and-reconciliation investigation in the Senate in A.D. 70, with Domitian present for the Flavians against senatorial informers under the preceding regimes. For detailed analysis see Rutledge 2001.

[91] E.g., Faustus Cornelius Sulla, husband of Claudius' daughter, and Rubellius Plautus (*Ann.* 14.57–59); Rudich 1993: 66–70.

[92] Tacitus describes the conspiracy in some detail (*Ann.* 15.48–74).

[93] See Bradley 1978: 71; Vervaet 2003. Tacitus claims that Nero had planned to visit Greece and the eastern Mediterranean in 64, but called it off (*Ann.* 15.36–37.)

tour would have lasted even longer than it did, had a freedman not arrived in late 67 to warn Nero of the dangers brewing in Rome.

During his Greek tour Nero did not forget about politics. He was by no means the only autocrat who feared conspiracy,[94] but in the mid-60s he seems to have suffered from a particularly severe strain of imperial anxiety. In the latter half of 66, right around the time of Cestius's expedition to Judaea, he began recalling powerful senatorial legates from their provinces. In spite of Corbulo's extraordinary service, or because of it, even he was summoned to Corinth to end his life. The same fate awaited the distinguished legates of Upper and Lower Germany, the Scribonius brothers (Dio 63.17.2–3). We do not know much about them, but Dio credits them with wealth, illustrious ancestry, and excellence. They may have been in their provinces for the same lengthy stretch (from ca. 60) as Galba in Spain.[95] Other senators accused them of complicity in the Beneventum conspiracy (Tacitus, *Hist.* 4.41). Nero asked them to visit and then played such unsettling mind games that they took their own lives.

That Galba in Spain did not receive the same treatment was perhaps only because, as Suetonius claims, he intercepted secret orders (*mandata*) authorizing Nero's procurators to assassinate him (*Galb.* 9.2). It has been suggested that Galba made his bid for empire not from unusual ambition, but simply from a fear of not acting[96] – the same motive that Tacitus attributed to Vespasian's bid for power (Tacitus, *Hist.* 2.76).

We would not know about the conspiracy against Galba if Suetonius had not written his imperial biography. Cestius never benefitted from such treatment, but we are entitled to suspect that he had similar worries. Perhaps attempts were made on his life. He was in much the same position as the others, brought out of retirement by Nero after Agrippina's removal (A.D. 59) to govern one of the most prestigious provinces. Cestius had every reason to be cautious about embarking on any kind of noticeable venture. He must have been as concerned as Galba about Nero's procurator in his province, who could turn informant in a moment. The details are lost to us, but these political realities must have factored into Cestius' calculations.

---

[94] One of Marc Antony's generals stopped pursuing the Parthians after successive victories, so as not to vex his boss (Plutarch, *Ant.* 34), and Gaius Sosius worried about how to win Antony's favour while avoiding his jealousy (Dio 49.23.2). Although Tacitus' father-in-law Agricola had much success in Britain, Dio (Epitome) relates that "Agricola for the rest of his life lived not only in disgrace but in actual need, because the deeds he had accomplished were too great for a mere general. Finally, he was murdered by Domitian for no other reason than this ... " (66.20.3).

[95] See Rudich 1993: 199–200 for possibilities. Eck (1985: 27, 125–28) weighs the arguments for a possible entry into office in 59/60, although evidence is clear only from 63.

[96] Rudich 1993: 223.

Cestius and his group?

Cestius was old. Apparently he had been a member of the Senate since A.D. 21, making his name under Tiberius in criminal accusations against high-ranking Romans (Tacitus, *Ann.* 3.36; 6.7.2).[97] He seems to have been elected praetor in 32. In 35 Tiberius honoured him with the consulship, alongside the eminent historian M. Servilius Nonianus, possibly at the young age of 38 (*Ann.* 6.31.1).[98] By A.D. 42 Cestius was in his third consulship (as suffect), thanks to Claudius' favour, which would place his second under Gaius Caligula. We know no details of Cestius' military experience, although Pliny mentions an ex-consul named Cestius just before Nero's time who liked to carry small Corinthian figurines "even in battle" (*Nat.* 34.48). Regardless of whether he is our man, Cestius likely had some military experience before his appointment to Syria in 63 (*Ann.* 15.25.3). He was in any case a man of impressive political standing and survival skills: consul under three quite different emperors and now holding a prestigious legateship under a fourth.

How old was he? To have met the qualifying age of 25 for the quaestorship in A.D. 21, Cestius must have been born not later than 4/3 B.C. Assuming that latest possible birthdate, he must have been 69 or 70 when he led the expedition to Judaea. That would put him in the same age bracket as the preceding Syrian legates, Ummidius Durmius Quadratus and Corbulo. Quadratus died in Syria after long service at age 71 or 72.[99] Cestius was also close to the age of Galba, who died at 70 (Chapter 1). Galba was reportedly plagued by weakness and infirmity such as arthritis.[100] Cestius was not likely to have been faring much better. When we think of this, his activities on horseback for weeks at a time and his escape from Beit-Horon seem quite impressive.

---

[97] See *PIR*[1] 571–572; *PIR*[2] 690–691). Although *PIR* attributes this account to Cestius' father, the arithmetic relating their two consulships (in 35 and 42, respectively) would be very difficult in that case. An inscription discovered after *PIR*'s completion indicates that the Cestius Gallus who was consul in 42 with C. Caecina Largus was then in his third consulship (*AE* 1982.199; Rutledge 2001: 213–14), strongly suggesting that he, legate of Syria from 63, was consul in 35. Several coins place Cestius in Antioch in A.D. 65/66 and 66/67; Mionnet 1806–1837; 5.169 nos. 189–90.

[98] Cestius' consulship of 35 is incidentally attested on an inscription concerning a charioteer, *CIL* 6.33950; cf. *AE* 1978.124; *IGRR* 1.495. On qualifying ages and senatorial career paths, see Talbert 1984: 16–23. Augustus had made it possible to become praetor at 29/30 rather than the 39/40 standard in the Republic. But praetors could not usually move to the consulship after the formal requirement of two further years (hence 32 rather than the Republican 42) unless they came from a patrician stock. Others were expected to serve in posts reserved for ex-praetors (e.g., legionary or provincial legate), with a two-year buffer between each. So the *effective* age of a consul remained close to the Republican norm of 42, at least one's late 30s. Cestius' holding his first at 38 suggests imperial favour.

[99] Having been quaestor in A.D. 14, he must have been born by 11 B.C. Cf. Syme 1981: 132.

[100] Tacitus, *Hist.* 1.6 ("weak and old"); Suetonius, *Galb.* 22–23 (gout, arthritis, age-related deformity); Plutarch, *Galb.* 16.4 ("old and feeble").

Cestius may have been part of the circle that promoted Vespasian. We saw in Chapter 1 that Vespasian (b. A.D. 9) flourished under Claudius and burnished that emperor's damaged legacy. Vespasian entered public life under Tiberius, as part of the coterie anchored by Claudius' mother Antonia (Chapter 3).[101] Antonia also favoured the Herodian family, especially Agrippa I. She took Alexander the Alabarch – brother of Philo and father of Tiberius Julius Alexander – as her personal financial manager.[102] Her clique of Roman and oriental elites would continue to be supported by Claudius at least until his last wife (and niece) and Nero's mother, Agrippina, came to hold sway in the court (until A.D. 49).[103] After Nero had Agrippina killed in 59, it may have been natural for him to return to those older men from his adoptive father's circle whom his mother had sidelined. Nevertheless, his terrible relations with the Senate could not have put them at ease.

Vespasian was a relatively young member of the circle, a decade junior to the others, but they all would have known each other. The older members reached great heights already in Tiberius' final years, once the toxic Praetorian Prefect L. Aelius Sejanus' terror was past (d. 31). Antonia, who had helped to expose Sejanus's conspiracy to her brother-in-law Tiberius, remained ascendant until Gaius' accession in 37.[104] She then committed suicide in exasperation, but received great posthumous honour from her son Claudius when he came to power. We have seen that Galba (b. December 23, 3 B.C.),[105] consul immediately after Sejanus (in 33), facilitated Claudius' rise to power, as did the Judaean Agrippa I in very concrete ways (January 41). Galba accompanied Claudius to Britain in 43, where Vespasian was also making his name, before receiving the proconsulship of Africa, which Vespasian would soon hold under Nero.[106] Claudius rewarded Galba with triumphal ornaments and three priesthoods (Suetonius, *Galb.* 8.1).

Corbulo was of the same vintage as Galba (b. 4 B.C.–A.D. 1). After holding the suffect consulship under Gaius (A.D. 39) – the emperor was married to his stepsister – he advanced under Claudius to the legateship of Lower Germany and proconsulship of Asia.[107] Young Domitian would marry Corbulo's

---

[101] Nicols 1978; Jones 1992: 3–12; Levick 1999: 10–22, 28–29; Vervaet 2003: 459 n. 115.

[102] Jones 1992: 3–12. Cf. Josephus, *Ant.* 18.143–46, 156–67 (Antonia and Alexander both fund Agrippa I in his poverty, she out of friendship with his late mother), 183–86 (Antonia tries to help the imprisoned Agrippa); 19.276 (Claudius frees Alexander, whom Gaius had imprisoned, in recognition of his status with Antonia).

[103] Jones 1992: 8–12. Agrippina was displeased with many of this group because they had opposed Claudius' marriage to her, his niece.

[104] Josephus, *Ant.* 18.181–82. Tacitus' account of the fall of Sejanus is missing from the end of *Annals* 5. Suetonius (*Tib.* 55, 65) portrays a thoroughly disgusting Tiberius, using Sejanus rather than being used by him. Dio 65/66.14 describes Caenis (Vespasian's lover) writing and erasing a letter from Antonia to Tiberius about Sejanus.

[105] Suetonius, *Galb.* 4.1.   [106] Plutarch, *Galb.* 3; Suetonius, *Galb.* 7; Tacitus, *Hist.* 1.49.

[107] Syme 1970b: 29–30, 38–39.

youngest daughter in 71, perhaps inadvertently assisting with his posthumous rehabilitation under the Flavians.[108]

Cestius (b. 4/3 B.C.), a contemporary of Galba and Corbulo, seems therefore to have belonged to the same circle. He held the ordinary consulship two years after Galba and had the honour of completing Claudius' consulship in 42 as the invasion of Britain was being planned.[109] Cestius, Galba, Corbulo, and Vespasian must have known each other fairly well.

This does not mean that all members of the circle, much less their children, got along. One important figure of the same time, who held the ordinary consulship between Galba and Cestius (in 34), was L. Vitellius: the legate in Syria (A.D. 35–39) who was so solicitous of Jerusalem and who dismissed Pilate (Chapter 4; *Ann.* 6.28.1). His press was poor, though perhaps from envy: He was remembered as a shameless flatterer of Gaius and then Claudius. The latter connection paid off when Claudius made him a virtual partner in power, giving him the ordinary consulship twice (43, 47) as well as the revived office of Censor, and leaving him to govern while the emperor was briefly in Britain (Suetonius, *Vit.* 2.4–5). Josephus quotes a letter from Claudius mentioning his fondness for Vitellius (*Ant.* 20.12). Still, Vitellius was accused of treason in A.D. 51 and felled by a stroke in his mid-fifties.[110] His son Aulus Vitellius (b. A.D. 12 or 15, *cos.* 48), Vespasian's hated predecessor, was vilified as Nero's man[111] and an undisciplined glutton lacking character.[112]

The connections between such powerful Romans and the native eastern elites are illustrated by the career of Tiberius Julius Alexander. He was one or two years younger than Vespasian, and his family had been integral to Antonia's group. After serving as Corbulo's war manager (*minister bello*; Tacitus, *Ann.* 15.28) in 63, he became Prefect of Egypt from mid-66. At Nero's death in 68 he was quick to lead his province in declaring allegiance to Galba, "whose light has shone upon us for the salvation of the entire human race."[113] But a year later, with Galba dead and Vitellius in power, he boldly administered the first oath of loyalty to the usurper Vespasian.[114]

When Vespasian had to put his Judaean campaign on hold following Nero's death, he sent Titus to pay his respects to Galba and receive new instructions from his old friend (*War* 4.498–99; cf. Tacitus, *Hist.* 1.10; 2.1–4). Titus'

---

[108] Suetonius, *Dom.* 1.3.   [109] Gallivan 1978: 407–8, 411–12.
[110] Tacitus, *Ann.* 12.42.3; Suetonius, *Vit.* 3.1.   [111] Rudich 1993: 225.
[112] Suetonius, *Vit.* 26; Tacitus, *Ann.* 12.4.
[113] From an edict of July 6, 68 (*OGIS* 2.669; translation in Levick 2000: 188), preamble.
[114] Josephus, *War* 4.616 (supports Vespasian); 5.45–46 (leader of Titus' forces, τῶν στρατευμάτων ἄρχων). Alexander's act had an enormous impact: Vespasian would date his rise to imperial power from July 1, A.D. 69, even though Vitellius was not removed until late December of that year, and he would not arrive in Rome until October of 70 (Suetonius, *Vesp.* 6.3).

decision to abort his trip when he heard of Galba's murder (January 69) seems to confirm the close connection. Titus' companion, Agrippa II, carried on regardless to greet the new emperor Otho, because the allied king had to serve whoever was in power. But Vespasian's relations with Otho, who was indirectly responsible for Galba's death, and with Vitellius were not at all the same (Tacitus, *Hist.* 2.1). Tellingly, the first reported action the Flavians would take in the Senate would be to restore Galba's imperial honours (Tacitus, *Hist.* 4.40.1).[115]

Corbulo's group would offer Vespasian vital support against Vitellius.[116] So would the former supporters of Galba in Pannonia and Moesia, from which Corbulo had taken two of his finest legions (*V* and *XV*). They in turn became the backbone of Vespasian's army, with Syria's Tenth, another favourite of Corbulo's. Hard-charging Antonius Primus, the legionary legate who became indispensable to Vespasian's success, had earlier been appointed by Galba (Tacitus, *Hist.* 2.86).

Although we cannot recover a fine-grained sense of these relationships, surviving indications suggest strong loyalties among the men who had come to prominence under Tiberius around Antonia Minor, had prospered together under Claudius before Agrippina and Nero, and had enjoyed close connections with eastern and especially Judaean elite families.

Although we know little about Cestius' own life, then, circumstantial evidence seems to place him in the Galba-Corbulo-Vespasian orbit. They all obliged young Nero when he appointed them to high-level service (how could they refuse?), but they remained vulnerable to senatorial informers and to freedmen and procurators of Nero such as Gessius Florus. In this context it is easy to understand the elderly Cestius' extreme caution at such a precarious time in relations between Nero and the senatorial class. He was in a difficult spot.

The sequel

According to Josephus, the "blunder of Cestius" was fateful for Jerusalem (*Life* 23–24). As the clamour for self-help was gaining momentum among Judaeans, this capable, well-disposed, and well-informed legate offered the best hope for an exit strategy. The more that Florus' activities inflamed tensions and Nero remained indifferent, the more Cestius appeared as the only one capable of stopping both procurator and Judaean vigilantes. In light of what that came

---

[115] Suetonius gives a different impression, claiming that the Senate voted a statue for Galba on the spot where he was slain in the forum. Vespasian vetoed it, "believing that assassins had been sent against him from Hispania to Judaea" (*Galb.* 23). It is possible that both claims are correct: the Flavians honoured Galba in principle, although Vespasian held back in this case out of pique. It is possible that this gossipy morsel from Suetonius is mistaken.

[116] Vervaet 2003.

later, the Judaeans' exclusion of Agrippa and then Cestius from Jerusalem was indeed fateful. But Cestius knew nothing of that at the time. He left Jerusalem in October 66 planning to return in force.

Cestius was still legate as Josephus began preparing Galilee's defences for inevitable punishment after the auxiliary massacre and legionary ambush (*Life* 373–74, 394–97). Josephus must therefore have assumed that he would be facing an army led by Cestius. The Sepphorites asked the legate to recognize their peaceful disposition by protecting their city from militant Galileans and Josephus, and Cestius obligingly sent a legionary garrison. He also assured them that he would soon return in person (*Life* 373, 394). Evidently, he was planning a campaign for the spring of 67. If so, he must have been in communication with Nero, from whom he may have requested the use of Corbulo's legions *V* and *XV* so as not to compromise Syria's frontier. He could reasonably hope that a decisive move in force against Judaea's militants would redeem his reputation. This time he would be prepared to do whatever was necessary, including a siege of Jerusalem. Still he could hope to finish the job by mid-67, given the still strong indications of popular support – and the absence of figures such as Simon bar Giora or John of Gischala from the later scene.

Nero decided, however, that the 70-year-old was not up to the task. He sent his companion in Greece, Vespasian, who had several advantages: he was a dozen years younger and had extensive command experience. But he was far less of a status threat and was accustomed to yielding his glory to others.[117]

If Cestius did request Nero's approval of a spring campaign, we must wonder whether he finally found the courage also to ask for Florus' removal. Josephus remarks that when leading Jerusalemites fled their city after Beit-Horon, realizing that it was becoming dangerous, some went to Cestius in Antioch in the company of Agrippa's cavalry-prefect Philip (*War* 2.556). Cestius proposed that they go and see Nero in Greece, instructing them to explain what had happened *and to accuse Florus*. The legate "hoped that Nero's fury against that man [Florus] would attenuate his own risks" (2.558). Josephus' later account in the *Life* gives a confusingly different picture of the episode (407–409), but it is enough to notice Josephus' awareness that Cestius was having difficulties with Nero after Beit-Horon and needed to deflect blame on the procurator.

The next thing we hear in Josephus, however, Nero is indeed blaming Cestius, whom he holds in contempt (*War* 3.1–3). Josephus makes no further mention of Florus, and we do not know how Nero judged *his* success with the revenue collection. According to Tacitus, Nero sent Vespasian to Syria when Cestius died. Tacitus is unsure, though, whether he died because of men's ordinary fate (i.e., natural causes) or through *taedium* – a word that could mean

---

[117] Bradley 1979.

simple weariness or rather "loathsomeness" – to Nero (*Hist.* 5.10). The latter possibility recalls Tacitus' remark about Caesennius Paetus, when Nero returned the Armenian portfolio to Corbulo because "Paetus had inspired disgust (*Paeti piguerat*)." Caesennius was for that reason anxious about returning to Rome, although in the event Nero limited his punishment to hearing some barbed jokes (*Ann.* 15.25).

Events at the end of Cestius' term (and life) were roughly these: the military catastrophe in Judaea (October 66), winter preparations for a new expedition in spring 67, Nero's appointment of Vespasian with a special command for Judaea (winter 67), Cestius' death in post (winter/spring 67), and Mucianus' arrival as Nero's new legate for Syria (summer 67, *War* 4.32). Given Cestius' disgrace and Roman aristocratic tradition, we might conjecture that he took his own life. Tacitus apparently did not know how he died, however, and if Josephus knew he did not say. We do not know either.

On the Roman side, at any rate, Cestius' humiliation set in motion a series of events.[118] Nero had to exact revenge, to restore Rome's honour and deterrent (= power; Chapter 3) and to re-establish a ruling consensus with local elites in the region.[119] As legate Cestius could attempt a diplomatic-military solution to inter-ethnic problems he understood, but after Beit-Horon any solution had to include visible punishment.

On the Judaean side, the consequences of the successful ambush were different for various groups. Many of those who were alarmed at what was sure to come fled the city – as people swim away from a sinking ship, in Josephus' derisive image (*War* 2.556). Statesmen like himself, however, were committed to seeing the troubles through no matter what the dangers or who was to blame (Chapter 2). Otherwise, even those who were skeptical about the resort to armed self-help were caught up in the exuberance, or pretended to be, so as not to seem traitors (2.562). We know in our world that people who feel oppressed can celebrate when a great power suffers defeat, even if they have no burning desire to fight them. Then too the mood was euphoric (*War* 3.9): "After the thrashing of Cestius, carried away by their unexpected success the Judaeans were unable to control the rush. As if set on fire by fortune, they carried the war yet further afield." A disastrous attempt on Ascalon would quickly drive home their limitations, however, and the folly of fighting on disadvantageous terms (3.9–28).

A modern historian's description of Boudica's forces seems apposite here:[120]

---

[118] Goodman (2007: 13–16, 425) persuasively makes this the watershed in Rome's dealings with Judaea.

[119] On values see Mattern 1999: 162–210; on restoring honour, Lendon 1997; on consensus, Ando 2000: 73–130.

[120] Webster's 1985: 93.

> The elation of the victorious Britons at their astounding success created a sense of wild euphoria, which for the moment obliterated any appreciation of the immediate realities and the need for rapid action to forestall or anticipate Roman reaction.

Being "carried away by fortune" was, all ancient readers knew, to give fortune hostages.[121]

The other important consequence of Beit-Horon involved Judaea's neighbours. When the residents of Damascus heard of Cestius' defeat, they reportedly lashed out at their Judaean minority, massacring an alleged 10,500. Other *poleis* with Judaean minorities likewise felt that they could settle scores with impunity. The citizens of Antioch turned violently against their Judaean minority, supposedly at the instigation of an opportunistic Judaean who denounced his own people.[122]

SYNTHESIS AND CONCLUSION: DID CESTIUS MANUFACTURE ENEMIES OF ROME?

We return, finally, to the questions posed at the beginning of this chapter. Although we know little about Cestius, we have seen enough to make the common statements about him implausible. His relentless involvement with Jerusalem and regional affairs, his personal energy in visiting Jerusalem in his old age, and his ongoing consultation with both Herodian royals and the city's priestly elite make it unlikely that he ever imagined Jerusalem or Judaeans to be in revolt against him or Rome. Certainly he seems not have known about a province of Judaea or an independent rebel state. Nor could he have intended his reluctant expedition in the early autumn of 66 to culminate in an assault on Jerusalem. His withdrawal, when he was shocked to find the gates closed against him, was his only rational move. Cestius was one of a few megastars in Rome's firmament. He must have had at least the average intelligence, experience, and political skills of ex-consuls entrusted with the province of Syria.

But he had to balance at least six concerns that might have given anyone insomnia: a mercurial young emperor at lethal odds with Cestius' peer group, the Parthian frontier, the great Corbulo to his north, serious regional antagonisms in the south, Nero's untouchable and yet supremely troublesome agent Florus, and the rapid developments in Jerusalem and Caesarea. I propose the following summary reconstruction.

---

[121] E.g., Polybius, *Hist.* 1.35.1–2; 2.4.3; 16.28.1; 36.13; 38.20–21; cf. Shorey 1921.

[122] *War* 7.46–53. At 7.52 Josephus remarks that the renegade Judaean "received soldiers from the Roman governor/commander." Cf. Philo on the attempt of prominent Alexandrians to exploit and enhance the antipathy of Gaius and the Flaccus toward the Judaeans as a cover for their own animosity (*Flacc.* 21–29).

On dispatch to their provinces, legates brought instructions (*mandata*) from the emperor, which they followed up with correspondence.[123] Cestius arrived in Syria with some sort of general guide from Nero, then corresponded with him occasionally, likely discussing the inter-ethnic unrest in the south.[124] Cestius brought up the importance of maintaining good relations with Jerusalem, but Nero dismissed his concerns about the Judaeans' importance (just as Gaius had needed persuading of this by Agrippa I).[125] This disdain may have been related to Nero's philhellenism, which perhaps predisposed him to favour the ancient *poleis* that had been under Jerusalem's dominance for so long. However that may be, Nero's contempt inspired Cestius to ask Jerusalem's chief priests for hard statistics. At the next Passover (65 or 66?) they produced what they called a conservative estimate of 2.7 million Judaeans coming in for Passover – an impossibly large number, supposedly extrapolated from the number of sacrificial victims (*War* 6.422–27). The priests may have given Cestius such a huge figure because it was also in their interest to convince Nero of Judaea's importance.[126]

Alongside his correspondence with the legate, however, Nero was influenced at least as much by the obsequious reports of his equestrian agents Albinus and Florus. These reports encouraged his disdain for Judaea with its non-Hellenic culture, long primacy over the *poleis*, and massive temple wealth, uniquely gathered from around the empire.

Cestius' most basic task was that of every governor: to cultivate harmonious relations with his *polis* elites, so that Rome's investment could flourish with minimal disturbance.[127] Jerusalem, which had for two centuries been more important than the other *poleis* of southern Syria and had a famously distinctive culture, merited his particular attention. Like his predecessors he understood the region's past, the grievances of non-Judaeans, and the hazards for Judaea that inevitably came with administration from Caesarea. So he monitored that situation closely, visiting Jerusalem when possible and otherwise relying on continuing dialogue with the city's priestly elite and royal family.

Florus' increasingly brutal revenue collection, on Nero's direct orders, was pushing the region into turmoil. Some Judaeans were understandably opting

---

[123] Millar 1966: 157–58; cf. Potter 1996.

[124] Compare Pliny's extensive correspondence with Trajan on matters great and small, also that of a predecessor in Syria, P. Petronius, with the emperor Gaius over the statue(s) he had been instructed to install in Jerusalem's temple and the resulting unrest (Philo, *Legat.* 207, 248, 254–60, 333–34; Josephus, *War* 2.202–3).

[125] Philo, *Legat.* 281–84.

[126] Nero's rejection of the appeal to make Caesarea Judaean, for example, might have reflected his disbelief in their importance.

[127] On the governor's responsibility to work closely with *polis* elites see Stevenson 1949: 34–35; Lintott 1993: 54–69; Swain 1996: 227–29; Lendon 1997: 194–236; Burton 2002; Meyer-Zwiffelhoffer 2002; Harland 2006; Revell 2009: 40–79; on the ruling consensus, Ando 2000: 73–276.

to protect themselves and even to retaliate as a deterrent, if they could not trust the procurator, legate, royal family, or emperor to provide security. Having been brokers of Rome's *imperium* for so long, they were now extremely vulnerable in the face of a hostile procurator commanding a vicious military. Florus was confident in his mission and expected some resistance, which he could quash with impunity. He also realized that Judaeans could not oppose him without seeming to oppose *Rome* – the very charge he was quick to raise with Cestius. Florus' own incentives lay in doing what Nero instructed. For this purpose, the region's resentment of Jerusalem was ripe for exploitation.

All of this Cestius must have understood. That the emergence of vigilante groups would be almost entirely on the Judaean side was particularly tragic. The Judaeans' enemies did not need to resort to force because the auxiliary was with them.

Because he did not believe Judaea to be in revolt, Cestius was loath to contemplate military action. Even when the royal pair reported their expulsion from the city, this meant only that the populace had lost patience with Florus and with Agrippa for preventing their embassy to Nero to plead their case and loyalty. In other words, all the familiar channels of redress were blocked. So the people of Jerusalem were increasingly tolerant of armed factions. At least they were standing up to the auxiliary and other Samarians, trying to protect the citizens in the immediate term while they awaited a more durable solution.

Jerusalem's elite felt the brunt of Florus' assaults, being the wealthiest with the most to lose, and so fully shared this outrage. Many or most of them also realized that taking up arms was a *cul-de-sac*. They pleaded with the king for urgent help. Agrippa and Berenice immediately visited Cestius in Beirut, and together they decided that forceful intervention was required to disarm the vigilante factions before they caused irreparable damage.

Their initial plan had two phases. First, Agrippa would send four cavalry squadrons immediately. Their mission was not to fight *against Jerusalem or its population* but to reach the city quickly, disarm the militants, reassure the population while confiscating all weapons, and stabilize the situation *until Cestius and Agrippa could arrive*. In the meantime, second, Cestius would put together a large force of legionaries, cavalry, and allied specialists to accompany the two men southward – also as soon as possible but after necessary preparation. This force would be redundant many times over, the largest that Cestius could assemble without compromising Syria's frontier. Once it reached Ptolemais and the south, its cavalry would deploy across the plains, showing Rome's colours and restoring calm everywhere, and leaving garrisons where needed. Cestius would deal with whatever problems he found along the way. But in the main Judaean centres of Sepphoris and Jerusalem he expected a very warm welcome from the *polis* leaders. The Judaean capital would be his final stop. There he would execute all the troublemakers identified by the leaders, consolidate relations with the aristocrats, and ensure that Agrippa and Berenice were peacefully reinstated.

The one thing Cestius could not do on his own authority was remove Florus. His best hope was to work around that problem: to isolate him as far as possible, hope for his quick replacement, and deal directly with the local population.

A short while after the expedition had left Antioch, however, the situation became immeasurably darker. Cestius received word that self-armed Judaeans had gone as far as to murder Jerusalem's auxiliary garrison and that the Caesarean situation had exploded in a massacre of the Judaean minority there. A week or two later as he neared Ptolemais, reports began to come in that Judaeans were launching reprisal attacks for Caesarea across the whole region south of Lebanon and over the Jordan. These and the affected *poleis*' reactions against their Judaean minorities were setting the region ablaze.

Cestius' original plan now required adjustment. (a) He would have to punish more Judaeans visibly and harshly, for several reasons: to show the Judaeans that Rome demanded a monopoly of force and rejected vigilantism, to dissuade other *poleis* and *ethnē* from further actions in retaliation, by showing them that Rome was handling it, and in general to restore Rome's honour and deterrent – especially with fitting retribution for the attacks on its auxiliary (no matter what the justification). An additional motive may have been to blood his soldiers, so to speak. There could be no real contest in a confrontation between legionaries and desperate local fighters. But it would be good training for his army to hunt down and if necessary kill such militants. (b) Second, because the militants were not a uniformed army with fixed bases, Cestius needed ways to draw out and make an example of all those who were willing to take up arms. (c) Third, none of this took away from Cestius' primary and ultimate need: to secure his working relationship with the *poleis* of his province, including Jerusalem and Sepphoris as well as Caesarea, Sebaste, Scythopolis, and all the other centres. He had to try to calm the seething hatred of neighbours and *polis* minorities as a basic condition of governance.

Task (a) may explain Cestius' willingness to let his soldiers loose on Judaean life and property as soon as they came within striking distance of western Galilee, across from Ptolemais. In *War* 3.133, Josephus will later describe Vespasian's brutality toward Galilean Gabara, soon after his arrival in the same area. Gabara is empty of fighting men and has shown no hostility, and Sepphoris has capitulated on behalf of Galilee (Chapter 6). Nevertheless, Vespasian allows his soldiers to kill anyone they find, regardless of age or sex, and to burn the villages. Josephus ascribes this to the soldiers' memory of "the outrage against Cestius" a few months earlier – namely, the ambush that concludes our story. The role of anger and vengeance in soldiers' morale has always been important, not least for recruitment. Commanders try to exploit this energy while channeling it productively for military purposes. Just as

Vespasian directed his legionaries' fury against Gabara, *while sparing the main population centres*, so perhaps Cestius let them torch empty Chabulon, Aphek Turris, and Lydda, *while preserving* Sepphoris, Jerusalem, and the populated towns. The devastation of Joppa and massacre of its population, even if the number 8,400 is inflated, might be explained as this kind of display violence, aimed at restoring Rome's deterrence.

The port of Joppa was a jewel in the Judaeans' crown, their only outlet to the sea, won by the Hasmoneans as we have seen. Cestius' utter destruction of the city, although the residents had caused not a moment's trouble, seems to have been calculated to drain the morale of would-be Judaean resisters, by driving home their hopeless situation. Look at what this commander is willing to do! Herod had once destroyed Joppa as he prepared to take control of Jerusalem, to avoid the prospect of a hostile stronghold at his rear (*War* 1.292). That may have been a factor here, but Josephus gives no hint of hostility from that quarter. The other settlements hit by Cestius, such as Chabulon with its fancy houses, were not destroyed for being hotbeds of militancy. The issue was not who was *guilty*, I would suggest, but rather which Judaean assets could be devastated for maximal impact at minimal risk. Shock and awe.

In these rapid early operations we see the value of Cestius' force configuration. The cavalry sweeps through the Narbatene villages (2.509) and cuts down those who resist them in Galilee (2.512). The rapid advance force to Joppa was likely mounted. In Galilee's broad valleys and the coastal plain, the cavalry enjoyed easy and complete dominance. It seems, again, that this must have been their planned function.

(b) Time was short. With autumn descending as he reached the south, Cestius had to make his brief expedition count. If he had come with gentleness on a listening tour, armed civilians could have lain low until he left. If he wanted to deal effectively with those bold enough to attack an auxiliary garrison, he needed to be provocative, to stir things up and shake out the would-be militants. When his army came slapping the faces of Judaeans, killing innocents and treating them with glaring injustice, he could expect draw out those who were inclined to fight. Leaving their walled cities in arms, they would mark themselves for destruction.

The tactic is familiar in asymmetrical conflicts today.[128] We noted Cestius' recruitment of untrained and expendable fighters from the northern towns, whose only qualification was hatred of Judaeans. Since he reportedly left 2,000

---

[128] Cf. the summary of an intelligence briefing (December 5, 2008) published by *The Guardian* (30 November 2010), www.guardian.co.uk/world/us-embassy-cables-documents/181529 (accessed December 9, 2011): "The international community should put intense pressure on the Taliban in 2009 in order to bring out their more violent and ideologically radical tendencies. This will alienate the population and give us an opportunity to separate the Taliban from the population."

of them to forage unprotected in Galilee after withdrawing his proper army, and they were quickly cut down by Judaeans (before the same number of militants were chased to Asamon and killed), it may be that they were designed as bait. They unwittingly enticed the rebels, by building their confidence and encouraging them to attack.[129] It was the military equivalent of a sting operation.

(c) The major Judaean *poleis*, however, called for a different approach. *Polis* leaders did not have the luxury of nurturing grievances based in emotion, ideology, or pride. We see Cestius' two-sided approach in Galilee. After he burns Chabulon for no apparent reason and ravages the (deserted) villages around Caesarea, he dispatches Caesennius Gallus to Sepphoris where he is warmly welcomed. The other towns follow suit. Cestius was not absolutely persuaded of Sepphoris' peaceful intent, I should note, for *Life* 30–31 mentions that he (or Caesennius) took hostages from there to coastal Dor as a guarantee of good behaviour. He was not naïve, but was making shrewd calculations at every turn. A measure of display violence in the mostly empty villages was, I am suggesting, intended to help him secure Judaean cities *without* bloodshed. Sepphoris' cooperative disposition, confirmed by material remains, would remain throughout the entire coming war.[130] It seems that he expected the same reception in Jerusalem, where, after all, his ties were much stronger.

We come now to a basic problem. If Cestius were confident of his ability to enter Jerusalem and there was little sign of anti-Roman or anti-Cestian sentiment when he began his expedition, where did all the militants come from, who were willing to attack his legionary column on the way in, kill Agrippa's messengers, bar Jerusalem's gates, and eventually ambush and massacre the Roman force? This is not a problem on the usual assumption that Judaea was in full revolt, but it becomes a question worth asking if one is willing to entertain the very different picture I have painted. If Jerusalem had consistently looked to the emperor and legate as protectors against regional enemies, and the populace had warmly received the legate and his tribune as friends, how could so many Judaeans be suddenly willing to take up arms against the legate and his legionaries, who had not been involved in their local disturbances? Does this not prove powerful *anti-Roman* sentiment?

---

[129] Herodotus tells a paradigmatic story in the same vein. The Persian Darius sacrificed a large number of expendable soldiers – "the least effective troops, whose loss will mean little" – to build the Babylonians' confidence and being them out of their walled city (3.154–60). Cf. Tacitus, describing Furius Camillus' use of an inadequate-seeming *Legio III Augusta* to bait African rebels (Tacitus, *Ann.* 2.52.3), and Poppaeus Sabinus' attempt to trap Thracian rebels by similar means (*Ann.* 4.49.1).

[130] *War* 2.511; *Life* 38, 104–11, 124, 232, 346, 373–80, 394 (they request and receive a garrison from Cestius Gallus), 411. On coins of A.D. 68 Sepphoris styles itself "city of peace" and *Neronias* (Meshorer 1982: 2.167–69). E. Meyers (2002) has argued that a deliberately filled-in fort complex from the period likewise reveals the city's peaceful intentions.

The answer may be so obvious that we miss it. Armies are trained to kill people and destroy property. Their task is to dominate populations physically and psychologically, by whatever means are necessary. They must never appear weak or uncertain but must give the impression that they will prevail with unstoppable strength. It is far better for them to err on the side of terror and fear than on the side of mildness. Whenever an army is injected among a foreign civilian population, accordingly, and the soldiers view the population as a potential enemy, whom they will also fear at a personal level, bad things are bound to happen.

When those bad things do happen, whether in controlled violence under orders or through soldiers' more extreme ad hoc violence, the invading force will manufacture enemies. Untold thousands of people in Afghanistan and Iraq who never had reason to hate the United States or Americans have been radicalized, as anyone can see in many documentaries and interviews, because of the presence of U.S. forces in their neighbourhoods. Not only the authorized home invasions, night raids, violent arrests, and incarceration without legal protection, but also the inevitable off-books instances of murder, robbery, assault, and rape of non-combatants cause profound hatred and the resolve of young men especially to get revenge (cf. Chapter 7). This is a universal phenomenon.

Cestius' expedition must have created *new* enemies of Rome among the Judaeans. Even according to Josephus' restrained and conventional account, his army destroyed many Judaean towns and villages, killing thousands of innocents of all ages. Judaean responses ran the predictable gamut. Political elites, no matter the outrage they also felt, pleaded for calm and struggled to maintain ties with the imperial power. They saw only a worse fate if they reacted violently and so tried to stifle their rage. But many others, typically younger men who felt both strong and honour-bound to protect or avenge their families and communities, became willing to fight to the death. It did not matter whether they could *win*. Of course they could not. But they had to *fight*, to resist, and to take revenge. This is not surprising, and it is easy to find examples of similar responses today.

The notion that Cestius created enemies of Rome on the spot challenges our comforting assumptions – about who is and is not in some essential way a terrorist, rebel, or guerrilla fighter. We assume that there is a fixed number of such people, that once they are gone that will be the end of them. In studying the first century, similarly, we want to know who *was pro-Roman* or *anti-Roman*, as though this was in their DNA, and whether they subscribed to philosophy number 2 or number 4. But this bent of ours does not map onto life as it is really lived. Like any invading army, Rome's legions were quite capable of creating instant enemies by their controlling presence, violence, and destructiveness. They needed only to kill a family or burn a house.

Before Cestius' expedition the Judaeans' problem had been that Rome's administration was proving incapable of protecting them against local enemies and Nero's equestrian agent. Everyone had assumed, from the legate's visits and ongoing efforts, that he understood – as indeed he likely did. Now, however, he and legions were *here* before them. Marching under offensive standards and banners, which Rome had previously kept out of Judaea (Chapter 3), they were killing and destroying at will. And the Judaean royal family were supporting them! It was outrage in response to Cestius' expedition, I am suggesting, and not some anti-Roman sentiment, that produced the opportunistic attacks of Judaean fighters on his army as it turned inland to enter Judaea, the murder of Agrippa's envoys, the legate's exclusion from Jerusalem, and the fateful ambush at Beit-Horon. Although many Judaeans in high positions could see no good outcome from such violent opposition, this turn to self-help when there seemed no alternative was inevitable.

This approach best explains, it seems to me, the complete surprise that faced Cestius and Agrippa as they ascended into the Judaean hills. Having imagined that they were doing away with many militants and simply intimidating the rest by their force, they had not reckoned on a violent reaction from those they had grievously harmed. They were still counting on the righteousness of their intervention and established relationships with Jerusalem. They were sure that the ruling classes would understand political necessity and the wisdom of cooperation. They did not anticipate the wave of outrage at the army's behaviour along the coast, which would keep Jerusalem's gates shut and force them into retreat. Those who hold a monopoly of professional military might rarely understand why their actions generate hatred among those they so righteously seek to control.

This inquiry has produced no new *knowledge* or facts about Cestius Gallus' fateful military intervention in Judaea. I hope to have illustrated instead the importance of thinking about history as *inquiry*, as the pursuit of defined problems and not as mere deduction or extrapolation from literary accounts. There is no point in trying to be specific about who thought or felt what and when in this case. Obviously we cannot know. I have tried to bring forward, rather, scenarios that would more plausibly explain how a conflict that was fundamentally regional and inter-ethnic, in which Rome's representatives were the trusted protectors of Judaean interests, suddenly generated deep anti-Roman sentiment. Once that emotion had taken hold, even for a brief time, it took on a life of its own. For some segments of the population there could be no turning back. They had gone too far either to surrender or to expect terms. They would have to flee or fight to the death. But Galillee had largely escaped this dilemma.

CHAPTER SIX

NERO'S WAR II: FLAVIANS IN GALILEE

Look, my father came into the region not to exact retribution from you for the Cestius affair, but to bring you to your senses. For you may be sure that if he had come for the removal of this nation, the appropriate thing would have been to race toward your root and immediately sack this city [Jerusalem]. Instead, he kept ravaging Galilee and the surrounding parts, granting you time for a change of heart. But to you, this example of humanity appeared as weakness, and you nourished your audacity on our gentleness.

Josephus' Titus to John and Simon in Jerusalem (*War* 6.338–40)

Josephus' Titus explains why Vespasian did not pursue a strategy we associate with Carl von Clausewitz (1780–1831).[1] The Prussian soldier-spy emphasized the need to concentrate forces on the enemy's "focal point of force and movement" (*Schwerpunkt*).[2] Commanders must resist temptations to divide their forces for small contests, which never decide a war and are hazardous besides: "In a word, the first principle is: *to act with as much concentration as possible*. The second principle is: *to act as swiftly as possible*; therefore to permit no delay or detour without sufficient reason."[3]

---

[1] Clausewitz's eight-volume work *On War* was published by his widow Marie (1832) a few months after his death from cholera at age 51.

[2] "ein Centrum der Kraft und Bewegung" 1883: 556 (Bk. 8, ch. 4). I have used the second German edition (1883), giving book and chapter number rather than page to facilitate tracking across editions. An accessible translation is Jolles 1950. Echevarria 2003 offers a corrective to overly mechanical interpretations of the *Schwerpunkt*.

[3] von Clausewitz 1883: 199, 578 (Bk. 4, ch. 11 and Bk. 8, ch. 9). I follow the translation of Jolles: 208, 609. For modern discussion see von Ghyczy, von Oetinger, and Bassford 2001: 134 with 129; Strachan and Herberg-Rothe 2007.

Josephus has Titus claim that because a concentrated assault on Jerusalem was the only sensible method of national punishment, Vespasian's decision to linger in the north proves that he was motivated by kindness (τὸ φιλάνθρωπον) and gentleness (ἡ πραότης).[4]

It is not necessarily so. Clausewitz had in view states with regular armies.[5] With irregular resistance fighters who were indistinguishable from ordinary folk, the Romans had either to annihilate the population or to drain the morale of potential militants (Chapter 3). Because they chose the latter, their aim became the reestablishment of control and domination at minimal risk. With psychological considerations paramount in both cases, the main difference between Vespasian's campaign and that of Cestius was that Vespasian had the time to be much more deliberate. He had nothing else to do but to suppress whatever revolt had been expressed in the massacre of the auxiliary garrison and the ambush of Cestius.

As we saw in Chapter 3, Liddell Hart proposed that the *indirect approach* was actually the essence of strategy. It kept the enemy off balance and in constant fear while forcing them to disperse their defences. The problem with taking this as an absolute principle (so Luttwak) is that a real-life enemy is neither static nor merely responsive, but will also be calculating, changing shape, and striking in ways that suit them.[6] So there is no single correct strategic concept, and we can debate even campaigns that look brilliant in retrospect.[7] In our war, an immediate attack on Jerusalem, thickly walled and high in the Judaean hills, would have been unnecessarily risky for Vespasian and needlessly raised the prospect of arousing new opposition elsewhere because of the special place of the holy mother-city in the hearts of Judaeans across the empire. Just as Titus' later invitations to surrender (Chapters 3, 7–8) reflect sound tactics more than personal benevolence, Vespasian's cautious entry via a mostly peaceful Galilee made sound strategic sense.

Summarizing military wisdom in the late fourth century, Vegetius wrote (3.9, my emphasis):

> Most important of all, he [the general] should deliberate whether it is expedient for the crisis to be prolonged or fought out more swiftly. For

---

[4] This is not necessarily Flavian propaganda. It is something plausible for Vespasian's son to say.

[5] See Honig 2011, contrasting Ludendorff's later "total war."   [6] Luttwak 2001.

[7] In World War II, commanders famously differed on the merits of overwhelming if predictable concentration (U.S. generals) over indirect incrementalism (British generals plus Roosevelt). The U.S. Chiefs began planning something like the later Normandy landings soon after their entry into the war. But because an invasion could not be ready until at least 1943, mid-term U.S. elections in 1942 and the need for results produced reluctant agreement on Operation Torch (first: Gymnast) via North Africa. For accounts of the debate, which has continued long since, see Ben-Moshe 1992: esp. 121–66, 197–224, 317–33 (critical of the decision taken) and Roberts 2008: e.g., 324 (sympathetic).

sometimes *the enemy hopes that the campaign can be ended quickly*, and if it becomes long-drawn out, is either reduced by hunger, or . . . through doing nothing significant is compelled to leave in despair.[8]

Why did Vespasian remain for a whole fighting season in Galilee? What was he actually doing there? Scholarship has produced two radically different alternatives, one of which has won general allegiance. We have usually followed Josephus in seeing the Galilean campaign as the "first phase of the war." After Cestius Gallus "went to Jerusalem to conquer it and thereby suppress the revolt" but failed, Israel Shatzman proposes, Vespasian took a deliberately harsher approach to the same problem of Judaean revolt:

> Vespasian adopted a different strategy: *a systematic suppression of every area* of the revolt would precede the battle for Jerusalem. His plan was to conquer region after region, to subdue every town and village in each region. The fighting was conducted methodically, carefully, and generally slowly. . . .[9]

This picture has a certain appeal: In retribution for what happened to Cestius, Vespasian wanted to stamp out every ember of rebellion throughout the land first.[10] But this is a hindsight view. Neither side could have known in the spring of 67, even if they had already thought of this as a Judaean-Roman war, that it would culminate with Jerusalem's destruction. Can we be so sure about Vespasian's intentions in and after Galilee? Should his actions there suggest scorched-earth preparation for the Judaean capital and suppression of a nation-wide revolt?

The only alternative I know to the common view is an awkwardly radical one from Richard Laqueur (1920). On the basis of passages in Josephus' *Life* (mid-90s A.D.), which he took to represent compositional strata from a document written in 67, Laqueur argued that there was no real war with Rome in Galilee. Galilee was dense with robbers, although many of these were intensely nationalist (a "national bolshevism"), and *this* banditry problem is what worried the Jerusalem leadership. Josephus was sent not as a war commander, but to deal with Galilee's bandit problem. He went native, however, succumbing to the temptations of power and the influence of his charges as a bandit chief himself. So he soon found himself facing the Flavians, who had likewise come to suppress banditry in Galilee, not to fight a war.[11] They would have left it there if the banditry had not then spread *from Galilee to*

---

[8] Trans. Milner 1996: 84 (my emphasis).   [9] Shatzman 2008: 84, emphasis mine.
[10] Cf. Smallwood 1982: 306–310; Sicker 2001: 152–54. These scholars do not impute an explicit strategy to Vespasian, but they do see the suppression of revolt in Galilee as his first major task.
[11] Laqueur 1920: 247–55, quotations from 253.

Judaea during the following winter, with arch-bandit John of Gischala's move southward (67/68).

Laqueur's hypothesis admirably avoids hindsight bias. His argument suffers fatally, however, from basing many acute observations and probing questions on his implausible reconstruction of compositional layers, over three decades of supposed sediment, in Josephus' *War* and *Life*.[12] Nor does he link all this convincingly with the actual tensions in the south, which we investigated in the previous two chapters. His hypothesis is oddly detached from those events.

Even if we grant that Jerusalem's leaders were preparing for retaliation for the Cestius debacle, however, Josephus' claim in *War* (2.573) that he immediately fortified Galilee's towns because "*he knew* that the Romans would first strike hard into Galilee" is not credible. For one thing it conflicts with the assertion of his Titus, that sound strategy would have targeted Jerusalem first. Cestius had easily pacified Galilee and installed a garrison in Sepphoris, so his anticipated return in the spring might have been expected to focus on the only place where he had faced surprising resistance: Jerusalem. Josephus' claim at *Life* 29, that he and some priestly colleagues in Galilee were instructed to "wait patiently to learn what the Romans would do" makes better sense than *War*'s bravado. *War*'s notion that he fortified the towns of Galilee in a single operation is also at odds with reason and contrary evidence.

What did Romans and Judaeans think they were doing in Galilee in 67? As we reconsider the evidence, we shall find reason to doubt that Vespasian intended a scorched-earth destruction of Galilee or even the systematic subjection of a region in revolt. We need to descend from abstract possibilities to the concrete and constantly changing conditions on the ground. If we are left with imagining motives in this respect, because we lack fine-grained evidence, at least we can channel our imaginings along more plausible lines.

Archaeology in the Galilee and Golan has been impressively productive over the past several decades. This is not the place for a survey,[13] but we can touch on the most important discoveries as part of an orientation. Then we shall examine Josephus' narratives before trying to imagine the events and motives that produced all these survivals.

I. GEOGRAPHICAL-ARCHAEOLOGICAL ORIENTATION

Not least because of its connections with Jesus of Nazareth and later rabbinic Judaism,[14] Galilee has been the scene of extensive archaeological labour. As the digging proceeds, synthetic interpretations of Galilean cultural identity

---

[12] See Mason 2001: xxx–xxxii.   [13] See Aviam and Richardson 2001; Leibner 2009.
[14] For sharp and largely cogent criticism of the use of Galilean archaeology in Jesus research, see Rappaport 2013: 140–62.

continue to appear.[15] Scholars try to interpret the archaeology in connection with both the literary evidence and social-scientific models in ways that are both suggestive and, by their nature, at odds and inconclusive.[16]

Sepphoris, Iotapata, Tiberias, Taricheae, and Gamala are the sites of greatest interest for us. Iotapata and Gamala are particularly valuable because they have not been significantly inhabited since A.D. 67. The latest finds there are usually from our period. With Sepphoris and Tiberias, by contrast, centuries of later habitation make it difficult to isolate clear pre-70 remains. Byzantine churches often reused material from the pre-70 period, but the later structures have often obliterated what came before. Figure 19 provides a view of Lower Galilee.

Sepphoris (Tzippori, Saffuriyeh) was founded at least several centuries before Josephus' time. It naturally commands much of lower Galilee from its location overlooking the main Beit-Netofa Valley to the north. The valley floor sits at 150 m (492 ft) above sea level. At 284 m (932 ft) above sea level, Sepphoris enjoys a fine view without being difficult to access. The rise to the summit is gentle. Within a few years of Pompey's conquest in 63 B.C., Sepphoris was recognized as the Judaeans' capital in the north (Chapter 4), a status it would retain through late antiquity. Excavations by several teams have exposed large areas of an impressive ancient city with broad streets, aqueducts, wealthy residential areas, public buildings, a theatre, spectacular mosaics and frescoes, and much else. Most of this dates from the second to the fifth centuries, alas, and mostly toward the latter half of that period.

The first-century *polis* is estimated to have hosted a population of not more than 12,000 in about 8 ha (20 acres) on the hilltop, before later expansions to the southeast.[17] It had a marketplace, and at the base of the hill the large public building and one of the two aqueducts appear to date from Antipas' time. The excavated theatre, 73 m (240 ft) in diameter, built into the bedrock of the northern slope and seating perhaps 4,500, seems to date from the second or third century, although it likely had a first-century precursor.[18] Although the

---

[15] For summaries of the archaeology, see Aviam and Richardson 2001; Aviam 2004, 2008; and Leibner 2009; for other analyses and syntheses, *inter alios* Freyne 1980, 1988, 2002, 2004; Goodman 1983; Horsley 1995, 1996; Edwards and McCullough 1997; Meyers 1999; Chancey 2002, 2005; Zangenberg, Attridge, and Martin 2007; and especially Jensen 2010.

[16] Sawicki 2000; Reed 2000; Crossan and Reed 2001; Arnal 2001. Moreland 2002 reviews recent scholarship. See Berlin 2002 and 2006 on the disappearance of fancy red-slip dishware, which she explains variously as the result of migration from Jerusalem in the earlier first century B.C., as the expression of anti-Roman sentiment (especially with Antipas as target), and as a move from individual to communal eating. These studies are cautionary: Although they might give the impression that archaeology proved widespread anti-Roman sentiment in Galilee, that explanation does not come from the dishes (cf. Jensen 2010: 237–39).

[17] Reed 2000: 69–77.

[18] Weiss first thought it early first century (1993: 1325–26) but revised his dating to early second century (2008: 2031).

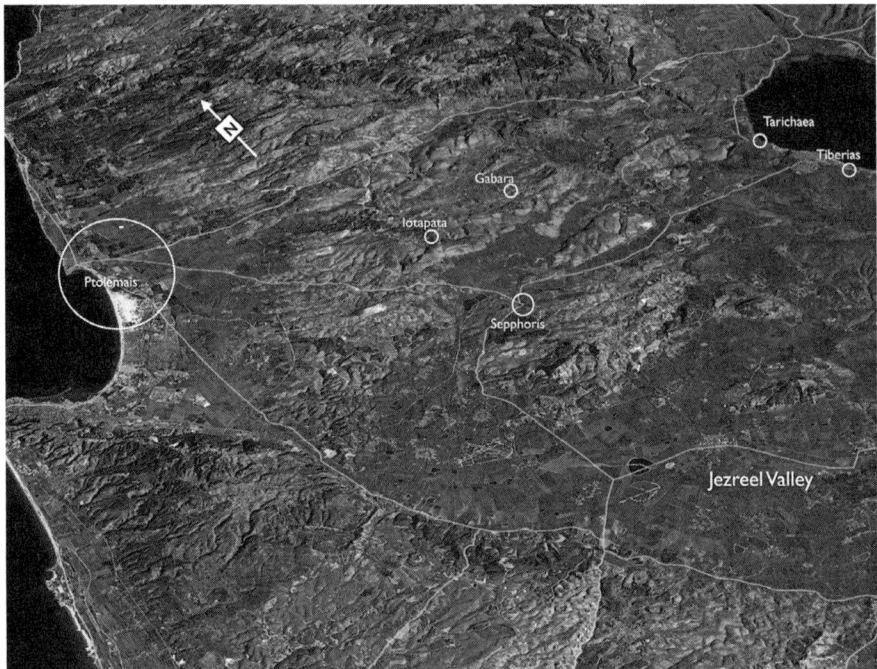

FIGURE 19. Lower Galilee, aerial from the southwest showing topographical features, Roman roads, and key sites in the Flavian campaign. Map courtesy of Richard Cleave (© RØHR Productions Ltd. & C.N.E.S.), with my annotations by permission.

astonishing excavations are not directly useful for the study of the first century, then, they help us to understand the size and situation of Galilee's capital.[19]

No walls have been found from pre-70 Sepphoris, but two finds appear to confirm Josephus' general portrait of the city as committed to peace with Rome. First, locally minted coins that date from Nero's fourteenth year (A.D. 67/68) and "the time of Vespasian" (as legate) call Sepphoris both *City of Peace* and *Neronias*.[20] Second, in one eminent and influential archaeologist's view the Hellenistic fortress complex in the city was deliberately filled in at this time to demonstrate Sepphoris' commitment to peace.[21]

About 5 km (3 mi) east of Sepphoris, just west of modern Kafr Kanna, is the ruin of Karm er-Ras, a small village. Salvage excavations in 1999–2006 revealed a fascinating picture of underground hiding places, dated precisely to the year 67 by revolt coins (Chapter 8). In one carefully hidden chamber

---

[19] After an initial effort in 1930/31, excavations began again in 1983, led by James Strange (University of South Florida), whose teams were complemented in 1985 by others led by Zeev Weiss (Hebrew University of Jerusalem) and Eric Meyers (Duke University). For an overview to 2000, see Aviam and Richardson 2001: 193–95. South Florida reports are at www.centuryone.org/sepphoris.html, Hebrew University reports at http://archaeology .huji.ac.il/Zippori/index.htm (accessed May 30, 2013).

[20] Meshorer 1982: 2.167–69; Miller 1984: 2–3.   [21] See Meyers 2002.

were discovered eleven intact dry-storage jars, each with a 28-litre (7.4 US gallon) capacity, suggesting an emergency shelter kitted out for long-term survival. A Latin inscription in one house's ruins records the presence of soldiers from the Tenth Legion *Fretensis* under Vespasian's command.[22] There are no signs of battle, however, and the lead excavator comments: "Once the neighboring Sepphoris capitulated to the Romans, the inhabitants of Karm er-Ras had no alternative but to surrender or leave the village to join the fighting factions."[23] The nature of the "fighting factions" in Galilee remains to be seen. From the archaeology we gather only that residents were storing supplies in security and that they left without fighting.

Excavations of ancient Tiberias, which lay south of the modern city on a strip of land 200–300 m (650–1,000 ft) wide, between Mt. Berenice and the lake, are ongoing.[24] In our period the town was roughly the size of Sepphoris or a bit smaller: 7 ha (17 acres) with a maximum population of 12,000.[25] Excavations have again exposed late Roman, Byzantine, and Muslim periods more vividly than the first century. A monumental city gate with round towers on each side has been dated to Josephus' time or earlier.[26] The gate seems to have been disengaged from any walls, marking the symbolic entry point. The same type is found in Gadara across the lake, which excavators have dubbed the "Tiberias-gate."[27] Tiberias enjoyed some "walls" from nature, in the lake to the east and Mt. Berenice to the west, but neither there nor in Taricheae (Migdal) to the north have the walls mentioned by Josephus been uncovered.

Figure 20 shows the remains of Tiberias' theatre at the base level, as restored in the second century. The lowest course of seats was cut from the natural slope of Mt. Berenice and so likely goes back earlier. Of interest for our story is the stadium, which plays a role in Josephus' accounts of both Tiberias and Taricheae.[28] In 2002 and 2005 Moshe Hartal unearthed sections of a 9-m (30-ft) thick curved wall, preserved to height of nearly 2 m (6 ft 6 in), north of Gai Beach. There is little doubt that this is the wall of the large stadium built by Herod Antipas, enclosing a circle of 39 m (128 ft) at one end. This was a salvage excavation, however, and the wall has been covered by the grounds of the hotel there.[29]

---

[22] Alexandre 2008. [23] Alexandre 2008: 77.

[24] An excellent topographical map is in Hirschfeld 1992: 221 fig. 16.1.

[25] Reed 2000: 69–77; Aviam and Richardson 2001: 196. [26] Foerster 1993.

[27] Hoffmann 2002: 113–15.

[28] Lämmer (1976: 43–54) hypothetically located the stadium northwest of the city, halfway to the village of Beit-Maon, on the basis of Josephus' account. He noted that in *War* 2.618–19 Josephus uses a term (βουνός) that suggests an earthen embankment rather than a stone wall (cf. Pausanias 2.27.5; 9.23.1 on Greek theatres).

[29] The Galei Kinnereit hotel. See Stepansky 2008: 2050; cf. Jensen 2010: 144–45.

FIGURE 20. Remains of Tiberias' first-century theatre, with orchestra and lowest level of seats built into the hillside, looking east-northeast, the Kinneret lake visible beyond. Author 2014.

Herod Antipas created Tiberias as a Judaean but Greek-style *polis* in A.D. 19–20.[30] The site had been a cemetery overlooking the lake, between much older Taricheae and the famous therapeutic springs of Hammat (Ammathus), ten or fifteen minutes' walk to the south, which now became part of Tiberias' *chōra*: the "the hot springs *of Tiberias*."[31] Antipas may have envisaged a Judaean version of Italy's Baiae, the shimmering hot-springs resort on the Bay of Naples, 400 km (240 mi) from Rome. He may have hoped that a reliable tourist industry, for the springs, would support the lake-based economy in trade with several other *poleis*. The future must have looked bright. The impurity-generating tombs had to be removed, however. Our Jerusalem priest Josephus describes the founding population as "scum" (σύγκλυδες), enticed there by free housing and improved status. But cultured Herodians and others also moved there and quickly formed the political elite. Some seem to have held Roman citizenship (*Life* 32–34; *Ant.* 18.36–38). The city soon had an elected council of 600, an executive Board of Ten, and an elected council-president, likely an annual post.[32]

---

[30] *War* 2.168; *Ant.* 18.36–39; Hoehner 1972: 92–100 (who unusually favours 23 as founding date); Bernett 2007: 221–29; Jensen 2010: 135–48 on Antipas' possible motives and political context.

[31] See *War* 2.614; Pliny, *Nat.* 5.71 (*Tiberiade aquis calidis salubri*). The rabbis of the Babylonian Talmud, writing centuries later when Tiberias had become the centre of learning in Palestine, routinely speak of the hot springs of Tiberias (*b. Shabb.* 40a-b. 147a; *Pes.* 8b, 41a; *Ḥull.* 8a, 106a). They also identify Hammat with Tiberias (*b. Meg.* 6a: "Ḥammat is Tiberias. And why is it called Ḥammat? On account of the hot springs [*Hammē*] of Tiberias").

[32] Jones 1971: 275–76; Schürer-Vermes 2.179–80. On the council see *Life* 169, 284, 300, 313, 381; on the president 134, 271, 278, 294, 300; on the Board of Ten 33, 69, 168, 296; *Ant.* 18.149 on another *polis* office once held by Agrippa.

The stadium and theatre prompt us to think about the kind of city Tiberias was. These facilities were for games, which in other *poleis* meant sacrifices to the Gods and male athletes competing nude. Games were so closely associated with Graeco-Roman culture that Herod's mere construction of a stadium in Jerusalem had caused an uproar, and it seems to have fallen into immediate disuse (*Ant.* 15.268–91).[33] Not so in Tiberias, where these facilities were regularly used. We do not know exactly what happened in them. But along with the city's Greek-style political institutions and location as a trade centre and the apparent remains of a gymnasium from A.D. 20–130 at the Hammat springs (where a synagogue would later be built),[34] the stadium and theatre *suggest* a Judaean city that was engaged with its foreign neighbours in both economic and cultural activities. Non-Judaeans were also a common sight on the streets, as we shall see. This brash young *polis*, named to honour the emperor Tiberius,[35] seems not to have been entirely scrupulous in terms of Judaean law and tradition,[36] perhaps leaving those concerns to the more conservative Taricheae/Migdal and Sepphoris.

Antipas gave Tiberias a tremendous boost by making it his capital, sidelining Sepphoris. Remains of his palace may have been found in a large building with an imported marble floor and magnificent view of the lake.[37] He issued large bronze coins to celebrate its founding and periodically thereafter through the 30s. On these coins he took the unprecedented step, in Judaean circles, of featuring the city name ensconced in a wreath.[38] He also located a bank and debt-record office or registry archive there, all of this a challenge to Sepphoris' prestige (*Life* 38; cf. *Ant.* 14.191). Tiberias was above all a port, and many or most residents made their livings in lake-borne business. Everyone seems to have had a boat, and the lake was ringed by harbours of other cities and towns – each with piers, a breakwater, and often a lakeside promenade. There were at least fifteen of these ports, including those of inland Hippos and Gadara in the Decapolis, on the southeastern shore.[39]

Most important among the nearby *poleis* was Gadara (modern Umm Qais, Jordan), which looked out over Lake Kinneret from a summit about 10 km (6 mi) southeast of the lake. The most important trade routes in the ancient world were those carrying luxury goods east and west. One ran through Nabataean Bostra via the Decapolis centres of Capitolias and Abila to Gadara, the last stop before the Jordan valley. From Gadara the caravans had two routes to the Mediterranean: via Scythopolis to Caesarea or, from A.D. 19, across the

---

[33] See Lämmer and Bernett 2007: 221–29 on the possible uses of the stadium.
[34] Dothan 1983: 10–19, esp. 16–18.
[35] The rabbis of the Talmud (*b. Meg.* 6a) prefer to link its Hebrew name (Teverya) with *tov* ("good"), "because its aspect is good."
[36] Bernett 2007: 221–29.   [37] Jensen 2010: 141–44.
[38] Meshorer 2001: 26–27 (nos. 75–90) with plate 49, 81–83.   [39] Nun 2008.

lake via Tiberias to Ptolemais. Because most goods would be headed to the northern Mediterranean, the Tiberias–Ptolemais route may have been preferred. Both Scythopolis and Tiberias could be seen from Gadara, and there were excellent connecting roads. That western outpost of the Orient could monitor the onward passage of goods.[40]

In addition to competing with its Galilean rival Sepphoris, ambitious Tiberias was thus built to play in the big league of these *poleis* around the lake. Its grand beginning and recent past under Antipas may be important for understanding its turn against King Agrippa II in the 60s.

Recent excavations at Migdal/Taricheae, Josephus' main centre in the east before he moved to Iotapata, have dramatically revised the impressions left by smaller digs in the 1970s. Those had found only a room identified as a synagogue and a modest area around it. Teams working over the past decade in two distinct areas have by contrast uncovered a remarkably large first-century town. It now seems that Taricheae began in Hellenistic-Hasmonean times on the shore of the Kinneret, then expanded significantly inland.[41] At the time of our war, the town and its revenue had recently been given to King Agrippa, along with Tiberias.

The name Taricheae suggests "pickling/preserving/salting" processes or facilities (ταριχεῖαι).[42] The geographer Strabo uses the word for other kinds of pickling, at times qualifying it with "of fish" (7.7.8; 11.2.4). He actually mentions our Galilean town as part of a wordplay (16.2.45): "In what is called *Taricheae*, the lake produces high-quality fish for pickling (ἐν ... ταριχείαις ἡ λίμνη μὲν ταριχείας ἰχθύων ἀστείας παρέχει), ... whereas the Egyptians use the bitumen for *the pickling of the dead*" (χρῶνται δ' Αἰγύπτιοι τῇ ἀσφάλτῳ πρὸς τὰς ταριχείας τῶν νεκρῶν). Apparently he confuses the Kinneret, which has no bitumen, with the bitumen-producing Dead Sea, which has no fish, but full marks to him for making geography interesting.[43]

In the southern area of Migdal/Taricheae the Franciscan excavators found grid-patterned streets, a large Hellenistic bath-house, and Roman-style public baths next to a public square and an ample residential area. In the northern zone Israel Antiquities excavators found streets arranged according to terrain

---

[40] See Hoffmann 2002: 98–100; Riedl 2003: 107 n. 371 discusses and rejects the suggestion that Gadarene coins featuring galleys suggest naval games on the lake; Nun 2008.

[41] In the large southern zone, on land belonging to the Franciscans, excavations were led by S. de Luca and A. Lena. Ground-penetrating radar supplemented the few excavated squares to reveal the town's great size. In the north, Mexican archaeologists M. Zapata Meza and M. Hernández Grajales worked with Israelis D. Avshalom-Gorni and A. Najar. See http://universidadanahuacsur.wordpress.com/2012/03/27/migdal-south-archaeological-excavations-universidad-anahuac-mexico-sur and www.antiquities.org.il/article_Item_eng .asp?sec_id=25&subj_id=240&id=1601&module_id=#as (accessed April 30, 2003).

[42] Cf. Herodotus 2.15, 113.

[43] Elsewhere Strabo confuses the Dead Sea with the now-gone western Lake Sirbonis (16.2.42).

and human need rather than a grid, another large residential area with at least three presumed ritual baths, a market, another large building (House of Dice) with mosaic floor and ritual bath, fishing weights, coins, and dishware. Most sensational is the exposed 120-m² (1,300 sq. ft) synagogue – the first known from pre-70 Galilee. It boasts a large entrance hall and square study hall. In the latter was found a remarkable carved limestone block, 0.6 m (2 ft) long, sitting on four feet and angled slightly upward, with vivid reliefs on each face. Mordecai Aviam has argued that this was the base of a wooden stand for reading sacred scrolls and that the reliefs are all temple-related, including mystical and zodiacal elements. The stone became instantly famous because it has the clear relief of a menorah on the façade seen by a viewer looking south toward Jerusalem.[44] These recent excavations show Taricheae to have been "a large, well established Jewish town" with an excellent port on the lake.[45]

Sitting midway between the Kinneret and the Mediterranean, 9 km (5.6 mi) north of Sepphoris across the Beit-Netofa Valley, is Iotapata, most famous as the scene of Josephus' surrender to Vespasian (Chapter 2). In its ancient past the town had apparently honoured someone called Iotapē, a Persian name common among queens of northern Syria and eastern Asia Minor.[46] On a pleasant hilltop in fertile countryside, with excellent drainage and dozens of natural caves and cisterns for cold storage of food and water, Iotapata was a fine site for a town. It was not a natural *fortress*, however. Sitting about 410 m (1,345 ft) above sea level, the spoon-shaped hill offered only about 5 ha (12.5 acres) of livable space on the summit, 175 m (570 ft) across at its widest point and 400 m (1,300 ft) from north to south. In normal conditions it might have accommodated 1,500–2,000 residents, perhaps hundreds more in a crisis if nearby villagers fled in.[47] The southward gradient (handle of the spoon) is gradual, dropping only about 1 m in 10. To the east the drop is precipitous, falling 70 m to the valley floor. To the west is a more gradual declivity, whereas the north/northwest rim of the spoon falls only about 15 m (50 ft) before flattening into the base of another hill. From Vespasian's angle of approach at the northwest, therefore, access was not difficult (Fig. 21). The site archaeologist Aviam writes that the Romans needed as a siege ramp to carry their men and equipment "one which would only cover the slope and create a moderate grade to accommodate movement of the siege engines" – no great feat of engineering.[48]

---

[44] Aviam 2013: 208–9.   [45] cf. Leibner 2009: 221–27; Aviam 2013: 206.

[46] Although the rabbis imagined that Iotapata went back to Joshua's time (*m. Arak.* 9.6), the variety of Hebrew transliterations (*Yatvat, Yotfat, Yodfat*) indicates that the name was not native (cf. Klein 1909: 50).

[47] Josephus' claim that 40,000 died at Iotapata while another 1,200 were taken prisoner (*War* 3.337) would be credible only if the town had a skyline of tightly packed twenty-story buildings.

[48] Aviam 2008a: 2077.

FIGURE 21. Looking northward across the gentle valley from Iotapata, to the likely hill where Vespasian arrayed his army to intimidate. Author 2009.

Iotapata is shielded in all directions, as Josephus remarks: "Concealed by a ring of other hills, it was completely invisible until one came right up to it" (*War* 3.160). To the south, the hill commonly called Asamon (Chapter 5), sitting 130 m higher than Iotapata (summit 540 m/1730 ft above sea level), conceals it from the Beit-Netofa Valley, and hills at least as high as Iotapata cover the other directions (Fig. 21).[49]

Iotapata has yielded clear evidence of Roman–Judaean warfare in 67. In several seasons of digging during the 1990s, excavators found remains of the assault ramp with arrows and *ballista* stones embedded in it. They confirmed two levels of fortification: a sturdy wall (ca. 1.2 m, 4 ft thick) from the Hasmonean period, surrounding the highest part of the summit only, and a much larger but less sturdy wall around the whole upper area from A.D. 67. Josephus' contemporaries used casemate construction where possible to fill in gaps the old wall and extend it. Aviam observes that the wartime wall looks to be an emergency construction, because it runs right over private residences and a pottery kiln, which had to be relocated. Remarkably, it does not appear to have had a gate. This would suggest extremely hasty building in a defensive crisis.

[49] Measurements are from the contour maps of the Survey of Israel (Merkaz li–Mapui Yisrael) at 1:25,000, in this case the map of Tsippori and region.

Casemate construction had been used by Herod for the apartments around the summit of Masada (Chapter 9) and the circumference of Herodium.[50] The idea was to build two parallel walls with a space in between, with occasional perpendicular walls creating rooms. The visible stretches of this construction at Iotapata are mainly on the vulnerable northwest side; perhaps this technique was not as feasible or necessary on the steeper slopes, where there is a single wall.[51] Casemate design was especially valuable in war, and we find parallels at Gamala. In peacetime the internal apartments could be used for accommodation or storage of food and fuel. In the face of imminent assault they could quickly be filled in with wood, earth, and/or stones to create an immensely thick defensive wall. The casemate at Iotapata was indeed filled in to deaden the blows of Vespasian's battering rams.[52]

Some residents dug underground rooms as hiding places. The entrance to one is marked by a little roof of gabled stones.[53] But the discovery of 35 *ballista* stones, 0.6–2 kg (1.3–4.5 lbs) in weight, and more than 60 arrowheads in and around the casemate walls, along with small hobnails from Roman soldiers' footwear, make clear how the siege ended.[54]

Although only a small area of Iotapata has been excavated, results thus far suggest that before the conflict this was an ordinary residential town populated by families leading normal lives. Pottery workshops and a large olive press were found, as well as human remains. Residential areas excavated in the east and north were mainly in the form of small apartments with floors of flat stone or beaten earth. A couple have plunging pools, stepped and plastered, taken to be ritual baths. Only a few luxury goods have been found, such as small gems and glassware. One excavated house stands out from the others for its relative luxury, boasting painted frescoes on the floor and three walls.[55]

Iotapata's location and topography would seem to have made it an ideal retreat for observing movements in central Galilee, perhaps also for guerrilla strikes at local enemies and for security from such enemies, who might have had small forces on comparable hilltops such as Gabara. The site could hardly have intimidated the Romans, however. Recall that the ad hoc unit under Caesennius Gallus had little trouble destroying militants who had seized the more imposing heights of nearby Asamon (Chapter 5), perhaps in a single afternoon. The stories about Placidus and Vespasian suggest that Iotapata was an easy mark, perhaps even an invitation to practise assault techniques in a low-risk environment. A wall was built rapidly and a Roman force took the

---

[50] Netzer 2013.
[51] For Iotapata's archaeology I depend gratefully on the site's principal excavator, Dr. Mordechai Aviam, both his writings (Aviam 2004: 110–15; 2008a, b) and his generous conversations during site visits (1998, 2009), although he bears no responsibility.
[52] Aviam 2008a: 2076–77.   [53] Aviam 2008b: 45.   [54] Aviam 2008a: 2077.
[55] Aviam 2008a: 2077.

site by storm. But what did it mean in context? Because Josephus used Iotapata before the Romans' arrival, as a base for his deadly conflicts with other Judaeans such as John and the Jerusalem delegation, it is possible that he first fortified the site at first as protection *against them*, reinforcing it later as the Romans arrived.[56]

Galilee lacked sites as dramatic as Masada, but several hills were higher and more difficult of access than Iotapata, including Asamon. Mt. Tabor in the Jezreel Valley was the highest, at more than 560 m (1,840 ft) above sea level, and towering 450 m (1,475 ft) above the surrounding valley.[57] Josephus claims to have walled that summit and stocked it with grain and weapons (*War* 2.573; *Life* 188).[58] Taking it would have been a much more difficult prospect, according to Josephus, had Placidus not combined diplomacy with deception to secure its surrender (*War* 4.54–61) – in a manner suspiciously close to that used by Antiochus III at the same location two and a half centuries earlier, according to Polybius (5.70.7).

A line drawn due east from the northern tip of the Sea of Galilee passes, after about 12 km (7.5 miles), just south of a ridge in the Golan Heights. As we now know (see the excursus to this chapter), its striking appearance attracted the name "Camel" in antiquity – Aramaic Gamala (Hebrew Gamla). About 2 km (1.25 miles) east of a bend in the Roman-era road that headed east from Bethsaida-Iulias (close to route 869 today), this was indeed a natural fortress. Josephus habitually calls it Fortress Gamala.[59] Its northward slope is the steeper one, dropping about 120 m (nearly 400 ft) from its 280 m peak in less than 200 m distance (ca. 660 ft), rendering it hard to attack and also impossible to build on. The residential town lay on the south-facing slope, where the gradient is half as steep although still imposing (Fig. 22).

Excavation has again exposed only 5 percent of the site, but the uncovered area provides vivid evidence of both the peacetime town with its stacked houses and the deadly assault by Roman legions that ended its life. After Gamala's founding, as early as the third century B.C., its residents were families pursuing ordinary lives. The town's main structures were solidly built from cut stones, suiting the location. Because of that and its unusual topography, Gamala did not see the need for a wall. The town had the usual range of wealth and status:

---

[56] M. Aviam, on whose expertise I rely heavily for Iotapata, is entirely innocent of this suggestion.

[57] Mt. Tabor occupies a similar position in relation to its plain as the citadel of Corinth in Greece (Acrocorinth) does to its surroundings.

[58] Josephus' walls have not certainly been found, although some scholars connect the remains of walls there with Josephus' time. Tabor was the site of an earlier Hellenistic fortress (Polybius 5.70.6); see Aviam 2004: 97–98. Although Josephus claims to have fortified the site, his notice – if our text is accurate – that the hill was nearly 4 miles high with a summit of more than 3 miles in circumference (*War* 4.55) is wildly exaggerated.

[59] *War* 1.105; *Ant.* 13.394; *Life* 47, 58–61, 179, 183, 398.

FIGURE 22. Gamala from the east, with residential area – synagogue, wartime wall, and breach – to the left, reconstructed tower in the lower centre, and small summit of the upper "camel hump" upper centre. Author 2009.

A three-level mansion (building 7000) has been found, along with a wide array of food-preparation and eating dishware, also remains of four olive-oil presses.[60] One public building of 320 m² (3,445 sq ft) with benches, Doric columns, and adjoining stepped pool – a multifunction community centre or synagogue[61] – marks the eastern boundary. Another nearly square building (15 by 16 m, 50 x 52.5 ft) was unearthed down the hill to the southwest.[62]

Gamala is famous for its final battle. Because it was undisturbed for many centuries, it is one of the richest and most vivid battle sites recovered from the Roman world. Many bits and pieces of Roman armour, about 100 bolt-projectiles from catapults, some 1,600 arrowheads (thousands more must have been gathered after the fighting), and nearly 2,000 *ballista* balls, fashioned from local rock by legionaries in the field, have been found. This ammunition was almost all discovered in a narrow strip either side of the eastern wall, which had been quickly constructed just before the final conflict. The ammunition had been fired from Roman positions on a small plateau about 300 m (1,000 ft) to the east.

[60] Berlin 2006; Syon and Yavor 2008: 1741.
[61] Runesson, Binder, and Olsson 2008: 8, 33–35; cf. *Life* 277 on public meetings in Tiberias' prayer-house – since it was the largest facility – and Levine 2000: 4–5, 54–55 et passim.
[62] Syon and Yavor 2008: 1741–42.

With Josephus' narrative as a guide, one can reconstruct the preparations that were made for the siege. A continuous wall was constructed from fieldstones to join up the outer walls of the eastern buildings. Inside the buildings, whose walls became part of the town wall, the outer wall was reinforced from the inside. In an apartment just above the community centre/synagogue), for example, residents filled in the space to a man's height. On the upper surface of this fill, several *ballista* balls were found.[63] The round tower that legionaries reportedly undermined on the morning of the final assault has been reassembled for viewing today (Fig. 22 centre front), and a clear breach-point in the wall, where the rams went through, was detected and reconstructed.

Uniquely among the northern wartime sites, Gamala has yielded a few crude, locally produced bronze coins. In contrast to the roughly 6,300 coins of other dates and origins found at the site, only seven of this type have turned up there, along with two that made their way elsewhere.[64] Numismatic evidence is always tantalizing because it holds the promise of revealing something about minters' intentions, but it is no simple problem to figure out what coins *mean*. The obverse of these coins shows a cup of some sort, an image reminiscent of one on the Jerusalem silver coins – whatever *that* is (see Chapter 8). Around it is a legend of five mixed palaeo- and square Hebrew letters, of inconsistent style and direction. The reverse has no image, but only a legend of seven letters without breaks. Everyone agrees that the producers lacked resources and skill, perhaps even literacy. But what do the coins say and mean?

On the basis of an early specimen, Meshorer concluded that the legend was modeled on that of Jerusalem's revolt coins and that it should be read as continuous script from front to back: "Of the Redemption of Holy Jerusalem."[65] The authority of the great scholar convinced many that Gamala saw itself as an outpost of nationwide revolt. It would be surprising, if that were so, that no Jerusalem coins are among the thousands found in Gamala, and a phrase running from front to back would be odd. But more recent research has shown that the coin's obverse actually appears to say "In [or of] *Gamla*."[66] A big difference! In this case, the front (obverse) would make its own statement, as we would expect. The script on the reverse is not yet decipherable.[67]

---

[63] Syon and Yavor 2008: 1739–40.

[64] Farhi 2006: 69; Arbel 2007: 265. One of the two, on the antiquities market, may also have been removed from Gamala.

[65] Meshorer 2001: 130–31.

[66] Farhi 2006: 72–74, winning over Syon (2007: 117), who notes that he and S. Gutmann had favoured this possibility in their original field work; also Lykke 2012: 231. Farhi excludes initial l- (for, effectively possessive) on the ground that the first letter is different from the fourth. That is clear, but can we be so exacting given the condition of the script? See also Pfann 2006 for this as the first city coin produced in Jewish territories.

[67] Farhi 2006: 74–75. He can identify three of the seven letters.

The newer reading suggests that these few coins were an assertion of identity and place, with no evident connection to Jerusalem. Why so few, and for what purpose: practical or symbolic? How large was the constituency for them? Against whom, if anyone, was this self-assertion directed? Some scholars have argued on the basis of the new reading that the most likely context was the long standoff between Gamala and its nominal master, King Agrippa II, in circumstances that we are about to review.[68] On this proposal the coins would be a statement of pride and possibly defiance in a royal territory, without reference to either Jerusalem or Rome.

Ḥorvat Kanaf in the Golan near Gamala, finally, offers a picture similar to that of Karm er-Ras near Sepphoris. This was a village of just 1.5 ha (3.7 acres) on a hillcrest 6 km (3.7 mi) southwest of Gamala and 4.5 km (3 mi) east of the Kinneret. After centuries of abandonment, it was occupied and fortified in the Hasmonean period. But around the time of the revolt against Agrippa (and the Flavian campaign), the residents fled, perhaps to Gamala. Among the extensive finds here there is again no evidence of battle.[69]

To summarize: The material evidence for Galilee and the Golan shows violent conflicts ending the habitation of Iotapata and Gamala at the time of our war in about A.D. 67. Aside from these two sites there is precious little evidence of disturbance, whether in Sepphoris and environs, Tiberias, Taricheae, Gischala, or Galilee's villages. Uzi Leibner's 2009 survey of fifty eastern-central sites from the Hellenistic through Byzantine periods confirms this picture. It finds that three villages were abandoned at about this time but that in general, regional settlement increased through the late first century.[70] As we examine Josephus' narratives, we must try to explain how there could have been such intense fighting in Iotapata and Gamala and so little elsewhere. What sort of *war* did the Flavians wage in Galilee and Golan?

II. LITERARY EVIDENCE: THE PREPARATORY PHASE (OCTOBER 66 TO APRIL 67)

The Galilean "war" falls into two phases: the half-year following Cestius' ambush in October 66 (Chapter 5), during which Judaeans prepared for an inevitable reaction by Cestius but had little contact with Roman forces, and the half-year that followed Vespasian's arrival in the spring of 67. Josephus' narratives mirror this break. The final section of *War* 2 covers the former period cursorily, while Josephus later devotes most of his autobiography (*Life* 17–412) to those months. That pre-Flavian period was marked by deadly internal-Judaean conflicts and skirmishes with Agrippa's royal forces. Because

[68] So Farhi 2006: 74; Arbel 2007: 268–75. [69] See Ma'oz 1993.
[70] Leibner 2009: 308–44.

of Josephus' literary shift of focus away from Jerusalem, we have no idea what became of Florus and his auxiliary in this period, although Galilee was nominally still in Caesarea's purview.

Our main interest is in the Flavian campaign, from March/April 67, for which *War* 3.1–4.120 provides the sole narrative. But we need to consider Josephus' accounts of the preceding six months for two reasons. First, *War* 3 assumes *War* 2 as context. Second, we need to understand the historiographical character of *War* 3, and for this the comparison of *War* 2 with the parallels in *Life* is revealing. It forces us to plunge in the cold water and face the fact of Josephus' literary freedom.

Two different stories: War 2 vs. Life

The two works tell different stories, in general and in detail. *War* 2 claims that the militants who defeated Cestius won over those members of Jerusalem's elite who had not fled the city, using persuasion or force (2.562) – a familiar couple in ancient writing.[71] The newly energized militants recognize two supreme leaders in the capital, who appoint "generals" of the same aristocratic type as themselves (Chapter 3) to command Idumaea, Judaea proper, and Peraea. Thirty-year-old Josephus, invisible in his narrative until this moment, appears fully formed. They send him to prepare Galilee and Gamala (*War* 2.566–68). The remainder of *War* 2 ignores the other regional generals to focus on this "command."

Upon arrival in Galilee, Josephus quickly sets up a government, appointing seventy elders as general administrators – compare Moses and the later Great Sanhedrin[72] – and seven in each town (*War* 2.570–71). He then turns to fortifications, building or strengthening the walls of seventeen named sites. In Sepphoris and Gischala he allows the residents to wall their own cities, in the latter case *instructing* local magnate John to handle it. In the other cases Josephus is personally on site as contractor, busily giving orders and sharing in the urgent physical work (2.572–75).

Once the fortifications are in place, our priest-general conscripts 100,000 young men and trains them on legionary lines (*War* 2.576–82). Placing them under tribunes, centurions, and decurions (!), he drills them in manoeuvres, signals, and tactics, and especially in discipline so to make them a match for their storied enemy. Of the 100,000 that enter this tough boot camp, 60,000

---

[71] Herodotus 8.111; Euripides, *Suppl.* 347; Thucydides 4.87.2; Isocrates, Phil. 10; Plato, *Apol.* 35d; *Pol.* 296b; 304d; *Gorg.* 517b; *Resp.* 411d; 488d; *Leg.* 722b; Xenophon, *Mem.* 1.2.10; *Symp.* 8.20; Demosthenes, *Alex.* 17.23.6; Dio Chrysostom, *Or.* 25.2; 30.14; 75.4; Plutarch, *Thes.* 24.3; *Rom.* 16.1; *Sol.* 16.2; *Them.* 21.2; *Tim.* 19.3; *Mar.* 29.3; Appian, *Bell. civ.* 3.6.42. Josephus features the pair elsewhere too: *War* 2.199, 562–63; 3.203; *Ant.* 4.17; 17.10; *Life* 42, 370.

[72] Cf. Num 11:16; *m. Sanh.* 1.5–6.

infantry, 350 cavalry, a corps of 4,500 mercenaries, and a personal bodyguard of 600 complete the training (2.583–84). NB: This force alone, which is only one of Judaea's seven regional armies, would – if it ever existed – outnumber the 60,000-strong army that Vespasian will bring (3.69). Josephus billets his army in the towns of Galilee. He details half the soldiers for security and the other half to find provisions (2.583–84), a neat plan recalling Polybius' description of the legions (10.16).

With his administration, fortifications, and trained army in place, Josephus is forced to divert his attention to internal challenges: from John of Gischala, the city of Tiberias, and the coalition in Jerusalem. These ructions occupy the sequel in *War* 2 (2.585–646) in support of the work's theme of debilitating civil strife (*stasis;* Chapter 2). Only after these internal fights are managed can Josephus return to preparing for the Roman invasion (2.647) – in Book 3.

In *Life*, written about twenty years later than *War*, Josephus goes to Galilee with a very different mandate. He is now part of a three-man committee of priests, with Joazar and Judas. Their shared task is to ensure that Galilee, which has not yet caught the south's martial fever, *does not* do so. Jerusalem's leaders dispatch these priests to observe and report. *Life* says nothing about war preparations or the other subtheatres and their "generals." Josephus and colleagues must keep the populace unarmed, reserving any weapons for those in charge. They do not want to fight, but must wait and see how the Romans respond to the Cestius debacle and Judaea's growing unrest (*Life* 28–30).

Josephus will eventually style himself a general in *Life*, it is true, because he grows into the role of commander or boss once his colleagues depart. Although he desperately wants to return to Jerusalem, he says, the locals force him to remain to look after them (204–212).[73] But his pacific mandate puts an entirely different complexion on things. He does not set up an administration, fortify towns, or train an army. In *Life*, the prospect of fortification results inadvertently from a clever ruse on his part. When he is caught trying to rescue some goods belonging to Agrippa II, which have been stolen by anti-Agrippa militants, he lies to the angry mob that he is planning to spend the proceeds on walls for Taricheae, a feint that forces him then to pledge walls for other places too (126–42, 187–88).

He has no reason in this account, given his mandate, to recruit an army. After a while we do find him with a bodyguard of 200 (*Life* 90), which becomes a force of 2,000 (118, 212–13). By *Life*'s halfway point he has acquired about 8,000 irregulars[74] and by the end of the book a round 10,000 (321, 331).

---

[73] Not until *Life* 97–98; then 123, 132, 135, 137, 176, 194, 205, 230–31, 249–51, 277, 341, 380, 393. The bulk of these (from 194) occur in the context of the delegation's attempt to remove Josephus – *as* a defective commander.

[74] Cf. *Life* 233 and 371: respectively, more than 3,000 or 4,000.

But he accumulates this force in the course of preventing banditry. *Life* 77–78 explains Josephus' dilemma in this respect. Unable to disarm the tough guys who are *raiding the townspeople*, he persuades the townsfolk to deal with the nuisance by paying him what is effectively protection money. He becomes a middleman, telling the thugs that if they want to see the money, they must stay out the towns. He will pay them, if they agree to return only in the case that he either defaults or summons them. It is a brilliant plan, at a stroke providing income for the robbers, peace for the townspeople, and a private army for him – paid by others. He is amazed at his cleverness, but there is no hint of raising an army to fight *Rome*.

Instead of training soldiers, *Life*'s Josephus and his colleagues fulfil their mission by gathering intelligence on Galilee's four main centres (*Life* 62–64). Sepphoris has pre-emptively concluded peace with Rome, since Cestius' expedition, and so presents no problems. Tiberias is factionalized and partly in arms, to the dismay of its Board of Ten, which remains loyal to the city's master, Agrippa II. Gischala has been fortified by its head man John, at his initiative because of attacks from neighbouring towns – not as in *War* at Josephus' direction. Finally, the stronghold of Gamala remains loyal to Agrippa (30–61). Josephus reassures the placid Sepphorites that he has not come to involve them in conflict. Having ascertained this Galilean situation, the priestly trio write to Jerusalem's leaders and await instructions. The latter ask them to remain for the time being and look after Galilee's populace (*Life* 62–63).

The rest of the story is Josephus' effort to do this in the face of changing circumstances. *Life* becomes rather confusing about Josephus' motives, in contrast to *War*'s consistent presentation of the bold general. This is largely because he finds that he must play a double game, particularly in Agrippa II's cities of Tiberias and Taricheae, where opposition to the king forces him to declare his loyalties. Although he postures as the king's friend, to *Life*'s literary audience/readership, and this may be borne out in reality by their cooperation as he wrote *War* (*Life* 364–67), in the story he must try to keep the anti-Agrippa militants on side by appearing to support them. This double game is a subset of the large-scale deception he attributes to Judaea's top leaders, who strongly oppose the move to armed self-help but must appear to support it, if they are not to become victims (*Life* 22).

Josephus sets his programme of deception in motion when he visits Tiberias, the only Galilean city initially reported to have a militant faction – albeit against King Agrippa. Perceiving the strong anti-royal sentiment among some, he concocts a ploy to win them over. He spins the yarn that the Jerusalem authorities have authorized him to destroy the lakeside residence of Herod Antipas, now belonging to Agrippa, because of its offensive images (*Life* 64–65). *Life*'s literary audience have enough clues to know that this mandate

is his invention.[75] In the story, Tiberias' pro-Agrippa eminent men are horrified, but with a wink Josephus persuades them to go along with his bluff (66;
cf. 32–34). He soon leaves Tiberias, satisfied that his trick has won him the
support of the rowdies, but it backfires. The anti-royals, now roused to action by
his eloquent encouragement, proceed to destroy and loot the lakeside residence,
killing their enemies and any foreigners they meet in the city while they are at it.
Mortified that they have taken his fiction so seriously, Josephus rushes back to
rescue the king's valuables, which he delivers to Agrippa's elite friends on the
council for safe keeping (*Life* 68–69; cf. 296). But the double game is on, and the
reader never quite knows where the façade ends. And Josephus will end up
fighting against royal forces in spite of his alleged disposition.

This must suffice as an overview of the very different spirit of the two
accounts. There are countless divergences in structure and detail, summarized
in Table 3. It compares seven events in *War* 2 with their closest parallels in *Life*,
showing the different sequence, narrative and causal logic, and internal differences. The Jerusalem-delegation episode, for instance, which *War* glides over
in a few sentences (2.626–32), not only forms the core of *Life* (189–335) but has
different motives, comes in a different place, and has different *dramatis personae*.
It is too easy to imagine that the two stories are *basically* compatible.[76] They are
not. We need to face the fact that Josephus could write entirely different
accounts of even important events in his life.

What is the historian to do? Scholars have tried to gain leverage with the
hypothesis that Josephus wrote *Life* in response to Justus of Tiberias, author of a
rival history that challenged Josephus' *War* and attacked him personally.[77] In
response to the challenge, Josephus conceded many of Justus' facts but not
their interpretation. The methodological payoff would be that one could then
treat *Life* as more reliable than *War* 2. It would be like a witness's revised

[75] I part company with most interpreters, who take this as Josephus' poorly concealed admission
of his anti-Roman stance: Luther 1910: 17–18; Drexler 1925: 97–98; Goodman 1987: 218;
Price 1992: 32; Vogel 1999. The keys are Josephus' framing language ("I started saying
that. . ."; 65), which flags a deception (cf. 22), and the sequel, in which he is surprised and
angry that his alleged instructions were acted upon.

[76] Rajak (1983: 147) recognizes "some disparities between the two accounts," but suggests that
they may be explained by the "common sense" view that a combination of greater
concentration and reminders in reading and conversation helped him to refine his
recollections.

[77] The basic hypothesis was suggested by Emil Schürer (1890; see Schürer–Vermes 1979–1987)
and Benedictus Niese (1896: 227), and worked out in detail by Niese's student Heinrich
Luther (1910), again by Hans Drexler (1925: 293–312) and Abraham Schalit (1933: 67–95).
The model was followed with minor adjustments by Hölscher (1916: 1994), Laqueur (1920:
78, 83), Thackeray (1929:16–7), Gelzer (1952: 89), Shutt (1961: 6), an early Rajak (1973),
Barish (1978: 64), an early Mason (1991: 316–24), and Rappaport (1994: 280–82). For a new
way of looking at Justus' possible influence, which takes account of the following, see
Rodgers 2006.

TABLE 3. *Comparative table showing the different ordering, causality, and content of the same episodes (in the preparatory phase of the Galilean conflict) in* War 2 *and* Life. *Episodes are listed in* War's *order, with their order in* Life *indicated by [number] in the right-hand column.*

War 2	Life
[1] 2.585–94: John is Josephus' implacable opponent. Poor, he generates income by swindling wealthy and profiteering in olive oil sold to "all the Judaeans of Syria." His motive is a despicable character.	[1] 70–76: John, most powerful man in Gischala, did not desire conflict with Rome. But opposes Josephus, generating money by *selling imperial grain* with permission of Josephus' priestly colleagues. Profiteers in olive oil sold to Judaeans of *Caesarea Philippi*.
[2] 2.595–610: Young Dabarittans rob Ptolemy, steward of King Agrippa, bring proceeds to Josephus: clothing, silver goblets, 600 gold pieces. He hands these to Annaeus, a prominent figure in Taricheae, for return to the king; they hold it. Accused of betrayal and threatened by 100,000 who surge toward his residence and set it on fire. Josephus awakened by 4 bodyguards. Going out to address the mob in posture of sorrow, lies that he will use the money for Taricheae's walls. This ploy divides audience, non-Taricheaens being upset that they will not benefit. So he promises walls for all.	[3] 126–44: Young Dabarittans relieve Ptolemy's *wife* of 4 pack mules, clothing, other treasures (not *War's*); bring haul to Josephus. He gives it to Dassion and Jannaeus, who secretly return it to the king. A posse of "some armed men" led by Jesus son of Sapphias arrive outside his house. Awakened by 1 bodyguard, who encourages him to suicide, Josephus goes to *hippodrome* and lies about plan to spend money on Taricheae's walls. This different speech stresses Taricheae's hospitality.
[3] 2.611–13: 2,000 unreconciled men pursue Josephus home. He invites their leaders inside, has them flogged within an inch of their lives, and releases them to a cowed mob.	[4] 145–48: He is not pursued home (speech succeeds). *Separate incident*: 600 bandits later set fire to house. Instead of inviting leaders in for flogging, he receives the "most audacious" man, whom alone he tortures. Josephus orders him to cut off his hand and suspend it from his neck before discharging him to horrified crowd.
[4] 2.614–25: John, behind the agitation, goes to Tiberias on pretext of visiting hot springs. Josephus escapes mob (and plot) by fleeing into a boat. When popular sympathy swings his way, he forbids revenge against John but persuades John's 3,000 followers to abandon him. Confined to Gischala and without support, John resorts to deviousness, arranging delegation from Jerusalem.	[2] 85–103: John foments revolt in Tiberias and Josephus escapes via boat. He restrains the Galileans from revenge. This parallels *War* (differently positioned), but John not confined to Gischala: he continues to harass Josephus. The conclusion of War's parallel is transferred to a later Tiberian revolt (370–72). Hence John's confinement cannot be motive for devious appeal to Jerusalem.
[5] 2.626–32: John appeals to Jerusalem, accusing Josephus of tyranny. Alarmed, they send mercenaries with 2,500 soldiers to retrieve Josephus dead or alive. Four eminences lead delegation: Ioesdrus son of Nomicus, Ananias Sadouki, and two *sons of Jonathan* named Simon and Judas. Galilee's	[6] 189–335: After the second Tiberias revolt here (contrast *War*) comes delegation from Jerusalem (*Life* 189–335). Four principal men have different names and relationships: two non-priest Pharisees (*Jonathan* himself and Ananias), a priest Pharisee (Joazar), and a young man of chief-priestly ancestry

TABLE 3. (*cont.*)

War 2	Life
poleis align with Jerusalem group. Josephus cleverly wins them back, humiliates the interlopers, and sends them packing.	(Simon). Though not even present in *War*, Jonathan leads here (200–201, 216–17, 226–32, 236, 245, 246, 249–52, 254, 260).
[6] 2.633–45: Tiberias defects from Josephus, requesting a garrison from Agrippa. Josephus subdues the city by ruse, commandeering 230 boats. Armada intimidates Tiberians into surrendering council of 600 plus 2,000 others, whom Josephus removes to Taricheae. The Tiberians blame Cleitus ("Mr. Famous"). Josephus orders a soldier to cut off the offender's hands. Frightened soldier refuses; Josephus becomes enraged, and Cleitus pleads to keep one hand. Josephus agrees–if he himself cuts off the other. Josephus boasts of suppressing revolt single-handedly.	[5] 155–74: Tiberias defects again, appealing to Agrippa for a garrison. Instead of commandeering 230 boats, Josephus orders each head of household in Taricheae to set sail with one helmsman. With this armada, he gradually removes the Tiberias' council and others. Cleitus is accused, but rather than calling out for permission to keep one hand, he is ordered by Josephus to cut off both (!), then magnanimously spared one.
[7] 2.645–46: Tiberias and Sepphoris defect again. Josephus allows soldiers to plunder them, to teach rebellious a lesson. He finally relents and orders his soldiers to return their plunder, to win back the people's affection.	[7] 373–89: Distinct and detailed accounts of further revolts in Tiberias and Sepphoris. Josephus emphasizes ingenious means by which he saved the cities from wrath of his Galileans. Does not mention the return of plunder, though he has mentioned it earlier in connection with Tiberias (333–35).

statement after shattering cross-examination: "OK, you're right, I did this, but I didn't mean. . . ." Whatever is admitted becomes historical gold.

The hypothesis is tantalizing, and it may be that some statements in *Life* concede Justus' claims, but overall the explanation lacks plausibility.[78] More-over, to read the work in this way one would have to ignore Josephus' indications of its purpose and structure as an appendix to the *Antiquities* (*Ant.* 20.262–66). Exhausted but self-congratulatory after completing the *Antiquities*, Josephus wants to celebrate his ancestry, precocious childhood and education, and character (cf. *Life* 430).[79] The digression against Justus, which comes late in the work and serves to swat him down, is presented as no more than that: "Having come this far in the narrative [i.e., near the end], I want to go through

---

[78] Cohen 1979 dealt with some by relativizing the role of Justus' challenge and historicizing it in relation to Tiberias' later history. For analysis see Mason 2001: xxvii–xxxiv.

[79] Neyrey 1994; cf. Chapter 2. A variation on the standard hypothesis was Laqueur's proposal that the *Life* originated in a context having nothing to do with Justus, in a report written by Josephus in Galilee, which he later revised to deal with Justus' challenge. The solution creates more problems than it solves (cf. Mason 2001: xiii–liii).

a few points against Justus. . . ." (336). Justus does not seem to have motivated the whole autobiography.

We are left with the unsettling reality that Josephus exercised great freedom in writing and did not like to retell a story the same way.[80] Because of that we cannot get beyond general statements. Somehow he found himself in Galilee as a consequence of Judaea's regional conflicts, apparently sent by Jerusalem's leaders. He had to manage some combination of worries about Cestius' coming reprisals, the hostility of Galilee's northern neighbours, disaffection with Agrippa II in his eastern towns, and the determination of city elites to protect their *poleis* and calm the populace.

The differences between *War* 2 and *Life*, which continue the pattern of divergence between *War* 1–2 and *Antiquities* 13–20 in general, should caution us about using *War* 3. If *Life* had continued to parallel *War* 3, it presumably would have departed from that work as much as it does from Book 2.

III. A ROMAN–JUDAEAN WAR IN GALILEE? UNDERSTANDING *WAR* 3–4

With this orientation to the scene and to the first phase of Galilean conflict, we now turn to survey *War* 3 and the beginning of Book 4, on the Flavians' northern campaign. There have not been many efforts – none of which I am aware – to interpret this as a narrative in terms of *War*'s character, plot, and rhetoric. The still-prevailing tendency has been to take it as a basic guide while challenging this or that claim. Our procedure, instead, will be to accept the story *for what it is* – a narrative by Josephus in mid-70s Rome – while posing our own historical questions.

War's portrayal of the Flavians in Galilee is like a play in three acts. The first and longest act (*War* 3.1–444) spotlights Josephus. It ends with the dramatic fall of his redoubt at Iotapata, his drawn-out surrender, and Vespasian's celebration of victory with his boon companion King Agrippa II. The second act begins while these men are celebrating. Hearing of unrest in Agrippa's eastern *poleis*, Vespasian undertakes a brief expedition to Lake Gennesar (Kinneret) to assist the king in restoring order. Requiring no sieges or protracted fighting, this act is over quickly (3.445–542). The third act involves clearing out three relatively remote fortresses (4.1–120): Mt. Tabor south of Galilee, John's Gischala in Upper Galilee, and Agrippa's fortress town of Gamala.

This summary already suggests that there is less of a "Galilean war" in *War* than meets the eye, a conclusion that agrees with the material remains. *War* 3

---

[80] Detailed explorations are in Laqueur 1920; Cohen 1979; Krieger 1994.

opens with the Judaeans' failed attack on Ascalon after the Cestius incident (3.9–28), followed by an excursus on Galilean geography (3.35–58) and another on the Roman army (3.70–109). After a concise account of Sepphoris' pre-emptive submission to Vespasian (3.30–34, 59), the bulk of the volume (3.141–408) is an entertaining portrait of the siege of Iotapata, viewed from Josephus' internal viewpoint. Nearly a fifth of the volume unfolds the drama of his surrender (3.340–442). By that point we are 80 percent of the way through. Book 3 mentions few other sites (briefly Sepphoris, Gabara, Tiberias, and Taricheae, Iapha, Joppa). Most of these *become* issues as a result of Sepphoris' capitulation: They were not part of a war against Rome. There is nothing here to suggest that Vespasian planned or executed a methodical reduction of Galilee, much less a scorched-earth rampage. *War* 4.1–120 opens with the statement that the few who remained in revolt *after Iotapata's fall* – Iotapata seeming an isolated centre of conflict – had surrendered at Taricheae (4.1).

To say it otherwise, *War* 3 describes virtually no fighting. The sites that remain after the unrest in Agrippa's cities – namely Gischala, Gamala, and Mt. Tabor – are handled within six weeks of Taricheae.[81] If we think about the historical reality behind Josephus' narrative, pushing aside his self-focus at Iotapata, it appears that the submission of Sepphoris was as decisive for Galilee in the spring of 67 as it had been during Cestius' expedition months earlier. The leading *polis* led the whole region in submission and that was (almost) good enough for the Roman commander. The rest amounts to individual and differently motivated security operations. A Galilean war this does not make.

Let us look more closely. Our first aim is to understand Josephus' story, although I shall intersperse critical observations in preparation for our reconstruction.

When Nero directed Vespasian to punish Judaea, the 57-year-old headed from Corinth to Syria by land, picking up Corbulo's Fifth Legion *Macedonica* and Syria's Tenth *Fretensis*. His 27-year-old son Titus caught a ship for Alexandria, where he assumed command of the Fifteenth Legion *Apollinaris*, which was lingering there after being released from Corbulo's service (*War* 3.8; Chapter 5). After visiting Antioch, still awaiting a new legate (Mucianus), Vespasian continued to Ptolemais opposite Galilee, the veterans' colony that was Cestius' earlier rallying point, to rendezvous with Titus coming north from Egypt.

---

[81] *War* 3.542 puts Taricheae's fall on 8 Gorpiaeus (Elul) and 4.63, 83 date the fall of Gamala to the 23rd of the following month, Hyperberetaeus (Tishri). However those dates should be aligned with our calendar, they were internally separated by only six weeks, four of which were occupied with the siege of Gamala.

Act I: Roman Galilee pacified

Even before Titus' arrival, Vespasian and Agrippa II are met in Ptolemais by "the inhabitants of Sepphoris," presumably a delegation of eminences from that *polis*. They have made the day's journey (30 km, 18 mi) northwest to welcome Vespasian and to leave no doubt about their unwavering allegiance, just as they had welcomed Cestius' representative in October. This preemptive action is the key to Galilee's whole situation, Josephus emphasizes, for Sepphoris is the region's largest *polis* and strategically crucial site. Eager to consolidate this decisive capitulation, Vespasian dispatches a super-legionary force of 6,000 infantry plus 1,000 cavalry to Sepphoris ahead of his main army. From there his cavalry can dominate Galilee's central Beit-Netofa plain (3.30–34, 59). Any conflict in Galilee is largely precluded.

War is admittedly inconsistent in describing Sepphoris' posture. Seventy years earlier the city had been home to some troublemakers (2.56), but in 66 the city welcomes Caesennius and Galilee's other towns follow (2.511; Chapter 5). Although the residents rush to welcome Vespasian, continuing their posture toward Cestius, Josephus makes the puzzling remark that in his preceding months as "general" the Sepphorites were *so eager for war* that they fortified their *polis* (2.574). However we explain it, that comment is at odds with all other evidence. At *War* 3.61 he claims that he built the city's walls, and credits *his* handiwork (not the 7,000 Roman soldiers there) for his later inability to take the city.[82] Likewise *Life* 188 includes Sepphoris among his fortifications.

Otherwise, *Life* offers an internally coherent picture of Sepphoris' ongoing struggle for *Roman protection* against Josephus and his armed Galileans. He arrives in Galilee to find Sepphorites hated by rural Galileans *because* of their Rome-friendliness (*Life* 30), and that stance remains pivotal to the story. Wealthy Sepphorites hire mercenaries to protect themselves (104–11, 123–24, 232). In his digression, refuting Justus' claim that he wanted to keep Tiberias loyal to Agrippa, Josephus cites Sepphoris as the model of a *polis* that remained staunchly faithful to Rome – refusing to permit its citizens to become involved in *Jerusalem's* issues (346–50). That Sepphoris never wavered from loyalty to Rome seems likely in view of its coins and material remains.

---

[82] Josephus claims that the Sepphorites tricked him into building walls *as they were awaiting Roman protection* (*Life* 347). When he heard that Sepphoris had appealed to Cestius, Josephus took the city by storm to prevent this, although he left out of compassion (373–80). The Sepphorites appealed again to Cestius. He eventually sent a garrison, which reached the city by marching past Josephus' outpost of Asochis at night. Josephus fled eastward to Garis and launched another attack. This was again successful, but again he withdrew (*Life* 394–97).

Sepphoris' Roman garrison is another puzzle caused by conflicting indications in *War* and *Life*. *War* taken by itself is clear enough: When Vespasian dispatches his 7,000-strong advance garrison from Ptolemais, the city already has a small garrison from Caesennius Gallus (Cestius' commander of the Twelfth Legion), apparently from the time of Cestius' recent expedition.[83] This Caesennius had become a significant figure in Josephus' Rome, and it might have been prudent to mention him.[84] *Life*, however, insists that the Sepphorites twice appealed to *Cestius Gallus* for a garrison, once *following* his expedition and again shortly before Vespasian's arrival. The city finally received both of the requested forces from Cestius, the second being a substantial force of cavalry and infantry (347, 373, 394). *Life* makes no mention of a garrison left by *Caesennius* Gallus during the first expedition, and it would be hard to understand the Sepphorites' repeated requests to Cestius if that had occurred. Conversely, it is hard to see why Vespasian's garrison would have been needed so urgently, as *War* claims, if Cestius had recently sent a *large* garrison as in *Life*.

Confusion of names may provide a solution. Only in these passages about Sepphoris' garrison does *Life* refer to the Syrian legate Cestius as *Gallus* (374, 394). Josephus normally calls him either Cestius Gallus or simply Cestius,[85] reserving the *cognomen* Gallus for Caesennius or other Galli. Vespasian reportedly puts his garrison under the command of one Placidus (*War* 3.59). This is Placidus' first appearance in *War*, but *Life* features a tribune named Placidus who served under *Cestius Gallus*. After his failed expedition, Cestius dispatches this Placidus to Ptolemais, to harass western Galilee and maintain pressure in preparation for Cestius' return in force (*Life* 213–15). Given that Cestius' Placidus is in Ptolemais as Vespasian arrives, his boss Cestius now dead, and that Vespasian puts a Placidus in charge of Sepphoris' new garrison, it seems most likely that they are the same man. That might help explain Josephus' confusion, his odd use of *Gallus* for the provincial legate being the clue. Because Placidus, the commander of Sepphoris' garrison, had served both Cestius and Vespasian, and because Cestius and Caesennius shared the name Gallus, perhaps he or his memory-aids or sources mixed everything up.[86] At any rate, we may

---

[83] *War* 3.31–34; cf. 2.511 and Chapter 5.

[84] Caesennius Gallus came from a consular family and was apparently consul under Vespasian, later appointed legate of Cappadocia-Galatia by Titus in 80–82. See Mason 2008: 361 n. 3119.

[85] *War* 1.20–21; 2.281, 333–34, 341, 499, 502–64 (24 times); 3.9, 133, 414; 5.41, 267, 302; 6.338, 422; 7.18; *Life* 23–24, 28, 31. Gallus is otherwise always Caesennius (*War* 2.510–13) or another man altogether (*War* 4.37; 7.92; *Antiquities* 14–15).

[86] A legionary tribune named Iulius Placidus would find fame in Rome as a Flavian partisan. He discover Vitellius on the last day of his life in a "shameful hiding-place," and handed him over to Flavian justice (Tacitus, *Hist.* 3.84), losing an ear in the process to one of Vitellius' German guards. Because this Placidus and the one in Sepphoris are tribunes in a Flavian legion, and the *cognomen* Placidus was not extremely common, though not rare (Kajanto

be confident of the crucial point that Galilee's leading *polis* welcomed Roman commanders and a large protective garrison, from a Gallus or a Vespasian.

Josephus' implication that all Galilee welcomed the Flavians with the leading city Sepphoris makes sense. As we have seen, Romans tended to see the provinces through their *poleis*.[87] As went the *polis*, so went its territory (*chōra*), and central Galilee was the *chōra* of Sepphoris. When Gabinius reorganized the government after Pompey's conquest, Sepphoris was one of only four Judaean regional centres west of the Jordan, with Jerusalem, Jericho, and Gazara (*War* 1.170). It had been temporarily eclipsed by Tiberias, but Nero's gift of that city to Agrippa II in 54/55 (*War* 2.252), making it part of Agrippa-land, allowed Sepphoris to resume its leading role for Galilee (cf. *Life* 37–39). In the same way that the destruction of Jerusalem would mean the effective conquest of Judaea, to be followed by celebration and triumph irrespective of the small and outlying sites that remained, so the submission of Sepphoris meant "Galilee welcomes Vespasian" – even if remnants of the fearful, the angry, and the visionary had fled to points east.

Sepphoris' representative position was not merely conceptual but also a practical reality. The installation of a 7,000-strong garrison there,[88] including 1,000 cavalry to roam the central plain and patrol the villages, spelled the end of feasible resistance in Galilee's lowlands. Josephus in his pose as general puts it vividly (*War* 3.60):

> Going out from both [their infantry and cavalry camps], and relentlessly overrunning the surrounding *chōra*, they brought serious trouble to Josephus and his men: if the latter did not budge from a city, the Romans ran rampant outside, while as often as they [Josephus' men] dared to push out, they were beaten back.

The Sepphoris garrison, "in their fury at Josephus' efforts, did not stop, night or day, ravaging their plains and despoiling the properties of the *chōra*" (3.62). There is no *fighting* here, even in our brave general's reports, but absolute Roman domination.

We might wonder why Josephus did not submit at this point, or flee, particularly if he went to Galilee with the pacific mission that *Life* describes. Any reasonable answer to that question – pride, fear that he would be

---

1982: 18, 262: particularly popular in Roman Spain), this may be our Placidus. The *PIR* entry "Placidus" suggests the link.

[87] E.g., Stevenson 1949: 34–35; Richardson 1976: 27–58; Lintott 1993: 54–69; Swain 1996: 227–29; Lendon 1997: 194–236; Burton 2002; Meyer-Zwiffelhoffer 2002; Harland 2006; Revell 2009: 40–79; Rogan 2011: 85–93.

[88] The Fifth, Tenth, and Fifteenth Legions, raised for the Judaean campaign, are all separately accounted for in the subsequent narrative (3.64–66, 411–12). Placidus, who has been operating in the region for some time, on the Syrian legate Cestius Gallus' order, might conceivably have brought legionary vexillations from Syria along and/or auxiliary cavalry.

maltreated, a sense of duty – highlights a point often missed. Every other significant figure in the area did submit or flee. One of the few things we can be sure about in Josephus' career is that he remained and put himself in the fight at Iotapata.

His description of the garrison's behaviour sounds plausible. Any Roman force in that position should and must have done roughly what he describes with dramatic flair: flaunting its control and shattering the will of any would-be enemy to resist. It is not clear that the garrison expected any resistance after the ready submission of Sepphoris – and many other towns – or that they encountered any.

When Josephus repeats that he could see from early on how things would turn out (*War* 3.136–37, 193–202), therefore, there is no reason to disbelieve this. Everyone else felt the same way, and without prophetic inspiration. With Romans controlling Lower Galilee, even those who had been exasperated by conflicts with the neighbouring towns or by the atrocities of Florus and his auxiliary reassessed their positions. The Romans were not in Sepphoris as hostile occupiers. In welcoming Vespasian the citizens had promised their eager support, as they would in such a situation: "If there is anything we can do. ..." (3.32). Josephus gives no details of what they did, but cooperative locals can always be found to assist powerful armies, especially with intelligence to identify potential threats. We might guess that some old scores were settled by such informants, not because we have specific evidence but because they always are.

Under Vespasian's command, "Mr. Gentle" (for this is the meaning of Placidus) terrorizes the area, killing any who were too weak to flee before his arrival (*War* 3.110). As we saw with Cestius, this was not contradictory behaviour, even from wise and respected commanders. In responding to rebellious Judaean actions (the massacre of the auxiliary and attack on Cestius), it was thought necessary to dominate and overawe the population with low-risk display violence. Burning empty villages was a high-impact technique for demonstrating control and ensuring urban compliance. So it was that with unbridled confidence Placidus decided to make a rapid assault on a town near Sepphoris, not because its still-resident families caused any problems but "supposing that he would take it easily in an assault, to get himself great fame among his superiors" (3.111), according to Josephus. The town was Iotapata.

With no Josephus around, Iotapata's intrepid residents came out to meet the force threatening their families, surprise it by some unknown means, and send the surprised legionaries fleeing to the safety of Sepphoris. We have no idea how they achieved this or indeed whether it happened. Perhaps Placidus brought only a small troop for the purpose and faced some small setback, prompting a rethink. In *War*, at any rate, it is the humiliation of Placidus that sets up the coming Clash of the Titans at the same site. The Titans are Vespasian and our author Josephus.

If the 7,000-strong garrison at Sepphoris already pacified Lower Galilee, the arrival of Vespasian, Titus, Agrippa, and the other kings with their 60,000-strong force anchored by three legions put the issue beyond doubt. Josephus' imaginary 60,000 Galilean force make themselves scarce: "[T]hey dispersed in flight not only before any battle, but even before catching sight of their adversaries" (3.129). Faced with comprehensive desertion, Josephus wisely "decided to withdraw as far as possible from the risks" – to Tiberias on Galilee's eastern edge (3.131). Not only was Tiberias far from Sepphoris. As part of Agrippa's kingdom, it was not on Vespasian's itinerary. Western Galilee's towns and villages had largely emptied from a perfectly understandable fear of the legions. We may detect a sting in Josephus' observation that Vespasian could find only very young or old men to kill, women and infants to enslave (3.132–34).

With Vespasian's massive army throwing its weight around, Josephus understands that the Judaeans' only hope lies in submission (3.136). Even as the "general" portrayed in *War*, he pens a sarcastic letter to Jerusalem: They must either send a clear directive to surrender, which is his preference, "or, if they had truly resolved on continuing the war, [they should] send a force that would be a match for the Romans" (3.139). No such force existed, of course; this is bitter sarcasm. Whether Jerusalem ever responded (or Josephus ever wrote such a letter) we shall never know. But the substance of Book 3 exists because Josephus leaves the safety of Tiberias to join the Galileans now trapped in Iotapata after Placidus' threatening move (3.142).[89]

With the principal city secure, Vespasian's first concern is to check on the "*polis* of Gabara" (3.132). The site is now identified with the unexcavated village of Arabah (Arabeh), about 6 km (3.73 mi) east-northeast as the crow flies from Iotapata north of the Beit-Netofa valley.[90] Gabara has already been mentioned as one of Galilee's four leading centres, which all deserted Josephus in his earlier conflicts with other Judaean leaders (2.629). That says nothing about its position now or toward Rome. *Life* describes Gabara as the most prominent town in Galilee after Sepphoris and Tiberias, and as partial to John

---

[89] Of many small problems: Josephus claims that he left Tiberias for Iotapata on 21 Artemisius (A.D. 67), or Iyyar (kept in April-May on the solar calendar by intercalation). At 3.339 (cf. 409) he says that Iotapata fell to the Romans on 1 Panemus (Tammuz), after the intervening month of Daesius (Sivan). Yet at 3.316 he claims that the siege ended on its 47th day. Given that lunar months had 29 or 30 days, the span between these dates would have been closer to 38 days, or perhaps 42 if one includes the days the Roman engineers used to prepare a road from Gabara (3.141–42).

[90] Aviam and Richardson 2001: 187.

of Gischala rather than Josephus in that earlier conflict.[91] Its prominence would explain why Vespasian wants to visit.

Finding Gabara empty of fighters, he decides to destroy it, killing any adult males he finds, enslaving others, and burning the deserted villages of the town's *chōra* (*War* 3.132–34). As a motive for this particularly angry visitation Josephus gives Vespasian's need to allow his soldiers' revenge for the attack on Cestius' legionaries (3.133). The destruction of deserted settlements does not constitute a Galilean *war*.

Given Galilee's capitulation and dearth of fighting-age men, Josephus must explain his heroic conflict with Vespasian at Iotapata. He says that the Roman commander has learned that "most of the combatants had fled there in concentration" and that "it was a fortified base of operations" (3.141). If Josephus' remark reflects any kind of reality, who were these assembled *fighters*? Several possibilities come to mind: remnants of Josephus' alleged army; men who had suffered loss in Cestius' earlier expedition or Vespasian's recent destruction, whether they had resisted or were enraged at losing property or relatives or were simply terrified to fall into Roman hands; those who rushed to Iotapata out of concern for the vulnerable population Placidus had harassed; or possibly some visionaries or pietists keen to die in a blaze of glory. But it is unnecessary to imagine the first or last groups.

The simplest explanation of Vespasian's motive is that, with no special knowledge of eager "fighters" at Iotapata, he merely deduced from Placidus' humiliating experience, with Placidus' encouragement, that Iotapata could use a good thrashing. If Iotapata's men had come out to resist his planned sack and if they caused him some embarrassment, that would be enough to have him incite Vespasian. From the Judaean side, it may be that some of those mentioned earlier decided to join the people of Iotapata, not because there was a war against Rome but from a combination of solidarity with those now endangered, outrage at atrocities elsewhere, and a feeling that there was no possibility of safe surrender in any case. Perhaps such people hoped that Josephus as a prominent Jerusalemite priest could help them to negotiate a safe corporate surrender.

Iotapata happened to be near Vespasian's route back to Sepphoris from Gabara, and his soldiers' blood was presumably still up from making a bonfire of that area. Perhaps he offered them still-inhabited Iotapata as a gruesome dessert. Although the terrain was hilly, and he had to bring his army over the intervening Yotvat range, it was a short distance made easier by his team of engineers. They took four days to widen and grade the road (3.141–42). Josephus implies in self-congratulation that Vespasian had expected to roll

---

[91] So *Life* 82, 123–24, 203, 233, 240.

over Iotapata quickly, with a vastly larger force than Placidus had. And Vespasian would have achieved this if Josephus had not been present, having courageously moved up from Tiberias to defend the populace.

Iotapata has not appeared in *War*'s description of Josephus' Galilean preparations, except in his list of the sites he fortified (*War* 2.573). *Life*, however, describes it as a town with which he has a uniquely close bond. It has been his base during his half-year in Galilee, especially since the arrival of the Jerusalem delegation sent to kill or capture him. When he is at Chabulon on Galilee's western edge, they move up to Gabara (*Life* 124, 235). Josephus counters by moving to Iotapata, a defensible site he finds loyal to him (*Life* 234–42). He later sends the enemies he captures in Tiberias to Iotapata for safe keeping (*Life* 332). This background may help to explain his concern for the townspeople when Vespasian puts them in his sights.

We might ask, again, why Iotapata did not surrender along with the other towns of central Galilee. The simplest solution is that *they did not realize* they had not surrendered with Sepphoris. They were not big enough to have sent a separate delegation to Vespasian Ptolemais. Josephus' descriptions assume that Iotapata was home to many families: women, infants, and senior citizens. He mentions a pregnant woman caught in the later fighting.[92] When Placidus tried to burnish his credentials by destroying Iotapata, its men fought with unexpected ferocity *because* "their home-town, wives, and children were in danger" (3.112). There is nothing here to suggest the presence of determined rebels. The town was part of Sepphoris' *chōra* and so its population may have assumed the same attitude as the capital. But once Placidus chose them, through no fault of theirs, for destruction, looting, rape, and killing, and they had deterred him, they had to expect a revisit. No matter what offers Vespasian might have extended, they could not have trusted him. They would have had every reason to fear a horrible death accompanied by violence and the rape of their women, even if in reality they would have been spared. Josephus refers repeatedly to their *despair of survival* as a motive for ferocious fighting (3.149, 153).

Some such scenario might best explain Josephus' decision to return, when he was safe in Tiberias and had no taste for confronting Rome. Namely, he knew what was likely to happen to the people and felt obligated to help, quite possibly hoping as a bona fide aristocrat to seek terms. He had diplomatic experience, after all, even in Nero's court (*Life* 13–16). This does not mean that Josephus expected to sacrifice his life. He admits that he tried to leave Iotapata soon after arriving, when he realized that he could not prevent the siege and coming destruction (3.193–203). The women, children, and aged men reportedly persuaded or forced him to stay as their only conceivable hope (3.201–202).

---

[92] *War* 3.246, 248, 261, 263, 336, 344.

Once again, any determined anti-Roman posture on the part of Galileans is difficult to find. It is an unnecessary supposition for imagining what happened in Iotapata,[93] a town of families and the only significant exception to Rome's easy domination of Galilee. This confrontation may have been simply a tragic situation created by the ego of Placidus.

We pass over Josephus' lengthy account of the contest at Iotapata, which serves mainly to exhibit his martial valour. Not only did he keep his poise while holding off the world's most imposing army, but his tiny and motley crew managed to injure and discomfit the mighty legions, even wounding Vespasian and throwing his army into panic.[94] It is hardly surprising that Josephus would see this period of his life as one to milk for proof of his character. Whatever happened exactly, and no matter how much we smirk at his retelling, it seems undeniable that he found himself leading one of very few standoffs against Roman legions in this war, outside the sieges of Jerusalem and the desert fortresses in the south.

Of particular interest is Josephus' claim that Vespasian adapted his tactics to the situation. He had no fixed plan, which he would execute mechanically. This flexibility is typical, as we have seen and will see again with Titus. Vespasian first tries no-risk intimidation, arraying his legions on a hillside opposite as he encircles Iotapata with infantry two deep and a ring of cavalry. There will be no escape, the visual message is, so they should give up (3.145–48). Seeing no possibility of either safe surrender or escape, however, the besieged resolve instead to fight all the harder (3.148–49). So Vespasian attacks Iotapata's meagre walls, but his forces are badly injured by sorties of the desperate Judaeans (3.150–57). Josephus then manages to supplement the walls to an alleged height of 9 m (30 ft). Seeing the difficulties posed by these new defences, Vespasian turns to a passive siege. His men are well provisioned and have plenty of room to move. As the summer heat becomes intense, they can wait for those in this hilltop prison to fall from thirst and hunger (3.178–80). When Josephus undermines Roman morale, however, by hanging out dripping clothes to fake an abundance of water, Vespasian returns to an active siege. The new assaults paradoxically raise Judaeans spirits by giving them what they covet: a chance to die fighting instead of a protracted end from hunger and thirst (3.188–89).

It is typical of Josephus to begin a story, bring it near a climax, then look away to another subject before concluding it (Chapter 2). After bringing the Iotapata story near its dramatic climax, he looks away at two smaller uprisings:

---

[93] Uniquely, because the uprising in nearby Iapha was reportedly in sympathy with Iotapata, not independent (3.289).

[94] *War* 3.236–37: an archer on Josephus' high rampart (3.174–75: 20 cubits or 9 m / 30 ft) managed to hit "the flat [sole?] of Vespasian's foot," which turned out to be a light wound.

at Iapha and on Samaria's Mt. Gerizim. The unexpected success of Iotapata in holding out for so long inspires Iapha (modern Yaphia) – 18 km (12 mi) due south, on the other side of Sepphoris – to put up resistance in solidarity (3.289).[95] The small town's double ring of walls looks like a superb defence until it becomes a death trap when the valiant townsmen are pinned between the two – with their families unable to let them back in without the Romans entering in force. The Romans have an easy time slaughtering the putative thousands trapped there – and destroying the town for good measure (3.297, 305). This is such an easy exercise that the legionary legate Trajan, father of the future emperor, sends to request the "help" of Titus, which is really a gesture to allow the commander's son some easy glory. It is a pathetic scene, which ends with women pelting the swarming legionaries with whatever they can find (*War* 3.303).

We wish we knew more about the Samarian disturbance, but Josephus has no sustained interest in it. His entire description is brief enough to quote (3.307–15).

> The Samarians did not remain untested by calamities either. After assembling on the mountain called Gerizim, which is sacred to them, they remained in place there, and both the fact of their gathering and their attitude held the threat of war. They were not in the least chastened by the disasters all around them, but against all reason were swollen up by their own weakness, uplifted and ready for trouble. To Vespasian it seemed best to anticipate the commotion and cut their ambitions short. To be sure, the whole of Samaria had been garrisoned with forts, but still the number of those who had come to that place and their level of organization were grounds for worry. So he sends in Cerealis, commander of the Fifth Legion, with 600 cavalry and 3,000 infantry.
>
> To him [Cerealis], with many of the enemy situated above [on Gerizim], it did not seem at all safe to go up on the mountain and engage them in battle. Instead, he surrounded the lower mountain with his force and kept watch on them through the entire day. But it happened that the Samarians, being without any source of water, were suffering from a scorching heat; it was summer time and they were unprepared with the necessary supplies. When some died of thirst that very same day, many others – preferring slavery to such an end – fled to the Romans.
>
> From this Cerealis deduced that those who still remained had been shattered by their torments, so he proceeded up the mountain. He arranged his force in a circle around the enemy and, at first, extended his right hand as a pledge. He appealed to them to save themselves, guaranteeing their safety if they would throw down their weapons. But when they would not be persuaded, he fell on them and killed them all –

---

[95] *Life* 230 and 270 suggest a close bond between these towns, at least in their positive dispositions toward Josephus.

11,600 in total. This was done on the twenty-seventh day of the month Daesius. Such were the calamities the Samarians experienced.

The story is fascinating for many reasons. By Josephus' count this group on Gerizim was twelve times as large as the one that would die on Masada – a huge number, especially if adult males only. They are not described as a faction or followers of a particular leader, though they may have been. Although Samaria had not participated in the revolt of 4 B.C. under Varus (*War* 2.69), as far as we know, Samarians are said to have been upset about the rule of Archelaus from Jerusalem (*War* 2.111) and about Pilate's long tenure, which ended following his attack at this very site, Gerizim (*Ant.* 18.85–89). Recall too that Claudius had executed three Samarian leaders on the advice of Agrippa II in connection with the Cumanus incident (*War* 2.445). Although Josephus has no interest in explaining the old enemy's viewpoint, the Samarians clearly had grievances under Rome. Because a big part of their grievance was Rome's favouritism toward Jerusalem, elements of their population may have harboured deeper *anti-Roman* sentiments than most Judaeans did. This incident is intriguing in any case.

Also noteworthy here is Josephus' description of Cerialis' incremental, low-risk procedure. This matches what we see of Roman commanders everywhere. Their tactics are flexible and determined mainly by psychological factors. They attack only when it is fairly safe to do so.

In spite of Josephus' strange reputation for flattery of the Romans, he by no means conceals their brutality as we have seen. So too when they finally invest Iotapata, after these digressions for Iapha and Gerizim, he writes: "because of the memory of what they had suffered during the siege [thanks to Josephus], they offered neither lenience nor mercy to anyone, but as they pushed the people down the precipice from the citadel they slaughtered them" (3.329). In their fury at those who had hidden in underground spaces, they spared no men, regardless of age, excepting only infants and women (3.336). Josephus' long surrender, which we discussed in Chapter 2, follows.

The most revealing part of Josephus' Galilean story for our purposes comes now, at the end of Act I. With Iotapata's fall, *Vespasian considers the submission of Galilee complete.* After Sepphoris' pre-emptive submission, at which most towns emptied, there remained only Iotapata to deal with – and it became a problem only because of Placidus' wounded pride. Iotapata had prompted a day of rage in Iapha, with predictably disastrous consequences. With Iotapata subdued, then, Galilee is truly settled. Vespasian withdraws his troops to rest, dividing the army between coastal Caesarea and Scythopolis, outside Galilee (3.411–13).

The commander himself opts for a vacation and relief from the rising summer heat as July begins, accepting the invitation of King Agrippa II. He is accompanied by a small force, perhaps those he considers deserving of special honour, in the refreshing shade of Agrippa's northern capital Panias (Caesarea Philippi). Like coastal Caesarea, this was a major site of imperial cult. Vespasian could feel at home. He offered sacrifices for the rapid submission of Galilee, which had been settled quickly and with little fighting or risk (3.443–44).

Act II: the little–big favour

Informed readers may be objecting that Vespasian's operations at Tiberias and Taricheae are also part of *War* 3 and the Galilean scene. That is true. But in Josephus' account, Vespasian initially has no concern about these royal territories. With the destruction of troublesome Iotapata, Roman Galilee is settled (*War* 3.443, my emphasis):

> Vespasian ... went over to the Caesarea called Philippi to have a look around the kingdom of Agrippa, because the king had enticed/induced him there, intending both to show hospitality to the general and his army with all the resources of his household and to treat, with their help, the disorders in *his sphere of rule*.

Only the first reason was on the invitation, it seems. Agrippa brings up the other matter while Vespasian is relaxing comfortably (*War* 3.445):

> When it was reported to him [Vespasian] that Tiberias was in rebellion and Taricheae was breaking away (ὡς δ᾽ αὐτῷ Τιβεριὰς μὲν νεωτερ-ίζειν ἀφεστάναι δὲ ἠγγέλλοντο Ταριχέαι) – for both were part of Agrippa's kingdom – and given that he had resolved upon subduing *Judaeans* wherever they were from (πανταχόθεν τοὺς Ἰουδαίους καταστρέφεσθαι διεγνωκὼς), he reckoned it an opportune moment for an expedition against those cities *for Agrippa's sake, as repayment for his hospitality* and to teach the cities a lesson for him (δι᾽ Ἀγρίππαν, ὡς εἰς ξενίας ἀμοιβὴν σωφρονίσων αὐτῷ τὰς πόλεις).

That is, Agrippa has become concerned about reports of opposition to him in these cities. While hosting Vespasian, he quietly solicits his help (2.443).

In Josephus' construction, the "rebelling" and "breaking away" in these cases are in relation to the king. Nero came to power on October 13 A.D. 54, and Josephus describes his gift of Tiberias and Taricheae, along with Iulias in Peraea, as an action of that emperor's first year (54/55 or 55/56?). With this move the prosperous lakeside cities were removed from supervision by the procurator in distant coastal Caesarea and given to the king, whose main territory was nearby to the north and east.[96] Agrippa II was only a decade

---

[96] *War* 2.252; *Ant.* 20.158–59. Cf. Kokkinos 2003: 172–79, showing that in Agrippa's coins a Tiberias era beginning in A.D. 55–56 is the only significant alternative to the king's main era from 60–61, used on coins from his capital (marking the expansion of Caesarea-Panias as Neronias).

older than teenaged Nero. Born and raised in Rome, as we have seen, he had been a significant figure in Claudius' court (*Ant.* 20.9) and Claudius had given him a starter kingdom at age 20. Nero, still under a tutelage of continuity with Claudius' later years, enlarged that territory with two Judaean lakeside centres.

In Josephus' narratives, Tiberias and Taricheae have never had problems *with Rome*. In *War*, Tiberias first appears as the scene of conflict between John of Gischala and Josephus, but the city's tendency is clear. Its leaders reject Josephus (sent as Judaean general) and appeal to Agrippa and the Romans against him. When Roman cavalry appear nearby and a force from Agrippa is en route, the leaders expel Josephus (2.632–34). He delights in telling how he then subdued them by craft, plainly the city's leaders wish to remain loyal to Agrippa. Still, when fleeing Vespasian's forces in western Galilee he can take refuge in Tiberias, which is an open and cosmopolitan city.

Life complicates matters as usual, although the big picture is similar. There Josephus finds Tiberias' council loyal to Agrippa, but also a faction of "insignificant people" bent on rebellion *against the king* (*Life* 31–43). As a *polis*, nevertheless, "the Tiberians had resolved to submit to the king and not to defect from the Romans" (391). Josephus' soliloquy against Justus, whom Josephus puts at the head of the anti-royal faction with his father, shows the complexity of attributing motives, for Justus had presented Josephus as the troublemaker in Tiberias (340). Even in Josephus' hostile portrait of him, council-member Justus does appear to have Agrippa's trust (357, 390, 393).

Josephus' supposedly watertight case that Justus desired war with Rome, in *Life*'s digression, is also revealing. With other Tiberians, he says, Justus was active in burning *the villages of Gadara and Hippos*. Because the Decapolis leaders complained to Vespasian about Justus when he reached Ptolemais, Josephus takes Justus' rebelliousness as proven (*Life* 341–43). But those local conflicts with neighbouring *poleis* are what we have come to expect (Chapter 4) and do not demonstrate opposition *to Rome*. John of Gischala was also engaged in such conflicts while he supposedly rejected an anti-Roman stance.[97] Otherwise, Josephus can only implicate Justus in Tiberias' brief confrontation with Vespasian (*Life* 352), but *War* portrays Tiberias' leadership as jumping into Vespasian's arms in that incident.

It is impossible to untangle all the knots of genuine conviction, rhetorical self-representation, recrimination, shifting alliances, and one-upmanship embedded in the Josephus–Justus conflict.[98] When Josephus admits that the Latin-named Justus "*pretended* to be in doubt about going to war" with Rome (*Life* 36), his charge against the Tiberian, we lose hope. Everyone is pretending all the time, especially Josephus (*Life* 21–23). Still, through all the dust and fog

---

[97] See Cohen 1979: 134.
[98] Rajak 1973 and Cohen 1979: 114–43, 216–21 are valiant attempts.

it seems that Tiberias' main leaders wished to remain loyal to Agrippa – or both Josephus' accounts would be unintelligible – notwithstanding anti-royal factions and a measure of popular sentiment.

Indeed, it seems that Tiberias' council sent delegates to welcome Vespasian and Agrippa in Ptolemais just as Sepphoris' council did. This was the only safe way for a *polis* to avoid suspicion of resistance or hostility.[99] *Life* 410 claims that when Decapolis leaders met Vespasian in Ptolemais (unmentioned in *War*), they complained about Tiberias' behaviour and blamed Justus. Vespasian believed them sufficiently to *hand Justus over* to Agrippa, who had little choice but to put him in chains for the moment. So Justus must have been present in Ptolemais, most likely as a council-member from Tiberias along with *polis* delegates from across the region. As we might expect, they were not only greeting the rulers but seizing the chance to put their preemptive spin on local conflicts.

For now, the main point is that Vespasian clearly distinguished between the province under Roman control, which had become his responsibility as he tried to redeem Cestius' shame, and the king's territories, which were Agrippa's to deal with and which now showed signs of anti-royal sentiment in spite of the official welcome at Ptolemais.

What was the problem in Agrippa's territories? Although the partly Herodian elite may have been happy when Nero presented the *polis* "as a gift to Agrippa," their distant relative, it rankled with others. The most basic qualities of a *polis* were the notional autonomy, self-direction, agency (ἐλευθερία, αὐτονομία, αὐτάρκεια), and prestige it offered its people, who treasured and guarded their citizenship.[100] A *polis* that served as a monarch's capital, as Tiberias under Antipas or Jerusalem under Herod, enjoyed the enhanced prestige of regional primacy. *Poleis* ruled by monarchs far away, as just another feather in their cap, were apt to feel humiliated. We have seen that leaders of several proud *poleis* complained bitterly about subjection to Herod's Jerusalem (*Ant.* 15.351–54). And many Greek *poleis* bristled with wounded pride under Roman rule.[101] In the mid-50s Tiberias and Taricheae became branches of Agrippa's kingdom based in Panias to the north.

---

[99]   E.g., *War* 2.213, 297, 318–25, 338; *Ant.* 16.14. Cf. the famous story of Alexander the Great as he drew near to Babylon. First the general Mazaeus and then the city treasurer rushed out to meet him, the latter covering the road to the city with flowers and silver altars burning incense. Alexander was pleased because this surrender of a major city and respected general would inspire everyone else to do the same (Curtius Rufus 5.1.17–18).

[100]   Hansen 1993a, 1993b, 2006: 39–47; McEvedy 2011.

[101]   Alexandria, the great capital now denied even its own council by Rome, may be the most famous case: Capponi 2005, 2011; Harker 2008. This issue lies at the heart of the problem "Greek cities /culture under Roman rule," which has attracted an enormous amount of research in recent decades. For basic issues see Bowie 1972; Swain 1996 with the *polis* orations of Dio of Prusa.

It may be that many citizens of Tiberias felt they had just been coming into their own, a quarter century after the demeaning exile of their beloved, resident, and long-ruling founder Antipas, when they were handed over to Agrippa. Just a year before the handover Claudius had permitted them to mint their own coins. The occasion was Claudius' thirteenth year, and the coins featured the city name enclosed in a wreath as in the glory days of Antipas.[102] Claudius would not live to complete his fourteenth year,[103] and one of Nero's first actions was to give the city to Agrippa II. Tiberias would issue city coins again only after Agrippa's death decades later, with renewed pride celebrating Trajan's rule and Tiberias' year 81 (= A.D. 99/100).[104] The pattern of coinage joins the literary evidence to suggest that Tiberians had no trouble whatsoever with Rome, under whom they had prospered. But Agrippa's lordship was an aggravation for many – even if the Herodian-inclined leaders were happy.

Josephus does not say exactly who resented Agrippa or why, but he signals potential grievances in the speech he writes for the demagogue Justus (38–39):

> You yourselves just happen to have been given to the younger Agrippa – as a gift from Nero! And because it submitted to Rome, Sepphoris immediately became the capital of Galilee, and both the royal bank and the archives, having been dismantled [here], are with them! Now is the time to welcome the [rural] Galileans as allies and take up weapons. They are eager to begin, because of the hatred they have toward the Sepphorites for maintaining loyalty to the Romans – and they have a large force to execute vengeance because of what they did.

Such rhetoric is no simple window on real conditions. What exactly the *royal* bank and archives were,[105] how they came to reside in Sepphoris, and how this was connected with Sepphoris' obsequious-seeming loyalty to Rome, or rural-Galilean anger, are fuzzy at best. Mainly it is confusing that these words against Agrippa should be given to someone who seems to have been his trusted agent.

---

[102] The coins are illustrated in Meshorer 2001: 261 (nos. 347–349a) with plate 77, discussion on 177–78.

[103] Claudius ruled thirteen years, eight months, twenty days (*War* 2.248).

[104] Kokkinos 2003: 175 uses this date to argue that Agrippa had *just* died (in 100). That may be so, but numismatics presents too many examples of gaps in the coinage of rulers or cities to make it dispositive.

[105] In the first-century Mediterranean world, there was no single system of banking. Money-lending was important to the economy, but took place in many contexts: among aristocratic friends in Rome, from private money-lenders at interest, or from banks associated with temples or states (Finley 1985: 53–7, 115–19; Stambaugh 1988: 106, 111, 117). Josephus' royal τράπεζα suggests a state-run bank. We might guess from the related "archives" or "records" that it lent money at interest (cf. *War* 2.427). Pliny remarks that a municipality in his province lent money at 9 percent but found few borrowers (*Ep.*10.54). 12% p.a. was common (Cicero, *Att.* 6.1).

The emotional force is nonetheless clear. Tiberians should feel humiliated at becoming playthings of Nero and his man-friend Agrippa, and this has something to do with *economic disadvantage*. Nothing suggests ongoing hatred of Rome, but only an indirect reflection on Nero as a result of these local conditions: "The hillbilly Galileans hate Sepphoris for its obsequiousness toward Rome, and we can take advantage of their farmers' brawn for our grievance."

We do not know what royal ownership of the lakeside cities entailed in commercial terms, but a transit tax on goods crossing in and out of the new royal zone seems likely.[106] Whatever extra bureaucracy or account-keeping was entailed might have annoyed business people, as such things do today. Perhaps the mechanisms of collection were as much of an irritant as the sums. That economic and trade issues were central may also be signalled by Josephus' remark that *sailors* and ingrates – not naval personnel but Tiberians earning their living on the lake – were eager to destroy the Herodian palace (*Life* 66). Although the issue there concerns images, that may represent Josephus' clever pretext – something the Jerusalem leadership could have been expected to worry about – which would give the anti-royals an excuse to act on a differently motivated hatred.

We cannot go farther, and this may be too far. Wherever we land in our speculations about the reasons for anti-Agrippan grievance in Tiberias, the fact remains that *War* 3 portrays Vespasian as concerned with Judaean sites in the Province of Syria under Roman administration as he takes over Cestius' operations. Cestius had been entirely satisfied with Sepphoris' submission for Galilee, while quickly chasing down irreconcilables and burning mostly empty villages; Vespasian followed the same pattern. Agrippa was a key ally and advisor for both men, and his territories had never been an issue. They had not been involved in Jerusalem's regional problems. When he was expelled from Jerusalem, tellingly, the king fled to the *safety* of his territories. In Tiberias, anti-Agrippa sentiment was found in pockets and grounded in local problems: Tiberias' loss of status under him a decade earlier, complications in commercial dealings with neighbours, possibly related violence from and toward Decapolis neighbours/rivals, and the old rivalry with Sepphoris. It is possible that Agrippa was blamed here also for not being more effective in the mother-city of Jerusalem, although Tiberias was not part of that struggle. With little or no evidence to constrain us, we may imagine many real-life possibilities.

As we ponder what was happening in the summer of 67, we see signs that factionalism in Tiberias had recently come to a head (cf. *Life* 32–42). Even still,

---

[106] In a story set several decades before the war in Galilee but written around the same time, Mark 2:14 mentions a tax-collector stationed at a toll booth by Capernaum, the first town on Herod Antipas' side of the Jordan River, which separated his territory from that of his brother Philip.

Vespasian will be officially welcomed in both Tiberias and Taricheae and will refrain from destroying them. Agrippa's concern seems to be about discord and fear of where it might lead, with perhaps the occasional incident providing evidence. Paradoxically, he may be responding to the effects of Josephus' clever ploy in claiming Jerusalem's support for action against the Herodian palace. The bold ransacking of the king's inherited residence and events energized by that, such as the robbery of his steward, would surely have seemed ominous to Agrippa.

The mysterious figure of Jesus son of Saphat draws attention here. When Vespasian reaches Tiberias, this Jesus appears as "the very head man of the swarm of bandits" in Tiberias, who promptly flees to Taricheae.[107] In *Life* 66, a certain Jesus son *of Sapphias* is the vigorous leader of the faction of sailors who loot the Herodian palace. But according to both *War* (2.599) and *Life* (134, 278, 294, 300), angry Jesus was "then president" (ἄρχων τότε) of Tiberias' council. Putting these notices together prompts the speculation that Agrippa had real reason for worry. Although the Council of Ten maintained close relations with him, a populist antagonist representing the interests of traders who had been elected to the rotating presidency of the council of 600 was bold enough to lead the aggrieved in vandalizing his royal possessions.

To summarize this reconstruction of what really lay beneath Josephus' accounts: Just as Vespasian was winding down his brief operations in Galilee, Agrippa's problems in Tiberias were growing for reasons peculiar to that city. After a period of relaxation with Vespasian, the king carefully raises the issue, over wine after dinner we might imagine. "I have this problem, you see. . . ." Vespasian: "Look, you have been so kind to us. Let me handle it. I have an army, and my soldiers will become soft if they sit around. They need exercise before winter. Let me take care of this." Agrippa: "You would do that for me?"

After gathering his dispersed forces, with a delighted Agrippa in tow,[108] Vespasian follows the usual plan. He brings his three legions and thousands of others close enough to be noticed from Tiberias, about 6 km (3.7 mi) away at Sennabris. He does not enter Tiberias, which would be a recipe for needless violence, but hopes to intimidate it into coughing up its agitators.[109] After allowing sufficient time for the citizens to grasp their situation, he sends just a fifty-strong cavalry troop to receive their submission and the offenders. He strictly forbids his soldiers to fight, even if provoked, so as not to damage his friend's charming city. The squadron leader arrives and orders his men to

---

[107] *War* 3.459, 452, 457, 498.
[108] Agrippa has no speaking parts but he is present: *War* 3.456; 4.14.
[109] On any location of Sennabris, it seems too far (several miles) distant for the army to have been "conspicuous" from Tiberias. See the excursus to this chapter. Josephus' claim could make sense if we imagine that such a large army with polished gear would have been noticed by scouts, sentries on hilltops, and those out on the lake.

dismount in a demonstration of peaceful intent. But before he can speak, Jesus' group rush out brandishing weapons, surprise the cavalrymen, and steal their horses. Tiberias' top echelon, realizing that this insult will surely bring retaliation, rush south to the Roman camp and appeal desperately to Vespasian, through Agrippa's good offices, to spare the city. It was not their fault. He agrees and now personally enters Tiberias, while again insisting that his soldiers harm nothing and touch no one for Agrippa's sake (3.453–61).

Jesus' group, meanwhile, are now isolated in keeping with Vespasian's plan, and flee 6 km (3.7 mi) up the shoreline to Taricheae. There again Vespasian follows the familiar pattern. He is determined to corral the agitators where he can punish them while sparing and duly intimidating the city.

Taricheae has figured in *War* 2 (as in *Life*) as Josephus' eastern base before his capture. He needed this resort because Tiberias rejected his moves toward war preparation. Taricheae's contrasting openness to Josephus might suggest that the much older community was even more amenable to anti-royal emotion. In any case, Josephus now portrays the town as a refuge for the disaffected from all corners, to the chagrin of the town's residents. Newcomers include "a crowd from Trachonitis, Gaulanitis, Hippos, and Gadara, mostly insurgents and fugitives, to whom war commended itself in view of their disgraceful actions in peacetime" (3.542). This large refugee element, which includes non-Judaeans,[110] imposes on the indignant people of Taricheae.

Josephus' elaboration, with a fine speech by Titus (3.472–84) and a geographical excursus on the lake area (3.506–21), does not disguise the fact that the submission of Taricheae is as rapid as that of Tiberias. Vespasian moves his camp from Tiberias half-way to Taricheae. Jesus' group, with characteristic boldness, charge out and attack his soldiers as they are building the camp, but are quickly chased to getaway boats they have prepositioned on the lakeshore – for the Roman soldiers have no boats. Vespasian, hearing that the rebels have assembled on the plain outside Taricheae, seizes this perfect situation for his cavalry. He sends Titus now with 600 horsemen. Titus is surprised by the strength of the enemy force, however,[111] and while awaiting reinforcements gives a speech to his dispirited troops.

---

[110] Those from Hippos and Gadara could be refugees from Judaean minorities, fleeing trouble that began after the massacre in Caesarea and the Judaean reprisals (*War* 2.459, 478). But at *Life* 112–13 Josephus describes *foreign* gentlemen from Agrippa's territories who cross into Galilee with their horses to help fight against the king. At *Life* 142 Josephus remarks in a speech in Taricheae that "this city, so hospitable toward foreigners, was eagerly accommodating such men as these, *who have left behind their native places and made common cause with our fortune.*" *Life* 372 speaks intriguingly of 1,500 "foreigners from the metropolis of Tyre" fighting for John.

[111] This need not mean that the rebels came close to matching Titus' 600, but only that he did not have the overwhelming advantage he might have expected, of perhaps 4 or 5 to 1.

That spurs them to a confident attack, and some rebels manage to flee inside the city walls. Understanding the turmoil this foreign element is producing in the city, Titus bypasses the flimsy town walls (built by Josephus) by leading his cavalry into the water and back inland again. Once inside, his soldiers kill ferociously and without discrimination until, satisfied that the culprits have either died or fled to the lake, Titus calls a halt (3.462–71, 485–96). His father, meanwhile, orders his soldiers to construct boats to deal with the waterborne refugees, who have nowhere to go (3.503–505, 522–31). An alleged 6,700 militants die in the ensuing bloodbath on the lake.[112]

This whole disturbance, which had begun with Tiberias' populist council-president Jesus, encouraged by Josephus' failed ruse, ends with Vespasian setting up a tribunal-platform in Taricheae to separate peaceable townsfolk from surviving troublemakers. Not wishing to lose the residents' goodwill, and always with an eye on Agrippa's continuing rule, he marches the convicted men in a guarded file to Tiberias. As we saw in Chapter 2, in spite of his public assurances he orders the 1,200 oldest and most useless executed, while sending the fittest 6,000 to Nero for labour on the Corinthian canal. In spite of the huge numbers given by Josephus, all these men are apparently outsiders to Taricheae.

And so Taricheae, which has never imagined war with Rome but has been caught up in some recent anti-Agrippa agitation and regional disaffection, is restored to its normal residents and royal favour. As Vespasian promised, the coastal cities have learned a lesson in loyalty (3.532–42). Agrippa is thrilled to have such a friend in need.

So ends *War* 3. It is simply not the story of a "Judaean-Roman war in Galilee," much less of Vespasian's scorched-earth destruction en route to Jerusalem. The Roman general has no expectation of fighting after Sepphoris' pre-emptive submission, which leaves his confident army with only patrols, confidence-building exercises, revenge for Cestius, and displays of force before beginning a long period of rest from July through the winter. Even after the hiccup at Iotapata caused by Placidus' pride, Roman Galilee is pacified by the end of June. The favour for Agrippa thus far costs Vespasian little.

Josephus dates the pacification of Taricheae to 8 Gorpiaeus (Elul), which seems to have been about September 5 that year (Fig. 23). This was more than two months (with Tammuz and Av intervening) after the fall of Iotapata (ca. June 30/July 1).[113] Tiberias and Taricheae seem to be over in a matter of days after the muster of the legions. This suggests that Vespasian indeed gave the hottest part of the summer, July and most of August, to resting his troops in

---

[112] This appears to be the best candidate for Vespasian's celebration of a recent *naval* victory in his coins (Kokkinos 2010: 9–10, 20; see Chapter 1).

[113] The new moon for Tammuz in that intercalated year was on June 30 (Julian), but we are allowing an extra day or two for sighting.

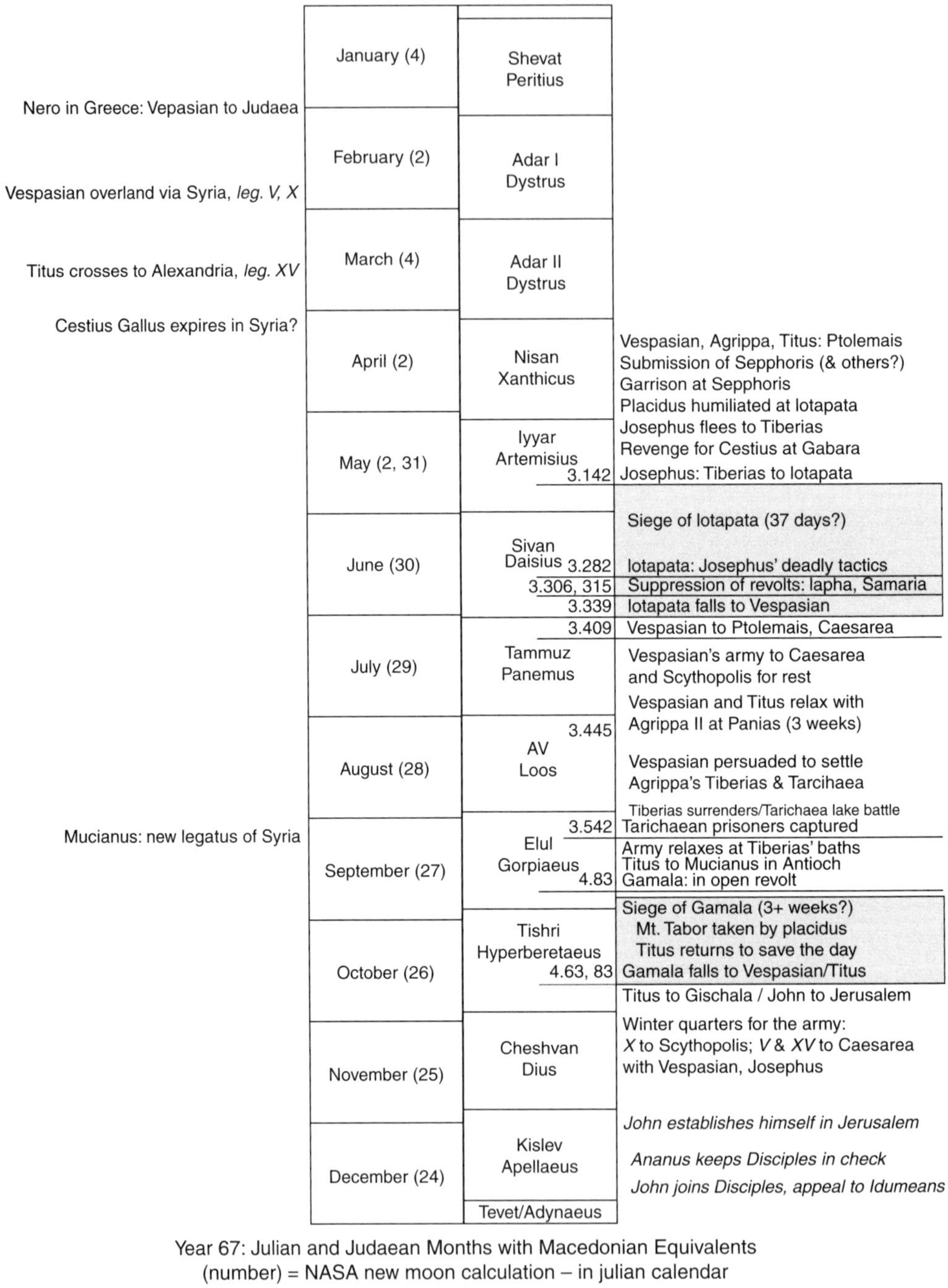

Julian	Judaean / Macedonian		Events
January (4)	Shevat Peritius		
February (2)	Adar I Dystrus		
March (4)	Adar II Dystrus		
April (2)	Nisan Xanthicus		Vespasian, Agrippa, Titus: Ptolemais Submission of Sepphoris (& others?) Garrison at Sepphoris Placidus humiliated at Iotapata
May (2, 31)	Iyyar Artemisius	3.142	Josephus flees to Tiberias Revenge for Cestius at Gabara Josephus: Tiberias to Iotapata
June (30)	Sivan Daisius	3.282 3.306, 315 3.339	Siege of Iotapata (37 days?) Iotapata: Josephus' deadly tactics Suppression of revolts: Iapha, Samaria Iotapata falls to Vespasian
July (29)	Tammuz Panemus	3.409	Vespasian to Ptolemais, Caesarea Vespasian's army to Caesarea and Scythopolis for rest Vespasian and Titus relax with Agrippa II at Panias (3 weeks)
August (28)	AV Loos	3.445	Vespasian persuaded to settle Agrippa's Tiberias & Tarcihaea Tiberias surrenders/Tarichaea lake battle
September (27)	Elul Gorpiaeus	3.542 4.83	Tarichaean prisoners captured Army relaxes at Tiberias' baths Titus to Mucianus in Antioch Gamala: in open revolt
October (26)	Tishri Hyperberetaeus	4.63, 83	Siege of Gamala (3+ weeks?) Mt. Tabor taken by placidus Titus returns to save the day Gamala falls to Vespasian/Titus Titus to Gischala / John to Jerusalem
November (25)	Cheshvan Dius		Winter quarters for the army: X to Scythopolis; V & XV to Caesarea with Vespasian, Josephus
December (24)	Kislev Apellaeus		John establishes himself in Jerusalem Ananus keeps Disciples in check John joins Disciples, appeal to Idumeans
	Tevet/Adynaeus		

Left-margin annotations (aligned to rows):
- Nero in Greece: Vepasian to Judaea — (January)
- Vespasian overland via Syria, *leg. V, X* — (February)
- Titus crosses to Alexandria, *leg. XV* — (March)
- Cestius Gallus expires in Syria? — (March/April)
- Mucianus: new legatus of Syria — (September)

Year 67: Julian and Judaean Months with Macedonian Equivalents
(number) = NASA new moon calculation – in julian calendar

FIGURE 23. Calendar of A.D. 67 showing Julian-Roman solar months aligned with Hebrew lunar (and equivalent Macedonian) months, with Josephus' dated events anchoring a sequence of others. Shading represents direct military confrontations.

welcoming places. Knowing that he could easily intimidate Tiberias, he marched there around the beginning of September with no special preparation or expectation of resistance.

A timeline that would make sense of Josephus' account, in sum (Fig. 23), has Vespasian in Ptolemais by mid-April of 67, where he receives welcoming embassies from all around before he has even formed up the army. By mid-May he has consolidated welcoming Sepphoris and with it Galilee's heartland. After Placidus' debacle at Iotapata he begins a siege there by late May and finishes it, thus pacifying Galilee beyond any doubt, by the end of June. After two months of negligible work apart from the siege, he takes a long vacation with Agrippa. The king's request leads him to reassemble his army at the end of August to perform the favour for his host before it is time for winter quarters.

After Taricheae, Vespasian takes advantage of his presence near Tiberias' famed hot-springs to refresh the army and build their morale (*War* 4.4).[114] They occupy the area of the baths and enjoy themselves greatly. Even including that rest period, the remaining sites will be cleared within six weeks of Taricheae.[115] Favours have a way of growing, however.

Act III: Gamala and the fortresses

I mentioned that the Galilean conflict spills over into *War* 4. Only at 4.120, with the surrender of Gischala, will Josephus claim that "Galilee was thus entirely subdued." Why did he not include these Galilean episodes in Book 3? It cannot be that he ran out of space (contrast *Apion* 1.320). The Greek word-counts of *War* 1 through 4 (see Chapter 2) show a rapid decline until Book 3, after which Book 4 grows by 3,377 words. That is roughly the size of the Galilee-Golan material in *War* 4 (= 3,162 words). Josephus could therefore have included this material in Book 3, simply reversing the sizes: Book 3 at 17,409 words and 4 at 14,462.

At least three considerations may have prompted him to keep the fortresses for the next volume. First, shunting them to Book 4 leaves the siege of Iotapata, his brilliant exploits, and his long surrender story as the highlights of Book 3. Tiberias and Taricheae, which were sub-glorious events for all concerned, are allowed to fill out that volume. Including the gripping drama of Gamala there would have risked diminishing Josephus' radiance. Second, the leftover fortresses provide a structural parallel that anticipates Book 7.

---

[114] Josephus has mentioned these springs without naming them at *War* 2.614, where John of Gischala uses a therapeutic visit as a pretext to foment anti-Josephan feeling in Tiberias. Cf. *Ant.* 18.36–37 (Antipas deliberately founded Tiberias "in the choicest part of Galilee" near these springs) and *Life* 85.

[115] By 22/23 Hyperberetaeus = Tishri around October 19/20 (*War* 4.63, 69, 83).

There, three fortresses also remain after Jerusalem's fall (Book 6) – Herodium, Machaerus, and Masada (4.555; 7.163–64, 252) – and again only Masada's capture will allow Josephus to declare the Judaean war fully over (7.408). In both cases, importantly, the fortresses are occupied mainly by those who have tried to *flee* the violence, especially women and children, whose end becomes tragic.[116] Third, placing Gischala's capture in Book 4 (4.84–120) allows Josephus to explain how John of Gischala, who will dominate the later narrative, made the fateful transition from Galilee to Jerusalem. That story creates much anticipation of famous John's activities.

To Gamala, then. The site has not appeared in *War* except in the list of sites captured by Alexander Jannaeus (104–76 B.C.: 1.105), being mentioned again only when Josephus receives it as defensive responsibility adjacent to Galilee. So he allegedly fortifies Gamala with walls, tunnels, and trenches (2.568, 574; 4.9). When he introduces the site's imminent fall, he says that, whereas other settlements in the Golan had confirmed their loyalty to King Agrippa (4.4), Gamala was holding out, its natural defences – better than those of Iotapata – attracting outside dissidents. Agrippa had already ordered the site besieged, in circumstances unclarified, but given his failure (4.10) Vespasian will deal with it as an addendum to his favour.

Gamala is much more prominent in *Life*. That story is broken up across the narrative and hardly lucid, but the main point for us is that its problems clearly have to do with local and personal struggles, not with animosity toward Rome. These struggles are bound up with the Babylonian Judaeans that King Herod had settled in the region (*Ant.* 17.23–30), their current star Philip son of Iakim (Jacimus), who is Agrippa's aide and prefect of the cavalry troop that the king dispatched urgently to Jerusalem (*War* 2.418–21), and Agrippa's Ituraean lieutenant Noarus/Varus, who took advantage of his short period as acting ruler to move against prominent Judaeans in the kingdom (Chapter 4).

According to *Life*,[117] after Philip's troop was released by Jerusalem's militants, ahead of the auxiliary massacre, he fled back north to Agrippa's territories. From a village near Gamala, he wrote to assure Agrippa that he had survived the trouble in Jerusalem. But Noarus, receiving Agrippa's letter in the king's absence, saw an opportunity to get rid of this Judaean rival. He executed the couriers who had brought Philip's letter on the brilliant charge that *they* had monstrously accused Philip of defecting to Jerusalem's rebels. He would not stand by and watch a fine soldier be tarnished by such accusations, which

---

[116] *War* 7.5–19 [7.5: "[Titus] having now settled everything pertaining to the war"], 23–25, 65, 67, 119–162.

[117] See Drexler 1925: 306–12; Cohen 1979: 160–69; J. J. Price 1991: 82–90. At *War* 2.437, the captured royal troops are freed. They remain in Jerusalem until at 2.556 Philip joins others fleeing Jerusalem and going to visit the recently defeated legate, Cestius.

he then propagated widely (*Life* 48–53). When the baffled Philip learned that his relatives were fleeing to Gamala's defences for protection against Noarus, he joined them in the fortress town.

Interestingly, they were inclined to assume that Noarus was acting with Agrippa's complicity, because their relations with Agrippa had soured for unknown reasons. Philip somehow persuaded them that their suspicions of his commander the king were unfounded and so he managed to keep Gamala loyal (*Life* 46, 61). Agrippa, however, infers that their flight to Gamala is an act of defiance. So, after removing Noarus, he sends Aequus Modius, a Roman military aide, to besiege Gamala (*Life* 114). When Philip discovers that his old friend Modius is conducting the siege, he writes to him. Modius, delighted to learn of his friend's survival and loyalty, in spite of the rumours, cheerfully informs Agrippa. The relieved king sends a cavalry escort to accompany Philip and the Babylonian Judaeans back to their homes (*Life* 179–84).

Now that Gamala is left with its own population, however, a certain Joseph son of Yair persuades the town's own leading men to defect *from the king* and arm themselves. The burghers of Gamala are not keen on this move and take some persuading, but Josephus presents the situation much as that in Tiberias and later Jerusalem. The leaders oppose rebellion, but energetic armed factions under charismatic leaders compel the nobles to show patriotic spirit – or face execution. Among the victims in Gamala are a Babylonian-Judaean relative of Philip's named Chares (*Life* 177, 186) and a certain Jesus, who happens to be Justus of Tiberias' brother-in-law (178, 186). The death-defying loyalty to Agrippa of these men, if it reflects reality, *might* suggest similar loyalties on the part of Philip and Justus.

Here is an oddity. The name Chares is rare in Josephus and appears only in connection with Gamala. Yet *Life* makes Philip's relative Chares a prominent victim of Gamala's militants, whereas *War* describes one Chares as the town's diehard leader in opposing Agrippa, and a victim of Vespasian's later assault (*War* 4.18, 68). Although these thus appear to be different men, can we be sure that Josephus knew who was who, given his Gallus confusions above? Another peculiarity is that *War* 4.81 has two adult daughters of Philip's sisters remaining in Gamala until its fall to the Flavians, becoming the only survivors and thus anticipating the two women who survive Masada (7.399).

Josephus' references to Gamala have enough twists to power giant speculative mills.[118] If Philip was keeping Gamala loyal to Agrippa, why did Modius besiege it? If they were friends, and just a few hundred metres apart, how could they not have known of each other for months? Why did some of Philip's relatives remain after his departure, in stubborn rebellion against Agrippa? What was

---

[118] See the judicious analysis of Price 1991.

Philip's relationship with *them*? It has tempted scholars to imagine that Philip himself, just as Noarus charged, actually joined anti-royal or anti-Roman militants. Because his troop had survived Jerusalem, he and the king by association would reportedly be accused of abetting the Judaean revolt. But the king's loyalty to Rome (in spite of anger at Florus) is hard to doubt, and his welcoming of Philip seems to settle that issue (*Life* 52, 407). Perhaps we must fall back on *Life*'s rich atmosphere of double games, hidden agendas, contradictory behaviour, and malicious accusations against rivals, along with Josephus' limitations, as a general explanation of the puzzles and contrary indications.

Although we cannot recover details, it seems that the issues at Gamala, as in Tiberias and Taricheae, concerned relations with Agrippa and not with the emperor, the Syrian legate, or even Florus far away in Caesarea.

When Josephus describes Gamala's fall, he adds the intriguing notice: "the revolt having begun on the 24th of the month Gorpiaeus (*War* 4.83)." This date, just two weeks after Taricheae's pacification, is in tension with his remark that Gamala had been a holdout from early on. It also seems not to include the whole business with Noarus and Philip (4.4). Josephus may be assuming that Gamala became a pressing issue after the reconciliation of Agrippa and Philip the previous autumn, only with the Flavians' action at Taricheae, when any still surviving opponents of Agrippa fled east to the remote fortress, dangerously supplementing a population that had once again resolved on conflict with the king.

War portrays the fall of Gamala, tragic-heroic though it was, as rapid. The story follows Josephus' pattern for fortress-like sites. It begins with a dramatic description of the geography, highlighting the walls and the difficulty of access (*War* 4.2–10; cf. 2.574). His portrait, which is germane to the story of Gamala's capture, matches well the archaeological finds:

> Both its sides and its face are cut off by inaccessible ravines, though the tail end provides relief from this harsh terrain where it clings to the mountain [on the east side]; then again, the locals have made this difficult of access too, by cutting a trench across it. The houses, which had been built onto that upright side, were packed in on one another in a frightful way. Suspended like that, the city looked as though it were crashing down upon itself, given the steepness. It inclined toward the south and the south-facing hill, stretching up to an enormous height, was also the citadel of the city, beyond which an unwalled precipice fell off [on the north side] into the deepest ravine. (*War* 4.6–8)

The Gamala episode also nourishes many themes of the work (Chapter 2). A Roman commander who moves quickly and confidently against Judaeans meets more vigorous resistance than expected. An initial repulse demoralizes Romans, calling for sober reflection, cautious planning, and a rousing commander-speech. The Judaeans display unimaginable heroism, if ultimately in a losing cause. The site is finally taken in a victory of Roman discipline and technical siege-craft, and the besieged meet their fate through battle, suicide, or the conquering army's vengeance.

Realizing that Agrippa has been unable to bring Gamala to heel, in that siege led by Modius, as we know from *Life* (*War* 4.4, 14), Vespasian moves his army up from the springs near Tiberias to the Golan plateau (4.4). Agrippa and his cavalry are still present, but Vespasian has sent Titus for talks with Mucianus in the north. Vespasian does not seem worried in the slightest. He camps his vast army on the hills around Gamala. He posts as many guards as the terrain allows and orders the Fifth and Fifteenth legions to build ramps on the east side. The Tenth, meanwhile, begins filling up the trenches and preparing level ground for an assault (4.13). As always, the intended psychological effect is paramount. Agrippa, the residents' ostensible sovereign, steps up to invite surrender in their native Aramaic (4.14). But as he bellows his no doubt masterful appeal, his arms extended, a Judaean has the temerity to nail his right elbow with a rock (4.14–15). So ends the diplomacy.

As at Iotapata, Vespasian adapts his tactics to the conditions. Seeing no hope of a quick surrender, he decides on a shock assault. His army breaks into the town on their first attempt through three breach-points. They surge in with trumpets blaring and war-cries (4.19–20), and the defenders yield. Whether by design or luck, however, the defenders quickly find themselves in an advantageous position, looming above the Romans on the steep slope. The Romans, pressed forward relentlessly by the mass pouring in behind them, can only advance uphill through narrow streets in single file, while armed Judaeans hurl deadly projectiles from above, which are bound to hit *someone*. Unable to turn around or to find shelter, the soldiers jump onto the wooden roofs of the "stacked" houses, which promptly collapse under their weight and create general mayhem. The legionaries had not expected casualties, but it is all they can do to regain their breach-points and flee this trap. Vespasian is personally caught in the melee and imperilled, although his poise enables him to make a step-by-step retreat while calming the soldiers around him (4.17–38).

The dejection resulting from this rout elicits a rousing speech from Vespasian, who blames the terrain and the soldiers' impetuosity – no credit to the Judaeans – and urges them on to a more methodical, more *Roman* effort (4.39–48). Although the people of Gamala are momentarily elated, they realize they have also forfeited any hope of safe surrender under terms. Those who have sufficient courage therefore *escape* via ravines and tunnels. Those who stay, we notice, do so because they are *terrified of being caught* and killed (4.50–53). This is a striking psychological observation, confirming that people will reject an immediate risk that *might* bring them safety for the *near certainty of a death* slightly postponed, because the immediate danger of bold action immobilizes them. Only a few of the frightened townsfolk who remain are even capable of bearing arms. And as later in Jerusalem, the few tough young fighters who do remain monopolize the scarce food supplies.

The end comes quickly. Three soldiers from the Fifteenth, among those assigned to the defensive tower on the northeast hill (Fig. 22), undermine it. The tower collapses in the early darkness of mid-October. Panicked residents hearing the din run in all directions. In this chaos the town's two militant leaders meet their ends: Joseph while trying to escape, Chares from a heart attack while recuperating from wounds received in the first assault (4.66–67). The rest is a story of unremitting slaughter against the weak remnants of Gamala's population. Uncharacteristically but notably, the slaughter is led by Titus, who has returned from his visit to Mucianus and become outraged that the army – under his father's command – has not yet succeeded. Entering with picked cavalry and infantry he wreaks vengeance (4.70–72): "From every side, the groaning of those being slaughtered was interminable, and blood was flooding over the whole city, pouring down the slopes" (4.72).

Vespasian then brings in the main force – or in imaginable reality, a fraction of it. The legionaries are so enraged by their earlier humiliation that they do not spare even infants, but seize toddlers and throw them from the high citadel (4.82). Although Judaeans do everything possible to hold them back, raining down rocks from a momentarily superior position, a tremendous gale unbalances those on the tiny summit and drives the Romans' projectiles against the defenders with added force (4.73–78). So it was that (4.79):

> Despairing of a safe outcome from any quarter, the masses took hold of their children and wives and threw themselves over the precipice into the ravine. This had been dug out to its lowest depth [as a defensive trench] beneath the citadel.

Given Josephus' dramatic exaggerations, we may incline to doubt even the core of the story. But Gamala's north side, although not a cliff, is steep indeed, especially from the highest small peak, and its floor today will have filled up over the centuries.

Anyone who doubts that civilians *can* react this way under such pressure, killing their families and themselves, should consider such well-documented examples as the murder-suicides of civilians during the U.S. occupation of Saipan Island in July 1944.[119] With its garrison of 31,600 Japanese soldiers, the island was also home to a large population of Japanese-Okinawan and Korean families. Most of the defending soldiers died in the American assault, frequently by suicide, with about two-thirds of the civilians.[120] The remaining civilians were understandably desperate. Matthew Hughes has argued that

---

[119] Burleigh 2010: 516.
[120] For the statistics and details, see Rottman 2002: 376–380 (379 for casualty numbers).

cultural stereotypes (e.g., "No Japanese will surrender"; "The Americans are giant demons who rape and torture") shaped this rare encounter between U.S. Marines and a civilian population.[121] Many civilians died by their own hands, some helped along by bullets from Japanese soldiers. Some soldiers exploded grenades under themselves. But an estimated 1,000 plunged to their deaths from the 61-m (200-ft) cliffs at Marpi Point on the island's north end, having run out of room to flee the American advance. Just as in Josephus' account of Masada (Chapter 9), fathers killed wives and children before taking their own lives. Footage of those scenes is easily available. Although Josephus' numbers are too large for the landscape (and Vespasian's army, about the size of the U.S. invasion force at Saipan, could not have entered little Gamala), the responses he describes accord with human experience.[122]

As for questions of motive and morale, Americans understood that the Japanese expectation of brutal treatment – not irrational given the Marines' reluctance to take prisoners in previous operations and liberal use of flame-throwers and explosive satchels, along with the recent innovation of napalm – played a large role in people's decision to kill themselves. Josephus regularly returns to the question of how *Judaeans thought* Romans would treat them if they surrendered as a crucial factor in deciding what they would do (Chapter 3). In the case of Gamala, he relates that, after those who held out their arms in surrender were savagely cut down, the rest despaired and jumped (4.78–79).

We turn finally to Gischala,[123] which was neither a possession of Agrippa nor of evident concern to Vespasian. Perhaps it was merely unfinished business. Josephus claims that most of the townspeople wanted nothing more than to farm their crops in peace. But some had been influenced by "a sizable bandit gang" from elsewhere, and by John, who thought that war would bring him personal power (*War* 4.84–86). Had these factors not prevented them, the Gischalans would have immediately sent emissaries declaring their submission. Even still, Vespasian does not simply attack this remote and populous town. How he heard of John's alleged ambitions we do not know. The obvious possibility is that Josephus suggested that the Flavians visit his old enemy.

After the bloodshed of Gamala, in any case, Vespasian dismisses his now tired infantry to winter quarters: the Tenth to Scythopolis and the others with himself to Caesarea. He sends Titus with a thousand horsemen to deal with John and Gischala (4.87–88), evidently expecting a quick capitulation. On his arrival, Titus finds John's little wall laughable. He could easily take the town by

---

[121] Hughes 2010.

[122] E.g., www.youtube.com/watch?v=eDUyouzmaU4 (accessed November 10, 2011).

[123] Rabbinic Gush Ḥalav (something like "dense area/block/centre of milk"; modern El-Jish (Arabic). For Gush Ḥalav in the rabbis see *j. Sheb.* 9.2.4.1c; *Meg.* 1.2.3l; *b. Pes. 53a*; *Men.* 85b.

storm if he wished, he observes, but he prefers to make an offer they cannot refuse (4.92–94). He gives a speech in the spirit of Thucydides' Melian Dialogue: "Your desire for freedom is very nice, but we are here and you have no options. You have seen others surrender (Sepphoris, Tiberias) and live to enjoy their possessions. So do the same. Or die – it's your call" (4.94–96).

I suggested that Josephus includes this episode in Book 4 as a lead-in to John's role in Jerusalem. The story displays the defining aspects of John's character in Josephus' portrait, treacherous and self-serving, that will later prove fatal for Jerusalem. Here John pretends to accept Titus' analysis of the situation as indeed obvious. But it is Friday afternoon, and he asks with moral force that his people be permitted to observe their sabbath (4.97–102). John's motive is fear, Josephus adds: He cannot trust the Romans to spare him (4.103).[124] Astonishingly – Josephus diplomatically shifts the responsibility from Titus to God's designs for John (4.104) – Titus accepts the pious request.

He goes much farther than even John recommends, indeed, leaving the town entirely unguarded as he rides off with his cavalry to Tyre's village of Kedasa (Kedesh) for dinner and a good sleep, more than 10 km (6 mi) away. He returns the next morning to find that he was fooled. John has absconded during a sabbath night with thousands of others and is now well on his way to Jerusalem. His character is such that he has abandoned those who could not keep up, especially women and children (4.106–11). Titus' 1,000 riders cannot catch John and his fit crew, but they do catch and kill 6,000 of the slower ones, while they courteously bring back 3,000 women and children (in wagons?). As always the numbers defy belief. In Gischala Titus is received with acclamations by the remaining townspeople. He allows them the quiet life they have desired, with a garrison for company (4.112–20).

Josephus' Galilee narrative: character and morale

Before proceeding to our reconstruction I would offer two general observations on *War* 3.1–4.120.

First, this is an integral and substantial part of the work. It advances the plot, complicates the characters (e.g., Vespasian, Titus, Josephus, John), and develops leading motifs. This observation may seem trite, but it has implications for our use of the story. Take the famous digression on the legions (3.70–109) and Vespasian's order of march (3.115–26). Historians tend to excise these as rare evidence for legionary practice, if not as proof that Josephus is

---

[124] *What* trouble is unclear, because John has figured as the opponent of (the rebel general) Josephus, who has confined him to Gischala at 2.632 and kept him out of the narrative since. At 4.85 we read that John has been inciting Gischala to rebellion, but what that means (flying black flags? throwing rocks at passersby?) is hard to picture.

trying to advocate Rome's invincibility.[125] But Josephus' arrangement, language, and emphases appear purposeful. "No disorder," he says, "interferes with their customary formation; no alarm confounds them; no fatigue exhausts them. And so their mastery over those [enemies] who lack a similar firmness always follows" (3.74).

By describing the legions in this glowing way, he achieves a number of things. First, he buffs his image as a statesman-historian in the tradition of Polybius, who had portrayed the Republican legions as the epitome of Rome's character (Polybius 6.19–42). Second, Josephus makes vivid what he and his Galileans are up against. Who could blame them for losing? The massive killing machine that forms up in Ptolemais easily explains why the whole region welcomes Vespasian, why Josephus' army dissolves, and why he flees to Tiberias. Third, these descriptions throw into stark relief the courage of the few who dare to face Rome, including his amazing self. Fourth, this framework sets up *War*'s later volumes, which routinely portray legionaries in disarray when facing the native spirit of Judaeans.

My other general observation is that Josephus, like Julius Caesar,[126] is well attuned to the psychological questions we considered in Chapter 3. In his picture of Placidus, whom he elsewhere claims personally to have intimidated before the Flavians' arrival (*Life* 215, 227), Josephus evokes the tribune's hope that "fear [or awe, δέος] would induce the other cities of Galilee to surrender, once the strongest had been taken" (3.111), before adding: "[H]e was much mistaken in this hope" (3.312). Because of Josephus' fortifications and Iotapata's courage, "Placidus finds himself too weak for an attack on the city and flees" (3.314).

It is Placidus' humiliating retreat that leads Josephus to describe Vespasian's order of march (3.115–26), which in turn sets up the contest between the two *real* generals at Iotapata: the Roman with every conceivable advantage, the Judaean left to his wits and divine aid. As soon as Vespasian's army is in Galilean territory, he parades it "with a view to creating terror [κατάπληξις] among the enemy while also offering the chance for reconsideration, in case they would change their minds before it came to blows" (3.127). This creates "in many regret [μετάνοια] for the revolt and in all terror [κατάπληξις]" (3.128). Most Judaeans would happily capitulate *if* they could trust the Romans, but they cannot (3.130). When Vespasian arrives outside Iotapata, again, he arrays his legions on the opposite hill – "trying to be as conspicuous as possible to the enemy, so as to create *panic* [ἔκπληξις]." The main purpose of

---

[125] For the latter, see Thackeray 1929: 27–28; Laqueur 1970 [1920]: 126–27. For the former, Goldsworthy 1996: 105–11; Keppie 1998: 197–98, where Josephus' "idealised account" of the army forms much of the conclusion; Gilliver 1999: 9 et passim.

[126] *Bell. gall.* 1.39–41; 4.34; 5.15–16.

Josephus' 30-ft wall is to block that demoralizing view. At *War* 3.175, in turn, his construction of the wall terrifies (καταπλήσσω) the Romans. The dripping-clothes deception causes "faint-heartedness and terror among the Romans" (ἀθυμία τῶν Ῥωμαίων καὶ κατάπληξις; 3.188), emotions increased when he deadens the impact of their rams by hanging sacks of chaff over the wall (3.222–25). The Judaeans' intrepid sorties and burning of siege-works *terrorize* the Romans (3.169, 177, 205–206, 227–35), and a Judaean archer's injury to Vespasian creates widespread *panic* (ἔκπληξις, 3.237). While the legionaries are breaching the wall, on the other hand, their war-cry creates *terror* (κατάπληξις) for the Judaeans (3.250). Odysseus-like Josephus orders his men to block their ears (3.259). In the later Taricheae story, again, the rebel fighters outside Taricheae create *terror* (κατάπληξις) among Titus' troops (3.471, 474).

One of Josephus' trenchant observations about Judaean morale is that they do not fight in hope of victory. They *know that they will die* if they fall into Roman hands; so they prefer to die as men retaining a vestige of control. Having attracted Rome's wrath, even if quite unintentionally, they fight with commitment *because* they have abandoned hope of living (3.152). Likewise, when Josephus resigns himself to remaining in Iotapata, he declares that the time for glorious action is "when there is no hope of a safe outcome" (3.204). With surrender off the table, the only options are dying on the enemy's terms or on their own (3.189). Josephus admonishes each man to enter the fray "not for the sake of saving the ancestral home, but for the sake of avenging it – as already destroyed. He should place before his eyes the slaughter of the elderly and the annihilation of the children and the women, which was at hand," and exact his *retribution in advance* (3.260–61).

Vespasian understands such motivation. That is why he cautions his legionaries not to emulate Judaean feats of daring. These are the actions of desperate men. Romans fight by choice and rely on method, skill, and discipline (3.210–11). In Josephus' hands, such an asymmetrical conflict becomes also a test of character on both sides.

IV. RECONSTRUCTION: ROMANS AND JUDAEANS IN GALILEE, A.D. 67

Impressions of the Flavian campaign in Galilee are inevitably shaped by our understanding of what preceded and followed it. The prevailing view sees it through the lens of the conclusion in Jerusalem, the triumph, and Josephus' mournful retrospective. A province of Judaea exploded in revolt after long-mounting tensions with Rome and boldly declared its independence. When the incompetent Cestius failed to stifle the revolt, Nero sent Vespasian.

Because Galilee was part of this national revolt, Vespasian methodically crushed it in preparation for the decisive attack on Jerusalem.

Approaching the evidence without such assumptions and asking different questions, I have argued that the common picture both assumes and explains too much. If we imagine how things looked to those at the time, screening out later developments and working from what had happened earlier, we can imagine a simpler picture. This does not come simply from reading Josephus' narrative. But the largely overlooked structure of *War* 3, distinguishing cleanly between a submissive Galilee and Agrippa II's restive cities, was not something he could easily have invented in Flavian Rome and with Agrippa as collaborator (Chapter 2). If we build tentatively from that basic framework, keeping in proportion his self-focus in *War* 3, drawing in archaeology and scraps of information from elsewhere, and using our historical–analogical imaginations, we might postulate the following sort of scenario.

As Nero's later reign repositioned the critical checks and balances that had protected Jerusalem from regional antagonism and envy, elements of the Judaean populace became extremely worried, and when they felt immediately vulnerable some turned to armed self-help. The legate Cestius continued to work with Jerusalem's leaders, understanding Florus' depredations and that the city was not in revolt. But he had to punish visibly those who had crossed the line into vigilantism and violence against the auxiliary, while showing all sides that he was in control. So his reluctant military intervention was a study in contrasts: killing and burning to strengthen his power of deterrence while hoping to consolidate his relationships with the main population centres. It almost worked. But in the brutal side of his programme, he unwittingly created many new and desperate Judaean enemies of Rome.

Vespasian, a younger alumnus of Claudius' court and Antonia Minor's salon, also realized that Judaeans, as Rome's most prominent friends in southern Syria, were not in revolt. Like Cestius he had no qualms about killing innocents and burning villages to make necessary points, and Nero had instructed him to punish Judaeans for the ambush of Cestius. But as soon as he and Agrippa II arrived in Ptolemais, *polis* elites from across the region rushed to welcome them, while pointing fingers at each other. This bickering was par for the course and to some extent encouraged by Roman leaders (Chapter 4). Sepphoris requested a large garrison to make their position clear, while ostentatiously submitting on behalf of Roman Galilee. Tiberias and Taricheae likewise welcomed their king, a crucial member of Vespasian's entourage, although Decapolis complained about Tiberian aggression with momentary success. So from Vespasian's perspective, there was no prospect of a *war* against Rome in Galilee. The region submissively welcomed him as it had Cestius before him. He garrisoned that area as well as Samaria and the central coastal plain as far as Caesarea – rapidly in the spring of 67.

Vespasian's tactics resembled those of Cestius, in keeping with the adages attributed to Augustus: "Make haste, slowly!" and "A thing is done quickly enough if it is done well."[127] There was no reason for unnecessary risks. Begin with overwhelming intimidation and proceed incrementally, responding to circumstances as needed. Villages empty of fighters and open plains were the best places for display violence. Captured prisoners could be treated according to whim and situation, but it was in Rome's interest to treat the *poleis*, their cooperative leaders, and their fixed assets with care, aiming for bloodless capitulation wherever possible. The main difference from Cestius' expedition was that Vespasian, beginning in early spring, had much more time.

Like his predecessor, nevertheless, he balanced the meaning-laden destruction with diplomatic approaches to the *polis* leaders. Gabara and its villages he allowed his soldiers to destroy in revenge for Cestius, as an outlet for a rage he needed to keep boiling though channeled, but he was exceedingly careful with Sepphoris and Agrippa's eastern *poleis*. Most villages emptied at the news of his army's arrival, but a few populations felt safe enough to remain, likely assuming they were covered by Sepphoris' effective diplomacy and lacking any intention to draw attention to themselves.

The constant presence of large military patrols filled with soldiers itching for a reason to exercise their might in the group created opportunities for disaster, however. Iotapata appears to be the clearest example. The tribune Placidus decided to attack the town with a modest patrol, because he could and possibly to take further revenge for his late commander Cestius. (NB: Placidus might have been caught in the ambush at Beit-Horon.) The momentary success of Iotapata's men in driving him away sealed their doom. When Vespasian reached Sepphoris, Mr. Gentle reported to him that Iotapata was one site that needed to be taught a lesson. So after his revenge attack on Gabara to blood his force, Vespasian's entire army appeared at Iotapata's door. Josephus had in the meantime heard of Placidus' menace and raced to his old base from the safety of Agrippa's territory (Tiberias). Knowing the townspeople, he went to see whether he could assist them in finding a way out. When he realized that Vespasian meant to erase the town and that he could not help them, he tried to flee but became trapped in a most unpleasant siege through June of 67.

Iotapata was, however, the only apparent exception to Vespasian's confirmation that Roman Galilee was peaceful – the very position Josephus had been sent to confirm (*Life*). After Iotapata's fall, Vespasian planned a lengthy period of rest and training for whatever would await his army in the very different situation of the Judaean hills the next summer. While Vespasian was relaxing with Agrippa, however, the king pleaded for help with his two

---

[127] *Festina lente* (σπεῦδε βραδέως) per Suetonius, *Aug.* 25.3. Also "a safe commander is preferable to a bold one."

lakeside cities, Tiberias and Taricheae. He was worried about the increased boldness of anti-royal agitators, especially the populist president of the *polis* assembly that year, who was encouraged accidentally by Josephus.

Vespasian aided the king by recalling his forces and making short and sharp visits to Tiberias and then Taricheae, rooting out Jesus and the other anti-Roman militants, identified by the *polis* leaders, without badly damaging either place. His favour would have to be extended to include Gamala, however, whose residents were in conflict with Agrippa, perhaps partly through a misunderstanding of Noarus' actions against the region's Judaeans. The natural fortress had attracted the last of the surviving disaffected – with angry and the fearful – from elsewhere.

Plainly Vespasian was in no hurry to head south, to the region of intense conflict among Jerusalem and its neighbours and the scene of attacks on auxiliary and legionary units. Benefits for Vespasian from the protracted and quiet year in Galilee might have included the following.

1. He might have been thrilled to be relieved of his role as cheerleader for the young artist-emperor on his Greek tour, to be back commanding tens of thousands of soldiers with absolute authority and no large threats to deal with.

2. Lower Galilee was almost paradisical for an invading army on such terms. It was temperate, luxuriant in crops and orchards, an easy place to find food and build shelter (*War* 3.42–47). There was relatively low risk of disease. Although there were likely malarial zones near the Jordan valley, the soldiers had no reason to linger there. Even during the siege of Iotapata they could rotate in and out, with Sepphoris or even Ptolemais a short distance away. And Vespasian could make full use of his army's many components – infantry, horse, archers, engineers – in such a varied landscape.

3. Opportunities for morale-building and skills training abounded. With the population basically cooperative, Vespasian could order brief and intense bouts of combat, entirely on his terms and with manufactured enemies if needed. Iapha was an easy day's work with a small walled town. Iotapata's month-plus siege[128] provided training in siege work, against a living enemy but in the most favourable environment imaginable.

4. Between these intense but low-risk engagements, the army enjoyed generous periods of recreation. Vespasian, the soldier's soldier, took every opportunity to offer them rest, even extended time commandeering Tiberias' renowned hot springs. These considerations would strengthen their feeling of comfort in the climate and culture, confidence, and mastery of the landscape as they prepared for whatever the south might have in store.

---

[128] Cf. *War* 3.142, 145, 339 for the length of the siege (Josephus departs Tiberias for Iotapata on 21 Artemisius, Vespasian's army arrives a day or two after his arrival, and the town falls on 1 Panemus, so about five weeks later), whereas 3.316, 406 cite a siege of forty-seven days.

5. Vespasian might have hoped, by prolonging his stay in the north, to draw out the more vigorous fighters from the south to Galilee's defence, where he could deal with them on his terms. The more men like Josephus he could isolate and eliminate up there, the easier his task would be in Judaea proper. Jerusalem could not have very many skilled fighters, after all, much less competent commanders. Titus thus made a fateful error in allowing John of Gischala's flight in the opposite direction. Jerusalem's militant factions must have understood these considerations, and that would explain why they made no effort to help protect rural Galilee. Vespasian would have to come to them and face them on their terms.

6. It is conceivable that Vespasian hoped to secure the submission of Jerusalem and Judaea proper, while he was still in Galilee and Samaria – that embassies would come to him and offer the capital city on terms of security. Why not? Why would they remain defiant when he was so clearly master of the land from the day of his arrival? A critical issue would be his treatment of those who surrendered. His conspicuous friendliness toward Sepphoris and Agrippa's cities in the north, once unburdened of their militants, was likely calculated in part to build a reputation for mercy for all those who willingly welcomed him in advance. That would give a kind of truth to Titus' alleged claim that Vespasian lingered in Galilee to give Jerusalem time to reconsider, although this would not have been from simple kindness. Of course there would need to be a reckoning for the assaults on Roman forces, but Vespasian could reasonably have hoped for embassies in Galilee of the kind he received in Ptolemais and later in Caesarea.

7. Galilee was politically safe for Vespasian. As long as he found little "victories" to keep him occupied, he could keep reporting his successes to Nero: scores of Judaean towns and villages destroyed, burned, subdued. If he was already concerned about Nero's survivability, which is quite possible given the atmosphere in Rome (Chapter 5), prolonging his time in Galilee would have been wise. He could delay investing much in a Judaean campaign, for uncertain and possibly dangerous political outcomes. He could wait to see what happened in Rome, and what the *meaning* of his little war would be for whoever was in power (Chapter 1).

Even as Vespasian's lengthy stay in Galilee brought him multiple benefits, it must have played havoc with Judaean morale. No Judaean could have anticipated where or how quickly the Romans would advance. For those in the Judaean hills the long wait must have been torture. Samaria was firmly in Roman hands, as we have seen: "the whole of Samaria had been garrisoned with forts" (3.309). Samaria's leaders must have quickly confirmed their peaceful intentions from the outset, as others had done, and welcomed garrisons.

This means that from the moment of his arrival in Ptolemais in spring of 67, Vespasian instantly dominated the whole country from Lebanon to Judaea's frontier, perhaps as close as 40 km (25 mi) from Jerusalem. The route south to Caesarea obviously presented no problems for him in mid-67, as he moved legions back and forth from Galilee at will. Idumaea was not yet part of a revolt (Chapter 7). So most of the land was under Roman control from Day One. Because Titus would not bring the legions to Jerusalem's walls for another *three years*, however, the long period of encirclement must have been agonizing. Residents of Jerusalem in particular could have had no idea what would become of them or when the sword might fall. They only knew that the Romans were not like to leave.

As Josephus focuses on his own activities in Galilee, he breaks away from Jerusalem. When he returns to it in *War* 4, we immediately see signs of extreme desperation and deep factionalism in the mother-city. It is not long before Jerusalem's chief priests are murdered and Simon bar Giora rampages through the frontier zones, while John of Gischala's arrival upsets alliances. We see a population in panic, its powerful men having gone too far to turn back, but violently disagreeing over how to proceed. The legions' occupation of Galilee and menacing presence nearby in Samaria must have contributed greatly, I would suggest, to the pressures generating this atmosphere. Judaea was under effective siege from the spring of 67.

The only two connections Josephus makes with Jerusalem in Book 3 concern himself, and both happen to mention plummeting morale in his home city. First, when his army dissolves and everyone is demoralized (πεπτώκοι τὰ φρονήματα; 3.130, 142), he writes to Jerusalem asking for support or instructions. Jerusalem's leaders know what is happening in Galilee and must be terrified, but they have nothing to offer. The other incident is darkly humorous but points the same way. News of Iotapata's fall makes Jerusalemites all the more despondent as they take in "the scope of the disaster" (3.432). According to *War*, they plunge into mourning for thirty days, thinking they have lost a heroic Josephus, but this rapidly turns to hatred when they learn he is alive and with the Romans. We may discount much of this, but the story plausibly suggests that Jerusalemites were acutely conscious of events in Galilee, with an eye to their own perils. If the Romans had suffered some terrible setback or political events had forced the Flavians to abandon the campaign, it would have brought enormous relief. Vespasian's immediate domination of the country and occasional displays of terrific violence, by contrast, must have paralyzed many people with fear.

Having pondered Vespasian's aims and interests in Galilee, we cannot meaningfully discuss those of a Judaean army and its command because there was none. We are limited to asking about Josephus' aims in Galilee. Was he a dedicated rebel against Rome, as Justus claimed (*Life* 340, 350)? Or was he hoping to enter into talks with Agrippa and Vespasian – to "betray" Galilee from the perspective of resolute militants (*Life* 129, 132)? How far did a sense of honour or duty toward the populace enter into his thinking? Did he change his attitude at different moments, ready to die in Galilee's defence while hoping for a safe conclusion (*Life* 17–29; cf. *War* 2.651)?

It seems to me that we may be fairly sure of two things. First, Josephus' personal motives are not recoverable in fine from his reports about himself. He confesses both his desire to flee and his programmatic duplicity, yet he energetically defends Iotapata. And he seems to oppose men who should be his kindred spirits in Sepphoris, Tiberias, and Gischala. These complications provide abundant material for speculation unfavourable to our author, but any cartoonish images of Josephus leave a sticky residue of much unexplained evidence. Without knowing the historical answers, I would suggest that the evidence is of a recognizable human being who found himself in extremely difficult circumstances, being pulled by competing motives and constituencies, and unavoidably having to present different faces to different people – all of that apart from his later literary interests.

Second, whatever strategic thinking Josephus may have managed would have depended on his assessment of Vespasian's moves and Jerusalem's responses. That was the only course open to him, even if he had not said so (*Life* 29). We find him, plausibly, writing letters to Jerusalem at key points, explaining developments and requesting guidance (*War* 3.138–40; *Life* 62, 266–70, 309–12). In the spring of 67 many possibilities were still open to Vespasian and Josephus alike, and neither could have known how things would go. But Josephus did not head to Tabor or Gamala or Asamon to barricade himself. Given that Iotapata was better suited to access and communication than a glorious last stand, and given his believable desire to leave when the situation became untenable, we might conclude that he went there to negotiate if possible, hoping to protect the victimized and vulnerable towns-folk he had come to know.

We can say something about what Josephus in Galilee was not. The evidence makes it difficult to understand why he should be singled out for cowardice. Any prospect of militant opposition to the legions in Lower Galilee's gentle terrain was practically hopeless from the start, even if there had been a desire for it. That is clear. The councils from Sepphoris, Agrippa's *poleis*, the Decapolis, and elsewhere followed the only sensible course in pre-emptively embracing the Flavians with their army. Jerusalem's leaders had no resources with which to defend any part of Galilee that found itself vulnerable. The great John of Gischala fled when he realized that he had been noticed. No matter what we might *speculate* about Josephus' character or motives, which we do not know, the actions of his life that no one has disputed make him one of very few who deliberately faced the Roman military . He could not have known that he would survive Iotapata. Would we like him better if he had fled like John and helped force Jerusalem's later destruction, leaving Iotapata's families to their devices? Or if he had found a sword to fall on?

We should be pleased that Vespasian did not follow Titus' Clausewitzian option and bypass Galilee for Jerusalem. Josephus would then have been left out of the picture: no defence of Iotapata, no surrender, and no *War* and *Antiquities* from Rome. Josephus' literary legacy is an unintended consequence of Vespasian's decision to linger in Galilee.

EXCURSUS TO CHAPTER 6: SITE IDENTIFICATION (TOPONYMY) IN GALILEE AND GOLAN

We have found reasons to doubt that Josephus always knew who was who or what was what. A related problem cannot, however, be laid at his door: whether *we* know where was where. He left no maps, but only names of sites, often with multiple Greek spellings in our manuscripts of his works. At best he offered rough distances between sites or general observations on their topography. But he omitted both compass directions and clear spatial indications, for which there was no precise language (as with modern grid coordinates). His audiences, which did not yet have our kind of map mentality, had enough information to enjoy the stories and their moral lessons. But if *we* are to think historically about the stories, we need to understand the geography.

When we use modern maps, or visit archaeological parks labelled *Gamala* or *Migdal (Taricheae)*, we might imagine that the ancient sites have somehow identified themselves.[129] Nothing could be farther from the truth. The recent revival of an old hypothesis concerning the location of Taricheae, about which "a violent dispute raged" in the nineteenth century, reminds us of the constant need to justify our assumptions.[130] Nineteenth-century scholars hoped that, with Josephus as guide, the Arabic names of Ottoman villages would preserve ancient names clearly enough to recover the sites. But some names (e.g., Jarash, Jamlah) were used often, and in some cases we do not know what Semitic consonants underlie Greek or Latin forms (e.g., with Cana). Ancient sites cannot in fact declare themselves. Historians must ask, explore, guess, and debate. Three important and interconnected cases for this chapter – Gamala, Taricheae, and Sennabris – illustrate the problem. There is now general agreement about their locations. But this was hard won and it has been challenged again. Thinking historically requires our constant attention to the problem: How do we *know*?

Josephus puts Taricheae 30 *stadia* (6 km, 3.73 mi) from Tiberias along the shore.[131] "Thirty *stadia*" may be formulaic for "an hour's walk" (Appendix A),

---

[129] Rainey and Notley 2006: 14–21.
[130] Kokkinos 2010 revives the hypothesis. The phrase is from Sukenik 1922: 102.
[131] *Life* 96, 132–34, 153, 155–57 (30 *stadia*), 163–68, 276 (he lines the road from Tiberias to Taricheae with messengers for relaying information), 280, 304.

but was the town north or south of Tiberias? Maps drawn until the 1920s locate Taricheae at the south end of the Sea of Galilee, very near or in the bronze-age town of Beit-Yerach (Ptolemaic Philoteria = Kh. al-Karak). This identification resulted mainly from Pliny's location of Taricheae at the south of the lake (*Nat.* 5.71).[132] Other reasons: It was about the right distance from Tiberias; its terrain could be understood as matching Josephus' description; and some scholars found a linguistic link between the last part of Hebrew Bei*tyerach* and the first part of Greek *Taricheae*.[133]

Until the early twentieth century scholarly opinion largely accepted this identification, although such luminaries as Charles W. Wilson (1877), Heinrich Graetz (1880), and Samuel Klein (1909) were doubtful.[134] Wilson rejected Pliny's notice because he found the topography of Beit-Yerach incompatible with the story of Vespasian's pacification of Taricheae. Graetz and Klein argued that Migdal Nunia ("Fish Tower") in rabbinic literature (*b. Pes.* 46a) was four Roman miles north of Tiberias (they emended the text), and that the similarity of names related to fish processing made Migdal the best candidate for Taricheae.[135] In a 1921 article, William F. Albright pursued the case against Pliny on a broad front, finally convincing most scholars to redraw the maps.[136]

Recently Nikos Kokkinos has argued for a return to the old view, locating Taricheae "up to 1.5 km north and north-west of Bet-Yerach," near the southern exit of the Jordan River by the modern Kinneret Moshav. Whereas in 1922 Eliezer Sukenik had declared that "every impartial reader of Josephus . . . sees at once from his descriptions that Taricheae must have been located north of Tiberias," dismissing Pliny's evidence as second or third hand,[137] Kokkinos thinks that Pliny offers crucial "primary evidence." Moreover, "A closer look at the Greek text of the Jewish historian [Josephus] shows that Taricheae *could only* have been located south of Tiberias."[138]

Josephus has been used to tip the scales for or against Pliny. Anticipating Kokkinos, the earlier scholars agreed that "crucial evidence for the location of Taricheae" comes from *War* 4.11.[139] That is where Vespasian begins his march

---

[132] Among many examples, see the matter-of-fact blending of Pliny with Josephus in the careful survey of V. Guérin 1868–1880: Pt. 3 vol. 1. 276–77.

[133] Merrill 1885: 135, who adds that comparing Beit-Yerach with Josephus' description "makes such a conclusion [of identity] almost if not absolutely certain." That would render the Greek meaning of the name ("pickling facilities") superfluous, however, and strangely so, given Strabo's belief that Taricheae was famous for fish-pickling and that the site on the lake identified as Taricheae (Migdal) *was* a known fish-pickling centre.

[134] The standard view is in Boettger 1879: 240, which includes a hesitant note in view of Wilson, just published. See Wilson 1877; Graetz 1880: 484–87; Klein 1909: 76–84.

[135] That is: Migdal Nunia (= "Fish Tower") resembles Taricheae (=“[Fish] Processing Place”).

[136] Albright 1921–1922: 29–45; Kokkinos 2010: 18–19. For the now-standard Albright view, see the reference works Grootkerk 2000: 239, 333; Leibner 2009: 217–19.

[137] Sukenik 1922: 102.   [138] Kokkinos 2010: 7, my emphasis.   [139] Kokkinos 2010: 15.

on Gamala by breaking camp from the hot springs by Tiberias at Hammat. But Josephus' previous reference to Vespasian's camp located it "between Tiberias and Taricheae" (*War* 3.462). Ergo (the argument goes), the hot springs – known to be south of Tiberias – sat between Tiberias and a Taricheae that must have sat farther south.[140]

This syllogistic argument skips a few steps, however. First, in Josephus' account the camp Vespasian establishes to strike at Taricheae seems closer to it than to Tiberias. He fortifies it with care *because* he is so near the enemy. They are so close that Jesus' group is able to rush out and attack the soldiers as they work. And when chased, they flee to boats prepositioned there outside Taricheae. The scene would not work well with the camp at Hammat and Taricheae located at the lake's south end.

A more basic problem is the mechanical logic of the argument: *War* 3.462 mentions *a camp* and 4.11 mentions *a camp*; since camp = camp the two are the same. But narratives change. Vespasian camps between Tiberias and Taricheae at 3.462 *in order to assault* the latter. That is a temporary site built for that purpose. On successful completion of that operation, Vespasian and his army *return to Tiberias* to deal with the captives in Tiberias' stadium. Now they are unquestionably near the hot springs (irrespective of Taricheae's location). Because the pre-Taricheae camp has fulfilled its purpose, the more natural assumption – especially given Vespasian's habit of refreshing his troops whenever possible – is well expressed by Albright: "Evidently Vespasian removed his camp from the plain above Taricheae to the hot springs of Tiberias, . . . where he gave his army a period of relaxation from the toils of war."[141] Vespasian's later departure from these springs to Gamala therefore offers no guide to *Taricheae's* location. The springs are not a fighting camp, but a place of relaxation after battle.

Against Pliny's claim, several passages in Josephus appear to place Taricheae near Migdal to the north. Most obviously, he describes the region south of Tiberias in some detail, and Taricheae does not appear there. At *Life* 42 he relates how Tiberians launched raids against nearby villages, which belonged to Gadara and Hippos of the Decapolis, "which happened to *lie on the frontier between Tiberias and the land belonging to the Scythopolitans*." The edge of Tiberias' *chōra* thus touches that of three Decapolis cities. That is the source of the complaints from Decapolis leaders against Justus of Tiberias.

The possibility that Josephus considered Taricheae so negligible a part of Tiberias' *chōra* that he did not mention it separately is highly unlikely. It was a

---

[140] See Guérin 1868–1880: Pt. 3 vol. 1, 279.

[141] Albright 1921–1922: 40, emphasis added. It is telling that military historian James Bloom, although he assumes Taricheae to have been south of Tiberias because (apparently) of reliance on older maps, as in the Loeb edition of Josephus, nevertheless infers from *War* 4.11 that Vespasian had camped his army at Hammat for recreation (2010: 136).

significant enough *polis* to be stormed by Caesar's assassin Cassius, who supposedly took 30,000 prisoners from there (*Ant.* 14.120). It was a toparchic centre (*toparchia*) with its own dependent villages (*War* 2.252), and it boasted such accoutrements as a hippodrome (*War* 2.599). As we have seen, Nero gave it as a distinct present to King Agrippa, separately from Tiberias and Iulias (*Ant.* 20.159), the villages of all three of these *poleis* being part of the gift. It is not plausible that Josephus overlooked Taricheae when describing Tiberias' *chōra* to the south.

Recall also Josephus' claim that Titus led his cavalry force into Taricheae by riding through the shallow water to bypass the wall, which extended to the shore (*War* 3.497). The Kinneret's depth varies dramatically, reaching its maximum of about 46 m (150 ft) in the northeast sector of the lake bed.[142] The drop from the shoreline is abrupt at most points. At the southern locale it is not as steep as some parts but still reaches a depth of 15 m (50 ft) very quickly.[143] Josephus' image of hundreds (dozens?) of horsemen cantering through shallow water suits the area of Migdal/Ginosar better.

Wilson and Albright thought that the decisive passage was Josephus' description of Vespasian's approach to Tiberias.[144] Titus brings the legion from Caesarea to rendezvous with Vespasian at Scythopolis, south of Tiberias – because "it is the largest [city] of the Decapolis *and a neighbour to Tiberias*" (*War* 3.446). The logic of the story is that Vespasian moves northward from Scythopolis against Tiberias, then continues to Taricheae in pursuit of rebels. How could Taricheae lie *between* Scythopolis and Tiberias? That question raises the problem of locating Sennabris.

Josephus has Vespasian bring his army from Scythopolis as far as Sennabris to intimidate Tiberias. Albright and others took Sennabris to be securely identified with the village of Eṣ-Ṣinnabrah (just north of Kh. al-Karak = Beit-Yerach) – close to Kokkinos' location of Taricheae.[145] Vespasian thus followed the road from Scythopolis up to the lake, camped at Sennabris, and sent the fifty-horse delegation ahead to Tiberias (*War* 3.448–49). Albright realized that Sennabris could not actually be seen from Tiberias, because the shoreline bulges eastward and steep hills rise in between, but he figured that Tiberias' many sailors would have spotted three legions nearby.[146] Because the Romans did not attack Taricheae until after Tiberias, on this plan, it must have been further north.

[142] See the topographic/bathymetric map of the Kinneret region in ben-Avraham et al. 1996: 536.
[143] Albright observed this on the basis of his field experience (1921–1922: 40).
[144] Wilson 1877: 11–12; Albright 1921–1922: 35–40.
[145] Albright 1921–1922: 36–37. A site of this name was the home of the dissident Muslim caliph Muʻawyia in the seventh century; Gil 1992: 78.
[146] Albright 1921–1922: 36. Kokkinos (2010: 14) nevertheless emphasizes the problem of visibility.

To make the southern location of Taricheae (at traditional Sennabris) plausible, Kokkinos must find another site for Sennabris as a staging camp before Tiberias. He locates it inland, west and slightly north of Tiberias near the Horns of Ḥattin. This is a bold move. Even those who argued for a southern Taricheae were sure that Sennabris was beside it in the south. But that would leave Vespasian's movements very puzzling. In Kokkinos' reconstruction, Vespasian did not take that direct road north to Tiberias from Scythopolis. Instead, he brought his force from Scythopolis in a clockwise motion, first to Sennabris *in the west*, then southeast to Tiberias on the shore, then finally *southward* in a large clockwise sweep to Taricheae.[147]

One problem with this is Josephus' explicit remark that Vespasian approached Tiberias *from the south*: He removes part of the *southern wall* to facilitate access (3.459). To deal with this problem, Kokkinos has Vespasian follow a circuitous path from the west, along Mt. Berenice, to approach the city from the south (after the northwest).[148]

Another problem is Josephus' description of the entire Jordan Valley region. He describes a long narrow valley straddling the Jordan River "from the village of Sennabris as far as [or up to] the Dead Sea" (*War* 4.455). This appears to put Sennabris at the southern end of the northern lake. That site indeed marks the end of the valley, after which the mountains rise abruptly, leaving only narrow ribbons of land along the shores. Rabbinic literature describes Beit-Yerach in a similar way – as the northern marker of the Jordan valley *and* coupling it with Sennabris.[149] Kokkinos is aware of this problem. His effort to explain it on the hypothesis of a western-inland Sennabris seems to me too strained.[150]

---

[147] Kokkinos 2010: 14–15.   [148] Kokkinos 2010: 15.

[149] In response to rabbis who traced the Jordan from Panias to the Dead Sea, "Rabbah b. bar-Hana said 'The Jordan is really only from Beit-Yerach and below'" (*b. Bekh.* 55a). Cf. Sukenik 1922: 102–3. For the pairing of Beit-Yerach and Sennabris, see *y. Meg.* 2:2, where the proposition that all the towns in a city's territory are included with the city (for the purpose of scroll-reading prescriptions) is qualified. *In spite of the close proximity* of these towns, they are autonomous (*shnei avtaliot*). Sukenik (1922: 106–7) quotes from *Ber. Rabba* 98.18 in agreement, although I am unable to find his quotation.

[150] Josephus says three things about this Jordan valley (4.455–58). (a) It extends from Sennabris to Lake Asphaltitis (ἀπὸ κώμης Γινναβρὶν διῆκον μέχρι τῆς Ἀσφαλτίτιδος). (b) it is 1,200 stadia long and 20 wide. (c) It is bisected by the river and "has lakes (λίμνας τε ἔχει) of different nature, the Asphaltitis and the Tiberian." Standard English, French, and German editions of Josephus take (a) to be confirmation of the accepted site for Sennabris *while* noting that the figure in (b), about 220 km, happens to match the whole distance including both lakes, whereas the valley from lake to lake is less than half that length (Thackeray, Loeb ad loc.; M–B 2.2: 224 nn. 130–31; Pelletier 3.228 n. 2). Kokkinos, assuming consistency against the consensus, insists that Josephus' valley must include the two lakes (2010: 14, "it is Josephus that we must trust . . ."), which means that Sennabris *cannot* be at the south end. There are problems. (i) If we did insist on consistency, surely Sennabris should then lie at the Kinneret's north end. (ii) The construction *A* διῆκον μέχρι τῆς *B* should mean that A goes *until* B, that is: the Jordan valley goes until Dead Sea; it ends where the other begins. (iii) Whereas Kokkinos uses ἔχω to trump that clear statement, the ἔχω phrase is actually the

A largely neglected passage of relevance is *Life* 398–406.[151] Josephus is there describing his exploits prior to Vespasian's arrival. In skirmishes with a royal force at the (undisputed) north end of the Kinneret near Bethsaida (precise location debated), he falls from his horse and fractures bones. He is taken to nearby Capernaum and then, under cover of darkness, *to Taricheae* (403–404). Agrippa's commander Sulla hears of Josephus' injury and takes advantage of his absence, but Josephus' soldiers rush from their commander's side to check Sulla, near Bethsaida-Iulias (405–406). This rapid movement of news and persons between the northern sites and Taricheae makes good sense only if Taricheae was nearby, and Migdal, 10 km (6 mi) from Capernaum, would fit the bill. If Taricheae were at the south end of the lake, we would need to imagine the injured Josephus being carried during the night past the towns of Migdal and Tiberias (why?), all the way to the south end, and then news and people traversing the entire length of the lake in each instance. The accepted northern site is preferable.

Taricheae's location is germane for locating a third site whose identification was insecure until surprisingly recently: Gamala. Nineteenth-century maps put this fortress east of the Kinneret on a parallel near the south end. That is because *War* 4.2 locates Gamala "opposite from Taricheae over the lake," and Taricheae was located on the southwest. In the late nineteenth century, Victor Guérin identified what we now call Hippos (Qal'at el-Ḥusn) *as Gamala*. He reasoned that this lofty ridge was across the lake from (a southern) Taricheae, and near Soganē in Agrippa's territory in the "Lower Golan" (*War* 4.2).[152] Remarkably enough, the first excavator of Hippos *thought* he was excavating Gamala.[153]

vaguer one: Without a clarifying prefix the verb is roughly as versatile as English "has," which has any number of senses. So (iv) there are other possibilities. The editors mentioned give both phraes their full weight: plausibly rendering ἔχω as "include" or similar, then describing the valley *sensu stricto* (from Sennabris to the Dead Sea), and then giving the distance, with the unsurprising consequence that Josephus used a relevant round distance he happened to know (1,200 *stadia*) without bothering to reconcile it with the valley description. Another possibility is that ἔχω means only that the valley *involves* two lakes, and that the whole business reaches 1,200 *stadia*. (v) We cannot figure out Josephus' *meaning* by comparing actual distances with his figures. His own figures for the Kinneret (140 *stadia* = 28 km, vs. the real ca. 20 km [*War* 3.506]) and Asphaltitis (580 *stadia* = 116 km vs. the real 80 km [4.482]) would give the two lakes nearly 50 percent too much of the entire 1,200 *stadia*. We cannot say that he must have had the river and two lakes in mind because of the agreement in overall actual distance, that is, if his constituent distances do not match the reality.

[151] This passage was used by Graetz as proof that Taricheae lay (4 miles) north of Tiberias (1880: 486). Albright mentioned it in a footnote (1921–1922: 40 n. 31).

[152] Guérin 1868–1880: Pt. 3, vol. 1, 317–21. He notes that the Arabic name of the site, Kal'at el-Ḥusn, meant "stronghold, fortress," recalling Josephus' characteristic way of mentioning Gamala. He concluded (my translation): "I believe that we are justified in definitively establishing the location of this famous town with total confidence" (p. 321).

[153] So German-American Gottlieb Schumacher (1888: 205), from the German Templar colony in Haifa: "If we compare Kul'at el-Ḥusn with the testimony of Josephus about Gamala, ... we can scarcely doubt the identity of these two places." He thought that Arabic *ḥusn* could mean both "horse" and "natural fortification," the former – crucial to its later identification

Other explorers, concerned about the mismatches between such a Gamala and Josephus' account, proposed a site farther inland, on the Ruqqad gorge, at El-Eḥdeb or nearby Tell ed-Dra', just north of the modern Syrian town of Jamlah/Jamleh, a site that also seemed to preserve the ancient Aramaic Gamala.[154] That location was preferred even after the widespread acceptance of Wilson's and Albright's arguments for a Taricheae north of Tiberias, because this Gamala was on roughly the same latitude, across the lake and far enough inland.

Only since the 1970s have scholars come instead to accept Es-Salama, which is about 12 km (7.5 mi) east of the Kinneret's northernmost point, as Gamala. After fourteen seasons of excavation, that site is now securely confirmed, and it has become one of Israel's most famous archaeological parks. Although Jamlah was enticing, people began to realize that it was too distant to be seen from Taricheae (18 km [11.2 mi]), and it was hard to imagine why Josephus would so greatly exaggerate that point. After the Six-Day War (1967) and with new access to the Golan Heights, Israeli scholars began to search for a better prospect. For the man who first identified Es-Salama as Gamala, a fundamental consideration was that he could see the lake and Taricheae (i.e., Migdal) from there.[155] It would be a rich paradox if Gamala had been correctly identified by its connection with the northern Taricheae, but that identification was itself mistaken and Taricheae was in fact at the south end of the lake.

Obviously I find the currently accepted locations of Taricheae and Sennabris the most plausible, and no one doubts Gamala. I have spent time with the issue because challenges like those from an eminent scholar such as Kokkinos are important and necessary to remind us that even such locations as that of now-famous Gamala are not mere *givens*. They are historical hypotheses, which we must construct in our imaginations to explain the evidence. Therefore we must always be open to reconsidering our identifications.

as Hippos ("horse" in Greek) – indicating only that his Gamala lay in the Hippene territory (p. 206).

[154] Schumacher's English editor rejected this identification of Gamala, citing Frei 1886: 130–32, who had pointed out the mismatches, identified this site with Hippos, and looked east to Jamlah (Dschamle) for Gamala (although he also looked in vain for Gamala near the north end of the Kinneret on the strength of Josephus' connection with Taricheae, which he already placed at Migdal, 121–22). In the mid-1920s Thackeray (Loeb Josephus, n. *a* to *War* 3.1) gave Kul'at el Ḥoṣn as the usual identification, offering Jamlah, "a day's journey east of the lake," as alternative.

[155] The man was Itzhaki Gal in 1968; see Syon 2010: 7–8.

CHAPTER SEVEN

JERUSALEM I: JOSEPHUS AND THE EDUCATION OF TITUS

This man, in the bloom of youth, destroyed the fierce tribes of Palestine by war.
Silius Italicus, *Punica* 605–606

The [Roman] soldiers held it to be terribly disgraceful if cunning should *always* prevail over valour, desperation over weapons, mass over expertise, Judaeans over Romans.
Josephus, *War* 6.20

Polybius relates a number of stories in which Greek and Roman generals capture seemingly unconquerable cities that are of no great value in themselves, but their conquest sends a message: This display of force generates power (Chapter 3). Because defenders trust their such strong walls and remote locations, their fall has a shattering didactic effect.[1] A general capable of doing *that* must be obeyed. Although Cestius and Vespasian fully exploited display violence to establish local power, as we have seen, Cestius' rebuff outside Jerusalem left the viability of this fortress *polis*, deep in Judaea's hills, an open question. Years later, after Titus had safely returned to Rome, his enablers would credit him with the unprecedented achievements of a fortune-blessed conqueror (Chapter 1). But that discloses nothing about his actual intentions in the spring of 70, his changing plans over time, or what transpired between his arrival in the spring of 70 and his departure from a city in ashes.

---

[1] Polybius 7.15.2–5 [Lagoras of Crete at Sardis], 3.18.3 [Aemilius Paullus at Dimale], 8.14.5 [Philip of Macedon at Acrolissus]; discussion in Marincola 2001: 127.

When Vespasian turned his attention to Jerusalem toward the end of 67, he must have prepared for various outcomes. Galilee had submitted instantly and Samaria was securely in hand (3.307–15). But how long the Judaean campaign would last and what it would entail depended on factors beyond Vespasian's control. Clearly he had to secure the Judaean mother-city in one way or another, but because he faced a human enemy his approach would need to be reassessed constantly. Would Jerusalem capitulate before his arrival, as Sepphoris had, and would its leaders request a garrison as protection against Judaean and neighbouring violence? Among other unknowables, the Flavians could not have known that a lightweight from Galilee, John, would soon become an intransigent leader in Jerusalem.

With respect to high Roman politics, Vespasian could not have imagined when he left ruined Gamala in October 67 that the still-young emperor would take his own life within a few months, launching a bloody civil war. He could not have known that his Judaean campaign would be put on indefinite hold as a consequence, its potential stakes changing constantly. He could not have known, above all, that within two years *he* would be emperor.

The Flavians could not even have been sure that they would survive this conflict, straightforward though it had been in Galilee. It would involve fighting, and both men were high-value targets. Leading from the front, Vespasian had been injured outside Iotapata,. During the first assault on Gamala his life had again been imperilled. Titus also had some dangerous situations behind him, and many more ahead. His horse had reportedly been killed beneath him at Taricheae, where he escaped only by seizing the mount of a fallen comrade. He would return to Rome with a permanent shoulder injury as a souvenir of Judaea. King Agrippa II and Nicanor were hit by projectiles while attempting to parley. A rock to the head would render Josephus unconscious, spawning rumours of his death.[2] If either Vespasian or Titus had been incapacitated or killed in such ways, the whole conflict would have developed very differently, and if Josephus had met his end, we might know little about the whole story.

Josephus imagines Titus' officers pressing just this point as they try to restrain him from dangerous activities: "He should have a thought for what fortune had made him, being master of the war and indeed of the whole world, and not try to discharge the duty of a private soldier" (*War* 5.88). He and his father must also have reckoned with their own mortality.

---

[2] Vespasian's arrow to the foot: *War* 3.236. Suetonius thinks it was a knee injury: *Vesp.* 4.13. Nicanor's wound: *War* 5.261. Josephus' rock to the head: *War* 5.541. Agrippa at Gamala: *War* 4.14. Titus' shoulder: Epit. Dio 65/66.5.1. Titus' horse: Suetonius, *Tit.* 4.3. Josephus recounts many incidents of Titus' perils and courage (e.g., *War* 5.52–65, 81–97). Literary dramatization does not change the underlying reality of serious risk in armed conflicts.

The same was true on the other side. Judaeans were the main targets of this Roman military operation, and they would have to deal with the prospect of death. John managed to escape to Jerusalem, insinuate himself into a position of influence, and lead the mother-city's resistance. But he could not have planned that, which required his lithe adaptation to changing circumstances along with considerable luck. What if Titus had killed him at their first meeting, which was entirely possible? Simon bar Giora was not on the Jerusalem scene through much of 68. He had many hazardous ventures ahead, any of which could have removed him from among the living. In the spring of 68 the city was still in the hands of chief-priestly leaders, who hoped to see the trouble through to a conclusion. They had no idea that they would soon be murdered – by Idumaeans, of all people.

Given the uncertainties facing all parties, with so much depending on the others' moves and on chance, asking about the commanders' intentions – or Rome's "policy toward Jerusalem" – can only be part of our investigative question. No doubt they *had* plans, perhaps even contingency plans B through K. At a minimum they hoped to retain operational control and force the enemy into submission. But Field Marshal Moltke's observation that planning does not survive contact with the enemy holds here as anywhere else.[3]

Our questions in this chapter and the next are more about the motives than the precise plans of both Roman and Judaean leaders as they approached the climactic conflict in Jerusalem. We also need to ask how the city came to be destroyed. We may not be able to answer our questions definitively with available evidence, but our task is to investigate responsibly. This chapter and the next constitute a single investigation of these questions. I have divided them for the reader's wellbeing.

This one is mainly a critical summary of *War* 4 to 6. I take the space for this because the story is far too complex to be summarized briefly or with simple propositions, such as "Josephus' bias is X or Y" (cf. Chapter 2). Only by coming to terms with some neglected twists and turns can we appreciate the evidence that will need explaining in our reconsideration. This does not mean that I consider my summary "objective." Objectivity would require reproduction in full. This is both an interpretative and a critical summary, which I hope will clarify enough of what is present and what is absent to assist our historical reflections. I conclude this chapter with initial probes of the most important groups and individuals on the Judaean side. Chapter 8 will then discuss evidence outside Josephus, including the coins produced between 66 and 70 and an alternative account of Titus and the temple, before moving to reconstructive scenarios.

---

[3] Hughes 2009: 45–47.

I. JOSEPHUS' STORY OF THE JERUSALEM SIEGE

Book 4 of Josephus' *War* describes the transition from the rise of violence in and around Jerusalem to the irretrievable *stasis* inside the mother-city, caused mainly by interloping outsiders, that will lead to the destruction of city and temple alike. This is the tyrant-led civil strife (στάσις οἰκεία) anticipated in the preface (1.10).

Book 4

War 4 opens with Flavian operations in Agrippa's Galilean cities and the Golanite fortress of Gamala, which we examined in the previous chapter. Jerusalem itself is still in the hands of its virtuous aristocratic leaders, who have been trying to manage the uncertain fallout from the ambush of Cestius, by both preparing defences – allegedly even appointing regional "generals" – and seeking paths to negotiation. By the end of *War* 4 everything has changed beyond recognition. These beloved leaders are dead, and desperate men from elsewhere are contending for power in Jerusalem, while Nero has committed suicide and Vespasian has been drawn into the Roman civil war.

In terms of Jerusalem's affairs, the first half of Book 4 belongs to John of Gischala (4.121–28), while the latter begins to focus on Simon (4.566–84). In Books 5 and 6 the personal conflict between these "tyrants" will define what Josephus calls *stasis*. But the latter half of Book 4 is to a surprising extent devoted to the civil war in Rome, which Vespasian boldly enters on the strength of his success in Judaea thus far (4.491–96, 545–49, 585–658). This comes after his lightning campaign in Peraea and Judaea and tightening of the cordon around Jerusalem early in A.D. 68, which Josephus flavours with a geographical digression on the exotic Jordan/Dead Sea area (4.366–490, 550–55).

The story of John's arrival in Jerusalem is filled with tragic if sometimes humorous irony. Although he has fled Gischala in the most ignoble way, Jerusalem naively receives him as a hero. The gullible deduce from his ability to leave Galilee alive that he has somehow bested the Romans, and must have a credible plan for them also (4.106–27). His fans include other desperate refugees who have recently poured into the city. Eleazar ben Simon's Zealot faction, which had been withering under the counter-measures of the senior chief priests, draws vital energy from these newcomers and especially from the energetic John. After executing many of Jerusalem's notables, including members of the royal family, this greatly strengthened coalition, dignified by its own priestly leadership, is able to take over the temple compound with its elevated position and gated access.[4]

---

[4] *War* 4.151, 225; cf. 5.5–6.

The former high priest Ananus II and some leading laymen, including Joseph ben Gorion, are still able to rouse much of the public against the violent outsiders and other priests.[5] But their position is undone by John, who allegedly uses a pretence of obsequious allegiance to the senior leaders to leak their plans to the Zealots. *War* gives the impression that John worms his way into Ananus' favour only now, although according to *Life* 192–96 he had old friends among Jerusalem's leaders. Having managed to become Ananus' negotiator with the Zealots, he tells them that Ananus has invited Vespasian into Jerusalem – an entirely plausible charge in view of the general pattern. If the Zealots are not prepared to acquiesce in that capitulation, he urges, they had better summon stronger help from outside against Ananus and his colleagues, and quickly. The only realistic source of armed help is Idumaea, its frontier about 10 miles (17 km) south of Jerusalem (4.208–32).[6] We have noted the Idumaeans' peculiar role in the war (Chapter 4), and we shall return to them after this summary.

The influx of outsiders is mostly ignored in discussions of Jerusalem's resistance, but Josephus blames them in large measure for the city's destruction – on the curiously practical ground that the large number of refugees would use up provisions that could have served the fighters (4.137). But his descriptions of them are frustratingly vague. He seems to have considered it enough for his audience to recognize a type: the "trouble-makers and seditious."

He does emphasize that Judaeans from elsewhere looked to the mother-city for security as Vespasian was quickly taking coastal Jamnia and Azotus in the spring of 68. Forced to decide how they would respond to the looming presence of his army – surrender, flight, or resistance – the inhabitants of Judaea's villages were in discord. Families disintegrated in these disputes and neighbours fell into strife, the young men being typically more willing to fight the invaders. Those who had an instinct to fight and those who simply feared contact with Romans or could not decide what to do flocked to the safety of Jerusalem (4.129–37). This description seems telling. Rather than die-hard or ideological anti-Romans, we see residents of the countryside who were minding their own business now overrun by an army, with all that entails, forced to a quick decision. Some try to surrender – we do not know their fate – while others flee, whether to buy more time to ponder their options or already resolved on resistance. Rome has again created potential enemies.

Josephus describes separately a stream of "bandits" who enter Jerusalem at the same time. The distinction may be rhetorically artificial, but in his account

---

[5] See Chapter 3 on these leaders.
[6] Herodium, 15 km (9 mi) south of Jerusalem, was near this frontier, although the principal Idumaean towns were closer to 40 km (25 mi) away.

these men are not like the mass of ordinary folk. With bloody-minded clarity they murder three prominent Herodians shortly after entering the city (4.138–46). They have a named leader, Yochanan ben Tzvi,[7] who personally cuts the throats of other upper-class men who are in chains awaiting trial – on the charge of intending to "betray" the city, or in other words seeking terms with Rome (4.145–46). We cannot see clearly behind the narrative veil, but the atmosphere of terror, divergent hopes and fears, and the murder of perceived traitors is vivid. It also fits a pattern running through *War* (Sepphoris, Tiberias, Taricheae). The domestic leadership seeks terms with their long-standing Roman allies while armed factions, partly from elsewhere, are no longer willing to trust Rome. The difference here is that Jerusalem, as both Judaea's mother-city and a well-fortified site, with the temple as a unique talisman and magnet for national affection, attracts many more of the unreconciled militants, the fearful, and the confused. Their presence overwhelms the city's leaders.

The violent newcomers join the priestly Zealots in transforming the inner temple into a fortress. Josephus does not explain what has become of its other occupants or even the currently serving high priest, Matthias son of Theophilus, who is invisible. His name appears incidentally in *Ant.* 20.223.[8] The intruders have no share in Jerusalem's tradition of appointing high priests from eminent families, a system of which the recent high priest Ananus II is a product. They proceed to elect their own high priest *by show of hands* – a democratic practice that Josephus will later connect with the biblical demagogue Korah, archetypal rebel against Moses and Aaron (*Ant.* 4.15–19). Josephus implies that these rough rustics try out several "high priests" elected in this fashion, abandoning each in turn (*War* 4.148–49).

They finally test the people's tolerance for mischief (*eirōneia*) by choosing a man by *lot*, a practice that even more radically repudiates the traditional system and royal prerogative. The lot happens to fall on a bumpkin of obscure priestly heritage, who according to our appalled narrator does not even understand what a high priest *is* (4.151–59). The man's name is given as Phanni.[9] His Hebrew name was presumably Pinchas (= Phineas), after the

---

[7] Josephus explains that "this man was called 'son of Dorcas' in the local language." Dorcas is Greek for gazelle or deer, and Josephus appears to mean that John's father had the equivalent name in Hebrew or Aramaic. Hebrew equivalents could be *Tzvi* (Zvi, gazelle) or *'Ayal* (deer). But why not simply transliterate the name, as he often does? If John's father's name were Tzvi, he might have balked at transliteration because Greek has no equivalent to *tz*, and any combination of a consonant (*s* or *z*) with *b* (for *v*) would have looked decidedly barbarian.

[8] *War* does mention a high priest or chief priest (ἀρχιερεύς) named Matthias, but he is a son of the eminent Boethus (4.574; 5.527).

[9] Phanas in *Ant.* 20.227, where Josephus calmly relates that he was the last to hold the office, "designated high priest by the insurgents during the war."

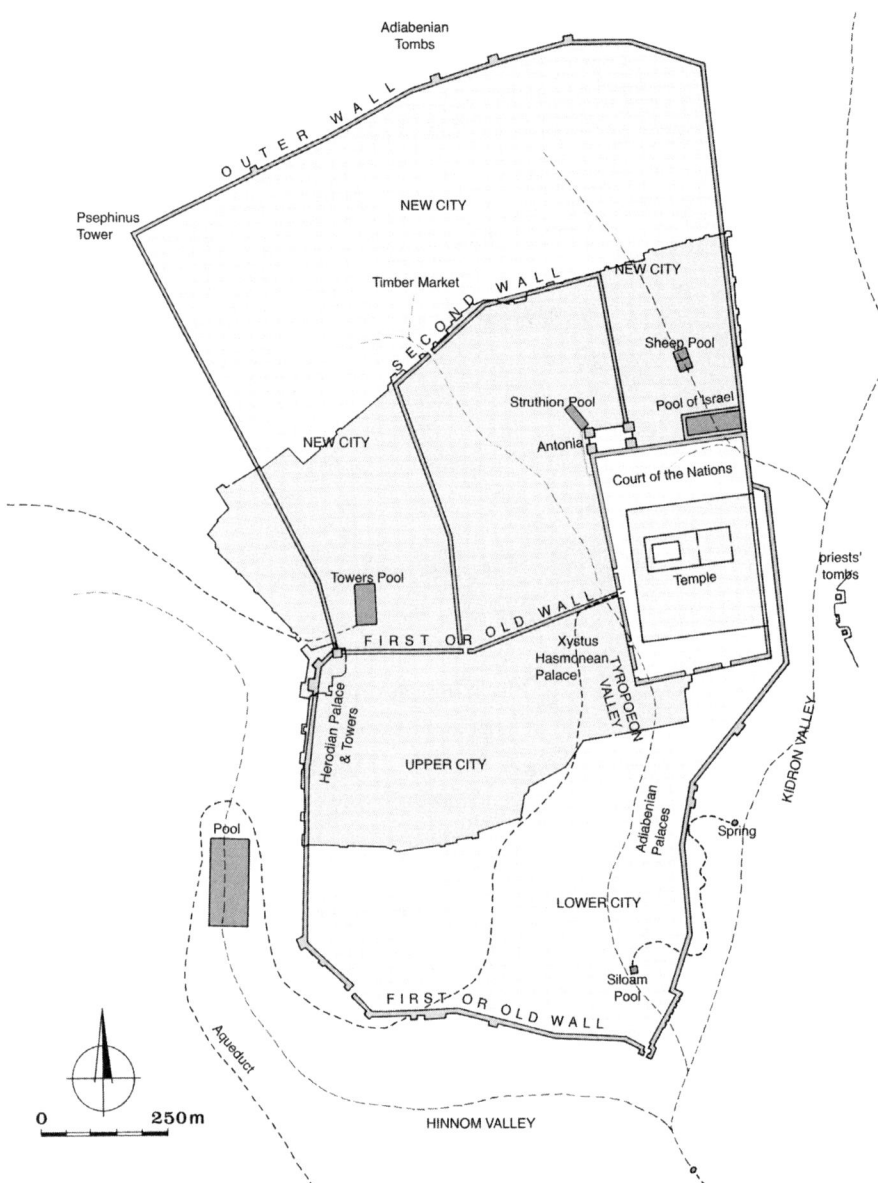

FIGURE 24. Plan of Jerusalem ca. A.D. 66, with the area of the modern Old City shaded. The diagram is © Leen Ritmeyer, the (permitted) annotations mine. For thoughtful challenges on several points see Kokkinos 2015 (summarized in his revisionist map, Figure 2).

biblical archetype of muscular zeal for the Law (Chapter 4). The experimental high priests do not appear elsewhere, and we might wonder whether Josephus has fabricated them for effect.[10]

[10] See Smallwood 1962: 31–32.

FIGURE 25. Model of first-century Jerusalem at the Israel Museum, from the south: Lower City and temple with Antonia in the background to the right, Upper city centre left, and New City in the distance northward. Author 2013.

Josephus does not label the new arrivals *Zealots*, although he soon has the populace and chief priests denouncing *as* Zealots those who have occupied the temple (4.160–61). They seem to include Eleazar ben Simon's group as well as the newcomers. The newcomers' ready access to the holy precinct and concern for (shall we say) reforming the high priesthood suggest connections with the dissident priests of *War* 2.409–10, whom Josephus may also have labeled "bandits" at 2.417, depending on the manuscript variant.[11] They may include rural priests.

So Jerusalem is becoming crowded. The arrival of an alleged 20,000 Idumaeans outside the walls (they would at least equal the size of the city's existing population by historical estimate),[12] in response to the Zealots' appeal, begins the central third of Book 4, which is also the narrative centre of *War* (Chapter 2). The Idumaeans demand entry on the premise that they have been called to *save the city from tyranny*, depredations, and betrayal – by Ananus and his group, they imagine. The chief priest Jesus' effort to correct the impressions, in an eloquent speech from the ramparts, only convinces the taciturn action-men that the smooth talker must be up to no good (4.233–82).[13] When a winter storm now breaks out (this is winter 67/68), Zealots are able to break out of the temple compound to open a gate for their sodden allies. The Idumaean fighters pour in, relieve their exhausted friends in the temple, and kill "thousands" in the outer court. Then it is their turn to hunt for aristocrats. They quickly dispatch the leaders Ananus and Jesus along with many others – more than 20,000 in Josephus' imagination. Victims include a putative 12,000 "well-born youth"

[11] He either calls them bandit-types (*lēistrikoi*) or [priestly] ministers (*leitourgoi*).
[12] See Geva 2014.   [13] On speech-making in Josephus, see Chapter 5.

whom the Zealots had failed to win over and therefore must die (4.314–44). Divided by 100 the numbers might enter the realm of plausibility.

When the Idumaeans' first flush of fury subsides, however, the Zealots' characterization of Jerusalem's distinguished men begins to give them pause. Their forebodings are confirmed by a deserter from the Zealots, who supposedly reveals the group's criminality and the innocence of those murdered. This leads the Idumaeans to abandon Jerusalem in disgust (4.345–52). On their way out they show their contempt by freeing the Zealots' 2,000 remaining prisoners, most of whom flee to the embrace of Simon bar Giora in the countryside (4.353). I have noted the literary artificiality of the Idumaean exodus (Chapter 2), given that they remain important in the story, under their original generals and allied with John.[14] They will also play the critical role in Simon's later entry and finally be recognized by Titus as "a major part of the war effort" (6.380).

As for John, he now "breaks free of the [Zealot] coalition" – apparently meaning that he staged a leadership coup – while managing to hold his base in the temple and adding the loyalty of the mysteriously lingering Idumaeans (4.389–97).

Vespasian's activities are ignored in the first half of *War* 4. As Josephus returns to them in the second half, some of what he says is by way of catch-up, back to early 68, and comes before episodes he has just narrated concerning Jerusalem. This problem, facing all writers who wish to keep simultaneous events in step *and* to tell coherent stories, can create confusion for the reader.

Judaea's response to Vespasian's arrival is very much like Galilee's had been, although in a negative image because of Jerusalem's unique position. Whereas in the north the principal *polis* of Sepphoris pre-emptively submitted for Galilee and the villages emptied, a pattern that will be repeated in Peraea, in Judaea the residents of countryside either surrender to Vespasian or flee to Jerusalem, which becomes a bastion of chaos and varying shades of potential resistance. Facing no trouble worth mentioning in the Judaean countryside, which he rapidly garrisons, Vespasian must quickly think about how he will crack Jerusalem.

Vespasian had gone to Caesarea from Agrippa's territories for the winter of 67/68 to plan the Judaean campaign with his commanders. In describing this, Josephus comes as close as he will to a discussion of Roman strategy (4.366–76). Much like Cestius' legates and tribunes in the summer of 66 (responding to Florus' letter), Vespasian's military men are confident in their strength and so advocate an immediate assault on Jerusalem. Their reasoning is that the city is in turmoil, its factionalism exacerbated by infusions of desperate

---

[14] See 4.566–70; 5.249; 6.380 with 4.233–35; also 5.290, 358; 6.92, 148, 378–81.

outsiders. If they wait, the Judaeans will have time to unite, making the Romans' task infinitely harder.

Vespasian responds with a caution typical of the Roman commanders we meet. What they really want, he mildly chastens, is to make a macho theatrical show of their skill and weapons. They do not realize that the course they advocate is needlessly *dangerous* (οὐκ ἀκίνδυνον, 4.368). As long as the inhabitants of Jerusalem are preoccupied with their bloody civil war, they are not forging weapons and armour, strengthening their walls, or training their army. They are not becoming a stronger enemy, but a weaker one. If they were together preparing for war, a quick strike would be warranted to halt their progress. But they are tearing themselves apart, which is good for us. Let them continue and exhaust themselves! If we strike now, our onslaught will instantly unite them against us. But God is handing them to us, without our needing to subject the army to both hardship and danger (ἀπονητὶ . . . ἀκινδύνως). We Romans care about two things equally: winning *and* safety (τὸ συμφέρον/κατόρθωμα/νίκη καὶ τὸ ἀσφαλὲς, 4.368, 370, 376). Our victory is not diminished if it comes without the hazards of combat (δίχα μάχης . . . τοῦ διὰ τῶν ὅπλων σφαλεροῦ, 4.372). Self-restraint and intelligence (ἐγκρατείᾳ καὶ συνέσει) are always preferable (4.373). So we shall wait until they are at their weakest. Instead of becoming *actors on their stage*, as your advice would have us do, we shall watch their bloody spectacle from the bleachers (4.371).

Vespasian's counsel suits Josephus' root theme of Judaean civil strife so patently that we may doubt that the Roman offered any such analysis. And how would Josephus know the exchanges in Vespasian's *consilium* with his commanders? All the same, Vespasian's purported caution matches well the approach taken by Cestius, by himself in Galilee, and later by Titus, in the tradition of strategic forethought associated with Augustus.

While Vespasian winters in Caesarea, many native Jerusalemites flee to him. They assure him that much of Jerusalem's real populace has remained loyal and would similarly like to make contact, but those trapped inside are being restrained by tyrants from outside who have killed the city's leaders. These fighters are preventing all who cannot afford bribes from leaving. The violent men have even ordered that corpses remain unburied on the road out of Jerusalem – recall Creon in the *Antigone* – as a grisly warning to defectors.[15]

In about February 68, the earliest moment for military activity after winter, Vespasian's first move is characteristically not against Jerusalem. He crosses Samaria to the north and the Jordan River into Peraea – the most neglected Judaean district in modern research. The wealthy elite of Peraea's largest town are among those who have sent an embassy to him in Caesarea, while

---

[15] *War* 4.377–88; cf. Sophocles, *Ant.* 1–38 re: Polyneices (a punishment in part for ostensible disloyalty in betraying Thebes to Athens).

dismantling their walls in a show of eager cooperation.[16] As the Romans are on the way to consolidate this area with a garrison, some local unreconciled men in the town panic and murder their most prominent man, abusing his corpse in the process. The standard pattern ensues: Vespasian garrisons the town without bloodshed and returns to Caesarea with his main army. He delegates the always eager Mr. Gentle (Placidus) to make an end of the town's belligerent refugees (4.413–19).

Placidus' 3,500-strong force, using a manoeuvre to draw his prey out of another village, cuts them down and burns the place. The survivors make for Jericho, west of the Jordan, terrifying all the villagers they meet along the way with news that the Romans are coming with a vengeance. Because no one imagines that a Roman force in this mood will worry much about distinguishing the guilty from the innocent, this news causes nearly everyone to panic and head for the river, which they are however unable to ford. Placidus catches up with them and destroys thousands, while also taking prisoners. The superfluity of corpses chokes the mighty river for some time (4.420–36).

Josephus' episode, although it is not his interest to elaborate on this, offers another example of Rome's instantly manufactured enemies. Peraeans who had never imagined opposing Rome were driven by fear to actions that made them look just like enemies to the Romans, who then assumed the roles of judge and executioner. The cycle expands as those who hear of this indiscriminate slaughter become more hardened enemies, for whom surrender to such brutal invaders is inconceivable.

As usual, Vespasian's army faces little or nothing in the way of combat. He needs to secure all the territory around Jerusalem, as a prelude to his inevitable confrontation of the capital, which has not yet indicated its submission in spite of the refugees' reports. Marching out from Caesarea at the first signs of spring (68), accordingly, he immediately secures all the towns of the inner plain and foothills: Antipatris (Aphek), Lydda (Lod), Iamnia (Yavneh), Thamna (Timnah), and Ammaus – this just 32 km (20 mi) west of Jerusalem, which becomes the Fifth Legion's camp (4.445). Finding Jericho mainly deserted, like most towns, he occupies it easily (4.451). By the end of May 68 he has established large garrisons, after occasional burning and the dispatch of weaker

[16] 4.413–18. The mss. call the place Gadara. As Thackeray explains (Loeb ad loc., n. *b*), this cannot be Decapolis Gadara (see the similar issue with Gerasa and Simon bar Giora). He suggests the prosperous town of Es–Salt (as-Sult), on the western edge of the mountains looking toward the Jordan valley. That would suggest Shunat-Nimrin (10 km south of Karama, Jordan) in the valley as the village to which the refugees flee. *Ant.* 13.375 may mention a *village* called Gadara in this area (the mss. show puzzlement). Name confusion is illustrated by the mss. of *War* 3.132, which give *Gadara* for *Gabara* ('Arabah) in Galilee. Josephus has not otherwise mentioned a capital for Peraea, which is largely desert (*War* 3.44), although Antipas had built a city named Iulias (orig. Livias) on the biblical site of Betharampha/Beit-Haram (2.168; Jones 1971: 275–77).

stragglers but no real fighting, in all the sites he needs to isolate Jerusalem (4.445–51, 486–90). Josephus' Roman audience should feel the terror of those trapped in and around the mother city. They are running out of air to breathe.

Here we must reckon with a problem in Josephus' chronology, which may have implications for understanding Vespasian's intentions (Figs. 26 and 27). Josephus is juggling several narrative strands: Vespasian's activities, Judaeans inside and outside Jerusalem, and affairs in Rome. His technique seems to catch up with him here. The problem emerges when we compare *War* 4.449, which has Vespasian camped at Ammaus on *2 Daesius* (late May) and securing Jericho and Adida a few paragraphs later (4.486–90), with 4.550, which says that he *moves out from Caesarea* on 5 Daesius. Given the absence of indicators to the contrary, scholars have understood this as a single campaign in the spring of 68.[17] But the dates plainly do not work on that assumption. Moreover, the intervening references to Otho and Vitellius in Rome (4.545–49, in A.D. 68/69), between the notices about 2 and 5 Daesius, seem to indicate that in the latter case we have passed into the spring of 69.[18] If Josephus expected his Roman audience to pay any attention to his month dates, and they were not mere spice to enhance his authoritative sound, he presumably expected them to know from his discussion of Roman events that he was now describing a new year in Judaea.

Already by May 68 (i.e., *War* 4.449 with 486–90), then, Vespasian has completely surrounded Jerusalem and is ready to do whatever will be needed, at a time of his choosing. At the beginning of June he returns to coastal Caesarea to plan the best approach (4.491). An extended stay in the Judaean hills, no matter what he decides to do, will require extensive logistical support. But while he is in Caesarea, around the end of June (assuming rapid couriers for official news), he learns of Nero's death. Because he is Nero's *legatus*, the news requires him to halt his preparations and await instructions from the new emperor Galba. Perhaps Josephus' Roman audiences remember that Galba took his time travelling to Rome from Spain, consolidating western provinces en route and reaching the capital only in October 68.[19] That might explain

---

[17] The English (Loeb-Thackeray), French (Pelletier), and German (M-B) editions of record, ad loc., all view 4.550 as a continuation from 4.449, 100 sections earlier, in spite of the references to Roman affairs and the impossibility of compressing all the intervening material (e.g., 4.486–490) in three days.

[18] Price (1992: 223) offers a clear and compelling analysis. Levick (1999: 39) reviews the problem of reconciling 4.550 (Vespasian leaves Caesarea on 5 Daesius) with 4.588 (he learns that Vitellius is emperor [from 17/18 April] on his return). My dating of Daesius a month earlier (5 Daesius: ca. May 14/15) eases the problem. It would be surprising if Vespasian had not heard after four weeks, although not impossible. Anyway, the simplest solution is Josephus' literary licence. Would Vespasian have cancelled this trip if he had just heard while climbing on his horse? Or perhaps 5 Daesius is a date connected in his notes with some minor event in the campaign, and Josephus uses it to provide a clear opening day.

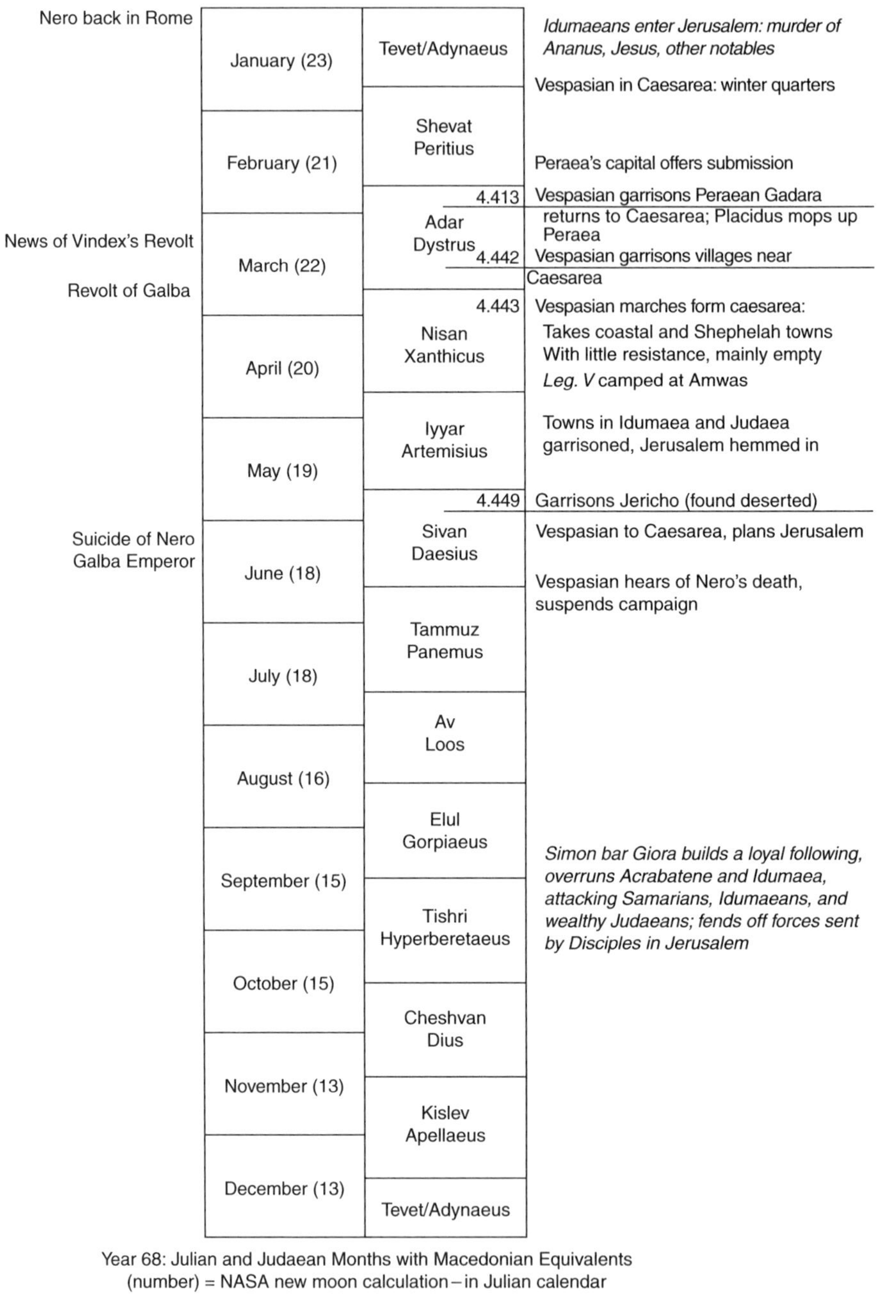

	Julian month	Judaean / Macedonian	Events
Nero back in Rome	January (23)	Tevet/Adynaeus	*Idumaeans enter Jerusalem: murder of Ananus, Jesus, other notables* Vespasian in Caesarea: winter quarters
	February (21)	Shevat Peritius	Peraea's capital offers submission
News of Vindex's Revolt Revolt of Galba	March (22)	Adar Dystrus — 4.413 4.442	Vespasian garrisons Peraean Gadara returns to Caesarea; Placidus mops up Peraea Vespasian garrisons villages near Caesarea
	April (20)	Nisan Xanthicus — 4.443	Vespasian marches form caesarea: Takes coastal and Shephelah towns With little resistance, mainly empty *Leg. V camped at Amwas*
	May (19)	Iyyar Artemisius — 4.449	Towns in Idumaea and Judaea garrisoned, Jerusalem hemmed in Garrisons Jericho (found deserted)
Suicide of Nero Galba Emperor	June (18)	Sivan Daesius	Vespasian to Caesarea, plans Jerusalem Vespasian hears of Nero's death, suspends campaign
	July (18)	Tammuz Panemus	
	August (16)	Av Loos	
	September (15)	Elul Gorpiaeus	*Simon bar Giora builds a loyal following, overruns Acrabatene and Idumaea, attacking Samarians, Idumaeans, and wealthy Judaeans; fends off forces sent by Disciples in Jerusalem*
	October (15)	Tishri Hyperberetaeus	
	November (13)	Cheshvan Dius	
	December (13)	Kislev Apellaeus	
		Tevet/Adynaeus	

Year 68: Julian and Judaean Months with Macedonian Equivalents
(number) = NASA new moon calculation – in Julian calendar

FIGURE 26. Calendar of A.D. 68 showing Julian-Roman solar months aligned with Hebrew lunar (and equivalent Macedonian) months, with Josephus' dated events anchoring the others listed.

why Vespasian delays everything now. Only toward the end of 68, perhaps November, does he send Titus and Agrippa II to greet Galba and receive orders. When they reach Corinth, however, toward the end of January after

[19] Morgan 2006: 38–43.

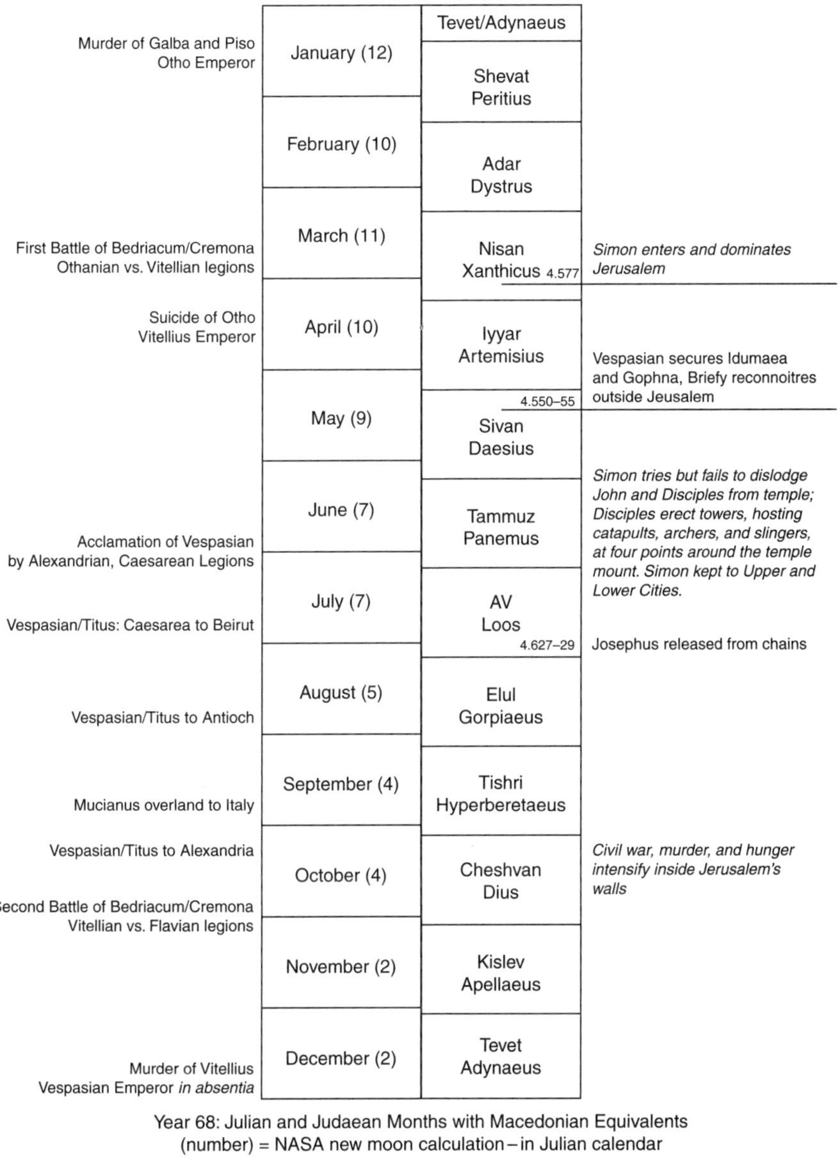

		Tevet/Adynaeus	
Murder of Galba and Piso Otho Emperor	January (12)		
		Shevat Peritius	
	February (10)		
		Adar Dystrus	
First Battle of Bedriacum/Cremona Othanian vs. Vitellian legions	March (11)	Nisan Xanthicus 4.577	Simon enters and dominates Jerusalem
Suicide of Otho Vitellius Emperor	April (10)	Iyyar Artemisius	Vespasian secures Idumaea and Gophna, Briefly reconnoitres
	May (9)	4.550–55	outside Jeusalem
		Sivan Daesius	
	June (7)	Tammuz Panemus	Simon tries but fails to dislodge John and Disciples from temple; Disciples erect towers, hosting catapults, archers, and slingers, at four points around the temple mount. Simon kept to Upper and Lower Cities.
Acclamation of Vespasian by Alexandrian, Caesarean Legions	July (7)	AV Loos 4.627–29	
Vespasian/Titus: Caesarea to Beirut			Josephus released from chains
	August (5)	Elul Gorpiaeus	
Vespasian/Titus to Antioch	September (4)	Tishri Hyperberetaeus	
Mucianus overland to Italy			
Vespasian/Titus to Alexandria	October (4)	Cheshvan Dius	Civil war, murder, and hunger intensify inside Jerusalem's walls
Second Battle of Bedriacum/Cremona Vitellian vs. Flavian legions	November (2)	Kislev Apellaeus	
Murder of Vitellius Vespasian Emperor in absentia	December (2)	Tevet Adynaeus	

Year 68: Julian and Judaean Months with Macedonian Equivalents
(number) = NASA new moon calculation – in Julian calendar

FIGURE 27. Calendar of A.D. 69 showing Julian-Roman solar months aligned with Hebrew lunar (and equivalent Macedonian) months, with Josephus' dated events anchoring the others listed.

delays from winter travel, they hear that Galba himself is dead (killed in mid-January 69). Agrippa continues on to greet his successor, whereas Titus turns back to consult with his father (4.497–502; see Chapter 5).

How long Vespasian leaves in place the forward camps he has established to choke Jerusalem is unclear. Apparently he leaves Idumaea largely unguarded toward the end of 68. When he returns in the spring of 69 to survey the situation, he must re-garrison Idumaea, now having Cerialis destroy Hebron, and secure camps along the crucial northern access from Samaria, at Gophna and Beit-el. In the spring of 69 he is able to ride right up to Jerusalem's walls, even with John and also Simon both inside, for a closer look (4.550–55). Here I would note again the injustice in blaming Cestius for not having assaulted and captured Jerusalem in October 66. Vespasian has made extremely elaborate preparations for encircling Jerusalem, but still he has no intention of making a quick and futile assault. He prefers to keep the city in a vice awaiting his final moves on his terms.

In the past year (68–69) Simon has been making a name for himself, in bold disdain of the Roman cordon. He has not been fighting *Romans*, to be sure, but has built his reputation as the man to be feared by Judaeans and Idumaeans. From late 66 through the winter of 67–68 he stays at Masada (2.652–64; 4.503–508). Finding this experience among (Josephus') *sicarii* depressing, because of their lack of spirit (cf. Chapter 9), once his nemesis Ananus II is dead in Jerusalem he springs back into the Judaean hills. There he quickly gathers a following, partly by freeing slaves and making extravagant promises to the poor. His resulting credibility attracts even men of standing. Full of confidence, he overruns Acrabatene on the Samarian frontier again, the area from which Ananus II had ejected him in late 66, and then Idumaea (4.503–37). Simon's fight is as usual with Judaea's neighbours. When Idumaea is betrayed to him by one of its own, he raids their land to feed his growing army (5.515–37). New forces from Jerusalem move against him, now from the Zealot faction under John's leadership, and manage to kidnap his wife as a bargaining chip. But his terrifying presence outside the walls results in her quick return (4.538–65). If only Titus had Simon on his side! After Simon's nuisance activity in the area, at any rate, in 69 Vespasian must re-secure Idumaea and the areas north of Jerusalem (4.550–55), even though he still has no immediate plans as he awaits developments in Rome.

The Idumaeans in Jerusalem now make a surprising move. Having tired of John's crew, they turn against them and chase them into the temple confines. They sack the Adiabenian palace south of the temple compound that he has used for his headquarters (4.567–68). Seeking a new coalition to deal with John, they join with what must be a tiny remnant of "chief priests" and propose the nuclear option: *admit Simon*. He is the only man capable of removing John (4.566–77). Says Josephus: "But God distorted their judgement for the worse, and they thought up a cure for their salvation that only brought a more ferocious destruction" (4.573). As soon as he is admitted, Simon confines John and the Zealots in the temple as hoped. His hosts are less pleased by his assumption of supreme command, which makes everything immeasurably worse (4.577–84). Josephus does not stress the point, but the story time happens to be Passover of 69 (4.577). The audience is being prepared for the catastrophe of Books 5 and 6.

Before we proceed to those volumes, we must glance at the closing section of Book 4, on the Roman civil war (especially from 4.585). By leaving Judaean affairs, this closing panel creates a frame with the opening (4.1–120), set in Galilee (Chapter 2). In Chapter 6 I suggested reasons for the Galilean spillover from Book 3 in Book 4's opening sections. The closing panel on Roman affairs offers relief from the growing sense of doom in Jerusalem while also heightening suspense. The audience must now wait for his harrowing account of the horrors they know are coming. A more prosaic reason for this post-Neronian Roman material is that it explains how Vespasian came to entrust Titus with the Jerusalem campaign, which will open Book 5.

Structure and language reveal that Josephus is doing much more than merely supplying information. He is bringing the Judaean and Roman civil wars into direct conversation. Just when Simon bar Giora reaches the height of his power, menacing Jerusalem from outside, Josephus makes the comparison: "Not only in Judaea were there civil strife and internecine war (στάσις ἦν καὶ πόλεμος ἐμφύλιος), but also in Italy" (4.545). After briefly covering the murder of Galba in the forum, Otho's war with Vitellius, who "craved kingship" just as John and Simon did (4.208, 390, 510), and Otho's suicide in defeat (4.545–49), Josephus returns to Simon's entry into Jerusalem (4.556–84) and remarks, "around this time terrible sufferings also enveloped Rome" (4.585). Just as John and Simon turn Jerusalem into a scene of bloody conflict and pollute the temple, so Vitellius and his rough German soldiers "made the whole of Rome into a military camp" (4.586). The switching back and forth, applying similarly charged language to Jerusalem and Rome, encourages his Roman audience to view both conflicts as species of the same genus. The Judaeans are not strange barbarians; their leaders face the same problems as those of every *polis*, of Rome itself. Josephus implicitly portrays himself as a man of the same cast as his cultured audiences (cf. Chapter 2). In addition, he points to what every intelligent person knows to be the real basis of the Flavian triumph, the victory over Roman rivals (Chapter 1).

Book 5

In contrast to these abrupt changes of scene in *War* 4, Books 5 and 6 focus with increasing resolution on Jerusalem. We want to look away as the picture becomes too clear, culminating in the lurid account of cannibalism (6.201–19). Josephus handles the imperative of narrative variety here by pausing for speeches, geographical digressions, and intensely vivid battle scenes, or by changing lenses from wide-angle to telephoto. While providing a measure of relief, these digressions also build suspense as the audience becomes impatient to see how things will progress toward the known outcome.

A pattern of "narrative – excursus – narrative – speech – narrative" creates five major sections in Book 5. The volume unfolds as Titus gradually comes to terms with the Judaean character and that of the stalwart mother city. When he first nears Jerusalem, he camps his men at Gibeah, 5 km (3 mi) north of the city, taking 600 cavalry with him to the northwest Psephinus tower (Fig. 24). He hopes that the mere sight of him with his impressive contingent will terrify the people into immediate submission (*War* 5.52–53). Perhaps the small advance unit is meant, at the same time, to minimize the fear of surrender.

Titus appears convinced that he can coax Jerusalem into submission – in narrative context because he is sure that much of the population is actually eager to flee the tyrants. When his friend Nicanor approaches the wall to offer terms and is hit by an arrow, Titus is infuriated (5.261). As we have seen (Chapter 3), he will try both exemplary violence and psychological intimidation to move the population. Only after repeated setbacks and the leaders' refusals of many invitations to surrender will he discuss with his generals the implementation of a proper siege, settling in and building ramps and an encircling wall (5.491–10). He has received waves of refugees, but despairs at the stubbornness of the militant leaders who persist. Book 5 is about the education of Titus.

By 5.136, where the first excursus begins, Josephus has established the essential conditions. He first summarizes the components of *stasis* inside Jerusalem (5.1–38). John has risen to supremacy over the Zealot-Galilean coalition, but Zealot founder Eleazar ben Simon reasserts himself and expels John from the inner temple. This temporarily creates a three-cornered *stasis*: Eleazar in the temple proper, John with numerical superiority in the outer court, and Simon controlling the Upper and Lower City. Josephus uses the *polis-stasis* framework to drive home his themes. The story is becoming saturated with the language of pollution, bloodshed, unholy sacrifice, carnage, impiety, suffering, mourning, and lamentation (e.g., 5.14–20). These are joined by the classic peril of hunger (*limos*)[20] as each faction burns grain stores to prevent their use by others (5.21–39).

With Vespasian now in Egypt and declared emperor, Titus is left to launch the war's final phase from Caesarea in the spring of A.D. 70. He has roughly the same allied and auxiliary forces that had served his father and the same three legions (*V Macedonica, X Fretensis*, and *XV Apollinaris*). But Vespasian seriously weakened these legions when he removed 5,000 of their best soldiers for the civil war in Italy under Mucianus (5.43–44). The shortfall is covered by

---

[20] E.g., Thucydides 3.57.3, 59.3; 4.40.1; 7.87.2.

vexillations from legions in Egypt and Syria: 2,000 from Alexandria and 3,000 from Syria (*IV Scythica* and *VI Ferrata*).

While those additions fill the gaps created for the civil war, Titus has also brought in from northern Syria the unlucky *XII Fulminata*, which had been humiliated under Corbulo and again recently under Cestius (Chapters 3 and 5). Given its apparent superfluity, we might speculate that he summons this legion for the same reason that may have motivated Cestius: to build its confidence with relatively safe combat experience, while significantly increasing his powers of intimidation. Josephus remarks that the newly rebuilt legion has a reputation for valour (we do not know how) *and* is eager for revenge (5.41).

The Judaean campaign will not, however, work out well for the Twelfth. They appear only one more time in *War*, in an incidental reference to their building of an ill-fated embankment (5.467). Josephus' silence might be thought accidental, but there are indications of continuing disgrace. First, their legion's commander is the only one not named. Should we understand that it was still Caesennius Gallus as under Cestius? That seems unlikely, and the silence becomes deafening when Titus holds his famous war council (6.237; Chapter 8) and Josephus names the legionary legates who participate – except the commander of the Twelfth. It is conceivable that Titus assumed their command (cf. 5.42), but that would be hard to square with their lack of visibility and especially his reported disdain for the legion. After Jerusalem's fall, according to Josephus, he gives the magnificent Tenth the honour of occupying the city as the new province's garrison and deems the Fifth and Fifteenth worthy of accompanying him to Egypt. The Twelfth he dismisses to the border with Armenia *because of their disgrace under Cestius*, which they have apparently done nothing to redeem (*War* 7.17–19). Perhaps Josephus' silence about the legate reflects his discretion in post-war Rome, where the man is likely to live and to own a signed copy of the book (*Life* 362; *Apion* 1.51). Passing over the rebuilt legion's actions under his command while blaming their reputation on what happened to their under Cestius might have been prudent.

Finally, the Prefect of Egypt, Tiberius Julius Alexander, famously the first governor to acclaim Vespasian,[21] joins Titus as his second-in-command and executive officer (5.39–46). Being now close to Vespasian's age (mid-50s), Tiberius Alexander will also be a mentor to Titus, who has recently turned 30.

---

[21] Josephus (*War* 4.601, 616–18) has the Alexandrian legions declare for Vespasian some days after those in Caesarea. Suetonius (*Vesp.* 6.3) and Tacitus (*Hist.* 2.79) agree that Alexandria was first, on July 1, and differ over whether Caesarea followed on July 11 or 3. Cf. the badly damaged *P. Fouad* 8 (Sherk 1988: no. 81), which mentions the Alexandrian acclamation of Vespasian as divine, saviour, benefactor, son of Ammon.

This part of Josephus' account is broadly confirmed by remarks in Tacitus (*Hist.* 5.1), who may have known *War* but if so used independent information as well. Tacitus explains that the donor legions from Alexandria were *III* (*Cyrenaica*) and *XXI* (*Deiotariana*), that the auxiliary element comprised twenty cohorts of infantry and eight cavalry wings (Josephus: "a considerable force"), and that the kings Agrippa II and Sohaemus accompanied Titus along with soldiers provided by Antiochus of Commagene. Tacitus also emphasizes the antipathy of Nabataean soldiers toward Judaeans ("with the usual hatred of neighbours"), supporting Josephus' description of their atrocities (*War* 5.551).[22]

Most interesting is Tacitus' claim that alert Romans volunteered to join Titus' war. Now that he was heir apparent, they spotted a golden opportunity to earn his favour in the trenches, thus positioning themselves for later honours in Rome. This too suggests that the Judaean campaign was not seen in Rome as particularly dangerous or uncertain of outcome. That point is further supported by Suetonius' report (*Vesp.* 6.4) that Vespasian's rival Vitellius sarcastically recommended to his German troops a safe and easy posting to Judaea.

Titus learned from Cestius, it seems, to avoid the Beit-Horon pass (5.39–53). He brings both Titus Frugius' Fifteenth, which is his own former legion (3.15; 7.19), with the Twelfth via Samaria to Gophna, a well-garrisoned site 22 km [13 mi] north of Jerusalem. The Fifth under Sextus Cerealis – he will become Judaea's first provincial legate – takes the southerly route via Ammaus (Emmaus/Amwas), where the legion established a base under Vespasian (4.444–45). Larcius Lepidus leads the distinguished Tenth on the longest march of all: east to the Jordan Valley and south to Jericho, where Vespasian had that legion establish a camp (under Trajan Senior), before ascending westward to Jerusalem (4.450).[23]

Approaching Jerusalem via these routes offered many advantages: maintaining several lines of communication and supply, so as not to endanger the operation if one failed, dispersing any enemy challenge, and securing a range of options for rapid retreat. Titus' caution is evident in other ways too. For example, the Fifth arrives many hours after the two that he brings, in the middle of the night. When he moves his army to Scopus, therefore, he leaves them in the rear to rest. When the Tenth arrives later that day, presumably rested after a camp stop, he has that elite force camp on the Mount of Olives, closest to Jerusalem and with a commanding view of the city (5.67–70).

The legionary pecking order hinted at by Josephus (cf. 5.269) makes it all the more impressive that Jerusalem's fighters immediately target the Tenth. It is nearest, but also at the top of a big hill. Titus was already surprised by a daring Judaean raid outside the walls during his preliminary appeal for surrender. In that

---

[22] See *War* 2.68–69, 76 for Varus and Chapter 5 for Cestius.
[23] On the commanders, see *War* 3.289; 6.237.

encounter he lost two cavalrymen and barely escaped himself, according to Josephus (5.54–66). Now, with the legions busy building camps above Jerusalem, the Judaean leaders take cognizance of their dire situation and join forces, bursting out of the eastern gate and up the Mount of Olives. In this rare display of unity (ὁμόνοια, opposite of *stasis*; 5.71–72), they achieve temporary success. At a huge tactical disadvantage, they charge up a steep hill against the world's finest soldiers, who have complacently laid aside their weapons for construction work. Thrown into confusion and even briefly ejected from their camp, the Tenth would have been imperilled had not Titus rushed over from Scopus with reinforcements to drive the Judaeans back *downhill*– excoriating his renowned soldiers for their "lack of manliness" (ἀνανδρία, 5.81).

One of *War*'s crucial dates comes now as the legions are digging in: It is Passover in A.D. 70 (5.99, 567). Although this is difficult to imagine, with tens of thousands of soldiers camped around the city, Josephus implies that the usual swelling of Jerusalem's population for the feast occurred this year. This is puzzling on several levels. If the pilgrims could gain access, how is it that Agrippa and his small force, led alone Titus and his, could not do so? How did all these Judaeans view their likely encounter with this massive army? How did they stroll past them into the city? For Josephus' account, at any rate, the main significance of the date is that the coincidence between Passover and the beginning of Titus' encirclement will multiply the number of Judaean victims at the end, as many will then become trapped within for the siege (6.420–29). Passover also provides a pretext for John to retake the inner temple and kill Zealot opponents there (5.100–105). Finally (Chapter 2), Passover's arrival intensifies the tragic irony.[24] As Josephus remarks pointedly here, the festival is supposed to celebrate the Judaeans' *liberation* (5.99), but the scene declares the very opposite.[25]

The Judaeans are not finished with harassing the Tenth Legion. When Titus gives them reinforcements, now using auxiliaries as guards while the legionaries finish building their camp, the Judaeans charge out again. They send the guards retreating *uphill* and again break through to the unarmed legionaries on the ridge, scattering them in panic. Only gradually does another intervention by Titus push them downhill in a fighting retreat (5.85–97).

This first section ends with glances at both sides and an encounter that bodes ill for the Romans. Titus levels the space between his army on Scopus and the city's northern wall (5.106–108), a huge engineering task that exposes his forces to close contact with the Judaeans. This is where an incident mentioned in Chapter 3 occurs. A small group of Judaeans appears outside the wall

---

[24] See Colautti 2002; Siggelkow-Berner 2011.

[25] Josephus can date things differently. *War* 5.302 makes the fifteenth day of the siege 7 Artemisius, which would mean that it began on 23 Nisan, after Passover.

pretending to be the only remaining militants, ejected by a majority that desires surrender – playing on Titus' hopes. Although he is learning skepticism, his soft-headed soldiers rush to the gates, only to be showered with projectiles. The Judaeans are gleeful as Titus becomes enraged. He would have executed the legionaries had there not been so many (5.109–35).

Leaving the Tenth on the Mount of Olives, Titus now brings the rest of the army (*V, XII, XV*) in to a safe distance of about four football fields from the northwest corner, near the modern Russian Compound, and the western side of the city's "waist" (across from Jaffa Gate) – close enough to be intimidating but beyond the range of Judaean projectiles (5.130–35).

Scholars have mainly scoured Josephus' lengthy description of Jerusalem and temple here (5.136–247) for historical information.[26] That is fine, but we should remember that this is no simple reporting. It is *reportage*, here with a military slant to explain both why the Judaeans take such confidence in their city and why the Romans will have such a difficult time. The opening words are heavy with the language of walls, fortified, unbridgeable chasms, enclosure, encircled, and hills. The next paragraph concludes: "On the outside, the city's two hills were enclosed by *precipitous chasms*, and because of the *cliffs* on each side it was *not accessible* from any point" (5.141). Josephus elsewhere exposes this as exaggeration. The very fact that his Judaeans are able to charge across the eastern valley and up the hill, assault the legionaries, and retreat back up Jerusalem's hill shows that the eastern wall is not *that* inaccessible. But the casual hiker today is impressed by the steepness of both sides, and Josephus is justified in observing the fortress-like situation of the city even if he exaggerates.

The innermost wall was "virtually untakeable," he says, and if Agrippa I had finished the outermost wall in the same way he had built its foundations, "the city could not have been taken" (5.143, 153). His description brims with figures about the height and thickness of walls, foundations of enormous ashlars set in bedrock, and the scores of sturdy towers. Then come the temple, a virtual fortress within the city, and the Antonia fortress towering over all of that ("built on rock, 50 cubits [75 ft, 24 m] in elevation, sheer drops on all sides," 5.238). The city and its temple thus embody the indomitable national character.

Josephus develops two other thematic groups here. Tragic lament is emphasized by reminders of the city that used to be, as he writes. Thus he recalls Herod's palace: "It is just not possible to portray the palace adequately, and the *memory of it brings agony*, recalling the enormous cost of the bandits' fire" (5.182). He also stresses the care with which the temple's sanctity was formerly guarded (5.190–247). Areas from which priests with mere physical blemishes used to be barred soon flowed with human blood and gore (5.227–30). The

---

[26] Cf. Levine 1994 and the scholarship he discusses.

excursus is not mere geography. He takes advantage of the narrative break to offer a portrait of the remarkable *polis* that is about to be devastated.

The middle part of Book 5 (5.248–359) takes the audience through Titus' capture of the two outer walls – after many setbacks. Josephus continues changing from Judaean to Roman perspectives, occasionally highlighting individual contests. He also gives long-awaited numbers for the Judaean factions, in schematic and inflated figures: Simon controls 10,000 men under fifty officers plus 5,000 Idumaeans under ten officers (i.e., 500-man cohorts) in the city; John has 6,000 in his largely Galilean faction under twenty officers (300-man companies?), now with Eleazar's 2,400 Zealots. Thus 15,000 rebel fighters dominate the upper and lower cities, while just over half that number (8,400) occupy the temple precincts. This is the *stasis* that portends Jerusalem's destruction (5.248–57; cf. 1.10).

On the Roman side, Titus plans to break into the New City suburb to reach the Antonia and from there the temple, via what seems the weakest point north of the Upper City (5.260). He sets up ranks of artillery, javelin throwers, and archers to keep Judaeans off the walls while the army builds embankments (5.26–70). He orders the felling of trees for construction material. The Judaeans show incredible bravery, however, not merely appearing on the ramparts but actually rushing out in bold raiding parties (5.275–87). The midnight crash of a Roman siege tower creates general panic among the legions (5.291–95), but with iron-cased towers they manage to drive Judaeans from the wall. Sending scaling parties to open the gates, they quickly enter the New City from the northwest (5.302). Once inside, Titus has his army clear the ground – partly rebuilt after Cestius recently burned the suburb – and he establishes a camp beyond Judaean bow-range.

The Romans try to keep up this momentum and quickly take the second wall, the fortress Antonia, and the northwest side of the temple mount. This throws Judaean courage into starker relief. Josephus points out the psychological importance, on both sides, of winning a commander's notice. He gives Simon due credit as an inspiring commander, for whom his fighters would gladly offer their lives. On the Roman side, a cavalryman wanting to impress Titus charges into a Judaean raiding party, killing two of the enemy's bravest. On both sides, determination to please the commander exceeds what physical strength could achieve (5.309–12). Again, however, Josephus contrasts Judaean courage with Roman risk-aversion (Chapter 2). This is where Titus admonishes his troops "to show their masculinity in ways that did not involve risk to themselves" (5.316).

Further illustrating Judaean boldness, Josephus describes a trick they use to delay the battering of the second wall. This is where Castor appears on the parapet with friends, arms raised in surrender, and "Titus, because of his simplicity, trusted him." Castor sends word to Simon that he could play these fools for ages (5.322). He wonders in a stage whisper where on earth he is going to put all the money he has with him. Only shrewd Josephus restrains those near him from rushing forward. A soldier who does so anyway is badly wounded (5.317–30).

Such diversions keep the story moving and entertaining while developing Josephus' themes. The cold realities are briefly told, however. Romans capture the second wall but immediately lose it again in the face of Judaean determination (5.331). Josephus attributes to the setback Titus – not because he lacks courage but because of his humane desire to spare the city, which leads him to order his soldiers not to harm anyone. Taking this for weakness, the Judaeans mount a sustained attack, although again Titus personally stands his ground and covers his soldiers' retreat with his skill in archery (5.331–41). He soon regroups for a more methodical attack, which dissipates the Judaeans' joy. This time he secures his gains, destroys much of the second wall, and prepares for an attack on the final remaining wall (5.342–47).

Having come this far so quickly, Titus pauses in the hope that the spectacle of a four-day parade will inspire surrender without further bloodshed (5.348–55; Chapter 3). Josephus agrees that this would have worked if the tyrants inside had not ruthlessly prevented escape. When his tactic does not work, Titus still hopes the Judaeans will be open to persuasion from their compatriot Josephus. His oration constitutes the fourth section of volume 5.

In Chapter 2 we saw that all of *War*'s speeches are *tours de force*: a statesman pulling out the stops and bending facts as needed. This is a clear example. When he cannot persuade the rebels with "direct advice" (You are losing, so give up!), Josephus turns to lofty rhetoric, supposedly finding conducive examples in the nation's past. Knowing that the militants take inspiration from biblical heroes and Hasmonean rebels, Josephus advances the remarkable thesis that those very ancestors all achieved their victories *without arms*, and that if they ever resorted to arms they failed (5.390). He offers five examples of success without arms and four disasters when they were used, concluding (5.399): "Thus, *in no case have arms been granted* to our nation, and the waging of war is *certainly* attended by defeat."

Given the biblical narrative of Israelite conquest and battles with neighbours, this comes as a surprise. Even such a friendly observer such as Hecataeus *praised* Moses' reputation (anachronistically) for training the nation in martial virtues and leading armies against surrounding nations (Diodorus 40.3.6–7; cf. *Apion* 1.200–204). For Josephus himself, elsewhere, the Judaeans' innate martial prowess is nothing to apologize for. He reconfigures Moses as a uniquely effective general (*Ant.* 2.241–53; cf. 300) and emphasizes Joshua's policy of exterminating all living beings – men, women, and children (*Ant.* 5.25–29, 45–48, 59, 62; cf. 39). The Hebrews' great success in battle is the basis of their reputation (*Ant.* 5.63), and *War* 1.34–69 has fully celebrated Hasmonean conquests. But the speech of *War* 5 deliberately suppresses all that, mentioning armed opposition to Antiochus IV only as though it represented *failure* (*War* 5.394). Josephus' radically pacifistic statement has an effect, as fancy rhetoric does, eliciting a flood of deserters. But this causes John and Simon to enact even harsher measures against such deserters (5.420–23).

By any calculation the Roman army was already close to its objective of dominating the city, with the northern half securely in hand. Josephus' Titus does not see it that way, however. The final section of Book 5 highlights how much he has learned about the toughness of the city and its defenders, even with just one wall to go. The climactic event in this section is his decision, following consultation with the generals, to build an 8-km (5 mi) encircling wall with thirteen forts built into it (5.507–10). This is something that Romans would usually do, *if* they were going to do it, at the beginning of a planned siege.[27] His consultation on the matter now suggests that he has become frustrated by clinging to the hope of a quick submission. These people will not capitulate even when his massive army is almost on top of them!

Titus vents his frustration at the many setbacks, thinking largely of the consequences for his reputation: "for the glory of success would be much diminished by a long span of time. Given enough time, of course, *everything* is doable, but where fame is concerned speed is vital!" (5.498). So Titus wants to wait no longer. He will make the Judaeans "entirely despair of rescue" by cutting off all conceivable avenues of resupply or exit (5.498–99). The Epitome of Dio remarks that Titus closed up tunnels that Judaeans had been using to reach distant points in the countryside (65/66.4.5). Titus' frustration matches the despondency of his the army: "The Romans were in a deep funk … Many despaired of taking this city with the customary machines" (5.490).

Titus has earlier ordered his four legions to build four separate embankments, two on the west, directed at the Upper City, and two on the north end leading to the Antonia and temple (5.356). This is another huge task, requiring vast amounts of scarce wood to frame the fill that creates the earthen ramps. Thousands of soldiers labour non-stop for seventeen days (5.466) – into early June 70. When the embankments are finally ready to support battering rams, victory seems very close.

But John has ordered his troops to tunnel out from the Antonia and undermine the two ramps in that sector, first supporting the earth above with their own wood frames before setting these alight and causing Titus' ramps above to collapse. Simon launches an even bolder attack in the other sector. His men dash out from the Upper City with burning torches and set the

---

[27] *War* 3.176–70 (Iotapata); 4.12–13 (Gamala); 7.275 (Masada). Although Josephus does not mention such a wall at Machaerus, it has been revealed by archaeology (see Chapter 9). On the practice in general see Campbell (2006: 33–37, 39–41, 99, 101, 124–27, 192–95), who notes Athenian and Spartan anticipations of the Roman practice.

battering rams and other siege machines on fire, from which the fire spreads to the ramp frames. His men tear through the Roman camp in a spree (5.466–90). Their daring intensifies Titus' consternation, and he castigates his legionaries again for their carelessness (5.486–87). Again.

On the Judaean side this final section of Book 5 has begun with a fine-grained description of the horrors caused by the tyrants inside, focusing on the population's gnawing hunger. With no grain to be found, individuals are stealing food from the mouths of family members, even mothers from infants. Armed men – not themselves starving yet, but to secure provisions – force their way into homes that they find locked, assuming that food is being protected inside. Those deemed guilty of concealing food are tortured, some with stakes driven up the anus, to make them reveal where they have hidden it (5.435).

These passages convey *War*'s progressively darkening tone. We have moved from urbane observations about *polis* life under stress with occasional bloodshed vaguely described in Book 2 to virtual hell on earth. By the end of Book 5 Josephus' dispassionate posture in earlier volumes has given way to high emotion and condemnation (5.442–44):

> To put it concisely, no other city has ever suffered such horrors, and no generation since time began has been more productive of evil. . . . They [the tyrants] confessed themselves to be what they actually were: slaves and scum and bastard cast-offs of the nation. They were the ones who overthrew the city and forced the Romans to register a gloomy success; they alone drew the reluctant fire onto the shrine.

We have only now reached the situation anticipated in *War*'s preface (1.10–11). Josephus drives home the sufferings of Jerusalem's people also by reverting to the Roman side. The few Judaeans who find the courage to steal out of the city and collect grain are caught and, given a natural tendency to avoid arrest, treated as Rome's prisoners (5.449). This means torture and crucifixion: hundreds of bodies hanging on stakes for those inside Jerusalem to observe, with hate-filled Roman soldiers devising entertaining death-poses (5.446–51). As usual, Josephus does *not* disguise Roman cruelty. Titus feels sorry for the victims, but what can he do? He is still trying to intimidate those inside (5.450–51).

After Titus authorizes the encircling wall to force either submission or starvation (5.499), which the army completes in a record-setting three days because of their eagerness to get it over with (5.509), Book 5 lurches to a close with tales of unspeakable cruelty. Death permeates the city. With burial no longer possible, insurgents rob and mutilate corpses before flinging them over the ramparts (5.512–26). Simon even kills his high-priestly sponsor, after murdering the man's sons in front of him. An effort by one of Simon's officers to open the city to Titus is punished by public execution (5.527–40). An interesting detail is that Josephus' parents (his father a distinguished priest according to *Life* 5) are still in the city and now arrested by the rebel leaders (5.541–47).

Reverting to the Roman side again: this is where Josephus tells how the Arab contingent cut open Jerusalem's deserters in hopes of finding gold coins, as Titus complains ineffectually (5.548–61). Inside the temple, John has resorted to shamelessly plundering every scrap of the holy temple's stores (5.562–66) – although much will mysteriously remain to the end. Josephus concludes with a reckoning of Judaean dead from the civil strife alone. More than 600,000 corpses (!) have been carried out through the gates, he says, an untold number thrown over the walls, and *still others* piled up in the abandoned houses of the wealthy (5.567–71). These numbers would be high if divided by 1,000.

Finally taking heart from his encircling wall, Titus builds bigger siege embankments concentrated on the Antonia fortress, which he has come to see as his best line of access, now via the temple (5.522–26). As always, he is constantly adapting his tactics.

Book 6

The completion of these new ramps, requiring wood from 18 km (11 mi) away, opens Book 6. The first paragraphs offer a grim summary (6.1–5):

> The sufferings of the Jerusalemites brought a more dire situation every day, while the insurgents became even more stimulated by the calamities, the famine turning to feed on them after [devouring] the populace. The sheer volume of piled corpses in the city was a spectacle to make one shudder, and it gave off the stench of disease, an impediment to those fighting in the raiding parties. For just as with a military column, ... those who wanted to advance had to trample on the bodies. As they trod on them they did not shudder, did not pity, did not reckon on the bad omen for themselves in this outrage against those who had fallen. Their hands soaked in the blood of compatriots, they rushed out to make war on "the enemy"! ... The Romans, for their part, though enduring constant hardship in the gathering of the needed wood, raised up the ramps in twenty-one days. ...

Although the Romans make steady progress, Josephus claims that they remain as apprehensive as the besieged. Judaeans understand that they must demolish the new earthworks or face death, while Romans realize that if the Judaeans manage to destroy these as they have the others, they will never take the city. The legionaries are exhausted, physically and spiritually, and there is no more material should these go up in flames (6.9–12). The Romans are actually the more disconsolate, according to Josephus, for while they feel every reverse against Jerusalem's mighty walls, the Judaeans are not disheartened even by terrible sufferings (6.13–14; see Chapter 2). The Romans therefore guard their new earthworks closely. Sure enough, John's faction rushes out, but this time they fail.

Book 6 has two main parts: a series of further engagements leading to Maria's cannibalism and, after that central episode, the spreading fire of purgation. Judaeans rarely leave the walls now, for they lack the strength (cf. 5.520). But they are no less valiant, and Josephus continues to emphasize Roman reverses and dejection.

The Romans use their four new ramps to batter the Antonia. They have initial success and, when they stop for the night, one (part?) of the walls even collapses by itself. But John's men, aware of that weakness in their defences, which they accidentally caused by their undermining, have quickly built another wall inside it. The Romans should make rapid headway against this flimsy new emergency wall, except that to reach it they must clamber over the massive jagged rubble of the fallen wall. No one dares to go first and face nearly certain death (6.23–32).

The discovery of the wall behind so unnerves the Romans that Titus must give another speech (6.33–53). The themes of his talk are masculinity, disgrace, and shame. It would be unmanly of him, he says, to give a speech if the task ahead were easy. But the situation is dangerous, calling for real men. He dwells on the fortitude of the Judaeans. His legionaries should see that *not* as reason to lose heart, but as a challenge to their own masculinity. "It would be disgraceful for *Romans*, and *soldiers of mine* ... to be worsted in either strength or spirit by *Judaeans!*" (6.38; see Chapter 2).

Noting the absolute necessity of taking Antonia, Titus segues to the glory of death in battle. Infinitely better than dying of disease and old age, it brings eternal renown and bliss in the afterlife (6.46–49). Josephus' Titus is a wordsmith, who plays with Greek to create an elegant invitation to noble death.[28] And although he has been talking as if this were a suicide mission, he steps back to reassure them, it is not *necessarily* so. "Those who show themselves *to be men* have it in their power to be saved from even the most uncertain operations" (6.50). His soldiers *might conceivably* find the undertaking bloodless. They will not know until they dare. And if only a handful should make it through, well, that should suffice to make the Judaeans capitulate (6.52). Finally he returns to practical matters, promising that he will amply reward the leader of any assault, while any who fall in such a brave effort will receive the "most enviable prize – valour" (6.53).

This brilliantly desperate speech does not stir the jaded legionaries. An auxiliary soldier volunteers, however, inspiring eleven others to join him. He courageously scales the wall, only to slip on a rock and die in a furious Judaean assault from above. Three of his comrades also perish and the other

---

[28] *War* 6.49. "Give" (*didonai*) and "pay back" (*apodōsomen*) are forms of the same verb, while "practical requirements" (*chreiais*) and "that which is necessary" (*chreōn*) share a common root. Thus: Since we shall in any case *pay back* this loan of life to fate (i.e., to "*what is necessary*" in the long term), would it not be nobler to *give* it *voluntarily* to the practical *necessities* of this moment?

eight make it back wounded (6.54–67). Respecting the man's courage, Josephus reflects on the unpleasant work of fortune.

His description of the next engagement recognizes courage on both sides. Twenty-one legionaries join two cavalrymen and a trumpeter in a truly bold initiative. In the middle of the night they noiselessly climb over the Antonia rubble, kill the first Judaean sentries in their sleep, and put the rest to flight. They then sound the trumpet, making the Judaeans think Romans have arrived in force. This wakes up Titus, who quickly arrives to lead his best men over the top (5.68–71). Josephus then gives both John's and Simon's forces credit for holding back the legionaries, with a "prodigious exhibition of both strength and spirit" – in Thackeray's fine rendering (6.72). This battle, which spills from Antonia to the fiercely defended entrances to the temple courts, lasts from about 3:00 a.m. to 1:00 p.m. Even in their woefully diminished state, the Judaeans confine the Romans to the Antonia that day.

Josephus mentions another ill-fated Roman, however, a centurion from a Bithynian auxiliary unit, whom he has come to know and respect. This man sees Judaeans prevailing and rushes forward, single-handedly driving them back. But his cleated boots slide on the smoothly paved stones and he lands on his back, immobilized by his armour as Judaeans beat him to death. Titus watches from the Antonia and is moved but is in no position to help, while the man's comrades are paralyzed by fear (6.81–90). Again Josephus identifies the excellent Judaean fighters: two from John's faction, three from Simon's (including an Idumaean), and two Zealots – named separately in these dispatches although apparently under John's command.

Titus now orders the "foundations of the Antonia" (apparently not the tower itself)[29] razed to make space for still another set of ramps, preparatory to a newly planned assault on the temple platform (6.93; cf. 149). Only at this late point, amazingly, does the temple's continual daily sacrifice (tamid) of two lambs, one in the morning and one at twilight (cf. Num 28:3–8), cease for lack of animals (6.94–95).[30] At Titus' direction, Josephus makes a final appeal to John to spare the temple and come out with his hands up, adding sarcastically: If anyone had deprived *John* of food, he would consider them an enemy. Yet here he is depriving *God* of food (with the end of the sacrifices)!

---

[29] From *War* 5.238–42, where Josephus distinguishes the glacis covered with smooth flagstones from "the tower," it is unclear what counted as "foundations." Presumably the glacis was the most obtrusive part of the structure, occupying a much larger area than the upright tower, which remains standing as an observation post for Titus long after the foundations are destroyed (6.133, 135, 145, 246, 249).

[30] Our manuscripts (dating from 900 years after Josephus' time) all mention a lack of *men* (*andrōn*) here. But because the sacrifices did not require many men, it is a reasonable conjecture that Josephus wrote about a lack of lambs (*arnōn*), the animals used for the *tamid*, a much more easily understood problem under siege conditions, and an early copyist misunderstood.

This argument does not convince John, but Josephus' words inspire remaining members of the priestly elite – perhaps because the sacrifices are finished – to desert. Titus moves them to a secure camp at Gophna in the north, far from the siege. He is soon forced to bring them back, however, when the rebel leaders use their disappearance as proof that Romans kill deserters (6.113–23; cf. Chapter 3). A short speech from Titus to John and Simon, translated by Josephus, is treated with the usual contempt (6.124–29). Titus then tries to repeat his success with the Antonia in a night-time assault on the temple court from the fortress's high position. Although he sends in as large a force as possible, only a few thousand can proceed through the bottleneck connecting the two structures, so he selects the best thirty from each century (6.131). They go in at around 3:00 a.m. again, but this time the Judaean sentries are awake and put up a fierce resistance. This ends around 11:00 a.m. in a draw, with the Romans *still* confined to the Antonia (6.147). Josephus names admirable fighters on both sides, again distinguishing the Judaeans by faction.

With his plan to use the Antonia as a route into the temple proving unviable because of the bottleneck, Titus reluctantly resorts to Plan D and orders his legions to build *yet another* four ramps. This time all four will be directed at the temple's outer court, with two approaching from the north and two from the western wall, north of the ("first") city wall protecting the Upper City. Josephus observes the challenges this poses for the exhausted Romans, who must now bring supplies from 20 km (12.5 mi) away, even as the Judaeans work feverishly to prevent their construction. The incorrigible Roman soldiers drop their guard again. When some cavalrymen take their horses to go foraging and leave them off the bridle, Judaeans appear out of nowhere and steal them – perhaps for meat.[31] Titus has one trooper executed for this carelessness (6.150–56).

In a desperate need for food, the Judaeans attempt yet another raid of the Tenth Legion's camp on Mount of Olives, but they are much weakened now, and the camp is securely defended. Hoping for surprise, they attack when the soldiers are at dinner, but this time they fail catastrophically. Josephus pictures a vignette: A strong – and flexible – cavalryman swoops down and grabs a fully armoured young Judaean by his ankle, carrying him upside-down to Titus (6.157–63).

It is now, in the debilitating heat of mid-July A.D. 70, that destructive fire is introduced to the temple precinct (6.164–65). It starts because the Judaeans, having lost the Antonia, decide to sever the colonnade connecting fortress and

---

[31] As non-ruminants, horses are not kosher (Deut 14:1–8). Yet one must wonder whether, with Jerusalem's besieged population starving and cannibalism becoming a possibility (6.200–213), captured horses would not be used for meat. Josephus will later charge John with having put food that was not permitted on his table (7.264).

temple. They had cut this four years earlier to prevent Florus' auxiliary from raiding the temple treasury via the Antonia, but quickly repaired it at Agrippa's urging (2.330–31, 403–405). Now they decide to burn through a 10-m (32.5-ft) section of the wooden ceiling and pull it down. To show that this does not worry them, the Romans themselves set fire to an even longer stretch, which the Judaeans also pull down (6.166).

Josephus now changes scene to the western gate of the city, behind which is the Upper City controlled by Simon. Again he focuses on an individual encounter. A Judaean named Jonathan, a small and ugly fellow lacking any distinction, comes out from the wall and abuses the besieging troops, challenging any of them to single combat – a reverse Goliath. Josephus divines that his challenge elicited three mental responses among the Romans: sneering contempt, fear, and reluctance to get involved with a crazy man. After a while the cavalryman Pudens rises to the challenge, presuming on the fellow's puny stature. Just as he is ready to deliver the decisive blow, however, Pudens is betrayed by fortune. He slips and falls, and Jonathan does him in. But then, while the ecstatic Judaean is performing a victory dance on the Roman's corpse, a centurion transfixes him with an arrow. Writhing in agony, Jonathan falls on top of his victim's body, "illustrating the very swift retribution (*nemesis*) that comes upon those who enjoy irrational good fortune in war" (6.176). Whatever basis it had in reality, the diverting episode is dense with biblical and classical precedents as well as Josephus' literary motifs.[32]

Now comes the final incident of Book 6's first half. While keeping up ostentatious efforts to destroy the ramps, the Judaeans secretly insert kindling-wood and bitumen into the upper spaces of the temple's western colonnade, between the beams and the ceiling. Then they noisily withdraw, giving the impression of going to rest. This entices incautious legionaries to throw up ladders against the western colonnade, walking straight into the trap. Once the roof is full of them, concealed Judaeans ignite the underside. The five ways in which the Romans die reprise the five ways in which Judaeans had died on the very same place in 4 B.C., with Romans burning the structure (*War* 2.49–50) – a parallel contributing to the work's large-scale symmetry (Chapter 2).

Josephus offers contrasting images of the doomed legionaries on the colonnade. A certain Longus, on the one hand, dismissing Judaean pledges of safety, bravely plunges a sword into his body (6.186–87). Artorius, on the other hand, survives by a cruel guile. Calling over his tent-mate Lucius and offering him all

---

[32] I demur here from Goldsworthy's appraisal (1996: 267): "the fullest complete account from our period of a duel of this nature." It *is* full, but full of what? For single combat in Homer see *Il.* 7.43–312 (Hector demands single combat, met initially by Achaean cowardice but ending in a fight with Ajax); 16.712–867 (Hector and Patroclus); 20.353–78 (Achilles demands single combat from the Trojans); 22.90–366 (Achilles and Hector).

his worldly possessions if Lucius will catch him when he jumps, Artorius persuades the man and jumps – saving his own life while freeing himself from obligation to the dead beneficiary under him (6.188–89). Josephus may intend a pun for his Roman audience in telling this story, for Artorius' Latin name means "the Squasher, the Compressor."[33]

It is unclear for us, who are blessed with maps unlike Josephus' audiences, where the Romans are supposed to be at this point. We assume that they remain outside the temple mount, against which the ramps have been built, for Josephus will soon describe another futile effort to gain the outer court (6.220–27). But the story just related puts the soldiers in the outer court, where they burn the remains of the northern colonnade (6.192) and on Titus' order fire the silver-coated gates of the inner temple complex with its porticoes (6.232–35). Artorius' jumping spot is relevant. If he leapt from the colonnade roof to the bottom of the Tyropoeon Valley, 30 m (100 ft) below, his chances of hitting Lucius were slim to none. If the Romans held the outer court, Lucius may have been only 12–13 m (40 ft) below him, on the temple platform – still a challenge and enough to crush the human shock absorber, but a more plausible gamble. Confusing topography is not unusual in Josephus, as we have seen.

Josephus now approaches the climactic episode of Jerusalem's horrors, returning to the hunger and its consequences (6.193–98):

> Of those throughout the city who were wasting away from the famine, a countless number were falling, and the sufferings that occurred were indescribable. In each house, if even some shadow of food should appear, there was war: the closest relatives raised their hands against one another, snatching away the miserable scraps needed for the soul's survival. Not even the dying were trusted to truly be in want, but the robbers searched also those who were expiring in case someone had food in the fold of his cloak and was faking his own death. Those who were gaping from hunger would stagger around like raving dogs, and go off rattling and smashing doors the way that drunks do, and in their confusion would burst into the same house two or three times in a single hour. Necessity was bringing *everything* to the mouth and they were collecting – and degrading themselves to eat – items that even dumb animals consider disgusting: in the end they did not hold themselves back from belts and sandals. . . . For some, food was a tuft of withered grass.

This is where Josephus introduces the aristocrat Maria, who has fled to the mother-city from Peraea (6.201–13; see Chapter 2). When Titus hears about the atrocity of her cannibalism, he concludes that "it was no longer possible to bring to reason those who had already suffered everything that, in order not to

---

[33] Artorius was, however, a common name.

suffer, it would have made sense to reform oneself" (2.219). With the population past saving, he must bury the city.

In a sharp departure from the attrition, indecisive engagements, innumerable setbacks, partial waves of desertions, and appeals for surrender until this point, events now move quickly. Battering rams are applied to the upper western wall of the temple mount, while on the north side the legionaries throw ladders up to the colonnades. With the advantage of elevation, the Judaeans throw the ladders back or stab the soldiers as they arrive, as in the movies. Josephus again credits courage on both sides, including even that of "the tyrant Simon's nephew" (6.220–27).

Titus now orders the gates of the central temple complex set on fire, abandoning his futile efforts to spare "foreign holy places" (6.198, 201). This biblically mandated temple structure, inside Herod's large Court of the Nations (approximately where the Dome of the Rock stands today), was a rectangular structure oriented roughly west to east. We cannot be sure of its appearance, and scholarly reconstructions differ.[34] A later rabbinic passage (*m. Midd.* 2.6) indicates nine monumental gates: four each along the north and south and one on the east. These were made of wood coated with silver and with gold fittings. The eastern part of the temple structure was the 61-m (200-ft) square of the rectangle called the Court of Women, into which the easternmost gates on the north and south opened, as did the eastern gate. At the western end, up fourteen or fifteen semicircular steps (about 3 m, 10 ft), was the massive bronze double door known as Nicanor's Gate, through which only Judaean males in a state of purity could pass.[35] When Titus orders these gates fired, then, it cannot be a matter of simply lighting matches. The heat must be intense enough to melt the silver, consume the wood inside, and spread from there to the inner temple's colonnade (6.233–35).

When the fire has done its preparatory work, Titus orders the flames extinguished and the legionaries to rest, while auxiliaries clear paths through the rubble for a final assault on the inner temple, the home of the Zealot faction and John's other forces. This is the point at which Titus holds his notorious council of war on the temple's fate. This is important enough to merit separate investigation in Chapter 8. In that story Titus decides to spare the temple as a symbol of Roman power. He rests most of his troops and himself for the final push to occupy the site intact, after the bravest auxiliary soldiers quench the fires.

---

[34] E.g., Ritmeyer 2006a: 131 and Patrich 2009: 56 fig. 27 both rely more heavily (than Fig. 8.5) on the Mishnah passage, but still they differ considerably.

[35] *War* 5.201; *Ant.* 15.418. The latter includes the awkward note that ritually pure priests entered the court through this gate *with their wives*.

But before 8:00 a.m. next day, the exhausted Zealots and Galileans inside the temple compound, seeing their imminent fate and with nothing left to lose, charge out through the still-smouldering gates and fight the auxiliary soldiers in the courtyard (6.244–48). Titus observes this from the Antonia and, seeing his men weakening against Judaean determination, sends in a mounted unit to contain the Judaeans in the temple – by about 11:00 a.m. Satisfied that this has worked, he calls it a day, planning to take the temple the next morning when the fires are out.

The Judaeans, however, burst out again to engage the soldiers tasked with extinguishing the fires. One of these, in the ensuing melee, grabs a burning timber. "Driven by some other-worldly impulse" and hoisted on a comrade's shoulders, he tosses it through a high window into the storerooms around the inner sanctuary that contains the Holy Place and Holy of Holies. The firebrand catches flammable material inside and flames shoot up (6.244–53).

A messenger rouses Titus, apparently from a siesta. He runs out in a panic, "just as he was," to extinguish the fire. He might have had a chance if he had not been followed by senior commanders and "the greatly agitated legions" (6.255), all them nervously primed for the final push. In the chaos the legionaries charge ahead and overrun the temple without awaiting orders, as usual. Titus screams and waves his arms about (6.256, 260), but the hysterical soldiers "recognize only fervour as their commander" (6.257) and pour into the temple, where some of them are trampled to death by their comrades' hobnailed boots. In addition to rage against their long-fought Judaean enemy, plunder is an irresistible attraction, for the treasury still surprisingly holds considerable wealth. Josephus claims that the legionaries' plundering led to a 50 percent drop in the local value of gold (6.317).

Titus can do little more than collar a centurion and spearman, ordering them to thrash a few private soldiers for disobedience. But it is a hopeless gesture. Someone sets alight the doors into the Holy Place, which go up in flames. Titus and his commanders give up and withdraw (6.260–66). This is Josephus' picture of Jerusalem's mighty conqueror.

Josephus redirects his focus to the Judaeans who are suffering, their shrieks and cries echoing off Peraea's hills across the Jordan Valley as the sanctuary burns and the thousands trapped inside are slaughtered. He also names exceptions. John and many of his militants force their way out and into the Upper City, not yet in Roman hands. (Again we wonder: How were they able to move so easily into the Upper City when the Roman army could not?) Several priests voluntarily leap into the flames.

Some 6,000 common folk, especially women and children, take refuge on the roof of the sole remaining colonnade, to the east. They do so because a false prophet has promised imminent divine deliverance. But legionaries burn the ceiling of that structure from below, bringing death to all (6.271–85). Josephus takes the opportunity to ridicule false prophets, many of whom the tyrants have co-opted to keep the simple folk loyal. This prompts a digression on the allegedly genuine omens from recent years that should have portended the city's *doom* – celestial signs and wonders coupled with eerie terrestrial phenomena (6.288–315).

As the legions infest the temple precinct, they begin to offer their familiar sacrifices to the Roman Gods represented by their standards. Titus has run out of mercy for Judaeans and, after regretting that he allowed a young priest to live, who outwitted him (again!), he orders the immediate execution of any Judaeans who show themselves (6.316–22).

Jerusalem's Upper and Lower Cities, inside the city's oldest wall south and west, remain untaken. But with the Romans now occupying the temple heights above, their fate is not in doubt. John, finding himself in his enemy Simon's area, joins with him in sending word to Titus to ask for terms. They agree to hand over the city if Titus allows them to pass through his lines with their families "into the desert" – presumably to a fortress (see Chapter 9). Titus, standing on the bridge over what we call Wilson's Arch, relishes the moment. He gives them a lecture on their behaviour and the impertinence of their request. His theme is Roman humanity (ἡ Ῥωμαίων φιλανθρωπία, 6.333), which he contrasts with their compulsive belligerence. Still Titus restrains his soldiers from cutting down the pair on the spot – because of his innate humanity (διὰ τὸ φιλάνθρωπον φύσει). The epigraph to Chapter 6 quotes from this speech: Vespasian's delay in Galilee from humanity (τὸ φιλάνθρωπον, 6.340, 341) is just one of several proofs offered by Titus, most of which concern his own behaviour. Given that Josephus wrote the speech as we have it, after the fact, we are not surprised that it echoes the orations he wrote for Agrippa II and his own character (e.g., 6.328–32), although it is crafted to suit the Roman. Titus is indeed willing to accept their surrender, he says, *even* now – but their safe departure is out of the question.

The tragic irony of the story reaches its apex here as these two *tyrants*, looking across the Tyropoeon valley at the flames consuming the temple, the result of their long and bloody civil war (*stasis*), request safe departure together – as though they had nothing to do with it (6.323–27, 351). In refusing to surrender, they proudly refer to an oath they have taken never to accept terms (6.351). But author and literary audience know that their actions in the service of "freedom" have brought only slavery or death to those around them. Titus' blanket claims about Roman humanity are also, however, at odds with Josephus' narrative. As usual, Josephus accentuates the psychological dynamics. The rebels request the parley, but Titus chooses the interpreter – possibly Josephus – and also speaks first to show that *he* is in charge (ὅπερ ἦν τεκμήριον τοῦ κρατεῖν, 6.327). Whatever happens now will be his decision. When John and Simon decline his offer of surrender on the spot, he advises them to fight for their lives (6.352–53).

On the next day his army has no difficulty moving out into the Ophel and Lower City, directly south of the temple, burning and destroying at will. Only at this point do the Adiabenian royals in Jerusalem, who have been involved in the fighting from the start (2.520) but remained vaguely in the background,[36] request protection from Titus. Other leading citizens try to ride their noble coat-tails. Titus, enraged that they have not surrendered before now, nevertheless agrees and will soon send them to Rome (6.356–57).

The Romans are now poised to overrun the Upper City, but (in spite of John's easy transfer there) this will be still be very difficult because of the terrain and a wall of some kind protecting the eastern slope. The rebel fighters now commandeer Herod's former palace, the spacious grounds of which had become a refuge for thousands of commoners, whom the militants blithely kill (6.358). They also now capture two Roman soldiers, in a scene I mentioned in Chapter 3. One they execute on the spot and parade around the Upper City. The other alertly claims to have crucial intelligence, which buys him a brief stay. When he is about to be beheaded, he makes a dash for the Roman ranks. Titus expels him from the legion for having been captured (6.359–62).

Titus proceeds to burn the now-deserted Lower City. Cautious to the end, he decides that an assault on the Upper City from that point, across Jerusalem's central valley, would be ill advised. So he orders a *fifth* series of four siege ramps to be constructed against the western wall of the Upper City (south of Jaffa Gate). These will give his legions direct access from high ground (Fig. 28). Auxiliaries and allies prepare secondary assault routes from the east side (6.363–77).

Here Josephus makes one of several revealing references to tunnels beneath Jerusalem, which the rebel leaders now consider their last possible refuge. They still think that they can wait out the Roman assaults for the moment, before making their escape via the same tunnels. To make this work, however, they must keep other Judaeans out of the tunnels. They are especially quick to kill anyone found hiding there with food (6.370–73).

The final and massive wave of surrenders comes now. Even the Idumaean fighters dispatch secret negotiators to Titus, who offers them amnesty in the hope of precipitating a collapse of rebel morale. But on their return, the five emissaries are killed by Simon's men, and he imprisons the Idumaean commanders. Nevertheless, tens of thousands of other Judaeans (!) overwhelm the sentries and surrender, as the ever-merciful Titus countermands his earlier order to kill everyone found.

---

[36] Cf. *War* 4.567; 5.474, contradicting Agrippa II's assertion (in a speech composed for him after the war) that Adiabene would want no part in this conflict.

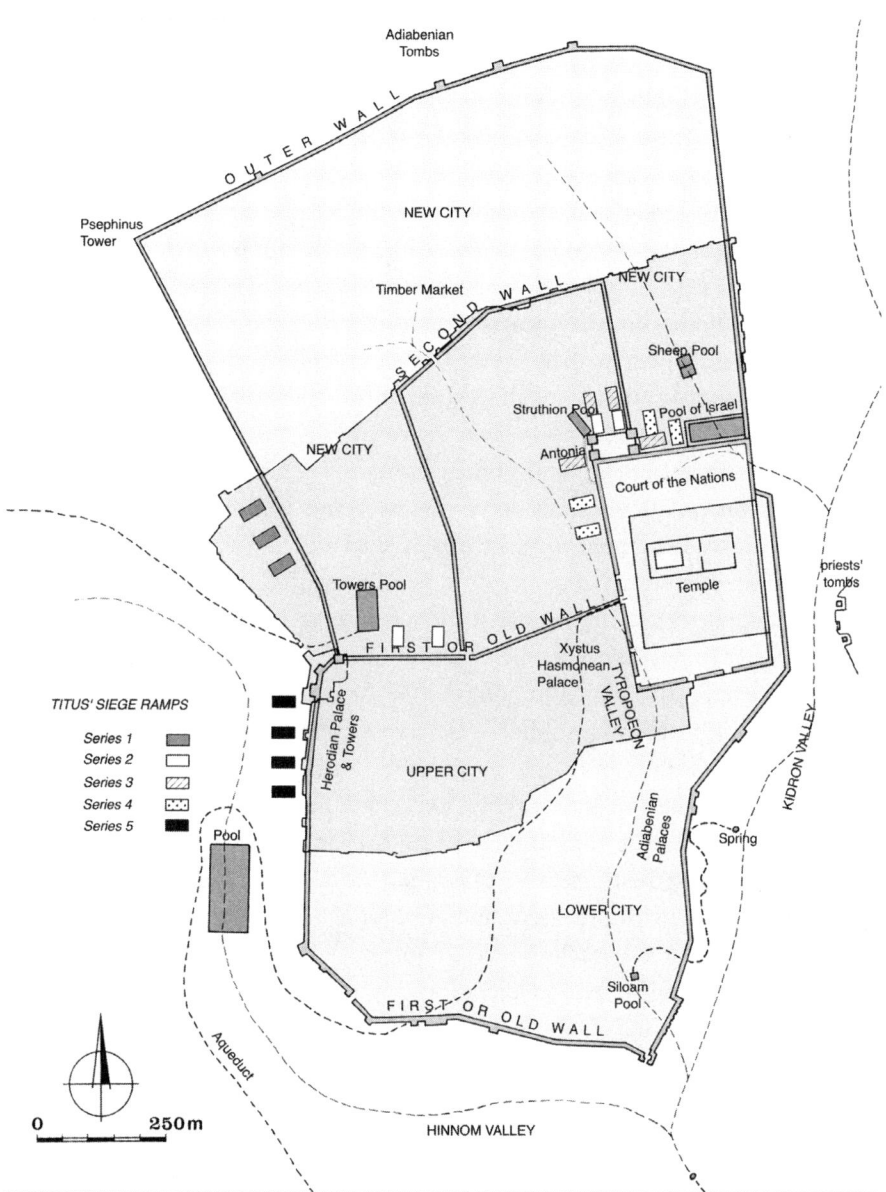

FIGURE 28. Plan of Jerusalem with Titus' five successive groups of siege ramps marked. Plan © Leen Ritmeyer, annotations (permitted) by the author

Josephus makes two noteworthy distinctions here. First, whereas Titus lets the refugees live *because of his character*, the legionaries do so because they are sated with killing and plunder, although they continue to ignore orders (6.383). Second, and more important, Titus allows the *original residents* of Jerusalem to remain free, after detaining them briefly, whereas "the other crowd" of those who have come from elsewhere he wants sold into slavery (6.384). This distinction between Jerusalem's actual residents (cf. 6.344) and outsiders recalls Taricheae and Gamala (Chapter 6). It is in keeping with Josephus' earlier claims that Jerusalem's population and leaders would have surrendered had the city not been overrun by outside strongmen and countless refugees.

An unnamed priest and the temple treasurer now manage to win Titus' favour by presenting him with, or disclosing the location of, hidden treasures: exquisite gold vessels, rare and expensive textiles, exotic spices, and ornaments (6.378–91). These were presumably reserved for the coming triumph, although I argued in Chapter 1 that even so they would hardly account for the treasures displayed then, much less for the construction of the Flavian Amphitheatre.

With the western siege works finally completed, Titus makes his last assault: The rams knock down sections of the wall and legionaries pour through. Josephus uses the moment to make fun of John and Simon, first for their want of courage – these tough guys tried to flee through holes in the wall, but their soldiers had deserted them – and then for their lack of intelligence. Not realizing that they could have held out for some time in the strong Herodian towers, they went down to the tunnels (6.392–402).

As soon as the Roman soldiers enter the Upper City they wreak havoc in the usual way: killing everyone they meet, looting, and burning. The commander allows them a day for this, then orders that only those who resist should be killed. Disobeying him, as usual, they kill the old and weak, keeping only the strongest males captive. Titus puts a trusted freedman in charge of guarding thousands of prisoners, and appoints "Fronto, one of his friends, to determine the fate that each deserved" (6.416). Under his tender mercies and prolonged assessment, 11,000 die of starvation – some denied food, some refusing it. Fronto selects the tallest and strongest for what they still assume will be Titus' (not Vespasian's) triumph. Of the rest, those under 17 are sold into slavery, while the mature men are assigned to labour projects in Egypt or to death-as-entertainment in Titus' coming eastern celebrations.

Josephus claims that 1.1 million Judaeans died in the siege of Jerusalem, *most having come from outside*, and that another 97,000 were taken prisoner. Admitting that his numbers will seem incredible, he cites the dodgy census that Cestius requested from the priests to convince Nero (6.414–28; Chapter 5). But the walled city, only about 2.5 km² (1 sq. mi), lacking high-rise buildings and including large public spaces, could not have accommodated more than about 20,000 to 30,000, perhaps 50,000 including all surrounding villages.[37]

---

[37] Geva 2014: 144–48, reviewing earlier estimates, considers 20,000 the high end.

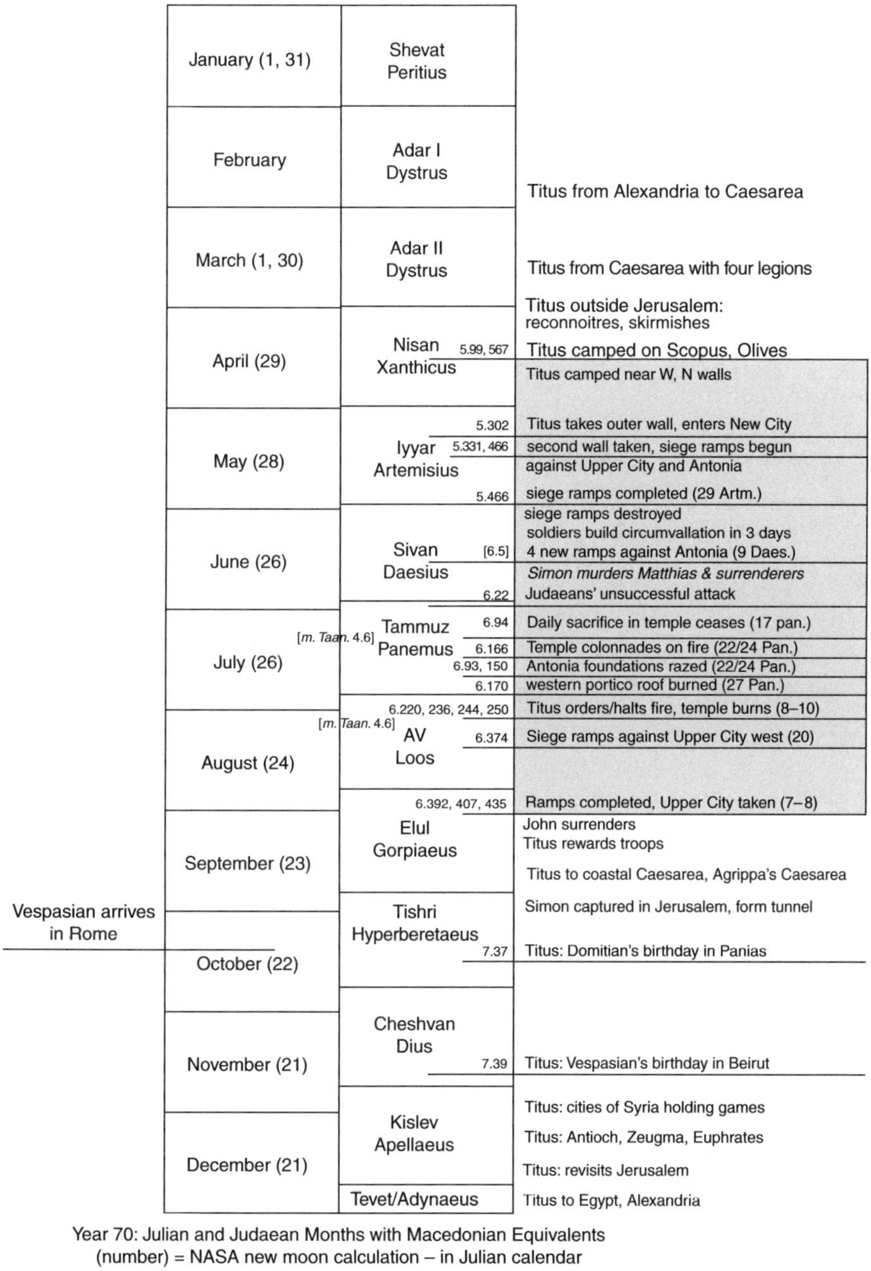

Julian month	Hebrew / Macedonian	NASA	Event
January (1, 31)	Shevat / Peritius		
February	Adar I / Dystrus		Titus from Alexandria to Caesarea
March (1, 30)	Adar II / Dystrus		Titus from Caesarea with four legions
April (29)	Nisan / Xanthicus	5.99, 567	Titus outside Jerusalem: reconnoitres, skirmishes / Titus camped on Scopus, Olives / Titus camped near W, N walls
May (28)	Iyyar / Artemisius	5.302 / 5.331, 466 / 5.466	Titus takes outer wall, enters New City / second wall taken, siege ramps begun / against Upper City and Antonia / siege ramps completed (29 Artm.)
June (26)	Sivan / Daesius	[6.5] / 6.22	siege ramps destroyed / soldiers build circumvallation in 3 days / 4 new ramps against Antonia (9 Daes.) / *Simon murders Matthias & surrenderers* / Judaeans' unsuccessful attack
July (26)	Tammuz / Panemus [m. Taan. 4.6]	6.94 / 6.166 / 6.93, 150 / 6.170	Daily sacrifice in temple ceases (17 pan.) / Temple colonnades on fire (22/24 Pan.) / Antonia foundations razed (22/24 Pan.) / western portico roof burned (27 Pan.)
August (24)	AV / Loos [m. Taan. 4.6]	6.220, 236, 244, 250 / 6.374 / 6.392, 407, 435	Titus orders/halts fire, temple burns (8–10) / Siege ramps against Upper City west (20) / Ramps completed, Upper City taken (7–8)
September (23)	Elul / Gorpiaeus		John surrenders / Titus rewards troops / Titus to coastal Caesarea, Agrippa's Caesarea
October (22)	Tishri / Hyperberetaeus	7.37	Simon captured in Jerusalem, form tunnel / Titus: Domitian's birthday in Panias
November (21)	Cheshvan / Dius	7.39	Titus: Vespasian's birthday in Beirut
December (21)	Kislev / Apellaeus		Titus: cities of Syria holding games / Titus: Antioch, Zeugma, Euphrates / Titus: revisits Jerusalem
	Tevet/Adynaeus		Titus to Egypt, Alexandria

Vespasian arrives in Rome *(between September and October)*

Year 70: Julian and Judaean Months with Macedonian Equivalents
(number) = NASA new moon calculation – in Julian calendar

FIGURE 29. Calendar of A.D. 70 showing Julian-Roman solar months aligned with Hebrew lunar (and equivalent Macedonian) months, with Josephus' dated events anchoring the others listed.

Once they discover the tunnels, the Romans begin to search for hideaways. John, who has been unable to find adequate food underground, emerges to surrender – around September 2 (Fig. 29). He will be reserved for the triumph and incarcerated "for life" (6.429–34).[38] Josephus anticipates the capture of Simon also, but holds that event over to Book 7 because it happens later – after Titus has celebrated with his soldiers, dispensed medals, and departed for recreation in Agrippa's territory. Simon seems a tougher character than John. He went underground prepared, with many days' provisions and accompanied by stone-workers with tools. He was not going to be limited by existing tunnels, but would dig out wherever necessary to escape. Alas, his food runs out before he can succeed. Even then he decides on a bold move. He emerges from the temple's former site, in white robes draped with purple, hoping to scare the daylights out of the superstitious legionaries. For a moment he succeeds, but they recover their senses and seize him. An officer delivers him to Titus in coastal Caesarea, from where Simon will travel to Rome as the triumph's chosen victim, the "enemy general" (7.26–36).

II. CRITICAL ASSESSMENT: KEY GROUPS AND INDIVIDUALS

To help us clarify what our historical scenarios will need to explain (Chapter 8), we now try to pull together Josephus' information concerning key groups and individuals involved in the siege.

A. General

War's complexities of plot and characterization combined with sometimes lurid detail are impressive. There are several things to say about this vividness. First, because similar kinds of things were part of every war, by Josephus' time a set of commonplaces for describing violence was shared by authors and audiences. These have been well synthesized by Viktor D'Huys,[39] and my summary is indebted to his.

Whereas some writers rejected gory detail as at odds with history's higher moral purposes, others reckoned its absence a betrayal of the truth mandate, for battles *did* spill blood. But opening the door to graphic violence could result in voyeuristic exploitation or turn history into tragedy. Polybius assumed the need for vivid description and illustrated it, but rejected emotion-rousing

---

[38] Whatever Josephus' phrase (ὁ δ' Ἰωάννης δεσμοῖς αἰωνίοις) means, we should not think of these perpetual bonds as a life sentence in a penitentiary; it is unlikely that John survived into his golden years. Corporal or capital punishments were the usual sentences, those in custody normally awaiting trial before such a verdict, although fit young prisoners of war might be sent to hard labour somewhere. One could languish in pretrial custody for years, in widely varying conditions according to personal status and situation. Erstwhile Roman ally King Jugurtha, thrown into Rome's dungeon at Marius' triumph, died after or because of starvation within a week (Plutarch, *Mar.* 12.3–4).

[39] D'Huys 1987.

devices (cf. Chapter 2). For him, only truly important battles merited a measure of gory-detail treatment, and in such rare cases the historian must be an eyewitness. There was no point processing others' accounts through one's own fertile imagination. Polybius' criteria are clear in his description of the siege of Abydus in 200 B.C. (16.30.2–3):

> This operation was not at all remarkable for its range of equipment or the variety of clever plans connected with the siege-works. . . . No, this is worthy of recollection and being passed along to posterity, if ever anything was, precisely because of the excellent character and extraordinary courage of the besieged.

Judging history by rhetorical criteria, however, critics typically invoked style and taste when they assessed literary portraits of violence.

Partly because we know about those concerns, we can become so preoccupied with the literary features of Josephus' reporting that we forget the awful realities that must have lain beneath it. Most of us are spared the experience of mass carnage, but vividly reported massacres in modern conflicts, from the Nazi *Einsatzgruppen* to Cambodia, Rwanda, Srebrenica, and Syria, resemble Josephus' portraits in striking ways. He was at least nearby for much of it and his *realistic* account – regardless of whether it is accurate in relation to specific actions – comes from hard experience of war's barbarity. The story is undeniably stylized. Simple reporting would not use such language as "compatriot slaughter," *stasis*, and lamentation, or formulaically stress the plight of women and children. But Josephus' colourful descriptions of fires, confusion, fear, and hunger are plausible even if they follow well-trodden paths. His cannibalism story illustrates this mixture of real life and literary craft. Famine and siege *did and do* produce cannibalism, even if he composed the story of Maria from a suite of literary models (Chapter 2).[40]

Quintilian, Josephus' contemporary in Rome, shows the influence of rhetoric on war writing. Insisting that all writing be "masculine and chaste, free from all artificial dyes" (8.3.6), he places weight on the importance of vivid representation (ἐνάργεια). Descriptions should be so clear that they turn the audience into virtual spectators (8.3.61–63). In a passage I mentioned for different reasons in Chapter 1, Quintilian uses the captured city as an example (8.3.67–70):

> No doubt, someone who says that "a city was captured" subsumes under that expression everything that such a misfortune entails, but this kind of brief report does not get through to *the emotions*. Now if you expand everything that this one word ["captured"] embodies, then: flames will appear spreading over houses and temples, and the crash of falling roofs and a confused noise of many cries will be heard: . . . there will be wailing

---

[40] See Chapman 2007.

of women and children and laments of old men preserved by a miserable fate to see that day. Then will come the pillaging of sacred and profane treasures, the hurrying of the plunderers back and forth. . . . So although, as I said, all these things are included in the "taking of a city," it is less impressive to say it at once like that than to elaborate everything. We shall achieve the vividness we are after *if we only provide verisimilitude*, and *we may even concoct fictitious incidents* of the kind that commonly occur.

Josephus was not one to say simply "Jerusalem was taken." Because his artistry is so compelling, we need to prod ourselves to keep thinking about *what he does not report.*

To take an obvious case, Josephus never hints at acts of rape, although it always accompanies armed conflict. In a later work he mentions the assumption that captured women will have been raped.[41] But as in most modern war films, no matter how violent their depictions of heroism, rape was not an acceptable subject for vivid representation. When Diodorus Siculus recounts the slaughter of fellow-citizens by Agathocles of Syracuse (early third century B.C.), he sounds much like Josephus as he describes the appalling ways in which men kill each other. He then makes a general comment about the violation of women, but steps back because "none of our readers wants to hear every detail, *when he knows full well what is involved.*" Men who boldly slaughter other men by day, he allows, "do not in addition require someone to elaborate on what they did by night" (19.8.4–5).[42] Without dropping even these hints, Josephus keeps his dramatic account within conventional bounds. It is, again, a highly selective story.

The detail that Josephus provides can deceive us into thinking that we have a comprehensive account. Whenever he stops to describe an encounter between two men, or to focus on a single raiding party, therefore, we should remember that he makes no mention of what was happening with the other tens of thousands. When he mentions the names of legates who attended the temple *consilium* (6.237), we might consider how little he says even about their activities, let alone about their tribunes and centurions, the allied commanders, and the common soldiers. We do not *even* hear about Agrippa II or the other allied kings or about Tiberius Julius Alexander, who had overall command of the army. That is a lot to be missing from the history of a war. Nor does Josephus describe communications among the Roman officer staff, their aims, views, and sentiments, specific unit assignments, accommodations, diet, physical and psychological disorders, or virtually anything of daily life.

---

[41] *War* 7.334, 377, 385; *Ant.* 3.276; 13.292; *Apion* 1.35; 2.212.

[42] For the contrast between vivid detail other violence and reluctance in connection with rape, see D'Huys 1987: 216.

We are not even clear about Josephus' location or activities during the siege (cf. Chapter 2): As we have seen, he opts to avoid almost all self-reference except where he can take centre stage.[43] When we learn incidentally that his parents and other family members were still in Jerusalem near the end, we might imagine that he was torn up as he sat among the besiegers. But he says nothing of that, or the vast bulk of what occurred day to day.

B. Groups and individuals

We now draw together Josephus' narrative threads concerning Jerusalem's main groups and individuals. We may pass by one label often associated with the war. We examined the term *sicarii* in Chapter 4 and will return to it in Chapter 9, but *sicarii* do not appear in the Galilean or the Judaean conflicts. The following groups and individuals figure significantly.

Eleazar son of Simon and his followers

Considering the frequency with which Zealots appear in *War*, and especially in scholarship, both the group and its early leader Eleazar present a surprising number of problems. Eleazar first appears near the end of *War* 2, where Josephus introduces the men supposedly elected to regional commands after Cestius' defeat. Eleazar has taken control of goods plundered from Cestius and also the public treasuries. The authorities keep him from power, however, on the ground that he is tyrannical. One proof is that "the Zealots under him were adopting the habits of spear-bearers [i.e., a tyrant's bodyguard]." In spite of this initial rejection, Eleazar gradually wins a following and hence a role in leadership because he is an "enchanter" (γόης), a term used of political demagogues with rhetorical skill,[44] and because those in charge need his resources (*War* 2.564–65).

At Eleazar's next possible appearance, John has arrived in Jerusalem and is encouraging the Zealots to seek help from the Idumaeans. Among the Zealot leaders are *the priests* Eleazar and Zacharias (4.224–25), and Eleazar "definitely seemed the most influential man among them" (4.225). The best manuscripts give this man's name as *son of Gion*, confusingly, although *War* 5.5 (referring to 4.151) says again that Eleazar *son of Simon* led the Zealots during this early factional strife. Given the frequent confusion over names in the manuscripts

---

[43] *War* 5.261, 325, 361, 375, 541–46; 6.96–99, 11, 118, 129, 365.
[44] Also *War* 2.264; 4.85; 5.317; *Ant.* 20.97, 160, 167, 188; *Apion* 2.145, 161. Cf. Plato *Soph.* 234c, 235a, 241b; *Euthyd.* 288b; *Pol.* 291c, 303c; *Gorg.* 483e; Demosthenes, *Cor.* 276; Polybius 4.20.5; Dionysius, *Ant. rom.* 11.25.4; *Is.* 4; *Thuc.* 6–7; Strabo 7.3.11; Dio of Prusa, *Or.* 2.19; cf. 32.11, 39; 77/78.34.

and it seems in Josephus' original composition, it is generally accepted that the son of Simon and the son of Gion are the same man: Eleazar the priest, leader of the Zealots.[45]

The rest of Eleazar's story is quick to relate, however, because he is one of many characters who disappear when Josephus has used them for what he needs. The passage just mentioned (5.5) reports Eleazar's break with John, when he finds submission to the younger Galilean intolerable. The higher position of Eleazar's base in the temple allows him to get the better of John for a while (5.10–12, 21), but John's men infiltrate the temple and reinstall the Galilean as leader of the Zealot faction (5.99–105). The last we see of Eleazar, he is commanding under John (5.250–51). Tacitus had heard that John killed Eleazar when he infiltrated the temple compound (*Hist.* 5.12), whereas Josephus has them fighting side by side. We do not know what became of Eleazar. Perhaps Josephus never learned either, or merely lost interest.

Zealots – or disciples

The Zealot faction is far more prominent in the story than its founder, and has remained so in subsequent Western history. As we have seen (Chapter 4), scholars formerly used the name Zealot for the whole (imagined) anti-Roman freedom movement, from Judas the Galilean in A.D. 6 if not from Pompey or the Maccabees. Farmer and Hengel charted a noble pedigree for the concept of zealotry, which they thought Josephus obscured. This began with biblical Phineas or Pinchas. A priest and grandson of Aaron, Phineas ran a spear through a prominent Israelite named Zimri and his Midianite wife. The Bible commends Phineas for this *jealous behaviour* on God's behalf (Num 25:11, 13), and his deed became paradigmatic of pure devotion to Torah.[46] In the Hasmonean court history we call *1 Maccabees*, the rural priest Mattathias is said to have "burned with jealous zeal (*ezēlōsen*) for the law, just as Phineas did in the case of Zimri" (2.24–26). The main qualification of the older use of Zealot that scholars have offered is to observe that Josephus does not use the term for "rebels" in general but reserves it for the priest-based faction of Eleazar taken over by John.[47] Nevertheless, there is still a general agreement with Farmer

---

[45] The visual difference was between ΓΙΩΝΟC and CIMΩNOC, not an implausible error, especially if the exemplar were blurred or scratched. Copyists of later (generally inferior) mediaeval manuscripts "corrected" to Simon. Alas, this means that *Gion* has text-critical principle in its favour (favouring the more difficult *and* the earlier reading), and the fourth-century Latin translator seems to have seen Gion in his Greek source. It remains possible that Josephus was confused or that the man had two names. Ilan and Price (1993–1994: 203–207) raise the "remote possibility" that Josephus confused the same man with Eleazar ben Ananias, although they concede problems in going that far.

[46] Cf. Sir 45:23; *b. Sanh.* 82a–b; *Vayikra [Exod] Rabb.* 33.4.

[47] E.g., Smith 1971, with Lake 1917.

and Hengel that Greek ζηλωταί (*Zēlōtai*) renders Hebrew *qanna'im* and that a party of this name in 66 and later probably traced its lineage to biblical Phineas via the Hasmoneans.[48]

The main problem with the common view is that it does not take full account of Josephus' rhetoric in using the term. This is a problem because he is our only source for a group that called itself "the Zealots."

A standard principle of translation is that we should avoid simple transliterations (e.g., humanity, dignity, province, virtue for *humanitas, dignitas, provincia, virtus*) wherever possible. That is because the transliterations have often picked up distracting baggage in centuries of English use that did not apply to the original Greek or Latin term, and the obvious-seeming equivalence obscures the differences. For similar reasons I recommend translating *zēlōtai* with an English term closer to its original Greek meaning, such as *Disciples*. English "zealot" has been decisively influenced by the very story we are examining, as traditionally remembered, with the result that nowadays the transliteration has connotations not present in Greek ζηλωτής (*zēlōtēs*).

In English a zealot is "a person who is fanatical and uncompromising in pursuit of religious, political, or other ideals."[49] Ten dictionaries at my fingertips all feature *uncompromising, extreme*, and/or *fanatical* as necessary traits of a "zealot." As it happens, the morning newspaper on the day I first drafted this section included an article denouncing an ex-Prime Minister's memoir as the work of a *zealot*. That was because the premier allegedly had "a mindset closer to a pathology than politics" and his book revealed a "dogmatic stupidity."[50] These are the connotations of English "zealot."

But Greek ζηλωτής (*zēlōtēs*) had nothing to with uncompromising dogma or fanaticism. European translations of Josephus decisively shaped the English, German, and French terms (*Zelot, zélote*). As Josephus himself observes, however, a *zēlōtēs* was an "emulator," "devoted follower," or "disciple" of something estimable, and this was a good and moral thing to be. The inherently favourable sense of the term underlies his wordplays, which require it to make sense. If we embed his distaste for this particular group in the very meaning of the Greek term and assume that being a *zēlōtēs* was bad (as being a zealot is), we entirely miss his point. And that is why we should translate rather than transliterate. If readers object that "disciples" is already taken for Christianity, I might suggest that the term rendered "disciples" for the gospels

---

[48] Hengel's elaborate case (2011: 150–229) has largely held in this respect.

[49] *New Oxford American Dictionary* (2005). The *OED* (second edition, 1989) has: "one who pursues his object with passionate ardour; usually *in disparaging sense*, one who is *carried away by excess of zeal*; an *immoderate* partisan, a *fanatical* enthusiast" (emphasis added).

[50] John Harris, "Blair the Zealot," *The Guardian*, Wed. Sept. 1, 2010.

(singular μαθητής) is perhaps closer to "students" or "learners."[51] *Zēlōtēs* has the stronger connotation of devoted emulation that goes with being a *disciple*.

The verb ζηλόω and noun ζῆλος occur frequently in ancient texts. The verb has the sense of rivalry in emulation. Plenty of other Greek words indicate plain old grudging, jealousy, envy, faction, and civil strife, but the lexicographer Ptolemy of Ascalon explains that "*zēlos* means emulation *of the good*, as when the child emulates the teacher."[52] In the only occurrence of *zēlos* in *War*, Eleazar ben Yair recognizes — unsurprisingly agreeing with Josephus (*Apion* 1.166; 2.280, 282) — that Judaea's laws are the *object of admiring emulation* (*zēlos*) by people of other nations (*War* 7.357). Cassius Dio likewise mentions foreigners enamoured of (*zēloō*) Judaean law (37.17.1). A *zēlōtēs* is a person who has fastened on such a model person or legal system or philosophy and disciplines himself to be a worthy follower. This agent noun appears most famously in a passage from Plato on the Seven Sages. Socrates remarks of them: "These men were all *disciples* and *lovers* and *students* of the Spartan training."[53] Aristotle observes that men who feel shame do not want to be seen by those who have emulated them (*zēloō*), because "*zēlōtai* are *by definition admirers*." The object of a *zēlōtēs*' emulation is assumed to be worthy and good.

This virtuous orientation is also clear in Josephus' use of *zēlōtēs* outside *War* 4–7. He calls Pythagoras, the Adiabenian royal family, and the Hasmonean Mattathias *zēlōtai* with approval because they admire and seek to follow Judaean laws (*Ant.* 12.271; 20.47; *Apion* 1.162), and he describes his younger self as a *zēlōtēs* of the supremely worthy ascetic Bannus (*Life* 11). He does not mean that he was a fanatic or narrow-minded, but that his admirable philosophical longings found satisfaction in emulation of this remarkable man. Elsewhere in *War* Josephus can similarly use *zēlōtēs* of those who strive to emulate men of *valour* (5.314; 6.59). It was good to be a *zēlōtēs*, whereas no one likes a zealot.

We need to understand this to catch Josephus' word plays. In the list of criminals prompted by his mention of *sicarii* at Masada (see Chapter 4), the *Zēlōtai* represented the apex of lawlessness, he says, *although their name would give no hint of this* (*War* 7.268–70):

> The group called Disciples ... excelled [in the lawlessness just described] ... for they faithfully *imitated every evil deed*; nor did human memory pass along any that existed in former times that they left aside as

[51] The case of the *Taliban* illustrates that the behaviour of groups can give otherwise merely descriptive labels unpleasant connotations. Their name also means "students" – a Pashto plural ending on the Arabic *talib* (student).

[52] Ptolemy, *Diff. verb.* 395 [Heylbut] end: ζῆλος μίμησις καλοῦ, οἷον ζηλοῖ τὸν καθηγητὴν ὁ παῖς.

[53] *Prot.* 342e–343b: οὗτοι πάντες ζηλωταὶ καὶ ἐρασταὶ καὶ μαθηταὶ ἦσαν τῆς Λακεδαιμονίων παιδείας.

unworthy of emulation (ἀζήλωτον). Even though they bestowed that appellation on themselves – *supposedly from emulating the good'* (ἀπὸ τῶν ἐπ' ἀγαθῷ ζηλουμένων) – either they were being ironic about all the people they mistreated in keeping with their beastly nature or they reckoned the greatest of evils as a "good."

The sarcasm works only on the assumption that people called *zēlōtai* ought to be of the most wholesome character.[54]

Who are Josephus' Disciples? The word's first occurrence (2.444) refers unproblematically to *Menachem's* devoted disciples. By itself the passage seems clear if ironic. Why would people latch onto *him*? Similarly sarcastic is the second appearance (2.564), referring to the disciples *of Eleazar* son of Simon (τοὺς ὑπ' αὐτῷ ζηλωτάς). He is glossed as an enchanter who bamboozles followers into "obeying him in all matters (αὐτῷ πειθαρχεῖν περὶ τῶν ὅλων)," turning them into his mindless tyrant-posse. From the third occurrence onward (*War* 2.651), however, Josephus drops any qualifiers and *The Disciples* appear thus. The "folly of those called Disciples" is pitted against the virtue of Ananus II, and when he comes to the story of Ananus' death, irony reaches its peak (4.324): The most admirable chief priests, who are practically worshiped (προσκυνούμενοί) by visitors from all over, are killed and cast out naked by *these* "Disciples" (of what?)! The idea seems to be that they should have made themselves disciples of men such as Ananus, but chose disgusting tyrants instead.

Zēlōtai disappear from Book 3, where Josephus is the main Judaean leader, to resurface in the passage concerning the violent men who enter Jerusalem from the countryside and form a terrorist bloc over the populace (4.135–61). Josephus remarks bitterly on the name: "for this is what they called themselves – *as though they were keen on emulating (zēloō) noble pursuits*, rather than excelling everyone in the most despicable of deeds" (4.161). He stresses again that the infiltrators have made themselves enemies of the men they *ought to have emulated*: the priestly elite

---

[54] Scholars occasionally suggest that Jesus of Nazareth's student Simon, "the one called *zēlōtēs*" in Luke-Acts (Luke 6:15; Acts 1:13), was a Zealot or militant of a Hengel-style freedom movement. Luke's source, Mark 3:18 (as Matt 10:4), calls the man instead "Simon the *Kananaios*," which might suggest a garbled Hebrew *qanna'* knowingly rendered *zēlōtēs* by Luke. The connection is noteworthy, but NT authors generally use *zēlōtēs* in the normal sense: as Paul in 1 Cor 14:12 (those keen on spiritual gifts); Gal 1:14 (of ancestral traditions); Tit 2:14 (of good deeds); 1 Pet 3:13 (of what is good); Acts 21:20; 22:3 (of God and the Law). Obviously, the historical Simon could not have been part of Eleazar's faction in 66–70 (Lake 1917; Smith 1971). Possible alternatives are (a) that his nickname *independently* picked up the Phineas-Hasmonean tradition linking *zēlōtēs* with *qana'*; (b) that, given other evidence for Luke's knowledge of Josephus, that author associated him with Josephus' *Zēlōtai* irrespective of chronology; or simply (c) that *Kananaios* refers to Simon's provenance or the like, which Luke found odd, and he tagged him *zēlōtēs* because he a particularly enthusiastic emulator/ disciple *of Jesus* – analogously with the "student whom Jesus loved" (specially) in John 13:23 etc.

(*War* 4.162, 193, 196–97). Handy with weapons, in stark contrast to the chief priests (4.197), these Disciples occupy the inner temple (4.201, 215–16) and attach themselves to unworthy dissident priests (4.225).

In most of *War*'s later occurrences, *Zēlōtai* has become a routine label for the faction led by Eleazar ben Simon and then by John.[55] As we have seen, Josephus counts them and cites their accomplishments as a definable group. *The Disciples* punch above their weight in influence, apparently because of their temple-priestly base and leadership.

Because Josephus is the only user of this label, however, questions like those connected with Latin *sicarii* (Chapter 4) unavoidably arise. Most basically, in its senses exploited by Josephus for the readers of his Greek text, *zēlōtai* has no close Hebrew or Aramaic equivalent. Second, did the group really call itself by such a *Greek* name? Greek specializes in emotions and motives, and readily constructs compound words to add nuance. Reserving a word group for *the emulation of a virtuous exemplar* was typically Greek. Ancient Semitic languages, although certainly sophisticated in their own ways and often lacking good Greek equivalents, did not have terms precisely matching the range of psychological abstractions possible in Greek. What did Josephus' Disciples call themselves and what did they mean by it?

When the translators of the Greek Bible (Septuagint, LXX) struggled to find equivalents for Hebrew terms, they often pressed into service words that had quite different senses in Greek. And Christians would later add *their* special complications to LXX terminology.[56] Some famous examples are νόμος (customary law) for *Torah* ([divine] instruction), διαθήκη (will, testament) for *bᵉrit* (covenant), ἁμαρτία (failure, shortcoming) for *ḥaṭṭa* (sin, violation of obligations); in the Christian world, δαίμονες (souls of the ancients or personal spirits) for *demons*, σωτηρία (rescue, preservation) for spiritual salvation, and πίστις (assurance, credence, confidence) for faith or belief.

Ζηλωτής is one such term given unusual connotations in the Greek Bible. All six references to a Ζηλωτής in the LXX refer to *God* – the very last person who *could* be a *zēlōtēs* or emulator of others in normal Greek.[57] In Greek-biblical usage, worship of other deities is prohibited because God is a *zēlōtēs*, which must mean in the context that God demands exclusive devotion *in rivalry with* competitors. Tellingly, Philo and Josephus both avoid this biblical description of God as a *zēlōtēs*, presumably because it would sound odd to their audiences. Josephus' *Zēlōtai* thus have no direct biblical precedent. He abuses their name

---

[55] Distribution of ζηλωτής: 55 of 59 occurrences are in *War*, 39 in Book 4 and 12 in Books 5 and 6. The verb *zēloō*, which never connects with a group, occurs only 4 of 16 times in *War*, the noun *zēlos* 1 of 8 times in *War*. *The Disciples* is thus a group name in *War* 4–6.

[56] Dodd 1935; Porter 1991; Walser 2001.

[57] Exod 20:5; 34:14; Deut 4:24; 5:9; 6:15; Nah 1:2; cf. Sir 9:1.

only on the basis of standard Greek usage. They foolishly devote themselves, he implies, *to men* who are utterly unworthy of their emulation.

But the Hebrew word that the Septuagint translates as *zēlōtēs* is the adjectival noun *qanna'*, which the Hebrew Bible also reserves for *God*: The phrase is always *'El* or *Yhwh qanna'*.[58] The cognate verb *qana'* ("to be jealous, envious") can overlap partially with the range of Greek *zēloō* ("jealously strive after, emulate"). That is probably why the translators chose this Greek word group for the whole semantic range in Greek. Still there are crucial differences. Wherever *qana'* has a favourable sense, it concerns *human-divine* relations, as when God is made jealous or humans become jealous/zealous on God's behalf.[59] When used in human-to-human relations, the word suggests plain and ugly envy or jealousy.[60] The Bible censures those who "envy" (*qana'*), in this human way. The objects of their envy are either the innocently successful or sinners with ill-gotten gains.[61] The Greek Bible renders all these passages with *zēloō and zēlos*, but the translation-Greek sense is very different from that of emulation of admirable persons or things.

What can we conclude about those whom Josephus mischievously calls *The Disciples*? A priest- and temple-based faction formed first around Eleazar ben Ananias in 66, as tensions with Florus came to a head and groups began arming themselves. Energized by the influx of rural priests in 67–68 and led by Eleazar ben Simon, they severed ties with foreigners for protection. It is entirely plausible that in doing so they looked to biblical Phineas, the noble executioner of Israelites who would consort with dangerous neighbours, and to Mattathias the Hasmonean for the same reason. If so, their Hebrew name might have had something to do with *qana'* as used in the Bible of Phineas. It would seem odd, however, if such biblicists called themselves by a term reserved in the Bible for God, whether in Hebrew or in Greek. At any rate, there is nothing in their name, presumed tradition, or behaviour to suggest that these people were motivated by anti-imperial grievances. They came into conflict with Rome as a result of regional strife, which persuaded them to arm themselves and look to God for protection.

Did they call themselves *Zēlōtai* in Greek? That is hard to imagine, first because they should have preferred a Semitic name and second because the Greek word would have suggested discipleship to *a man* such as Eleazar, which was surely not the point of their Hebrew/Aramaic name. The simplest

---

[58] Exod 20:5; 34:14 (twice); Deut 4:24; 5:9; 6:15; cf. *'El qanno'* at Josh 24:19, rendered verbally in the LXX (ζηλώσας οὗτος) and Nah 1:2, rendered ζηλωτής.

[59] Num 11:29; Deut 32:16, 21; 1 Kgs 14:22; 19:10.

[60] Gen 26:14 (Philistines envy Isaac's wealth); 30:1 (Rachel envies Leah's fertility); 37:1 (Joseph's brothers envy him); Num 5:12–31 (a man overcome by a spirit of jealousy for a wife suspected of adultery).

[61] Prov 23:17; 24:1, 19.

explanation of Josephus' sarcastic references seems to be that, although he knew of a Hebrew name with perhaps biblical connotations – "Pinchas' Divine Jealousy Party" or the like – as a Greek writer *he* decided to saddle them with *Zēlōtai* because this partial equivalent offered room for satire. In other words, he invented *The Disciples* from his Phineatic contemporaries to heap scorn on their allegiances, and his modern translators created ancient *Zealots*.

John of Gischala

Josephus' character John well illustrates how little we know about even central figures. Tacitus mentions John as one of three, ultimately two, rebel leaders in Jerusalem, mistakenly lending him Simon's surname Bargioras (*Hist.* 5.12). The Epitome of Dio ignores him, perhaps deducing from Simon Bargiora's execution in the triumph that he was the only rebel general (65/66.7.1). Josephus' Roman audience in the 70s would presumably have known about John from the recent triumph. He makes no effort in *War* to soften John's reputation as a despicable fellow (2.585–89): "the slipperiest and craftiest of all those distinguishing themselves in wretched behaviour during those times. ... and extremely bloodthirsty when there was a hope of gain." In Chapter 2 we noted Sallustian parallels. John's later activities in *War* are on a continuum with the treacherous character he establishes in Books 2 and 4.

That we cannot recover much of the real John from this is indicated by *Life*'s casual mention of John's brother. This Simon was John's trusted link with the Jerusalem council, and a man influential enough in his own right to make convincing representations, with alleged bribes, to these dignitaries (*Life* 190, 195–196). We might have guessed that this important sibling would have accompanied John to Jerusalem (*War* 4.106–27). Yet *War* says not a single word about *Simon* son of Levi.

Between *War* and *Life* we have enough information to be puzzled about John's motives. Josephus indicates a perpetual hostility between Gischala and Tyrian Kedasa, 10 km (6 mi) away (*War* 2.429; 4.105), but claims without explanation that many of John's followers were *Tyrians* (*War* 2.588; *Life* 372). What was his relationship with Tyrian and Decapolis centres? And was John a Levite? In *War* his father is called *Lēios* (*War* 2.575, 585), a name that seems related to field crops (*lēion*) – the main activity of Gischala's residents (*War* 4.84) – or possibly plunder (*leia*). But in *Life*, not long after Josephus' harsh comments about Levites in *Ant.* 20.116–18, he gives the father's name as "Levite" (*Lēoueis*). Is this a joke or a pun? Did John come from a family of farmers, bootleggers, or Levites? And what were his own ambitions? How did his close ties with Jerusalem's elite originate? Had he ever given much thought to Rome? Did his outlook evolve greatly from 67 to 70? Was his intention in fleeing from Gischala to escape only the imminent threat in Roman hands, hoping later to sue for terms from a safe position with the rest of Jerusalem, or was he resolved on fighting Rome to the death? If so, why and with what rationale? Josephus implies that few of his followers made it to Jerusalem (4.115, 121), but then later speaks of the corps (*syntagma*) of *Galileans* – his Tyrians have disappeared – who raised him to power (4.558). Still later John is in command of 6,000, not counting Disciples under him (5.250).

I omit many more questions to spare the reader. My point is that John is a puzzle.[62] Consider one laudable recent effort to explain the evidence coherently. U. Rappaport proposes that John was originally a member of Galilee's urban elite, indeed the eminent figure in Gischala, and a political moderate. Like his Jerusalem friend Simon ben Gamaliel and like Josephus, he had no reason to oppose Rome. When Vespasian sent Titus with 1,000 cavalry to take Gischala, it was not because he regarded John as a threat or a rebel leader. John's conflicts with nearby towns had been local concerns. Once the Romans were in country, however, John felt that Josephus' defensive efforts had been an embarrassing "sham." Although his views were moderate, he wanted to be among more serious leaders in Jerusalem, not trapped far away under Josephus. Although he would have much preferred another course of events, in the circumstances John "was probably convinced that Jerusalem, where God's intervention might bring eschatological expectations to their consummation, would be preferable as a battle-ground for the Jews."[63]

In Rappaport's reconstruction, John's arrival in Jerusalem marked a major turning point. His natural allies there were the moderate leaders, who were planning to seek terms with Rome. They welcomed him as the ally they knew him to be. But Josephus' accusation of treachery reflects the reality that John had become disturbed when he realized that the elite ignobly "looked forward to surrendering."[64] Having to choose between his moderate instincts and the Zealot perspective that had elsewhere taken hold in Jerusalem, he came to reflect that his earlier problems with non-Judaean neighbours in the north were part and parcel of an undesirable imperial situation, and so he made new friends among the Zealots (Disciples). He was won over to their war of national liberation, which would depend on Jerusalem's strong walls and the hope of divine intervention.[65]

Many parts of this reconstruction are attractive, and it brings a real humanity to John's life. Rappaport refreshingly accepts that we lack the information to reach confident conclusions. Even in such a thoughtful account, however, we

---

[62] Rappaport 1982. I have not had a chance to study Rappaport 2013, but a quick read suggests that it follows the same *basic* lines (especially: John made fateful new choices once in Jerusalem, 118–19).

[63] Rappaport 1982: 486.   [64] Rappaport 1982: 488–89.   [65] Rappaport 2013: 118–19.

meet the usual problems of explaining evidence and assuming too much. Rappaport's main criterion for finding secure material is that, where Josephus had no reason to "lie" or to "invent," we may accept his claims. Thus John "probably" saw Jerusalem as the end-time battleground because the speech that Josephus gives him on arriving in Jerusalem suggests this. John tells his adoring listeners about the circumstances of his escape, declaring that the Romans have no hope against the walls of Jerusalem. Even if they had "wings" they could not surmount these walls (*War* 4.125–27). Rappaport proposes that, because these words "are no discredit to him [John]" and therefore do not stem from Josephus' anti-John polemic, they have "the ring of truth." John's real "national-religious views" likely find expression here, and this implies his expectation of an eschatological showdown in Jerusalem.[66]

It seems to me, rather, that John's saying about Rome, which Josephus crafts for him, is fully part of Josephus' highly sarcastic portrait of him as a rotten liar. In Josephus' words, "Without so much as a blush at having abandoned his friends, going around to each group John kept inciting them to war by the hopes he raised, painting a picture of Roman weakness ..." (4.126). The temple's alleged impregnability is the apex of John's *deception*, therefore hardly free of our author's bias. His claim is all the more ironic because "wings" (Greek *ptera*) were precisely what the Romans would bring to bear, in the form of cavalry *alae* (wings), to destroy these defences. Jerusalem's great walls are a theme in Josephus, as we have seen, most clearly featured in his excursus on the city's impregnability.[67] *War*'s final reference to them is given to Eleazar ben Yair at Masada (7.375):

> And where is now that great city, the mother-city of the entire Judaean race, *the one fortified all the way around with so many walls, which had so many fortresses and large tower structures protecting it*, which could barely contain all the implements prepared for war, and which had so many tens of thousands of men fighting for it?

Because Josephus makes such a point of a misguided trust in Jerusalem's walls as the central motive for the prolongation of the conflict, when he has John singing from that same song sheet, we should be very cautious about finding John's *real* views here. In any case, it is hard to get from there to Jerusalem as eschatological battlefield.

It does seem clear that John began in Gischala as a wealthy local concerned mainly with his town's well-being in the regional context, and we may be sure that he ended up in Jerusalem, resisting Titus' legions until the end. *Conceivable* explanations of the transition are many. For example, what if Josephus in Roman custody identified John, his own recent nemesis, as an enemy whom

---

[66] Rappaport 1982: 487.   [67] *War* 5.153; cf. 259, 282–83, 300, 364, 374; 6.400–13; 7.2.

the Flavians needed to capture? Or perhaps John's Decapolis neighbours targeted him in this way? When Titus arrived outside Gischala to arrest him, in either case, John might have had good reason to fear surrender. So he fled to Jerusalem, where at least he would buy significant time and protection. Once there, having added the undeniable humiliation of Titus to whatever he feared before, he could not support those who were advocating submission. He was now in far greater jeopardy than he had been originally. If John was going to be involved with Jerusalem's armed factions, moreover, his only security lay in being at the top of the heap, the same motive that allegedly inspired men to seek imperial power. In short, perhaps John felt that he had no serious option after fleeing Galilee – which he may have done simply from fear as the target of his enemies – but to fight to the end. There is no direct evidence for most of this reconstruction, or any other, but it is an economical hypothesis that would explain the scattered evidence we have for his transition from Gischala's leading man to a determined and terrified holdout behind Jerusalem's walls, who tries even at the end to bargain his way out of Roman custody.

Simon son of Gioras from Gerasa

A heavy layer of dust likewise coats the figure of Simon bar Giora, who would play the role of "enemy general" in the triumph.[68] A rare gold coin minted at Lugdunum in 71 portrays Vespasian in his triumphal chariot, heralded by a trumpeter and with a manacled and bearded prisoner ahead, over the legend "Triump[h] Aug[ustus Vespasian]" (Fig. 30). If the image is realistic, the prisoner is most likely *Titus'* captive Simon.[69] I mentioned that both Tacitus and Dio know him also as a (or the) Judaean rebel chief.

Appearing only in *War*, Simon does not benefit from the ounce of redemption that John enjoys in *Life*. He appears consistently as the most ruthless tyrant imaginable, first gaining notoriety as the man who captured much of Cestius' baggage train (2.521). Curiously, Josephus also credits Eleazar son of Simon – Simon bar Giora's later enemy – with holding Cestius' plunder (2.564), although this possibly refers only to the spoils from the main ambush (2.554). *War* 2 highlights Simon's future importance in an ominous closing note (2.652–54): Ananus and his circle dispatch a force against Simon because of the havoc he is wreaking on the borders of Judaea and Samaria while he plunders wealthy Judaeans. When Ananus moves against him, Simon flees to Masada. From that base he and certain *sicarii* terrorize both nearby Judaeans and Idumaeans in their constant search for fresh food.

---

[68] Josephus, *War* 6.433; 7.36, 153–55; Tacitus, *Hist.* 5.12; Dio 65/66.7.1.
[69] Mattingly 1977: 28 and pl. X no. 6; Deutsch 2010a.

FIGURE 30. Gold *aureus* of Vespasian, from Lugdunum (Lyons) celebrating his triumph with bound Judaean prisoner ahead.© Trustees of the British Museum (ref. 1864,1128.255). The Museum's date of A.D. 71 is more likely than Meshorer's (2001: 186) 70, which would have anticipated the event. This is apparently from the collection of nineteenth-century explorer F. C. de Saulcy.

The next we see Simon, he is welcoming 2,000 ex-prisoners of the Disciples, freed by the Idumaeans. He remains implacably opposed to these temple-based Disciples. Many of their victims are men of means, and some of the freed prisoners who run to Simon are wealthy (4.353).

At 4.503 Josephus reintroduces Simon as the son of one Gioras from Gerasa, offering a rare comment on his personal traits: a younger man than John, physically stronger and more daring although less cunning.

Here Josephus picks up the story about Simon's retreat to Masada. The experiment ends when he decides that these *sicarii* are too lethargic (Chapter 9). On hearing of Ananus' death (early 68), he heads to the Judaean hills (4.508). In spite of the anticipatory notice in Book 2, only now does his army harass Idumaea, after overrunning Acrabatene and much of Jerusalem's *chōra* (4.509–38), ahead of the Flavian advance. Along the way he craftily enlarges his following "by declaring freedom for slaves and bonuses for free persons." Simon (or Josephus) takes a leaf from the Achaean leader Diaeus in the 140s B.C, who promised manumission of slaves and suspension of debts to quickly recruit a loyal force.[70] Simon's army of "low-lifes from everywhere" (4.508) allows him to repel an expedition sent by Jerusalem's Disciples, who are becoming increasingly anxious about his power.

The Disciples, we noted, try to subdue him by kidnapping his wife. This backfires when Simon arrives outside Jerusalem's walls, "just like a wounded beast" and – with much greater effectiveness than the legions – terrifies the

---

[70] See Polybius 38.11.9–10, 15.2–4, 7, with Fuks 1970.

Disciples (4.538–44). Simon seizes, tortures, and kills Jerusalemites of any age he finds outside, all but gnawing at their corpses in his rage (4.541). He chops off hands and sends amputees into the city, threatening that he will knock down the walls and slaughter every living soul if they did not return his woman. There are shades here of Achilles' rage at losing *his* woman in the *Iliad* (1.1–205), suggesting perhaps not so much the loss of a match made in heaven as the disrespect of stealing a man's most intimate possessions.

With Simon lowering, and Jerusalem's inhabitants exasperated by the brutalities of John and the Disciples, the Idumaeans switch sides and persuade Matthias the chief priest to invite Simon in as a strong antibiotic against the infection from Gischala (4.556–84).

On the reasonable assumption that Josephus' portrait of Simon is not entirely fair, historians have tried to resurrect a nobler figure as leader of the Jerusalem revolt. Cecil Roth offered:

> It seems certain that these Jewish patriots fighting against Rome were motivated by profound religious as well as patriotic feelings. . . . That Simon bar Giora considered himself as being to some extent a religious teacher is nowhere indicated in our sources, but is by no means improbable. . . .[71]

Notice the slide from seeming certainty to *not being utterly improbable*. Other scholars have found slivers of evidence that Simon really was a social revolutionary and/or consciously messianic figure.

Otto Michel's 1968 article is representative. The renowned German translator of Josephus found in Simon not a *classical* messianic idea, in the absence of suggested Davidic descent, but a fresh idea drawn from Isaiah 9:5 of a physically powerful hero (Hebrew *gibbor*) who would establish the law of God by means of war.[72] Because the Jerusalem leaders and a chief priest invited him in they *must* have seen something admirably pious in him.[73] Michel tries to expose Josephus' portrait as a willful distortion. What Josephus denigrates as brutal measures was merely the *disciplina* required of a military commander fighting for survival. They were necessary to maintain morale – a virtue in contrast to John's loose behaviour, Josephus' description of which Michel accepts at face value.[74] That Simon was a social revolutionary Michel considers clear from his attacks on the wealthy and freeing of slaves.[75] He finds a messianic consciousness implied by Simon's final appearance as a ghostly presence emerging from the tunnels beneath the temple site. Clearly Simon was offering himself as a sacrificial victim, in something of a parallel to Jesus of Nazareth. All of this Josephus suppressed, partly because he did not want a martyr tradition to grow around Simon.[76]

---

[71] Roth 1960: 53. [72] Michel 1968: 402–403. [73] Michel 1968: 404.
[74] Michel: 404–405. [75] Michel: 402. [76] Michel 1968: 406–407.

Michel's arguments have been ably dismantled by Gideon Fuks.[77] The problem is that they heavily massage a few elements in Josephus' account while ignoring others, such as Simon's brutality toward *the lower classes* and attraction of upper-class men. Fuks points out that if Simon had thought of himself as a messiah, Josephus might have wanted to air that claim to serve his general mockery of such types.[78] Fuks is himself not unsympathetic to the search for reliable data in Josephus, however; he criticizes Michel and others for their arbitrariness in selection.

Although I agree with Fuks on the latter point, I recommend viewing all of these apparent data first as contributions to Josephus' narrative (Chapter 2). If we wanted to find significance in Simon's revolutionary or messianic potential, that is, we would need to explain similar motifs elsewhere in Josephus. In our post-Marxist world we incline to see references to debt release as evidence of class conflict,[79] but then we may miss Josephus' *pattern* of alleging such behaviour of demagogues. Early in the revolt, for example, the faction led by Eleazar ben Ananias struggles against "the powerful and the chief priests" (2.422). Eleazar's insurgents attack the royal and high-priestly residences. They conceive the clever idea of burning the public record office (2.427–28):

> hurrying to obliterate the contracts of those who had lent out money and to cut off the collection of the debts, *so that they might add to their number the horde* of those who had received assistance, and raise up with impunity the deprived against the well-heeled. So after those in the record-office had fled, they lit the fire.

Ancient writers assumed that cunning leaders knew how to manipulate the masses in such ways. Josephus assumes that non-elite citizens – not only the destitute but also those with large loans – are likely to join in any burning, looting, and mayhem that sounds advantageous to them.[80] In the last chapter we saw Justus of Tiberius, explicitly portrayed as a demagogue, concocting economic arguments to spur unrest among Tiberians (*Life* 38–40). In Josephus, tyrants and demagogues exploit human weakness and emotion constantly.[81] Although some *may have been* genuine social reformers, class warfare in the

---

[77] Fuks 1985/88: 106–119.   [78] Fuks 1985/88: 119.

[79] E.g., Faulkner 2004, which welds many such references into an economic explanation of the war against Rome.

[80] Cf. *War* 7.54–62, where Josephus describes a fire in Antioch (A.D. 71), which consumed the record office and archives. Although falsely blamed on Judaeans, it was started by "rotters" hoping to evade their debts (7.61).

[81] Those most likely to have taken sizable loans were presumably not the destitute, because lenders would not throw away money on borrowers who had little chance of repaying on schedule. Borrowers were more likely businessmen, artisans, and traders needing to expand their businesses or purchase rights; see the contracts in the Egyptian papyri, *CPJ* 20, 23, 25, 26, 149, 411, 413, 414, 488 (loans of a year, more or less, with interest up to 12 percent); also Luke 16:1–8, where the larger debts are owed by men of means.

post-industrial sense was not in the cards. We have no way of discovering refined social motives from such stock narratives.

The same problem faces any effort to find a messianic consciousness in Simon. Josephus generally avoids the messianic language found in some post-biblical and Christian texts. Most ancient audiences, especially in Rome, were allergic to the idea of monarchy portrayed as such.[82] Josephus shares the values of his class and place. He ridicules diadems and pretenders to thrones, whether they be shepherds and slaves, sons of Herod, or the later Hasmoneans, not sparing even Rome's emperors.[83] He typically characterizes political trouble-makers as *tyrants* and would-be *despots* who like to surround themselves with a "spear-carrying" bodyguard. Some of them wear purple. Converting any of this into evidence that such individuals had a genuine messianic consciousness would be daring indeed.

Other puzzles include Simon's patronym, *son of Giora*, and his origin in *Gerasa*. Although the significance of "Giora" has been debated, most scholars agree that his father was a "convert." Aramaic *giora*, equivalent to Hebrew *ger*, means "stranger, alien, sojourner, foreigner, or immigrant." (Josephus might privately have enjoyed the pun: a *ger* from *Ger*asa.) We notice foreigners when they are *among us*, and that was the sense of these terms: *foreigners over here*. The Bible has some ninety-three occurrences of *ger*. Two-thirds are in the Penta-teuch, where laws are given for the fair treatment and obligations of aliens residing in Israel. The Greek Bible usually renders *ger* as *prosēlytos*, from which we get English *proselyte*. Although the meaning of the Greek adjective is uncomplicated ("[one who has] come to, over, arrived at [here]"), non-Judaean writers found no use for that form (*prosēlytos*). It does not appear in surviving classical literature and Josephus also avoids it.[84] The Latin equivalent (adj. *advena*, vb. *advenio*) did find ample usage because Romans had many opportunities to mention, with distaste, foreigners who had *come over here*.[85]

We think of "proselytism" as belonging to the sphere of religion, which leads us to translate Giora as *convert*, but in the first century the categories were different.[86] What we call conversion was closer to a change of citizenship or new ethnic identity, as the biblical Ruth memorably put it: "Your people will

---

[82] See Cassius Dio 53.17.2 (third century), noting the perseverance of this horror, even though a *de facto* Roman monarchy has existed for centuries.

[83] See Mason 2009b, 2012b.

[84] In the 9,000 or so Greek texts in the TLG database (www.tlg.uci.edu), only the undated grammarian Ptolemy (*Diff. voc.* P. 407 ln. 26) uses it, quite incidentally of those who have come into slavery for some reason or other.

[85] Of many examples, Plautus, *Aul.* 3.1; *Poen.* 1031; Cicero, *Pis.* 70; *Tusc. disp.* 5.34; *Leg. agr.* 2.94; *De orat.* 1.250; Livy 10.8.6; 34.61.7; Pliny 10.127; Seneca, *Herc. fur.* 917; Tacitus, *Dial.* 7.4; *Ann.* 11.24; *Hist.* 2.2. Romans also used *advena* also to describe someone incompetent through lack of experience, a dilettante.

[86] Smith 1963: 61–64; Masuzawa 2005; Cavanaugh 2009; Nongbri 2013.

be my people, and your God my God."[87] The name Giora appears inscribed on several ossuaries (bone boxes) in the Jerusalem area from our period, signifying a foreign-born adopter of Judaean laws who moved or was buried there.[88] The most famous case of such realignment involved the Adiabenian royals. The three men called *giora* in the funerary inscriptions all happen to have taken the Hebrew name Yehuda (= Judas), celebrating their new identities. At least two Yehudas known from rabbinic literature are also called *gerim* (plural of *ger*), and described as newcomers (*ger 'ammoni*, Ammonite alien).[89] Perhaps Simon's father was also a Yehuda?

War 4.503 says that Simon was "a Gerasene by origin." An ancient audience might assume that this was the famous Decapolis city (modern Jarash), home of orators and the mathematician Nicomachus.[90] Josephus also knows other Gerasas, however. In a passage shortly before this one (4.486–89), he describes Vespasian's destruction of a certain Gerasa to complete Jerusalem's encirclement in Judaea (4.490), which cannot therefore be the Decapolis Gerasa. Other candidates for this Gerasa include Gezer or Gazara (by a common transposition) near the edge of the western coastal plain.[91] Simon first appears around Beit-Horon, attacking Cestius' expedition on its way inland (2.521). South of that used to be another Arab village of Jarash, about 19 km (12 mi) from both Jerusalem and Beit-Horon, near the Cave of the Twins.[92] Some prefer the modern village of Jureish for Simon's Gerasa, 35 km (21.75 mi) northeast of Jerusalem in Acrabatene. That is where he becomes active after the attack on Cestius, returning again after Ananus' death (2.652–53, 504, 511).[93] Then again, his alleged violence, burning, and plundering in that area (2.652–53; 4.511) might suggest that this was not his home.

We also do not know whether Simon's family or only he personally was associated with Gerasa. If it was the family's town, Decapolis Gerasa (Jarash) is a plausible site after all, for it once had a large Judaean community on good terms with the other citizens (*War* 2.480).[94] It might have been the sort of environment in which Simon's non-Judaean father could

---

[87] Ruth 1:16. Cf. Philo, *Virt.* 102–103: Moses had us welcome newcomers "because they have left behind *blood-affiliation, ancestral ways, customs, sacred rites and temples of the Gods, the gifts and honors too*, having undertaken a noble migration."

[88] Avni, Greenhut, Ilan 1994: 215.

[89] The naming pattern on ossuaries as in the literature (although not the significance proposed here) is pointed out by Avni, Greenhut, and Ilan 1994: 215. Rabbinic passages: *m. Yad.* 4:4 and *b. Moed Katan* 9a.

[90] The orators are mentioned by Philo of Byblos (in Stephanus, Jacoby 3c.790F, frag. 34).

[91] See Bergmeier 1998.

[92] Conder and Kitchener 1880 (Sheet 17: Ku), noted merely as "a small village on a spur" in Conder and Kitchener 1883: 25.

[93] See Fuks 1985/88: 11–13 and notes for supporting references.

[94] So Stern 1973: 146 n. 39.

encounter and become attracted to Judaean culture. Josephus claims, after all, that such attraction was common in the *poleis* of Syria (*War* 2.463, 560). Or perhaps the father moved the family, or Simon himself moved, to a Judaean *Jarash*.

Whatever Simon's place of origin, an economical picture of the historical man might be along these lines. As a strong youth from a new Judaean family, he was particularly alert to threats from the neighbouring populations. He made himself a tough enforcer, patrolling the frontiers and funding his efforts with plunder, also from wealthy Judaeans who were appalled at his behaviour. When Cestius entered the Judaean hills, having shown callous disregard for Judaean life and property and having destroyed Joppa, Simon and his men were ready to attack the legion's poorly guarded baggage train. This action further alienated him from Jerusalem's leaders at the time, who were hoping for terms with Rome, and they took energetic measures to chase him away. More fatefully, Simon was marked from an early point for Roman punishment by the raid on Cestius. Whether he had attacked the column from angry impulse or a longer-term vision of some kind we cannot know. But with good reason to think that he could never surrender, he had a powerful incentive, if quite different from John's, to fight to the finish.

It is remarkable that in Simon we appear to have a first-generation Judaean, possibly the first boy circumcised in his family, who became *the central figure* in the Judaean war against Titus. His centrality is all the more impressive because of the young Adiabenian royals, also recent emigrés to Jerusalem from a family that had newly embraced Judaean law and life.

The Adiabenians

In *War*'s preface Josephus remarks that "the fate of the regions to the east [was uncertain], with some in hope of [their] acquisition, but others in anxiety over [their] removal" (1.4). This appears to suggest that some in the Parthian empire hoped to *acquire* Judaea, presumably with southern Syria and Nabataea. In Chapter 3 we reviewed relations between Romans and Parthians. What about Judaeans and Parthians?

Relations appear to have remained close. There was no hard border between their worlds; movement back and forth was easy. Judaeans in Parthia needed regular contact with the mother-city for legal interpretation, in which Jerusalem's priests were paramount authorities, and for the calendar: The new moon announced in Jerusalem apparently had to be conveyed by messenger and bonfire.[95] Parthia's Judaeans contributed the half-shekel tax for the temple

---

[95] So *m. RH* 1.3–9; *b. Pes.* 3a; *RH* 18a. This is the origin of two-day celebrations of feast days for Diaspora Jews – to cover any question about the correct day.

and two of their fortified cities, Nehardea and Nisibis, stored the treasure securely until the annual caravan to Jerusalem.[96] Parthia's Judaeans also seem to have visited the mother-city no less frequently than their compatriots on the Roman side.[97] Their bond might be reflected in the violent revolt under Trajan (A.D. 116–117), which was arguably triggered by that emperor's reduction of Nisibis while subduing Mesopotamia.[98]

In this general scene Adiabene was a special case. Located not far from the Parthian winter capital of Ctesiphon on the Tigris, it seems to have had a Judaean minority for centuries.[99] Josephus has a particular interest in the royal family's embrace of Judaean law in the 30s (*Ant.* 20.17–96). Jacob Neusner proposed that Adiabene's leaders had a political motive in addition to any other, hoping to unite Judaean communities from Jerusalem eastward under their patronage.[100] Such an effort would mirror Herod's efforts to bring Parthia's Judaean populations under his influence. According to Josephus, the Adiabenian royals' adoption of foreign laws put King Izates II in danger from his local aristocracy but also secured him divine protection (*Ant.* 20.34–48, 75–91). The family flourished and the Parthian King Artabanus gave Nisibis to Izates in gratitude for support at a critical moment (*Ant.* 20.68).

Whatever their motives, Izates and his mother Helena became prominent benefactors of Jerusalem. She made a pilgrimage during a famine in the 40s (*Ant.* 20.49–53; cf. Acts 11:29–30), after which she remained and built a palace on Jerusalem's southeastern hill (*War* 5.253; *Ant.* 20.49–53),[101] and Izates sent his five sons to be educated in Jerusalem (*Ant.* 20.71). Given that Josephus was born in 37, his Adiabenian contemporaries must have been known to him in the small circles of Jerusalem's upper class.

Soon after she returned to Adiabene, following Izates' death in the mid-50s, Queen Helena died. The bodies of mother and son would be buried in the tomb complex 0.5 km (0.3 mi) north of Jerusalem's old city known as the "Tombs of the Kings" or Royal Caverns.[102] Pausanias has a remarkable description of her tomb, claiming that its door opened automatically once a

---

[96] *Ant.* 18.311–13. Josephus' description places Nisibis near Nehardea, which has led to the proposal that it was a different Nisibis from the famous one in northern Mesopotamia. That may be, although given the unfamiliarity of the place and the absence of modern mapping in antiquity, it is at least as likely that Josephus does not have a clear picture of the geography and/or has expressed himself poorly.

[97] Acts 2:9 describes a Feast of Weeks (Shavuot, Pentecost) in the 30s at which "Parthians, Medes, Elamites, and residents of Mesopotamia" were present with western pilgrims. Josephus describes merchants and traders from Judea spending time in Parthia, including at Charax Spasinou, a port for trade with the Far East (*Ant.* 20.34–35, 43).

[98] See ben Zeev 2005.   [99] Neusner 1969: 1.13.   [100] Neusner 1969: 1.60–70.

[101] Ben-Ami and Tchekhanovets 2011 report on a large and expensive structure in the Givati parking area of the modern city, which they believe could be an Adiabenian palace.

[102] Josephus, *War* 5.55, 119; *Ant.* 20.95–96.

FIGURE 31. One section of the elaborate tomb complex of the Adiabenian royal family, a short walk northeast of the ancient city. A decorated sarcophagus generally agreed to have been Queen Helena's (now in the Louvre) was found here. Author 2009.

year (8.16.4–5). Titus would destroy that complex as his army rolled down from Mount Scopus in 70, although the underground tombs remain (Fig. 31). Helena's presumed sarcophagus resides in Paris's Louvre Museum.

Relations remained close thereafter. Other members of the royal family built palaces in Jerusalem (*War* 4.567; 5.252–53). As we have seen, Josephus gives Adiabenians a leading role in the ambush of Cestius (*War* 2.520). Titus revealingly complains that, as the rest of the world was sending embassies to congratulate Vespasian, Judaeans were sending embassies "across the Euphrates, with a view to revolution" (*War* 6.343). The timing here is interesting: not 66 or 67, but late 69 or early 70. This would suggest a desperate appeal for help, perhaps also diplomatic, in protecting Jerusalem. We have no idea what came of such representations, if they occurred. At least resident Adiabenians were involved in both attacking Cestius' force after its depredations and later defending Jerusalem. If Josephus' language is accurate, Titus took them to Rome, perhaps on the same ship as Josephus (*Life* 422), as hostages for Adiabene's future cooperation (*War* 6.357).

The Idumaeans

In Chapters 3 and 4 we have discussed the Idumaeans from various angles: their role in the Hasmonean expansion, complex ethnic identity and loyalties, defection from Judaea's military after Herod's death, crushed secessionist bid, potential role as fighters in the war, and apparent absence from Jerusalem's ongoing regional struggles. It remains to assess their role in the developing revolt from 66 to 70. Alan Appelbaum has tried to reassemble "the Idumaean War" from Josephus' fragmentary notices and proposed that he uses the term Idumaean not to describe real people and events as much as to invoke an ethnic stereotype of "bloodthirsty thugs."[103] His study is insightful, but I would like to ask simply, in light of the material in this chapter, about Idumaean motives and interests in finally joining Jerusalem's struggle.

Josephus finds no reason to mention Idumaeans in the seventy years between their departure and secessionist bid after Herod's death and the defeat of Cestius. At that time, the process that sends Josephus to Galilee allegedly sees three men appointed generals for Idumaea: two chief priests and the experienced soldier Niger the Peraean (2.566). Appelbaum, assuming that they did what Josephus did in Galilee, commanding armies, sees this as the beginning of Idumaea's involvement in the war.[104] But Josephus' military command was either nonexistent (*Life*) or rapidly vanishing (*War*). Given that the "generals" for Idumaea disappear (NB: When the Idumaeans enter Jerusalem, they are under native commanders), we should not assume much about the real nature of their efforts. If three were thought necessary for Idumaea, so far from the Romans' direction of approach and beyond Jerusalem, their portfolio might have been diplomatic – for example, to coordinate moves with Jerusalem so as not to undermine its negotiations with Rome. Whatever they really did, as we know from Josephus' varying accounts of his own mission, he would have been capable of schematizing it as "generalship" for the sake of that passage.

I would emphasize that the Idumaeans do not seem to have been involved in Jerusalem's regional conflicts, where their martial skill would surely have been welcomed. This impression comes not only from Josephus' failure to mention such activities. More than that, Idumaeans appear among the principal *targets* of such Judaeans as Tolmai, Simon and his followers, and the residents of Masada (Chapter 4). When the Disciples request Idumaean help, Josephus presents this as a clever idea by John, not as the most obvious thing in the world. The Idumaeans have not flocked to Jerusalem of their own initiative, as Judaeans elsewhere have, but need to be specifically invited – and then they are locked out at the beginning.

In appealing for their help, John and the Disciples portray themselves as tyrannized by an elite ready to accept a Roman garrison (4.228–29). When the Idumaeans arrive, they declare that their "mother-city" (*mētropolis*) Jerusalem has always "opened its gates to all foreigners to worship" (4.275) and now is being outrageously shut up: "We *Idumaeans* will preserve the house of God

---

[103] Appelbaum 2009: 9–10.   [104] Appelbaum 2009: 13.

and fight preventively for *our common home*" (4.281). We see here the juxta-position of a proudly distinct ethnic identity and a shared cultic centre, a situation possibly comparable with that of Sidonians in Idumaea and Shechem (Chapter 4).

Idumaean commitment to the temple and city might have something to do with loyalty to Herod, who built these structures in such grand style and under whom their grandfathers had served. They might even consider themselves duty-bound guardians of Herod's temple: Jerusalem's Ghurkas or Sikhs, or a Swiss Guard with a pledge to protect the sanctuary – not ordinarily but by heritage a special force needed in time of crisis. We should not press Josephus' language, but in combination with circumstantial evidence it certainly suggests that Idumaeans do not *simply* consider themselves Judaeans. They might regard themselves rather among Judaea's victimized neighbours in many respects, in spite of having a common cult – perhaps very roughly in the way that Christianized nations in Africa and the Far East can be unquestioningly devoted to Christian faith while at some odds with the former imperialist nations that brought Christianity to them. (And they might consider themselves purer devotees than peers in the originating countries.) Simple models of human identity and loyalty rarely match the reality.

The Idumaeans' reported relationship with Simon is most perplexing. He relentlessly attacks their territory, devastating and burning it (4.529–37). Yet when he enters Jerusalem not long afterward, it is with the support of the Idumaean fighters. What motives and shifts of outlook, if any, lie behind this? Are the soldiers in the city aware of what has been happening at home? What do they hope for as the war progresses? And why do they persist until nearly the end? Have they gone too far to turn back, or do they see themselves as duty-bound guardians of the temple, who are free to seek terms, like the last of the priests, only when the sanctuary is in flames (6.378–81)? They are some of this war's most intriguing players.

Perhaps the most impressive point from our survey is that a wide range of outsiders – Judaean villagers, John and his Galileans, Simon bar Giora's varied followers, Adiabenian royals, and large numbers of Idumaean fighters – become central players in Jerusalem. The original residents of Jerusalem largely flee and and many of their leaders are murdered in the early phases of the struggle.

CONCLUSION: JERUSALEM PART I

In this chapter we have laid the groundwork for Chapter 8 with a critical summary and preliminary analysis of *War* 4 to 6. Our main conclusions are these.

1. Josephus' narrative is complex, not the working out of a simple idea or argument. Books 4 through 6 reach the dramatic climax of the story we surveyed in Chapter 2. His language, themes, structures, and devices continue to develop through these volumes.

2. Josephus did not and could not report *most* of what was going on. Even the most important groups and personalities (Disciples, Idumaeans, Adiabenians, Eleazar, John, Simon) receive few speaking parts or roles. There is no direct path, therefore, from his narrative to the complexity of real life then.

3. Four threads become especially prominent in this part of Josephus' narrative.

   a. The Flavians continue the risk-averse approach that they began in Galilee, following Cestius' plan. They engage only on their terms and operate as long as possible in open territory under their control, with all options available. From the moment of Vespasian's arrival at Ptolemais they dominate the land outside Jerusalem's immediate territory. So they take their time, blocking all routes to external help, degrading all possible resources, and very gradually tightening the noose after consolidating Peraea to the east. This terrifying isolation largely works. It inspires surrender or flight to the only remaining sites, unconquerable Jerusalem or – barely mentioned yet – the desert fortresses, an attractive option for refugee families (Chapter 9). The Romans keep their risk of casualties to a bare minimum, steadily building the army's confidence and morale while leeching that of the Judaeans, who are indeed terrorized and desperate.

   b. Vespasian's war, lasting to the summer of 69 (Book 4), continues his approach in Galilee. Dio remarks that "Vespasian was in no sense reckless" and that his prudence made him look like a candidate for imperial power.[105] In spite of the occasional blunder claimed by Josephus, as at Gamala, he shows himself a cagey commander who fights cautiously and on his terms. His strong suit is intimidation through manoeuvre. He accepts the eager submission of Peraea's capital and quickly chases down militants in the countryside, albeit manufactured enemies, to support dominance with ruthlessness. If Galilee in 67 provided little combat, Judaea and Peraea in 68 and 69 furnished none worth mentioning. Vespasian approaches Judaea circuitously and with great care from strong bases in Samaria, the coastal plain, Peraea, and Idumaea. He can tighten the noose this far without logistical challenges or other noticeable risks. Even the major towns are empty of fighting-age males.

   c. Whether Titus used his father's plans for Jerusalem or modified them significantly with Tiberius Alexander, his approach to the Judaean capital was very similar, hopeful of an early conclusion that would not risk

---

[105] Epit. Dio 64/65.8.3a, 3.2.

Roman blood, although he was prepared to escalate the conflict incrementally as needed, all the way to a full siege and assault. An important consideration was his fame, which recommended Jerusalem's rapid submission. When that did not happen, he quickly gained the city's northern half. He then balanced morale-crushing assaults, demonstrations, and bursts of extreme violence with a conspicuously decent treatment of refugees and invitations to surrender in safety. Josephus diplomatically credits Titus' *humanitas*, although we may call it sensible tactics.

d. Between the winter of 67/68 and spring of 70, the regular population of Jerusalem was largely overtaken by refugees. Given similar phenomena elsewhere (Iotapata, Tiberias, Taricheae, Tabor, Gamala), we suspect a literary device here: Good residents are overwhelmed by militants. But Tacitus, with at least some independence, makes a similar claim: "[T]heir numbers grew tremendously with the influx from the downfall of other cities" (*Hist.* 5.12). Josephus does not exactly thematize this issue, but provides the evidence while stressing other points about John, Jerusalem's walls, the Idumaeans, Simon, Titus' distinction between Jerusalemites and outsiders, or the tragedy of pilgrims being trapped. If there is a deliberate apologetic pattern here, scholars have missed it and all but universally view the siege of Jerusalem in Josephus and in reality as a conflict between Jerusalem and Rome (Chapters 4, 8). From what we have seen in Josephus and in other evidence for Simon and John in particular, it is hard to avoid the impression that Jerusalem itself would have capitulated, had it not been for the large numbers of desperate men who fled to Jerusalem from elsewhere and who could not surrender.

CHAPTER EIGHT

JERUSALEM II: COINS, COUNCILS, CONSTRUCTIONS

In the preceding chapter we surveyed Josephus' account of the Flavian war in Judaea/Peraea and offered a preliminary analysis, rethinking the motives and outlooks of the main groups and individuals that appear. In this chapter we consider the most important evidence outside Josephus. Then we turn to the real-life scenarios that might best answer our questions about Judaean and Roman aims and explain the evidence that has survived.

Archaeological work in Jerusalem since 1967 continues to generate stunning results. We have repeatedly seen the need, however, to interpret, contextualize, and explain all survivals from the past. They do not declare their own meaning or significance.

Beneath the Umayyad, Byzantine, and Hadrianic layers, structures of King Herod's Jerusalem are sometimes recoverable, and archaeologists have also found artefacts of the city at war.[1] Nahman Avigad directed excavations in the Jewish Quarter, comprising the eastern half of the Upper City, as that area was being rebuilt after 1967. His work exposed the sumptuous dwellings of the city's wealthiest pre-70 neighbourhood, on the large western slope facing the temple mount (Fig. 32). The half-dozen houses that dominated that space included a palatial mansion with three terraces on the slope, a frescoed wall,

---

[1] See in general Avigad 1976, 1983; Geva 2000; Levine 2002; Ritmeyer 2006a and 2006b; Galor and Avni 2011: 205–324 (for the Roman period, among the others covered in this excellent book).

FIGURE 32. Mosaic floor, storage vessels, and furnishings including high and low stone table from mansion house in pre-70 Upper City. Wohl Archaeological Museum, Jerusalem. Author 2014.

Latin-inscribed wine jars, and a peristyle courtyard that would have been at home in Pompeii. These residences belonged to wealthy priests, who needed to remain in a state of ritual purity for their work in the temple, and partly for that reason we see an abundance of locally produced stone vessels – stone and glass do not transmit ritual impurity – as well as private ritual baths (Fig. 32).

The so-called Burnt House was found in this wealthy neighbourhood. It is connected with the priestly family of Katros, known from the Talmud, by an inscribed stone weight found in the lower level. It boasted a stone-paved courtyard and a large but unknown number of rooms. The seven nonresidential rooms exposed on the (under)ground level include a kitchen, ritual bath, and workshop spaces, perhaps for perfume/incense manufacture for temple use, with stone tables and vessels, ovens, inkwells, oil lamps, and much pottery. This house was consumed by a raging fire, possibly intensified by oil stored there. In addition to the remains already mentioned, excavation has uncovered coins (including one from A.D. 69), the partial arm skeleton of a woman in her mid-twenties, and an iron spearhead propped in a corner, which may have belonged to a fighter based in the house.

Given the evidence considered in Chapter 7, we should not imagine a wealthy family living here in comfort and peace until the moment that Roman soldiers burst through the door. Jerusalem had been in turmoil for three or four years before Titus' army arrived for the siege. This Upper City area had been the centre of violent struggle between the auxiliary and Judaean elites and among contending Judaean factions since 66, coming under Simon's control after his admission to the city. Even if we discount Josephus' drama, it is inherently likely that factional strife, desperate hunger, and gang brutality reached a peak in the months before and during the siege. Rich families would have been prime targets in such strife, even if Josephus had not repeatedly said so. The Upper City was also the last neighbourhood to be taken by Titus, after five months of siege and after the temple's fall. The residents of this great house must therefore have lived in terror for many months or years. We cannot be sure how or when their home first came to be burnt or who was occupying it at the end, although its destruction was evidently finished off by the Roman invasion in late August of 70.

Benjamin Mazar's excavations along the southern and western walls of the temple mount revealed hundreds of pieces of worked stone, many of them large, from the upper walls and colonnades brought down by the temple's destruction. Analysis has shown that column fragments and decorative pieces burned under intense heat – ca. 800°C (1472°F) – and that some are coated in human or animal bone dust.[2] An unusual dig, running since 2004, involves the careful sifting of thousands of tons of debris removed from the former temple mount during development work by the Muslim trust (*Waqf*) in 1999–2000. Finds to date from that material include coins from the revolt years and the jamb of a gate from the temple.[3]

All of these material survivals help us to imagine the horrible realities underlying Josephus' horrifying narrative. The discovery of underground caverns and tunnels has a similar effect (Chapter 3). Even such details as chisel marks on the ashlars in the lower courses of the Herodian retaining wall might show the futile efforts of Roman soldiers to chip away at these massive, immovable stones of the master course.[4]

These remains confirm massive destruction at the end of this period and help us to imagine the pervasive fear and desperate efforts at escape. As valuable as they are, however, none of these remains gives us much insight into specific events, groups, or personalities of 66 to 70. From a period shortly after the conflict, similarly, stamped roof tiles amply confirm the presence of the Tenth Legion on Jerusalem's western hill.[5] But little of this promises understanding of persons or groups and their motives. For these questions, the coins produced in Jerusalem between A.D. 66 and 70 have proved the most tantalizing. Because the production of every single coin in antiquity required a swing of the hammer to create a particular symbol and script, Jerusalem's wartime coins have seemed to offer the hope of calling back to life the real groups that produced them.

---

[2] Shimron and Peleg-Barkat 2010: 56–62.   [3] Shanks 2005: 14–15.   [4] Bahat 1994: 181.
[5] Geva 2000: 18–19.

1. WHAT DO THE COINS TELL US?

Scholars have used the beautiful silver denominations and abundant bronze coinage produced in wartime Judaea to illuminate Josephus' narrative but also to challenge it. Numismatics is an increasingly specialized subdiscipline, becoming ever more technical as technology advances. I am no specialist. My aim is to review basic issues and debates in relation to the coins and to make the simple point, above all, that they do not tell us what happened. As always, we need to use our imaginations to think of the possible conditions that produced them. To understand the debates we need first to recall how coins were produced and clarify what we mean by "coins of the first Jewish revolt."

By the time the Roman empire expanded into Syria and Judaea, although payment in kind was still possible and practised in some cases, coinage had been long established as the principal means of exchange. The four standard metals were gold, silver, and the copper-alloys brass and bronze. Coins were valued in principle for their intrinsic ("melt") worth, although adjustments in weight and metal purity had rendered the lower-value coins *subsidiary*. They had become tokens representing an assigned value, like modern coins.[6] Gold and silver coins did not need to declare their denominations, which were obvious from their metal and size. So the space they offered was used for symbolic images and legends. Coins were usually dated, however, by the year of the issuing city or one or more rulers. Valuing coins according to material and size permitted both the continuing use of very old coins and cross-fertilization of coins from different places around the eastern empire. A silver *drachma/denarius* had currency anywhere, no matter which *polis* or province had produced it, and even small bronzes from Judaea have been found as far away as Athens and Spain.[7]

The few imperial mints kept a monopoly on gold coinage and the central messaging from Rome (cf. Chapter 1). Provincial governors, allied kings, and important *poleis* were permitted to produce coins in silver and especially in copper alloys. Along with images reflecting the city or region, these typically honoured the imperial family with portraits and legends. Gaza, Ascalon, Tyre, Sidon, Berytus, and Antioch, the principalities to the north (Philip, Antipas, Agrippa I and II), and several Decapolis cities (e.g., Pella, Gadara, Gerasa) produced their own *polis* coins. We saw in Chapter 6 that Claudius granted Tiberias this right shortly before his death, although it ended with the city's transfer to Agrippa II the next year, and in Chapter 4 that equestrian governors in Caesarea avoided human or animal portraiture from evident respect for Judaean custom.

---

[6] Lönnqvist 2009: 247–51.

[7] Meshorer 2001: 176. On old coins see Avigad 1976, who notes that specimens from centuries earlier were still being used in pre-70 Jerusalem.

With the gold and silver coins, their purity, weight, and regulation of supply determined their value. If certain coins of this class had the purchasing power of their size and type, for example, but 5 percent or 10 percent less precious-metal content than the standard, those who spent them or traded them for higher-purity coins scored a bonus. In the 30s B.C., Marc Antony issued debased silver *denarii* to help fund his military campaigns, dropping their weight from 3.9 to 3.4 grams *and* their purity from 99 percent to 85 percent. As these coins continued to circulate for decades alongside higher-quality specimens, people naturally tried to spend Antony's coins and hoard the better ones, fulfilling Gresham's Law.[8] It has been argued that Nero's debasement of his silver coinage to a standard matching Antony's was meant to increase the money supply by removing this incentive to hoard.[9] The most extreme case of value manipulation was Tiberius' isolation of Egyptian currency from regional markets, by cutting the silver purity of its *drachma* to only about 33 percent.[10]

The Province of Syria, which is most relevant for us, had two main provincial mints. The one in Antioch, the capital, produced silver coins of roughly 70 percent purity. This was so low that their four-drachma (*tetra-drachm*) piece, which should have been worth four Roman *denarii*, would often bring only three in exchange. These coins appear to have traded exclusively in the northern half of the province, perhaps being rejected elsewhere.[11] The mint at Tyre also served the south. For reasons that are unclear but must have included great civic pride, Tyre produced coins from 126 B.C. to A.D. 66 that were almost pure silver bullion, at 97 percent or higher levels of purity. The obverse of these attractive coins bore the image of Tyre's God Melqart (= Baal = Herakles), their reverse an eagle with Herculean symbols and the proud inscription "Of Tyre the Holy and Inviolable."[12] That slogan refers to the city's undying satisfaction in having been granted honorific recognition by the Seleucid King Demetrius II in 141 B.C., as he was desperately shoring up support for his claim to the throne. Judaea's old enemy Tyre seems to have been the first *polis* outside the Greek heartland to receive this august title, which remained central to its identity through the Roman period.[13]

---

[8] Modern states have faced the reverse problem, when the melt worth of silver in coins *surpassed* their declared value, prompting citizens to remove them from circulation for their metal value. That is why the U.S. Coin Act of 1965 replaced the silver in quarters with cheaper alloys. Canada soon followed, with the result that a pre-1968 Canadian quarter is now worth many times its face value: www.coinflation.com/canada (accessed December 1, 2012) shows the fluctuating values.

[9] Comparette 1914. Cf. Pliny, *Nat.* 33.47 on Nero's new gold standard (45 instead of 40 to the pound). See generally on debasement and currency controls, Howgego 1995: 111–35.

[10] Burnett 1992: 688–713, Cf. Capponi 2005: 157–68, and Bagnall 2009: 189–90.

[11] Butcher and Ponting 2009: 59–61.

[12] See, e.g., the specimen in the British Museum, ref. 1874,0703.2.   [13] Rigsby 1996: 481–85.

What Greeks called a *tetradrachm* – recall that coins did not name their denominations – counted in Judaean areas as the *shekel*, and their smaller two-drachma (*didrachm*) piece was therefore a half-shekel. As it happens, the Tyrian silver coinage has been found mainly in Judaea. Rome's loyal ally Herod was permitted to produce copper-alloy coins, but for larger expenses his kingdom also used the high-quality Tyrian coinage.[14] Not only that, but Jerusalem authorities declared it the *only* acceptable silver currency, also for the half-shekel dues paid into the temple annual by adult Judaean males around the world.[15] One function of the gospels' "money-changers" must have been to sell these Tyrian silvers to pilgrims.[16] The impact of this currency is well attested in inscriptions, documents, and rabbinic references, as well as the coin finds.[17] When Josephus accuses John of profiteering in Galilee, he remarks that John was using Tyrian *tetradrachms* to buy up large quantities of olive oil (*War* 2.592).

Ancient "mints" were simple affairs, requiring no machinery. Many minting spaces were needed only occasionally and could be repurposed when coins were not being produced.[18] The production process required first making blank metal discs (flans or planchets). Workers drilled shallow hollows into chalk-limestone or clay tablets to produce moulds connected by small channels. Then they poured molten metal into the moulds and covered the stone tray with a flat lid. When the metal cooled and hardened inside, the lid was removed, the ribbons of coins were ejected, and the connecting metal bits (trunnions) were cut and filed off, leaving blank round discs.

Meanwhile, the engravers (celators) had cut approved images and legends into hard metal dies. They had to do this backwards, as though in a mirror (but there were no clear mirrors), so it required a high level of skill. Because each die was cut by hand, it was unique: Images and letters would have slightly different shapes, angles, and sizes. These differences allow modern analysts to identify coins produced from the same die.

The die for the *obverse* ("heads") was secured in a workbench or anvil for stability. The operator would lay a blank flan on this die and hold the reverse die – a metal punch with the image for the "tails" side fixed on the end – above it. He might have used a stand or tongs for this. Then with a single hammer blow, ideally, he would strike the coin, instantly engraving both sides with the die impressions. Sometimes he missed. Many surviving specimens betray double strikes to correct mistakes.[19]

---

[14] Hendin with Kreindler 2010: 476–82. On Meshorer's hypothesis that Tyrian shekels were produced in Jerusalem, see later.

[15] Cf. Exod 30:13–15 with Josephus, *Ant.* 3.194–96; *m. Bech.* 8.7.

[16] Jeremias 1969: 32–33 with *m. Shek.* 1.1–3.

[17] Cf. *m. Bech.* 8.7 and the overview in Syon 2004: 157–67.   [18] Howgego 1995: 27.

[19] Howgego 1995: 24–38.

This basic background is necessary if we are to understand some debates about Judaea's wartime coinage in silver and bronze. To begin with, both were produced from blank planchets – rather than by overstriking existing coins as Judaeans of the later Bar-Kochba Revolt would do. An unusual feature of both types is that they declare their denominations. The silver issues are engraved *Shekel of Israel* or *Half-Shekel*, and the odd *Quarter-Shekel* has been found.

Declaring these values takes up the space for a legend on the obverse, surrounding the image of some kind of vessel on a vertical stem with a pedestal base on short legs. Half-way up that stem is a small protrusion. The degree to which the top of the vessel protrudes beyond its bowl-shaped body varies from one die and year to another. The thicker-lipped versions are so extreme as to suggest that that the rim was a cover rather than part of the vessel.[20] Although the vessel is most often described as a *chalice*, many representations show that it would be hard to drink from, with such a broad rim and/or large beaded lip (Figs. 33–34).[21] Meshorer compares a vessel of the same shape on the table in the Arch of Titus relief (Fig. 1), agreeing with Romanoff that it is not a chalice but rather the cup for measuring the first-harvest grain for sacrifice at Passover: the *omer*.[22]

In the space above the mystery vessel and below the legend sits one of the first five letters of the Hebrew alphabet, *aleph* to *he*, which doubled as numbers. Here they represent years 1 through 5. We know this because, from the *bet* (= Year 2) series onward, that counting letter is preceded by the letter *shin*, which the bronze coins spell out as *shanah* (year).

The writing on both silver and bronze coins is in palaeo-Hebrew, an ancient script that had long since been replaced by the square letters of Aramaic and classical Hebrew. These legends might have been unreadable to many users, recognizable only as very old Hebrew. The moneyers were evoking the nation's ancient past, just as the Hasmonean coin-makers had done two centuries earlier. Likewise the use of *Israel*,[23] rather than the ethno-political *Judaea* of common discourse, added to that aura of antiquity and highlighted the nation's internal perspective. For us, incidentally, it casts further doubt on the suggestion that there was a rebel state of Judaea (Chapter 4).[24]

---

[20] A. Reifenberg (1973: 31–32) concludes that it is a *cover*, citing m. *Sukk.* 4:10; *Ter.* 8:4 on the need to protect wine being separated for offering to the priests from snakes.

[21] Romanoff 1943: 440–44.

[22] Meshorer 2001: 117–18; Romanoff in previous note. Cf. *m. Men.* 10.

[23] Gen 32:28; 35:10; 49:2–28.

[24] Goodblatt 2006: 121–39 argues that the rebels called their "state" Israel, although he admits that the evidence is not clear. In my view, the references to Israel here and elsewhere (also "restoration of Israel" language in various places) make the best sense with in light of our knowledge that Israel and Zion were familiar ancient, biblical names for the people and (elements of) their land. It is conceivable that Israel was the name of a budding state but the evidence does not tell us this.

FIGURE 33. Silver shekel from Year 1 (A.D. 66–67): *Shekel of Israel / Jerusalem is Holy*, with defective spelling and relatively crude imagery. © The Trustees of the British Museum (ref. 1927,1219.1).

FIGURE 34. Example of a silver shekel from Year 2 (A.D. 67–68): *Shekel of Israel / Jerusalem the Holy*, with plene spelling and more elegant images. © The Trustees of the British Museum (ref. 1881,0606.1).

On the reverse of the silver coins is a form matching the obverse's geometry. Here the figure has a triple stem supporting three fruits or blossoms, the uppermost matching the position of the year-letter on the obverse. The stem branches right and left, terminating in the fruit/blossom. In many examples this reverse figure is impressively symmetrical, as wide as it is high and with the right/left termini in the 3:00 and 9:00 positions. The palaeo-Hebrew perimeter inscription on this side reads "Jerusalem is Holy" on the Year 1 coins, and "Jerusalem the Holy" in Years 2 through 5. The Year 1 coins use a defective spelling, dropping the final *yod* from *Yerushalayim* to produce *Yerushalem* and omitting the middle *vav* and definite article *he* from "the holy" ([*ha*]*qadoshah*). The more skilled or experienced engravers of later years were able to include all these letters in the same space. Their changes accompany a general refinement and simplification from Year 2 onward.[25]

The image on the reverse is no more self-explanatory than its obverse partner, even though both are expertly executed, especially on later specimens. Nineteenth-century scholars thought that the rectilinear form with blossoms represented the budding of the high priest Aaron's staff with blossoms and almonds (Num 17:8). By 1903, however, Théodore Reinach was dismissing that notion and stating confidently that it was "a branch of lily with three flowers."[26] Earlier Judaean coins had featured lilies and often in threes. In 1960, Leo Kadman categorically rejected that interpretation, declaring it "beyond doubt" that P. Romanoff was right to see the image as "three pomegranates *in their transition from blossom to fruit.*"[27] Recently, Robert Deutsch has discarded the notion of *natural* pomegranates, arguing that the straight upright and stylized representation suggest, after all, the high priest's staff.[28] He thus returns us to the earliest proposals, but with stylized pomegranates rather than blossoms. These images are not self-interpreting.

The silver coinage was, we may objectively state, manufactured to a high standard. This has always been recognized, but sophisticated means of testing in recent years make the question measurable. In test samples, Deutsch found that the silver coins sustain over 98 percent purity through the first four years, dropping only slightly in Year 5, thus exceeding the fineness of the famed Tyrian shekels. He further notes the consistency and near perfection of the die-striking, and near absence of off-centre specimens. The extraordinary effort and quality combine with a limited distribution pattern – almost exclusively in Jerusalem and Masada – to persuade Deutsch that the silver coins were never meant for ordinary use but for the payment of the half-shekel temple tax.[29]

As for the volume of production, Goldstein and Fontanille studied 747 samples, counting eighty-one shekels from Year 1, 258 from Year 2, 128 from Year 3, thirty-three from Year 4, and only nine from Year 5. Year 2 was thus the high point, after which production fell dramatically. Surviving half-shekels

---

[25] There is considerable variety among the Year 1 dies, in their depiction of the vessel (ranging from tall and thin to squat), their shaping of the letters, and their relation of the legend to the figure. See the composite images in Goldstein and Fontanille 2006: 17.

[26] Reinach 1966 (1903): 12–13. On the importance of lilies for Judaean coinage, see Romanoff 1944: 301–307.

[27] Kadman 1960: 87. Emphasis added.   [28] Deutsch 2010a: 52.   [29] Deutsch 2010b, 2010c.

reveal a more consistent pattern through the first three years (seventy-six, eighty, seventy-eight), before dropping sharply in the last two (three, one).[30] With access to many more (1,225) silver coins, tracked down from museums, catalogues, and private collections, Deutsch found basically the same relative distribution.[31]

These patterns make the best sense, most scholars agree, if the years indicated on the coins began from Nisan (March-April) of 66. Although production would have begun only late in that year, the producers counted their Year 1 from the spring. Year 4 thus ran from April 69 to March 70. Because Year 5 began with the arrival of Titus' army for the siege in April 70, and coin production must have ended in August at the latest, it is not surprising that Year 5 specimens are so few.[32]

This all seems to work. It is, however, a reminder of the recalcitrance of our sources that Josephus describes Nisan (= Xanthicus) 69, which should be the first month of Year 4 on this explanation, as part of *the third year of the war* (*War* 4.577). If he was not being careless, he may have reckoned the war's first year from Vespasian's arrival in early 67[33] or from Cestius' defeat in October 66, and/or reckoned with a year beginning in Tishri (September/October). At *Ant.* 1.81 he observes that Moses' law begins the calendar of *sacred festivals* in Nisan, but preserves "the primary/original arrangement" for business and trade – apparently meaning the autumnal new year indicated in the Mishna (*RH* 1:1), which remains the Jewish New Year today.

That the coins do not simply *tell us* even what we have come to agree on is well illustrated by the history of debate about dating these coins. The eminent Reinach could not imagine why or how Jerusalem's mint could have produced coins before the massacre of the auxiliary garrison, which he dated to September 66. Because the temple had fallen within four years of that date, he could not accommodate five years of coins in the war against Rome.[34] Along with other eminences (F. de Saulcy, F. W. Madden, H. Graetz), therefore, he dated them to another period of Jerusalem's proud independence, beginning in 139 B.C. when the Seleucid Antiochus VII (Sidetes) granted the Hasmonean Simon the right to mint coins (1 Macc 15.6).[35]

Although the calendar now accepted obviates Reinach's objection by backdating Year 1 to spring 66, that debate remains instructive because Reinach himself had converted from the wartime to the Hasmonean dating. He wrote an elegant defence of his new position in 1903. Sir George F. Hill

---

[30] Goldstein and Fontanille 2006: 14.   [31] Deutsch 2010b, 2010c.   [32] Kadman 1960: 54.

[33] He can speak of the war beginning with the Flavians' arrival (*War* 7.46), but also of various earlier starting points in 66 (e.g., 2.284).

[34] Reinach 1966 [1903]: 12–13.

[35] It is unclear how long that permission lasted (1 Macc 15:27).

wrote a supportive appendix, and his wife translated the book. Just a decade later, however, Hill published a forceful argument for the Roman-war dating, based on differences in epigraphic style between the silver coins and Hasmonean bronzes and similarities between the Jerusalem silvers and wartime bronzes.[36] The decisive proof came in the 1960s, when Year 1–2 silver shekels were found in almost new condition alongside Tyrian shekels dating as late as A.D. 65, in a hoard from Silwan in southeast Jerusalem. Only this evidence compelled A. Reifenberg to abandon the Hasmonean camp, where he had stubbornly remained long after Hill's work.[37]

No scholar today doubts that wartime Jerusalem produced these beautiful silver shekels, but it is not a self-evident fact. It is the hypothesis that best explains the new condition of these coins found in a hoard that must be dated to 65 or later. The historical significance of the coins is another issue, also far from obvious, as we shall see presently.

The bronze coins have a different profile and present their own problems. They survive in vastly greater quantities, estimated in the hundreds of thousands, although the number is uncountable because of their global dispersion. In spite of that abundance, they have been found only for Years 2 through 4, and the huge number of survivals makes it unlikely that examples from Years 1 or 5 will be found. Moreover, they change significantly between Year 3 and Year 4.

The bronze coins of Years 2 and 3 are very similar. Instead of declaring their value, perhaps because they looked so much like other *prutot* used in the region,[38] they spell out their date in full words (e.g., *shanat shtayim*, "Year Two") on the obverse, in palaeo-Hebrew characters, around the figure of a two-handled wine-storage jar (amphora). On the reverse is the legend "freedom of Zion" (*ḥerut Tziyon*) around a descending vine leaf. Like *Israel*, *Zion* is a resonant ancient name largely opaque to contemporary non-Judaeans.[39]

The Year 4 bronzes are puzzling. On the one hand, they continue the pattern of a central symbol surrounded by a legend in ancient script indicating the year. Their letter shapes deviate noticeably, however, from those of both the silver currency and the Year 2 and 3 bronzes (especially in *aleph* and *vav*, somewhat in *tsaddi*). Like the silvers but *unlike* the other bronzes, they indicate three denominations: "Year 4, Half" and "Year 4, Quarter," and on the smallest simply "Year 4."[40] Given that the Hebrew word for "eighth" (*sh'mini*)

[36] Hill 1914: xciii.   [37] cf. Kadman 1960: 42; Reifenberg 1973: 28–33.

[38] So Kadman 1960: 99.

[39] Cf. 2 Sam 5:7; 1 Kgs 8:1; 19:21, 31. *Zion* appears 154 times in the Hebrew Bible and is a particular favourite in the prophetic books. It was also favoured by the biblicizing author of 1 Maccabees (4.37, 60; 5.54; 6.48, 62; 7.33; 10.11; 14.27). Zion does not appear in Philo or Josephus. NT texts have it seven times, although usually in citations of the prophets.

[40] See the Year 4 bronze (eighth) in the British Museum, ref. 1885,1001.11.

requires five wide letters, the denomination is probably omitted here for space reasons. The coin would clearly be an eighth in the same series. The standard view is that they are fractions of a *shekel*, struck in bronze because their producers lacked silver.[41] That sensible hypothesis prompts further questions, however: Who produced them and under what circumstances? And why create these fractions only now in Year 4?[42]

These Year 4 bronzes have stimulated fascinating debates. We noticed uncertainty as to whether the vessel on the silver shekel is a chalice or an *omer* bowl, or something else altogether (manna pot, laver).[43] A similar image, minimizing the stand part (perhaps for reasons of space), appears on the tiny bronze "eighth." Goldstein and Fontanille propose that it might have nothing to do with temple rituals, but could be a symbolic cup of imminent salvation (Ps 116:13).[44] Why not? But how could we *know*? More importantly, what is at stake in its interpretation?

As for the legends, the change from "freedom of Zion" in Year 3 to "for the redemption of Zion" in Year 4 brings out the inner theologian in scholars. We are convinced that the difference is *profoundly* meaningful, but we cannot agree about the meaning. Baruch Kanael took the Year 4 bronzes (alone) to be Simon bar Giora's currency. For him the change from *freedom*, a "mainly political" conception, to *redemption* showed Simon's new influence. He "stood at the head of a Messianic movement": Redemption is obviously a "religious and Messianic" term.[45] Contrast Romanoff: "The messianic idea, on the whole, did not yet enter the minds of the people."[46] For Kadman, differences of vision or personality among leaders had nothing to do with it. Rather:

> *Herut* means political freedom, while the word *Geula* – redemption – has a much more profound and all-embracing meaning. It expresses desire for the ingathering of the exiles and even messianic hope. At the beginning of the fourth year, the Jews in Jerusalem enjoyed *Herut*, . . . but *Geula* – redemption – was only a matter of hope.

Redemption was thus the grander *aspiration*, in Kadman's view, building on the *achievement* of freedom by 69.[47] For Meshorer, on the contrary, the shift reflects increasingly *dire straits*. Whereas *freedom* signified early Judaean victories

---

[41] For the *communis opinio* see Meshorer 2001: 129; for the still-open discussion see Goldstein and Fontanille 2006: 28.

[42] This Year 4 bronze is © Trustees of the British Museum (1885,1001.11).

[43] Romanoff 1943: 440–44; but Kadman 1960: 84–87.

[44] Goldstein and Fontanille 2006: 26.   [45] Kanael 1953: 20.

[46] Romanoff 1942: 5–6. Emphasis added.

[47] Cf. Romanoff 1942: 7 n. 19 – a long note on the uncertainty of dating (emphasis added): "If we assume that the 'Simon' coins belong to the year four of the First Revolt, *they are surely significant* and *may reflect a definite change* in the leadership of the war or *a definite religious tendency* in the fourth year of the First Revolt against the Romans."

by the sword, the grim outlook and suffering of Year 4 meant that Jerusale-mites could *only* hope for divine intervention, which is to say redemption.[48] The passage Meshorer cites to illustrate this *Year-4* desperation, however, actually belongs to *Year 5* and the siege under Titus. Year 4 (spring 69–spring 70) was reportedly free of direct engagement with Roman forces, although Jerusalem was encircled and mired in civil conflict.

Goldstein and Fontanille stand Meshorer's view on its head:

> Immediately we are struck with the perception that freedom does not necessarily imply confrontation and can conceivably be obtained by mutual consent, possibly as a result of negotiation, whereas redemption denotes salvation *or a forced release* from a status of war and oppression. In other words, a different philosophy altogether might have been at play.[49]

The only point that emerges clearly from these discussions is that scholars can be as creative as anyone in sermonizing on *redemption* and *freedom*.

But is the change *so* meaningful? The Year 4 bronzes came with many changes – in size, denomination, and imagery – so why would their producers not also refresh the motto? Elsewhere in biblical-Judaean sources, *freedom* and *redemption* are so close as to be interchangeable, the latter (*ge'ula*) often meaning liberation, or freeing. Recall that Meshorer understood the obverse of the half-dozen Gamala coins to read "For *Redemption*," in sympathy with Jerusalem (Chapter 6), but they are from 66/67 (Year 2), before the change in the bronzes.[50] And when the Bar-Kochba Revolt broke out two generations later, its leader Simon bar Kosiba struck coins with the legend "Year One of Israel's *Redemption*" before changing to Year 2 to "of Israel's *Freedom*."[51] Did he not grasp the difference?

In a biblical passage on the paradigmatic event of Israel's freedom, the Exodus, God says to Moses (Exod 6:6):

> Therefore say to the children of Israel, "I am the Lord, and I shall *bring you out from under the burden* of Egypt, and I *shall free [or deliver, ve-hiẓalti] you from their slavery*, and I *shall redeem [or liberate, ve-ga'alti] you* by my outstretched arm and by mighty acts of judgment."

Similarly the Psalms (e.g., 106:10):

> He *delivered* them [*va-yoshi'em*] from the hand of the enemy;
> He *redeemed* / *liberated* them [*va-yig'alem*] from the hand of the adversary.

How deep is the difference?

---

[48] Meshorer 2001: 127–28.   [49] Goldstein and Fontanille 2006: 21.
[50] Meshorer 2001: 130–31. The inscriptions are far from clear; cf. Hendin 2010: 364 and Chapter 6.
[51] Meshorer 2001: 140–61.

The verb behind the coins' redemption motto, *ga'al*, has biblical roots. It is used of the strong family member (*go'el*) who helps in time of need, the relentless advocate who will do whatever is necessary: to clear debts, buy back a seized field, or pay a ransom or fee (Lev 25:25–54; 27:13–33). Such a relative might become the avenger of shed blood, should the need arise (Num 35:12–27). Because the subject of the verb is often a human being, we need not assume that a redeemer is divine, as in Christian usage. Why could the coins' producers not have seen *themselves* as the agents of redemption, as Jerusalem's protectors and avengers – with divine aid of course?

Judaean wartime coinage has similarities to that of the Batavian revolt (A.D. 69–70), whose leaders produced a silver coinage. Some issues appear to celebrate their stunning early victory over the legions *V Alaudae* and *XV Primigenia*, and others bear nationalistic legends and themes.[52] Similarities with Judaean coins include pride in the motherland (Jerusalem; Gaul/Gallia), evocative local symbols (palm, vine, lulav and etrog; boar, grain, Celtic torc, trumpet), the freedom motif (*ḥerut*; *libertas*), and the divine alliance with those who save and avenge their people (*ge'ula*; Mars Ultor). Especially interesting is the Gallic invocation of help from Mars *Adsertor* (or *assertor*), for an *assertor* is more or less a *go'el* (one bringing *ge'ula*): a champion, advocate, deliverer, redeemer, and restorer of liberty.[53] The Latin word overlaps with *vindex*, the name of the governor under Nero, Julius Vindex, who used *Adsertor* on his coins.[54] In comparison with the Batavian coins, however, the Jerusalem silvers are very restrained.

Debates about the life setting of the Year 4 bronzes remain. Hill accepted the wartime dating for the silver shekels, as we have seen, but dated these bronzes to the Hasmonean Simon, whereas Reinach, attributing the silvers to the Hasmoneans, thought war with Rome the obvious context for the Year 4 bronzes.[55] Nowadays everyone dates them to the war, and the debate turns on whether they were the common coin of Jerusalemites or minted by Simon bar

---

[52] Mattingly (1977: 26–27) deduces that the coins featuring Gallia (Gaul personified) on the obverse, other Gallic symbols, and the language of freedom, concord, and divine assistance – all without any reference to an emperor or contender, the Senate, the Roman people, or the army – "with high probability" come from the Batavian rebels themselves. Most telling is the coin bearing a helmeted head on the obverse, glossed only as "Champion of Liberty," with Victory and Gallic symbols (boar, grain ears) on the reverse and a reference to the Fifteenth Legion, which surrendered to rebels in this revolt. See also Sutherland and Carson 1984: 201–202, 214, and plate 24 nos. 130–31.

[53] See Mattingly 1977: 26–27.

[54] See Mattingly and Sydenham 1966: vol. 1, 199 n. 3, with earlier references.

[55] Reinach 1966 (1903): 43–44. Kadman (1960: 47) overlooked Reinach when he claimed in 1960 that "all books on Jewish numismatics" until 1945 (with one other exception) agreed with Hill's assignment to Simon the Hasmonean. Again, it was find-spots and physical contexts that decided the issue, when Year 4 bronzes were discovered alongside those of Years 2 and 3 at Masada in 1949 (Kadman 1960: 48).

Giora away from the temple. Reinach, calculating Year 4 (69–70) as that of the siege, his year beginning in the autumn, reckoned that "all the reserve of silver and gold, formerly hoarded in the treasury of the Temple, had been exhausted by the necessities of war." Jerusalemites were faced with a currency crisis, and the emergency (obsidional) bronze series had to be produced for daily needs.[56] Kadman and Meshorer, using a different calendar, correlated the appearance of the Year 4 bronzes with the sharp drop in the number of Year 4 silvers and likewise inferred a dearth of available silver.[57]

Kanael, however, stressed in light of Josephus that 69 was the year in which Simon bar Giora entered Jerusalem. In his view, however (here ignoring Josephus), Simon was "riding the crest of a wave of messianic enthusiasm" energized by the death of Nero in 68 and Vespasian's diversion from Judaea.[58] Although Simon controlled much of Jerusalem, the temple with its bullion remained in the hands of others: "Since Bar Gioras had no silver at his disposal for minting purposes, he was compelled to use copper."[59] Goldstein and Fontanille take a similar view and link it with their die analysis, which showed that the side they identified as obverse suffered at least as much damage as the reverse. That unusual situation arose because Simon's group had to use mobile dies, lacking such a stable facility as the traditional one in the temple compound. This created more instability with the obverse dies.[60] Also accepting the Year 4 bronzes as Simon's, finally, Rappaport speculates that the change of motto reflects the civil strife he encountered once inside Jerusalem, and the hope of his faction to recover the temple from John and the Disciples. *Their* victory in civil war was the hoped-for "redemption."[61]

If my reader is bewildered, that is a rational response. The scholarship is acute and perceptive. My point in surveying a few important studies is not primarily to poke fun, but to drive home the methodological point that this evidence needs both interpretation and historical explanation. Even where we now agree, our confidence results from testing and narrowing hypotheses. These reflections bring us back to the crucially important silver shekels. Do they *impose* a certain understanding of the war and its origins?

---

[56] Reinach 1966 (1903): 44.
[57] Kadman 1960: 98–101; Meshorer 2001: 124, 129–30. Meshorer compared the Nabataean kingdom's shift to bronze coins when silver supplies were low.
[58] Kanael 1953: 19.   [59] Kanael 1953: 20.
[60] Goldstein and Fontanille 2006: 23–25. This conclusion depends on identifying the obverse and reverse. They agree with common opinion (Kadman 1960: 128–32; Meshorer 2001: 124–25) that in the case of the Year 4 bronzes, the side stating the year is the reverse. This view rests mainly on the similar appearance of the vessel on silver reverses and one side of the *eighths*. It seems to me that treating the Year side of all these coins as the obverse produces more consistent interpretations in all respects, including the larger number of dies used for the *reverse* in the Year 4 coins.
[61] Rappaport 2007: 112.

In a provocative 2003 article, James McLaren argued that the Year 1 silver shekels furnish decisive evidence of a specific group's actions *and motives* in the first year of the war and that this evidence plainly contradicts Josephus. McLaren understands Josephus, however, as trying to minimize the role of priests in the revolt: "According to Josephus, the motive of the aristocratic priests was to prevent the war from getting out of hand. . . . Here the coinage undercuts this reconstruction."[62]

McLaren argues methodically to make the case seemingly airtight. He confirms that silver coins begin in the first year of the conflict and come from Jerusalem. They must therefore come from the temple, the only place that had such high-quality silver for new flans. McLaren proposes that these coins were needed to cover temple expenses and to allow payment of the temple tax because wartime conditions had made access to the customary Tyrian shekels uncertain. Beyond economic necessity, however, he stresses the revolutionary nature of minting silver coins without Rome's permission, an act made all the bolder by the care and pride that went into producing these nationalist issues.[63] McLaren asks in effect who had the motive, opportunity, and state of mind to produce the Year 1 silver coins: access to the temple stores, eagerness to assert Jerusalem's freedom, a view of the temple as national rallying point, a powerful interest in seeing the temple tax paid, and a calendar dating years from Nisan.

Not wanting to become "entangled" in Josephus' narrative, McLaren nevertheless extracts three "key events" from Josephus: Gessius Florus' attempt to raid the temple treasury; the decision of priests led by Eleazar son of Ananias to halt the sacrifice for foreigners; and the earliest period of factional strife, which produced a priest-led coalition of leaders.[64] These provide sufficient evidence that *leading priests* produced the silver coins. Josephus is thus exposed as a deceiver: "Whoever minted these coins did so, at least in part, as an act of defiance against Rome." Josephus' account, allegedly of a priestly leadership determined to end the revolt, must therefore be a "substantial distortion."[65] The coins tell us a different story. They "lay to rest Josephus' explanation" by revealing a coordinated war effort led by the senior priesthood. McLaren even wonders how the captive Josephus, in striving (he thinks) to conceal priestly aristocratic involvement, could have explained such an obvious affront to his Roman captors.[66]

The problem with this case is that most of it is devoted to only one premise of the many needed for the argument: that the silver shekels issued from Jerusalem's temple in 66. This McLaren argues clearly and convincingly. But the other necessary premises receive little attention and would be much more difficult to sustain: that Josephus tries to divorce priests from the revolt, that

[62] McLaren 2003: 150–51.   [63] McLaren 2003: 144–45.   [64] McLaren 2003: 148–49.
[65] McLaren 2003: 151.   [66] McLaren 2003: 152.

production of coinage was chiefly an act of revolt (irrespective of context), that the priesthood was a more or less unified block, and above all that one can infer intentions or aspirations of public figures from their coins or other public actions.

The problem with the last premise we began to discuss in Chapter 2: It is much easier to observe what public leaders do and say than to discern their motives or feelings. The worldwide consternation caused by the disclosure of diplomatic correspondence that was meant to remain top secret, by WikiLeaks and others, and all the apologizing that follows, makes the point with sufficient force. Public actions and private thoughts are different things. It is easy to show that a public figure declared war, signed a treaty, gave a speech, approved a bill, advocated a position, or (under monarchies) issued coins. It is, for example, easy to learn that the U.S. Congress voted overwhelmingly on Friday, October 11, 2002, to authorize President George W. Bush to attack Iraq, a vote the administration cited as proof that "America speaks with one voice."[67] But only rigorous investigation could uncover what individual members actually felt when they voted – three weeks before the 2002 mid-term congressional elections and subject to huge pressures from various quarters.[68] Public figures rarely if ever give speeches or take public actions *merely* to divulge their innermost views. Recall Liddell Hart's distinction between prophets, whose concern is authentic self-expression, and *leaders*, who have no business doing that (Chapter 2).

We can all agree that silver coins issued from the temple in 66. Especially in times of crisis, when leaders' lives may hang in the balance if they depart from public sentiment, they must keep a finger on their constituents' pulse. Examples abound from every period, in modern times from the Soviet Union, pre–World War II Germany, the Middle East, and the U.S. Congress.[69] But if political dissembling and obfuscation are both normal and necessary, inferring attitudes from public expressions including coins is a doubtful procedure.

Even if it were clear that those in charge of the temple's bullion in late 66 were Ananus II and his colleagues (this is far from clear), one could imagine reasons why *they* might have issued such silver coins. It probably was illegal,[70] but not at the same level of illegality as slaughtering the auxiliary garrison or ambushing and massacring Cestius' legion, acts for which Jerusalem's leaders

---

[67] The House of Representatives voted 296–133, the Senate 77–23: http://articles.cnn.com/2002-10-11/politics/iraq.us_1_biological-weapons-weapons-inspectors-iraq?_s=PM:ALLPOLITICS (accessed December 10, 2012).

[68] See Isikoff and Corn 2006: 21–32.

[69] For society's mid-level leaders and professionals saying what was necessary in pre-war Germany, see abundant examples in Evans 2005: 234–320. For parallels in wartime Japan, see Trefalt 2003: 16. In democracies even heads of government must often compromise with popular sentiments they do not share.

[70] It would not have been illegal if Jerusalem had been minting silver coins all along, as Meshorer thought.

were going to be held accountable. However we understand the coinage, it was part of a larger vortex of events. Josephus claims, in a single passage, that these leaders *both* made active war preparations *and* hoped to wind the conflict down, without expecting his audiences to object: "But that's a contradiction!" (*War* 2.648–51). He expected political awareness on the part of his Polybius-informed audiences. If the Judaean leaders could produce armour and genuinely prepare for conflict while *hoping* to end the war without massive bloodshed, why could they not have produced coins if coins were needed?

Would the captured fighter Josephus – captured from a battlefield in which he had been fighting Romans – really have been embarrassed for the Flavians to learn that, along with the Judaeans' fortifications, armour production and long resistance, and their massacres of auxiliary and legionary soldiers, they had gone so far as *to mint coins*?

As for the possibility that Josephus wished to separate the priesthood from revolt, I have proposed a rather different interpretation of his *War* (Chapters 2 and 4). Here I would emphasize only that *he* is the one who describes the temple-based opposition to Rome and the priest-led government, of which his own position in Galilee – as a high-ranking priest – is a subset (e.g., *War* 2.648–49). *War*'s opening sentence declares that he is a priest who fought Rome until he was forced to stop (*War* 1.1–3), and his military exploits are central to his status in that work. So it is hard to imagine that he hopes to absolve himself or others of his class. He does not simply portray the chief priests as wishing to end the war immediately. He claims that his virtuous type of leader, while certainly considering the war dangerous and doomed, prepared for it with commitment so that if terms could not be reached, it would be honourably conducted.[71] Had Ananus lived, according to Josephus, he would have found a way to reach terms with Rome *or the Judaeans would have fought a better war* (*War* 4.320–21). The issue, I have proposed, is not pro- or anti-Roman ideology. Josephus wrote as a pragmatic statesman guided by political-moral concerns.

Uriel Rappaport, in responding to McLaren, focuses on the question of the coins' producers. He begins from the continuity of the silver shekels in appearance, message, and quality over the whole five years, though these were apparently times of violent upheaval in Jerusalem's leadership. If the first series (66–67) *had* expressed the aspirations of Ananus II and his colleagues, he asks, why did the violent coup that removed those men from office have no effect in the later coins (67–68)? Would we not expect a change in symbols and legends once the more radical groups had taken charge?

Rather than finding the shekels proof against Josephus, Rappaport thinks that a careful reading of Josephus best explains them. It was the Zealot

---

[71] *War* 2.648–51; 4.320–21; cf. Polybius 15.10–16; 36.7.3–5; cf. Plutarch, *Mor.* [*Praec.*]. 800d–e; Eckstein 1995: 214–18; Millar 2006a.

(Disciple) faction, he observes, that controlled the inner temple from the start in Josephus' account. Temple commandant Eleazar son of Ananias had sufficient priestly support to halt foreigners' sacrifices that first year, against the wishes of older priests and Pharisees (*War* 2.409–17). The temple was then held by Eleazar ben Simon's followers and later John (4.147–215). That priest-based Zealot faction, opposed to the senior priesthood and removing them with the help of outsiders, never lost the inner temple. Even Simon could not dislodge them in 69. So it must have been this priestly faction that created the coinage in 66 and continued producing it throughout. That is why it does not significantly change.

Rappaport points out, moreover, that the legends and symbols chosen by this group were very restrained. Such beautiful coins must have been designed to appeal to all Jerusalemites, even Ananus' group initially. Everyone needed money, and this was the new coinage from those in control of the temple. Rappaport argues, however, that such fine coins were not likely made to facilitate payment of temple dues into the treasury. The half-shekel obligation may have fallen into abeyance. If not, it would have been strange for the authorities to exhaust their high-quality bullion and technicians' expertise on coins they would receive back. More likely, also in view of the find spots outside the temple, these pieces were meant to pay suppliers around Jerusalem for such temple requirements as sacrificial animals, incense, wine, olive oil, and tradesmen's wages. With Judaea in crisis, I.O.U. notes would have been useless. The coins' high quality might have been required to reassure suppliers.

Rappaport also finds a basic continuity in the bronzes, in spite of the Year 4 changes. He proposes that Simon bar Giora's group, which never had access to the temple bullion, was responsible for all of them. The differences between the two types he explains by their changing locations: outside Jerusalem in Years 2 and 3, in the Upper City from Year 4.[72] As often in this speculative area, this happens to reverse Goldstein and Fontanille's argument that the Year 4 dies reflect a newly *mobile* mint.

In sum, whereas McLaren finds in the silver coins of Year 1 decisive proof that Jerusalem's priests were defiant rebels, undermining what he sees as Josephus' effort to shield the priesthood from war complicity, Rappaport counters that it was the very priests *Josephus portrays* as militant who likely produced the silver coins. It seems to me that, of these possibilities, Rappaport's hypothesis has the greater explanatory power. I have emphasized that these coins were (a) produced in contexts of political turmoil and (b) were public media driven by political need, not vehicles for self-expression.

---

[72] Rappaport 2007: 105–106, 109–11, 114.

I close this section with four further observations.

First, we need to ask how much one can communicate through coins. Ancient historians naturally seek *the meaning* of every survival, including coin symbols and legends. That is our job. But where is meaning supposed to reside in coins: in the *inner thoughts* of their designers? In what a given *audience* might reasonably decode? In the evocation of a certain emotion or atmosphere, rather than a proposition? Whenever an authority produces coins, after all, they must put *something* on them. State-produced coinage typically includes national symbols and emblems of authority. In Canada these include the beaver, maple leaf, and loon – to the amusement of foreigners. How many coin users engage in exegesis? Did the users of Jerusalem's coins meditate on them and think that a particular symbol meant *this and not that*? Or would they simply have been happy that they had some silver coins?

Christopher Howgego, after summarizing academic debates on the general question of meaning in ancient coins, steers a middle course between currency as propaganda and the complete dismissal of any intended meaning. He observes, however, that in the clearest case we know of an ancient population's pondering coin imagery – when Antiochenes objected to the bulls and altars on Julian's coins in the fourth century – they entirely *misread* the symbols' intent.[73]

Second, in interpreting Jerusalem's wartime coinage we might consider what is *missing*, or options not taken. The Flavian coins we discussed in Chapter 1 convey unmistakable ideas of conquest and victory, supported by ubiquitous weapons, Victory images, trophies, *Iudaea capta* and similar mottoes, mounted warriors, triumphal scenes, and soldiers in battle dress towering over the defeated foe. We get it. Martial themes are also clear on the Batavian coins featuring the captured legion *XV Primigenia*, although it is admittedly not certain that these were products of the revolt. Again, L. Clodius Macer began minting coins while commanding two legions in Carthage. Although his specific intentions remain unclear, his coins convey obvious martial themes: a warship or legionary standards and eagle.[74] Not to be outdone, 70-year-old Galba highlighted his military prowess in spirited poses, wearing a muscled cuirass and holding the reins of a rearing horse.[75]

Nothing remotely similar appears on Jerusalem's coins. Granted the Judaean prohibition of human images, we might have expected at least swords, shields, and helmets on what we call "revolt" coinage. The long-used Tyrian shekels are more overtly aggressive, with Hercules, the eagle, the club, and the

---

[73] Howgego 1995: 62–87 (74) with Socrates 3.17 and the notice in Julian's response, *Misop.* 355d.

[74] See the silver *denarii* of Clodius Macer in the British Museum, e.g., refs. 1837,1030.22 and 1843,1024.78.

[75] See the *denarius* of Galba from A.D. 68 in the British Museum (ref. 1920,1215.1).

"inviolable" slogan. The Jerusalem coins portray a pearled bowl of some sort, palm trees, citrons, and willows, with a nearly tourism-like appeal. *Lulav* and *etrog* were among the most obvious, comforting symbols for Judaeans, found abundantly elsewhere. There is nothing radical or warlike about them.[76] The high-priest's staff, if that is what it is, ends in fruit or flower, reminding us perhaps of peaceful protestors offering flowers to soldiers. It seems the visual equivalent of porridge, comforting but bland. The silver coins do not remotely suggest an idea of holy war.

There is a time to rally spirits for war and a time to say "Keep calm and carry on." The Jerusalem silver coins appear to do the latter. If so, we should rethink the circumstances and intentions behind their production.

Third, the relationship between the Tyrian and Jerusalem shekels is tantalizing. Some early rabbinic literature considered the two types comparable.[77] There we have high-quality silvers celebrating "Tyre, holy and inviolable" with the proud symbols of that ancient *polis*, and used chiefly in Judaea and Jerusalem's temple but ceasing production around A.D. 66. Then here we have equally fine (or slightly better) silver issues of the same denominations, proclaiming "Jerusalem the holy" with ancient Judaean symbols, used in the same area *from* 66.[78]

Meshorer ingeniously proposed that Tyrian shekels had actually been Jerusalem's currency, produced first as Herod's coinage (from 18 B.C.) and continuing until the outbreak of war when the Jerusalem shekels took their place. That hypothesis would have answered several questions[79] while also explaining the Tyre-Jerusalem continuity.[80] It is, however, one hypothesis from the great numismatist that has found *no* traction with others.[81] Most specialists have attributed the end of Tyre's coinage to regional issues in the north, in particular the new dominance of Antioch's less pure currency. It seems that it was part of Nero's currency programme to introduce new eagle-bearing silvers in Antioch, offering an alternative to Tyre's expensive coins in preparation for shutting down that mint as too expensive.

---

[76] Cf. Leon 1960: 196, 208–22, 221–22; Setzer 2006: 69–70; Trebilco 2006: 78; Levine 2006: 524, 542, 546.

[77] Jeremias 1969: 33 discussing *m. Bech.* [mistakenly printed *Ber.*] 8.7; *t. Ket.* 13.3, 275; with *b. BK* 97b.

[78] I drafted this chapter before seeing Lykke 2012: 234–38, which discusses more fully an undeniable relationship between the Tyrian and Jerusalem silver coinage.

[79] Meshorer's hypothesis would have explained why such a major ally of Rome as Herod was not invited to produce silver coinage (viz., he was, but chose to preserve the well-regarded Tyrian silver), why the Tyrian coins are found mainly in Judaea, and why (in Meshorer's view) they changed noticeably from 18 B.C.

[80] Meshorer 2001: 75–78.

[81] E.g., Levy 1995, 2005; Butcher and Ponting 2009: 65. No specialist I know, at least, not even those (according to private conversation) who studied with Meshorer, supports his Jerusalem hypothesis. The principal objection seems to be the sheer oddity that Jerusalem would mint (and be permitted to mint) coins in the name of another city.

Nero's involvement in both the currency changes of the north and the raids in Jerusalem at around the same time raises the prospect of a link between the two in the minds of Jerusalemites, even if we cannot clarify the nature of the link. In any case, the gradual disappearance of Tyrian coinage from 65 onward must have created problems for Jerusalem, which depended on it so heavily. If we consider that the decision of influential Jerusalem priests to sever the temple's ties with foreigners in 66 (*War* 4.409–10; Chapter 4) roughly coincides with the emergence of Jerusalem's new coinage, we might imagine the general circumstances that required a new currency.

We want to regard the creation of Jerusalem silver coins as a free ideological choice, but the city *could not* have continued using Tyre's coins. They had either to adopt the hated Nero's new Antiochian coins of 30 percent less silver purity or – in the context of rampant violence caused by neighbours and Nero's agents – begin producing their own coins of unimpeachable quality.

Finally, perhaps we should focus less on the *ideas* held by the coins' makers and more on the requirement that anyone in power (at any time) keep their populace feeling calm and reassured in the midst of turmoil. Even groups that come to power through radical upheaval or coup usually move quickly to reassure everyone that everything is under control. A city in panic does not help anyone. Jerusalem did not seek turmoil: Aggression came to it from neighbouring populations aggrieved at its long dominance, from a Samaria-raised auxiliary, and from Nero's brutal revenue collection, against which Jerusalem reacted in various ways. The priests controlling the silver might naturally have used coins as a way of reassuring the people of their internal stability, without expecting scrutiny of the chosen symbols and text choices. Their use of old scripts, some nice words about the city, and comforting symbols would show that everything was under control. In spite of all the *unsought* turmoil and violence around them and recently in Jerusalem's very heart, the holy places, temple service, and supreme office were in safe hands and the all-important sacrifices to God would continue uninterrupted. Not a call to holy war but an important sign of stability amidst unwanted distress.

Even the cruder bronzes of Years 2 to 4 may reflect little more than hope for the restoration of Jerusalem's freedom – "freedom" meaning regional primacy and the centre of rule as under Herod, Archelaus, and Agrippa I, the kind that Jerusalemites longed for in A.D. 6 and 44. It is noteworthy that all the coins focus on Jerusalem, or Zion, and so may have to do with the root question of Jerusalem's regional status and relations with neighbours.

II. TITUS AND THE DESTRUCTION OF JERUSALEM

We turn now to a different kind of evidence outside Josephus. His effort to distance Titus from the temple's destruction, which is clear from *War*'s preface through Book 6, has most often been seen as part of his alleged programme to flatter the Flavians. The assumption is that he wanted to *shield Titus from blame*, just as he supposedly wished to exculpate his priestly class. In the case of Titus, scholars have been able to offer a competing ancient narrative, which claims that in the war council described in *War* 6, Titus actually declared his intention to destroy the temple. Since the 1860s that other account has usually been preferred to Josephus' putative flattery of the Flavians and used much like the coins to expose his narrative as a whitewash. I have offered reasons for rejecting the impressions of Josephus' *War* that feed these assumptions and for doubting that his picture of Titus at the temple's burning could be construed as flattering (Chapters 1, 2, 4). Here we must turn to that other ancient text, to ask about its nature and historical value.

From a methodological perspective, I emphasize, the most curious thing is that we should cling *to any text* for our understanding of the past. We have consistently distinguished between real life and any literary representation. What follows is not therefore an endorsement of Josephus. It challenges the proposal, however, that an early fifth-century Christian text offers a better and less distorted account of events in A.D. 70 Jerusalem.

We took note of Titus' war council in the previous chapter while surveying the content of *War* 6. Now we may look more closely. Titus' army has finally captured the temple's outer court. Learning of Maria's cannibalism, he promises to bury the city. An unsuccessful effort to invade the inner temple leads him to order its gates and colonnades burned (6.229–36). When the burning has lasted a day, he summons an ad hoc council of senior officers to discuss the sanctuary's fate (*War* 6.237–43):

> And when they had gathered – six of the highest-ranked: Tiberius Alexander, prefect of all the forces, Sextus Cerealius leading the Fifth Legion, Larcius Lepidus the Tenth, and Titus Frigius the Fifteenth, and with them Fronto Haterius, camp commander of the two [partial] legions from Alexandria as well as Marcus Antonius Iulianus, procurator of Judea; after these were assembled the various procurators and tribunes – he convened a *consilium* concerning the shrine.
>
> To some of them it seemed appropriate to resort to the law of war. For the Judaeans would never stop their rebellious activities as long as the shrine remained, *to which they rally from everywhere.* Some advised, on the contrary, that *if* the Judaeans should abandon it and place no weapons in it, he should preserve it, whereas [only] if they climbed up on it to wage war should he burn it down, because in that case it would be a fortress and no longer a shrine – and in the sequel the impiety would belong to those who had forced [this outcome] and not to themselves [the Romans].
>
> But Titus declared that even if the Judaeans should climb up on it and wage war, he would not take vengeance on the inanimate objects instead of the men involved. There was no way that he was going to burn down

such a great work as this, because that would only bring harm to the Romans themselves, even as it would be an ornament to their power [*imperium*, ἡγεμονίας] as long as it remained. Full of confidence now, Fronto, Alexander, and Cerealius quickly sided with this opinion.

So he dissolves the council and, after directing the commanders to rest the other forces, so that he would have reinvigorated men at his disposal in the battle lines, he ordered the select men of the [auxiliary] cohorts to clear a path through the ruins and to extinguish the fire.

Some commanders named here, at least, were active in Rome while Josephus was writing *War*. Some were presumably among those commanders who "had fought along with [Vespasian and Titus]" who received handmade copies of *War* (cf. *Life* 362; *Apion* 1.51).[82] We do not know the limits of their tolerance for fabrication, but events involving them were not a zone of free creativity. I have stressed his literary freedom, but it was of course constrained when it involved the interests of his powerful contemporaries (Chapter 2).

The question of a temple's fate was one that any army besieging a city would have to consider. One did not attack temples without good reason, although good reason could be found if needed. Consider the emperor Tiberius' review of Greek temples' claims to inviolability in A.D. 22, described by Tacitus as an important task that the emperor delegated to the Senate (*Hist.* 3.60–63). Tiberius worried that a universal principle of temple asylum was being abused. Slaves, debtors, and murderers would simply flee to sanctuaries and hope to be untouchable. The Senate called in each major temple's representatives in succession. They recognized a basic right to preserve the sanctity and customary usages of the shrine *as long as* this privilege was not abused and temples remained sites of sacred activity.[83] The Romans thus recognized no absolute right of asylum, if a temple was functioning as a criminal hideout or, certainly, as a military fortress resisting Rome.

In his account of Titus' *consilium* Josephus describes three opinions according to a typical literary scheme of two poles plus a middle position.[84] Although it is usually the middle position that is moderate and therefore best, here Titus occupies one of the poles. Some officers want the temple destroyed in any case, noting the "law of war" clearly permits its destruction (*War* 6.238–39). The decisive issue is that its destruction would crush Judaean morale. The middle position basically agrees, with the proviso that *if* the Judaeans can be induced to surrender the sanctuary rather than use it for protection, there is no reason to destroy it (6.239–40). Titus' position is extreme and unconditional:

---

[82] Cotton and Eck 2005.

[83] Rigsby 1996: 1–29 has many useful insights, and he finds Tiberius' review to mark the end of asylum grants to Greek cities, after nearly three centuries and about 90 known grants.

[84] The most famous case is *Ant.* 13.171–73 on the three views of fate (all, none, or some), but the device is a common way of summarizing opinions, e.g., at *War* 6.169–70.

He *will not* burn down "such an extraordinary construction" (τηλικοῦτον ἔργον). His concern with psychological impact is on a different level, with an eye on his future imperial responsibilities. The removal of this temple would principally harm *the Romans*, once the conflict is over, whereas its preservation would be "an ornament of [Rome's] *imperium* as long as it endured" (κόσμον τῆς ἡγεμονίας αὐτοῦ μένοντος; 6.241). Josephus does not explain this, but his Titus may have in view particularly the widely distributed Judaean population in Syria and far beyond that Josephus mentions often. Sparing their sole international sanctuary would avoid needless provocation and win admiration for their restraint.

With his extremely concise remark – these are not minutes of the meeting but a literary configuration – Josephus' Titus convinces the commanders from Egypt and the legate of the Fifth. Perhaps Josephus leaves the others still unconvinced for the sake of realism; perhaps he was present and this reflects reality. At any rate, Titus' view is now firm. They adjourn and he orders the fires extinguished. But as we have seen, a soldier's impetuosity (under divine control) thwarts Titus' intention.

We do not know how many versions of this meeting circulated in Josephus' time, originating from the participants, or how important it seemed among many such meetings. The alternative version that has enchanted scholars does not come from Josephus' time. It was written in Latin, 330 years after the event (in A.D. 401), the same interval that separates us from 1685. It was by a Christian chronicler and hagiographer from western Gaul (France) named Sulpicius Severus. He was writing in a world that had been Christian for generations. Even though his account is very late and very Christian, it continues to fascinate. Why?

Sulpicius' account has a familiar ring to the reader of Josephus, but it differs in crucial ways. I have italicized some phrases for comment later.

> 2.30.6 After calling a *consilium*, Titus *is said* to have deliberated, first, whether he should bring down a sanctuary *of such extraordinary construction* [*an templum tanti operis*]. For it seemed to some [*nonnullis videbatur*] that a consecrated shrine more famous than all human works ought not to be wiped out. Preserved, it would furnish evidence of Roman restraint; demolished, *an enduring relic of Roman cruelty.* 7 Others, by contrast, also Titus himself [*at contra alii et Titus ipse*], reckoned that the temple above all must be brought down, with the result that *the religion [religio] of the Judaeans and Christians would be eliminated more completely.* [He/they said:] "In fact these religions [*religiones*], though opposed to each other, *nevertheless proceeded from the same ancestors* [or originators, *isdem . . . auctoribus*]. The Christians emerged from the Judaeans. So, *with the root eliminated, the offshoot will quickly vanish.*"
>
> 8 Thus, with God's approval and everyone's minds being inflamed, the temple was demolished, *three hundred and thirty-one years ago.* This latest

> overthrow of the temple and harshest captivity of the Judaeans, which sees them refugees from their ancestral land and scattered across the circle of the earth, are *a daily proof to the world of their having been punished for nothing other than the impious hands they laid on Christ*. Although they have often been reduced to captivity at other times because of their sins, nevertheless they have never faced a punishment of slavery for more than 70 years.

In an 1861 study, Jacob Bernays made a new and vigorous case for the historical value of Sulpicius' version.[85] He argued that, although the text is very late, this passage with its very different presentation of Titus' view has its origins in a lost passage in Tacitus' *History*, and that Tacitus took his information from another participant in the *consilium*. Sulpicius then discovered the story in his copy of Tacitus and preserved it, although that section of Tacitus has been lost to us, and unwittingly bequeathed us a compelling alternative to Josephus' white-wash of Titus.

Eminent historians from Theodor Mommsen onward endorsed Bernays' analysis[86] and built arguments about Flavian intentions or policy on the foundation of Titus' resolve to destroy the temple – dismissing Josephus as a Flavian lackey.[87] T. D. Barnes wrote in the 1970s: "The proof was first formulated by Jacob Bernays in 1861, and the only attempt to gainsay it must be pronounced a hopeless failure."[88] Barnes tried to strengthen Bernays' case by identifying what seemed telltale Tacitean vocabulary in Sulpicius.[89] Barnes' 2005 essay, "The Sack of the Temple in Josephus *and Tacitus*" (notice the title), again builds on Bernays to propose three distinct stages of Flavian historiography.[90] A contribution from James Rives in that same 2005 volume

---

[85] On Bernays' place in scholarship, see Bach 1974.

[86] Mommsen 1894: 5.539 and n. 1: Sulpicius/Tacitus helps to show that the burning of the temple was the result of a Flavian *Programme*, not chance.

[87] The long n. 15 in Leoni 2007: 42–43, lists scholars who see Josephus' account as a whitewash of Titus, with greater or lesser influence from Bernays' hypothesis.

[88] Barnes 1977: 228; cf. 2005: 134: ". . . Bernays' proof that Severus used Tacitus' account of the sack of the Temple in 70 is incontrovertible. . . ."

[89] Barnes 1977: 227 and n. 13: proposing *at contra* ("by contrast," *Chron.* 2.30.7) and citing Tacitus, *Ann.* 4.28. The problem is that Sulpicius' *at contra* turns up frequently in Cicero and other definitive authors, *except* Tacitus, whose phrase (which is only there) is *at contra reus*. For the simpler phrase, see Cicero (*Pro Quinct.* 75; *Pro Rosc.* 131; *Verr.* 2.5.66; *Pis.* 95; *Fin. bon.* 156; *Tusc. disp.* 1.5; *Ep. fam.* 4.4.2); Sallust (*Cat.* 54; *Bell. iug.* 4.7; 15.3; 25.6; 36.2); Lucretius (1.466, 570, 1087; 2.235, 392, 400, 424, 713; 3.25, 191, 198, 201; 4.95, 625, 661, 843, 976); Ovid and pseudo-Ovid (*Ars amat.* 2.604; *Hal.* 31, 118); Petronius (*Sat.* 124.1 [254]); younger Seneca (*Oed.* 962; *Dial.* 4.11.2; 7.12.2; 10.16.4; *Clem.* 1.17.3; *Ep. mor.* 33.8; 70.28; 81.23; 97.11; 100.7; 107.4, 12; *Nat. quaest.* 1.3.1, 6; 3.6.2; 5.2.1; 7.5.1); elder Pliny (5.42; 7.186; 31.127; 34.18); Statius (*Theb.* 12.709); and Quintilian (*Inst. or.* 2.15.11). The phrase might better be called Ciceronian, Sallustian, Lucretian, or Senecan (and in keeping with Sulpicius broad classical inclinations), not noticeably Tacitean.

[90] Barnes 2005: 143.

builds partly but significantly on Bernays, arguing that Vespasian had taken a policy decision to destroy Jerusalem's temple. Rives' commendable interest is in problematizing the ancient phenomena we lump together as *religion*, arguing here that Vespasian wanted to remove the Judaean *cult*, which was anomalously exclusive and creating dual loyalties, but that he had no problem with synagogue-based Judaism in the Diaspora, which was accommodated to ethno-political life throughout the empire.[91] Because Sulpicius' account continues to have such an impact, it is necessary to scrutinize the evidence.[92]

Bernays' pivotal assumption is that Sulpicius did *not* use Josephus. If he were rewriting Josephus more than three centuries later, obviously, his passage would have no value for the first century. Bernays was sure of this because he could not fathom why, if the pious monk *had* known Josephus, he would have presented Titus as anti-Christian and would not have borrowed Josephus' emphasis on God's role in destroying Jerusalem, a Christian staple.[93] His puzzlement overlooks, however, Sulpicius' pronounced *theme* of pre-Constantinian persecution by Rome's emperors. Second, Bernays assumed that Josephus to be a mouthpiece of the Flavians, as many did in his day. Supposing that the Flavians must have been starting to worry that Titus' destruction of Jerusalem would threaten their image as mild rulers, he figured that Josephus must have been tasked with spreading word of Titus' gentle restraint.[94] *That* is why Josephus wished to keep Titus from the temple's destruction.

In tracking down Sulpicius' source for the *consilium*, if it was not Josephus, Bernays thought the lost part of Tacitus' *Histories* Book 5 most likely, because we know that it included more on Jerusalem's fall. But where did Tacitus find *his* information for that section? He would not have turned to Josephus, given his hatred of Jews (*Judenhass*).[95] But Josephus mentions one Marcus Antonius Julianus, the "procurator of Judaea" in 70, as a participant in the consultation, and in the latter half of the second century the Christian writer Minucius Felix mentions an Antonius Julianus as author of a work *On the Judaeans* (*Oct.* 33). Bernays joined the dots and thought it likely that Josephus' Antonius of 70 later

---

[91] Rives 2005: 147. Rives' argument is much fuller, but Tacitus' presentation of Titus' determination (known via Sulpicius) is an important foundation for his isolation of Josephus (misleading, on Titus' reluctance).

[92] E.g., S. Schwartz 2006: 30 (*Cambridge History of Judaism*), consciously building on Rives, though his summary – the Flavians "understood themselves to be stamping out Judaism" and leaving only "private mores" untouched – may not align precisely with Rives' argument (2005: 154–55, 157–58).

[93] Bernays 1861: 48–61 on the war council, 52–53 on this point. He notes that *other* Christian writers had turned the emperor Tiberius into an admirer of Christianity (via Pilate) and seems to think that Sulpicius would have preferred this route with Titus if a source had not countered it.

[94] Bernays 1861: 48–52.   [95] Bernays 1861: 55–56.

wrote a book on Judaeans, which must have included the temple consultation, that Minucius refers to the same author, that Tacitus took the *consilium* story from Antonius, and that although Tacitus' version is lost, Sulpicius rescued it from his copy of Tacitus.[96]

Bernays did not claim that Sulpicius made no changes, but there was not much he had to deny to Tacitus in the core of *Chron.* 2.30.6–7 – not even the concern with Christianity, which he took to be Tacitean. Overlooking the close parallel in Sulpicius' Hadrian story, he imagined Tacitus writing that Titus wished to eradicate the Christians' root in Jerusalem. Still, he thought that Tacitus must have named the council participants (NB: as Josephus does), rather than using Sulpicius' "some" and "others," and must have spoken of *superstitiones* rather than the later Christian-sounding *religiones*. Further, the Roman commander could not have spoken about the Jerusalem temple's fame *beyond all human constructions* (NB: a theme of Josephus' *War*). Finally, Bernays thought he could detect vestigial phrases from Tacitus, although neither his examples nor Barnes' addition to the Tacitean stock is compelling.[97]

Bernays concluded by asking readers *to choose* one of these accounts: one written "under Titus' eyes by his devoted darling Josephus, at a time when the emperor was valued and wanted to be valued for his mildness," or one written by a reliable and independent Roman historian, when the simple truth about Titus could be told.[98]

Within a year, Bernays was answered in an overlooked essay by the Professor of Latin at Harvard, Charles (Karl) Beck. Beck doubted some of Bernays' assumptions, first that the Flavians ever felt a need to apologize for Jerusalem. Why and to whom? He made a general case for Josephus' reliability and even-handedness, citing testimony from eminent scholars of the day. He also stressed that Josephus, living in Rome, could not have attributed to powerful Romans

[96] Bernays alertly spotted two men named Marcus Antonius with a Judaean connection. But Marcus Antonius was a very common name. It belonged to the lover of Cleopatra and rival of Octavian, of course, but Antony's father and grandfather had shared it too, and Antony gave it to all the many in the eastern empire who received their freedom from his hand. The third-century emperors we know as Gordian I, II, and III were, each one, a *Marcus Antonius* Gordianus. As for Julianus, it is by far the most commonly attested *cognomen* of its type, constructed from family names (via Caesar's Julian clan), with some 800 known occurrences (Kajanto 1982: 34–35, 148). So the name M. Antonius Iulianus was rather like Robert E. Jones or John B. Smith in the twentieth century.

[97] Bernays 1861: 58–59. Sulpicius calls the Jerusalem shrine *consecrated* (2.30.6: *aedem sacratam*) rather than *sacred* (e.g., *Chron.* 2.10.1, *sacrae aedis*). Tacitus often uses *quippe* ("in fact") in indirect speech, which Sulpicius does here and not elsewhere. But Sulpicius does use *quippe* eight other times (*Chron.* 1.19.4, 42.2, 53.3; 2.15.4, 21.3, 28.3, 32.4, 46.6) and Sulpicius rarely cites *indirect speech*. His two small volumes must cover everything from Creation to his day, affording little space to report speech. For Barnes, see n. 90.

[98] Bernays 1861: 59.

positions that they knew to be wrong.[99] Finally, given Sulpicius' evident freedom with his *biblical* sources,[100] which Bernays had conceded, Beck saw no reason to doubt that the *consilium* passage was nothing other than a tendentious rewriting of Josephus.

I would observe that Sulpicius even changes *Tacitus*. The Roman historian had described Otho's suicide (*Hist.* 2.49) and Vitellius' murder by Flavian partisans (*Hist.* 3.84–86), whereas Sulpicius turns these around: Otho was killed (*Chron.* 2.30.2) and Vitellius killed himself (2.30.3). A writer who could take such liberties with both Tacitus and the Bible was surely capable of changing Josephus in similar ways.

Beck agreed with Bernays on the methodological point, however: "[T]he accounts of Josephus and Sulpicius contradict each other; they cannot be reconciled ...; *we must choose one and reject the other.*"[101] This need to *choose* has dogged scholarship ever since. Tommaso Leoni has reviewed the research (absent Beck) and shown the scholarly preference for Sulpicius/Tacitus because of Bernays. Leoni sees himself standing nearly alone with Tessa Rajak in valuing Josephus over the "inextricable tangle of inconsistencies and distortions" in Sulpicius.[102] He highlights a contradiction in the assumption that Josephus was Titus' lackey. For if Titus had coerced him into writing such a flattering account, it would be hard to explain the large number of "slips" that Titus missed. As Beck observed, Josephus was not "in a position to lie blatantly to readers who were well-informed about the facts."[103]

My contribution to the discussion has two sides. First, as Rajak briefly proposed,[104] we may be sure that Sulpicius rewrites Josephus and therefore has no independent value. Second, the historian's task is not to find a *trustworthy account* to follow. The first is important enough for our question that I shall elaborate.

To understand Sulpicius' passage, some context is needed.

1. Although classically educated, Sulpicius was a deeply committed Christian writing in the service of his faith. He is famous for his biography of Martin of Tours, which is filled with miracle accounts. He shared with that saint-in-waiting a devotion to the monastic life and a suspicion of worldly values or powers. In the *Sacred Chronicle*, our text, Sulpicius uses his classical education to swaddle the divine story in blankets of a secular weave, to support its truth claims.

2. His preface conveys the spirit of the chronicle. Composed at the request of eager inquirers, he allows (cf. Josephus, *Ant.* 1.5–10), it will be mainly a

---

[99] Beck 1862: 27–40 for these arguments.   [100] See Beck 1862: 25–26.
[101] Beck 1862: 38 (emphasis added); cf. 40, reprising Bernays: "Whom do you believe, readers?"
[102] Rajak (1983: 206–10) offered trenchant criticism of Bernays. In the year that Leoni's article appeared, Goodman (2007: 441–42) expressed his decided preference for Josephus' version.
[103] Leoni 2007: 49.   [104] Rajak 1983: 208.

summary of sacred events from scripture (*Chron.* 1.1). For the period since the crucifixion of Christ, however, he must supplement that story. He will need to work with "worldly historians" (*historicis mundialibus*) for this, whereas for the sacred material he is a mere channel of divine truth and no author (*auctor*, 1.1). This distinction is sharp. When he comes to the origins of Christianity after King Herod, he will not include the gospels and Acts because he does not want to taint their sublimity by making them touch profane history (2.27.3).

3. As Rajak stressed, two of the *Chronicle*'s key themes are the divine destruction of Jerusalem in 70 and the persecution of Christians by successive Roman rulers (1.1). Sulpicius numbers these persecutions, beginning with Nero's (2.28). Persecutors include "Vespasian's son Domitian," Trajan, Hadrian (2.31), Marcus Aurelius, Septimius Severus, Decius, Diocletian, and Maximian (2.32). The inventory ends only with Constantine (2.33.1).

4. Roman persecutions are a subset of Sulpicius' theme of the *cruelty of worldly leaders* toward the pious. When referring to kings, rulers, and their decrees he reflexively adds "cruel" and "bloodthirsty."[105]

5. In Sulpicius' view, Jews and Christians were indistinguishable to Roman rulers until the time of Hadrian. When emperors acted against Jews, they were really after Christians. Remarkably, he separates Hadrian's war against *the Judaeans*, which he presents as an understandable police action to stop their plundering of Syria and Palestine (2.31.3), from Hadrian's construction of Aelia Capitolina on the site of Jerusalem. Sulpicius does not even mention the Bar-Kochba revolt that this action provoked, in spite of its enormous toll on Roman forces.[106] He detaches Aelia Capitolina from Jewish issues altogether:

> At this time Hadrian [Adrian], *supposing that he would eliminate the Christian faith* by means of an outrage in that place, set up likenesses of demons both in the temple and in the place of the Lord's suffering. And because Christians were thought to come mostly from the Judaeans – for the church at Jerusalem had no priest except from the circumcision – he ordered a cohort of soldiers to maintain a constant guard so as prevent all Judaeans from approaching Jerusalem.

For Sulpicius it is all about Christians all the time. His handling of Hadrian's war is a stunning Christian revision of a watershed event in Jewish history. But that episode is also very close to his account of Titus and Jerusalem's destruction. In both cases, Roman cruelty targets Christians.

6. Although Sulpicius does not identify his sources, he knew Josephus' *War* either directly or at second hand, whether in Greek or via the recent Latin translation. This is clear because the chapter that includes Titus' temple consultation begins

---

[105] E.g., *Chron.* 1.13.3, 35.2, 5, 37.2, 54.3; 2.16.8, 23.5, 27.4, 28.2, 29.2, 30.6, 50.7.
[106] See Eck 1999b: 76–89.

with a clear précis of *War* 5 and 6, which my reader will recognize from the summary of Josephus in Chapter 7:

> 2.30.3 Meanwhile the Judaeans, hemmed in by the siege – since no opportunity for either peace or surrender was given them – were perishing in desperation from famine, and the streets began to be filled with corpses everywhere, for the duty of burying them had been overridden. Why, having dared to eat everything of a disgusting kind, they did not spare even human bodies. . . . 4 So the Romans broke in on the exhausted defenders. As it happened, everyone had assembled at that time, from the countryside and from the other towns of Judaea, for the day of the *Pascha* [Passover]: no doubt it pleased God that this impious people should be given over to destruction at the very season in which they had put the Lord on a cross. 5 For a while the Pharisees held their ground bravely before the temple until at last, with minds bent on death, they flung themselves into the flames of their own accord. The number of those killed is related to have been 1,100,000, with fully 100,000 captured and sold.

Sulpicius' Christian overlay is clear – Jesus' crucifixion as the cause of Judaean punishment – but Josephus' voice provides this material: the hopeless situation of those trapped in Jerusalem, those from outside trapped by the Passover/*Pascha* siege (cf. *War* 6.420), the crushing famine, the piling up of corpses, the horror of cannibalism, bravery marked by leaps into the flames (*War* 6.280), and the numbers of dead and prisoners, which he admits are "related" by someone. The one who relates them is Josephus (*War* 6.420).[107]

Even Sulpicius' three sentences on the *consilium* (2.30.6–7) are obviously borrowed from Josephus, with the roles adjusted to suit Sulpicius' themes. It is unimaginable that two independent authors could, from the thousands of events occurring outside Jerusalem in 70, choose the same meeting and *then* present it in almost precisely the same form and language. Verbal echoes of Josephus[108] include Sulpicius' *tanti operis* (2.30.6) in relation to the temple's grandeur, a phrase from the Latin *War* that represents Josephus' Greek τηλικοῦτον ἔργον (6.241). Both authors use the artfully mismatched construction "it seemed to some. . . . but others advised,"[109] and both highlight the consequences for Rome's reputation of preserving or destroying the temple.

[107] Rajak (1983: 208) also stresses this agreement in figures.

[108] The Latin translation of *War*, completed shortly before Sulpicius wrote, helps one see similarities. Alas we have no published text, but manuscripts are increasingly available online, for example, the ninth-century St. Gallen Codex 627 at www.stgallplan.org/ stgallmss/viewItem.do?ark=p21198-zz0026dh5s (accessed July 1, 2013). Our passage is on codex p. 216, left column.

[109] Rather than "some said, but others said" or "it seemed to some, but seemed to others." Thus Josephus τοῖς μὲν οὖν ἐδόκει . . . τινὲς δὲ παρήνουν; Latin *War, alquis.. videbatur; nonnulli monebant*; Sulpicius: *nonnullis videbatur . . . alii censebant.*

Using a commander's *consilium* to focus issues happens to be a narrative trait of Josephus. Recall that Cestius "took counsel with his commanders" before sending Neapolitanus to Jerusalem (*War* 2.334). At Taricheae Vespasian holds a *consilium* to decide what to do with the captured militants (3.532–36). In Caesarea he rejects his generals' recommendation of a rapid assault on Jerusalem in a *consilium* (4.366–77). Titus himself has recently convened a *consilium* on the question of surrounding Jerusalem with a wall (5.491–501). The *consilium* on the temple is entirely characteristic of *War*. Like the others, however, it is included not merely because it happened but because it serves a literary purpose. It breaks the narrative with a vignette that encapsulates contending views and in this case strengthens Josephus' claim that the temple's fall was divine work. Contrary to the triumphal propaganda, it happened in spite of Titus.

When Sulpicius reports that Titus "is said" (*fertur*) to have deliberated in this way, therefore, we know *who* said it: Josephus. Sulpicius reworks the story to advance his theme of Roman *crudelitas* toward Christians via Judaeans. Titus overrides his generals here and resolves on the temple's destruction in Sulpicius because, sharing the cruel imperial gene, he wants to eradicate *Christians*. Sulpicius knew where to find source material. Josephus was by far the most famous authority for this war, as Tacitus was for Roman-imperial matters (*Chron.* 2.28–29).

In case the reader doubts that Sulpicius would have changed Josephus' account so dramatically, I would point out that another Christian author did something similar. I am not aware that he has been mentioned in this context. Writing after Julian's failed effort to rebuild the temple (A.D. 361–363), a generation before Sulpicius, the writer we call Pseudo-Hegesippus insisted on the finality of the temple's destruction: It is "not restorable" because the Judaeans have permanently offended its Protector – by killing Christ (*De excid.* 5.32). These common Christian sentiments anticipate Sulpicius.

The preface to Pseudo-Hegesippus' five-volume history of Jerusalem's fall gives explicit credit to "the excellent narrator Josephus," while griping that:

> In his own discourse he clearly showed himself to be a partner in the treachery of the Judaeans (*consortem . . . perfidiae Iudaeorum*). This [treachery of theirs] he made clear enough by describing their suffering. . . . He mournfully bewailed the bloodshed, but he did not comprehend *the cause* of the bloodshed. (*De excid.* praef.)

He will have no qualms about altering Josephus' account.

Pseudo-Hegesippus' treatment of the temple consultation, although it plainly draws from *War* 6, significantly changes Josephus' story (*De excid.* 5.42). When Titus orders the temple gates fired he immediately has qualms of pity. That is why he calls his commanders together. Only two views are aired in this version of the council: a consensus view, which Titus had until recently shared, that the temple must be destroyed, and Titus' developing doubts. Only this growing doubt leads him to ponder (as in Josephus) that saving the temple would benefit Rome. But since he is *alone* in his doubts, in this version, against the unanimous position of his generals, he makes *no decision*. He decides to mull it over until the next day (*tractatum in posterum diem*). This means that his soldiers do not contravene Titus' orders when they burn the temple in the next day's skirmishes. They are simply following the previous direction, which Titus has not countermanded. In this version his decision becomes irrelevant and it is never given.

It is easy to imagine Pseudo-Hegesippus' possible motives for these changes. Titus' delay makes sense when he alone has doubts.[110] Perhaps the author finds improbable Josephus' claim that Roman soldiers blatantly ignored their commander. Titus does not look as impotent and undignified here. Freedom to rewrite well-known stories was at the heart of the rhetorical enterprise (Chapter 2). Given Josephus' own reluctance to retell episodes in the same way, we might imagine that *he* would have changed his *consilium* account had the opportunity arisen. Pseudo-Hegesippus was exercising his freedom in the explicit service of Christian theology, and so was Sulpicius.

This does not mean that we can return, comforted, to Josephus. Even if we could be sure that Titus expressed more or less what Josephus attributes to him at the end of some meeting on a particular day, how much could that tell us about Titus' views or a Flavian *policy*? Not very much, for several reasons.

First, the purpose of such a meeting was not to declare Titus' or Vespasian's policy. Issuing orders did not require consultation.[111] *Consilia* were convened for deliberation. Military and political leaders would gather their friends (*amici*: senior advisors) for a frank airing of opinions. Emperors often held *consilia*, a legacy from Republican days, to seek out trusted advice: "The Romans had an immemorial tradition that men in positions of responsibility should not take decisions alone."[112] When Augustus convened the *consilium* to decide Herod's succession, he allowed each party to present its case before he made that difficult decision (*War* 2.25–38, 93–100). Notice Josephus' language at Titus' earlier council on the circumvallation: *After all opinions had been voiced*, he tried to persuade his officers of his view. Only after winning their agreement did he issue orders for dividing up the work (5.502). Likewise he says that the temple *consilium* is convened "to bring forward *for discussion* the question of the shrine" (6.238). All views are solicited and given. In the end Titus convinces only three

---

[110] Cf. Caesar, *Bell. civ.* 1.65.5 (*rem in posterum diem distulerunt*); Livy 8.32.14 (*ut rem in posterum diem differret*); 10.40.1; 26.17.12; 32.36.2; Curtius Rufus, *Alex. magn.* 6.11.9.

[111] Cf. Schürer-Vermes 1.506–7 n. 115: If there had been an order from Vespasian, "the Council of War would have been superfluous."

[112] Crook 1955: 4.

named commanders, although everyone must fall in with his decision (6.242–43). The *consilium* ensures that decisions are not rashly made, that cautionary or countervailing advice will be heard. But this means that the commander's viewpoints are *evolving and open* in relation to the changing circumstances.

Second, even a transcript or recording of the meeting, which we do not have, could tell us only what the participants expressed on that hot Jerusalem morning. It would not tell us what they had felt three days before or afterward. Opinions must have been in constant flux. Within the story, Titus himself had recently changed direction to insist that Jerusalem be buried (6.216–19), for there was no benefit in trying "to spare foreign sanctuaries" (6.228). He had ordered the inner temple gates lit up. Then, before the final assault, he rethinks matters again and asks for a full airing of views. The dynamic narrative itself speaks against ossifying one moment as a *policy* or innate conviction.

Third, participants in important meetings do not necessarily say what they feel inside. We have probably all said things in meetings that we did not necessarily believe with every fibre. We might speak as devil's advocate, or strategically. In high politics leaders are notoriously cagey, especially in the proverbial "frank exchange of views."[113]

Fourth, scholars who have been skeptical of Josephus' account are right to be skeptical, but I would align things differently. Josephus' presentation of Titus' insistence on sparing the temple clearly serves *his* aims, not Flavian propaganda (Chapter 2). He is consistent in asserting *both* that Titus destroyed the temple, which was perfectly obvious to everyone after the triumph, and that Titus did not intend this, contrary to ongoing and indispensable Flavian messaging. Both claims appear in *War*'s prologue (1.10, 27–28; cf. 5.444; 6.266; *Ant.* 20.250), and he cannot have thought them contradictory, as modern scholars incline to do. Josephus resorts often to the theme of Rome's inability to destroy Jerusalem.[114] It was the Judaean God who used Rome as cleansing agent, to purge his shrine of the pollution of native civil strife and bloodshed. Josephus makes this realistic in portraying the nice but ineffectual Titus' futile efforts to stop the burning.[115] As we have seen, his Titus witnesses emphatically that it was not *his* doing (6.410–13; cf. 1.10–11). Josephus' picture of the commander resting late in the day, hearing of the fire, and flailing about while his screams are ignored (6.254–58) does not support the Flavian image.

Instead of looking for a story on which we can stretch out and relax, we need to recognize that we do not know what happened without investigating and imagining. If we pose the open question, "How did Titus come to destroy

---

[113] Roberts 2008 is alert throughout to the strategies of Churchill (especially), Roosevelt, and their military chiefs in their secret, supposedly frank talks.

[114] E.g., *War* 6.220–28, 411.   [115] *War* 6.249–66, 346.

the temple?" and imagine real-world scenarios, both our inquiry and result will look different from an approach built on trying to verify Josephus or Sulpicius. Let us take as our starting point for Titus' initial plans and as our end-point Jerusalem's destruction by his army. Our question is how Titus moved from Point A to Point B.

We can establish our starting point with a thought experiment. Suppose that Nero had not died in June 68 and Vespasian had continued his campaign as he planned, completing the cordon around Jerusalem by the end of May 68, planning the Jerusalem campaign in June, then advancing to the city in July to execute the plan. John was then a newcomer in Jerusalem and Simon was far from the scene. If Jerusalem had capitulated in the late summer, walls intact, would *Vespasian* have demanded that the city and temple be destroyed? To what purpose? If the surviving aristocratic leadership could have been restored, it seems unthinkable that Vespasian would have ordered city and temple demolished, in cold blood as it were. If that assumption is correct, and Titus' task was to continue his father's plan, would *he* have resolved to destroy Jerusalem and its temple following a quick surrender? It seems not.

That Titus hoped for Jerusalem's quick submission is suggested by general conditions, by Cassius Dio, and by many indications in Josephus. Dio's Epitome mentions that the legionaries were soon exhausted and lacking water as the heat intensified (Dio 65/66.4.5; cf. Chapter 3). They had no bombs, rockets, or close air support, of course, and early capitulation was far preferable to the hazards of assaulting massive walls and high internal fortresses. Recall that, after battering the Antonia's walls and seeing one wall collapse – a major success – Titus' soldiers were still imperilled because it was dangerous to climb over the massive rubble, and those who attempted it were fatally exposed (6.23–32, 54–67). Similarly, after Titus' initial order to burn the temple gates, he had to assign auxiliary cleanup crews to clear a path for the legions. As we see in the case of Monte Cassino in 1944, attackers' destructiveness can work against them by creating deadly obstacles. For these reasons and many others, it was preferable that cities and fortresses built with costly feats of engineering return to Roman control – as at Herodium, Machaerus, and Masada – without needing to be destroyed. If Titus had hoped to garrison Jerusalem, as Cestius and Vespasian had garrisoned Sepphoris, he should have preferred that the magnificent walls remain in place.

There were also political considerations. If damage to Jerusalem was minimal, the Flavians would be better positioned to restore the historic Jerusalem-Rome connection, which had proven so effective in southern Syria for over a century. They also needed to put relations between Judaeans and their neighbours on a sound footing again, deflating the hostilities that had generated the war, with Florus and the Samarian auxiliary out of the picture. This would have recommended treating the Judaean *mētropolis* with due firmness, against elements of the population that had resorted to arms, but leaving it intact if possible (cf. *War* 7.107–109). Even if Vespasian *had* wanted to dismantle the Judaean cult (so Rives), would it not have been preferable to occupy the site and establish the new cult in it, as Antiochus IV had done and Hadrian would do?

And what about King Agrippa and Berenice? The close Herodian siblings, who were present with Titus or accessible to advise throughout the siege, would surely have wanted the city, temple, and its elite leaders to survive. Jerusalem was not only their second home but the source of their status. Agrippa might well have been hoping to return as king, in the tradition of his fathers. They had a palace with exclusive views across the Tyropoeon Valley from the sanctuary, which they frequently renovated.[116] Agrippa had responsibility for the temple and the honour of appointing the high priests. He customarily mediated between the city elite and Rome's *legati* as well as with emperors, providing vital services recently to both Cestius and Vespasian.[117] He remained Titus' close associate (4.498–500), providing him with even more soldiers for 70 (5.42). Berenice and Titus may have been an item already, and she would soon live with him for years.[118] Did these important figures have no say or sway in the future of Jerusalem?[119]

When Titus arrived outside Jerusalem in 70 he could have had no idea of what lay ahead, but we have grounds for imagining that he hoped for a quick resolution with minimal risk on his side or destruction needed on the other.

At the other end of the conflict, we know that Titus destroyed Jerusalem and the temple without evident regrets. Tacitus agrees with Josephus in describing the temple as a virtual fortress occupied by Eleazar's and John's fighters (*Hist.* 5.12: *in modum arcis propriique muri, labore et opere ante alios*). As we have seen, Titus' legionary commanders agree that "the law of war" made it a fair target: "once a fortress, no longer a shrine" (*War* 6.239). In Titus' final speech to John and Simon he also insists that the "law of war" permitted the temple's destruction, because of their actions, although he had preferred to save it (6.346). We may be confident that the Flavians had no more qualms about Jerusalem's temple than earlier Romans had felt over temples in Corinth

---

[116] *War* 2.2.310–14, 333–34, 405, 426, 595; *Ant.* 20.189–95.

[117] *War* 2.500–502; 3.29, 443; 4.14–15.

[118] Suetonius, *Tit.* 7.1; Tacitus, *Hist.* 2.2; Cassius Dio 65/66.15.4, 18.1. Smallwood says (1981: 386) that they were already "known to be in love" in 68 on the strength of Tacitus' remark that some people took Titus' return from the Galba trip to be sped along by his passion for the queen. Even though Tacitus mentions it to challenge the notion, such reported gossip more than a generation later is not a firm foundation.

[119] Graetz (1949: 2.307) emphasized Berenice's influence on Titus generally, and credited it for his decision not to destroy the temple.

or Carthage. The Flavian triumph made this clear, even exaggerating the number of burning sanctuaries (*War* 7.144–45; Chapter 1). Recall the centrality of the temple furniture in the parade and on the surviving arch, as well as Vespasian's coveting of these objects (*War* 7.158–61). The Epitome of Dio shows a Roman perspective in having Titus eager to lead the charge into the temple, *forcing* his superstitious and reluctant soldiers to advance (65/66.6.2). The Flavians were not sorry about their destruction of Jerusalem or its temple. They exploited it to the full.

Between Titus' initial hope for a quick resolution and Jerusalem's comprehensive destruction, it is economical to imagine that his course was *not clear* as each day dawned. His actions depended on those of the besieged and their leaders. He presumably continued to hope for submission as early as possible because the longer the operation continued, the greater his risks and the greater the likelihood of unforeseen disasters from nature or accident, even if the enemy was not able to cause him much distress. The need for hot food, clean water, and salutary accommodations imposed enormous logistical requirements (Chapter 3). Josephus' narrative is also easiest to understand, although he does not explore strategic questions as such, if Titus came to Jerusalem with a range of options available and changed course as needed. The continued resistance of Jerusalem may have generated frequent *consilia* and perhaps daily informal conversations with senior staff.

Just as the periodic waves of refugees could not have been predicted, John and Simon might have decided at any moment to surrender. Titus therefore *could not* have had a fixed plan, impervious to developments. It seems to have taken him months to decide on the encircling wall, after consultation (5.491). He could make or commission warm rhetorical appeals, but his methods included display crucifixions. Although we have no access to the realities of Titus' mind, or the minds of any other players, we should assume constant re-evaluation on all sides.

To help us think realistically about how the temple came to grief, we might consider the far better-documented destruction of another famous sanctuary in wartime.

Destruction of a holy site: Monte Cassino 1944

I refer to the Allied campaign outside Italy's Monte Cassino early in 1944, which saw the controversial destruction of the ancient and world-famous abbey on the summit.[120]

---

[120] What follows is culled from Majdalany 1957; von Senger 1963; Ellis 1984; Colvin and Hodges 1994; Hapgood and Richardson 2002; Hoyt 2002; Parker 2003; Clark 2006; Clark 2007 [1950]; Caddick-Adams 2013. There are many other studies and relevant memoirs.

Following a successful sweep through North Africa, Allied forces invaded Sicily and the lower Italian mainland in September 1943. Rome would fall in June 1944, but during the intervening months the Allies faced enormous hardship, working their way up Italy's boot. After a series of fighting retreats, the Germans had dug in deeply on the Gustav Line at Monte Cassino, and there the Allied attack ground to a halt. Fighting for mere inches through the bitter winter of 1943/44, their exhausted and undermanned units faced terrible losses. Route 6, which they were following to Rome, made an abrupt left turn at this mountain spur, before resuming its journey along the Liri River Valley. The S-shaped route presented huge obstacles: not only the Rapido River streaming across it, whose plain had been deliberately flooded by the defenders, but also the mountains themselves. From their positions high atop these hills, German forces enjoyed complete tactical command with an embarrassment of Allied targets below.

Although it was not the highest summit, the crown of the ridge where the highway turned was Monte Cassino. On its 520-m (1700-ft) peak sat a fortresslike monastery, with walls 3 m (10 ft) thick at their base and 46 m (150 ft) high – much like those of Herod's temple in Jerusalem. Founded by St. Benedict in the sixth century, the abbey housed his burial crypt along with numerous invaluable manuscripts and pieces of art. The structure had been rebuilt several times following earthquakes, and the building that stood in 1944 dated from the sixteenth century.[121] In the valley below, the Allied advance came to a standstill for almost half a year.

On the morning of February 15, 1944, Allied air forces destroyed the abbey on Monte Cassino in a massive bombardment. More than 200 planes dropped hundreds of tons of high-explosive and incendiary bombs, although the lower wall foundations were so solid that they remained upright (Fig. 35).[122] This modern campaign benefits from a range of independent and overlapping evidence that could make an ancient historian weep in envy:[123] personal memories strengthened by site visits to retrace movements; official histories of participating units and their war diaries; memoirs by commanders on both sides; interviews with hundreds of soldiers and such key noncombatants as the Abbot's secretary; personal diaries and letters from enemy dead and prisoners of war; mounds of dated memoranda, telephone logs, official correspondence, propaganda leaflets, press reports, and newsreel footage from war reporters.[124] Even with that abundance of evidence, however, the military significance of

---

[121] Incidentally, the abbey contained (and contains) the only known manuscript – a twelfth-century copy – of Frontinus' work on aqueducts, written in Josephus' time.

[122] Parker 2003: 181–82.

[123] Majdalany 1957; Ellis 1984; Colvin and Hodges 1994; Hapgood and Richardson 2002; Parker 2003; Pugsley 2004; Caddick-Adams 2013.

[124] See, e.g., the fifteen pages of sources listed at the end of Ellis 1984: 515–29.

FIGURE 35. Benedictene abbey on Monte Cassino from Cassino town below. Author 2012.

the abbey's bombing, its timing, and the question of responsibility have remained hazy and controversial. A brief look at the destruction of Cassino and its abbey, aided by this abundance of documentation, will help us to think realistically about Titus' situation.

When fortifying their line from late 1943, the Germans had decided not to use the abbey. The Vatican had reached an agreement with German and Allied commanders to respect religious structures of historic importance. Field Marshall A. Kesselring ordered that the monastery be excluded from Italy's defensive positions. Tenth Army commander General H. von Vietinghoff, his subordinate, happened to be a devout Catholic. He personally assured the abbey's seventy monks that he would not use the site, in part to deprive the Allies of any reason to bomb them. And General F. von Senger und Etterlin, who was tasked with defending Cassino itself, was not only a Catholic but a lay member of the Benedictine Order, and apparently as opposed to the Nazi leadership as a senior German officer could be.[125] A number of his junior officers were also observant Catholics, and he posted sentries to prevent soldiers from entering the compound. The Germans were deeply dug in on

[125] Von Senger 1963: 179–258. It is proper to be skeptical about his post-war self-descriptions, but see Caddick-Adams 2013: 304–305 for the case that von Senger understood military service in Christian ethical terms and was indeed opposed to the Nazis.

the slopes around the monastery and the higher hills nearby, then, but not in the abbey grounds.

On the Allied side, American Lt.-Gen. Mark Clark, commander of the Fifth Army, claimed consistently that he was against bombing the abbey. This was not for religious reasons, which may have had greater weight with the defending Germans, but from military and partly political considerations. Clark was convinced by air reconnaissance that the summit was not being used defensively. If he bombed it, however, he was certain that the Germans would need to occupy the ruins, creating an even stronger defensive barrier.[126] Bombing was imprecise at best, and the summit of Cassino was small, so Clark was also concerned about civilian casualties in surrounding villages and the inevitable propaganda campaign that would descend on the killers of innocents who also destroyed an ancient sacred site. For all these reasons, Clark's early plans avoided a frontal attack on the central hilltop. He wanted to outflank it right and left. His superior, British General Harold Alexander, had also ordered that the abbey be spared, albeit with the Roman-like qualification that "Consideration for the safety of such areas will not be allowed to interfere with military necessity."[127]

On the basis of intentional German and Allied policy alike, then, the abbey should have survived. Yet it was destroyed. Why? It fell because of a series of decisions and actions, each tinged with chance or luck. I discuss this example not in order to draw direct or allegorical parallels, but because Cassino's well-documented fate furnishes a caution against thinking in artificially simple terms and binary choices: "If Titus did X, he *must have* wanted Y." It is undeniable that Mark Clark ordered the bombing of Cassino and that it was destroyed, but it also seems clear that he did not wish to destroy it – and that this preference was not because he was nice.

Clark's plan for outflanking Cassino in the river plains to the left and mountains to the right came to grief when his army sustained terrible losses and morale plummeted in the winter conditions of January 1944. He was forced to consider a more direct assault on the massif. Here I must mention a few names to give an idea of the competing interests involved. After the first line of troops took thousands of casualties, new units arrived to replace them. These included a New Zealand Corps under Gen. B. C. Freyberg, a World War I hero, with divisions under Generals Kippenberger and Tuker. Freyberg and Tuker wanted the abbey attacked immediately, but Clark refused for the reasons mentioned. To the new commanders, it was immaterial whether the site was being occupied by soldiers: For them it was *the psychological centre* of the German line. Given the scale of Allied casualties, they would not ask their

---

[126] Clark 2007: 248–50.   [127] Cf. Hoyt 2002: 133–34.

men to repeat the same exercise under the same conditions and expect a different result. It was imperative *on grounds of morale* that the "monster in the sky" be removed. Another consideration was that air power was the one area in which the demoralized Allies enjoyed unquestioned superiority. It only made sense to exploit that advantage in a spectacular way to charge morale.[128]

Tuker easily persuaded Freyberg, who tried relentlessly to win over Clark. As chance would have it, when the moment of decision came Clark was away visiting the new beachhead at Anzio to the north and unavailable. When his Chief of Staff received the call from Freyberg, he in turn called Clark's boss Alexander, assuring him that Clark would oppose the bombing. But the Briton Alexander deferred to his divisional generals from the Commonwealth, partly because he too understood the need to fight with highly motivated troops who could see an end in sight. The order would have to come from Clark, but Alexander made it clear that he supported Freyberg and Tuker. When Clark returned from Anzio and discovered what had transpired, he felt ambushed. But he had little choice.[129] Bad weather postponed the bombing, which gave him a chance to try dissuading Alexander, but the latter was firm and Clark gave the order.[130]

The bombardment was supposed to trigger an immediate rush of Allied ground forces through the Gustav Line, taking advantage of the expected German shock. Units had advanced cautiously into the hills above Cassino to exploit the opening, occupy the summit, gain a new vantage-point against the other hills, and enable the rest of the Fifth Army massed in the valley below to pour through Cassino town below. These two lines would join up in the Liri Valley past Cassino, with a clear run northward to Rome. But it was not to be. The unexpectedly early bombing runs destroyed the monastery indeed, but the ground forces were not ready to exploit it. And the Germans recovered with remarkable speed to occupy the abbey ruins. Clark's nightmare scenario took shape before his eyes. The Germans established an even more lethal defense, where they would hold out for three more months at huge cost to the Allies.

The bombing of Cassino's monastery is a cautionary tale on several levels. First, it demonstrates that in military operations it makes little sense to talk of a "policy" impervious to changing conditions. Changing factors, due to nature (the bombers chose the early date because of a favourable weather forecast) and psychological perception (e.g., frustration at miscommunication and lack of progress, Clark's perception of insufficient courage among subordinates, changes of key personnel and interpersonal tensions) affect or even determine daily tactical decisions.

Second, although subsequent analysts have singled out the abbey, debating whether it was in fact used by German forces and what benefit came from

---

[128] Parker 2003: 165–74.   [129] Clark 2007: 250–51.   [130] Parker 2003: 169–172.

bombing it, Matthew Parker emphasizes that this question did not much concern the British commanders who wanted it bombed. "To them, the building and the hill were a single military objective and could not be separated."[131] The abbey was only a means to an end. Perhaps the same was true of Jerusalem's temple. Our priestly historian was understandably preoccupied with the fate of the temple, but we might guess from hints in his narrative that the advancing Romans regarded the temple as part of a larger objective and not a separate military question – in spite of the *consilium*. Only after Titus abandoned his initial efforts at a more direct assault on Simon's Upper City, after he changed course to approach via the Antonia's elevated position, did the temple mount become his pathway to the Upper City, where Simon, now John, and the Idumaeans remained.

Third, Cassino offers support for the principle that we cannot draw valid inferences about people's intentions from their actions, even from direct orders they might give. We would require extraordinary evidence – diaries are helpful although not infallible – to reconstruct the feelings of an individual.[132] General Eisenhower was placed in command of the North African campaign ("Torch"), which resulted in Cassino from 1942, and he executed his task with memorable élan. He confided to a British general, however, that he considered the whole plan "unsound strategically." That did not stop him from doing his job "in a spirit of loyalty."[133] Who could have guessed Eisenhower's deep misgivings, if we judged only from his actions and public statements, which were fully behind the operation? Prime Minister Churchill seems to have deliberately misled even his closest allies about *his* thoughts, for strategic purposes.[134] A notice here or there that someone said or did X in a meeting tells us nothing at all about their inner views or hopes.

Fourth, even central players in complex events remember things differently. Clark's published memoir omits Tuker's role, for example, placing sole responsibility for the bombing decision on Freyberg.[135] But we now know that Tuker was crucial to the decision.

Finally, given the worldwide consternation that followed the abbey's bombing, we might have assumed that the paramount issue was *blame* for an

[131] Parker 2003: 173.
[132] E.g., in Clark's published memoir he honours Freyberg's war record and suggests only that he might have been difficult for the British to handle (2007 [1950]: 190, 238), whereas in candid remarks elsewhere he called him a prima donna and objected to having to work with him (in Ellis 1984: 161).
[133] Eisenhower speaking to the British General John Kennedy, quoted by Roberts 2008: 287–88.
[134] See Roberts (2008: 303–309) on Churchill's feint in seeming to give up on the Mediterranean strategy, apparently in order to force others to make the case.
[135] Clark (2007: 251–52) mentions Freyberg's agreement with an unnamed divisional commander, but Freyberg is the key figure.

impious or uncivilized action, just as scholars have tended to assume that Josephus needed to *exculpate* Titus. But reality is more complicated. Although German propaganda indeed exploited the bombing of the abbey as uncivilized, German commanders had always assumed that the Allies would bomb the abbey if they considered it militarily necessary, as they themselves would have done in the same position. Churches had been destroyed throughout Europe, the mission and the lives of soldiers always taking priority. No important figure was going to blame Clark if the bombing had been necessary, as long as civilians had been warned to leave (as they were).[136] He had to be much more concerned about apparent recklessness with his soldiers' lives, for which he faced a congressional investigation. Clark regretted the bombing not from piety or moral scruple, but because it seemed injurious to his military and political aims.[137]

Claims that a commander wanted to spare a site that he in fact destroyed are thus not necessarily contradictory, much less a whitewash. In the case of Titus, the assumption that Josephus wished to shield Titus from *blame* for the very thing on which his fame rested is hard to credit.

CONCLUSION: A HYPOTHETICAL RECONSTRUCTION

In these two chapters we have reviewed Josephus' account of events from late A.D. 67 to 70 (*War* 4–6), along with the salient material evidence, while taking soundings in scholarship at various points. Against this background we may now return to our questions about Judaean and Flavian aims in Jerusalem and Judaea proper. Our aim is to imagine real-life scenarios that would best explain the surviving evidence with as few needless assumptions as possible.

Judaeans

Judaean concerns continued to be centred in the mother-city, where the problems had always been. Galilee and Peraea submitted to Rome immediately. The Idumaeans had not lifted a finger to help Jerusalem with its local conflicts. These arose from Jerusalem's relations with aggrieved neighbours from the Decapolis to Ascalon via Samaria. They were exacerbated by Florus and his eager auxiliary, and had led to Cestius' intervention with disastrous consequences. When coins began to appear from Jerusalem and environs in 66,

---

[136] This was another intervention of chance. Leaflets were dropped, but missed their target. When one was found, its interpretation was debated (intimidation?), and the abbey was bombed before everyone could leave (Parker 2003: 175).

[137] Clark 2007: 249: "Not only was the bombing of the Abbey an unnecessary psychological mistake in the propaganda field, but it was a tactical military mistake of the first magnitude. It only made our job more difficult, more costly. . . ."

they also focused on Jerusalem/Zion. Jerusalem had been the regional hegemon, not only under the Hasmoneans but with Roman favour under King Herod, Archelaus, and Agrippa I. Claudius and the early Nero were steadily increasing the power of Agrippa II, who seemed on a track to restore Jerusalem's monarchy, as he would have succeeded his father if Agrippa I had lived longer. The intervening shifts of power to Caesarea in A.D. 6 and 44 were perilous for Jerusalem (Chapter 4). A decade into Nero's reign, local animosities joined with a disdainful emperor's priorities and a neutralized legate in Antioch to make Jerusalem and Judaeans physically vulnerable, in an unprecedented way and with little hope in sight from any plausible quarter.

In the late summer of 66, after a succession of horrors during the previous year or more, a priestly group led by those tasked with temple security – the temple commandant and his circle – advocated severing the institution's ties with non-Judaeans. This group may well have taken inspiration from biblical Phineas and the Hasmoneans; it is entirely plausible that they attracted a Hebrew name connected those figures' jealous protection of God's temple from auxiliary assault. Some turned to armed self-help, joining in the massacre of Jerusalem's brutal garrison and, after the benevolent Cestius' expeditionary force burned Judaean property and massacred compatriots, the ambush of his army. Increasingly isolated, and forced to deal with a currency crisis created by Nero's closure of the Tyrian mint, they used the temple stores of silver bullion to create beautiful coins of *Jerusalem the Holy*. Their purposes included providing a currency of unquestionable value for meeting the needs of Jerusalem and its temple and reassuring Jerusalem's populace (and others) in the midst of such unwanted turmoil. Perhaps they expected that, when everything was sorted out – on Nero's removal, a more effective legate in Antioch, and/or Agrippa II restored to rule – the coin issue would resolve itself in a general political settlement.

This group in the temple would turn out to be the most stable element in Jerusalem as the conflict with Cestius and then the Flavians grew, and the composition of the populace changed dramatically. When Nero's avenging army arrived in Ptolemais under Vespasian, it was clear to most Judaeans that their best hope for survival lay in rapid submission. Their recent humiliations and grievances notwithstanding, Jerusalem's chief-priestly leadership and much of the citizenry intended to do what Sepphoris, Tiberias, Samaria, and the Decapolis elites and the rest of the region had done, and what Peraea would do as Vespasian drew closer.

The leaders of Jerusalem faced a unique situation, however. No other *polis* had lost as much or become as vulnerable. But none had as much explaining to do after the violence against the auxiliary, Agrippa, and Cestius' force. The leaders could not simply hope to greet Vespasian and see everything return to normal. There would have to be a reckoning. Negotiations would be delicate at best after all that had transpired. Perhaps the biggest challenge of all was that many Judaeans from elsewhere were fleeing to the protection of the mother-city.

As the Flavians advanced from Galilee southward (67–68), Jerusalem increasingly became a magnet for all those who could not (they thought) or would not surrender to a Roman army. Some fled there from outrage at the violence of Cestius, having lost loved ones and property, some out of uncertainty and postponing the moment of decision, some because they feared they had done things in actions against Florus, the garrison, and/or Cestius that would be punished, some from the general fear that rational people have about yielding to foreign forces that view them as the enemy. For women and children, rape and abuse were always serious risks, and their men preferred to postpone the risk as long as possible. Many may have hoped that Jerusalem's leaders would find a way to work out terms with Vespasian, but it was far safer for these to come about officially at the *polis* level, to cover all Judaeans, than for individuals to approach the Roman lines and hope for mercy.

Josephus' story of Peraea furnishes an example of the Romans' continual creation of enemies even as they tried to end the revolt. Like great powers generally, they took little notice of the effects of their actions on the populace, assuming that the population comprised either *friends* or *enemies*. As Placidus' army arrived, villagers who had been minding their own business fled in fear because of rumours of his intent. But the very act of fleeing made them seem deserving of death. The cycle of grievance and despair was set in motion.

Some such combination of reasons would explain why so many fled to Jerusalem, without any assumption that they all sought an apocalyptic intervention or the like. Jerusalem's massive structures and few gates also made the city vulnerable to control by small groups, however, as Cestius' exclusion had shown. Small but intensely motivated groups could dominate the city if they controlled the gates. Some newcomers' leaders were resolute from the start about not surrendering, because they could expect nothing pleasant. Persuading the martially competent Idumaeans to join them, they staged a violent coup in the winter of 67–68 against the city's established leadership, which was planning to seek terms with Rome. This prompted more Jerusalemites who had the means to leave to flee en masse to Vespasian, now in Caesarea, hoping for the best. In Jerusalem the leaders of armed factions predictably began arguing intensely about matters of policy, style, and personal leadership. Violence erupted among them from time to time. Some of these leaders presumably viewed themselves as victims of events they had not desired, but saw no alternatives to violence. Some or most of the priests remained devoted to the temple's sanctity and tried to secure it, as did the Idumaeans, who were willing to die to protect it.

Although it is possible that some of Jerusalem's new leaders and factions nurtured visions of angelic intervention or a Parthian invasion, no evidence requires such hypotheses or would be better explained by them. When we see groups defying greater powers, we often wonder, "What do they hope to achieve?" In some cases the depth of their grievance and loss means that they see resistance as the only honourable course, irrespective of its outcome. In some cases, they know that they have been branded as criminals or worse, rightly or wrongly, and can expect death, perhaps after terrible torture, should they find themselves in others' hands. Resisting, if necessary to the point of death, at least gives them a measure of control over their life and death.

When Vespasian's army began to stir from Caesarea in the early spring of 68, beginning its sweep around and through Jerusalem's *chōra*, residents of the towns and villages were forced to make decisions, regardless of ideology. Would they rush to the Romans pre-emptively, risk a surrender when the army arrived, or flee to Jerusalem? For those who wished to surrender, the only way to do this with any hope of safety was en masse and pre-emptively, preferably via an official embassy of their civic leaders – as in Sepphoris, Tiberias, and the other centres. The year 68 began with a similar initiative from Peraea – albeit at the cost of the head man's life. For those who lacked civic representatives able to do this – given the mother-city Jerusalem's paralysis –they were faced with risking more personal surrender or flight, to the temporary safety of Jerusalem or perhaps beyond to the desert fortresses, to buy extended time.

This human inundation in Jerusalem transformed its composition. It soon hosted thousands of refugees from Galilee, Idumaea, and the *chōra*, with their varied fears and hopes, perhaps the occasional vision. The sometimes violent conflicts and domination of the weak by the strong constituted the civil war (*stasis oikeia*) that appalled Josephus, the factional leaders becoming his *tyrants*. None of them had the slightest intention of facing the legions in pitched battle, or in guerrilla warfare after Vespasian's arrival. Once Titus' army was immediately outside and there was little left to lose, however, many would leave the walls in sorties – with undeniable courage – to make a siege as difficult as possible. Who knew whether the Romans could be persuaded to give it up? Although the factional leaders knew that much of the population inside might prefer to take their chances in surrender, prospects of safe surrender for the leaders had become remote. If they were willing to use lethal force to keep people in the city, as Josephus insists, this would not be entirely surprising.

The Flavians

On the Roman side, Vespasian had perhaps allowed himself the campaigning seasons of A.D. 67 and 68 to complete his assignment from Nero, settling the disturbances in Syria that Cestius had unwittingly inflamed. He would take as long as needed, but things moved quickly. Galilee submitted with the rest of the region except Jerusalem immediately upon his arrival. He was able to use the summer and autumn of 67 roaming around there and Samaria at will – with brief operations at Iotapata and then in aid of Agrippa II. All this served to heighten the sense of terror in Judaea, so Vespasian was in no hurry to reach the south.

While his army gained confidence, it was creating a nearly unbearable strain in the south among those awaiting his arrival. They had nowhere to go, with even Caesarea a legionary stronghold and the plains under patrol, and destroyed Joppa garrisoned since Cestius' time. Whatever the Judaeans decided, calm deliberation was not in the cards. Panic must have greatly raised the temperature inside Jerusalem's walls as they waited. By the spring of 68 Vespasian easily dominated Jerusalem's *chōra*.

He used the first half of the season to encircle the mother-city, establishing garrisons without resistance before withdrawing to Caesarea to plan for Jerusalem. We can only wonder how different the Jerusalem operation would have looked if he had proceeded as planned. Would there have been a siege or would he have been able to induce an early surrender? The latter seems more likely, given the unsettled state and the absence of Simon. Would Vespasian have needed to destroy much of the city? If the other sites are any guides, an early capitulation would have led him to occupy and garrison Jerusalem largely intact. From such actions a triumph for Nero would have never have been a prospect.

When Titus restarted Vespasian's Jerusalem campaign after the long hiatus in the spring of 70, it seems that his father's cordon still largely held. He could march straight to Jerusalem's walls. Depots and garrisons were in the next-biggest towns. Many of those who had fled to Jerusalem had been stewing there for two years or more, and even Simon with his force had been inside for half a year. Titus might well have expected the people, their nerves utterly frayed, to welcome an offer of terms. We do not know what if any contact had been maintained between the city and the Flavians, perhaps with Agrippa and Berenice as intermediaries, between mid-68 and 70. Some efforts seem likely.

Without his father to advise him, Titus brought ample support to ensure that things would end well for him: a spare legion in rehabilitation (*XII*) and a wealth of experience in his senior commanders, with Tiberius Julius Alexander *in loco patris* and Fronto Haterius as well as Agrippa II, the other kings, and the likes of Josephus among high-ranking prisoners. Titus' aim seems to have been to seize, pacify, and garrison Jerusalem. Everything else was *Auftragstaktik*: tactics adjustable to the mission.[138] Even in bare outline, his actions in Josephus' account suggest someone determined to adapt, improvise, and overcome. He changed his approach nimbly, after regular consultation with

---

[138] See Caddick-Adams (2013: 23) on the Prussian-German preference for giving senior officers a mission (*Auftrag*) rather specific orders (*Befehle*).

his advisors. This is most obvious in his five successive configurations of siege ramps. There was no single plan.

There seems no reason to imagine that Titus had a *policy* concerning the city or temple, any more than Vespasian had one in 68. However the temple came to burn, on Titus' hard-fought path from the north wall to the Lower and Upper City, its destruction was not likely a matter of *policy*. If he had hoped to save the temple, it was not from love or sentiment, but for military advantage in the present – to avoid creating obstructive rubble, fire, and smoke – and for political advantage afterwards. If Titus decided to bring it down, that would have been a tactical choice as events unfolded. When the structure went up in flames, in any case, Titus shed no tears. His army used the higher ground to dominate the Lower and Upper City and end the conflict. Soon he was off on an extravagant celebratory tour, which would culminate in his joint triumph in Rome with Vespasian (Chapter 1). Titus was happy to exploit what had happened, as part of the myth of Flavian origins. But he could not have planned it.

CHAPTER NINE

A TALE OF TWO ELEAZARS: MACHAERUS AND MASADA

> A few grey *federales* say,
> They could have had him any day.
> They only let him go so long
> Out of kindness, I suppose.
>
> Townes van Zandt, *Pancho and Lefty*

No site in modern Israel receives more attention than Masada, the striking mesa at the southwest end of the Dead Sea's main basin. And none offers more food for thought concerning the relationship between history and tradition (Chapter 1). Although Masada's meaning as a national icon has increasingly been questioned,[1] the site continues to be seen as a symbol of the heroic struggle for national freedom. In 1932, 60-year-old German academic Adolf von Schulten and a former general named Adolf Lammerer camped below the hilltop for a month to study the Roman siege works. They were inspired by the thought that "the heroic struggle for the Fatherland has been and remains one of the most distinguished objects of historical research and writing."[2] In 2001, when Masada became Israel's first UNESCO World Heritage Site, the

---

[1] Ben-Yehuda 1995; 2002 (which should be read with Ben-Tor 2009: 269–309); also Zerubavel 1994.

[2] von Schulten 1933: 2: "Denn der Heldenkampf für das Vaterland ist und bleibt eines der vornehmsten Objekte historischer Forschung und Darstellung."

criterion was still that Masada symbolized "the continuing human struggle between oppression and liberty."[3]

What happened to create this image? That question is entangled with interests other than historical curiosity. Before and after Israel's creation in 1948, fascination was intense. Masada hosted thousands of hikers from the embryonic state. A preliminary survey in 1955 and 1956 prepared for full-scale excavations from 1963 to 1965. The latter were of exceptional duration, intensity, thoroughness, and international exposure. It helped that they were led by Yigael Yadin: soldier, Chief of Defence Staff, and archaeologist, later founder of a political party and Deputy Prime Minister. Yadin's patriotic interpretation of the stunning discoveries, especially in his popular book, helped to secure Masada's position in Israel's and the world's imagination.[4]

The line between plausible reality and inspiring story quickly became blurred. American aviator-sailor-author Ernest K. Gann novelized Josephus' brief Masada story in *The Antagonists* (1971), which Boris Sagal then brought into American living rooms as the eight-part television series *Masada* (1981). He used British actors to play the Roman imperialists, Americans for the death-defying Jewish patriots under Eleazar.

Historical scholarship could not indulge so obviously in emotional stakes, but it often seemed to pit heroic freedom-fighters against imperial enforcers just as clearly. Scholars debated exactly how the freedom-fighters died and what this might say about their moral character. Did they actually kill themselves, as the despicable turncoat Josephus claimed, rather than fight boldly to the end? Yadin's popular book, and still more a description of the excavation by his translator, army officer and civil servant M. Pearlman (*The Zealots of Masada*, 1967), seemed only to be extracting Masada's patriotic aura from plain historical facts. It *was* an episode of stirring heroism, which needed only to be told to move people.

Pearlman opened his account of Yadin's excavation with a sketch of these known historical facts. Because of his impression of what happened at Masada, I quote a few sentences as our starting point:

> ... Titus slaughtered thousands of Jewish prisoners and *took the rest of the captives as slaves to Rome.* But not all. *A few managed to escape, and they were determined to continue the fight. They were led by Eleazar ben Yair and were called Zealots.* ... Eleazar and his band *made their painful way eastward from Jerusalem* across the Judean desert. *Their sufferings were great. Some had been wounded in the Jerusalem fighting.* There was no shelter from the hot sun. ... They had almost no food and very little water. ... *They chose*

---

[3] See the Report of the World Heritage Committee, 25th session, December 11–16, 2001, at http://whc.unesco.org/archive/repcom01.htm#1040 (accessed August 1, 2009).

[4] This spirit infuses Yadin's illustrated book (1966). For Yadin's career see Silberman 1993.

this harsh route precisely because they knew they would not be followed by the enemy – certainly not so quickly. They chose it for another reason as well. At the journey's end lay the rock of Masada, and at Masada *they believed they could hold out for a long time against the might of Rome.*

All through the rest of A.D. 70, 71, and the first part of 72, the Zealots continued to occupy Masada and *harry the Roman authorities whenever they could, as well as disrupt Roman rule in the area.* At first the Romans paid little attention to them, . . . ignoring them as one would a gnat. *But as the Zealot raids continued,* the gnat became a bee and then *a wasp with a painful sting, and the Romans began to take notice. . . . What annoyed the Romans even more than their losses in the Zealot raids was the harm to their prestige. . . .*[5]

In this picture the Romans have a clear motive for brutal action against Masada. They have become seriously annoyed that these diehard enemies, who slipped through their fingers in Jerusalem, are still causing them relentless problems.

The great author on strategy E. Luttwak said similar things, using the supposed three-year Roman campaign against Masada as Exhibit A of the determined imperial mindset:

The Jewish War had essentially been won, and *only Masada was still holding out*; but this *spark of resistance* might *rekindle at any time the fire of revolt.* . . . The *entire three-year operation*, and the very insignificance of its objective, *must have made an ominous impression* on all those in the East who might otherwise have been tempted to contemplate revolt.[6]

Every claim I have italicized in these two quotations, which is to say their main content, conflicts with our evidence and with any historical plausibility. Far from being the only hold-out, Masada was one of three fortified sites that the Flavians deliberately ignored while dealing with Jerusalem. The Judaean War that mattered to them was over with Jerusalem's fall (Chapters 1, 7–8). And when successive governors of Judaea finally got around to the three desert fortresses, some years later, they placed a higher priority on Herodium and Machaerus, leaving Masada until last. Most residents of these fortresses were not refugees from the siege of Jerusalem in 70. Eleazar had arrived at Masada in 66, before the Flavians' arrival in Galilee and even before Cestius' expedition. Such people had fled the Jerusalem area before any conflict with Rome. The Romans, for their part, paid them little attention for years afterward.

Scholars have elevated Masada's role perhaps in part because the spectacularly elevated site is so inspiring, and its visible remains in situ are easier to

---

[5] Pearlman 1967: 8–9, 11–13 (my emphasis). The reprint date of 2004 on my copy shows its enduring popularity.

[6] Luttwak 1976: 3–4 (emphasis mine). Luttwak is illustrating the Romans' limited use of *force* to project *power*.

populate with ancient inhabitants than continuously inhabited and overbuilt Jerusalem. I shall propose that Masada does indeed epitomize the war with Rome, but the war as we have reconstructed it and not as tradition and myth would have it. The site provides plentiful evidence, which is best explained on the hypothesis that many Judaean groups and especially *families* fled Jerusalem's growing violence before the arrival of the Romans. That Roman military operations occurred at Machaerus and Masada is undeniable, given the literary and material evidence. But what *kind* of operations were these and for what purposes?

Particular questions driving our investigation in this chapter are as follows. Who were the Judaeans who occupied these fortresses and what were their aims in doing so? What were the Romans' aims in eventually taking the fortresses back as provincial strongholds? And what happened in the final days and hours of Judaean occupation, when Roman forces came to seize them? In order to understand the evidence and imagine the real-life possibilities, we need to consider several other issues: the nature, purpose, and past uses of these desert fortresses; the identity of their inhabitants before and after 70; the Roman siege camps, walls, and ramps; and the dates, durations, and difficulty levels of the sieges.

Given Masada's unique fame, it can be surprising to learn that Josephus describes its entire siege, from initial planning of the ramp to the breach of the wall, in seven Greek sentences, or a single paragraph on two small-format pages of the Loeb Classical Library edition (7.304–19). His account of Machaerus, although it is virtually unknown to the public, is only slightly fuller (7.190–209). More important than size is placement: Josephus puts Machaerus first. He compares and contrasts the two stories, generally to the advantage of Machaerus' Judaean defenders.[7] After a glance at the two sites' geographical settings, we shall consider Josephus' story along with the material remains to help us rethink what happened at these places.

I. MACHAERUS AND MASADA: GEOGRAPHICAL CONTEXTS AND FEATURES

The Dead Sea environment we see today is different from that of the first century, although we are not sure how. Since the 1930s, this lake, the lowest surface on earth, has dropped some 23 m (80 ft) to about 415 m below sea level, with most of the loss occurring since 1970. It continues to fall at the alarming

---

[7] Concluding that Bassus conquered Machaerus and the Jordan Grove before Silva took Masada does not require uncritical acceptance of Josephus. Silva was Judaea's long-serving governor (ca. 73–78?), who became ordinary consul in 81 under Titus. Josephus could not plausibly have assigned his military achievements to Bassus.

rate of about a metre (3 ft 3 in) each year. Its shape has changed accordingly. The "tongue" peninsula known as the Lashon (Lisan), which used to protrude from the Jordanian side, is now a wide land bridge. What used to be the shallower basin south of this tongue, visible in atlases of Bible times, would be dry today were it not for the evaporation pools carefully maintained there.

The Dead Sea's level has not been dropping consistently since antiquity, which is why we cannot be sure of the first-century situation. Geological study suggests fluctuations. Until about 5100 B.C. Mt. Sedom, 200 m (220 yds) above the lake near the south end, was apparently submerged, although in subsequent periods the lake rose and fell.[8] There are reasons, ranging from saltwater-created caves to isotope analysis of Carbon-13 in the ramp wood, to think that the water level was somewhat higher in the first century than it is now, in a slightly cooler and wetter climate. One study puts the level around − 330 m (−1,080 ft), a remarkable 85 m or 280 ft higher than at present, although others consider −375 m (−1,230 ft) more plausible.[9] In any case, we should not assume that what we see today looks just like the first-century lake and surrounding landscape. The changes in water level affect settlements on the western shore most of all, where the shoreline slopes gradually into the water, especially in the northwest area near Qumran. Settlements on the west side may have been only half or a third of their present distance from the water's edge in the first century.

The positions of Masada and Machaerus relative to each other have of course not changed. If we take En Gedi on the west as a rough midpoint along the Dead Sea's 80-km (50-mi) length north to south, Machaerus is roughly as far north of that point (13 km, 8.1 mi) on the east side as Masada is south of it on the west (14.5 km, 9 mi). Machaerus is farther inland, though, and the terrain is entirely different. East of the lake, hills rise abruptly to a high plateau. Inland the terrain continues to rise, with occasional sharp drops, until at a crow's-fly distance of 7 km (4.5 mi) we reach Jebel al-Mishnaqa. The peak of this hill is 700 m (2,300 ft) above sea level and 1,100 m (3,600 ft) above the Dead Sea. Here the Hasmonean Alexander Jannaeus established a place of refuge, which King Herod later transformed into a characteristic royal redoubt. Machaerus, as we know it from Greek texts, sits on a ridge 650 m (0.4 mi) long, aiming northwest, like a compass needle with a bulge in its middle. On each side of that ridge − northeast and southwest − a steep ravine falls 150 m

---

[8] Klein 1982: 67–94; Frumkin, Magaritz, Carmi, and Zak 1991; Frumkin and Elitzur 2002: 334–42.

[9] For the higher estimates, see C. Klein 1982: 89–92. Her conclusions are moderated by Frumkin, Magaritz, et al. (1991) and by Issar and Yakir 1997: 70 on Klein. See now Lev-Yadun, Lucas, and Weinstein-Evron 2010: The wood used for the ramp did not come from the Masada region and says nothing about the climate *there*. To a non-specialist, the other evidence still seems to indicate a cooler and wetter ancient climate.

(500 ft) to the valley floor. The bulge in the middle of the compass needle is a nearly square hill with rounded corners, rising almost 50 m (165 ft) above the main arrow-ridge and providing a westward view to the Dead Sea, even to Jerusalem if the air is clear (Fig. 36).[10]

Josephus explains that Herod enclosed a large part of Machaerus' hillside with walls and towers, establishing a town there. Archaeology locates this town on the northeastern slope, which is the gentlest one although still quite steep. The hillside construction is reminiscent of Gamala (Chapter 6). Remains of houses, walls, and towers there have been unearthed. The summit of Machaerus, roughly a football field shortened by a fifth and squared, hosted Herod's palace. This he secured by adding a third rectangular tower on the west side – to the existing Hasmonean towers at the southeast and northwest. This arrangement recalls the tetrapyrgion (four-tower) design he favoured in Herodium and Jerusalem's Antonia.[11] Perhaps there was not room or need here for a fourth.

In spite of the summit's constrained area, Herod laid on his usual amenities: a full bath system, a 20 x 15 m (66 x 50 ft) peristyle enclosure graced by ornate columns, two large dining rooms (*triclinia*) at 100 m² each (1,075 sq. ft), another courtyard, and private rooms with decorated stucco walls and mosaic floors.[12] This complex was not a fighting fortress, but a secure and comfortable place of refuge. Herod's paramount concern for security is obvious from the large towers and the amount of space devoted to storerooms for long-term stays.

Nor was the water supply neglected. To the southeast of Machaerus is a hill (Jumeijme) from which Herod brought an aqueduct into two cisterns, an upper one from which water was hauled to the reservoirs on the summit and a lower one serving the town.[13] A Herodian (and later) tomb complex, of a typical Judaean kind with *kokhim*-style burial spaces and signs of ossuary use, has been found 300 m across the valley to the west.[14]

In A.D. 71 or 72 Sextus Lucilius Bassus took over from Sextus Vettulenus Cerealis as governor (*legatus Augusti pro praetore*) of the new province of Judaea. Cerealis had ably commanded the Fifth Legion during the war, and stayed on as the province's first legate with the distinguished Tenth as his army.[15] He would soon rise to high office in Rome, as suffect consul and curator of public works, before proceeding to more prestigious provincial governorships.[16] His successor Lucilius Bassus had been instrumental in the Flavians' rise to power in

---

[10] Vörös 2010.

[11] Josephus, *War* 7.172–76. Cf. Strobel 1974: 136–44; Corbo and Loffreda 1981; Vörös 2013: 236–58.

[12] See Corbo and Loffreda 1981, especially the fold-out plan of the upper fortress between pp. 272 and 273; Vörös 2013: e.g., 252–53.

[13] Vörös 2013: 279–94.   [14] Vörös 2013: 143–52.   [15] So *War* 7.5, 163.

[16] Eck 1970: 92–93.

FIGURE 36. The situation of Machaerus, oriented northwest toward the Dead Sea. Dr. Győző Vörös (of the Hungarian Academy of Arts (Director of the Machaerus Research Project) has superimposed a reconstruction of the ancient site on an aerial photograph by Dr. David L. Kennedy. I am grateful to both for permission to use the image.

a different theatre. Appointed by Vitellius to command the Roman fleets at Ravenna and Misenum, Bassus inspired his navy to defect to the Flavian cause.[17] His devastating desertion forced the Second Battle of Cremona/ Bedriacum in October 69, which set the stage for the victory of Flavian forces over Vitellius that December.[18] As a reward for this huge service, Vespasian made Bassus a praetor in 71, which qualified him to govern the new little

[17] Two surviving diplomas, issued to marines on discharge, show that Lucilius Bassus was still commanding the fleets in April 71 (*CIL* 3.850, 851; 10.897); cf. Newton 1901: 8, 21–23.
[18] Nicols 1978: 79, 163.

FIGURE 37. The hill of Machaerus today, from approximately where Bassus' camp would have been (Jumeijme). The collapsed aqueduct foundation is visible in the lower centre (parallel stone walls). Author 2012.

province of Judaea the next year. Having taken Machaerus in 72 or 73, however, Bassus died suddenly in his post.[19]

After surveying the terrain around Machaerus, Josephus relates, Bassus decided to build a siege ramp on the land-saddle to the southeast, where the aqueduct entered the town, which was the only plausible access route (*War* 7.190). The remains of aqueduct and ramp are visible today (Figs. 36–37). In his study of the Roman siegeworks, August Strobel proposed that the Judaean defenders destroyed the aqueduct as a precaution against tampering with their water supply.[20] They could rely on the water in their cisterns for some time.

Archaeology reveals a second substantial embankment, unmentioned by Josephus, at the northwestern end of the ridge. This ramp begins from a higher level (above 650 m) than that on the southeast and rises 20 m (66 ft) over a length of 100 m (330 ft) toward the rounded square hill. Then it stops abruptly, however, leaving a sizable gap before the summit. Strobel suggested that Bassus began his assault in the southeast, with the hillside town as his target, but when he saw that the Judaeans were concentrated in the summit, he changed his mind and began an embankment on the northwest to reach the top more

[19] Werner Eck (1999a) has identified his name from the tiny fragment of a building inscription in the Abu Gosh area west of Jerusalem.
[20] Strobel 1974: 138.

directly.[21] That seems a reasonable explanation of the remains, but we might also imagine other scenarios. It could have made tactical sense, as it eventually did for Titus in Jerusalem, to seize the highest ground first –via the northwest ramp – and dominate the town from there, a project abandoned when it was no longer needed. Or, giving the defenders two simultaneous assault points to worry about could have been a deliberate tactic to divide defensive efforts.

Bassus apparently enclosed the town with an encircling wall, with periodic towers, to keep the enemy from fleeing. Neither this wall nor the embedded camps have been preserved with the clarity of their Masada counterparts, but enough remains visible to indicate the lines. The wall was a rectangle, stretched toward the northwest so that two of its sides could sit on the crests of the hills opposite Machaerus. Because the facing ridge on the southwest side is significantly closer, the siege wall was closer there. Along the wall were as many as fifteen camps, double Masada's number and perhaps reflecting the need for more frequent smaller posts in this varied terrain, where visibility was obscured. Machaerus' hilly environment may also have enabled the defenders there to exit via hidden places and harass the Romans.

An estimated 120 *ballista* balls, at least a dozen arrowheads, a spearhead, and other small-weapon finds provide further evidence of the Roman assault.[22] Most of the 130 or so coins found thus far at Machaerus – small bronzes, badly corroded in most cases – come from the period of this war.[23]

Whereas Machaerus was thus ensconced in nature's folds and creases east of the rift valley, Masada sat proudly erect and solitary in full view of the flat coastal road west of the lake, like a great stranded ship.[24] Between the lake and Masada's base today, the land rises gradually with fascinating rock formations. Again, this distance may be twice what it was in the first century. Visitors to the summit enjoy an unobstructed vista to the north, east, and south. Masada is a mesa or butte: a roughly flat-topped hill with sheer drops all around. The stunning effect is created by its abrupt 360-m (1,180-ft) rise from the eastern plain, in silhouette against the desert sky. The summit is only 59 m (194 ft) above general sea level – one-twelfth the height of Machaerus in absolute terms – but that is irrelevant for its position in relation to much lower surroundings. Especially to those approaching from the north and east, the hilltop must have looked intimidating for a force contemplating an assault (Fig. 38).

[21] Strobel 1974.
[22] Vörös 2013: 129, supplemented by personal correspondence, for which I am most grateful.
[23] Vörös 2013: 71, 102, 320. Curiously, no Herodian coins have been found. E.g., seventy-one of the ninety-six coins from the 1978–1981 excavations are from the war period, while eighteen are Hasmonean, with little else.
[24] Jacobson (2006: 99–117) suggests that Herod's northern palace was deliberately modeled on a large pleasure ship.

FIGURE 38. Aerial view of Masada from the south, showing the difference in level between the northern summit, where the main buildings are, and the emptier lower level. Casemate-wall apartments are clearly visible around the perimeter except at the northern palace. The natural spur (and Silva's ramp) is left. Courtesy of Todd Bolen and bibleplaces.com (tb121704262).

Yet Masada does not seem to have caused Flavius Silva consternation, any more than Bassus had been unnerved by Machaerus. The flatness of the coastal plain made it relatively easy to bring in supplies and to build an encircling wall and camps on the east side. Heavier supplies were apparently brought from Hebron through the interior, not 50 km (30 mi) by road.[25] Hard work, to be

---

[25] Richmond (1962: 153) observes that the relationship between Camp D, which marked the end of the route from En Gedi at the northeast of the siege operations, and Silva's main Camp F, close to the ramp operations on the northwest, makes it unlikely that heavy supplies requiring wagons came via the shore route. They would have had to be conveyed up an 82-m (270-ft) hill outside the circumvallation. The 2-m (6.5-ft) wide track found on this slope

sure, but not extraordinary for legionaries, especially if undertaken before the hottest summer months.

Just as the imposing Machaerus could be approached from its inland side with *relative* ease, so could Masada, except here the inland side was to the west. There the mesa sat between two deep ravines, which swooped around it carrying brief but heavy winter torrents to the lake. On that rugged west side, the summit was only about 88 m (290 ft) above the valley floor, most of that difference being covered by a natural rock spur created by the fork in the wadis and the rush of water over millennia. This natural "ramp" reached about 80 percent of the way to the summit.[26] Josephus describes the ascent as a relatively easy route to the top, and the one normally used. For that reason, King Herod blocked the path at the bottom with a tower.[27] When Josephus describes Silva's siege constructions, he minimizes the value of this natural spur. But it must have been an important factor in the Hasmonean choice of this hilltop as a fortress, cut off from the surrounding land except by one highly visible and easily blocked path. There were three or four other possible routes to the summit, all of them winding and laborious: a steep path up the southern face; the Water Path(s) around the north face by the collection cisterns; and the famed Snake Path that zigzags up the eastern face.[28]

Every siege presented unique challenges, whether from elevation, difficult terrain from marshes to barren rock, climate, lack or surfeit of water, or sheer isolation. At Masada the inhospitable environment and difficulty of bringing in adequate water, food, and wood would presumably have been bothersome indeed. The dryness might also have brought advantages, however, minimizing the risks of spoilage and malaria that came with damper environments. Reliable sunshine and lack of tree cover provided excellent visibility, putting any human movement in stark relief against the desert's light brown. Temperatures in March/April can exceed 30°C (86°F) today, but they are normally lower and the ancient climate may have been cooler. Silva seems to have expected the siege to be over, as indeed it would be, before the furnace temperatures exceeding 40°C (104°F) of summer.

Although the site of Masada is imposing, then, there is no reason to think that it unnerved Roman commanders any more than Machaerus or Jerusalem

has hairpin bends unsuitable for wagons. Single pack animals would have carried food and water from En Gedi up these tracks, heavier supplies having come perhaps from Hebron.

[26] Gill 1993: 569–70.

[27] *War* 7.281, 293. Josephus puts this tower a round 1,000 cubits (1,500 ft, 460 m) from the western edge. If we cut the distance to about two-thirds it would be in the vicinity of what are now called the Engineers' or Construction Yard and Silva's Camp E, well beyond the beginning of the spur, which is only about 200 m (656 ft) from the summit. The full distance would reach to the level area hypothetically assigned to camp followers' shops and services (*canabae*).

[28] Ben-Tor 2009: 23–27.

had done. Josephus' brisk account of the siege's progress (*War* 7.275, 304–10) certainly suggests no great setbacks.

The summit of Masada is shaped like a rough diamond oriented toward the north-northeast, 634 m (2,080 ft) on its long axis and 306 m (1,004 ft) at the widest point. This gives an area of about 8 hectares (20 acres), in contrast to Machaerus' 0.65 ha (1.6 acres). Although it looks flat from below, the summit itself rises from its lowest point in the south to reach its highest points at the centre and north. Herod concentrated his buildings on the higher ground, leaving the south and east largely empty except for their perimeter casemate wall. This area could be observed from the comparable heights of what is now called Mt. Eleazar in honour of the siege defender, 400 m (0.25 mi) to the south. The substantial area and varied topography of Masada's summit created the possibility for different groups to live there with some degree of separation. In Herod's time, the royal family had been able to stay with friends in splendid isolation from the garrison around the perimeter.

Like Machaerus, Masada was a place of refuge for the king, his family, and entourage, not a military fort, and so the summit is dominated by palaces and amenities.[29] To the west of three small villas, Herod's main western palace sprawled over 3,345 m² (36,000 sq ft). It contained at least three wings: royal residential, service, and storage/administration. The luxury of the appointments, from the massive cooking stoves to a beautiful Persian rug-like mosaic floor, testify to the comfort in which Herod expected to maintain his family on the rare occasions when they stayed there.[30]

The jewel in Masada's crown is the opulent structure we now call the northern palace. Spilling over the northern cliff in three terraces, even its remains after two millennia are breathtaking. This feat of engineering shows again that the site was a place of royal refuge: "for rest and relaxation, for leisure and pleasure, a place from which one could enjoy the wondrous scenery," as the excavator Yadin put it.[31] From here the king – and the later wartime refugees – could see for miles and anticipate trouble coming from Jerusalem, the Dead Sea, or Nabataea. For all its grandeur, the hanging palace was designed for a very small group of people. Its three levels with their elaborate bath system, vast storage rooms on the top, and Pompeian frescoes in vivid colour could have accommodated only the monarch and a few friends.[32] It may be misleading to call these terraces a *palace*.

Josephus describes only one palace on the summit. For reasons I do not entirely understand, scholars usually assume that he has this "northern palace"

---

[29] The point was emphasized by Yadin (1966: 42–49, 59–62, 117–40).
[30] Yadin 1966: 117–34.   [31] Yadin 1966: 47, speaking of the lowest terrace.
[32] Yadin 1966: 62.

in mind.[33] Basic aspects of his portrait, however, fit the large western palace better. He describes a unified structure on a single plane with many internal rooms, which the Romans later found to contain many hundreds of bodies.[34] The early British explorers who prepared the nineteenth-century *Survey of Western Palestine* remarked of this "western" palace's remains: "The position is exactly that in which Herod's palace is described by Josephus."[35] Josephus may have regarded the northern terrace structure as a satellite of the main precinct, and not considered it a palace itself.

In general, Herod's architecture on Masada matches his constructions elsewhere. Even in such a remote place he spared no expense, apparently employing Roman architects and engineers.[36] As at Machaerus, security provisions took three main forms: an abundant supply of food and water, weapon stores for the garrison, and fortification. All three of these were valued also by the later wartime residents.

We noted the large cisterns and aqueduct at Machaerus. At Masada the water system is astonishing.[37] Along the northwest slope of the hill, not far from the ramp, are two rows of hewn cisterns: four below and eight above. In each case a large window opens into an enormous reservoir, each from 12 to 15 m (40–50 ft) in height and 15 to 17 m (50–56 ft) wide. Each holds between 2,500 and 4,200 m^3 (660,000–1.1 million gallons). Most were cut in a rectangular plan, and all were plastered and had staircases cut in the bedrock. Given the nearly rainless environment, they were filled by an ingenious means. Dams diverted into the cisterns the brief winter torrents that flood the two wadis in January-February. Situated on the northwest face and well below the summit, the cisterns would suffer relatively little evaporation. Water was hauled from them as needed to reservoirs on the summit.[38]

As for the warehouses, Josephus claims that Herod had stored enough grain for years, with huge quantities of wine, oil, legumes, and dates. These were reportedly found in usable condition a century later by the *sicarii* from Jerusalem. Even the Roman soldiers in 73/74 supposedly still found edible

---

[33] Yadin 1966: 46; Cohen 1982: 394–95 and n. 30 ("His description of the northern palace contains several inaccuracies"); Ben-Tor 2009: 51–65.

[34] Josephus emphasizes the palace's western location: It was built "on/at the ascent from the west, below the walls of the summit, though inclining toward the north"; it was large and strong, with towers at the corners, and contained many apartments, colonnades, and baths; a path led up *from* the palace to the highest point (7.289–90). The path to Masada from the west goes "to the palace and the highest summit" (7.305). Although the most impressive baths are undoubtedly those near the northern palace, the western palace had a bath chamber (Ben-Tor 2009: 105–8). For the bodies see 7.405–406.

[35] Conder and Kitchener 1881–1884: 3.420.   [36] Roller 1998: 95–100.

[37] Ben-Tor 2009: 69–72.

[38] Yadin 1966: 26–29. Avi-Yonah et al. (1957: 54–59) reported seeing a 40-m section of a dam-aqueduct structure, west of the Leuke, which diverted the seasonal torrents.

food (*War* 7.296–97). Josephus claims that Herod stored enough weapons for 10,000 men, along with supplies of various metals for workshops. The number seems like enormous overkill, but if he did leave a guard of 800 to protect his family (*War* 1.267), it is not implausible. In the summer of 66 this armoury was reportedly famous enough to be raided by Jerusalemites in desperate need of weapons to fight the auxiliary garrison and each other (2.433–34).

Josephus claims that Herod reserved most of the summit for agriculture, the topsoil being exceptionally rich and productive (*War* 7.288). All non-palatial accommodations were therefore kept to the edges and incorporated into a perimeter casemate wall (see Chapter 7). Excavation indicates that this wall was added only in the final phase of construction, after the central palaces and other fixtures were completed.[39]

Archaeology has exposed the casemate around the entire perimeter, except where the northern villa spills over the cliff.[40] It thus ran for about 1,290 m (0.8 mi), discounting small bends. Roughly every 40 m (131 ft) stood a rectangular tower, rising one storey above the rooms. Where there was a tower, the wall was thickened on the inner side to allow guards to walk around the tower during patrols. The wall is made of local stone, with a plaster of white lime applied outside and one of brown earth inside, to create smooth surfaces. The outer wall is on average 1.4 m (4.6 ft) thick, about 50 percent larger than the inner one. The seventy apartments that have been found in the casemate might have housed 500 or 600 altogether in reasonable comfort. They were spacious: 4 m (13 ft) in width and estimated height, and from nearly 10 m (33 ft) to 37 m (121 ft) in length. Certainly the larger apartments – nine are longer than 30 m (98.5 ft) – could have accommodated an extended family or a military unit.[41] This appears to be where Herod housed most of his soldiers.

In addition to casemate accommodation, there was room for several dozen families or others in a second storey above the large western palace, in the smaller palaces and grand rooms (perhaps built for Herodian officials and staff), and in the residential complexes of the buildings we number 7, 9, and 11 to 13.[42] When the later wartime occupants occupied the site with their families, they both added some flimsier structures and subdivided existing rooms.[43]

Like all autocrats, King Herod was perpetually alert to internal and external threats. That was one important reason to build such places of secure refuge for himself and his family. He did *not* build them to facilitate military confrontations and we should not think of them as forts like those on later Roman

---

[39] Netzer 1991a: 358. For casemate walls see Chapter 6.   [40] Ben-Tor 2009: 75–82.

[41] Netzer 1991a: 604–7. In pondering the reason for the casemate construction (p. 607), Netzer does not consider Josephus' explanation but wonders only about a provision for military or animal housing or other storage needs.

[42] Netzer 1991a: 319–83.   [43] Netzer 1991a: 325, 336, 339–40, 344–59.

frontiers or in the U.S. Civil War. Although Machaerus and Masada were near the frontier with Nabataea, they were unlikely scenes of battle. They were not part of a defensive line, facing comparable fortresses across a border. Distance *from Jerusalem* seems to have been more of a concern than proximity to Nabataea. They were as remote as Herod could be in the southern heartland of his kingdom. Internal enemies would have had to undertake extraordinary labours and logistical planning to strike at him in such places. Herod did not envisage war against Rome. He seems to have calculated that in any other imaginable crisis, which would most likely emanate from Jerusalem or another subject city, he and his family would be safe as long as they could reach one of these sites. His potential enemies, internal or external, were not likely to make war on him. More likely threats were kidnapping and assassination in the case of his dependents, assassination for the king himself. The desert retreats were effective defences in such cases.

II. THE STORY IN JOSEPHUS

Josephus introduces Machaerus (1.161–72), Masada (1.237–38), and Herodium (1.265) early in *War* 1. Their reappearance in Book 7 strengthens the sense of ring composition (Chapter 2). The Masada story of Book 7 explicitly recalls events from Herod's time from Book 1, concerning Marc Antony's "enslavement" to Cleopatra and Herod's fear of the same queen (7.300–302).[44] Josephus ponders the paradox that a fortress built by a staunch Roman ally should become the last scene of Judaean-*Roman* conflict (7.303).

According to Josephus, the three strongest Hasmonean fortresses had been Machaerus, Hyrcania, and Alexandrium. Those were the sites where the dynasty kept its treasures, where the last Hasmonean hid for safety while resisting the arrival of Roman rule, and where Herod built his desert refuges. Of those three, only Machaerus figures in the war, the other two perhaps being too deep in Idumaea and Samaria, respectively.[45]

In writing of the war Josephus treats Herodium, Machaerus, and Masada as a group. After Vespasian's pacification of southern Syria, these three alone remain aside from Jerusalem (*War* 4.555). Vespasian ignores them completely, however, to concentrate his efforts on the mother-city, the nerve-centre of Judaean trouble. The desert retreats will remain irrelevant until a much later time and the Flavians' war is decidedly over in 70 (Chapter 1).

The story of Herodium, 15 km (9 mi) south of Jerusalem, Josephus concludes in a mere phrase (7.163). Ehud Netzer, Herodium's late and lamented excavator, argued that Herod destroyed his own impressive structures at the

---

[44] Cf. *War* 1.243, 279, 359–67, with 389–91.
[45] See *War* 1.161, 167; *Ant.* 13.417; 14.89; 16.13; cf. Shatzman 1991: 95–97.

site in his final years, creating as his mausoleum the distinctive artificial cone we see today.[46] Archaeology indicates reoccupation of the site around the time of our war, and it is even possible that the vigorous destruction of the reddish limestone sarcophagus widely (not universally) taken to be Herod's tomb was conducted by Simon's men in their rampages of 67–68. If that is so, they may have acted more from anti-Idumaean than anti-Roman sentiment, but we have no idea who smashed the sarcophagus.[47] The site had reportedly become a stronghold of Idumaean fighters, from whom Simon of bar Giora's fighters took it without a fight in mid-68 (4.518–20, 539). For the Romans in 72, it seems to have been a similarly minor handover, requiring a fraction of Bassus' army.[48]

The siege and capitulation of Machaerus, with a follow-up operation at the mysterious Jordan Grove,[49] then dominate Josephus' story (7.163–215). After those episodes he pauses to describe other contemporary events (7.216–54) before continuing with Masada. The two remaining fortresses thus function as a literary pair. Both were introduced as Hasmonean fortifications developed by Herod. Josephus emphasizes the strength of Machaerus. Along with Alexandrium and Hyrcania, Machaerus was seized by Hasmonean rebels after Pompey's arrival. Gabinius destroyed all three Hasmonean fortresses (57 B.C.) to prevent such reuse, because the Romans could not garrison them at that time (1.161, 167). Aristobulus II again tried to make a last stand from a base in Machaerus' ruins, but he was captured (1.171–74).[50]

That background anticipates Josephus' description of Bassus' motives in taking Machaerus in 72/73 (7.164–65):

> [Bassus] resolved to bring the fight to Machaerus. It was absolutely necessary that this fortress be taken out so that it could not entice many to rebellion, *because of its strength*. For the nature of the site was more than sufficient to furnish those who held it with the confident hope of security [or "salvation"], those who came against it with apprehension and alarm.

From Hasmonean times until its end, Machaerus is singled out for its uniquely secure situation. It must therefore be occupied by the governing power or rendered unusable.

---

[46] Netzer et al. 2013: 157–60.

[47] See Foerster 2013 for a detailed description. With other prominent archaeologists he is hesitant, in the absence of clear evidence, to identify the box as Herod's.

[48] Josephus' language is vague, but his sentence structure at 7.163–64 implies a contrast between the minor forces used at Herodium and Bassus' assembling of the whole provincial army, anchored by the Tenth Legion.

[49] The name *Iardes* is cognate to the Hebrew for Jordan (*Yarden*), often held to derive from the verb *yarad*: to descend (given the significant drop in elevation along the river's course). This Jordan Grove could have been any wooded area in the fertile river valley, presumably near its southern end, close to Machaerus.

[50] *Antiquities* adds material on Machaerus: 13.417; 14.83–96.

Masada's character, use, and reputation appear rather differently in Josephus. The site plays no role in Hasmonean defence or vestigial defiance of Rome. We hear about its Hasmonean fortification only in long retrospect, when Silva is about to take it in 73/74 (7.285). At its first mention (*War* 1.237) Josephus reports that Masada was the strongest *of* the Judaean fortresses briefly seized by the Nabataean king. Its later use would involve essentially the safe keeping of Herodian royal women, families, and possessions against threats from Cleopatra (*War* 7.300–303).

In the case of Cleopatra, Herod's concern was not that she would lead an army against him. *War* 1.360–62 describes trumped-up charges that she brought to Antony against various strong men in Syria and Arabia, hoping that her lover would "get rid of them" so that she could have their territories (cf. *Ant.* 15.77). Such men were handled discreetly, however: an accident while bathing, a nasty case of food poisoning, or finding themselves in the bedroom with a knife-wielding assassin when their bodyguards had taken the evening off. Cleopatra removed two of Herod's neighbours by such stealthy means, being careful to avoid spectacle, much less open warfare (1.440; cf. 228). But Herod, whose father had been poisoned by neighbouring rivals (*War* 1.223–26), was himself a skilled practitioner of the black arts.

Given the king's concern about assassins from within or without, Jerusalem was not a secure environment for him. He needed places where he could retreat in moments of heightened threat, where his bodyguard would be able to see human figures for miles. Herodium, Machaerus, and Masada fit the bill. At Masada, he and a few dozen of his family and friends could live happily with a large bodyguard, food, water, shelter, weapons, and all conveniences. Any conceivable attackers would be visible long before they arrived. And any effort to scramble up the steep hillsides could be repelled with little effort by such well-armed guards above. Even an attacking military unit, if it somehow came to that, would have great difficulty finding shelter from the blazing sun and heat, not to mention water and food.

Josephus gives examples of Masada's use, which illustrate the site's value. When the Parthians struck against Jerusalem in 40–39 B.C., they enjoyed the support of many Judaeans who favoured the Hasmoneans and opposed Rome-connected Herod. The king "ordered his mother and brothers and the young woman to whom he was betrothed [Mariamme], with her mother and the youngest of her brothers," to Masada, while he and his attendants held back the Parthian "barbarians" (1.264). Some 9,000 joined his procession through Idumaea to the desert fortress, although he had to send most of them away (1.266). When Herod reached Masada, he left his brother Joseph and a garrison of 800 "for the women" as he went off in search of support (1.267). The Parthians were then frustrated because they desperately wanted to capture Herod's women. Such prizes were a great humiliation to the enemy and a potent bargaining chip. But Herod's women were safe and unreachable on the summit of Masada, even by a skilled Parthian force below (1.273).

Herod's quest led him to Rome, where the Senate appointed him king. The Parthians' Judaean client was the Hasmonean Antigonus. While Herod was away, Antigonus undertook to besiege the king's family at Masada. They remained impervious, however, their only vulnerability on that desert summit being a shortage of water. They were saved by a timely rainfall, which filled the cisterns on the summit (1.286–87). This vulnerability accounts for Herod's construction of Masada's water system when he returned.

It is also worth noting that, in contrast to Masada's later residents, the Herodian garrison force reportedly made effective forays against the besieging troops, according to Josephus, and that Joseph could contemplate an escape with 200 guards to seek Nabataean assistance (1.287). When Herod returned from Rome, his priority was "the liberation of his family members from the siege," which he soon accomplished (1.292–94). Again, the site was a place of safety for families and other possessions, not the place where a bold man of action such as Herod would spent a great deal of time by choice.

This image of the fortresses as refuges for royal families is consistent in Josephus. A telling example comes in *Antiquities* 15. When Octavian defeats Antony and Herod leaves to make peace with the victor in Rhodes, the king again sends his mother, sister Salome, and brother Pheroras to Masada. Pheroras is instructed to assume control of the kingdom should he not return (*Ant.* 15.183–84). Relations between Herod's family and that of his wife Mariamme are catastrophic, following the king's murder of Mariamme's young brother. The grieving mother, Alexandra, enjoys great popular sympathy. So Herod deposits Mariamme and her family at Alexandrium, on the border of Samaria, far from the rest of the family at Masada (*Ant.* 15.185–86). Herod himself remains above it all.

Machiavelli advised princes to build fortresses for protection against *internal* opponents: "The prince who has more to fear from the people than from foreigners ought to build fortresses, but he who has more to fear from foreigners than from the people ought to leave them alone" – although the safest situation, he added, was not to be hated by one's people in the first place.[51] Herod used the desert fortresses in this way against a combination of enemies, for the Parthians worked through local clients.

More immediate context for the fall of these two desert fortresses comes in *War* 2 and 4. Machaerus' story is simple. As regional tensions after conflicts with the auxiliary flare in mid-66 (Chapter 4), Judaeans capture the desert

---

[51] *Prince* 20.6.

fortresses from their (presumably) auxiliary garrisons.[52] Some take and destroy Hyrcania, west of the Dead Sea (near Mar Saba monastery). In Machaerus, the town's existing Judaean residents, whose relations with the auxiliary must be deteriorating in connection with Jerusalem's problems, persuade the garrison to leave under a pledge of safe conduct as they take over the summit (2.485–86). This account raises questions, but the sequence of events is reasonably clear.

Masada's capture is more violent. After King Agrippa's failed speech and expulsion in the summer of 66 (Chapter 5), armed factions begin to form in Jerusalem and one group rushes to Masada in search of good weapons. They capture the fortress by stealth, secretly, or unnoticed (λάθρα), and butcher the auxiliary garrison (*War* 2.408). Later Josephus recalls with similar language that Eleazar ben Yair and his *sicarii* took the summit by cunning, craft, or deception (δόλῳ, 7.297). These words might suggest concealed access routes or perhaps a night-time assault with surprise and/or decoy. Or perhaps Josephus did not know what had happened, but surmised that any group of irregulars that succeeded in taking Masada from professional soldiers must have done so by cunning.

The next we hear of Masada (2.433–34), Eleazar ben Yair's relative Menachem is again raiding Herod's armoury to collect weapons for use against the auxiliary garrison in Jerusalem. That Menachem's group gain easy entry suggests, to us who can join up Josephus' scattered remarks, that Masada was already in the hands of Menachem's relative Eleazar. At 2.441–47 Josephus claims that when Menachem's group is ambushed by Eleazar ben Ananias's faction in Jerusalem, Menachem having killed Eleazar's father Ananias, some of Menachem's followers escape (again "by stealth") to Masada. Menachem dies in the ambush, but those who reach Masada (ca. August 66) include Eleazar ben Yair, flagged by Josephus as the "future tyrant of Masada" (2.447).[53] This early departure from Jerusalem, well before Cestius' expedition, seems to mark the beginning of ongoing wartime habitation of the site by Judaean refugees.

Machaerus and Masada both reappear in *War* 4. Describing the "war, tyranny, and civil strife" that descended on Jerusalem after the violent coup,[54] Josephus here adds a fourth evil: banditry (4.399–405). This erupted throughout Judaea, he says, but it was exemplified by the refugee *sicarii*:

---

[52] Although it is conceivable that such garrisons comprised legionaries, the legions apparently stayed out of Judaea in ordinary times (*Ant.* 18.120–22); it is easier to suppose that these were detachments of the auxiliary based in Caesarea.

[53] Josephus does not clarify this, but Josephus' remarks would make sense if Eleazar ben Yair's group took Masada from the Roman garrison, which then made it logical for Menachem to look there for weapons. Eleazar returned with him to Jerusalem and, when Menachem was killed, escaped with his group back to the desert stronghold.

[54] For this trio, see Plato, *Resp.* 470b. It is a slight variation on the more programmatic triad of war, civil strife, and *famine* (*War* 1.27; 4.137; 6.13, 205), itself a supplement to the ubiquitous pair: war (external) and civil strife (internal).

> A very strong fortress was not far from Jerusalem, fitted out by our ancient kings *as a repository for their stuff and for the security of their persons in the turmoil of war*. It was called Masada. Having taken possession of it in the meantime, those called *sicarii were overrunning the neighbouring territories*, though procuring for themselves nothing more than was necessary *because their anxiety prevented them from greater plunder*. So when they learned that the Roman army was idle [i.e., from June 68], whereas on their own side the Judaeans in Jerusalem were torn by civil strife and tyranny, they applied themselves to bolder ventures.

We should not miss the irony here. Rather than fighting Judaea's enemies or preparing Jerusalem's defences, these tough guys (*sicarii*) limit themselves to raiding nearby Judaean villages because they are afraid to venture farther. Most heinously, during the very festival of Passover, the men of Masada launch a vicious raid on En Gedi to steal its excellent produce. Those who are able to flee do so, but the Masada men kill a reported 700 women and children (4.401–406). Idumaeans to the west must also protect themselves against Masada's marauders (4.516).

Josephus emphasizes the disgrace of killing fellow Judaeans in a summary statement (7.255):

> They banded together against *those who wished to submit to Rome* [NB: not against Romans] and in every way regarded them as enemies: seizing their goods, rounding up their cattle, and setting fire to their homes. For, they asserted, they were *in no way different from foreigners*, who so ignobly forfeited the Judeans' hard-won freedom and openly admitted that they chose slavery under the Romans.

The group had become powerfully disdainful of Rome, quite possibly because of Nero's depradations, auxiliary behaviour, and the legate's failure to protect them – compounded by the later violence of his own force. But they have fled the troubles, and their problem or justification for violence is that other Judaeans hope to continue with life as normal under Rome.

Machaerus appears twice in this period, although much more briefly and only for Josephus to say that Vespasian ignored the site – planting seeds of literary anticipation for Book 7. The Flavians ignore "bandits" at such sites because their exclusive military and political concern is the mother-*polis* Jerusalem (4.439, 555).

Here in *War* 4 is the vignette concerning Simon bar Giora on Masada, which I mentioned in Chapter 7. After being expelled from Acrabatene by Ananus in late 66, it seems, Simon seeks a haven for himself *and the women of his family*. For this he naturally chooses Masada (4.503–508). The refugees who have recently established a base there are suspicious of the newcomer and keep him at a distance from their families, in the lower part of the fortress. Perhaps

TABLE 4. *Table comparing the sieges of Machaerus and Masada stories in Josephus'* War.

Machaerus	Masada
War 7.163–64: New legate Bassus, succeeding Cerealis, concentrates forces for a strike on fortress Machaerus (Greek συνάγω, στρατεύω, φρούριον).	*War* 7.252: Silva succeeds Bassus, he concentrates forces for a strike on fortress Masada (Greek συνάγω, στρατεύω, φρούριον).
164: reason for Bassus' action: the *strength of this fortress* might induce further revolt. Whoever held it felt emboldened.	252: reason for action: *only this fortress remains*. Digression on rogues' gallery during war, greater criminality than *sicarii* (253–74).
165–70: description of site's natural properties: precipitous drops on three sides, access on inland side (here east). Digression on deadly rue plant (178–89).	279–84: description of site's natural properties: precipitous drops on three sides, access on inland side (here west).
171–177: history of site's use and development, emphasizing King Herod's fortifications, palaces, cisterns, stores of weapons.	285–302: history of site's use and development, emphasizing Herod's fortifications, palaces, cisterns, and storehouses; also weapons (for 10,000) and food stores—anticipating Masada's end.
190: Roman commander begins the siege ramp by filling up inland ravine.	304–307: Roman commander begins the siege ramp by filling up inland ravine.
196–209: Judaean leader is named Eleazar	253–258: Judaean leader is named Eleazar

this means the south end of the summit, less likely the valley below. After a while they come to trust him, however, and invite him to join in their marauding. Simon enthusiastically participates for a while. But being young, strong, and daring he cannot see why they spend all their time in such trivial raids. He tries to inspire them to greater exploits but these *sicarii* are not keen, "for they, *accustomed to being in their fortress*, just as if it were an animal's den, were afraid to stray far from it" (4.507). As soon as he hears that Ananus is dead, Simon abandons these chicken hawks. He is willing to risk the exposure of his wife and family, their security having been his main reason for fleeing to Masada in the first place. The temporary kidnapping of his wife by the Disciples (Chapter 7) shows that he had good reason for taking them to Masada. Once he has left, the slow-moving family become easier targets.

Josephus, in sum, portrays Masada's wartime Judaean inhabitants as family men seeking the security of the former royal refuge for their women and children. Fearing the bloody factionalism in Jerusalem and no doubt the expected Roman reprisals, and proven wise repeatedly by first Cestius' and then Vespasian's expeditions, they remove themselves from the fray to this remote, fortified site built by ancient rulers "as a repository for their stuff and for the security of their persons" (*War* 4.399). They hope to escape Judaea's current troubles and ride out the storm in security. The main problem is finding fresh food, and this forces them to some kind of arrangement with local villages. According to Josephus that arrangement is often one of robbery.

As we approach Josephus' accounts of the two sieges, we are prepared by the fortresses' different pasts for a study in contrasts, and that is what we find. The table in Table 4 summarizes the parallels in his account.

This kind of symmetry throws into relief the different characters of the residents in each fortress and their respective Eleazars. At Machaerus they have a clear plan with two options: defence or terms of safe surrender (7.191–93). Six years after taking this site (*War* 2.485–86), the Judaeans are for unexplained reasons living among foreigners (ξένοι; 7.191, 206). We can only wonder how such people came to live in a Judaean-rebel town – *if* that is what it was understood to be. Perhaps the foreigners had been there all along, unmentioned in the earlier narrative. Josephus claims that with Bassus' arrival, the Judaeans separate themselves from these foreigners and *seize* the upper fortress, while confining the foreigners to the lower town (7.191–92). Why should they need to seize the summit only now? Who has occupied it from 66 until now? Perhaps the seizing of the summit here is a clumsy flashback: They took the fortress in 66 (7.192) but only now cut themselves off from the other townsfolk (7.191). Imagining the real-life events is confusing for the reader of Josephus' scattered notices who tries to visualize the lived reality. But that is not unusual, as we have seen.

If we do not demand to know the real conditions in relation to earlier notices, the present narrative by itself is clear enough. When Bassus arrives, the Judaeans lock themselves in the walled summit and force the town's foreigners, whom they disdain, to stay in the more exposed lower town (7.191–92). They do this to delay their own peril, Josephus claims, because a Roman assault would have to reach the lower town first, giving them time to negotiate a surrender should it come to that. Do they assume that the Romans want only the fortress and not revenge and/or that the Romans are intent on fighting only militants? Are the foreigners of the lower town their human shields? However Josephus' indications of motive should be nuanced, he presents the Judaeans of Machaerus as shrewdly planning a safe exit and credits their forethought (πρόνοια, 7.192).

Although they are willing to capitulate if necessary, however, the Judaeans are not quick to take that option. Being innately tough, they want first to try their strength and see whether they can repel Bassus (7.193). Perhaps they hope to demoralize these Romans in the desert and persuade them that their hill is not worthwhile? Or they might resist long enough that a failure of Roman logistics will cause a temporary retreat, allowing them to escape. Josephus does not explain the goal of resistance, but stresses only that the daring defenders harass the Romans as they try to build siege works. They rush out in spirited forays, risking their lives time and again. "Many of them were killed, but they also eliminated many Romans" (7.193). Perhaps the surrender plan is only in Josephus' mind, in view of what eventually transpired, and what he describes here is genuine desperation of the kind we have seen in Iotapata and Jerusalem, where there is no hope of surrender but only a choice of ways to die.

Josephus ascribes the Judaeans' courage largely to their young leader Eleazar, who is "bold and daring and vigorous in strength" (7.196). His example inspires the others.[55] Being the first one out to fight and last to withdraw, wreaking Josephus-like havoc on the Roman earthworks while nobly protecting his comrades, Eleazar galvanizes Machaerus' defenders (7.197). He is finally undone, in a typical twist of fortune, by that same courage. One day he lingers too long outside the wall and is captured. In a trick to force the Judaean surrender, the Romans make out that they are about to crucify him. Eleazar has so many relatives and supporters inside, who cannot imagine going on without him, that they immediately make a deal. They will hand over the fortress in exchange for their young champion. Bassus honours his word and, astonishingly, the Judaeans depart with their lives (7.205, 209).

The only ones deliberately killed in the story are the unlucky foreigners, who have been caught up in what seems a Judaean conflict. When they see that the Judaeans have fled under an agreement that did not include them, they find themselves without a plan. Josephus does not explain why they could not have surrendered or simply evacuated the site earlier. When they hear of the Judaean-Roman deal, in any case, they see their only hope of escape from the legion outside in bolting during the night. Perhaps they know the legionaries' reputation and simply fear that the army's presence will mean bad things for them and their families, as the only ones remaining for rape and pillage.

With a lack of moralizing commentary, Josephus relates that their plan to flee is betrayed *by the Judaeans* – whether because the latter begrudge their neighbours' safety, he wonders, or because they fear that they would be held responsible (7.207). Either way, they somehow alert Bassus' army that the others are planning to leave, and only their boldest make it out alive: a reported 1,700 men die, while their women and children are enslaved. They were justified in trying to escape.

Josephus' account of Machaerus' fall includes much that seems highly implausible. Nonmilitant non-Judaeans are massacred by Romans for no apparent reason, while they allow the Judaeans who have fought and killed

---

[55] I cannot follow Chapman here (1998: 121): "It is important . . . to realize, especially in light of the representation of the Sicarii in the Masada account later, that any actions or attributes related to the verb τολμάω [be bold, audacious] carry a negative, not positive, connotation." Although most of Josephus' 312 uses of this word's cognates do imply impudence or rashness, often against divine instruction (e.g., *Ant.* 1.14, 16, 73, 113), everything depends on context. Contrast *Ant.* 1.155; 2.116; 6.375–76. In this episode Eleazar's boldness inspires everyone else (cf. *War* 2.469; 3.22, 152, as frequently in relation to Josephus' actions at Iotapata).

Roman soldiers to leave in peace. That the Judaeans could have planned a neat two-stage scheme of ferocious fighting followed by safe retreat defies imagination. The story does, however, further Josephus' literary interests (Chapter 2), and it makes for drama. He describes the Judaeans' death-defying courage, resourcefulness, and foresight. They are not heroes and their perpetuation of a pointless fight does not come across as a moral example, but they do display the typical trait of holding death in contempt. The improbabilities here should remind us again of his freedom with all parts of the narrative.

Immediately after Machaerus' fall comes an equally neglected episode: the battle of the Jordan Grove (7.210–15).[56] It merits attention for the sake of context but also because it shows further twists in Josephus' thematic repertoire. Bassus proceeds to this unidentified thicket because of reports that refugees from the sieges of Jerusalem and Machaerus – those he has just allowed to leave – have fled there. Now he is determined to eradicate them. He first surrounds the wood with his cavalry, to catch anyone fleeing, then has his infantry cut down the trees to deprive the refugees of cover. This forces them to make a bold – and rather noble (τι γενναῖον) – attempt to break out. Coordinating their charge against the horse-mounted pursuers, they manage to prolong the conflict for a while. But all 3,000 are soon cut down, against Roman losses of only twelve.

This action recalls an episode I mentioned in Chapter 6 in connection with civilian suicides: the actions of Japanese soldiers on Saipan when U.S. Marines stormed the island in July 1944. The 3,000 soldiers caught there, their ammunition exhausted, decided on a concerted rush at the U.S. lines. Against well-armed and armoured Marines they could brandish only knives tied to bamboo poles. They too were cut down to the last man, although their surprising tenacity cost the Americans dearly.[57] There are parallels also among civilian prisoners facing certain death. In August and October 1943, the Jewish inmates of Treblinka and Sobibor who had been kept separate from the majority killed on arrival realized that the imminent closure of those camps meant their doom. They planned concerted charges for the exits, as thier only possible hope of survival or at least their preferable way to die. In the event they managed to surprise their well-armed SS and Ukrainian guards. Of some 850 prisoners at Treblinka II, half were shot in the escape and hundreds more when the Germans cordoned off a 5-km perimeter. But about 100 survived. At Sobibor half of the 600 prisoners survived the initial

---

[56] The form in Josephus (7.210), appearing only here in ancient literature, is Ἰάρδην [δρυμόν]. Because of the accusatives in the context (following ἐπὶ), this is reasonably taken as the accusative of (an otherwise unknown) Ἰάρδης. But the printed form happens to represent the Hebrew *Yarden*, Jordan. Although Josephus elsewhere has Ἰορδάνης for the river, he may simply have given the Hebrew name here, in which case it would not be accusative.

[57] Kennedy 1999: 817.

escape, although 100 were caught in the forest and killed.[58] These examples are relevant to the Jordan Grove incident but also for thinking about what may have happened at Masada.

Josephus names one high-value target of the Romans in the Jordan Grove. Judas son of Ari had escaped from Jerusalem through underground tunnels (7.214–15). Josephus has earlier mentioned him as one of two brothers with leadership roles in the Disciples faction who distinguished themselves for bravery (6.92). But the second time he mentions Simon, Judas is gone (6.148), perhaps having fled to Machaerus or directly here to the thicket.

The story of the Jordan Grove again invites many questions and some observations. It is far from clear what motives these diverse refugees had. Most were apparently adult males able to fight and/or afraid to surrender. In contrast to his descriptions of Machaerus and especially Masada, Josephus neither mentions nor assumes the presence of women and children. The scene of refugees living for months in the woods and their final act suggests few if any families. Had they been conducting guerrilla raids from this hideaway? Were others known refugees from Jerusalem, like Judas? Were most fleeing Roman forces or conflicts with other Judaean factions? What became of their families? Did some resolve to fight because their family members had been killed? Particularly puzzling are the refugees from Machaerus, given that Bassus has just let them depart under a pledge. Is he going back on his word, or does he feel that some have abused his trust by regrouping here? Or is his promise of safety only a ruse to gain the fortress (cf. Vespasian's promises to Josephus at Iotapata, Chapter 2), which he may ignore once it is in his hands? Or are these refugees a different group, who had fled Machaerus at an earlier point? We have no idea.

Bassus' felling of trees is also noteworthy. The desert environments of Machaerus and Masada had few trees, and Bassus would need timber for a siege of Masada. If he was planning that now, as seems likely, he would not likely have squandered such resources. He might have scored a double benefit by clearing the Jordan Grove, wherever it was, and collecting the wood for Masada.

The so-called *sicarii* of Masada provide a stark contrast, in Josephus' *War*, to the fighters at both Machaerus and the Jordan Grove. They do not pursue either of the courses exhibited here: *either* courageously fighting *or* planning a safe surrender. Those at Masada venture beyond their lofty retreat only to plunder and kill fellow Judaeans, when the Romans are nowhere around. Otherwise they sit behind Masada's defences with their families. Even as they watch thousands of superbly equipped soldiers arrive, encircling them with a

---

[58] Mazower 2008: 391. For details, see Arad 1980.

wall and camps, Josephus gives no hint of defensive or other moves. Under a steadily intensifying artillery barrage, they do nothing. In all his other siege accounts – his own project at Iotapata, Gamala, Jerusalem, Machaerus, the Jordan Grove, even the encounters at Iapha and Taricheae – the Judaeans make bold defensive efforts, no matter how dire their predicament. Groups besieged in walled cities or fortresses had some advantages (Chapter 3), and a lucky arrow or stone might kill or incapacitate an enemy general. But Josephus mentions nothing like this for Masada, and depending on how one reads the archaeology, it may agree with this silence. Whereas the Machaerus episode combines clever forethought with vigorously courageous action, Masada offers neither.

Instead we have words, lots and lots of words. Most of the Masada story comprises speeches. This is where Josephus locates the last of *War*'s great orations, a two-part humdinger by Eleazar ben Yair. This eloquent Eleazar is a very different character from his laconic and rather Spartan namesake at Machaerus.

III. THE SPEECHES OF ELEAZAR BEN YAIR

Having expeditiously constructed a ramp and siege tower (*War* 7.305–10), Silva's army is presently at the summit entrance to Masada, pounding the wall with a ram. Here they discover the sole defensive achievement of the defenders: a thick wood-and-earth wall inside the casemate. Realizing that this will absorb the ram's strikes for some time, Silva sensibly decides to set fire to its wooden in-fill. The wind temporarily favours the Judaeans, but then quickly turns against them, setting the entire wall ablaze (7.315–19). (Recall the sudden wind that turns against the Judaeans at Gamala.) But by now night is falling. (Recall the nightfall that ended the Judaean ambush of Cestius.) Letting the fire blaze away, the Romans return to their camp to prepare for a full-scale assault at daybreak. (Recall Titus' burning of the inner temple gates and then resting before advancing.) It is in this brief respite on the summit that Eleazar ben Yair turns to oratory.

Scholarship on Masada has taken some peculiar directions.[59] First, it has ignored most of the context, notably Machaerus. Second, in reading the Masada episode it has fastened on the speeches and the resulting mass suicide. This interest may rest on the doubtful assumption that the speeches reveal Josephus' ideas.[60] A common view seems to be that the speeches, which visitors often can hear being read by tour groups on the summit, report actual

---

[59] For reviews of fundamental scholarship see Feldman 1975 and 1984: 763–90; for more recent work, Chapman 1998: 107–68; Brighton 2009: 2–17.

[60] Lindner 1972: 21–48.

words spoken. Yadin's popular book is a striking example. He devotes his
chapter on "The Dramatic End" almost entirely to quoting Eleazar's speech,
with the briefest justification: "It seems appropriate to include here the *detailed
description of that dramatic event* in the words of Josephus" (my emphasis).[61]

Third, analysis of the speeches has largely amounted to scouring them for
signs of *Josephus'* positive or negative appraisal, sometimes with the aid of
outside texts – Plato, tragedy, Hellenistic consolation literature, or the failed
Stoic opposition to the Roman regime – as a criterion. The question is
whether Josephus portrays them as heroes or as villains.[62] Public and academic
interest in Masada alike has been preoccupied with his moral appraisal, on the
apparent assumption that it might somehow help *us* to admire or dislike these
people.[63] In that vein, many scholars have found hints of nobility or more,
even if this is at odds with Josephus' plainly censorious judgments of *sicarii*
generally.[64] While himself trying to get past all such polarities, David
Ladouceur posed the central question, "Why did he include so detailed and
stirring a record of apparent heroism on the part of a group whom he had
opposed?"[65] A recent popular study posits that Masada was a turning point in
Josephus' personal views: right here in the narrative, the erstwhile Flavian
stooge rediscovers his patriotism as he describes Masada's defenders.[66] Archaeology has played a fundamental role in such discussions, whether in seeming to
support an account that ennobles these Judaeans or in contradicting Josephus
and ennobling those whom he is understood to disparage.

In pursuing the good/evil binarism, it seems to me, we have embarked on
the wrong train and found ourselves unable to get off, therefore dooming
ourselves to pointless debates. First, whatever Josephus thought of the people
of Masada could surely not be a guide for us. Second, his account of them, as
almost everywhere else, is more complicated than the labels *good* or *bad* allow.
He writes as an urbane statesman exploring human complexity on a broadly
tragic canvas. Although he is capable of reducing figures to two-dimensional
rottenness (e.g., Simon bar Giora or *War*'s John), and of constructing thin

---

[61] Yadin 1966: 232–37 (232).
[62] On the contents and connections of the Masada speeches see Morel 1926 (an array of classical
allusions); Lindner 1972: 21–48 (emphasizing biblical substructure and thematic coherence
with Josephus' other speeches; Ladouceur 1980, 1987 (Plato and a strong association with
Stoic teaching on suicide in the Flavian-Roman environment; Eleazar's speech an *antilogos* to
Josephus' speech against suicide in *War* 3); Luz 1983 (Hellenistic consolation stories);
Chapman 1998: 135–68 (introducing game theory amongst other interesting suggestions).
[63] Especially Yadin 1966: 15. Cf. Feldman (1984: 777): "Josephus' account makes heroes of the
Sicarii" – and since he is generally hostile to *sicarii*, such a heroic account must be *true*.
[64] Cohen (1982: 405) portrays Josephus as the founder of the Masada myth: "even Josephus
forgot [having recounted their crimes] that he wished to heap opprobrium, not approbation,
on them."
[65] Ladouceur 1980: 246.   [66] Seward 2009: 247–59.

cardboard scenes (wailing women with children, unnamed youths), his important efforts at characterization are much more humanly complex. Third, he calls the people involved here *sicarii*. We have seen reasons to think that this is not an actual group name. It is in any case an unmistakable fear-word (Chapter 4). If we think of the connotations for his Roman audience and realize that he keeps calling these people "murderers, assassins, cut-throats" while describing their robbing and killing of fellow Judaeans, we see how hard it is to imagine that he is praising them. But this does not mean that he is simply despising them.

The bandit society they create for their families in the desert, before the Roman war begins in earnest, furnishes Josephus' fullest example of the *sicarii* type.[67] In describing their speeches and actions, he is neither undergoing a conversion before our eyes ("Maybe these murdering cut-throats weren't so bad!")[68] nor piling on ad nauseam what he has made perfectly clear ("They *are* bad people who have made deadly choices"). All that is clear. But he uses the story of their end to do more interesting things, exploring human complexity, foible, and contradiction.

Do the speeches, finally, carry Josephus' own ideology? In Chapter 2 we considered his paradoxical stance toward speechifying. Like other critics of rhetoric he affects to regard plain talk as the masculine way. But because the masses are moved by great speeches, and that is not going to change, virtuous leaders must be *capable* of producing extemporaneous gems on cue. Josephus makes no apology for his own rhetorical brilliance, even when he admits that it is a con required by circumstances.[69]

His own character has used the two-part model that Eleazar employs. At the siege of Jerusalem Josephus first goes around the walls of Jerusalem urging the people that it is futile to resist (5.362–74). When all he got for his straight-talk was abuse and projectiles, "he turned to forays into the national history," and brought a wave of defections (5.375–419).

Eleazar follows the same pattern. He first tries masculine talk, singling out for the purpose his toughest men, who should be able to handle it (7.323–36). To them he says plainly, in my paraphrase:

> Look men, we started on this path because we could accept no master but God, and now we are in the final act. God is obviously supporting the Romans, while we have fallen afoul of his plans. We have nowhere to turn except to the one ultimate action of free men, which will atone

---

[67] See Brighton 2009: 93–140. Of *War*'s fifteen uses of *sicarius*, eight concern the residents of Masada (2.400, 516; 7. 254–54, 262, 275, 297, 311) while five relate to affairs in Egypt and Cyrene.

[68] Yadin (1966: 15): Josephus was overwhelmed by the heroism of these nationalist fighters.

[69] E.g., *War* 2.337–407 (Agrippa), 604–10; 3.354–91; 5.362–414; *Life* 17–22.

for our errors: We must take our own lives. This will show that we are *men*, who prefer death to slavery. We must first do away with our wives and children, to spare them violation and slavery, and destroy our property to keep it from Roman hands. And we should leave some food, to show that we acted from *courage* and not from starving desperation. So, let us arise and help each other to die.

This direct appeal to male virtue has mixed results, however. Many comrades, although they have been dispatching *other people's* families with little concern, are "rather soft" when it comes to their own, and especially to themselves. Notice the assumption that Masada is a community of families. Many of these tough men begin crying, and Josephus highlights Eleazar's frustration (7.339–40):

> When he saw these people acting like cowards, and their souls collapsing at the scale of the plan, Eleazar became afraid that this lot would, with their howling and weeping, cause even those who had heard his words with resolve to behave like women. So he did not relax his appeal, but raised himself up and, full of great purpose, made an effort with *more brilliant words* – on the immortality of the soul.

Here comes the big speech. What does it say about these cruel assassins (*sicarii*) that Eleazar cannot win them over with truth, but must raise his rhetorical game to overcome their "womanish" sentiment?

Eleazar now faces the ultimate debating-school challenge, with a legion at the gate and his most stalwart comrades reduced to mush. He must overcome their squeamishness about killing their families and themselves by defending the extraordinary thesis that life and not death is humanity's misfortune (7.343). This would have made nonsense of the whole political-freedom agenda, and it is not a position Eleazar ever thought of before. But it must be argued now if he is to move his audience. And so his night-time oration in the desert becomes a *tour de force*, surveying Greek and Indian philosophy in an appeal that would still be read on Masada in the twenty-first century (7.350–52). Finally, Josephus' humour tinges even this tragic situation as Eleazar miscalculates again and overshoots his mark. He cannot finish his masterpiece because his men rush forward as one, now suddenly eager to take their lives (7.389).[70] What a speech!

As usual with *War*'s orations, this one exaggerates or contradicts claims Josephus makes elsewhere. He seems to highlight this by having Eleazar assert a fact and then qualify it. We are invited to watch the wheels turning as he makes his bad case appear the right one. To prove that inscrutable divine

---

[70] How did Josephus know what Eleazar *planned* to say? Did one of the women survivors make notes and observe that the formal symmetry was not satisfied by a peroration?

judgement has overtaken them, he cites events in Caesarea: Judaeans were attacked *without provocation* (7.362)! He pauses: "But someone will say that there was a longstanding quarrel with the Caesareans" (7.363). Well yes – and the someone is our narrator Josephus. All right, Eleazar responds to his own criticism (7.364), but what about Scythopolis? *That* was an atrocity against Judaeans! But Josephus has described the Scythopolitans' actions as a response to Judaean reprisal attacks for Caesarea. Eleazar catalogues the suffering of Judaean minorities in Syria, before having to concede that none of these attacked Judaeans *in their own land* (7.389), which reminds the audience that he is referring to defences against Judaean raids.[71] Josephus' earlier account certainly does expose Judaean suffering, but he embeds it in a complex picture of regional resentment and conflict. As an orator in this desperate situation, however, Eleazar must present a cleaner and less complicated picture if he is to stir the men to the necessary deed.

Eleazar tries to valorize their position by claiming that they have been motivated by the fight for Jerusalem's recovery. Who could believe, he movingly asks (7.375–77), that the mother-city, the fortress founded by God with its rings of impregnable walls and myriads of armed defenders, would now lie in ashes? "But since a not ignoble hope – that maybe somehow we might be able to take revenge on the enemy for her sake – has cheated us, having now vanished and abandoned us alone to our fate, let us hasten to die nobly" (7.380). In *War*'s context, this claim is astonishing. If they had intended to fight for Jerusalem, there were many opportunities before now, years after its destruction, but the *sicarii* on Masada have made no moves in that direction. Only now, with a legion having finally caught up with them, does he mention their dedication to saving Jerusalem, which they abandoned before Cestius Gallus' expedition in 66. In context, this appears to be biting sarcasm from Josephus. Eleazar and his group never had a plan for Jerusalem or its future. That is the problem. They are self-deluded out there on the rock, trying to console themselves that their actions are virtuous.

Eleazar's bravest men, just moments before reduced to jelly by his direct call for self-immolation, are now so transported by his eloquence that they cannot let him finish (7.389–93):

> *Filled with some uncontrollable urge, indeed possessed by spirits*, they went off, each one struggling to get ahead of the other, *supposing this* to be a demonstration of his courage and prudence, that he not be seen among the last [to act]. So great was the desire (ἔρως) for slaughter, of wives and of children and of themselves, that *overcame* them. And when it came to

---

[71] Josephus has Eleazar give casualty figures of 18,000 for Damascus and 60,000 for Alexandria (7.367), whereas Josephus as narrator had 10,500 (2.561) and 50,000, respectively (2.497) – the latter toll again prompted by Judaean attacks amidst simmering ethnic tension (2.490–93).

the deed itself they were not cowed, *as one might have imagined*, but they pursued intently *the resolve they had found while listening to Eleazar's words*, though certainly emotion and tender affection toward their own remained with them all. But reason [i.e., Eleazar's compelling case], which had seemed to offer the best counsel for those dearest to them, won out.

So two things happened together: They hugged and greeted their wives, and took their children in their arms, planting final kisses on them and welling up with tears, and at the same time, as though this were being done by the hands of complete strangers, they carried out the plan on which they had resolved, having the atrocities they were going to suffer from their enemies as consolation for the necessity of this killing. In the end, no one was found to be unequal to such boldness, but all of them ran through their closest relations. Miserable victims of necessity, for whom the killing of their wives and children with their own hands seemed the lightest of evils!

Unable to bear their grief, the men then burn their possessions in piles and devise a plan for killing themselves. A select group of ten dispatch the others, after each man positions himself with his dead family members. Of the remaining ten, the man chosen to be last kills the other nine and sets fire to the palace before plunging a sword into himself (7.394–97).

There are no heroes here, but nor is Josephus' emphasis on mere villainy.[72] These are pathetic individuals and the whole scene is moving. Josephus' appeal to pity and fear, and his elaboration of tender familial emotion in the face of violence, are hallmarks of tragedy (see Chapter 2). This is an insane world of war, civil strife, and desperation, in which normal virtues and affections are inverted, as he pointedly observes. Josephus holds his audience's faces toward the horrifying scene, stressing the unbearable contrast between natural affections and the deeds they are forced by their predicament to execute. They have been, we are not allowed to forget, manipulated or even *possessed* by Eleazar's speech.

Consider, incidentally, how odd it is that Josephus should allow a young woman, and a relative of Eleazar at that, to escape with her five children, unmissed (7.399). This is convenient because she, said to be unusually intelligent for a woman, can then relay her careful notes on Eleazar's speech to the Romans (7.404). If everyone had died, one would ask how Silva or Josephus knew what had happened. But given the systematic plan of killing, with each husband and father concerned that his loved ones be spared ordeals in Roman hands, and with each gathering with his family, how did it happen that these relatives *of Eleazar* were missed? Where were this woman's husband and father?

---

[72] Here I agree with Ladouceur 1980, 1987 and Chapman 1998, although from a somewhat different perspective.

That the women hid is not implausible, but surely their responsible male would have had to search energetically for them. Was the plan put on hold while men searched for their hiding relatives? Did the man in this case look only briefly and say "Well, I can't find mine. Let's get on with it"? The story, as often, is schematic and artificial in its mechanics, although acute in its exposure of human nature and motives – its main concern after all.

Most impressively, the final encounter of the Roman soldiers with these women and children, whose vulnerability was the main reason for the final act of self-destruction, presents no trauma. Eleazar's profound and lethal fears were misplaced.

IV. HEROES OR VILLAINS?

Were we determined to find heroes and villains in Josephus' narrative, we would do well to remember similar episodes elsewhere. Eleazar is anticipated, as we saw in Chapter 4, by Simon of Scythopolis (*War* 2.469–76). When Scythopolis is under attack from "brutalized" Judaean raiders (2.458) seeking vengeance for Caesarea, Simon defends his *polis* alongside other Scythopolitans, displaying great valour (2.470). Is he wrong to do so? It seems his only option and he handles it virtuously. But Josephus indicts him for shedding the blood of fellow-Judaeans – those who brutally attacked Scythopolis – and when the Scythopolitans then turn against their Judaean minority Simon must reflect on his *crime*. As the ungrateful Scythopolitans are poised to kill him with his family, he makes a speech acknowledging the *curse* he lives under, before running through his father, mother, wife, and children before plunging a sword into his body: "This should be at once *both* a worthy penalty, in view of *my pollution*, and praise for my manly courage, in order that none of my adversaries might boast about having butchered me or brag at my having fallen" (*War* 2.473). On Masada, Eleazar likewise follows his elaborate confession of *sicarii* crimes with the recognition that he is facing "divine anger for the many injustices that we, being crazed, dared to perpetrate *against our compatriots*" (7.332). Like Simon, however, he is concerned that the enemy not receive *credit* for his killing (7.326, 331–32, 359–61). That both men face the final act with resolve – in full recognition of their disastrous failings – does not make them heroes.[73] I do not mean to compare them in other respects, for their situations are different. My point is only that the two accounts bring forward aspects of the work's pervasive ethos of tragic complexity, which defies easy labelling.

[73] Ladouceur (1980: 247) observed that in classical literature it is almost expected that enemies' deaths will be given a "melodramatic and heroic" treatment.

This is not to deny a general sort of message, well known to all statesmen of Josephus' kind. Namely, "freedom" is the finest of aspirations, but absolute freedom has not been possible in Judaea for centuries. Those who preach radical freedom are dangerous tyrants, merely taking advantage of common grievances to enslave others with their impossible promises. Their actions only create destructive civil war and the overthrow of serious leaders of integrity and wisdom. The end of their programme is death for all. Eleazar is the last representative of this lethal persuasion on Judaean soil – in Josephus' *War*.

The same moral complexity remains in the less familiar story that follows Masada, concerning certain *sicarii* in Alexandria (*War* 7.407–19). Josephus makes clear the *insanity* of their programme. They undertake revolutionary schemes and murder respected Judaean officials (7.410–11). Their "freedom" language is madness (*aponoia*), but still they draw peaceable Judaeans into their "crimes" (7.412–13). In spite of this clear verdict, Josephus gives also these *sicarii* unstinting credit for the ways in which they meet their inevitably horrible ends. "There was not a single person who was not astonished at their fortitude and – call it what you will: insanity or strength of purpose" (7.417). He dilates on this courage, which could be seen even in their children, "not one of whom could be prevailed upon to name Caesar as master" (7.419). Josephus may have such Judaeans in mind when, in his last known work, he reflects on the fortitude shown by *Judaeans* in the recent war (*Apion* 1.43–44; 2.272). We see the same tension when he describes (the monstrous) John of Gischala's recruitment of fighters "who excelled in condition of body, determination of soul, and expertise in wars "(2.590). In *Antiquities* the paradigm for masculine character is King Saul. But he too receives complex assessment. He blatantly violates divine commands and slides into murderous tyranny, yet he merits an encomium as the paragon of male courage and contempt for death.[74] This complexity is characteristic of Josephus.

The line that, more than any other, has given the impression that Josephus heroizes the residents of Masada comes when the legionaries enter the summit on the morning of Nisan 15. But this too should be read in context. The fires having burned out, the soldiers throw up gangways and charge through the breach. Finding no one, they are at a loss. Assuming the Judaeans to be hiding from them, they walk around calling out for someone to fire at (7.402–406). The surviving women carefully emerge from their hiding places, and one begins to recount the speech of Eleazar and its outcome. The soldiers "had trouble listening to her, not crediting the scale/scope of the boldness" (7.404–405: τῷ μεγέθει τοῦ τολμήματος ἀπιστοῦντες). But they had to accept her account, when she showed them hundreds of bodies in the palace.

---

[74] Cf. *Ant.* 6.100–104, 137–39, 142–56, 166, 256–68, and 343–50.

Josephus remarks that although the Judaeans were their enemies, the Romans took no pleasure in the sight: "[T]hey were amazed/astonished at the nobility of the plan and at their resolute contempt for death – by these actions in such straits" (7.406).

These perfectly human reactions, given the large number of women and children who lie dead before them, give power and depth to the story. First came disbelief: "You're saying that all the men killed their children and wives, and themselves? No!" Then, on seeing the bodies, astonishment: "They actually did it. We didn't think such a thing was possible – or, that *these* people had it in them." Finally, a common recognition among combat soldiers, who see the enemy doing something they themselves would not contemplate: "Well, that's incredible, killing your families and yourself for the sake of honour and not begging for your lives." In context, the soldiers' amazement cannot imply Josephus' judgment that these were noble individuals. Their end only shows what Eleazar was able to persuade them to do. The soldiers were amazed, certainly, but not necessarily admiring.

One small feature of the Masada narrative helps to show Josephus' care with the aspects that concern him most. At 7.398–401 he concludes the story: Everyone died, with the exception of the two women and five children, for a total of 960, and "this *pathos* transpired on the 15th of the month Xanthicus." This might seem to be just another of *War*'s dates, provided to enhance the sense of authority and knowledge.[75] But of course Nisan 15 was the first day of Passover,[76] the festival that is central to Josephus' programmatic contrast between declared freedom and tyrannical bloodshed (6.428).[77] If he had intended to valorize Masada's residents, he passed over a golden opportunity in silence. The Romans breach the wall on Nisan 14, the very day of slaughtering Passover lambs. They withdraw to prepare the next morning's attack just when these men *should* be eating the Passover seder with their families. Instead, Eleazar launches into his speeches about the need for *family killing*. The potential for moral elaboration was huge. Given that he has explained Passover and its customs elsewhere,[78] it is doubtful that he intended the mere mention of this date to inspire exegesis among his audiences.[79] Josephus himself seems deliberately tight-lipped, letting Judaeans in his

---

[75] E.g., *War* 2.284, 315, 430, 440, 528, 555; 3.142, 282, 306, 315, 339, 409, 542; 4.63, 69, 83, 413, 449, 550, 577, 654; 5.99.

[76] *Ant.* 1.81; 2.311, 318; 3.248.   [77] See Colautti 2002 and Chapter 2.

[78] *War* 2.10, 224, 244, 280; 4.402; 5.99; 6.290, 422–23, 428;   *Ant.* 3.248–51;5.20; 9.263–64; 10.70–71; 17.213–14; 18.29, 90; 20.106.

[79] I cannot follow Chapman's proposal (1998: 154–55) that the date "is as loaded with meaning in this text ... as the date of the destruction of the temple," bringing *aqedah* traditions into play, or Colautti (2002: 120, 128), who suggests that Josephus *forces* the connection with Passover. It seems to me that the date could not be more incidental or unadorned.

audience feel the pathos but avoiding any move to sermonize in favour of Masada's residents as victims.

Let us turn now to Masada's material remains.

V. MASADA: SOME RELEVANT ARCHAEOLOGY

Yadin's excavation in 1963–1965 produced a wealth of material, which we cannot begin to cover adequately. Eight oversized volumes by scores of contributors, decades in the making, now comprise the final reports.[80] They provide countless examples of our working principle that evidence is not self-interpreting. I do not mean that the remains can be made to say whatever we wish, but only that they do not *tell us* what happened. We must interpret and then interrogate the evidence to discover its possibilities. Here we can register only the few items most relevant for our questions about the aims of Masada's defenders and the Romans' intentions in moving against the site.

Coins from many periods and places have been found at Masada: a dozen from the third century B.C., more than 100 produced under Alexander Jannaeus (104–76 B.C. – the "Jonathan" who fortified the site), nearly 400 from Herod's reign (37–4 B.C.), 170+ from the ethnarchy of Archelaus (4 B.C.–A.D. 6), over 500 from the prefects and procurators of Judaea, the largest and latest group from Festus' time (A.D. 58/60–62), and more than 100 from King Agrippa I (A.D. 41–44). About sixty coins from neighbouring Nabataea (dated through the first century) have turned up, along with small counts from regional *poleis*, mostly from the time of Claudius and Nero: Antioch, Tyre, Sidon, Dora, Caesarea, Ascalon, Caesarea Philippi, Scythopolis, Tiberias (under Trajan), Sebaste, Gerasa, Canata, Alexandria. Nearly 800 other coins cannot be identified because of their poor condition.[81]

For us the most important coins are more than 2,300 examples of wartime Judaean issues in silver and bronze (Chapter 8): seventy-three of the silver issues from Years 1 to 5, the rest bronzes from Years 2 to 4.[82] These are most abundant for Year 2, in other words April 67 to March 68 (1,664 specimens), and Year 3 (491). There are relatively few (103) from Year 4, which ended in the spring of 70. The silver coins were found in three hoards: one hidden in a cloth bag beneath a floor, one in a bronze cup, and one possibly hidden in a casemate wall but found strewn on the floor. Discovery in hoards is normal for silver coins, because they tended to be gathered and stored because of their value. Given that Year 5 was the year of Jerusalem's siege, reduced to

---

[80] *Masada I–VIII, The Yigael Yadin Excavations 1963–1965: Final Reports* (1989–2007). See Bibliography. Ben-Tor 2009 is a judicious précis with much added insight, alongside a defence and explanation of Yadin's views.

[81] Meshorer 1989; 2001: 132–33.   [82] Ben-Tor 2009: 212–14.

the period from April to August of A.D. 70, it is noteworthy that three shekels from Year 5 found their way to Masada, from during or after the siege.

If Josephus' account of the core group's arrival under Eleazar in 66 reflects reality, newcomers must have continued to arrive from Jerusalem through the following years. The coins might suggest that the largest influx came in Years 2 through 4 (= 67–69), which corresponds to the period before the Flavians arrived in the south, their quick subjugation of Judaea causing general flight from the villages, and the period in which the campaign was frozen for the Roman civil war. Ahead of the Roman advance, while many fled to Jerusalem to buy time, some families fled to the remotest place they knew. Recall that Simon bar Giora came to Masada *with his wife and family* in the winter of 66/67, the time of the Year 2 coins. Then again, people may have arrived later carrying Year 2 coins.

Simon's case also reminds us that people came to Masada *and left*. There is no reason to suppose that everyone who fled there remained a long time, let alone until the bitter end. The majority might have sought temporary security, first from Jerusalem's violence and then from the Roman advance, while they decided what to do. From there they might have left for greener pastures in Egypt, the Parthian world, or even Galilee after its safe capitulation. Recall the people Josephus describes as "from the faction/sedition of the *sicarii*, who had been enabled to flee" to Alexandria (7.410), where they resumed their destructive activities against other Judaeans (7.410–12) – more than 600 (7.416). This flight from Judaea could have come at any point. They might have chosen Egypt in the 50s, instead of Masada in 66, or if they were connected with the core of the Masada group, stayed only briefly at the desert refuge before leaving for Egypt.

From the abundant material evidence found there, Ronny Reich has fashioned a portrait of life on the summit before the siege. He focuses on the distribution patterns of the 3,560 coins, 384 spindle whorls, and roughly 230 appliances for baking and cooking.[83] These last are of two kinds: cylindrical ovens for baking bread with ambient heat and square-shaped stoves for cooking over fires. The visitor today can still see a few examples *in situ*. Whorls are the small stone discs with holes in the middle for spinning yarn. The wooden sticks that went inside have long since perished. Because spinning and weaving were women's activities, the distribution of these objects is considered a particularly reliable marker of women's presence, supplementing the evidence for baking and cooking – also usually women's work but done by men if necessary. Several dozen loom weights, used in the spinning process, have also

---

[83] Reich 2001; 2003; full catalogue and descriptions of the whorls in Reich 2007.

been recovered. And it turns out that many of the textiles found – about 2,000 fragments, of which only 122 have been published – were produced on site using.[84]

Most of these "gendered" objects, including bronze cooking utensils and woven baskets along with cosmetic items such as eyeliner containers and sticks, combs, and brooches, were found in the casemate apartments around the summit's perimeter,[85] as were hundreds of storage casks (typically 325 ltr/86 U.S. gallon) and large jars (ca. 25 ltr/6.6 U.S. gallon).[86]

Reich argued that this distribution indicates the presence of different groups on wartime Masada.[87] Concentrations of coins *and* whorls together turned up in the casemate apartments and in a large structure (Building 9) in the north-central area. In other places were coins but few whorls, while in others, notably the western palace and Buildings 11 and 12, hardly any coins or whorls. Reich posited at least three categories of resident, each living somewhat separately on the large summit. The vast majority were families, whose women cooked and made clothes. But there were also single male refugees, who used money but did not spin wool, and a segregated male community whose members neither used much money nor made cloth.

In a subsequent article Reich confirmed these results by showing that the family complex in Building 9 and the casemate rooms had separate stoves and ovens, as one would expect with families, whereas the dwellings he had associated with the communal ascetics had just one oven per building, or a few in one place, strongly suggesting communal food preparation. The building he had interpreted as comprising separate apartments for single male refugees (Building 13), by contrast, had baking and cooking installations "spread around with no apparent order."[88] Guy Stiebel has since identified a large Roman-style oven in the western palace, prompting yet further questions about social diversity on the summit.[89]

For our inquiry Reich's most pertinent conclusion is that from 66 until the final siege, Masada was "a camp of displaced persons." It was not a "Zealot" stronghold but rather a place for different kinds of refugees, whose various needs were catered for by a stable central administration.[90] The scheme may seem too neat or skewed to suit other evidence related to Qumran scrolls and "Essenes," and other explanations may be possible. Certain activities might have been confined to particular areas for reasons now lost to us, other than simple demographic distribution. But Reich's focus on families is the only economical explanation of so much material and literary evidence. His picture of a displaced persons' camp with many families, anchored by a core group

[84] Ben-Tor 2009: 226–35.   [85] Yadin 1966: 144–54.   [86] Ben-Tor 2009: 129–40.
[87] Ben-Tor (2009: 224–26) reaches similar conclusions independently, it seems.
[88] Reich 2003: 152.   [89] Stiebel 2011.   [90] Reich 2001: 162.

from Jerusalem but open to other visitors, matches Josephus' assumption (he does not make an explicit issue of it) that the adult males at Masada were concerned mainly about their women and children (*War* 7.338, 389–95). Reich's proposal about an ascetic community has less in its favour, although it is possible.

If there is substance behind Josephus' report that Simon and John tried to bargain with Titus for "a way out through his circumvallation wall *with their wives and children*, for they would *go off into the desert* and leave the city to him" (*War* 6.351; Chapter 7), it seems likely that they were hoping to provide security for their families at Masada, as far as possible from Roman attention.

The ordinariness of family life on the summit is confirmed by a bill of divorce found there. In Aramaic, it was issued in the mid-autumn of 71: Joseph son of Naksan dissolved his marriage to Miriam daughter of Jonathan. In this document, which anticipates the rabbinic divorce decree known as the *get*, both parties are said to be "living at Masada."[91] Following their split, Miriam apparently left for another equally remote part of the desert.[92] A much-discussed curiosity of this document is its opening date, "On the first of Marcheshvan, Year Six at/in (*b^e*) Masada." As with the coins (Chapter 8), scholars have read much theology into this formula, supposing for example that it:

> attests to the messianic expectations and aspirations of the occupants of Masada, who continued to use the era initiated at the time of the First Revolt even after the destruction of Jerusalem and the Temple. Whoever dated this bill of divorce … hoped that the situation would still change for the better.[93]

A more economical hypothesis is suggested by the formula itself. This was the sixth year *of the settlement at Masada*, counting from 66, and of the creation of a Judaean community there after the garrison's removal. In the absence of a general dating system, and given that they would not have wished to date their lives by an enemy *polis* era or by Vespasian's rule, a Masada "city year," so to speak, would have been logical. Messianism is hardly necessary to explain such a routine-seeming date on a legal document.

A tantalizing fragment of palaeo-Hebrew text found at Masada features the words *Har Gerizim* (Mount Gerizim). Because it is written as a single word in the usual Samarian way, some scholars have identified it as a hymn written by a Samarian to honour their sacred mountain.[94] It then becomes possible that Masada's mix of refugees included even Samarians, Judaea's long-standing

---

[91] This is *p. Mur.* 19. See Yardeni 2000: 1.131 (transcription) and Friedman 2011 (interpretation in light of the later traditional divorce document).

[92] Eshel 2002: 159.   [93] Eshel 2002: 159.

[94] So Talmon 1999: 143–45. Cf. Ben-Tor 2009: 206–208.

enemies. War can make strange allies, and we have noted the massacre of
pietist Samarian rebels on Gerizim during Vespasian's campaign (*War*
3.307–15; Chapter 6). Then again, the mere name *Hargerizin* does not prove
this to be a Samarian text. The site might have been mentioned here because
of *anti-Samarian* animus.[95]

Piety is another area potentially illuminated by archaeology. Excavators
have found the remains of a synagogue, ritual baths (*miqva'ot*), tiny leather
boxes containing essential texts (*tefillin*), and various biblical and non-biblical
scrolls. Sixteen fragments of Hebrew texts have been found, nearly half
biblical: from Genesis, Leviticus (2), Deuteronomy, Ezekiel, and Psalms (2).[96]
The rest are of *Ben Sira* and *Jubilees* (otherwise known from biblical apocrypha
and pseudepigrapha), apocryphal renditions of biblical Genesis and Joshua, and
unidentified texts (including the Samarian fragment). A fascinating debate
concerns the relationship between texts found at both Masada and in
Qumran's caves. Did members of the "Qumran community" (often identified
with the Essenes known from Philo, Pliny, and Josephus) flee to Masada? The
issue turns on one's view of the Qumran site and whether it hosted a pietist
community in the first place, on the connection between its residential site and
the caves in which the scrolls were found, and on the status of otherwise
unknown texts found in the caves – whether they are sectarian products from
Qumran or copies of works circulating more widely.[97] At least nineteen ritual
baths (*miqvaot*) have been identified, two-thirds of which were built by the
wartime residents, and a number of basins for ritual handwashing.[98] Several
pieces of pottery have tags connected with tithing or the cleanness of vessels.
One names the son of a high priest, apparently Ananias, possibly as the
certifying authority.[99] Among the textiles, no mixture of wool and linen has
yet been found – suggesting care in observance of biblical prohibition.[100]

---

[95] See Tov 2000; discussion in Kartveit 2009: 241–43, supporting H. Eshel's argument for a
curse on Samaria.

[96] Ben-Tor 2009: 198–208.

[97] Netzer 1991a: 633–34. Tov (2000: 64–72) finds "typical Qumran orthography and
morphology" in one Masada text, and argues that Qumran was the source of many texts at
Masada. But L. H. Schiffman observes (1994: 355): "When a manuscript of this text [*Songs of
the Sabbath Sacrifice*] was found at Masada, it was initially suggested that some Qumran
sectarians who had taken part in the Great Revolt escaped to Masada. . . . However, study of
the remaining Masada texts makes it clear that the Masada corpus contained a number of
texts parallel to those found in the Qumran collection. Apparently, these were commonly
known works that circulated widely in Palestine. . . ." Yadin 1966: 173–74 and Ben-Tor
2009: 204–5 argue that a solar calendar was followed by Qumran-Essene sectarians on
Masada. But see Stern (2001: 4) on the variety of solar and lunar calendars. For a classic
presentation of the Qumran site and its relation to the Scrolls, see VanderKam 1994; for
recent diversity of opinion, Galor, Humbert, and Zangenberg 2006; for altogether different
interpretations of the Qumran site, Magen and Peleg 2007; Stacey and Doudna 2013.

[98] Grossberg 2007.   [99] On the last of these categories see Naveh 1989: 32–39.

[100] Ben-Tor 2009: 227–28.

It is difficult to know what inferences we should draw from all this. Most or all of these features would be expected among Judaeans generally. *Tefillin* are prescribed in Deut 6:6–9 and well known elsewhere. Ritual baths are amply attested in Judaean areas. Synagogues were communal meeting places, with cut benches for sitting (Chapter 6). Beneath the floor of Masada's meeting space, next to a section of the casemate wall at the northwest end, were found separate fragments of the biblical books Deuteronomy and Ezekiel, which confirm its use for the study of sacred texts, but this does not exclude other uses. Yadin argued that the synagogue went back to Herod's time; Stiebel and Netzer thought it had earlier been a stable.[101] These finds certainly help us envisage the daily life of Masada's residents; they do not identify them with a particular party or sect.

We look to archaeology also for help in understanding Masada's defensive posture, though again the evidence does not speak for itself. For example, excavators found small piles of heavy rounded boulders, weighing on average 45 kg (100 lbs). The largest pile was in the casemate wall above the Snake Path, a smaller one in the casemate room 1039 above the paths leading up from the cisterns just north of the siege ramp. Both the great weight of the rocks and their location suggests that they were designed for rolling down the slopes, to dissuade anyone making the ascent.[102] Although they could surely ruin such a soldier's day, they were useless against a besieging army.[103] They were not exactly spherical, and even if they had been, their course would have been unpredictable on descents such as the Snake Path. Legionaries used screens to defend against such objects as they worked on ramps, and they could sidestep one-time efforts. The small piles discovered on the summit (not on the ramp) might have been there from Herod's day. Evidently they were not deployed.

Incoming projectiles, by contrast, have been found in abundance: hundreds of round stones, for example, apparently launched by Roman *ballistae*. Of fifty complete samples (hundreds are broken), 85 percent are orange-to-grapefruit-sized, weighing 0.6–3 kg (1.3–7 lbs), although one weighs a frightful 22 kg (50 lbs) and two are around 13.5 kg (30 lbs). The use of light shot suggests that the Romans were targeting humans rather than hoping to damage the walls in this way. Josephus claims that, once they had their siege tower in place, they used torsion-driven bolt-throwers and *ballistae* to keep the walls clear of defenders (*War* 7.309).[104] That makes sense.

But there are many puzzles and debates. At a point about 100 m (330 ft) north of the ramp's junction with the summit, the straight line of the casemate

---

[101] Yadin 1966: 184–86; Netzer and Stiebel 2008: 1937.   [102] See Yadin 1966: 156, 162–63.

[103] Cf. Ben-Tor 2009: 242–43.

[104] On all this see Holley 1994: 349–63. Stiebel and Magness (2007: 31) infer from the absence of any identifiable bolts, given that the other ammunition is found in abundance and that bolts are found at other sites, that the Romans did not use catapults and bolts.

wall ends at locus 1038, which is one of the tower rooms, and the room just mentioned (1039) abuts it from the side as the wall shifts direction eastward. This locus 1039 was found to have layers of soil containing all kinds of objects: baskets, fabrics, coins, documents in Hebrew, Greek, and Latin, and beneath them larger rolling stones and hundreds of *ballista* balls. Netzer argued that, because the papyri must have been gathered up and tossed in by Roman soldiers following Masada's fall, the ammunition beneath must have come from the defenders. Given the large number of stones left sitting in nearby areas, he did not think that Romans had gathered just these balls into that space. For Netzer, their high concentration there and their random findspots in the room (not neatly piled), suggests that they fell from above. He proposed that the defenders had their own *ballista* artillery, sitting on the roof of 1038 and firing outward. In the defenders' last days, they had to dismantle the wooden beams of the casemate roofs to create the internal wooden wall mentioned by Josephus at the top of the ramp. When they dismantled the roof here, they let their *ballista* balls piled on the higher level fall to the ground.

Netzer's reconstruction would provide unique evidence of active resistance by Masada's residents.[105] In an essay for the final-report volumes, however, A. Holley raises a number of objections.[106] First, he thinks it unlikely that Masada's defenders could have built a *ballista*, a technically exacting piece of equipment with machined elements. Recall that Judaeans in Jerusalem could not operate the artillery they had captured from Cestius (*War* 5.268). Second, with a typical range of about 400 m (1300 ft), such a weapon could have reached Roman Camp E and part of F, which was Silva's headquarters. It is inconceivable, Holley argues, that the Romans would have built camps in the enemy's shooting range. They must have satisfied themselves quickly that the Judaeans had no such capability. Holley considers it more plausible that the concentration of stones in locus 1039 resulted from concentrated Roman firing around that area, where we would have expected them to aim.[107]

Similar uncertainty surrounds the hundreds of arrowheads found on the summit, more than a thousand armour scales, remains of spears, and bits of scabbard.[108] The arrowheads are mostly of a similar type: iron trilobate (three-bladed rather than flathead) with barbs (ends of the blade angled back to make removal difficult) and tangs (to insert in the wooden shaft), in a wide range of sizes and individually made. More than 200 were found in the western palace, gathered in piles near signs of fire, another 80 or so in the lower northern palace.[109] Yadin argued that the defenders' only useful weapons against the Romans below were bows and arrows, explaining why spears and swords have

---

[105] See Netzer 1991a: 416–22.   [106] Holley 1994: 349–63.   [107] Holley 1994: 362.
[108] Yadin 1966: 55–57, 97–100.   [109] Stiebel and Magness 2007: 22–24.

not been found.[110] Magness and Stiebel point out, however, that these arrow-heads were too soft to penetrate armour. They were better suited to hunting animals or targeting unarmed persons.[111] Given that arrowheads were not found below the summit, perhaps Masada's residents manufactured these for hunting or for use in their local food-gathering raids. Re-examination of Yadin's dig reports also led Magness and Stiebel to propose that, rather than being sites where the inhabitants burned their arrows with other possessions (*War* 7.335), the fire spots were actually the remains of *arrow-production* facilities. Masada's residents forged their own iron in furnaces creating temperatures of 1200°C.[112]

Other potentially relevant discoveries, including human remains, also have no definitive explanation yet. This is partly because the original finds had to be moved, creating disputes remain about what exactly was found where.[113]

How many fighters were there on Masada? Given the coming and going, many unattached young men likely left the site before Silva arrived. If they were mobile and had options, why would they sit there? Their departure in the years and months before the siege, as Bassus began rolling up Judaea's fortresses, might explain Josephus' impression that mature men had families – even if Reich is correct that single men had been present earlier. We do know of one male divorcee in 71.

Given Josephus' tendencies with numbers, we naturally guess that his figure of 960 dead is inflated. But it is not a round thousand (or 10,000) and could perhaps come from an official report. If we took it as a hypothetical maximum and assumed that most men present at the end were attached to families, there might have been somewhere between 150 to 300 men capable of fighting.[114] The one family we hear about had five children, suggesting one fighting-age male in seven persons, and we have no idea whether grandparents might have been present. And these were *potential* fighters. We have no reason to think that people went to Masada with the intention of fighting Romans. Quite the opposite, it seems: They went to avoid fighting. Estimates of 500 or 600 fighters apparently rest on the assumption that most residents each had at most a spouse, but the literary and material evidence alike speak against that.[115]

---

[110] Yadin 1966: 97–100.   [111] Stiebel and Magness 2007: 23.

[112] Magness 1992; Stiebel and Magness 2007: 24; Ben-Tor 2009: 248–50.

[113] E.g., Yadin 1966: 54–56; Zias 1998; Ben-Tor 2009: 241–53, 299–307.

[114] Even if the families were American-standard husband, wife, and two children, 1,000 persons would yield only 250 adult males.

[115] Gichon 2000: 542–43: in addition to the *two men* he counts per family of five, producing 300 fighters, "[a] further 300 were (to my mind), single, as is to be expected in a siccarian force." He also works from an initial total of 1,200, allowing for casualties by the end of the siege while accepting Josephus' 960 who died at the end.

The number of available male defenders becomes very small indeed when we consider essential daily tasks, once the siege had begun and a futile defence or at least surveillance was imperative: keeping watch around the perimeter in shifts, monitoring the Snake Path and the smaller entrances in some strength against night-time breach (assuming a willingness to fight to the death), labouring to maintain families, and possibly manufacturing crude weapons.[116] Risking the few available bodies in raiding parties outside the walls, or even rising above the walls to fire a pointless arrow, would have been an unacceptable risk. Gichon estimates that, with an estimated thirty artillery pieces, the Romans could have maintained a withering rate of fire on a 100-m (330-ft) stretch of the northwest wall above the ramp, "one shot hitting every 3.3 meters [10+ ft] of its length, every 5 minutes."[117]

If Masada's residents made little effort to fight as the siege took shape, as it seems, that would be no reflection on their courage. It may simply be that they had gone there with no intention of fighting, that there were too few of them – without training or equipment – to do anything useful. What happened, then, at the end?

VI. THE FINAL DAYS

Other aspects of Masada's archaeology may have a bearing on the final days. Here I should mention what Yadin considered "the most dramatic find of the whole dig": twelve broken pieces of pottery (ostraca) discovered near the entrance to the northern storehouses, with names inscribed on them, one reading "ben Yair." In the excitement of those days Yadin thought that he had stumbled on the lots Josephus claims were used to select the last ten executioners (7.395–96), in dramatic confirmation of the story.[118] Two main objections have since been raised. First, many other pottery fragments with individual names, lists of names, and single letters or groups of letters have been found, but these are understood to be the remains of stores or ration administration.[119] Why take this group of shards alone, which inconveniently numbers twelve anyway, to be *lots*?[120] Second, we cannot take Josephus' account, least of all Eleazar's speeches and everything that follows from them, as a record of events.

---

[116] See Roth 1995: 95–96.   [117] Gichon 2000: 2.545.   [118] Yadin 1966: 197–201.

[119] The issues are reviewed by Naveh 1989: 12–45, esp. 28–31.

[120] Ben-Tor (2009: 157–59, 297–99) clarifies Yadin's view (that he was not sure about the lots) and defends it: One of the twelve names was not finished and so that lot might not have been used, and the remaining eleven might include one for the commander, not counted among the ten. But Josephus' account disallows a separate lot for ben Yair (7.395–96). Once we change his story to include eleven, why not thirty? Why imagine the lots at all? (Who or what are we defending? What is really at stake?)

The layers of ash and charred wood beams revealed by Yadin's excavations are suggestive. In some ash piles were found remains of personal belongings: clothing, sandals, furnishings, and storage vessels. In store rooms, hundreds of smashed clay storage jars were found that had contained wine, oil, and flour. Casemate 1045, on the northwest end by the synagogue, shows evidence of a major fire. Yadin took all this as confirmation of Josephus' story: Before taking their lives the defenders destroyed their goods (*War* 7.394).[121] Not all storage rooms had been burned, however. Recall Eleazar's directive that some supplies be left so that the Romans could see that the Judaeans died by choice (7.335–36).[122]

On the basis of further excavations in the mid-1980s, Netzer offered a new explanation. He estimated that only 10 percent of Masada's built area was burned and stressed that the affected areas are not contiguous. This is hard to explain if the wooden roofs were in place, for they would have facilitated the fire's spread. Netzer solved that problem together with another one: the wood–and–earth wall that burned as Eleazar gave his speeches (7.310–15). Where did that wood come from? Observing that there was nowhere else on the summit to find "beams," Netzer proposed that the defenders dismantled room ceilings for this internal wall. Hence, a fire started in one stone-built room could not have spread to the next, and this would explain the irregular burn patterns.[123] Not all the roofs were dismantled, however. Some were left until the end, for example in the large room in the western palace with the beautiful mosaic floor. Josephus' claim that the last man standing set a great fire "in the palace" (7.397) suggested to Netzer that the final burning destroyed the rooms that still had ceilings.

This is a brilliant solution to the problems Netzer identified, although we cannot be sure. If Reich is correct, some ceilings would have been dismantled earlier for fires needed in food preparation – although the dried dung of the doves maintained in Masada's columbaria could fuel small fires. Further, Netzer's image of the defenders' inner wall is difficult to support. He imagined 4,000 beams of 4–5 m (13–16 ft) stacked at right angles to the stone wall, behind these the earthen fill, and behind that a stack of hundreds of shorter beams (3+ m, 10 ft), also perpendicular to the wall. He calculated from the amount of wood available on the summit (given room sizes) that this wall would have been an astonishing 18.5 m (60 ft) deep, 21.5–24.5 m (70–80 ft) long, following the course of the wall, and 7–8 m (23–26 ft) high – nearly double the casemate height. To achieve this, the defenders would have had to dismantle the existing inner wall and roof of the casemate.[124]

---

[121] Yadin 1966: 95–96, 155, 200 (with photographs).   [122] Yadin 1966: 97.
[123] Netzer 1991b.   [124] Netzer 1991b: 24.

Gichon noted problems with this reconstruction. Given that the Romans had the summit in clear silhouette and under fire, how could they have been surprised to find such a massive wall? How could they have missed the dismantling of the roof, and how were the Judaeans able to achieve it under constant fire? Above all, why would the defenders not have taken the simpler route of filling in the casemate to make the most of structural strength? Gichon proposed that the wood-and-earth wall was built *within* the casemate, the work thereby screened from Roman eyes.[125] Josephus' claim that the beams were laid "lengthwise" in a series, with their ends (literally "cuts") joined, seems to mean that they were laid end to end. Josephus describes the apartments constructed inside (Greek ἔνδον) the casemate wall (*War* 7.287), and so his claim that the wooden wall was built "[from] within (ἔνδοθεν)" (7.311) suggests fill in the same place. He says that the defenders laid two parallel rows of wooden beams, with the space of a wall between them, which they filled with earth (7.312). To keep it packed in and prevent it from collapsing to the open sides, shorter beams were laid periodically at right angles (*War* 7.312–14). Josephus' description seems to support Gichon, and it requires rather less wood than Netzer's reconstruction.

However their lives ended, it is plausible that Masada's desperate inhabitants filled in the casemate wall facing the ramp. It would have been a sensible move to delay things, even in futility. I have said that Masada was not regularly inhabited after the siege. The Roman army seems to have left a garrison for a time, however, and a group of fifth-century Christian monks removed much of the ruined casement structure, right about where Josephus locates the breach, to build their own rooms, walls, and corridors (loci 1031 to 1023, with courtyard 1014 and church to the east), along a stretch of 43 m (140 ft).[126] Those renovations removed a great deal of potential evidence. Again, the recoverable remains do not speak for themselves, and we must be willing to doubt every part of the story and reimagine the reality.

Whereas archaeologists working on the summit have found material remains that most find at least amenable to Josephus' narrative, research on the ramp has generated radical doubt. A visitor to Masada today easily gains the impression that the conspicuous ridgeback hill to the west is the *Roman ramp* because that is how it is called for convenience.[127] But we have seen that nature had created a large spur there before Silva arrived. The present ridge rises from about 17 m below sea level to 47 m above it, its 225 m hypotenuse being about 74 m in length on a gradient of 17 degrees. The ridge reaches to about 13 m below the summit.[128]

---

[125] Gichon 2000: 545.   [126] See Netzer 1991a: 427–38; Ben-Tor 2009: 255–68.
[127] Cf. Conder and Kitchener 1881–1884: 3.418–19: Silva raised "an artificial mound some 300 feet high" over the natural limestone promontory.
[128] Gill 1993: 570.

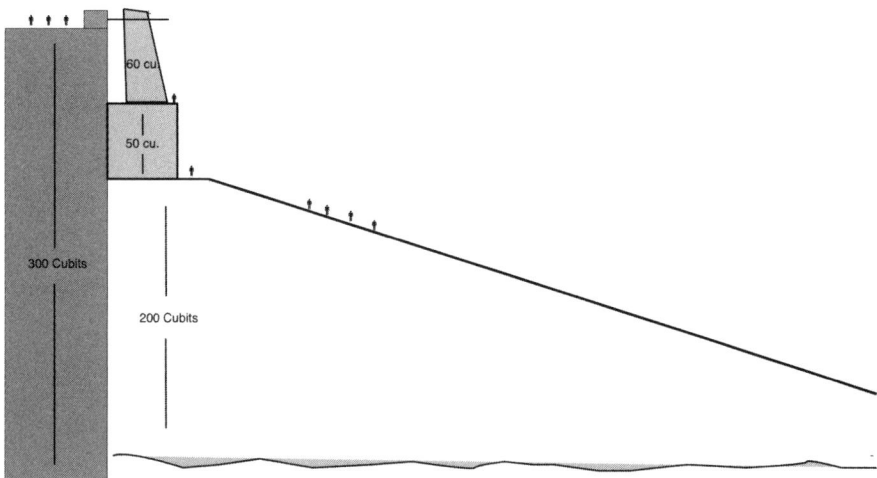

FIGURE 39. The implications of Josephus' schematic description of Silva's ramp, stone platform, and siege tower (*War* 7.305–309).

Josephus, who was settled in Rome at the time of the Masada campaign,[129] gives a simple, schematic, and impossible account of Silva's engineering work (*War* 7.305–309). Although at one point he mentions the easy western access path to the summit present in Herod's time, he seems to forget about that when describing Silva's ramp. There he relates that a natural projection of white rock, which Silva chose as the base for his ramp, was 300 cubits (ca. 137 m, 450 ft) below the summit. Silva therefore did three things (Fig. 39). To cover two-thirds of this gap he built a sloped embankment, using wood as usual to frame and stabilize the soil-and-gravel fill. Then, because he needed a large flat surface to support the battering ram and siege tower, he built a 50-cubit (23 m, 75 ft) cube-shaped stone platform on the top end of the embankment. One might presume that the siege tower and ram would be winched up for a horizontal run at the wall on the top of this cube. Its surface was still 50 cubits (23 m, 75 ft) short of the summit, however. According to Josephus, Silva made up the rest with a huge 60-cubit (27.5 m, 90 ft) siege tower. Once in position on the cubed platform, it would have protruded 10 cubits (5 m, 16.3 ft) above the summit, enabling the soldiers stationed in its uppermost level to see and fire over the wall.

There are at least four problems with this description. First, the real gap between the valley floor and the summit is about 33 percent smaller than Josephus remembers or guesses: ca. 90 m (300 ft) rather than his 137 m. Second, no evidence remains of such a massive stone cube.[130] Third, Josephus puts

---

[129] I find highly implausible Shahar's proposal (2004: 203–27) that Josephus returned for the sieges of Machaerus and Masada; reasons are in Mason 2007.

[130] Roth (1995: 106 n. 136) observes that some nineteenth-century explorers reported seeing cut stones at the top, although these were more likely connected with the wall. Cf. Conder and Kitchener 1881–1884: 3.417–19.

three things on the cubic platform: artillery pieces (7.308), siege tower (7.309), and "in addition a large [battering] ram" (7.310). His language suggests that the ram was a separate engine, as normal, but if so it would have sat far below the summit wall. For that reason, scholars tend to help him by placing it within the tower (Fig. 39). But where? If on the top level, we should wonder about the stability of the 90-ft structure; if on a lower level, it still would not reach the wall. And Josephus' explicit placement of *artillery* inside the tower makes it difficult to accommodate a ram: "a tower of 60 cubits was assembled, entirely clad in iron, out of which the Romans [were] shooting with many bolt-firers and *ballistae*. . . ." (7.310).

Fourth, the biggest problem with Josephus' picture is that the natural spur reached far higher than he suggests. In their 1932 survey, Schulten and Lammerer measured Masada's summit as 365 m (1,200 ft) above Dead Sea level in their day (−385 m). Approaching from the western side, they found that the natural spur rose from the 295 m to the 350 m level on this grid, abutting the cliff some 15 m (50 ft) below the summit. So the legion's task would have been to straighten the ascent while adding as much as 25 m (82+ ft) to its depth, with sufficient width to produce a 25-m-wide ramp of consistent grade for the machines and troops. Once the natural hill had been supplemented in this way, the multistorey tower, constructed in an engineering yard on site, made up the shortfall. Their reconstruction left no room, however, for Josephus' cubic platform. Schulten and Lammerer reasoned that the tower must have had an angled base, precisely matching the 17-degree grade of the hill. That would be extraordinary indeed.

A brief but important article by Israeli geologist Dan Gill (1993) confirmed the essential points of their study by an analysis of the spur's composition. Gill stressed the problems this created for Josephus' account. Not only was there no platform, but even the Germans' modest estimate of Roman labour was too great. Gill reckoned that Silva "would have had no need to raise the spur much higher [than its natural height] along most of its length."[131] His diagram suggests a top-up of 7 or 8 m (23–26 ft) at most.

The results of a 1995 excavation of the ramp by Ben-Gurion University archaeologists Benjamin Arubas and Haim Goldfus take us yet farther from Josephus' description. Assuming that Silva built the structure to storm the perimeter wall, following Josephus' account, earlier studies had assumed that erosion accounted for the difference between what we see now, which is close to the natural spur, and what Silva left. Arubas and Goldfus resolved to understand the ramp on the basis of material remains alone, putting aside

[131] Gill 1993: 570.

Josephus' account. With Schulten, they emphasize that a siege embankment would have needed to be much wider than the current ridge to carry troops and engines. If we postulate a 25-m width (with Schulten), then the hill we see today has only about *a third* of the needed volume. But two-thirds of the hill could not plausibly have been lost to erosion here alone, given that no other formations in the area have suffered so dramatically. Arubas and Goldfus conclude that the existing remains at the site cannot be dramatically different from what Silva left. But this means that he never completed a usable siege ramp, much less the massive crowning cube. This in turn would explain the surprising absence of evidence for any fighting in the ramp area, in contrast to the ground outside Gamala or Iotapata.[132]

This is not the place, and I am not the archaeologist, to debate the merits of each group of material remains and its interpretation. I have surveyed this important work of archaeologist colleagues because historical scenarios must take account of it. In the case of the famous ramp, archaeology may provide a reference point for the doubt we bring in principle to all of Josephus' (or others') literary accounts. Perhaps this ramp, as more visibly the northwest embankment at Machaerus, was never completed – or used.

VII. DATE AND DURATION OF THE SIEGE

Before turning to historical scenarios that might account for all of this, we must consider two very basic issues: the date and duration of the siege.

The year in which it occurred has been creeping steadily from Niese's 72 to Schürer's 73 and now Werner Eck's 74. Even a year later (75) is conceivable.[133] Why the uncertainty? Josephus dates the fall of Masada to Xanthicus 15 (Passover), which was April in 73 or late March in 74, but he does not indicate the year. Most twentieth-century scholars agreed with Schürer that the year had to be 73.[134]

The reasoning was as follows. Between Josephus' accounts of Machaerus/ Jordan Grove and Masada, he describes Commagene's loss of independence and incorporation into Syria. He dates this to Vespasian's fourth year, which ran from July 1, 72 to June 30, 73 (*War* 7.219). His wording might suggest that it was early in that year, in the latter half of 72. Then Silva arrives to replace the deceased Bassus (7.252), and Masada falls to him in early spring. Then, immediately after the fall of Masada Josephus describes events in Alexandria when a certain Lupus was governor (7.420). When Lupus reported these

---

[132] Arubas and Goldfus 2008, 2010.
[133] Schürer 1898–1901: 1.639–40 n. 139 (cf. 605–6 n. 16) demolished Niese's dating system (counting imperial years in Jewish way, from Nisan 1), which put the fall of Masada in 72.
[134] Schürer 1898–1901: 1.638–39.

disturbances, Vespasian ordered him to destroy the Judaean satellite temple at Leontopolis. "Shortly after" he closed the temple, Lupus died and was succeeded by Paulinus (7.434). We know from an inscription that Ti. Iulius Lupus was Egypt's Prefect in February–March of A.D. 73.[135] Everything seemed to fall into place, then, if Silva replaced Bassus in 72 and Masada fell in April 73, after which other *sicarii* created problems in Alexandria during Lupus' governorship, later in 73.

Although this chronology *could* fit Josephus' narrative, the story does not require it.[136] Even if Josephus is correct that the Commagene affair occurred in Vespasian's fourth year, it does not follow that the next event he mentions – Silva's arrival – occurred immediately. Likewise on the other side, although Lupus was Egyptian Prefect in the spring of 73, we do not know that he was not still Prefect in 74 or later. We know only that Aeternius Fronto, who seems to have replaced Lupus' successor Paulinus, was in post by late 78.[137] Lupus might have remained in office until 75 or later. Further, Josephus dates only the result of *sicarii* activity to Lupus' governorship, without saying how long this had been occurring. Josephus traces the *sicarii* of Egypt to Judaean origins (7.410), but we have seen that they may have gone there at any time from the late 50s or 60s. Josephus' evidence is not as dispositive as the usual reading suggests.

In favour of 74 is a pair of inscriptions found in the 1950s, in Silva's Italian hometown of Urbs Salvia, which honoured the local celebrity for his provision of an amphitheatre. (Modern Urbisaglia honours Flavio Silva with a prominent boulevard.) These inscriptions do not mention Masada, and their significance for that siege went unnoticed until W. Eck subjected them to scrutiny. He pointed out that both list Silva's honours, in standard *cv* fashion, beginning with the most recent achievements:[138]

> L. Flavius Silva Nonius Bassus, tribe Velina, consul [81], *pontifex* [member of an important priestly college], *legatus Augusti pro praetore* in the province of Judaea, adlected among the patricians by the divine Vespasian and the divine Titus while censors, adlected by the same among the praetors, legate of the *legio XXI Rapax*, tribune of the plebs, quaestor, tribune of *legio IIII Scythica*, on the three-man committee for jails and policing, *praetor quinquennalis* [a magistracy in Urbs Salvia]. ...

Eck observed that the two honours immediately preceding Silva's Judaean legateship, patrician and praetor status, seem to have been granted by Vespasian

[135] *SEG* 20.651.
[136] On what follows, see Campbell 1988: 156–58; Cotton 1989; Cotton and Geiger 1989: 21–23; Schwier 1989: 45–48; Ben-Tor 2009: 253–54.
[137] Cotton 2007: 157–59.
[138] Eck 1969; 1970: 93–111; the two inscriptions, which have basically the same content (but some different word fragments) are in *AE* 1969/70:183a and 183b.

and Titus as censors. But Vespasian revived the office of *censor* only around April 73. If Silva received these honours while the Flavians were censors, therefore, he could not have been an ex-praetor and legate in Judaea in time for a siege that ended in the month the censorship began, April 73. His siege of Masada must have ended in the spring of 74.

Critics have responded that the inscriptional evidence *could* still be compatible with 73.[139] Silva's offices may not follow a strict sequence: Perhaps the inscription lists the two "adlections" together for the sake of efficiency, and only the patrician adlection occurred while they were censors. Silva could have been praetor, and thus eligible for legateship, earlier. Or perhaps he was in Judaea in 72–73 and enrolled among the patricians in 73–74 while absent from Rome. Eck noted the absence of parallels for adlection *in absentia*, but this does not mean that it could not have happened.

But what is at stake? Efforts to save 73 assume that Josephus implies this date. We have seen that he does not. If we remove that constraint, Eck's reading of the inscriptions seems the more natural one.[140] In further illustration of the complexities, however, Hannah Cotton has both defended Eck's arguments in general and tossed a new spanner in the works. A fragment of Latin papyrus found in Masada's casemate room 1039 addresses Iulius Lupus. If this is the Egyptian prefect *and if* he received the letter at Masada, then the siege must have been underway in 72–73, if he progressed to the Prefectship of Egypt in the spring of 73. Cotton concedes, however, that these may be different Lupuses, that such a rapid jump from Judaean desert service to Prefect of Egypt seems awkward, and that the letter may not have been received at Masada (someone there might have drafted a letter to Lupus in Egypt and not sent it).[141]

In short, we cannot be certain whether Masada fell in 73 or 74, although it seems to me that 74 requires less force in explaining the evidence.

The year of the siege does not make a great deal of difference. If it were 74, it would further strengthen the picture we would have anyway of Rome's lack of concern about the remote site. The question of the siege's length and difficulty level of the siege, by contrast, is germane for our understanding of intentions and morale on both sides. The intimidating effect of the site on modern visitors creates an assumption that the Tenth Legion faced an extraordinarily tough slog, even if Josephus' brisk description does not suggest such Herculean labour.

In a 1934 review of Schulten's Masada study, C. F. C. Hawkes and I. A. Richmond challenged his estimate of a six-month siege: "two months . . .

---

[139] See especially Jones 1974; Bowersock 1975.

[140] Schürer-Vermes (1.515), relying on Eck, is emphatic: "the fall of Masada must belong in spring A.D. 74, at the earliest."

[141] Cotton 1989, corresponding closely to Cotton and Geiger 1989: 23. The letter in question is no. 724 in the latter collection, which she discusses separately on 62–67.

seem ample for the whole operation."[142] Jonathan Roth came up with similar conclusions in an exacting study of the logistical requirements, which he weighed against workload norms and the size of the available force. Estimating 8,000 soldiers plus 2,000 slaves and another 3,000 conscripted porters and using productivity rates attested elsewhere – 1 cubic metre of construction per day per man for earth or stone – Roth calculates that everything *could* have been completed in under four weeks.[143] Allowing for delays and problems, nine weeks would be plenty. He splits the difference and suggests a seven-week siege.[144]

Roth strengthens this proposal with several other considerations. First, from a strategic and logistical point of view, Silva must have wanted this over quickly. Maintaining his army in the desert would have required hundreds of donkey-loads of food and water over long distances each day. Against a tiny number of poorly equipped defenders, who may have enjoyed an abundant supply of food and water, a rapid assault would have been the only way to maximize his advantage. Second, there is no material or literary evidence of deterrence from the summit. Third, the remains of the Roman camps show that they were not built for winter use, with drainage ditches or storehouses. Their low stone walls suggest tent foundations rather than barrack walls. Such considerations convince Roth that Silva both planned and executed a quick operation.

While agreeing that Silva *wanted* it over quickly, Gichon sees the task as much larger and posits a minimum of six months.[145] He thinks that the siege ramp required nearly three times as much volume as Roth estimates, over and above the natural spur (about 100,000 cubic m rather than Roth's 37,500), dismissing Gill's "faulty drastic conclusions" – although Roth followed Schulten and Lammerer. Gichon imagines a rate of progress less than a fifth of Roth's estimate (only 0.18 cubic m per man per day) and also believes that there must have been intensive Judaean bombardment of the legionaries as they worked.[146]

We cannot resolve these issues definitively, but the general movement has been away from old assumptions of a long and exhausting siege (even two or three years: see the opening of this chapter) toward minimizing the labour and time involved. Given our new understanding of how much the natural spur contributed, Roth's careful argumentation shows that Silva could have executed the operation in a few weeks.[147] If the spur's contribution was so

---

[142] Hawkes and Richmond 1934: 75.   [143] Roth 1995: 91–95.   [144] Roth 1995: 98–110.

[145] Gichon 2000: 541–554.

[146] Gichon 2000: 541, 546. Oddly he dates this from late 74 to the spring of 75. This appears to be a simple mistake, because he also claims to support Eck.

[147] Also Ben-Tor 2009: 291–95, and that without doubting that the ramp was completed and taking Josephus' numbers (of soldiers and defenders) as basically correct.

prominent *and* Silva never completed a ramp (Arubas and Goldfus), even the shorter estimates could be too long. If Silva wanted to avoid the area's winter torrents (January–February) on one side and extreme summer heat on the other, he would have gone to Masada in late February or early March and expected to complete his work by mid-April – precisely when Schulten and Lammerer stayed in 1932 (March 4 to 31) for the same reasons.[148] In A.D. 74, Josephus' end date of Nisan 15 fell around April 11.

The question of the campaign's duration is important mainly because working through the evidence helps us to think about plausible historical scenarios. We now return to our questions about Judaean and Roman aims in going to Masada and about the final events.

VIII. RECONSTRUCTION

Judaean aims

We can say with some confidence that Masada's wartime residents did not flee there in order to fight Romans. From the beginnings of the revolt in 66, a refuge designed for a few royal personages and their treasures came to house hundreds of ordinary people. The large population of refugee families did not change the character of the place, however, as a sanctuary sited as far as possible from danger. Anyone who wished to fight foreigners had to do what Herod and Simon bar Giora did: *leave* Masada and go to find the enemy.

When Josephus remarks that Herod's fortified sites (*War* 4.555), or Masada (4.504), were in the hands of "bandits," his label is not mere slander. Those who defected from civil society to live in anti-states led by strongmen and following their own rules without accountability were by ancient definition *bandit* domains.[149] From this perspective, Masada was a bandit society. Its inhabitants had fled there to create a community with its own rules and the charismatic leadership of Eleazar ben Yair. It was free from the authority of the mother-city, whether Jerusalem was led by its traditional chief priests or by the Disciples faction that overthrew them. The community sustained itself, as bandit societies did, by armed intimidation of neighbouring towns. Masada was a community of *families*, however, with women and children forming the majority of its population. In addition to Eleazar's core group, all sorts of others apparently came and went, looking for temporary security. These various

---

[148] Schulten 1933: 4.

[149] See Isaac 1984 (who emphasizes the importance of bandit suppression in legionary tasks); Shaw 1984, 1993, 1995 (who emphasizes the instability of bandit identities in changing power structures, and the vertical social dimensions of banditry); van Hooff 1988 (on social banditry); and Grünewald 2004: 1–32 (on the common bandit type in Roman law), 98–100 on the Babylonian-Judaean bandit states.

groups and individuals did not always share aims and attitudes, as we see in the brief stay of the Simon bar Giora family.

How did the many who fled there think it would end? Rome had built its reputation for "peace and security" on an efficiently brutal handling of bandit and pirate societies – the reason for Pompey's eastern campaigns in the 60s B.C. In a system that required submission to Rome's *imperium*, bandit groups living outside the order were intolerable. Herod and his family had begun their services to Rome by clearing much of the countryside of bandits.[150] But there were always questions of scale and cost-benefit analysis in pursuing bandits. Pompey's campaigns were necessary because of serious threats in the east. Through the first century, nevertheless, substantial bandit societies remained in the mountainous landscapes of the Syrian frontier, Lebanon's Bekaa valley, and Egypt. As long as they were isolated from population centres, outlaws were often left to themselves for long periods. But a new sheriff who decided it was time for law and order could move against them swiftly and harshly at at any time. That seems to have happened with Judaea's desert fortresses.

How long did Masada's refugees expect to live in peace? If the siege came in the spring of 74, the founding group had lived there without disturbance for nearly eight years: enough for a B.A., M.A., and a good start on the Ph.D. This was plenty of time for them to become comfortable, marry, divorce, and raise families. There must have been many pregnancies. In a cave on the southern cliff face Yadin found what he counted as twenty-five human skeletons, including a foetus in the sixth or seventh month.[151] Given the high rate of infant and maternal mortality even under favourable conditions in antiquity, we cannot know how many newborns survived. But Josephus' image of small children in their father's arms (7.391) suggests that many births were successful.

As they reached the temporary security of Masada, each family or individual could not have known how long he or she would stay. It was home for the moment and the residents would need to see how the conditions suited them. The long years since 66 when legions remained far away must have nurtured the hope that they could stay indefinitely. The request of Simon and John to flee into the desert (6.351) assumes that Romans were not bothered about such refuges. Those who tired of Masada had plenty of opportunity between 66 and 74 to find other homes. Why not resettle in the Parthian world, Egypt, or Galilee – if one had the mobility, resources, and contacts to do so?

Some of Masada's residents in 73/74 may have harboured apocalyptic hopes, but we have no clear evidence of that and need not suppose it. It is simplest to imagine that the families still there in 73/74 had simply hoped to continue

---

[150] Isaac 1984: 176–77.   [151] Ben-Tor 2009: 299.

unmolested. Having fled there during Judaea's troubles, they had made a home and had reason to think it could last. Masada's physical situation must have inspired a feeling of security, especially as long as the men were able to bring in fresh food and supplies, for the children especially. When Silva's army finally approached in the spring of 74, we may imagine that they were surprised and had to decide quickly what to do next.

Roman aims

Although we have no access to Roman commanders' thoughts, the picture we have built from Cestius, Vespasian, and Titus suggests a similar approach to Herodium, Machaerus, and Masada. Namely, the Romans did not send their precious legions on fools' errands, but used them with deliberation and caution. They looked for ways to make a low-risk investment of force yield an oversized projection of power. In suppressing the Judaean revolt, accordingly, the Flavians concentrated all but exclusively on the *poleis* and ultimately on Jerusalem, the locus of turmoil. The desert fortresses were not important for the Judaean campaign (*War* 4.555). The Flavians could have taken these remote sites whenever they wished, but there was no reason to undertake pointless operations with no yield in fame or power.

Most telling in this regard is that after the big prize was won, even though Titus remained in Syria for months with legions at his disposal, which had nowhere else to be, he *still* ignored the desert fortresses. He did not even bother with Herodium, just half a day's march from Jerusalem across easy terrain and there for the taking.[152] Titus apparently thought that it was not an issue, no matter who was doing what there. It did not merit even mild Roman exertions. Then after Titus left the region, through the whole period of Cerealis' governorship with the crack Tenth Legion under his command (ca. December 70–71/72), he too made no move against the desert fortresses. We can only conclude that they did not matter.

When Bassus became the province's second legate, he may have taken the same view. In consolidating his province and rebuilding its infrastructure, however, he would sooner or later need to garrison the fortifications. Any government must either control strongholds in its territory, if only as a matter of accounting for resources, or to put them beyond use for others. It was unwholesome for Roman rule to permit bandit fiefdoms to thrive if something could be done about it. When Bassus did get around to the fortresses, however, he seems to have preferred the voluntary surrender of their inhabitants. With his overwhelming forces he could have wreaked terrible vengeance

---

[152] 14.4 km or 9 mi via the straight road to Bethlehem, 12.5 km (7.5 mi) straight from Jerusalem to Herodium.

on their small populations. That he chose not to do so, at Herodium or Machaerus, might suggest that he did not want to aggravate the recently pacified population, producing new martyrs and grievances, or simply that he did not want to waste even a few of his own men in such attacks.

But he *did* want his fortresses back and he would take them. It was up to the occupants how things would go.

Bassus might have had practical aims for his army. As we have seen, Roman legionary training occurred on the job.[153] The Tenth Legion and the province's new auxiliary cohorts might have needed training by now, after their lengthy postwar rest and new recruitment. Allowing provincial soldiers to become soft was a known danger previously associated with Syria's legions.[154] The legions were feared, but their lethal skills did not magically appear with the uniform. They had to be learned and tested. Marching out to desert sites in full gear, prepared for whatever would happen, building encircling walls, camps, towers, and earth ramps, and improvising responses was ideal training and physical conditioning. Here was a real human "enemy" of some description (as in Vespasian's Galilee), but not one that posed a serious threat. Low-risk manoeuvres in recovering the fortresses would build the soldiers' confidence and *esprit de corps* along with their technical competence.

In Josephus' account, the Machaerus and Masada expeditions feel very different from the Jerusalem siege – a mammoth and exhausting project through a long and dispiriting summer, which necessitated constant tactical revisions. Clarity of purpose and speed of operation make them seem compact exercises with assured outcomes. Bassus receives a quick surrender at Herodium and a delayed one at Machaerus. How he "brought over" the former we do not know, but it may have required little more than showing up in force (*War* 7.163).

Bassus' reported assembly of the province's entire army for Machaerus and Masada, perhaps the better part of 8,000 legionaries and auxiliaries, may have been calculated to have the same overwhelming effect in more difficult and remote locations. Machaerus was a much more demanding proposition than Herodium. We do not know how much effective opposition Bassus faced there. It may be that the encircling wall and ramps were built as much for the soldiers' practice as to speed along the conclusion.

It is remarkable that Bassus accepted the surrender of that fortress, as Josephus and the unfinished ramp suggest. Perhaps this was merely a tactic to recover the fortress with little risk – and then chase down the refugees in open terrain. Roman forces would not likely have allowed people who had violently resisted and taken legionaries' lives to go in peace. The alleged slaughter of the lower townsfolk remains a puzzle on various levels.

---

[153] Parker 1928: 224–28; Webster 1985: 120–21; Keppie 1998: 28–29, 47, 59–60.
[154] Tacitus, *Ann.* 13.35.1–3, concerning Corbulo's energetic reforms.

When Bassus died, Silva took over his methodical recovery of the fortresses, with Masada the only one left. If Silva's expedition fell in late February to April 74, the army would have been well recovered from its exertions under Bassus. If he continued with Bassus' approach, Silva should have been willing to let Masada's families leave, as long as they peacefully abandoned the fortress site. Those who rejected Roman magnanimity he would have punished with untroubled conscience. This is a pattern we have seen repeatedly, as when Cerialis invited the Samarians' surrender but massacred without hesitation those who rejected his appeals (*War* 3.307–15). In Idumaea, the same commander was reportedly planning a siege of Capharabis when its inhabitants threw open their gates and came with olive branches. Cerealis accepted their gesture, whereas in Hebron, having had to force his way in, he killed everyone but small children and burned the city (*War* 4.552–54).

This brings us to the main question of what happened to the refugee families on Masada. They undoubtedly witnessed the terrifying sight of a professional army arriving in its columns, armour, and weapons dazzling in the desert sun, and countless followers and slaves trailing with untold numbers of animals, carts, and war machines. What were they to do now? They might have heard about Machaerus and the Jordan Grove in the previous year and might have seen advanced scouting or engineering parties from the Tenth.[155] But even if they had been thinking of leaving, as so many had left before them, what were they to do as the army approached? If they fled, would they not be vulnerable to the army? If they walked out to surrender, what were the prospects of safety for either men or women and children? They did not have a *polis* council, and at least some of their leaders had been involved in actions against the auxiliary in 66.

What happened?

Josephus' description of the group self-immolation received a huge endorsement from Yadin's archaeological work. Energetic challenges came already in the late 1960s from the scholar-journalist Trude Weiss-Rosmarin.[156] Charging Yadin with reading Josephus naïvely, she claimed that typical Roman behaviour suggested a different outcome. She also insisted that because Jewish (i.e., rabbinic) tradition abhorred suicide, pious Jews could not have done this. Weiss-Rosmarin saw an obvious alternative. Silva's army completed the ramp, battered down the wall, poured onto the summit, and massacred everyone.

---

[155] Gichon (2000: 542) envisages a broad preparatory campaign in the area from En Gedi in the north to En Boqeq in the south, to deprive Masada of its food sources.

[156] Weiss-Rosmarin (PhDs in Semitics, philosophy, and archaeology) was editor of the *Jewish Spectator*, and her articles are scattered in that periodical. The most accessible summary, which is scrupulously fair, is in Feldman 1975. He provides a synthesis in nineteen points (232–35) before tackling each in respectful detail (235–47).

Josephus, whom she viewed as a mouthpiece of the Flavian regime, *covered up* Silva's atrocities for the same reason that people commonly assumed he *concealed* Titus' destruction of the temple: to make the Romans look better. He flattered Silva by suggesting that his mere arrival at Masada was terrifying enough to make the *sicarii* take their own lives.[157]

In a characteristically thorough response, Louis Feldman produced ancient examples of Jewish suicide in comparable circumstances and addressed the rabbinic-legal issues. His most telling points concerned Flavius Silva, a distinguished figure in Rome when Josephus was writing *War* – he would be consul in 81 – and hence a curb on literary freedom. Because military glory was the most coveted basis for a Roman official's prestige and not easy to come by, if Silva had engaged in any fighting, even a slaughter, that would have been a claim to martial glory. Josephus could not have cheated him of this glory by having Masada's residents already dead when he arrived.[158] Indeed, Feldman thought, Josephus probably consulted Silva's own field notes for his account.[159] Something like the self-killing described by Josephus must have occurred, therefore, with due allowance for literary dramatization.

Shaye Cohen refined the discussion with an essay that remains a clinic in method. Although writing in tribute to Yadin, Cohen challenged his inferences from the archaeology while rejecting any simple scheme of collective suicide.[160] He surveyed sixteen Graeco-Roman parallels for communal self-destruction, which included killing of family members and pre-emptive destruction of property by those caught in an unwinnable siege. From these accounts he concluded that such stories were often exaggerated, with "all" reportedly being killed in spite of evidence for survivors, that these dramas are a "stock motif" in historical literature and for Livy in particular, and that they are usually told with a certain admiration for the victims' resolve. Livy could admire personal suicide but not the killing of family members.[161] Against this background, Cohen concluded that in Josephus "the general tone of the narrative is favourable" to the *sicarii*.[162]

In probing what actually happened, Cohen found Josephus in conflict with both archaeology and historical plausibility. We pass over the small matters he raises and even two of the three more substantial ones: on Josephus' location of the palace, which he thought confused,[163] and the prospect that 960 killing

---

[157] K. Atkinson (2007: 356) adds a twist. Although some of Masada's residents may have fought, he says, "[t]he absence of mass graves leads to the conclusion that the Romans likely captured the majority of Masada's defenders."

[158] See Feldman 1975: 235–36, 244.   [159] *Life* 342, 358, 366; *Apion* 1.56.

[160] Cohen 1982.   [161] Cohen 1982: 389–92.   [162] Cohen 1982: 393.

[163] As I noted earlier, Cohen understood Josephus' palace (7.397, 405) to be the northern one, hence too small for 960 bodies. I have suggested that Josephus assumed the "palace" in his evidence to be the large (western) one he knew from the site.

themselves, which he found implausible.[164] Most importantly, Cohen considered Josephus' whole picture of the Romans' overnight delay incredible. Rejecting that removes the possibility of Eleazar's speech and the collective self-killing. The Romans, Cohen argued, had every incentive to push through at the moment of the breach. Withdrawal would only have created the worry of an overnight watch for fleeing defenders. Cohen also doubted that the legionaries could have failed to hear the screams and see the fires in Josephus' account, so as to be so dumbfounded the next morning.[165]

I have suggested that withdrawal to allow the "huge volume of fire" (*War* 7.315–19) in the casemate to burn through was not so strange, especially as night was falling at the end of a long day's work. It was normal. But Cohen's methodical doubt is entirely appropriate.

He agreed with Feldman, nevertheless, that Josephus' freedom must have been constrained by Silva's presence in Rome. He tried to strengthen this observation with the argument that *War* 7 appeared after Silva's consulship in 81.[166] But he also pointed out, importantly, that Silva's criterion would not have been factual accuracy. As long as the Roman commander looked good, the Silva base was covered. This insight allowed Cohen to conjecture that those on Masada had a *variety* of responses to the (assumed) Roman breach and charge onto the summit. *Some* probably burned their possessions and killed their families and themselves. That action by a few would be enough to explain Josephus' story. Others would have fought to the death, however, and still others would have tried to hide out in caves. Cohen adds that Silva himself could not have known what had transpired before he entered the summit. He could only have made deductions from what he found there. Writing in Rome, Josephus was free to work up his source material into a dramatic story, as long as he made Silva appear diligent and efficient. By turning to stock motifs of mass suicide under siege from classical historiography, however, Josephus *accidentally* infused the story of the *sicarii* with a sense of nobility.[167] I have offered aforementioned reasons for doubting this last point.

---

[164] Cohen reckoned (1982: 394) that the twenty-five skeletons reported by Yadin in the cave on the southern cliff must have gone there alive, against Yadin's own proposal that Roman soldiers tossed them in there. Since Cohen wrote, the skeletons have become true bones of contention. J. Zias (1998: 64) has argued that 220 bones were found, far too few for twenty-five persons (a human having 206 bones); that one skeleton was found nearly intact in a burial pose, whereas the other bones are cracked and likely brought in by wild animals; and that the presence of pig bones makes it highly unlikely that they were even Judaeans. These might be the remains of Roman soldiers. A curious addendum to *Masada IV* (1994) on "The Human Skeletal Remains from the Northern [sic] Cave at Masada – A Second Look" (366–67) is a confusing stew. This committee-written effort adds ominously that the pig bones show "the desecration of Jewish skeletal remains by antagonistic and unsympathetic forces," contradicting Zias (one of its authors) four years later. For later perspectives on the controversy, see Ben-Tor 2009: 299–303.

[165] Cohen 1982: 395–97.   [166] Cohen 1982: 399–401. See Chapter 2 for critique.

[167] Cohen 1982: 404–405.

Two questions that Josephus does not explicitly raise and that do not appear in scholarship, although they are important for any reconstruction, are whether Silva attempted to take the summit by any path other than the ramp and whether he offered terms of surrender. We might guess at affirmative answers to both.

As for offers of surrender, it seems that all his predecessors preferred peaceful submission. In the case of Masada, Josephus has Eleazar say (7.383):

> We, thinking highly of our courage [or manliness], revolted from the Romans and did not respond *even when, now at the last, they were urging us to a course of safety* [or salvation].

What could this mean? Although it has been taken to refer to Titus' appeals outside Jerusalem (e.g., 6.350–51),[168] Eleazar was not present there. His language ("*now at the last*") suggests rather that Silva has offered – or Josephus imagines that he would have offered – terms. Eleazar will not oblige the Roman because he does not trust him, as Josephus did not trust Vespasian's invitations and most characters are rightly suspicious of such offers. Eleazar envisions only *horrors* awaiting those who "fall into Roman hands," making no distinction between deliberate surrender and being taken prisoner in combat: "Who would not pity the mass of those who have fallen into Roman hands? Who would not rush to his death before suffering the same things as those people?" For all alike he conjures up grisly scenes of torture on the rack, prisoners half-eaten by animals and left alive for a second round, and victims longing for death but unable to find it (7.372–73; cf. 324, 334).

Of course many Judaeans *had* surrendered without facing such horrors, some even after fighting. Josephus is a clear example, and we noted that the surviving women and children in his story surrender without incident. Josephus' literary audience were entitled to wonder whether Eleazar's imaginings about Roman mistreatment were not the product of a fevered mind trapped in its alternative reality.

We have reason to guess that Silva offered terms of surrender, as was usual in cases of non-resisting populations, if only to simplify his own work – and irrespective of what he planned to do with those who surrendered.

The possibility that Silva attempted to seize the summit by means other than the main ramp links up with the possibility that he never completed the ramp itself. Arubas and Goldfus do not speculate about why he stopped, other than to observe that "the siege apparatus had already fulfilled its purpose and the work on the construction of the ramp ceased. . . ."[169] That would make sense, but *how* had the siege fulfilled its purpose? If they are correct, something must

---

[168] So Thackeray, ad loc. (Loeb).

[169] Arubas and Goldfus 2010, quotation p. 30. I am grateful to the authors for letting me see an advance copy and draft translation.

have happened, on the summit or on the Roman side or both, to change the situation. There are at least two kinds of possibilities in each location.

1. Silva may have used other means of access to the summit, introducing soldiers by stealth and killing or capturing Eleazar. Recall that Masada's current residents were there because their fighters had seized the site from a military garrison, in an operation Josephus describes as "stealth" (2.408). If irregular fighters could take the summit from professional soldiers by stealth, then surely a massed professional army with specialist units could take it from a group of families in the same way. The large force camped to the east (Camps A, B, and C) implies that Silva carefully monitored the Snake Path and that he would have looked for ways to exploit it. Recall that Gamala reportedly fell when three soldiers of the Fifteenth undermined a tower under cover of darkness (*War* 4.62–69) and that two dozen men of the Fifth made a decisive night-time assault on the Antonia (6.68–80). Why would Silva not send a squad to Masada's summit during the night via one of the alternative routes? If such a team did enter the fortress and ingloriously murder sleeping families, he might have preferred Josephus' version.

2. If Eleazar saw the end drawing closer daily, with no possibility of safe escape or surrender, and if he were convinced that the residents' best option *was* to take their own lives, that should have dawned on him long before the night of 14 Nisan. He could not have calibrated the timing so finely, for he could not have known how or when the end would come from the Roman side. Why wait until the *very last minute* and risk the very capture and torture of families that supposedly motivated self-immolation? It is conceivable that Silva halted construction of the ramp because the Judaeans, or at least Eleazar and other leaders, had killed themselves at some earlier point. Josephus' version would give Silva a more satisfyingly dramatic finish.

These options assume that Eleazar and his group had ruled out surrender or fighting. If they did not, two other kinds of options come into view.

3. Perhaps, like those in the Jordan Grove and the foreigners at Machaerus (cf. Saipan, Sobibor, and Treblinka), once the residents of Masada saw the legionaries in vast numbers all around, they saw their best chance in a coordinated charge in all directions, the men using whatever weapons they could fashion and the women doing their best to shelter the children, in the desperate hope that *some* would reach safety. Most would have been captured and some killed, even if a few found temporary safety in caves. If anything like this happened, Silva might have preferred Josephus' version, in which he plays a dutiful, vigorous, and humane commander.

4. The very simplest hypothesis, given the likelihood that Silva offered terms, is that Masada's inhabitants accepted his appeal and surrendered. That would explain why he halted construction of the ramp – for much the same reason as Bassus stopped work at Machaerus. How could we then explain Josephus' account? What if the Judaeans accepted his terms and came down the Snake Path or ladders thrown up from ramp to summit, the women clutching children and the men

terrified, and Silva or some of his soldiers violated the pledge of safety? These things happen almost routinely in Josephus' story, the fear of insincerity is ubiquitous.[170] Every large military conflict, certainly the world wars, witnessed many episodes of surrendering prisoners being killed (Chapter 3).[171] Orders to ignore pledges of safety can come from senior commanders, but often they result from spontaneous decisions or impulsive behaviour among subalterns and ordinary soldiers. Even if Silva did not order it, but soldiers disobeyed his orders (cf. under Titus), the outcome might have seemed inglorious for Silva: He had either ordered a massacre of women and children or been unable to stop one. Either way, Josephus' account, painted in classical siege-story hues, might have been altogether more satisfactory.

These are only a few possibilities. Many others and many combinations are possible. My purpose has been to think through the evidence and try to explain it in plausible ways. It will inevitably be objected, "But there is no evidence!" Quite right. But where *would we* find evidence of such events? Josephus' wonderful drama is demonstrably erroneous in its testable claims. His description of the siege ramp is far from *any* possible reality. The speeches that dominate the account are his historically implausible creations. And his description of Masada's final moments is as geometrically schematic as the siege ramp and platform. *Each* man kills his wife and children; ten men kill the others; one kills the nine and then himself. Our task as historians is to ask our questions, interpret the evidence, and try to explain it in economical ways.

Finally, could there be hidden evidence of mass self-destruction at Masada in Pliny the Elder? I opened Chapter 1 with a passage from Pliny on Judaea's balsam tree (*Nat.* 12.111–13): "The Judaeans vented their rage on it *just as they did on their own lives.*" Gichon proposed that this remark "makes the best sense if we assume that Pliny was reminded of the Masada mass suicide, when commenting on the Zealots (sic) practicing in the balsamum plantations 'scorched earth' policy, because he knew that those plantations were near Masada."[172] This explanation is possible, but Pliny's language might more simply reflect the Roman sentiment, in a work dedicated to Jerusalem's conqueror Titus, that Judaeans must have been bent on self-annihilation in general when – as everyone in Rome thought – they had audaciously revolted against Rome.[173]

CONCLUSIONS

The desert retreats of Herodium, Machaerus, the Jordan Grove, and Masada caused the Roman governors of the new Province of Judaea no great unease.

---

[170] *War* 2.54, 524; 6.350–51; *Ant.* 20.160–61; *Life* 216, 246–47, 294–302. On the garrison: *War* 2.430–56 and Chapter 4.

[171] Burleigh 2010: 360–93.   [172] Gichon 2000: 542 n. 11.

[173] So Murphy 2004: 113–21, 127.

They waited until the war was long over, their troops were well rested, and the second postwar governor was in office before moving against any of them. These moves appear to have had more to do with the tasks of governing than urgent military necessity.

Both Machaerus and Masada were mainly inhabited by families at this point, the potential fighters among them being too few to be of concern to Roman officials. They were bandit societies in the Roman sense of being autonomous outlaw groups that, in the case of Masada, violently imposed on others. But the provincial legates' long delay and the high percentage of women and children present in the sites suggest that the Romans' concern was to recover their fortresses with as little trouble as possible. Other benefits of such operations were related to keeping the province's military fit, trained, and confident. They would methodically force the occupying families to leave, practising all manner of siege warfare as needed.

For Judaeans, these old royal properties were places of refuge, capable of providing their families with food, water, and security. Their promise lay in their distance from centres of violence, especially the Jerusalem area. Machaerus might have attracted more men without wives and children, and those who took to the Jordan Grove may have been virtually all male. At Masada, most residents were women and children, the men supporting their families with periodic raids on nearby settlements. We see no evidence of a resolve to fight Romans at these sites; anyone wishing to do so would have had to go elsewhere. Having lived on the summit for many years, the residents presumably hoped they could remain indefinitely. But Rome eventually needed the fortresses back.

Whatever happened at the end, which we cannot know, is easier to conceive of in the ordinary terms of fear, pride, and miscommunication between people of very different culture than by resort to extraordinary visions or feats of heroism. And that is all the evidence requires. It seems most likely, for example, that in an expedition he hoped would be quick at Masada in the spring of 74, Silva offered terms of surrender to Masada's families and these were accepted for lack of alternative – although some residents may have killed themselves out of abject fear. That is why he stopped work, as it seems, on the ramp. But something went amiss in communication, as it so often did. Whatever embarrassment resulted would not need to be recorded for posterity. For Josephus, it was enough that the tragedy of these families, under the leadership of a bandit refugee from Jerusalem, had ended badly. Giving these people more political intentionality than their desert refuge merited, he elevated their story to become part of his great literary production. Flooding it with classical themes and oratory, he made it a fitting end-piece for his long meditation on political freedom in Judaea, radical programmes that ended only in death.

CONCLUSIONS

It is time to review our main results. Since I have emphasized the importance of thinking about historical method, I first summarize the method and then the substantive conclusions it has produced.

METHOD

While writing these chapters I have imagined a critical voice objecting: "Your prattling about historical method doesn't make any difference, does it? You have cited passages from Josephus and material remains in support of your reconstruction, choosing your favourites and ignoring others, just as everyone else does!" In case my readers have heard the same voice, or perhaps they own it, I would like to explain in light of the foregoing chapters. A metaphor may help.

We usually approach Josephus as we would a house made of brick and stone. We can see the materials from which the house is constructed. If we are interested in some small part of that structure – in Pontius Pilate, the upper priesthood, the causes of the war – we look at what Josephus has done with that part and suspect that we could do better. In building his house, we believe, he had a skewed perspective and/or unimaginative vision: fealty to the Flavians or some pathetic effort to exculpate his kind from war guilt. But no one doubts that he used excellent materials, and they don't make them like that any more! So our best bet is to dismantle his house and salvage those materials for our building. We can identify good material through a combination of intuition and educated guesswork about its provenance: Is this a brick that he himself made ad hoc, a solid older one, or a piece of excellent stone? To help us decide, we use the principle that whatever does not seem to fit his building design is likely older and not made by him. Even better, not too far from Josephus' house are piles of loose bricks – fragmentary material remains – that are wonderful for us because they do not belong to any existing structure. They are free for us to use along with the best bits from Josephus as we build a more robust structure.

Having stretched the metaphor to breaking point, I shall leave it there. My implicit criticism is directed at all of us, myself included. When we have become curious about the human past we have tended to simplify the task by looking for usable or reliable bits, facts or "givens" with which we can confidently build. We have seen in every chapter – on the Flavian triumph, Josephus' *War*, the causes of the real war, Cestius' expedition through Judaea, Vespasian's campaign in Galilee, Titus and Jerusalem, or the inhabitants of Masada – the tendency to consult Josephus' account, remove the blocks that seem made only for his final construction, and build with the others.

There are at least two problems with this, however. First, it forecloses the nearly infinite possibilities of the real lives once lived. If we focus on making something of the existing material, for example, we are more likely to ask why Cestius really abandoned Jerusalem *rather* than inquiring into the man's context, position, and aims. We are more likely to debate whether Josephus' or Sulpicius' description of Titus' war-council is *the reliable one* for us to build with, rather than asking more open-endedly how Titus came to destroy Jerusalem's temple and imagining any number of possibilities.

Second, by treating material survivals or passages from Josephus as reusable stones, we misunderstand what we are looking at. When he wrote *War*, Josephus produced something much more like a modern film. A long and sometimes boring film by modern standards, perhaps, but a visual masterpiece by ancient standards, intended for dramatic visualization. It was thus the ancient equivalent of film: an artistic creation to entertain and inform sometimes live audiences by vividly recreating scenes of high drama, political intrigue, and bloodshed. The intricately crafted narrative is carefully proportioned with incisive speeches and diverting portraits of landscapes or of irenic philosophers. Our producer, writer, director, and leading man created the story to convey urgent truths about what had recently happened in Judaea and its causes. But the truths in questions were chiefly moral. They concerned character, political wisdom, battling demagoguery in the *polis*, and the purity and pollution of sacred areas. He expected his creation to be judged as a balanced unity by the criteria of moral insight and aesthetics. His audiences were not in a position to re-examine his use of evidence and he had no interest in proving mere facts.

The historical method for which I have argued is not my creation. As far as I know it is simply history, as usually practised in fields of the ancient past that have no Josephus to beguile us, or such spectacular archaeological finds to dazzle us. In those fields it may be more obvious that it is up to the historian to formulate problems, open investigations, and test hypotheses. That is what I have tried to do here.

I have tried, in other words, to distinguish between the *interpretation* of whatever has survived, which is in front of our eyes, and our *imagining* of the lost past that produced these remains. Instead of breaking off some bits from a text such as Josephus' *War* and tossing away the rest, I have argued that the whole creation needs explaining. The same holds for the five years of silver coinage from wartime Jerusalem or any other relevant survival.

Readers uncomfortable with the insubstantial feel of the film metaphor might prefer another. Historians are scientists, *if* science can be understood to mean the methodical pursuit of knowledge (*scientia, Wissenschaft*). The differences between history and other sciences lie not in our critical and questioning disposition, which is common to all, nor in the need for imagin-ation, but in what we are attempting to know. In our case this is human thought and action in the past. The nature of our evidence is different from that of the natural sciences, and this must affect the confidence of our results. But we are all diagnosticians, looking at symptoms – or evidence – and trying to explain what created the things we can directly study. Like physicians, we seek first the most commonly attested kinds of causes in shared human experi-ence, moving to the rare and extraordinary only if it is required.

Scholars invested in the study of Roman Judaea have constructed impressive paradigms of apocalypticism, messianism, prophecy, anti-imperialism, economic oppression, and so on. We tend to assimilate the evidence to these paradigms. Without excluding any of these causes, I have tried to investigate crucial moments in the war and the evidence for them by looking *first* for the simplest, or most analogically complete, explanations. Although it is *possible* that Cestius uniquely reached the legateship of Syria as a bumbler, we should prefer to explain the evidence, direct and circumstantial, in more contextually familiar and human ways. Although it is possible that Simon bar Giora emerged from beneath the destroyed temple wearing purple to reveal his inner messianic consciousness, he might have been trying his best to escape. Although Judaea may have been under a spell of unique anti-Roman zealotry for generations, with people calling themselves the Fourth Philosophy and Latin *sicarii* all over the place, less nervous-making explanations of the surviving evidence are possible.

MANUFACTURED ENEMIES

One example of a common human phenomenon that is generally overlooked in the rush to high-level explanations I have inelegantly called the *manufacture of enemies*. I use this phrase to describe Judaeans and others who had no reason in normal life to hate Romans, but suddenly appear willing to risk their lives fighting them. Jerusalem's residents benefitted from uniquely close relations with Rome and protested vigorously when their status as Rome's agents was about to end in A.D. 6. But when the legions under Cestius, Vespasian, and Titus arrived sixty years later they found many Judaeans locked up in the capital and some willing to fight to the death. Given that virtually all the towns of southern Syria and their populations instantly submitted and even welcomed Roman and royal-Agrippan forces, why did a few people in Galilee and more in Jerusalem become enemies to the death? By manufactured enemies, I am suggesting four related situations.

First, "to the person carrying a loaded gun, everything looks like a target," the saying goes. When an army is inserted among a foreign population with alien customs, dress, and language, and the soldiers are told that this population is their potential enemy, they will tend to treat them with fear, suspicion, and aggression. For all they know, elements of the populace are watching for a chance to kill them. Soldiers will stay in the security of their camp as far as possible and close to the unit. They are likely to treat any suspicious-looking activity, even if it is fear-driven (such as rapid flight), as oppositional. Because their mission requires them to dominate the field absolutely, they will err on the side of strength and intimidation.

Josephus' account of Peraea, whatever lay behind it in reality, illustrates the phenomenon clearly. When Vespasian garrisons the welcoming capital, villagers who formerly had no concern with Rome and were minding their own business flee in a panic ahead of this powerful and alien army in their world. They rush the Jordan River because of frightful rumours about what the Romans' arrival might mean, apparently hoping to reach Jerusalem for temporary safety in numbers. But because they flee, they look like enemies and are pursued, trapped, and killed. And their fears may have been justified, given the fate of Gabara and Iotapata among other places in the north.

Second, elements of the invaded population will become objectively militant, or "radicalized," *as a direct consequence* of the army's arrival. The presence of Cestius' or the Flavians' legions and cavalry in the south was not like that of legions permanently stationed in northern Syria or outside Alexandria. In those places, although bad things could and did happen, legionaries were a familiar sight and part of the social fabric, taking informal spouses and raising families, sometimes helping to solve local disputes. An army deployed on a war footing, in sharp contrast, had to show physical and psychological dominance. They brought the ancient version of shock and awe: burning, destruction, and pillaging, often enough with rape and torture. Armies are trained to kill people and break things, and when located fearfully among a foreign population that is what they tend to do. Even with a highly restrained and disciplined force, it does not take many "bad apple" incidents for a terrified population to magnify or generalize the threat.

Some segment of the occupied population, at any rate, will have suffered tangible loss: injury to themselves and loved ones, night-time raids, loss and occupation of property, sexual violation, humiliation generally. Some will therefore pledge themselves to oppose the occupiers, even to death. We see this already in the responses to Florus' auxiliary. Many or most Judaeans may have viewed that grievance as a separate issue from Jerusalem's relations with Rome, as King Agrippa and the legate Cestius apparently did, but the phenomenon intensifies with Cestius' expedition. Daring anti-Roman militants now appear from nowhere to ambush the column, presumably from a strong sense of grievance and hatred. These actions first occur immediately after Cestius' force has destroyed Galilean villages and massacred putative thousands of men, women, and children. Simon bar Giora, from a newly Judaean family, dares to attack Cestius' trailing baggage train as his expedition heads toward Jerusalem. It seems easiest to suppose that his fighters were responding to the immediately preceding outrages.

Third, although we tend to be cynical about categories of honour and shame in public discourse, we should not discount the possibility that some who persisted in opposing Rome acted from a social-moral code that is no longer obvious to us. The high priest Jesus, as Josephus fancied it, expressed ideas worth pondering (*War* 4.49–50):

> It is not easy now to be reconciled with the Romans *even if we wanted that*, given that the [rapid] subjection of Galilee has *made them contemptuous*. Anyway, to court them when they are now so close by would bring on us a *shame more grievous than death*. Look, to speak for myself, I certainly might have preferred peace to death. But once I had embarked on war and entered the fray, *[I prefer] death with reputation intact* to living as a captive.

Regardless of whether Jesus said any such thing, these were thinkable thoughts. The values are not ours, but we can understand them. If Jerusalem had welcomed the Flavians when they first arrived in Ptolemais – along with Sepphoris, the Decapolis, Tiberias, and many others – that would have been honourable, because this option was freely chosen and preserved a modicum of self-respect. But to surrender *now*, when our *inability* to resist has been fully exposed in Galilee, and we have waited until they are on our doorstep, would amount to disgraceful begging. So we are trapped, and the only honourable course left is to fight.

Finally, much of an occupied population will be afraid to surrender, even if they are repeatedly invited to do so with generous assurances given. They will be reluctant for sensible reasons (Chapters 3 and 6). It *is* a fearful prospect to approach massed groups of heavily armed men. When foreign soldiers take over towns and villages, why would families, women, and children trust them? And *to whom* should they surrender if they wish to do so safely, especially women with children whose male guardians are not present? If the resident population have heard about brutality elsewhere, what basis do they have for confidence? Women run the serious risk of rape. If a young man has thrown a stone or fled to a fortress, or his family members have, he might see no option but fighting, flight, or suicide. But all of these new and desperate choices have become real only *because* the foreign army is suddenly present.

The only mode of surrender likely to be safe is the representation of a *polis* by its leading figures on behalf of all citizens and residents of the *chōra*. This takes forethought, however. It requires a courageous face-to-face meeting with the Roman side, preferably with high-ranking Judaean mediators such as Agrippa II at Ptolemais. The commander can then cooperate with the *polis* leaders to provide a garrison instructed to be careful of the citizens' well-being, although even this by no means rules out individual incidents.

These various kinds of manufactured enemies, which are well attested in human conflict and suggested by Josephus' occasional remarks, are likely to have played a significant role in reactions to each successive Roman incursion, from Cestius and Vespasian through to Bassus and Silva. Even or especially such central figures as John, Simon, and Eleazar ben Yair – as Eleazar stresses in his final speech – could not see surrender with their families as a viable option, even if it was in reality. To the extent that these ordinary human considerations adequately explain events, higher-order hypotheses about ingrained and ideological anti-Romanism become unnecessary.

WHAT HAPPENED? AN ECONOMICAL RECONSTRUCTION

Our main concern has been to investigate, and we have little ground for confidence in particulars, but I owe the reader a summary of the overall picture that our investigations have yielded. What follows is not a *result* that I have shown to have happened. It is an effort to imagine, as economically as possible in relation to evidence, the general causes and course of the Judaean-Roman War.

Judaea entered the Roman period as regional hegemon. It remained an integral part of Rome's province of Syria from Pompey to Vespasian (64/63 B.C.–A.D. 67/70), becoming an independent province only after the war although effectively from Vespasian's arrival. The century before Pompey had seen the small, landlocked, and vulnerable hinterland of Jerusalem expand its *chōra* with stunning success. A series of Hasmonean rulers leveraged Seleucid decline to dominate their environment both politically and culturally.

The surrounding populations reacted variously, in some cases acquiescing while dissenters fled, in others resisting and facing destruction. Most fatefully, the Hasmoneans razed the Samarian capital, the ancient temple on Mt. Gerizim, and some proud cities of the Decapolis. Ascalon alone remained defiant and outside the Hasmonean orbit. This expansion created powerful resentments, and Pompey was greeted as a liberator when, in the name of Rome, he pruned Judaea's reach to nearly pre-Hasmonean (post-Exilic) size, restoring the affected populations with their *polis* infrastructures.

Within a couple of decades, the political marvel that was Herod's family had risen to prominence. Successive Roman leaders found in them their best option for a broker in the cultural mosaic of southern Syria. Herod was handed an even larger kingdom than the Hasmoneans had won by conquest, now as a Rome-sponsored monarch in Jerusalem. His outlook and operational mode were the antithesis of Hasmonean precedents in many ways. He not only made no attempt to Judaize the neighbours; he ostentatiously fostered their distinctive institutions, cultures, and cults. He showed particular love to Samaria and Idumaea, the large zones north and south of Judaea. Even his benign form of rule from Jerusalem generated resentment from within and without, although Jerusalem's prosperity and political success over a third of a century set an unavoidable standard.

On Herod's death, in spite of appeals from both disgruntled neighbours and Jerusalem's sidelined aristocracy, Augustus preferred to keep trying Judaean monarchy as his governing instrument in southern Syria. Honouring his friend's will, he took a gamble and assigned Herod's three young sons portions of the kingdom. With Philip and Antipas in the north, the gamble paid off in even longer periods of tranquillity. Alas, the one failure was in the crucial heartland, where Archelaus managed only a decade before Augustus had to accept the pleas of Samarian and Jerusalem-priestly elites.

His removal of Archelaus brought a fateful shift in Jerusalem's position. The only remaining element of Herod's multi-ethnic army, now to become the auxiliary force based in Caesarea under an equestrian official, was basically Samarian. If Samarian soldiers and leaders could influence their prefect, they could hope to restore their long-injured pride when opportunities arose. The Judaean populace, alive to the dangers in this loss of regional primacy, responded with a mass protest in A.D. 6. The high priest who had led the call for change, Joazar, calmed things long enough to see Jerusalem's integration into Syria, but popular fears had been set in motion. The temple authorities set up a guard and commandant, because they did not trust the auxiliary garrison tasked with maintaining order in the fortress next to the temple. Struggles with this garrison involved numerous issues, such as the care of the high priest's garments. Jerusalem's regional status remained the central question during the next six decades.

Emperors and their legates in Syria apparently viewed the shift to Caesarea as ad hoc and reversible, if a suitable Herodian monarch could be found. Why they did not move Philip or Antipas to Jerusalem we do not know. But descendants of Herod continued to live in Rome, with better imperial access than any other elites from the area we know about. Until a suitable monarch could be nurtured, however, everything depended on the equestrian in Caesarea maintaining peace and protecting the newly vulnerable Jerusalem.

Samarians immediately tested the new situation (A.D. 7 or 8) in the bones incident, presumably with the complicity of the garrison. The first incumbent's removal (A.D. 9) may have been related to his failure there. Tiberius' man Pontius Pilate, however, seems to have been careful about protecting Jerusalem, and remained in place a long time.[1] He built or extended an aqueduct for Jerusalem and efficiently handled regional troublemakers in collaboration with the city elite. Whether he was a nice man we do not know, but his coins and behaviour seem designed not to offend Judaean law and custom. Pilate was eventually removed in 37 because of *Samarian* complaints about routine brutality toward them. The legate L. Vitellius, who sent him packing, was evidently solicitous of Jerusalem, visiting regularly at Passover and dispensing favours in recognition of warm loyalty.

After Herod's grandson Agrippa had played an extraordinary role in Claudius' accession (A.D. 41), the new emperor gave him a restored monarchy in Jerusalem. This kingdom rivalled his grandfather's, and he had a teenage son in waiting to succeed him. Although a monarchy in Jerusalem was apparently preferred by Rome – combining trusted friendship, economy of investment, efficiency, and manageable tensions – this was bitterly disappointing for the neighbours, especially for Samarians and their auxiliary after a generation of freedom. They were now back under Jerusalem's thumb. When Agrippa died suddenly in 44, the celebrations of Samarians and auxiliary were exuberant. They had been freed not only from Agrippa I but, because his son was too young to succeed, from Jerusalem for the foreseeable future.

Claudius returned the region to the pre-Agrippa model. His first equestrian appointee to Caesarea was under strict orders to rein in the auxiliary; the second was a prominent Judaean from Alexandria. Claudius might well have been grooming Agrippa II for a renewed monarchy in Jerusalem. He gave the 20-year-old a small kingdom, which he began steadily to expand. Claudius' next appointment to Caesarea, Felix, was personally requested by the Judaean high priest. His relatively lengthy term might suggest that he was meant to be a caretaker until Agrippa II was ready, as might his marriage to Agrippa's sister Drusilla.

The equestrian governor before Felix was Judaea's nightmare, however, and a warning of things to come. Ventidius Cumanus (48–52) did not intervene when Samarian villagers and his auxiliary killed or harassed Judaeans. When he proved unable to protect them, some Judaeans turned to armed self-help, striking hard

---

[1] Agrippa (b. 11/10 B.C) was old enough to be tested by rule, but Tiberius perhaps thought that Pilate was a safe enough pair of hands to leave in place as long as possible, while there may have been questions about the young royal's character.

at nearby Samarian villages. Seeing the escalation, Cumanus finally intervened – but against Judaeans only. If the Judaeans had gone as far as killing auxiliary soldiers, the "Judaean-Roman War" could have begun then. What prevented the explosion in 51/52 was the involvement of the legate and emperor. The former sent his equestrian subordinate to give an account to Claudius, who harshly punished the Samarians, the auxiliary, and the equestrian.

There is no need to deny *some* measure of anti-Roman sentiment among Judaeans ever since 63 B.C., although it has left few if any traces. And one could presumably have found resentment among Samarians, Ascalonites, Gadarenes, Scythopolitans, and Nabataeans. But such grumbling does not usually start wars against great powers. The Judaean-Roman conflict broke out, I have argued, not from anti-Roman ideas or dreams among the uniquely favoured Judaean population, but from the sort of thing that more commonly drives nations to arms: injury, threats of more injury, perceived helplessness, the closure of avenues of redress, and ultimately the concern for survival.

The teenaged Nero's early reign from A.D. 54 at first changed little in southern Syria. He confirmed Felix while adding choice Judaean cities on Lake Kinneret to Agrippa II's kingdom. But once he reached maturity around 59/60 and shed his overseers by various means, Nero took a much-discussed turn. He became increasingly obsessed with art and revenue, the need for the latter exacerbated as his government weakened through fire, fear, and intrigue. In the early 60s he sent Lucceius Albinus and then Gessius Florus with a mandate to transfer as much money as possible to the imperial treasury.

Florus found an auxiliary force more than willing to assist, with the impunity granted as agents of the emperor. So began a rapid series of assaults, insults, and atrocities in Jerusalem. The political climate had changed radically in a few years, and this affected the position of the legate in Syria, who was responsible for Jerusalem. Cestius Gallus made every effort to maintain his close and productive partnership with Judaean elites, especially the royal siblings. But he was now helpless against Nero's designs and agents. The legate was stymied, while Agrippa II and Berenice had lost their standing with this bold young emperor.

In spite of appeals from leaders for calm and patience, many Judaeans felt that again they had no alternative to armed self-help. They could not wait and tolerate plunder of the temple, robbery, and even murder at the hands of Florus' goons. Florus tried to sell Cestius on the notion that a revolt was brewing, but Cestius knew better and delayed military intervention.

Caesarea was a flashpoint. The regional seat of Roman culture and administration, home of the auxiliary (in the absence of a Jerusalem monarchy), and centre of imperial cult, its prosperous Judaean minority felt increasingly vulnerable amidst the aggressive changes after Agrippa's death, Cumanus' indifference, and now Florus. This emperor was still only in his twenties and might rule for decades. His next equestrian agent might be no improvement. If Nero was not likely to place Agrippa II on Jerusalem's throne and the intolerable situation had to continue indefinitely, the Judaean elite would use every channel to have Caesarea recognized as a Judaean city. That would at least help to keep the prefect and auxiliary based there respectful of Judaean law and tradition. Nero's answer was a clear *No*. Departing from his predecessors in many well-known ways, he reportedly held the Judaeans in contempt, not believing that they should be so important in the region. His decision on Caesarea was a signal that he did not care about Judaean claims or their regional plight in relation to the auxiliary. Because the legate and the royals were unable to intervene effectively, Judaeans again saw no recourse but to protect themselves. In Jerusalem, a younger circle of priests around the temple commandant reached a turning point. They would protect the temple, symbolically at least, by cutting it off from all foreign access. This was against the counsel of senior priests and Pharisees, who understood the grievance well enough and were suffering more than most as targets, but thought such a move would worsen their image and situation.

Growing sentiment against Florus and the auxiliary began to overwhelm such caution. It was practically dangerous for members of the elite to seem less than resolute in standing up for the city and people. When Agrippa stonewalled against a popular demand for on an embassy to Nero (en route to Greece) – to demand Florus' removal and *show that* Jerusalem was *not in revolt against Rome* – the king was driven from the city. Groups began to arm themselves against all eventualities, immediately against the auxiliary.

Banished Agrippa immediately reported this dangerous turn to Cestius. From about the end of July 66, king and legate began planning a major legionary intervention to sideline the auxiliary, reassure non-Judaeans that Rome was in control, assert their monopoly of armed force, and punish any who had taken up arms. They knew that the auxiliary and Florus were the problem, but a subject population could under no circumstances use violence against a Roman force. For the sake of regional stability and for Nero's eyes, Cestius would have to make a show of punishing culprits, while quietly trying to restore the ruling consensus with Jerusalem's and other elites.

Cestius now had to thread several needles, showing a strong hand while creating peace. The danger of confusing his audiences and signals was great. Then word reached him of the garrison massacre in Jerusalem, the slaughter in Caesarea, and Judaean retaliations for the latter. Cestius had to intensify the punitive side of the expedition, allowing his legionaries to burn and destroy (mostly emptied) Judaean villages. But Sepphoris welcomed his garrison and assisted him in identifying militants. His intimidating measures became more severe as he moved southward, climaxing in the destruction of Joppa. But still he and Agrippa expected to be welcomed in Jerusalem.

By the time Cestius turned inland toward Jerusalem, however, he had manufactured enough enemies that groups of Judaean fighters were willing to assault his baggage train. This aggression came as a shock. There was no point turning back now, however. Cestius and Agrippa still hoped to be welcomed eagerly by Jerusalem's relieved elite. Their exclusion from the city seemed incredible. When Cestius realized that he would not be admitted, now in mid-October and with no provisions for a long stay, he turned back for Antioch. Evacuating the now unfriendly Judaean hills in haste, however, he suffered a costly ambush in the notorious pass at Beit-Horon.

Once back in Antioch, humiliated and disgraced, Cestius immediately began planning a different kind of visit in the spring to settle the Jerusalem issue once and for all. He was sure that he retained the trust of the Jerusalem elite, mediated via Agrippa. At Sepphoris' request, he sent them a large garrison in anticipation, also a cavalry force to Ptolemais to monitor Galilee. Jerusalem's leaders for their part, whatever their personal wishes, knew that harsh retaliation for Beit-Horon and the garrison slaughter were a matter of time. Fierce debates erupted about the best way forward. But in the meantime, Nero had lost faith in Cestius and dispatched the nonthreatening but seasoned Vespasian. Agrippa II would continue as his key local advisor.

As soon as Vespasian arrived in Syria (early in 67), nearly the entire region welcomed him and Agrippa II, declaring their peaceful intentions. Delegates came from Judaean Sepphoris on behalf of Galilee, Tiberias among the king's dependencies, the Decapolis cities, Samaria, and the coastal towns. Even before Titus had arrived with his legion, his father enjoyed nearly complete territorial control. Any potential regional *war* was largely over in principle at this point. As his army ranged undisturbed across Galilee, Samaria, and the coastal plain to Caesarea, many or most villagers deserted their homes in droves from fear. Many were afraid to risk falling into the legionaries' hands. Vespasian allowed his army a measure of display violence, now to include demonstrable vengeance for Cestius' losses. Judaean land and property suffered terribly, but because people had time to flee – to Sepphoris, King Agrippa's territories beyond Vespasian's purview, or points farther east – relatively few lives were lost.

Before Vespasian reached Galilee, his commander in the Sepphoris garrison had created a problem at Iotapata. He reported these "hostiles" to Vespasian, and Iotapata was marked for punishment. Josephus, who had fled far away to the safety of Agrippa's Tiberias, returned to the imperilled town. He seems to have hoped to negotiate terms, but found himself trapped there in the town's defence. He held out until the town fell, before being captured in circumstances that would haunt his legacy.

Aside from the aberration of Iotapata, Galilee remained settled. The few empty towns assaulted by Roman forces were targets of opportunity, chosen to demonstrate control, intimidate the population, and exercise the forces. Immediately following Iotapata, Vespasian took a long celebratory break and rested his troops in the summer of 67. He seems to have intended that his army would remain in camp or billet through the winter, but his host Agrippa requested help against anti-royal activists in his cities of Tiberias and Taricheae.

Vespasian recalled his army and dealt with these cities in short order, without needing to besiege or destroy them. Agrippa's fortress town of Gamala, to which refugees had fled in a puzzling mix of circumstances, although the main issues there were between Agrippa and his subjects, was Vespasian's last favour for the king. This required some weeks. Meanwhile, Gischala had appeared on his radar. Young Titus, sent to receive its submission and apparently to arrest John, inadvertently allowed him to flee to Jerusalem.

As Vespasian moved south to Caesarea (winter 67/68), the pattern of preemptive submissions continued. The leaders of Peraea and Judaean towns offered submission, even as the villages again emptied from fear of the army. Jerusalemites of means also rushed to Vespasian. Their native leaders were seeking a safe way for the *polis* to submit, but their situation was complicated. Jerusalem had already become a haven for refugees, including some such as John who could not or would not surrender. The ruling elite could not simply capitulate, and they faced a serious dilemma. Along with the perils they faced in the city for any perception of betrayal, their reception by Vespasian was not a given. They had much explaining to do.

While the city leaders were making their plans, the arrival of more armed factions made their handwringing superfluous. An emerging coalition of Disciples (Zealots) appealed to Idumaeans, who had a complicated relationship with Jerusalem, to defend the temple. The Idumaeans answered the call and murdered the chief-priestly leaders. Along with the other newcomers they dramatically changed the city's profile. From A.D. 68 onward, Jerusalem was in the hands of factions, mainly from elsewhere, who could not easily turn back.

Vespasian's nearly immediate domination of southern Syria makes it difficult to accept either that a province of Judaea revolted or that the wartime coins reveal an independent rebel state from 66 to 70 (Chapters 4, 7). From the spring of 68 at the latest, only the walled city of Jerusalem and its agricultural hinterland were not under direct Roman control. Whatever notional independence a distressed Jerusalem now enjoyed could not be well captured by the phrase "free state." Jerusalem and its hinterland must have been in abject terror, not knowing what the Romans would do or when. Vespasian was in no hurry.

Roman commanders habitually sought the least risky path to their goals. In early 68 Vespasian showed off his domination by tightening his cordon around it, no doubt *hoping* for a quick capitulation but not risking resources. In June, with everything but the walled city itself in his hands, he returned to Caesarea to plan its capture. He had every reason to expect submission by that summer's end. Nero's death, however, forced him to suspend operations and await direction. The two years that followed before Titus' siege must have been a period of prolonged trauma for those in Jerusalem. Internal suffering led them eventually to welcome Simon, a daring man feared by both the earlier leaders and the Disciples. His entry created rigidly demarcated zones inside the city and even more serious conflict.

When Titus arrived outside Jerusalem in the spring of 70, in the company of Agrippa, Tiberius Alexander, Josephus, and many others, he again hoped for a rapid surrender. Some of those inside deserted, and he quickly took the northern wall. More deserted, but he could not persuade the militant leaders or much of the populace, trapped between rival psychological appeals. Titus tried every tactic he knew to sap their morale while encouraging defection. He had no fixed plan, except that he had to take Jerusalem. The militant leaders and their closest supporters had no hope of success, but were certain now that surrender was no option. In the end, the unyielding resistance of John, Simon, and the Idumaeans required him to destroy most of the city in phases. As his army moved finally through the temple courts toward the Lower and Upper City, the inner temple, which had been John's stronghold, went up in flames.

With Jerusalem's fall the war was over as far as the Flavians were concerned. Vespasian had always had one aim, the submission of Jerusalem with whatever punishment seemed necessary in the circumstances, but time was on his side. It only helped him to prolong and intensify the Judaeans' agony. Most of southern Syria and most Judaeans in the province wanted no part of a showdown with the legions, no matter how intense the grievances that had led them to act against Florus and Cestius. As a result, there was little fighting, even of a guerrilla kind – little in 67 and apparently none in 68 or 69 (Fig. 40). Jerusalem was the only real exception, and that is because the holy city had become the repository of hopes and fears among many varied groups and individuals who fled there – not so much the city's native population.

Jerusalem's fall was a godsend to the Flavians and a Roman Senate eager to please them and support a stable new government. A famous city destroyed and a province added to Rome's *imperium*, even with such artifice, could plausibly serve as the basis of a triumph and a strong new regime. Vespasian shrewdly declined the offer of a separate triumph so as to clothe himself in, or co-opt, his son's glory. Their message-men drooled at the possibilities: A fierce

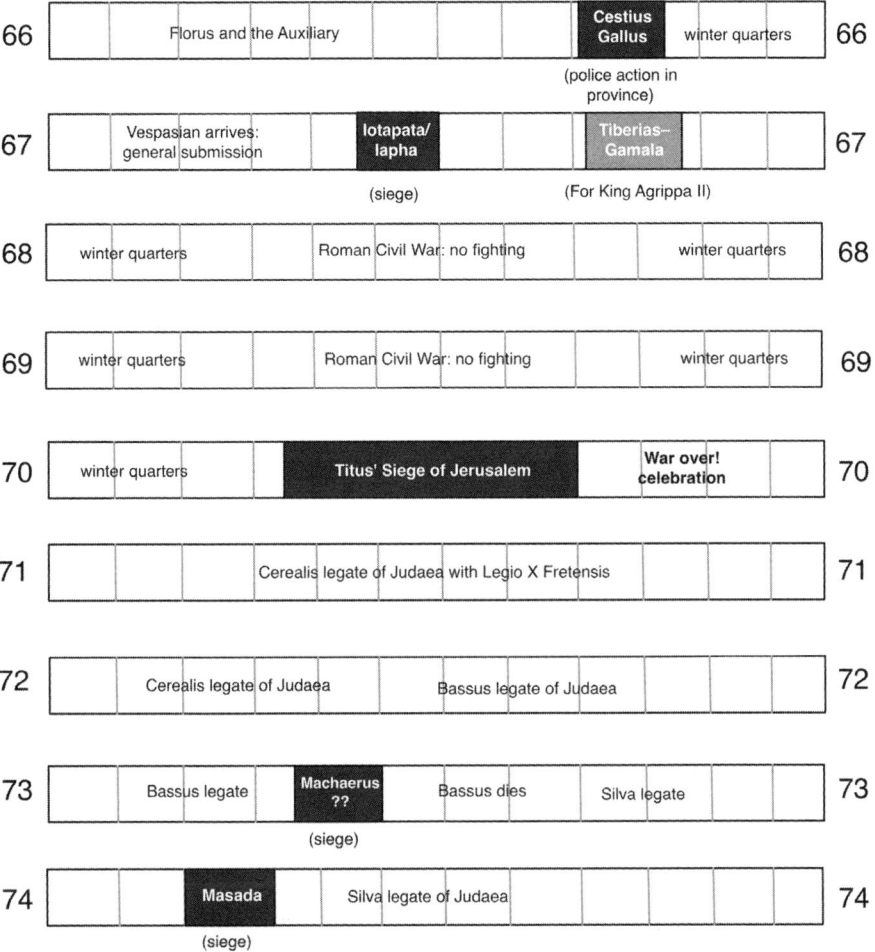

FIGURE 40. Chart showing episodes of known combat during the "Jewish-Roman War." Not
included: burning of empty villages, killing of the defenceless, or establishment of garrisons. Dark
shading indicates operations within the Flavians' mandate, lighter shading Flavian assistance to
King Agrippa II – with opposition to him in his territories.

tribe and strong city never before conquered had been taken by Titus! The
representations quickly lost all connection with reality. The eventual retaking
of Judaea's desert fortresses, where families had fled to *escape* encounters with
Rome's legions, magnified the tragic chasm between intentions and
consequences.

APPENDIX A

JOSEPHUS' DISTANCES IN *STADIA*

If we wanted to approach Josephus with the question "Is his work accurate?" his distances would be an obvious place to start. His distances have often been used to successfully identify sites: Josephus claims that A is 30 *stadia* (ca. 6 km) from B, but if a candidate for B is actually 37.5 *stadia* (ca. 7.5 km) from A, we look for a better option.[1] Here as always we need to understand the nature of our evidence before using it in historical reasoning.

Josephus nowhere explains his method or sources for indicating distance. His main unit of distance measurement is the *stadion*, and if we review all occurrences of numbered *stadia* (plural) in his works, some general patterns suggest themselves. The word appears 121 times in total, although in a few cases it refers to a *stadium* facility or to an undefined number ("many *stadia*" etc.). Below are all the passages that give numbered *stadia* as measurements. The figures down the left side are not ordinals. They are the numbers of *stadia* given by Josephus in the corresponding passages to the right.

1:	*Ant.* 15.415; *Life* 399
2:	*War* 2.189; 5.133, 134, 270; *Ant.* 7.225, 243
3:	*War* 3.245; 5.68; *Ant.* 20.95
4:	*Ant.* 9.225; 15.400; *Life* 64, 322
5:	*Ant.* 20.169; *Life* 398
6:	*War* 4.533; 5.70, 192
7:	*War* 2.528; 3.146; 5.68; 7.286; *Ant.* 19.340
10:	*Ant.* 5.20
20:	*War* 1.403, 425; 3.521; 4.107, 467, 659; *Ant.* 5.140; 7.34, 312; 10.114; 15.297; *Life* 118, 265, 395
30:	*War* 2.386, 551; 3.447, 521; 4.3, 44, 615; 5.51; 7.101, 217, 284; *Ant.* 5.139; 12.408; 19.6; *Life* 157, 281, 349
33:	*War* 5.159
40:	*War* 3.506; 5.508; *Ant.* 7.283; 8.303; *Life* 234
50:	*War* 2.516; *Ant.* 5.20; 13.175; *Apion* 1.197
60:	*War* 1.265, 419; 2.188, 291, 338; 4.3, 474; *Ant.* 4.112; 5.4; 14.359; 15.324; *Life* 115, 214, 349
70:	*War* 1.673; 4.467; *Ant.* 12.369
80:	*Ant.* 13.276; 17.199
90:	*War* 5.523; 6.5; *Ant.* 18.365

[1] E.g., Kokkinos 2010: 14. Kokkinos employs many arguments for relocating Senanbris and Taricheae but distance is one.

100:	*War* 2.188; 6.151, 375; *Ant.* 18.179; 20.113
120:	*War* 2.188; 3.510, 515; 4.456; 7.229; *Life* 349
140:	*War* 3.506
150/	*War* 4.474, 482; *Ant.* 13.390
160:	
180:	*War* 7.426
200:	*Ant.* 18.60
230:	*War* 4.456
300:	*War* 4.613; *Ant.* 9.7; 15.168
400:	*War* 2.175
520:	*War* 3.10
580:	*War* 4.482
600:	*War* 1.79; *Ant.* 13.312
2000:	*War* 4.610
3600:	*War* 4.610

From this inventory several patterns become clear. These are all the more impressive because the references are taken from all over Josephus' corpus. They therefore reflect his habits of thinking and writing, rather than a conscious device used in a single context. The patterns are significant because in reality, of course, the distance between any two points, A and B, will fall unpredictably along a continuum. If some sites are 1, 2, 3, 4, 5, 6, or 7 *stadia* from each other, just as Josephus claims, then others should be 13, 31, 47, 148, and 212 *stadia* apart. But that is not what we find. Once he gets close to 10 *stadia*, he stops trying to be so specific.

Here are some patterns.

(1)   All single digits from 1 to 7 are well represented, but then nothing until 10. This suggests that once the figure was near 10, 10 was close enough.

(2)   The finer and smaller measurements mainly relate to distances in the vicinity of Jerusalem or in Lower Galilee, the two scenes that Josephus would have known intimately from daily walking over many years.

(3)   For distances of 10 *stadia* or greater, Josephus almost invariably uses multiples of 10 as intervals – 10 *stadia* roughly equating to 2 km (1.25 mi). Remarkably, every multiple of 10 up to 100 is represented, but *no* in-between figures above 10: no 25 or 18. The sole exception is the 33-*stadia* circumference of Jerusalem's third wall, the foundations of which were laid by King Agrippa I when Josephus was a boy of 5 or so (*War* 5.159). As an aristocrat from the city, he must have grown up knowing this number as the sort of figure that one might share with visitors. With that sole exception, multiples of 10 will do.

(4)   From 100 upward the same pattern continues, now on the 100-scale. Josephus uses every 100-*stadia* increment except 500, with hardly any stops between the hundreds. When he does rarely offer an intermediate stop, it is always multiple of 20 or 30. But after 600 we find nothing until 2000.

(5)   Whereas Josephus has an easy and accurate knowledge of distances around Jerusalem and in Lower Galilee, his estimates for distances between remoter places

can be wildly inaccurate, even if he has visited one or more of the sites in question. This is no criticism of him. I could do no better. Here are some examples:

    a.   *War* 2.188: Ptolemais is 120 *stadia* north of Carmel (in reality about 75) and 100 stadia south of the Ladder of Tyre (correct).

    b.   *War* 3.10: Ascalon is 520 *stadia* from Jerusalem (in reality about 350 *stadia* or 70 km).

    c.   *War* 4.474: Jericho is 150 *stadia* from Jerusalem, and 60 from the Jordan (in reality about 115 from Jerusalem and 38 from the Jordan).

    d.   *War* 4.610: Alexandria (Plinthinē) to Pelusium is 3600 *stadia* by boat (in reality about 2400–2500 *stadia*, 500 km or 300 mi).

    e.   *Ant.* 9.7: En Gedi sits 300 *stadia* from Jerusalem (in reality about 200 *stadia* [40 km] as the crow flies, ca. 225 *stadia* [45 km] by road).

    f.   *Ant.* 13.312: Strato's Tower (Caesarea) is about 600 *stadia* from Jerusalem (in reality about 500 *stadia* or 100 km by Roman road).

    g.   *Ant.* 18.249: Baiae in Italy is 5 *stadia* from Puteoli (actually about 60 *stadia* or 12 km).

(6) Josephus not only favours multiples of 10 and 100 *stadia* but also shows a marked preference among these for multiples of 3. Along with the convenient 20 *stadia* (4 km or 2.5 mi), thus, he has a taste for 30, 60, and 120 (also 600 and 3600) *stadia*.

(7) When describing particular regions, he may use similar figures for the distances from a central Point A, such as Ptolemais, to radial points B, C, and D, at the cost of accuracy. This suggests that he may use a mnemonic measure based in 30 or 60 *stadia* (cf. *War* 2.188; *Life* 214).

(8) The favoured root figure of 30 *stadia* may mean in effect "an hour's march." It would thus be equivalent to the Persian parasang (παρα-σάγγης), discussed by ancient authors.[2] This might help to explain Josephus' remarkable claim that Mt. Tabor (Itabyrion) stood 30 *stadia* high (*War* 4.55), which would put it in aircraft space. He would have meant perhaps that it took an hour to walk up.[3]

A good example of all these points is *Life* 349, where Josephus is railing against Justus of Tiberias for having led his city in revolt against Rome, when it was so close to large non-Judaean *poleis* that it could have joined them in remaining loyal without danger: "Your native place, ... 30 *stadia* away from Hippos, 60 from Gadara, and 120 from Scythopolis." This is a highly schematic picture. Josephus' distances translate as 6 km (3.73 mi) to Hippos, 12 km (7.5 mi) to

---

[2] E.g., Herodotus 2.6 (= 30 *stadia*); 5.52–53; Xenophon, *Anab.* 1.7.15; 2.4.10; 4.5.10; *Cyr.* 3.3.28; 4.2.20; Pliny 6.124. See Albright 1921–1922: 41.

[3] Suggested by Albright 1921–1922: 41.

Gadara, and 24 km (15 mi) to Scythopolis. The actual distances are nearly 10 km to Hippos' harbour (but 12 km to the hilltop *polis*), the same 10 km to Gadara's harbour (18 km to Gadara itself), and 35 km to Scythopolis.

The *stadion* was usually reckoned at 600 feet. But since the length of a *foot* varied from place to place, *stadia* varied significantly, from the Phoenician *stadion* of 220.5 m to the Olympic at 177.8 m (i.e., 723.5 vs. 583 ft), via the Ptolemaic (211.6m) and Italian (185.2 m) – a potential difference of 40 m per *stadion*. And Pliny the Elder claimed that the geographer Eratosthenes used a *stadion* of only 158.7 m (calculated as 1/40 of an Egyptian *schoinos* = 1,200 royal cubits), whereas a Persian or Chaldaean *stadion* was about 198.4 m (1/32 of a *schoinos*).[4]

With due regard for such complications, we can nevertheless get a sense of Josephus' intended distances by comparing his *stadia* measurements for the places with which he was most familiar, in Lower Galilee and Jerusalem, with the actual distances, which we can measure today. That exercise yields the result that his *stadia* are very close to 200 m, hence roughly matching the Persian/Chaldaean *stadion* (198.4 m). Dividing his distances by 5 therefore gives the approximate number of kilometres, and dividing it by 8 gives a rough equivalent in imperial/American miles. Again, however, this formula yields only the distances that he has in mind, not necessarily the correct distances.

[4] Pliny, *Nat.* 12.53. See Lelgemann 2004.

BIBLIOGRAPHY

Ahl, F. 1984. "The art of safe criticism in Greece and Rome," *American Journal of Philology* 105: 174–208.

Ahrensdorf, O. J. 1997. "Thucydides' realist critique of realism," *Polity* 30: 231–65.

Albright, W. F. 1921–1922. "Contributions to the historical geography of Palestine," *The Annual of the American School of Oriental Research in Jerusalem* 2: 1–46.

Alcock, S. E., J. F. Cherry, and J. Elsner. 2001. *Pausanias: Travel and Memory in Roman Greece.* Oxford: Oxford University Press.

Alexandre, Y. 2008. "The archaeological evidence of the Great Revolt at Karm er-Ras (Kfar Kanna) in the Lower Galilee," in Guri-Rimon 73–79.

Alföldy, G. 1995. "Eine Bauinschrift aus dem Colosseum," *ZPE* 109: 195–226.

Alföldy, G. 1999. "Pontius Pilatus und das Tiberieum von Caesarea Maritima," *Scripta Classica Israelica* 18: 85–108.

Allmand, C. T. 2011. *The De re militari of Vegetius: The Reception, Transmission and Legacy of a Roman Text in the Middle Ages.* Cambridge: Cambridge University Press.

Alston, R. 1995. *Soldier and Society in Roman Egypt: A Social History.* London: Routledge.

Alston, R. 1998. *Aspects of Roman History, AD 14–117.* London: Routledge.

Ando, C. 2000. *Imperial Ideology and Provincial Loyalty in the Roman Empire.* Berkeley: University of California Press.

Anonymous. 1855. "Money vs. merit – English promotion," The *New York Times*, August 20.

Anonymous. 2010. "Escape clause: where Jews fled from Roman destruction beneath the streets of Jerusalem," *BAR* 36:3 (May/June): 45–47.

Antonius, G. 1938. *The Arab Awakening: The Story of the Arab National Movement.* Beirut: Khayats.

Appelbaum, A. 2009. "'The Idumaeans' in Josephus' *The Jewish War*," *JSJ* 40: 1–22.

Arad, Y. 1980. "The Nazi concentration camps," *Proceedings of the Fourth Yad Vashem International Historical Conference*, Jerusalem, January 1980, online at www.jewishvirtuallibrary .org/jsource/Holocaust/resistyad.html.

Arbel, Y. 2007. "The Gamla coin: A new perspective on the circumstances and date of its minting," in S. Malena and D. Miano (eds.), *Milk and Honey: Essays on Ancient Israel and the Bible in Appreciation of the Jewish Studies Program at the University of California, San Diego.* pp. 257–75. Winona Lake: Eisenbrauns.

Arnal, W. E. 2001. *Jesus and the Village Scribes: Galilean Conflicts and the Setting of Q.* Minneapolis: Fortress.

Arreguin-Toft, I. 2001. "How the weak win wars: A theory of asymmetric conflict," *International Security* 26: 96–98.

Arubas, B. and H. Goldfus. 2008. "Masada, the Roman siege works," *NEAEHL* 5: 1937–39.

Arubas, B. and H. Goldfus. 2010. "Masada from the Roman point of view: The excavations of the siege works," in S. Yona (ed.), *Or Le-Mayer: Studies in Bible, Semitic Languages, Rabbinic Literature, and Ancient Civilizations presented to Mayer Gruber on the Occasion of his Sixty-fifth Birthday*, pp. 19–32. Beer-Sheva: Ben Gurion University Press [Hebrew].

Ascough, R. S., P. A. Harland, and J. S. Kloppenborg. 2013. *Associations in the Greco-Roman World: A Sourcebook.* Berlin: W. de Gruyter.

Atkinson, K. 2004. *I Cried to the Lord: A Study of the Psalms of Solomon's Historical Background and Social Setting*. Leiden: Brill.

Atkinson, K. 2007. "Noble deaths at Gamla and Masada? A critical reassessment of Josephus' accounts of Jewish resistance in light of archaeological discoveries," in Z. Rodgers (ed.), *Making History: Josephus and Historical Method*, pp. 349–71. Leiden: Brill.

Attridge, H. W. 1976. *The Interpretation of Biblical History in the Antiquitates Judaicae of Flavius Josephus*. Missoula: Scholars.

Avi-Yonah, M., N. Avigad, Y. Aharoni, I. Dunayevsky, S. Gutman. 1957. "The Archaeological survey of Masada 1955–1956," *Israel Exploration Journal* 7: 1–60.

Aviam, M. 2004. *Jews, Pagans and Christians in the Galilee. 25 Years of Archaeological Excavations and Surveys: Hellenistic to Byzantine Periods*. Rochester: University of Rochester Press.

Aviam, M. 2008a. "Yodfat." *NEAEHL* 5: 2076–78.

Aviam, M. 2008b. "The fortified settlements of Josephus Flavius and their significance against the backgrounds of the excavations of Yodefat and Gamla," in Guri-Rimon, pp. 39–54.

Aviam, M. 2013. "The decorated stone from the synagogue at Migdal: a holistic interpretation and a glimpse into the life of Galilean Jews at the time of Jesus," *NovT* 55: 205–20.

Aviam, M. and P. Richardson. 2001. "Appendix A: Josephus' Galilee in archaeological perspective," in S. Mason (ed.) *Flavius Josephus: Translation and Commentary, vol. 9: Life of Josephus*, pp. 177–201. Leiden: Brill.

Avigad, N. 1976. "How the wealthy lived in Herodian Jerusalem," *BAR* 2: 1, 23–32, 34–35.

Avigad, N. 1983. *Discovering Jerusalem: Recent Archaeological Excavations in the Upper City*. Nashville: Thomas Nelson.

Avni, G., Z. Greenhut, and T. Ilan. 1994. "Three new burial caves of the Second Temple Period in Aceldama (Kidron Valley)," in H. Geva (ed.) *Ancient Jerusalem Revealed*, pp. 206–18. Jerusalem: Israel Exploration Society.

Bach, H. I. 1974. *Jacob Bernays: ein Beitrag zur Emanzipationsgeschichte der Juden und zur Geschichte des deutschen Geistes im neunzehnten Jahrhundert*. Tübingen: J. C. B. Mohr.

Bagnall, R. S. (ed.). 2009. *The Oxford Handbook of Papyrology*. Oxford: Oxford University Press.

Bahat, D. 1994. "The Western Wall tunnels," in H. Geva (ed.) *Ancient Jerusalem Revealed*, pp. 177–90. Jerusalem: Israel Exploration Society.

Baker, J. N. L. 1963. *The History of Geography: Papers*. Oxford: Blackwell.

Ballif, M. and M. G. Moran (eds.). 2005. *Classical Rhetorics and Rhetoricians: Critical Studies and Sources*. Westport, Conn.: Greenwood.

Balsdon, J. P. V. D. 1979. *Romans and Aliens*. Chapel Hill: University of North Carolina Press.

Baltrusch, E. 2002. *Die Juden und das römische Reich: Geschichte einer konfliktreichen Beziehung*. Darmstadt: Wissenschaftliche Buchgesellschaft.

Bar-Kochva, B. 1976. "Seron and Cestius at Beith Horon," *PEQ* 108: 13–21.

Bar-Kochva, B. 1992. *Pseudo-Hecataeus on the Jews*. Berkeley: University of California.

Barclay, J. M. G. 2006. *Against Apion (Flavius Josephus: Translation and Commentary*, ed. S. Mason, vol. 10). Leiden: Brill.

Barnes, T.D. 1971. *Tertullian: A Historical and Literary Study*. Oxford: Clarendon.

Barnes, T. D. 1977. "The fragments of Tacitus' 'Histories,'" *Classical Philology* 72: 224–31.

Barnes, T. D. 2005. "The sack of the Temple in Josephus and Tacitus," in J. Edmondson, S. Mason, and J. Rives (eds.) *Flavius Josephus and Flavian Rome*, pp. 129–44. Oxford: Oxford University Press.

Barish, D. A. 1978. "The autobiography of Josephus and the hypothesis of a second edition of his *Antiquities*," *Harvard Theological Review* 71: 61–75.

Barrett, A. A. 1989. *Caligula: the Corruption of Power*. New Haven: Yale University Press.

Barrett, A. A. 1991. "Claudius' British Victory Arch in Rome," *Britannia* 22: 1–19.

Barth, F. 1969. *Ethnic Groups and Boundaries: The Social Organization of Culture Difference*. Boston: Little, Brown.

Bartoli, P. S. and G. P. Bellori. 1685. *Admiranda romanarum antiquitatum ac veteris sculpturae vestigia. . . .* Rome: Iacobus de Rubeis.

Barton, C. 2001. *Roman Honor: the Fire in the Bones.* Berkeley: University of California Press.

Bar-Yosef, E. 2001. "The last crusade? British propaganda and the Palestine campaign, 1917–18," *Journal of Contemporary History* 36: 87–109.

Basu, B. D. 1927. *The Consolidation of the Christian Power in India.* Calcutta: Prabasi.

Baumgarten, A. I. (ed.). 2002. *Sacrifice in Religious Experience.* Leiden: Brill.

Beacham, R. 2005. "The emperor as impressario: Producing the pageantry of power," in Galinsky (ed.), *Cambridge Companion,* pp. 151–74.

Beagon, M. 1992. *Roman Nature: the Thought of Pliny the Elder.* Oxford: Clarendon Press.

Beall, T. S. 1988. *Josephus' Description of the Essenes illustrated by the Dead Sea Scrolls.* Cambridge: Cambridge University Press.

Beard, M. 2003. "The triumph of Flavius Josephus," in Boyle and Dominik, *Flavian Culture,* pp. 543–59.

Beard, M. 2007. *The Roman Triumph.* Cambridge, Mass.: Belknap/Harvard University Press.

Beck, C. 1862. "Bernays's chronicle of Sulpicius Severus," *Christian Examiner* 72: 22–40.

Beck, I. 1971. *Die Ringkomposition bei Herodot und ihre Bedeutung für die Beweistechnik.* Hildesheim: Georg Olms.

Bederman, D. J. 2001. *International Law in Antiquity.* Cambridge: Cambridge University Press.

Beebe, H. K. 1983. "Caesarea Maritima: Its strategic and political importance to Rome," *Journal of Near Eastern Studies* 42: 195–207.

Beer, F. A. 1996. *Post-Realism: The Rhetorical Turn in International Relations* East Lansing: Michigan State University Press.

Begg, C. T. 1993. *Josephus' Account of the Early Divided Monarchy (AJ 8,212–420): Rewriting the Bible.* Leuven: Leuven University Press; Uitgeverij Peeters.

Ben-Ami, D. and Y. Tchekhanovets. 2011. "Has the Adiabenian royal family 'palace' been found?" in Galor and Avni, *Unearthing Jerusalem,* pp. 231–39.

Ben-Avraham, Z., U. ten Brink, R. Bell, and M. Reznikov. 1996. "Gravity field over the Sea of Galilee: Evidence for a composite basin along a transform fault," *Journal of Geophysical Research* 101: 533–44.

Ben-Moshe, T. 1992. *Churchill, Strategy and History.* Boulder: Lynne Rienner.

Ben-Yehuda, N. 1995. *The Masada Myth: Collective Memory and Mythmaking in Israel.* Madison, University of Wisconsin Press.

Ben-Yehuda, N. 2002. *Sacrificing Truth: Archaeology and the Myth of Masada.* Amherst, N.Y., Humanity Books.

Ben-Tor, A. 2009. *Back to Masada.* Jerusalem: Israel Academy of Sciences.

Bentwich, N. D. M. 1914. *Josephus.* Philadelphia: Jewish Publication Society of America.

Ben Zeev, M. P. 1993. "The reliability of Josephus Flavius: The case of Hecataeus' and Manetho's accounts of Jews and Judaism. Fifteen years of contemporary research (1974–1990)," *JSJ* 24: 215–34.

Ben Zeev, M. P. 1998. *Jewish Rights in the Roman World: The Greek and Roman Documents Quoted by Josephus Flavius.* Tübingen: Mohr Siebeck.

Ben Zeev, M. P. 2005. *Diaspora Judaism in Turmoil, 116/117 CE: Ancient Sources and Modern Insights.* Leuven: Peeters.

Bergmeier, R. 1993. *Die Essener-Berichte des Flavius Josephus: Quellenstudien zu den Essenertexten im Werk des jüdischen Historiographen.* Kampen: Kok Pharos.

Bergmeier, R. 1998. "Die Leute aus Essa," *ZDPV* 113: 75–87.

Berlin, A. 1997a. "Archaeological sources for the history of Palestine. Between forces: Palestine in the Hellenistic period," *Biblical Archaeologist* 60: 2–51.

Berlin, A. 1997b. "From monarchy to markets: The Phoenicians in Hellenistic Palestine," *BASOR* 306: 75–88.

Berlin, A. 2002. "Romanization and anti-Romanization in pre-revolt Galilee," in A. Berlin and A. Overman (eds.), *The First Jewish Revolt: Archaeology, History, and Ideology,* pp. 57–63. London: Routledge.

Berlin, A. 2006. *Gamla I: The Pottery of the Second Temple Period: The Shmarya Gutmann Excavations, 1976–1989*. IAA Reports 29. Jerusalem: Israel Antiquities Authority.

Berlin, I. 2002. *Liberty: Incorporating Four Essays on Liberty*, ed. H. Hardy. Oxford: Oxford University Press.

Bernays, J. 1861. *Ueber die Chronik des Sulpicius Severus: ein Beitrag zur Geschichte der classischen und biblischen Studien*. Berlin: Wilhelm Hertz.

Bernett, M. 2007. *Der Kaiserkult in Judäa unter den Herodiern und Römern*. Tübingen: Mohr Siebeck.

Bernhardi, F. von. 1914 [1912]. *Germany and the Next War*. New York: Chas. A. Eron.

Beyer, K. 1986. *The Aramaic Language, Its Distribution and Subdivisions*. Göttingen: Vandenhoeck & Ruprecht.

Bickerman, E. J. 1980 [1968]. *Chronology of the Ancient World*. London: Thames and Hudson.

Bickerman, E. J. 1988. *The Jews in the Greek Age*. New York: Jewish Theological Seminary.

Bilde, P. 1988. *Flavius Josephus between Jerusalem and Rome: His Life, His Works and Their Importance*. Sheffield: Sheffield Academic Press.

Bird, H. W. 1994. *Aurelius Victor: De Caesaribus*. Liverpool: Liverpool University Press

Birley, E. 1989. "Some legionary centurions," *Zeitschrift für Papyrologie und Epigraphik* 79: 114–28.

Birt, T. 1882. *Das antike Buchwesen in seinem Verhältniss zur Litteratur*. Berlin: Hertz.

Bishop, M. C. and J. C. N. Coulston. 2006. *Roman Military Equipment*, rev. edn. Oxford: Oxbow.

Black, M. 1974. "Judas of Galilee and Josephus' 'Fourth Philosophy,'" in O. Betz, K. Haacker, and M. Hengel (eds.), *Josephus-Studien: Untersuchungen zu Josephus, dem antiken Judentum und dem Neuen Testament*, pp. 45–54. Göttingen: Vandenhoeck & Ruprecht.

Blewitt, O. 1850. *A Hand-book for Travellers in Central Italy*. 2nd edn. London: John Murray.

Bloch, M. 1992 [1941]. *The Historian's Craft*, trans. P. Putnam. Manchester: Manchester University Press.

Bloch, R. S. 2002. *Antike Vorstellungen vom Judentum: der Judenexkurs des Tacitus im Rahmen der griechisch-römischen Ethnographie*. Stuttgart: F. Steiner.

Bloom, J. J. 2010. *The Jewish Revolts against Rome, A.D. 66–135: A Military Analysis*. Jefferson NC: McFarland & Co.

Blumell, L. 2008. "Social banditry? Galilean banditry from Herod until the outbreak of the first Jewish Revolt," *Scripta Classica Israelica* 27: 35–53.

Boatwright, M. T. 2000. *Hadrian and the Cities of the Roman Empire*. Princeton: Princeton University Press.

Boers, H. 1975–1976. "The form critical study of Paul's letters: I Thessalonians as a test case," *NTS* 22: 140–58.

Boettger, G. 1879. *Topographisch–Historisches Lexicon zu den Schriften des Flavius Josephus*. Leipzig: L. Fernau.

Boffo, L. 1994. *Iscrizioni Greche e Latine per lo Studio Della Bibbia*. Brescia: Paideai.

Bohrmann, M.. 1989. *Flavius Josephus, the Zealots and Yavne: Towards a Rereading of the War of the Jews*. New York: Peter Lang.

Bond, H. K. 1998. *Pontius Pilate in History and Interpretation*. Cambridge: Cambridge University Press.

Bonfante Warren, L. 1970. "Roman triumphs and Etruscan kings: the changing face of the triumph," *JRS* 60: 49–66.

Boon, G. C. and C. Williams. 1967. *Plan of Caerleon, Isca; Legio II Augusta*. Cardiff: National Museum of Wales.

Boucher, D. 1998. *Political Theories of International Relations: From Thucydides to the Present*. Oxford: Oxford University Press.

Bowersock, G. W. 1971. "A report on Arabia Provincia," *Journal of Roman Studies* 61: 219–242.

Bowersock, G. W. 1975. "Old and new in the history of Judaea," *JRS* 65: 180–85

Bowersock, G. W. 1978. *Julian the Apostate*. Cambridge, Mass.: Harvard University Press.

Bowie, E. L. 1970. "The Greeks and their past in the Second Sophistic," *Past and Present* 46: 3–41.

Boyle, A. J., and W. J. Dominik (eds.) 2003. *Flavian Rome: Culture, Image, Text.* Leiden: Brill.

Bradley, K. R. 1978. "The chronology of Nero's visit to Greece A.D. 66/67," *Latomus* 37: 61–72.

Bradley, K. R. 1979. "Nero's retinue in Greece, A. D. 66/67," *Illinois Classical Studies* 4: 154–56.

Brandon, S. G. F. 1970. "The defeat of Cestius Gallus: A Roman legate faced the problem of the Jewish revolt," *History Today* 20: 38–46.

Braudel, F. 1958. "Histoire et science sociale: la longue durée," *Annales: Economies, Sociétés, Civilisations* 13: 725–53.

Braund, D. 1984. *Rome and the Friendly King: The Character of the Client Kingship.* London: Croom Helm.

Braund, S. 2009. *De Clementia: Edited with Text, Translation, and Commentary.* Oxford: Oxford University Press.

Bremmer, J. 1994. *Greek Religion.* Oxford: Oxford University Press.

Bricault, L. and J. Leclant. 2001. *Atlas de la diffusion des cultes isiaques (IVe s. av. J.-C. – IVe s. apr. J.-C.).* Paris, Diffusion de Boccard.

Bricault, L., M. J. Versluys, and P. G. P Meyboom (eds.) 2007. *Nile into Tiber: Egypt in the Roman World. Proceedings of the IIIrd International Conference of Isis Studies, Leiden, May 11–14 2005.* Leiden: Brill.

Bricault, L. 2013. *Les cultes isiaques dans le monde gréco-romain.* Paris, Les Belles Lettres.

Brighton, M. 2009. *The Sicarii in Josephus's Judean War: Rhetorical Analysis and Historical Observations.* Atlanta: Society of Biblical Literature.

Broadhurst, L. 2005. "Melito of Sardis, the Second Sophistic, and 'Israel,'" in W. Braun (ed.) *Rhetoric and Reality in Early Christianities,* pp. 49–74. Waterloo: Wilfrid Laurier University Press.

Brooke, G. and P. R. Davies (eds.). 2002. *Copper Scroll Studies.* JSPSup. 40. Sheffield: Sheffield Academic Press.

Broshi, M. 1982. "The credibility of Josephus," *JJS* 33: 379–84.

Brown, C., Nardin, T., and Rengger, N. (eds.). 2002. *International Relations in Political Thought.* Cambridge: Cambridge University Press.

Brüne, B. 1913. *Flavius Josephus und seine Schriften in ihrem Verhältnis zum Judentume, zur griechisch-römischen Welt znd zum Christentume.* Gütersloh: Bertelsmann.

Brunt, P. A. 1965. "Reflections and British and Roman imperialism," *Comparative Studies in Society and History* 7: 267–88.

Brunt, P. A. 1975. "The administrators of Roman Egypt," *JRS* 65: 124–47.

Brunt, P. A. 1977. "Josephus on social conflicts in Roman Judaea," *Klio* 59: 149–53.

Brunt, P. A. 1983. "*Princeps* and *Equites,*" *JRA* 73: 42–75.

Buckle, H. T. 1903 [1857]. *History of Civilization in England,* 3 vols. London: Henry Frowde.

Burkert, W. 1985. *Greek Religion.* Cambridge, Mass.: Harvard University Press.

Burleigh, M. 2010. *Moral Combat: A History of World War II.* London: Harper Collins.

Burnett, A., Amandry, M., and Ripollès, P. P. 1992. *Roman Provincial Coinage, vol. 1, pt. 1.* London: British Museum.

Burr. D. 2004. "The Antichrist and the Jews in four thirteenth-century Apocalypse commentaries," in McMichael and Myers (eds.), *Friars and Jews,* pp. 23–38.

Burrell, B. 1993. "Two inscribed columns from Caesarea Maritima," *ZPE* 99: 287–95.

Burton, G. 2002. "Government and the provinces," in J. Wacher (ed.) *The Roman World, 2 vols,* pp. 423–39. London: Routledge.

Butcher, K. 2003. *Roman Syria and the Near East.* London: British Museum.

Butcher, K. and M. Ponting. 2009. "The silver coinage of Roman Syria under the Julio-Claudian emperors," *Levant* 41: 59–78.

Bytwerk, R. 2005. *Paper War: Nazi Propaganda in One Battle, on a Single Day, Cassino, Italy, May 11, 1944.* New York: Mark Batty.

Caddick-Adams, P. 2013. *Monte Cassino: Ten Armies in Hell.* London: Arrow.

Campbell, D. B. 1986. "Auxiliary artillery revisited," *Bonner Jahrbücher des Landesmueums in Bonn* 186: 117–32.

Campbell, D. B. 1988. "Dating the siege of Masada," *ZPE* 73: 156–58.

Campbell, D. B. 2005. *Roman Siege Warfare*. Oxford: Osprey.

Campbell, D. B. 2006. *Besieged: Siege Warfare in the Ancient World*. Oxford: Osprey.

Campbell, J. B. 1984. *The Emperor and the Roman Army: 31 BC–AD 235*. Oxford: Clarendon.

Campbell, J. B. 1993. "War and diplomacy: Rome and Parthia, 31 BC–AD 235," in J. Rich & G. Shipley (eds.) *War and Society in the Roman World*, pp. 213–40. London: Routledge.

Cape, R. W. Jr. 1997. "Persuasive History: Roman rhetoric and Historiography," in W. J. Dominik (ed.), *Roman Eloquence: Rhetoric in Society and Literature*, pp. 212–28. London: Routledge.

Capponi, L. 2005. *Augustan Egypt: The Creation of a Roman Province*. London: Routledge.

Capponi, L. 2010. "Hadrian in Jerusalem and Alexandria in 117," *Athenaeum* 98: 489–502.

Capponi, L. 2011. *Roman Egypt*. Bristol: Bristol Classical Press.

Carlsson, S. 2010. *Hellenistic Democracies: Freedom, Independence and Political Procedure in Some East Greek City-States*. Stuttgart: Franz Steiner Verlag.

Carr, E. H. 2001 [1961]. *What Is History?* 50th anniversary edition. Introduction by R. J. Evans. London: Palgrave Macmillan.

Cartledge, P. 2002a. *The Greeks: A Portrait of Self and Others*. Oxford: Oxford University Press.

Cartledge, P. 2002b. *The Spartans: An Epic History*. New York: Pan Macmillan.

Cary, E. 1914–1927. *Dio's Roman History*, 9 vols. Cambridge, Mass.: Harvard University Press.

Castagnoli, F. 1941. "Gli edifici rappresentati in un rilievo del sepolcro degli Haterii," *Bollettino della Commissione Archeologica comunale di Roma* 69: 59–69.

Castriota, D. 1995. *The Ara Pacis Augustae and the Imagery of Abundance in Later Greek and Early Roman Imperial Art*. Princeton: Princeton University Press.

Cavanaugh, W. T. 2009. *The Myth of Religious Violence: Secular Ideology and the Roots of Modern Conflict*. Oxford: Oxford University Press.

Chamberlain, H. S. 1910. *Foundations of the Nineteenth Century*, trans. J. Lees, introduction Lord Redesdale, 2 vols. London: John Lane.

Champion, C. B. 2004. *Cultural Politics in Polybius's Histories*. Berkeley: University of California Press.

Champlin, E. 2003. *Nero*. Cambridge, Mass.: Harvard University Press.

Chancey, M. A. 2002. *The Myth of a Gentile Galilee*. Cambridge: Cambridge University Press.

Chancey, M. A. 2005. *Greco-Roman Culture and the Galilee of Jesus*. Cambridge: Cambridge University Press.

Chapman, H. H. 1998. *Spectacle and theater in Josephus's Bellum Judaicum*. PhD dissertation, Stanford University. http://pace-ancient .mcmaster.ca/york/york/dissert.htm?id=11

Chapman, H. H. 2006. "Paul, Josephus, and the Judean nationalistic and imperialistic policy of forced circumcision," *Ilu Revista de Ciencias de las Religiones* 11: 131–55.

Chapman, H. H. 2007. "Josephus and the cannibalism of Mary (BJ 6.199–219)," in J. Marincola (ed.) *A Companion to Greek and Roman Historiography*, pp. 419–26. Oxford: Blackwell.

Chapman, H. H. 2009. "What Josephus sees: The Temple of Peace and the Jerusalem temple as spectacle in text and art," *Phoenix* 63: 107–30.

Chazan, R. 2006. *The Jews of Medieval Western Christendom, 1000–1500*. Cambridge: Cambridge University Press.

Cheesman, G. L. 1914. *The Auxilia of the Roman Imperial Army*. Oxford: Clarendon.

Ciancio Rossetto, P. 2000. "Arcus Titi (Circus Maximus)," in M. Steinby (ed.) *Lexicon Topographicum Urbis Romae*, 6 vols. Rome: Edizione Quasar.

Clark, E. A. 2004. *History, Theory, Text: Historians and the Linguistic Turn*. Cambridge, Mass.: Harvard University Press.

Clark, L. 2006. *Anzio: The Friction of War. Italy and the Battle for Rome 1944*. London: Headline Review.

Clark. M. 2007 [1950]. *Calculated Risk*. New York: Enigma Books.

Clarke, K. 1999. *Between Geography and History: Hellenistic Constructions of the Roman World*. Oxford: Clarendon Press.

Coarelli, F. 1984. *Roma Sepolta*. Rome: Quasar.

Coarelli, F. 1993. "Arcus ad Isis," in M. Steinby (ed.) *Lexicon Topographicum Urbis Romae: Volume Primo: A-C*. Rome: Quasar.

Coarelli, F. and A. Gabucci. 2001. *The Colosseum*. Los Angeles: J. Paul Getty Museum.

Cohen, G. M. 2006. *Hellenistic Settlements in Syria, the Red Sea Basin, and North Africa*. Berkeley: University of California Press.

Cohen, S. J. D. 1979. *Josephus in Galilee and Rome: His Vita and Development as a Historian*. Leiden: Brill.

Cohen, S. J. D. 1982. "Masada: Literary tradition, archaeological remains, and the credibility of Josephus," *JJS* 33: 385–405.

Cohen, S. J. D. 1999. *The Beginnings of Jewishness: Boundaries, Varieties, Uncertainties*. Berkeley: University of California Press.

Cohn, N. S. 2012. *The Memory of the Temple and the Making of the Rabbis*. Philadelphia: University of Pennsylvania Press.

Colautti, F. M. 2002. *Passover in the Works of Josephus*. Leiden: Brill.

Coleman, K. M. 2002. "Euergetism in its place," in Lomas and Cornell, *Bread & Circuses*, 61–88.

Colledge, M. 1967. *The Parthians*. London: Thames & Hudson.

Collingwood, R. G. 1994 [1946 posth.]. *The Idea of History*, rev. edn., ed. J. van der Dussen. Oxford: Oxford University Press.

Collins, J. J. 1997. *Apocalypticism in the Dead Sea Scrolls*. London: Routledge.

Collins, J. J. 2009. "The Essenes in Josephus: The sources of his information," in Z. Rodgers et al. (eds.) *A Wandering Galilean: Essays in Honour of Seán Freyne*, pp. 51–72. Leiden: Brill.

Collins, R. F. 1984. *Studies on the First Letter to the Thessalonians*. Leuven: Leuven University Press.

Colpe, C. 1974. "Die Arsakiden bei Josephus," in O. Betz, M. Hengel and, K. Haacker (eds.) *Josephus-Studien: Untersuchungen zu Josephus, dem Antiken Judentum and dem Neuen Testament*, pp. 97–108. Göttingen, Vandenhoeck & Ruprecht.

Colvin, D. and R. Hodges. 1994. "Tempting providence: The bombing of Monte Cassino," *History Today* 44: 13–20.

Comber, M. 1997. "Re-reading the Roman historians," in Bentley (ed.), *Companion to Historiography*, 43–56.

Comparette, T. L. 1914. "Debasement of the silver coinage under the Emperor Nero," *American Journal of Numismatics* 47: 1–11.

Conder, C. R. and H. H. Kitchener, with C. Wilson. 1881–1884. *The Survey of Western Palestine*, 4 vols. with 26 sheet maps. London: Palestine Exploration Fund.

Condor, J. E. 2010. "The tomb of the Haterii: The significance of the Sacra Via Relief." Paper presented to the Classical Association of the Middle West and South, March 26, 2010, Oklahoma City.

Comte, A. 1896 [1830–1842]. *The Positive Philosophy of Auguste Comte*, 3 vols., trans. and condensed by Harriet Martineau. London: George Bell & Sons.

Conte, G. B. 1994. *Latin Literature: A History*, trans. J. B. Solodow et al. Baltimore: Johns Hopkins University Press.

Corbeill, A. 2004. *Nature Embodied: Gesture in Ancient Rome*. Princeton: Princeton University Press.

Corbo, V., and Loffredo, S. 1981. "Nuove scoperte all fortezza di Macheronte. Rapporto preliminare all quarta campagna di scavo: 7 settembre–10 ottobre 1981," *Liber Annus Studium Biblicum Franciscanum* 31: 257–86.

Cotton, H. M. 1989. "The date of the fall of Masada: The evidence of the Masada Papyri," *ZPE* 78: 157–62.

Cotton, H. M. 1991. "Fragments of a declaration of landed property from the Province of Arabia," *ZPE* 85 (1991) 263–267.

Cotton, H. M. 1999. "Some Aapects of the Roman administration of Judaea/Syria-Palaestina," in W. Eck (ed.) *Lokale Autonomie und römische Ordnungsmacht in den kaiserzeitlichen Provinzen: Kolloquien des*

Historischen Kollegs, pp. 75–91. Munich: Oldenbourg.

Cotton, H. M. 2007. "The impact of the Roman army in the Province of Judaea/Syria Palaestina," in L. de Blois and E. L. Cascio (eds.) *The Impact of the Roman Army (200 BC–AD 476)*, pp. 393–408. Leiden: Brill.

Cotton, H. M. and J. Geiger with J. D. Thomas. 1989. *Masada II: The Latin and Greek Documents* in *Masada I–VIII*.

Cotton, H. M. and W. Eck. 2005. "Josephus' Roman audience: Josephus and the Roman elites," in J. C. Edmondson, S. Mason and J. B. Rives (eds.), *Flavius Josephus and Flavian Rome*, pp. 37–52. Oxford: Oxford University Press.

Craig, C. 2003. *Glimmer of a New Leviathan: Total War in the Realism of Niebuhr, Morgenthau, and Waltz*. New York: Columbia University Press.

Crane, G. 1998. *Thucydides and the Ancient Simplicity: The Limits of Political Realism*. Berkeley: University of California Press.

Crawford, R. M. A. 2000. *Idealism and Realism in International Relations: Beyond the Discipline*. London: Routledge.

Creative Commons license www.archeocommons .net/cms/index.php?option=com_con tent&view=article&id=5%3Aliseo-cam pense-tra-mito-e-archeologia-ricostru zione-di-un-percorso-urbano&catid=7% 3Acc-by-nc&Itemid=10&lang=en.

Cribiore, R. 2001. *Gymnastics of the Mind: Greek Education in Hellenistic and Roman Egypt*. Princeton, NJ: Princeton University Press.

Crook, J. A. 1955. *Consilium Principis: Imperial Councils and Counsellors from Augustus to Diocletian*. Cambridge: Cambridge University Press.

Crossan, J. D. and J. Reed. 2001. *Excavating Jesus: Beneath the Stones, Behind the Texts*. New York: Harper San Francisco.

Crown, A. D. and R. Pummer. 2005. *A Bibliography of the Samaritans*. Lanham, MD: Scarecrow Press.

Curran, J. R. 2007. "The Jewish War: some neglected regional factors," *The Classical World* 101: 75–91.

Curtis, V. S. and S. Stewart (eds.). 2007. *The Age of the Parthians*. London: I. B. Tauris.

Dąbrowa, E. 1993. *Legio X Fretensis: A Prosopographical Study of Its Officers (I-III C. A.D.)*. Stuttgart: Franz Steiner.

Dąbrowa, E. 1996. "The commanders of Syrian legions, 1st–3rd C. A.D.," in D. L. Kennedy (ed.), *The Roman Army in the East*, pp. 277–96.

Dąbrowa, E. 1998. *The Governors of Roman Syria from Augustus to Septimius Severus*. Bonn: R. Habelt.

Dalberg-Acton, J. E. E. 1907. *The History of Freedom and Other Essays*, eds. J. N. Figgus and R. V. Laurence. London: Macmillan.

Davies, P. J. E. 2004. *Death and the Emperor: Roman Imperial Funerary Monuments from Augustus to Marcus Aurelius*. Austin: University of Texas Press.

Dawson, D. 1996. *The Origins of Western Warfare: Militarism and Morality in the Ancient World*. Boulder: Westview Press.

Deacy, S. and K. F. Pierce. 1997. *Rape in Antiquity*. London: Duckworth in association with the Classical Press of Wales.

Debevoise, N. C. 1938. *A Political History of Parthia*. Chicago: University of Chicago Press.

Degrassi, A. 1954. *Fasti Capitolini*. Aug. Taurinorum: In aedibus Io. Bapt. Paraviae.

Delia, D. 1991. *Alexandrian Citizenship during the Roman Principate*. Atlanta: Scholars.

Delitzsch, F. 1921. *Die Grösse Täuschung*. Stuttgart and Berlin: Deutsche Verlags-Anstalt.

den Hollander, W. 2014. *Josephus, the Emperors, and the City of Rome: From Hostage to Historian*. Leiden: Brill.

Deutsch, G. N. 1986. *Iconographie de L'Illustration de Flavius Josèphe au Temps de Jean Fouquet*. Leiden: Brill.

Deutsch, M. E. 1924. "Pompey's three triumphs." *Classical Philology* 19: 277–79.

Deutsch, R. 2010a. "Roman coins boast 'Judaea Capta,'" *BAR* 36 (1): 51–53.

Deutsch, R. 2010b. *The Coinage of the First Jewish Revolt, 66–73 C.E.* Paper presented at the symposium, "The Jewish War against Rome (66–70/74): Interdisciplinary

Perspectives," Qumran Institute, University of Groningen, October 21, 2010.

Deutsch, R. 2010c. *The Coinage of the First Jewish Revolt against Rome*. Paper presented in the colloquium, "Judaea and Rome in Coins," at Spink and Son Ltd., London, U.K., September 14, 2010.

D'Huys, V. 1987. "How to describe violence in historical narrative," *Ancient Society* 18: 209–50.

Diehl, J. 2011. "Anti-imperial rhetoric in the New Testament," *Currents in Biblical Research* 10: 9–52.

Diehl, J. 2012. "Empire and Epistles: anti-Roman rhetoric in the New Testament Epistles," *Currents in Biblical Research* 10: 217–63.

Dignas, B. and Trampedach, K (eds.). 2008. *Practitioners of the Divine: Greek Priests and Religious Officials from Homer to Heliodorus*. Washington, DC: Center for Hellenic Studies.

Dindorf[ius], L. 1870. *Historici Graeci Minores*. Leipzig: Teubner.

Dmitriev, S. 2011. *The Greek Slogan of Freedom and Early Roman Politics in Greece*. Oxford: Oxford University Press.

Dodd, C. H. 1935. *The Bible and the Greeks*. London: Hodder & Stoughton.

Dodge, H. 1999. "Amusing the masses," in D. S. Potter and D. J. Mattingly (eds.) *Life, Death, and Entertainment in the Roman Empire*, pp. 205–55. Ann Arbor: University of Michigan.

Donnelly, J. 2000. *Realism and International Relations*. Cambridge: Cambridge University Press.

Dothan, M. 1983. *Hammath Tiberias, vol. 1: Early Synagogues and the Hellenistic and Roman Remains*. Jerusalem: Israel Exploration Society/University of Haifa.

Drexler, H. 1925. "Untersuchungen zu Josephus und zur Geschichte des jüdischen Aufstandes," *Klio* 19: 277–312.

Duckworth, G. E. 1962. *Structural Patterns and Proportions in Vergil's Aeneid: A Study in Mathematical Composition*. Ann Arbor: University of Michigan.

Dunn, J. D. G. 2003. *Jesus Remembered*. Grand Rapids: Eerdmans.

Dušek, J. 2012. *Aramaic and Hebrew Inscriptions from Mt. Gerizim and Samaria between Antiochus III and Antiochus IV Epiphanes*. Leiden: Brill.

Dyson, S. L. 1971. "Native revolts in the Roman Empire," *Historia: Zeitschrift für alte Geschichte* 20: 239–274.

Eberhardt, B. 2005. "Wer dient Wem? Die Darstellung des flavischen Triumphzuges auf dem Titusbogen und bei Josephus (*B.J.* 7.123–62)," in Sievers and Lembi, *Josephus and Jewish History*, 257–77.

Echevarria, A. J. 2003. "Clausewitz's center of gravity: it's not what we thought." *Naval War College Review* 56 (Winter): 108–23.

Eck, W. 1969. "Die *Eroberung* von Masada und eine neue Inschrift des L. Flavius Silva Nonius Bassus," *Zeitschrift für die Neutestamentliche Wissenschaft* 60: 282–89.

Eck, W. 1970. *Senatoren von Vespasian bis Hadrian*. Munich: Beck.

Eck, W. 1985. *Die Statthalter der germanischen Provinzen vom 1.–3. Jahrhundert*. Bonn: Rheinland.

Eck, W. 1999a. "Sextus Lucillius Bassus, der Eroberer von Herodium, in einer Bauinschrift von Abu Gosh," *SCI* 18: 109–120.

Eck, W. 1999b. "The Bar Kokhba revolt: the Roman point of view," *JRS* 89: 76–89.

Eck, W. 2001. "Spezialisierung in der staatlichen Administration des römischen Reiches in der hohen Kaiserzeit," in L. de Blois (ed.) *Administration, Prosopography and Appointment Practices in the Roman Empire*, pp. 1–23. Amsterdam: Gieben.

Eck, W. 2003. *The Age of Augustus*. 2nd edn. Oxford: Blackwell.

Eck, W. 2007. *Rom und Judaea: fünf Vorträge zur römischen Herrschaft in Palaestina*. Tübingen: Mohr Siebeck.

Eck, W. 2011. "Die römischen Repräsentanten in Judaea: Provokateure oder Vertreter der römischen Macht?" in M. Popović (ed.) *The Jewish Revolt against Rome: Interdisciplinary Perspectives*, pp. 45–68. Leiden: Brill.

Eckstein, A. M. 1990. "Josephus and Polybius: a reconsideration." *Classical Antiquity* 9: 175–208.

Eckstein, A. M. 1995. *Moral Vision in the Histories of Polybius*. Berkeley: University of California Press.

Eckstein, A. M. 2006. *Mediterranean Anarchy, Interstate War, and the Rise of Rome*. Berkeley: University of California Press.

Edelman, D. V. 2005. *The Origins of the "Second" Temple: Persian Imperial Policy and the Rebuilding of Jerusalem*. London: Equinox.

Edmondson, J. C. (1987). *Two Industries in Roman Lusitania: Mining and Garum Production*. Oxford: Archaeopress/B.A.R.

Edwards, D. R. and C. T. McCollough. 1997. *Archaeology and the Galilee: Texts and Contexts in the Graeco-Roman and Byzantine Periods*. Atlanta: Scholars.

Edwell, P. M. 2008. *Between Rome and Persia: The Middle Euphrates, Mesopotamia, and Palmyra under Roman Control*. London: Routledge.

Ehlers, W. 1939. "Triumphus," *PWRE* 2nd series 13th Halbband (= 7.1), 493–511.

Eichholz, D. E. 1951. "Galen and his environment," *Greece & Rome* 20: 60–71.

Elizabeth (Tonna), C. 1845. *Judæa Capta*. New York: John S. Taylor & Co.

Ellis, J. 1984. *Cassino, the Hollow Victory: the Battle for Rome, January–June 1944*. London: Aurum.

Elukin, J. 2007. *Living Together, Living Apart: Rethinking Jewish-Christian Relations in the Middle Ages*. Princeton: Princeton University Press.

Erasmo, M. 2004. *Roman Tragedy: Theatre to Theatricality*. Austin: University of Texas Press.

Erdkamp, P. (ed.). 2007. *A Companion to the Roman Army*. Oxford: Blackwell.

Erim, K. T. 1982. "A new relief showing Claudius and Britannia from Aphrodisias," *Britannia* 13: 277–81.

Eshel, H. 2002. "Documents of the First Jewish Revolt from the Judean Desert," in Berlin and Overman, *The First Jewish Revolt*, 157–63.

Esler, P. S. 1995. "God's honour and Rome's triumph," in P. S. Esler (ed.) *Modelling Early Christianity: Social-scientific Studies of the New Testament*, pp. 239–58. London: Routledge.

Evans, M., and A. Ryan (eds.). 2000. *The Human Face of Warfare: Killing, Fear and Chaos in Battle*. St. Leonards: Allen & Unwin.

Evans, R. J. 2005. *The Third Reich in Power*. London: Penguin.

Falls, C. 1928–1930. *Military Operations: Egypt and Palestine*, 3 vols. "History of the Great War based on Official Documents." London: Imperial War Museum.

Fantham, E. 1996. *Roman Literary Culture: From Cicero to Apuleius*. Baltimore: Johns Hopkins University Press.

Farmer, W. R. 1973 [1956]. *Maccabees, Zealots, and Josephus*. New York: Columbia University Press.

Faraone, C. A. and F. S. Naiden (eds.). 2012. *Greek and Roman Animal Sacrifice: Ancient Victims, Modern Observers*. Cambridge: Cambridge University Press.

Faulkner, N. 2004. *Apocalypse: The Great Jewish Revolt against Rome AD 66–73*. Stroud: Tempus.

Favro, D. 1996. *The Urban Image of Augustan Rome*. Cambridge: Cambridge University Press.

Favro, D. 2005. "Making Rome a world city," in Galinsky (ed.), *Cambridge Companion*, pp. 234–63.

Feeney, D. 2007. *Caesar's Calendar: Ancient Time and the Beginnings of History*. Berkeley: University of California Press.

Feldherr, A. 1998. *Spectacle and Society in Livy's History*. Berkeley: University of California Press.

Feldman, L. H. 1975. "Masada: A critique of recent scholarship," in J. Neusner (ed.), *Christianity, Judaism, and Other Greco-Roman Cults: Studies for Morton Smith at Sixty*, pp. 218–48. Leiden: Brill.

Feldman, L. H. 1984. *Josephus and Modern Scholarship, 1937-1980*. Berlin: W. de Gruyter.

Feldman, L. H. 1990. "Some observations on the name Palestine," *HUCA* 61: 1–32.

Feldman, L. H. 1993. *Jew and Gentile in the Ancient World: Attitudes and Interactions from*

Alexander to Justinian. Princeton: Princeton University Press.

Feldman, L. H. 1998a. *Studies in Josephus' Rewritten Bible*. Leiden: Brill.

Feldman, L. H. 1998b. *Josephus's Interpretation of the Bible*. Berkeley: University of California.

Feldman, L. H. 2001. "Financing the Colosseum," *BAR* 27 (4): 20–31, 60.

Feldman, L. H. and Hata, G (eds.). 1987. *Josephus, Judaism, and Christianity*. Detroit: Wayne State University Press.

Feldman, L. H. and Hata, G (eds.). 1989. *Josephus, the Bible, and History*. Detroit: Wayne State University Press.

Ferguson, N. 1998. *The Pity of War*. London: Penguin.

Ferris, I. M. 2000. *Enemies of Rome: Barbarians through Roman Eyes*. Stroud: Sutton.

Ferris, I. 2009. *Hate and War: the Column of Marcus Aurelius*. Stroud: The History Press.

Finkelstein, I. 2008. "Jerusalem in the Persian (and Early Hellenistic) Period and the Wall of Nehemiah," *Journal for the Study of the Old Testament* 32: 501–20.

Fischer, D. H. 1970. *Historians' Fallacies: Toward a Logic of Historical Thought*. New York: Harper & Row.

Fischer, M., Isaac, B., and Roll, I. 1996. *Roman Roads in Judaea II. The Jaffa-Jerusalem Roads*. Oxford: Archaeopress.

Flower, H. 2008. "Remembering and forgetting Temple destruction: the destruction of the Temple of Jupiter Optimus Maximus in 83 BC," in G. Gardner and K. Osterloh (eds.) *Antiquity in Antiquity: Jewish and Christian Pasts in the Greco-Roman World*, pp. 74–92. Tübingen: Mohr Siebeck.

Foakes Jackson, F. J. 1930. *Josephus and the Jews: The Religion and History of the Jews as explained by Flavius Josephus*. London: Society for Promoting Christian Knowledge.

Foerster, G. 1993. "Excavations in the south of the City [Tiberias]." *NEAEHL* 4.1470–73.

Foerster, G. 2013. "Sarcophagi from the mausoleum unearthed at Herodium," in Rozenberg and Mevorach, *Herod the Great*, pp. 266–77.

Foerster, G. and Y. Tsafir [sic, for Tsafrir]. 2002. "Skythopolis–Vorposten der Dekapolis," in Hoffmann and Kerner, *Gadara–Gerasa*, 72–87.

Forde, S. 1995. "International relations and the science of realism: Thucydides, Machiavelli, and Neorealism," *International Studies Quarterly* 39: 141–60.

Fournier, A. 1903. *Napoleon the First: a Biography*, trans. M. B. Corwin and A. D. Bissell, ed. Ed. G. Bourne. New York: Henry Holt and Co.

Fowler, D. 2000. *Roman Constructions: Readings in Postmodern Latin*. Oxford: Oxford University Press.

Franke, T. 1991. *Die Legionslegaten der römischen Armee in der Zeit von Augustus bis Traian*. 2 vols. Bochum: Universitätsverlag N. Brockmeyer.

Franke, T. 1996. "Review of *Legio X Fretensis. A Prosopographical Study of Its Officers (I–III c. A.D.)* by Edward Dąbrowa," *Gnomon* 68: 236–40.

Franxman, T. W. 1979. *Genesis and the Jewish Antiquities of Flavius Josephus*. Rome: Biblical Institute Press.

Fraser, P. M. 1972. *Ptolemaic Alexandria*, 3 vols. Oxford: Clarendon.

Frei, A. 1886. "Beobachtungen vom See Genezareth," *ZDPV* 9: 81–145.

Frend, W. H. C. 1974. "Review of T. D. Barnes' Tertullian: a historical and literary study," *CR* 24: 72–76.

Freyberg-Inan, A. 2004. *What Moves Man: The Realist Theory of International Relations and Its Judgment of Human Nature*. Albany: State University of New York.

Freyne, S. 1980. *Galilee from Alexander the Great to Hadrian, 323 B.C.E. to 135 C.E.: A Study of Second Temple Judaism*. Wilmington: M. Glazier; Notre Dame: University of Notre Dame Press.

Freyne, S. 1988. *Galilee, Jesus and the Gospels: Literary Approaches and Historical Investigations*. Philadelphia: Fortress.

Freyne, S. 2002. *Galilee and Gospel: Collected Essays*. Leiden: Brill.

Freyne, S. 2004. *Jesus, a Jewish Galilean: A New Reading of the Jesus Story*. Edinburgh: T. & T. Clark.

Freyne, S. 2009. "Review of Steve Mason, *Josephus, Judea and Christian Origins: Methods and Categories*," *Review of Biblical Literature* 27 November: [www.bookreviews.org]: www.bookreviews.org/bookdetail.asp?TitleId=7010&CodePage=4130,6945,7010,1649,4648,481.

Friedman, S. 2011. "The Jewish Bill of Divorce – from Masada onwards," in A. I. Baumgarten et al. (eds.), *Halakhah in Light of Epigraphy*, pp. 175–83. Göttingen: Vandenhoeck & Ruprecht.

Frothingham, A. L. 1912. "Who built the Arch of Constantine? Its history from Domitian to Constantine," *American Journal of Archaeology* 16: 368–86.

Frova, A. 1961. "L'Iscrizione di Pontio Pilato a Cesarea." *Rendiconti Istituto Lombardo (Accademia di Scienze e Lettere)* 95: 419–34.

Frumkin, A., Magaritz, M., Carmi, I., and Zak, I. 1991. "The Holocene climatic record of the salt caves of Mount Sedom Israel," *The Holocene* 1: 191–200

Frumkin, A., and Elitzur, Y. 2002. "Historic Dead Sea level fluctuations calibrated with geological and archaeological evidence," *Quaternary Research* 57: 334–42.

Frye, R. N. 1962. *The Heritage of Persia*. London: Weidenfeld and Nicolson.

Frye, R. N. 1967. "Parthia and Sasanid Persia," in F. *Millar* et al. (eds.) *The Roman Empire and Its Neighbours*, pp. 249–69. London: Duckworth.

Fuks, A. 1970. "The Bellum Achaicum and its social aspect," *Journal of Hellenic Studies* 90: 78–89.

Fuks, G. 1985/1988, "Some remarks on Simon bar Giora," *SCI* 8–9: 106–119.

Fung, Y.–L. 1948. *History of Chinese Philosophy*, ed. D. Bodde. New York Macmillan.

Funke, P., and N. Luraghi (eds.). 2009. *The Politics of Ethnicity and the Crisis of the Peloponnesian League*. Washington, DC: Center for Hellenic Studies.

Gabriel, R. A., and Boose, D. W. Jr. 1994. *The Great Battles of Antiquity: A Strategic and Tactical Guide to Great Battles That Shaped the Development of War*. Westport, CT: Greenwood.

Gagniart, P. 2007. "The late republican army (146–30 BC)," in P. Erdkamp, ed., *A Companion to the Roman Army*, pp. 80–95. Oxford: Blackwell.

Galinsky, K. 1996. *Augustan Culture: An Interpretive Introduction*. Princeton, NJ: Princeton University Press.

Gallivan, P. 1981. "The Fasti for A. D. 70–96," *Classical Quarterly* 31: 186–220.

Galor, K. and G. Avni (eds.). 2011. *Unearthing Jerusalem: 150 Years of Archaeological Research in the Holy City*. Winona Lake: Eisenbrauns.

Galor, K., J.-B. Humbert, and J. Zangenberg (eds.). 2006. *Qumran, the Site of the Dead Sea Scrolls: Archaeological Interpretations and Debates*. Leiden: Brill.

Gantz, T. 1993. *Early Greek Myth: A Guide to Literary and Artistic Sources*. Baltimore: Johns Hopkins University.

Garfinkel, Y. 2011. "The birth and death of biblical minimalism," *BAR* 37 (3): 46–53, 78.

Garraghan, G. J. and J. Delanglez. 1946. *A Guide to Historical Method*. New York: Fordham University Press.

Geier, J. 1999. "Vietnam: the soldier's revolt," *The International Socialist Review* 9. www.isreview.org/issues/09/soldiers_revolt.shtml, accessed August 21, 2010.

Gehrke, H.-J. 1985. *Stasis: Untersuchungen zu den inneren Kriegen in den griechischen Staaten des 5. und 4. Jahrhunderts v. Chr.* Munich: C. H. Beck.

Gelzer, M. 1952. "Die Vita des Josephos," *Hermes* 80: 67–90.

Gergel, R. A. 1988. "A late Flavian cuirassed torso in the J. Paul Getty Museum," *The J. Paul Getty Museum Journal* 16: 5–24.

Gergel, R. A. 2001. "Costume as geographic indicator: Barbarians and prisoners on cuirassed statue breastplates," in L. Sebesta and L. Bonfante (eds.) *The World of Roman*

Costume, pp. 191–212. Madison: University of Wisconsin.

Geva, H. (ed.). 2000. *Ancient Jerusalem Revealed*, revised and expanded edn. Jerusalem: Israel Exploration Society.

Geva, H. 2014. "Jerusalem's population in antiquity: A minimalist view," *Tel Aviv* 41: 131–50.

Ghiretti, M. 1985. "Lo 'status' della Giudea dall'età Augustea all'età Claudia," *Latomus* 54: 751–66.

Gibson, S. and D. M. Jacobson. 1994. "The oldest datable chambers on the Temple Mount in Jerusalem," *BA* 57: 150–60.

Gichon, M. 1981. "Cestius Gallus's campaign in Judaea," *PEQ* 113: 39–62.

Gichon, M. 1986. "Aspects of a Roman army in war according to the *Bellum Judaicum* of Josephus," in P. W. Freeman and D. L. Kennedy (eds.), *The Defence of the Roman and Byzantine East*, pp. 287–310. Oxford: BAR.

Gichon, M. 2000. "The siege of Masada," in Y. Le Bohec and C. Wolff (eds.), *Les Légions de Rome sous le Haut-Empire*, 3 vols: 2.541–54. Paris: de Boccard.

Gil, M. 1992. *A History of Palestine, 634–1099*. Trans. E. Broido. Cambridge: Cambridge University Press.

Gill, D. 1993. "A natural spur at Masada," *Nature* 364: 569–70.

Gilliver, C. M. [= K.] 1999. *The Roman Art of War*. Stroud: Tempus.

Gilliver, K. [= C. M.] 2007. "The Augustan reform and the structure of the imperial army," in P. Erdkamp (ed.), *A Companion to the Roman Army*, pp. 183–200. Oxford: Blackwell.

Ginzburg, C. 1991. "Checking the evidence: The judge and the historian," *Critical Inquiry* 18: 79–92.

Giovannini, A. 1996. "Die Zerstörung Jerusalems durch Titus: Eine Strafe Gottes oder eine historische Notwendigkeit?" In P. Barceló (ed.), *Contra quis ferat arma deos? Vier Augsburger Vorträge zur Religionsgeschichte der römischen Kaiserzeit*, pp. 11-34. Munich: E. Vogel.

Glass, C. 2014. *Deserter: A Hidden History of the Second World War*. London: William Collins.

Gleason, M. W. 1995. *Making Men: Sophists and Self-presentation in Ancient Rome*. Princeton: Princeton University Press.

Glick, L. B. 1999. *Abraham's Heirs: Jews and Christians in Medieval Europe*. Syracuse, N.Y.: Syracuse University Press.

Gobineau, A. 1915 [1853]. *The Inequality of Human Races*. London: Heinemann.

Goldstein, I. and J. P. Fontanille. 2006. "A new study of the coins of the first Jewish revolt against Rome, 66–70 C.E.," *ANA [American Numismatic Association] Journal* 1 (2): 8–32.

Goldstein, J. A. 1984. *The Anchor Bible: 2 Maccabees*. New York: Doubleday.

Goldsworthy, A. K. 1996. *The Roman Army at War 100 BC –AD 200*. Oxford: Oxford University Press.

Goldsworthy, A. K. 2000. *The Fall of Carthage: The Punic Wars 265–146 BC*. London: Weidenfeld & Nicolson.

Goldsworthy, A. K. 2003. *The Complete Roman Army*. London: Thames & Hudson.

Goodblatt, D. 2006. *Elements of Ancient Jewish Nationalism*. Cambridge: Cambridge University Press.

Goodchild, R. G. 1949. "The coast road of Phoenicia and its Roman milestones," *Berytus* 9: 91–127.

Goodman, M. D. 1983. *State and Society in Roman Galilee, A.D. 132–212*. Totowa, NJ: Rowman & Allanheld.

Goodman, M. D. 1987. *The Ruling Class of Judea: The Origins of the Jewish Revolt against Rome AD 66–70*. Cambridge: Cambridge University Press.

Goodman, M. D. 2007. *Rome and Jerusalem: The Clash of Ancient Civilizations*. London: Penguin.

Grabbe, L. L. 1992. *Judaism from Cyrus to Hadrian. 2 vols.* Minneapolis: Augsburg Fortress.

Graetz, H. 1880. "Notizen zur Topographie Palästinas," *Monatsschrift für Geschichte und Wissenschaft des Judenthums* 29: 481–95.

Graetz, H. 1949 [1893]. *History of the Jews*. 6 vols. Philadelphia: Jewish Publication Society of America.

Grajetzki, W. 2011. *Greeks & Parthians in Mesopotamia and Beyond, 331 BC–224 AD*. Bristol: Bristol Classical Press.

Grant, M. 1916. *The Passing of the Great Race, or, the Racial Basis of European History*. New York: Charles Scribner's Sons.

Green, P. 1990. *Alexander to Actium: The Historical Evolution of the Hellenistic Age*. Berkeley: University of California Press.

Green, P. 2007. *The Hellenistic Age: A History*. New York: Modern Library.

Gregoratti, L. 2012. "The importance of the mint of Seleucia on the Tigris for Arsacid history: Artabanus and the Greek Parthian cities," *Mesopotamia* 47: 129–36.

Griffin, M. T. 1984. *Nero: The End of a Dynasty*. London: Batsford.

Griffiths, M. 1992. *Realism, Idealism, and International Politics: A Reinterpretation*. London: Routledge.

Grossberg, A. 2007. "The *Miqva'ot* (ritual baths) at Masada," *Masada VIII*, 95–126.

Gruen, E. S. 1976. "The origins of the Achaean war," *Journal of Hellenic Studies* 96: 46–69.

Gruen, E. S. 1978. "Review of *The Grand Strategy of the Roman Empire from the First Century A.D. to the Third* by Edward N. Luttwak," *Journal of Interdisciplinary History* 8: 563–66.

Grünenfelder, R. 2003. *Frauen an den Krisenherden: eine rhetorisch-politische Deutung des Bellum Judaicum*. Münster: LIT.

Grünewald, T. 2004. *Bandits in the Roman Empire: Myth and Reality*, trans. J. Drinkwater. London: Routledge.

Gschwind, M. 2006. "Raphaneae," in *Jahresbericht 2005 des Deutschen Archäologischen Instituts* [*Archäologischer Anzeiger*], 285–86.

Gschwind, M. 2007. "Raphaneae," in *Jahresbericht 2006 des Deutschen Archäologischen Instituts* [*Archäologischer Anzeiger*], 185–87.

Gschwind, M. 2008. "Raphaneae," in *Jahresbericht 2007 des Deutschen Archäologischen Instituts* [*Archäologischer Anzeiger*], 265–67.

Gschwind, M. 2011. "Raphaneae," in *Jahresbericht 2010 des Deutschen Archäologischen Instituts* [*Archäologischer Anzeiger*], 277–78.

Guérin, V. 1868–1880. *Description géographique, historique et archéologique de la Palestine: accompagnée de cartes détaillées*, 3 parts in 7 vols. Paris: à l'imprimerie impériale [repr. 1969, Amsterdam: Oriental Press].

Günther, A. 1922. *Beiträge zur Geschichte der Kriege zwischen Römern und Parthern*. Berlin: C. A. Schwetschke & Sohn.

Günther, H. F. K. 1930. *Rassenkunde des jüdischen Volkes*. 2nd edn. Munich: J. F. Lehmann.

Gurval, R. A. 1995. *Actium and Augustus: The Politics and Emotions of Civil War*. Ann Arbour: University of Michigan.

Gussmann, O. 2008. *Das Priesterverständnis des Flavius Josephus*. Tübingen: Mohr Siebeck.

Habicht, C. 1998 [1985]. *Pausanias' Guide to Ancient Greece*. Berkeley: University of California Press.

Habinek, T. N. 1998. *The Politics of Latin Literature: Writing, Identity, and Empire in Ancient Rome*. Princeton: Princeton University Press.

Hadas-Lebel, M. 2006 [1990]. *Jerusalem against Rome*, trans. R. Fréchet. Leuven: Peeters.

Hall, E. 1989. *Inventing the Barbarian: Greek Self-Definition through Tragedy*. Oxford: Clarendon Press.

Hall, J. M. 1997. *Ethnic Identity in Greek Antiquity*. Cambridge: Cambridge University Press.

Hall, J. M. 2002. *Hellenicity: Between Ethnicity and Culture*. Chicago: University of Chicago Press.

Hall, L. J. 2004. *Roman Berytus: Beirut in Late Antiquity*. London: Routledge.

Halleck, H. W. 1846. *Elements of Military Art and Society*. New York: D. Appleton & Co.

Hallote, R. S. and A. H. Joffe. 2002. "The politics of Israeli archaeology: Between 'nationalism' and 'science' in the age of the Second Republic," *Israel Studies* 7: 84–116.

Halsey, F. W. (ed.). 1920. *The Literary Digest History of the World War*. 10 vols. New York: Funk & Wagnalls.

Hannah, R. 2005. *Greek and Roman Calendars: Constructions of Time in the Classical World.* London: Duckworth.

Hansen, M. H. (ed.). 1993a. *The Ancient Greek City-State: Symposium on the Occasion of the 250th Anniversary of The Royal Danish Academy of Sciences and Letters, July, 1–4 1992.* Copenhagen: Munksgaard.

Hansen, M. H. 1993b. "The *Polis* as a citizen-state," in Hansen (ed.), pp. 7–29.

Hansen, M. H. 2006. *Polis: An Introduction to the Ancient Greek City-State.* Oxford: Oxford University Press.

Hansen, M. H. and T. H. Nielsen (eds.). 2004. *An Inventory of Archaic and Classical Poleis: An Investigation Conducted by The Copenhagen Polis Centre for the Danish National Research Foundation.* Oxford: Oxford University Press.

Hanson, V. D. 1989. *The Western Way of War: Infantry Battle in Classical Greece.* New York: A. A. Knopf.

Hapgood, D., and Richardson, D. 2002. *Monte Cassino: The Story of the Most Controversial Battle of World War II.* Cambridge, Mass.: Da Capo.

Har-El, M. 1981. "Jerusalem & Judea: roads and fortifications," *BA* 44: 8–19.

Hardwick, M. 1989. *Josephus as an Historical Source in Patristic Literature through Eusebius.* Atlanta: Scholars.

Harker, A. 2008. *Loyalty and Dissidence in Roman Egypt: The Case of the Acta Alexandrinorum.* Cambridge: Cambridge University Press.

Harland, P. A. 2003. *Associations, Synagogues, and Congregations: Claiming a Place in Ancient Mediterranean Society.* Minneapolis: Fortress.

Harland, P. A. 2006. "The declining *Polis*? Religious rivalries in ancient civic Context," in L. E. Vaage (ed.) *Religious Rivalries in the Early Roman Empire and the Rise of Christianity*, pp. 21–49. Waterloo: Wilfrid Laurier University Press.

Harlow, M. and R. Laurence. 2002. *Growing Up and Growing Old in Ancient Rome: A Life Course Approach.* London: Routledge.

Harris, J. 2010. "Blair the Zealot: a mindset closer to pathology than politics," *The Guardian*, Wednesday Sept. 1, *Main* section, p. 31.

Harris, W. V. 1989. *Ancient Literacy.* Cambridge Mass.: Harvard University Press.

Hart, H. St.-J. 1952. "Judaea and Rome: The official commentary," *Journal of Theological Studies* 3: 172–98.

Hartog, F. 1988. *The Mirror of Herodotus: The Representation of the Other in the Writing of History*, trans. J. Lloyd. Berkeley: University of California Press.

Hata, G. 1975. "Is the Greek version of Josephus' 'Jewish War' a translation or a rewriting of the first version?" *JQR* 66: 89–108.

Hawkes, C. F. C. and A. A. Richmond. 1934. "Review of Adolf Schulten, *Masada: Die Burg des Herodes und die römischen Lager*," *Journal of Roman Studies* 24: 72–75.

Hellems, F. B. R. 1902. *Lex de Imperio Vespasiani: A Consideration of Some of the Constitutional Aspects of the Principate at Rome.* Chicago: Scott, Foresman and Co.

Hempel, C. G. 1942. "The function of general laws in history," *Journal of Philosophy* 39: 35–48

Henderson, J. 1998. *Fighting for Rome: Poets and Caesars, History and Civil War.* Cambridge: Cambridge University Press.

Hendin, D. 2010. *Guide to Biblical Coins*, 5th edn. New York: Amphora.

Hengel, M. 1989 [1961]. *The Zealots: Investigations into the Jewish Freedom Movement in the Period from Herod I until 70 A.D.*, trans. David Smith. Edinburgh: T. & T. Clark.

Hengel, M. 2011. *Die Zeloten: Untersuchungen zur jüdischen Freiheitsbewegung in der Zeit von Herodes I. bis 70 n. Chr.* 3rd edn., R. Deines and C.-J. Thornton (eds.). Tübingen: Mohr Siebeck.

Herz, P. 2002. "Sacrifice and sacrificial ceremonies of the Roman Imperial Army," in A. I. Baumgarten (ed.) *Sacrifice and Sacrificial Ceremonies of the Roman Army*, pp. 81–100. Leiden: Brill.

Herzl, T. 1896. *Der Judenstaat.* Berlin: Jüdischer Verlag.

Heylbut, G. 1887. "Ptolemaeus ΠΕΡΙ ΔΙΑΦΟΡΑΣ ΛΕΞΕΩΝ," *Hermes* 22: 388–410.

Hickey, W. 1995 [1810]. *Memoirs of a Georgian Rake*, ed. R. Hudson. London: Folio Society.

Hill, G. F. 1914. *Catalogue of Greek Coins in the British Museum, vol. 27: Palestine*. London: British Museum.

Hirschfeld, Y. 1992. *A Guide to Antiquity Sites in Tiberias*. Jerusalem: Israel Antiquities Authority.

Hjelm, I. 2004. *Jerusalem's Rise to Sovereignty: Zion and Gerizim in Competition*. London: T. & T. Clark International.

Hjelm, I. 2010. "Mt. Gerizim and Samaritans in recent research," in M. Mor and F. V. Reiterer (eds.), *Samaritans: Past and Present. Current Studies*, pp. 25–41. Berlin: de Gruyter.

Hobsbawm, E. J. 1972. *Bandits*. Harmondsworth: Penguin.

Hock, R. F., E. N. O'Neil, et al. 2002. *The Chreia and Ancient Rhetoric: Classroom Exercises*. Leiden: Brill.

Hoehner, H. W. 1972. *Herod Antipas*. Cambridge: Cambridge University Press.

Hoffmann, A. 2002. "Topographie und Stadtgeschichte von Gadara/Umm Qais," in Hoffmann and Kerner, *Gadara–Gerasa*, 98–124.

Hoffmann, A. and S. Kerner (eds.). 2002. *Gadara–Gerasa und die Dekapolis*. Mainz: Philipp von Zabern.

Hölkeskamp, K.-J. 1996. "Exempla und *mos maiorum*: Überlegungen zum kollektiven Gedächtnis der Nobilität," in H.-J. Gehrke and A. Möller (eds.), *Vergangenheit und Lebenswelt: soziale Kommunikation, Traditionsbildung und historisches Bewusstsein*, pp. 301–38. Tübingen: Gunter Narr.

Holley, A. E. 1994. "The ballista balls from Masada," *Masada IV*, 349–65, in *Masada I–VIII*.

Holmes, R. 2011. *Soldiers: Army Lives and Loyalties from Redcoats to Dusty Warriors*. London: Harper.

Hölscher, G. 1916. "Josephus," in A. F. Pauly and G. Wissowa (eds.) *Paulys Realenzyklopädie der classischen Altertumswissenschaft,* Vol. 18, cols. 1934–2000. Munich: A. Druckenmüller.

Hölscher, T. 2006. "The transformation of victory into power: from event to structure," in S. Dillon and K. E. Welch (eds.), *Representations of War in Ancient Rome*, pp. 27–48. Cambridge: Cambridge University Press.

Hölscher, T. 2009. "Monuments of the Battle of Actium: propaganda and response," trans. C. Nader, in Edmondson, *Augustus*, pp. 310–23.

Honig, J. W. 2011. "The tdea of total war: from Clausewitz to Ludendorff," *Proceedings of the National Institute for Defense Studies* [Japan], Tenth Forum, Tokyo, 14 September, 29–41. www.nids.go.jp/english/event/forum/e2011.html (accessed 30 August 2013).

Honigman, S. 2003. "*Politeumata* and rthnicity in Ptolemaic and Roman Egypt," *Ancient Society* 33: 61–102.

Hopkins, K. 1983. *Death and Renewal*. Cambridge: Cambridge University Press.

Hopkins, K. and M. Beard. 2005. *The Colosseum*. London: Profile Books.

Hornblower, S. 1987. *Thucydides*. London: Duckworth.

Hornum, M. B. 1993. *Nemesis, the Roman State & the Games*. Leiden: Brill.

Horsley, R. A. 1979a. "Josephus and the bandits." *Journal for the Study of Judaism* **10**: 37–63.

Horsley, R. A. 1979b. "The Sicarii: Ancient Jewish 'terrorists,'" *Journal of Religion* 59: 435–58.

Horsley, R. A. 1993. *Jesus and the Spiral of Violence: Popular Jewish Resistance in Roman Palestine*. Minneapolis: Fortress.

Horsley, R. A. 1995. *Galilee: History, Politics, People*. Valley Forge: Trinity Press International.

Horsley, R. A. 1996. *Archaeology, History, and Society in Galilee: The Social Context of Jesus and the Rabbis*. Valley Forge, Pa.: Trinity Press International.

Horsley, R.A. 2003. *Jesus and Empire: The Kingdom of God and the New World Disorder*. Minneapolis: Fortress.

Horsley, R.A. 2008. "Jesus and empire," pp. 75–96 in Horsley, ed., *In the Shadow of Empire: Reclaiming the Bible as a History of Faithful Resistance*, Louisville: Westminster John Knox.

Horsley, R. A. and Hanson, J. S. 1988. *Bandits, Prophets, and Messiahs: Popular Movements at the Time of Jesus*. New York: Harper & Row.

Howgego, C. J. 1995. *Ancient History from Coins*. London: Routledge.

Hoyt, E. P. 2002. *Backwater War: The Allied Campaign in Italy, 1943–1945*. London: Praeger.

Hudon, W. 1996. "Religion and society in early modern Italy – old questions, new insights," *American Historical Review* 101 1996: 783–94

Hughes, D. J. (ed.). 2009. *Moltke on the Art of War: Selected Writings*. New York: Random House.

Hughes, M. 2010. "When soldiers kill civilians: the battle for Saipan, 1944," *History Today* 60 (2): 42–48.

Huitink, L. and J. W. van Henten. 2009. "The publication of Flavius Josephus' works and their audiences," *Zutot* 6: 49–60.

Iggers, G. G., et al. 2008. *A Global History of Modern Historiography*. Harlow: Pearson Longman.

Ilan, T. and J. J. Price. 1993–1994. "Seven onomastic problems in Josephus' *Bellum Judaicum*," *JQR* 84: 189–208.

Inowlocki, S. 2006. *Eusebius and the Jewish Authors: His Citation Technique in an Apologetic Context*. Leiden: Brill.

Isaac, B. H. 1984. "Bandits in Judaea and Arabia," *HSCP* 88: 171–203.

Isaac, B. H. 1992. *The Limits of Empire: The Roman Army in the East*, rev. ed. Oxford: Clarendon Press.

Isaac, B. H. 1998. *The Near East under Roman Rule: Selected Papers*. Leiden: Brill.

Isikoff, M., and D. Corn. 2006. *Hubris: The Inside Story of Spin, Scandal, and the Selling of the Iraq War*. New York: Three Rivers.

Issar, A. S., and Yakir, D. 1997. "Isotopes from wood buried in the Roman siege ramp of Masada: The Roman period's colder climate," *BA* 60: 101–106.

Itgenshosrt, T. 2005. *Tota illa pompa: der Triumph in der römischen Republik*. Göttingen: Vandenhoeck & Ruprecht.

Jacobson, D. M. 2006. "The northern palace at Masada – Herod's ship of the desert?" *PEQ* 138: 99–117.

Jampoler, A. C. A. 2005. *Sailors in the Holy Land: The 1848 American Expedition to the Dead Sea and the Search for Sodom and Gomorrah*. Annapolis: Naval Institute Press.

Jaroés, K. 2002. *In Sachen Pontius Pilatus*. Mainz: von Zabern.

Jenkins, K. 1995. *On "What Is History?" From Carr and Elton to Rorty and White*. London: Routledge.

Jensen, M. H. 2010. *Herod Antipas in Galilee: The Literary and Archaeological Sources on the Reign of Herod Antipas and its Socio-Economic Impact on Galilee*. 2nd edn. Tübingen: Mohr Siebeck.

Jensen, W. M. 1978. *The Sculptures from the Tomb of the Haterii (Volumes I and II)*, Unpublished PhD Dissertation, University of Michigan.

Jeremias, J. 1969. *Jerusalem in the Time of Jesus: An Investigation into Economic and Social Conditions during the New Testament Period*. London: SCM.

Joes, A. J. 1996. *Guerrilla Warfare: A Historical, Biographical, and Bibliographical Sourcebook*. Westport, Conn.: Greenwood.

Johnson, W. A. 2010. *Readers and Reading Culture in the High Roman Empire: A Study of Elite Communities*. Oxford: Oxford University Press.

Johnson, W. A. and H. N. Parker. 2009. *Ancient Literacies: The Culture of Reading in Greece and Rome*. Oxford: Oxford University Press.

Jokilehto, J. 1999. *A History of Architectural Conservation*. Oxford: Butterworth-Heinemann.

Jones, A. H. M. 1940. *The Greek City: from Alexander to Justinian*. Oxford: Clarendon.

Jones, A. H. M. 1971. *The Cities of the Eastern Roman Provinces*. 2nd edn. Oxford: Clarendon.

Jones, B. W. 1992. *The Emperor Domitian*. London: Routledge.

Jones, C. P. 1971. *Plutarch and Rome*. Oxford: Clarendon.

Jones, C. P. 1974. Review of W. Eck's *Senatoren von Augustus bis Vespasian*. *American Journal of Philology* 95: 89–90.

Jones, C. P. 2002. "Towards a chronology of Josephus," *Scripta Classica Israelica* 21: 113–31.

Jones, S. 1997. *The Archaeology of Ethnicity: Constructing Identities in the Past and Present*. London: Routledge.

Jonsson, P. 2008. "'Arc d'Atlanta' . . . or a new bit of kitsch?" *The Christian Science Monitor*, July 7.

Jordan, K. C. 2002. "Right for the wrong reasons: S. L. A. Marshall and the ratio of fire in Korea," *The Journal of Military History* 66: 136–137.

Josephus Jitta, D. 1919. *The Renovation of International Low on the Basis of a Juridical Community of Mankind*. The Hague: Martinus Nejhoff.

Josephson, J. A. 2012. *The Invention of Religion in Japan*. Chicago: University of Chicago Press.

Jossa, G. 2001. *I gruppi giudaica ai tempi di Gesù*. Brescia: Paideia.

Kadman, L. 1960. *The Coins of the Jewish War of 66 to 73*. Tel Aviv: Schocken.

Kajanto, I. 1982 [1965]. *The Latin Cognomina*. Rome: Bretschneider.

Kanael, B. 1953. "The historical background of the coins 'Year four . . . of the redemption of Zion,'" *BASOR* 129: 18–20.

Kartveit, M. 2009. *The Origin of the Samaritans*. Leiden: Brill.

Kasher, A. 1988. *Jews, Idumaeans, and Ancient Arabs*. Tübingen: Mohr Siebeck.

Kasher, A. 1990. *Jews and Hellenistic Cities in Eretz-Israel*. Tübingen: Mohr Siebeck.

Kellum, B. A. 1982. *Sculptural Programs and Propaganda in Augustan Rome: the Temple of Apollo on the Palatine and the Forum of Augustus*. Cambridge, Mass.: Harvard University Press.

Kennedy, D. L. 1996. "Parthia and Rome: Eastern perspectives," in D. L. Kennedy (ed.) *The Roman Army in the East*. Ann Arbor: Journal of Roman Archaeology.

Kennedy, D. L. 2006. "Demography, the Population of Syria and the Census of Q. Aemilius Secundus," *Levant* 38: 109–24.

Kennedy, D. L. (ed.). 1996. *The Roman Army in the East*. Ann Arbor: Journal of Roman Archaeology.

Kennedy, D. M. 1999. *Freedom from Fear: the American People in Depression and War, 1929–1945*. Oxford: Oxford University Press.

Kennedy, G. A. 2003. *Progymnasmata: Greek Textbooks of Prose Composition and Rhetoric*. Leiden: Brill.

Kennell, N. M. 1995. *The Gymnasium of Virtue: Education & Culture in Ancient Sparta*. Chapel Hill: University of North Carolina Press.

Keppie, L. 1998. *The Making of the Roman Army: From Republic to Empire*. London: Routledge.

Klein, C. 1982. "Morphological evidence of lake level changes, western shores of the Dead Sea," *Israel Journal of Earth Sciences* 31: 67–94.

Klein, S. 1909. *Der Beraijta der vierundzwanzig Priesterabteilungen: Beiträge zur Geographie und Geschichte Galiläas*. Kirchhain: Max Schmersow.

Kleiner, F. S. 1990. "The Arches of Vespasian in Rome," *Mitteilungen des Deutschen Archäologischen Instituts, Römische Abteilung* 97: 127–36.

Kletter, K. M. 2005. *The Uses of Josephus: Jewish History in Medieval Christian Tradition*. Unpublished PhD Dissertation, University of North Carolina, Chapel Hill.

Knight, W. 1896 [1876]. *The Arch of Titus and the Spoils of the Temple*. 2nd edn. London: Religious Tract Society.

Knox, N. 1972. "On the classification of ironies," *Modern Philology* 70: 53-62.

Knust, J. W. and Z. Varhelyi (eds.). 2011. *Ancient Mediterranean Sacrifice*. Oxford: Oxford University Press.

Köberlein, E. 1962. *Caligula und die ägyptischen Kulte.* Meisenheim: Anton Hain.

Koester, C. 1989. "The origin and significance of the flight to Pella tradition," *CBQ* 51: 90–106.

Kokkinos, N. 1998. *The Herodian Dynasty: Origins, Role in Society and Eclipse.* Sheffield: JSOT.

Kokkinos, N. 2003. "Justus, Josephus, Agrippa II and his coins," *Scripta Classica Israelica* 22: 163–80.

Kokkinos, N. 2010. "The location of Tarichaeae: North or south of Tiberias?" *PEQ* 142: 7–23.

Kokkinos, N. 2012. "The Prefects of Judaea 6-48 CE and the coins from the Misty Period 6-36 CE," in D. M. Jacobson and N. Kokkinos (eds.) *Judaea and Rome in Coins 65 BCE–135 CE*, pp. 85–112. London: Spink.

Kokkinos, N. 2015. "Aspects of Jerusalem under Herod," in *Eretz-Israel: Archaeological, Historical and Geographical Studies* 31: 79–109.

Kraeling, C. H. 1942. "The episode of the Roman standards at Jerusalem," *Harvard Theological Review* 35: 263–89.

Kraus, A. S. and Woodman, A.J. 1997. *Latin Historians, Greece and Rome: New Surveys in the Classics.* Oxford: Oxford University Press.

Krause, J-U. and Witschel, C (eds.). 2006. *Die Stadt in der Spätantike—Niedergang oder Wandel?* Stuttgart: Franz Steiner.

Krehbiel, E. B. 1916. *Nationalism, War and Society: A Study of Nationalism and Its Concomitant, War, in Their Relation to Civilization; and of the Fundamentals and the Progress of the Opposition to War.* New York: Macmillan.

Kreissig, H. 1970. *Die sozialen Zusammenhänge des judäischen Krieges: Klassen und Klassenkampf im Palästina des 1. [ersten] Jarhunderts vor Unserer Zeit.* Berlin: Akademie-Verlag.

Krieger, K.-S. 1994. *Geschichtsschreibung als Apologetik bei Flavius Josephus.* Tübingen: Francke.

Krieger, K.-S. 1995. "Pontius Pilatus – ein Judenfeind? zur Problematic einer Pilatusbiographie," *Biblische Notizen* 78: 63-83.

Künzl, E. 1988. *Der römische Triumph: Siegesfeiern im antiken Rom.* Munich: C. H. Beck.

Labbé, G. 2012. *L'affirmation de la puissance romaine en Judée (63 avant J.-C.–136 après J.-C.).* Études anciennes: Série latine, 74. Paris: Les Belles Lettres.

Ladouceur. D. J. 1980. "Masada: a consideration of the literary evidence," *Greek, Roman, and Byzantine Studies* 21: 245–60.

Ladouceur. D. J. 1987. "Josephus and Masada," in L. H. Feldman and G. Hata (eds.), *Josephus, Judaism, and Christianity*, pp. 95–113. Detroit: Wayne State University Press.

Lämmer, M. 1976. "Griechische Wettkämpfe in Galiläa unter der Herrscchaft des Herodes Antipas," *Jahrbuch der deutschen Hochschule Köln 1976.* Schorndorf: Hofmann-Verlag: 37–67.

Lake, K. 1917. "Simon Zelotes." *HTR* 10: 57–63.

Landau, T. 2006. *Out-Heroding Herod: Josephus, Rhetoric, and the Herod Narratives.* Leiden: Brill.

Lanfrey, P. 1886. *The History of Napoleon the First,* 4 vols. 2nd edn. London: Macmillan & Co.

Lape, S. 2010. *Race and Citizen Identity in the Classical Athenian Democracy.* Cambridge: Cambridge University Press.

Laqueur, R. 1909. "Über das Wesen des römischen Triumphs," *Hermes* 44: 215–36.

Laqueur, R. 1920. *Der jüdische Historiker Flavius Josephus: ein biographischer Versuch auf neuer quellenkritischer Grundlage.* Giessen: Münchow. English translation by C. Disler, *The Jewish Historian Flavius Josephus* (2005), ed. S. Mason, online at http://pace.mcmaster.ca/york/york/studies-ext.htm.

Larson, J. 2007. *Ancient Greek Cults: A Guide.* London: Routledge.

Le Bohec, Y. 1994. *The Imperial Roman Army,* trans. R. Bate. London: Routledge.

Le Bohec, Y. and C. Wolff, eds. 2000. *Les légions de Rome sous le haut-empire: actes du congrès de Lyon (17–19 Septembre 1998).* Paris: Diffusion de Boccard.

Leach, E. W. 2006. "Freedom and immortality in the tomb of the Haterii," in E. D'Ambra and G. Métraux (eds.) *The Art of Citizens, Soldiers, and Freedmen in the Roman World*, pp. 1–17. Oxford: Archaeopress.

Lebow, R. N. 2003. *The Tragic Vision of Politics: Ethics, Interests, and Orders.* Cambridge: Cambridge University Press.

Leibner, U. 2009. *Settlement and History in Hellenistic, Roman, and Byzantine Galilee: An Archaeological Survey of the Eastern Galilee.* Tübingen: Mohr Siebeck.

Leiter, B. 2004. "The hermeneutics of suspicion: recovering Marx, Nietzsche, and Freud," pp. 74–105 in B. Leiter, (ed.), *The Future for Philosophy.* Oxford: Clarendon.

Lelgemann, D. 2004. "On the ancient determination of the meridian arc length by Eratosthenes of Kyrene," FIG Working Week 2004 (May 22–27, 2004), online at www.fig.net/pub/athens/papers/wshs1/wshs1_1_lelgemann.pdf. Accessed 1 December 2011.

Lémonon, J.-P. 1981. *Pilate et le gouvernement de la Judée: textes et monuments.* Paris: J. Gabalda.

Lendon, J. E. 1997. *Empire of Honour: The Art of Government in the Roman World.* Oxford: Clarendon Press.

Lentz, A. 1867. *Grammatici Graeci recogniti et apparatu critico instructi,* 3 parts in 8 vols. Leipzig: Teubner [repr. Hildesheim: G. Olms, 1965].

Leon, H. 1960. *The Jews of Ancient Rome.* Philadelphia: Jewish Publication Society.

Leoni, T. 2007. "'Against Caesar's wishes': Flavius Josephus as a source for the burning of the Temple," *JJS* 58: 39–51.

Leoni, T. 2009. "The text of Josephus's works: an overview," *JSJ* 40: 149–84.

Lerner, J. D. 1999. *The Impact of Seleucid Decline on the Eastern Iranian Plateau: The Foundations of Arsacid Parthia and Graeco-Bactria.* Stuttgart: Steiner.

Lerner, L. S. 2002. "Narrating over the ghetto of Rome," *Jewish Social Studies* 8: 1–38.

Lev-Yadun, S., D. S. Lucas, and M. Weinstein-Evron. 2010. "Modeling the demands for wood by the inhabitants of Masada and for the Roman siege," *Journal of Arid Environments* 74: 777–85.

Levick, B. 1999. *Vespasian.* London: Routledge.

Levick, B. 2000. *The Government of the Roman Empire: A Sourcebook.* 2nd edn. London: Routledge.

Levick, B. 2001. *Claudius.* London: Routledge.

Levick, B. 2010. *Augustus: Image and Substance.* Harlow: Pearson.

Levine, L. I. 1974. "The Jewish-Greek conflict in first century Caesarea," *Journal of Jewish Studies* 25: 381–97.

Levine, L. I. 1994. "Josephus' description of the Jerusalem Temple: *War, Antiquities,* and other sources," in F. Parente and J. Sievers (eds.), *Josephus and the History of the Greco-Roman Period,* pp. 233–46. Leiden: Brill.

Levine, L. I. 2000. *The Ancient Synagogue: The First Thousand Years.* New Haven: Yale University Press.

Levine, L. I. 2002. *Jerusalem: Portrait of the City in the Second Temple Period (538 B.C.E.–70 C.E.).* Philadelphia: Jewish Publication Society/Jewish Theological Seminary of America.

Levine, L. I. 2006. "Jewish archaeology in late antiquity: Art, architecture, and inscriptions," in S. T. Katz (ed.), *Cambridge History of Judaism,* 4 vols, vol. 4, pp. 519–55. Cambridge: Cambridge University Press.

Levy, B. E. 1995. "Tyrian shekels: the Myth of the Jerusalem mint," *Society for Ancient Numismatics* 19: 33-35.

Levy, B. E. 2005. "Later Tyrian shekels: dating the 'crude' issues; reading the controls," in C. A. Asins, C. M. Alonso, and P. O, Morán (eds.), *XIII Congresso Internacional de Numismática, Madrid, 2003: actas–proceedings–actes,* vol. 1, pp. 885–90. Madrid: Ministerio de Cultura.

Lewis, A. T. and C. Short. 1945. *A Latin Dictionary.* Oxford: Clarendon.

Liddell Hart, B. H. 1941. *The Strategy of the Indirect Approach.* London: Faber and Faber.

Liddell Hart, B. H. 1948. *The German Generals Talk.* New York: William Morrow.

Liebl, U. 1997. *Die Illustrierten Flavius-Josephus-Handschriften des Hochmittelalters.* Frankfurt am Main: Peter Lang.

Linder, A. 2009. "'The Jews too were not absent ... carrying Moses's Law on their shoulders': the ritual encounter of pope and Jews from Middle Ages to modern times," *JQR* 99: 323–95.

Lindner, H. 1972. *Die Geschichtsauffassung des Flavius Josephus im Bellum Judaicum.* Leiden: Brill.

Lintott, A. W. 1982. *Violence, Civil Strife and Revolution in the Classical City, 750–330 BC.* London: Croom Helm.

Lintott, A. W. 1993. *Imperium Romanum: Politics and Administration.* London: Routledge.

Lodge, H. C. 2006. "'Speech against the League of Nations,' August 12, 1919, Washington DC," in J. Ciment, M. Hickey, and T. Russell (eds.) *The Home Front Encyclopedia: United States, Britain, and Canada in World Wars I and II, 3 vols.* Santa Barbara: ABC–CLIO.

Lönnqvist, K. 2009. *New Perspectives on the Roman Coinage of the Eastern Limes.* Saarbrücken: VDM Verlag Dr. Müller.

Loomis, L. R. (ed.). 1916. *The Book of the Popes (Liber Pontificalis), vol. 1: To the Pontificate of Gregory I.* New York: Columbia University Press.

Luce, T. J. 1977. *Livy: The Composition of His History.* Princeton: Princeton University Press.

Lüdemann, G. 1980. "The successors of pre-70 Jerusalem Christianity: a critical evaluation of the Pella-tradition," in E. P. Sanders et al. (ed.) *Jewish and Christian Self-Definition*, 3 vols, vol 1, pp. 161–73. Philadelphia, PA: Fortress Press.

Lusnia, S. 2006. "Battle imagery and politics on the Severan Arch of the Roman Forum," in Dillon and Welch, *Representations of War*, 272–99.

Luther, H. 1910. *Josephus und Justus von Tiberias: ein Beitrag zur Geschichte des jüdischen Aufstandes.* Halle: Wischan & Burkhardt.

Luttwak, E. N. 1976. *The Grand Strategy of the Roman Empire.* Baltimore: Johns Hopkins University Press.

Luttwak, E. N. 2001. *Strategy: The Logic of War and Peace*, revised and enlarged edition. Cambridge, Mass.: Belknap Press of Harvard University Press.

Luz, M. 1983. "Eleazar's second speech on Masada and its literary precedents," *Rheinisches Museum für Philologie* 126: 25–43.

Lykke, A. 2012. *Reign and Religion in Palestine: The Political Instrumentalization of Sacred Iconography in the Hellenistic-Roman Period on the Basis of the Numismatic Evidence,* PhD dissertation, Klassische Archäologie, Universität Wien.

MacMullen, E. 1966. *Enemies of the Roman Order: Treason, Unrest, and Alienation in the Empire.* London: Routledge.

MacMullen, R. 2003. *Feelings in History.* Claremont, CA: Regina Books.

Mader, G. 2000. *Josephus and the Politics of Historiography: Apologetic and Impression Management in the Bellum Judaicum.* Leiden: Brill.

Magen, Y. [=I.]. H. Misgav, and L. Tsefania. 2004. *Mount Gerizim Excavations I: The Aramaic, Hebrew and Samaritan Inscriptions*, trans. E. Levin and M. Guggenheim. Jerusalem: Israel Antiquities Authority.

Magen, Y. [=I.]. 2008. *Mount Gerizim Excavations II: A Temple City*, trans. E. Levin and C. Ebert. Jerusalem: Israel Antiquities Authority.

Magen, Y. [=I.]. undated. "The Temple on Mount Gerizim," Israel Antiquities Authority website www.antiquities.org.il/article_Item_eng.asp?sec_id=36&sub j_id=286), accessed 15 April 2012.

Magen, Y. [=I.], and Peleg, Y. 2007. *The Qumran Excavations 1993–2004: Preliminary Report,* Judea and Samaria Publications 6. Jerusalem: Israel Antiquities Authority.

Magness, J. 1992. "Masada: Arms and the man," *BAR* 18: 58–67.

Magness, J. 2001. "The cults of Isis and Kore at Samaria-Sebaste in the Hellenistic and Roman periods," *HTR* 94: 157–77.

Magness, J. 2002. *The Archaeology of Qumran and the Dead Sea Scrolls.* Grand Rapids: Eerdmans.

Majdalany, F. 1957. *Cassino: Portrait of a Battle.* London: Cassell.

Mallinson, A. 2010. *The Making of the British Army: From the English Civil War to the War on Terror.* London: Bantam.

Mann, J. C. 1979. "Power, force and the frontiers of empire," *JRS* 69: 175–83.

Mann, J. C. and M. M. Roxan. 1983. *Legionary Recruitment and Veteran Settlement during the*

Principate. London: Institute of Archaeology.

Ma`oz, Z. U. 1993. "Kanaf, Ḥorvat," in *NEAEHL* 3: 847–850.

Marcus, J. R. 1999 [1938]. *The Jew in the Medieval World: A Source Book, 315–1791,* revised edn., ed. Marc Saperstein. Cincinnati: Hebrew Union College Press.

Marincola, J. 1997. *Authority and Tradition in Ancient Historiography.* Cambridge: Cambridge University Press.

Marincola, J. 2001. *Greek Historians.* Oxford: Oxford University Press.

Marincola, J. 2003. "Beyond pity and fear: the emotions in history," *Ancient Society* 33: 285–315.

Marincola, J., ed. 2011. *Greek and Roman Historiography.* Oxford: Oxford University Press.

Marrou, H. I. 1956. *A History of Education in Antiquity.* Madison: The University of Wisconsin Press.

Marsden, E. W. 1969. *Greek and Roman Artillery: Historical Development.* Oxford: Clarendon.

Marshall, S. L. A. 1947. *Men against Fire: the Problem of Battle Command.* New York: William Morrow & Co.

Martineau, H. 1848. *Eastern Life, Present and Past.* Complete in One Volume. Philadelphia: Lea and Blanchard.

Marx, K. 1904 [1859]. *A Contribution to the Critique of Political Economy,* trans. N. I. Stone. Chicago: Charles H. Kerr.

Mason, H. J. 1970. "The Roman government in Greek sources: the effect of literary theory on the translation of official titles," *Phoenix* 24: 150–59.

Mason, S. 1991. *Flavius Josephus on the Pharisees: A Composition-Critical Study.* Leiden: Brill.

Mason, S. 1994. "Josephus, Daniel, and the Flavian House," in F. Parente and J. Sievers (eds.) *Josephus and the History of the Greco-Roman Period.* Leiden: Brill.

Mason, S. 2001. *Flavius Josephus: Translation and Commentary, vol. 9: Life of Josephus.* Leiden: Brill.

Mason, S. 2003a. *Josephus and the New Testament.* 2nd edn. Peabody, Mass.: Hendrickson.

Mason, S. 2003b. "Flavius Josephus in Flavian Rome: Reading on and between the lines," in Boyle and Dominik, *Flavian Culture,* 559–90.

Mason, S. 2005a. "Figured speech and irony in T. Flavius Josephus," in J. Edmondson, S. Mason, J. Rives (eds.) *Flavius Josephus and Flavian Rome,* pp. 244–88. Oxford: Oxford University Press.

Mason, S. 2005b. "Of audience and meaning: reading Josephus' *Bellum Iudaicum* in the context of a Flavian audience," in J. Sievers and G. Lembi (eds.) *Josephus and Jewish History in Flavian Rome and Beyond,* pp. 70–100. Leiden: Brill.

Mason, S 2007a. "Essenes and lurking Spartans in Josephus' *Judean War:* from story to history," in Z. Rodgers, (ed.), *Making History: Josephus and Historical Method,* pp. 219–61. Leiden: Brill.

Mason, S. 2007b. "Yuval Shahar, *Josephus Geographicus,*" *Henoch* 29: 159–66.

Mason, S. 2008. *Flavius Josephus: Translation and Commentary, vol. 1b: Judean War 2.* Leiden: Brill.

Mason, S. 2009a. *Josephus, Judea, and Christian Origins: Methods and Categories.* Peabody, Mass.: Hendrickson.

Mason, S. 2009b. "Of despots, diadems, and *Diadochoi:* Josephus and Flavian politics," in W. J. Dominik, J. Garthwaite, and P. A. Roche (ed.), *Writing Politics in Imperial Rome,* pp. 323–49. Leiden: Brill.

Mason, S. 2011. "Speech-making in ancient rhetoric, Josephus, and Acts: messages and playfulness. Part I," *Early Christianity* 2: 445–67.

Mason, S. 2012a. "Speech-making in ancient rhetoric, Josephus, and Acts: messages and playfulness. Part II," *Early Christianity* 3: 147–71.

Mason, S. 2012b. "The importance of the latter half of Josephus' *Antiquities* for a Roman audience," in G. Hata and A. Moriya (eds.), *Pentateuchal Traditions in the Ancient World,* 129–53. Leiden: Brill.

Masuzawa, T. 2005. *The Invention of World Religions, or, How European Universalism was*

Preserved in the Language of Pluralism. Chicago: University of Chicago Press.

Mattern, S. P. 1999. *Rome and the Enemy: Imperial Strategy in the Principate.* Berkeley: University of California.

Mattingly, H. 1910. *The Imperial Civil Service of Rome.* Cambridge: Cambridge University Press.

Mattingly, H. 1977. *The Coinage of the Civil Wars of 68–69 A.D.* New York: Attic Books.

Mattingly, H. and E. A. Sydenham et al.. 1966. *The Roman Imperial Coinage,* 10 vols. London: Spink & Son.

Maude, F. N. 1907. *War and the World's Life.* London: Smith, Elder & Co.

May, J. M. 1988. *Trials of Character: the Eloquence of Ciceronian Ethos.* Chapel Hill: University of North Carolina Press.

Mazower, M. 2008. *Hitler's Empire: How the Nazis Ruled Europe.* London: Penguin.

McDonald, A. H. 1975. "Theme and style in Roman historiography," *JRS* 65: 1–10.

McDonnell, M. 2006. *Roman Manliness: Virtus and the Roman Republic.* Cambridge: Cambridge University Press.

McEvedy, C. 2011. *Cities of the Classical World: An Atlas and Gazetteer of 120 Centres of Ancient Civilization,* ed. D. S. Oles. London: Allen Lane.

McGing, B. C. 2010. *Polybius' Histories.* Oxford: Oxford University Press.

McGushin, P. 1992. *Sallust: the Histories. Volume I. Books i-ii.* Oxford: Clarendon.

McGushin, P. 1994. *Sallust: the Histories. Volume II. Books iii-v.* Oxford: Clarendon.

McKechnie, P. 2005. "Judaean embassies and cases before Roman emperors, AD 44-66," *Journal of Theological Studies* 56: 339-61.

McLaren, J. S. 1998. *Turbulent Times? Josephus and Scholarship on Judaea in the First Century CE.* Sheffield: Sheffield Academic Press.

McLaren, J. S. 2003. "The coinage of the first year as a point of reference for the first Jewish revolt (66–70 CE)," *SCI* 22: 135–52.

McMichael, S. J. and S. E. Myers (eds.). 2004. *Friars and Jews in the Middle Ages and Renaissance.* Leiden: Brill.

Mearsheimer, J. J. 2001. *The Tragedy of Great Power Politics.* New York: W. W. Norton & Co.

Mearsheimer, J. J. 2011. *Why Leaders Lie: The Truth about Lying in International Politics.* New York: Oxford University Press.

Mearsheimer, J. J. 2014. "Getting Ukraine wrong," *International New York Times* Opinion section, March 14.

Meimaris, Y. E. et al. (eds.). 1992. *Chronological Systems in Roman-Byzantine Palestine and Arabia: The Evidence of the Dated Greek Inscriptions.* Athens: The National Hellenic Research Foundation/Research Centre for Greek and Roman Antiquity; Paris: Diffusion de Boccard.

Mellor, R. 1993. *Tacitus.* London: Routledge.

Mellor, R. 1999. *The Roman Historians.* London: Routledge.

Melville, C. H. 1912. *Military Hygiene and Sanitation.* London: Edward Arnold.

Mercer, C. 1999 [1870]. *Journal of the Waterloo Campaign.* London: Da Capo Press.

Merrill, S. 1885. "The stations of David's census officers," *Quarterly Statement of the Palestine Exploration Fund,* January: 134–37.

Meshorer, Y. A. 1982. *Ancient Jewish Coinage.* New York: Amphora Books.

Meshorer, Y. 1989. "The coins of Masada," in J. Aviram, G. Foerster, and E. Netzer (eds.) *Masada I. The Yigael Yadin Excavations 1963–5. Final Reports,* pp. 71–132. Jerusalem: Israel Exploration Society.

Meshorer, Y. 2001. *A Treasury of Jewish Coins from the Persian Period to Bar Kokhba.* Jerusalem: Yad ben-Zvi.

Meyer, C. 2009. *Getting Our Own Way: 500 Years of Adventure and Intrigue: The Inside Story of British Diplomacy.* London: Weidenfeld & Nicolson.

Meyer-Zwiffelhoffer, E. 2002. *Politikōs Archein: zum Regierungsstil der senatorischen Statthalter in den kaiserzeitlichen griechischen Provinzen.* Stuttgart: Franz Steiner.

Meyers, E. 1999. *Galilee through the Centuries: Confluence of Cultures.* Winona Lake: Eisenbrauns.

Meyers, E. M. 2002. "Sepphoris: City of peace," in A. M. Berlin and J. A. Overman (eds.) *The First Jewish Revolt: Archaeology, History, and Ideology*, pp. 110–20. London: Routledge.

Michel, O. 1968. "Studien zu Josephus: Simon bar Giora," *New Testament Studies* 14: 402–408.

Milano, A. 1963. *Storia degli ebrei in Italia*. Turin: Giulio Einaudi.

Millar, F. 1966. "The emperor, the Senate and the provinces," *JRS* 56: 156–66.

Millar, F (ed.). 1967. *The Roman Empire and its Neighbours*. New York: Delacorte.

Millar, F. 1977. *The Emperor in the Roman World, 31 BC–AD 337*. Ithaca: Cornell University Press.

Millar, F. 1990. "The Roman *Coloniae* of the Near East: A study of cultural relations," in H. Solin and M. Kajava (eds.), *Roman Policy in the East and Other Studies in Roman History*. Helsinki: Finnish Society of Science and Letters.

Millar, F. 1993. *The Roman Near East, 31 B.C. – A. D. 337*. Cambridge, Mass.: Harvard University Press.

Millar, F. 2005. "Last year in Jerusalem: Monuments of the Jewish war in Rome," in J. Edmondson, S. Mason, and J. Rives (eds.) *Flavius Josephus and Flavian Rome*, pp. 101–128. Oxford: Oxford University Press.

Millar, F. 2006a. "Polybius between Greece and Rome," in F. Millar, *Rome, the Greek World, and the East, vol. 3: The Greek World the Jews, and the East*, eds. H. M. Cotton and G. M. Rogers, pp. 91–105. Chapel Hill: University of North Carolina Press.

Millar, F. 2006b. "The Roman *Coloniae* of the Near East: a study of cultural Relations," in F. Millar, *Rome, the Greek World, and the East, vol. 3: The Greek World the Jews, and the East*, eds. H. M. Cotton and G. M. Rogers, pp. 164–222. Chapel Hill: University of North Carolina Press.

Miller, S. S. 1984. *Studies in the History and Traditions of Sepphoris*. Leiden: Brill.

Milner, N. P. 1996. *Vegetius: Epitome of Military Science*. Liverpool: Liverpool University Press.

Mionnet, T. E. 1806–1837. *Description de Médailles antiques, grecques et romaines, avec leur Degré de Rareté et leur Estimation: Ouvrage Servant de Catalogue à une Suite de plus de vingt mille Empreintes en Soufre, Prises sur les Pièces originales*. 15 vols. Paris: Imprimerie de Testu, Imprimeur de l'Empereur.

Mitchell, T. J. 1931. *Medical Services: Casualties and Medical Statistics of the Great War*. History of the Great War based on Official Documents. London: Imperial War Museum.

Moehring, H. R. 1957. *Novelistic Elements in the Writings of Flavius Josephus*. PhD dissertation, University of Chicago.

Moehring, H. R. 1984. "Joseph ben Matthia and Flavius Josephus," *ANRW* 2.21.2.864–917.

Moll, S. 2010. *The Arch-Heretic Marcion*. Tübingen: Mohr Siebeck.

Molyneux, J. H. 1993 (ed.). *Literary Responses to Civil Discord*. Nottingham: University of Nottingham.

Momigliano, A. 1976. "Review of T. D. Barnes' *Tertullian: A Historical and Literary Study*," *JRS* 66: 273–76.

Momigliano, A. 1977. "Historicism revisited," in A. Momigliano, *Essays in Ancient and Modern Historiography*, pp. 365–73. Oxford: Blackwell.

Mommsen, T. 1887. *The Provinces of the Roman Empire from Caesar to Diocletian*, trans. W. P. Dickson. 2 vols. New York: Charles Scribner's Sons.

Mommsen, T. 1894. *Römische Geschichte*, 5 vols. Fourth edition. Berlin: Weidmann.

Montefiore, H. 1962. "Sulpicius Severus and Titus' council of war," *Historia* 11: 156–70.

Monten, J. 2006. "Thucydides and modern realism," *International Studies Quarterly* 50: 3–25.

Montgomery, J. A. 1920–1921. "The religion of Flavius Josephus," *JQR* 11: 277–305.

Morel, W. 1926. "Eine Rede bei Josephus," *Rheinisches Museum für Philologie* 75: 106–15.

Moreland, M. 2002. (Review Article) "*Archaeology and the Galilean Jesus: A Re-examination of the Evidence* by J. L. Reed / *Crossing Galilee: Architectures of Contact in the Occupied Land of Jesus* by M. Sawicki / *Jesus and the*

Village Scribes: Galilean Conflicts and the Setting of Q by W. E. Arnal," *JBL* 121: 757–66.

Morgan, C. 2009a. "Ethnic expression on the Early Iron Age and Early Archaic Greek mainland. Where should we be looking?" In T. Derks and N. Roymans (eds.) *Ethnic Constructs in Antiquity: The Role of Power and Tradition*, pp. 11–36. Amsterdam: University Press.

Morgan, C. 2009b. "The archaeology of *Ethnē* and ethnicity in the fourth-century Peloponnese," In P. Funke and N. Luraghi (eds.) *The Politics of Ethnicity and the Crisis of the Pelopponesian League*, pp. 148–82. Washington, DC: Center for Hellenic Studies.

Morgan, G. 2006. *69 A.D.: The Year of Four Emperors*. Oxford: Oxford University Press.

Morgenthau, H. 1954. *Politics among Nations: The Struggle for Power and Peace*. 2nd edn. New York: Knopf.

Mountford, L. M. 1898. "The Kaiser in Jerusalem: The city's great reception to Emperor William's party," *New York Times* November 27.

Muecke, D. C. 1969. *The Compass of Irony*. London: Methuen.

Müller, K (ed.). 1841–1870. *Fragmenta Historicorum Graecorum* (= *FHG*), 5 vols. Paris: Didot.

Murphy, T. M. 2004. *Pliny the Elder's Natural History: The Empire in the Encyclopedia*. Oxford: Oxford University Press.

Murray, J. O. 1891. *Francis Wayland*. Boston: Houghton, Mifflin and Company.

Myerly, S. H. 1996. *British Military Spectacle: From the Napoleonic Wars through the Crimea*. Cambridge, Mass.: Harvard University Press.

Myers, E. A. 2010. *The Ituraeans and the Roman Near East: Reassessing the Sources* (Cambridge: Cambridge University Press.

Naiden, F. S. 2013. *Smoke Signals for the Gods: Ancient Greek Sacrifice from the Archaic through Roman Periods*. Oxford: Oxford University Press.

Nash-Williams, V. E. 1940. *The Roman Legionary Fortress at Caerleon, Monmouthshire*. Cardiff:

National Museum of Wales; University of Wales.

Nauta, R. R. 2002. *Poetry for Patrons: Literary Communication in the Age of Domitian*. Leiden: Brill.

Navy League of the United States. 1915. *Seven Seas* (now *Seapower*) 2: November, 27–28.

Netzer, E. 1991a. *Masada III. The Yigael Yadin Excavations 1963–1965. Final Reports: The Buildings, Stratigraphy and Architecture*. Jerusalem: Israel Exploration Society.

Netzer, E. 1991b. "The last days and hours at Masada," *BAR* 17: 20–32.

Netzer, E. 2008. "Herodium," *NEAEHL* 5.1778–80.

Netzer, E. et al. 2013. "Herodium," in Rozenberg and Mevorach (eds.), *Herod the Great*, pp. 126–65.

Netzer. E. and G. D. Stiebel. 2008. "Masada," *NEAEHL* 5.1935–37.

Neusner, J. 1969. *A History of the Jews in Babylonia, 3 vols. Vol. 1: The Parthian Period*. Leiden: E. J. Brill.

Newton, H. C. 1902. *The Epigraphical Evidence for the Reigns of Vespasian and Titus*. Cornell Studies in Classical Philology 16. New York: Macmillan.

Neyrey, J. H. 1994. "Josephus' vita and the encomium: a native model of personality," *JSJ* 25: 177–206.

Nickau, K. (ed.). 1966. *Ammonii Qui Dicitur Liber de Adfinium Cocabulorum Differentia*. Leipzig: Teubner.

Nicols, J. 1978. *Vespasian and the Partes Flavianae*. Wiesbaden: Franz Steiner.

Niebuhr, R. 1932. *Moral Man and Immoral Society: A Study in Ethics and Politics*. New York: Charles Scribner's Sons.

Niese, B. 1896. "Der jüdische Historiker Flavius Josephus," *Historische Zeitschrift N. F.* 40: 193–237.

Nongbri, B. 2013. *Before Religion: A History of a Modern Concept*. New Haven: Yale University Press.

Noy, D. 2000. *Foreigners at Rome: Citizens and Stranger*. London: Duckworth / Classical Press of Wales.

Nun, M. 2008. "Ports of Galilee: Modern drought reveals harbors from Jesus' time," in Biblical Archaeology Society (ed.), *The Galilee Jesus Knew*. Washington DC: Biblical Archaeology Society, 14–26.

Ogilvie, R. M. 1980. *Roman Literature and Society*. London: Penguin.

O'Gorman, E. 2000. *Irony and Misreading in the Annals of Tacitus*. Cambridge: Cambridge University Press.

Opper, T. 2008. *Hadrian: Empire and Conflict*. Cambridge, Mass.: Harvard University Press.

Orlin, E. M. 2002. *Temples, Religion and Politics in the Roman Republic*. Leiden: Brill.

Paget, J. C. 2010. *Jews, Christians and Jewish Christians in Antiquity*. Tübingen: Mohr Siebeck.

Paine, T. 1793. *The Age of Reason*. Various editions.

Panzram, S. 2002. "Der Jerusalemer Tempel und das Rome der Flavier," in Hahn (ed.), *Zerstörungen des Jerusalemer Tempels*, pp. 167–82.

Parker, H. M. D. 1928. *The Roman Legions*. Oxford: Clarendon.

Parker, M. 2003. *Monte Cassino: The Story of the Hardest-fought Battle of World War Two*. London: Headline.

Parkin, T. G. 1992. *Demography and Roman Society*. Baltimore: Johns Hopkins University Press.

Patrich, J. 2009. "538 BCE–70 CE: the temple (*Beyt Ha-Miqdash*) and its mount," in O. Grabar and B. Z. Keda (eds.), *Where Heaven and Earth Meet: Jerusalem's Sacred Esplanade*, pp. 36–71. Jerusalem; Austin: Yad Ben-Zvi; University of Texas Press.

Paul, G. M. 1993. "The presentation of Titus in the *Jewish War* of Josephus: Two aspects." *Phoenix* 47: 56–66.

Pearlman, M. 1967. *The Zealots of Masada: Story of a Dig*. Herzliya: Palphot.

Pearson, B. 1971. "1 Thessalonians 2:13–16: A Deutero-Pauline interpolation," *HTR* 64: 79–94.

Pekáry, T. 1987. "*Seditio*: Unruhen und Revolten im römischen Reich von Augustus bis Commodus," *Ancient Society* 18: 133–50.

Pelikan Pittenger, M. R. 2008. *Contested Triumphs: Politics, Pageantry, and Performance in Livy's Republican Rome*. Berkeley: University of California Press.

Pelling, C. 2000. *Literary Texts and the Greek Historian*. London: Routledge.

Pfann, S. 2006. "Dated bronze coinage of the sabbatical years of release and the first Jewish city coin," *Bulletin of the Anglo-Israeli Archaeological Society* 24:101–113.

Pfanner, M. 1983. *Der Titusbogen*. Mainz: Philipp von Zabern.

Phang, S. E. 2001. *The Marriage of Roman Soldiers (13 B.C.–A.D. 235): Law and Family in the Imperial Army*. Leiden: Brill.

Pitcher, L. 2009. *Writing Ancient History: An Introduction to Classical Historiography*. London: I. B. Tauris.

Plass, P. 1988. *Wit and the Writing of History: the Rhetoric of Historiography in Imperial Rome*. Madison: University of Wisconsin Press.

Platner, S. B. and T. Ashby. 1929. *A Topographical Dictionary of Ancient Rome*. London: Oxford University Press.

Pollard, N. 2000. *Soldiers, Cities, and Civilians in Roman Syria*. Ann Arbor: University of Michigan.

Porter, S. E (ed.). 1991. *The Language of the New Testament: Classic Essays*. Sheffield: JSOT.

Potter, D. S. 1996. "Emperors, borders, and their neighbours: The scope of imperial *Mandata*," in Kennedy (ed.), *Roman Army*, 49–66.

Potter, D. S. 1999. *Literary Texts and the Roman Historian*. London: Routledge.

Povoledo, E. 2012. "Technology identifies lost color at Roman Forum," *New York Times* (New York edition), 25 June, p. C3.

Price, J. J. 1991. "The enigma of Philip ben Jakimos," *Historia* 11: 77–94.

Price, J. J. 1992. *Jerusalem under Siege: The Collapse of the Jewish State, 66–70 C.E.* Leiden: Brill.

Price, J. J. 2008. "The failure of rhetoric in Josephus' *Bellum Judaicum*," *Ramus* 36: 6–24.

Project Runeberg (http://runeberg.org/nfcc/).

Pummer, R. 1987. *The Samaritans*. Leiden: Brill.

Pummer, R. 2009. *The Samarians in Flavius Josephus*. Tübingen: Mohr Siebeck.

Pummer, R. 2010. "Samaritanism – a Jewish sect or an independent form of Yahwism?" in M. Mor and F. V. Reiterer (eds.), *Samaritans: Past and Present. Current Studies*, pp. 1–24. Berlin: de Gruyter.

Purcell, N. 1996. "Pliny," in *OCD*[3]: 1197.

Rabinovich, A. 2011. "At Yadin's side," *The Jerusalem Post Magazine*, April 28, 2011. Accessed online May 1, 2011: www.jpost .com/Magazine/Features/Article.aspx? id=218262

Rainey, A. and S. Notley. 2006. *The Sacred Bridge: Carta's Atlas of the Biblical World*. Jerusalem: Carta.

Rajak, T. 1973. "Justus of Tiberias," *Classical Quarterly* 23: 345–68.

Rajak, T. 1983 [repr. 2002]. *Josephus: the Historian and his Society*. London: Duckworth.

Rajak, T. 1998. "The Parthians in Josephus," in J. Wiesehöfer (ed.), *Das Partherreich und seine Zeugnisse*, 309–324. Stuttgart: Franz Steiner.

Rajak, T. 2005. "Josephus in the Diaspora," in J. Edmondson, S. Mason, and J. Rives (eds.), *Flavius Josephus and Flavian Rome*, pp. 79–99. Oxford: Oxford University Press.

Rappaport, U. 1969. "Les Iduméens d'Egypte," *Revue de Philologie, de littérature et d'histoire ancienne* 43: 73–82.

Rappaport, U. 1981. "Jewish–pagan relations and the revolt against Rome in 66–70 C.E.," in Levine (ed.), *Jerusalem Cathedra*, pp. 1.81–95.

Rappaport, U. 1982. "John of Gischala: from Galilee to Jerusalem," *JJS* 33: 479–93.

Rappaport, U. 1994. "Where was Josephus lying – in his *Life* or in the *War*?" in F. Parente and J. Sievers (eds.), *Josephus and the History of the Greco–Roman Period,* pp. 279–89. Leiden: Brill.

Rappaport, U. 2007. "Who minted the Jewish war's coins?" *Israel Numismatic Research* 2: 103–116.

Rappaport, U. 2013. *John of Gischala: From the Mountains of Galilee to the Walls of Jerusalem.* The author's electronically circulated translation, by R. Toueg (with J. Pastor and G. Silberman), of his *Yohanan mi-Gush Halav: me-Hare ha-Galil el Homot Yerushalayim* (Haifa: University of Haifa Press [Hotsa'at ha-Sefarim], 2006) [Hebrew].

Rashidi, K. 2006. *The Iron Cage: the Story of the Palestinian Struggle for Statehood.* Boston: Beacon.

Ravid, B. 2012. "*Cum Nimis Absurdum* and the Ancona auto-da-fé revisited: Their impact on Venice and some wider reflections," *Jewish History* 26: 85–100.

Rawlinson, G. 1889. *The Seventh Great Oriental Monarchy, or, The Geography, History, and Antiquities of the Sassanian, or New Persian Empire.* London: Longmans Green & Co.

Reed, J. L. 2000. *Archaeology and the Galilean Jesus: A Re-examination of the Evidence.* Harrisburg: Trinity Press International, 2000.

Reelant, A. 1716. *[Hadriani Relandi] de Spoliis Templi Hierosolymitani in Arcu Titiano Romae conspicuis.* Utrecht [Tajecti ad Rhenum]: Willem Brodelet.

Reich, R. 2001. "Women and men at Masada: some anthropological observations based on the small finds (coins, spindles)," *ZDPV* 117: 149–62

Reich, R. 2003. "Baking and cooking at Masada," *ZDPV* 119: 140–58.

Reich, R. 2007. "Spindle whorls and spinning at Masada," *Masada VIII*, 171–194.

Reich, R. and E. Shukron. 2011. "The ool of Siloam in Jerusalem of the late second Temple period and its surroundings," in Galor and Avni, *Unearthing Jerusalem*, pp. 241–55.

Reifenberg, A. 1973. *Ancient Jewish Coins*, 6th edn. Jerusalem: Rubin Mass.

Reinach, T. 1966 (1903). *Jewish Coins*, trans. Mary Hill. London: Lawrence & Bullen.

Remini, R. 2001. *Andrew Jackson and His Indian Wars.* New York: Viking.

Renan, J. E. 1898 [1863]. *Renan's Life of Jesus*, trans. W. G. Hutchinson. London: Walter Scott.

Report of the World Heritage Committee, 25th session, December 11–16, 2001, at http:// whc.unesco.org/archive/repcom01. htm#1040 (accessed August 1, 2009).

Revell, L. 2009. *Roman Imperialism and Local Identities.* Cambridge: Cambridge University Press.

Rhoads, D. M. 1976. *Israel in Revolution, 6–74 C.E.: A Political History Based on the Writings of Josephus*. Philadelphia: Fortress.

Rich, J. W. 2009. "Augustus, war and peace," in Edmondson, *Augustus*, 137–64.

Richardson, J. 1976. *Roman Provincial Administration*. London: Macmlllan.

Richardson, J. 2008. *The Language of Empire: Rome and the Idea of Empire from the Third Century BC to the Second Century AD*. Cambridge: Cambridge University Press.

Richardson, P. 1996. *Herod: King of the Jews and Friend of the Romans*. Columbia: University of South Carolina Press.

Richlin, A. 1992a. *Pornography and Representation in Greece and Rome*. Oxford: Oxford University Press.

Richlin, A. 1992b. *The Garden of Priapus: Sexuality and Aggression in Roman Humor*. Oxford: Oxford University Press.

Richmond, I. 1962. "The Roman siege-works of Masada, Israel," *JRS* 52: 142–55.

Rickard, J. N. 2003. "The Canadian Army and fighting power," *The Army Doctrine and Training Bulletin* 6: 33–42.

Ricoeur, P. 1970. *Freud and Philosophy*. New Haven: Yale University Press.

Riedl, N. 2003. *Gottheiten und Kulte in der Dekapolis*. PhD dissertation, Freie Universität Berlin.

Rigsby, K. J. 1996. *Asylia: Territorial Inviolability in the Hellenistic World*. Berkeley: University of California Press.

Ritmeyer, L. 2006a. *The Quest: Revealing the Temple Mount in Jerusalem*. Jerusalem: Carta.

Ritmeyer, L. and K. 2006b. *Secrets of Jerusalem's Temple Mount*. Revised edn. Jerusalem: Washington: Biblical Archaeology Society.

Rives, J. B. 1999. *Tacitus: Germania*. Oxford: Oxford University Press.

Rives, J. B. 2005. "Flavian religious policy and the destruction of the Jerusalem temple," in Edmondson, Mason, and Rives, pp. 145–66.

Roberts, A. 2008. *Masters and Commanders: The Military Geniuses who led the West to Victory in WW II*. London: Penguin.

Roberts, A. 2009. *The Storm of War: A New History of the Second World War*. London: Penguin.

Rocca, S. 2009. *The Army of Herod the Great*. Oxford: Osprey.

Rodgers, Z. 2006. "Justice for Justus: A reexamination of Justus of Tiberias' role in Josephus' autobiography," in B. McGing and J. Mossman (eds.), *The Limits of Ancient Biography*, 169–92. Swansea: The Classical Press of Wales.

Rogan, J. 2011. *Roman Provincial Administration*. Stroud: Amberley.

Rogers, C. L. 1992. *The Topical Josephus: Historical Accounts That Shed Light on the Bible*. Grand Rapids: Zondervan.

Roller, D. W. 1998. *The Building Program of Herod the Great*. Berkeley: University of California Press.

Roller, D. W. 2003. *The World of Juba II and Kleopatra Selene: Royal Scholarship on Rome's African Frontier*. London: Routledge.

Romanoff, P. 1942. "Jewish symbols on ancient Jewish coins," *JQR* 33: 1–15.

Romanoff, P. 1943. "Jewish symbols on ancient Jewish coins (continued)," *JQR* 33: 435–44.

Romanoff, P. 1944. "Jewish symbols on ancient Jewish coins (continued)," *JQR* 34: 299–312.

Romer, F. E. 1998. *Pomponius Mela's Description of the World*. Ann Arbor: University of Michigan Press.

Ronen, I. 1988. "Formation of Jewish nationalism among the Idumaeans," in A. Kasher (ed.), *Jews, Idumaeans, and Ancient Arabs: Relations of the Jews in Eretz-Israel with the Nations of the Frontier and the Desert during the Hellenistic and Roman Era (332 BCE-70 CE)*, pp. 214–20. Tübingen: Mohr Siebeck.

Rorty, R. 1989. *Contingency, Irony, and Solidarity*. Cambridge: Cambridge University Press.

Rossini, O. 2006. *Ara Pacis*. Milan: Electa.

Roth, C. 1946. *The History of the Jews of Italy*. Philadelphia: Jewish Publication Society of America.

Roth, C. 1960. "Simon bar Giora: Ancient Jewish hero: A historical reinterpretation," *Commentary* 29 (1): 52–8.

Roth, E. 1973. *Preußens Gloria im Heiligen Land: die Deutschen und Jerusalem*. Munich: Georg D. W. Callwey.

Roth, J. P. 1995. "The length of the *siege of Masada*," *SCI* 14: 87–110.

Roth, J. P. 1999. *The Logistics of the Roman Army at War (264 B.C.-A.D. 235)*. Leiden: Brill.

Roth, J. P. 2009. *Roman Warfare*. Cambridge: Cambridge University Press.

Rottman, G. L. 2002. *World War II Pacific Island Guide: A Geo-Military Study*. Westport, Conn.: Greenwood.

Roullet, A. 1972. *The Egyptian and Egyptianizing Monuments of Imperial Rome*. Leiden: Brill.

Rudich, V. 1993. *Political Dissidence under Nero: The Price of Dissimulation*. London: Routledge.

Rudich, V. 1997. *Dissidence and Literature under Nero: The Price of Rhetoricization*. London: Routledge.

Runesson, A., D. D. Binder, B. Olsson. 2008. *The Ancient Synagogue from Its Origins to 200 C.E.: a Source Book*. Leiden: Brill.

Runnalls, D. 1997. "The rhetoric of Josephus," in S. E. Porter (ed.), *Handbook of Classical Rhetoric in the Hellenistic Period 330 BC–AD 400*, pp. 737-54. Leiden: Brill.

Rüpke, J. 2007. *Religion of the Romans,* trans. R. Gordon. Malden, Mass.: Polity.

Russell, D. A. 1966. "On reading Plutarch's Lives," *Greece and Rome* 13: 139.

Rutledge, S. H. 2001. *Imperial Inquisitions: Prosecutors and Informants from Tiberius to Domitian*. London: Routledge.

Sacks, K. S. 1990. *Diodorus Siculus and the First Century*. Princeton: Princeton University Press.

Sallares, R. 2002. *Malaria and Rome: A History of Malaria in Ancient Italy*. Oxford: Oxford University Press.

Saller, R. P. 1982. *Personal Patronage under the Early Empire*. Cambridge: Cambridge University Press.

Saller, R. P. 1983. "Martial on patronage and literature," *The Classical Quarterly* 33: 246-57.

Saller, R. P. 1994. *Patriarchy, Property, and Death in the Roman Family*. Cambridge: Cambridge University Press.

Salles, C. 1992. *Lire à Rome*. Paris: Les Belles Lettres.

Samuel, A. E. 1972. *Greek and Roman Chronology: Calendars and Years in Classical Antiquity*. Munich: C. H. Beck.

Sandgren, L. D. 2010. *Vines Intertwined: A History of Jews and Christians from the Babylonian Exile to the Advent of Islam*. Peabody: Hendrickson.

Sartre, M. 2005. *The Middle East under Rome*. Cambridge, Mass.: Belknap / Harvard University Press.

Sawicki, M. 2000. *Crossing Galilee: Architectures of Contact in the Occupied Land of Jesus*. Harrisburg: Trinity Press International.

Schäfer, P. 2003. *The History of the Jews in the Greco-Roman World*. London: Routledge.

Schalit, A. 1933. "Josephus und Justus," *Klio* 26: 67–95.

Schalit, A. 1969. *König Herodes: der Mann und sein Werk*. Berlin: De Gruyter.

Schechter, R. 2003. *Obstinate Hebrews: Representations of Jews in France, 1715–1815*. Berkeley: University of California Press.

Scheidel, W. 2001. *Death on the Nile: Disease and the Demography of Roman Egypt*. Leiden: Brill.

Scheidel, W. 2004. "Creating a metropolis: A comparative demographic perspective," in W. V. Harris and G. Ruffini (eds.), *Ancient Alexandria between Egypt and Greece*, pp. 1–32. Leiden: Brill.

Scheidel, W. and S. J. Friesen. 2009. "The size of the economy and the distribution of income in the Roman Empire," *Journal of Roman Studies* 99: 61–91.

Scheidgen, A. 2002. *Die Gestalt des Pontius Pilatus in Legende, Bibelauslegung und Geschichtsdichtung vom Mittelalter bis in die frèuhe Neuzeit: Literaturgeschichte einer umstrittenen Figur*. Frankfurt am Main: Peter Lang.

Schiffman, L. H. 1994. *Reclaiming the Dead Sea Scrolls*. Philadelphia: Jewish Publication Society.

Schippmann, K. 1980. *Grundzüge der Parthischen Geschichte*. Darmstadt: Wissenschaftliche Buchgesellschaft.

Schlatter, A. 1910. *Wie sprach Josephus von Gott?* Gütersloh: Bertelsmann.

Schlatter, A. 1932. *Die Theologie des Judentums nach dem Bericht des Josefus*. Gütersloh: Bertelsmann.

Schmitt, R. 1998. "Parthische Sprach- und Namenüberlieferung aus arsakidischer Zeit," in J. Wiesehöfer (ed.) *Das Partherreich und Seine Zeugnisse*, pp. 163–204. Stuttgart: Franz Steiner.

Schneider, R. M. 1998. "Die Faszination des Feindes: Bilder der Parther und des Orients in Rom," in J. Wiesehöfer (ed.) *Das Partherreich und Seine Zeugnisse*, pp. 95–146. Stuttgart: Franz Steiner.

Schreckenberg, H. 1972. *Die Flavius-Josephus-Tradition in Antike und Mittelalter*. Leiden: Brill.

Schreckenberg, H. 1977. *Rezeptionsgeschichtliche und Textkritische Untersuchungen zu Flavius Josephus*. Leiden: Brill.

Schreckenberg, H., and Schubert, K. 1992. *Jewish Historiography and Iconography in Early and Medieval Christianity*, Compendia Rerum Iudaicarum ad Novum Testamentum. Assen: van Gorcum; Philadelphia: Fortress.

Schulten, A. von. 1933. *Masada: die Burg des Herodes und die römischen Lager, mit einem Anhang: Beth-Ter*. Leipzig: J. C. Hinrichs (Sonderdruck *ZDPV* 56: 1–185).

Schumacher, G. 1888. *The Jaulan: Surveyed for the German Society for the Exploration of the Holy Land*. London: Richard Bentley.

Schuol, M. 2000. *Die Charakene: ein Mesopotamisches Königreich in Hellenistisch-parthischer Zeit*. Stuttgart: Franz Steiner.

Schürer, E. 1874. *Lehrbuch der neutestamentlichen Zeitgeschichte*. Leipzig: J. C. Hinrichs.

Schürer, E. 1890. *Geschichte des jüdischen Volkes im Zeitalter Jesu Christi*. 2nd edn. Leipzig: J. C. Hinrichs.

Schürer, E. 1898–1901. *Geschichte des jüdischen Volkes im Zeitalter Jesu Christi*. 3rd–4th edn. Leipzig: J. C. Hinrichs.

Schürer, E. 1979–1987. *The History of the Jewish People in the Age of Jesus Christ*, eds. G. Vermes, F. Millar, and M. Goodman. 3 vols. in 4. Edinburgh, T. & T. Clark.

Schwartz, D. R. 1990. *Agrippa I: The Last King of Judaea*. Tübingen: Mohr Siebeck.

Schwartz, D. R. 1992. *Studies in the Jewish Background of Christianity*. Tübingen: Mohr Siebeck.

Schwartz, D. R. 2007. "'Judaean' or 'Jew'? How should we translate IOUDAIOS in Josephus?" in J. Frey, D. R. Schwartz, and S. Gripentrog (eds.) *Jewish Identity in the Greco-Roman World: Jüdische Identität in der Griechisch-römischen Welt*, pp. 3–28. Leiden: Brill.

Schwartz, D. R. 2008. *2 Maccabees*. Berlin: Walter de Gruyter.

Schwartz, S. 1986. "The composition and publication of Josephus's *Bellum Iudaicum* Book 7," *HTR* 79: 373–86.

Schwartz, S. 1990. *Josephus and Judaean Politics*. Leiden: Brill.

Schwartz, S. 1993. "A note on the social type and political ideology of the Hasmonean family," *Journal of Biblical Literature* 112: 305–9.

Schwartz, S. 2006. "Political, social, and economic life in the land of Israel, 66–c. 235," in S. T. Katz (ed.), *Cambridge History of Judaism, 4 vols*, vol. 4, pp. 23–50. Cambridge: Cambridge University Press.

Schwier, H. 1989. *Tempel und Tempelzerstörung: Untersuchungen zu den theologischen und ideologischen Faktoren im ersten jüdisch-römischen Krieg (66–74 n. Chr.)*. Göttingen: Vandenhoeck & Ruprecht.

Sear, F. 1982. *Roman Architecture*. Ithaca, NY: Cornell University Press.

Segev, T. 2000. *One Palestine, Complete: Jews and Arabs under the British Mandate*, trans. Haim Watzman. London: Abacus.

Segre, B. 2001. *Gli Ebrei in Italia*. Florence: Giuntina.

Seigne, J. 2002. "Gerasa–Jerasch—Stadt der 1000 Säulen," in Hoffmann and Kerner, *Gerasa–Gadara*, 6–22.

Semenchenko, L. 2002. *Hellenistic Motifs in the Jewish Antiquities of Flavius Josephus*. PhD dissertation, Department of History, Russian Academy of Sciences [Russian].

Setzer, C. 2006. "The Jews in Carthage and Western North Africa, 66–235 CE," in S. T. Katz (ed.), *Cambridge History of Judaism, 4 vols*, vol. 4, pp. 68–74. Cambridge: Cambridge University Press.

Seward, D. 2009. *Jerusalem's Traitor: Josephus, Masada, and the Fall of Judea*. Cambridge, Mass.: Da Capo.

Shahar, Y. 2004. *Josephus Geographicus: The Classical Context of Geography in Josephus*. Tübingen: Mohr Siebeck.

Shanks, H. 2005. "Sifting the Temple Mount dump: finds from the first temple period to modern times," *BAR* 31 (4): 14–15.

Shatzman, I. 1991. *The Armies of the Hasmonaeans and Herod: from Hellenistic to Roman Frameworks*. Tübingen: Mohr Siebeck.

Shatzman, I. 1999. "The integration of Judaea into the Roman empire," *Scripta Classica Israelica* 18: 49-84.

Shatzman, I. 2008. "Vespasian and the conquest of the Galilee: the performance of a Roman general in war," in O. Gur-Rimon (ed.) *The Great Revolt in the Galilee*, 81–90. Haifa: Hecht Museum, University of Haifa.

Shatzman, I. 2010. "Review of J. Richardson's *The Language of Empire: Rome and the Idea of Empire from the Third Century BC to the Second Century AD*," *Scripta Classica Israelica* 29: 128–32.

Shaw, B. D. 1984. "Bandits in the Roman empire," *Past and Present* 105: 3–52.

Shaw, B. D. 1993. "Tyrants, bandits, and kings: personal power in Josephus," *JJS* 44: 176–204.

Shaw, B. D. 1995. "Josephus: Roman power and responses to it," *Athenaeum* 83: 357–90.

Shenoy, S. 2006. *Josephus' Jewish War as a narrative five-act tragedy*. Ph.D. dissertation, Australian Catholic University, School of Theology.

Sherk, R. K. 1988. *The Roman Empire: Augustus to Hadrian*. Cambridge: Cambridge University Press.

Sherwin-White, A. N. 1963. *Roman Society and Roman Law in the New Testament*. Oxford: Clarendon Press.

Shimron, A., and O. Peleg-Barkat. 2010. "New evidence of the royal stoa and Roman flames," *BAR* 36 (2): 56–62.

Shorey, P. 1921. "Τύχη in Polybius," *Classical Philology* 16: 280–83.

Shutt, R. J. H. 1961. *Studies in Josephus*. London, S.P.C.K.

Sicker, M. 2001. *Between Rome and Jerusalem: 300 years of Roman-Judaean Relations*. London: Praeger.

Siggelkow-Berner, B. 2011. *Die jüdischen Feste im Bellum Judaicum des Flavius Josephus*. Tübingen: Mohr Siebeck.

Silberman, N. A. 1993. *A Prophet from amongst You: The Life of Yigael Yadin: Soldier, Scholar, and Mythmaker of Modern Israel*. Reading, Mass.: Addison-Wesley.

Smallwood, E. M. 1962. "High priests and politics in Roman Palestine," *Journal of Theological Studies* 13:14–34.

Smallwood, E. M. 1981. *The Jews under Roman Rule from Pompey to Diocletian: A Study in Political Relations*. Leiden: Brill.

Smith, M. 1971. "Zealots and sicarii, their origins and relation," *Harvard Theological Review* 64: 1–19.

Smith, R. R. R. 1988. "*Simulacra Gentium*: the ethne from the Sebasteion at Aphrodisias," *JRS* 78: 50–77.

Smith, W. C. 1963. *The Meaning and End of Religion: A New Approach to the Religious Traditions of Mankind*. New York: Macmillan.

Smoler, F. 1989. "The secrets of the soldiers who didn't shoot," *American Heritage* 40: 37–45.

Sonnabend, H. 1986. *Fremdenbild und Politik: Vorstellungen der Römer von Ägypten und dem Partherreich in der Späten Republik und frühen Kaiserzeit*. Frankfurt: Lang Verlag.

Spano, G. 1906. "Sul rilievo sepolcrale degli Aterii rappresentante alcuni edifici di Roma," *Atti della R. accademia di Archeologia, Lettere e Belle arti di Napoli* 24: 229–62

Spencer, H. 1896 [1872]. *The Study of Sociology*. New York: Appleton.

Spiller, R. J. 1988. "S. L. A. Mashall and the ratio of fire," *Journal of the Royal United Services Institute* 133: 67–71.

Spilsbury, P. 1998. *The Image of the Jew in Flavius Josephus' Paraphrase of the Bible.* Tübingen: Mohr Siebeck.

Spilsbury, P. 2003. "Flavius Josephus on the rise and fall of the Roman Empire," *Journal of Theological Studies* 54: 1–24.

Sprague, R. K. 1968. "*Dissoi Logoi* or *Dialexeis*," *Mind: A Quarterly Review of Psychology and Philosophy* 77 no. 306: 155-67.

Sprague, R. K. 1972. *The Older Sophists.* Columbia, SC: University of South Carolina Press.

Stacey, D. and G. Doudna. 2013. *Qumran Revisited: A Reassessment of the Archaeology of the Site and Its Texts.* Oxford: Archaeopress.

Stambaugh, J. E. 1988. *The Ancient Roman City.* Baltimore: Johns Hopkins University Press.

Stamper, J. W. 2005. *The Architecture of Roman Temples: The Republic to the Middle Empire.* Cambridge: Cambridge University Press.

Starke, M. 1828. *Travels in Europe Between the Years 1824 and 1828, Adapted to the Use of Travellers. . . .* London: John Murray.

Starr, R. J. 1987. "The circulation of texts in the ancient world," *Mnemosyne,* ser. 4, 40: 213–223.

Steinberg, A. 2008. "Secret passage discovered under ancient Jerusalem," *BAR* 34 (4): 20.

Stepansky, Y. 2008. "Tiberias." *NEAEHL* 5.2048–53.

Sterling, G. E. 1992. *Historiography and Self-Definition: Josephus, Luke-Acts, and Apologetic Historiography.* Leiden: Brill.

Stern, M. 1973. *Encyclopaedia Judaica Yearbook 1973.* Jerusalem: Encyclopaedia Judaica.

Stern, S. 2001. *Calendar and Community: A History of the Jewish Calendar, Second Century BCE – Tenth Century CE.* Oxford: Oxford University Press.

Stevenson, G. H. 1949. *Roman Provincial Administration till the Age of the Antonines.* Oxford: Blackwell.

Stewart, D. 1989. "The hermeneutics of suspicion," *Journal of Literature and Theology* 3: 296–307.

Stewart, N. 1951. "Divide and rule: British policy in Indian history," *Science and Society* 15: 49–57.

Stiebel, G. D. 2011. "'Meager bread and scant water' – food for thought at Masada," in A.I. Baumgarten, H. Eshel, R. Katzoff, and Sh. Tzoref (eds.), *Halakhah in Light of Epigraphy,* pp. 283–303. Göttingen: Vandenhoeck & Ruprecht.

Stiebel, G. D. and J. Magness. 2007. "The military equipment from Masada," *Masada VIII,* 1–94, in *Masada I–VIII.*

Stoll, O. 2007. "The religions of the armies," in P. Erdkamp (ed.) *A Companion to the Roman Army,* pp. 451–76. Oxford: Blackwell.

Stover, T. 2012. *Epic and Empire in Vespasianic Rome: A New Reading of Valerius Flaccus' Argonautica.* Oxford: Oxford University press.

Stow, K. R. 1977. *Catholic Thought and Papal Jewry Policy, 1555–1593.* New York: Jewish Theological Seminary of America.

Stow, K. R. 1992. *Alienated Minority: The Jews of Medieval Latin Europe.* Cambridge, Mass.: Harvard University Press.

Stow, K. R. 1995–1997. *The Jews in Rome.* 2 vols. Leiden: Brill.

Stow, K. R. 2006. *Jewish Dogs: An Image and Its Interpreters. Continuity in the Catholic-Jewish Encounter.* Stanford: Stanford University Press.

Stow, K. R. 2007. *Popes, Church, and Jews in the Middle Ages: Confrontation and Response.* Aldershot: Ashgate.

Strachan, H. and A. Herberg-Rothe (eds.). 2007. *Clausewitz in the Twenty-First Century.* Oxford: Oxford University Press.

Strobel, A. 1974. "Das römische Belagerungswerk um Machärus: Topographische Untersuchungen," *ZDPV* 90: 128–84.

Sufian, S. M. 2007. *Healing the Land and the Nation: Malaria and the Zionist Project in Palestine, 1920–1947.* Chicago: University of Chicago Press.

Sukenik, L. [E]. 1922. "The ancient city of Philoteria (Beit-Yeraḥ)," *The Journal of the Palestine Oriental Society* 2: 101–109.

Sutherland, C. H. V. 1951. *Coinage in Roman Imperial Policy 31 BC–AD 68.* London: Methuen.

Sutherland, C. H. V. and R. A. G. Carson. 1984. *Roman Imperial Coinage, vol. 1: From 31 B.C. to A.D. 69*, revised edition. London: Spink.

Sutherland, J. T. 1932. *India in Bondage*. New York: Lewis Copeland.

Swain, S. 1996. *Hellenism and Empire: Language, Classicism, and Power in the Greek World, AD 50–250*. Oxford: Clarendon.

Syme, R. 1939. *The Roman Revolution*. Oxford: Oxford University Press.

Syme, R. 1970a. "Domitius Corbulo," *JRS* 60: 27–39.

Syme, R. 1970b. *Ten Studies in Tacitus*. Oxford: Clarendon.

Syme, R. 1979–80. *Roman Papers*, eds. E. Badian and A. R. Birley. Oxford: Clarendon Press.

Syme, R. 1981. "Governors dying in Syria," *ZPE* 41: 125–44.

Syme, R. 1995. *Anatolica: Studies in Strabo*. Oxford: Clarendon Press.

Syon. D. 2004. "*Tyre and Gamla: A Study in the Monetary Influence of South Phoenicia on Galilee and the Golan in the Hellenistic and Roman Periods*." PhD dissertation, Hebrew University of Jerusalem.

Syon, D. 2007. "Yet again on the bronze coins minted at Gamala," *Israel Numismatic Research* 2: 117–22.

Syon, D. and Z. Yavor (eds.). 2010. *Gamla II: The Architecture: The Shmarya Gutmann Excavations 1976–1989*. IAA Reports 44. Jerusalem: Israel Antiquities Authority.

Syon, D. and Z. Yavor. 2008. "Gamala." *NEAEHL* 5.1739–42.

Talbert, R. J. A. 1984. *The Senate of Imperial Rome*. Princeton: Princeton University Press.

Talmon, S. 1999. "Hebrew fragments from Masada," in S. Talmon and Y. Yadin (eds.) *Masada VI. The Yigal Yadin Excavations 1963–1965. Final Reports: Hebrew Fragments from Masada and the Ben Sira Scroll from Masada*, pp. 1–149. Jerusalem: Israel Exploration Society.

Taylor, A. J. P. 1979. *How Wars Begin*, London: Hamish Hamilton.

Taylor, J. E. 2006. "Pontius Pilate and the Imperial Cult in Roman Judaea," *New Testament Studies* 52: 555–82.

Taylor, P. R. 1994. "Valerius' Flavian *Argonautica*," *Classical Quarterly* 44: 212–35

Tcherikover, V. A. and Fuks, A. (eds.). 1957–1963. *Corpus Papyrorum Judaicarum*, 3 vols. Cambridge, Mass: Harvard University Press.

Thackeray, H. St. J. 1929. *Josephus: the Man and the Historian. New York: Jewish Institute of Religion*.

Thesaurus Linguae Graecae (TLG), online at www.tlg.uci.edu

Thomas, R. 2000. *Herodotus in Context: Ethnography, Science and the Art of Persuasion*. Cambridge: Cambridge University Press.

Thompson Crawford, D. J. 1984. "The Idumaeans of Memphis and the Ptolemaic Politeumata," in M. Gigate (ed.) *Atti del XVII Congresso Internazionale di Papirologia*, pp. 1069–75. Naples: Centro internazionale per lo studio dei papyri ercolanesi.

Thompson, D. J. 1988. *Memphis under the Ptolemies*. Princeton: Princeton University Press.

Timpe, D. 2011. "*Memoria* and historiography in Rome," trans. M. Beck, in Marincola (ed.), *Greek and Roman Historiography*, 151–74.

Tov, E. 2000. "A Qumran origin for the Masada non-biblical texts?" *Dead Sea Discoveries* 7: 67–69.

Townend, G. 1962. "The Consuls of A. D. 69/70," *Classical Philology* 83: 113–29.

Trebilco, P. 2006. "The Jews in Asia Minor, 66–c. 235 CE," in S. T. Katz (ed.), *Cambridge History of Judaism, 4 vols*, vol. 4, pp. 75–81. Cambridge: Cambridge University Press.

Trefalt, B. 2003. *Japanese Army Stragglers and Memories of the War in Japan, 1950–1975*. London: Routledge.

Turcan, R. 1996. *The Cults of the Roman Empire*. Oxford: Blackwell.

Turner, E. W. 1954. "Tiberius Iulius Alexander," *JRS* 44: 54–64.

Ulf, C. 2009. "The Development of Greek ethnê and their ethnicity: an anthropological perspective," in P. Funke and N. Luraghi (eds.) *The Politics of Ethnicity and the Crisis of the Peloponnesian League*, pp. 215–49. Washington, DC: Center for Hellenic Studies.

Ullman, L. and J. J. Price. 2002. "Drama and history in Josephus' *Bellum Judaicum*," *Scripta Classica Israelica* 21: 97–111.

Ullmann-Margalit, E. 2008. "Spotlight on scroll scholars: Dissecting the Qumran-Essene hypothesis," *BAR* 34 (2): 63–67, 86.

UNESCO, Report of the World Heritage Committee, 25th session, December 11–16, 2001, at http://whc.unesco.org/archive/repcom01.htm#1040, accessed August 1, 2009.

van Creveld, M. 2008. *The Culture of War*. New York: Ballantine.

VanderKam, J. C. 1994. *The Dead Sea Scrolls Today*. Grand Rapids: Eerdmans.

van Groningen, B. 1963. "EKDOSIS," *Mnemosyne* 16: 1–17.

van Hooff, A. J. L. 1988. "Ancient robbers: Reflections behind the facts," *Ancient Society* 19: 105–24.

Vasta, M. (2007) "Flavian visual propaganda: Building a dynasty," *Constructing the Past* 8, Issue 1, Article 10. Available at: http://digitalcommons.iwu.edu/constructing/vol8/iss1/10 (accessed October 1, 2013).

Vermes, G. 1981. *Jesus the Jew: A Historian's Reading of the Gospels*. Minneapolis: Fortress.

Versnel, H. S. 1970. *Triumphus: An Inquiry into the Origin, Development and Meaning of the Roman Triumph*. Leiden: Brill.

Vervaet, F. J. 1999. "*CIL* IX 3426: a new light on Corbulo's career, with special reference to his official mandate in the east from AD 55 to AD 63," *Latomus* 58: 574–99.

Vervaet, F. J. 2000. "Tacitus, *Ann.* 15, 25, 3: A revision of Corbulo's *imperium maius* (AD 63–AD 65?)," in C. Deroux (ed.), *Studies in Latin Literature and Roman History*, vol. 10, pp. 260–98. Collections Latomus 254. Brussels: Latomus.

Vervaet, F. J. 2002. "Domitius Corbulo and the senatorial opposition to Nero," *Ancient Society* 32: 135–93.

Vervaet, F. J. 2003. "Domitius Corbulo and the rise of the Flavian dynasty," *Historia – Zeitschrift für Alte Geschichte* 52: 436–64.

Villalba i Varneda, P. 1986. *The Historical Method of Flavius Josephus*. Leiden: Brill.

Vivanti, C. 1995. "The history of the Jews in Italy and the history of Italy: *Die Konstruktion der jüdiscen Geschichte* by Heinrich Graetz," *Journal of Modern History* 67: 309–57.

Vlassopoulos, K. 2007. *Unthinking the Greek Polis: Ancient Greek History beyond Eurocentrism*. Cambridge: Cambridge University Press.

Vogel, M. 1999. "Vita 64–69, das Bilderverbot und die Gailäapolitik des Josephus," *JSJ* 30: 65–79.

von Bernhardi, F. 1914a. *Britain as Germany's Vassal*, trans. J. Ellis Barker. London: William Dawson and Sons. Original: *Unsere Zukunft: ein Mahnwort an das Deutsche Volk* (Stuttgart 1912).

von Bernhardi, F. 1914b. *Germany and the Next War*. New York: Chas. A. Eron. Original: *Deutschland und der nächste Krieg* (Stuttgart 1912).

von Bernhardi, F. 1914c. *How Germany Makes War*, trans. Hugh Rees. London: Hodder and Stoughton. Original: *Vom heutigen Kriege* (Stuttgart 1911).

von Clausewitz, C. 1883 [1832]. *Vom Kriege*. 2nd edn. Berlin: Richard Wilhelm.

von Fritz, K. 1954. *The Theory of the Mixed Constitution in Antiquity: A Critical Analysis of Polybius' Political Ideas*. New York: Columbia University Press.

von Ghyczy, T., B. von Oetinger, and C. Bassford (eds.). 2001. *Clausewitz on Strategy: Inspiration and Insight from a Master Strategist*. New York: John Wiley and Sons.

von Senger und Etterlin, F. 1963. *Neither Fear nor Hope: The Wartime Career of General Frido von Senger und Etterlin, Defender of Cassino*. London: Macdonald.

Vörös, G. 2010. "The Herodian fortified Palace: overlooking the Dead Sea in Transjordan," *Liber Annuus* 60: 349–61.

Vörös, G. 2013. *Machaerus I: History, Archaeology and Architecture of the Fortified Herodian Royal Palace and City overlooking the Dead Sea in Transjordan*. Milan: Terra Santa.

Walbank, F. W. 1972. *Polybius.* "Sather Classical Lectures" 42. Berkeley: University of California Press.

Walbank, F. W. 2002. *Polybius, Rome and the Hellenistic World: Essays and Reflections.* Cambridge: Cambridge University Press.

Wallace-Hadrill, A. 2005. "Mutatas Formas: The Augustan Transformation of Roman Knowledge," in Galinsky (ed.), *Cambridge Companion*, 55–84.

Walser, G. 2001. *The Greek of the Ancient Synagogue: An Investigation on the Greek of the Septuagint, Pseudepigrapha and the New Testament.* Lund: Lund University Press.

Walton, A. 1924. "The date of the Arch of Constantine," *Memoirs of the American Academy in Rome* 4: 169–80.

Waltz, K. N. 1979. *Theory of International Politics.* New York: McGraw-Hill.

Warde Fowler, W. 1903. "Polybius' conception of *Tyche*," *Classical Review* 17: 445–49.

Warde Fowler, W. 1913. "Passing under the yoke," *CR* 27: 48–51.

Wardman, A. 1976. *Rome's Debt to Greece.* London: P. Elek.

Wardy, R. 2009. "The philosophy of rhetoric and the rhetoric of philosophy," in E. Gunderson (ed.), *The Cambridge Companion to Ancient Rhetoric*, pp. 43–58. Cambridge: Cambridge University Press.

Warry, J. 1998. *Warfare in the Classical World: War and the Ancient Civilizations of Greece and Rome.* London: Salamander.

Watson, G. R. 1969. *The Roman Soldier.* London: Thames & Hudson.

Wayland, F. 1860 [1835]. *The Elements of Moral Science.* Abridged. Boston: Gould and Lincoln.

Weber, W. 1921. *Josephus und Vespasian: Untersuchungen zu dem Jüdischen Krieg des Flavius Josephus.* Berlin: W. Kohlhammer.

Webster, G. 1978. *Boudica: the British Revolt against Rome AD 60.* London: Routledge.

Webster, G. 1985. *The Roman Imperial Army of the First and Second Centuries A.D*, 3rd edn. London: A. & C. Black.

Weiss, Z. 1993. "Sepphoris." *NEAEHL* 4: 1324—28.

Weiss, Z. 2008. "Sepphoris." *NEAEHL* 5.2029–35.

Welch, J. W. 1981. *Chiasmus in Antiquity: Structures, Analyses, Exegesis.* Hildesheim: Gerstenberg.

Welch, K. E. 2006. "Introduction," in S. Dillon and K. E. Welch (eds.) *Representations of War in Ancient Rome*, pp. 1–26. Cambridge: Cambridge University Press.

Welch, K. E. 2007. *The Roman Amphitheatre: From Its Origins to the Colosseum.* New York: Cambridge University Press.

Wellesley, K. (2000). *The Year of the Four Emperors.* London: Routledge.

Whealey, A. 2003. *Josephus on Jesus: The Testimonium Flavianum Vontroversy from Late Antiquity to Modern Times.* New York: Peter Lang.

Wheeler, E. F. 2007. "The army and the *Limes* in the east," in P. Erdkamp (ed.) *A Companion to the Roman Army*, pp. 451–76. Oxford: Blackwell.

White, P. 1975. "The friends of Martial, Statius, and Pliny, and the dispersal of patronage." *Harvard Studies in Classical Philology* 79: 265–300.

White, P. 1978. "*Amicitia* and the profession of poetry in early imperial Rome." *Journal of Roman Studies* 68: 74–92.

Whitman, C. H. 1965. *Homer and the Heroic Tradition.* Cambridge MA: Harvard University Press.

Whittaker, C. R. 1994. *Frontiers of the Roman Empire: A Social and Economic Study.* Baltimore: Johns Hopkins University Press.

Wiedemann, T. E. J. 1986. "The *Fetiales*: a reconsideration," *CQ* 36: 478–90.

Wiedemann, T. E. J. 1996a. "Tiberius to Nero," in A. K. Bowman, E. Champlin, A. Lintott (eds.) *CAH vol. 10: The Augustan Empire, 43 B.C.–A.D. 69*, pp. 198–255. Cambridge: Cambridge University Press.

Wiedemann, T. E. J. 1996b. "From Nero to Vespasian," in A. K. Bowman, E. Champlin, A. Lintott (eds.) *CAH vol. 10: The Augustan Empire, 43 B.C.–A.D. 69*, pp. 256–82. Cambridge: Cambridge University Press.

Wilamowitz-Moellendorff, U. von. 1982 [1921]. *History of Classical Scholarship*, trans. A.

Harris, ed. H. Lloyd-Jones. Baltimore: Johns Hopkins University Press.

Williams, C. A. 1999. *Roman Homosexuality: Ideologies of Masculinity in Classical Antiquity.* Oxford: Oxford University Press.

Williamson, G. A. 1964. *The World of Josephus.* Boston: Little Brown.

Wilson, C. W. 1877. "The sites of Taricheæ and Bethsaida," *Palestine Exploration Fund Quarterly Statement* 9: 10–13.

Wilson, S. G. 1995. *Related Strangers: Jews and Christians 70–170 C.E.* Minneapolis: Fortress, 1995.

Winter, P. 1961. *On the Trial of Jesus.* Berlin: De Gruyter.

Wiseman, T. P. 1998. "The publication of *De Bello Gallico*," in Welch and Powell (eds.), *Caesar as Artful Reporter*, pp. 1–7.

Wolski, J. 1993. *L'Empire des Arsacides.* Acta Iranica 32. Leuven: Lovanii.

Wolters, A. 1990. "Apocalytic and the copper scroll," *JNES* 49: 145–54.

Wood, H. 1972. *The Histories of Herodotus: An Analysis of the Formal Structure.* Mouton: The Hague Press.

Woodman, A. J. 1988. *Rhetoric in Classical Historiography: Four Studies.* London: Croom Helm.

Woolf, G. 2006. "Pliny's Province," in T. Bekker-Nielsen (ed.) *Rome and the Black Sea Region: Domination, Romanization, Resistance*, pp. 93–108. Aarhus: Aarhus University Press.

Wright, G. R. H. 1985. *Ancient Building in Southern Syria and Palestine.* 2 vols. Leiden: Brill.

Wright, D. 2000. "Tertullian," in P. F. Esler (ed.), *The Early Christian World*, 2 vols., pp. 1027–47. London: Routledge.

Yadin, Y. 1966. *Masada: Herod's Fortress and the Zealots' Last Stand.* London: Phoenix.

Yadin, Y., and Naveh, J. 1989. "Masada I: The Aramaic and Hebrew Ostraca and Jar Inscriptions," in *Masada I–VIII*.

Yarden, L. 1991. *The Spoils of Jerusalem on the Arch of Titus: A Re-investigation.* Stockholm: Paul Åströms.

Yardeni, A. 2000. *Textbook of Aramaic, Hebrew and Nabataean Documentary Texts from the Judaean Desert and Related Material.* 2 vols. Jerusalem: Magnes.

Yardley, J., and Heckel, W. 1997. *Epitome of the Philippic History of Pompeius Trogus, Vol. 1: Books 11–12: Alexander the Great.* Oxford: Oxford University Press.

Yardley, J. and W. Heckel. 2001. *Quintus Curtius Rufus: The History of Alexander*, rev. edn. London: Penguin.

Yarshater, E. (ed.). 1983. *The Cambridge History of Iran. Vol. 3: The Seleucid, Parthian and Sasanian Periods.* 2 vols. Cambridge: Cambridge University Press.

Yavetz, Z. 1975. "Reflections on Titus and Josephus," *Greek, Roman, and Byzantine Studies* 16: 411–432.

Yeager, S. M. 2004. "'The siege of Jerusalem' and biblical exegesis: writing about Romans in fourteenth-century England," *The Chaucer Review* 39: 70–102.

Zagorin, P. 2005. *Thucydides: An Introduction for the Common Reader.* Princeton: Princeton University Press.

Zaho, M. A. 2004. *Imago Triumphalis: The Function and Significance of Triumphal Imagery for Italian Renaissance Rulers.* New York: Peter Lang.

Zangenberg, J., H. W. Attridge, and D. B. Martin (eds.). 2007. *Religion, Ethnicity and Identity in Ancient Galilee: A Region in Transition.* Tübingen: Mohr Siebeck.

Zanker, P. 1988. *The Power of Images in the Age of Augustus.* Ann Arbor: The University of Michigan Press.

Zeitlin, S. 1965. "Masada and the sicarii," *JQR* 55: 299–317.

Zeitlin, S. 1967. "The sicarii and Masada," *JQR* 57: 251–70.

Zerubavel, Y. 1994. *Recovered Roots: Collective Memory and the Making of Israeli National Tradition.* Chicago: University of Chicago Press.

Zias, J. 1998. "Questioning Masada: whose bones? Were they really Jewish defenders? Did Yadin deliberately obfuscate?" *BAR* 24: 40–45, 64–66.

Zias, J., Segal, D., and Carmi, I. 1994. "The human skeletal remains from the northern

[sic] cave at Masada – a second look," in J. Aviram, G. Foerster, E. Netzer, and A. Paris (eds.) *Masada IV. The Yigael Yadin Excavations 1963–1965. Final Reports*, pp. 366–67. Jerusalem: Israel Exploration Society.

Ziegler, K. H. 1964. *Die Beziehungen zwischen Rom und dem Partherreich*. Wiesbaden: Steiner.

Zumpt, A. W. 1859. *Studia Romana, sive de delectis antiquatum romanorum captibus commentationes quattuor*. Berlin: Ferdinand Duemmler.

Zunz, O., ed. 1985. *Reliving the Past: The Worlds of Social History*. Chapel Hill: University of North Carolina Press.

BIBLIOGRAPHICAL ABBREVIATIONS

ABD   D. N. Freedman (ed.), *Anchor Bible Dictionary*, 6 vols. (New York: Doubleday, 1992).

AE   *L'année epigraphique* (Paris: Ernest Leroux, 1888–).

CIL   *Corpus Inscriptionum Latinarum*) Berlin: Berlin-Brandenburgische Akademie der Wissenschaften, 1863–).

CPJ   V. A. Tcherikover and A. Fuks (eds.), *Corpus Papyrorum Judaicarum*, 3 vols. (Cambridge, Mass: Harvard University Press, 1957–1963).

ILS   H. Dessau (ed.), *Inscriptiones Latinae Selectae*, 3 vols. in 5. 4th edn. (Dublin: Weidmann, 1974 [1892]).

Jacoby   F. Jacoby (ed.), *Die Fragmente der grieschischen Historiker*. 3 vols. in 15 (Berlin: Weidmann, 1923–1959).

Loeb Josephus   H. St. J. Thackeray, Josephus in Nine Volumes, "Loeb Classical Library" 203 and 210 (London: William Heinemann; Cambridge, Mass.: Harvard University Press, 1927–1965).

LSJ   H. G. Liddell, R. Scott, and H. Stuart Jones, *Greek-English Lexicon*, 9th edn. (Oxford: Oxford University Press, 1940).

Masada I–VIII.   J. Aviram, G. Foerster, and E. Netzer (eds.), *Masada I–VIII: The Yigael Yadin Excavations 1963–1965. Final Reports* (Jerusalem: Israel Exploration Society, 1989–2007).

M-B   O. Michel and O. Bauernfeind (eds.), *De bello judaico, der jüdische Krieg: griechisch und deutsch*, 3 vols. in 4 (second, corrected edition; Munich: Kösel/Darmstadt: Wissenschaftliche Buchgesellschaft, 1962-1969).

NEAEHL   E. Stern et al. (eds.), *New Encyclopedia of Archaeological Excavations in the Holy Land*. 4 volumes (Jerusalem: Israel Exploration Society, 1993); *Supplementary Volume* (= 5), 2008.

OCD[3]   S. Hornblower and A. Spawforth (eds.), *Oxford Classical Dictionary,* 3rd edn. (Oxford: Oxford University Press, 1996).

OGIS   C. F. W. Dittenberger (ed.), *Orientis Graeci Inscriptiones Selectae*, 2 vols. (Hildesheim: G. Olms, 1960 [Leipzig: Hirzel, 1903–1905]).

Pelletier   A. Pelletier (ed.), *Josèphe, Guerre des Juifs*. 3 vols., "Collection des Universités de France [Budé]" (Paris: Les Belles Lettres, 1975–1982).

PIR   E. Klebs, H. Dessau, P. von Rohden, and Deutsche Akademie der Wissenschaften zu Berlin, *Prosopographia Imperii Romani Saec. I. II. III.* 3 vols. (Berlin: Georg Reimer, 1897).

PIR² | Preussische Akademie der Wissenschaften and Berlin-Brandenburgische Akademie der Wissenschaften. *Prosopographia Imperii Romani Saec. I. II. III.* 3 vols. 2nd edn. (Berlin and Leipzig: W. de Gruyter, 1933).

Schürer-Vermes | Emil Schürer, *The History of the Jewish People in the Age of Jesus Christ*, 3 vols. in 4, revised by Geza Vermes et al. (Edinburgh: T. & T. Clark, 1979–1987).

SEG | *Supplementum Epigraphicum Graecum*. Vols. 1–25: 1923–1971 (Leiden: van Nijf). Vols. 26–: 1979– (Amsterdam: J. C. Gieben; now Leiden: Brill).

SIG | W. Dittenberger (ed.), *Sylloge Inscriptionum Graecarum*. 3rd edn. (Leipzig: S. Hirzel, 1915–24).

INDEX OF MODERN AUTHORS

INDEX TO HISTORICAL PERSONS, GROUPS, AND PLACES

INDEX OF TEXTS, INSCRIPTIONS, AND PAPYRI